Road map symbols

Motorways

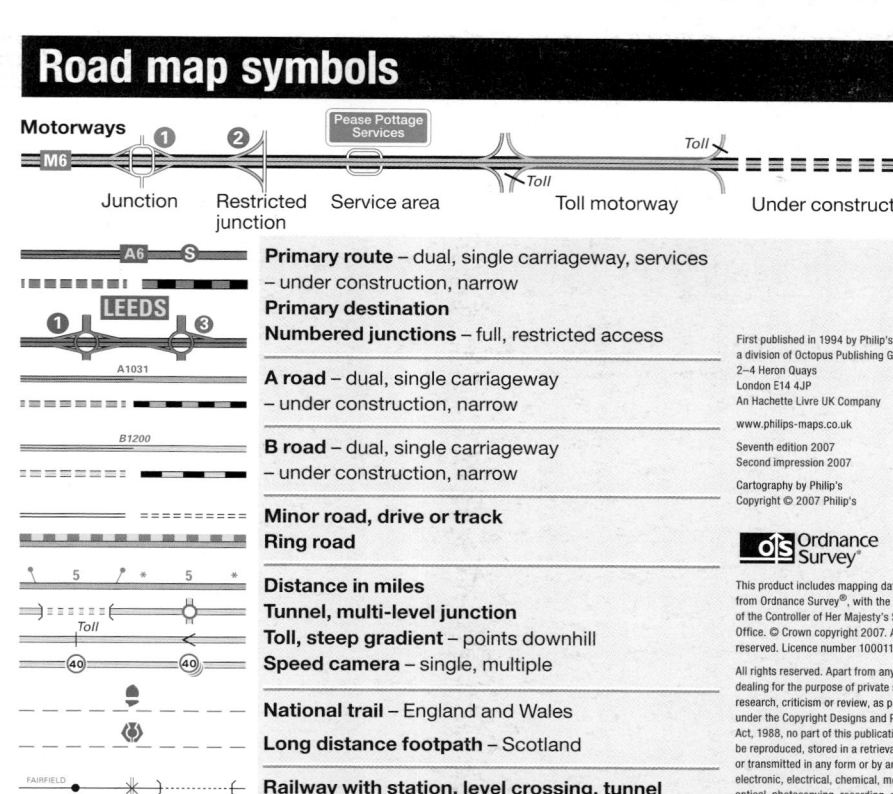

M6 — Junction **1** — Restricted junction **2** — Service area (Pease Pottage Services) — Toll motorway (Toll) — Under construction

A6 / S	**Primary route** – dual, single carriageway, services – under construction, narrow
LEEDS	**Primary destination**
1 **3**	**Numbered junctions** – full, restricted access
A1031	**A road** – dual, single carriageway – under construction, narrow
B1200	**B road** – dual, single carriageway – under construction, narrow
	Minor road, drive or track
	Ring road
5 · 5	**Distance in miles**
	Tunnel, multi-level junction
Toll (40) (40)	**Toll, steep gradient** – points downhill **Speed camera** – single, multiple
	National trail – England and Wales
	Long distance footpath – Scotland
FAIRFIELD / ALRESFORD	**Railway with station, level crossing, tunnel** **Preserved railway with station, tramway**
	National boundary **County or unitary authority boundary**
	Car ferry, catamaran **Passenger ferry, catamaran** **Hovercraft, freight ferry** **Internal ferry** – car, passenger
	Principal airport, other airport or airfield
	Area of outstanding natural beauty – England and Wales, **Forest park, National park, National scenic area** – Scotland, **Regional park**
	Woodland
	Beach – sand, shingle
R. SEVERN 6 12	**Navigable river or canal** **Lock, flight of locks, canal bridge number**
▲965 ✕1066 HOLTON HEATH MILLENNIUM STADIUM P&R	**Viewpoint, spot height** – in metres **Site and date of battle, RAC or AA telephone box** **National nature reserve, major sporting venue** **Shopping village, park and ride** **World Heritage site, caravan site, camping site**

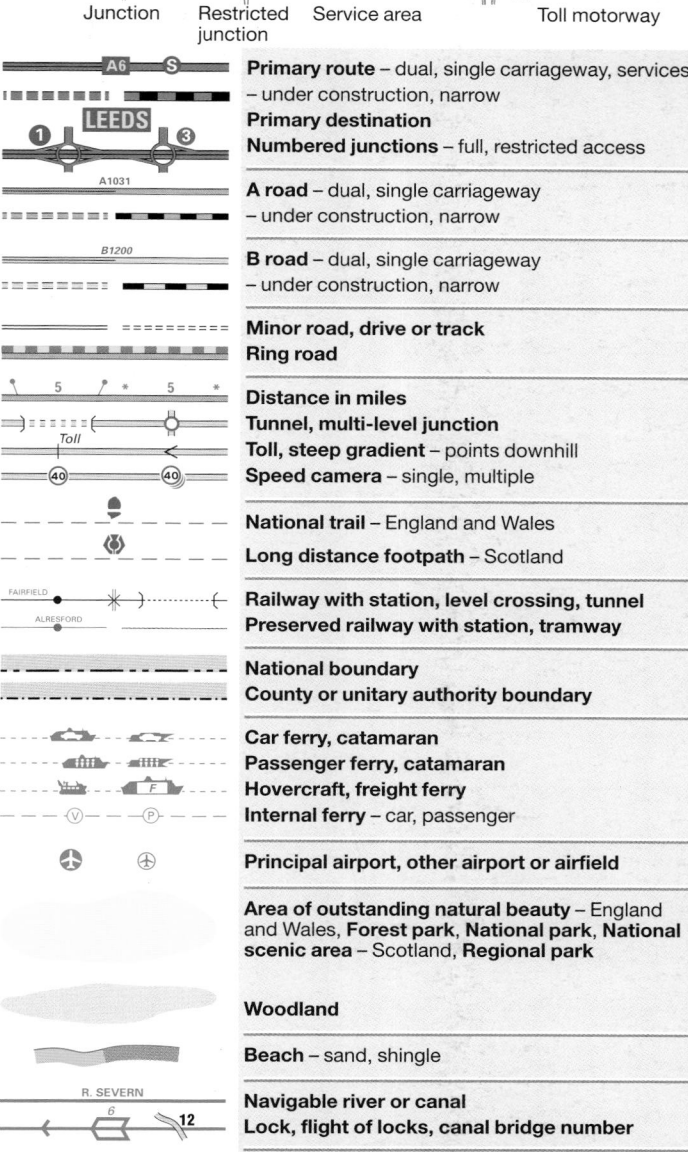

Tourist information 1: 100 000 road maps

✠ Abbey or priory	⛳ Golf course	🚂 Preserved railway
🐬 Aquarium or dolphinarium	⛴ Historic ship	🎭 Theme park
🏛 Art gallery	🏚 House	**Tourist information centre**
✕ Art collection or museum	🏡 House and garden	i – open all year
🐦 Bird sanctuary or aviary	🏛 Local museum	i – open seasonally
🏰 Castle	⚓ Marina	⊕ Transport collection
✝ Cathedral	◆ Maritime museum	★ Viewpoint
⛪ Church of interest	Military museum	△ Youth hostel
🏕 Country park – England and Wales	▦ Motor racing circuit	🐘 Zoo
🏕 Country park – Scotland	ⓟ Picnic area	**Ancient monument**
🐄 County show ground	✕ Racecourse	**Earthwork**
🐑 Farm park	🏺 Roman antiquity	**Windmill**
❀ Garden	⚐ Safari park	**Watermill** **Other place of interest**

Tourist information 1: 200 000 road maps

✝ Abbey, Cathedral or Priory	❀ Garden	✕ Racecourse
🏛 Ancient monument	⛳ Golf course	🏺 Roman antiquity
🐬 Aquarium	⛴ Historic ship	⚐ Safari park
🏛 Art gallery	🏚 House	**Tourist information centre**
🐦 Bird collection or aviary	🏡 House and garden	i – open all year
🏰 Castle	⚓ Marina	i – open seasonally
⛪ Church of interest	▦ Motor racing circuit	△ Youth hostel
🏕 Country park – Scotland	🏛 Museum	🐘 Zoo
🐑 Farm park	🚂 Preserved railway	✦ Other place of interest

First published in 1994 by Philip's
a division of Octopus Publishing Group Ltd
2–4 Heron Quays
London E14 4JP
An Hachette Livre UK Company
www.philips-maps.co.uk

Seventh edition 2007
Second impression 2007

Cartography by Philip's
Copyright © 2007 Philip's

This product includes mapping data licensed from Ordnance Survey®, with the permission of the Controller of Her Majesty's Stationery Office. © Crown copyright 2007. All rights reserved. Licence number 100011710

All rights reserved. Apart from any fair dealing for the purpose of private study, research, criticism or review, as permitted under the Copyright Designs and Patents Act, 1988, no part of this publication may be reproduced, stored in a retrieval system, or transmitted in any form or by any means, electronic, electrical, chemical, mechanical, optical, photocopying, recording, or otherwise, without prior written permission. All enquiries should be addressed to the Publisher.

To the best of the Publisher's knowledge, the information in this atlas was correct at the time of going to press. No responsibility can be accepted for any errors or their consequences.

The representation in this atlas of any road, drive or track is no evidence of the existence of a right of way.

Data for the speed cameras provided by PocketGPSWorld.com Ltd.

Information for Tourist Attractions in England supplied by the British Tourist Authority / English Tourist Board.

Information for National Parks, Areas of Outstanding Natural Beauty, National Trails and Country Parks in Wales supplied by the Countryside Council for Wales.

Information for National Parks, Areas of Outstanding Natural Beauty, National Trails and Country Parks in England supplied by the Countryside Commission.

Data for Regional Parks, Long Distance Footpaths and Country Parks in Scotland provided by Scottish Natural Heritage.

Data for National Scenic Areas in Scotland provided by the Scottish Executive Office. Crown copyright material is reproduced with the permission of the Controller of HMSO and the Queen's Printer for Scotland. Licence number C02W0003960.

Gaelic name forms used in the Western Isles provided by Comhairle nan Eilean.

Information for canal bridge numbers supplied by GEOprojects (UK) Limited.

Printed in Spain by Cayfosa-Quebecor.

Ordnance Survey®

PHILIP'S NAVIGATOR® Britain

Contents

Route-finding system

Town names printed in yellow on a green background are those used on Britain's signposts to indicate primary destinations. To find your route quickly and easily, simply follow the signs to the primary destination immediately beyond the place you require.

Below Driving from Totnes to Berry Pomeroy, follow the signs to Paignton, the first primary destination beyond Berry Pomeroy. These will indicate the most direct main route to the side turning for Berry Pomeroy.

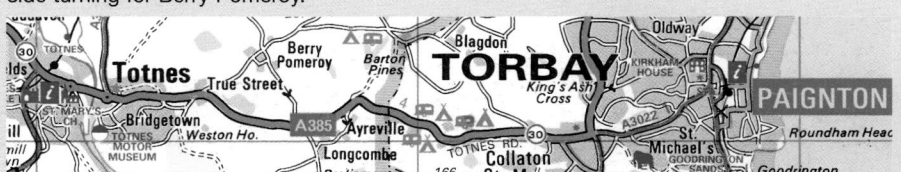

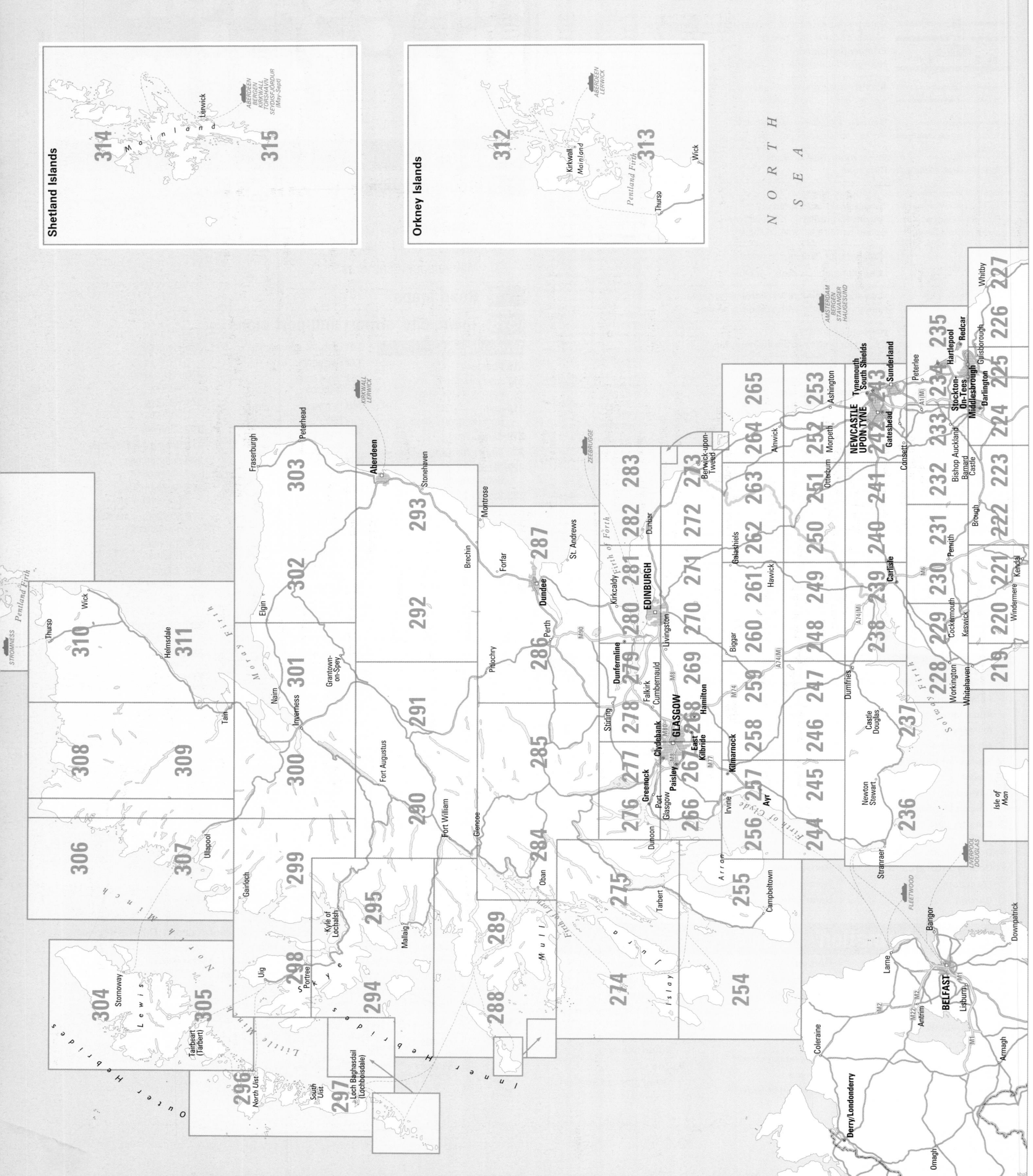

IRISH SEA
ENGLISH CHANNEL
ST. GEORGE'S CHANNEL
Cardigan Bay
Bristol Channel
Strait of Dover
LONDON
BIRMINGHAM
MANCHESTER
LIVERPOOL
LEEDS
SHEFFIELD
BRADFORD
NOTTINGHAM
LEICESTER
COVENTRY
WOLVERHAMPTON
STOKE-ON-TRENT
DERBY
KINGSTON UPON HULL
BRISTOL
CARDIFF
SOUTHAMPTON
PLYMOUTH
DUBLIN
Isles Of Scilly
Calais
Dieppe
Boulogne-sur-Mer
Le Touquet-Paris-Plage
Wexford
Waterford
Douglas

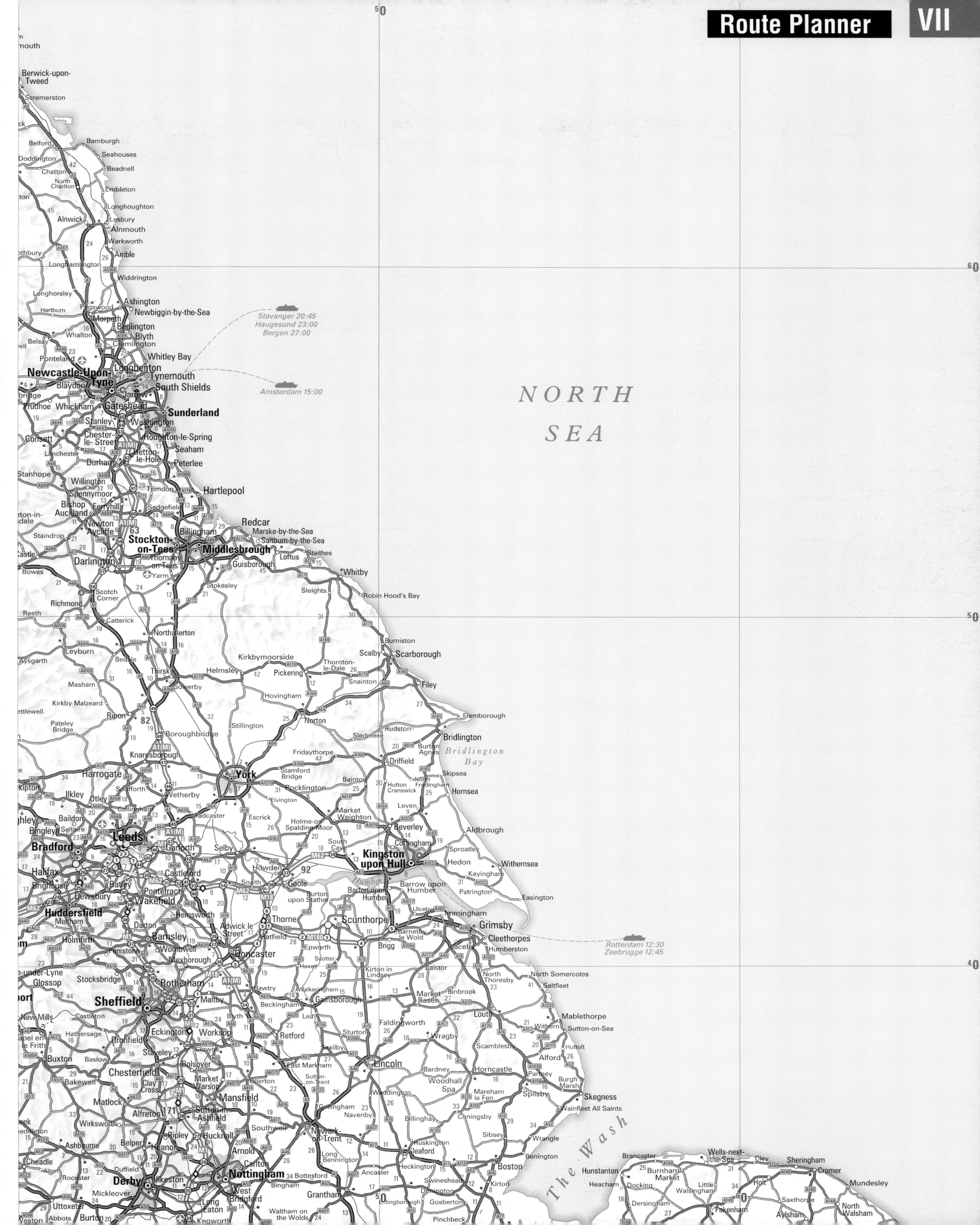

NORTH

SEA

Stavanger 20:45
Haugesund 23:00
Bergen 27:00

Amsterdam 15:00

Bridlington Bay

Humber

Rotterdam 12:30
Zeebrugge 12:45

The Wash

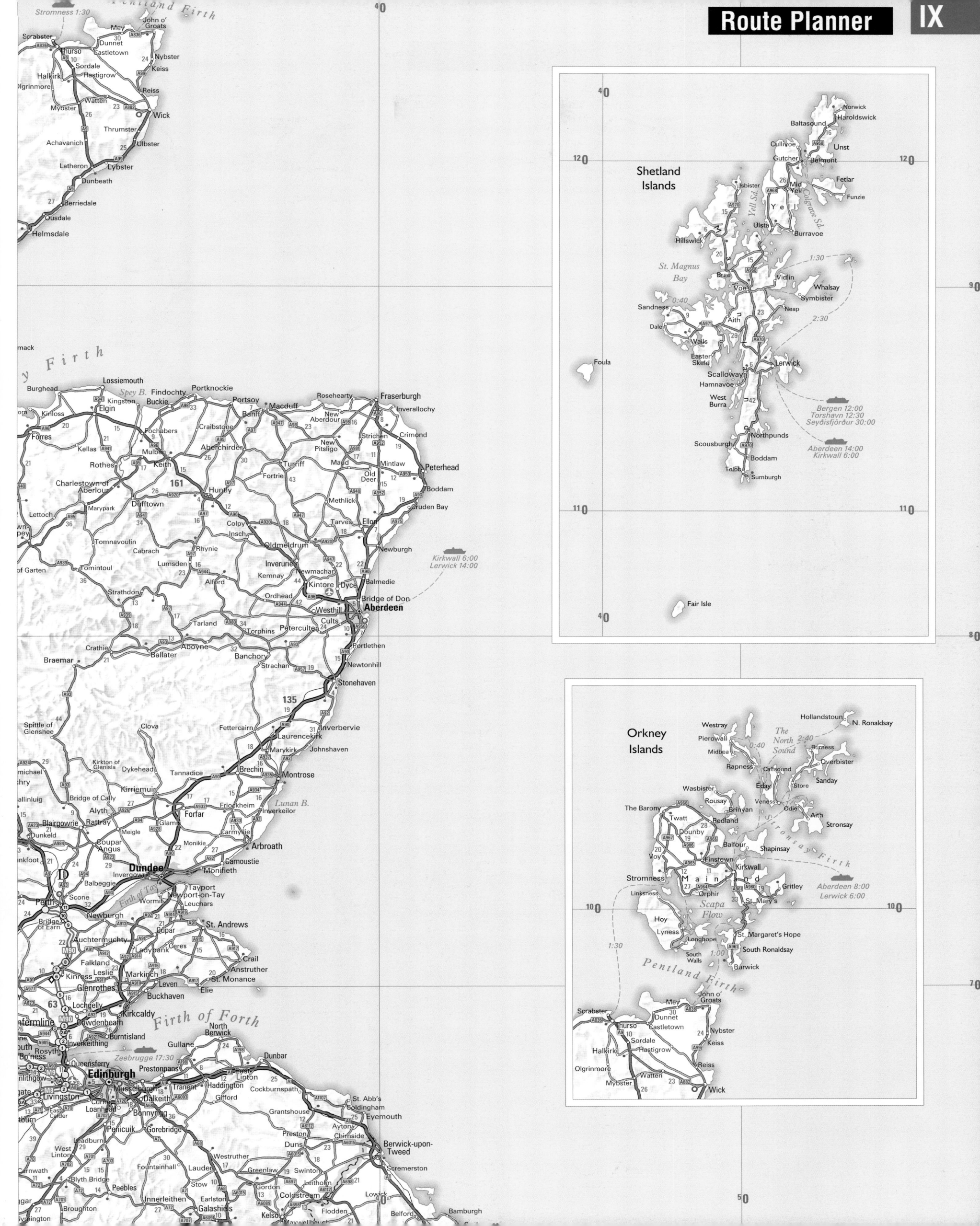

Distance table

How to use this table

Distances are shown in miles and kilometres with estimated journey times in hours and minutes.

For example: the distance between Aberdeen and Birmingham is 420 miles or 676 kilometres with an estimated journey time of 8 hours, 30 minutes.

Estimated driving times are based on an average speed of 60mph on Motorways and 40mph on other roads. Drivers should allow extra time when driving at peak periods or through areas likely to be congested.

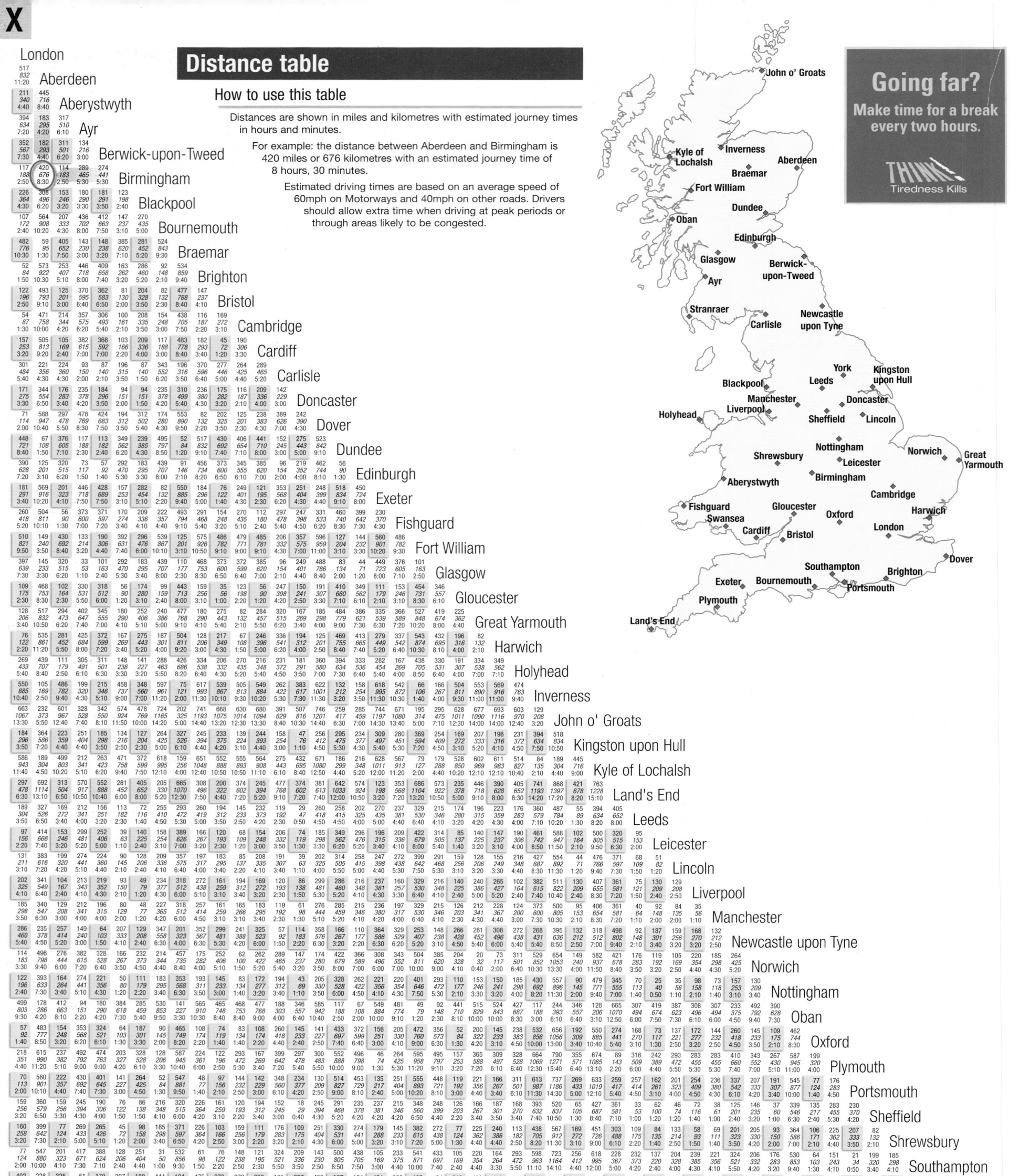

Mobile speed camera sites

The vast majority of speed cameras used on Britain's roads are operated by safety camera partnerships. These comprise local authorities, the police, Her Majesty's Court Service (HMCS) and the Highways Agency.

This table lists the sites where each safety camera partnership may enforce speed limits through the use of mobile cameras or detectors. These are usually set up on the roadside or a bridge spanning the road and operated by a police or civilian enforcement officer. The speed limit at each site (if available) is shown in red type, followed by the approximate location in black type.

Abbreviations

adj	adjacent
btwn	between
Dr	Drive
Ind Est	Industrial Estate
jct	junction
j/w	junction with
nr	near
o/s	outside
opp	opposite
rdbt	roundabout
twds	towards

England

Avon and Somerset

Bath and North East Somerset, Bristol, North Somerset, Somerset, South Gloucestershire

M32
60 Bristol Stadium

A4
30 Bath, Newbridge Rd
30 Bristol, Anchor Rd
30 Bristol, Totterdown Bridge
50 Nr Keynsham, Keynsham Bypass jct A4175 Durley Hill
50 Portway
30 Portway, nr A4176 Bridge Valley Rd

A4/B4054
30 Bristol, Avonmouth Rd

A30
50 Cricket St Thomas
30 East Chinnock
40 Roundham
40 Yeovil, Hospital Rdbt
30 Yeovil, Sherborne Rd

A37
30 Bristol, Wells Rd (nr jct Airport Rd)
30 Bristol, Wells Rd (nr St Johns La)
60 Chilthorne Domer (east)
50 Emborough
30 Gurney Slade (north)
60 Lydford to Bristol
40 Lydford to Yeovil
60 Nr Podimore, Fosse Way, north of Podimore Rdbt
30 Shepton Mallet

A38
40 Aztec West, nr Bradley Stoke Way
30 Bathpool
40 Bedminster Down, Bridgwater Rd
40 Bristol, Bedminster Down Rd nr Bishopsworth Rd
30 Bristol, Bedminster Down Rd/West St
30 Bristol, Cheltenham Rd/Gloucester Rd, nr Cranbrook Rd
30 Bristol, Gloucester Rd nr B4052 Ashley Down Rd
30 Bristol, Stokes Croft nr Bond St
40 Churchill – Langford
40 Cross
30 East Reach/Toneway
40 Filton, Gloucester Rd (north) nr B4057 Gypsy Patch Lane
50 Heatherton Grange
40,30 North Petherton
40 Patchway, Gloucester Rd nr Highwood Rd
50 Pawlett (south)
50 Redhill
30 Rooks Bridge (east)
30 Taunton – Bridgwater
30 Taunton, Wellington Rd (inbound)
30 Taunton, Wellington Rd (outbound)
30 West Huntspill (north)

A39
30 Ashcott
30 Bilbrook
30 Bridgwater, Bath Rd
30 Bridgwater, North Broadway nr A38 Taunton Rd
30 Bridgwater, North Broadway/Broadway/ Monmouth St
30 Chewton Mendip
40 Coxley nr Wells
50 Green Ore (south)
40 Horsey, Bath Rd
30 Quantock Rd
30 Walton

A46
60 Bath to Wickwar Rd
40 Dunkirk

A303
50 Buckland St Mary
50 Downhead nr Ilchester

A303/A3088
70 Cartgate Rdbt

A357
30 Templecombe

A303/A358
60 Southfields Rdbt

A358
60 Ashill
30 Donyatt
30 Henlade, nr M5 jct 25
40 Hornsbury Mill
40 Pen Elm (south)
30 Staplegrove Rd
30 Taunton Deane, Priorswood Rd
30 Taunton, Greenway Rd

A359
30 Mudford (north)

A361
30 Doulting
40 Durston
60 Frome Bypass
30 Othery
30 Pilton
30 West Pennard

A362
40 Terry Hill

A367
30 Bath, Green Park Rd
30 Bath, Bear Flat
30 Radstock, Wells Rd

A369
40 Abbots Leigh
60 Easton-in-Gordano, Martcombe Rd nr M5 jct 19

A370
30 Cleeve Village
30 Congresbury, Station Rd, Bristol Rd
30 Flax Bourton nr B3130
40 Long Ashton Bypass, Bristol End
50 West Wick, Somerset Avenue, west of M5 jct 21
30 Weston-super-Mare, Beach Rd
50 Weston-super-Mare, Herluin Way nr Winterstoke Rd
50 Weston-super-Mare, Somerset Avenue (central reservation)
50 Weston-super-Mare, Somerset Avenue, jct Moor Lane
30 Weston-super-Mare, Winterstoke Rd

A371
30 Draycott
40 Priestleigh (south)
30 Winscombe, Sidcot Lane nr jct A38,

A372
30 Aller

A378
30 Curry Rivel
40 Wrantage

A403
40 Avonmouth Docks

A420
30 Bristol, Lawrence Hill
30 Kingswood, Two Mile Hill Rd, Regent St
30 Old Market, nr Temple Way/Bond St
30 Redfield, Church Rd
30 St George, Clouds Hill Rd/Bell Hill Rd
30 Warmley, High St London Rd nr A4175 Bath Rd
60 Wick, Tog Hill

A432
30 Bristol, Fishponds Rd nr B4048 Lodge Causeway
30 Bristol, Fishponds Rd nr B4469 Royate Hill
30 Bristol, Fishponds Rd with B4469 Muller Rd
30 Bristol, Stapleton Rd nr jct A4320 Easton Way
40 Hambrook, Badminton Rd nr A4174 Avon Ring Rd
40 Kendleshire
30 Yate, Station Rd/B4059 Stover Rd

A3027
30 North St/East St

A3029
40 Bristol, Avon Bridge

A3039
30 Devonshire Rd

A3088
30 Yeovil, Lysander Rd

A3259
30 Monkton Heathfield

A4018
30 Bristol, Black Boy Hill/ Whiteladies Rd
30 Bristol, Cribbs Causeway jct 17 M5
30 Bristol, Westbury Rd nr B4054 North View
30 Bristol, Whiteladies Rd into Queens Rd
30 Westbury on Trym, Falcondale Rd

A4044
30 Bristol, Temple Way/ Redcliffe Way

A4081
40 Catbrain

A4162
30 Bristol, Sylvan Way/Dingle Rd/Canford Lane

A4174
50 Avon Ring Rd nr jct 1 M32
30 Bristol, Hartcliffe Way
40 Bristol, Hengrove Way/ Airport Rd nr Creswicke Rd
50 Filton, Filton Rd/Avon Ring Rd nr Coldharbour Lane
40 Filton, Station Rd, nr Great Stoke Way

A4320
30 Bristol, at A4 Bath Rd nr Sandy Park Rd

B3124
30 Clevedon, Walton Rd

B3130
30 Nailsea, Stockway (north)/ Chapel Avenue
30,40 Wraxall

B3133
30 Clevedon, Central Way

B3139
30,40 Mark Causeway
30 Chilcompton

B3140
30 Berrow, Coast Rd

B3141
30 East Huntspill

B3151
30 Compton Dundon
30 Ilchester
30 St, Somerton Rd

B3153
30 Keinton Mandeville (east Somerton)

B3170
30 Shoreditch Rd

B3440
30 Weston-super-Mare, Locking Rd/Regent St/Alexandra Parade

B4051
30 Bristol, Park Row/Perry Rd

B4054
30 Sea Mills, Shirehampton Rd

B4056
30 Bristol, Northumbria Drive/Linden Rd/Westbury Park
30 Bristol, Southmead Rd nr Pen Park Rd
30 Bristol, Southmead Rd nr Wellington Hill

B4057
30 Bristol, Crow Lane nr A4018 Passage Rd
30 Gypsy Patch Lane nr Hatchet Rd
50 Winterbourne Rd nr B4427 Gloucester Rd

B4058
30 Bristol, Frenchay Park Rd
30 Winterbourne, Winterbourne Hill/High St

B4059
30 Yate, Goose Green Way

B4060
30 Yate, Station Rd/Bowling Hill/Rounceval St

B4061
30 Thornbury, Bristol Rd

B4465
30 Mangotsfield, Broad St

B4465
30 Staple Hill, Staple Hill Rd/High St nr Forest Rd

Unclassified
30 Bristol, Bishopsworth, Whitchurch/Hareclive Rd
30 Bristol, Bishport Avenue
30 Knowle Bristol, Broadwalk
30 Bristol, Hengrove, Hawkfield Rd nr A4174 Hartcliffe Way
30 Bristol, Kingsway
30 Bristol, Long Cross, Lawrence Weston
30 Bristol, Stoke Hill/Stoke Rd nr Saville Rd, Clifton
30 Bristol, Sturminster Rd
30 Bristol, Whitchurch Lane nr Dundry Rd
30 Little Stoke, Little Stoke Lane
30 Taunton, Cheddon Rd
30 Taunton, Chestnut Drive
30 Taunton, Lisieux Way
30 Taunton, Trull Rd
50 Watergore, Harp Rd
30 Yeovil, Combe St

Bedfordshire and Luton

A5
60 Battlesden
40 Hockcliffe
60 Kensworth

A6
60 Gravenhurst, Barton Rd
30 Kempston, Ampthill Rd
30 Luton, New Bedford Rd
60 Pulloxhill, Barton Rd
60 Silsoe, Barton Rd

A421
50 Brogborough
60 Link Rd

A428
30 Bedford, Bromham Rd
30 Bedford, Goldington Rd

A505
30 Dunstable, Luton Rd
60 Leighton to Linslade Bypass

A507
30 Ridgmont, High St East
30 Ridgmont, High St West
60 Shefford, nr New Rd

A603
30 Bedford, Cardington Rd
30 Bedford, Lovell Rd
40 Willington

A1081
60 Luton, Airport Way

A4146
40 Leighton Buzzard, Billington Rd

A5120
40 Houghton Regis, Bedford Rd
30 Toddington, Station Rd

A5134
30 Kempston, High St

B530
60 Houghton Conquest

B1040
30 Biggleswade, Potton Rd

Unclassified
30 Bedford, Roff Avenue
30 Bromham, Stagsden Rd
30 Clapham, Highbury Grange
30 Cranfield, High St
30 Eaton Bray, Bower Lane
30 Flitwick, Ampthill Rd
30 Flitwick, Dunstable Rd
30 Heath and Reach, Woburn Rd
30 Leighton Buzzard, Heath Rd
30 Luton, Crawley Green Rd
30 Luton, Grange Avenue
30 Luton, Leagrave High St
30 Luton, Marsh Rd
30 Luton, Park Viaduct
30 Luton, Waller Avenue
30 Luton, Whitehorse Vale
30 Slip End, Markyate Rd

Berkshire

see Thames Valley

Buckinghamshire

see Thames Valley

Cambridgeshire

A14(E)
70 2km west of A1 Brampton Hut
70 East/Westbound

A15
30 New Fletton, London Rd

A47
60 Thorney Toll

A141
60 Clews Corner
60 Warboys
60 Wimblington/Doddington Bypass

A142
60 Soham Bypass
60 Witchford Bypass

A605
60 Elton, Bullock Rd
40 Kings Dyke

A1073
60 Eye Green, Peterborough Rd

A1123
60 Bluntisham, Needingworth Bypass

A1123
40 St Ives, Houghton Hill
40 Wiburton Village

A1307
70 Bartlow crossroads
30 Hills Rd
60 Linton Bypass

B645
40 Tilbrook Bends

Cheshire

A50
30 Grappenhall, Knutsford Rd
30 Knutsford, Manchester/ Toft Rd
30 Warrington, Long Lane

A54
60 Ashton, Kelsall Rd

A56
40 Lymm, Camsley Lane

A57
40 Paddington, New Manchester Rd

A523
30 Poynton, London Rd

A532
30 Crewe, West St

A533
40 Middlewich, Booth Lane

A537
50 Macclesfield, Buxton Rd nr Wildboarclough

A5019
30 Crewe, Mill St

A5032
30 Whitby, Chester Rd

A5034
60 Mere, Mereside Rd

A5104
30 Chester, Hough Green

B5071
30 Crewe, Gresty Rd

B5078
30 Alsager, Sandbach Rd North

B5082
30 Northwich, Middlewich Rd

B5132
30 Ellesmere Port, Overpool Rd

B5463
30 Little Sutton, Station Rd

B5470
30 Macclesfield, Rainow Rd

Unclassified
30 Burtonwood, Lumber Lane
30 Ellesmere Port, Overpool Rd
30 Fearnhead, Harpers Rd
30 Hough Green, Prescot Rd
30 Howley, Battersby Lane
40 Runcorn, Astmoor Rd
30 Runcorn, Boston Avenue
30 Runcorn, Clifton Rd
30 Runcorn, Halton Rd
30 Runcorn, Heath Rd
30 Runcorn, Northwich Rd
30 Runcorn, Warrington Rd
30 Vale Royal, Woodford Lane (St John's Drive)
30 Whitecross, Lovely Lane
30 Widnes, Birchfield Rd
30 Widnes, Hough Green Rd
30 Wilmslow, Hough Lane
40 Winsford, Bradford Rd

Cleveland

Darlington, Hartlepool, Middlesbrough, Redcar and Cleveland

A171
50 Redcar, Charltons

A172
40 Middlesbrough, Morton Rd from crossroads to St Lukes
30 Middlesbrough, Morton Rd from Longlands to St Lukes
40 Middlesbrough, Stokesley – from Guisborough Rd jct to Captain Cooks Crescent

A177
50,60 Stockton, Durham Rd

A178
30 Seaton Carew, The Front

A179
30 Hartlepool, Easington Rd/Powlett Rd

A689
50 to 40 Hartlepool, from Sappers Corner

B1380
40 Middlesbrough, from Marton Crossroads to Ormesby Rd
30 Redcar, Eston

Unclassified
30 Dormanstow, Broadway
30 Eaglescliffe, Yarm Rd
30 Hartlepool, Catcote Rd
40,30 Hartlepool, Coronation Drive
30 Hartlepool, Owton Manor Lane and Wynyard Rd
30 Hartlepool, Oxford Rd
30 Hartlepool, Raby Rd
30 Hartlepool, Throston Grange Lane
30 Hartlepool, Winterbottom Avenue
30 Middlesbrough, Acklam Rd
40 Middlesbrough, Acklam Rd from Blue Bell to the Crematorium
30 Middlesbrough, Mandale Rd
30 Middlesbrough, Ormesby Rd
30 Middlesbrough, Trimdon Avenue
30 Ormesby, Normanby Rd
30 Redcar, Bankfields Rd
30 Redcar, Carlin How
30 Redcar, Church Lane
30 Redcar, Flatts Lane
30 Redcar, Greenstones Rd
30,40 Redcar, Kirkleatham Lane
30 Redcar, Marske High St
30 Redcar, Normanby Rd
30 Redcar, Ormesby Bank
30 Redcar, Redcar Lane
30 Redcar, Redcar Rd
30 Redcar, Stanghow Rd
30 Redcar, West Dyke Rd
30 Seaton Carew, Seaton Lane
30 Seaton Carew, Station Lane
40 Stockton, Bishopton Avenue
30 Stockton, Bishopton Rd West
30 Stockton, Darlington Lane
30 Stockton, Harrogate Lane
30 Stockton, Junction Rd
30 Stockton, Thames Rd
30 Stockton, Thornaby Rd
30 Stockton, Whitehouse Rd
30 Thornaby, Acklam Rd
30 Thornaby, Cunningham Drive

Cumbria

M6
70 Brunthwaite
70 Capplerigg
70 Cowperthwaite
70 Tebay

A6
60 Garnett Bridge/ Hollowgate
30 Kendal, Milnthorpe Rd
30 Kendal, Shap Rd
30 London Rd
30 Penrith, Scotland Rd
60 Thiefside

A7
60 Westlinton Crossroads

A65
30 Kendal, Burton Rd
40 Kirby Lonsdale, Devils Bridge
60 Kirkby Lonsdale, Hollin Hall to Hornsbarrow

A66
60 Brigham/Broughton to Chapel Brow
60 Crackenthorpe
60 Dubwath/Bass Lake
60 Sandford Rd Ends
60 Troutbeck/Mungrisdale
60 Warcop, Brough Hill

A69
60 Aglionby
60 Scarrow Hill

A74
70 Kendal, Floriston

A590
60 Bouth Rd Ends
60 Haverthwaite/Backbarrow
70 Heaves/Levens/Gilpin
60 Newlands

A592
30,40 Rayrigg Rd

A595
60 Broughton, Wreaks End
30 Carlisle, Wigton Rd
60 Red Dial, Greenhill Hotel
60 West Woodside/ Curthwaite Jct
40 Whitehaven, Loop Rd

A596
60 Micklethwaite

A683
60 Middleton to Cautley

A685
30 Kendal, Appleby Rd

A686
60 Edenhall to Meathaw Hill

A5087
30 Ulverston

B5277
30 Grange, Lindale Rd

B5299
40 Carlisle, Dalston Rd

Unclassified
30 Carlisle, Durdar Rd / Blackwell Rd
30 Barrow in Furness, Abbey Rd
30 Barrow in Furness, Michelson Rd

Derbyshire

A6
30 Allestree
30 Alvaston to Raynesway
40 Ambergate, Matlock Rd nr Chase Rd
30 Bakewell
40 Bakewell, Buxton Rd nr Holme Lane
30 Belper
40 Darley Dale, Dale Rd North nr The Parkway
40 Darley Dale, Dale Rd North opp The Parkway
30 Derby, London Rd
30 Fairfield, Fairfield Rd nr North Rd
40 Matlock Bath to Matlock, Dale Rd nr St John's Rd
40 Matlock Bath to Matlock, Dale Rd opp No. 138
40 Rock Corner, Buxton Rd
50 Taddington to Buxton

A52
30 Derby, Ashbourne Rd
40 Mackworth

A53
30 Buxton, Station Rd o/s Railway Station
30 Buxton, Station Rd opp Railway Station

A57
30 Glossop, Dinting Vale nr Primary School
30 Glossop, Dinting Vale opp Dinting Lane
30 Glossop, High St West nr Glossop Brook Rd

A61
30 Chesterfield, Derby Rd nr Herriot Drive
30 Chesterfield, Derby Rd nr Langer Lane
50 Stretton, Main Rd nr B6014
50 Stretton, Main Rd nr Straw Lane

A444
30 Overseal, Acresford Rd nr Valley Rd
30 Overseal, Burton Rd nr Lullington Rd
30 Stanton, Woodland Rd nr Piddocks Rd
30 Stanton, Woodland Rd opp Park Rd

A511
40 Bretby, Ashby Rd East nr Greary Lane
30 Hatton, Station Rd
30 Swadlincote, Ashby Rd nr Field Lane
30 Swadlincote, Burton Rd nr Eureka Rd
30 Swadlincote, Burton Rd nr Lincoln Way
30 Swadlincote, Burton Rd nr Sandcliffe Rd
30 Swadlincote, Burton Rd nr Springfield Rd
30 Woodville, Burton Rd nr Sorrel Drive
30 Woodville, High St nr Butt Lane

A514
30 Derby, Osmaston Rd nr Keble Close
30 Derby, Osmaston Rd nr Shaftesbury St
30 Derby, Osmaston Rd opp Cotton Lane
30 Hartshorne
30 Shelton Lock, Chellaston Rd nr Shelton Drive
30 Swadlincote
40 Swadlincote to Hartshorne
30 Ticknall

A516
30 Uttoxeter, New Rd

A601
30 Derby, Abbey St

A608
30 Heanor, Church St nr Hands Rd
30 Heanor, Heanor Rd nr Peatburn Ave
30 Heanor, Mansfield Rd adj Watson Ave
30 Heanor, Mansfield Rd opp Watson Ave
30 Langley Mill, Station Rd adj Aldred's Lane
30 Smalley

A609
30 Ilkeston, Nottingham Rd opp Ashdale Rd
30 Ilkeston, Nottingham Rd opp Little Hallam Lane
30 Kilburn to Horsley Woodhouse

A610
40 Codnor Gate
40 Ripley, Nottingham Rd nr Brittain Dr

A615
60 Tansley to Wessington

A616
30 Clowne
30 Creswell

A617
40 Bramley Vale
40 Glapwell to Pleasley

A6175
30 Holmewood
30 North Wingfield

A618
30 Killamarsh, Rotherham Rd

A619
50 Barlborough, Worksop Rd nr Van Dyks Hotel
40 Brimington, Chesterfield Rd opp Lansdowne Rd
30 Brimington, Ringwood Rd nr Foljambe Rd
30 Chesterfield, Chatsworth Rd nr Chatsworth Ave
30 Chesterfield, Chatsworth Rd opp Church View
30 Chesterfield, Chatsworth Rd opp Haddon Close
30 Hollingwood, Chesterfield Rd opp Ringwood Hall
40 Mastin Moor, Worksop Rd nr Norbriggs Rd
40 Mastin Moor, Worksop Rd nr Renishaw Rd
30 Middlecroft, Chesterfield Rd nr Ringwood Ave
30 Staveley, Chesterfield Rd nr Middlecroft Rd
50 Whitwell Common, Worksop Rd opp Highwood Lane
50 Whitwell, Barlborough nr Southgate Bungalows
50 Whitwell, Clinthill Lane o/s Southgate Bungalows

A623
30 Stoney Middleton

A624
40 Hayfield, Chapel Rd nr Church
40 Hayfield, Chapel Rd nr New Mills Rd

A632
30 Bolsover
30 Bolsover, Langwith Rd
30 Calow, Top Rd o/s No.33
30 Calow, Top Rd o/s No.62
40 Duckmanton, Chesterfield Rd nr Staveley Rd
40 Duckmanton, Chesterfield Rd opp Arkwright Arms Pub
30 Langwith, Main Rd nr Langwith Drive
30 Langwith, Main Rd nr Whaley Rd
30 Matlock

A5111
40 Derby, Harvey Rd nr Cockayne St North
40 Derby, Harvey Rd nr Neilson St
40 Derby, Harvey Rd nr Wyndham St
40 Derby, Harvey Rd o/s Newsagents
40 Derby, Osmaston Park Rd nr Arkwright St

A5250
30 Derby, Burton Rd
30 Littleover, Burton Rd

A6005
30 Draycott to Breaston
30 Long Eaton, Derby Rd opp Russell St
30 Long Eaton, Nottingham Rd nr Charlton Ave
30 Long Eaton, Nottingham Rd opp Cleveland Ave
30 Spondon, Derby Rd nr Derwent Rd
30 Spondon, Derby Rd o/s Asda
30 Spondon, Nottingham Rd nr Angler's Lane

A6007
30 Codnor to Heanor
30 Heanor, Ilkeston Rd nr Westfield Ave
40 Ilkeston, Heanor Rd nr Broadway
40 Ilkeston, Heanor Rd nr Hospital
40 Ilkeston, Heanor Rd nr Woodside Crescent
40 Shipley, Hardy Barn o/s No.64
40 Shipley, Hassock Lane North nr Algrave Hall Farm
40 Shipley, Hassock Lane South nr Pitt Lane

A6096
30 Kirk Hallam, Ladywood Rd nr Godfrey Dr
30 Kirk Hallam, Ladywood Rd nr Goole Ave
30 Spondon, Dale Rd nr Dreyfus Close
30 Spondon, Dale Rd nr Wood Rd
30 Spondon, Dale Rd opp Sandringham Dr

B5010
30 Sandiacre, Derby Rd adj Brook St
30 Sandiacre, Derby Rd adj Friesland Drive
30 Sandiacre, Derby Rd adj Woodside Rd

B5036
30 Cromford, Cromford Rd

B5353
30 Newhall, Park Rd

B6002
30 Sandiacre, Longmoor Rd nr Springfield Ave
30 Sandiacre, Longmoor Rd o/s No.108
30 Sandiacre, Longmoor Rd nr Queen's Drive

B6019
30 Alfreton, Mansfield Rd nr Prospect St
30 South Normanton, Mansfield Rd nr Carter Lane West
30 South Normanton, Mansfield Rd nr Storth Lane
30 South Normanton, The Common nr Market St
30 South Normanton, The Common nr The Hamlet

B6051
30 Chesterfield, Newbold Rd
30 Newbold, Newbold Rd

B6052
30 Eckington, High St nr j/w School St
30 Eckington, West St nr j/w Fanshaw Rd
30 Whittington

B6056
30 Eckington, Dronfield Rd opp Ravenscar Rd
30 Marsh Lane, Main Rd nr School Lane
30 Marsh Lane, Main Rd o/s No.45

B6062
30 Chinley

B6179
30 Little Eaton
40 Lower Kilburn
50 Lower Kilburn to Little Eaton
30 Ripley to Marehay

B6407
30 Shirebrook, Portland Rd adj Ashbourne St
30 Shirebrook, Portland Rd opp Ashbourne St

B6540
30 Long Eaton, Tamworth Rd nr Charles St
30 Long Eaton, Tamworth Rd nr Wyvern Ave
30 Long Eaton, Tamworth Rd opp Draycott Rd
30 Long Eaton, Tamworth Rd opp No.559
30 Long Eaton, Tamworth Rd opp Shaftesbury Ave

Unclassified
30 Chaddesden, Nottingham Rd nr No.427 (Cemetery)
30 Chaddesden, Nottingham Rd nr Pentagon Island
30 Chaddesden, Nottingham Rd o/s No.590 (Cherry Tree)
30 Charlesworth, Long Lane
30 Chesterfield, Boythorpe Rd
30 Chesterfield, Linacre Rd
30 Chesterfield, Old Rd
30 Denby, St Lane
30 Derby, Blagraves Lane
30 Derby, Kedleston Rd
30 Derby, Stenson Rd
30 Langley Mill, Upper Dunstead Rd
30 Shardlow, London Rd
40 Stenson Fields, Stenson Rd
30 Swadlincote, Hearthcote Rd

Devon and Cornwall

A30
60 Chiverton Cross
70 Highgate (Eastbound)
70 Highgate Hill
40 Sowton
60 Temple

A38
70 Bittaford Straight, Wrangaton
70 Deep Lane
70 Lee Mill, Lee Mill On-slip
70 Lower Clicker Tor
70 Smithaleigh
70 Smithaleigh, Smithaleigh Overbridge
70 Wrangaton, Bittaford Straight

A39
60 Barras Moor
30 Camelford, Valley Truckle
40 Perranarworthal, nr Truro

A361
50 Ashford
30 Barnstaple, Eastern Avenue
40 Knowle
30 Knowle (Westerland)
30 Wrafton

A374
30 Ebford
40 Plymouth, Plymouth Rd (Inbound)
40 Plymouth, Plymouth Rd (Outbound)
30 Torpoint, Anthony Rd

A376
30 Exmouth, Exeter Rd

A377
30 Copplestone
30 Crediton, Western Rd
30 Exeter, Alphington Rd

A379
30 Brixton Village
30 Paignton, Dartmouth Rd
30 Starcross
30 Starcross, The Strand
30 Teignmouth, Teignmouth Rd
30 Torquay, Babbacombe Rd
30 Yealmpton

A380
40 Kingskerswell, Newton Rd

A381
30 Newton Abbott, East St

A385
30 Collaton St Mary, Totnes Rd
30 Totnes, Ashburton Rd

A386
60 Chubb Tor
30 Plymouth, Outland Rd
60 Plymouth, Roborough Down
40 Plymouth, Tavistock Rd

A388
30 Kelly Bray

A390
60 Penstraze
60 Sticker Bypass

A394
40 Kenneggy Downs

A396
30 Rewe
30 Stoke Canon, Exeter Rd

A3015
30 Exeter, Topsham Rd

A3047
30 Carbis Bay
30 Pool, Trevenson Rd
30 Tuckingmill

A3058
30 Trewoon

A3064
30 Plymouth, St Budeaux Bypass

A3075
60 Rosecliston

B3165
30 Raymonds Hill, Crewkerne Rd

B3174
30 Ottery St Mary, Barrack Rd

B3183
30 Exeter, Heavitree Rd
30 Exeter, New North Rd

B3212
30 Exeter, Dunsford Rd
30 Exeter, Pinhoe Rd

B3213
30 Wrangaton Village, nr South Brent

B3233
30 Barnstaple, Bickington Rd

B3250
30 Plymouth, North Hill

B3284
60 Liskey
30 Liskey, Perranporth
30 Chudleigh, Station Hill

B3396
30 Plymouth, Milehouse Rd

Unclassified
30 Avonwick Village
30 Buddle Lane, Exwick Rd
30 Elburton, Haye Rd
30 Exeter, Exwick Lane
30 Fraddon Village, nr Indian Queens
60 Goss Moor, Castle an Dinas
30 Honicknowle, Shakespeare Rd
30 Ivybridge, Exeter Rd
40 Monkton Village
30 Paignton, Colley End Rd
30 Paignton, Preston Down Rd
30 Plymouth, Beacon Park Rd
30 Plymouth, Church Hill
30 Plymouth, Devonport Rd
30 Plymouth, Eggbuckland Rd
30 Plymouth, Glen Rd
30 Plymouth, Honicknowle Lane
30 Plymouth, Honicknowle Lane (North)
30 Plymouth, Lipson Rd
30 Plymouth, Mannamead Rd
30 Plymouth, Molesworth Rd
30 Plymouth, North Prospect Rd
40 Plymouth, Novorrossiysk Rd
30 Plymouth, Pomphlett Rd
30 Plymouth, Southway Drive
30 Plymouth, St Levan Rd
30 Plymouth, Tamerton Foliot Rd
30 Plymouth, Union St
30 Plymouth, Weston Park Rd
30 Plymouth, Wolseley Rd (Both Directions)
30 Plympton, Glen Rd
30 Saltash, Callington Rd
30 St Judes, Grenville Rd

Dorset

A30
70 Babylon Hill
40 Shaftesbury, Long Cross

A31
40 Winterbourne Zelston

A35
60 Bridport, Crabb Dykes nr Whiteway Cross
60 btwn Morden Mill & Slepe
70 Christchurch Bypass
60 Dorchester, Friary Press
60 Kingston Russell
60 Lyndhurst Rd
50 Lytchett Minster, Bakers Arms
30 Poole, Upton Rd
40 Sea Rd South
60 Vinney Cross

A37
60 Holywell Cross
60 Long Ash Lane
60 Staggs Folly

A338
50 Cooper Dean, Wessex Way
70 Spur Rd

A348
40 Bear Cross, Ringwood Rd

A349
40 Poole, Gravell Hill

A350
50 Holes Bay Rd to Sterte Rd
60 Poole Rd
70 Poole, Upton Country Park
30 Stourpaine, Shashton Rd

A352
30 Wool, Dorchester Rd

A354
30 Dorchester Rd Manor Rdbt
40 Redlands, Dorchester Rd
60 Ridgeway Hill, Dorchester Rd
30 Upwey, Dorchester Rd
30 Weymouth, Buxton Rd
30 Whitechurch, Winterbourne

B3065
30 Poole, Pinecliff Rd
30 Poole, The Avenue

B3073
40 West Parley, Christchurch Rd
30 Wimborne, Oakley Hill

B3074
30 Poole, Higher Blandford Rd

B3081
30 Ebblake, Ringwood Rd

B3082
60 Bradbury Rings, Blandford Rd

B3092
n/a Gillingham, Colesbrook

B3157
30 Lanehouse Rocks Rd
50 Limekiln Hill
30 Portesham

B3369
30 Poole, Sandbanks Rd
30 Poole, Shore Rd

Unclassified
30 Blandford, Salisbury Rd
30 Bournemouth, Branksome Wood Rd
30 Bournemouth, Crabery Avenue
30 Bournemouth, Littledown Avenue
30 Bournemouth, Southbourne Overcliff Drive
30 Poole, Old Wareham Rd
30 Portland, Weston Rd
40 Staplehill, Wimbourne Rd
30 Upton, Poole Rd
30 Weymouth, Chickerell Rd

Durham

A66
Bowes Moor/Galley Bank/Greta Bridge

A67
Conniscliffe

A167
Chester-le-St, North Lodge
Darlington, North Rd
Durham, Whitesmocks and Tollhouse Rd

A690
Crook, Low Willington to West Rd
Durham, West Rainton

A1086
Crimdon to Horden

B6188
Dipton, New Kyo to Flint Hill

B6280
Darlington, Yarm Rd

B6282
Bishop Auckland, Etherley and B6284 Ediscum Garth

B6288
Spennymoor/A167 Croxdale

Unclassifed
Darlington, McMullen Rd
Durham, Finchale Rd
Peterlee, Essington Way

Essex

A12
Braintree, Overbridge nr Kelvedon Interchange

A13
30 Castle Point, High St (Hadleigh twds London)
30 Leigh on Sea, London Rd
Southend, Bournes Green Chase
Southend, North Shoebury Rd
Southend, Southchurch Boulevard

A113
30 Epping, High Rd

A120
Little Bentley, Pellens Corner

A121
30 Epping, High Rd
30 Loughton, Goldings Hill (j/w Monkchester Close)
Loughton, High Rd
Waltham Abbey, Farm Hill Rd
Waltham Abbey, Sewardstine Rd

A126
30 Grays, London Rd
30 Tilbury, Montreal Rd

A128
Chipping Ongar, High St
30 Ingrave/Herongate, Brentwood Rd

A129
30 Basildon, Crays Hill
Billericay, Southend Rd
Rayleigh, London Rd
30 Wickford, London Rd
Wickford, Southend Rd

A130
30 Canvey Island, Long Rd
South Benfleet, Canvey Way

A133
30 Elmstead Market, Clacton Rd

A133
Little Bentley, Colchester Rd

A134
40 Great Horkesley, Nayland Rd

A137
30 Lawford, Wignall St

A1016
30 Chelmsford, Waterhouse Lane

A1017
30 Sible Hedingham, Swan St

A1023
30 Brentwood, Chelmsford Rd
30 Brentwood, London Rd
30 Brentwood, Shenfield Rd

A1025
40 Harlow, Third Avenue

A1060
Little Hallingbury, Lower Rd

A1090
30 Purfleet, London Rd
30 Purfleet, Tank Hill Rd

A1124
30 Colchester, Lexden Rd

A1158
30 Westcliff on Sea, Southbourne Grove

A1168
30 Loughton, Rectors Lane

A1169
40 Harlow, Southern Way

A1205
40 Harlow, Second Avenue

B170
Loughton, Roding Lane
Chigwell, Chigwell Rise

B172
Theydon Bois, Coppice Row

B173
Chigwell, Lambourne Rd

B184
40 Great Easton, Snow Hill

B186
30 South Ockendon, South Rd

B1002
30 Ingatestone, High St

B1007
30 Billericay, Laindon Rd
40 Chelmsford, Stock Rd

B1007
30 Billericay, Stock Rd

B1008
30 Chelmsford, Broomfield Rd

B1013
30 Hawkwell, High Rd
30 Hawkwell, Main Rd
30 Hockley/Hawkwell, Southend Rd
Rayleigh, High Rd
30 Rayleigh, Hockley Rd

B1014
30 South Benfleet, Benfleet Rd

B1018
30 Latchingdon, The St
30 Maldon, The Causeway

B1019
30 Hatfield Peveral, Maldon Rd

B1021
Burnham on Crouch, Church Rd

B1022
30 Colchester, Maldon Rd
30 Heckfordbridge, Maldon Rd
30 Maldon, Colchester Rd
30 Tiptree Heath, Maldon Rd

B1027
30 Clacton-on-Sea, Valley Rd/Old Rd
30 St Osyth, Pump Hill
40 Wivenhoe, Brightlingsea Rd

B1028
30 Wivenhoe, Colchester Rd
30 Wivenhoe, The Avenue

B1033
30 Kirby Cross, Frinton Rd

B1335
40 South Ockendon, Stifford Rd

B1352
Harwich, Main Rd

B1383
30 Newport, London Rd
Stansted Mountfitchet, Cambridge Rd

B1389
30 Witham, Colchester Rd
30 Witham, Hatfield Rd

B1393
30 Epping, Palmers Hill

B1441
30 Clacton-on-Sea, London Rd

B1442
30 Clacton-on-Sea, Thorpe Rd

B1464
30 Bowers Gifford, London Rd

Unclassified
40 Alresford, St Osyth Rd
30 Aveley, Purfleet Rd
Aveley, Romford Rd
30 Barstable, Sandon Rd
30 Basildon, Ashlyns
40 Basildon, Cranes Farm Rd (j/w Honywood Rd)
Basildon, Crayhill Rd
30 Basildon, Felmores
Basildon, London Rd, Wickford
30 Basildon, Vange Hill Drive
30 Basildon, Whitmore Way
30 Basildon, Wickford Avenue
30 Billericay, Mountnessing Rd
30 Bowers Gifford, London Rd
30 Braintree, Coldnailhurst Avenue
30 Brentwood, Eagle Way (nr j/w Clive Rd twds Warley Rd)
30 Buckhurst Hill, Buckhurst Way/Albert Rd
30 Canvey Island, Dovervelt Rd
30 Canvey Island, Link Rd
30 Canvey Island, Thorney Bay Rd
Chadwell St Mary, Brentwood Rd
30 Chadwell St Mary, Linford Rd
30 Chadwell St Mary, Riverview
30 Chelmsford, Baddow Rd
30 Chelmsford, Chignall Rd
30 Chelmsford, Copperfield Rd
Chelmsford, Galleywood Rd
30 Chelmsford, Longstomps Avenue
30 Clacton-on-Sea, St Johns Rd
30 Clacton, Kings Parade
30 Clacton, Marine Parade East
30 Colchester, Abbots Rd
30 Colchester, Avon Way
30 Colchester, Bromley Rd
Colchester, Ipswich Rd
30 Colchester, Old Heath Rd
30 Colchester, Shrub End Rd
30 Corringham, Southend Rd
30 Corringham, Springhouse Rd
Danbury, Maldon Rd
30 Daws Heath, Daws Heath Rd
30 Eastwood, Green Lane j/w Kendal Way
30 Eastwood, Western Approaches j/w Rockall
30 Grays, Blackshots Lane
30 Grays, Lodge Lane
Grays, London Rd (nr Angel Rd)
Grays, London Rd (nr Bransons Way)
40 Harlow, Abercrombie Way, twds Southern Way
40 Harlow, Howard Way
30 Hullbridge, Coventry Hill
30 Laindon, Durham Rd
30 Laindon, Nightingales
30 Laindon, Wash Rd
Langdon Hills, High Rd
30 Leigh on Sea, Belton Way East
30 Leigh on Sea, Belton Way West
30 Leigh on Sea, Blenhelm Chase
30 Leigh on Sea, Grand Parade/Cliff Parade
30 Leigh on Sea, Hadleigh Rd
30 Leigh on Sea, Highlands Boulevard
30 Leigh on Sea, Manchester Drive
30 Leigh on Sea, Mountdale Gardens
30 Leigh on Sea, Western Rd
30 Loughton, Alderton Hill
30 Loughton, Loughton Way
Loughton, Valley Hill
30 Maldon, Fambridge Rd
30 Maldon, Holloway Rd
30 Maldon, Mundon Rd
30 Pitsea, Rectory Rd
30 Prittlewell, Kenilworth Gardens
30 Prittlewell, Prittlewell Chase
30 Rayleigh, Bull Lane
Rayleigh, Downhall Rd
30 Rayleigh, Trinity Rd, nr Church Rd
30 Rochford, Ashingdon Rd
30 Rochford, Rectory Rd
Rush Green, St Osyth Rd
30 Shoeburyness, Ness Rd
30 South Woodham Ferrers, Hullbridge Rd
30 South Woodham Ferrers, Inchbonnie Rd
30 Southend on Sea, Lifstan Way
Southend, Bournemouth Park Rd
30 Southend, Hamstel Rd
Southend, Western Esplanade/Westcliff on Sea
30 Southend, Woodgrange Drive j/w Sandringham Rd
30 Springfield, New Bowers Way
30 Stanford le Hope, London Rd
30 Tendring, Burrs Rd, Clacton
Tendring, Harwich Rd, Wix Arch Cottages to Cansey Lane
Theydon Bois, Piercing Hill
30 Thorpe Bay, Barnstaple Rd
30 Thorpe Bay, Thorpe Hall Avenue
Waltham Abbey, Paternoster Hill
Weeley Heath, Clacton Rd
30 West Thurrock, London Rd
30 Westcliff on Sea, Chalkwell Avenue
30 Westcliff on Sea, Kings Rd
30 Wickford, Radwinter Avenue
30 Witham, Powers Hall End
30 Witham, Rickstones Rd

Gloucestershire

A38
40 Twigworth

A40
60 Andoversford
50 Churcham
60 Farmington
40 Gloucester Rd
60 Hampnett
60 Hazleton
60 Northleach
60 The Barringtons
60 Whittington Area

A46
30 Ashchurch
40 North of Nailsworth

A48
60 Stroat

A417
70 Burford Jct
40 Corse, Gloucester Rd
70 Dartley Bottom
40 Lechlade
30 Maisemore
40 North of Hartpury

A419
40 Oldends Lane to Stonehouse Court

A429
60 Nr Bourton-on-the-Water
40 Fossebridge

A430
40 Hempsted Bypass

A435
60 Colesbourne

A436
60 Jct with B4068

A4013
30 Gloucester, Princess Elizabeth Way
30 Gloucester, Princess Elizabeth Way (Arle)

A4019
50 Uckington

A4136
40 Brierley
40 Coleford, Lower Lane
40 Harrow Hill
40 Little London

A4151
40 Steam Mills

A4173
30 nr St Peters School

B4008
40 Hardwicke, Bristol Rd south of Tesco rdbt
30 Olympus Park Area, Bristol Rd
30 Stonehouse, Gloucester Rd

B4060
30 Katharine Lady Berkeley's School

B4215
50 South east of Rudford
50 South of Newent Bypass

B4221
30 Picklenash School
40 Kilcot Village

B4226
60 Speech House

B4228
30 Coleford, Old Station Way
40 Perrygrove

B4231
30 Bream, Coleford Rd

B4633
30 Cheltenham, Gloucester Rd

Unclassified
30 Gloucester, Abbeymead Avenue
30 Gloucester, Barrow Hill
30 Gloucester, Chesterton Lane
30 Gloucester, Parkend Fancy Rd
30 Gloucester, St Georges Rd
30 Gloucester, Swindon Lane
30 Gloucester, Wymans Lane
30 Lydney, Highfield Rd
40 Minchinhampton Common
30 Siddington
40 Tewkesbury, Gloucester Rd

Greater Manchester

A6
Manchester, Stockport Rd
Salford, Manchester Rd

A34
Manchester, Birchfield Road

A49
Marus Bridge, Warrington Rd

A56
Bury, Bury New Rd
Bury, Walmersley Rd
Bury, Whalley Rd

A57
Manchester, Hyde Rd
Salford, Liverpool Rd
Tameside, Manchester Rd

A58
Bury, Bury & Bolton Rd
Bury, Rochdale Rd

A62
Manchester, Oldham Rd
Oldham, Oldham Rd
Oldham, Oldham Way

A575
Salford, Walkden Rd

A580
Salford, East Lancashire Rd

A627
Oldham, Chadderton Way
Oldham, Ashton Rd

A662
Manchester, Ashton New Rd

A663
Oldham, Broadway

A664
Manchester, Rochdale Rd

A665
Bury, New Rd
Bury, Radcliffe New Rd

A666
Bolton, Blackburn Rd
Bolton, St Peter's Way
Salford, Manchester Rd

A667
Bury, Ringley Rd West

A5103
Manchester, Princess Parkway/Road

A6010
Manchester, Alan Turing Way

A6044
Prestwich, Sheepfoot Lane
Prestwich, Hilton Lane

A6053
Radcliffe, Dumers Lane

A6104
Blackley, Victoria Avenue

B6196
Ainsworth, Church Street
Ainsworth, Cockey Moor Rd

B6213
Tottington, Turton Rd

B6214
Greenmount, Brandlesholme Rd
Holcombe, Helmshore Rd
Holcombe Brook, Longsight Rd

B6226
Horwich, Chorley Old Rd

Unclassified
Ashton on Mersey, Ashton Lane
Bolton, Chorley Old Rd
Bolton, Hardy Mill Rd
Bolton, Hulton Lane
Bolton, Lever Park Avenue
Bolton, Plodder Lane
Bolton, Stitch Mi Lane
Bredbury, Ashton Rd
Bury, Croft Lane
Bury, Higher Lane
Bury, Stand Lane
Bury, Walshaw Rd
Manchester, Blackley New Rd
Manchester, Kingsway
Manchester, Mancunian Way
Oldham, Abbey Hills Rd
Oldham, Manchester Rd
Rochdale, Bagslate Moor Rd
Rochdale, Broad Lane
Rochdale, Bury Old Rd
Rochdale, Caldershaw Rd
Rochdale, Edenfield Rd
Rochdale, Halifax Rd
Rochdale, Heywood Old Rd
Rochdale, Hollin Lane
Rochdale, Manchester Rd
Rochdale, Queens Park Rd
Rochdale, Shawclough Rd
Rochdale, Smithybridge Rd
Rochdale, Todmorden Rd
Rochdale, Wildhouse Lane
Salford, Belvedere Rd
Salford, Langley Rd
Stockport, Birdhall Lane
Stockport, Bridge Lane
Stockport, Buxton Rd
Stockport, Chester Rd
Stockport, Councillor Lane
Stockport, Dialstone Lane
Stockport, Harrytown
Stockport, Jacksons Lane
Stockport, Kingsway
Stockport, Longhurst Lane
Stockport, Marple Rd
Stockport, Sandy Lane
Stockport, Schools Hill
Stockport, Strines Rd
Stockport, Styal Rd
Stockport, Wellington Rd North
Tameside, Mossley Rd
Tameside, Mottram Old Rd
Tameside, Mottram Rd
Tameside, Stamford Rd
Tameside, Stamford Street
Trafford, Church Rd
Trafford, Edge Lane
Trafford, Glebelands Rd
Trafford, Hope Rd
Trafford, Mosley Rd
Trafford, Norris Rd
Trafford, Park Rd
Trafford, Seymour Grove
Trafford, Warburton Lane
Trafford, Westinghouse Rd
Wigan, Almond Brook Rd
Wigan, Bickershaw Lane
Wigan, Bolton Rd
Wigan, Chaddock Lane
Wigan, Chorley Rd
Wigan, Crow Orchard Rd
Wigan, Lily Lane
Wigan, Newton Rd
Wigan, Pemberton Rd
Wigan, Scot Lane
Wigan, Victoria Street
Wigan, Wigan Rd

Hampshire and Isle of Wight

A3
70 Liphook
30 Petersfield

A27
40 Fareham (east and west bound)
30 Fareham, Portchester Rd (eastbound)
30 Fareham, Portchester Rd (westbound)
30 Fareham, The Avenue

A30
30 Blackwater
30 Hook, London Rd

A32
30 West Meon

A33
50 Basingstoke
50 Chandlers Green
50 Sherfield on Loddon
50 Southampton, Millbrook Rd (western end of Flyover to Regents Park Rd)
30 West Quay Rd

A35
50 Totton

A325
40 East Hampshire (south)
70 Farnborough, Farnborough Rd
40 Rushmoor (north)

A334/B2177
40 Wickham

A335
30 Eastleigh

A337
30 New Forest (east)
40 New Forest (west)

A338
40 New Forest (south and north bound)

A339
60 Lasham

A340
30 Basingstoke
30 Tadley

A343
30 Hurstbourne Tarrant

A3020
40 Blackwater Rd

A3024
40 Bursledon Rd
30 Northam Rd to southern river bank

A3054
30 Newport, Fairlee Rd
30 Wootton / Lushington Hill, High St

B3037/A335
30,40 Eastleigh

B3055
40 New Forest

B3395
30 Sandown, Culver Parade

Unclassified
30 Apse Heath
30 Binstead Hill
30 Brading, High St New Rd
30 East Cowes, Victoria Grove/Adelaide Grove
30 East Cowes, York Avenue
40 Fareham, Western Way
30 Fleet, Reading Rd South
30 Newport, Staplers Rd/Long Lane
30 Portsmouth, Northern Rd (north and south bound)
40 Southampton, The Avenue (north and south bound)
30 Swanick, Swanick Lane
50 Totton / Redbridge, Redbridge Flyover

Herefordshire

see West Mercia

Hertfordshire

A119
30 Hertford, North Rd

A409
30 Bushey, Heathbourne Rd

A411
30 Bushey, London Rd
30 Elstree, Barnet Lane
30 Watford, Hempstead Rd

A414
40 Hemel Hempstead, St Albans Rd
40 Hertford, Hertingfordbury Rd

A505
30 Hitchin, Cambridge Rd

A600
30 Hitchin, Bedford Rd

A602
40 Hitchin, Stevenage Rd
40 Stevenage, Broadhall Way
40 Stevenage, Monkswood Way

A1000
40 Bishops Stortford, Barnet Rd

A1057
40 Hatfield, St Albans Rd West
30 St Albans, Hatfield Rd

A1170
30 Turnford, High Rd

A4125
40 South Oxhey, Sandy Lane
30 Watford, Eastbury Rd

A4145
30 Watford, Tolpits Lane

A4147
30 Hemel Hempstead, Leverstock Green Rd

A4251
30 Bourne End, London Rd

A5183
30 St Albans, Frogmore Rd

A6141
60 Letchworth, Letchworth Gate

B156
30 Cheshunt, Goffs Lane

B176
30 Cheshunt, High Street

B197
30 Baldock, London Rd
30 Stevenage, North Rd

B462
30 Bushey, Aldenham Rd

B487
30 Harpenden, Redbourn Lane
40 Hemel Hempstead, Queensway

B488
40 Tring, Icknield Way

B556
30 Potters Bar, Mutton Lane

B1004
30 Bishops Stortford, Windhill

B1197
30 Hertford, London Rd

B1502
30 Hertford, Stansted Rd

B4505
30 Bovingdon, Chesham Rd

B4630
30 St Albans, Watford Rd

B5378
30 Elstree, Allum Lane
40 London Colney, Shenleybury

B6426
30 Hatfield, Cavendish Way

Unclassified
30 Cheshunt, Hammond St Rd
30 Hemel Hempstead, Bennetts End Rd
30 Hemel Hempstead, High Street Green
30 Hemel Hempstead, Long Chaulden
30 Hoddesdon, Essex Rd
30 Letchworth, Pixmore Way
30 Royston, Old North Rd
30 South Oxhey, Hayling Rd
30 St Albans, Sandpit Lane
30 Stevenage, Clovelly Way
30 Stevenage, Grace Way
40 Stevenage, Gresley Way
30 Watford, Radlett Rd
30 Watford, Whippendell Rd
30 Welwyn Garden City, Heronswood Rd
30 Welwyn Garden City, Howlands

Humberside

East Riding of Yorkshire, Hull, North East Lincolnshire, North Lincolnshire

M180
70 North Lincolnshire, West of River Trent

A18
60 North East Lincolnshire, Barton St Central
60 North East Lincolnshire, Barton St North
60 North East Lincolnshire, Barton St South
30 North Lincolnshire, Wrawby

A63
50 East Riding, Melton
40 Hull, Castle St
40 Hull, Daltry St Flyover

A161
30 Belton

A163
30 Holme on Spalding Moor

A164
30 Leconfield

A165
30 Beeford
40 East Riding, Coniston
30 Freetown Way
40 Holderness Rd
30 Skirlaugh

A180
70 Great Coates Jct

A614
40 Holme on Spalding Moor
30 Middleton on the Wolds
60 Shiptonthorpe, north of rdbt
60 Shiptonthorpe, south of the village

A1033
40 Thomas Clarkson Way
30 Thorngumbald, Main St
30 Withernsea

A1077
30 Barton

A1079
50 Barmby Moor
30 Bishop Burton
30 Hull, Beverley Rd (Desmond Ave to Riverdale Rd)
40 Hull, Beverley Rd (Sutton Rd to Mizzen Rd)

A1084
30 Brigg, Bigby High Rd

A1174
30 Dunswell
30 Woodmansey

B1206
30 Barrow, Wold Rd

B1230
40 Gilberdyke
40 Newport

B1398
40 Greetwell

Unclassified
30 Ashby, Grange Lane South
30 Ashby, Messingham Rd
30 Belton, Westgate Rd
30 Beverley, Hull Bridge Rd
30 Bilton, Main Rd
30 Bridlington, Kingsgate
30 Bridlington, Quay Rd/St John's St
30 Broughton, High St
30 Cleethorpes, Clee Rd
30 East Halton, College Rd
30 Goole, Airmyn Rd
30 Grimsby, Cromwell Rd
30 Grimsby, Great Coates Rd
30 Grimsby, Laceby Rd
30 Grimsby, Louth Rd
30 Grimsby, Waltham Rd
30 Grimsby, Weelsby Rd
30 Hessle, Beverley Rd
30 Hornsea, Rolston Rd
30 Howden, Thorpe Rd
30 Hull, Anlaby Rd
40 Hull, Boothferry Rd
30 Hull, Bricknell Avenue
30 Hull, Greenwood Avenue
30 Hull, Hall Rd
30 Hull, John Newton Way/Bude Rd
30 Hull, Leads Rd
30 Hull, Marfleet Lane
30 Hull, Marfleet Lane/Marfleet Avenue
30 Hull, Priory Rd
30 Hull, Saltshouse Rd
40 Hull, Spring Bank West
30 Hull, Wawne Rd
30 Humberston, Tetney Rd
30 Immingham, Pelham Rd
70 Laceby Bypass
30 Preston, Station Rd
30 Scunthorpe, Ashby Rd
30 Scunthorpe, Cambridge Avenue
30 Scunthorpe, Cottage Beck Rd
40 Scunthorpe, Doncaster Rd
30 Scunthorpe, Luneburg Way
40 Scunthorpe, Queensway
30 Scunthorpe, Rowland Rd
30 South Killingholme, Top Rd
30 Yaddlethorpe, Moorwell Rd

Kent and Medway

A2
70 Canterbury
60 Dover, Guston
70 Dover, Lydden
40 Medway, London Rd

A20
70,40 Dover, Dover Rd/Archcliffe
40,50 Tonbridge and Malling, London Rd

A21
70 Sevenoaks Bypass
60 Tonbridge and Malling, Castle Hill
60 Tunbridge Wells, Key's Green

A25
30 Sevenoaks, Seal Rd

A26
40 Tonbridge and Malling, Maidstone Rd

A28
40 Ashford, Ashford Rd

A224
30 Sevenoaks, Tubs Hill

A225
30 Sevenoaks, Sevenoaks Rd

A226
50 Gravesham, Rochester Rd/Gravesend Rd through Chalk
50 Gravesham, Rochester Rd/Gravesend Rd through Shorne
40 Gravesham, Rochester Rd/Gravesend Rd through Higham

A227
30 Gravesham, through Culverstone Green
40 Gravesham, through Istead Rise
30 Gravesham, through Meopham Green

A228
40 Medway, Ratcliffe Highway

A229
50 Maidstone, Bluebell Hill
40,30 Maidstone, Linton Rd/Loose Rd
30 Medway, City Way
40 Tunbridge Wells, Angley Rd (Hartley Rd)

A249
70 Maidstone, Chalky Rd/Rumstead Lane, South St
70 Swale, Chestnut St

A253
30 Thanet, Canterbury Rd West

A256
70 Dover
30 Dover, London Rd
40 Thanet, Haine Rd

A258
50 Dover, Dover Rd

A259
40 Shepway
60 Shepway, Guldeford Lane
30 Shepway, High St

A262
30 Ashford, High St

A268
30 Tunbridge Wells, Queen St

A289
50 Medway, Medway Tunnel
70 Medway, Wainscott Bypass

A290
30 Canterbury, Blean

A291
30 Canterbury, Canterbury Rd

A292
30 Ashford, Mace Lane

A2033
30 Shepway, Dover Rd

A2990
60 Canterbury, Old Thanet Way

B258
30 Dartford, Barn End Lane

B2015
40 Nettlestead Green, Maidstone Rd

B2017
30 Tunbridge Wells, Badsell Rd

B2067
60 Ashford, Ashford Rd
30 Ashford, Woodchurch Rd

B2071
30 Shepway, Littlestone Rd

B2097
30 Rochester, Maidstone Rd

B2205
30 Swale, Mill Way

Unclassified
30 Canterbury, Mickleburgh Hill
30 Canterbury, Rough Common Rd
30 Dartford, Ash Rd/Hartley Rd
30 Gravesham, Sole St
30 Medway, Beechings Way
30 Medway, Esplanade
30 Medway, Maidstone Rd
30 Medway, St End Rd
30 Medway, Walderslade Rd
30 Sevenoaks, Ash Rd/Hartley Rd
30 Swale, Lower Rd
30 Thanet, Shottendane Rd

Lancashire

A6
40 Broughton, Garstang Rd (north of M55)
30 Chorley, Bolton Rd
30 Fulwood, Garstang Rd (south of M55)
30 Fulwood, Garstang Rd, north of Blackpool Rd
30 Lancaster, Greaves Rd
50 Lancaster, Scotforth Rd nr Burrow Lane Bailrigg
30 Preston, North Rd
30 Preston, Ringway

A56
30 Colne, Albert Rd
30 Colne, Burnley Rd
30 Nelson, Leeds Rd

A59
60 Gisburn, Gisburn Rd
50 Hutton, Liverpool Rd
30 Preston, New Hall Lane

A65
40 Lancaster, Cowan Bridge

A570
40 Scarisbrick, Southport Rd, Brook House Farm

A581
40 Ulnes Walton, Southport Rd

A583+A5073
30 Blackpool, Whitegate Drive/Waterloo Rd

A583+B5266
30 Blackpool, Church St/Newton Drive

A584
30 Blackpool, Promenade
30 Lytham, West/Central Beach
30 Warton, Lytham Rd

A584+A587
30 Blackpool, Promenade/Fleetwood Rd

A587
30 Blackpool, East/North Park Drive
30 Cleveleys, Rossall Rd/Crescent East

A588
60 Pilling, Head Dyke Lane
60 Wyre, Lancaster Rd, Cockerham at Gulf Lane

A666
30 Darwen, Blackburn Rd
30 Darwen, Bolton Rd nr Cross St
30 Darwen, Duckworth St

A671
30 Read, Whalley Rd

A674
30 Cherry Tree, Preston Old Rd

A675
50 Belmont, Belmont Rd (south of village)
50 Darwen, Belmont Rd, north of Belmont Village
60 Withnell, Bolton Rd (Dole Lane to Calf Hey Bridge)

A680
40 Edenfield, Rochdale Rd

A682
60 Barrowford, Gisburn Rd nr Moorcock Inn
30 Brierfield, Colne Rd
40 Crawshawbooth, Burnley Rd
60 Gisburn, Gisburn Rd
60 Gisburn, Long Preston Rd

A683
30 Lancaster, Morecambe Rd

A5073
30 Blackpool, Waterloo Rd

A5085
30 Lane Ends, Blackpool Rd

A5209
30 Newburgh, Course Lane/Ash Brow

A6068
50 Barrowford, Barrowford Rd

A6114
30 Burnley, Casterton Avenue

A6177
50 Haslingden, Grane Rd West of Holcombe Rd
50 Hyndburn, Haslingden Rd/Elton Rd

B5192
30 Kirkham, Preston St

B5251
30 Chorley, Pall Mall

B5254
30 Lostock Hall, Leyland Rd/Watkin Lane
30 South Ribble, Leyland Rd (north of Talbot Rd to A59 Golden Way Rdbt, Penwortham)

B5256
30 Leyland, Turpin Green Lane

B5269
40 Goosnargh, Whittingham Lane

B6231
30 Oswaldtwistle, Union Rd

Unclassified
60 Belmont, Egerton Rd
30 Blackburn, East Park Rd
30 Blackburn, Whalley Old Rd, west of Railway Bridge
30 Blackpool, Dickson Rd, Queens St to Pleasant St
30 Briercliffe, Burnley Rd
30 Darwen, Lower Eccleshill Rd
60 Galgate, Bay Horse Rd
30 Nelson, Netherfield Rd
30 Preston, Lytham Rd
30 Preston, St Georges Rd
30 St Anne's, Church Rd to Albany Rd, nr High School

Leicestershire and Rutland

A1
70 Empingham, Great North Rd
70 Stretton, Great North Rd

A5
60 Hinckley, Watling St (B578 to M69)
50 Hinckley, Watling St (M69 to A47)
70 Sharnford, Watling St (Highcross to B4114)

A6
40 Birstall, Loughborough Rd
40 Leicester, Abbey Lane
30 Leicester, London Rd (Knighton Drive)
30 Loughborough, Derby Rd
40 Oadby, Glen Rd/Harborough Rd

A47
60 Barrowden, Peterborough Rd
60 Bisbrooke, Uppingham Rd
30 Earl Shilton, Hinckley Rd
40 Houghton on the Hill, Uppingham Rd
30 Leicester, Hinckley Rd
30 Leicester, Humberstone Rd
50 Morcott, Glaston Rd
50 Skeffington, Uppingham Rd
50 Tugby, Uppingham Rd

A50
70 Hemmington to Lockington
40 Leicester/Glenfield, Groby Rd/Leicester Rd
30 Woodgate

A426
50 Dunton Bassett, Lutterworth Rd
40 Glen Parva, Leicester Rd
60 Lutterworth, Leicester Rd
60 Whetstone, Lutterworth Rd

A444
60 Fenny Drayton, Atherstone Rd
30 Twycross Village, Main St
60 Twycross, Norton Juxta

A447
60 Cadeby, Hinckley Rd
40 Ravenstone, Wash Lane

A512
30 Loughborough, Ashby Rd
40 Shepshed, Ashby Rd Central

A563
30 Leicester, Attlee Way
30 Leicester, Colchester Rd/Hungarton Boulevard
30 Leicester, Glenhills Way
40 Leicester, Krefield Way
30 Leicester, New Parks Way

A594
30 Leicester, St Georges Way

A606
60 Barnsdale, Stamford Rd
60 Leicester, Broughton/Old Dalby
60 Tinwell, Stamford Rd

A607
30 Leicester, Melton Rd
30 Melton, Norman Way
70 Thurmaston, Newark Rd
60 Waltham on the Wolds, Melton Rd
60 Waltham/Croxton Kerrial, Melton Rd

A4304
40 Market Harborough, Lubbenham Hill

A5199
30 Leicester, Welford Rd
30 Wigston, Bull Head St
30 Wigston, Leicester Rd

A5460
40 Leicester, Narborough Rd

A6004
30 Loughborough, Alan Moss Rd

A6030
30 Leicester, Wakerley Rd/Broad Avenue

A6121
30 Ketton, Stamford Rd

B568
30 Leicester, Victoria Park Rd

B581
30 Broughton Astley, Broughton Way

B582
30 Blaby, Little Glen Rd

B590
30 Hinckley, Rugby Rd

B591
60 Charley, Loughborough Rd

B676
60 Freeby, Saxby Rd

B4114
40 Enderby/Narborough, Leicester Rd/King Edward Avenue
30 Leicester, Sharnford

B4616
30 Leicester, East Park Rd

B4666
30 Hinckley, Coventry Rd

B5003
40 Norris Hill, Ashby Rd

B5366
30 Leicester, Saffron Lane

B5350
30 Loughborough, Foreset Rd
30 Loughborough, Nanpantan Rd

Unclassified
30 Barrow upon Soar, Sileby Rd
30 Blaby, Lutterworth Rd
30 Ibstock, Leicester Rd
30 Leicester, Fosse Rd South
30 Shepshed, Leicester Rd

Lincolnshire

A15
60 Ashby Lodge
60 Aswarby

A15-B1191
60 Dunsby Hollow

A16
60 Boston, Boston Tytton Lane
40 Burwell
60 Deeping Bypass
60 Grainsby to Holton-le-Clay
60 North Thoresby

A17
60 Fleet Hargate
60 Hoffleet Stow
60 Moulton Common

A52
60 Bridge End
60 Horbling and Swaton
60 Ropsley

A153
40 Billinghay
50 Tattershall

A158
50 Scremby to Candlesby

A631
60 Hemswell
60 West Rasen, Dale Bridge

B1188
30 Branston
60 Canwick, Highfield House
60 Potterhanworth

London

M11
Chadwell

M25
Egham
Elmbridge, Byfleet
Hillingdon
Hillingdon, Colnbrook
Runneymeade
Spelthorne
Wraysbury

A3
Kingston Bypass
Wandsworth, Kingston Rd

A4
Hounslow, Brentford, Great West Rd
Hounslow, Great West Rd

A5
Barnet, Hendon Broadway
Brent, Edgware Rd

A10
Enfield, Great Cambridge Rd
Hackney, Stamford Hill

A13
Barking and Dagenham, Alfreds Way
Barking and Dagenham, Ripple Rd
Dagenham, Ripple Rd
Newham, Alfreds Way

A20
Bexley, Sidcup Rd
Bromley, Sidcup Bypass
Greenwick, Sidcup Rd

A21
Lewisham, Bromley Rd

A22
Croydon, Godstone Rd

A40
City of Westminster, Westway
Ealing, Perivale
Ealing, Western Avenue
Hammersmith and Fulham, Westway
Hillingdon, Ruislip, Western Avenue

A110
Enfield, Enfield Rd

A124
Newham, Barking Rd

A205
Richmond upon Thames
Richmond upon Thames, Upper Richmond Rd West

A213
Bromley, Croydon Rd

A214
Wandsworth, Trinity Rd

A215
Croydon, Beulah Hill

A217
Croydon, Garratt Lane

A219
Hammersmith and Fulham, Scrubs Lane

A222
Bromley, Bromley Rd

A232
Sutton, Cheam Rd

A298
West Barnes, Bushey Rd

A312
Hillingdon

A315
Hounslow, High St

A406
Barking and Dagenham, Barking Relief Rd
Barnet, North Circular Rd
Redbridge, Southend Rd

A501
Camden, Euston Rd

A503
Haringey, Seven Sisters Rd

A3220
Wandsworth, Latchmere Rd

A4006
Brent, Kenton Rd

B178
Barking and Dagenham, Ballards Rd

B272
Sutton, Foresters Rd

B278
Sutton, Green Lane

B279
Sutton, Tudor Drive

Unclassified
Barnet, Oakleigh Rd South
Bexley, Abbey Rd
Bexley, Bellegrove Rd
Bexley, Erith Rd
Bexley, Farady Avenue
Bexley, King Harolds Way
Bexley, Lower Rd
Bexley, Penhill Rd
Bexley, Pickford Lane
Bexley, Well Hall Rd
Bexley, Woolwich Rd
Brent, Crest Rd
Brent, Hillside
Brent, Kingsbury Rd
Brent, Kingsbury, Fryent Way
Brent, Sudbury, Watford Rd
Brent, Wembley, Watford Rd
Brent, Woodcock Hill
Bromley, Beckenham Rd
Bromley, Burnt Ash Lane
Bromley, Crystal Palace Park Rd
Bromley, Elmers End Rd
Bromley, Main Rd
Bromley, Sevenoaks Way
Bromley, Wickham Way
City of Westminster, Great Western Rd
City of Westminster, Millbank
City of Westminster, Vauxhall Bridge Rd
Croydon, Addiscombe, Long Lane
Croydon, Brigstock Rd
Croydon, Coulsdon, Coulsdon Rd
Croydon, Coulsdon, Portnalls Rd
Croydon, Thornton Rd
Ealing, Greenford, Greenford Rd
Ealing, Horn Lane
Ealing, Lady Margaret Rd
Ealing, Ruislip Rd
Ealing, Southall, Greenford Rd
Ealing, Uxbridge Rd
Eastcote, Field End Rd
Enfield, Fore St
Forest Hill, Stanstead Rd
Forest Hill, Stanstead Rd
Greenwick, Beresford St
Greenwick, Court Rd
Greenwick, Creek Rd
Greenwick, Glenesk Rd
Greenwick, Rochester Way
Greenwick, Rochester Way
Greenwick, Woolwich Church St
Hackney, Clapton Common
Hackney, Seven Sisters Rd
Hackney, Upper Clapton Rd
Hammersmith and Fulham, Fulham Palace Rd
Hammersmith and Fulham, Uxbridge Rd
Hammersmith and Fulham, Westway
Haringey, Belmont Rd
Haringey, Bounds Green Rd
Haringey, Seven Sisters Rd
Haringey, White Hart Lane
Harrow, Alexandra Avenue
Harrow, Harrow View
Harrow, Harrow Weald, Uxbridge Rd
Harrow, Honeypot Lane
Harrow, Porlock Avenue
Harrow, Watford Rd
Havering, Chase Cross Rd
Havering, Eastern Avenue
Havering, Eastern Avenue East
Havering, Hall Lane
Havering, Hornchurch, Parkstone Avenue
Havering, Ockenden Rd
Havering, Romford, Brentwood Rd
Havering, Wingletye Lane
Hillingdon, Cowley, Cowley Rd
Hillingdon, Cowley, High Rd
Hillingdon, Harefield, Church Hill
Hillingdon, Hayes, Kingshill Avenue
Hillingdon, Hayes, Uxbridge Rd
Hillingdon, Northwood Hills, Joel St
Hillingdon, Park Rd
Hillingdon, Stockley Rd
Hillingdon, Uxbridge, Cowley Rd
Hounslow, Bedfont, Hatton Rd
Hounslow, Great West Rd
Hounslow, Hanworth, Castle Way
Hounslow, Harlington Rd West
Islington, Holloway Rd
Islington, Seven Sisters Rd
Islington, Upper St
Kensington and Chelsea, Barlby Rd
Kensington and Chelsea, Chelsea Embankment
Kensington and Chelsea, Chesterton Rd
Kensington and Chelsea, Holand Park Avenue
Kensington and Chelsea, Holland Villas Rd
Kensington and Chelsea, Kensington Park Rd
Kensington and Chelsea, Kensington Rd
Kensington and Chelsea, Ladbroke Grove
Kensington and Chelsea, Latimer Rd
Kensington and Chelsea, Royal Hospital Rd
Kensington and Chelsea, Sloane St
Kensington and Chelsea, St Helens Gardens
Kingston upon Thames, Kingston Rd
Kingston upon Thames, Manor Drive North
Kingston upon Thames, Richmond Rd
Lambeth, Atkins Rd
Lambeth, Brixton Hill
Lambeth, Brixton Rd
Lambeth, Clapham Rd
Lambeth, Herne Hill Rd
Lambeth, Kennington Park Rd
Lambeth, Kings Avenue
Lambeth, Streatham High Rd
Lewisham, Brockley Rd
Lewisham, Brownhill Rd
Lewisham, Burnt Ash Hill
Lewisham, Lee High Rd
Lewisham, Lewisham Way
Lewisham, Westwood Hill
Merton, Central Rd
Merton, Colliers Wood, High St
Merton, Hillcross Avenue
Merton, London Rd
Merton, Martin Way
Merton, Ridgway Place
Merton, West Barnes Lane
Newham, Barking Rd
Newham, Romford Rd
Newham, Royal Albert Dock, Spine Rd
Newham, Royal Docks Rd
North Dagenham, Rainham Rd
Redbridge, Hainault, Manford Way
Redbridge, Woodford Avenue
Redbridge, Woodford Rd
Richmond upon Thames, Kew Rd
Richmond upon Thames, Sixth Cross Rd
Richmond upon Thames, Uxbridge Rd
Southwark, Albany Rd
Southwark, Alleyn Park
Southwark, Brenchley Gardens
Southwark, Camberwell New Rd
Southwark, Denmark Hill
Southwark, Kennington Park Rd
Southwark, Linden Grove
Southwark, Old Kent Rd
Southwark, Peckham Rye
Southwark, Salter Rd
Southwark, Sunray Avenue
Streatham, Streatham High Rd
Sutton, Beddington Lane
Sutton, Cheam Common Rd
Sutton, Maiden Rd
Sutton, Middleton Rd
Tower Hamlets, Bow Rd
Tower Hamlets, Cambridge Heath Rd
Tower Hamlets, Homerton High Rd
Tower Hamlets, Manchester Rd
Tower Hamlets, Mile End Rd
Tower Hamlets, Upper Clapton Rd
Tower Hamlets, Westferry Rd
Waltham Forest, Chingford Rd
Waltham Forest, Hoe St
Waltham Forest, Larksall Rd
Wandsworth, Battersea Park Rd
Wandsworth, Garratt Lane
Wandsworth, Upper Richmond Rd
Woolwich, Woolwich Church St

Norfolk

A10
60 Stow Bardolph
60 Tottenhill/Watlington

A11
60 Attleborough Bypass
70 Ketteringham
70 Roundham
70 Snetterton
70 Wymondham/Bestthorpe

A12
70 Hopton

A17
60 Terrington St Clement

A47
60 East Winch
60 Emneth
60 Honington/Easton
50 Lingwood/Acle
60 Mauthby/Halvergate
60 Narborough
70 Postwick
70 Pullover Rdbt
60 Scarning
60 Swaffham/Sporle
70 Terrington St John
70 Tuddenham
60 Wendling/Framsham

A140
60 Aylsham
60 Dickleburgh Moor
60 Erpingham
60 Long Stratton/Tivetshall St Mary
60 Newton Flotman
40 Newton Flotman/Saxlingham Thorpe
30 Norwich, Harford Bridge
40 Roughton village
70 Scole Bypass
60 St. Faiths

A143
60 Billingford/Brockdish

A146
60 Hales

A148
60 Bodham
60 Fakenham Bypass
40 King's Lynn, Grimston Rd
60 Pretty Corner
50 Thursford

A149
70 Caister Bypass
60 Catfield
40 Catfield/Potter Heigham
30 Hunstanton
60 Kings Lynn/Nth Runcton
60 Knights Hill
60 Little Snoring
60 Roughton (N and S Repps)
60 Sandringham
50 Wayford Bridge East
50 Wayford Bridge West/Smallburgh

A1065
60 Hilbrough
60 South Acre
60 Weeting with Broomhill

A1066
60 Rushford
60 South Lopham
40 Thetford, Mundford Rd

A1067
50 Bawdeswell
60 Morton/Attlebridge

A1075
60 Wretham (heath)

A1082
30 Sheringham

A1122
60 Swaffham/Beachamwell

A1151
60 Rackheath/Wroxham

B111
30 East Harling

B1108
30 Norwich, Earlham Rd

B1135
50 Wymondham/Wreningham

B1149
60 Horsford Woods

B1150
50 Scottow
50 Westwick

B1152
60 Orby

B1332
50 Ditchingham

Unclassified
70 Caister, High St/Norwich Rd
30 Caister, Ormesby Rd
60 Drayton, Reepham Rd
30 Shipdham, High St
30 Walton

North Yorkshire

A1
70 Catterick

A59
60 Beamsley

A64
70 Malton

A65
60 Clapham
60 Settle

Unclassified
30 Tunstall, Main St

Northamptonshire

A5
60 DIRFT to County Boundary
60 Norton/Whilton Crossroads
30/40 Towcester Racecourse to A43

A6
60 Burton Latimer Bypass

A14
70 Kelmarsh
70 Kettering Junctions 7-10

A43
60 Laxton Turn to A47 Duddington
60 Mawsley to A14 Junction 8 (inc Mawsley spur)
70 Towcester to M1 Junction 15a

A45
60 M1 Junction 16 to Weedon
60 Stanwick to Raunds

A361
60 Byfield to Chipping Warden

A422
60 Brackley West to A43

A428
60 East Haddon
30/60 Great Houghton to Yardley Hastings

A508
30 Northampton, Plough Gyratory
30 Northampton, St Georges Avenue to Holly Lodge Rd
30 Northampton, St Peters Way to Georges Avenue
30/60 Northampton, Stoke Bruerne to A5
70 Northampton, Wootton Flyover to M1 Junction 15

A509
60 Wellingborough to Isham

A605
40/60 Thrapston to Warmington

A4256
30 Daventry, Eastern Way

A4500
40/60 Great Billing to Earls Barton
30 Northampton, Abington Park to York Rd
30 Northampton, Park Avenue to Booth Lane South
30 Northampton, Weedon Rd to Duston Rd

A5076
40 Northampton, Mere Way
40 Northampton, Great Billing Way South

A5193
30/40 Wellingborough, London Rd

A6003
50/60 Kettering to Corby

A6014
40/60 Corby, Oakley Rd

B569
50 Irchester to Rushden

B576
60 Desborough to Rothwell

B4038
30/60 Rugby Rd

B4525
40/60 Welsh Lane

B5385
60 Watford to West Haddon

Unclassified
30 Brackmills Industrial Estate
30 Northampton, Grange Rd

Northumbria

Gateshead, Newcastle-upon-Tyne, North Tyneside, Northumberland, South Tyneside, Sunderland

A1
60 Berwick Bypass, Dunns Jct (N)

A68
60 Colt Crag

A69
60 Haltwhistle Bypass
70 Hexham, Two Mile Cottage

A167
30 Newcastle, Stamfordham Rd

A182
30 Sunderland, Houghton Rd

A183
30 Broadway, Chester Rd

A186
40 Denton Burn, West Rd
30 Newcastle, City Rd at Beamish House
40 Newcastle, West Rd at Turret Rd
30 Newcastle, Westgate Rd at Elwick Row

A189
70 Cramlington, High Pitt
70 Cramlington, Spine Rd
30 South Gosforth, Haddricks Mill Rd

A191
30 Benton, Whitley Rd

A193
30 Wallsend, Church Bank

A194
40 Simonside, Newcastle Rd

A196
30 Blackclose Bank

A690
30 Sunderland, Durham Rd
50 Sunderland, Stoneygate, Houghton, Durham Rd

A694
30 Gateshead, Rowlands Gill, Station Rd
40 Gateshead, Winlaton Mill (Spa Well Rd)

A695
60 Gateshead, Crawcrook Bypass
40 Prudhoe Jct B6395

30 Belsay Village
60 Blaxter Cottages
60 Kirkwhelpiington
60 Otterburn Monkridge

A697
60 Morpeth, Heighley Gate
60 Northumberland

A1018
30 Sunderland, Ryhope Rd, Irene Avenue

A1058
30 Newcastle, Jesmond Rd at Akenside Terrace

A1068
30 Amble Ind Est

A1147
30 Stakeford, Gordon Terrace

A1171
30 Cramlington, Dudley Lane

A1290
30 Sunderland, Southwick, Keir Hardie Way

A1300
30 South Tyneside, Nook, Prince Edward Rd

A6085
40 Newcastle, Lemington Rd

A6127
30 Gateshead, Barley Mow, Durham Rd

B1288
40 Gateshead, Leam Lane/ A195

B1296
30 Gateshead, Sheriffs Highway, QE Hospital
30 Gateshead, Sheriffs Highway, Split Crow Rd

B1298
30 South Tyneside, Boldon Colliery, New Rd

B1301
30 South Tyneside, Dean Rd (John Clay St)
30 South Tyneside, Laygate, Eglesfield Rd

B1316
30 North Tyneside, Lynn Rd

B1318
30 North Tyneside, Seaton Burn, Bridge St

B1426
30 Gateshead, Felling, Sunderland Rd

B1505
30 North Tyneside, West Moor, Great Lime Rd

B6315
30 Gateshead, High Spen, Hookergate Lane

B6317
30 Gateshead, Ryton, Main Rd
30 Gateshead, Whickham Highway

B6318
60 Whitchester, Military Rd
60 Whittington Fell, Military Rd

B6324
40 Newcastle, Stamfordham Rd southeast of Walbottle Rd

B6918
30 Newcastle, Woolsington Village

Unclassified
30 Ashington, Station Rd
30 Benton, Coach Lane
30 Gateshead, Blaydon, Shibdon Bank
30 Gateshead, Crawcrook, Greenside Rd
30 Gateshead, Felling, Watermill Lane
30 Gateshead, Whickham, Fellside Rd
30 Gateshead, Askew Rd West
30 Hebburn, Campbell Park Rd
70 Nafferton Eastbound
60 Newcastle, Dinnington Rd North Brunton Lane
40 Newcastle, West Denton Way east of Hawksley
30 North Shields, Norham Rd
30 South Tyneside, Harton Lane
40 South Tyneside, Hedworth Lane, Abingdon Way
40 Sunderland, Farringdon, North Moor Lane
40 Sunderland, North Hylton Rd, Castletown Way
30 Sunderland, Silksworth Rd, Rutland Avenue
30 Sunderland, Springwell Rd
30 Sunderland, Warwick Terrace

30 Wallsend, Battle Hill Drive
30 Whiteleas, Nevinson Avenue

Nottinghamshire

A1(T)
70 East Markham (Northbound)

A52(T)
40 Clifton Boulevard

A60
30 Carlton in Lindrick
30 Mansfield, Nottingham Rd
60 Market Warsop/Cuckney
30 Nottingham, Bellar Gate to Woodthorpe Drive
30 Nottingham, London Rd
50 Ravenshead
30 South, Nottingham

A609
30 Nottingham, Ilkeston Rd/Wollaton Rd/Russell Drive

A610
30 Nottingham, Bobbers Mill

A611
30 Annelsey, Derby Rd
30 Nottingham, Hucknall Rd

A612
30 Southwell, Nottingham Rd

A614
60 Arnold, Burnt Stump

A617
40 Mansfield, Chesterfield Rd South

A620
40 Retford, Welham Rd

A631
50 Beckingham Bypass
50 Beckingham, Flood Plain Rd
50 Beckingham, nr Wood Lane
60 Gringley to Beckingham, nr Mutton Lane
50 West of Beckingham

A6005
30 Nottingham, Castle Boulevard/Abbey Bridge/ Beeston Rd

A6008
30 Nottingham, Canal St

A6130
30 Nottingham, Gregory Boulevard
30 Nottingham, Radford and Lenton Boulevards

A6200/A52
30 Nottingham, Derby Rd

B679
30 West Bridgford, Wilford Lane

B682
30 Nottingham, Sherwood Rise/Nottingham Rd/ Vernon Rd

B6004
40 Arnold, Oxclose Lane

B6010
30 Giltbrook, Nottingham Rd

B6011
30 Hucknall, Annesley Rd/ Nottingham Rd/Portland Rd

B6020
30 Rainworth, Kirklington Rd

B6040
30 Worksop, Retford Rd

B6166
30 Newark on Trent, Lincoln Rd/Northgate

B6326
40 Newark on Trent, London Rd

Unclassified
30 Newark, Balderton, Hawton Lane
30 Nottingham, Beechdale Rd/Wigman Rd
30 Nottingham, Bestwood Park Drive
Nottingham, Radford Boulevard/Lenton Boulevard
30 Nottingham, Ridge Way/Top Valley Drive

Oxfordshire

see Thames Valley

Shropshire

see West Mercia

Somerset

see Avon and Somerset

South Yorkshire

A18
60 Doncaster, Slay Pits to Tudworth, Epworth Rd
40 Doncaster, Carr House Rd/Leger Way

A57
40,60 Anston, Sheffield Rd/Worksop Rd
60 Rotherham, Worksop Rd
60 Sheffield, Mosborough Parkway

A60
60 Tickhill, Doncaster Rd
30,60 Tickhill, Worksop Rd

A61
30 Cutting Edge, Park Rd
30,40 Sheffield, Chesterfield Rd/Chesterfield Rd South
30,40 Sheffield, Halifax Rd
30 Sheffield, Penistone Rd

A614
60 Thorne, Selby Rd

A618
40 Wales Bar, Mansfield Rd

A628
30,40 Barnsley, Cundy Cross to Shafton Two Gates
40,60 Barnsley, Dodworth
40 Penistone, Barnsley Rd

A629
60 Barnsley, Wortley
30 Burncross, Hallwood Rd/Burncross Rd
40 Rotherham, New Wortley Rd
30,40 Rotherham, Wortley Rd/Upper Wortley Rd

A630
30,40,60 Dalton/Thrybergh, Doncaster Rd
30,40,60 Doncaster, Balby Flyover to Hill Top
40 Doncaster, Wheatley Hall Rd
40,50 Rotherham, Centenary Way

A631
40 Brinsworth, Bawtry Rd
30,40 Hellaby/Maltby, Bawtry Rd/Rotherham Rd
50 Rotherham, West Bawtry Rd
40 Wickersley/Brecks, Bawtry Rd

A633
30 Athersley South, Rotherham Rd
40 Monk Bretton, Rotherham Rd
30 Wath upon Dearne, Sandygate
30,40 Wombwell, Barnsley Rd

A635
30,40,60 Barnsley, Doncaster Rd/Saltersbrook Rd

A638
40 Doncaster, Bawtry Rd
40,50 Doncaster, Great North Rd/York Rd

A6022
30 Rotherham, Swinton

A6101
40 Sheffield, Rivelin Valley Rd

A6102
30,40 Hillsborough/Deepcar, Manchester Rd/Langsett Rd

A6109
40 Rotherham, Meadow Bank Rd

A6123
40 Rotherham, Herringthorpe Valley Rd

A6135
40 Sheffield, Ecclesfield Rd/Chapeltown Rd

B6059
30,40 Rotherham, Kiveton/ Wales

B6089
40 Thorn Hill/Greasbrough, Greasbrough Rd/ Greasbrough St

B6096
30 Barnsley, Wombwell to Snape Hill

B6097
30,60 Wath upon Dearne, Doncaster Rd

B6100
30 Barnsley, Ardsley Rd/ Hunningley Lane

B6411
30 Thurnscoe, Houghton Rd

B6463
60 Tickhill, Stripe Rd

Unclassified
30 Armthorpe, Hatfield Lane/Mill St
30 Armthorpe, Nutwell Lane
30 Barnsley, Pogmoor Rd
30 Bolton upon Dearne, Dearne Rd
30 Doncaster, Melton Rd/Sprotbrough Rd
30 Doncaster, Urban Rd
30,60 Edlington/ Warmsworth, Broomhouse Lane/Springwell Lane
40,60 Finningley, Hurst Lane
30 Grimethorpe, Brierley Rd
30,60 Rotherham, Fenton Rd
30,40 Rotherham, Haugh Rd
30 Rotherham, Kilnhurst Rd

30 Stainforth, Station Rd
40 Wath upon Dearne, Barnsley Rd
30 Wheatley, Thorne Rd

Staffordshire

A5
60 A5127 to A38 – Wall Island to Weeford Island
60 Brownhills, Watling St
60,70,60,30 btwn A34 Churchbridge and The Turf Pub Island (B4154)
50 Cannock, Watling St
50,40 from A38 to Hints Lane
70 from A461 to A5127 (Muckley Corner Island to Wall Island Lichfield/ Tamworth)
60,70,60 Hanney Hay/ Barracks Lane Island to Muckley Corner Island
50 M6 jct 12 to A460/A4601 Island
50,30 South Cannock, A460/ A4601 to A34 Longford Island to A34 Bridgetown
60 Wall, Watling St
60 Weeford, Watling St

A34
30 Cannock North, North of Holly Lane jct to A34/ B5012 rdbt
30,50,30 Cannock South to County Boundary
30 Cannock South, A34 from south of jct A5 Walsall Rd to north of jct with Jones Lane
40 Newcastle North, from Wolstanton Rd/Dimsdale Parade west Island to Milehouse Lane/B5367
30,40 Newcastle Rd btwn Hanford Island to London Rd Bowling Club
40 Newcastle South, Barracks Rd to Stoke City Boundary
70,40 Newcastle under Lyme to Talke, btwn Wolstanton Rd/Dimsdale Parade West Island to Jct of A500
30,40 Stafford South, from A449 jct to Acton Hill Lane Jct
30 Stafford, btwn A5013 and A518
40 Stafford, Queensway
40,30 Stone Rd from jct of Longton Rd/A5035 to Handford Island/A500
40,30 Stone Rd Redhill (A513/A34) island to Lloyds Island, Eccleshall Rd
30,60 Talke, Jct A500 to Jct A5011

A38
40 Alrewas, btwn Rradley Lane and Wychnor Lane
70 btwn London Rd Lichfield and A5121 Burton
70 btwn Weeford Island and Bassetts Pole Island (Community Concern Site)

A50
30 Kidsgrove, btwn City Boundary and Oldcott Drive
30 Kidsgrove, Liverpool Rd
30 Stoke on Trent, Victoria Rd btwn Leek Rd and City Rd

A51
60 btwn Armitage Lane Rugeley and A515 nr Lichfield
30,40,60 Lichfield, from A5127 Birmingham Rd to Heath Rd
30 Lichfield, Tamworth Rd
50 Pasturefields, A51 from south of jct with Amerton Lane to south of Hoomill Lane
40,30 Rugeley North, from A51 jct with Bower Lane to island of A460 Sandy Lane and B5013 Elmore Lane
30,40 Rugeley South, from south of island of A460/ Sandy Lane and B5013 Elmore Lane to Brereton Island
30 Tamworth, A51 Tamworth Rd/Dosthill Rd from south of jct with Peelers Way to jct with A51 Ascot Drive
60,40,50 Weston, btwn New Rd and 500m past Sandy Lane (going north)

A52
30 Stoke on Trent, Werrington Rd – btwn jct of B5040 to half mile east of Brookhouse Lane (Ashbank)
30,40 Stoke, Werrington Rd, btwn Brookhouse Lane and Kingsley Rd

A53
40,30,40,60 Endon, from A53 Leek New Rd from jct with Nursery Avenue to jct with Dunwood Lane
60,40,30 Longsden, from A53 jct with Dunwood Lane to A53 jct with Wallbridge Drive

A444
30 Stanton Rd – St Peters Bridge to Derbyshire boundary

A449
70,40 Coven, btwn Station Drive by Four Ashes to just before M54 island
40 Coven, Wolverhampton Rd
60,70 Gailey, btwn Rodbaston Drive and Station Drive
60 Galley, Wolverhampton Rd
40 Penkridge, Lynehill Lane to 0.5mile north of Goodstation Lane
30 Stafford, Lichfield Rd to Gravel Lane

A454
50 Trescott, Bridgenorth Rd btwn Brantley Lane and Shop Lane

A458
40,50 Gilberts Cross, btwn Six Ashes Rd, Six Ashes and Morfe Lane

A460
30 Rugeley, A460 from A51/A460 jct of Sandy Lane/Hednesford Rd to south of jct A460 Stile Cop Rd

A500
40 btwn M6 jct 16 and A34

A511
40,30 Burton North, btwn Anslow Lane to island of A5121
30 Burton South, island of A5121 to Brizlincote Lane (by Derbyshire boundary)

A518
30 Stafford, btwn M6 and Bridge St
30,40 Stafford, Riverway to Blackheath Lane

A519
40 Newcastle, Clayton Rd – from south of A519 Clayton Rd/Friars Wood and Brook Lane to rdbt on A519

A519
30 Woodseaves, btwn Moss Lane and Lodge Lane (Community Concern Site)

A520
30 Sandon Rd btwn Grange Rd and A50
30 Weston Rd – from north of the A50 to City boundary (Park Hall) through Meir and Weston Coyney

A522
50,40 Beamhurst, btwn Fole Lane and Grange Rd, nr Uttoxeter

A4601
30 Cannock, btwn A34 Walsall Rd jct to Longford Island A5
30 Old Hednesford Rd btwn jct with A5190 Lichfield Rd and jct with A460 Eastern Way
30,40 Wedges Mill, Longford Island twd jct 11 to just before Saredon Rd

A5005
Stoke on Trent, Lightwood Rd btwn A520 and A50

A5013
30 Stafford, Eccleshall Rd btwn A34 and M6

A5035
30 Trentham, Longton Rd btwn Trentham Rdbt A34 and A50 jct at Longton

A5121
30 Burton, Derby Rd
50,40,30 Burton, from Island Junction with B5108 Branston to Borough Rd
30,40 Burton, from jct with Byrkley St, Horninglow to jct with Hillfield Lane
30 Burton, Wellington Rd

A5127
30 Lichfield, Trent Valley Rd
30 Lichfield, from jct with Upper St John St towards Streethay (incs change in speed limit over railway bridge)

A5189
30 Burton, St Peters Bridge
30,40 Burton, from Wellington Rd jct along St Peters Bridge to Stapenhill Rd rdbt

A5190
30 Burntwood, Cannock Rd from Attwood Rd to Stockhay Lane Jct
30 Cannock, Cannock Rd
30,40,60 Cannock, from Five Ways Island to Hednesford Rd

B5027
30 Stone Rd btwn Byrds Lane and Springfield Rd

B5044
30 Silverdale, btwn Sneyd Terrace and the jct of the B5368 (Church Lane/ Cemetery Rd)

B5051
30 btwn Sneyd Hill Rd and Brown Edge
30 Stoke on Trent, Ford Green Rd

B5066
30 Hilderstone, btwn B5027 and Hall Lane
60 Sandon, Sandon Rd btwn A51 and Salt Lane
30 Stafford, Sandon Rd btwn A513 and Marston Rd

B5080
30,40 Tamworth, Pennine Way btwn B5000 and Pennymoor Rd

B5404
40,30 Tamworth, from Sutton Rd to jct of A4091 (Coleshill Rd/Fazeley Rd)
30 Tamworth, Watling St btwn jct with A51 and A5

B5500
30 Audley btwn Barthomley Rd and Park Lane (Community Concern Site)
30,40 Bignall End/Bignall Hill, btwn Boons Hill Rd and Alsager Lane

Unclassified
30 Burntwood, Church Rd btwn Rugeley Rd and Farewell Lane
30 Burton on Trent, Violet Way/Beauford Rd btwn A444 and A511
30 Burton, Rosliston Rd btwn A5189 St Peters Bridge and County Boundary by Railway Bridge
30 Cannock, Pye Green Rd
30 Cedar Rd btwn Crackley Bank and B5500 Audley Rd
30 Cheadle Rd btwn Uttoxeter Rd and Quabbs Lane
40 Cresswell, Sandon Rd btwn Severley Green Rd and Uttoxeter Rd
30 Hednesford, Rawnsley Rd btwn A460 and Littleworth Rd
30,40 Leek New Rd – btwn B5049 Hanley Rd and B5051 jct with A53 at Endon
30 Oxford Rd/Chell Heath Rd btwn A527 and B5051
30 Stoke on Trent, Chell Heath Rd
30 Stoke on Trent, Dividy Rd – btwn B5039 and A52

Suffolk

A11
50 Barton Mills Elveden
40 Elveden Cross Rds Elveden, Chalk Hall Worlington

A12
40 Blythburgh Kelsale
30 Little Glemham
50 Little Glemham, North Lound
40 Marlesford
40 Melton Saxmundham

A14
Exning Newmarket Rougham

A134
40 Barnham
30 Little Welnetham Long Melford
40 Nowton

A137
30 Brantham

A140
50 Thwaite
40 Wetheringsett

A143
30 Bury St Edmunds
30 Chedburgh
40 Stanton
40 Stanton Bypass
40 Stradishall, Highpoint Prison

A144
30 Ilketshall St Lawrence

A145
40 Felixstowe, Trinity Avenue

A146
50 Barnby Bends

A1065
40 Eriswell Mildenhall North of RAF Lakenheath

A1071
40 Boxford Hadleigh, Lady Lane

A1088
30 Honington

A1092
30 Cavendish
30 Clare
40 Glemsford, Skates Hill

A1101
30 Flempton
30 Mildenhall
50 Shippea Hill

A1117
30 Lowestoft, Saltwater Way

A1120
30 Stonham Aspal

A1156
30 Ipswich, Norwich Rd

A1156
40 Nacton

A1214
40 Ipswich, London Rd

A1302
30 Bury St Edmunds

A1304
Newmarket, Golf Club

A1307
40 Haverhill

B1078
30 Barking
30 Needham Market

B1106
30 Fornham

B1113
40 Bramford

B1115
40 Chilton

B1384
30 Carlton Colville

B1385
30 Corton

B1438
30 Melton Hill

B1506
40 Kentford Moulton

Unclassified
30 Felixstowe, Grange Farm Avenue
30 Felixstowe, High Rd
30 Ipswich, Ellenbrook Rd
30 Ipswich, Foxhall Rd
30 Ipswich, Landseer Rd
30 Ipswich, Nacton Rd
30 Kesgrave, Ropes Drive

Surrey

A23
30 Horley, Brighton Rd
40 Salfords, Brighton Rd

A31
60 Hogs Back, (Central and Eastern Sections)

A308
50 Staines Bypass

Unclassified
30 Staines, Kingston Rd

Sussex

A24
30 Worthing, Broadwater Rd nr Cecilian Avenue

A27
70 Angmering, Hammerpot n/side
60 Firle, Firle Straight
70 Shoreham, Holmbush

A29
30 Aldingbourne, Westergate St/Elmcroft Place
30 Aldingbourne, Westergate St/Hook Lane
40 Bognor, Shripney Rd

A259
30 Bognor, Hotham Way
30 Brighton, Marine Parade/ Eaton Place
30 Fishbourne, Main Rd
30 Saltdean, Marine Drive

A280
40 Patching

A281
30 Horsham, Guildford Rd

A283
30 Northchapel
30 Pulborough, Lower St

A285
30 Petworth, Station Rd

A2031
30 Worthing, Offington Lane/Rogate Rd
30 Worthing, Offington Lane/The Plantation

A2032
30 Worthing, Littlehampton Rd nr Little Gables

A2280
40 Eastbourne, Lottbridge Drove

B2093
30 Hastings, The Ridge

B2104
30 Hallsham, Ersham Rd

B2138
30 Fittleworth, Lower St

B2166
30 Bognor, Aldwick Rd

Unclassified
30 Bognor, Hawthorn Rd/Amberley Drive
30 Brighton, Ditching Rd/Balfour Rd
30 Brighton, Falmer Rd Woodingdean
30 Crawley, Breezhurst Drive
30 Crawley, Gatwick Rd nr Hazlewick Flyover
30 Crawley, Gossops Drive
30 Crawley, Manor Royal/ Faraday Rd
30 Heathfield, Hallsham Rd
30 Horsham, Pondtail Rd/Haybarn Drive
30 Horsham, Pondtail Rd/Pondtail Close
30 Hove, New Church Rd/Wish Rd
30 Hove, Shirley Drive/Onslow Rd
30 Shirley, Shirley Drive/ Shirley Rd
30 Worthing, The Boulevard

Thames Valley

Bracknell Forest, Buckinghamshire, Milton Keynes, Oxfordshire, Reading, Slough, West Berkshire, Windsor and Maidenhead, Wokingham

A5
70 Wolverton
70 Bletchley

A30(T)
30 Sunningdale, London Rd

A34
70 Radley
70 Kennington

A40
60 Cassington
70 Forest Hills

A41
70 Buckland

A44
50 Kiddington with Asterleigh

A338
50 Hungerford

A361
30 Chipping Norton, Burford Rd
60 Little Faringdon

A404
70 Little Marlow, Marlow Bypass

A413
60 Swanbourne
60 Weedon
60 Hardwick
60 Wendover Bypass

A421
70 Tingewick Bypass
60 Wavendon

A422
50 Radclive cum Chackmore

A509
70 Newport Pagnell
60 Emberton Bypass

A4074
60 Dorchester
50 Nuneham Courteney

A4095
40 Freeland, Witney Rd

A4130
60 Nuffield
40 Remenham Hill

A4155
30 Shipiake

A4260
50 Shipton on Cherwell, Banbury Rd
60 Rousham, Banbury Rd
60 Steeple Aston

B4009
50 Ewelme

B4011
60 Piddington

B4494
60 Leckhampstead

Unclassified
30 Abingdon, Drayton Rd
30 Abingdon, Oxford Rd
30 Aylesbury, Buckingham Rd
30 Aylesbury, Gatehouse Rd
30 Aylesbury, Oakfield Rd
30 Aylesbury, Tring Rd
30 Aylesbury, Walton St
30 Aylesbury, Wendover Rd
30 Barkham, Barkham Rd
60 Beenham, Bath Rd
30 Blackbird Leys, Watlington Rd
30 Bletchley, Buckingham Rd
40 Bracknell, Bagshot Rd

- 50 Bracknell, Nine Mile Ride
- 30 Bracknell, Opladen Way
- 30 Buckingham, Stratford Rd
- 50 Burnham, Bath Rd
- 30 Chalfont St Peter, Gravel Hill
- 40 Chipping Norton, London Rd
- 40 Curbridge, Bampton Rd
- 40 Denham, North Orbital Rd
- 30 Denham, Oxford Rd
- 40 Earley, 30 London Rd
- 30 Great Missenden, Rignall Rd
- 60 Hardmead, Newport Rd
- 30 Hazelmere, Sawpit Hill
- 30 High Wycombe, Holmers Farm Way
- 30 High Wycombe, Marlow Hill
- 30 High Wycombe, New Rd
- 30 High Wycombe, West Wycombe Rd
- 60 Hungerford, Bath Rd
- 30 Kidlington, Oxford Rd
- 60 Kintbury, Bath Rd
- 30 Long Crendon, Bicester Rd
- 40 Maidenhead, Braywick Rd
- 70 Milton Keynes, Woughton on the Green, Standing Way
- 30 Milton Keynes, Avebury Boulevard
- 30 Milton Keynes, Midsummer Boulevard
- 30 Milton Keynes, Silbury Boulevard
- 30 Monks Risborough, Aylesbury Rd
- 30 Oxford, Church Cowley Rd
- 30 Oxford, Headington Rd
- 30 Oxford, London Rd
- 30 Oxford, Windmill Rd
- 30 Reading, Berkeley Avenue
- 30 Reading, Castle Hill
- 30 Reading, Kings Rd
- 30 Reading, Park Lane
- 30 Reading, Vastern Rd
- 30 Reading, Wokingham Rd
- 30 Slough, Buckingham Rd
- 30 Slough, Cippenham Lane
- 40 Slough, London Rd
- 30 Slough, Parlaunt Rd
- 30 Slough, Sussex Place
- 60 Speen, Bath Rd
- 30 Stanford in the Vale, Faringdon Rd
- 40 Sunninghill, Brockenhurst Rd
- 30 Tiddington, Oxford Rd
- 40 Tilehurst, Bath Rd
- 30 Wantage, Charlton Rd
- 70 Winkfield, Bagshot Rd
- 30 Witney, Corn St
- 30 Wokingham, London Rd
- 60 Wroxton, Stratford Rd

Warwickshire

A5
- 50 North Warwickshire, Grendon to Hinckley
- 60 Rugby, Churchover

A45
- 50 Rugby, nr Ryton

A46
- 60 Stratford upon Avon, nr Snitterfield
- 60 Warwick, nr Stoneleigh

A47
- 30 Nuneaton and Bedworth, Hinckley Rd
- 40 Nuneaton and Bedworth, Longshoot, Nuneaton Radial Route

A422
- 30 Stratford upon Avon, Stratford, Alcester Rd

A423
- 60 Rugby, nr Marton
- 30 Rugby, Marton
- 60 Stratford upon Avon, nr Fenny Compton
- 60 Stratford upon Avon, South of Southam

A425
- 30 Stratford upon Avon, Ufton
- 30 Warwick, Radford Semele

A426
- 30 Rugby, Dunchurch Rd
- 60 Stratford upon Avon, nr Stockton

A428
- 30 Rugby, Binley Woods
- 60 Rugby, Church Lawford
- 40 Rugby, Long Lawford

A429
- 60 Stratford upon Avon, Stretton on Fosse
- 60 Stratford upon Avon, Wellesbourne

A435
- 40 Stratford upon Avon, Mappleborough Green

A439
- 50 Stratford upon Avon, Stratford to A46

A446
- 60 North Warwickshire, Allen End

A452
- 60 Warwick, Greys Mallory
- 60 Warwick, Heathcote

A3400
- 50 Stratford upon Avon, Alderminster
- 60 Stratford upon Avon, Little Wolford
- 40 Stratford upon Avon, North of Henley in Arden
- 50 Stratford upon Avon, Pathlow

A4091
- 60 North Warwickshire, Middleton

A4189
- 60 Stratford upon Avon, Outhill to Lower Norton

B4089
- Stratford upon Avon, Alcester, Arden Rd

B4098
- 40 North Warwickshire, Corley, Tamworth Rd

B4100
- 60 Stratford upon Avon, Gaydon

B4110
- 60 Warwick, Bishops Tachbrook

B4112
- 40 Nuneaton and Bedworth, Nuneaton Radial Route, Ansley Rd

B4113
- 30 Nuneaton and Bedworth, Hilltop, Nuneaton Radial Route

B4114
- 60 North Warwickshire, Church End
- 30 Nuneaton and Bedworth, Ansley Common, Coleshill Rd
- 30 Nuneaton and Bedworth, Tuttle Hill
- 60 Rugby, Burton Hastings, Lutterworth Rd

B4429
- 40 Rugby, Ashlawn Rd

B4455
- 60 Rugby, Fosse Way south of Princethorpe

B5414
- 30 Rugby, Clifton Rd

Unclassified
- 30 Nuneaton and Bedworth, Donnithorne Avenue
- 30 Warwick, Primrose Hill

West Mercia

Herefordshire, Shropshire, Telford and Wrekin, Worcestershire

A5
- 60 Aston towards Oswestry
- 60 Aston towards Shrewsbury
- 60 Moreton Bridge towards Chirk
- 60 West Felton

A40
- 50 Pencraig

A41
- 40,60 Albrighton Bypass
- 60 Chetwynd
- 60 Prees Heath
- 40 Tern Hill
- 60 Whitchurch Bypass

A44
- 40 Wickhamford towards Broadway
- 30 Worcester, Bromyard Rd towards Bromyard

A46
- 50 Beckford, Cheltenham Rd
- 60 Evesham Bypass

A49
- 60 Ashton towards Leominster
- 60 Ashton towards Ludlow
- 60 Dorrington
- 30 Dorrington towards Shrewsbury
- 40 Herefordshire, Harewood End

A417
- 40 Ledbury, Parkway

A442
- 40 Crudgington

A456
- 30 Blakedown
- 30 Newnham Bridge towards Tenbury Wells

A458
- 40 Morville
- 30 Much Wenlock
- 30 Shrewsbury, The Mount towards Town Centre

A465
- 60 Allensmore

A483
- 30 Pant

A491
- 60 Bromsgrove, Sandy Lane nr Hagley
- 50 Bromsgrove, Stourbridge Rd

A528
- 30 Shrewsbury, Ellesmere Rd towards Town Centre

A4103
- 60 Hereford, Lumber Lane towards Lugg Bridge
- 60 Hereford, west of Lumber Lane towards Great Malvern
- 40 Newtown Cross towards Hereford
- 60 Ridgeway Cross towards Hereford
- 50 Stiffords Bridge to Storridge
- 50 Stiffords Bridge towards Worcester

A4104
- 30 Welland, Drake St
- 30 Welland, Marlbank Rd

A4110
- 30 Hereford, Three Elms Rd towards City Centre
- 40 Hereford, Three Elms Rd towards Leominster

A5064
- 30 Shrewsbury, London Rd

B4096
- 30 Lower Marlbrook, Old Birmingham Rd

B4211
- 30 Great Malvern, Church St

B4349
- 60 Clehonger

B4373
- 40 Telford, Castlefield Way
- 40 Telford, Wrockwardine Wood Way

B4386
- 30 Shropshire, Mytton Oak Rd

B4638
- 30 Worcester, Woodgreen Drive

B5060
- 40 Telford, Castle Farm Way

B5061
- 40 Telford, Holyhead Rd

B5062
- 30 Shrewsbury, Sundorne Rd

B5069
- 30 Shropshire, Gobowen Rd

Unclassified
- 30 Hadley, Britannia Way
- 30 Hereford, Yazor Rd
- 30 Newport, Wellington Rd
- 50 Pencraig, towards Monmouth
- 50 Pencraig, towards Ross on Wye
- 30 Redditch, Birchfield Drive
- 40 Redditch, Coldfield Drive
- 30 Redditch, Studley Rd
- 30 Redditch, Studley Rd towards Park Farm
- 30 Shrewsbury, Monkmoor Rd
- 30 Shropshire, Longden Rd (Rural)
- 30 Snedshill, Holyhead Rd
- 30 Telford, Britannia Way
- 30 Telford, Hollinsgate
- 40 Telford, Stafford Park 1
- 30 Telford, Trench Rd

West Midlands

Birmingham, Coventry, Dudley, Sandwell, Solihull, Walsall, Wolverhampton

A5
- 60 Brownhills, Watling St
- 50 Cannock, Watling St
- 60 Wall, Watling St

A41
- 40 Albrighton Bypass towards Wolverhampton
- 40,60 Albrighton, Albrighton Bypass towards Newport

A46
- 70 Stoneleigh, Kenilworth Bypass

A51
- 30 Lichfield, Tamworth Rd
- 60 Weeford, Watling St

A446
- 60 Allens End, London Rd
- 60 Bassetts Pole, London Rd

A449
- 40 Coven, Wolverhampton Rd
- 60 Gailey, Wolverhampton Rd

A4177
- 60 Hasley Knob, Honiley Rd

A5127
- 30 Lichfield, Trent Valley Rd

B4065
- 30 Ansty, Main Rd

B4098
- 40 Fillongley, Coventry Rd
- 60 Fillongley, Tamworth Rd

B4101
- 40 Tanworth, Broad Lane

B4103
- 30 Kenilworth, Castle Rd
- 30 Kenilworth, Clinton Lane

B4109
- 40 Bulkington, Coventry Rd

Unclassified
- 30 Ash Green, Royal Oak Lane
- 30 Ash Green, St Giles Rd
- 30 Ash Green, Vicarage Lane
- 30 Coleshill, Station Rd

West Yorkshire

A58
- 40 Leeds, Easterley Rd

A61
- 40 Leeds, Scott Hall Rd
- 60 Rothwell, Wakefield Rd northbound carriageway lamp post 140
- 40 Rothwell, Wakefield Rd southbound carriageway jct Castlefields
- 60 Rothwell, Wakefield Rd southbound carriageway nr Wood Lane lamp post 124

A62
- 30 Huddersfield, Manchester Rd

A64
- 40 Leeds, York Rd

A616
- 30 Huddersfield, Woodhead Rd

A629
- 50 Elland, Calderdale Way southbound carriageway north of Huddersfield Way
- 50 Halifax, Keighley Rd
- 40 Shelley, Pennistone Rd

A636
- 30 Wakefield, Denby Dale Rd southbound carriageway jct Cotton St

A638
- 50 Ossett Bypass westbound carriageway layby location lamp post 39

A638
- 30 Wakefield, Dewsbury Rd eastbound carriageway jct Broadway

A644
- 30 Mirfield, Huddersfield Rd

A646
- 30 Portsmouth, Burnley Rd jct Durn St
- 30 Todmorden, Halifax Rd jct Hallroyd Rd

A651
- 40 Birkenshaw, Bradford Rd

A652
- 30 Batley, Bradford Rd
- 30 Batley, Bradford Rd opp Hampson St
- 30 Batley, Bradford Rd opp no.253 Lucas Yard
- 40 Birstall, Bradford Rd

A653
- 40 Shaw Cross, Leeds Rd

A657
- 30 Shipley, Leeds Rd eastbound carriageway nr jct Cragg Rd
- 30 Shipley, Leeds Rd westbound carriageway jct Little Cote Farm

A6025
- 50 Elland, Park Wood, Elland Rd

A6038
- 40 Baildon, Otley Rd opp lamp post 117

B6145
- 30 Bradford, Greenside, Thornton Rd
- 30 Bradford, Thornton, Thornton Rd

B6269
- 40 Shipley, Cottingley Cliffe Rd westbound carriageway jct New Brighton

Unclassified
- 30 Huddersfield, Dalton, Long Lane o/s No.144
- 30 South Elmsall, Minsthorpe Lane jct Ash Grove
- 30 South Kirby, Minsthorpe Lane jct Minsthorpe twds A180 jct Minsthorpe Vale
- 60 Walton, Wetherby Rd

Wiltshire and Swindon

M4
- 70 approx 1.8km west of jct 15
- 70 approx 6.9km east of jct 15
- 70 at jct 15
- 70 approx 3km east of jct 16
- 70 approx 8.4km west of jct 16
- 70 approx 3.1km east of jct 17
- 70 approx 8.3km east of jct 17

A4
- 40 Froxfield
- 60 West Overton

A30
- 40 Fovant
- 60 The Pheasant

A36
- 60 Brickworth
- 60 Hanging Langford
- 50 Knook
- 30 Salisbury, Wilton Rd
- 60 south of Whaddon
- 60 Stapleford to East Clyffe

A303
- 50 Chicklade
- 60 Parsonage Down
- 60 Willoughby Hedge

A338
- 40 Bosscombe
- 30 nr Little Woodbury
- 60 nr Southgrove Copse

A342
- 60 Chirton to Charlton
- 30 Ludgershall, andover Rd
- 50 Lydeway

A346
- 60 Chiseldon Firs
- 60 Whitefield

A350
- 60 Heywood
- 70 Pretty Chimneys

A354
- 40 Coombe Bissett

A360/A344
- 60 Airmans Corner

A361
- 60 Inglesham
- 60 nr Blackland Turning
- 70 nr jct with B3101
- 60 nr Shepherds Shore
- 30 Southwick
- 30 Trowbridge, Frome Rd
- 60 west of Beckhampton

A363
- 30 Bradford on Avon, Trowbridge Rd
- 30 North Bradley, Woodmarsh
- 40 Trowle Common

A419
- 70 Cricklade
- 70 nr Covingham
- 70 Widhill

A420
- 60 Giddeahall to Ford

A3026
- 40 Ludgershall, Tidworth Rd

A3028
- 40 Durrington, Larkhill Rd

A3102
- 30 Calme, Oxford Rd
- 30 Lyneham
- 30 Melksham, Sandridge Rd
- 30 Wootten Bassett

A4259
- 50 nr Coate
- 40 Swindon 2, Queens Drive (nr to jct with Rushton Rd)

A4361
- 60 Broad Hinton
- 60 Uffcott Xrd
- 30 Wroughton, Swindon Rd

B390
- 60 Maddington Farm

B3105
- 30 Hilperton, Hill St/Marsh St

B4006
- 40 Swindon, Marlborough Rd

B3098
- 30 Bratton

B3106
- 30 Hilperton, Hammond Way

B3107
- 30 Bradford on Avon, Holt Rd

B4006
- 30 Stratton St Margaret, Swindon Rd
- 30 Swindon, Whitworth Rd

B4040
- 50 Leigh

B4041
- 30 Wootten Bassett, Station Rd

B4143
- 30 Swindon, Bridge End Rd

B4192
- 50 Liddington

B4289
- 40 Great Western Way nr Bruce St Bridges

B4553
- 40 Swindon, Tewkesbury Way

B4587
- 30 Swindon, Akers Way

Unclassified
- 30 Corsham, Park Lane
- 30 Swindon, Ermin St
- 30 Swindon, Merlin Way
- 30 Swindon, Moredon Rd
- 30 Trowbridge, Wiltshire Drive

Worcestershire

see West Mercia

Wales

Mid and South Wales

Blaenau Gwent, Bridgend, Caerphilly, Cardiff, Carmarthenshire, Merthyr Tydfil, Monmouthshire, Neath Port Talbot, Newport, Pembrokeshire, Rhondda Cynon Taff, Swansea, Torfaen, Vale of Glamorgan

M4
- 70 1.1km east of Jct33 where Llantrisant Rd crosses M4
- 70 1.5km east of Jct37
- 70 2km east of Jct35
- 70 at Jct36 overpass
- 70 Cherry Orchard Overbridge Jct30-32
- 70 Llanmartin
- 70 Rhiwbina Hill overpass (Jct30-32)
- 50 Toll Plaza

A40
- 60 Buckland Hall, Brecon to Abergavenny
- 70 from 1.2km east to 100m west of Bancyfelin Jct
- 70 Johnstown, Carmarthen to St Clears
- 60 Llanhamlac, Brecon to Abergavenny
- 60 Llansantffried Jct
- 70 Mitchel Troy
- 70 Monmouth, opp. Llangattock Lodge
- 60 Rhosmaen, Llandeilo
- 60 Scethrog, Brecon to Abergavenny
- 40 Trecastle
- 60 Whitemill

A40 to B4302
- 30 Rhosmaen, jct to N

A44
- 60 Forest Bends
- 30 Llanbadarn Fawr
- 60 Llanfihangel Nant Melan
- 60 Sweet Lamb, West of Llangurig
- 60 The Gwystre opp Gwystre Farm

A48
- 70 300m South of Bristol House Layby to Pont Abraham Rdbt
- 30 Baglan, Dinas Baglan
- 30 Belle Vue, Cardiff Rd
- 50 Berryhill
- 40 Bonvilston
- 40 Brocastle
- 30 Castleton
- 70 Cowbridge Bypass
- 40 Crosshands to Cwmgwili
- 70 Cwmgwili, Pontarddulais Rd Jct.to Bristol House Layby
- 70 from 1.7km west to 300m east of Llanddarog Jct
- 70 from 1.8km west to 300m east of Foelgastell Jct
- 70 from 700m east to 2.2km west of Nantycaws Jct
- 40 Langstone
- 30 Pontarddulais, Bolgoed Rd
- 30 Pontardulais, Carmarthen Rd
- 30 Pontardulais, Fforest Rd
- 30 Port Talbot, Margam Rd (Rhanallt S)
- 30 St Nicholas

A438
- 40 Three Cocks

A449
- 70 Llandenny
- 70 Llantrissent nr Usk
- 70 nr Coldra

A458
- 60 Cefn Bridge
- 60 Llanfair Caereinion (Neuadd Bridge)
- 40 Trewern

A465
- 60 btwn Aberbaden and Llanfoist
- 60 llanfoist nr Abergavenny
- 50 Llanelly
- 40 Pandy
- 50 Pandy (50mph area)
- 60 Trilley Mill nr Abergavenny

A466
- 40 High Beech Rdbt to Old Hospital
- 30 Llandogo
- 30 Monmouth, Redbrook Rd
- 30 St. Arvans
- 30 Tintern

A467
- 60 Abertillery
- 40 Blaina
- 70 Danycraig, Risca
- 40 Warm Tum (changing from 40 to 30 soon)

A468
- 30 Machen Village

A469
- 70 Caerphilly, Lower Rhymney Valley Relief Rd
- 30 Tir-Y-Birth

A470
- 70 Abercynon (southbound)
- 70 at Aberfan overbridge
- 30 at Cilfynydd
- 70 at overbridge of Cilfynydd
- 60 Brecon to Merthyr (Storey Arms)
- 40 Cardiff, Manor Way
- 30 Erwood
- 60 Erwood South
- 40 Llandinam to Caersws Jct
- 40 Llandinam Village
- 60 Llanidloes to Llandinam
- 30 Llyswen
- 30 Newbridge on Wye
- 60 Newbridge to Rhayader
- 70 nr Taffs Well North
- 70 nr Taffs Well South
- 60 Powys, Beacons Reservoir
- 70 Rhydyfelin overbridge, Dynea Rd
- 60 South of Builth (Aberduhonw)
- 60 South of Builth (Abernant)
- 60 South of Builth (Ysgiog)

A472
- 30 Hafodrynys
- 30 Maescwmmer
- 60 Monkswood
- 30 Usk Bridge to Old Saw Mill

A473
- 30 Bridgend, Bryntirion Hill
- 30 Pencoed, Penybont Rd

A474
- 30 All the village of Glanaman
- 40 Alltwen, Graig Rd
- 30 Ammandford to Portamman, Heol Wallasey Jct
- 30 Glanffrwd Est Jct. to Garnant
- 30 Heol-Y-Gors
- 30 Neath, Penywern Rd
- 30 Rhyd y Fro, Commercial St

A475
- 40 Llanwnen
- 40 Lampeter, Pentrebach, County Rd

A476
- 30 Carmel to N at Temple Bar
- 40 Carmel, Stag and Pheasant
- 30 Ffairfach, 30 mph to the Square
- 30 Gorslas, Cross Hands Rdbt to the Phoenix Inn
- 40 Gorslas, The Gate
- 30 Heol Bryngwili, Cross Hands
- 30 Llannon, Erw Non Jct to Clos Rebecca Jct
- 30 Swiss Valley, Thomas Arms, Llanelli to North
- 30 Upper Tumble, Llannon Rd and Bethania Rd

A477
- 40 Bangeston to Nash Fingerpost Roadworks
- 30 Llanddowror

A478
- 30 Clunderwen
- 30 Llandissillio
- 30 Pentlepoir

A479
- 30 Bronllys

A482
- 30 Aberaeron, Lampeter Rd
- 30 Cwmann, North
- 30 Cwmann, South
- 30 Village of Llanwrda

A482 and A475
- 30 Lampeter

A483
- 60 Abbey Cwm Hir Jct
- 30 Ammanford, Tycroes to Villiers Jct
- 30 Ffairfach, N to Llandeilo Bridge
- 30 Llandeilo, Rhosmaen St

A483
- 50 Garthmyl, Refail Garage
- 60 Garthmyl, Welshpool
- 60 Llandrindod, Midway Bends
- 60 North of Crossgates

A484
- 40 Bronwydd Village
- 30 Burry Port
- 30 Cenarth
- 40 Cwmffrwd
- 30 Cynwyl Elfed
- 30 from 80m west of New Rd Jct, east to N N.C.E
- 40 Idole, from 200m s.w. of B4309 Jct south to N
- 30 Llanelli, Sandy Rd
- 60 Llanelli, Trostre Rdbt to Berwick Rdbt
- 60 Pembrey
- 30 Pembrey, Danybanc Jct to St Illtyds Rise Jct
- 40 Pentrecagel
- 40 Rhos
- 40 Saron

A485
- 40 Alltwalis
- 30 Cwmann, from the A482 Jct N
- 40 Llanllwwni
- 30 Llanybydder (North)
- 30 Llanybydder (South)
- 40 Peniel

A487
- 40 Approach to Llanrhystud from the south
- 30 Central Aberaeron
- 30 Central Aberystwyth
- 30 Ceredigion, Bow St
- 30 Eglwyswrw
- 40 Furnace
- 30 Llanarth
- 30 Llanfarian
- 30 Newgale
- 30 Newport
- 40 Penglais Hill/Waunfawr
- 40 Penparc, Trunk Rd
- 40 Rhydyfelin
- 30 Rhydypennau
- 30 Talybont

A489
- 60 Caersws Jct to Penstrowed
- 60 Kerry, County Rd, Glanmule Garage
- 40 Newtown, west of Hafren coll
- 60 Penstrowed to Newtown

A4042
- 60 Llanover

A4046
- 40 Ebbw Vale (nr Tesco's)
- 30 Ebbw Vale, College Rd
- 30 Waynllwyd

A4048
- 30 Argoed
- 30 Blackwood (Sunnybank)
- 30 Cwmfelinfach Village
- 30 Hollybush
- 30 Pontllanfraith, Blackwood Rd

A4054
- 30 Edwardsville, Nantddu, Tec
- 30 Merthyr Vale, Cardiff Rd

A4061
- 30 Ogmore Vale, Cemetery Rd

A4066
- 40 Broadway
- 40 Llanmiloe, Pendine
- 40 Pendine, Llanmiloe
- 30 Pendine, Marsh Rd

A4067
- 60 Abercraf
- 60 Crai

A4068
- 30 Cwmtwrch, Bethel Rd
- 30 Cwmtwrch, Heol Gleien

A4069
- 30 Llandovery, Broad St
- 30 Llangadog, East
- 30 Llangadog, North, Station Rd
- 30 Llangadog, South
- 30 Station Rd to the Remploy Factory

A4074
- 30 Milford Haven, St Lawrence Hill

A4075
- 30 Pembroke

A4076
- 30 Carew
- 30 Johnston

A4093
- 30 Glynogwr

A4102
- 30 Gellideg, Swansea Rd

A4106
- 30 Porthcawl, Newton Nottage Rd
- Porthcawl, The Porthway

A4107
- 30 Abergwynfi, High St

A4109
- Aberdulias, Main Rd
- 30 Crynant, Main Rd
- 30 Glynneath
- 30 Seven Sisters, Dulais Rd

A4118
- 60 Fairwood Common

A4119
- 50 Llantrisant, Mwyndy Cross

A4120
- 30 Aberystwyth

A4138
- 30 Hendy, Loughor Bridge to 40mph speed limit
- 40 Talyclun, from the 30mph at Hendy to the B4297 Jct

A4139
- 30 Pembroke
- 30 Pembroke Dock
- 30 Tenby

A4216
- 30 Cockett, Cockett Rd

A4221
- 60 Caehopkin

A4222
- 30 Cowbridge, Abertin Rd
- 30 Maendy

A4226
- 40 Barry, Five Mile Lane

A4233
- 30 Ferndale, The Parade

B4181
- 30 Bridgend, Coity Rd

B4223
- 30 Ton Pentre, Pentwyn Rd

B4235
- 60 Gwernesney nr Usk

B4242
- 30 Pontneddfechan, Gwyn Neath

B4245
- 30 Caldicot Bypass
- 30 Langstone, Magor Rd
- 60 Leechpool
- 30 Rogiet, Caldicot Rd
- 30 Undy

B4254
- 30 Penpedairheol, Pengam Rd

B4265
- 30 St Brides Major

B4281
- 30 Kenfig Hill, High St

B4282
- 30 Bridgend, Bridgend Rd and Castle St
- 30 Bryn, Measteg Rd

B4290
- 30 Skewen, Pen-yr-Heol and Crymlyn Rd

B4295
- 40 btwn Gowerton and Penclawdd
- 60 btwn Penclawdd and Llanrhidian

B4297
- 40 Bynea, Lougher Bridge Rdbt to Station Rd Jct
- 30 Capel Hendre
- 30 Fforest
- 30 Llanedi
- 30 Llangennech, Cleviston Park Jct to Park Lane Jctct
- 30 Llwynhendy, from Capel Soar to the Police Station

B4301
- 30 Bronwydd Village

B4302
- 30 Talley

B4303
- 30 Llanelli, Dafen Rdbt to Felinfoel Rdbt

B4304
- 40 Llanelli, Copperworks Rdbt to Morfa Rdbt
- 30 Llanelli, Lower Trostre Rd Rdbt to Trostre Rd Rdbt

B4306
- 30 Bancffosfelen, Heol Y Banc
- 30 Llangendeirn
- 30 Pontyberem, Llanon Rd

B4308
- 40 Penmynnydd

B4309
- 30 Five Roads

B4310
- 30 Drefach, Heol Caegwyn
- 40 Nangaredig, Station Rd

B4312
- 30 Johnstown, from the Square to N
- 30 Llangain

B4314
- 30 Narberth
- 30 Pendine

B4317
- 30 Carway, East
- 30 Carway, West
- 30 Ponthenri, Myrtle Hill
- 30 Pontyberem, Heol Capel Ifan
- 30 Pontyberem, Station Rd

B4320
- 30 Hundleton

B4322
- 40 Pembroke Dock, Pembroke Rd

B4325
- 30 Neyland

B4328
- 30 Whitland, Trevaughan

B4333
- 30 Cynwyl Elfed (North)
- 30 Hermon
- 30 Newcastle Emlyn, Aber-arad

B4336
- 30 All the village of Llanfihangel Ar Arth
- 30 Llandysul, Pont-tyweli

B4337
- 30 Llanybydder (East)
- 30 Llanybydder (West)
- 40 Talsarn

B4347
- 30 Newcastle Village

B4350
- 60 Glasbury to Hay on Wye, County Rd

B4436
- 40 Kittle, Pennard Rd

B4459
30,40 Pencader
B4524
30 Corntown
B4556
30 All the village of Caerbryn
30 Blaenau, Penygroes Rd
30 Pengroes, Norton Rd
B4560
30 Beaufort, Ebbw Vale, Llangynidr Rd
B4591
30 High Cross, Risca Rd
B4598
60 Horse and Jockey nr Abergavenny
60 Llancayo
B4599
30 Ystradgynlais
B4622
30 Broadlands Link Rd
Unclassified
Aberbargoed, Bedwwellty and Coedymoeth Rd Jct
30 Abercwmboi, Park View Terrace
30 Abercynon, Abercynon Rd
30 Abergavenny, Hereford Rd
30 Abergwili, Ambulance Station to the Bypass Rdbt
30 Abertillery, Gwern Berthi
30 Ammanford, Layby outside Saron Church, Saron Rd
30 Ammanford, New Rd and Pantyffynnon Rd
30 Argoed, Penylan Rd
30 Barry, Barry Rd
30 Barry, Buttrills Rd
30 Barry, Gladstone Rd
30 Barry, Holton Rd
30 Barry, Jenner Rd
30 Beddau, Bryniteg Hill
30 Beddau, Gwaunmiskin Rd
30 Betws, Betws Rd
30 Betws, Maesquarre Rd
30 Birchgrove, Birchgrove Rd
40 Bishopston, Northway
30 Brackla, Brackla Way
30 Bridgend Ind Est, Kingsway
30 Bridgend Ind Est, North Rd
30 Bridgend Ind Est, South Rd
30 Bridgend Ind Est, Western Avenue
30 Bridgend Inner Bypass
30 Bridgend, Coychurch Rd
30 Bridgend, Pen-Y-Cae Lane
30 Britton Ferry, Old Rd
30 Brynamman, Brynamman Rd
30 Brynmawr, Beaufort Hill and High St
30 Brynna, Brynna Rd
30 Caerleon, Ponthir Rd
30 Caerleon, Usk Rd
30 Caerphilly, 2 Llanbradach
30 Caerphilly, Kendon Hill
30 Caerphilly, Mountain Rd
30 Caldicot, Chepstow Rd
30 Cardiff, Circle Way E/W Llanedeym
30 Cardiff, Cyncoed Rd
30 Cardiff, Excalibur Drive
30 Cardiff, Heol Isaf
30 Cardiff, Leckwith Rd
30 Cardiff, Newport Rd
30 Cardiff, North Rd
30 Cardiff, Pencisely Rd
30 Cardiff, Penylan, Colchester Avenue
30 Cardiff, Rhiwbina, Heol y Deri
30 Cardiff, Rhyd-y-pennau Rd
30 Cardiff, Roath, Lake Rd East/West
30 Cardiff, Rumney, Wentloog Avenue
30 Cardiff, St Fagans Rd
30 Cardiff, Willowbrook Drive
30 Carmarthen, Lime Grove Avenue and Fountain Head Tce
30 Cefn Criwber, Cefn Rd
30 Cefn Glas, Liangewydd Rd
30 Cefn Glas, Merlin Crescent
30 Cefncoed, High St
30 Cefncoed, Vaynor Rd
30 Cefneithin
30 Ceredigion, Cardigan, North
30 Ceredigion, Llandysul Central
30 Ceredigion, New Quay Central
30 Church Village, Main Rd
30 Cilfynydd, Cilfynydd Rd
30 Clydach, Pontarddawe Rd
30 Clydach, Vadre Rd
30 Cockett, Cwmbach Rd
30 Coity, Heol Spencer
60 Coldharbour, Usk to Raglan Rd
30 Cowbridge, Primrose Hill
30 Crofty, New Rd
30 Crumlin, Hafodyrynys Hill
40 Cwmbwria, Carmarthen Rd
30 Cwmgovilon
30 Cwmgwili
30 Cwmgwili, Thornhill Rd
30 Deri, New Rd
30 Derwen Fawr, Rhy-Y-Defaid Drive
30 Dinas, Dinas Rd
30 Dowlais, High St
30 Drefach, Heol Blawnhirwaun
30 Ebbw Vale, Letchwworth Rd
30 Ebbw Vale, Newchurch Rd
30 Ebbw Vale, Steelworks Rd
30 Farm Shop, Pentregethin Rd
30 Felinfoel, Llethri Rd
30 Ferndale, Highfield Jct
30 Ferndale, Oakland Terrace
30 Fforest Fach, Carmarthen Rd
40 Five Mile Lane
30 Fochrie, Olgivie Terrace
30 Foelgastell
30 Forden
60 from 120m s.e. of Heol Login for 1.2km s.e. along Nantycaws Hill
40 Gelligaer, Church Rd
30 Gelli, Gelli Ind Est
30 Gelli, Gelli Rd
30 Gilwern, Cae Meldon (aka Ty Mawr Lane)
30 Gorseinon, Frampton Rd
30 Gorslas, Pengroes Rd
30 Haverfordwest, New Rd/Uzmaston Rd
30 Heath, Maescoed Rd
30 Hendreforgan, Gilfach Rd
30 Hopkinstown, Hopkinstown Rd
30 Jersey Marine, New Rd
30 Johnstown, St Clears Rd
30 Killay, Goetre Fawr Rd
30 Llanelli, Denham Avenue
30 Llanelli, Heol Goffa (from the A476 Jct to the A484 Jct)
30 Llanfihangel Ar Arth (South)
30 Llangonoed, Bridgend Rd
30 Llangyfelach, Swansea Rd
30 Llangynwyd, Bridgend Rd
30 Llanharan, Brynna Rd
30 Llanharen, Bridgend Rd
60 Llanhenock, Caerleon to Usk Rd – Apple tree farm
30 Llantrisant, Cross Inn Rd
50 Llantwit Major Bypass
30 Llantwit Major, Llanmaes Rd
30 Maesteg, Heol Ty-With
30 Maesteg, Heol-Ty-Gwyn
30 Malpas, Rowan Way
30 Merthyr Tdyfil, Brecon Rd
30 Merthyr Tdyfil, Goatmill Rd
30 Merthyr Tdyfil, Goitre Lane
30 Merthyr Tdyfil, Gumos Rd
30 Merthyr Tdyfil, Heol-Tai-Mawr
30 Merthyr Tdyfil, Heolgerrig Rd
30 Merthyr Tdyfil, Pant Rd
30 Merthyr Tdyfil, Plymouth St
30 Merthyr Tdyfil, Rocky Rd
30 Merthyr Tdyfil, The Walk
30 Milford Haven, Priory Rd
40 Milford Haven, Thornton Rd
40 Monmouth, Bend at Green Farm
30 Monmouth, Devauden Village
30 Monmouth, Dixton Rd
30 Monmouth, Hereford Rd
30 Monmouth, Magor (West)
60 Monmouth, Parkwall
30 Monmouth, Usk Bridge to Llanbadoc
30 Morriston, Caemawr Rd
30 Morriston, Clasemont Rd
30 Mount Pleasant, Cardiff Rd
30 Mountain Ash, Llanwonno Rd
30 Mountain Ash, Miskin Rd
30 Mountain Ash, New Rd
30 Nantgarw, Oxford St
30 Nash Village, West Nash Rd
30 New Tredegar, White Roase Way
30 Newbridge, Park Rd
30 Newport, Allt-Yr-Yn Avenue
30 Newport, Caerleon Rd (east of Beaufort Rd)
30 Newport, Chepstow Rd nr Aberthaw Rd
40 Newport, Chepstow Rd nr Royal Oak Hill
30 Newport, Corporation Rd
30 Newport, Lighthouse Rd
30 Newport, opp Power Station, Risca Rd
30 Newport, Rhiwderin
30 Newport, Wharf Rd
30 North Cornelly, Heol Fach
30 Pembroke, Merlins Bridge
30 Pencoed, Felindre Rd
30 Pendarren, High St
30 Pendine
30 Penrhiwceiber, 2 Penrhiwceiber Rd
40 Pentrecagel
30 Ponthir, Caerleon Rd
30 Pontllanfraith, Bryn Rd
30 Pontyclun, Cowbridge Rd
30 Pontymister, Welsh Oak PH
30 Pontymister, Welsh Oak PH
30 Pontypool, Little Mill
30 Pontypridd, The Broadway
40 Porthcawl, Bridgend Rd
30 Porthcawl, Fulmar Rd
30 Rassau, Reservoir Rd
30 Rhondda Cynon Taff, Tonteg Rd
30 Rhymney, Llys Joseph Parry (nr Farmers Arms)
30 Rhymney, Wellington Way
30 Risca, Cromwell Rd
30 Risca, Holly Rd
30 Risca, Waun Fawr Park Rd
30 Rogerstone, Pontymason Lane
30 Sandfields, Village Rd
30 Saron Village, Dyffryn Rd
30 Skewen, Burrows Rd
30 St Athan, Cowbridge Rd
30 Steynton
30 Sully, Haynes Rd
30 Sully, South Rd
30 Swansea, Fabian Way
30 Swansea, Grovesend
40 Swansea, Mumbles Rd (A4067) Sketty Lane to St Helens Sports Gr.
30 Swansea, Mynydd Newydd Rd, Caemawr Rd, Parry Rd, Vicarage Rd (Heol Ddu to Clasemont Rd)
30 Swansea, Peniel Green Rd (nr Station Rd o/s TOTAL Garage)
60 Tiers Cross
30 Ton Pentre, Maindy Rd
30 Tonteg, Church Rd
30 Tonyrefail, Gilfach Rd
30 Tonyrefail, Penrhiwfer Rd
30 Torfaen
30 Treboeth, Llangyfelach Rd
30 Tredegar, Vale Terrace
30 Trelewis, Gelligaer Rd
30 Upper Boat, Cardiff Rd
Upper Church Village, Pen yr Eglwys
30 Usk, Porthycame St
30 Vale of Glamorgan, Pen-y-turnpike Rd
30 Waungren, Pentre Rd
30 Whitland (East), Spring Gardens
30 Whitland (west)
30 Whitland, Market St
30 Whitland, North Rd
30 Wick, St Brides Rd
30 Willowtow, Gwaun Helyg Rd
30 Ynystawe, Clydach Rd
30 Ynyswdre, Heol-Yr-Ysgol
30 Ynysybwl, New Rd

North Wales

Ceredigion, Conwy, Denbighshire, Flintshire, Gwynedd, Isle of Anglesey, Powys, Wrexham

A5
30 Holyhead
A5/A5025
50 Holyhead to Llanfachraeth
A470
30,60 Conwy Valley
40,60 Dolgellau
40,60 (30 at rdbts) Llandudno to the A55
30,40,60 Tal-y-waenydd to Congl-y-wal (Blaenau)
A483/A5
60 Ruabon to Chirk
A487
30,40,50,60 Caernarfon to Dolbenmaen
30,40,60 Penmorfa to Gellilydan
A494
40,60 Bala to Glanrafon
30 Llyn Tegid, Bala
40,60 Ruthin to Llanferres
A496
30,40,60 Harlech to Llanbedr
A499
30,40,60 Pwllheli
A525
40,60 Denbigh to Ruthin
30,40,60 Llanfair Dyffryn Clwyd to Llandegla
30,60 Wrexham to Minera
30,40,60 Wrexham to Redbrook Maelor
A534
30 Holt Rd
A539
30,60 Llangollen, Mill St
30,40,60 Trevor to Erbistock
A541
30 Mold Rd
30,40,60,70 Mold to Caergwrle
30,40,60,70 Wrexham to Cefn-y-bedd
A541/525
30,40,60 St Asaph to Bodfari
A545
30,40 Menai Bridge to Beaumaris
A547
30,40,50 Colwyn Bay
30,40,60 Prestatyn to Rhuddlan
30 Rhyl, Vale Rd/Rhuddlan Rd
A548
30,40 Abergele to Kinmel Bay
30 Abergele, Dundonald Avenue
30,40,50,60,70Gronant to Flint (Oakenholt)
30,40 Rhyl to Prestatyn
A549
30,60 Mynydd Isa to Buckley
A550/B5125
30 Hawarden
A4086
30,40,60 Cwm-y-glo to Llanrug
A4212
60 Graig Las/Tryweryn to Trawsfynydd
A4244
60 Ty Mawr to Cym-y-glo
A5025
30,40,50,60 Amlwch, Menai Bridge
A5104
30 Coed-Talon to Leeswood
A5112
30,40 Llandygai to Bangor
A5119
30,50,60 Mold to Flint
A5152
30,60 Bala
30 Chester Rd
30,40 Rhostyllen
B4545
30,40 Kingsland to Valley
B5108
30,60 Benllech
B5109
30 Llangefni
B5113
30 Colwyn Bay, Kings Rd/Kings Drive
B5115
30 Llandrillo, Llandudno Rd
30,40 Llandudno Promenade to Rhos Point
B5118
30 Rhyl Promenade
B5120
30 Prestatyn, Pendyffryn Rd
B5129
30,60 Kelsterton to Saltney Ferry
B5420
30 Menai Bridge
B5425
30,60 Llay, New Rd
B5443
30 Rossett
Unclassified
30,40,60 Johnstown
30,60 Kinmel Bay, St Asaph Avenue
30,40,60 Menai Bridge to Gwalchmai

Scotland

Dumfries and Galloway

A74(M)
70 Cogries
A7
60 Langholm
A76
Auldgirth
60 Closeburn
30 Dumfries, Glasgow Rd Gateside
A77
60 Balyett
60 Cairnryan
60 Whiteleys
A701
30 Moffat
60 Mollinburn/St Anns
A709
60 Burnside
A711
50 Beeswing
30 Kirkcudbright
A716
60 Stoneykirk
A718
60 Craichmore
B721
30 Eastriggs

Fife

A91
Deer Centre to Stratheden Jct
Guardbridge to St Andrews
Melville Lodges to St Andrews
A92
Cadham to New Inn
Cardenden Overbridge to Chapel
Cowdenbeath to Lochgelly
Crossgates to New Inn
Melville Lodges to Lindifferon
New Inn to Tay Bridge
Rathillet (south) to Easter Kinnear
A823
Dunfermline, Queensferryroad
Dunfermline, St Margaret Drive
A907
Dunfermline, Halbeath Rd
A911
Glenrothes to Leslie
Glenrothes to Milton
A914
Edenwood to Cupar
Forgan to St Michaels
Kettlebridge
New Inn to Cupar
Pitlessie to Clushford Toll
A915
Checkbar Jct to Percival Jcts
A921
Kirkcaldy, Esplanade
Kirkcaldy, High St/Path
Kirkcaldy, Rosslyn St
Kirkcaldy, St Clair St
A977
Kincardine, Fere Gait
A985
Culross (west) to C38 Valleyfield
Kincardine to Rosyth
Rosyth, Admiralty Rd
Waukmill to Brankholm
B914
Redcraigs to Greenknowes
B942
East of Collinsburgh
B980
Rosyth, Castlandhill Rd
B981
Cowdenbeath, Broad St
Gosshill to Ballingry
Kirkcaldy, Dunnikier Way
B9157
Bankhead of Pitheadle to Kirkcaldy
Orrock to East Balbairdie
Sheriff Rdbt to Kirkcaldy
White Lodge Jct to Croftgary
Unclassified
Buckhaven, Methilhaven Rd
Dunfermline, Townhill Rd
Glenrothes, Formonthills Rd
Glenrothes, Woodside Rd
Glenrothes, Woodside Way
Kirkcaldy, Hendry Rd
Leven, Glenlyon Rd
Methil, Methilhaven Rd

Lothian and Borders

East Lothian, Edinburgh, Midlothian, Scottish Borders, West Lothian

A8
40 Edinburgh, at Ratho station
A7
60 Crookston
NSL Galashiels, Buckholmside to Bowland
30 Hawick Sandbed to Galalaw
30 Stow to Bowland
A68
30 Jedburgh
NSL Soutra Hill
A70
30 Edinburgh, Balerno between Bridge Rd and Stewart Rd
A71
30 Breich
30 Polbeth
A72
NSL Borders, Holylee nr Walkerburn
NSL Castlecraig nr Blyth bridge
30 Peebles, Innerleithen Rd
A90
40 Edinburgh, Southbound from Burnshot flyover to Cammo Rd
A697
30 Greenlaw and south approach
NSL Orange Lane
NSL Ploughlands to Hatchednize
A697/8
30 Coldstream
A698
NSL Ashybank
NSL Crailinghall
A699
40 Maxton Village
A701
NSL Blyth Bridge to Cowdenburn
30 Rachan Mill, Broughton to A72
A702
NSL Dolphinton to Medwyn Mains
A703
30 Eddleston and approaches
NSL Leadburn to Shiplaw
30 Peebles to Milkieston
30 Peebles, Edinburgh Rd
A705
30 between Whitburn and East Whitburn
A706
30 Whitburn, Carnie Place
A720
50 Edinburgh, City Bypass, east of Gogar Rdbt
A899
50 btwn Lizzie Bryce Rdbt and Almond Interchange
50 South of Deer Park Rdbt
A6091
NSL Melrose bypass
A6105
30 Gordon and approaches
B6374
30 Galashiels, Station Bridge to Lowood Bridge
Unclassified
30 Edinburgh, Bruntsfield place btwn Thorneybauk and Merchiston place
40 Edinburgh, Comiston Rd btwn Oxgangs Rd and Buckstone Dr
40,60 Edinburgh, Frogston Rd west btwn Mounthooly loan and Mortonhall gate
30 Edinburgh, Lower Granton Rd btwn Granton Square and Trinity Rd
30 Edinburgh, Muirhouse Parkway
40 Edinburgh, West Approach Rd btwn Morrison St Link and Dundee St
30 Edinburgh, West Granton Rd
30 Whitburn, West Main St

North East Scotland

Aberdeen, Aberdeenshire, Moray

A90
40 Aberdeen, Midstocket Rd to Whitestripes Avenue Rdbt
60 btwn bend at South of Leys and Bogbrae
60 btwn Bogbrae and north of Bridgend
70 btwn Candy and Upper Criggie
60 btwn Jct with B9032 and A98 at Fraserburgh
70 btwn Laurencekirk and north of Fourdon
70 btwn Mill of Barnes and Laurencekirk
60 btwn St Fergus and access Rd to Bilbo
70 Dundee to Aberdeen Rd at Jct with B9120 Laurencekirk
70 north of Newtonhill Jct to South of Schoolhill Rd
60 Peterhead and St Fergus, btwn A982 North Rd
60 Peterhead, btwn north of Bridgend and Blackhills
70 Portlethen to South Damhead (southbound), south of Schoolhill Rd
70 south of Schoolhill Rd, Portlethen to South Damhead (northbound)
A92
60 btwn Johnshaven and Inverbervie
60 btwn rdside of Kinneff and Mill of Uras
A93
30 Aboyne
40 at Banchory eastbound from Caravan Site
30 at Banchory westbound from Church
60 btwn Cambus O'May and Dinnet
60 btwn Dinnet to Aboyne
60 btwn Kincardine O'Neil and Haugh of Sluie
A95
30 Cornhill
60 btwn 30mph at Keith and Davoch of Grange
A96
60 btwn East Mill of Carden at B9002 Jct and north of Pitmachie
60 btwn Forgie and A98 Jct at Fochabers
60 btwn north of Pitmachie and Jct with A920 at Kirton of Culsalmond
30 Haudigain rdbt to Chapel of Stoneywood
60 Mosstodloch to Lhanbryde (East)
40 South Damhead to Midstocket Rd
A98
30 Banff
60 btwn Carnoch Farm Rd, Buckie and 30mph at Cullen
60 btwn Fochabers 30mph and Mill of Tynet
60 Buckle, btwn Mill of Tynet and Barhill Rd Jct
A941
60 btwn 30mph at Lossiemouth and 40mph at Elgin
60 btwn Clackmarras Rd and South Netherglen
60 btwn Glassgreen and Clackmarras Rd
60 from South Netherglen and Rothes
A947
60 btwn Mains of Tulloch Jct and Fyvie
A947
60 btwn Newmachar and Whiterashes
A948
60 btwn Ellon to Auchnagatt
A952
60 btwn New Leeds and Jct with A90 at Cortes
B9040
60 btwn Silver Sands Caravan Park to Jct with B9012
B9089
60 from Kinloss and crossroads at Roseisle Maltings
Unclassified
30 Aberdeen, Beach Boulevard to Links Rd
30 Aberdeen, Beach Boulevard to Wales St
30 Aberdeen, Great Northern Rd
30 Aberdeen, Great Southern Rd
30 Aberdeen, King St
30 Aberdeen, Springhill Rd
30 Aberdeen, St Machar Drive
40 Aberdeen, Wellington Rd
40 Aberdeen, West Tullos Rd

Northern Scotland

Highland, Orkney, Shetland, Western Isles

A9
Altnasleanach by Inverness
Caulmaillie, Golspie, Sutherland
Cuaich by Dalwhinnie
Daviot, by Inverness
Fearn, by Tain
North Kessock jct (both directions)
North of Dalwhinnie junction
nr Dalwhinnie
South of the Mound, by Golspie
A82
Altsigh Youth Hostel, by Inverness
Drumnadrochit, Temple Pier
Invergarry Power Station
Kingshouse Hotel, Glencoe
White Corries, Rannoch Moor, Lochaber
A87
West of Bunloyne jct
A95
by Grantown on Spey, Congash
Drumuillie by Boat of Garten
North of Cromdale
A96
East Auldearn jct, by Nairn
Gollanfield, by Nairn
Nairn, West Auldern Jct
West of Allanfearn jct, by Inverness
A99
Hempriggs, south of Wick
A834
Dingwall, nr Foddarty Bridge
Dingwall, Strathpeffer Rd
A835
Inverlael straight nr Ullapool
A939
Ferness to Grantown, Spey Rd
B9006
Sunnyside, Culloden, Inverness

Strathclyde

Argyll & Bute, East Ayrshire, East Dunbartonshire, East Renfrewshire, Glasgow, Inverclyde, North Ayrshire, North Lanarkshire, Renfrewshire, South Ayrshire, South Lanarkshire, West Dunbartonshire

M74
Abington, Jct 13 (northbound)
A70
East Tarelgin
A73
Airdrie, Carlisle Rd
A76
New Cumnock, nr Lime Rd
A78
Fairlie, Main Rd
A82
Bridge of Orchy
Milton, Dunbarton Rd
A85
west of Tyndrum
A89
Airdrie, Forrest St
A706
South of Forth
A730
Rutherglen, Blairbeth Rd
A737
Dairy, New St/Kilwinning Rd
A749
East Kilbride Rd btwn Cathkin Rd and Cairnmuir Rd
A807
Bardowie, Balmore Rd
A814
Dunbarton, Cardross Rd
A815
nr Ardkinglass
B768
Rutherglen, Burnhill St
B803
Airdrie to Glenmavis, Coatbridge Rd
B814
Duntocher Rd
B8048
Kirkintilloch, Waterside Rd
Unclassified
Bargeddie, Glasgow Rd
Barrhead, Aurs Rd
Bishopbriggs, Woodhill Rd
Clydebank, Glasgow Rd
Coatbridge, Townhead Rd
Drymen Rd/Duntocher Rd
East Kilbride, Maxwelton Rd at Kirkoswald (South)
Johnstone, Beith Rd
Neilston, Kingston Rd
Newton Mearns, Mearns Rd
Paisley, Glasgow Rd nr Newtyle Rd
Rutherglen, Glasgow Rd
Rutherglen, Mill St
Troon, Craigend Rd

Tayside

Angus, Dundee, Perth & Kinross

A9
60 Inverness to Perth road, nr Balnansteuartach
70 Perth to Inverness road, nr Inveralmond Industrial Estate
70 Stirling to Perth road, btwn Broom of Dalreoch and Upper Cairnie
70 Stirling to Perth road, Tibbermore jct
A90
40 Dundee nr Fountainbleau Drive, Forfar Rd
70 Dundee to Perth road, Walnut Grove to Inchyra
70 Dundee to Perth road, west of Longforgan village
50 Dundee, Kingsway
50 Dundee, Swallow rdbt to Strathmartine Rd rdbt
A91
60 Milnathort to Devon Bridge
A92
60 Arbroath to Montrose
30 Dundee btwn Arbroath Rd and Craigie Avenue, Greendykes Rd
40 Dundee, East Dock St
A93
60 Guildtown to Blairgowrie
60 Old Scone to Guildtown
A94
60 Scone to Coupar Angus
A822
60 Crieff to Braco
A923
60 Blairgowrie to Tullybaccart
A933
60 Colliston to Redford
A935
60 Brechin to Montrose
A972
40 Dundee, Kingsway East to Pitairlie Rd
A977
60 Kinross to Crook of Devon
B961
30 Dundee, Drumgeith Rd
B996
60 Kinross to Kelty
Unclassified
30 Dundee, Broughty Ferry Rd
30 Dundee, Charleston Drive
30 Dundee, Laird St
30 Dundee, Old Glamis Rd
30 Dundee, Perth Rd
30 Dundee, Strathmartine Rd

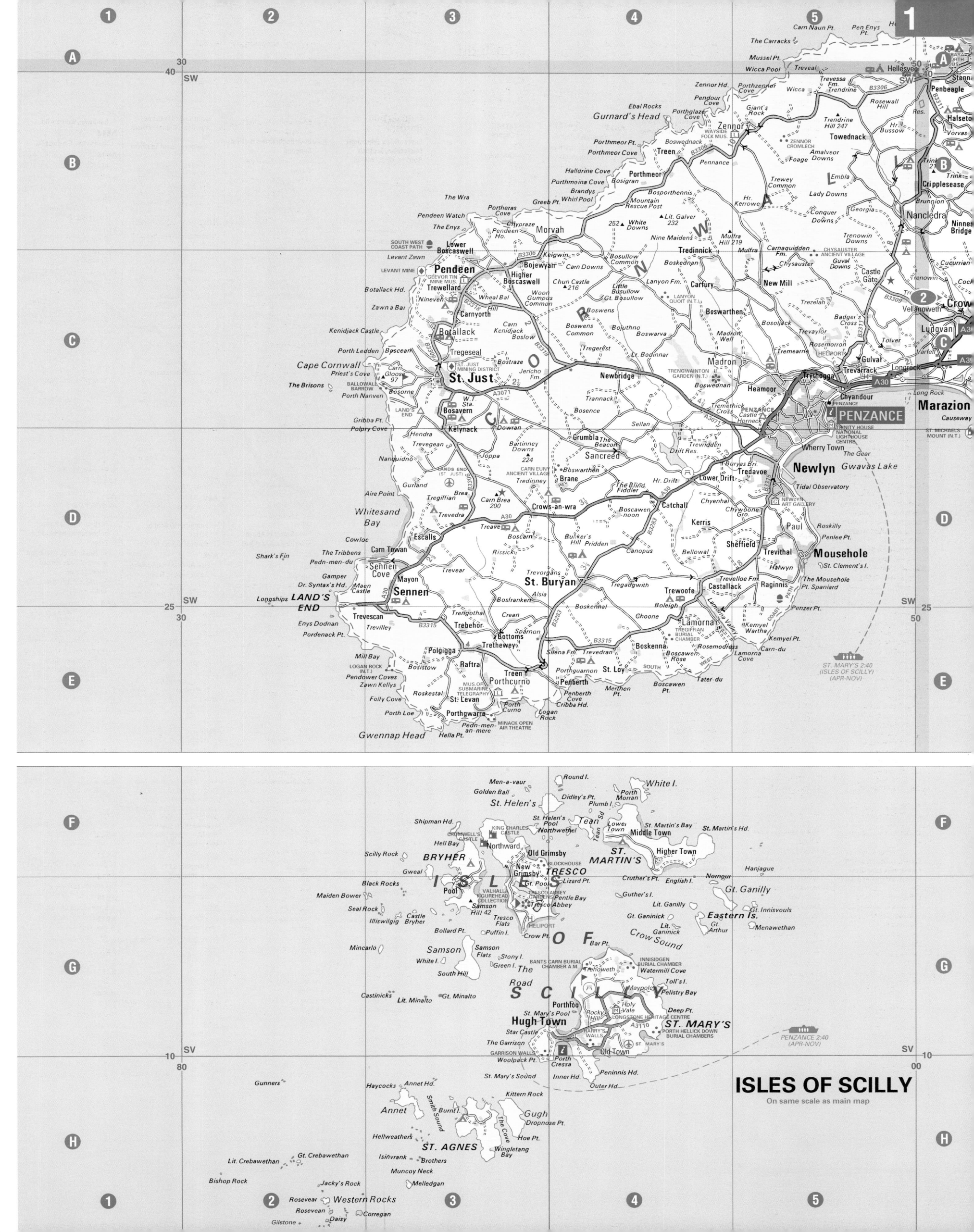

ISLES OF SCILLY

On same scale as main map

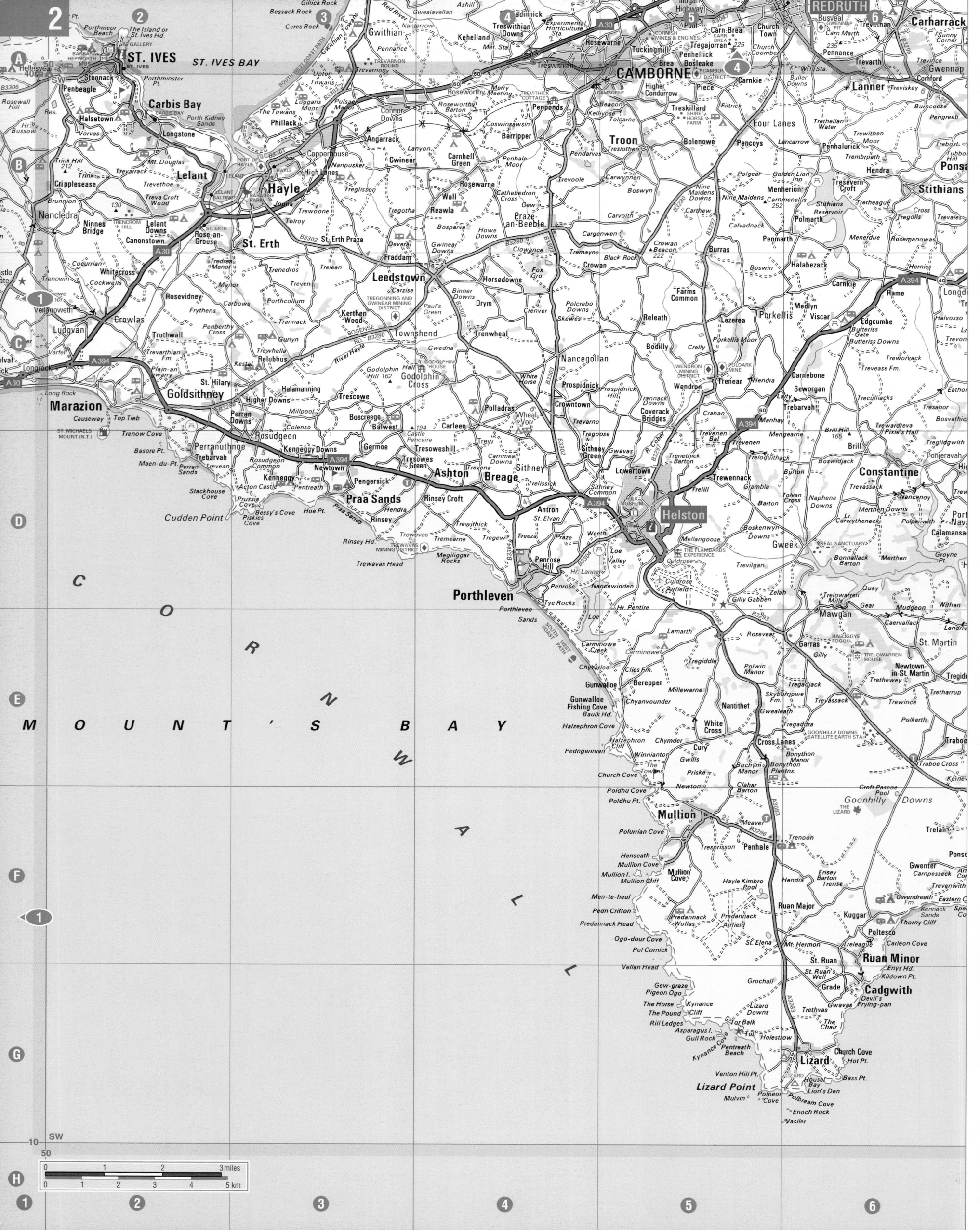

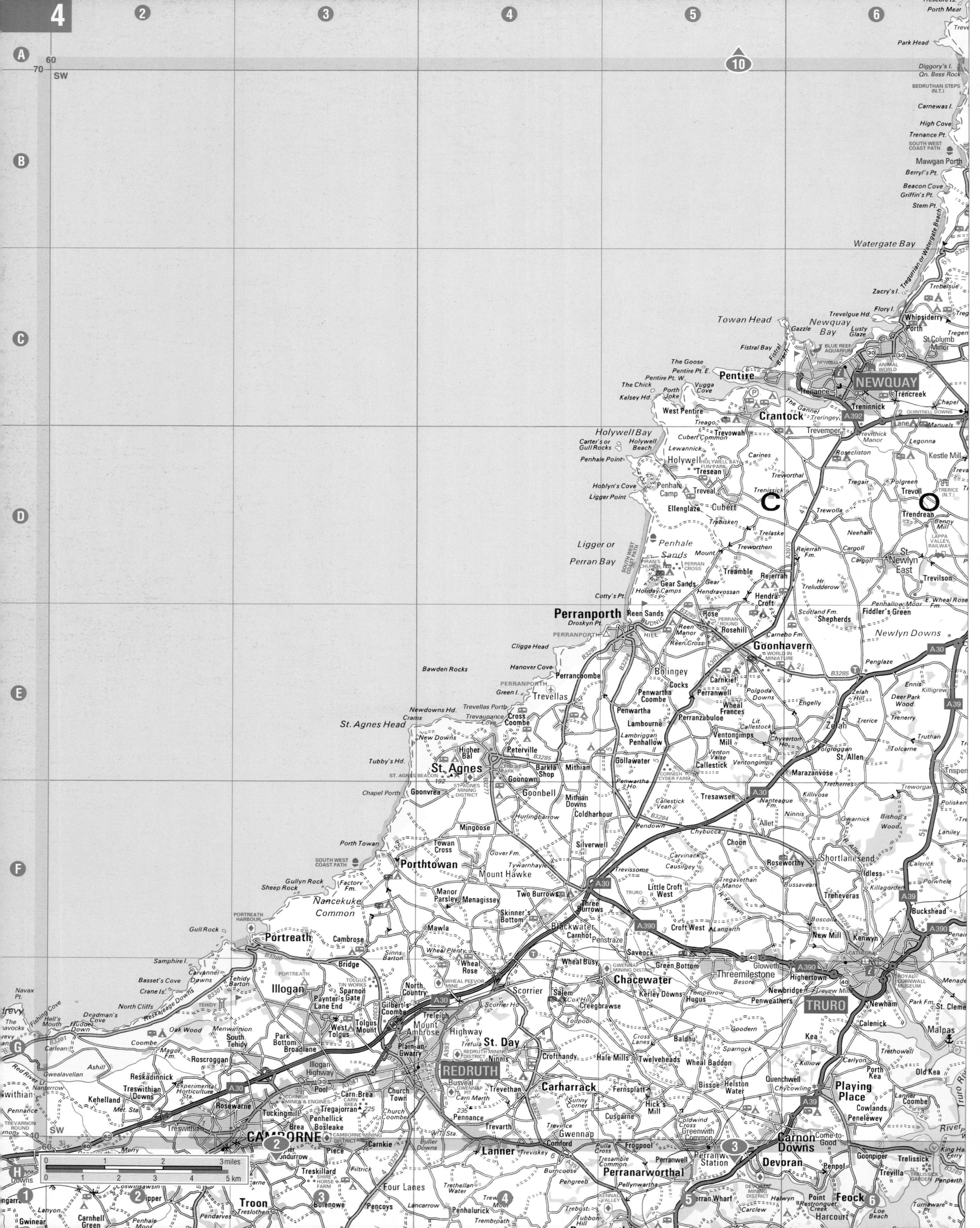

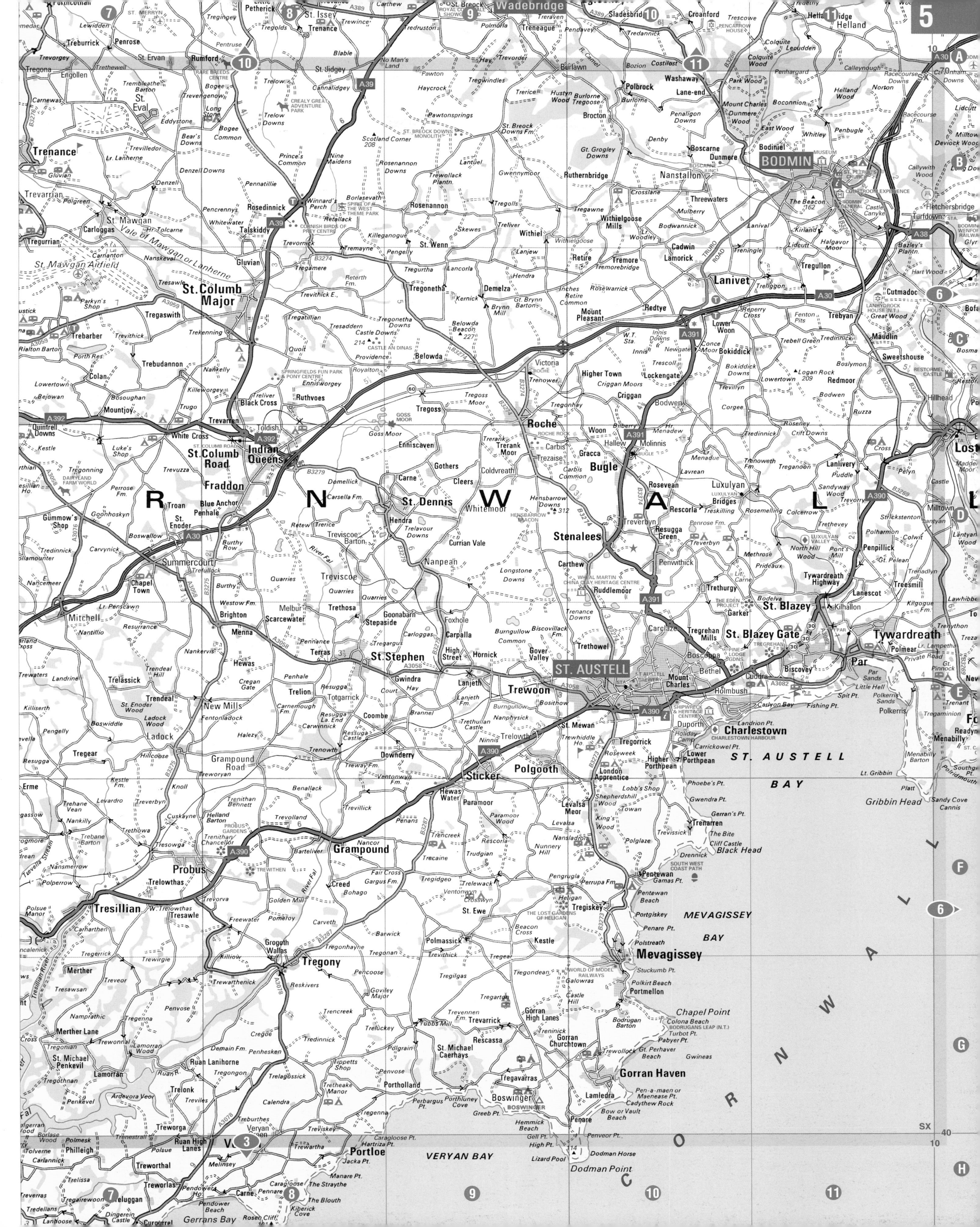

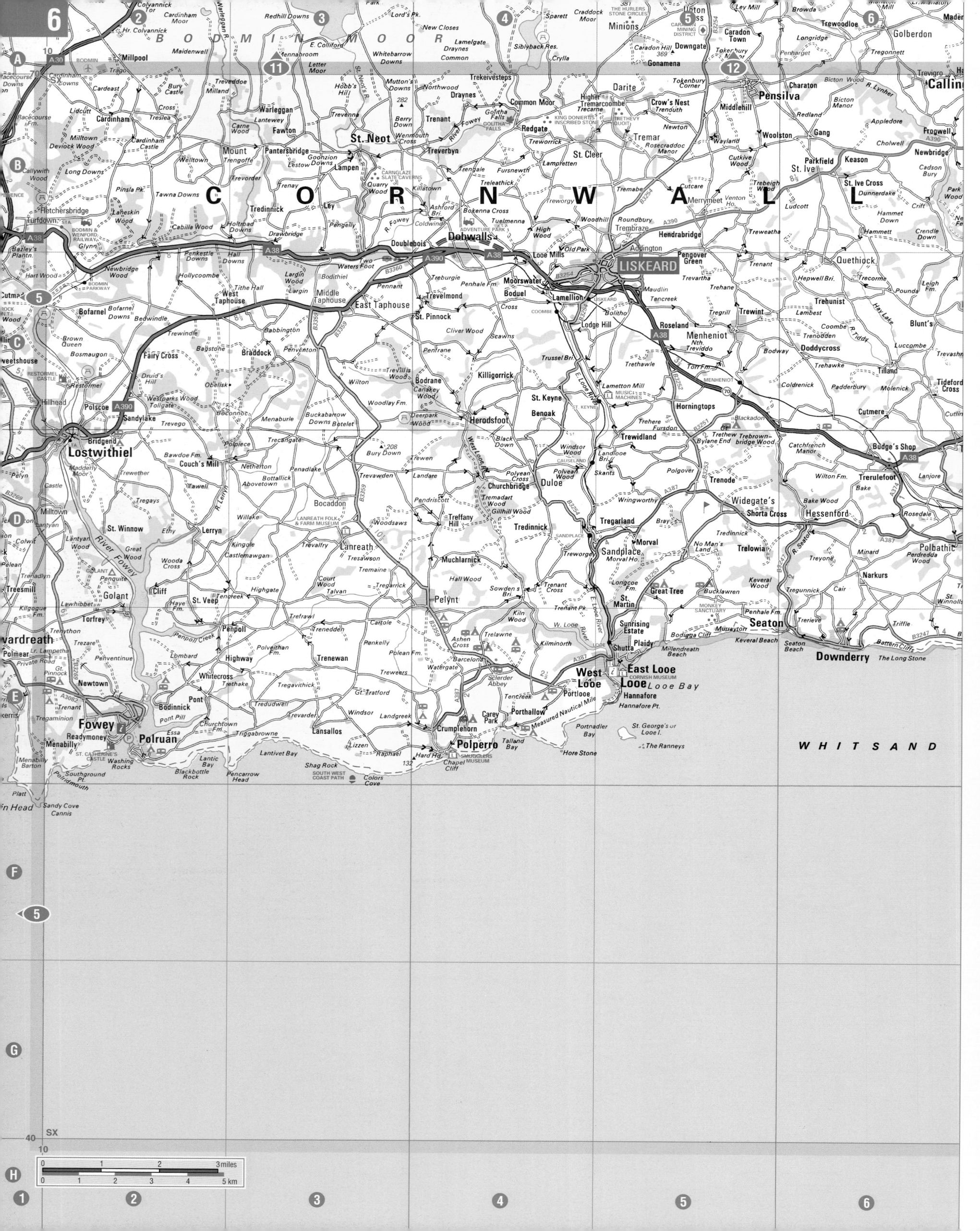

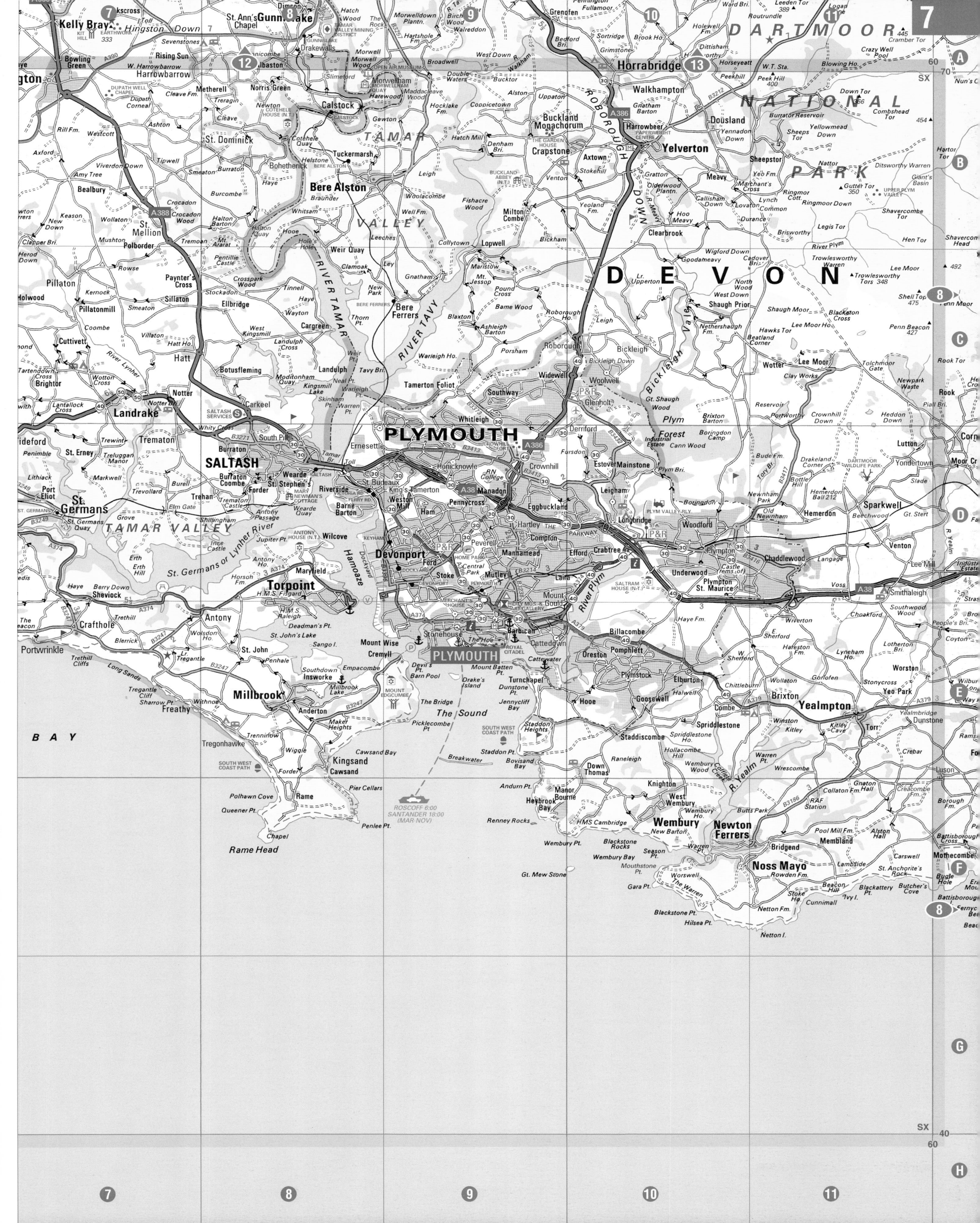

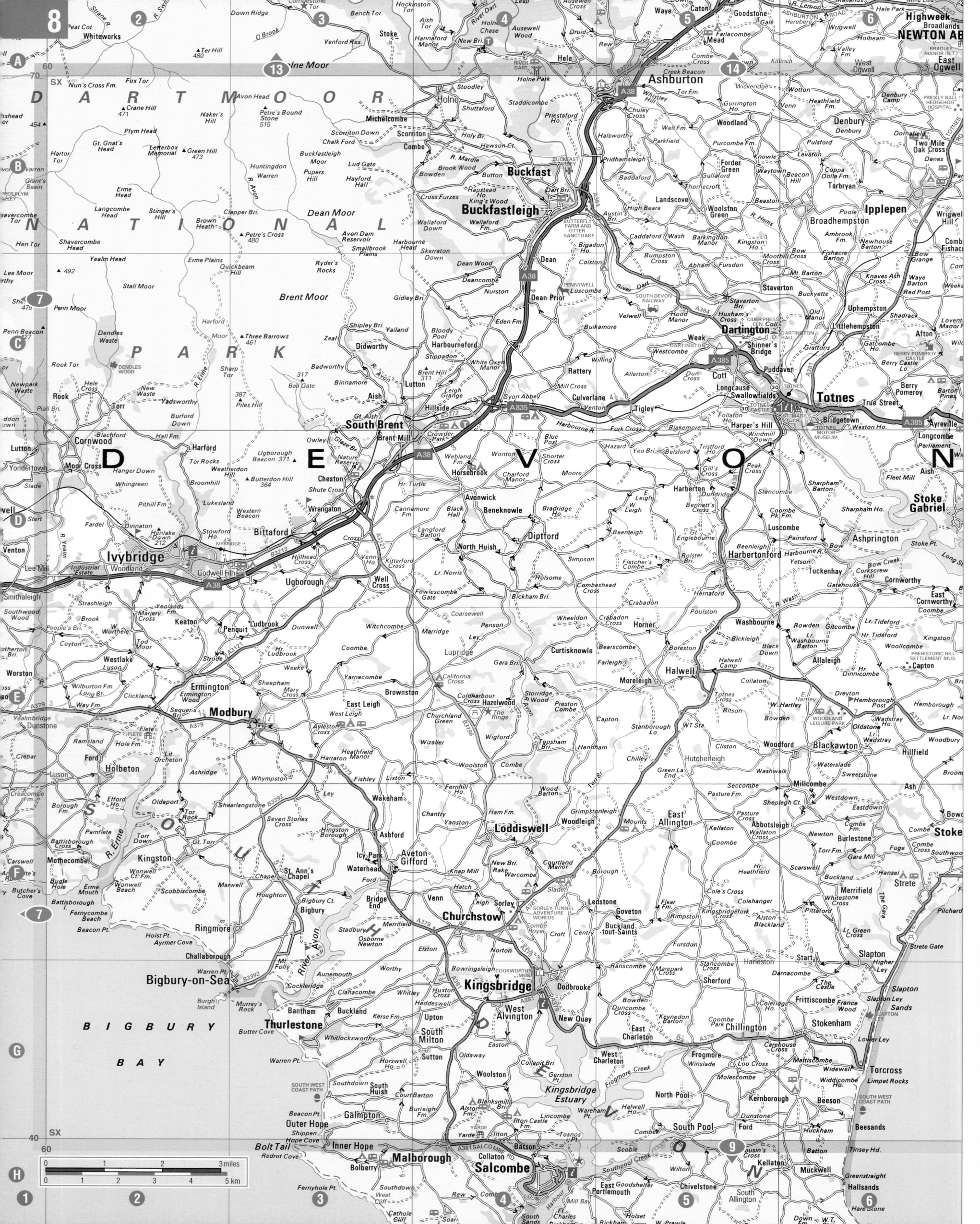

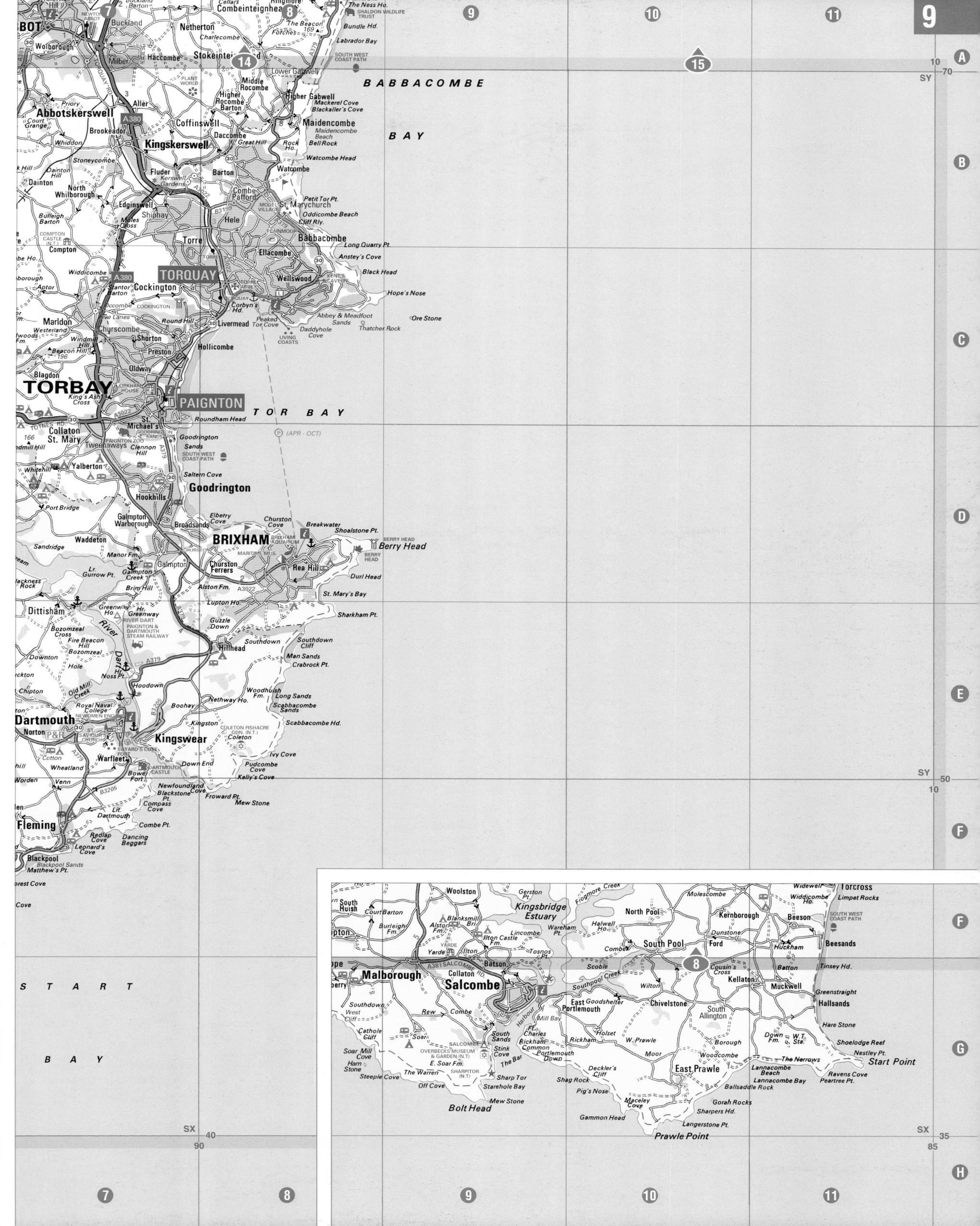

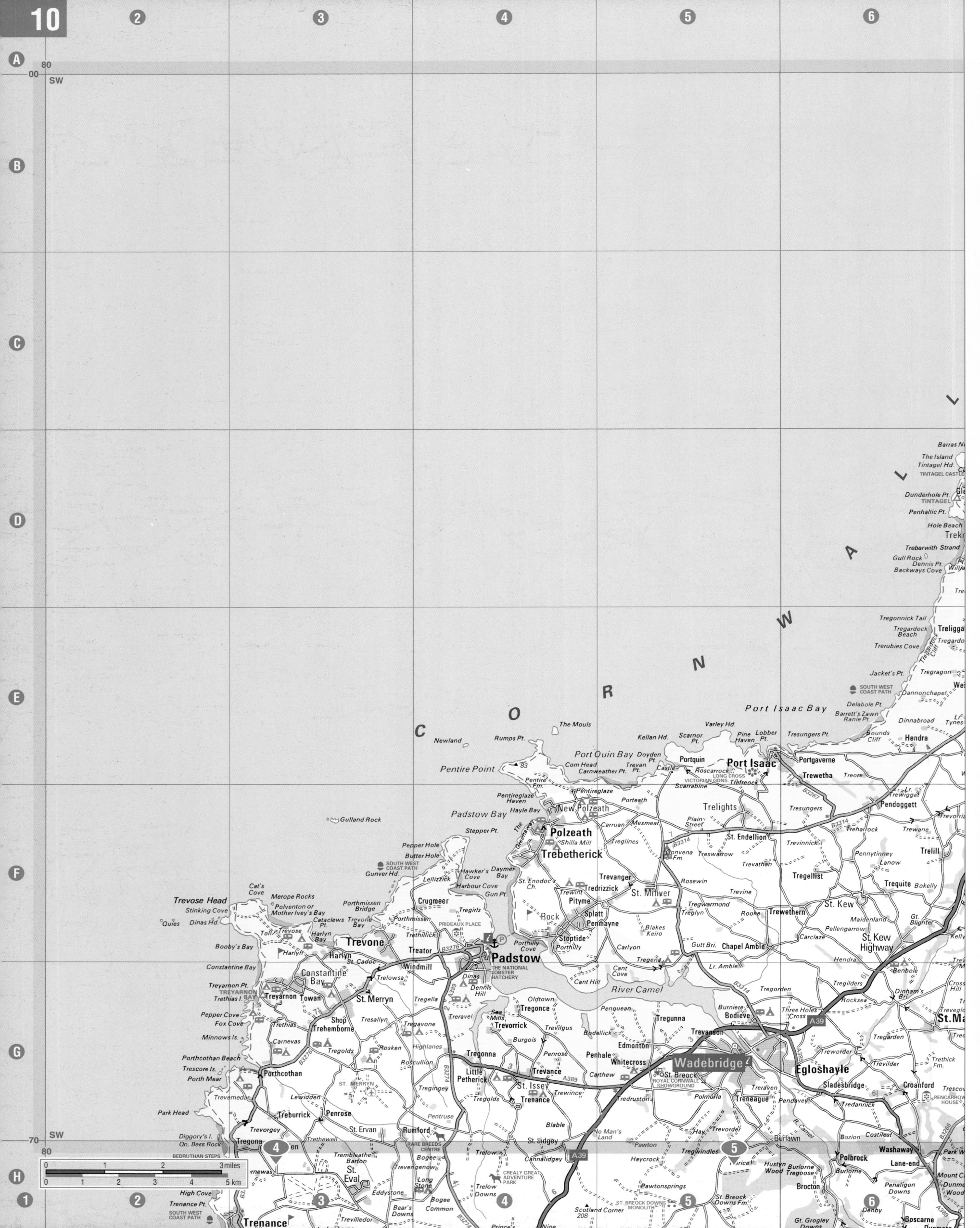

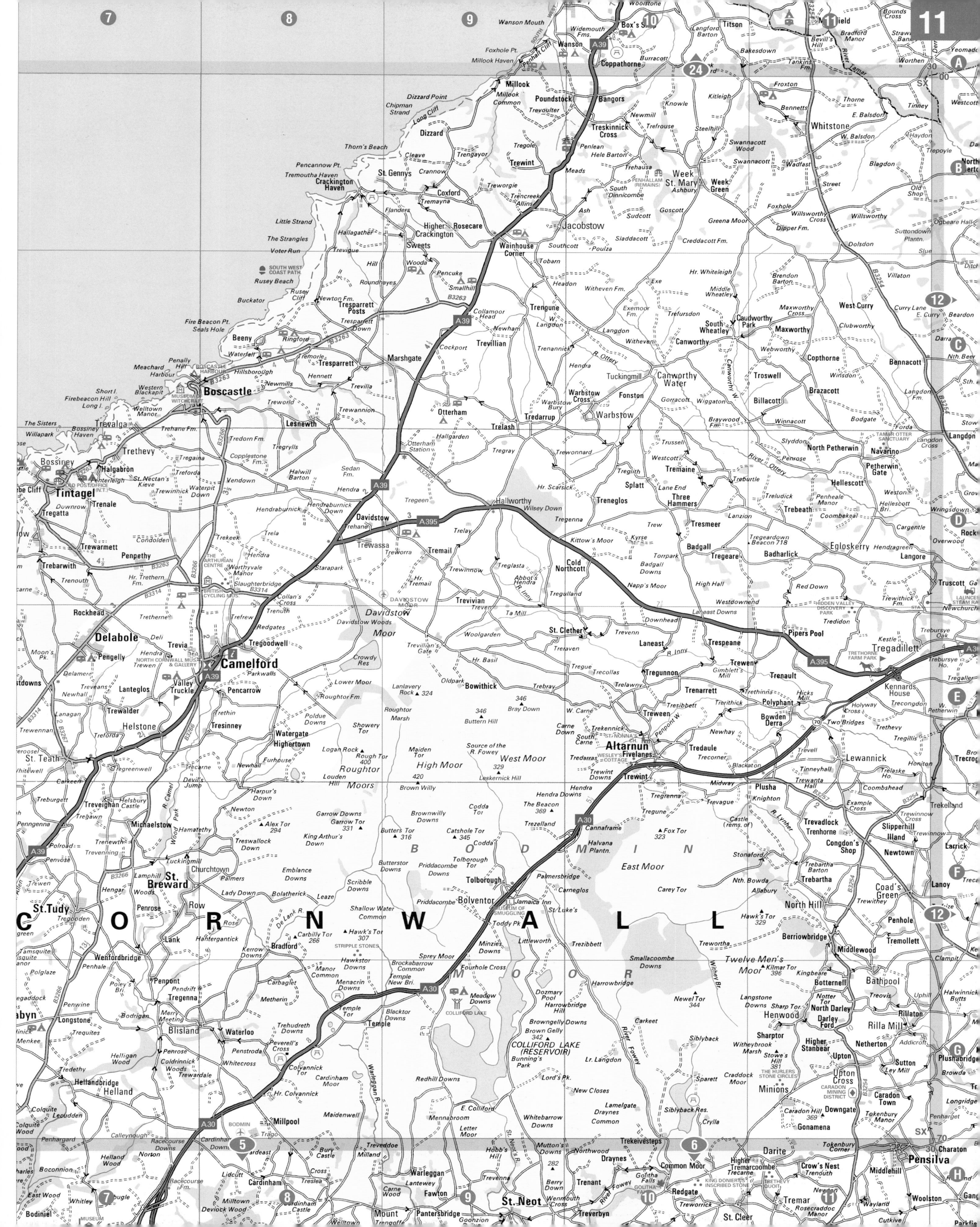

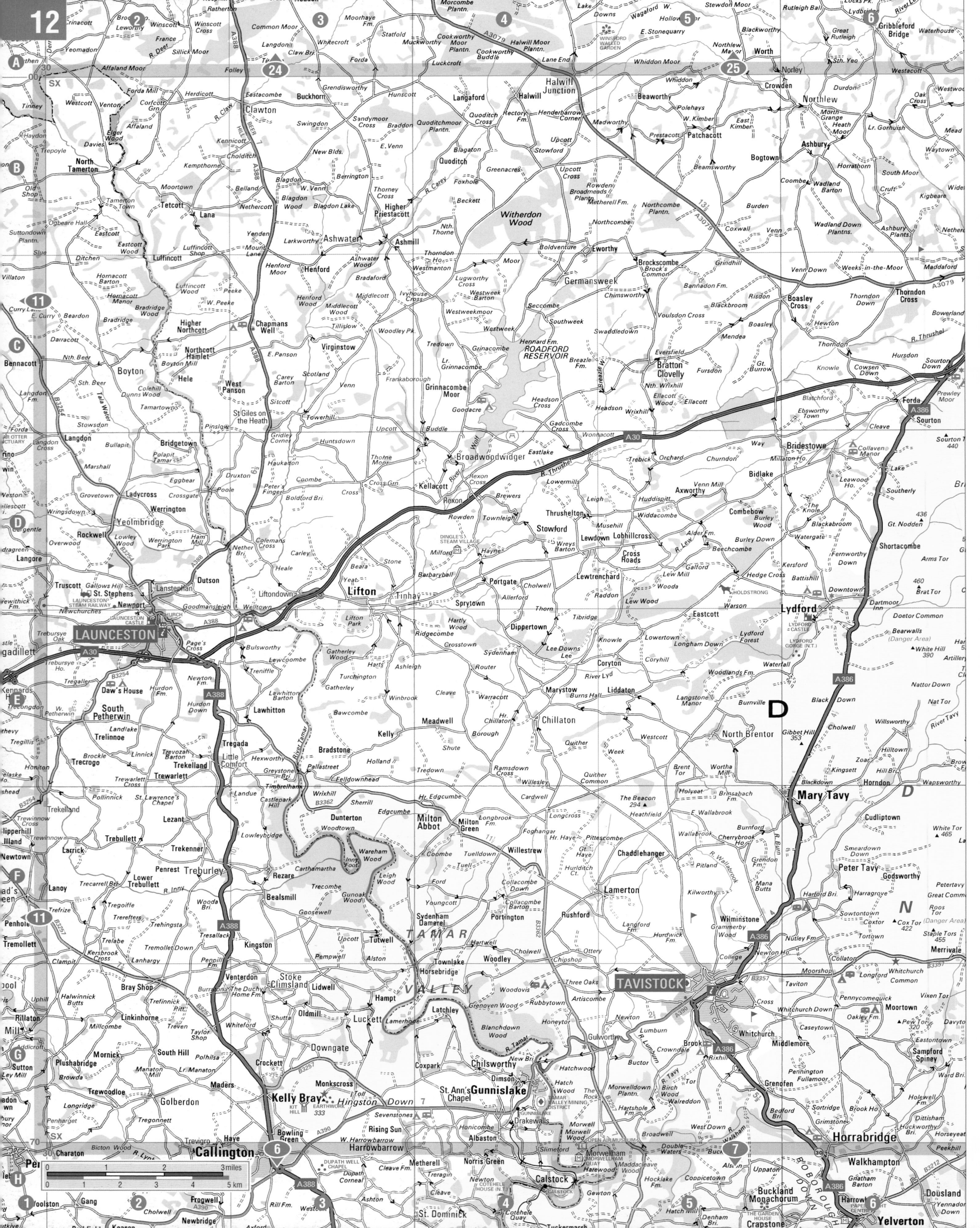

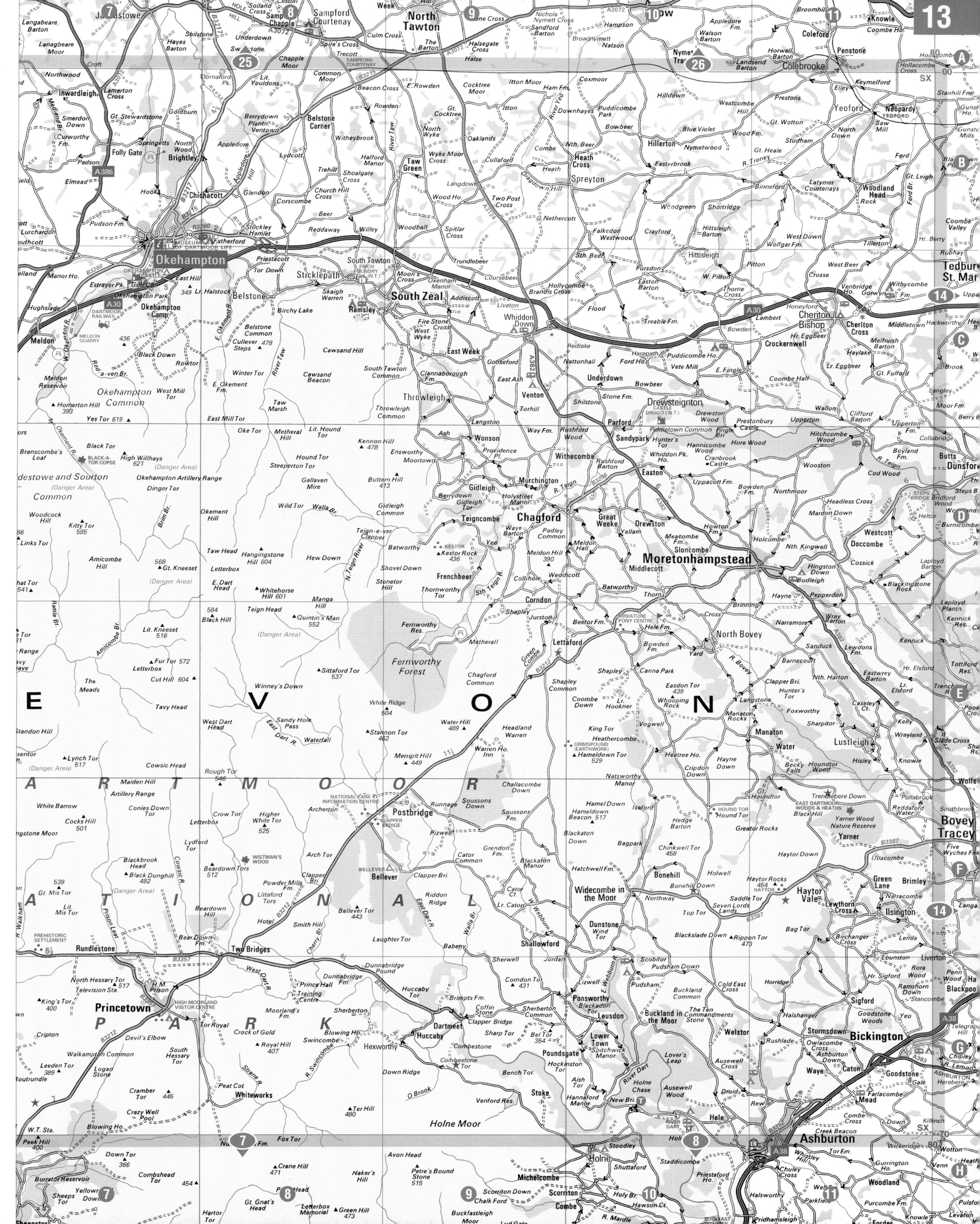

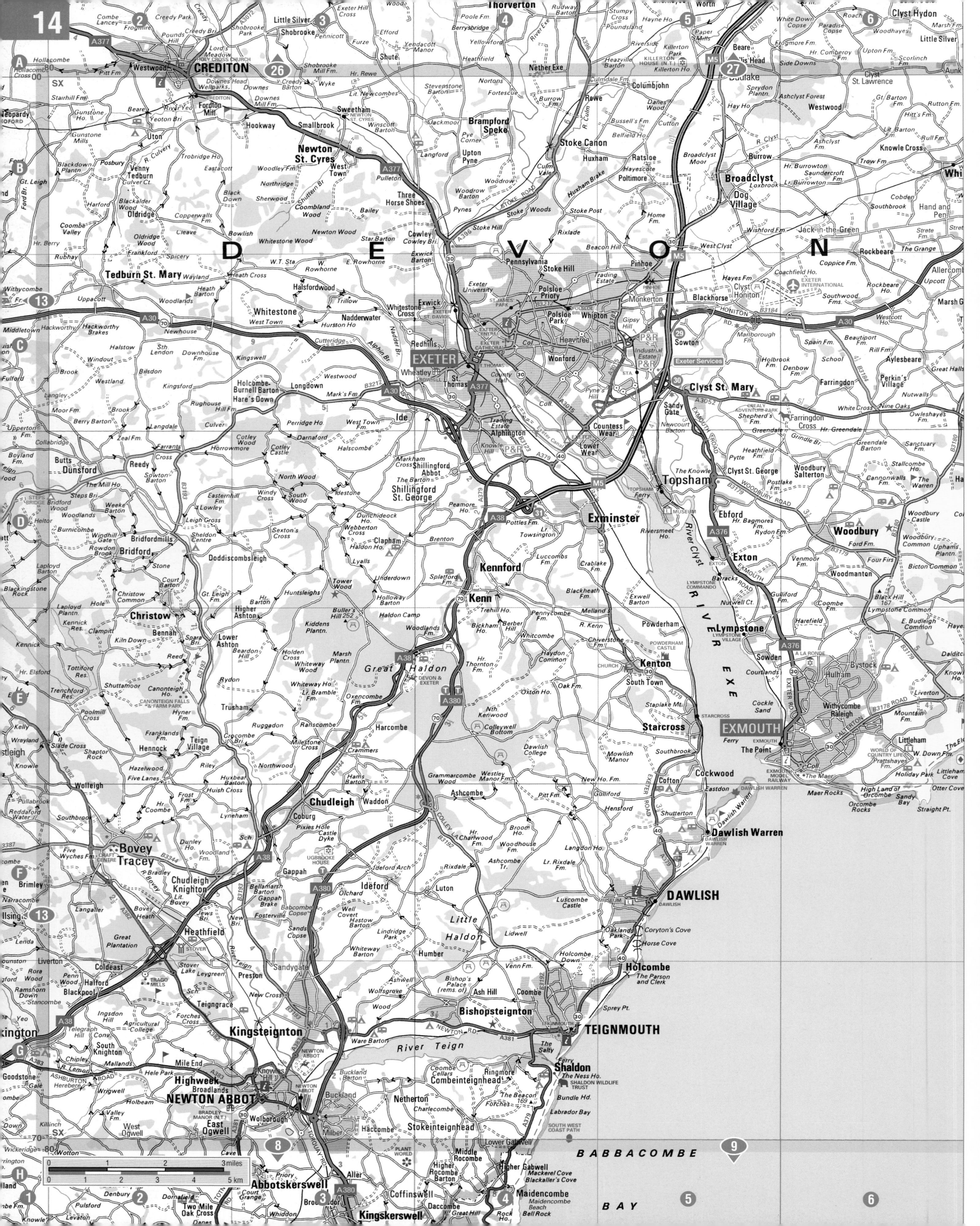

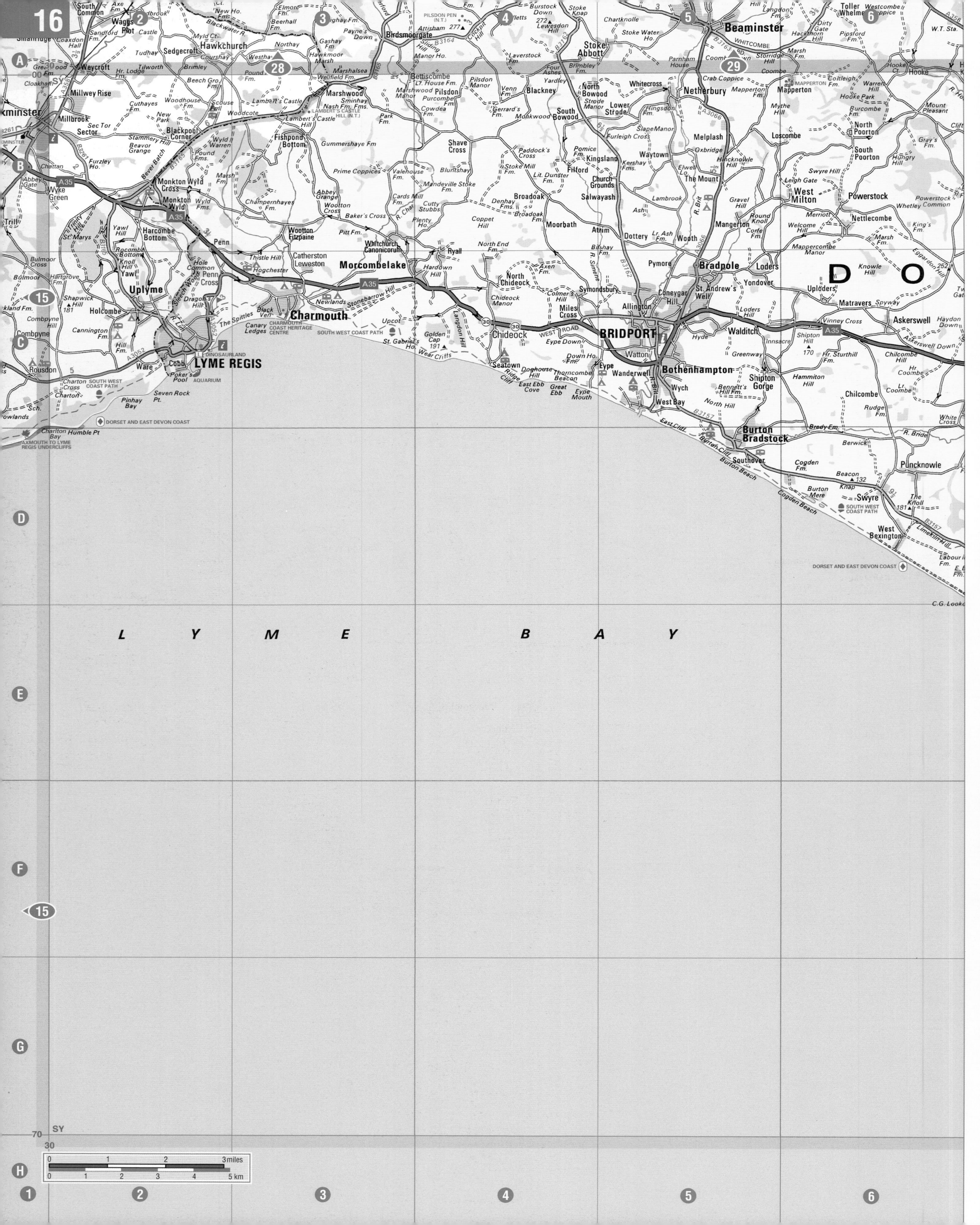

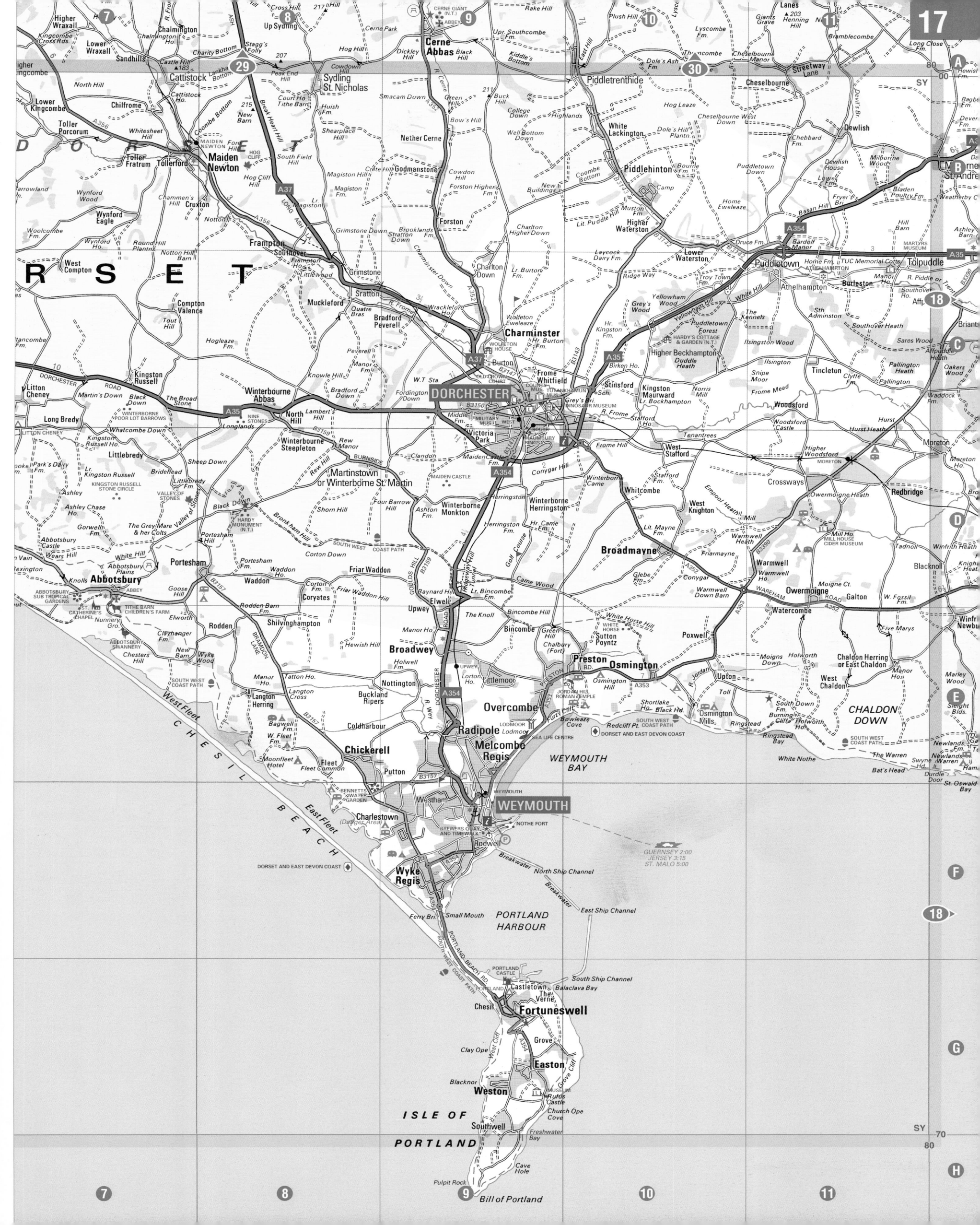

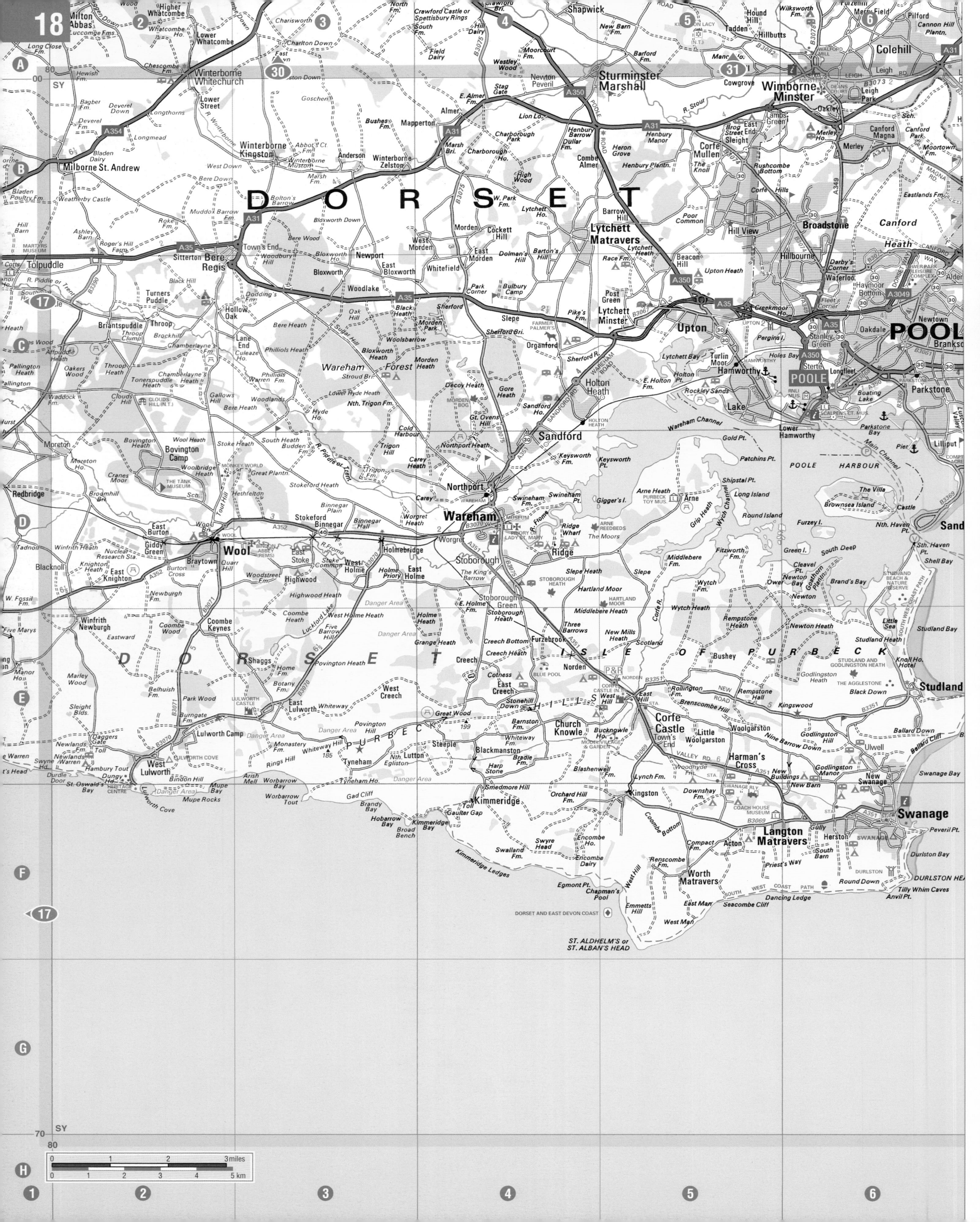

BOURNEMOUTH

CHRISTCHURCH

NEW FOREST

POOLE BAY

CHRISTCHURCH BAY

Ferndown

Stapehill

Bournemouth International Airport

Sway

New Milton

Lymington

Boscombe

Southbourne

Hengistbury Head

Milford on Sea

Barton on Sea

Highcliffe

Mudeford

The Needles

Totland

Alum Bay

Old Harry

The Foreland or Handfast Pt.

CHERBOURG 4:15
GUERNSEY 2:30
JERSEY 3:45 (APR-OCT)
ST. MALO 5:25
CHERBOURG 2:15 (MAY-SEPT)

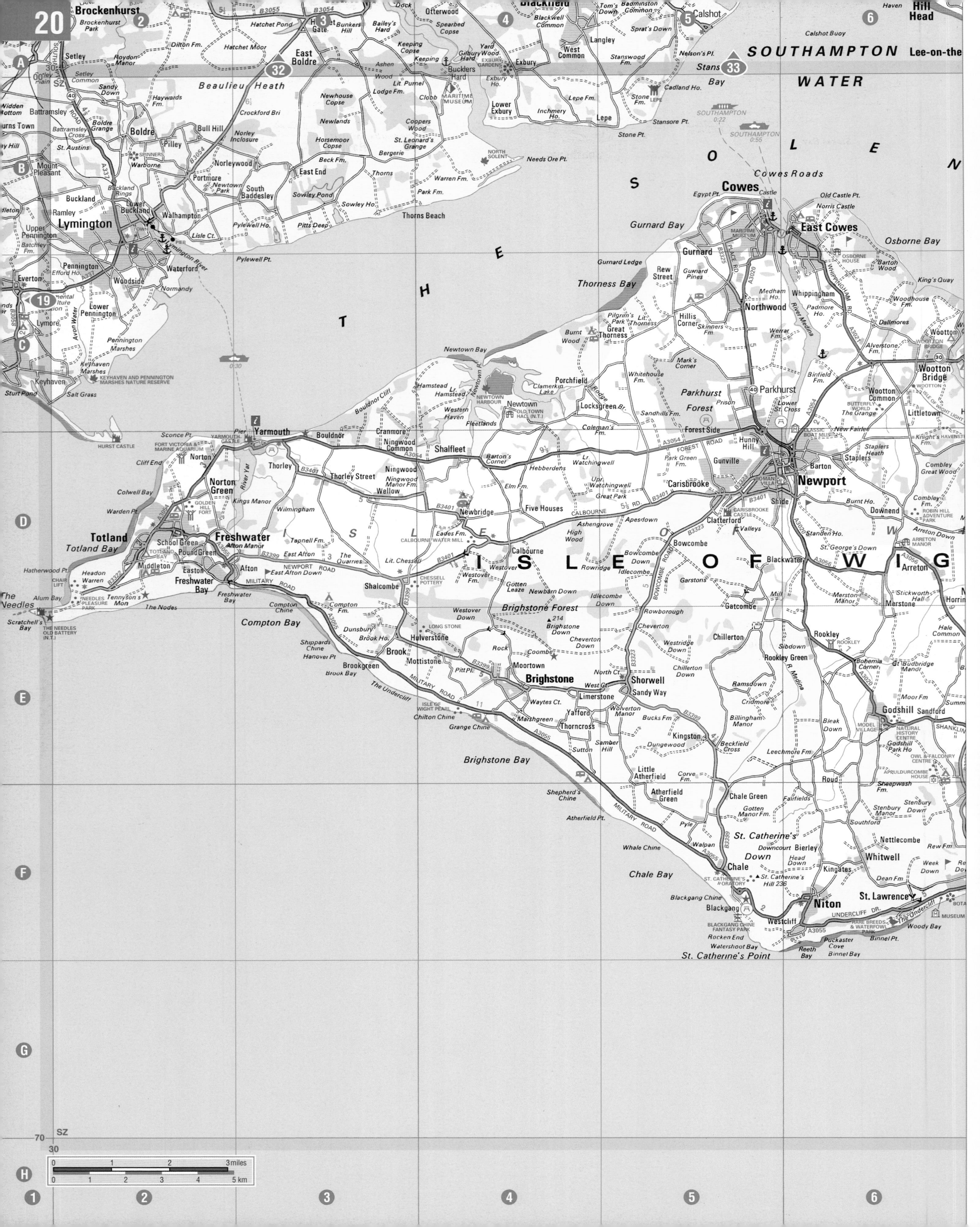

SPITHEAD

GOSPORT 8 PORTSMOUTH PORTSEA LAND 9

Solent

Brownsdown Pt. Brownsdown Privett Alverstoke Clayhall

Stokes Bay

Gilkicker Pt.

(Passenger only)
0:10

Southsea

BLUE REEF AQUARIUM CASTLE MUSEUM

Spit Sand Fort

Horse Sand Fort

No Man's Land Fort

Ryde Roads
PIER HEAD Pier
Ryde Esplanade
Ryde Ryde East Sands

Fishbourne QUARR ABBEY Kite Hill Quarr Hill Binstead Newnham Haylands Swanmore Appley Puckpool Pt. WIRELESS MUSEUM Spring Vale Nettlestone Pt. Seaview Elmfield Pondwell Nettlestone Bullen Horestone Pt. Priory Bay The Priory Node's Pt. St. Helen's Fort

Smallbrook Fm. Upton SMALLBROOK JUNC. Bartlett's Green Park Fm. St. Helen's Ch. The Duver St. Helens Hill Fm. Bembridge Pt. Bembridge Harbour Bembridge

Whitefield Fm. Gate Ho. Whitefield Wood Ashey West Ashey Fm. E. Ashey Hardingshute Carpenters Harbour Fm. MARITIME MUSEUM Ethel Pt. Lane End Foreland

Nunwell Fm. ISLE OF WIGHT WAX WORKS R. Yar Steyne Cross

Ashey Down NUNWELL HO. BEMBRIDGE WINDMILL (N.T.) SANDOWN ROAD Hillway Long Ledge

Brading BRADING ROMAN VILLA Bembridge Down BEMBRIDGE FORT Culver Down Whitecliff Bay

Mersley Down Mersley Fm. Kern Brading Down Adgestone Yarbridge Morton Yaverland Culver Cliff

Langbridge Alverstone Hill Fm. ISLE OF WIGHT ZOO Red Cliff

Queen's Bower SANDOWN DINOSAUR ISLE ISLE OF WIGHT (SANDOWN)

Winford Branstone Sandown Pier SANDOWN BAY

Apse Heath Lake Lake

Ninham Lit. Stairs Pt.

Apse Manor Fm. Shanklin Pier
Whiteley Bank Winstone SHANKLIN Shanklin Chine SHANKLIN CHINE

St Martin's Down 235 Shanklin Down

Wroxall Luccombe Village Luccombe Bay Luccombe Chine

Wroxall Manor Fm. Nansen Hill 235 Dunnose Bonchurch Monks Bay Horseshoe Bay

Ventnor Ventnor Bay Steephill OF SMUGGLING HISTORY

Thorney 11 Itchenor Westlands 80 00 A

Copnor 10 et HAYLING ISLAND Manor Ho. Gable Head To Bury 34 CHICHESTER HARBOUR Bra

Baffins EASTERN Milton Eastney Ft Cumberland Sinah Common West Town Westfield Menghan Selsmore Eastoke Pilsey I Shipton Green West Wittering East Wittering

West Winner East Winner Hayling Bay South Hayling EAST HAYLING LIGHT RLY. Eastoke Point Black Pt. Cakeham Manor Ho. B

Stocker's Lake Rookwood East Head Walnut Tree Ho.

Brackleshar

22

CAEN 6:00 CHERBOURG 4:45 LE HAVRE 7:30 ST MALO 8:45 D

GUERNSEY 6:30 JERSEY 10:00 BILBAO 35:00

E

F

G

SZ 70 80

H

7 8 9 10 11

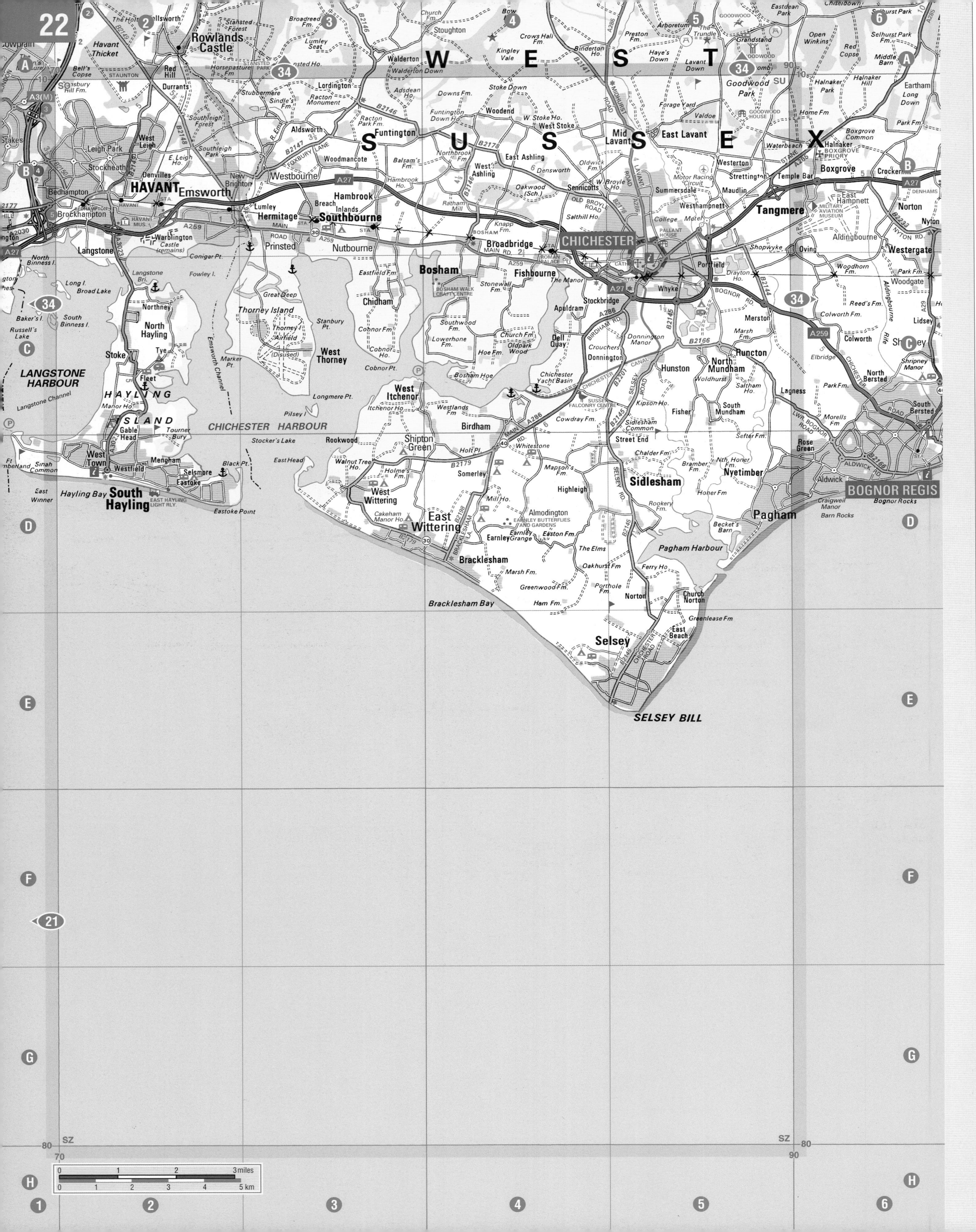

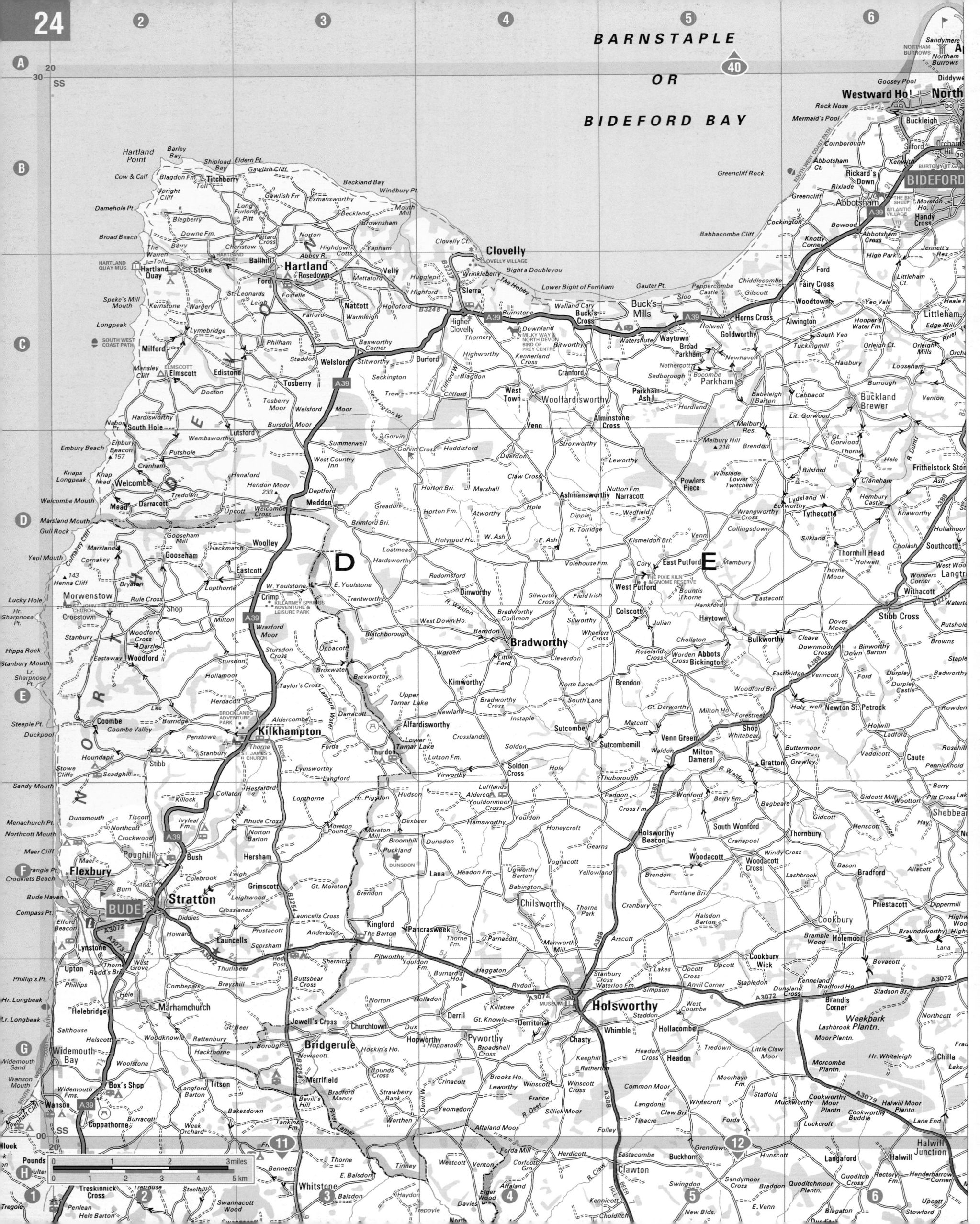

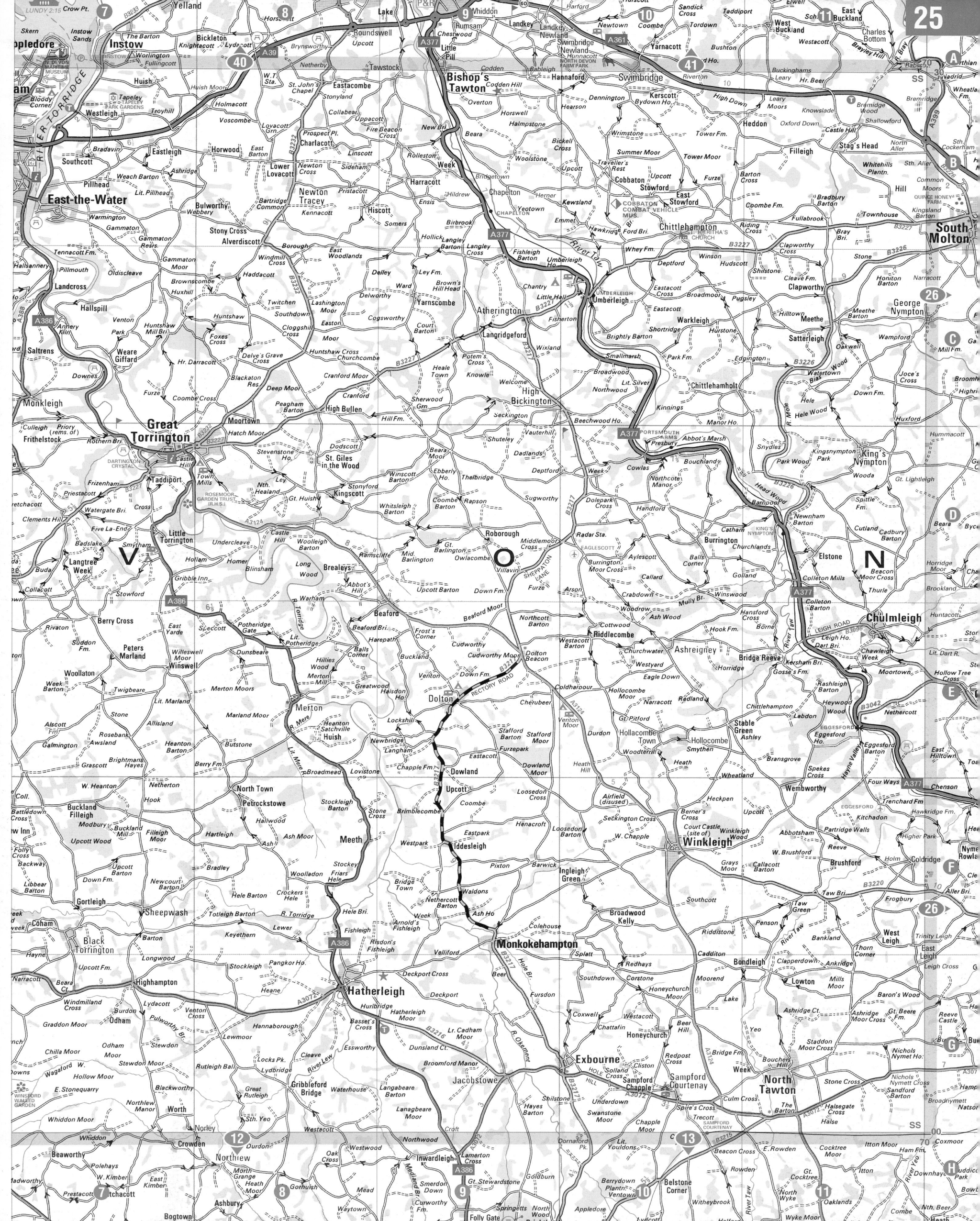

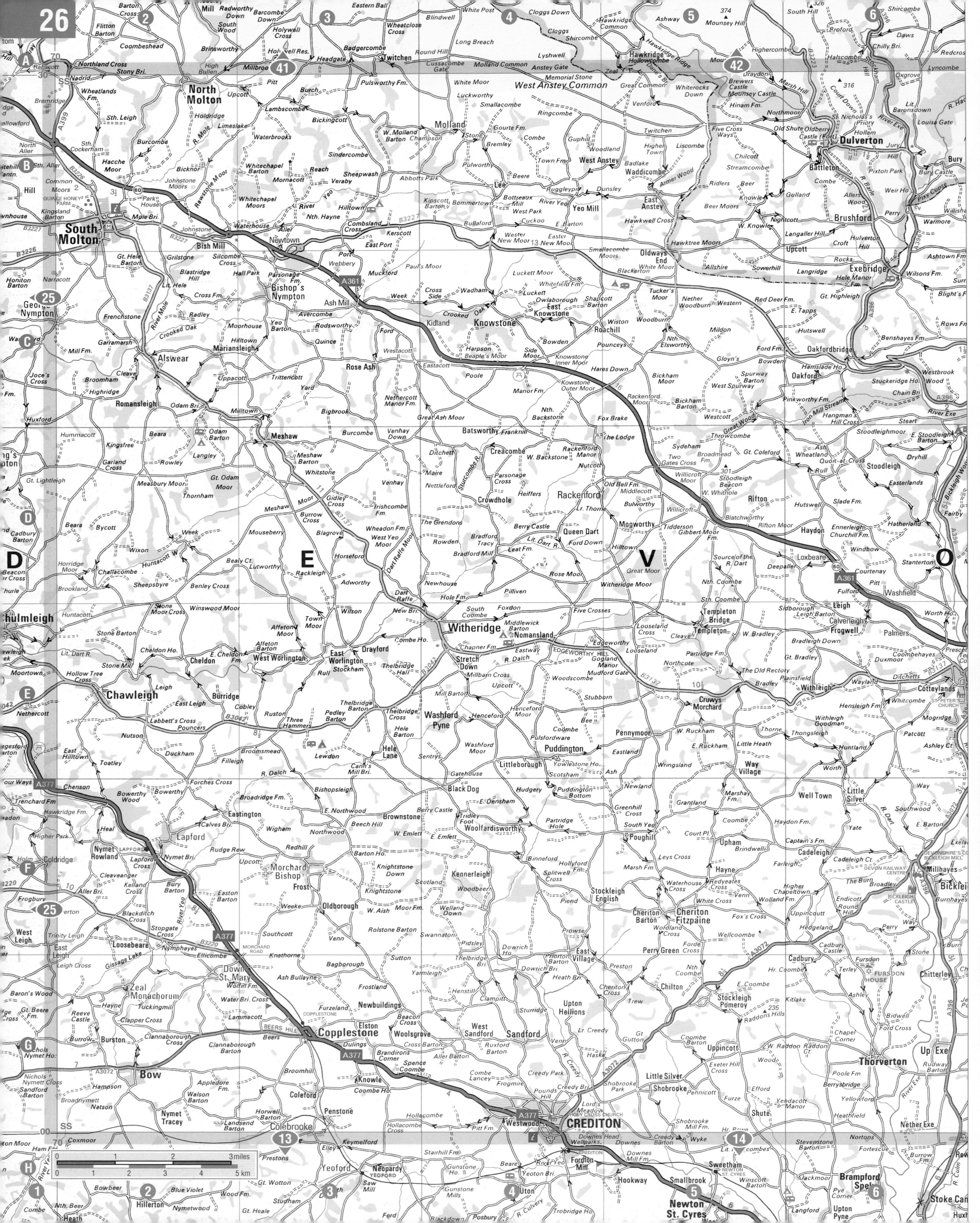

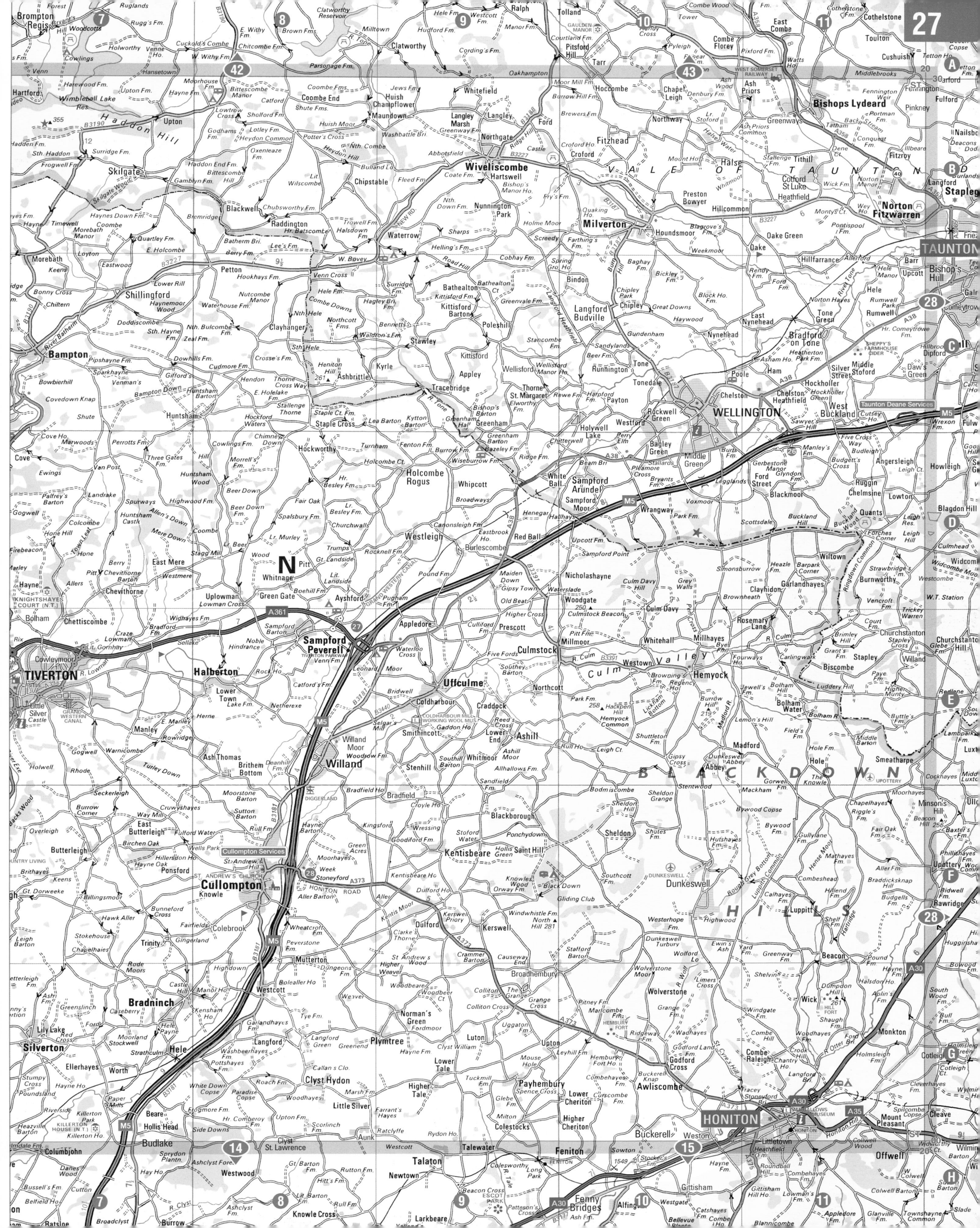

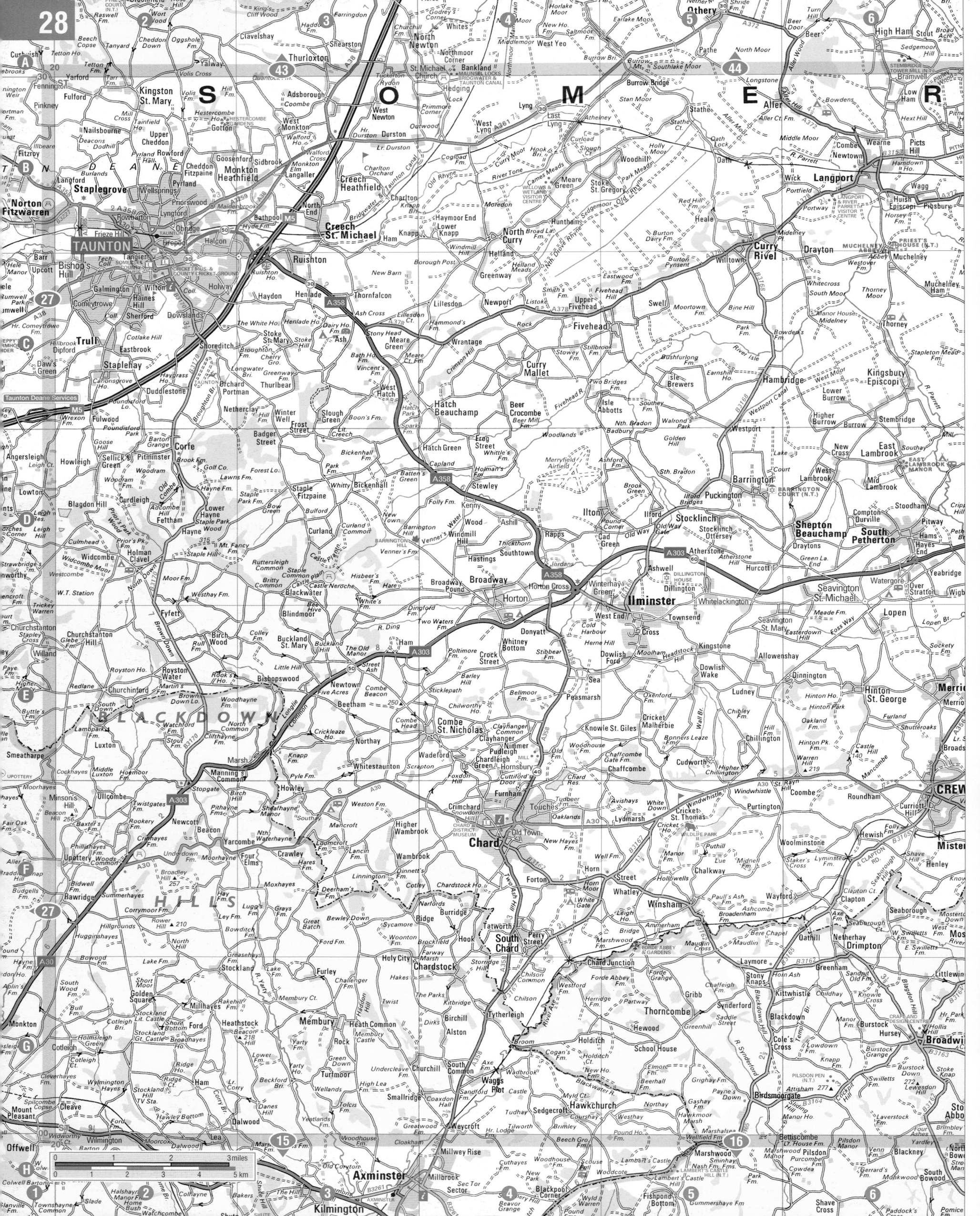

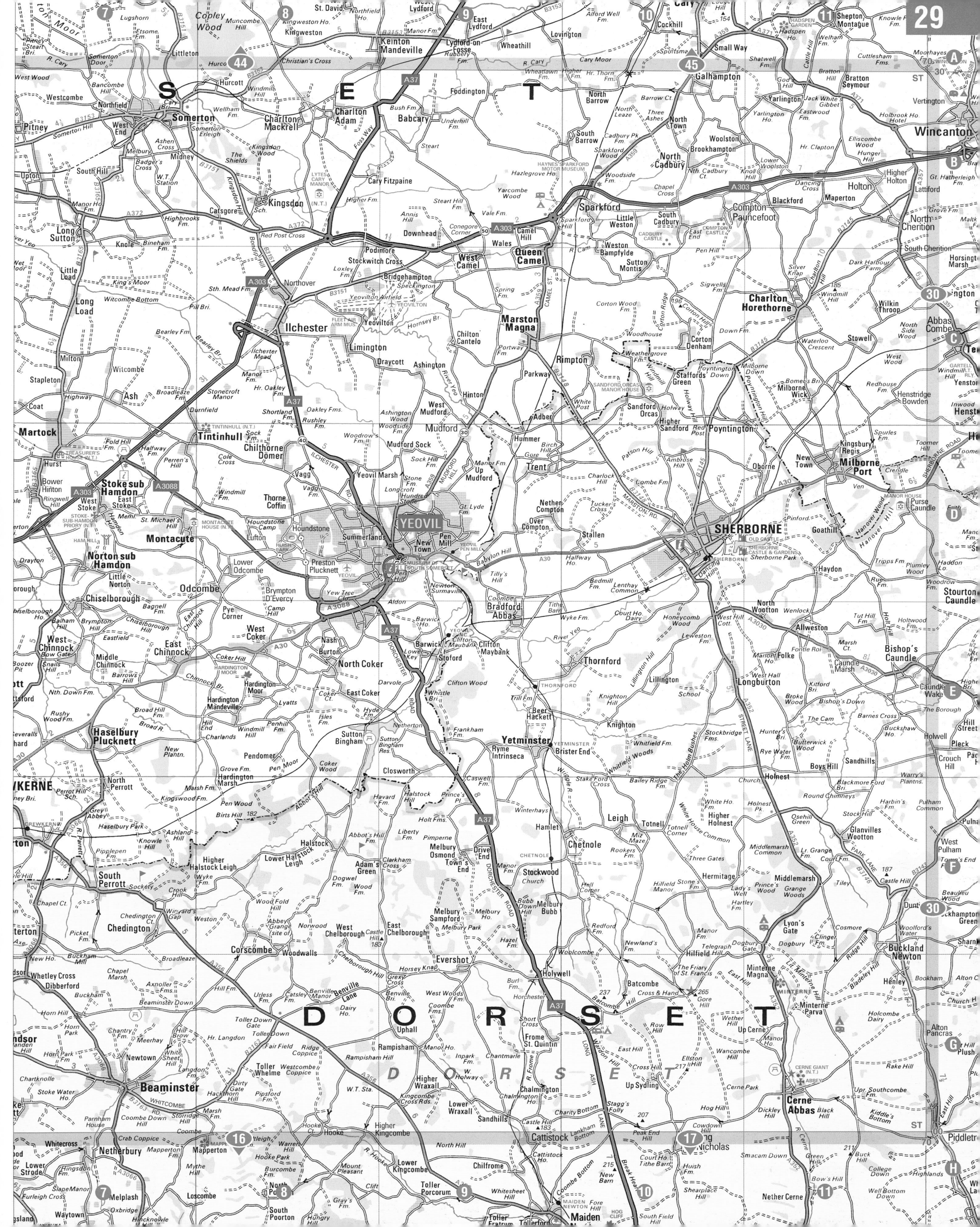

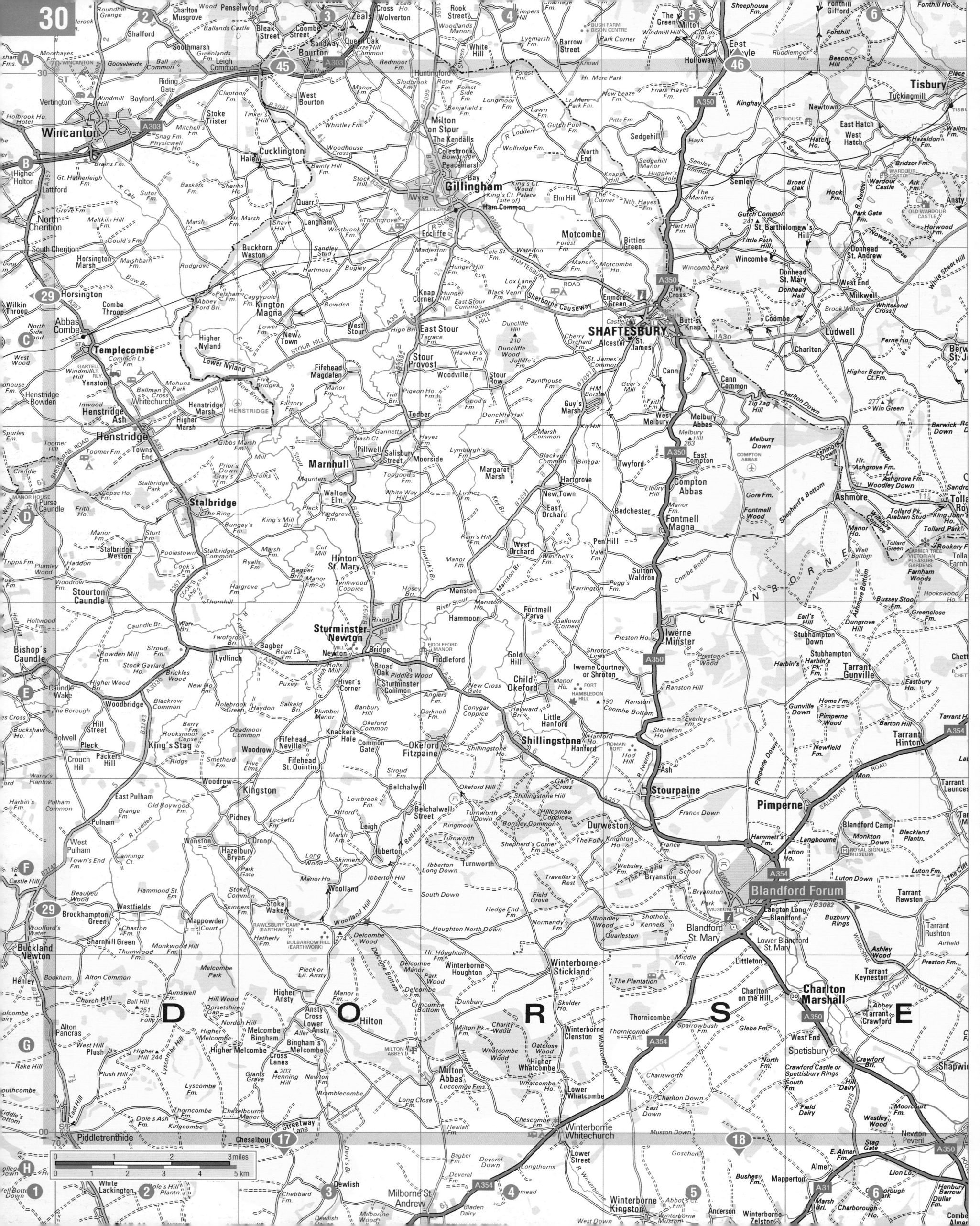

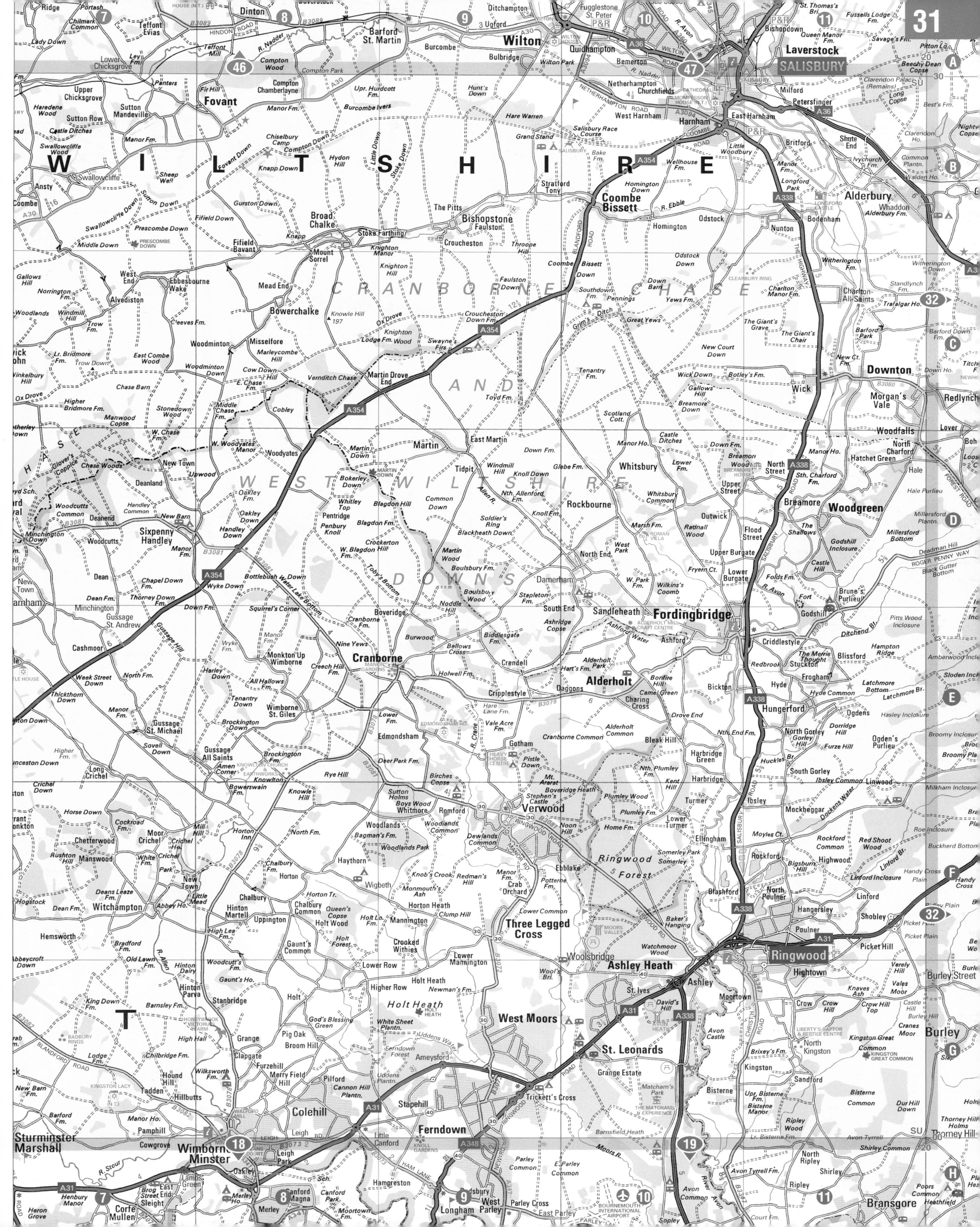

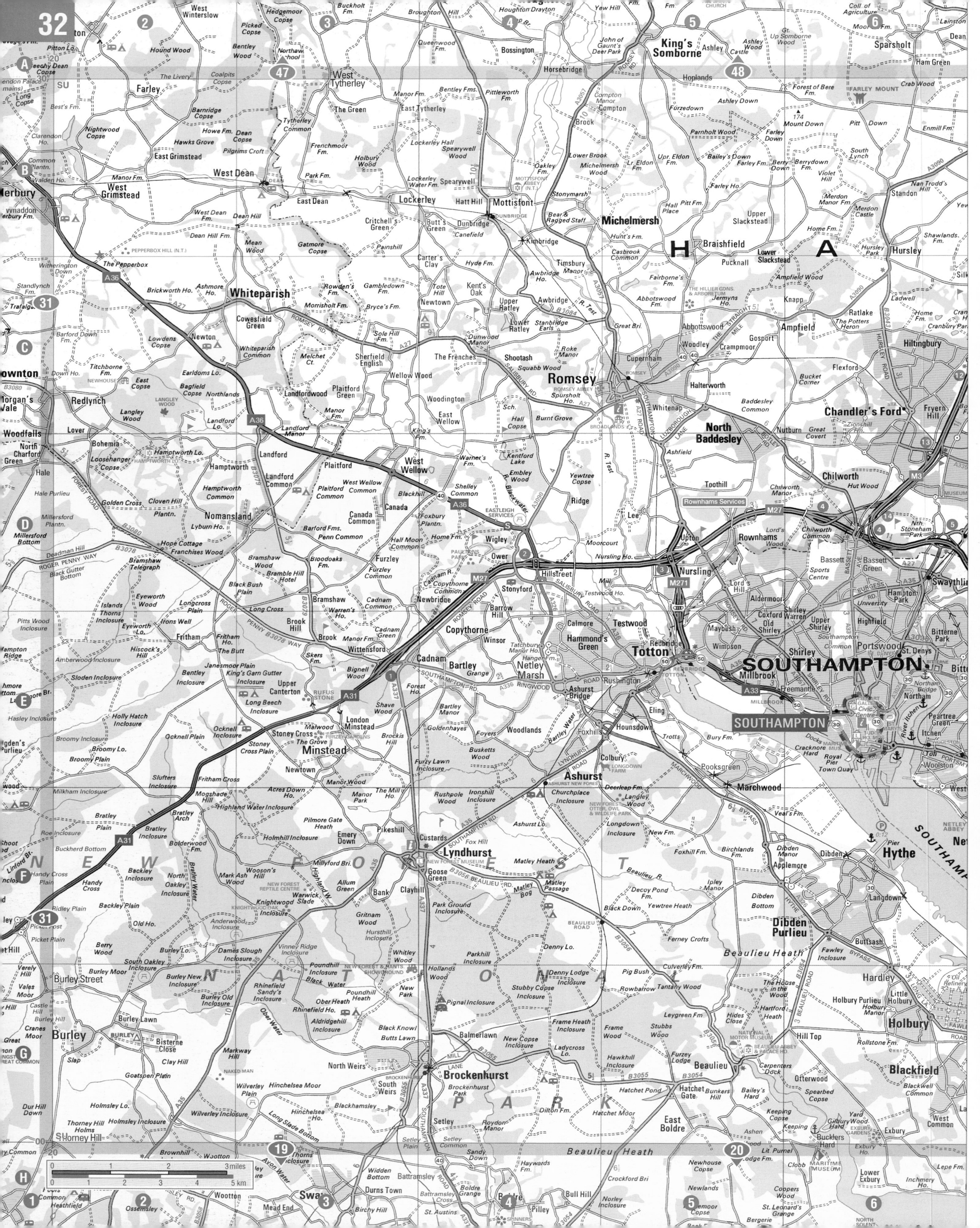

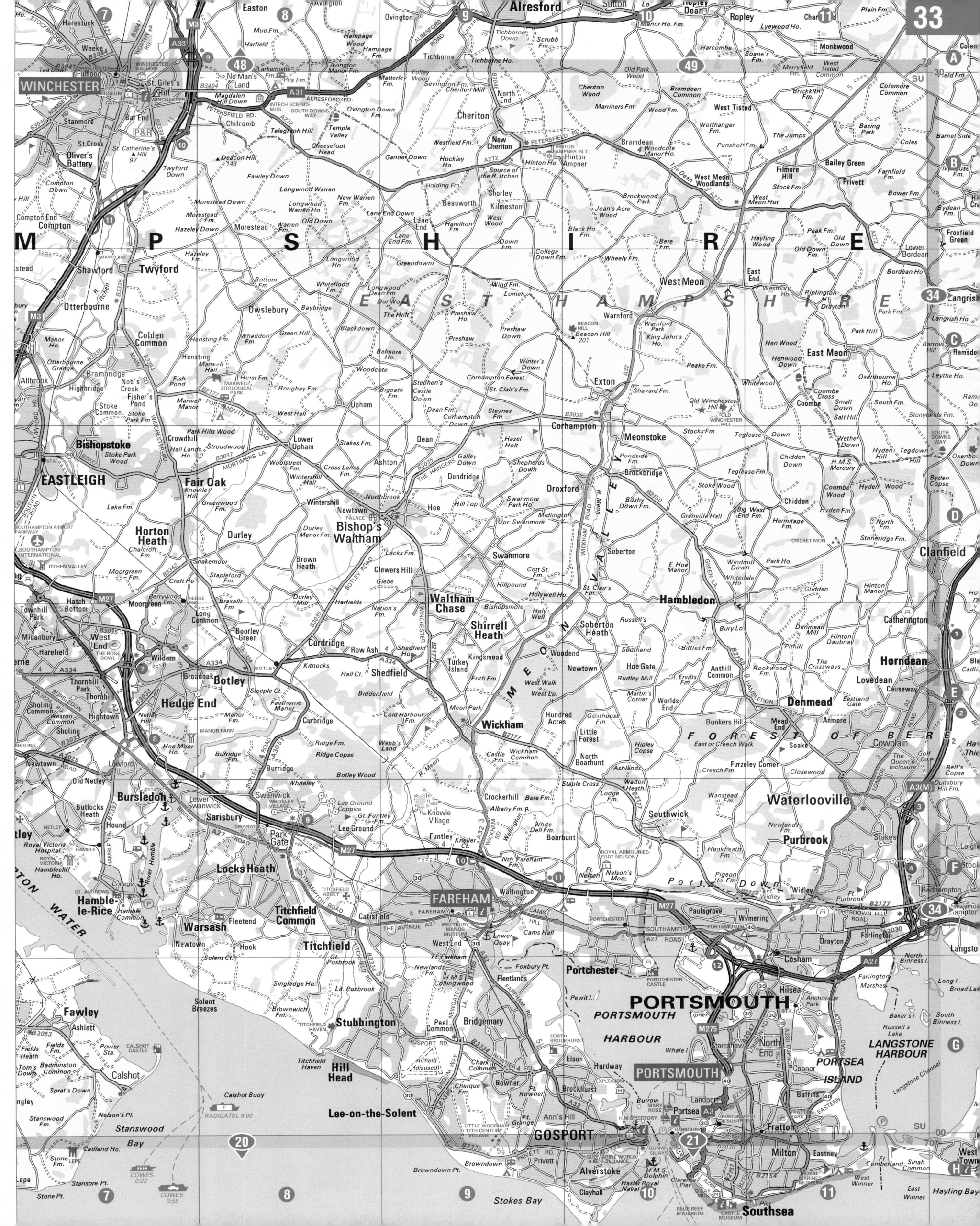

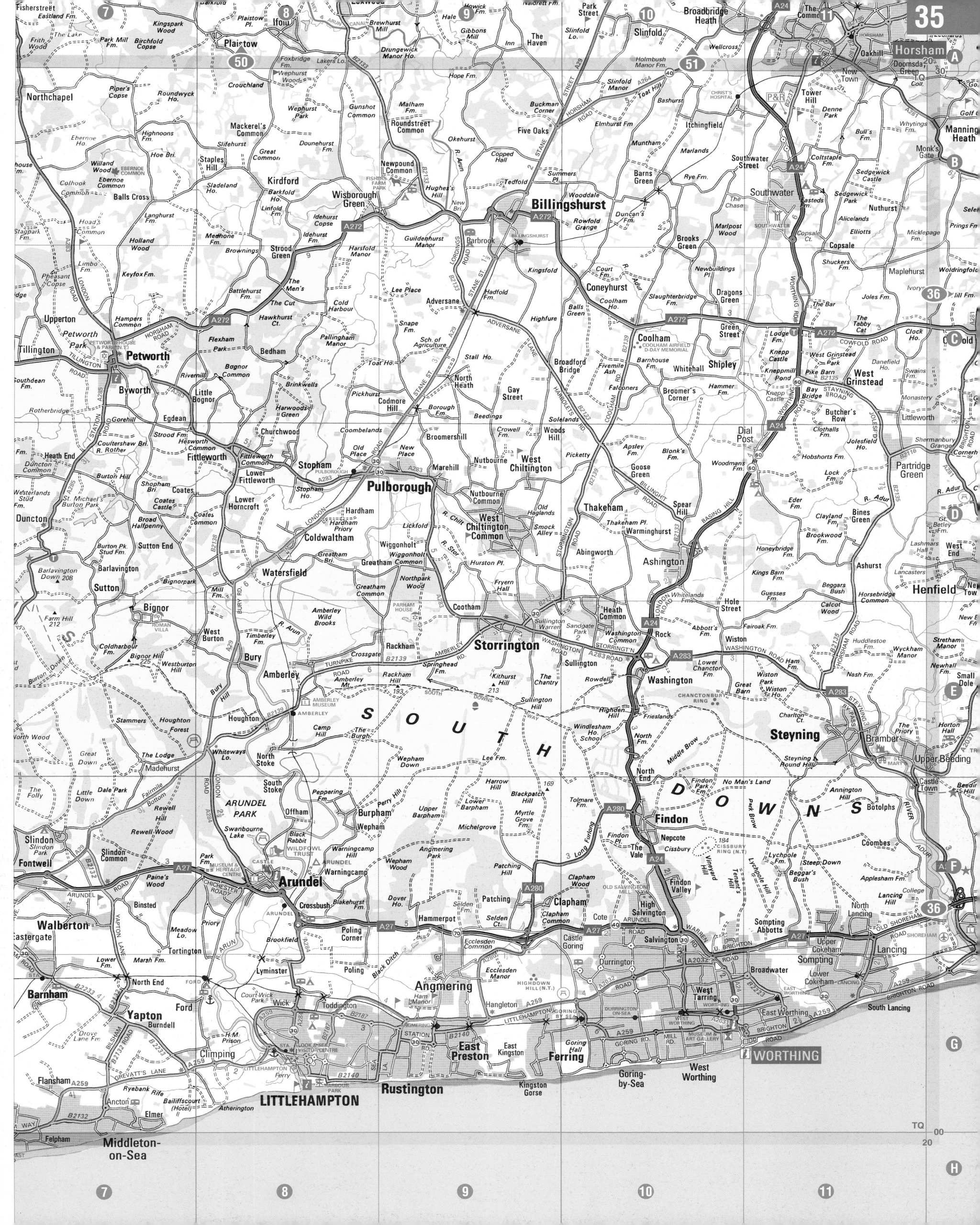

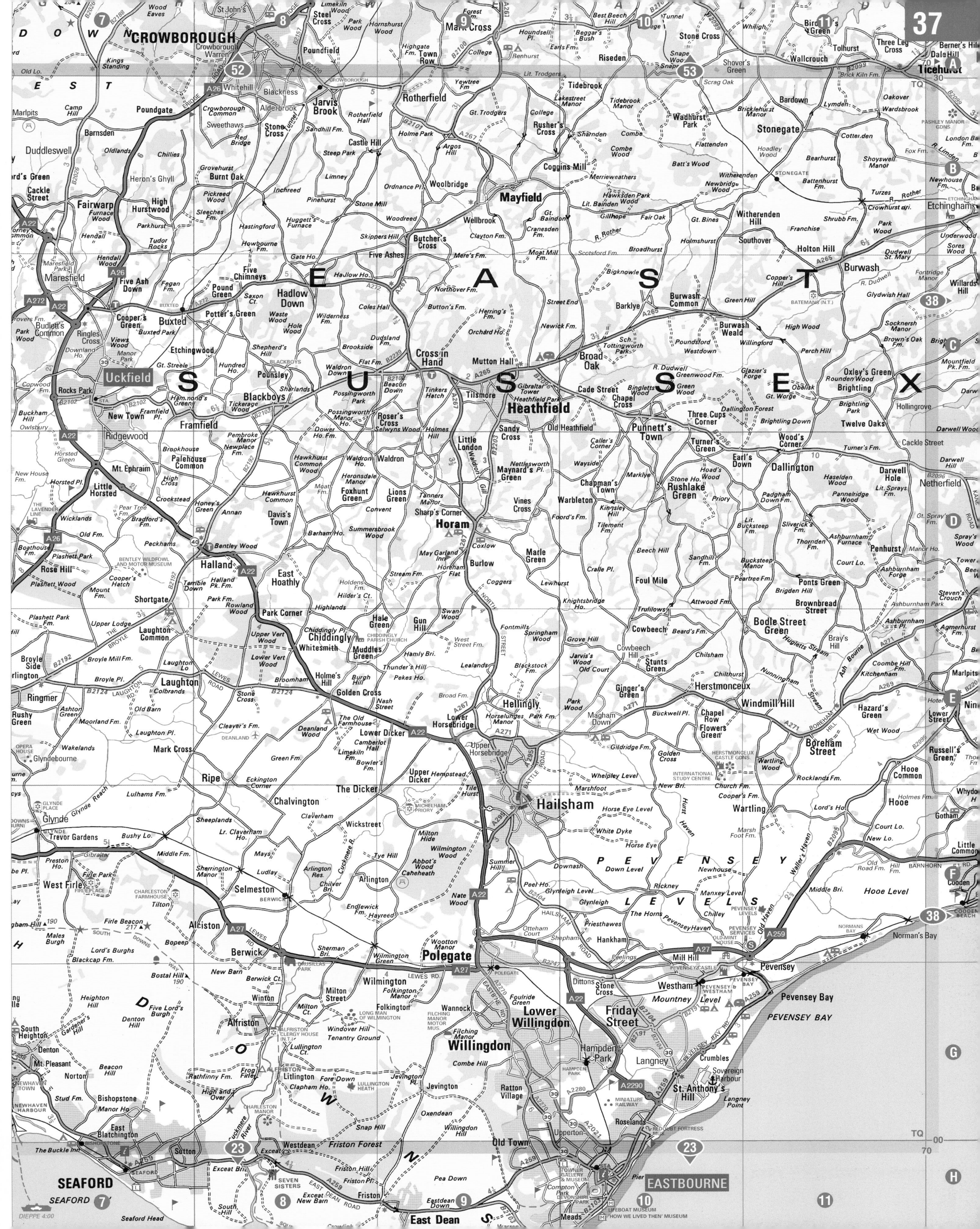

THE DOWELS

Heron Wood
Park Hill
Horne's Place Chapel

KENT

Appledore

Snargate
Godhall
Bowdell
Fairfield Ct.
Becket Fm.
Fairfield
Poplar Hall
Dean Ct.

Brenzett
Ivychurch
Brenzett Green
Whitehall Fm.
Moat Ho.
Lit. Appledore

ROMNEY

Newchurch
Ham Mill Fm.
Wey Street Fm.
Will's Fm.
Newbarn
Gammons Fm.
Orgarswick Fm.
Manor Ho.
Norwood Fm.
Rookelands

Stockbridge Ho.
Millbank
Poplar Ho.

Snave
Willow Fm.
Lodgeland
Pickney Bush

MARSH

North Fording Ho.
Melon Fm.
Haffenden Fm.
St. Mary in the Marsh
Blackmanstone Bri.
Sellinge Fm.

STA.
DYMCHURCH MARTELLO TOWER
Dymchurch
Martello Towers

Camp
Martello Tower

Brenzett Pl.
AERONAUTICAL MUS.
Blue Ho. Fm.
Rheewall Fm.
Yoakes Ct.
Goose Fm.
Honeychild Manor
Slinches

Holiday Camp

St. Mary's Bay

Mislenham
STRAIGHT LANE

New Sewer
All Saints'Ch (Remains)
Bush Fm.
Old Romney
Warren Ho.

Brookland
White Kemp Sewer
New Building
Hook Ho.

WALLAND

Blue Ho.
Old Cheyne Ct.
Wheelsgate
Caldecot
Hawthorn Corner

STA.
New Romney
ROMNEY SANDS

Littlestone-on-Sea

Greatstone-on-Sea

Offen's Fm.
Guldeford La. Corner
ane Ct.
deford
Barn Fm.
Little Cheyne Ct.
Lr. Agney
Little Scotney

MARSH

Westbrook Fm.
Westbroke Ho.
Belgar
Jack's Ct.

ROMNEY SANDS
Holiday Village

enny Ho.

Point Fm.
Holiday Camp
Camber
Camber Sands
Broomhill Sands
Scotney
Pigwell
The Forelands
Holmstone
Danger Area
Lydd Ranges
The Wicks
South Brooks
Wall Fms.
Jury's Gap
Sewer

Lydd
LYDD
Denge Marsh
Boulderwall
Dengamarsh Fm.
DUNGENESS
Denge Beach

Lydd-on-Sea

The Pilot

RYE BAY

Power Sta.
STA.
Signal Sta.
DUNGENESS
OLD DUNGENESS LIGHTHOUSE

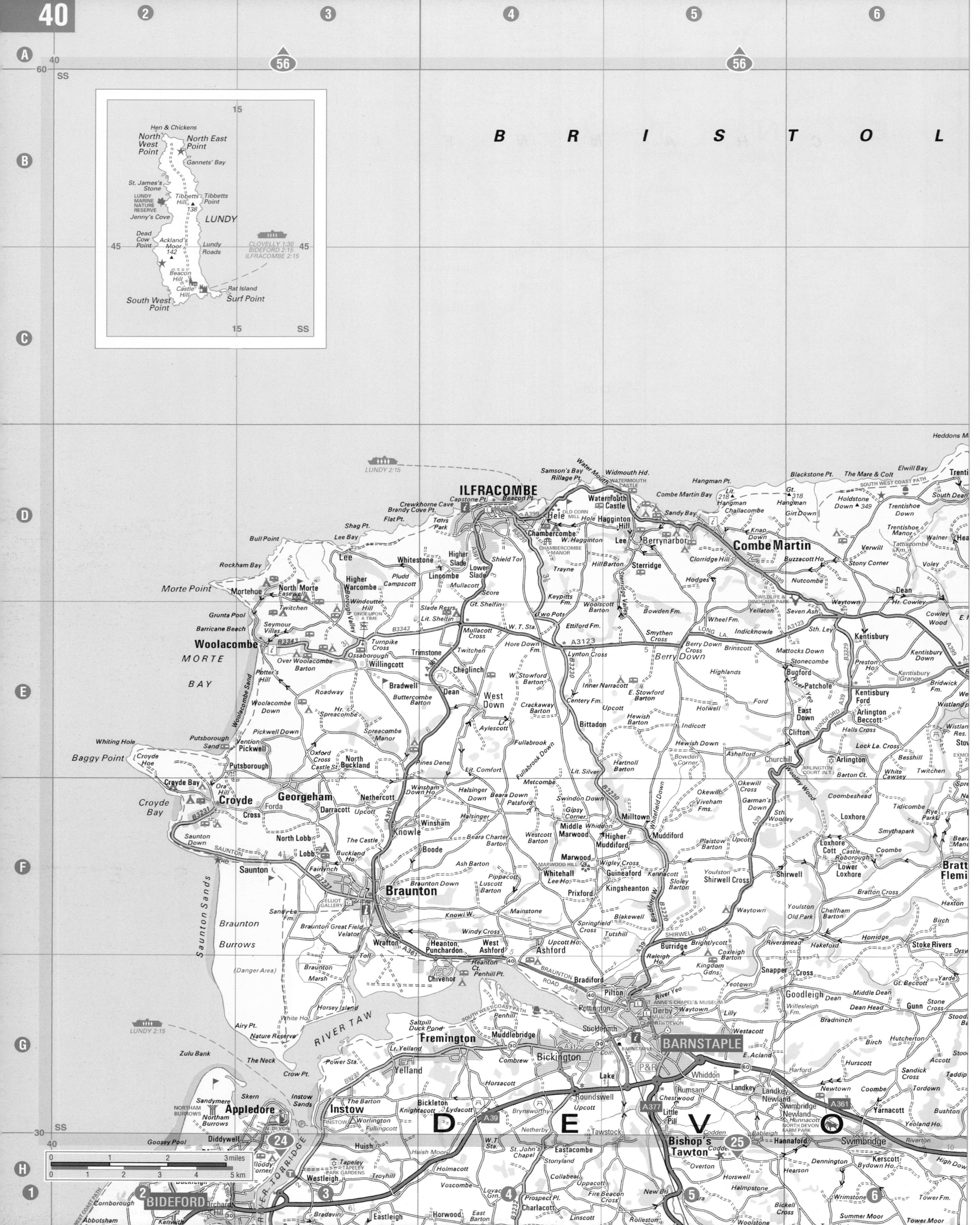

B R I S T O L

LUNDY 2:15

ILFRACOMBE

Woolacombe

MORTE
BAY

Baggy Point

Croyde
Bay

Braunton

Braunton
Burrows

Combe Martin

LUNDY 2:15

RIVER TAW

Fremington

BARNSTAPLE

Appledore

Instow

BIDEFORD

D E V O

**Bishop's
Tawton**

0   1   2   3 miles
0 1   2   3   4   5 km

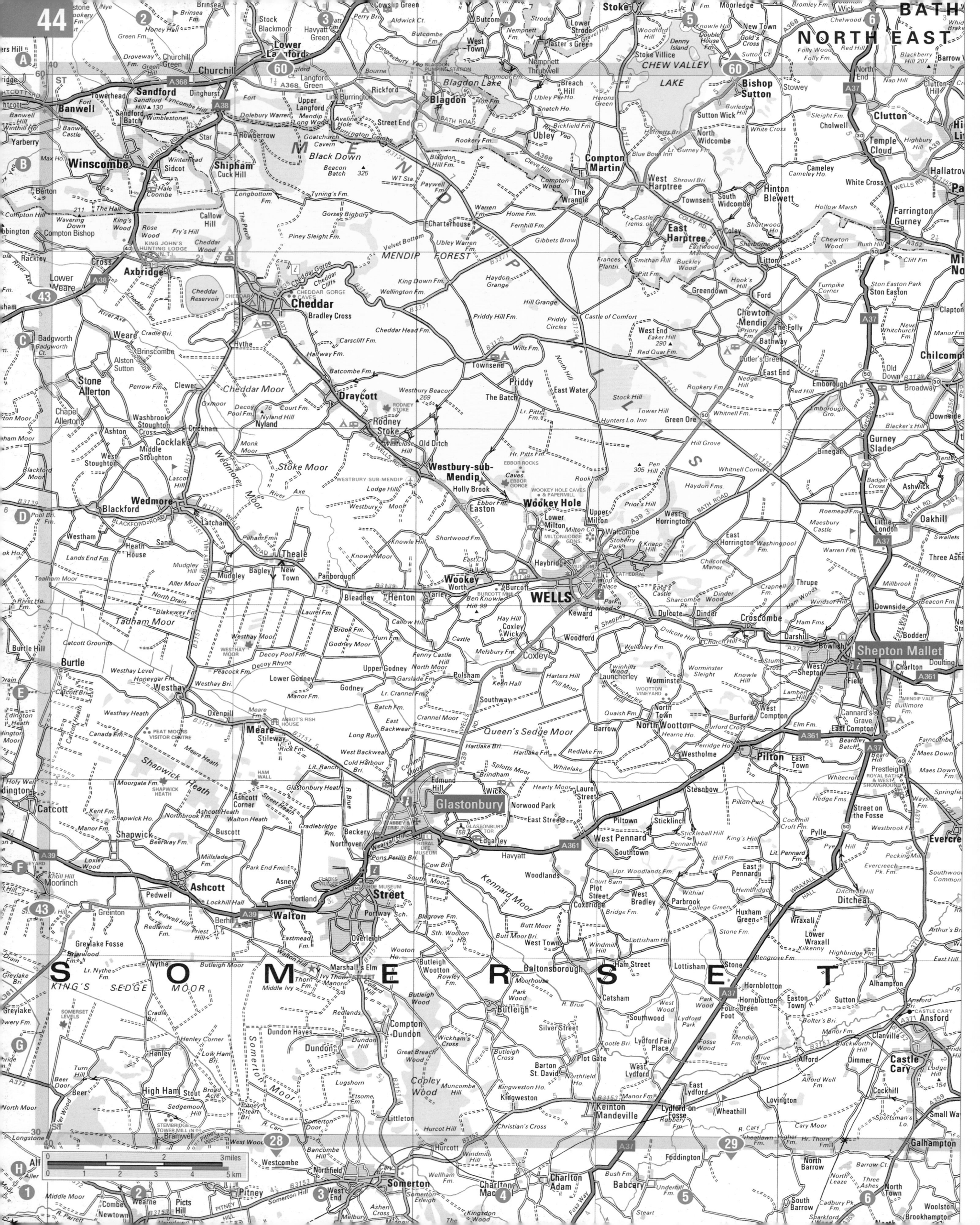

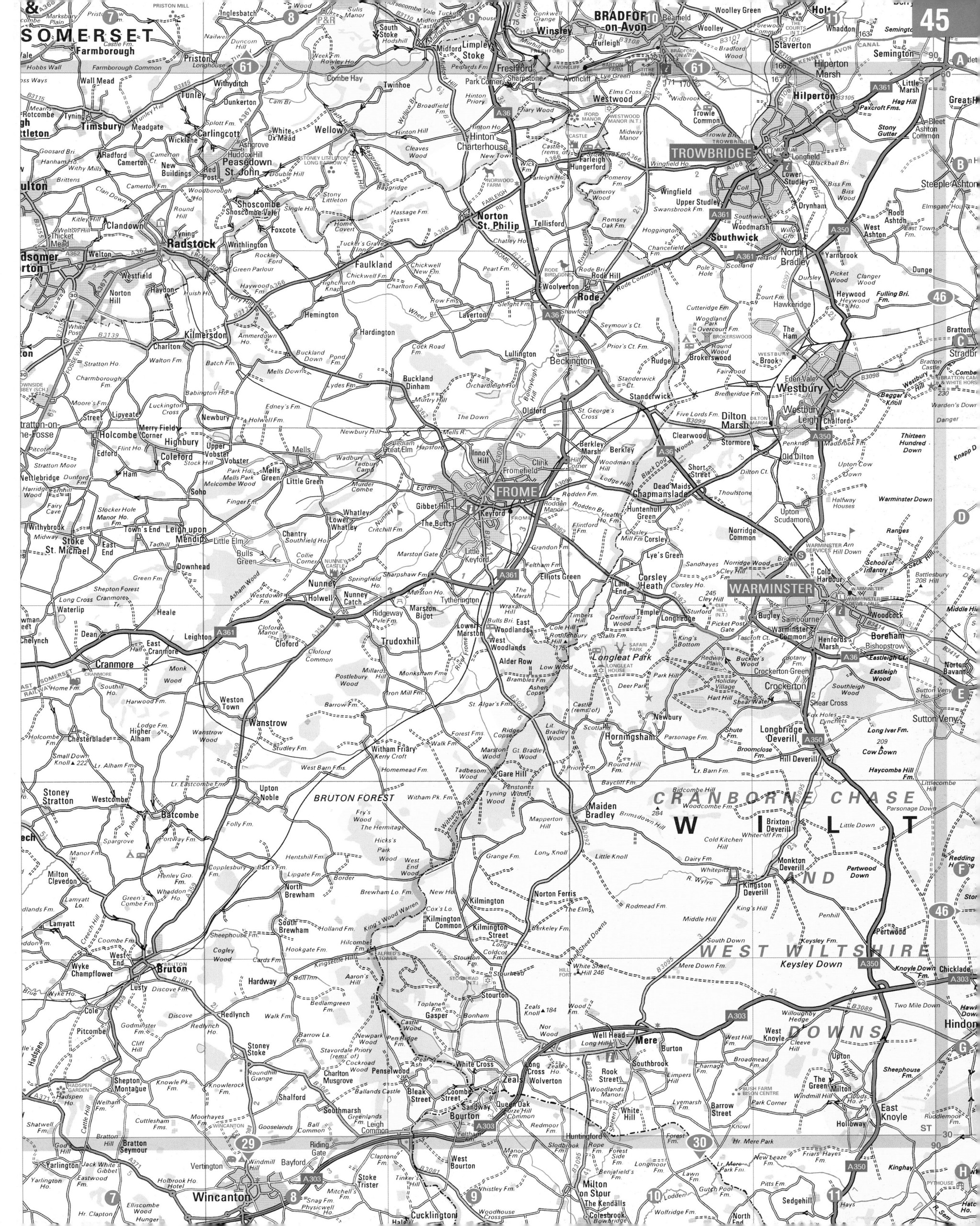

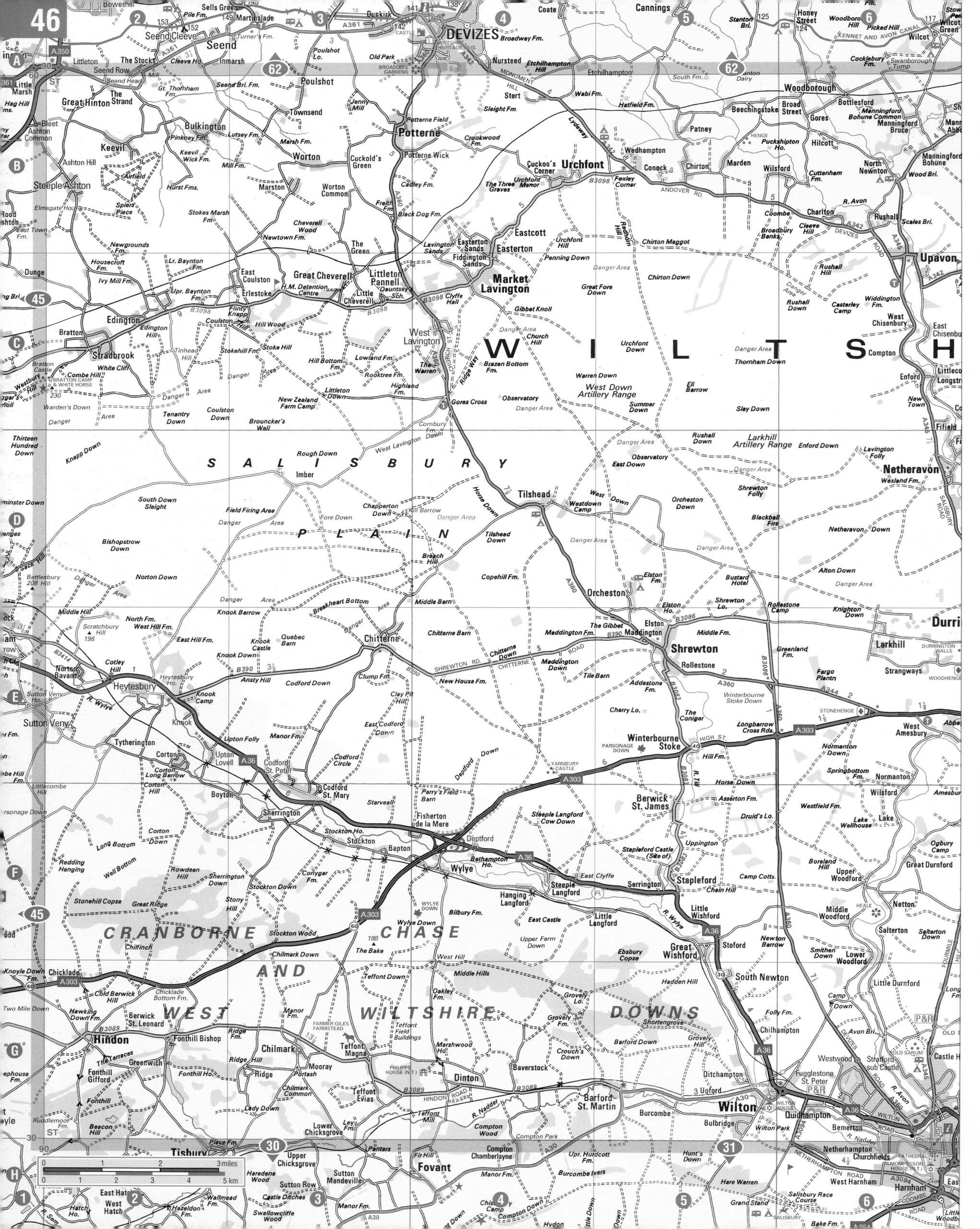

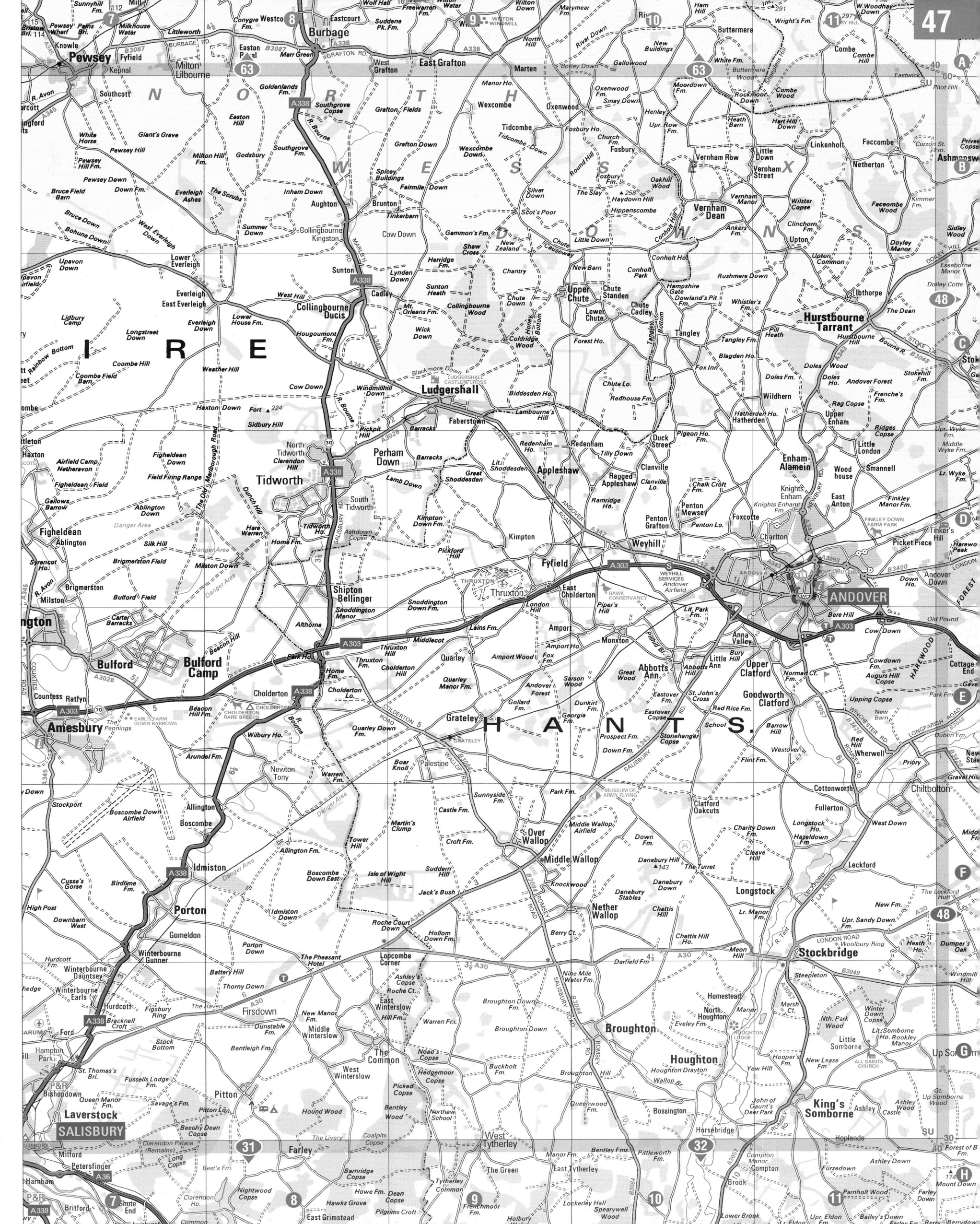

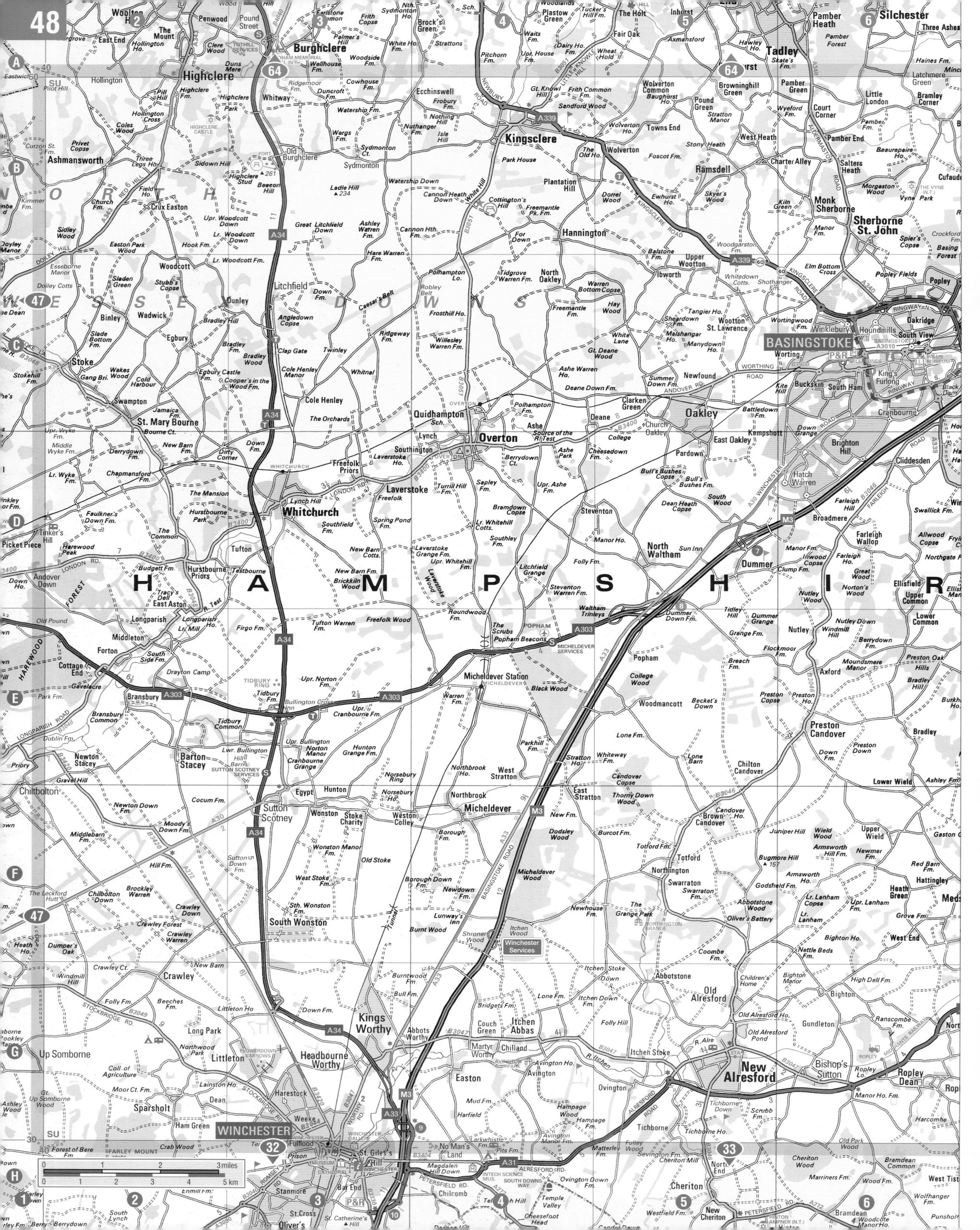

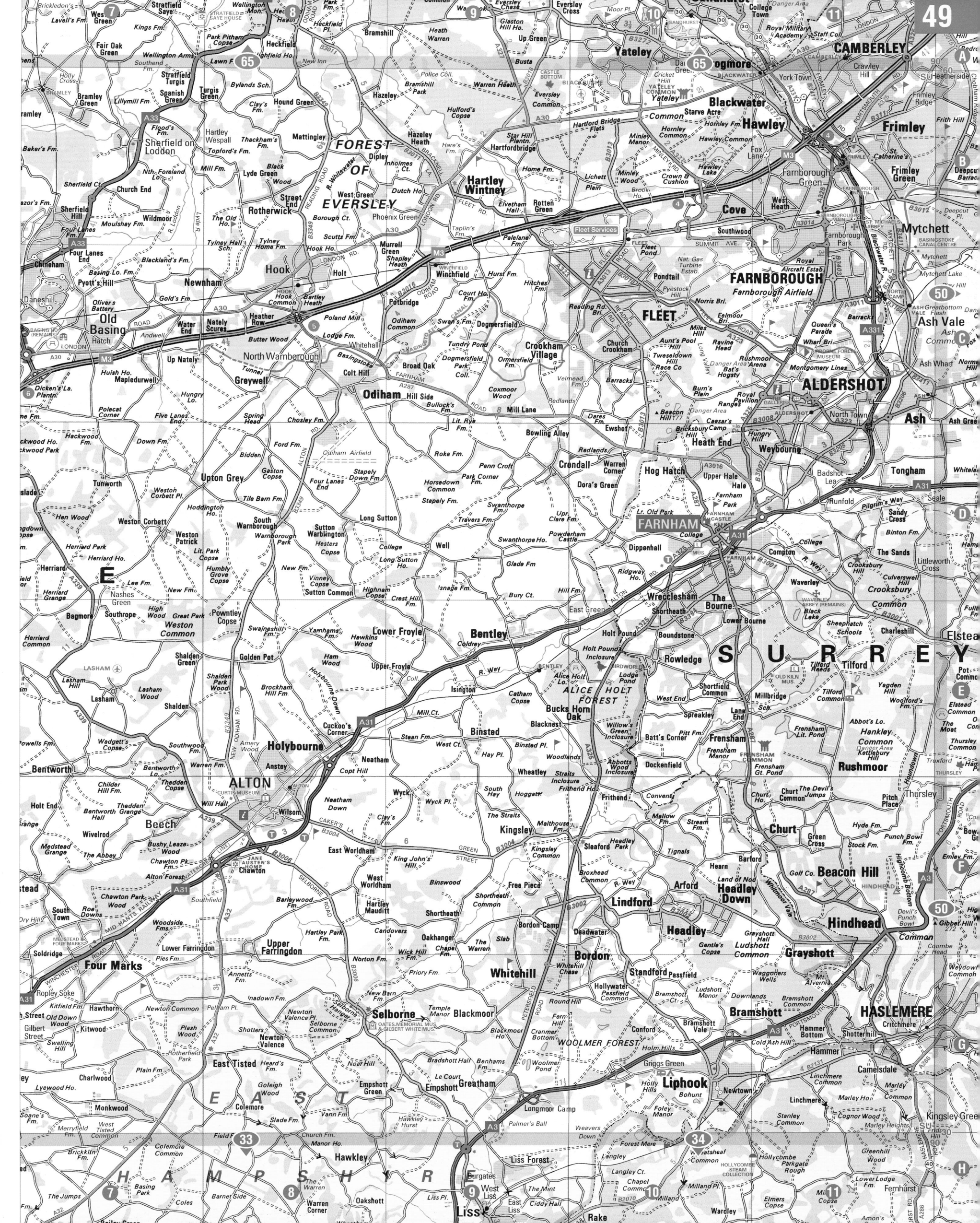

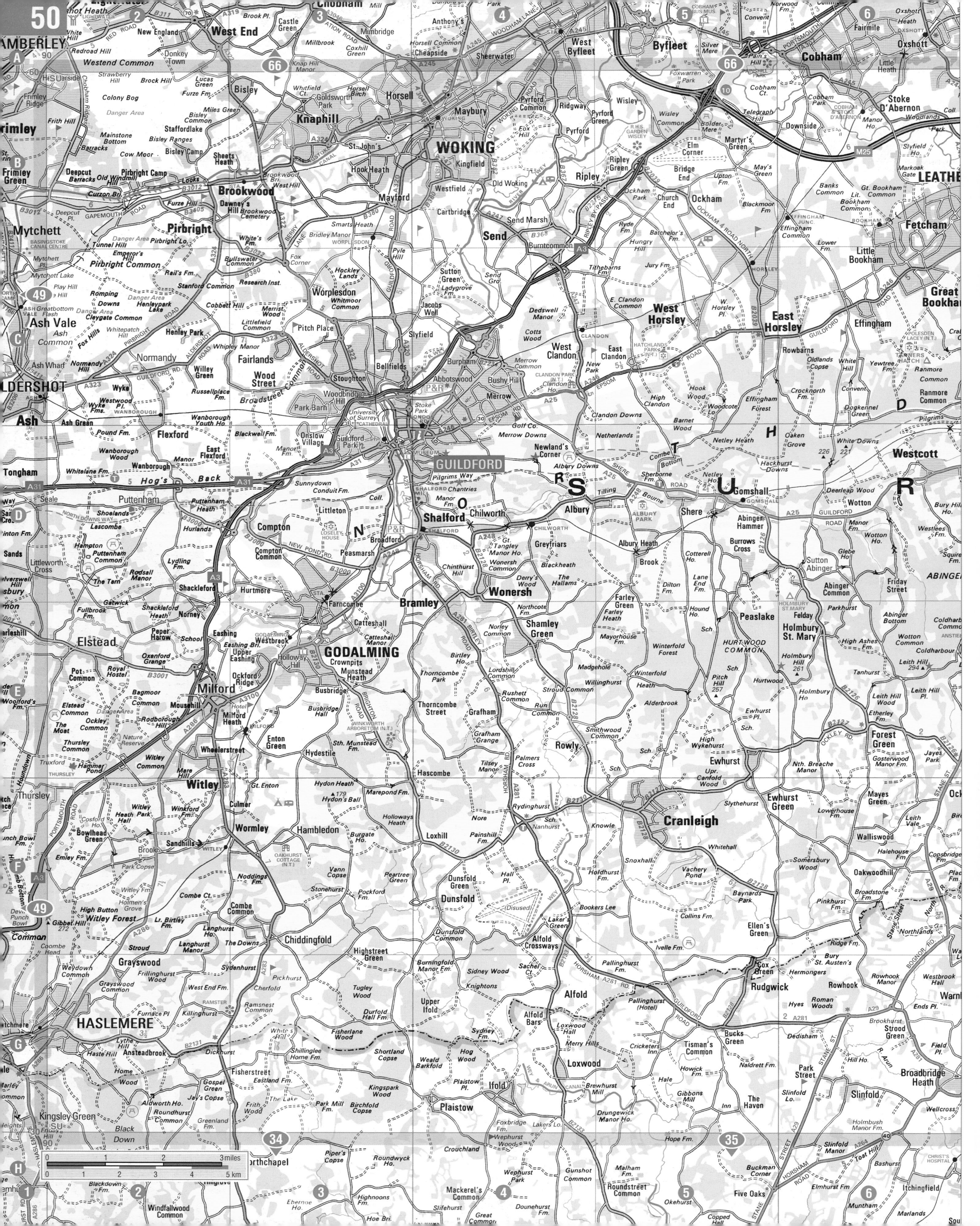

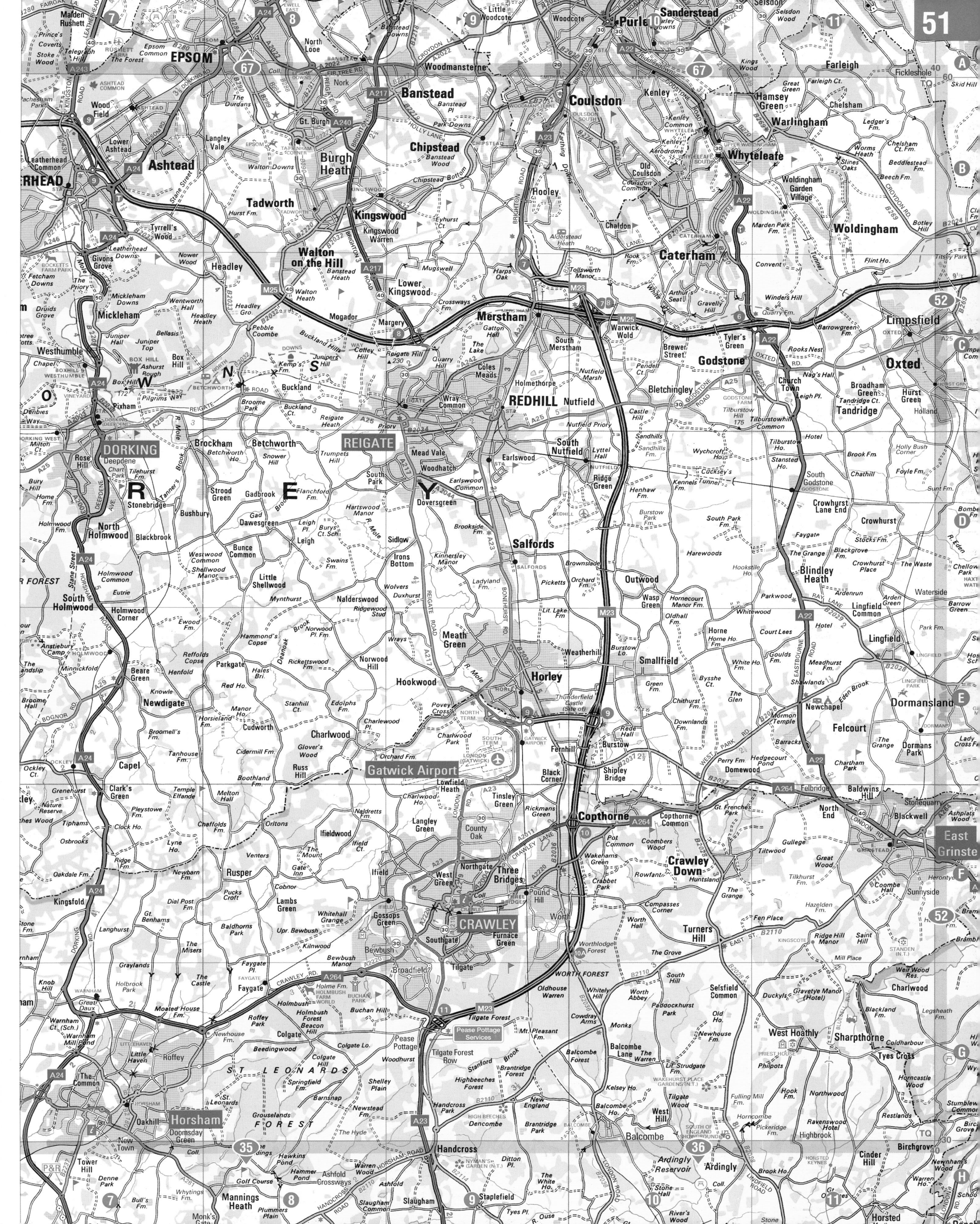

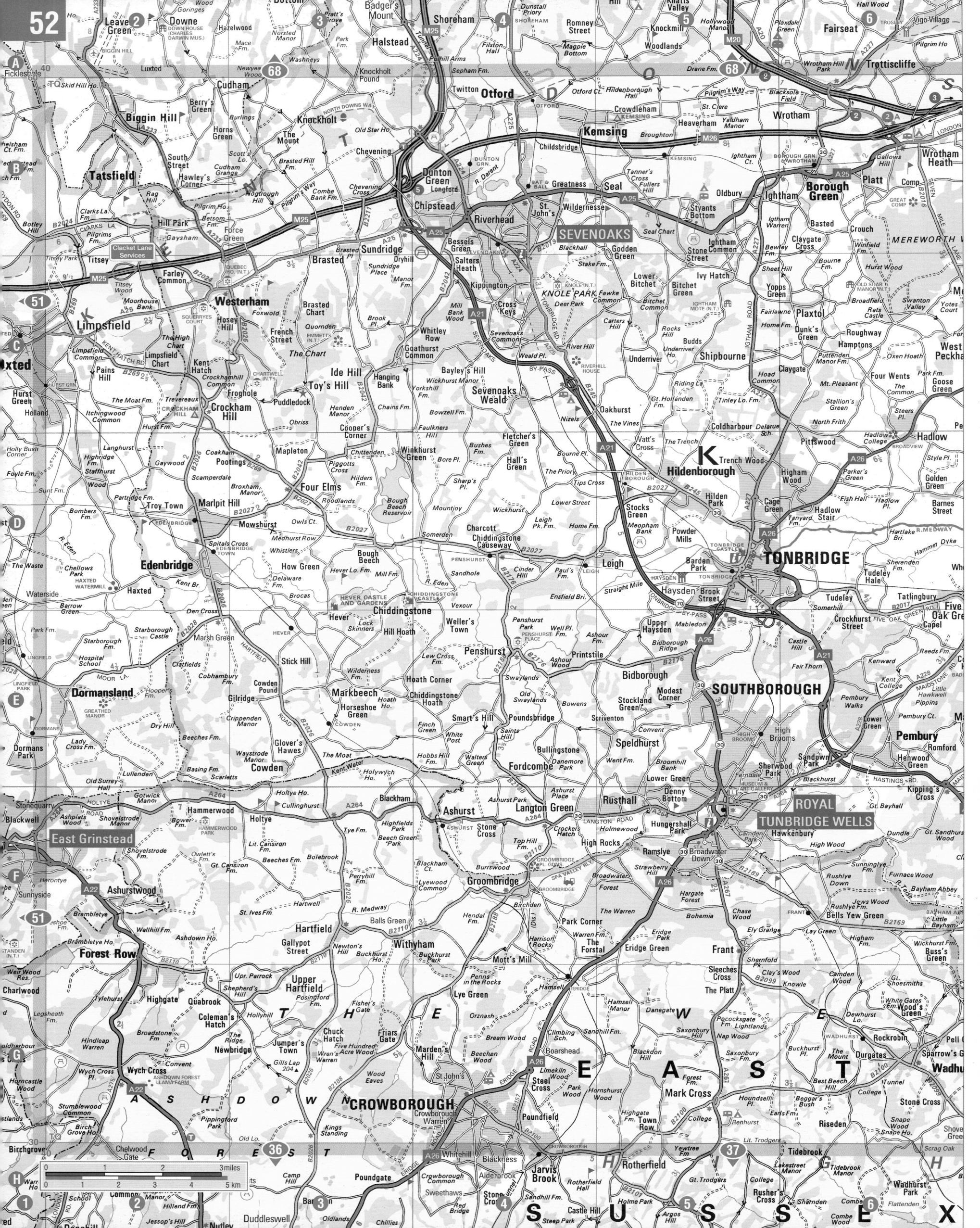

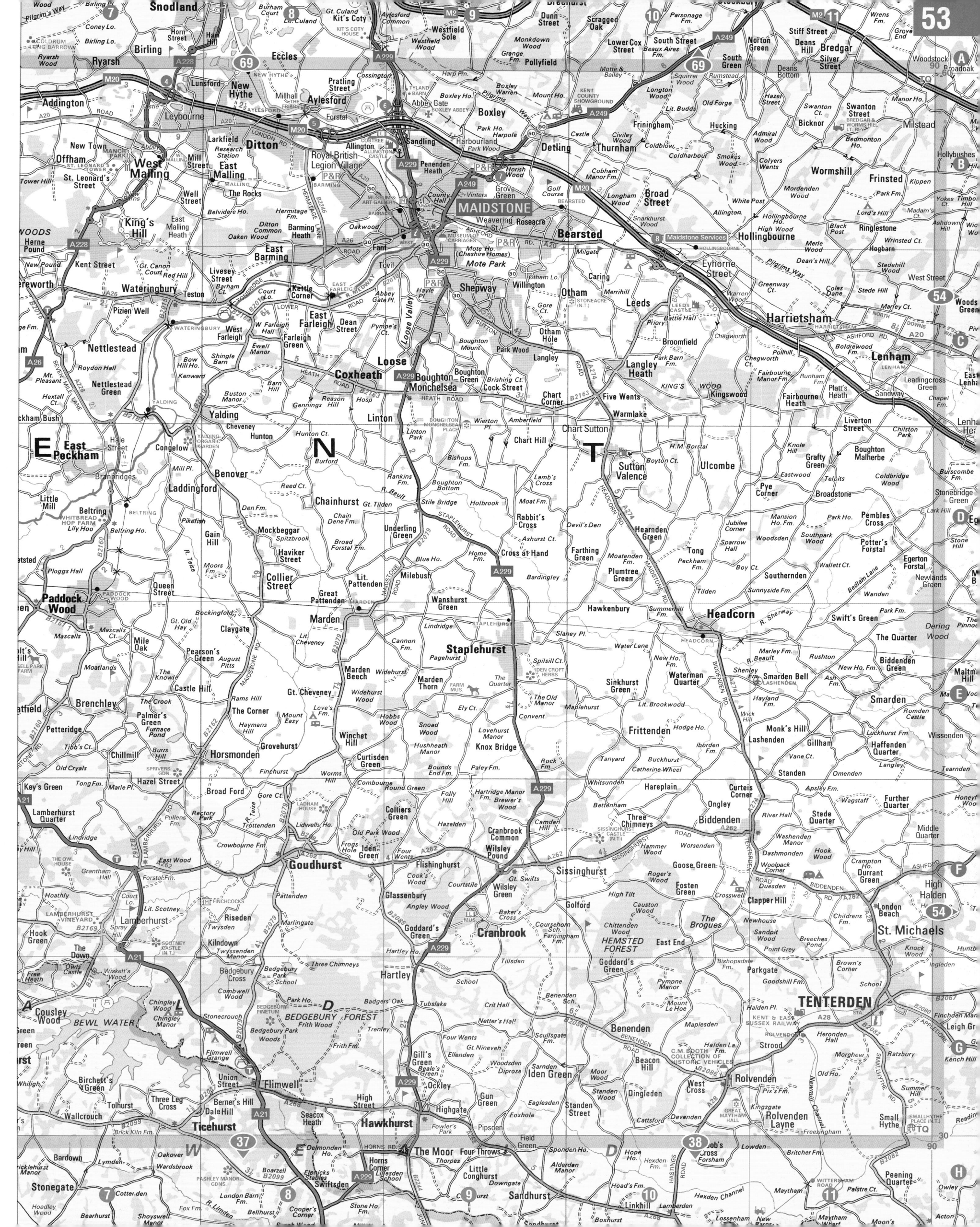

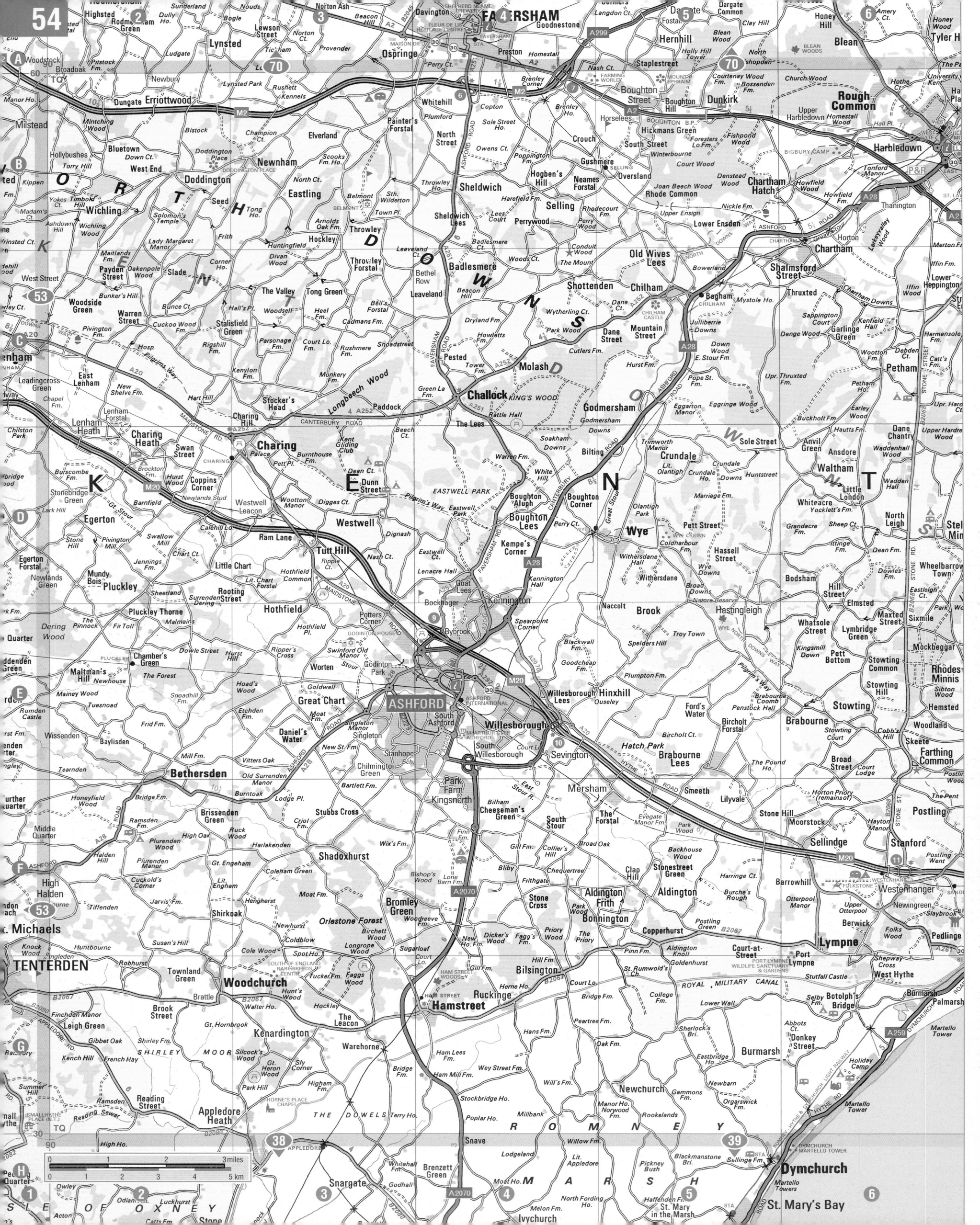

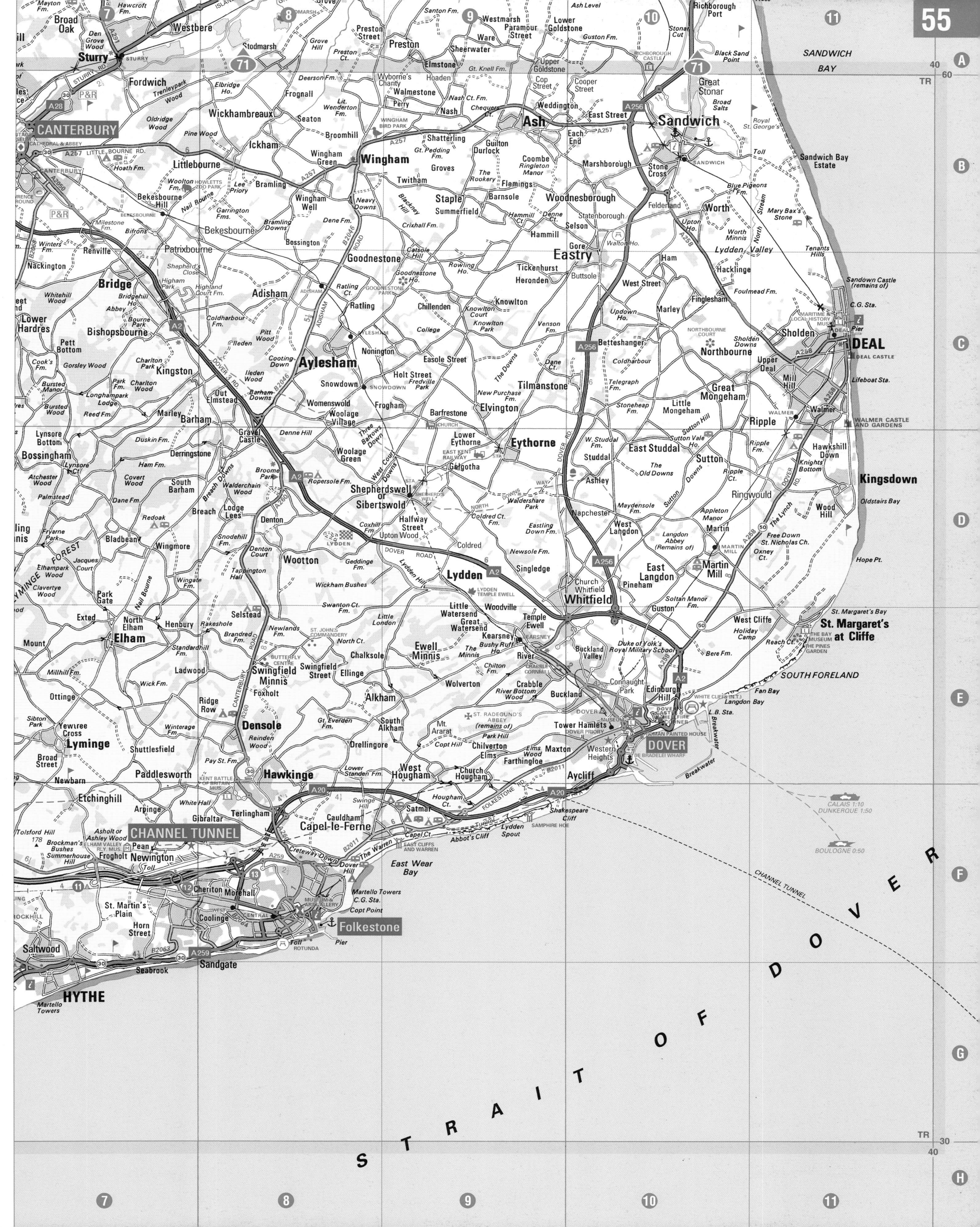

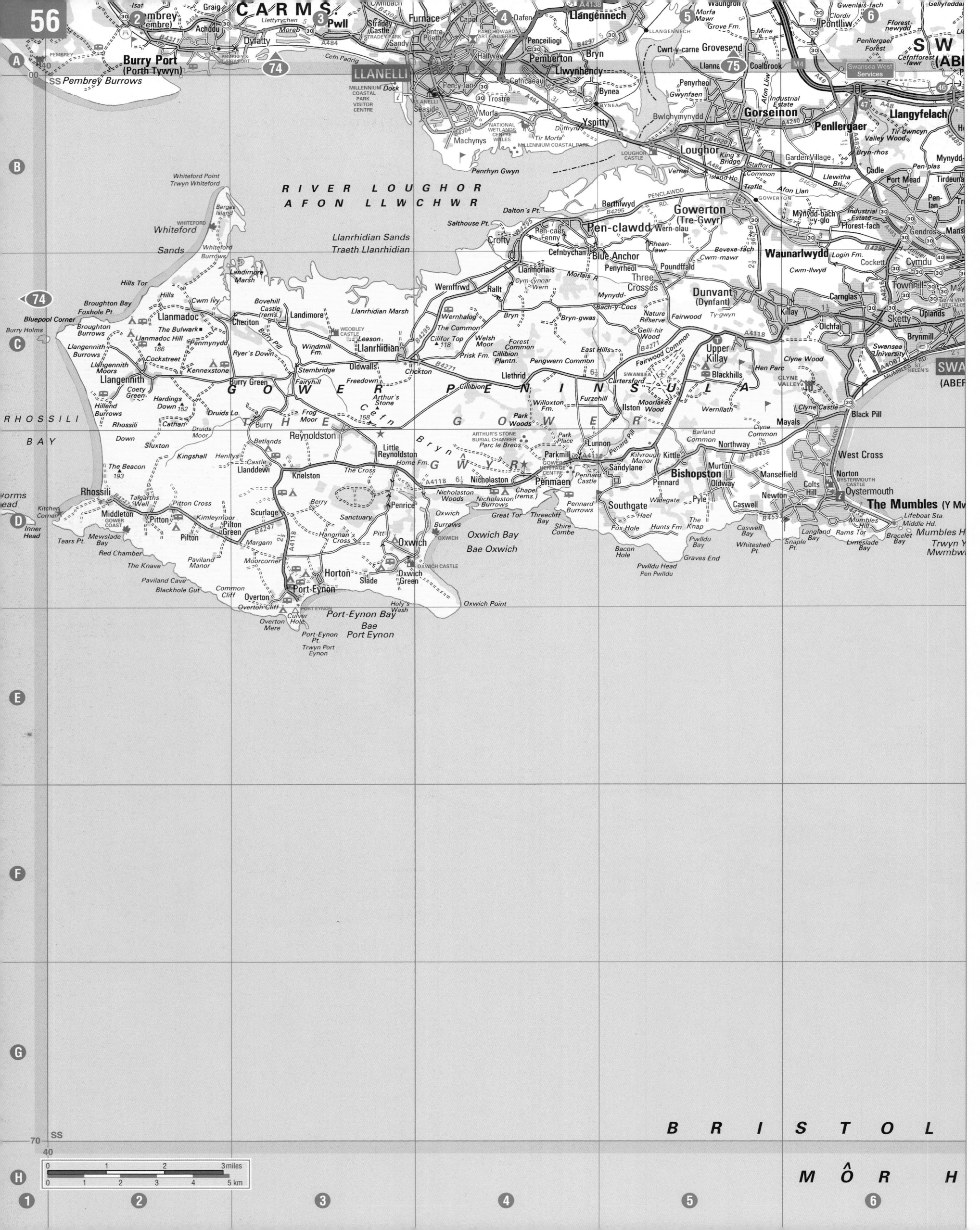

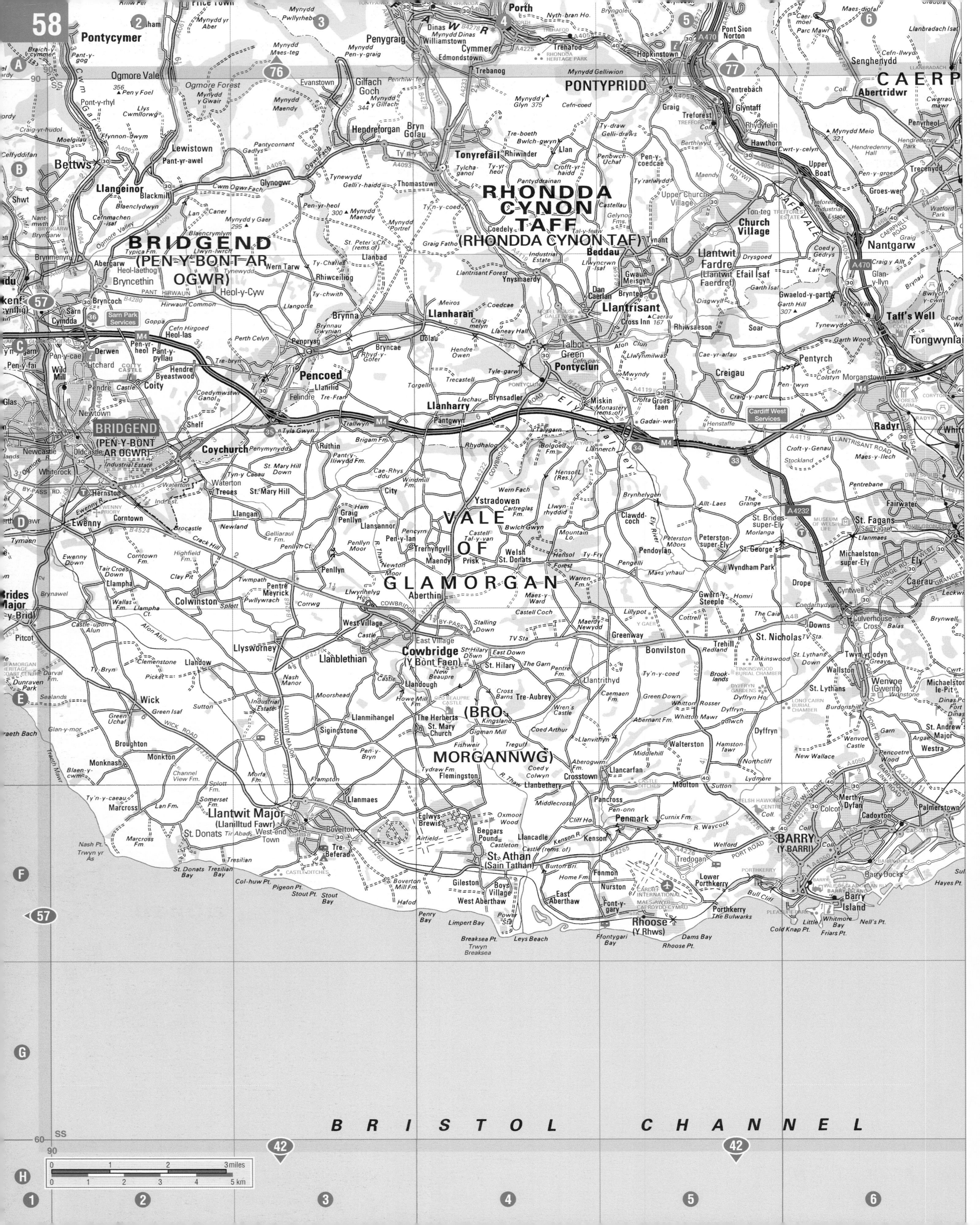

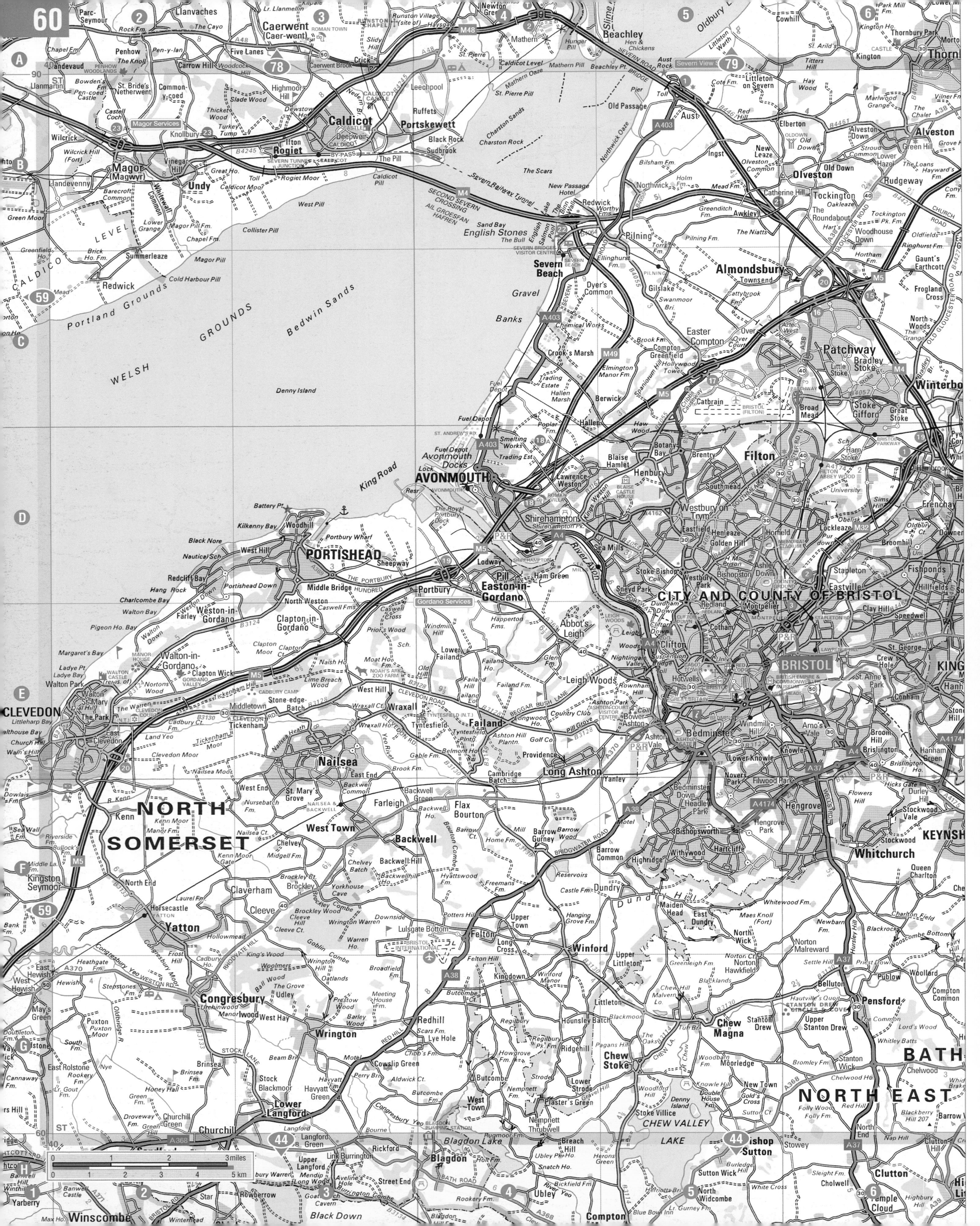

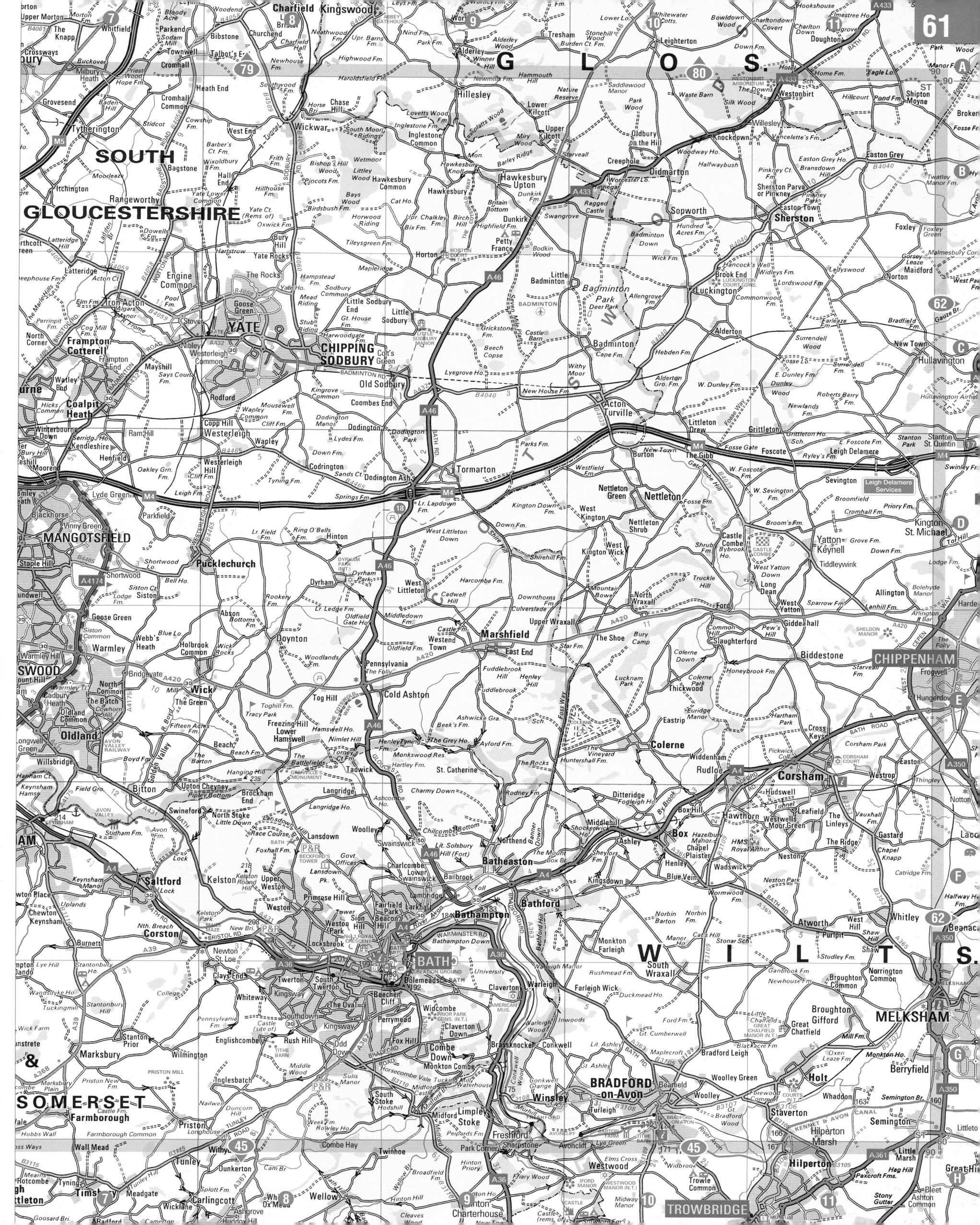

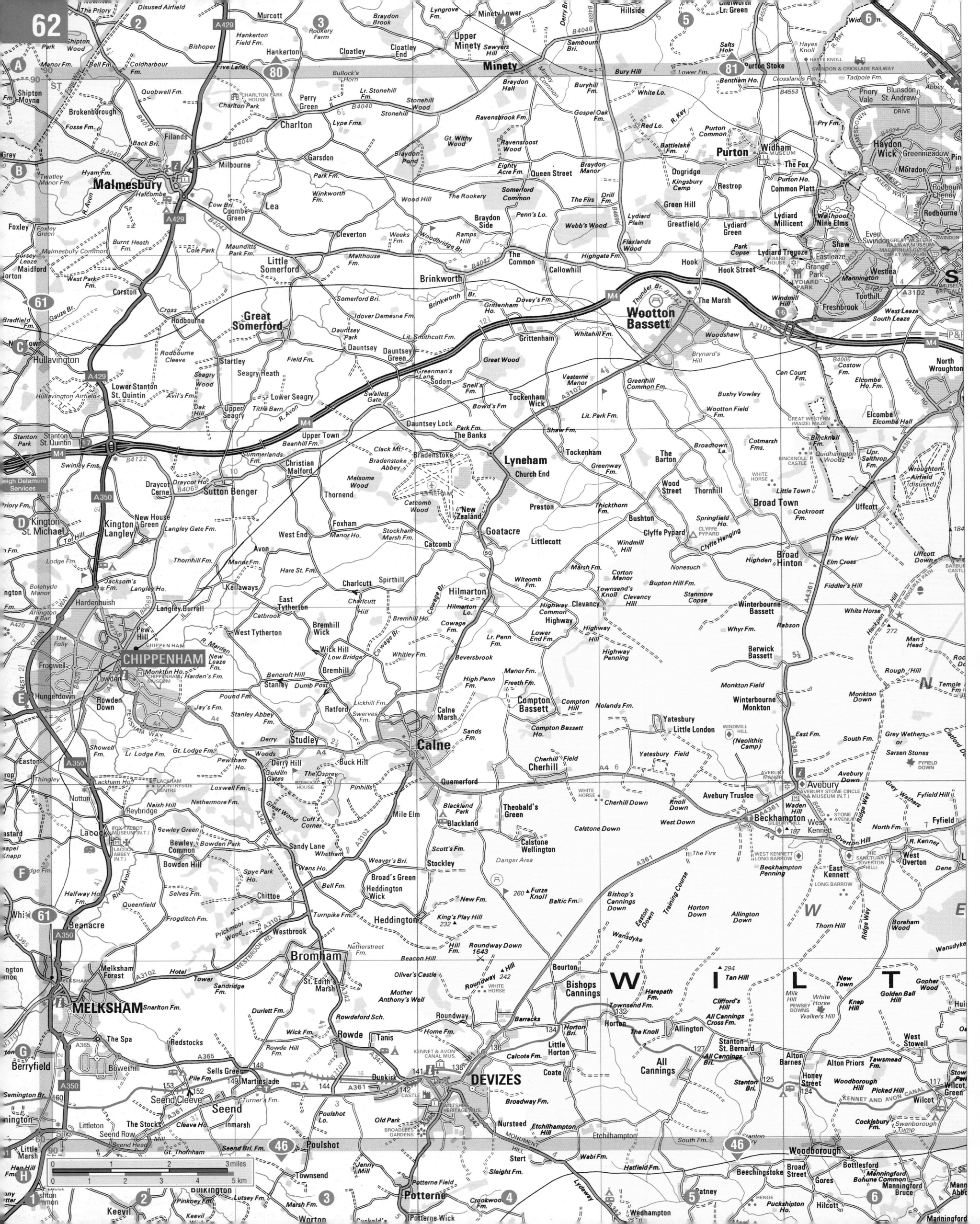

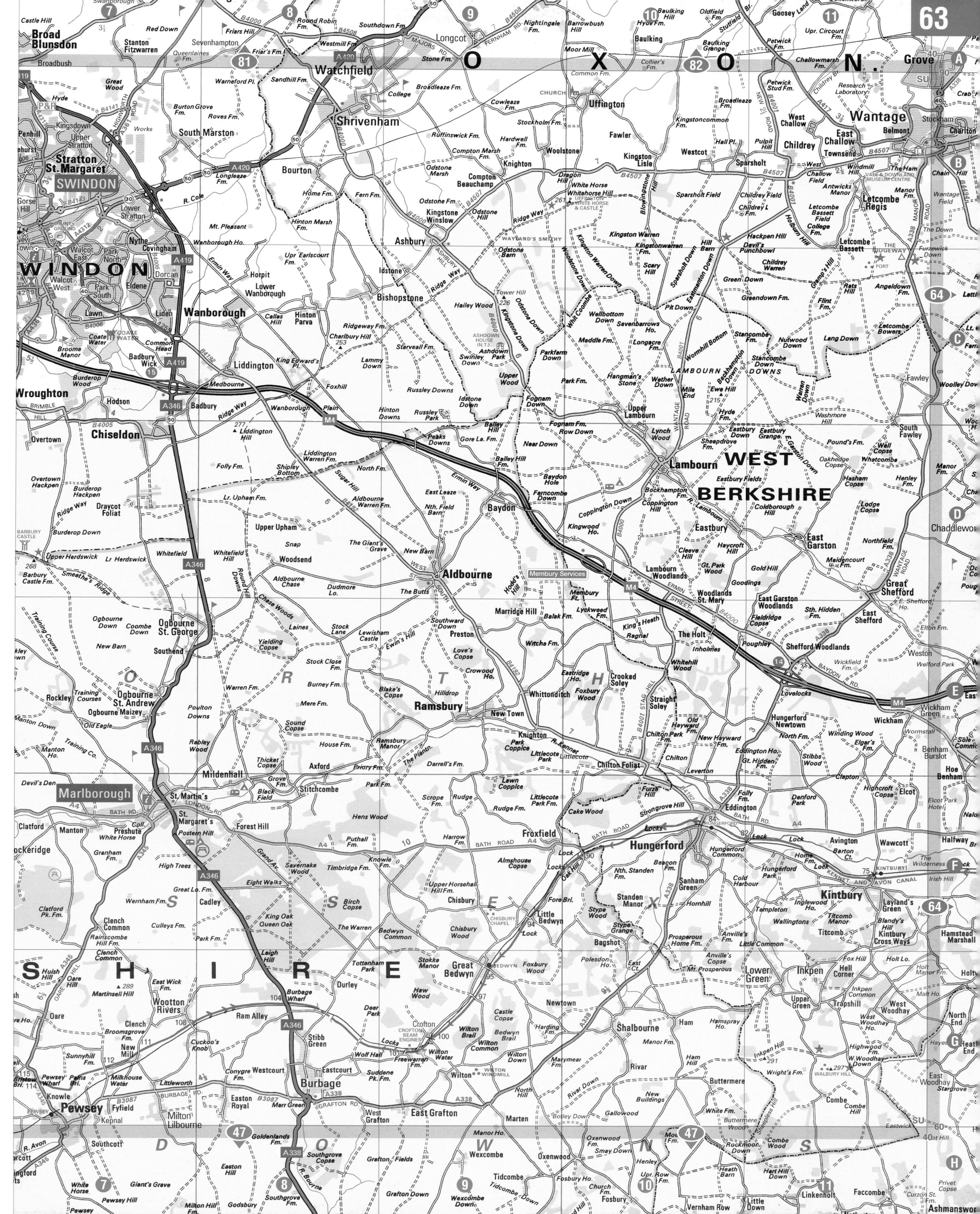

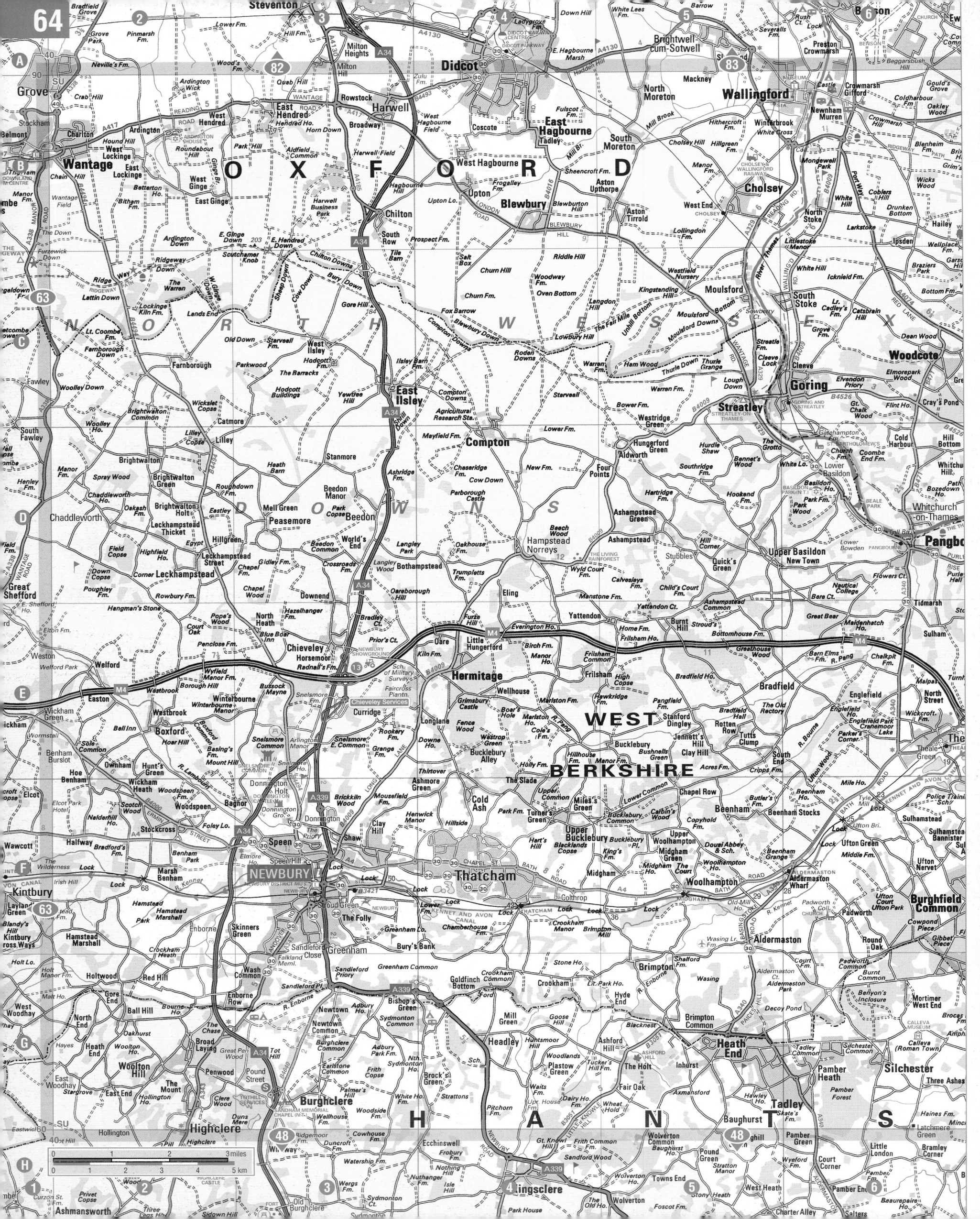

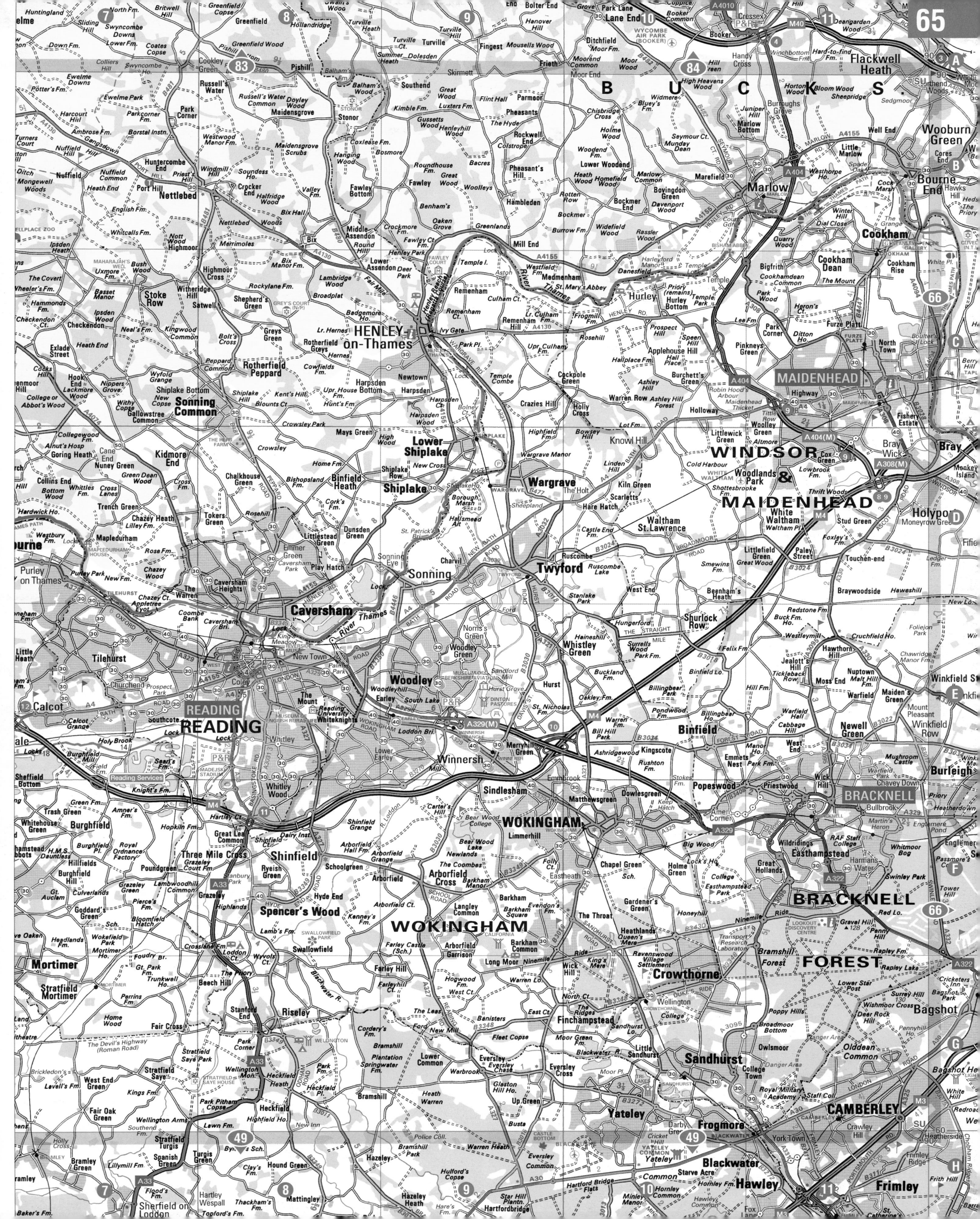

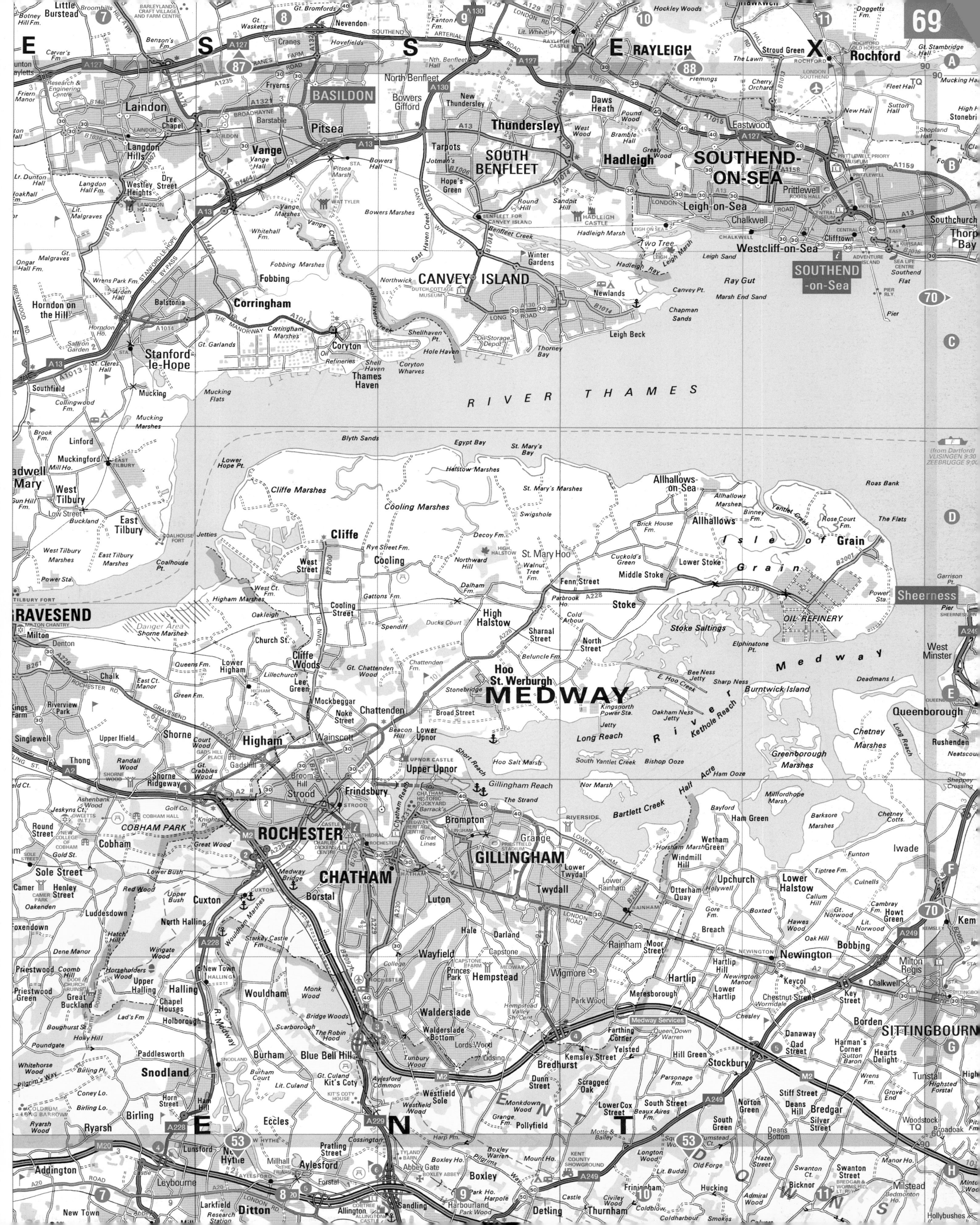

A
40
90
TR

N O R T H   S E A

B

C

D

E

Long Nose Spit
Fulsam Rock   Walpole Rocks   Palm Bay   Foreness Pt.
Botany Bay
MARGATE   Cliftonville   White Ness
Nayland Rock   The Bay
St. Mildreds Bay   SHELL GROTTO
OLD TOWN HALL MUSEUM   Kingsgate
Westgate on Sea   DREAMLAND   NORTH
Grenham Bay   Epple Bay   Hartsdown   FORELAND
Minnis Bay   WESTGATE   MARGATE   Northdown   Lighthouse
Castle   Westbrook   Reading
Birchington-on-Sea   Garlinge   Street
RECULVER TOWER   Salmestone   North Cliff
AND ROMAN FORT   Reculver   Woodchurch   Grange   St. Peters
C.G. Lookout   Gt. Brooksend Fm.   QUEX   Hengrove   Nash Ct.   BROAD
HERNE BAY   Bishopstone   Plumpudding   HOUSE   Lydden   STAIRS
Island   Waterloo   ISLE OF   Westwood   Upton   DICKENS HOUSE
Hillborough   Chambers   Shuart   Brooks   Tower   Vincent   Bromstone   MUSEUM
Studd   Beltinge   Wall   Potten   End   Acol   Fm.   THANET   South
Hill   Hawthorn   Little   Street   Hale   Cheeseman's   Manston   Haine   Northwood   Cliff
Corner   Grays   Monkton   Fm.   Dumpton Gap
Greenhill   A299   Under the   R. Wantsum   Rd. Fm.   Clev   SPITFIRE &   Newington   DUMPTON PARK
Hunters   Wood   Marshside   St. Nicholas Ct.   Mount   Ct.   HURRICANE   Manston   Dumpton
WAY   Forstal   Broomfield   Chislet   Boyden   St. Nicholas   Pleasant   Alland   MUSEUM   East
Lower   Marshes   Gate   at-Wade   Grange   Cliff
West   Herne   Strode   Ford   Quarry   KENT   RAMSGATE
End   Bullockstone   Herne   Park   Highstead   Shelvingford   A28   A253   Way   INTERNATIONAL   BOULEVARD
Herne   Millbank   Gilling Drove   Sarre   Gore   A253   Thorne Fm.   St. Lawrence   MARITIME MUS.
Bleangate   Common   Maypole   Old Tree   Sarre   Street   Monkton   St. Lawrence   Clinton   RAMSGATE
Chitty   Penn   Hoo   Marshes   Sevenscore   Cliffs End   Pegwell   Harbour
West Blean Wood   Hoath   Chislet   Sarre   Minster   Durlock   ST. AUGUSTINE'S   West Cliff   MOTOR MUSEUM
Hicks   Knave's   Hollow   Wall End Wall   Sheriffs Ct.   CROSS   OOSTENDE 4:00
Blaxland   Forstal   Ash   Chislet   Street   MINSTER   PEGWELL
Fm.   Forstal   Monkton   Docker   Minster   (ABBEY REMAINS)   BAY
West Blean Wood   Buckwell   Marshes   Hill   Marshes   A256
House   Rushbourne   Plucks   Ebbsfleet   Pegwell
Calcott   Manor   Upstreet   Gutter   Ebbsfleet   Fm.   Bay
Mayton   Vale Fm.   Tile   Site of the Saxon Landing   Stonelees
Fm.   Hersden   Lodge Fn.   A28   RIVER STOUR   A.D. 449   SANDWICH &   Ness
Hawcroft   ROAD   West   East   PEGWELL BAY
Fm.   Little Stour   Stourmouth   Stourmouth   SHELL   Richborough
Broad   Den   ISLAND   Grove   Ash Level   Port
Oak   Grove   STODMARSH   Santon Fm.   Black Sand
Sturry   Wood   Westbere   Stodmarsh   Grove   Westmarsh   RICHBOROUGH   Point   SANDWICH
A2   Grove   Hill   Lower   Guston Fm.   CASTLE   BAY
Fordwich   STURRY RD.   Preston   Paramour   Goldstone   Stonar
P&R   Trenleypark   Street   Preston   Street   Upper   Cut
CANTERBURY   Wood   Ct.   Preston   Sheerwater   Goldstone   Stonar   Broad
7   Elbridge   Deerson Fm.   Ware   55   Salts
Oldridge   Ho.   Elmstone   Gt. Knell Fm.   Royal
Wood   Wickhambreaux   Frognall   Wyborne's   Hoaden   Cop   Cooper   St. George's
Pine Wood   Seaton   Charity   Nash Ct. Fm.   Street   Street   A256   Toll
8   WINGHAM   Perry   Chequers   Weddington   Sandwich Bay Estate
Wingham   9   BIRD PARK   Nash   East Street   Sandwich
Littlebourne   Ash   10   11
A257   A257   Littlebourne   Guilton   Each   Broad
Shatterling   Durlock   End   A256
Coombe   Marshborough

F

G
60
TR

H

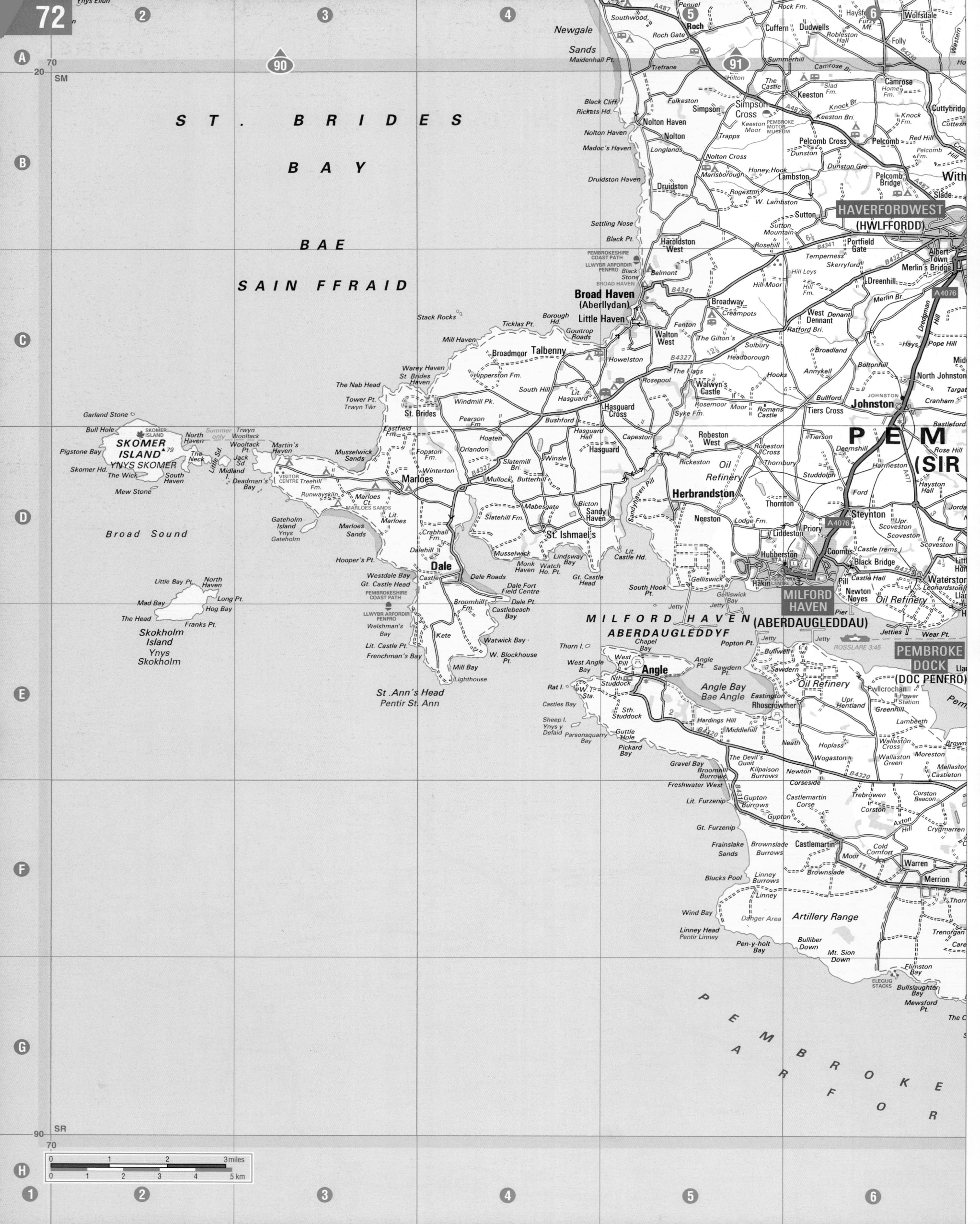

ST. BRIDES

BAY

BAE

SAIN FFRAID

Newgale
Sands
Maidenhall Pt.

Southwood
Roch
Roch Gate
Cuffern
Dudwells
Rock Fm.
Wolfsdale

Trefrane
Hilton
The Castle
Keeston
Slad Fm.
Knock Br.
Camrose Home Fm.
Camrose

Black Cliff
Rickets Hd.
Folkeston
Simpson
Simpson Cross
Keeston Moor
PEMBROKE MOTOR MUSEUM
Knock
Keeston Bri.
Pelcomb Cross
Pelcomb
Red Hill
Cuttybridge
Cottess

Nolton Haven
Nolton
Nolton Cross
Trapps
Dunston
Dunston Gro.
Pelcomb Bridge

Madoc's Haven
Longlands
Honey-Hook
Lambston
Slade
With

Druidston Haven
Marloesborough
Druidston
Rogeston
W. Lambston
HAVERFORDWEST (HWLFFORDD)

Settling Nose
Black Pt.
Sutton
Sutton Mountain
Rosehill
Portfield Gate
Albert Town
Merlin's Bridge
Llan

Haroldston West
Temperness
Skerryford
Dreenhill
Merlin Br.
A4076

PEMBROKESHIRE COAST PATH
LLWYBR ARFORDIR PENFRO
Black Stone
BROAD HAVEN
Belmont
Hill Leys
Hill Fm.
Hill Moor
Broadway
Creampots
West Dennant
Denant
Dredgman Hill

Broad Haven (Aberllydan)
Little Haven
Borough Hd.
Goultrop Roads
Walton West
Fenton
The Gilton's
Solbury
Broadland
Hays
Pope Hill

Ticklas Pt.
Mill Haven
Broadmoor
Talbenny
Howelston
Rosepool
Headborough
B4327
Hooks
Annykell
North Johnston
Boltonhill

Stack Rocks
St. Brides Haven
Hipperston Fm.
South Hill
Lit. Hasguard
Rosemoor Moor
The Flags
Walwyn's Castle
Tiers Cross
Romans Castle
Johnston
PEM (SIR

The Nab Head
Warey Haven
Pearson
Bushford
Hasguard
Hasguard Cross
Syke Fm.
Robeston West
Bastleford

Tower Pt.
Trwyn Twr
St. Brides
Windmill Pk.
Hoaten
Hasguard Hall
Capeston
Robeston Cross
Tierson
Rose Fm.
Deemshill

Garland Stone
Eastfield Fm.
Orlandon
Slatemill Bri.
Winsle
Hasguard
Oil Refinery
Thornbury
Rickeston
Harmeston
Haybush Hall

Bull Hole
SKOMER ISLAND
North Haven
Summer only
Trwyn Wooltack
Martin's Haven
Fopston Fm.
Mullock
Butterhill
Herbrandston
Studdolph
Ford

SKOMER ISLAND YNYS SKOMER
Pigstone Bay
The Neck
Little Sd.
Jack Sd.
Midland
Treehill Fm.
Winterton
Marloes
Sandy Haven
Sandyhaven Pill
Neeston
Lodge Fm.
Steynton
Upr. Scoveston
Scoveston
Jorda

Skomer Hd.
The Wick
South Haven
Deadman's Bay
VISITOR CENTRE
Runwayskiln
Marloes Ct.
Mabesgate
Bicton
Thornton
Priory
A4076
Ft. Scoveston

Mew Stone
Gateholm Island Ynys Gateholm
Lit. Marloes
LIT. MARLOES SANDS
Slatehill Fm.
St. Ishmael's
Liddeston
Coombs
Castle (rems)

Broad Sound
Marloes Sands
Crabhall Fm.
Musselwick
Lindsway Bay
Lit. Castle Hd.
Hubberston
Black Bridge
Waterston

Hooper's Pt.
Dalehill
Monk Haven
Watch Ho. Pt.
Gt. Castle Head
Gelliswick
Castle Hall
Leonardston
Hon

Little Bay Pt.
North Haven
Westdale Bay
Gt. Castle Head
Dale
Castle
Dale Roads
South Hook Pt.
Gelliswick Bay
MILFORD HAVEN
Newton Noyes
Oil Refinery

Mad Bay
Long Pt.
PEMBROKESHIRE COAST PATH
LLWYBR ARFORDIR PENFRO
Dale Fort Field Centre
Dale Pt.
Hakin
Pill
Jetties
Wear Pt.

The Head
Hog Bay
Welshman's Bay
Broomhill Fm.
Castlebeach Bay
MILFORD HAVEN (ABERDAUGLEDDAU)
Jetty

Skokholm Island Ynys Skokholm
Franks Pt.
Lit. Castle Pt.
Frenchman's Bay
Kete
Watwick Bay
W. Blockhouse Pt.
ABERDAUGLEDDYF
ROSSLARE 3:45
PEMBROKE DOCK (DOC PENFRO)

Mill Bay
Lighthouse
Thorn I.
Chapel Bay
Popton Pt.
Jetty
Jetty

St. Ann's Head
Pentir St. Ann
West Angle Bay
West Pill
Angle
Angle Pt.
Sawdern
Bullwell
Sawdern Pt.
Oil Refinery
Pem

Rat I.
W. Sta.
Nth Studdock
Angle Bay
Bae Angle
Eastington
Rhoscrowther
Upr. Hentland
Greenhill
Power Station

Castles Bay
Sth. Studdock
Hardings Hill
Middlehill
Neath
Hoplass
Wogaston
Wallaston Cross
Lambeeth
Brown

Sheep I.
Ynys y Defaid
Guttle Hole
The Devil's Quoit
Kilpaison Burrows
Newton
Wallaston Green
Moreston
Mellastor
Castleton

Parsonsquarry Bay
Pickard Bay
Gravel Bay
Broomhill Burrows
Castlemartin Corse
B4320
Axton
Crygmarren

Freshwater West
Lit. Furzenip
Gupton Burrows
Corseside
Trebrowen
Corston Beacon
Corston

Gt. Furzenip
Gupton
Cold Comfort

Frainslake Sands
Brownslade Burrows
Castlemartin
Moor
Warren
Merrion

Blucks Pool
Linney Burrows
Brownslade

Wind Bay
Linney
Artillery Range
Thorn

Linney Head
Pentir Linney
Danger Area
Pen-y-holt Bay
Bulliber Down
Mt. Sion Down
Trenorgan
Care

Flimston Bay
ELEGUG STACKS
Bullslaughter Bay
Mewsford Pt.
The C

P E M B R O K E   F O R

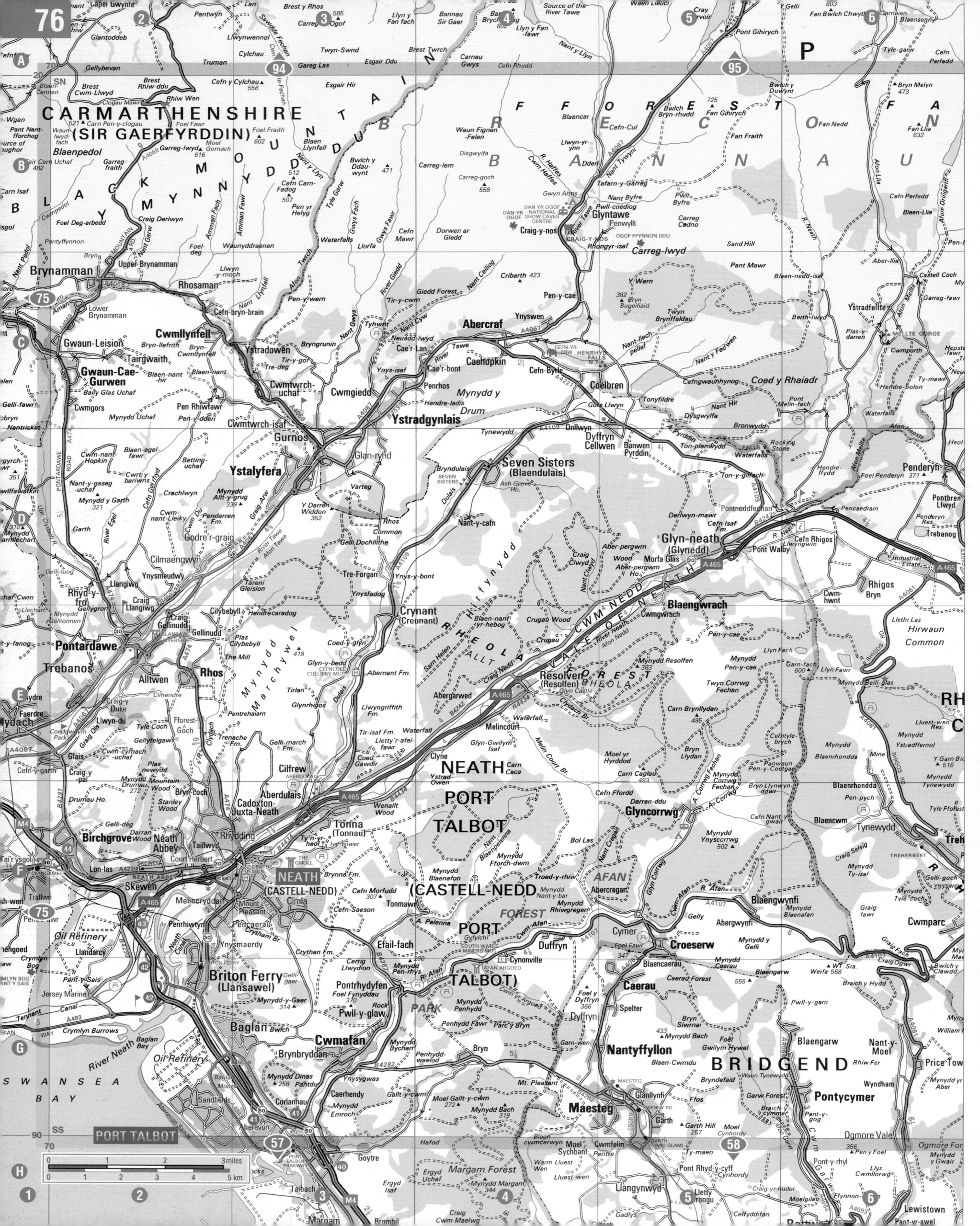

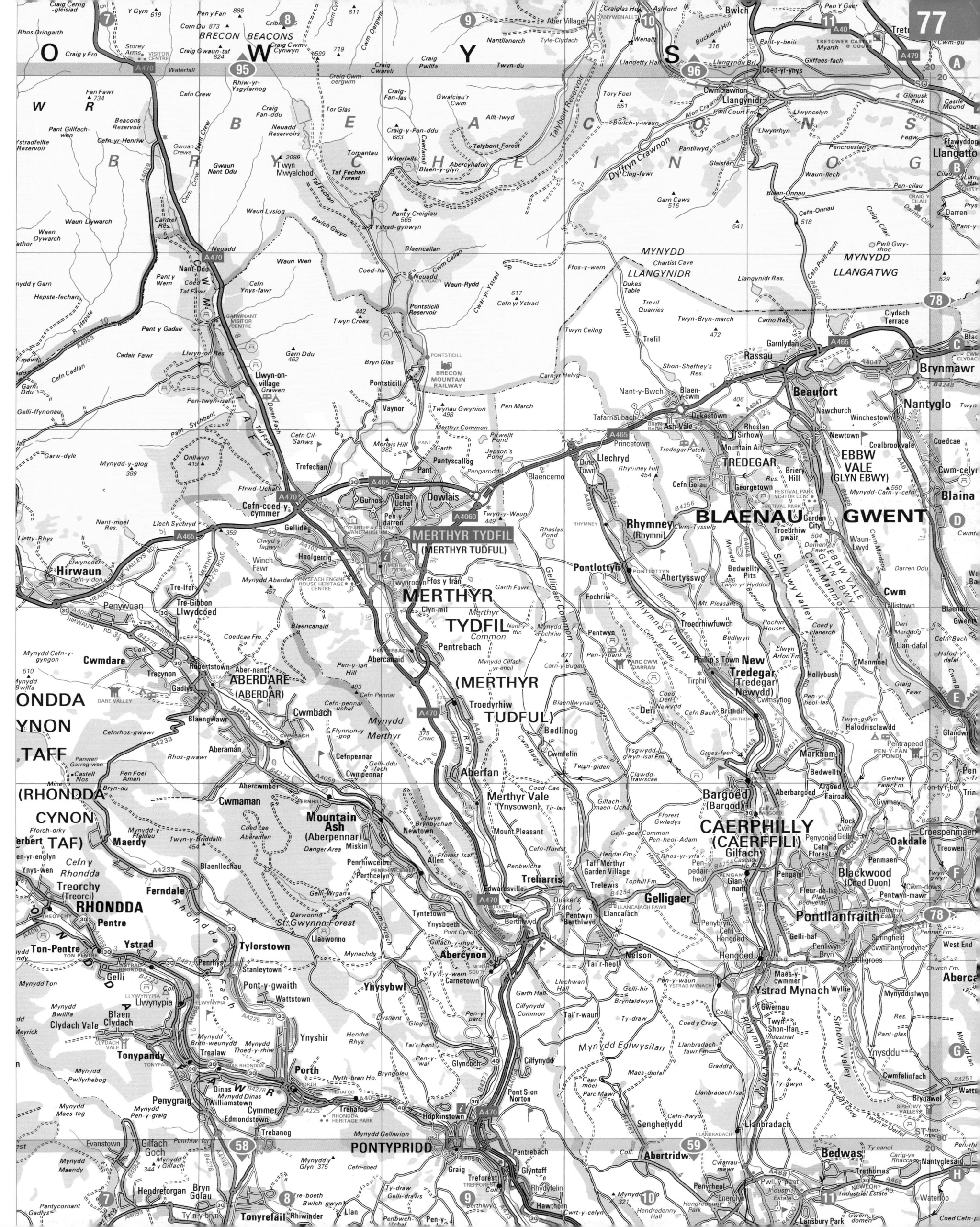

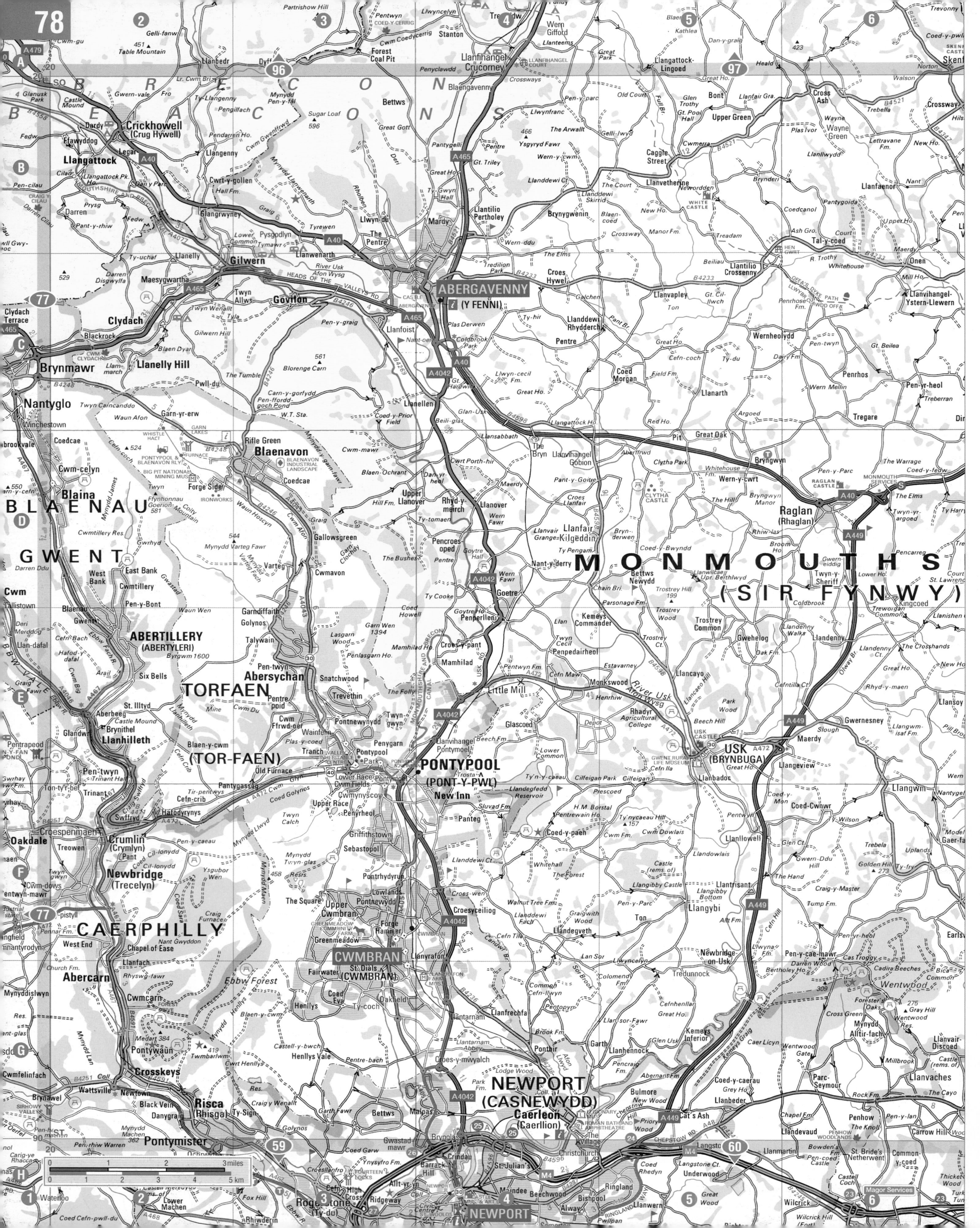

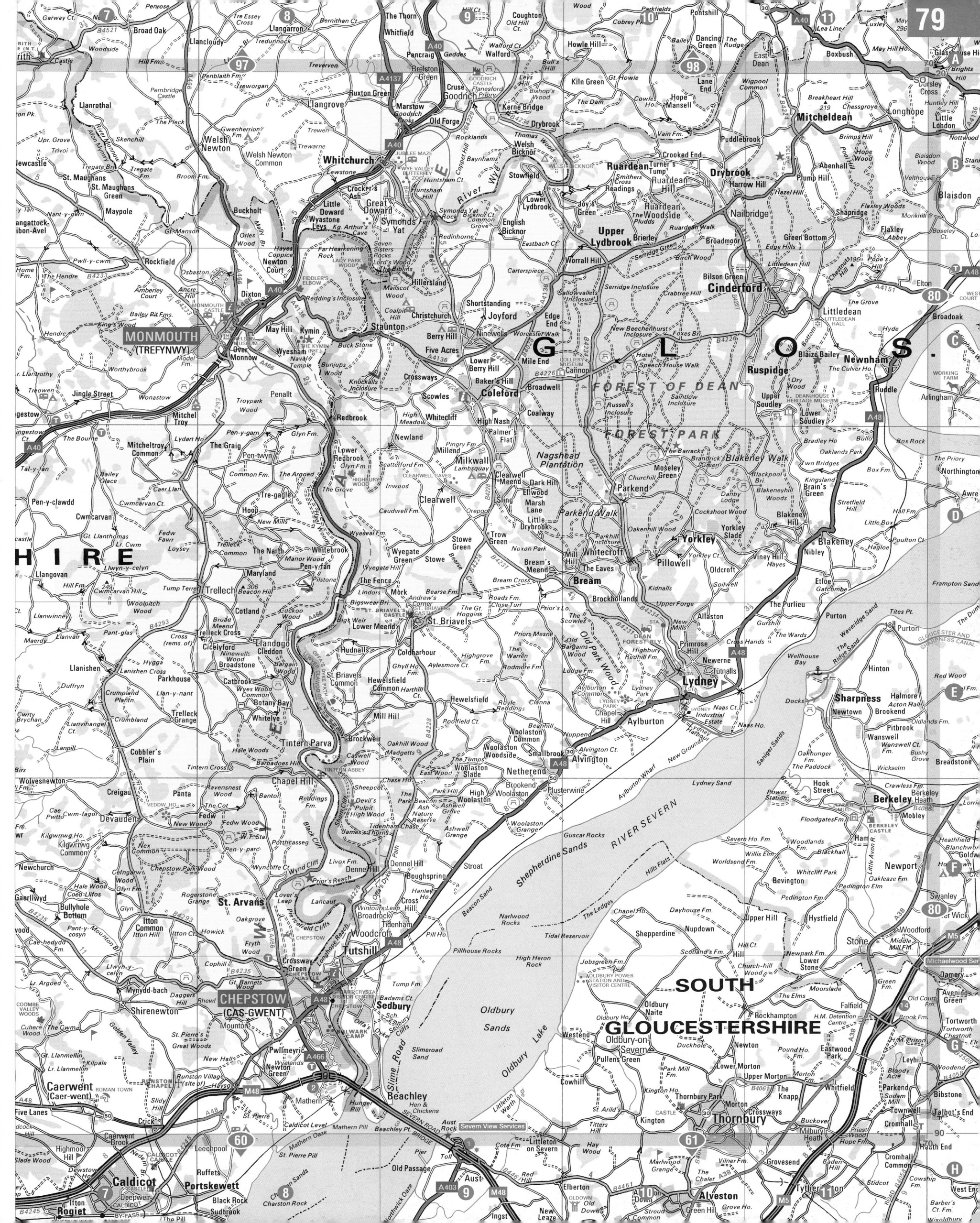

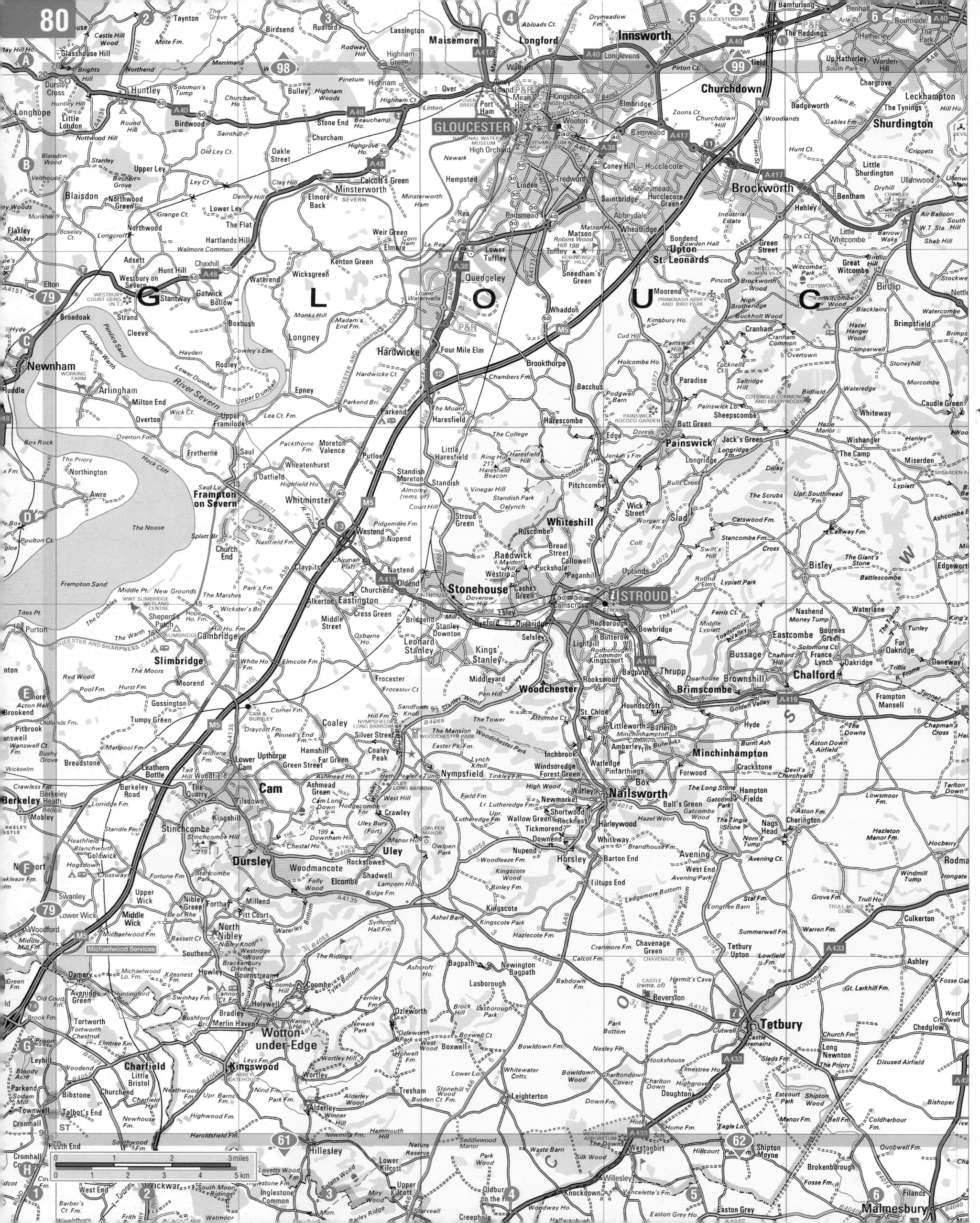

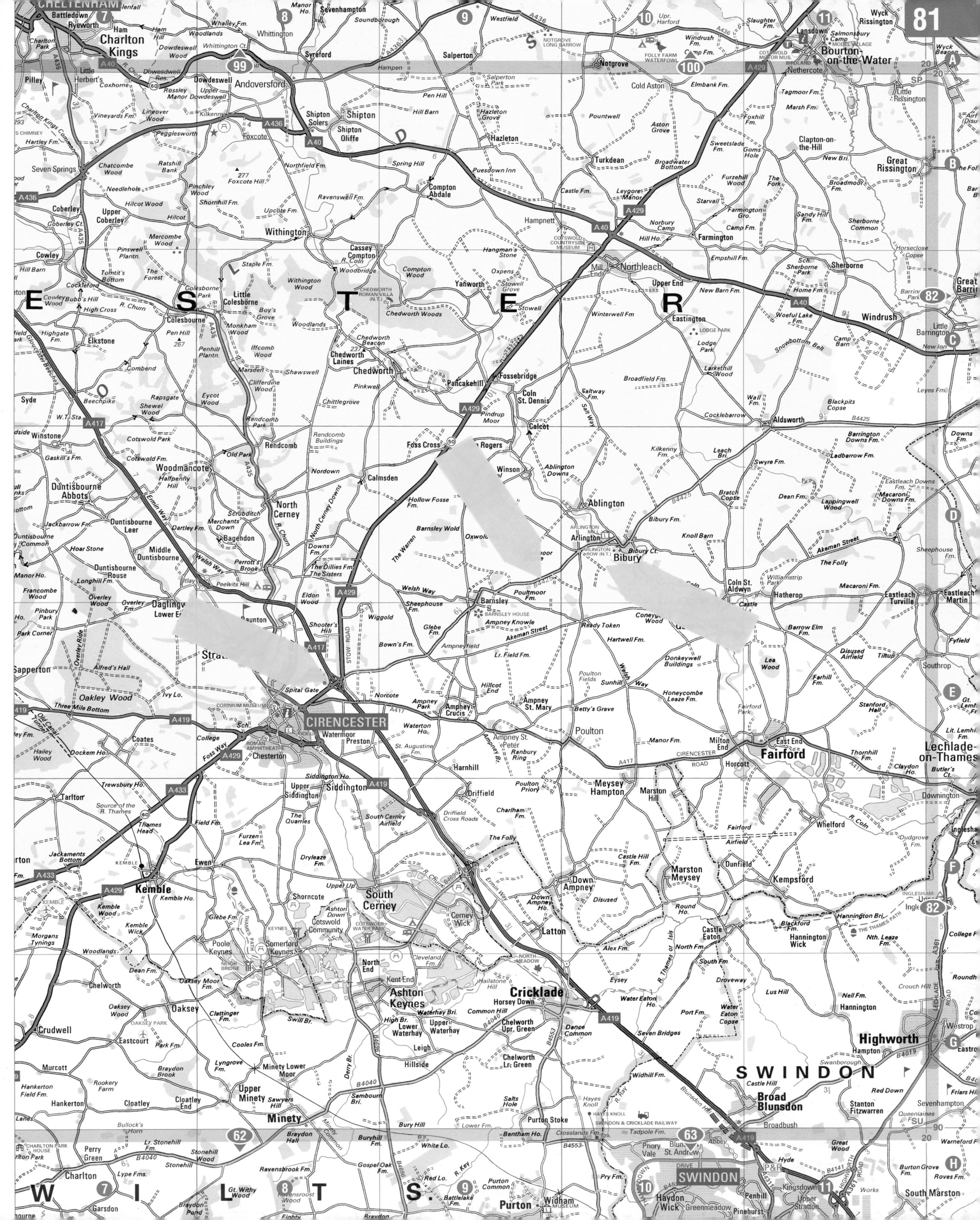

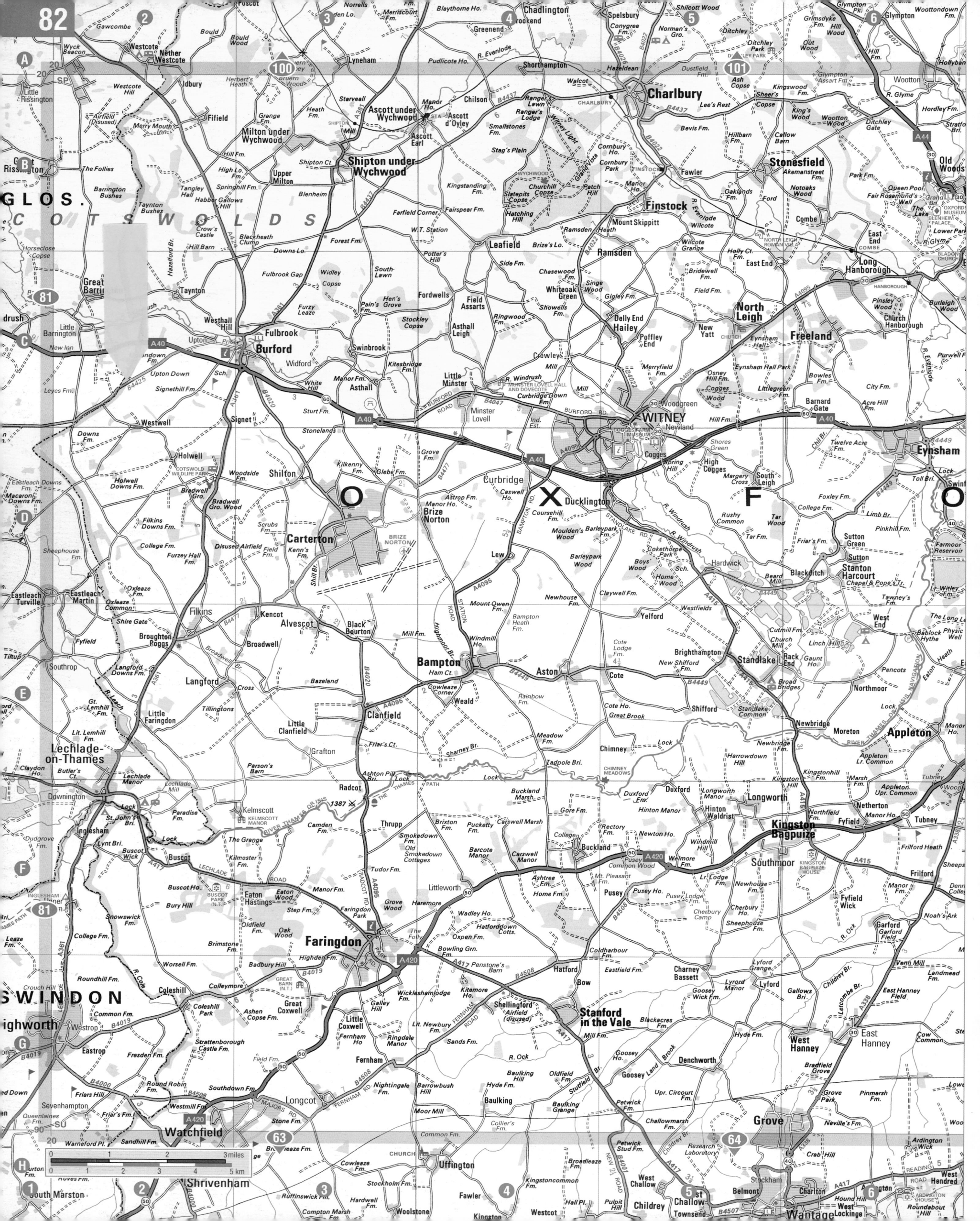

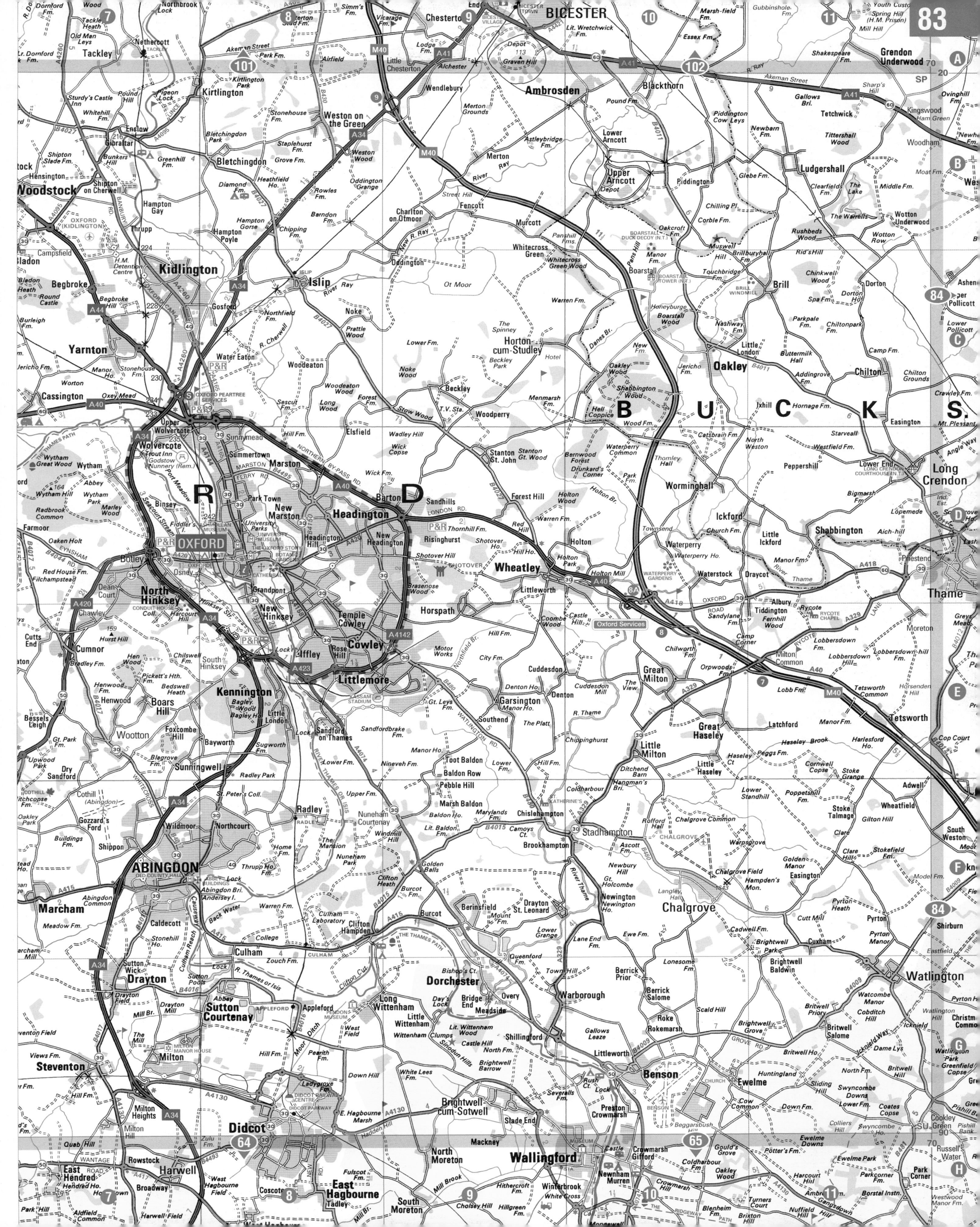

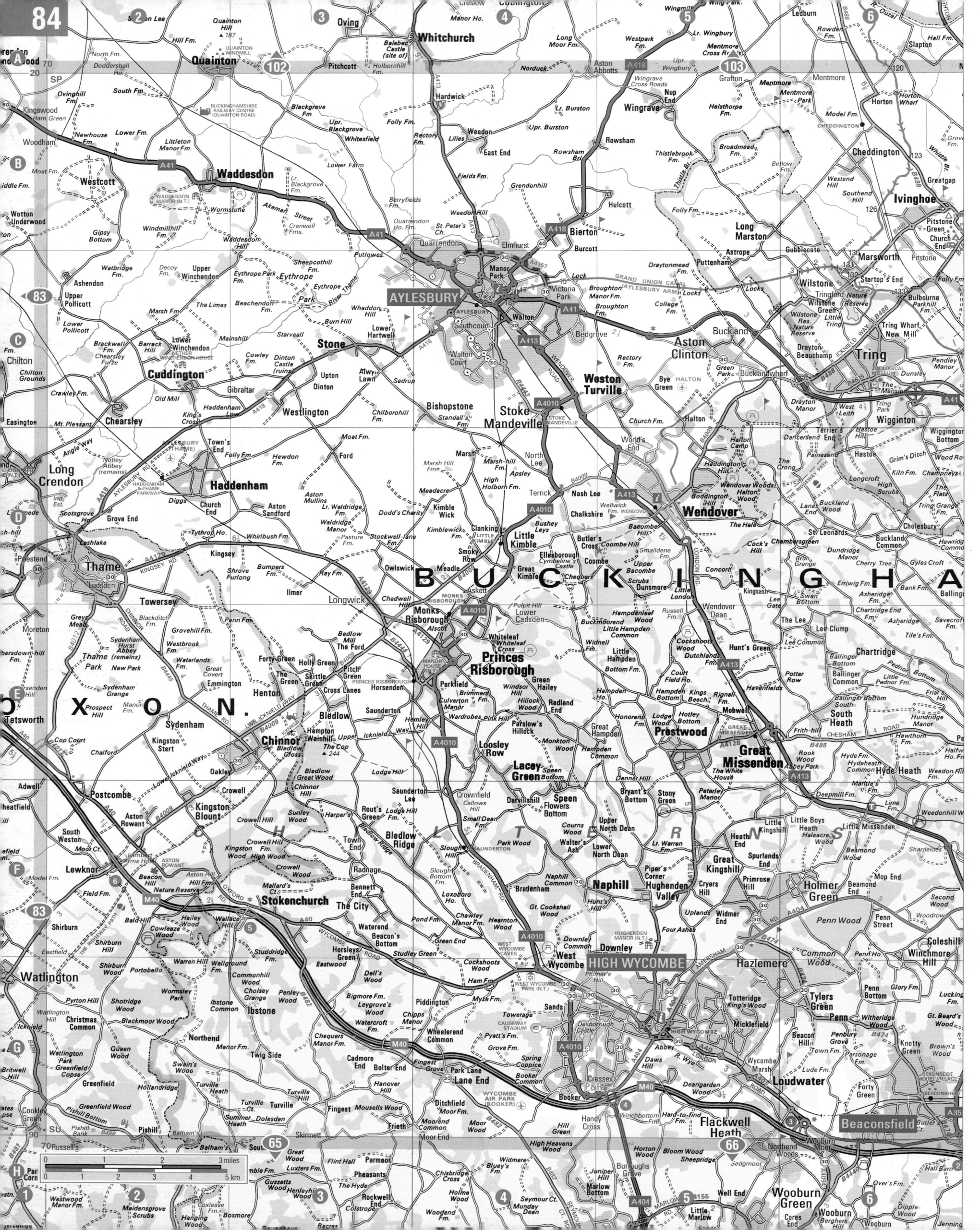

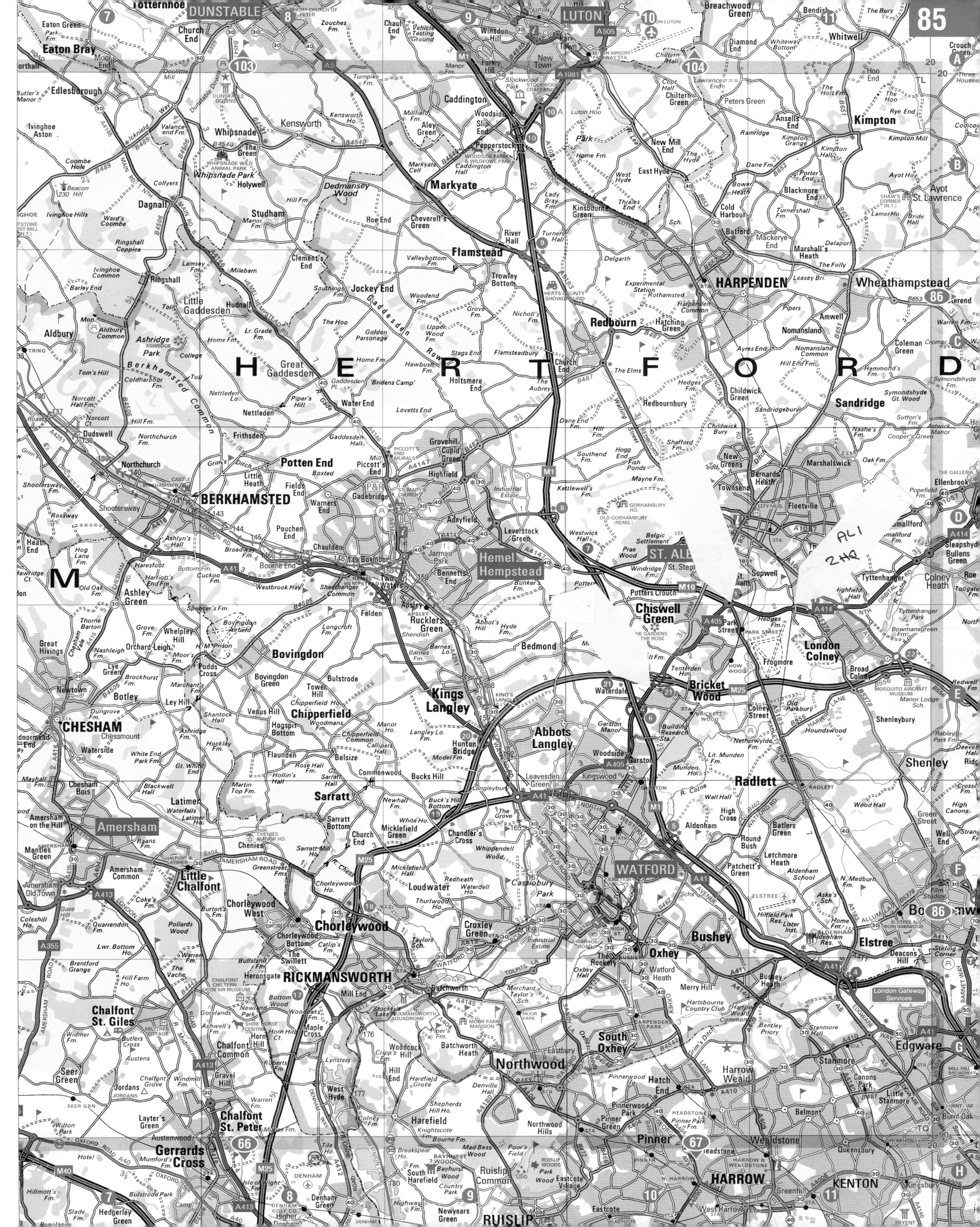

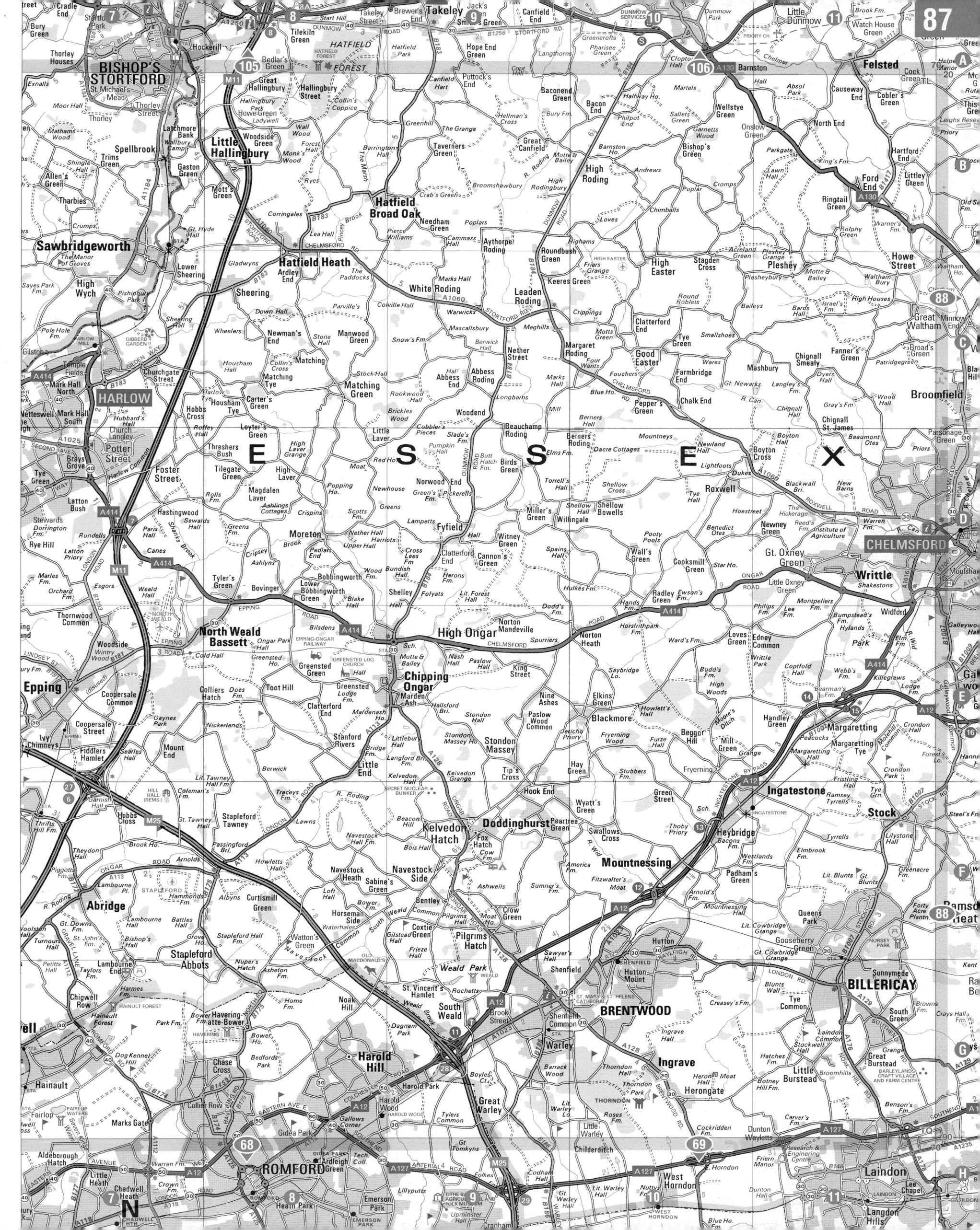

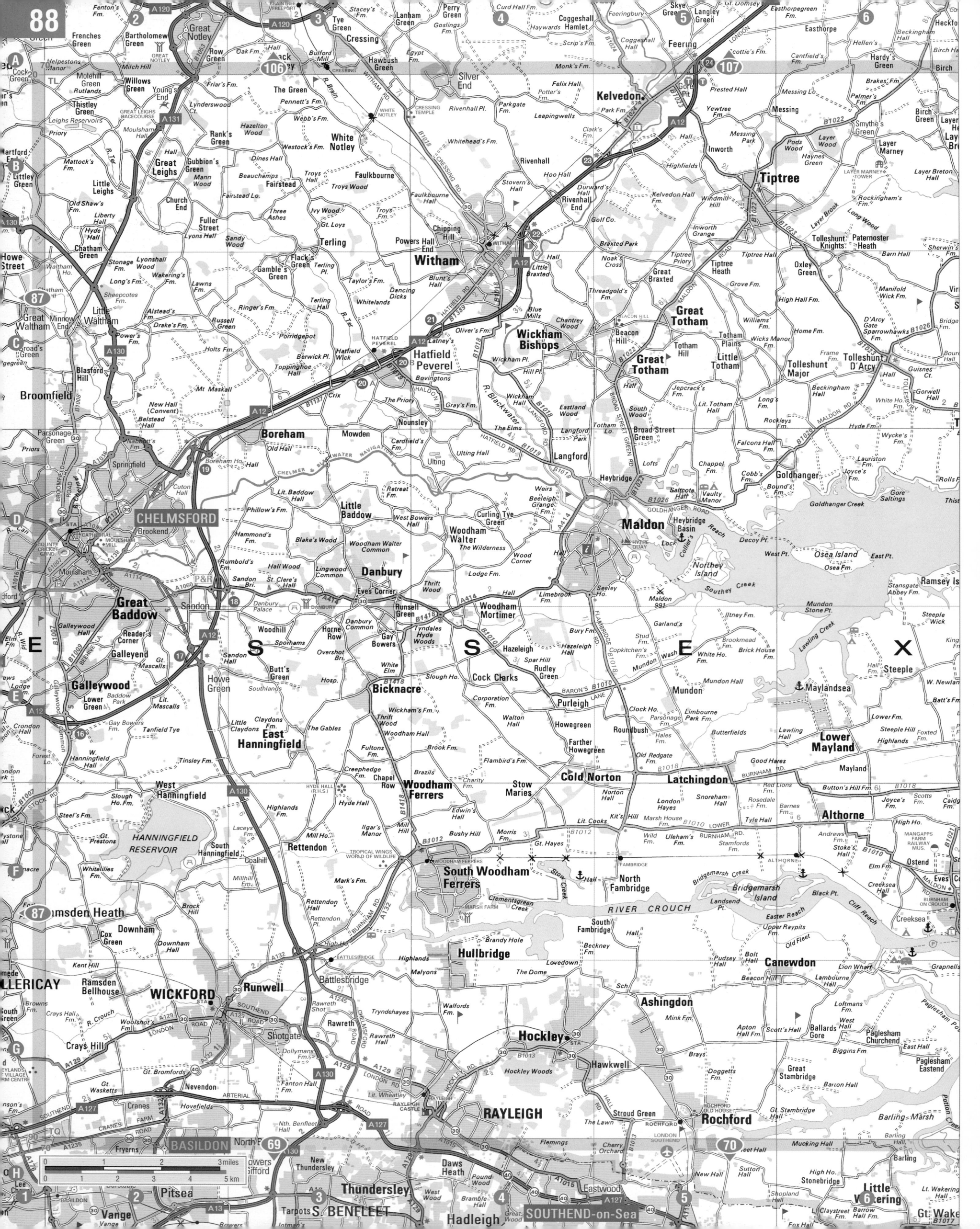

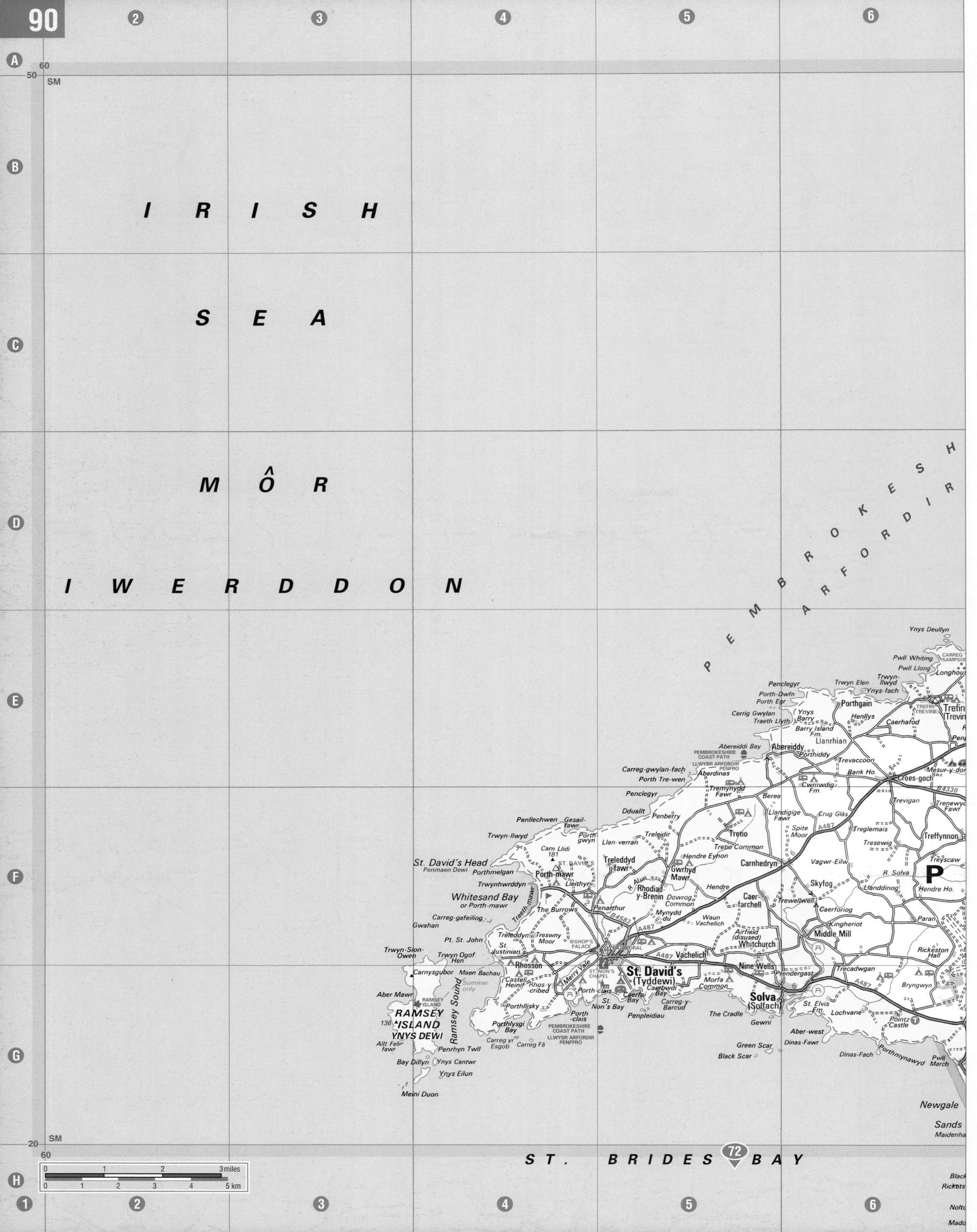

I R I S H

S E A

M Ô R

I W E R D D O N

P E M B R O K E S H
ARFORDIR

Ynys Deullyn

Pwll Whiting
Pwll Llong   CARREG
                    SAMPSON
Penclegyr   Trwyn Elen
Porth-Dwfn   Ynys-fach   Trwyn-
Porth Egr   llwyd   Longhous
Cerrig Gwylan   Ynys   Porthgain   TREFIN   Trefin
                Barry   (TREVINE) Trevin
                Island   Henllys
        Traeth Llyth Barry Island Caerhafod
                          Fm.
    Abereiddi Bay Abereiddy Llanrhian
PEMBROKESHIRE   Porthiddy
COAST PATH   Trevaccoon   Pen
Carreg-gwylan-fach LLWYBR ARFORDIR   Mesur-y-dor
Porth Tre-wen   PENFRO   Bank Ho.   Croes-goch
                Aberdinas   B4330
            Tremynydd   Cwmwdig   Berea   Trevigan
Penclegyr   Fawr   Fm.   Trenewy
            Dduallt Penberry   Llandigige Crug Glâs Fawr
Penllechwen Gesail-   Fawr   Treleidir Tretio   Spite   A487 Treglemais
Trwyn-llwyd   fawr   Porth-   Tretio Common Moor   Tresewig Treffynnon
            Carn Llidi gwyn Llan-verran
            181   Treleddyd   Hendre Eynon   Vagwr-Eilw
St. David's Head ST. DAVID'S -fawr   Gwrhyd   Treyscaw
Penmaen Dewi Porthmelgan   Mawr   Hendre   Skyfog   Handdinog Hendre Ho. P
Trwynhwrddyn   Porth-mawr   R. Alun   R. Solva
    Whitesand Bay   Lleithyr   Rhodiad Dowrog   Caer-   Paran
    or Porth-mawr   y-Brenin Common farchell
Carreg-gafeiliog The Burrows   Mynydd Waun   Trewellwell Caerforiog Kingheriot
Gwahan   Penarthur du   Vachelich   Rickeston
        Pt. St. John Treleddyn Treswny BISHOP'S   Airfield   Hall
Trwyn-Sion- St.   Moor   PALACE   (disused) Middle Mill
  Owen   Justinian   CATHEDRAL A487 Vachelich   Whitchurch
    Trwyn Ogof   Rhosson   Nine Wells   Trecadwgan
       Hen   St. David's   Prendergast
  Carnysgubor Maen Bachau   (Tyddewi)   Bryngwyn
Aber Mawr   Summer Castell Rhos-y- Caerbwdi   Morfa
            only Heinif -cribed Bay   Common   Solva
        RAMSEY   St. Non's Chapel Carreg-y- (Solfach) St. Elvis
        ISLAND   St.   Porth-clais Barcud   Fm.
RAMSEY ISLAND Porthlisky Non's Bay Penpleidiau The Cradle Gewni Lochvane
YNYS DEWI 136 Porthlysgi   PEMBROKESHIRE   Aber-west   Pointz
Allt Felir Bay   Bay Carreg yr COAST PATH   Green Scar   Castle
  fawr   Esgob Carreg Fâ LLWYBR ARFORDIR Black Scar Dinas-Fawr Porthmynawyd Pwll
    Penrhyn Twll   PENFRO   Dinas-Fach   March
Bay Dillyn Ynys Cantwr   Black Scar
        Ynys Eilun   Newgale

    Meini Duon   Sands
                                                      Maidenha

S T .   B R I D E S   (72) B A Y

Black
Rickets

Nolto

Mado

0   1   2   3 miles
0 1 2 3 4 5 km

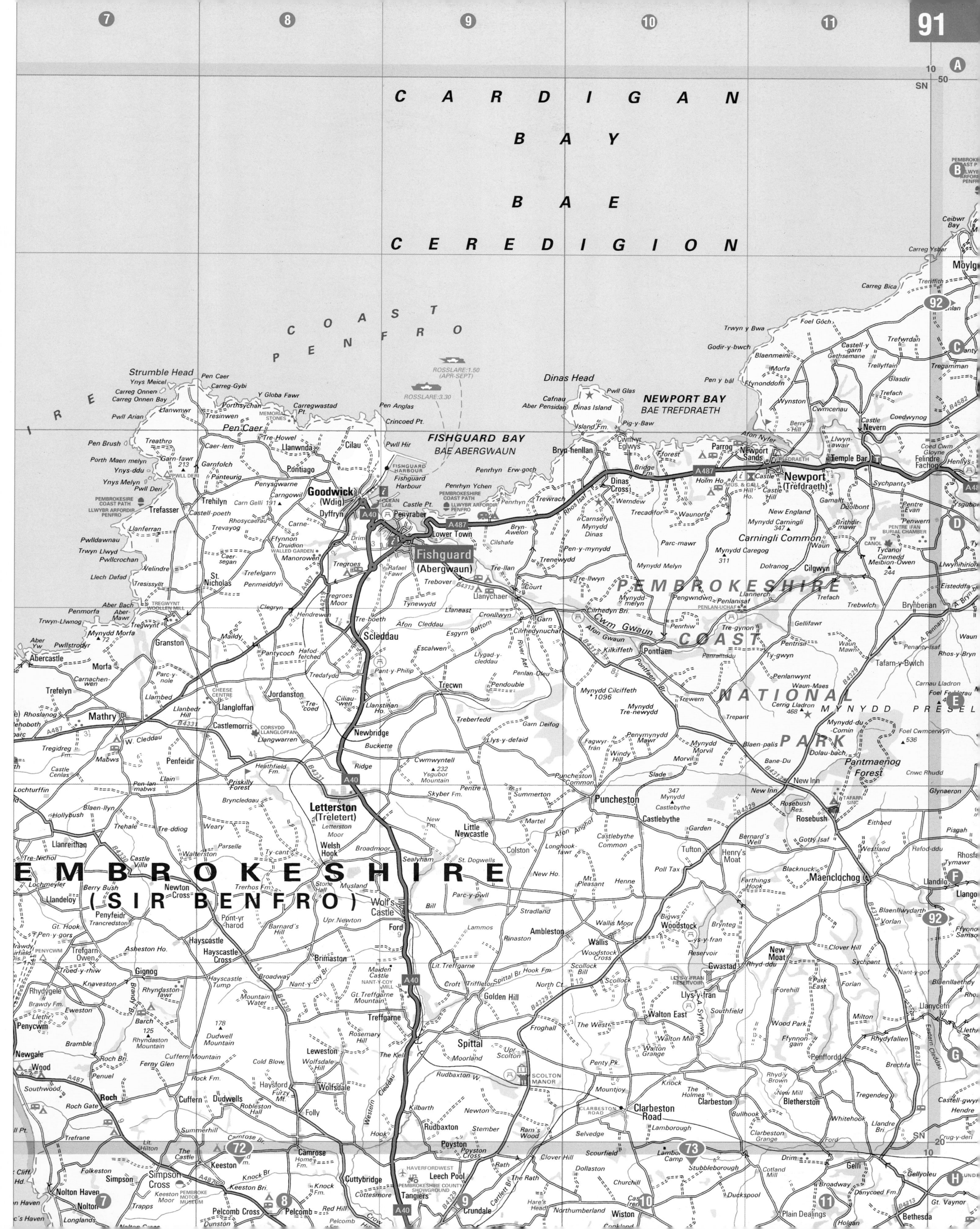

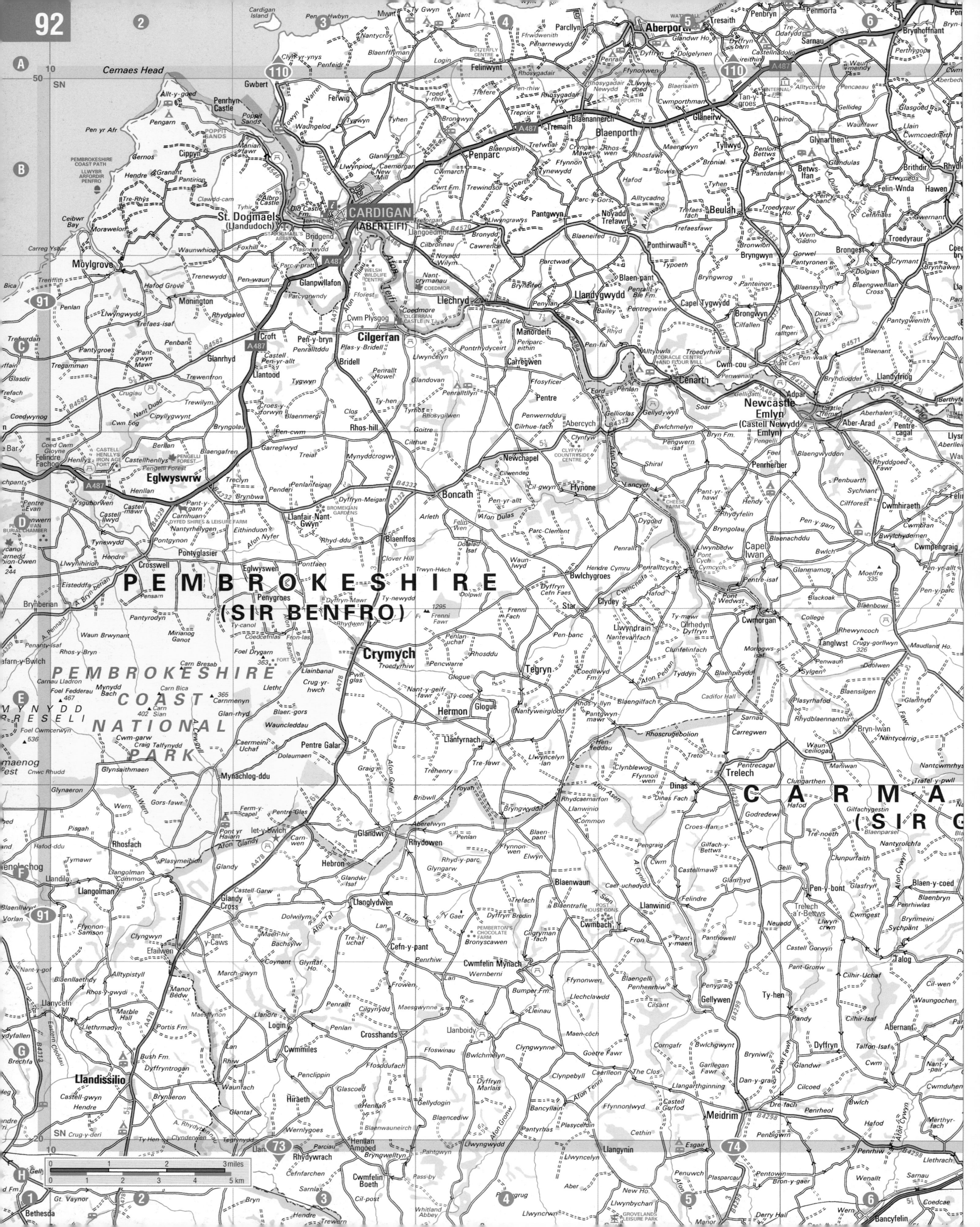

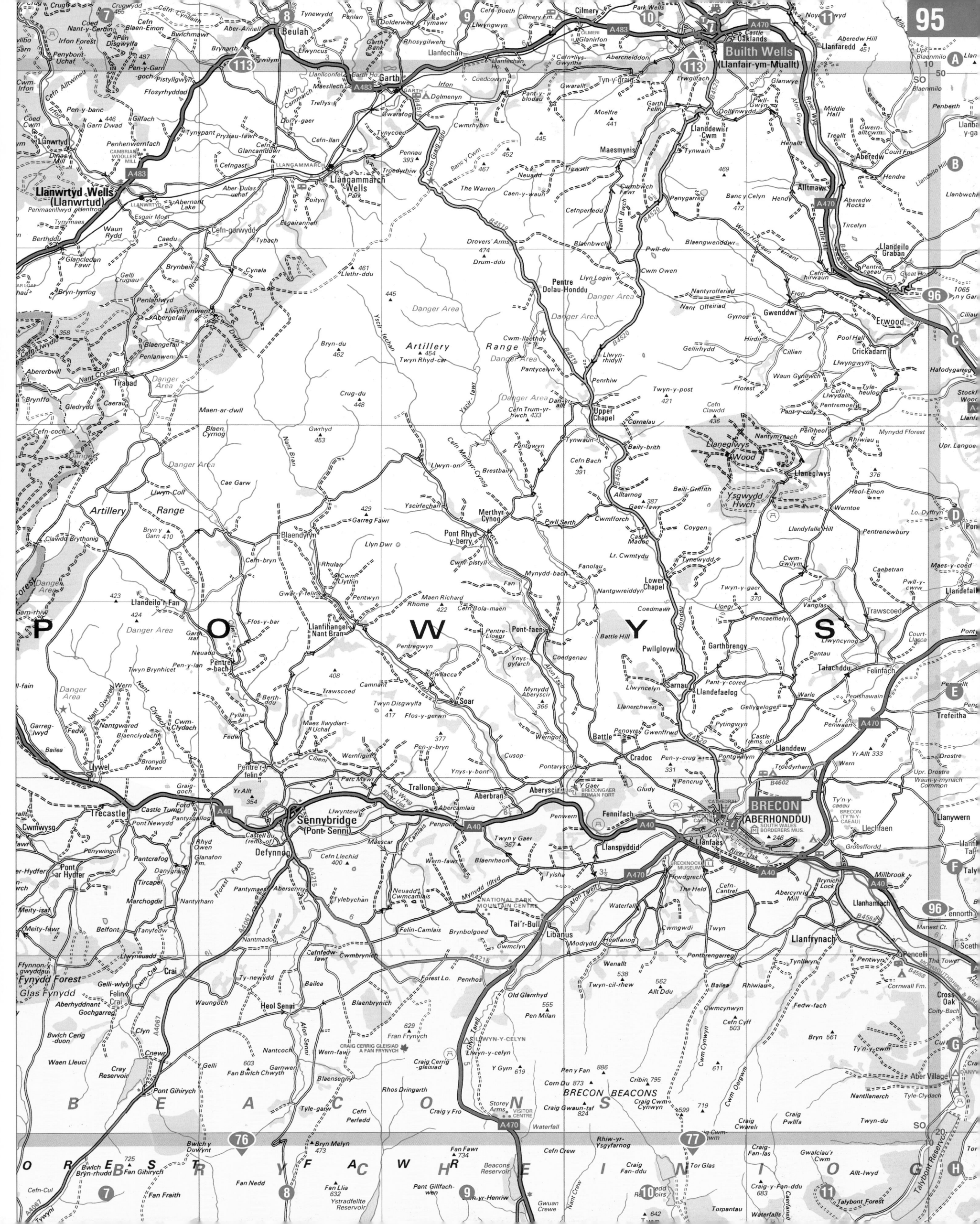

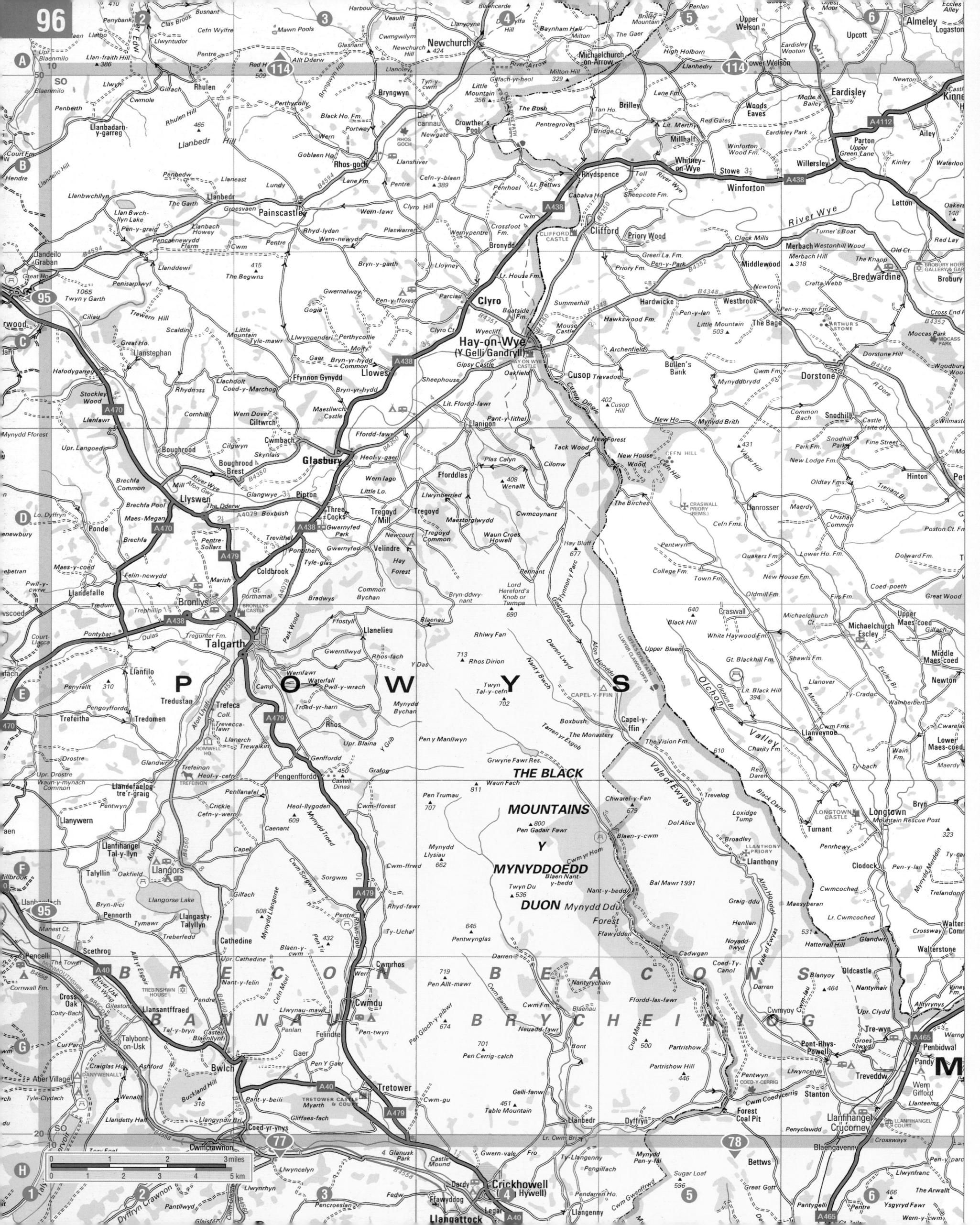

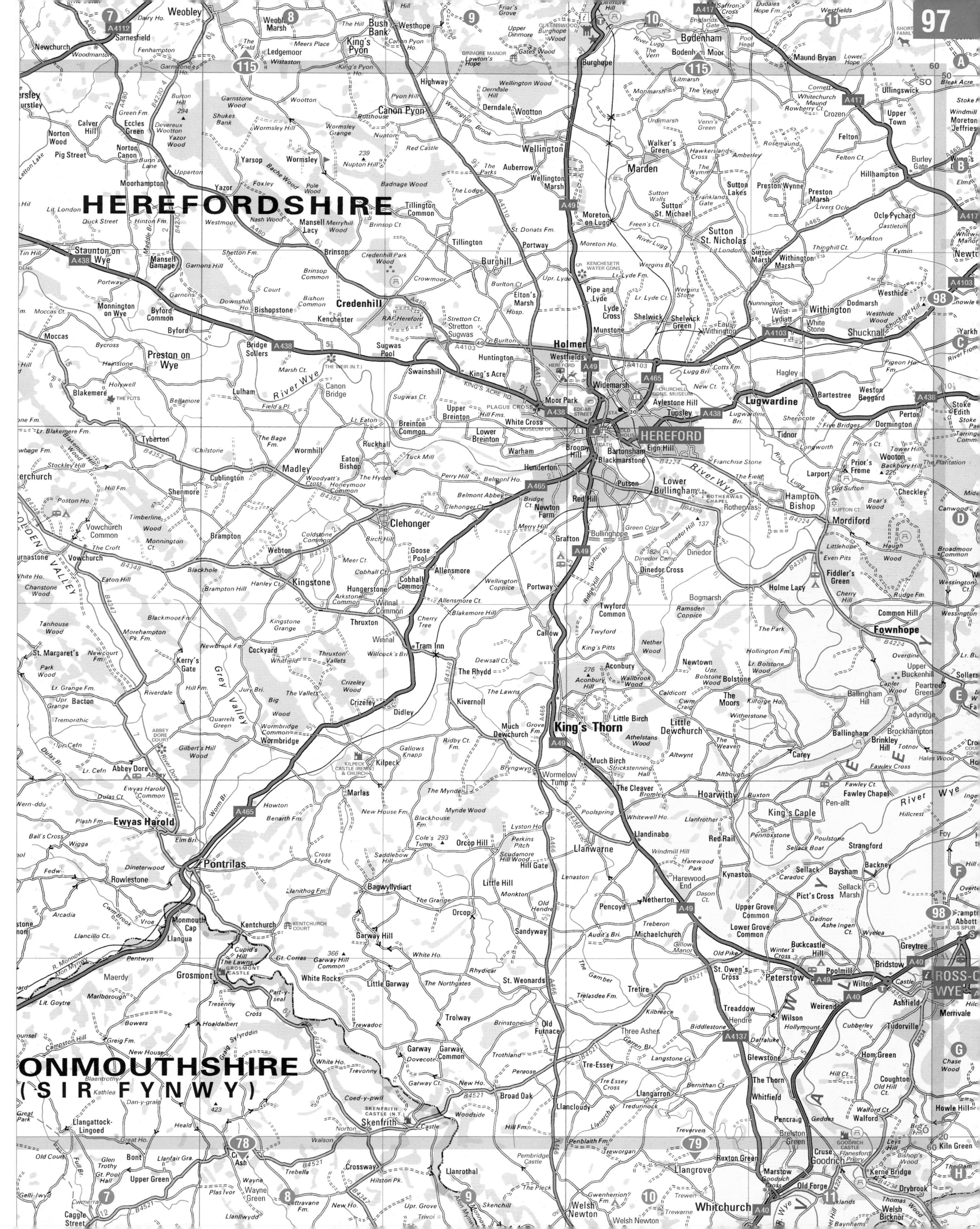

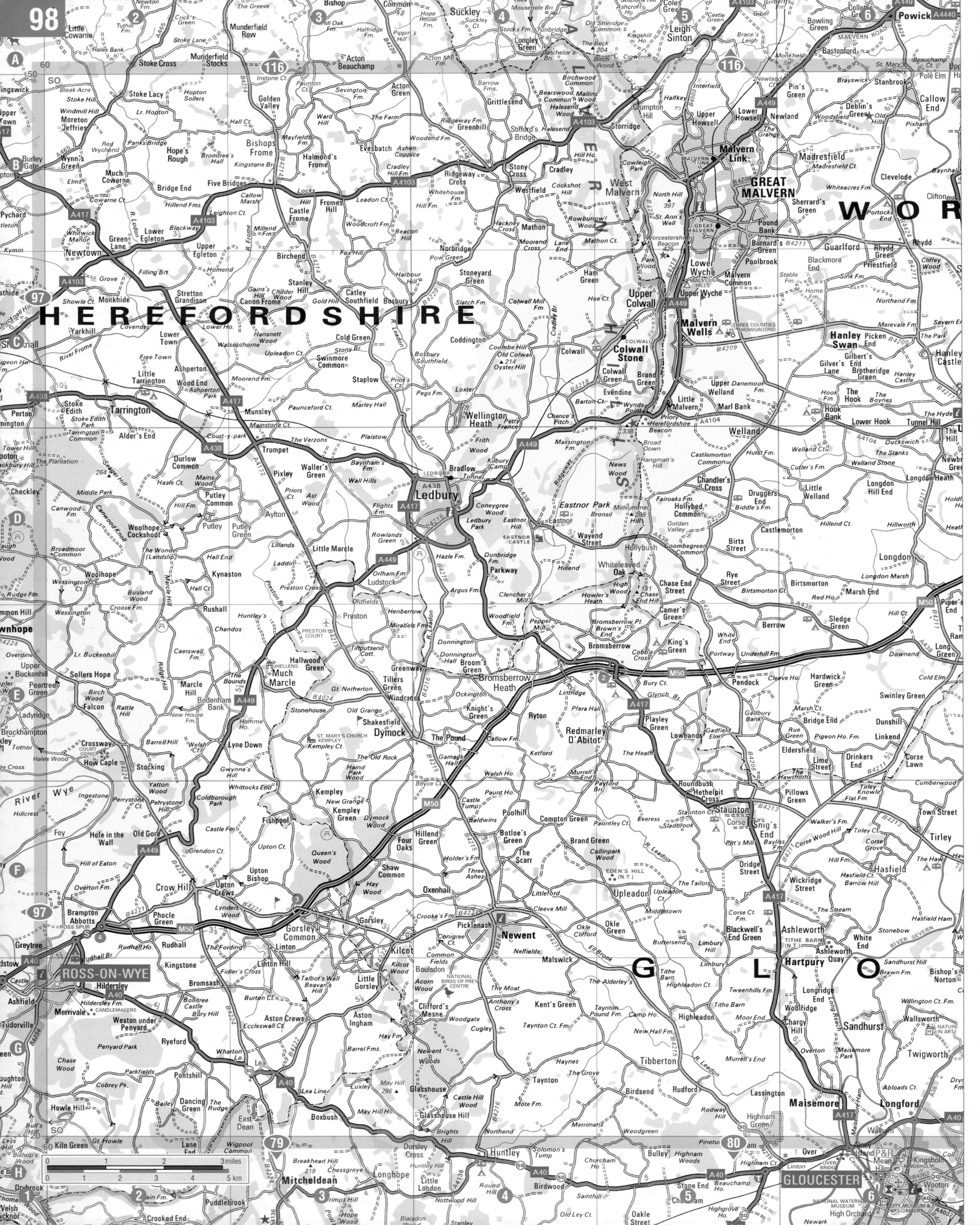

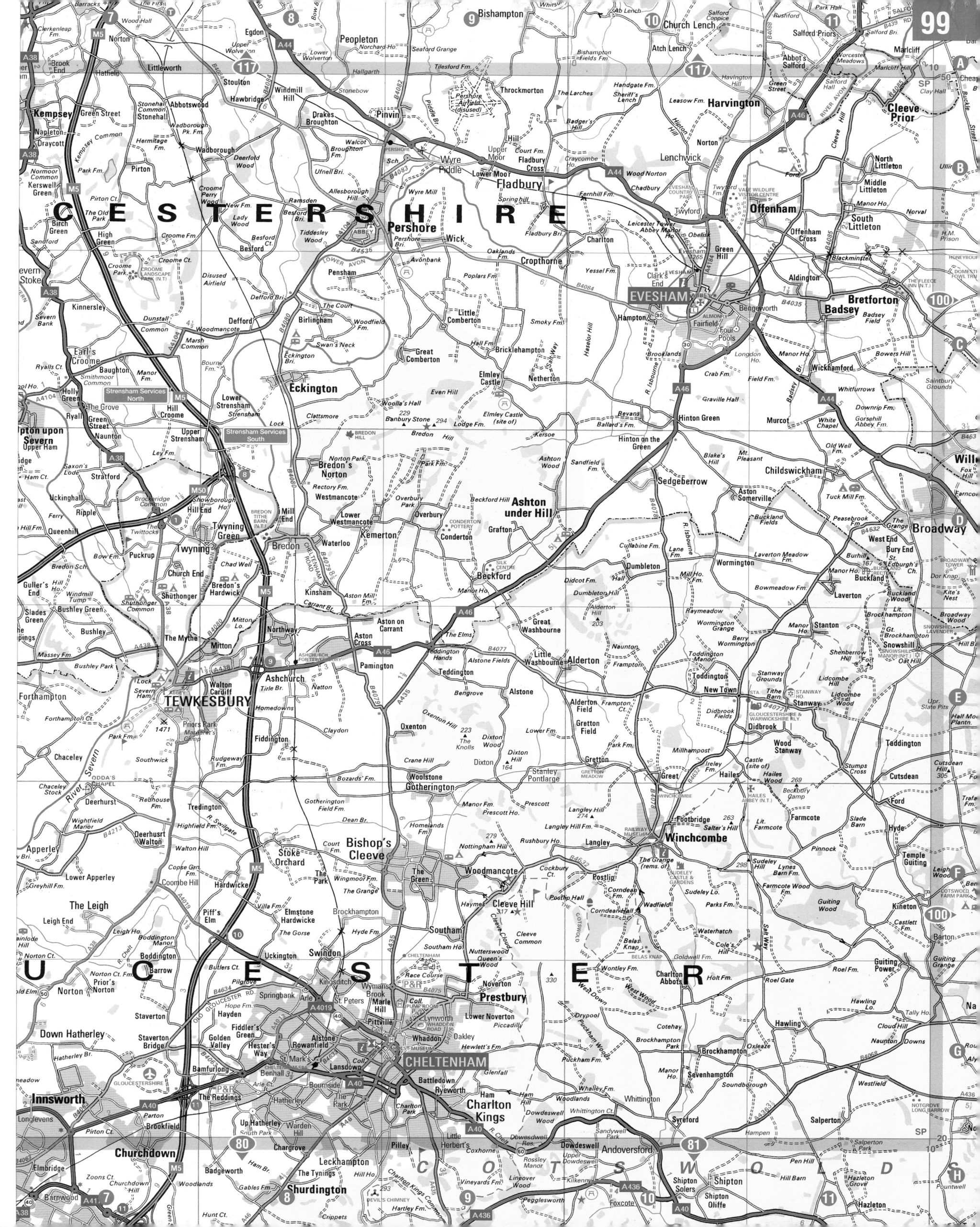

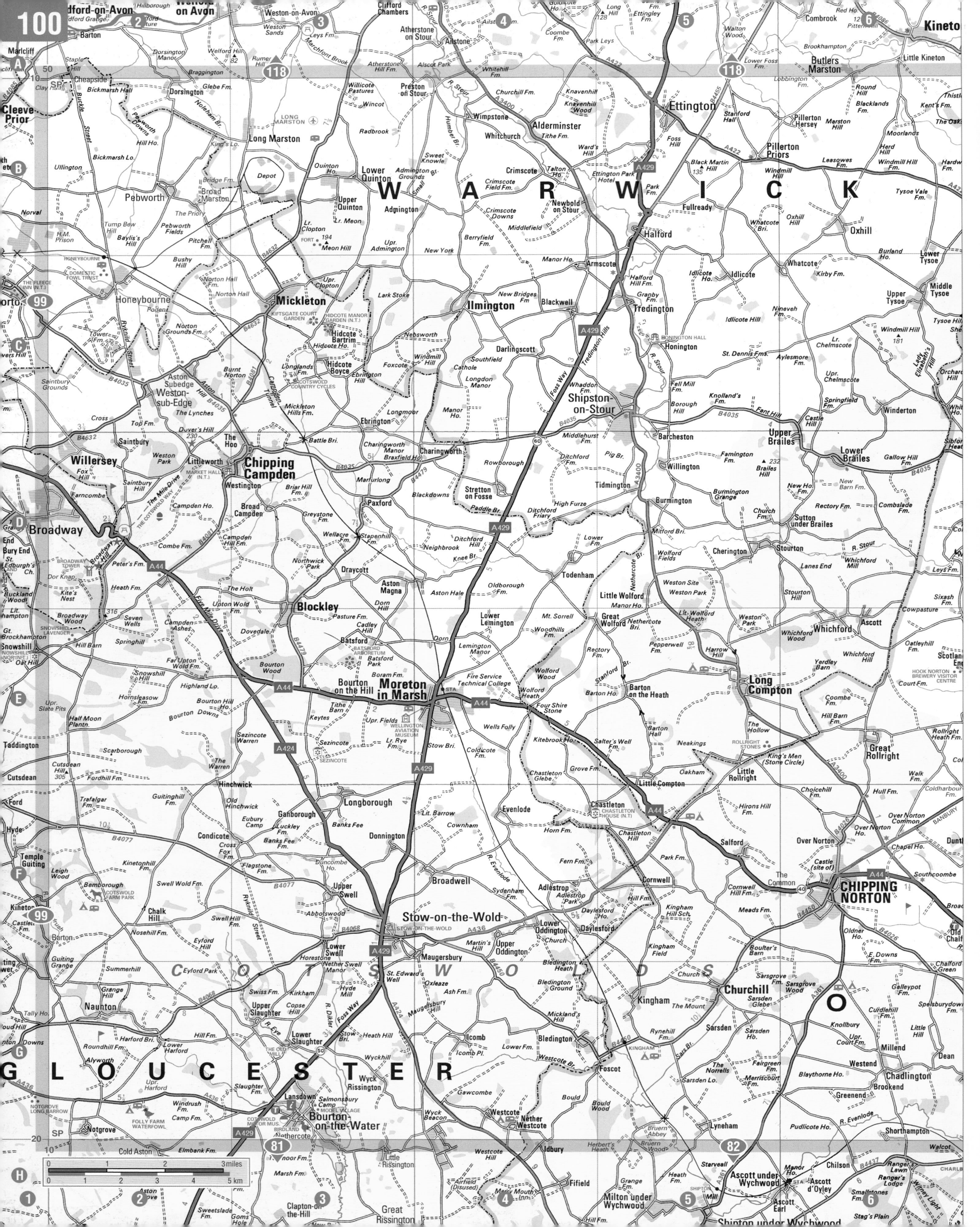

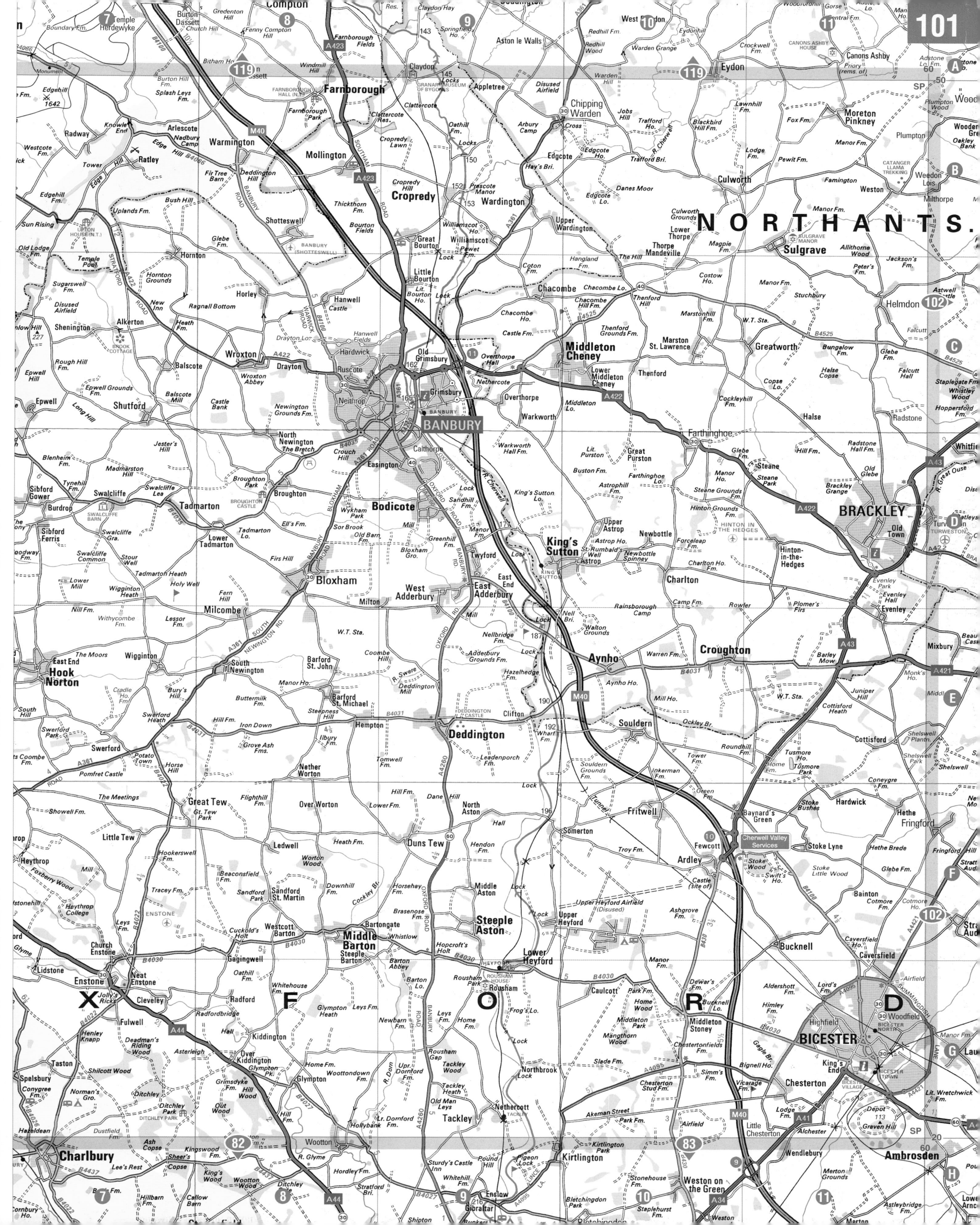

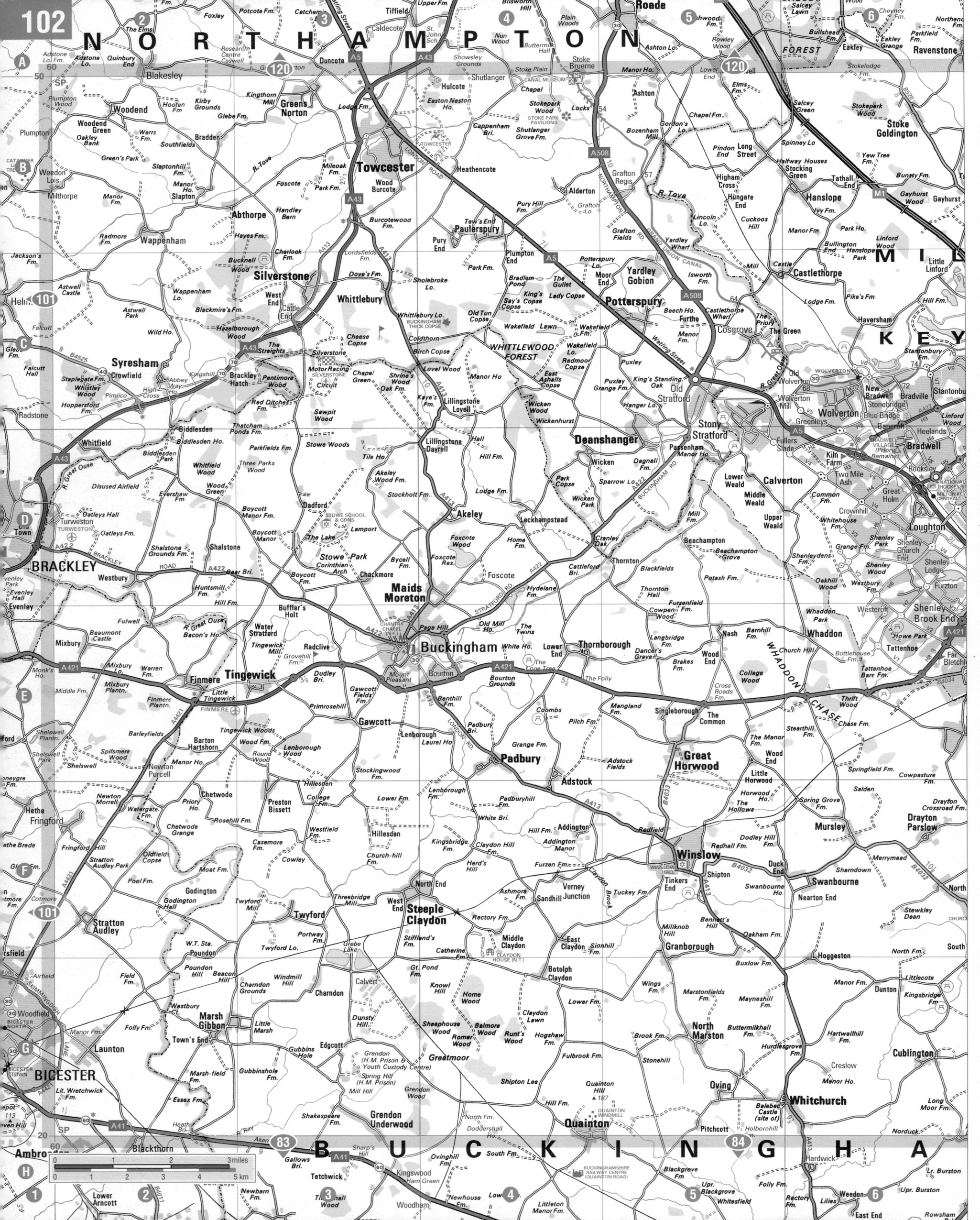

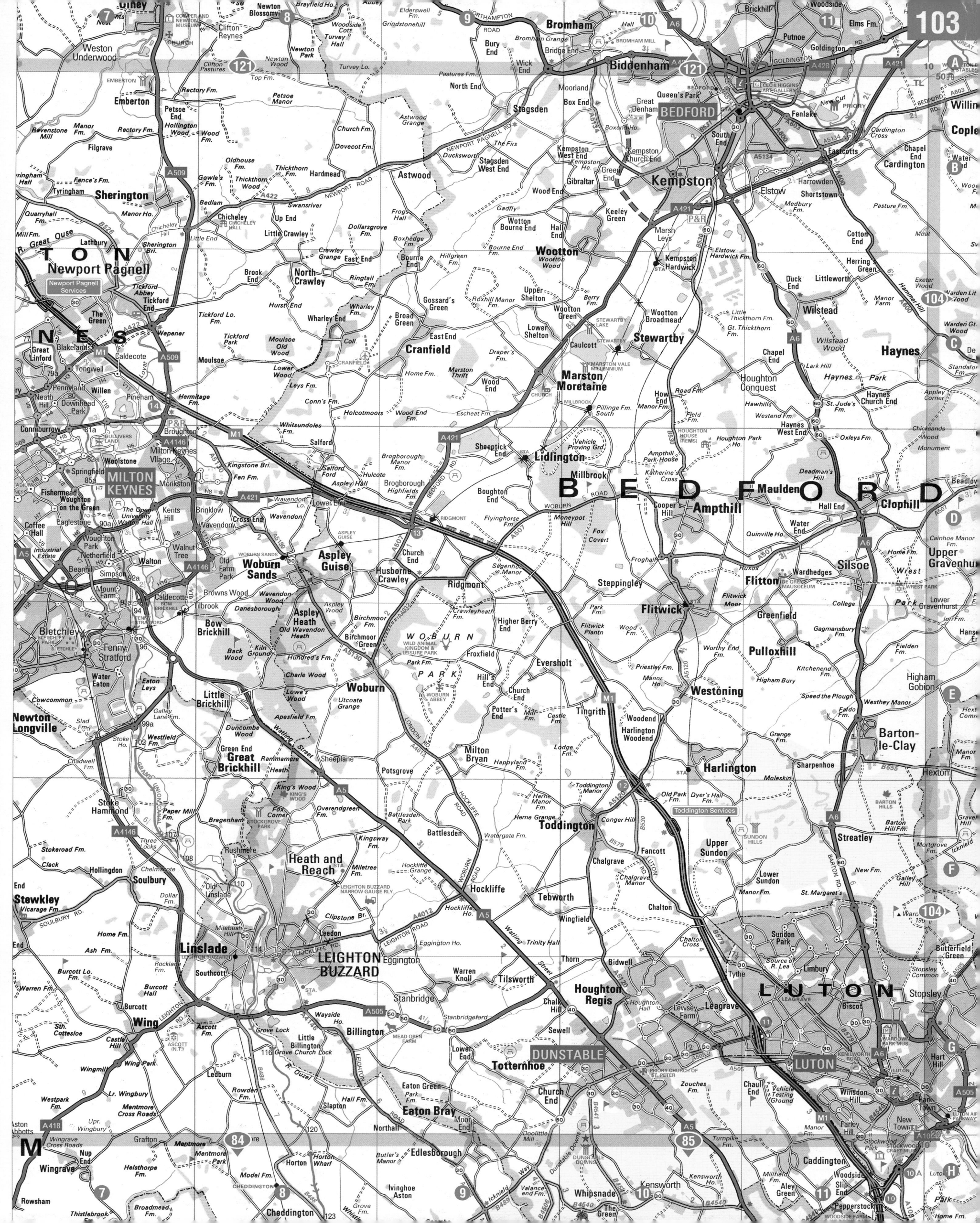

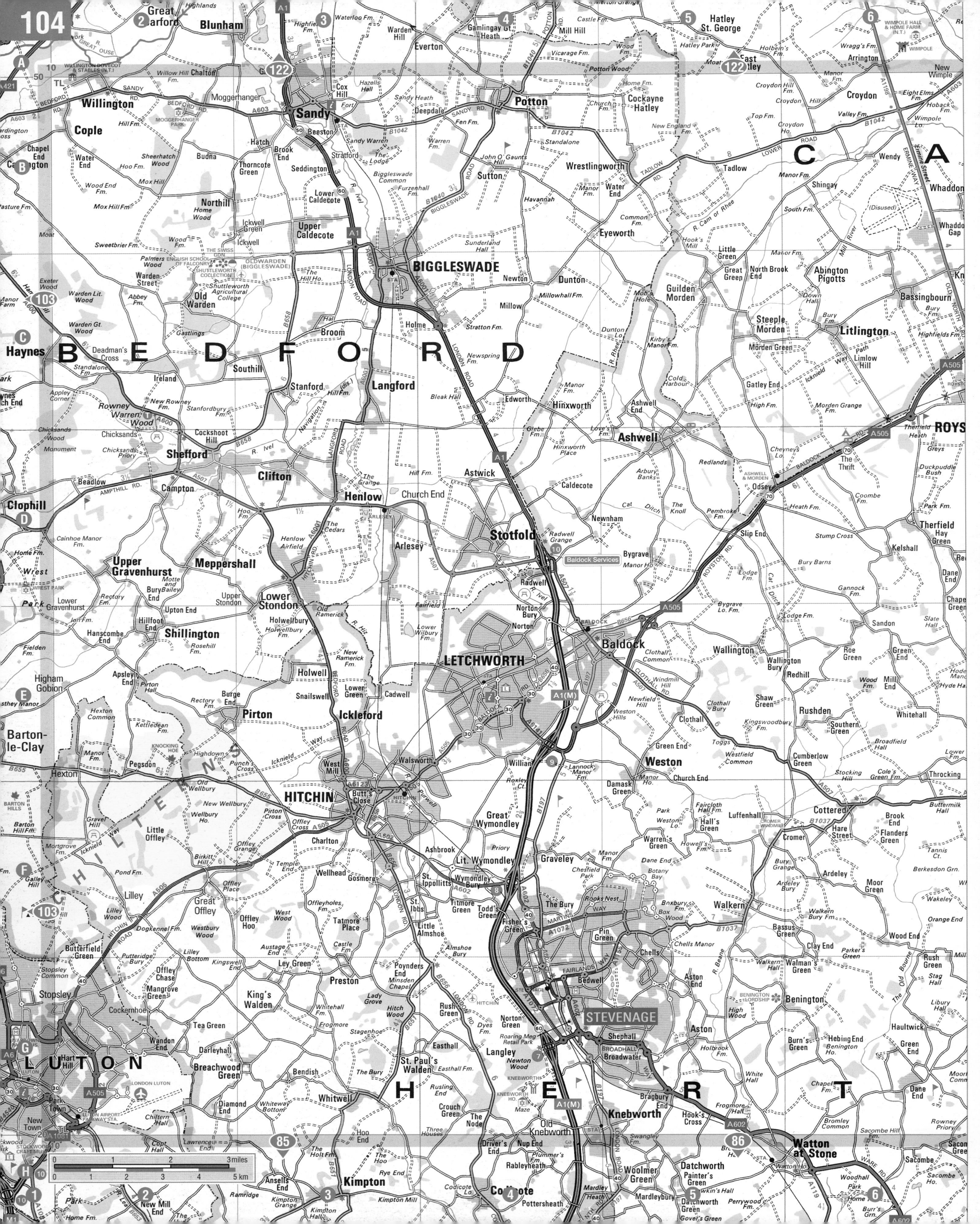

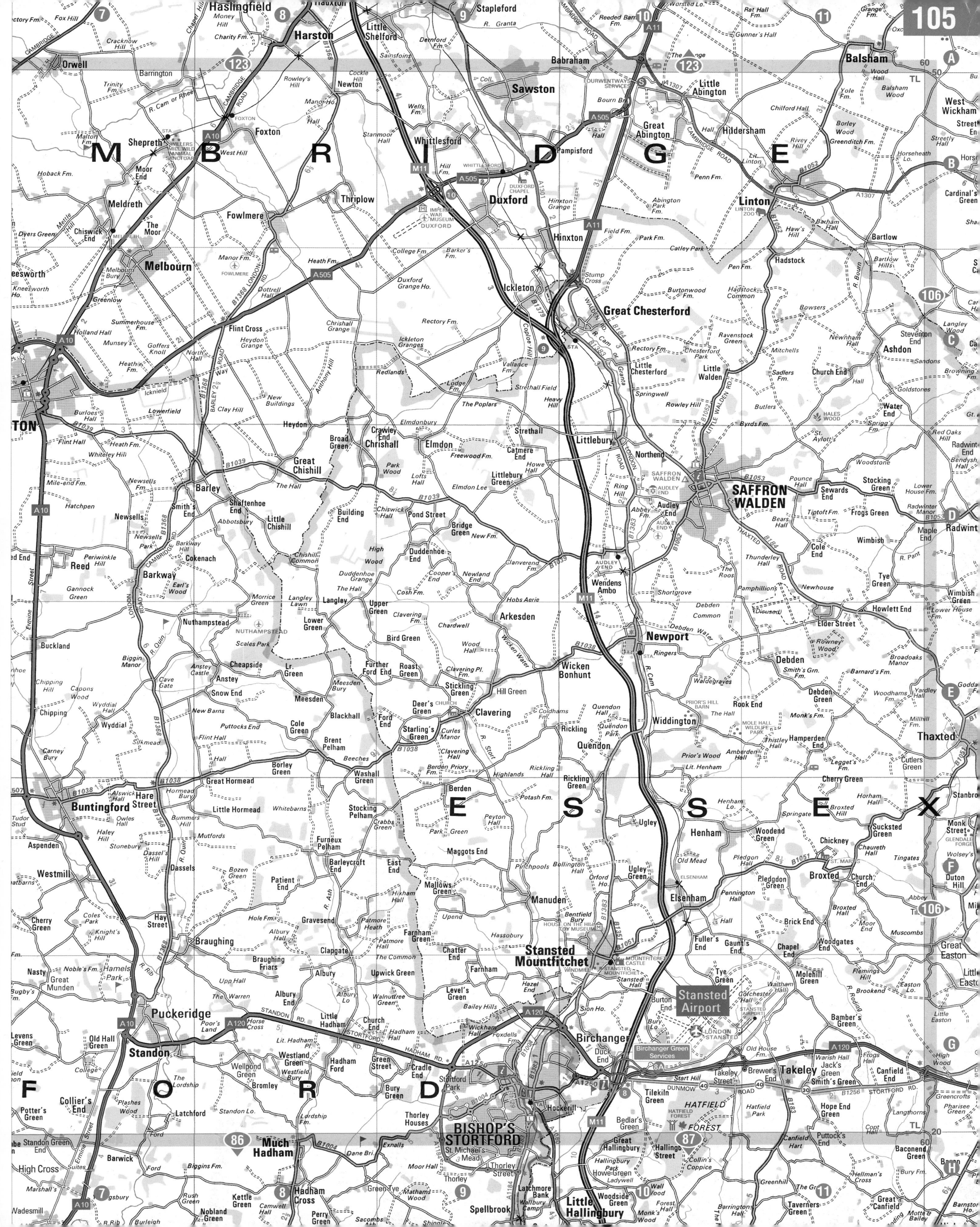

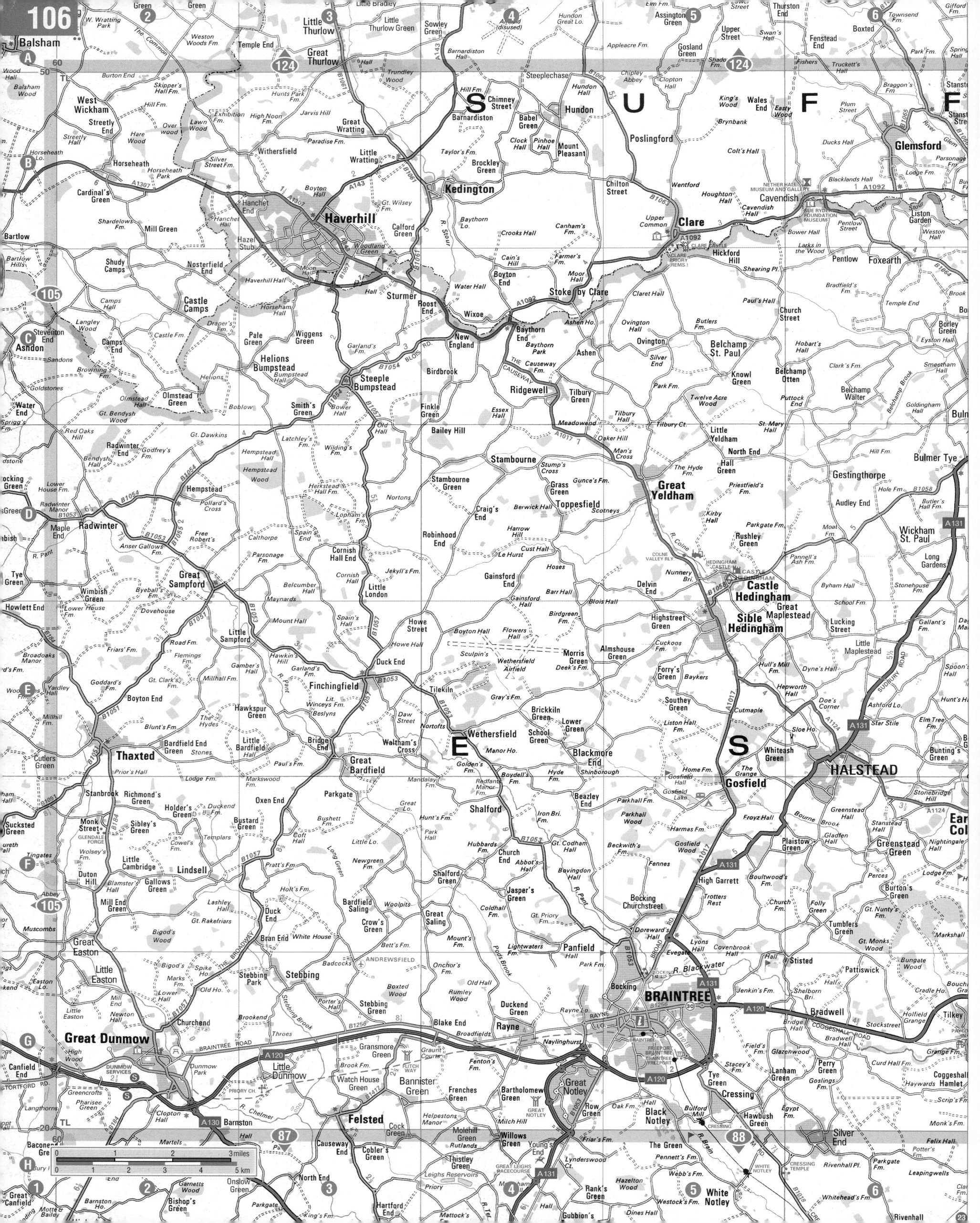

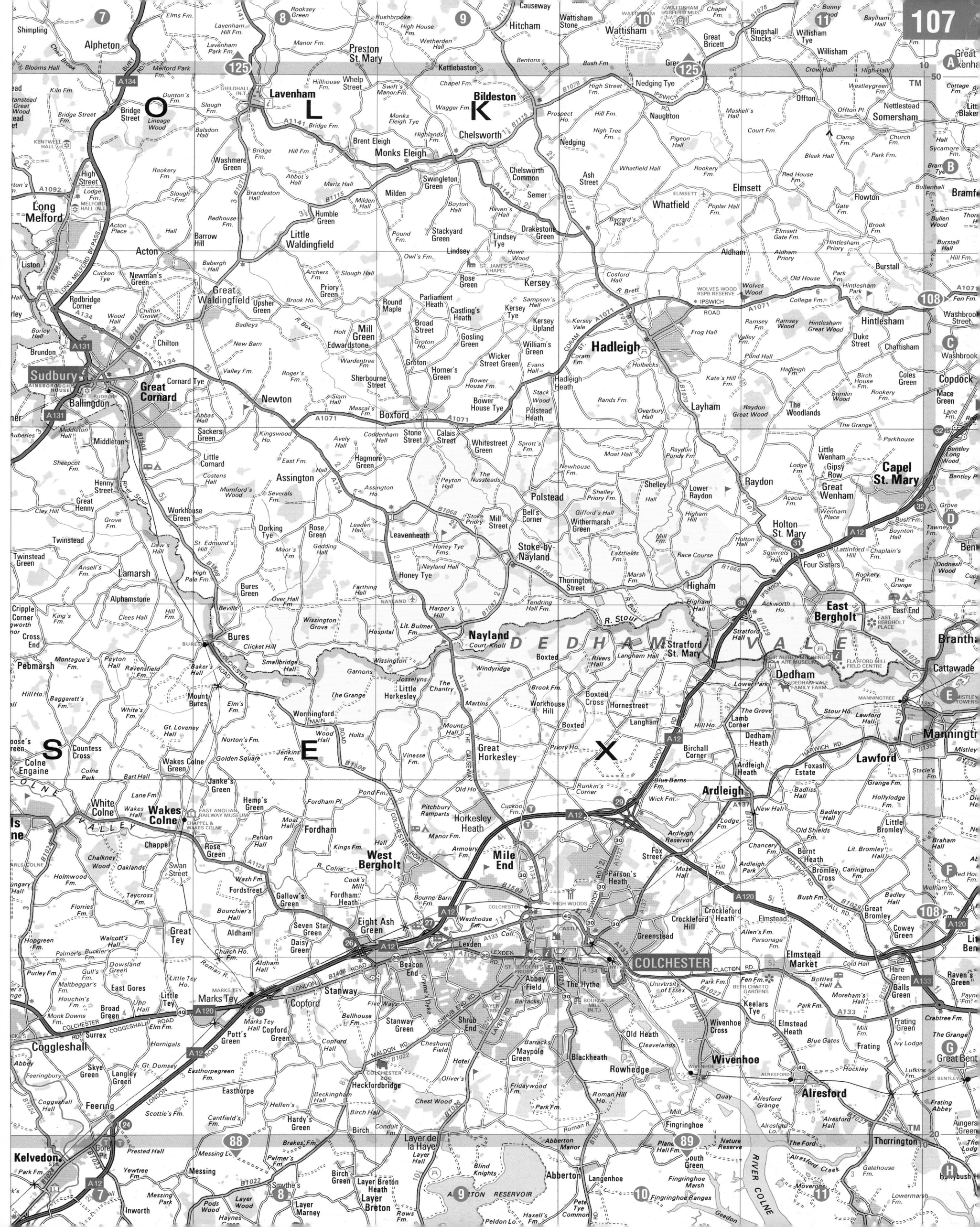

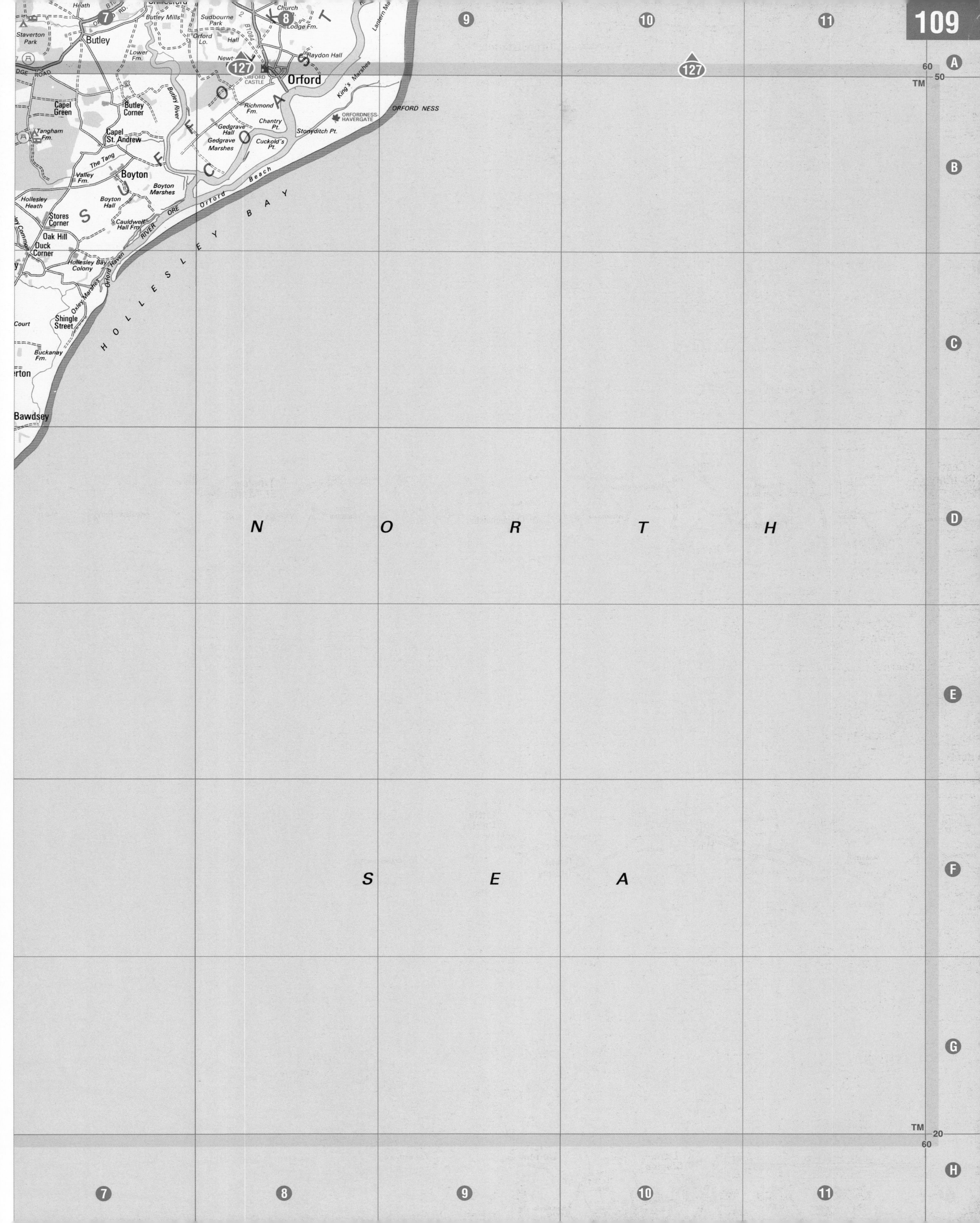

N O R T H

S E A

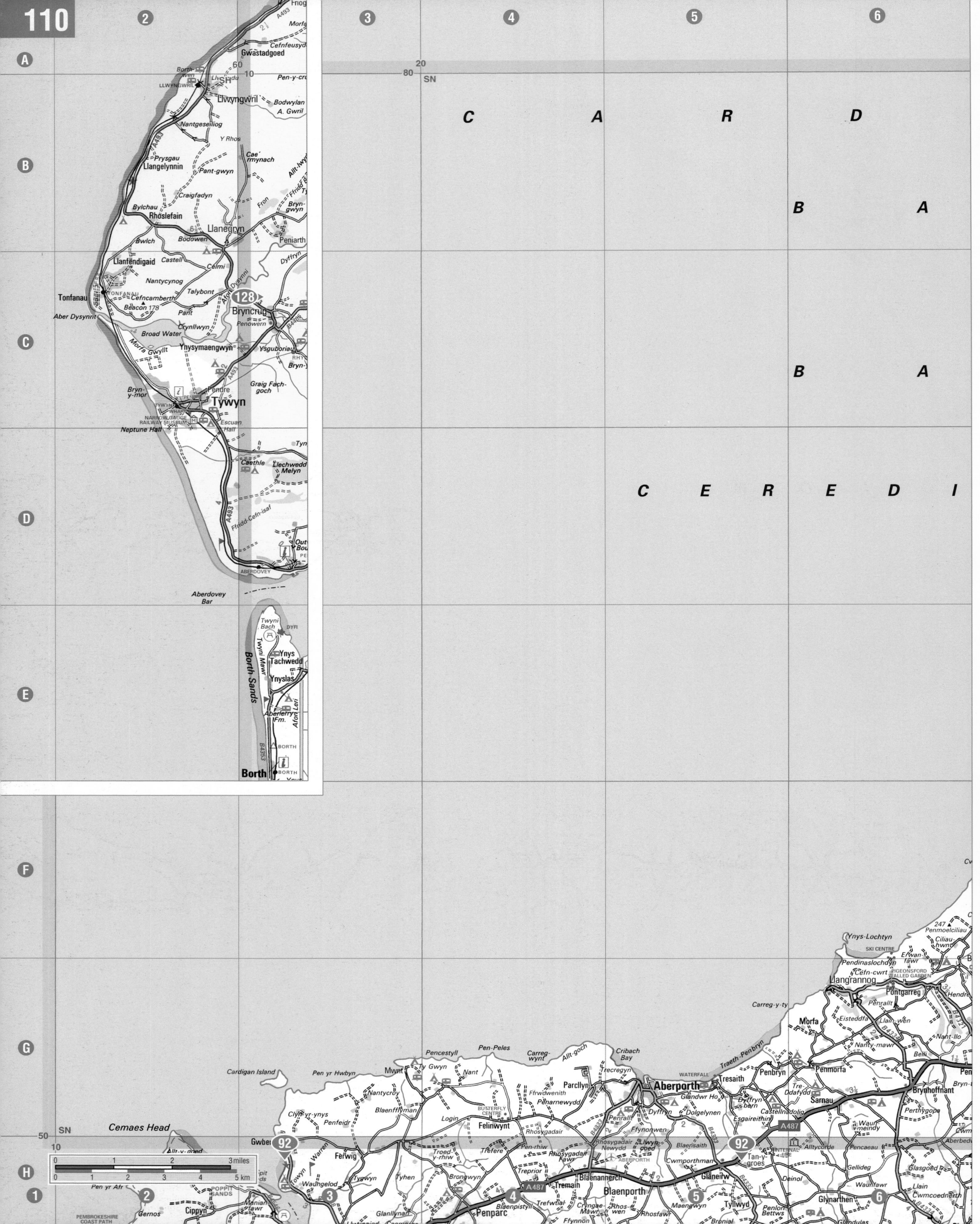

A

B

C

D

E

F

G

H

A493
Morfa
Cefnfeusyd
Gwastadgoed
60 10
20
80 SN
Pen-y-cru
Borth-
wen
LLWYNGWRIL
SH
Llwyngwril
Bodwylan
A. Gwril
Nantgeselliog
Y Rhos
Cae rmynach
Prysgau
Allt-lwyd
Llangelynnin
Pant-gwyn
Fron
Fridd Ty
Bryn-
gwyn
Craigfadyn
Bylchau
Rhoslefain
Llanegryn
Peniarth
Bwlch
Bodowen
Dyffryn
Llanfihangid
Castell
Celri
Nantycynog
Talybont
Aber Dyfi
Tonfanau
TONFANAU
Cefncamberth
128
Beacon 178
Pant
Bryncrug
Broad Water
Crynllwyn
Penowern
Morfa Gwyllt
Ynysymaengwyn
Ysguboriau
RHY
Bryn-
Graig Fach-
goch
Bryn-
y-mor
Pendre
i
Tywyn
NARROW GAUGE
RAILWAY MUSEUM
Escuan
Hall
Neptune Hall
Caethle
Tyn
Llechwedd
Melyn
A493
Ffridd-Cefn-isaf
Out
Bou
PE
ABERDOVEY
Aberdovey Bar
Twyni
Bach
DYFI
Ynys
Tachwedd
Twyni Mawr
Ynyslas
Borth Sands
Aberlefri
Fm.
Afon Leri
B4353
BORTH
i
BORTH
Borth

C   A   R   D

B   A

B   A

C   E   R   E   D   I

247
Penmoelciliau
Ynys-Lochtyn
Ciliau
SKI CENTRE
Erwan
fawr
Pendinaslochdyn
Cefn-cwrt
PIGEONSFORD
WALLED GARDEN
Llangrannog
Pontgarreg
Carreg-y-ty
Penrallt
Hendre
Morfa
Eisteddfa
Llain-wen
Nant-llo
Nanty-mawr
Cardigan Island
Pen-Peles
Carreg-
wynt
Cribach
Bay
Traeth-Penbryn
Penbryn
Penmorfa
Bryn-
Pencestyll
WATERFALL
Tresaith
Trecregyn
Pen yr Hwbyn
Mwnt
Nant
Aberporth
Pen y Gwyn
Allt-goch
Glandwr Ho.
Tre
Ddafydd
Nantycroy
Parcllyn
Penarnewydd
Ffrwdwenith
Dyffryn
Dolgelynen
Castellnadolig
Sarnau
Brynhoffnant
Clyn yr ynys
BUTTERFLY
CENTRE
Blaenfflyman
Login
Penfeidr
Ffynonwen
Rhosygadair
Newydd
Blaensaith
Esgaireithin
A487
Waur
meindy
Pencaeau
Aberbed
Cemaes Head
SN 50 10
Gwbert
92
Trefere
Troed-
y-rhiw
Rhosygadair
Fawr
Cwmporthman
Llwyn-
coed
ABERPORTH
Rhos-
Tan-y-
groes
A487
INTERNAL
Alltycorde
Ferwig
Penrhiw
Blaensaith
92
Pen yr Afr
Gernos
Gwel
Tywyn
Waughgelod
Tyhen
Bronwyn
Treprior
Blaenannerch
Glaneirw
Gelliдеg
Glasgoed
Deinol
Llain
Cwmcoednefn
PEMBROKESHIRE
COAST PATH
POPPIT
SANDS
Cippyn
Mwnt
Maniar
fawr
Glanllynan
Tremain
A487
Blaenpistyll
Trefwtial
Penparc
Blaenporth
Cryngae
Mawr
Rhos
Maengwyn
Tyllwyd
Penlon
Bettws
Waunfawr
Glandulas
Ffynnon
Bronia

0   1   2   3 miles
0   1   2   3   4   5 km

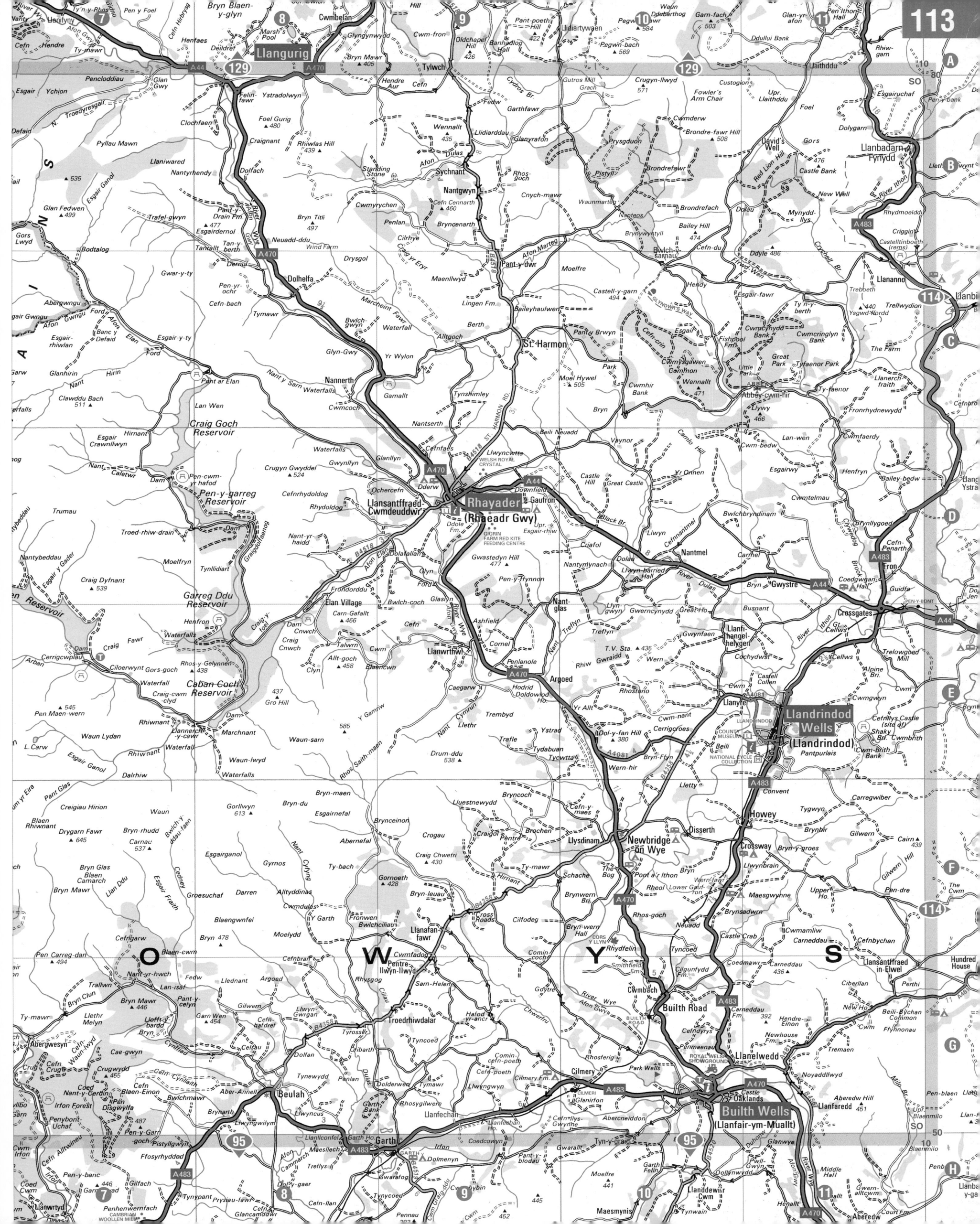

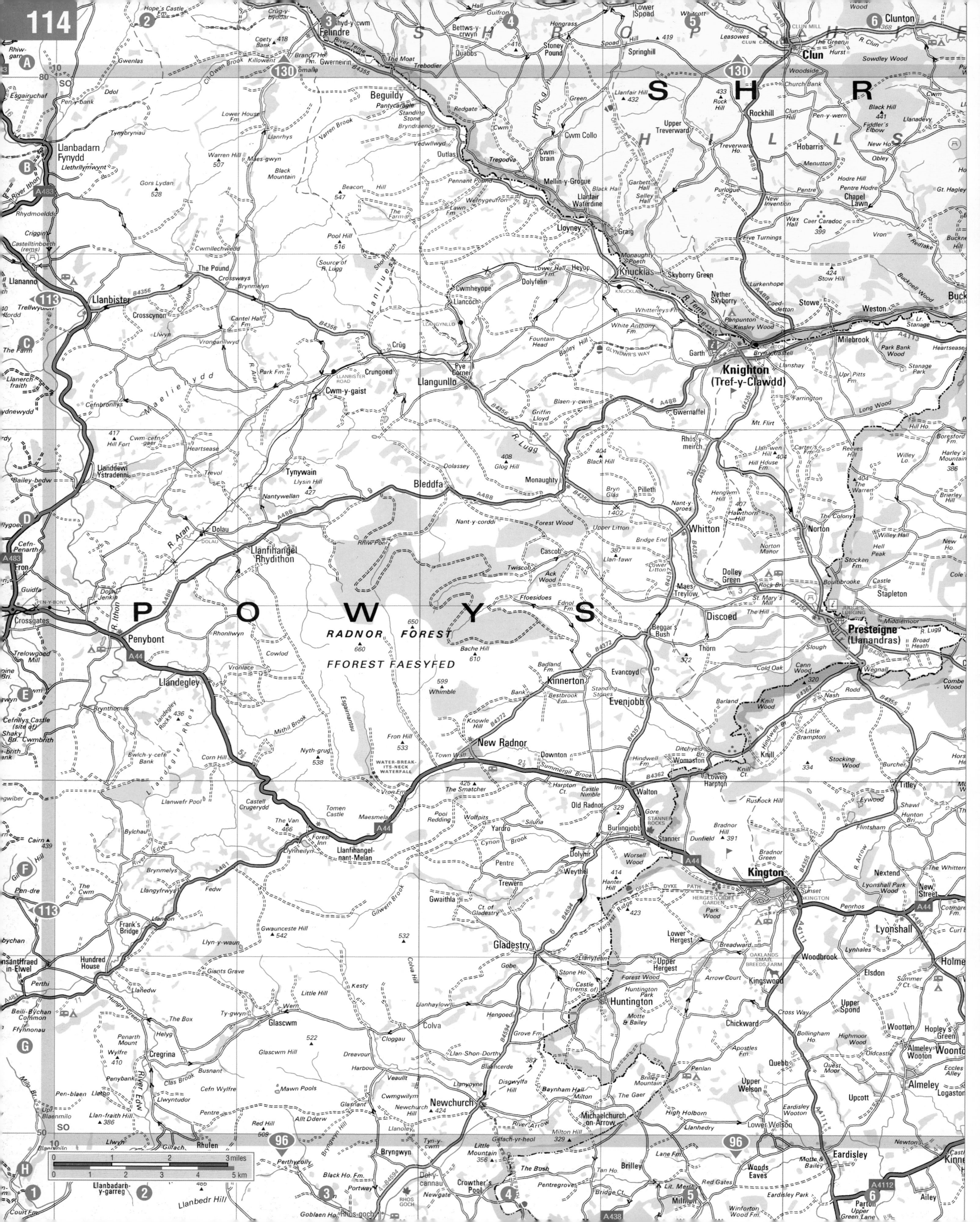

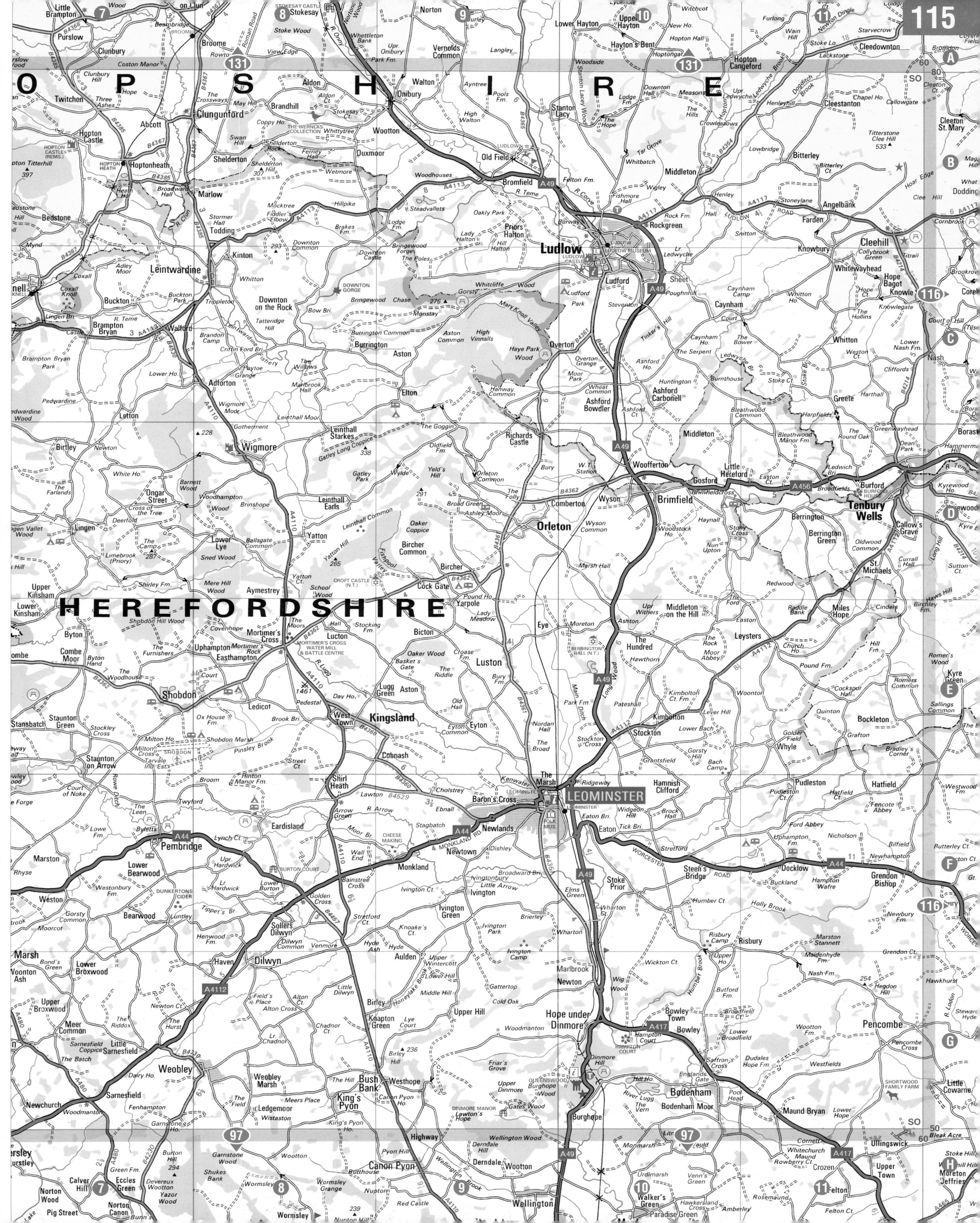

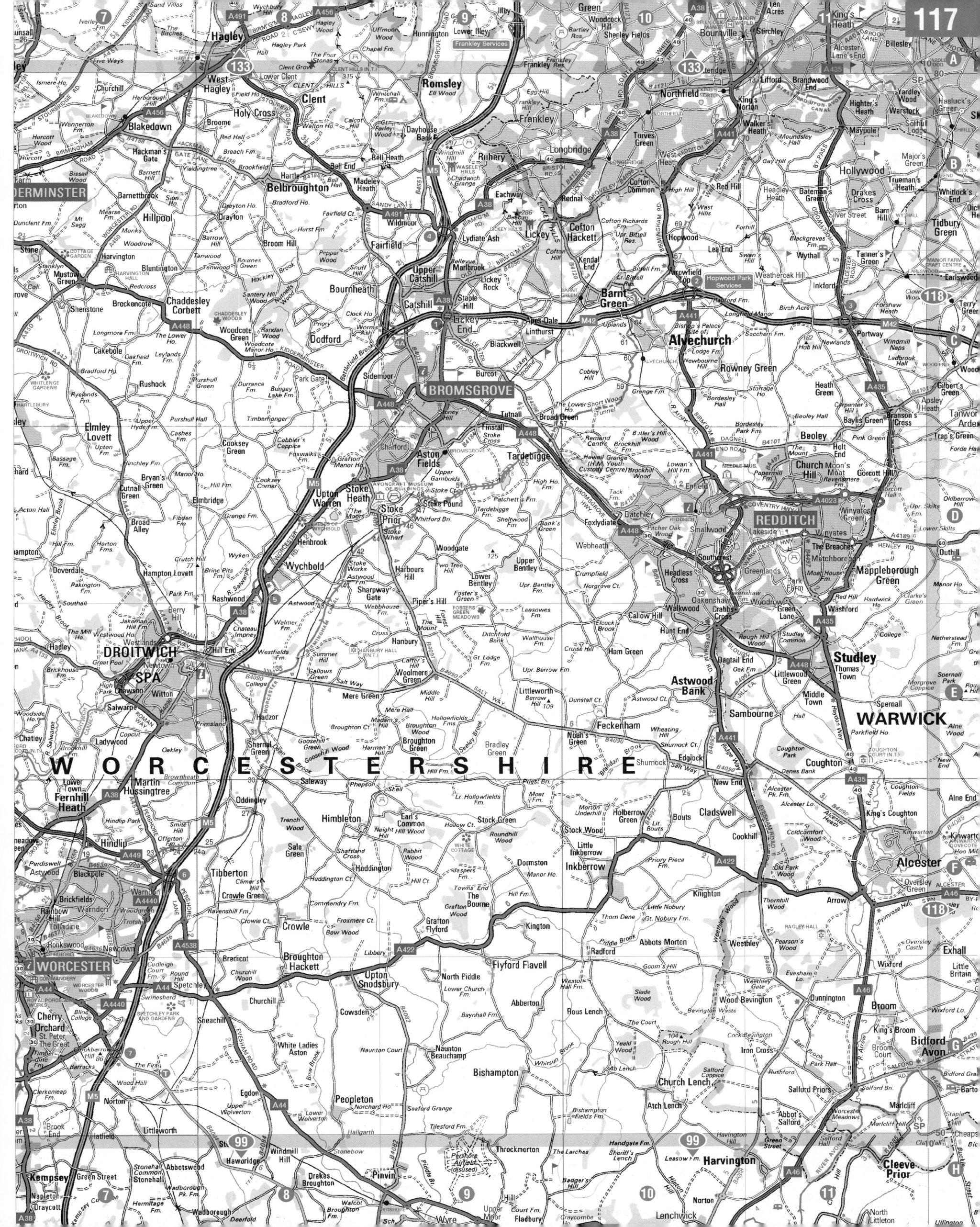

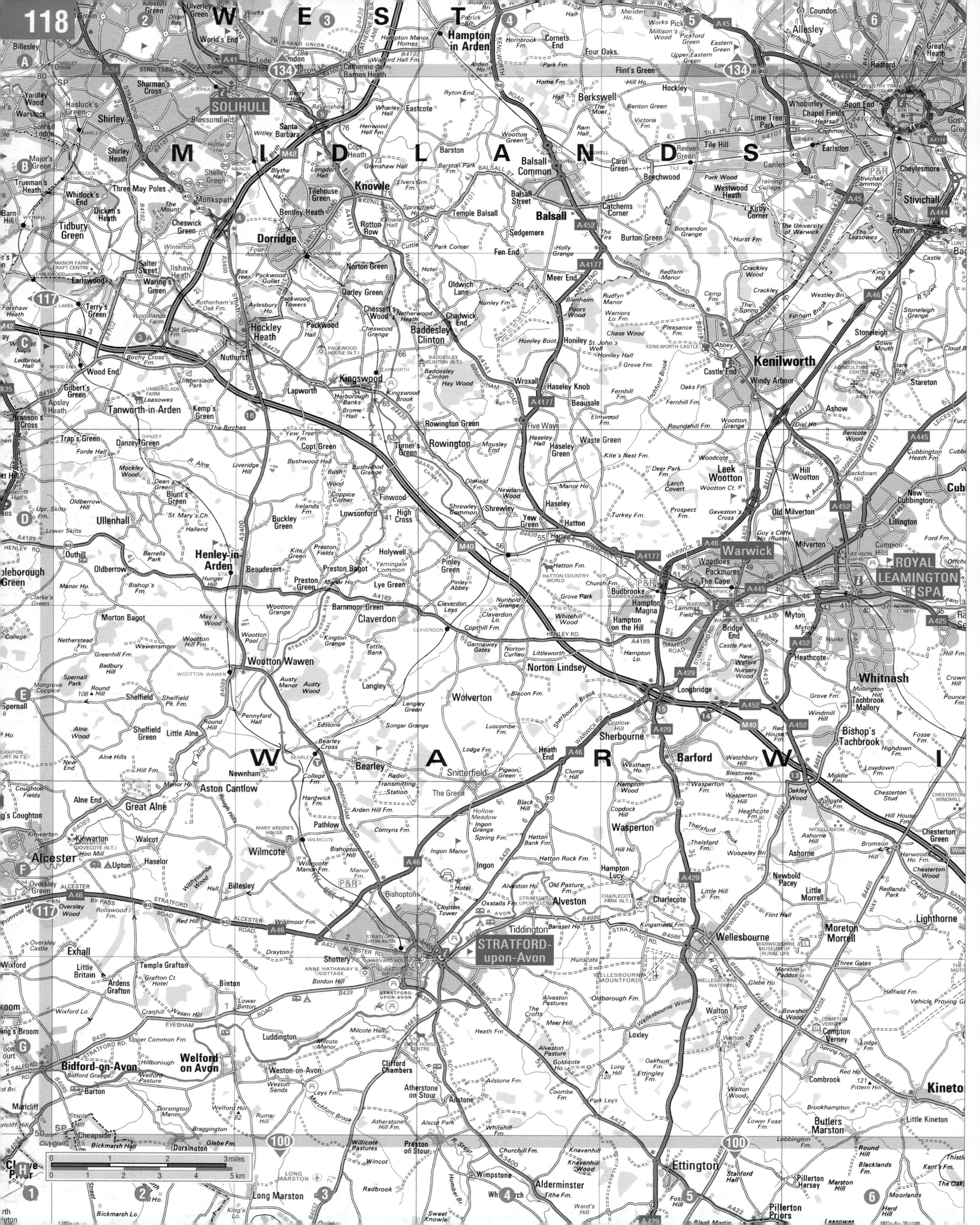

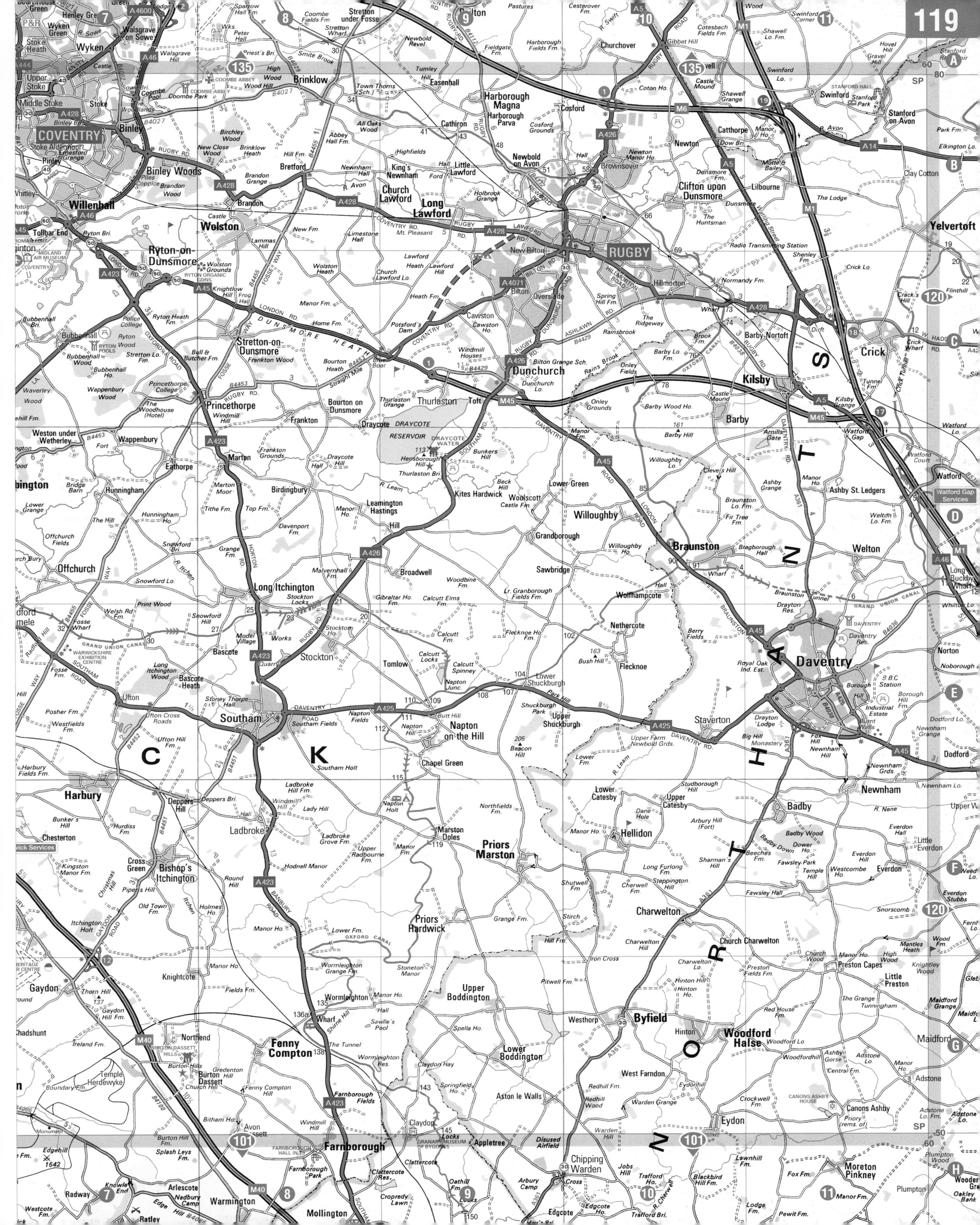

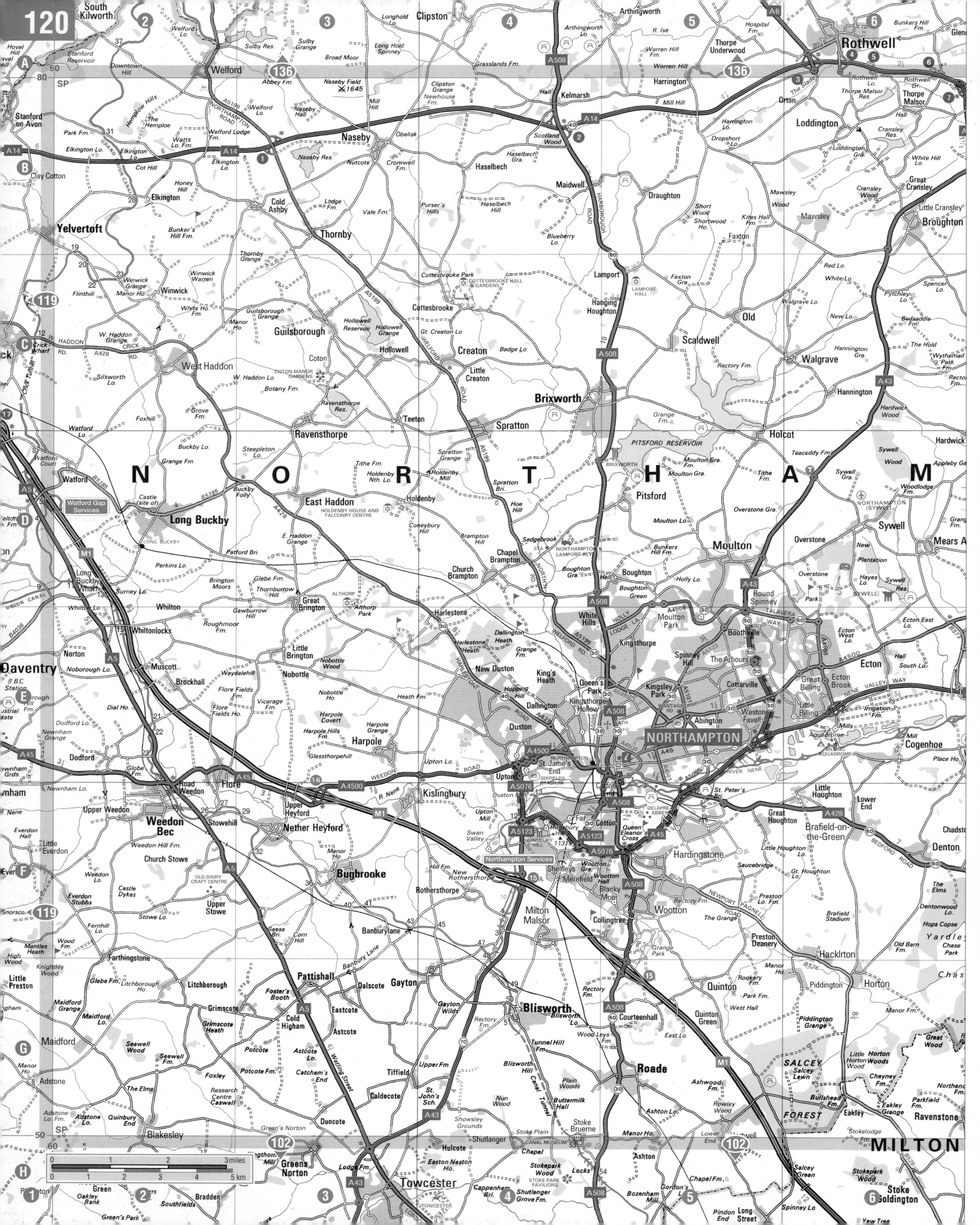

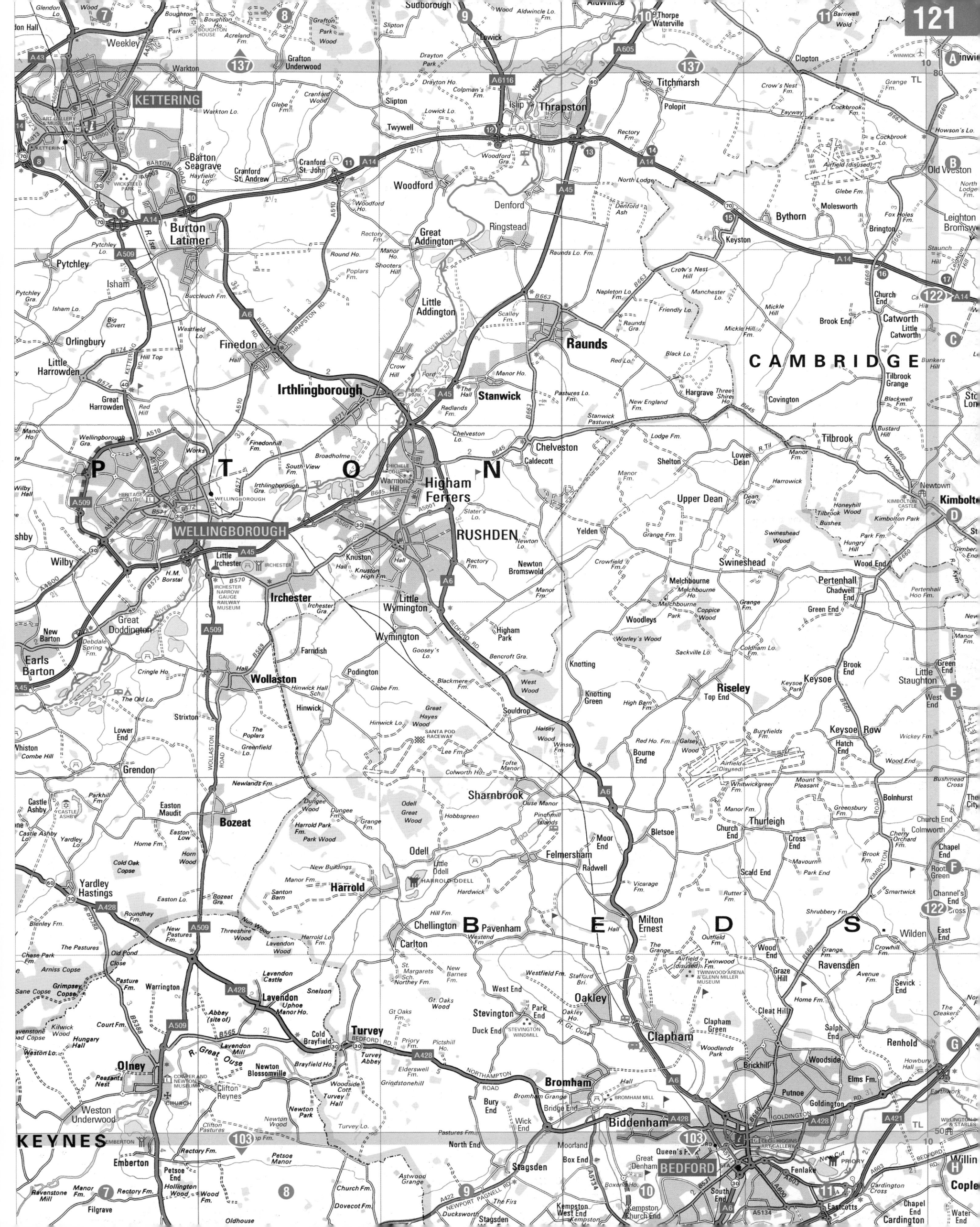

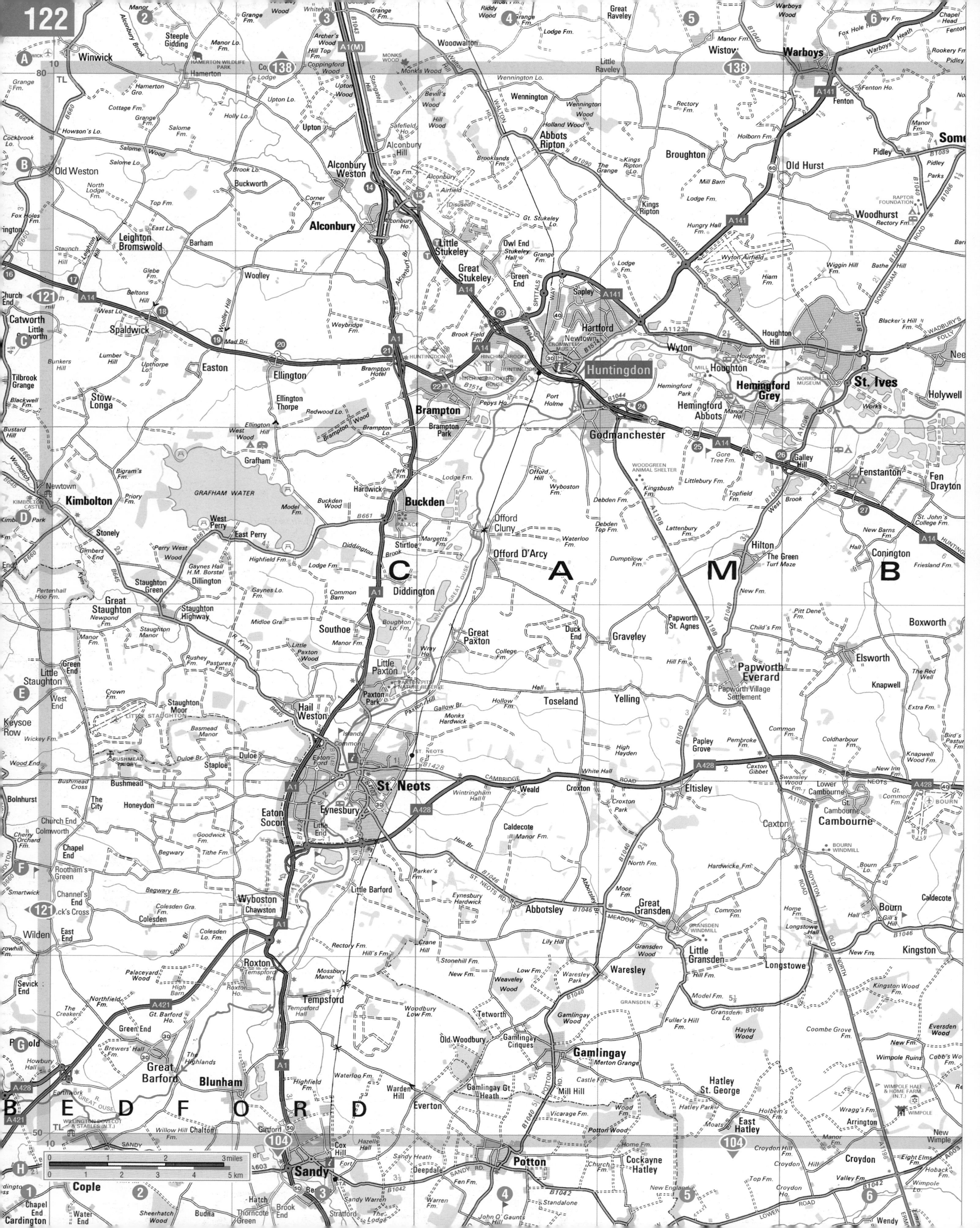

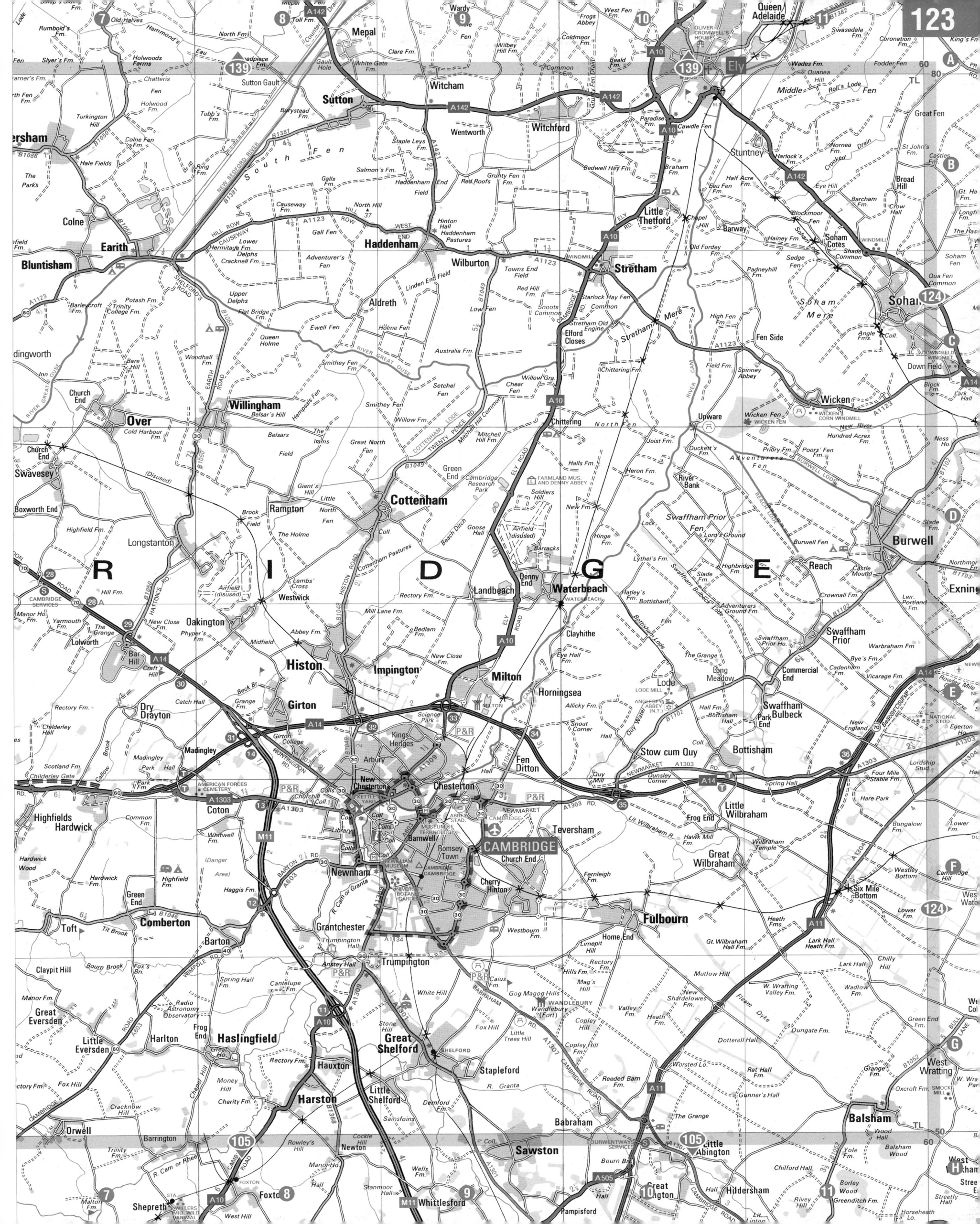

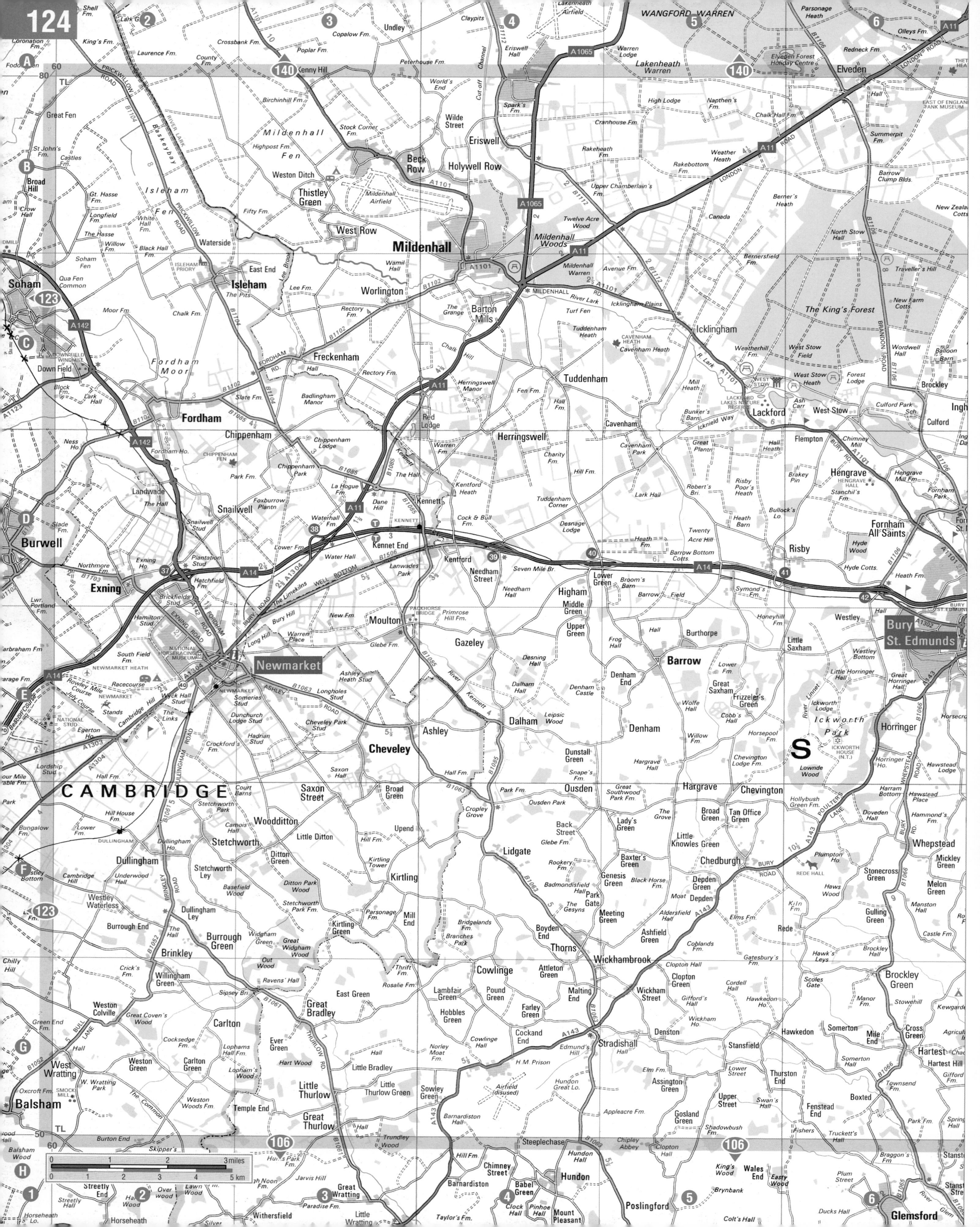

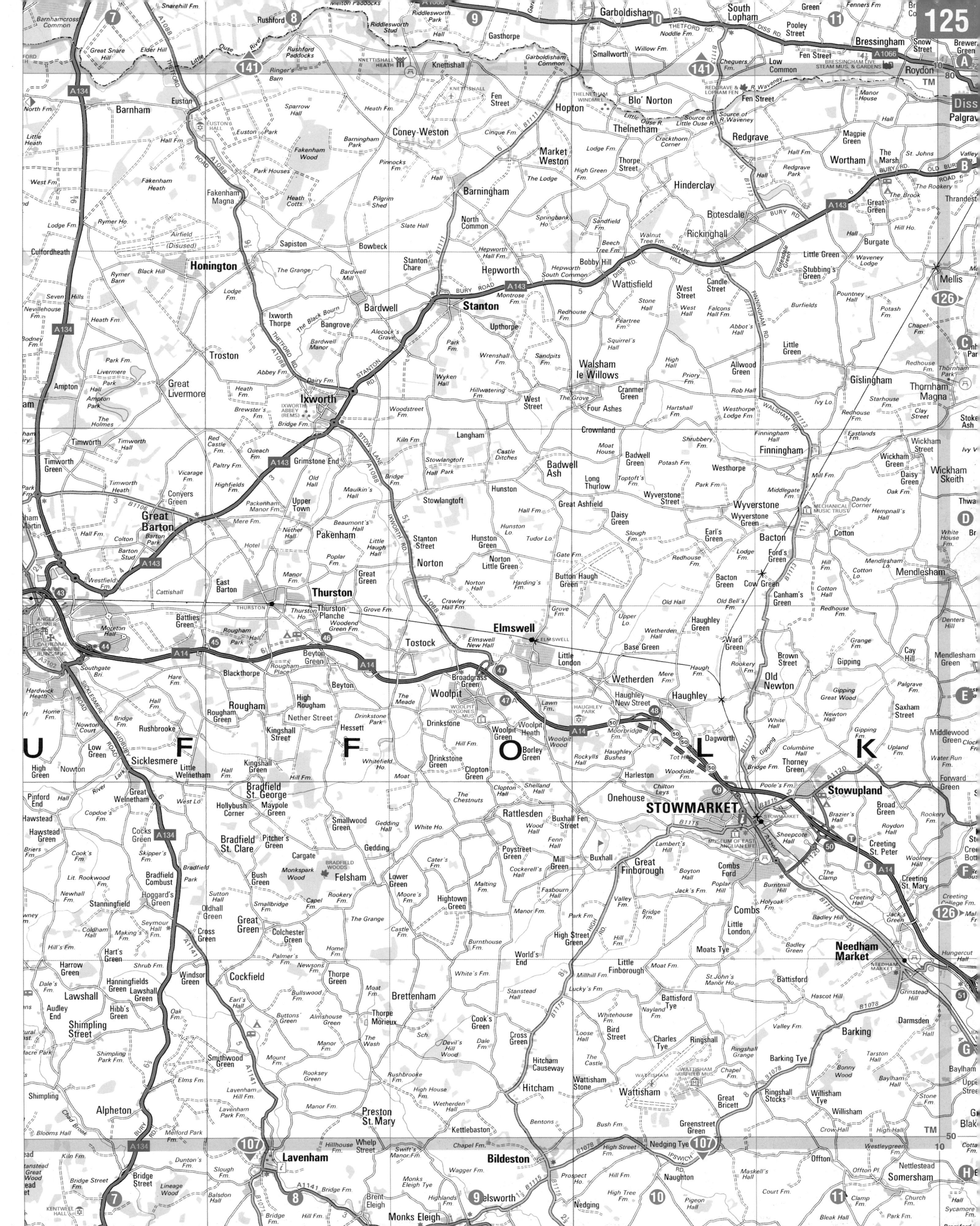

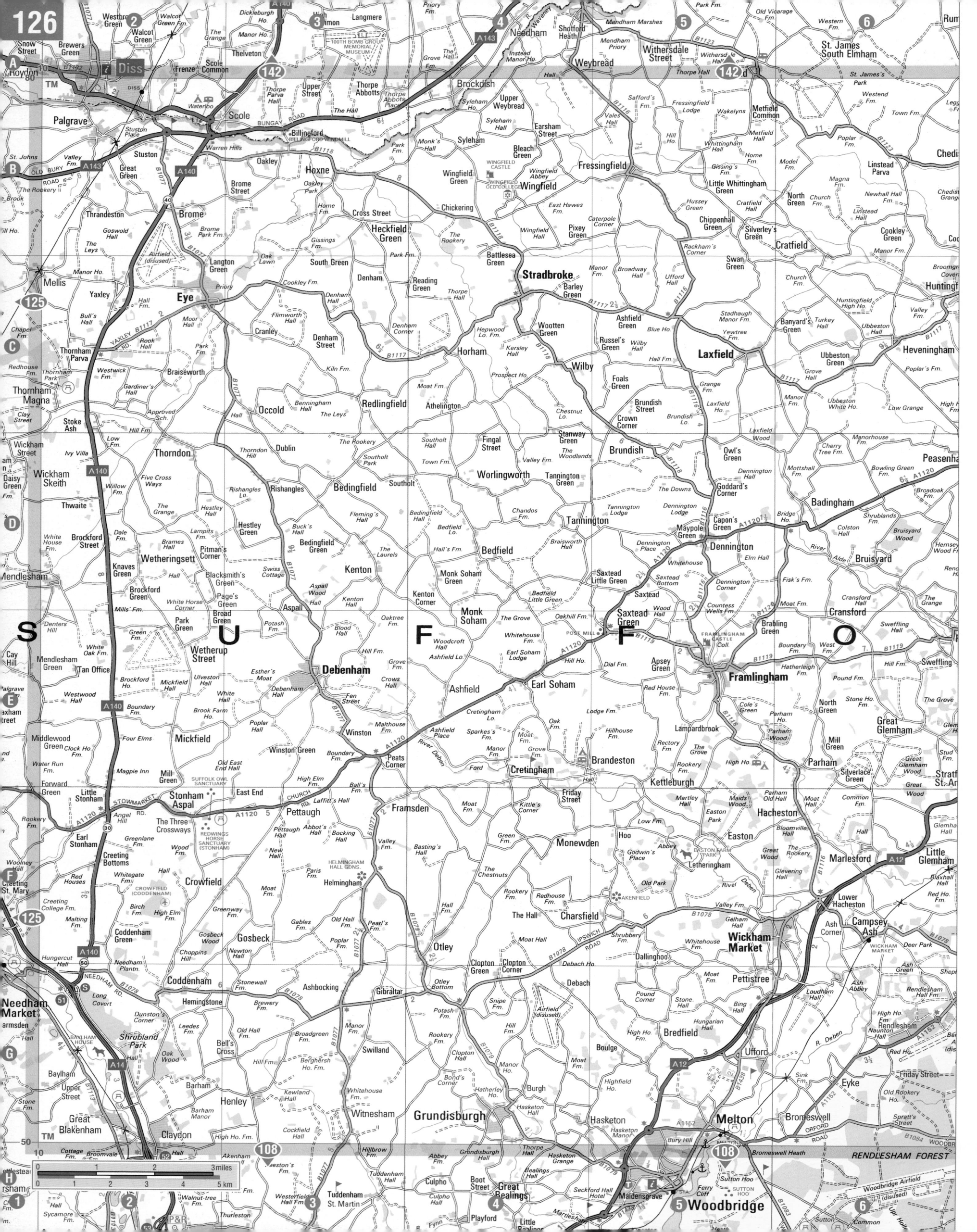

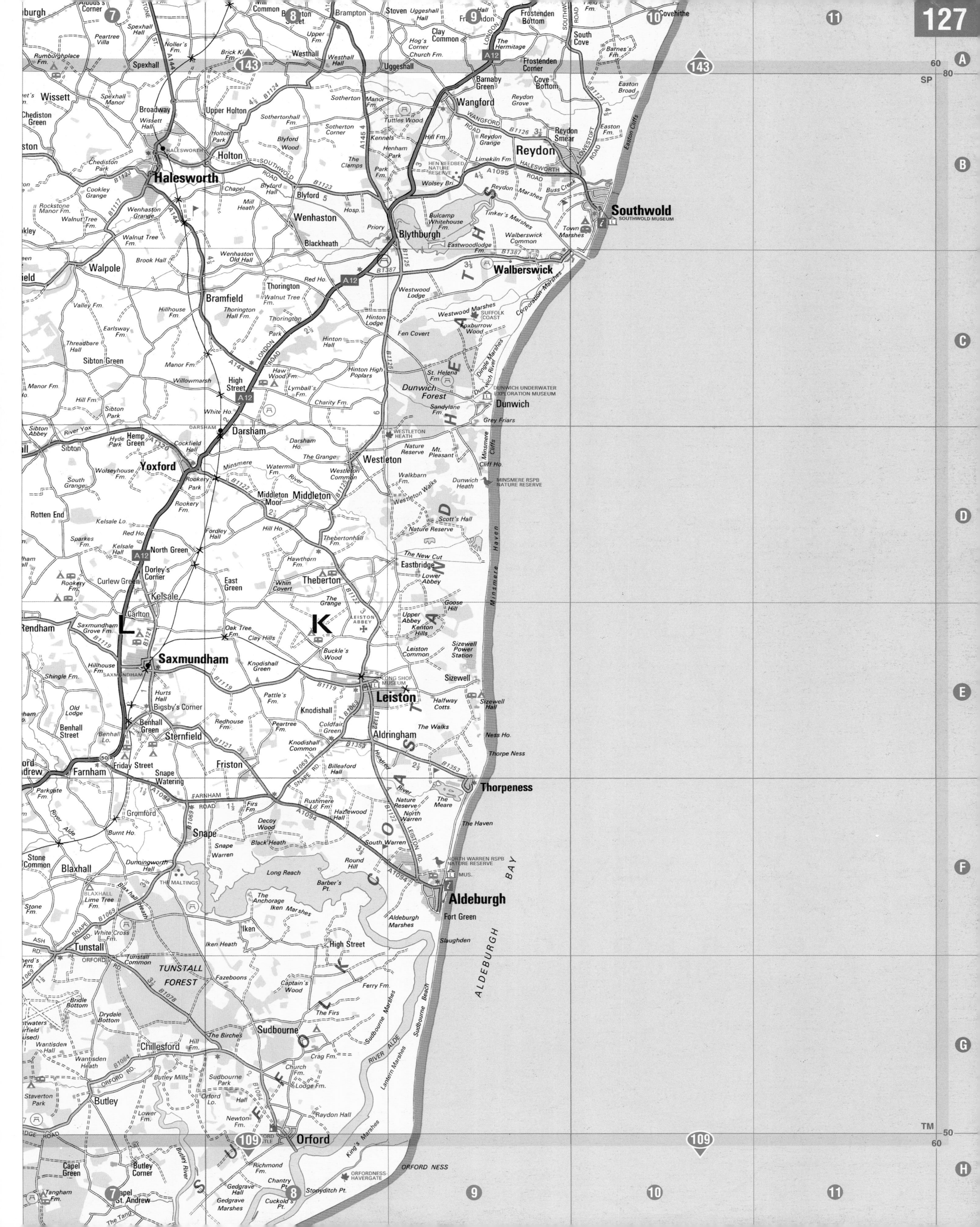

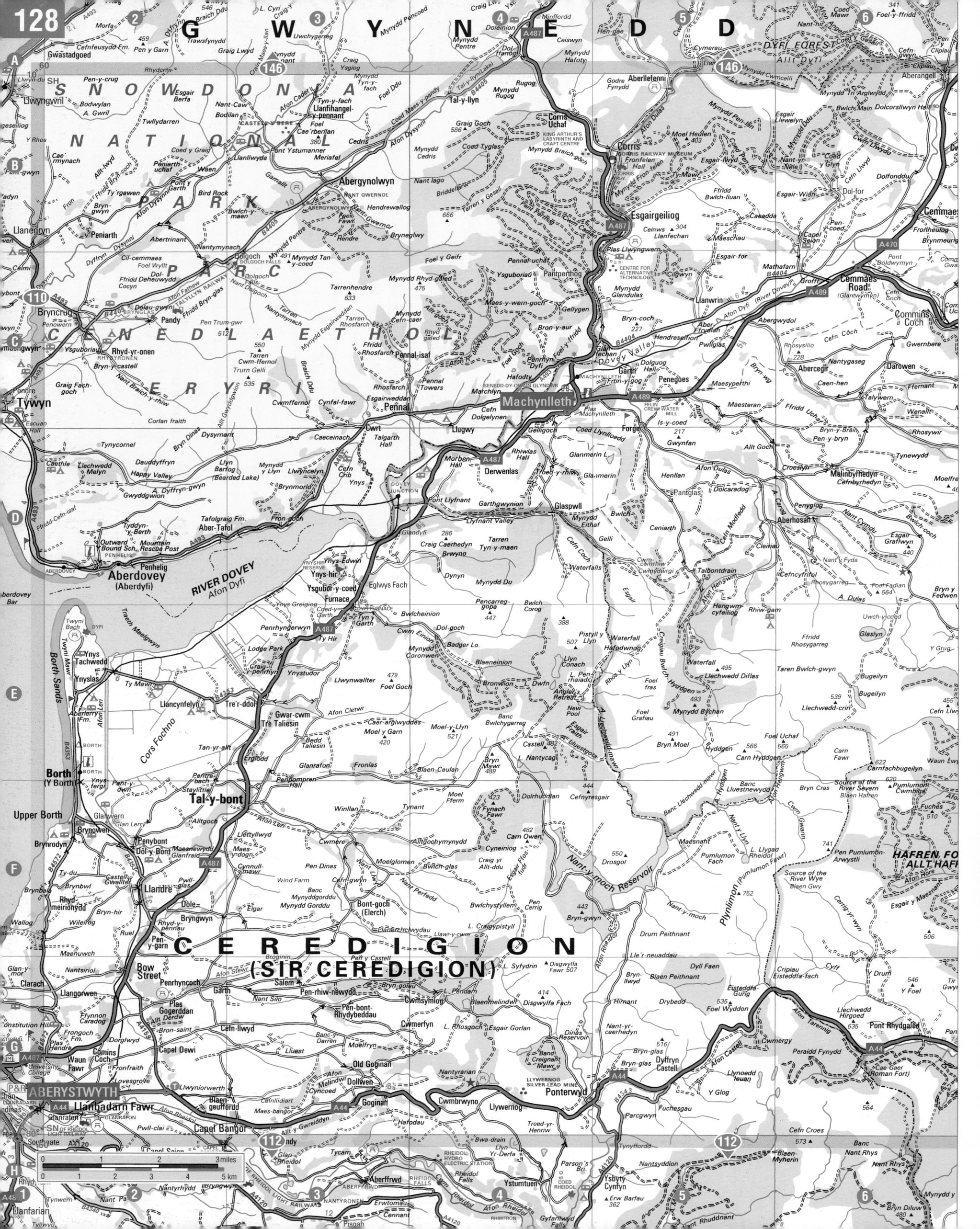

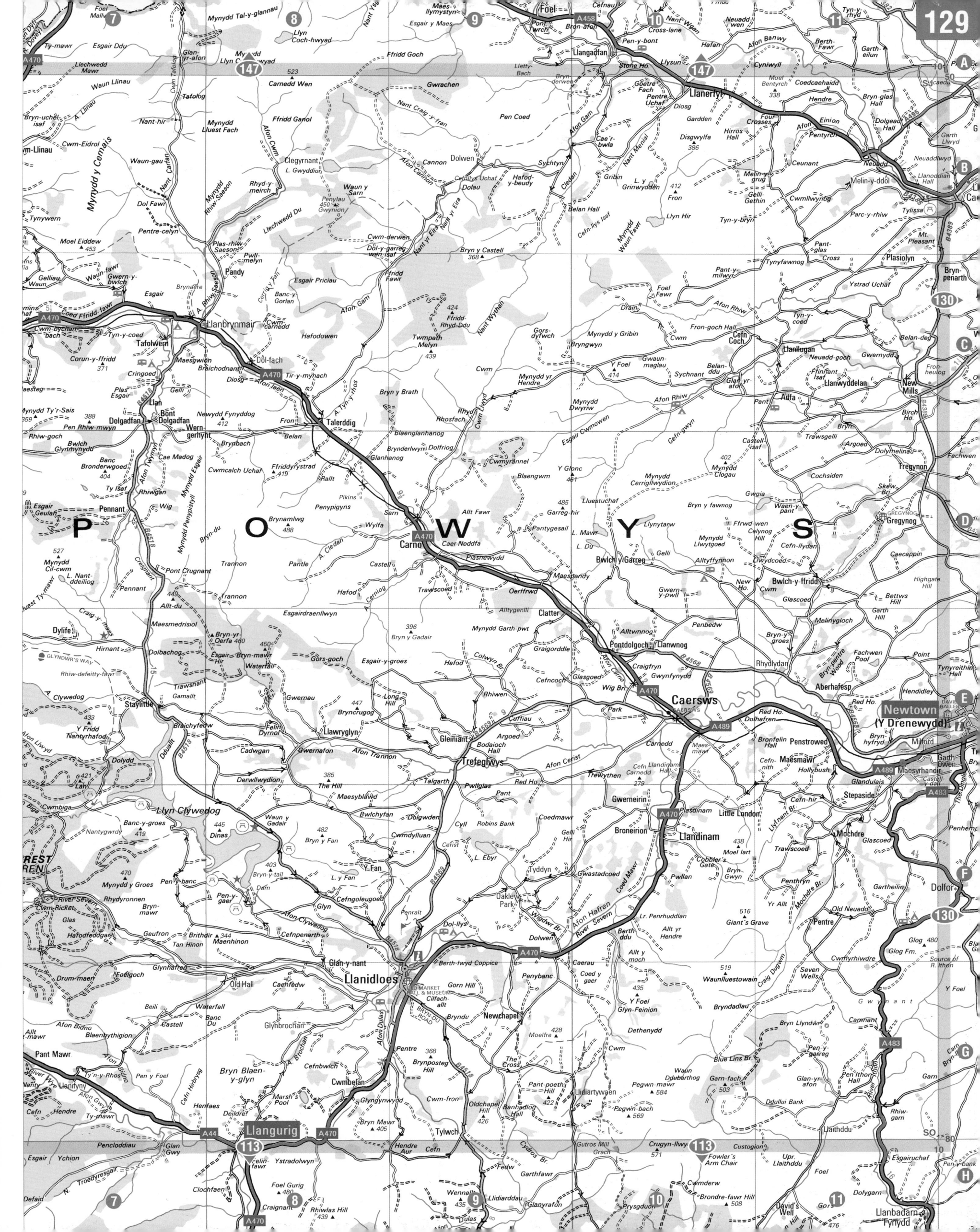

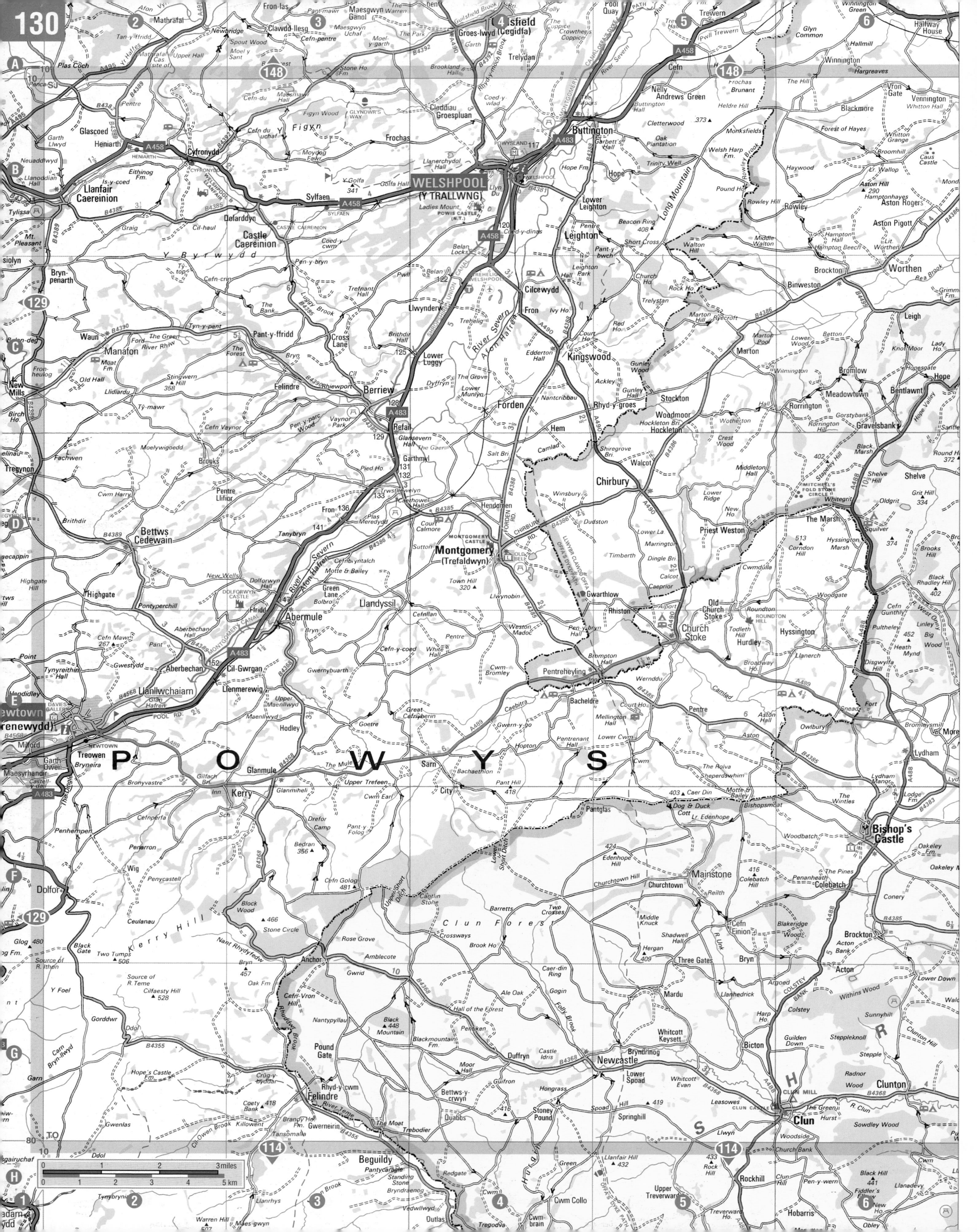

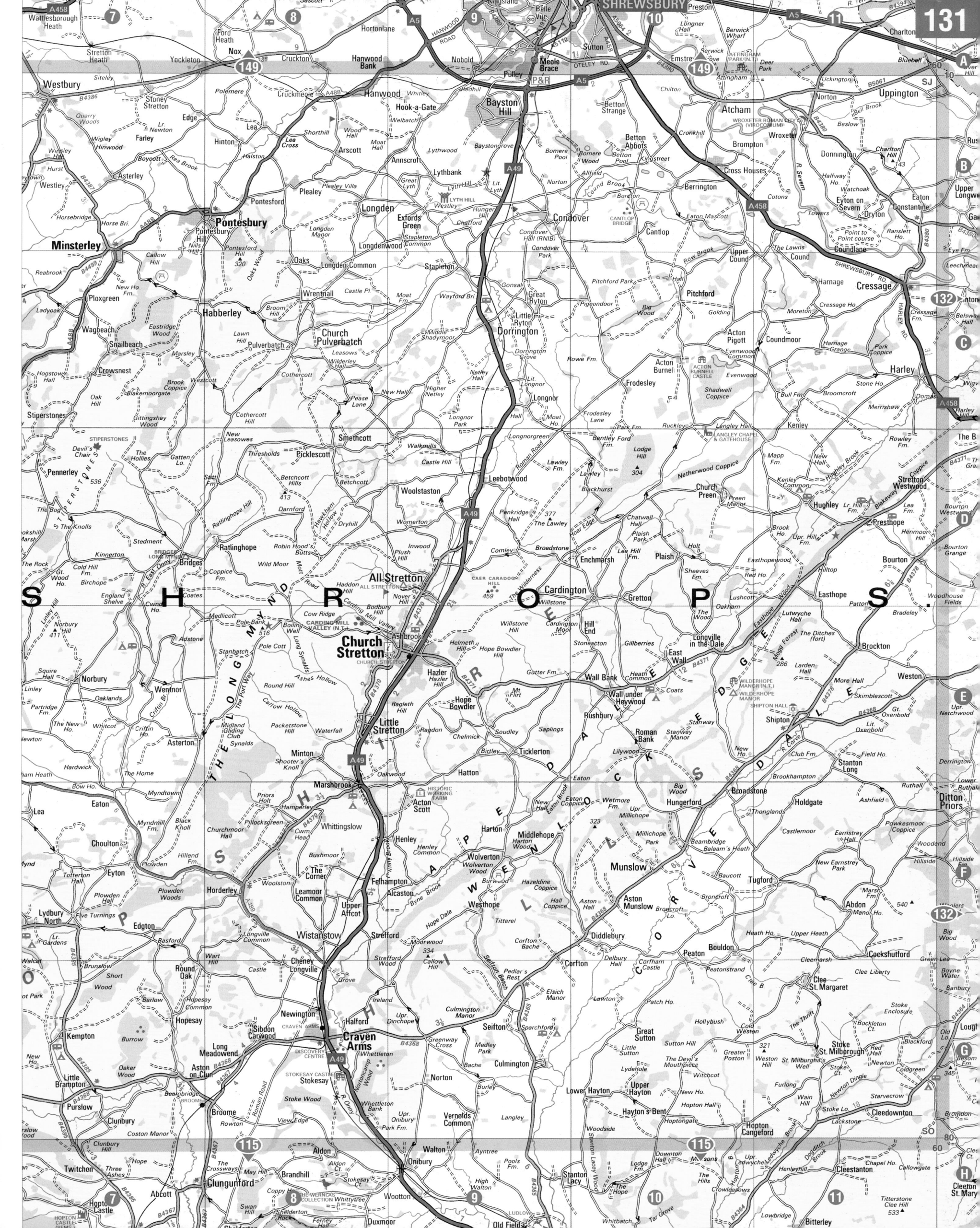

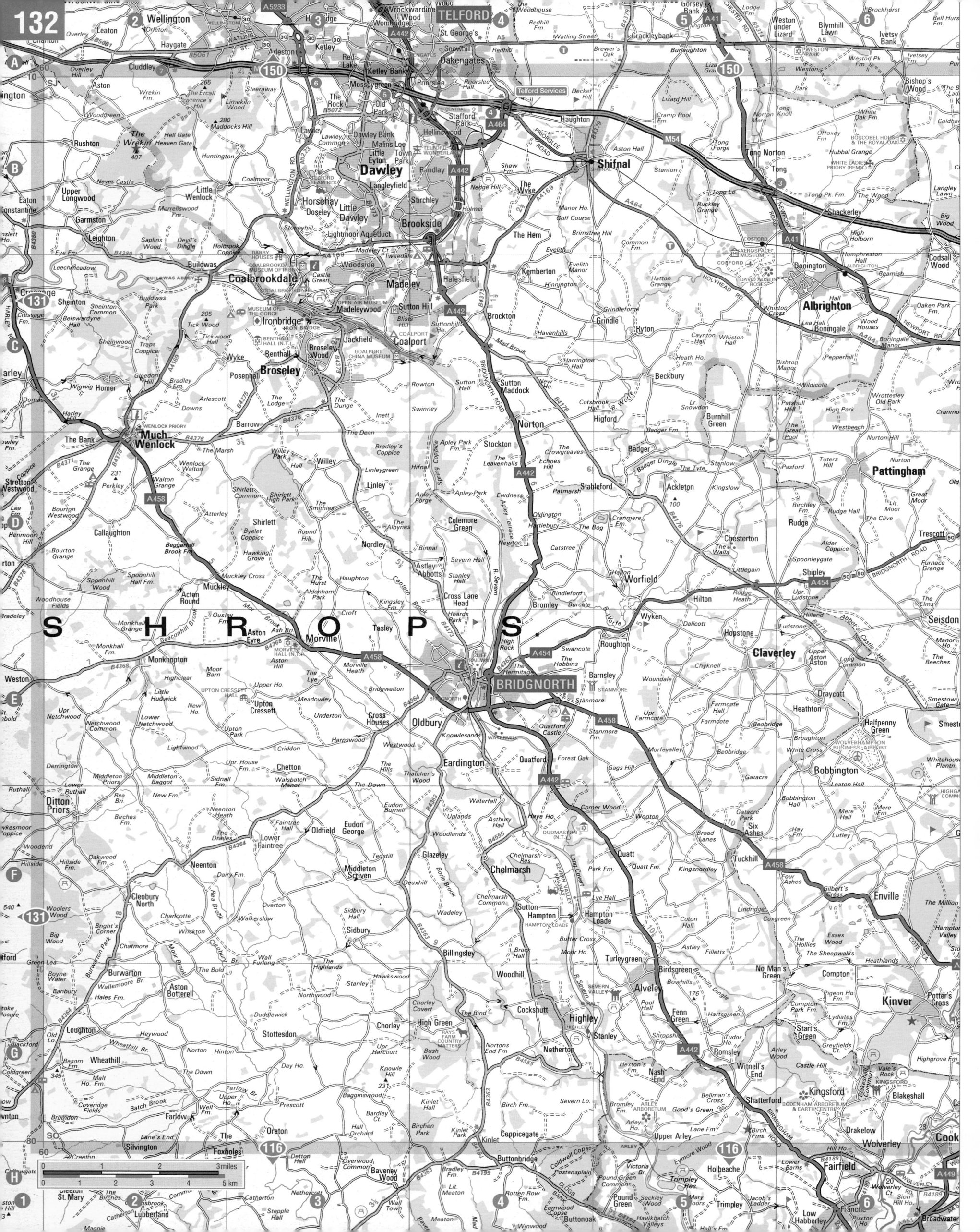

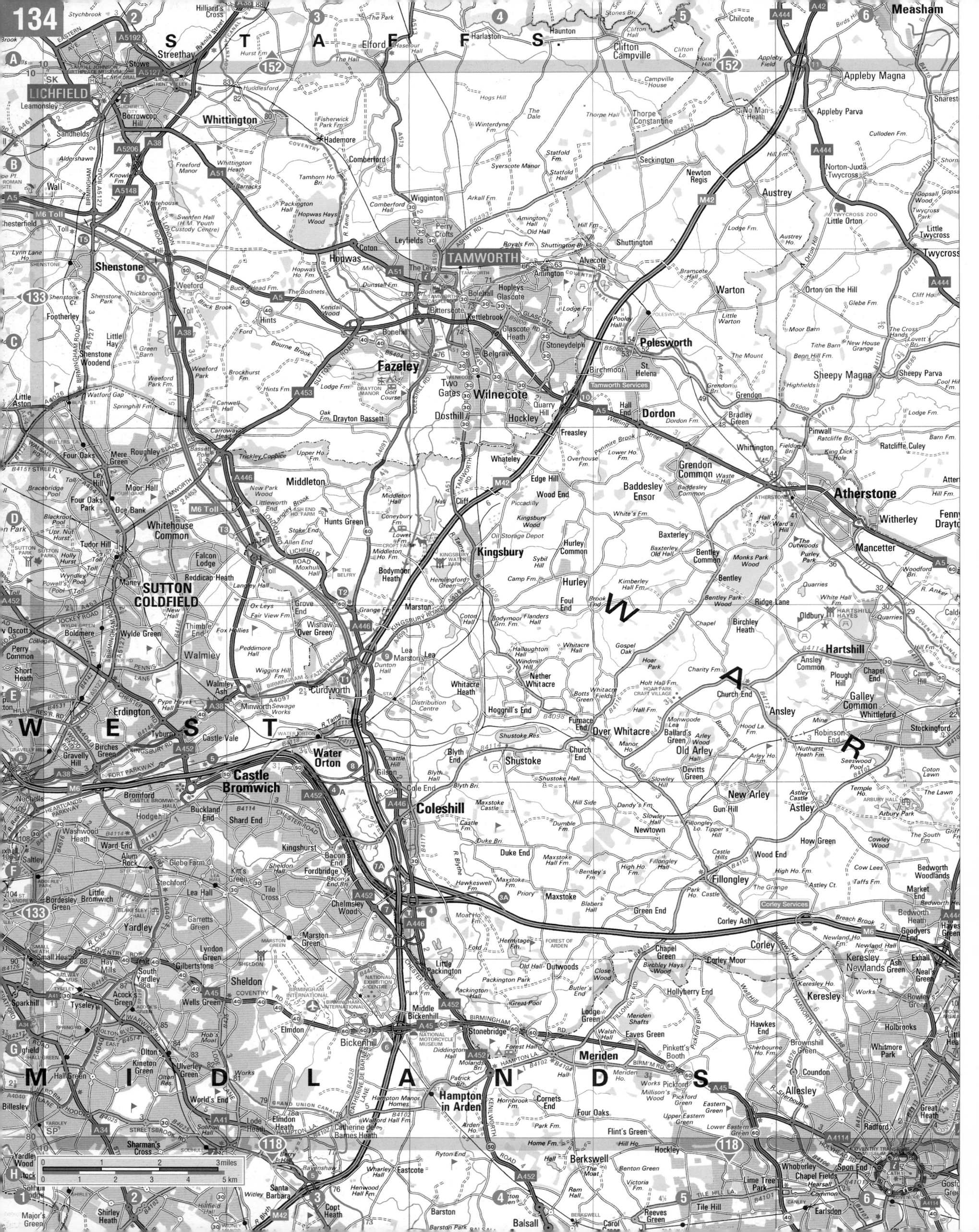

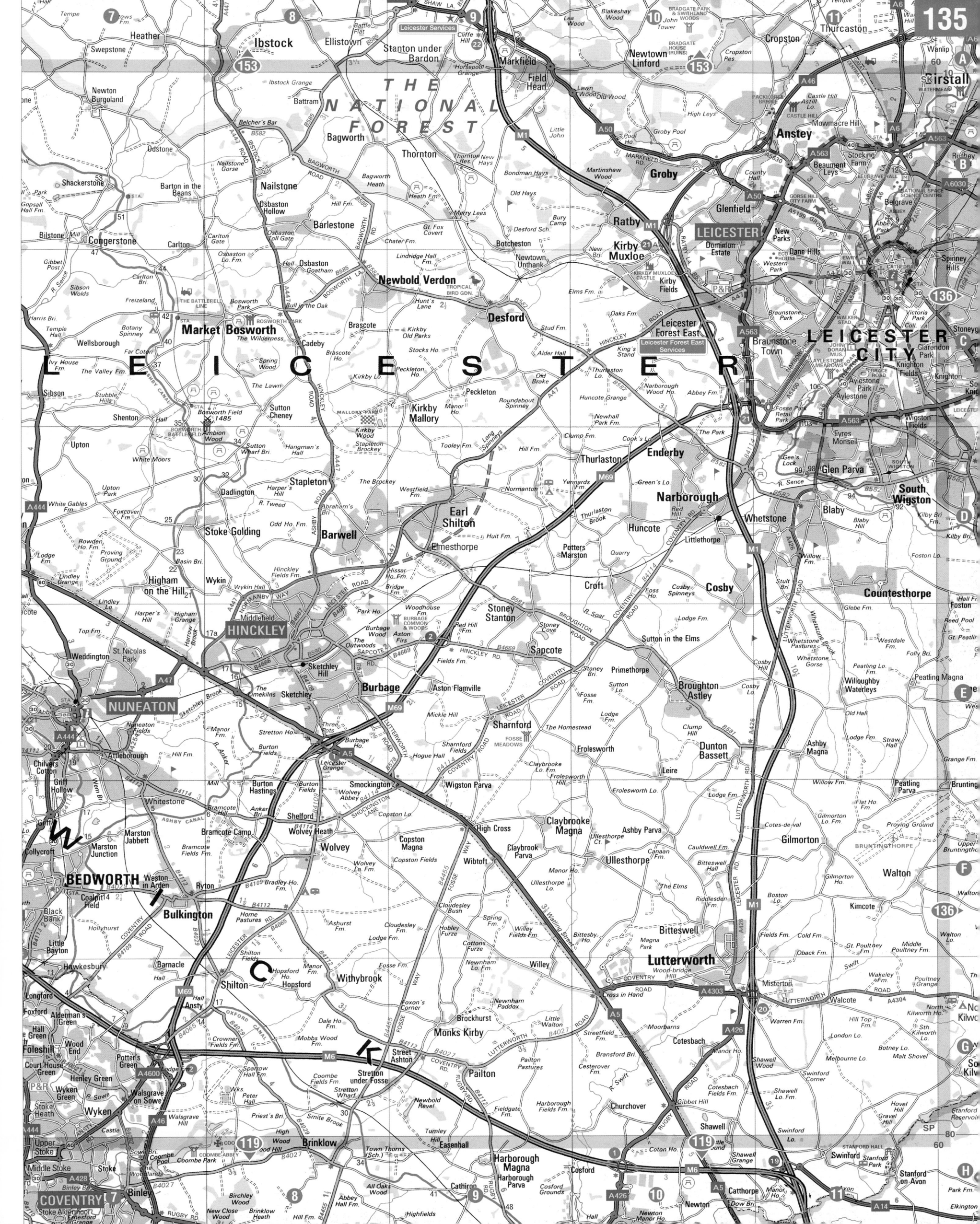

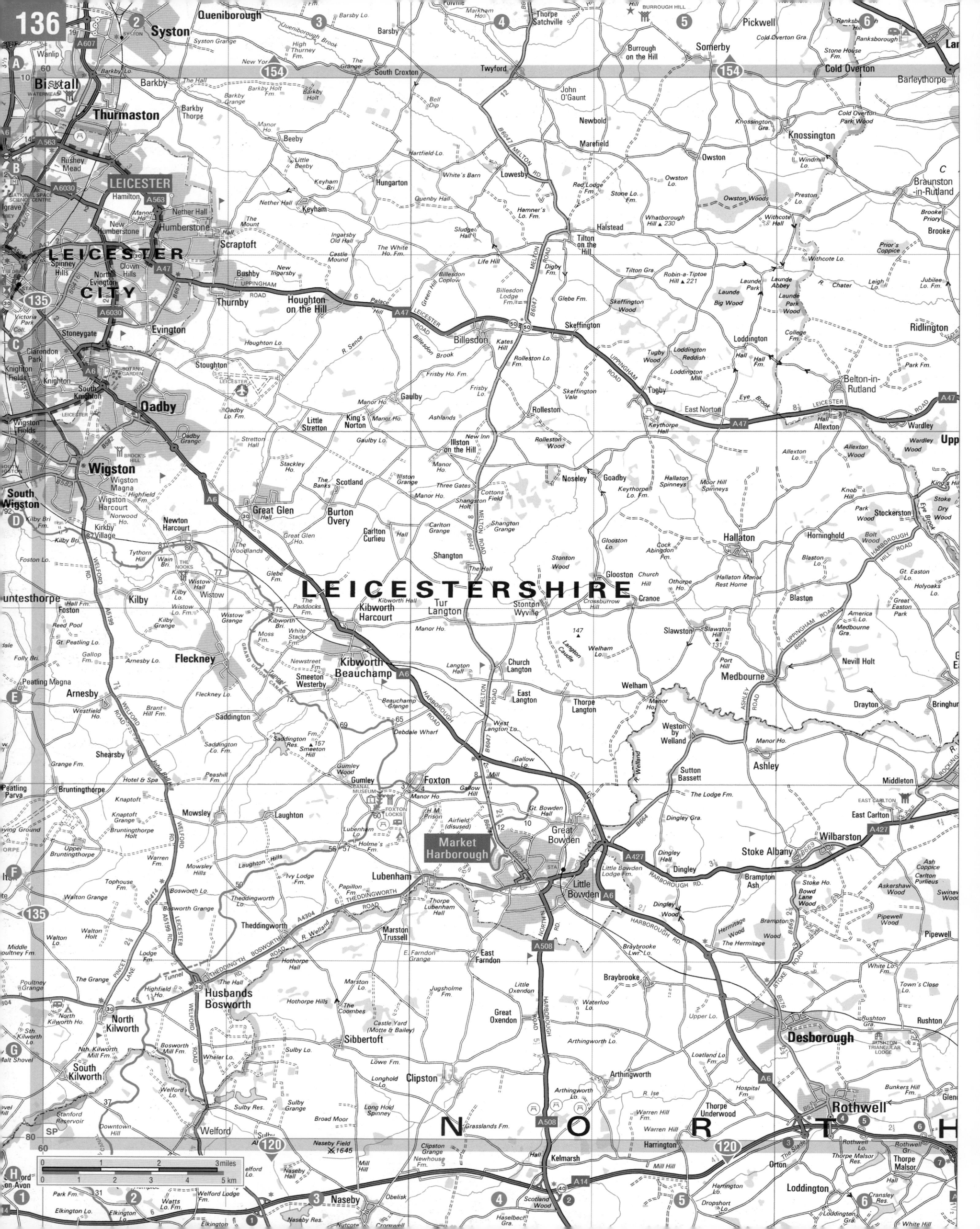

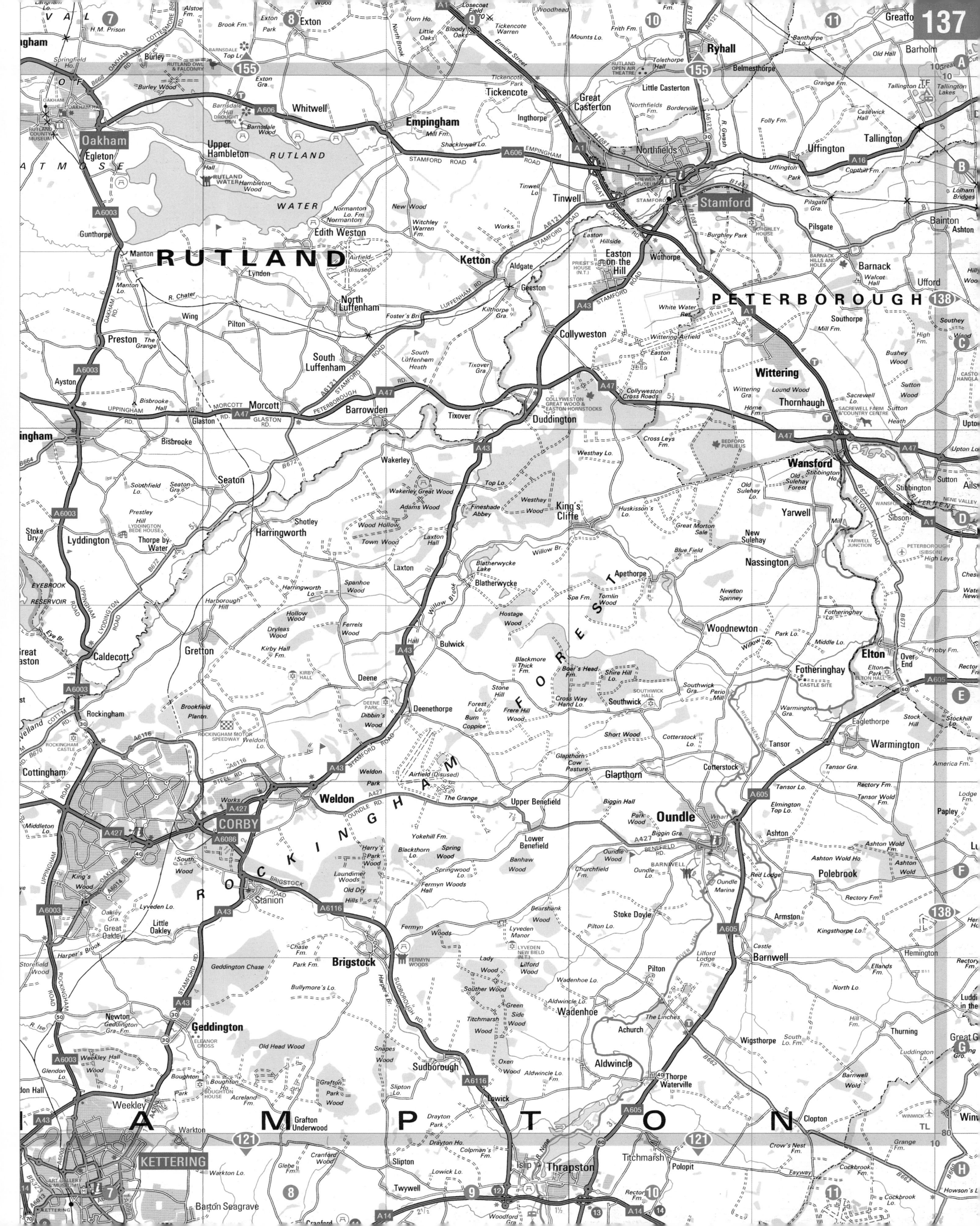

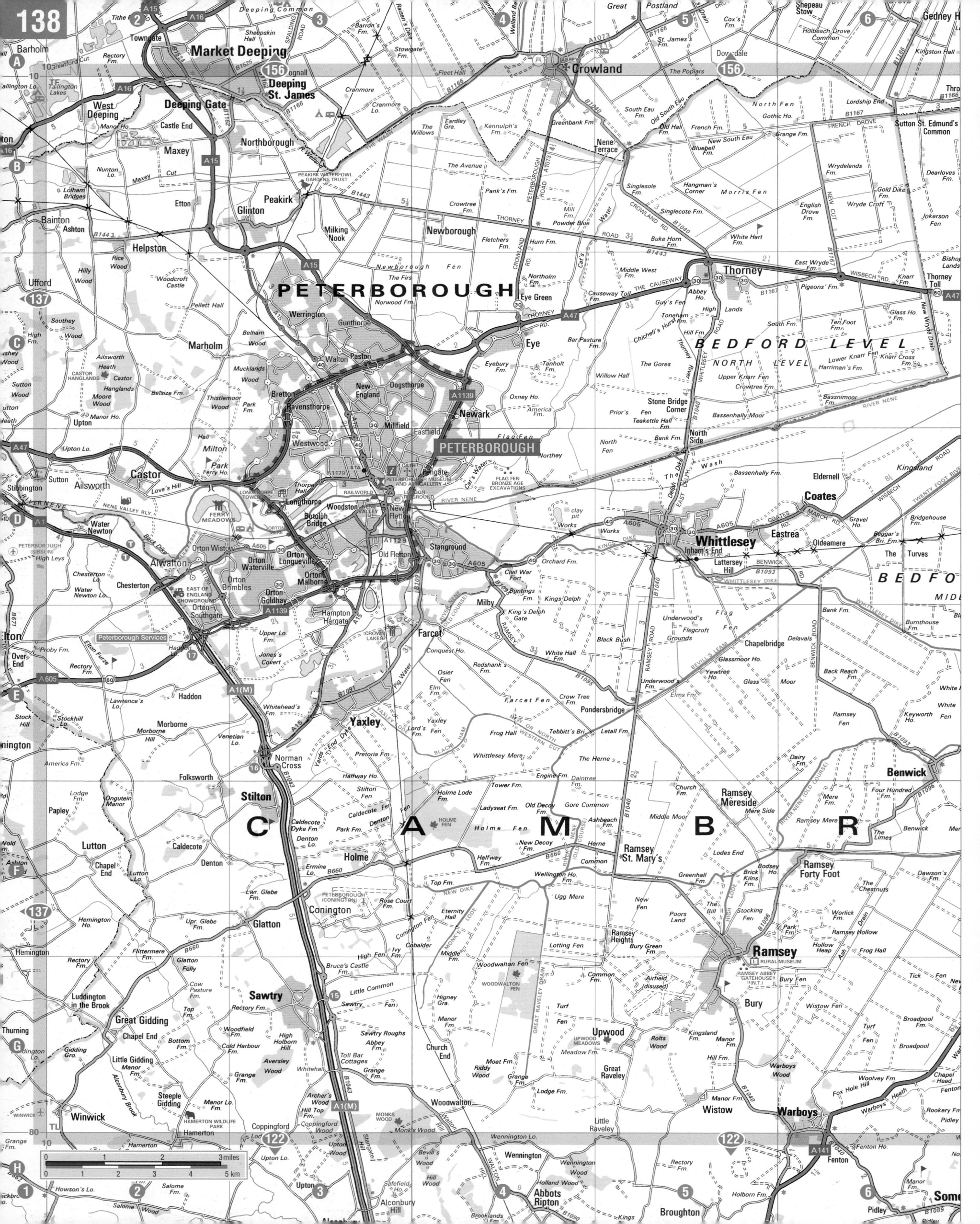

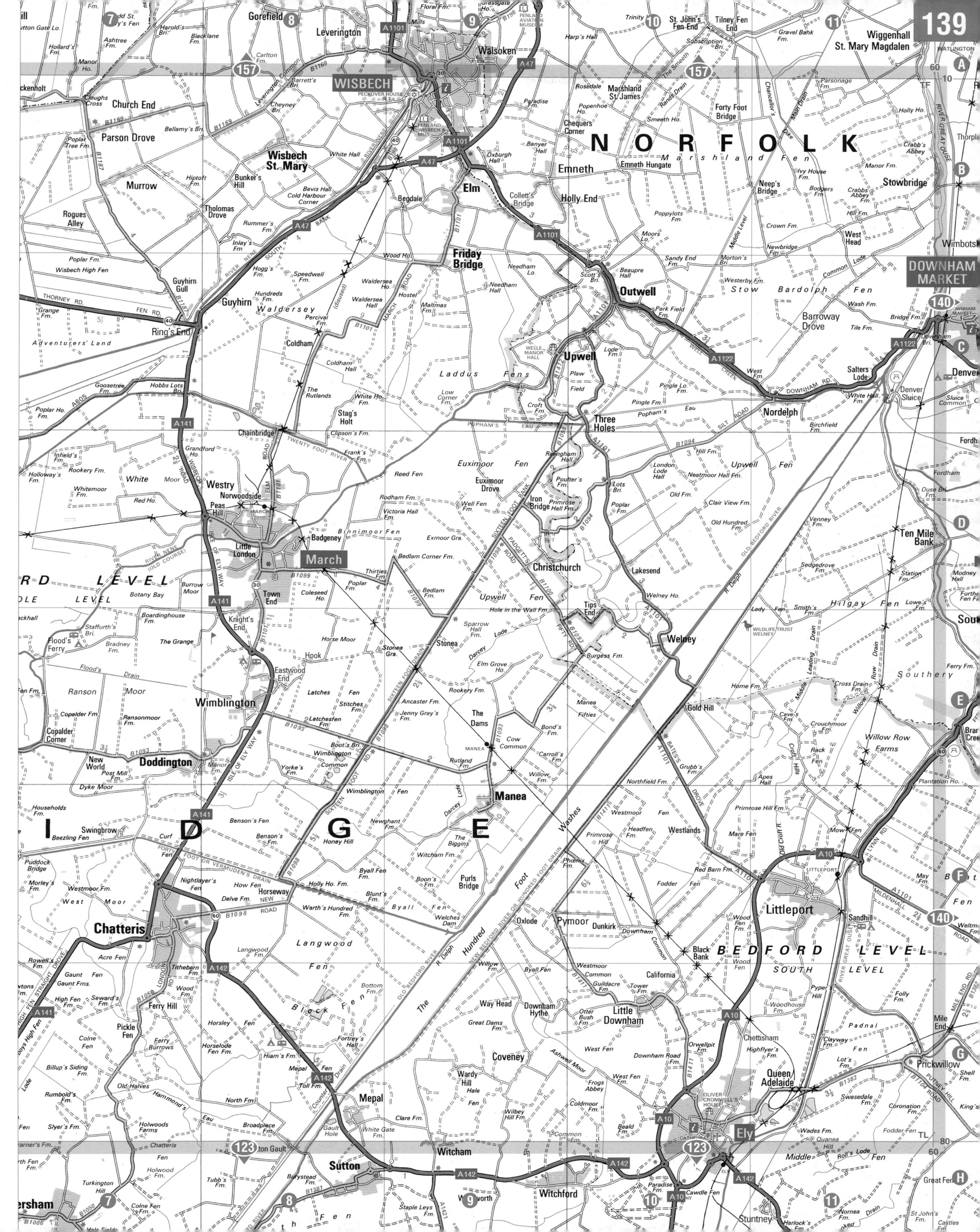

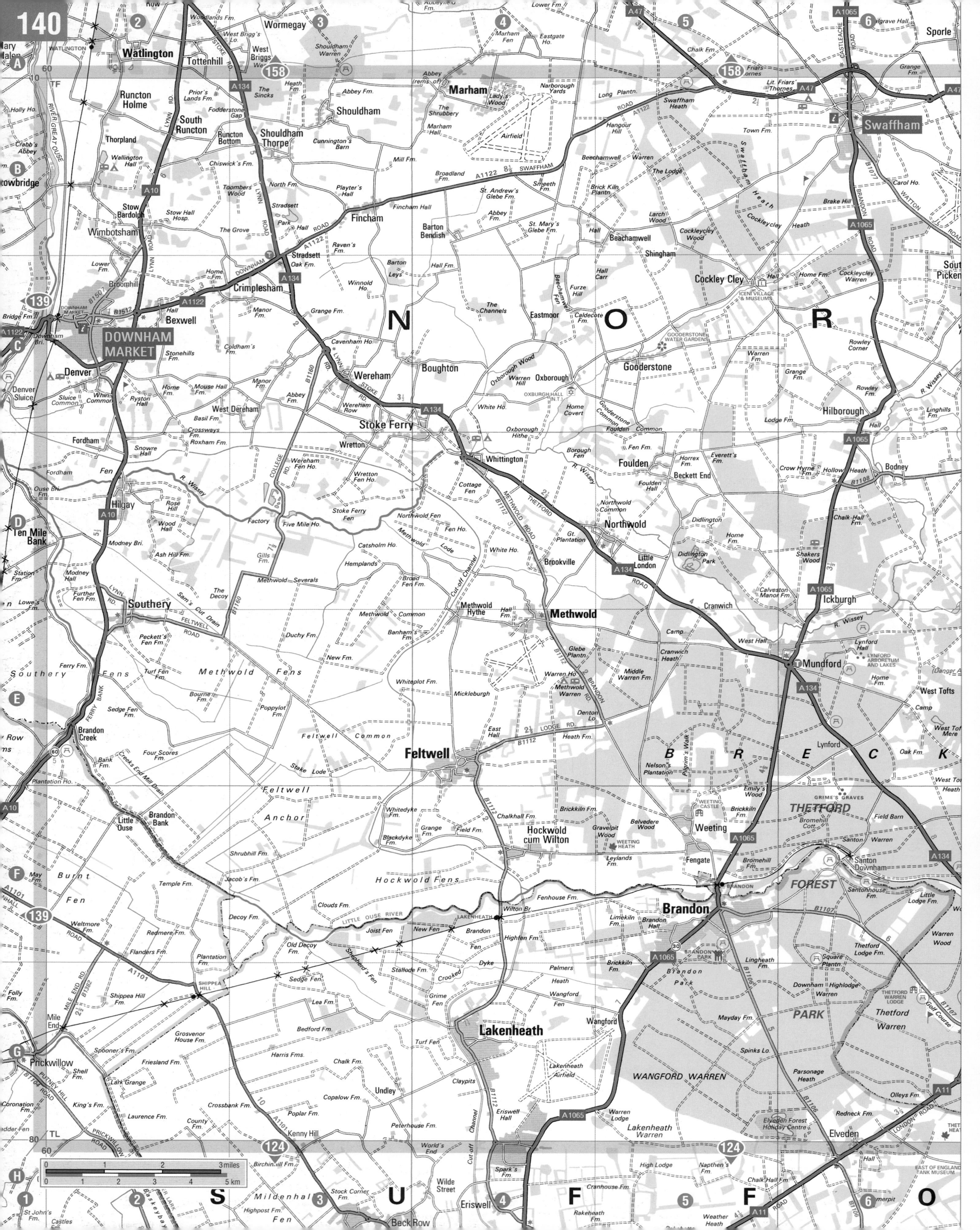

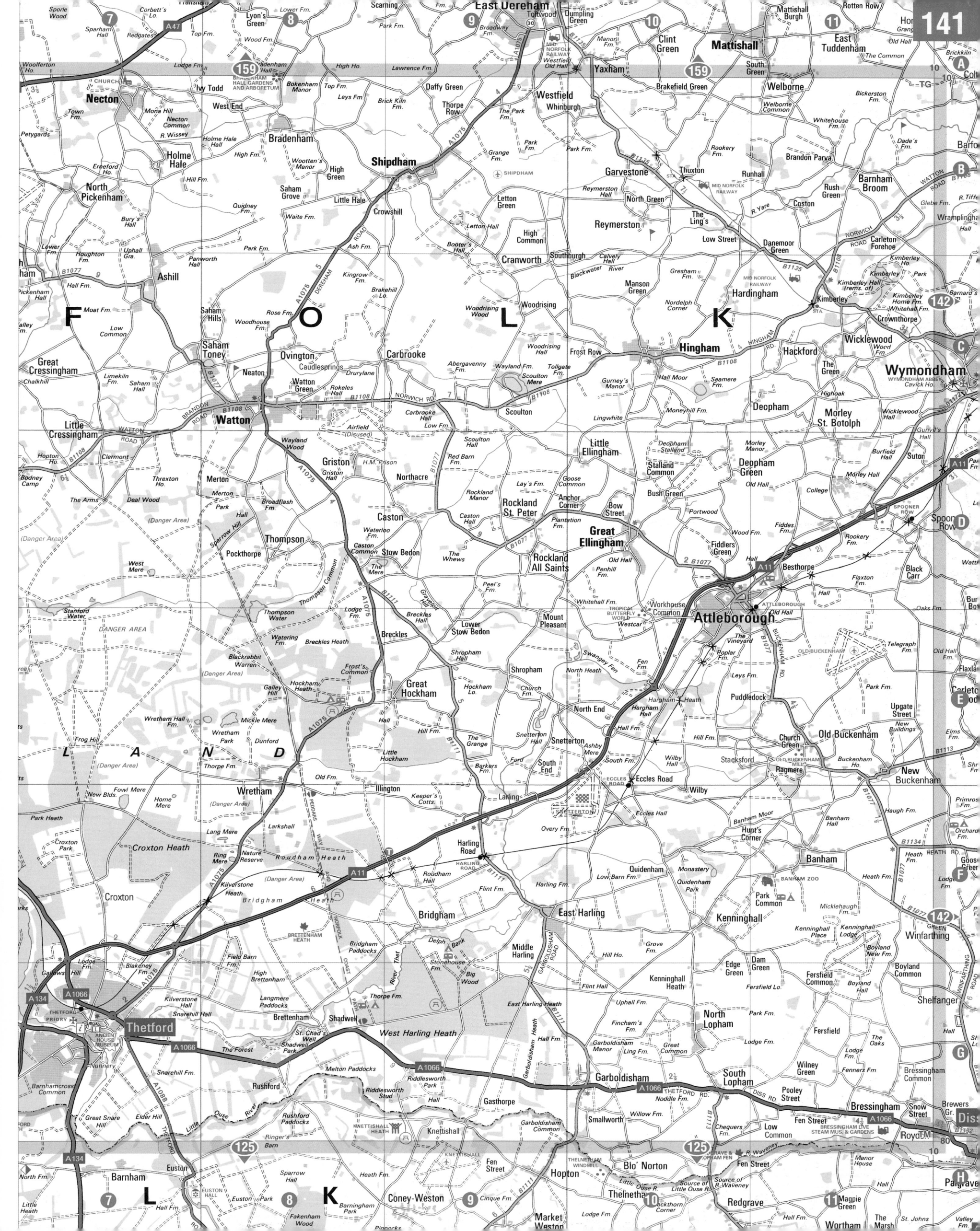

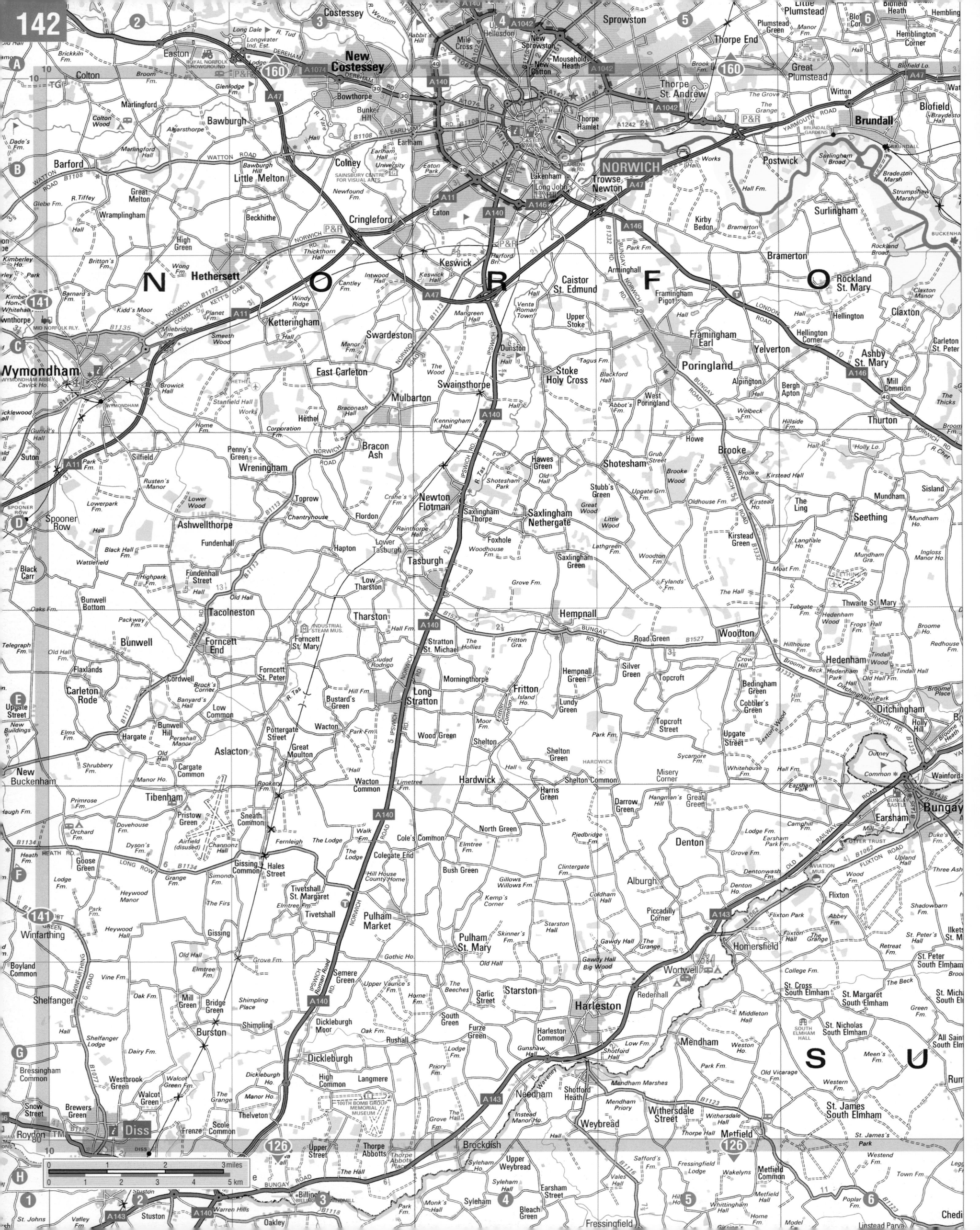

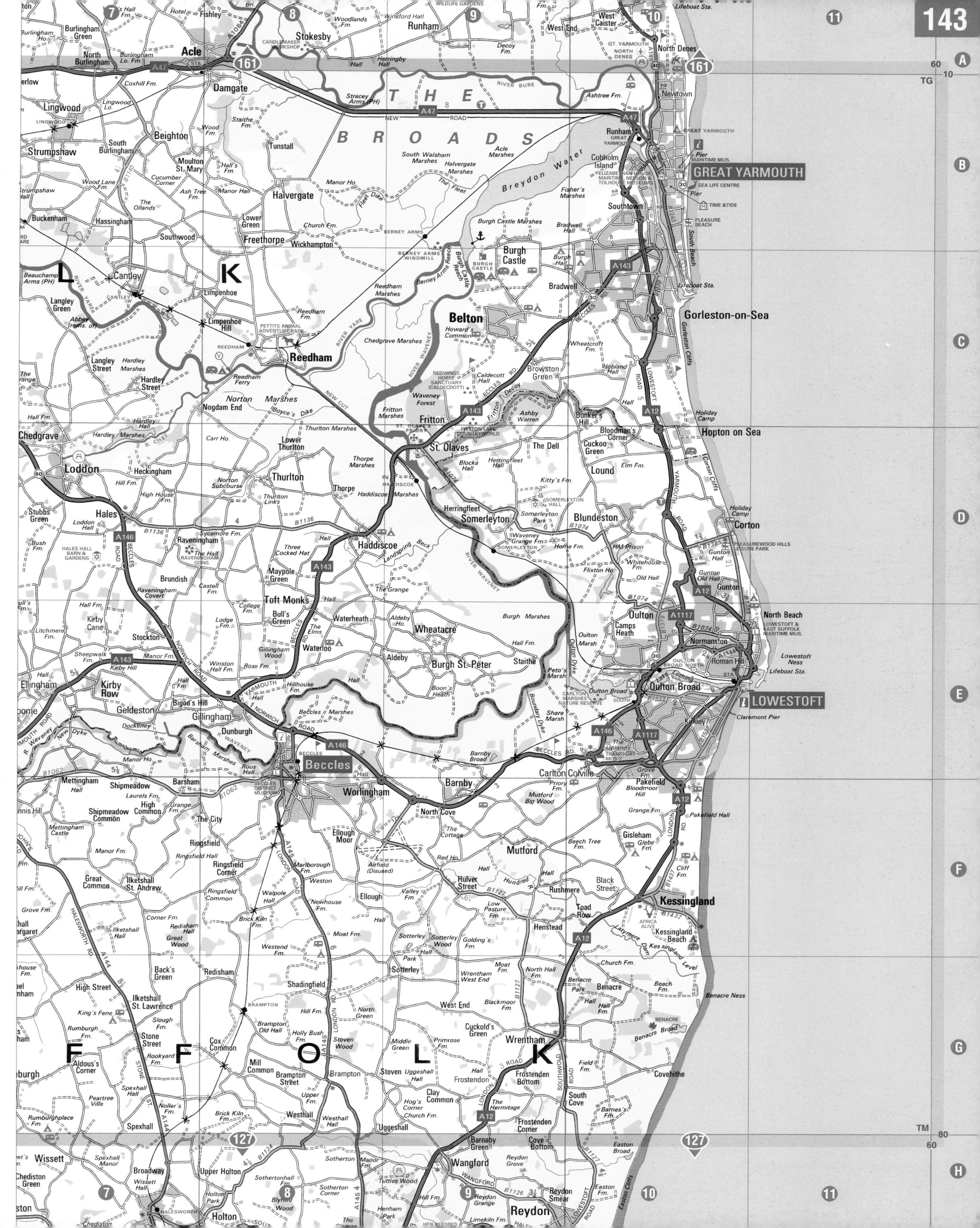

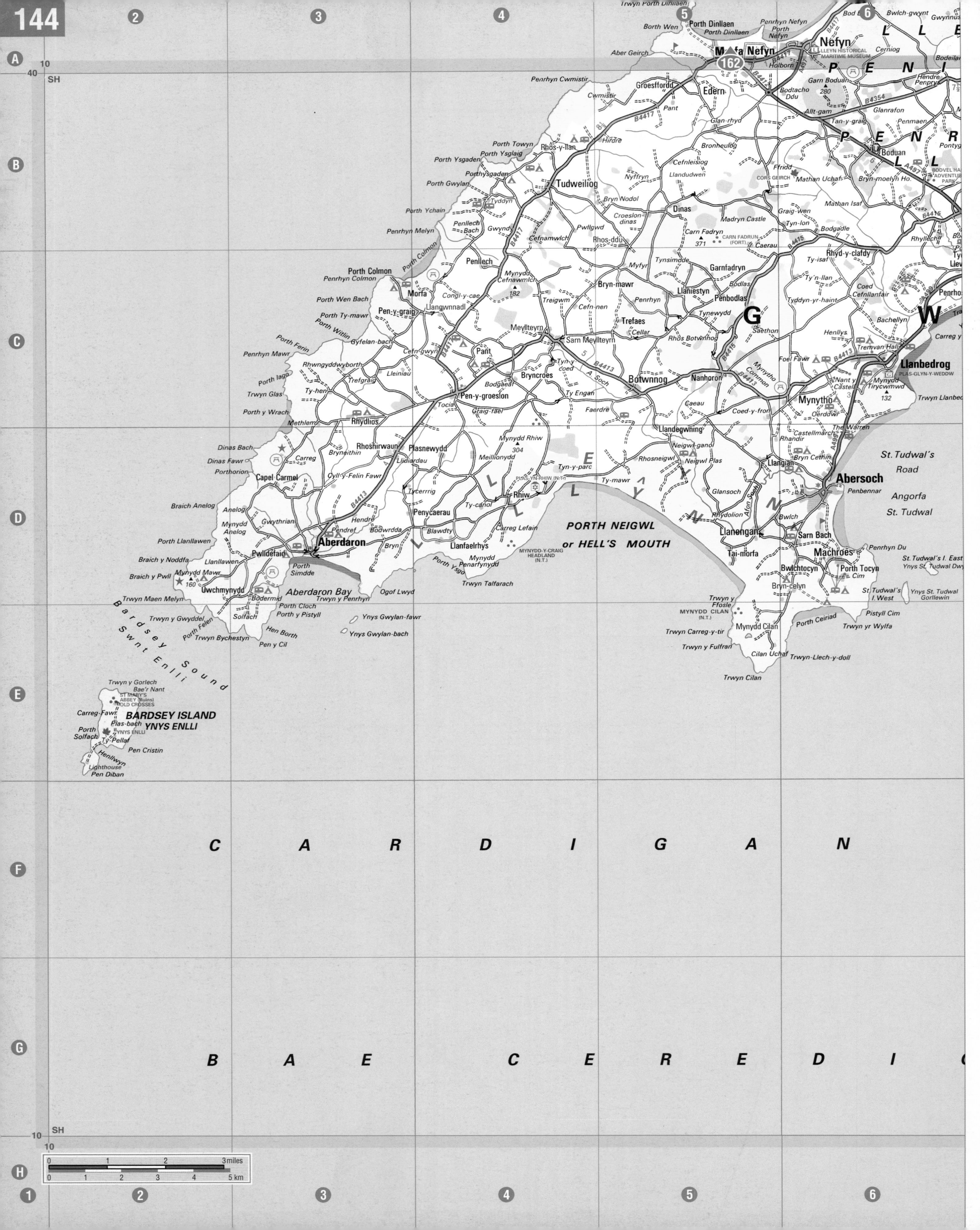

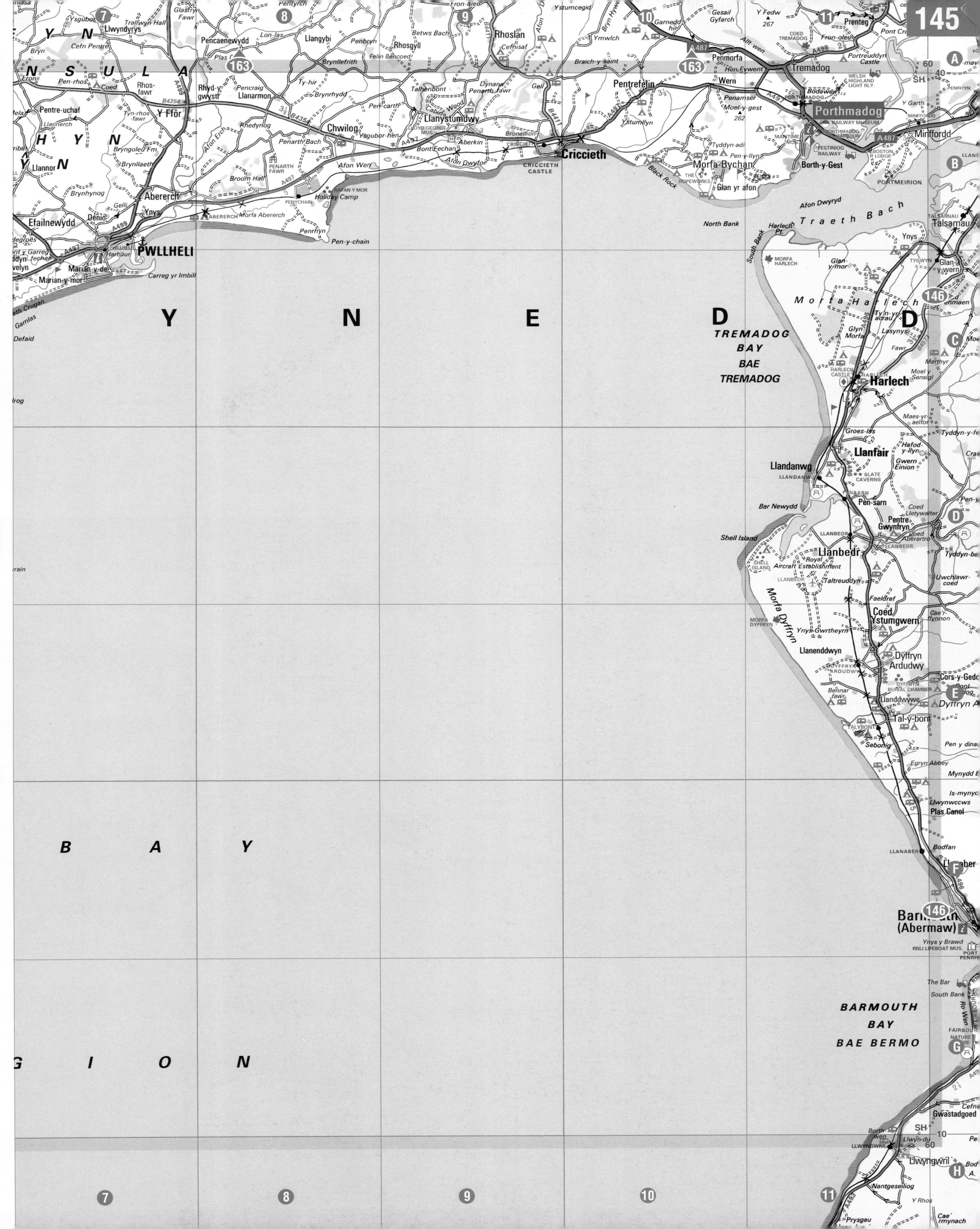

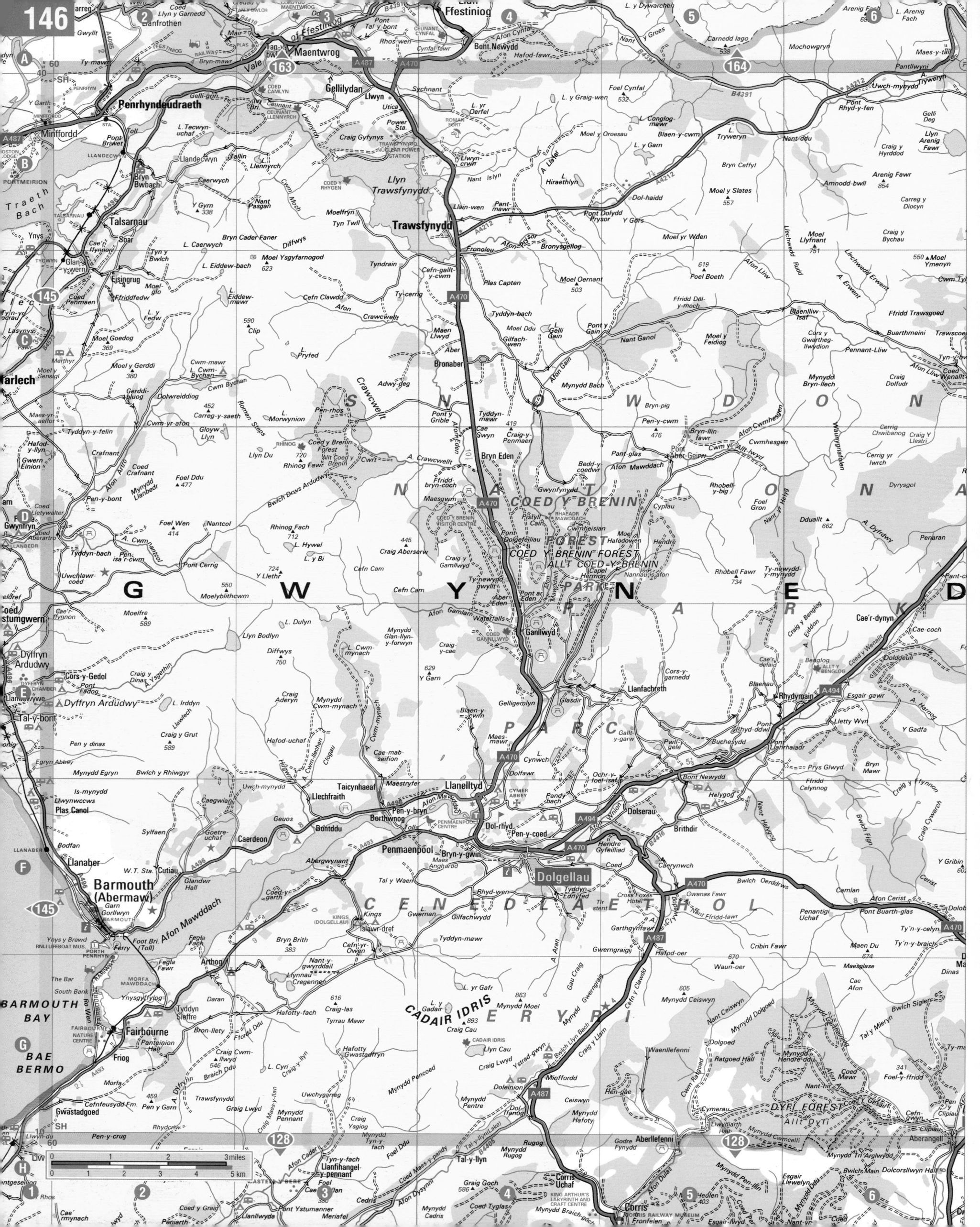

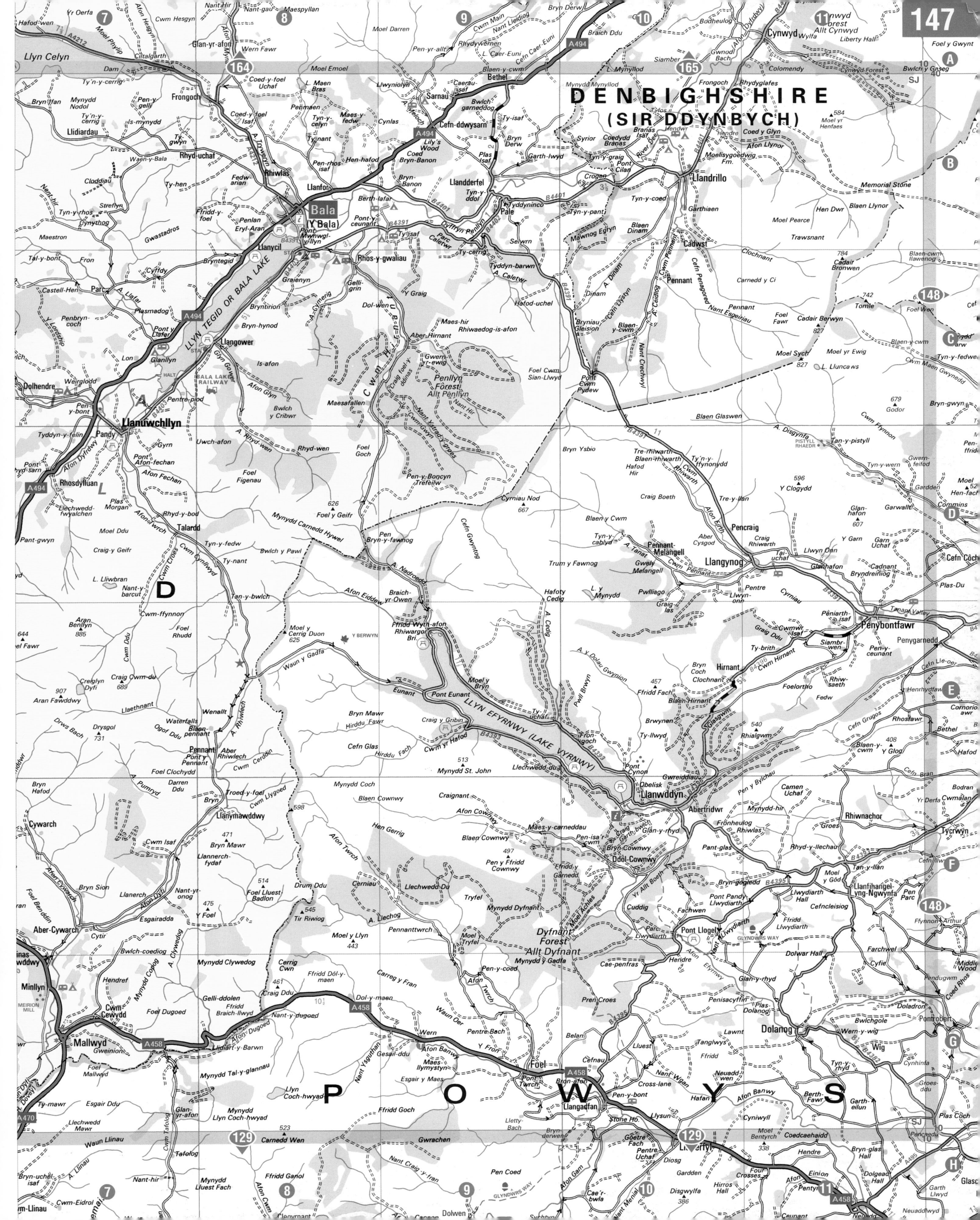

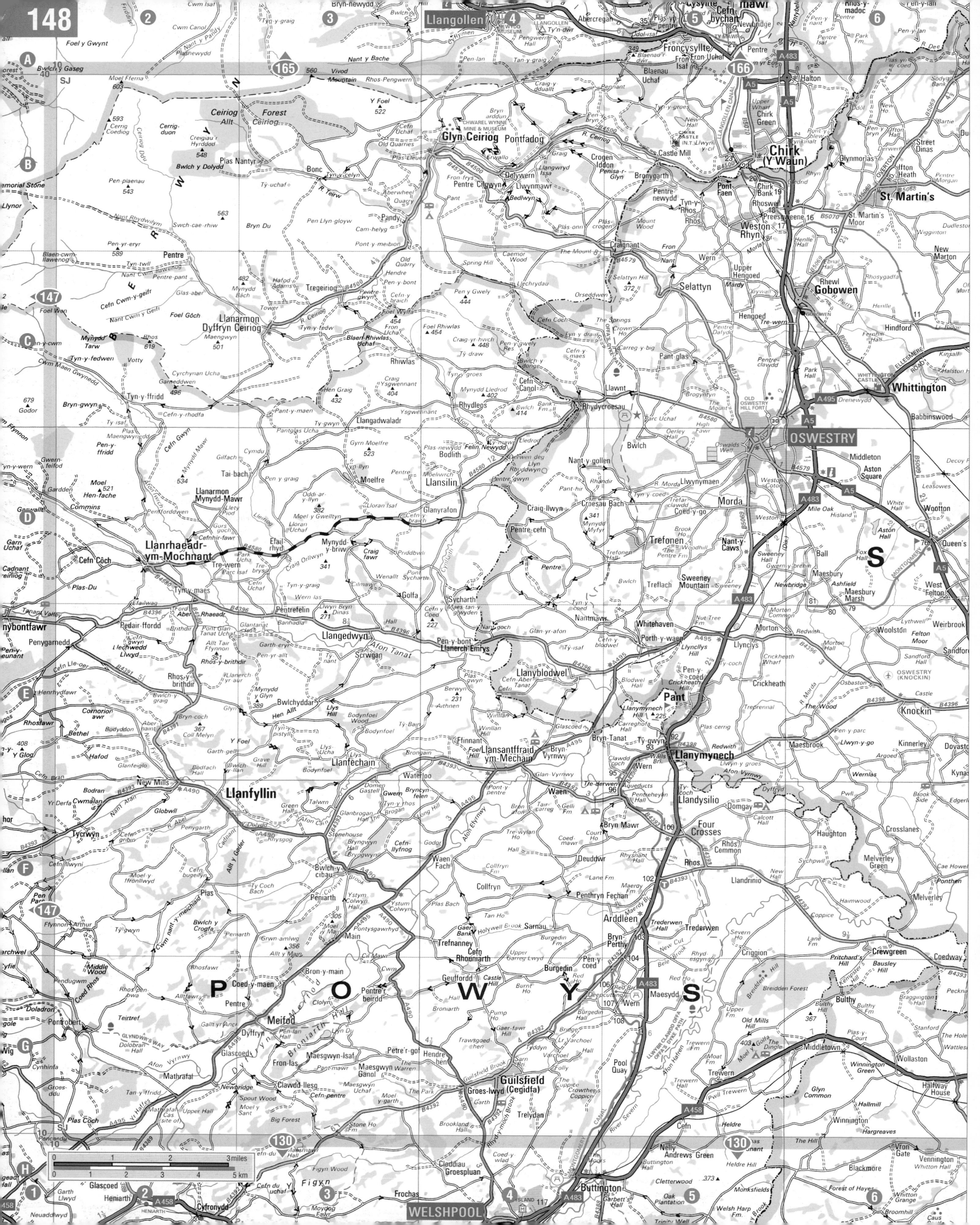

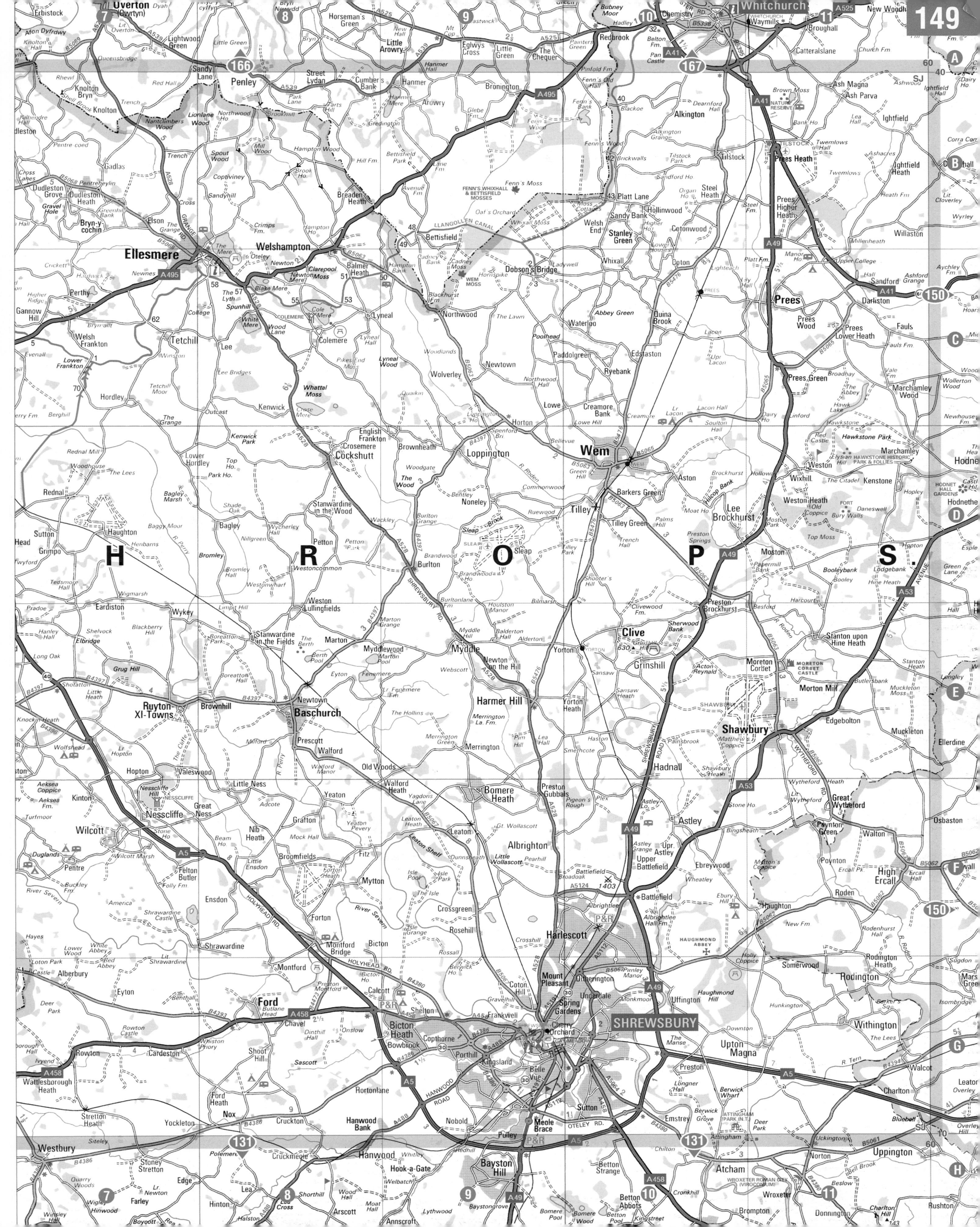

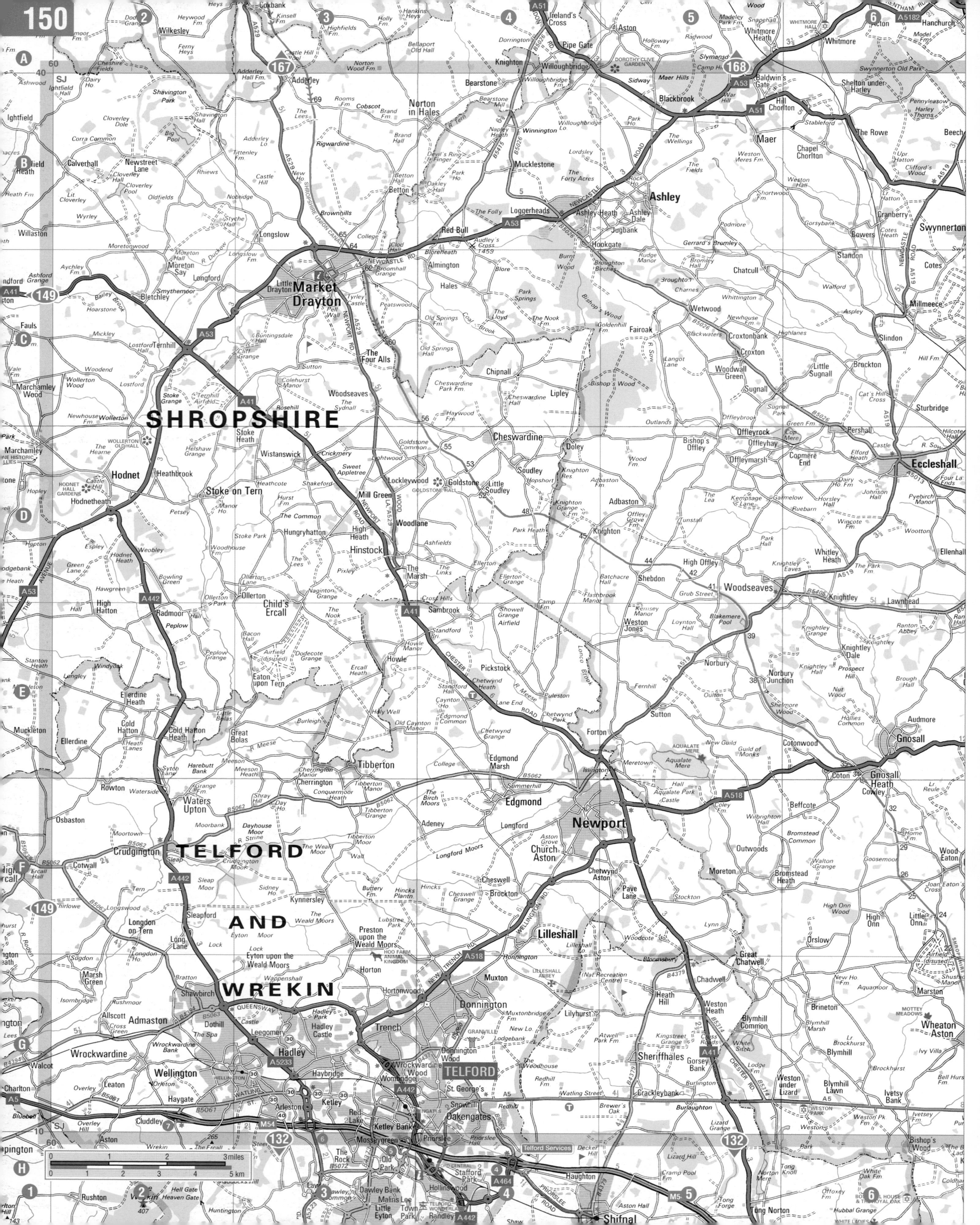

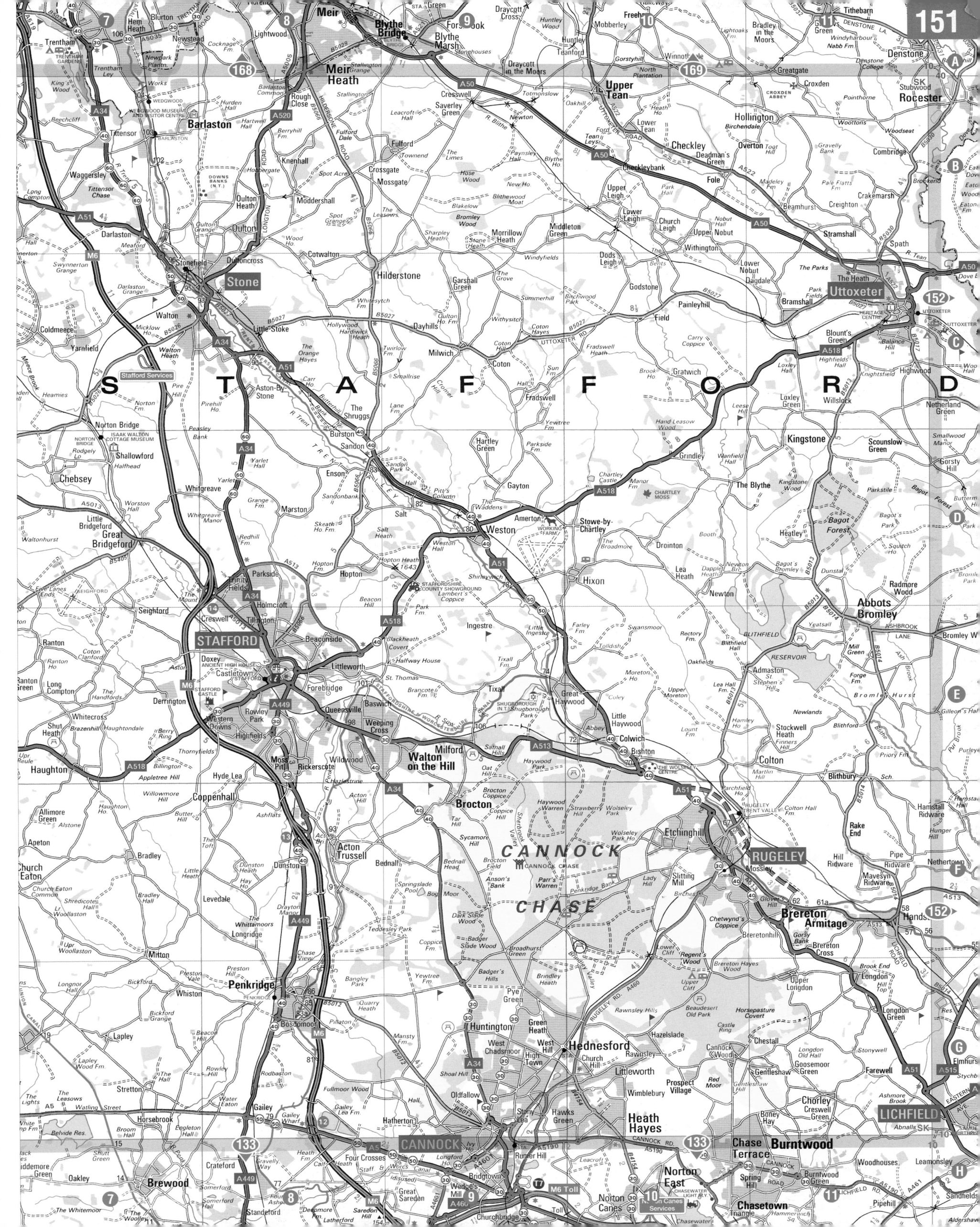

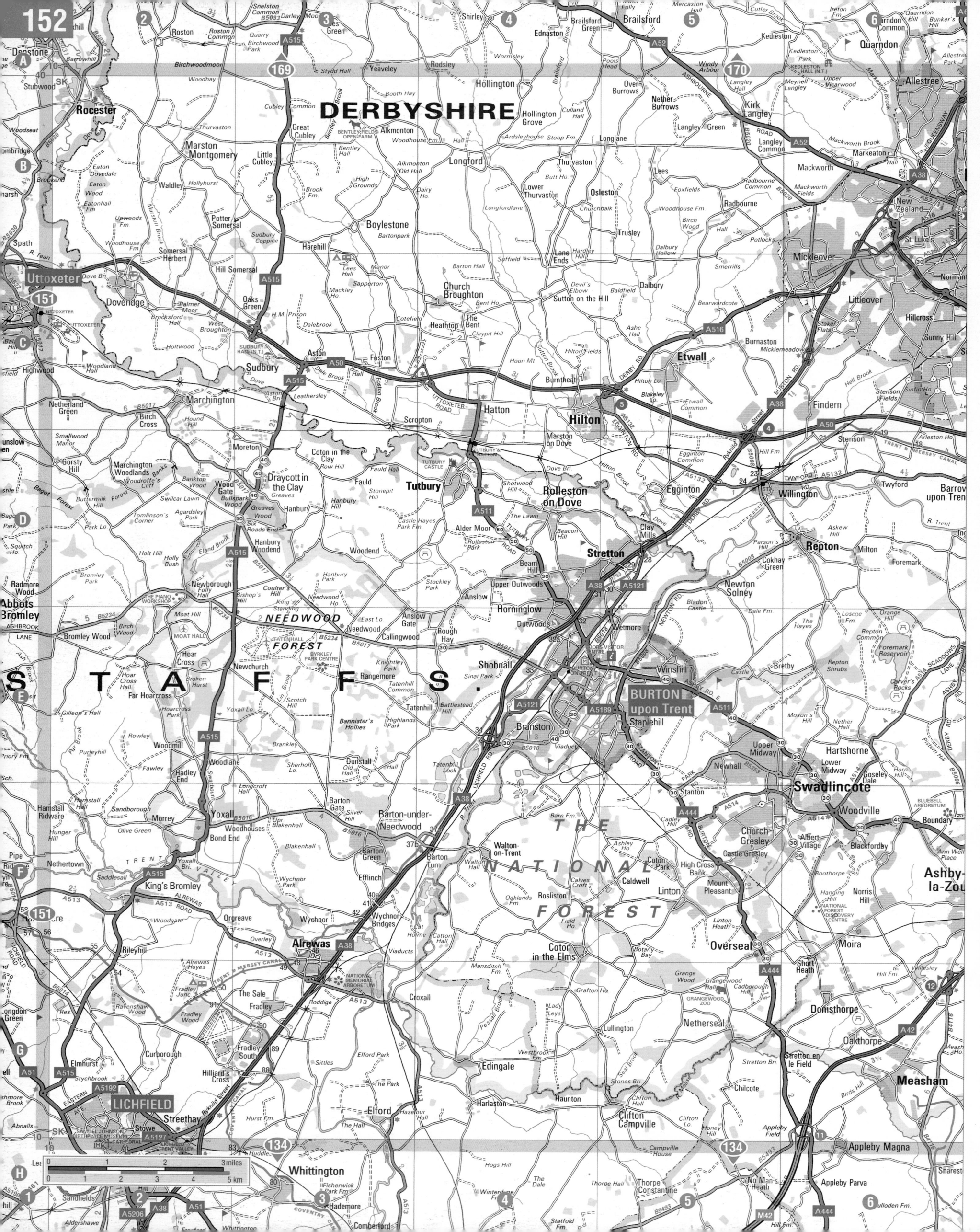

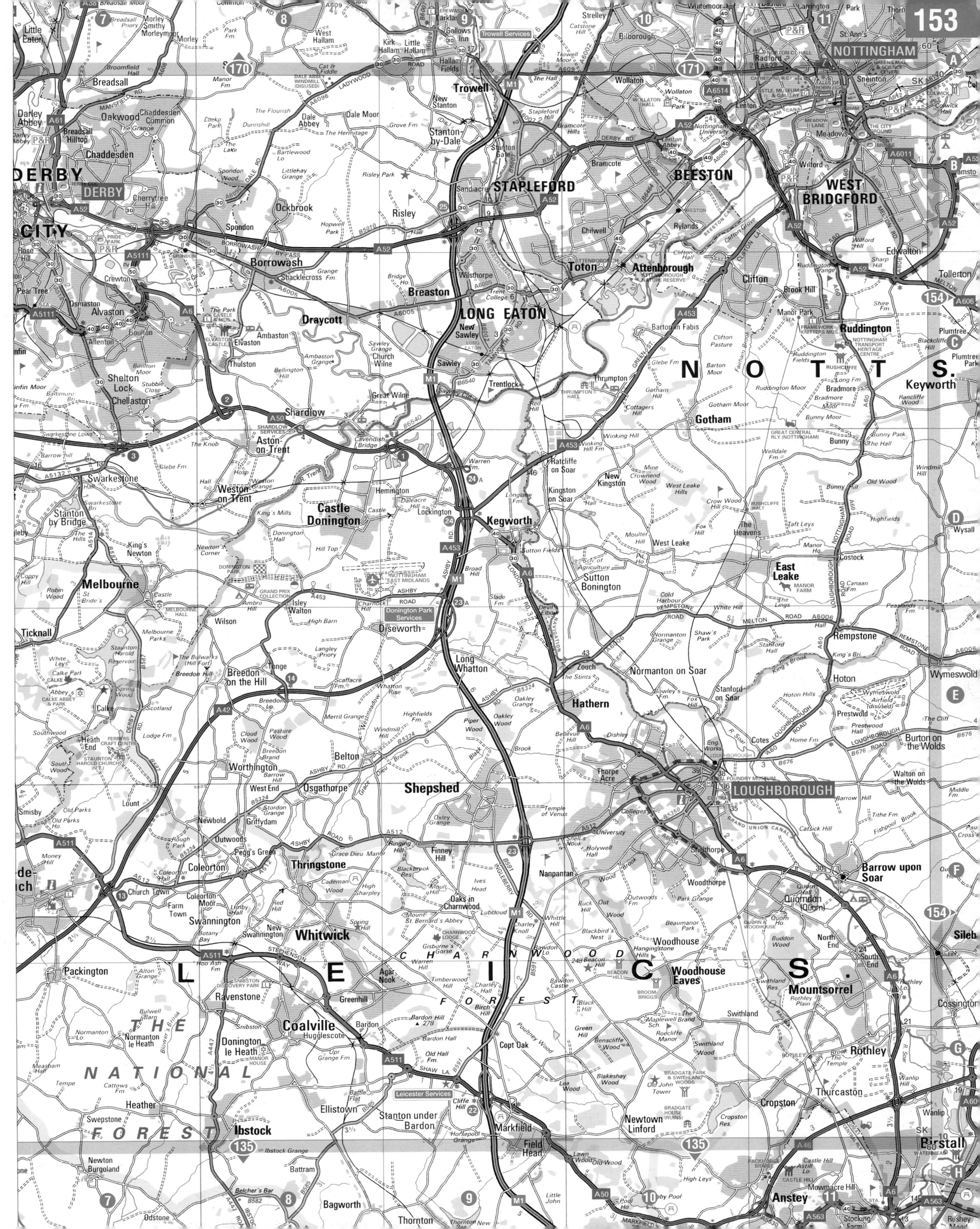

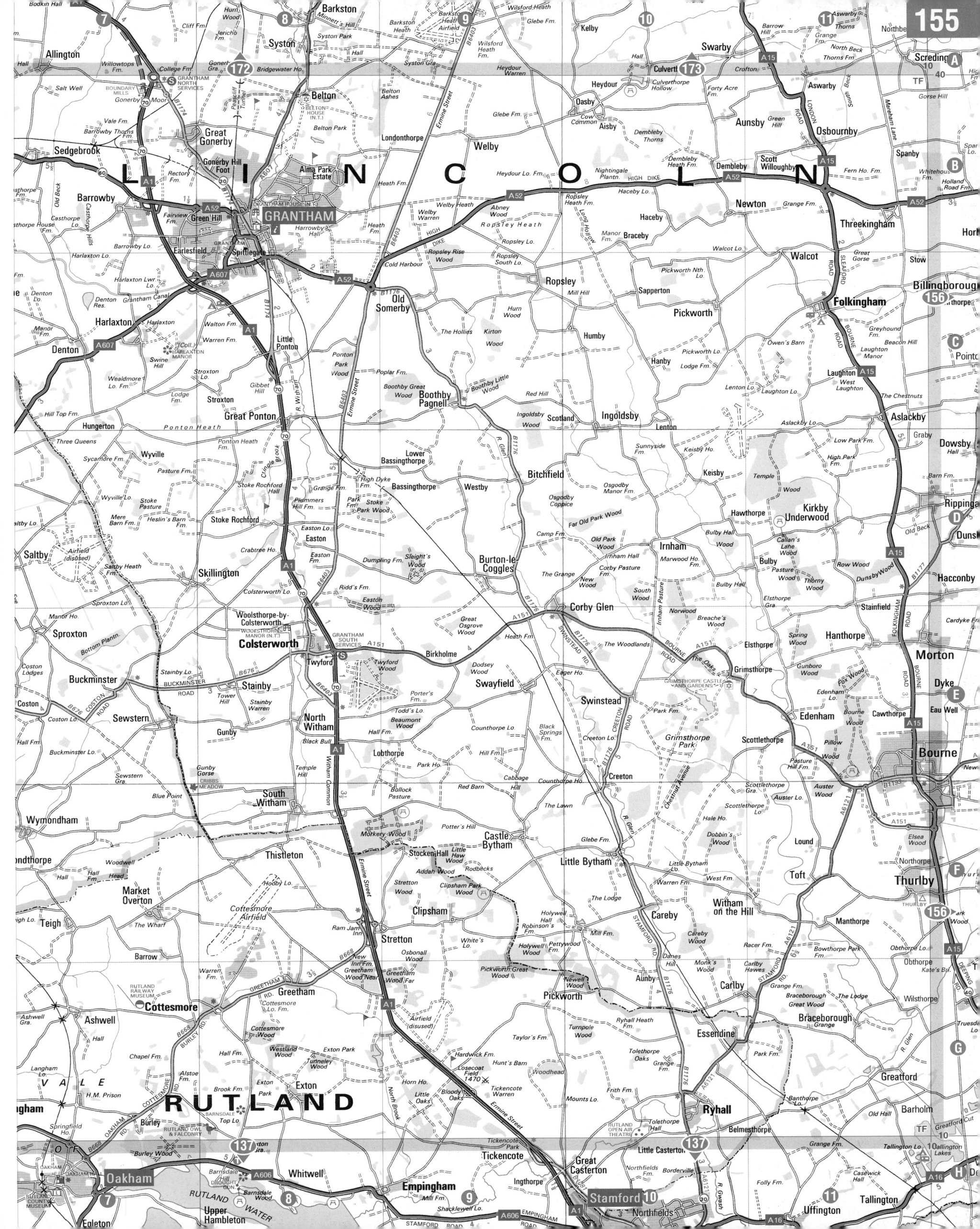

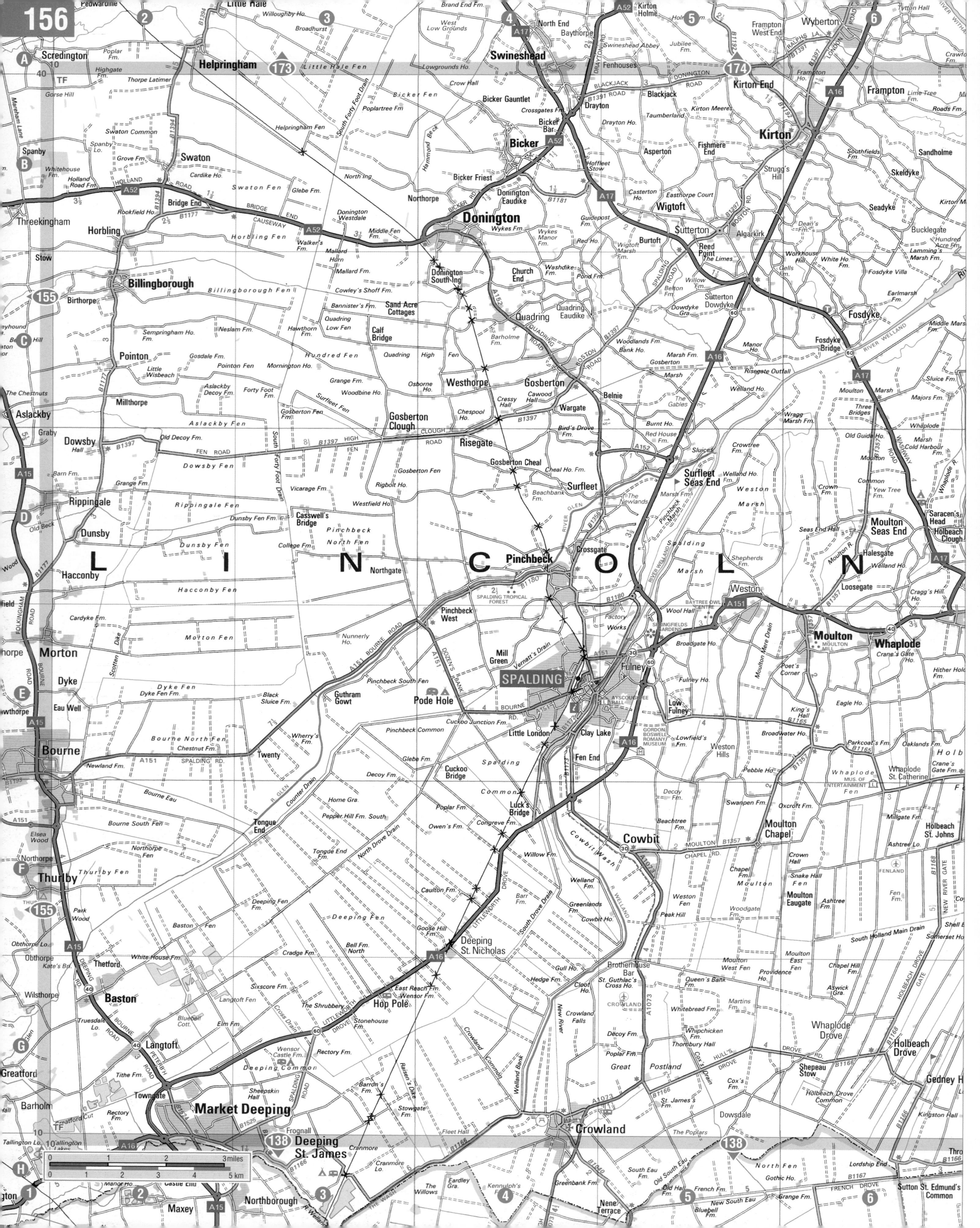

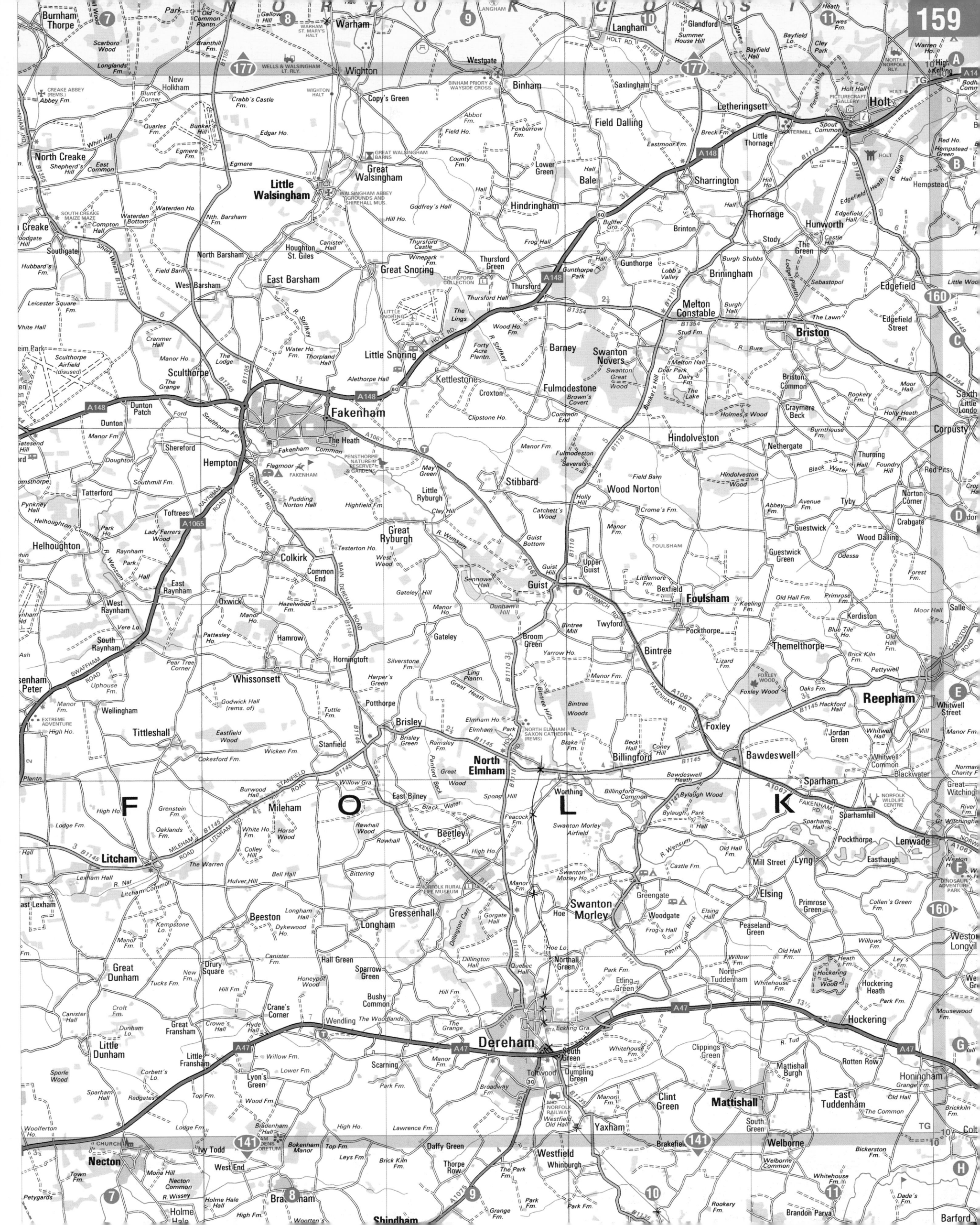

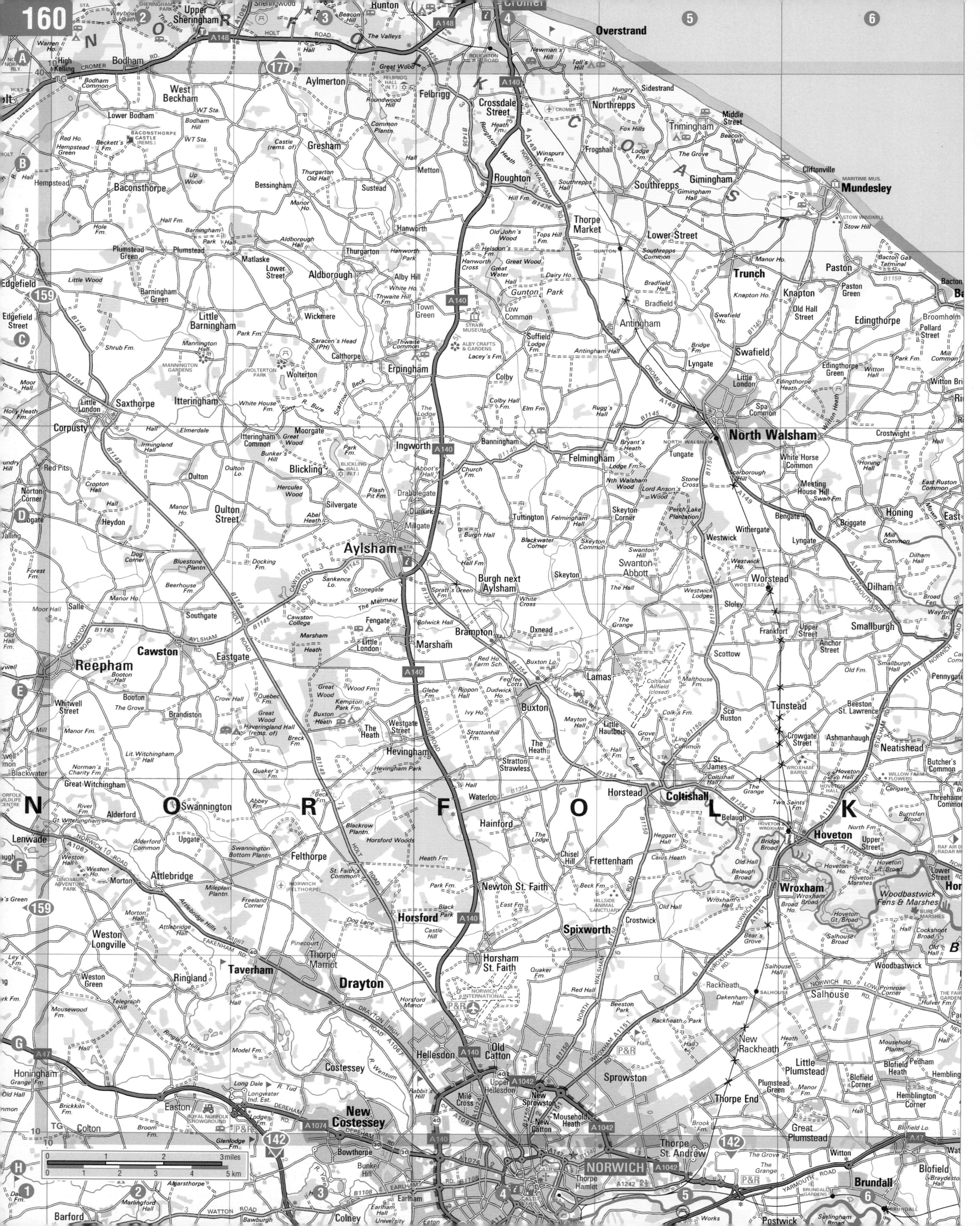

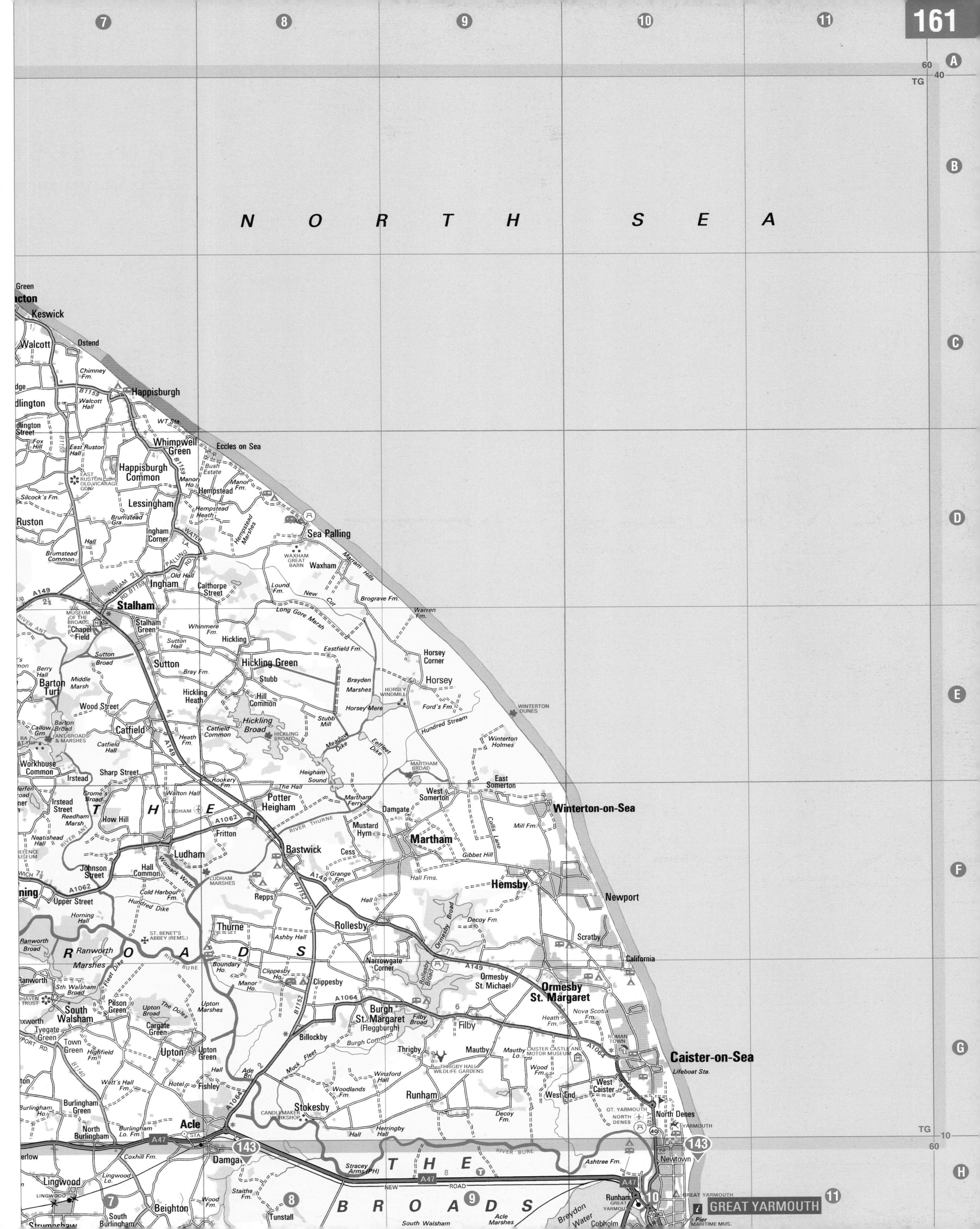

N O R T H   S E A

THE BROADS

GREAT YARMOUTH

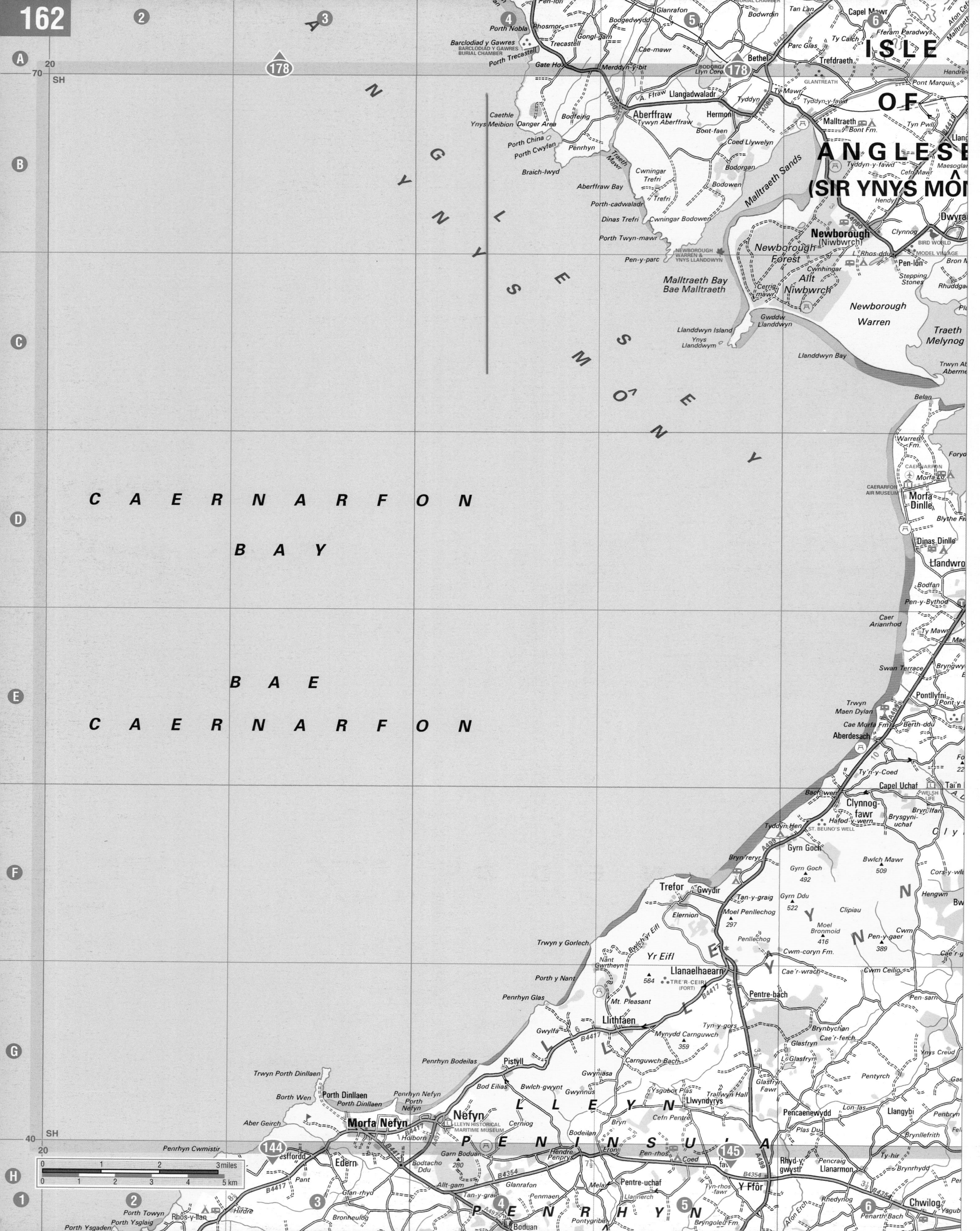

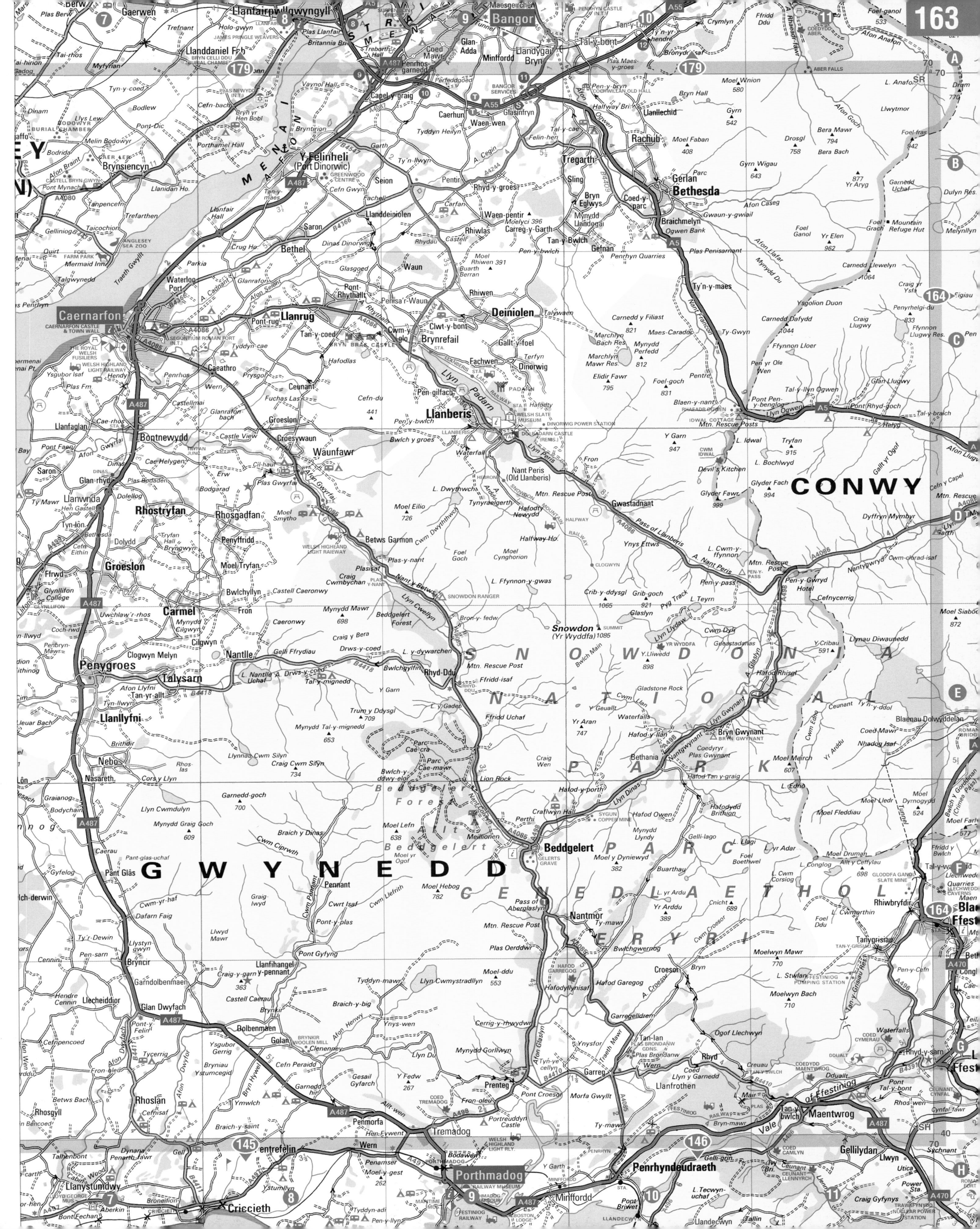

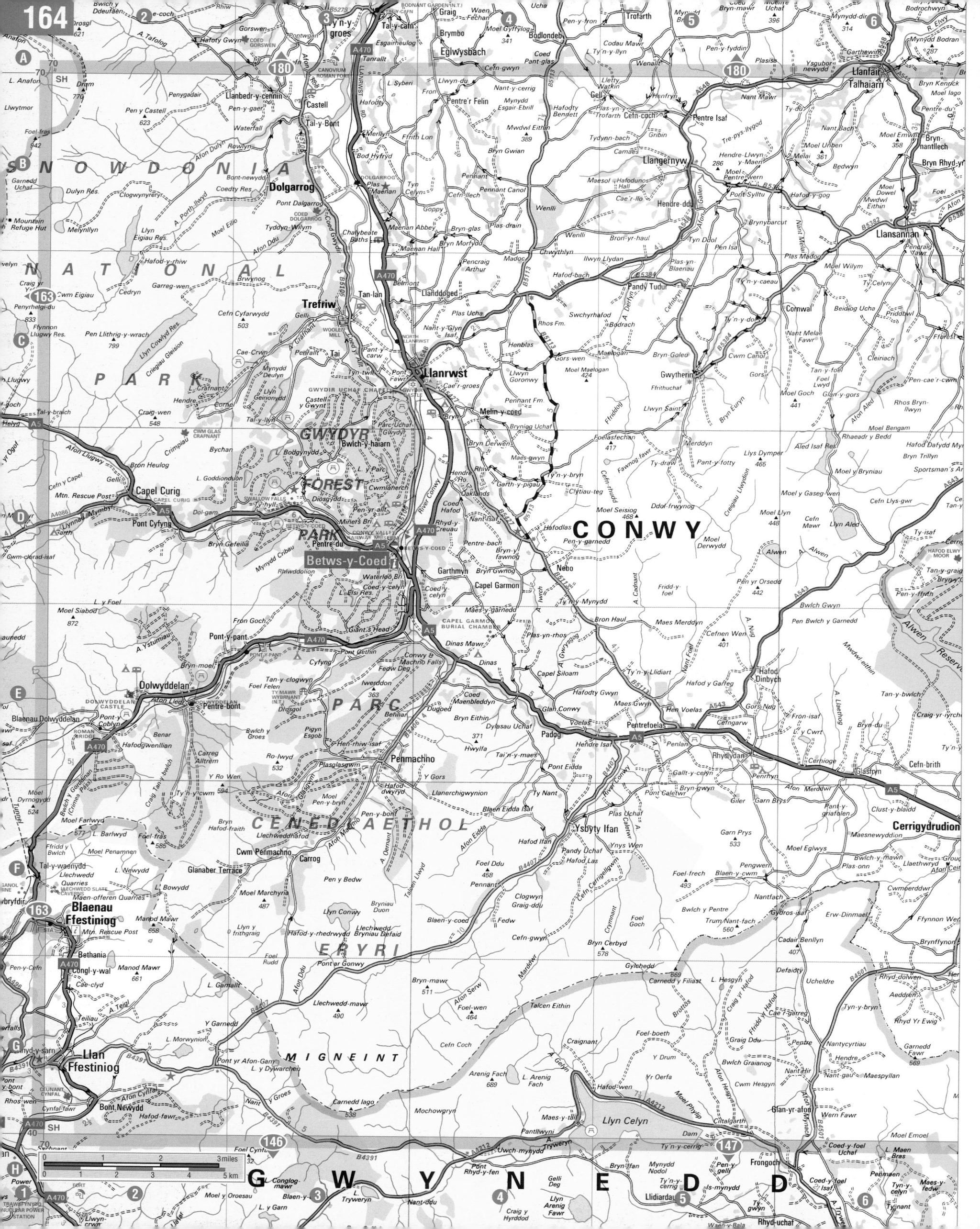

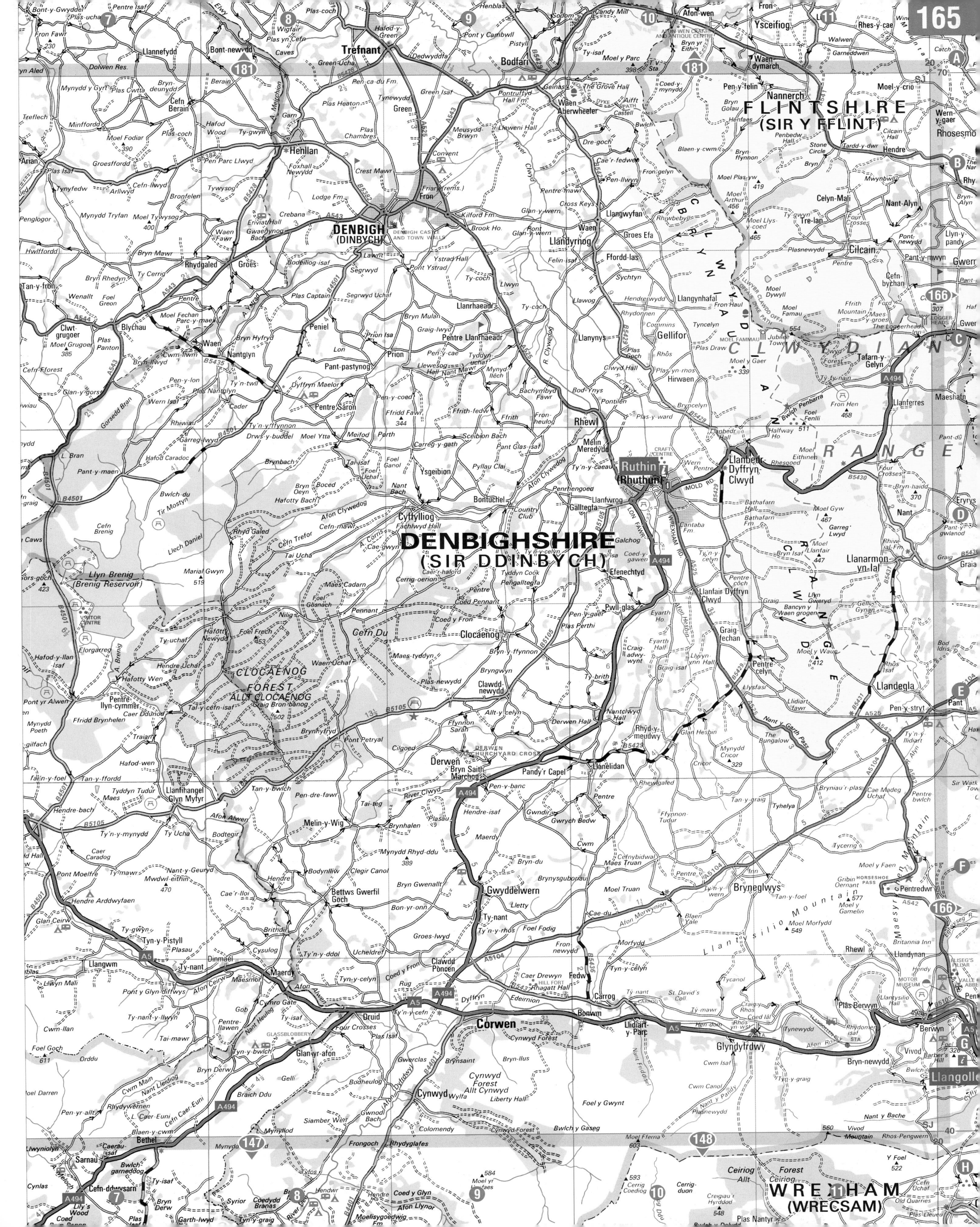

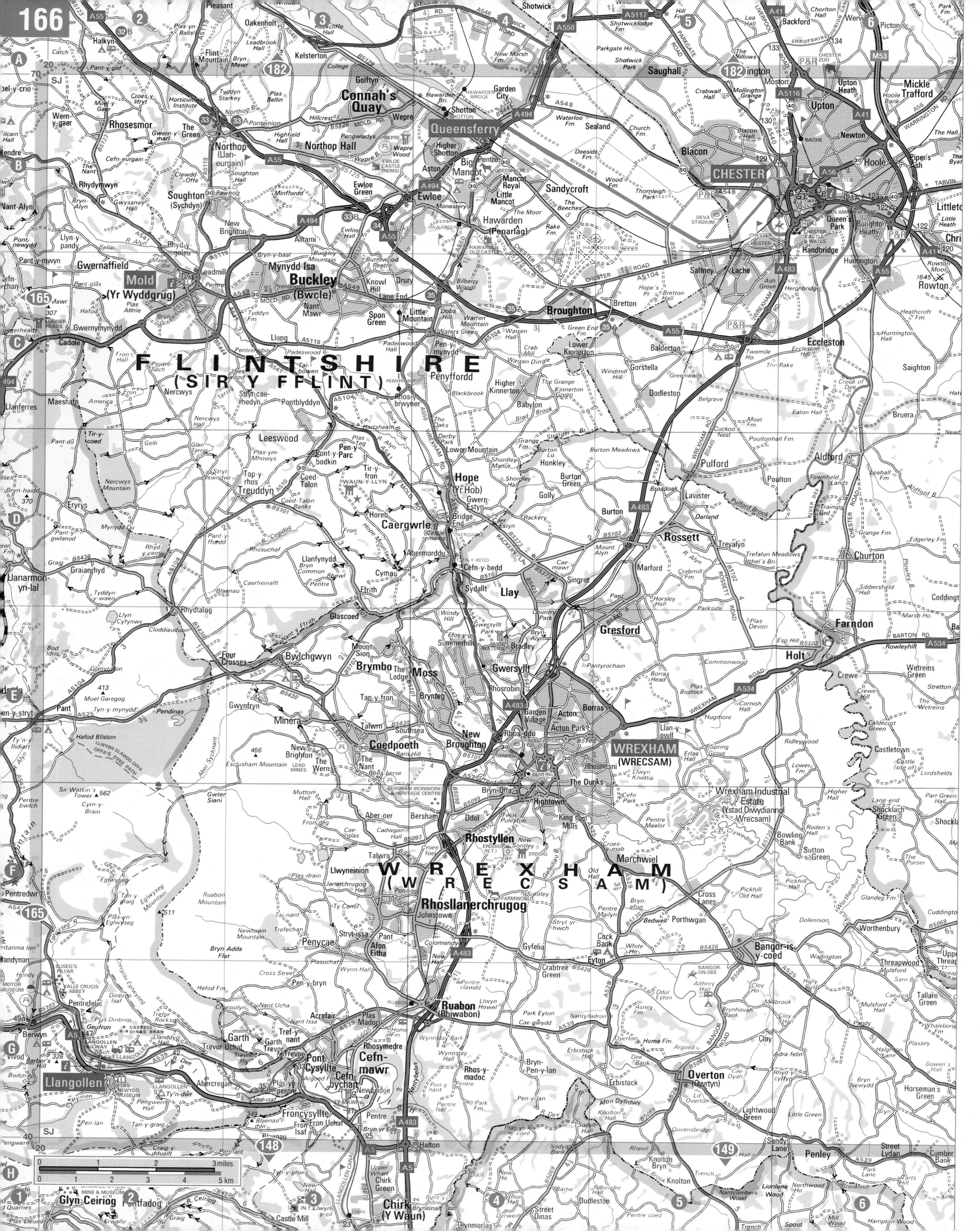

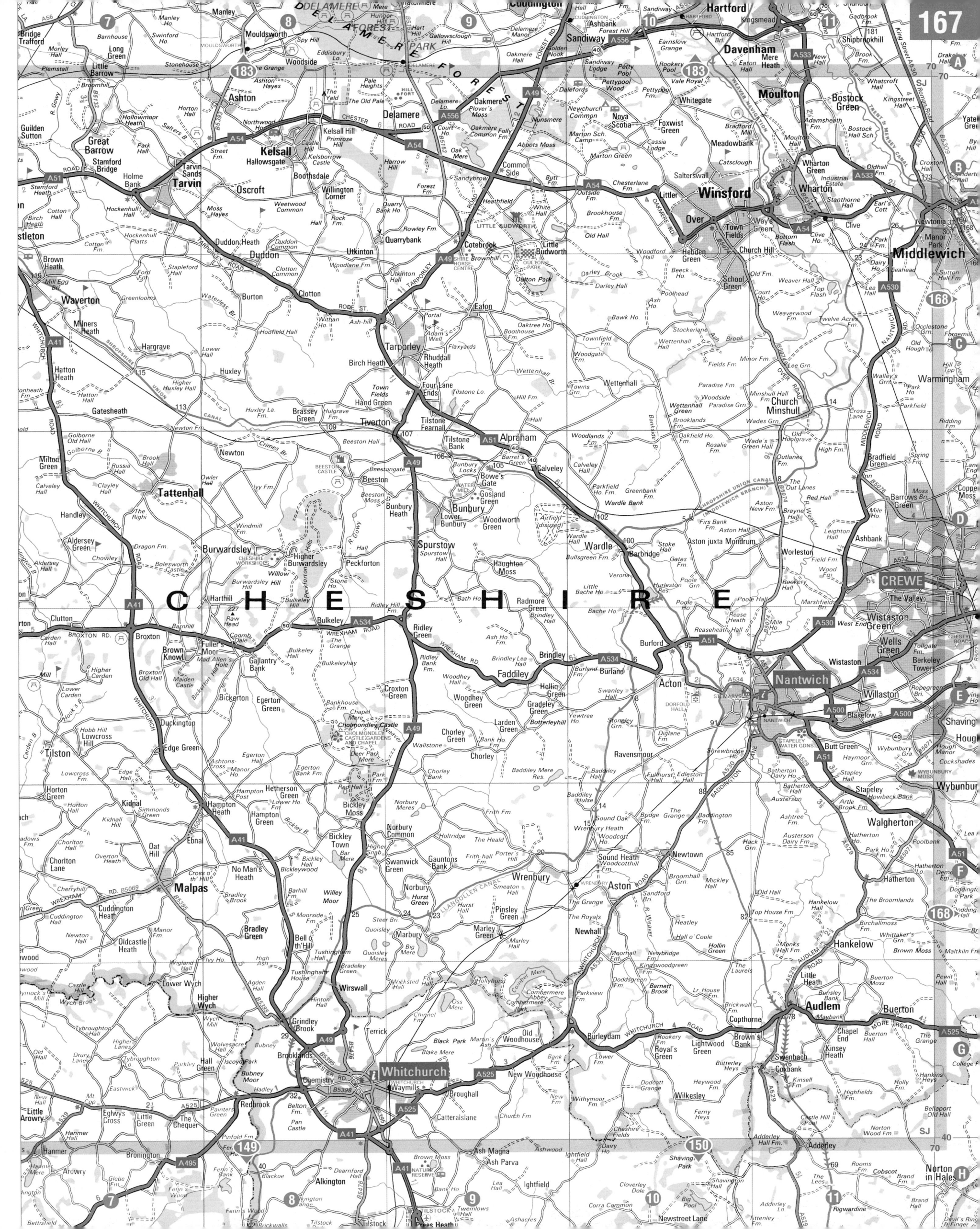

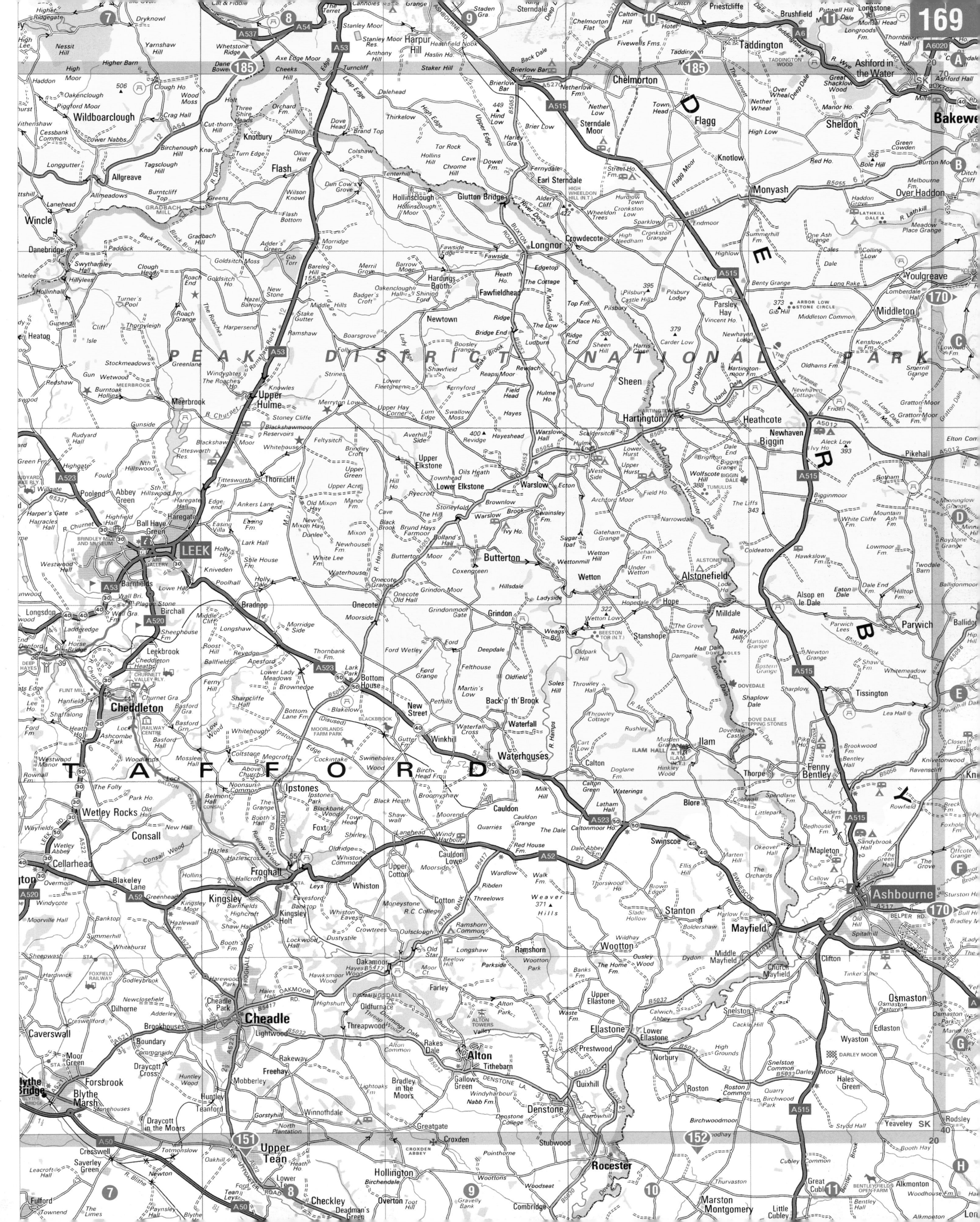

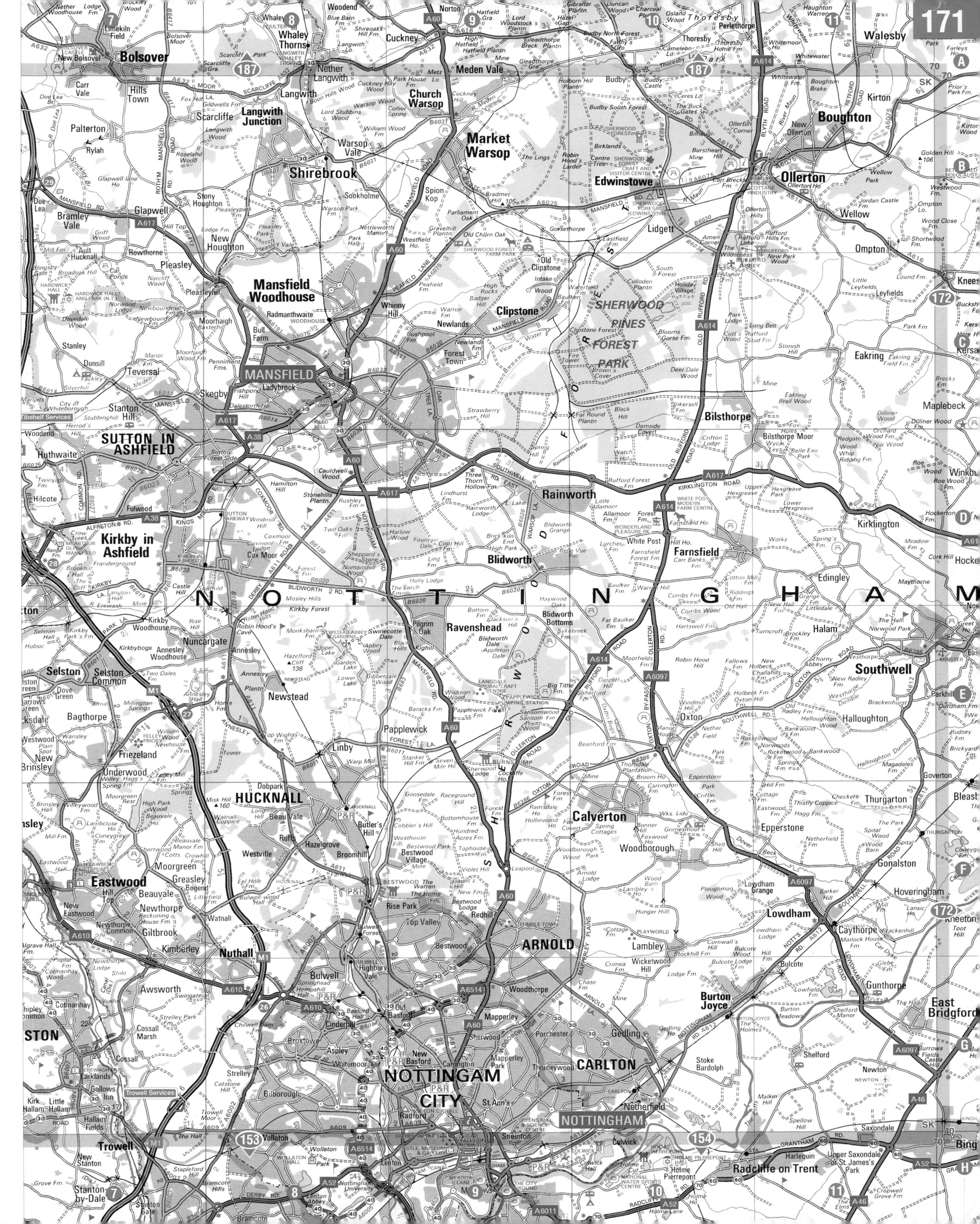

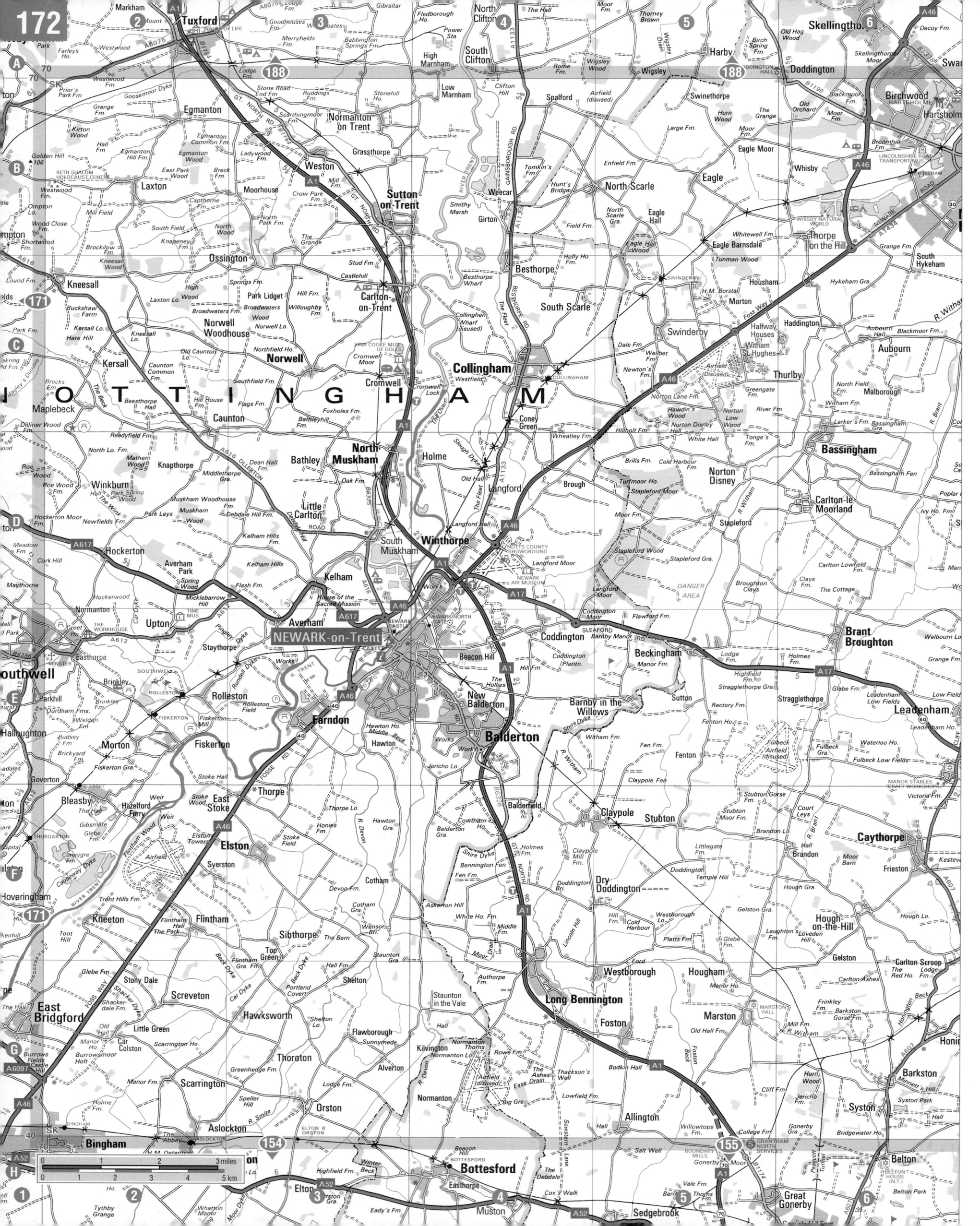

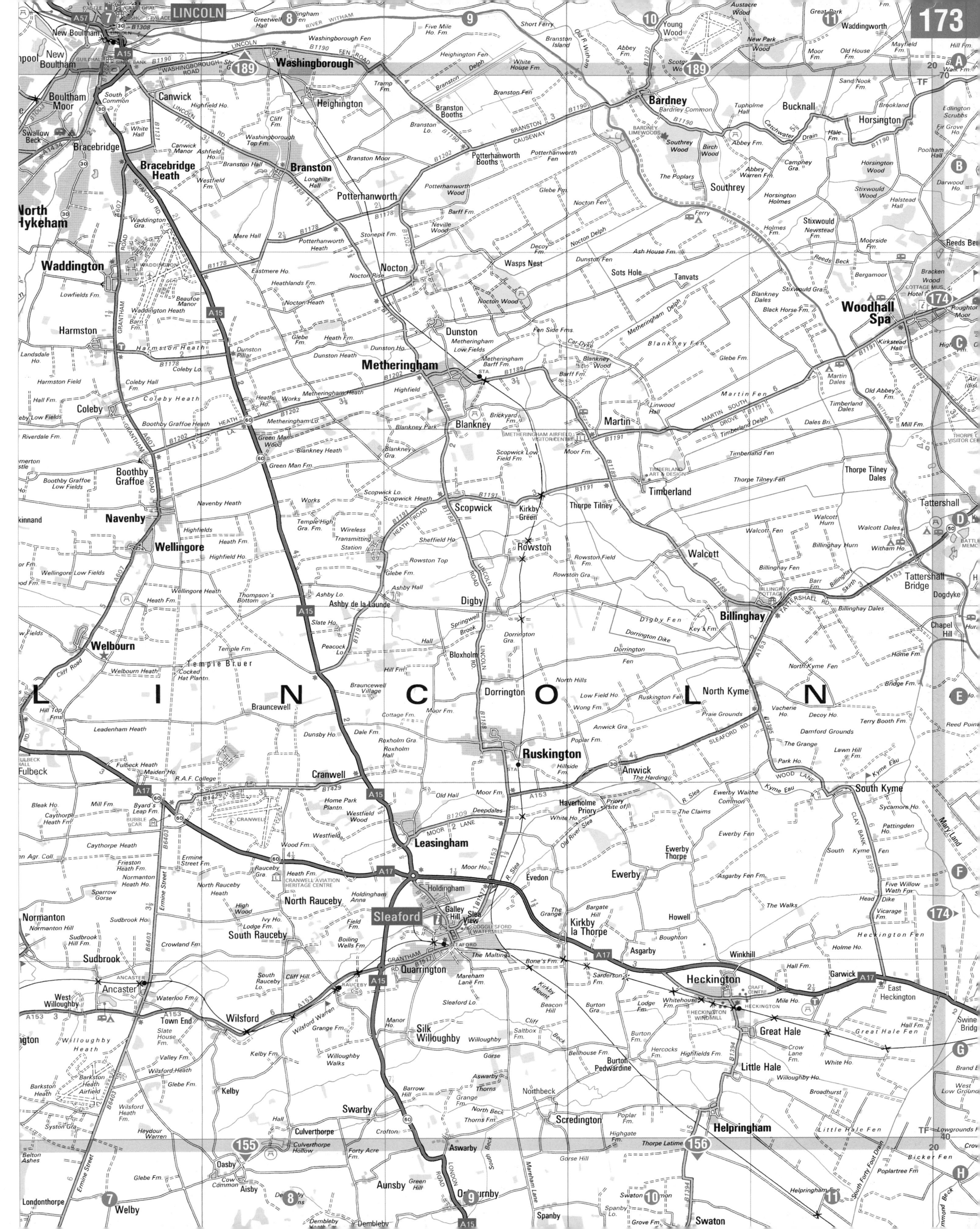

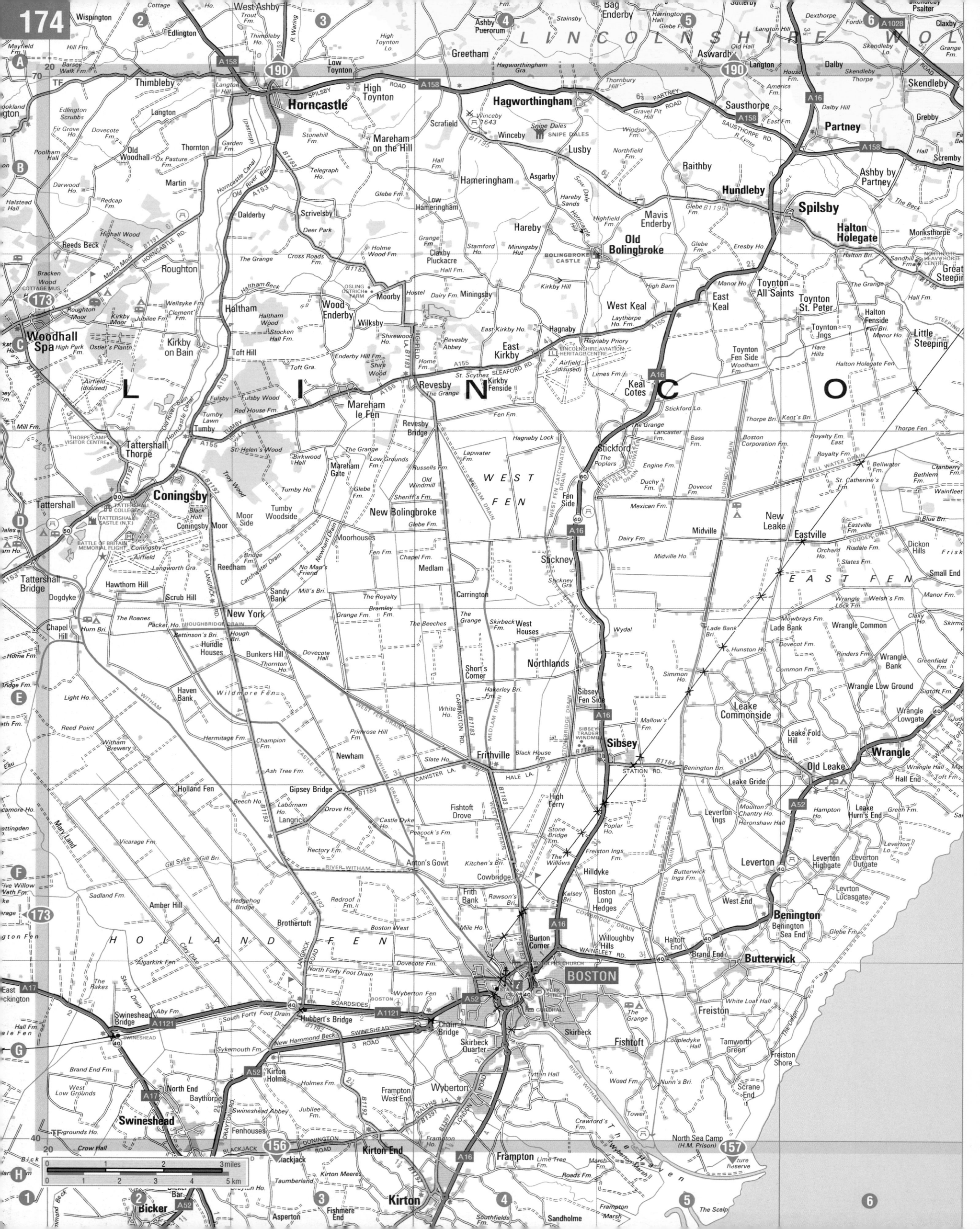

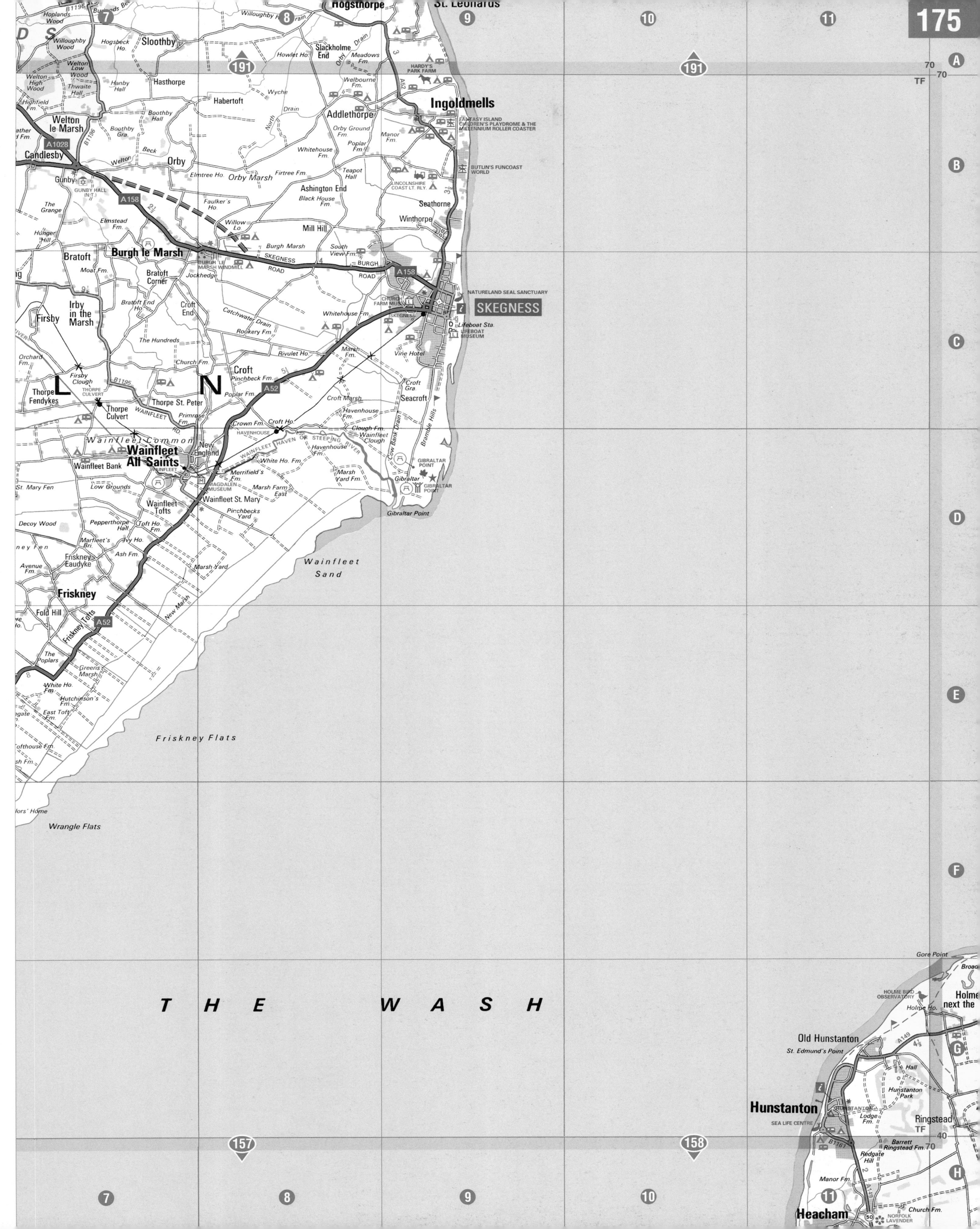

THE WASH

SKEGNESS

Ingoldmells

Hogsthorpe   St. Leonards

Hunstanton

Old Hunstanton

Heacham

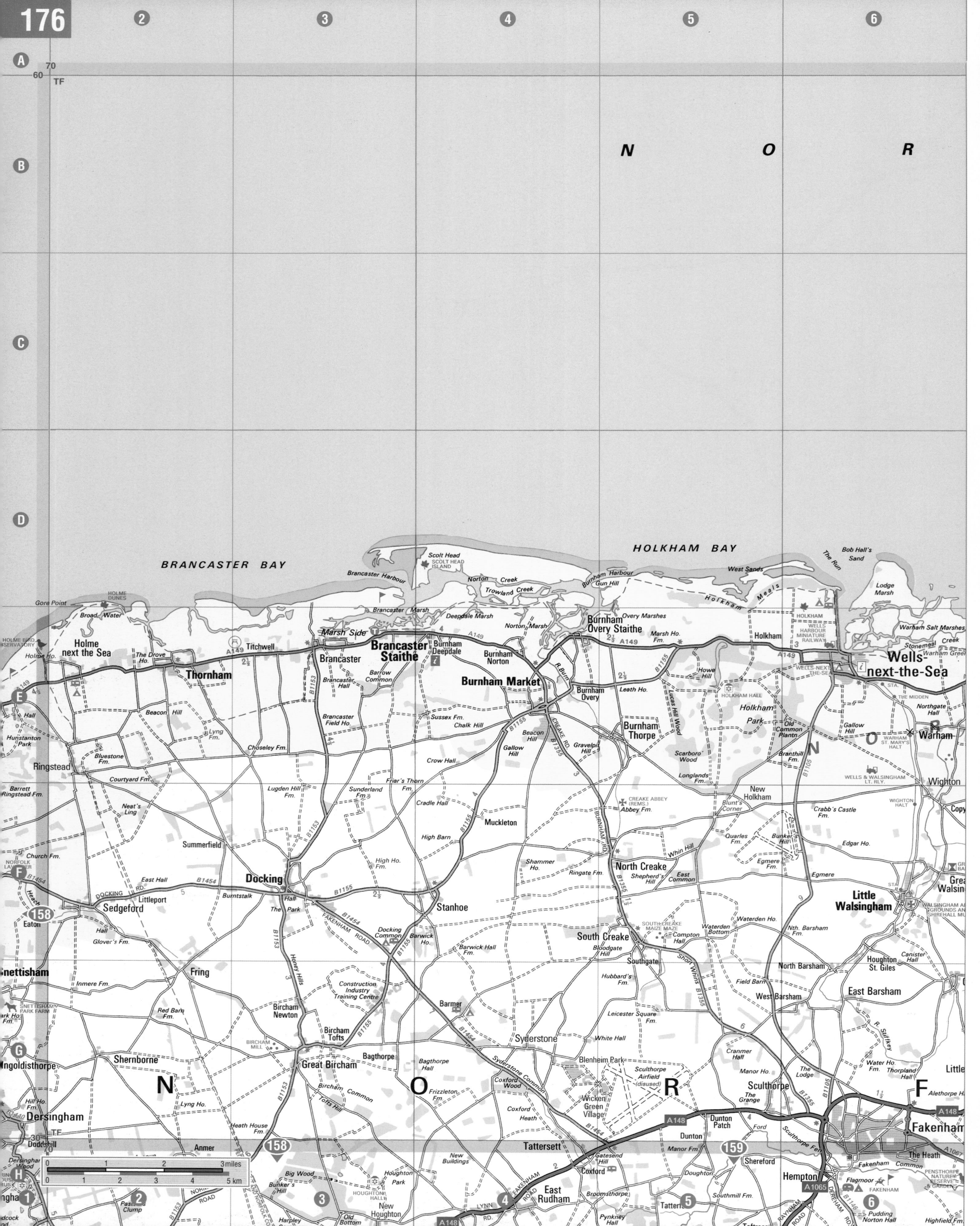

NORTH SEA

Blakeney Point

Cabbage Creek

Blakeney Harbour

BLAKENEY

Stiffkey Salt Marshes

Morston Salt Marshes

Agar Creek

Blakeney Eye

Cley Eye
Bird Sanctuary

Fresh Marshes
CLEY MILL

PEDDARS WAY AND NORFOLK COAST PATH

COAST RD.

Warborough Hill

Camping Hill

Stiffkey Greens

Morston

Greencroft

BLAKENEY
GUILDHALL

A149

Cley next
the Sea

Salthouse

MUCKLEBURGH
COLLECTION

Sheringham

NORFOLK
SHIRE
HORSE CENTRE

Stiffkey

R. Stiffkey

Warborough
Hill

Cockthorpe

Langham

Blakeney

Wiveton

Newgate

Bard Hill

Warborough
Hill

Muckleburgh
Hill

Weybourne

NORTH NORFOLK
RAILWAY

A149

Sheringham
Priory

West Runton

WEST
RUNTON

East
Runton

Cromer

Muck
Hill

F O L K   C O

Sparrow
Hill

The Downs

B1156

Glandford

Gravelpit
Hill

Salthouse
Heath

Kelling

Telegraph
Hill

Lowes
Fm.

Kelling Heath

WEYBOURNE

HALT

Weybourne
Heath

The Dales

Sheringham
Hall

SHERINGHAM

Sheringwood

A1082

A149

Beeston
Regis

Row
Heath

Beacon
Hill

WEST
RUNTON

Muck
Hill

E

A148

Westgate

Summer
House Hill

Bayfield
Lo.

Cley
Park

Holt Hall

High
Kelling

CROMER

Bodham

RD.

The Valleys

B1436

BINHAM PRIORY &
WAYSIDE CROSS

Binham

Saxlingham

HOLT RD.

Bayfield
Hall

Warren's
Ho.

Bodham
Common

Lower Bodham

Bodham
Hill

West
Beckham

East
Beckham

WT Sta.

Aylmerton

Roundwood
Hill

FELBRIGG
HALL
(N.T.)

Great Wood

Felbrigg

Metton

Letheringsett

PICTURECRAFT
GALLERY

Holt

Spout
Common

WATERMILL

Red Ho.

Hempstead
Green

Beckett's
Fm.

WT Sta.

Castle
(rems. of)

Gresham

Common
Plantn.

Field Dalling

Abbot
Fm.

Field Ho.

Foxburrow
Fm.

Breck Fm.

Little
Thornage

B1110

HOLT

Baconsthorpe
CASTLE
(REMS.)

Hempstead

Up
Wood

Baconsthorpe

Thurgarton
Old Hall

Bessingham

Sustead

County
Fm.

Eastmoor Fm.

A148

Hall
Ho.

Hall

Edgefield Heath

R. Glaven

Hole
Fm.

Plumstead
Green

Plumstead

Hall Fm.

Manor
Ho.

Thurgarton

160

Lower
Green

Bale

Sharrington

Hill
Ho.

Thornage

Hunworth

Stody

Edgefield
Heath

Little Wood

Matlaske

Lower
Street

Gresham

Hanworth

Bullfer
Gro.

Brinton

The
Green

Hall

Barningham
Park

Hall

Aldborough
Hall

Hanworth
Park

Hindringham

Hall

Frog Hall

Gunthorpe

Burgh Stubbs

Castle
Hill

Lodge Plantn.

Sebastopol

Edgefield

Plumstead
Green

Barningham
Green

Aldborough

Alby Hill

White Ho.

A140

Thursford
Castle

Winepark
Fm.

Thursford
Green

Thursford
Collection

Gunthorpe
Park

Lobb's
Valley

Briningham

Burgh
Hall

Edgefield
Street

B1149

Little
Barningham

Wickmere

Thwaite Hill

Town
Green

Great Snoring

Thursford

Thursford Hall

A148

B1354

2½

Melton
Constable

B1354
Stud Fm.

The Lawn

Little Wood

Mannington
Hall

Saracen's Head
(PH)

Thwaite
Common

Erpingham

LITTLE
SNORING

The
Lings

Wood Ho.
Fm.

Melton Hall

Deer Park

R. Bure

Moor
Fm.

MANNINGTON
GARDENS

WOLTERTON
PARK

Wolterton

Barney

Swanton
Novers

Briston

Shrub Fm.

Park Fm.

Snoring

Kettlestone

Forty
Acre Plantn.

Swanton
Great
Wood

Swanton
Great
Wood

Dairy
Fm.

The
Lake

Briston
Common

Craymere
Beck

Edgefield
Street

B1354

Holly Heath
Fm.

Little
London

Saxthorpe

Itteringham

White House
Fm.

R. Bure

Ford

Calthorpe

Thwaite
Common

The
Lodge

Croxton

Fulmodestone

Brown's
Covert

Holmes's Wood

Rookery
Fm.

Park
Fm.

Blickling

BLICKLING
HALL
(N.T.)

Abbot's

HOLT RD.

Clipstone Ho.

Common
End

Burnthouse
Fm.

Corpusty

Moorgate
Fm.

Itteringham
Common

Ingworth

A140

159

Hindolveston

Nethergate

Thurning
Hall

160

Oulton

Great
Wood

Bunker's
Hill

30

May
Green

Manor Fm.

Fulmodeston
Severals

Field Barn
Fm.

Hindolveston
Wood

Black Water

Foundry
Hill

Red Pits

Irmingland
Hall

Hall

Oulton
Lo.

Park
Fm.

Hercules
Wood

Flash
Pit Fm.

Drabblegate

Little
Ryburgh

Clay Hill

Stibbard

Wood Nor.

Holly
Fm.

Catchett's Fm.

Crome's Fm.

Abbey
Fm.

Avenue
Fm.

Tyby

Norton
Corner

Cropton
Hall

Dulton

Manor
Fm.

Oulton
Street

Silvergate

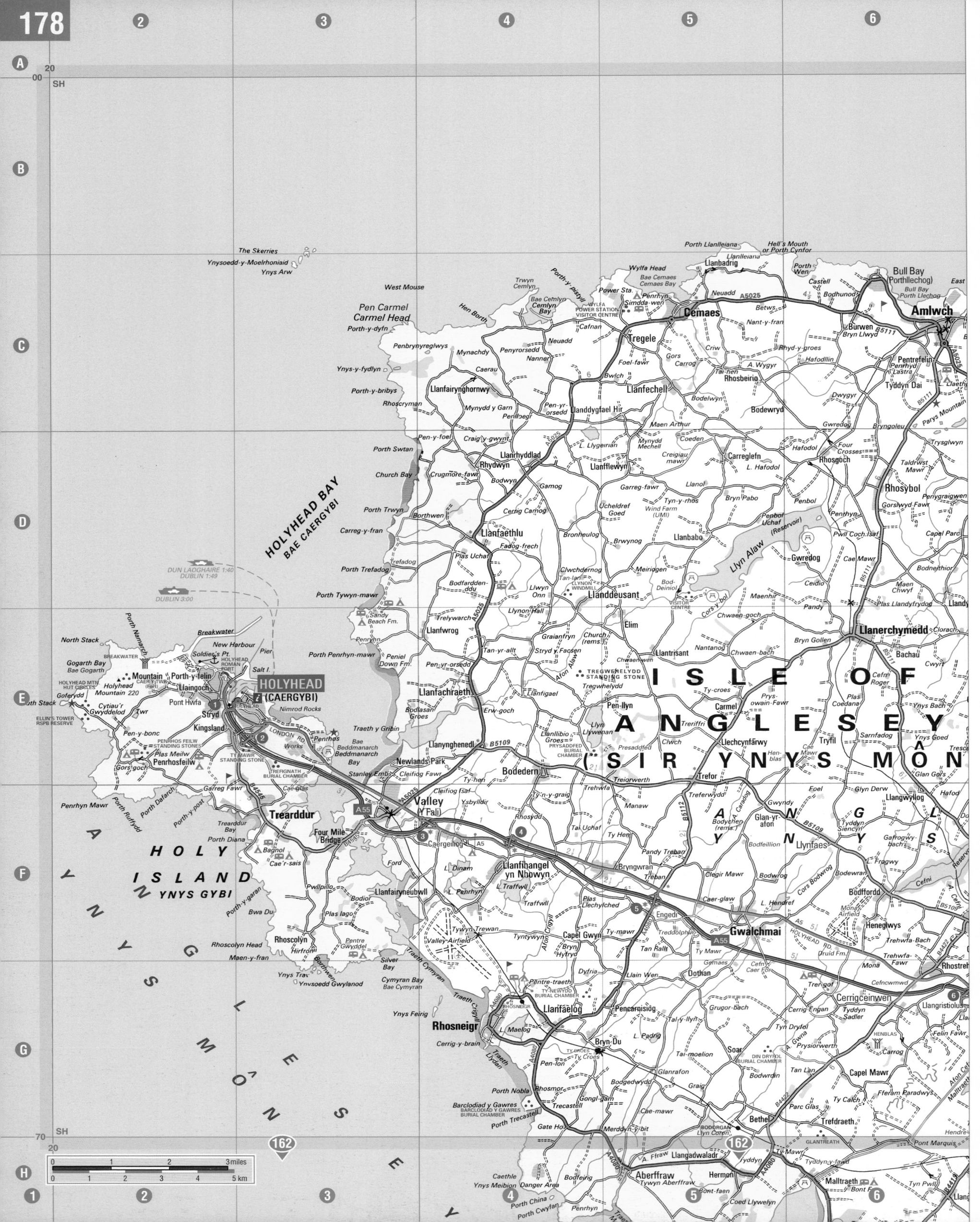

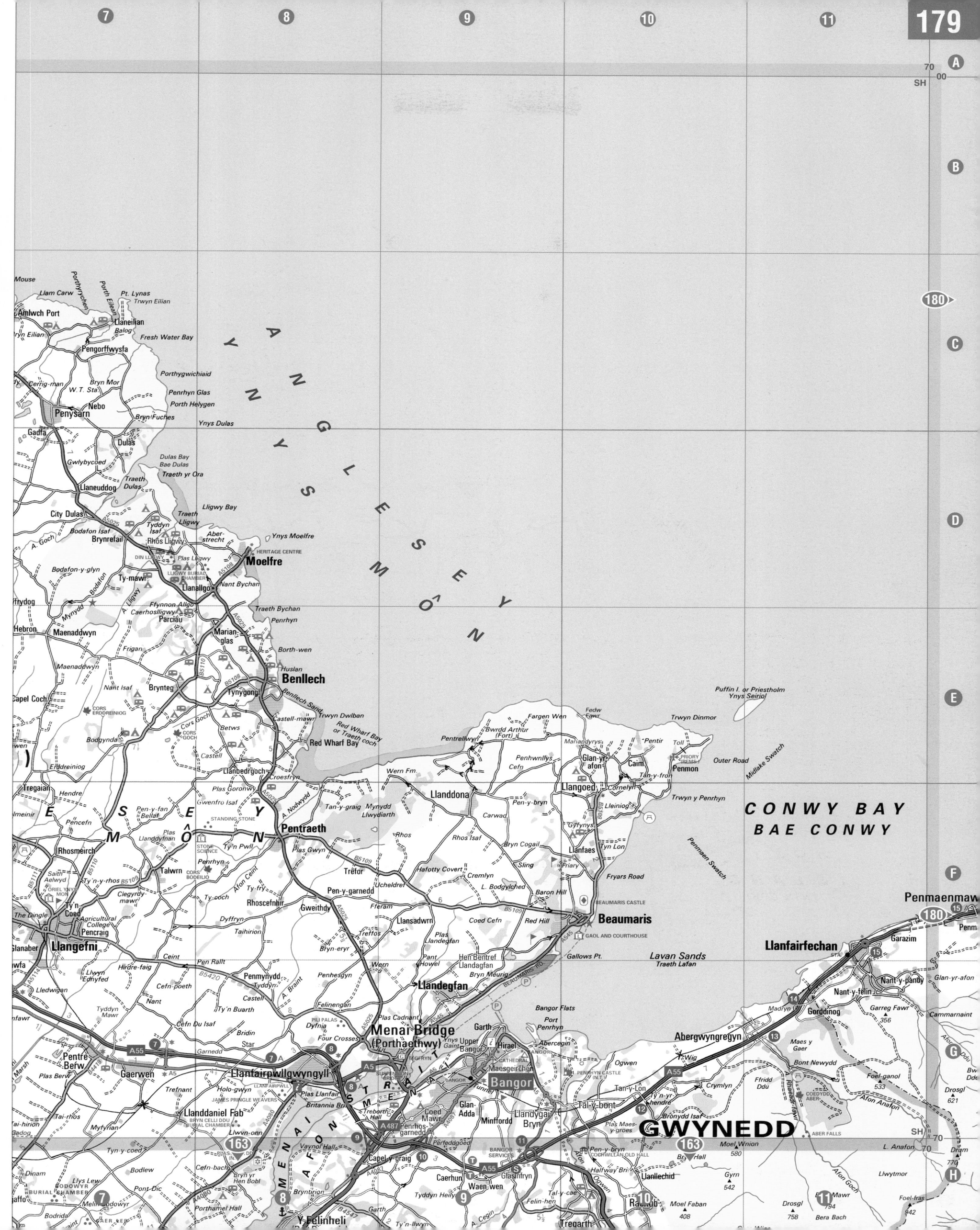

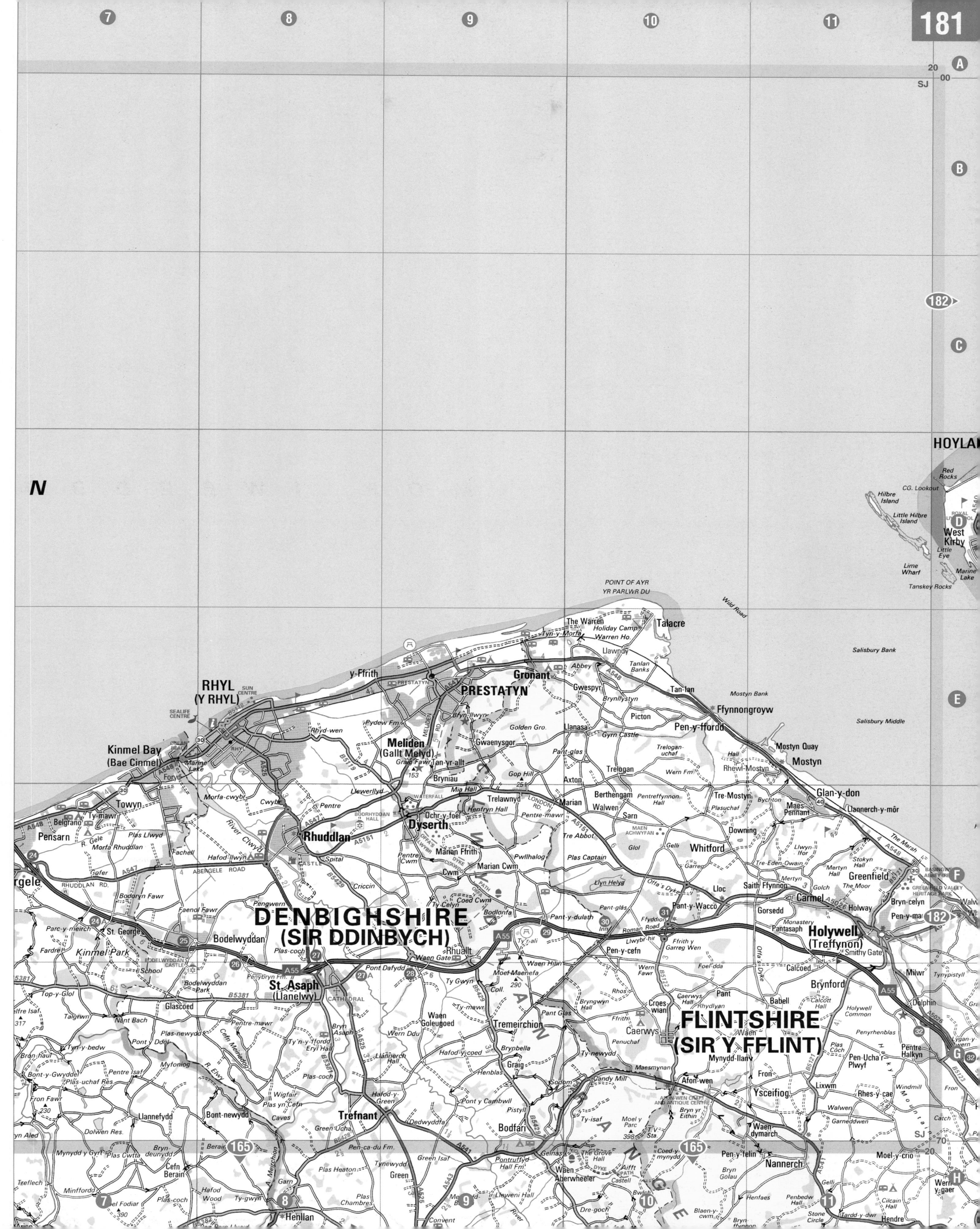

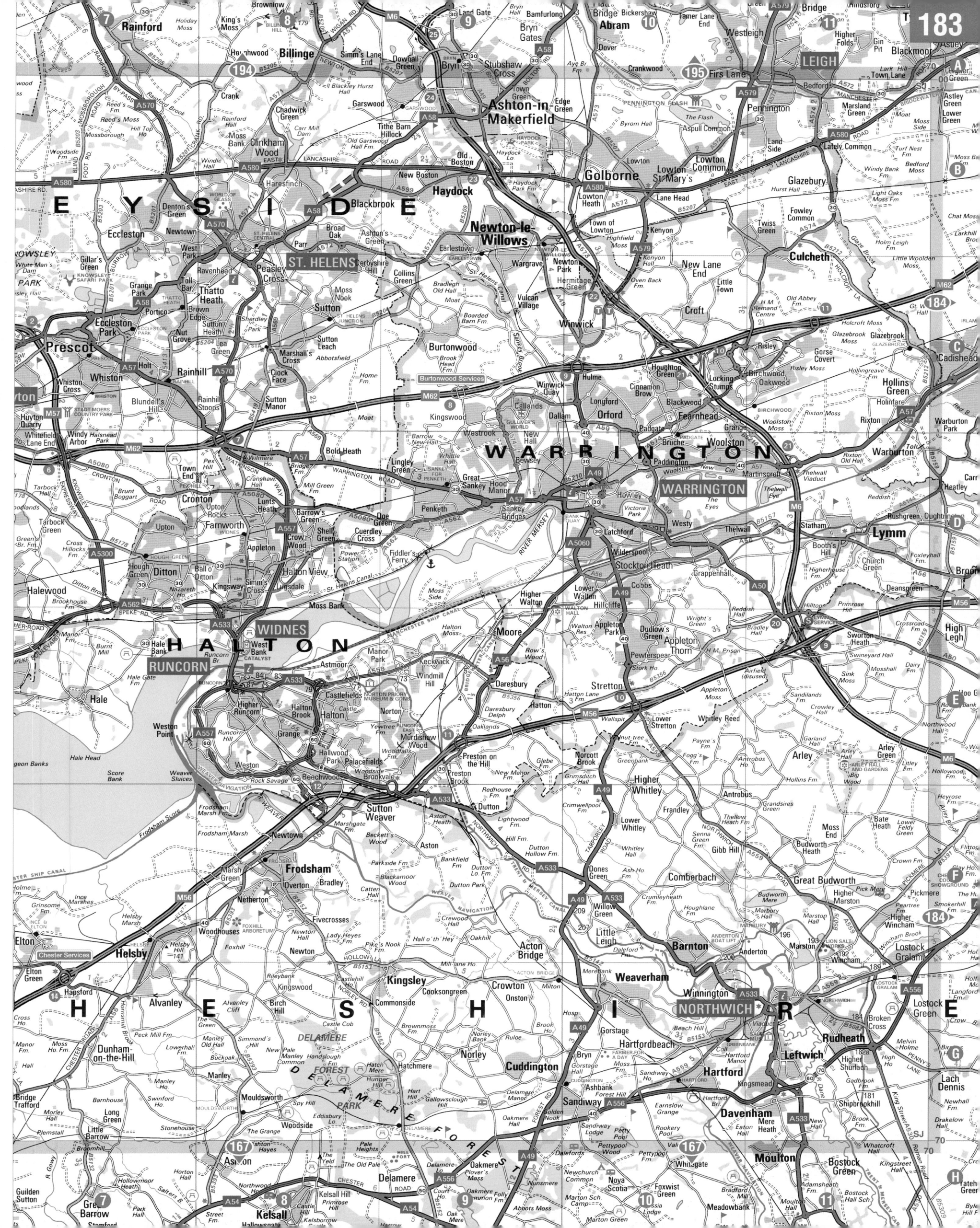

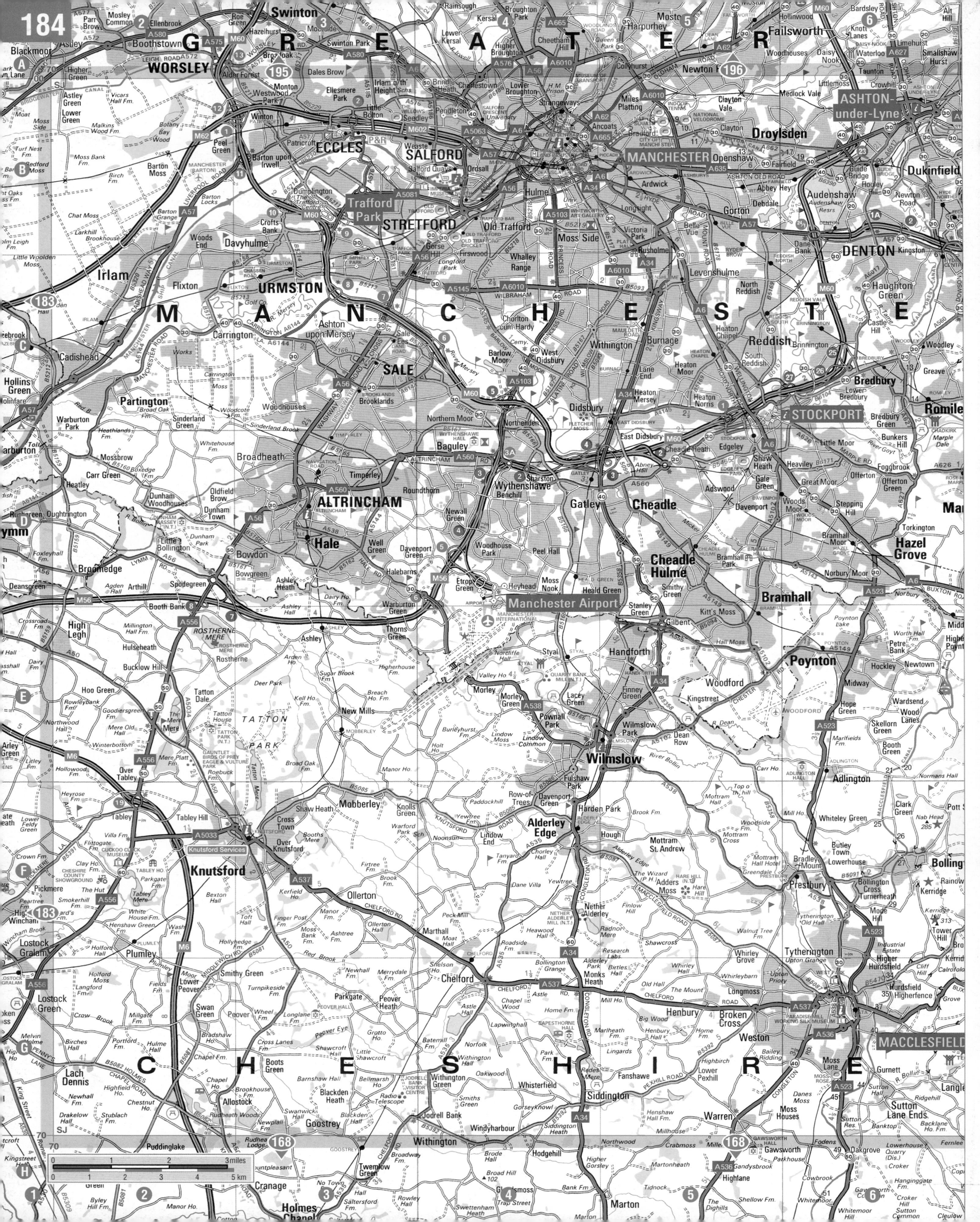

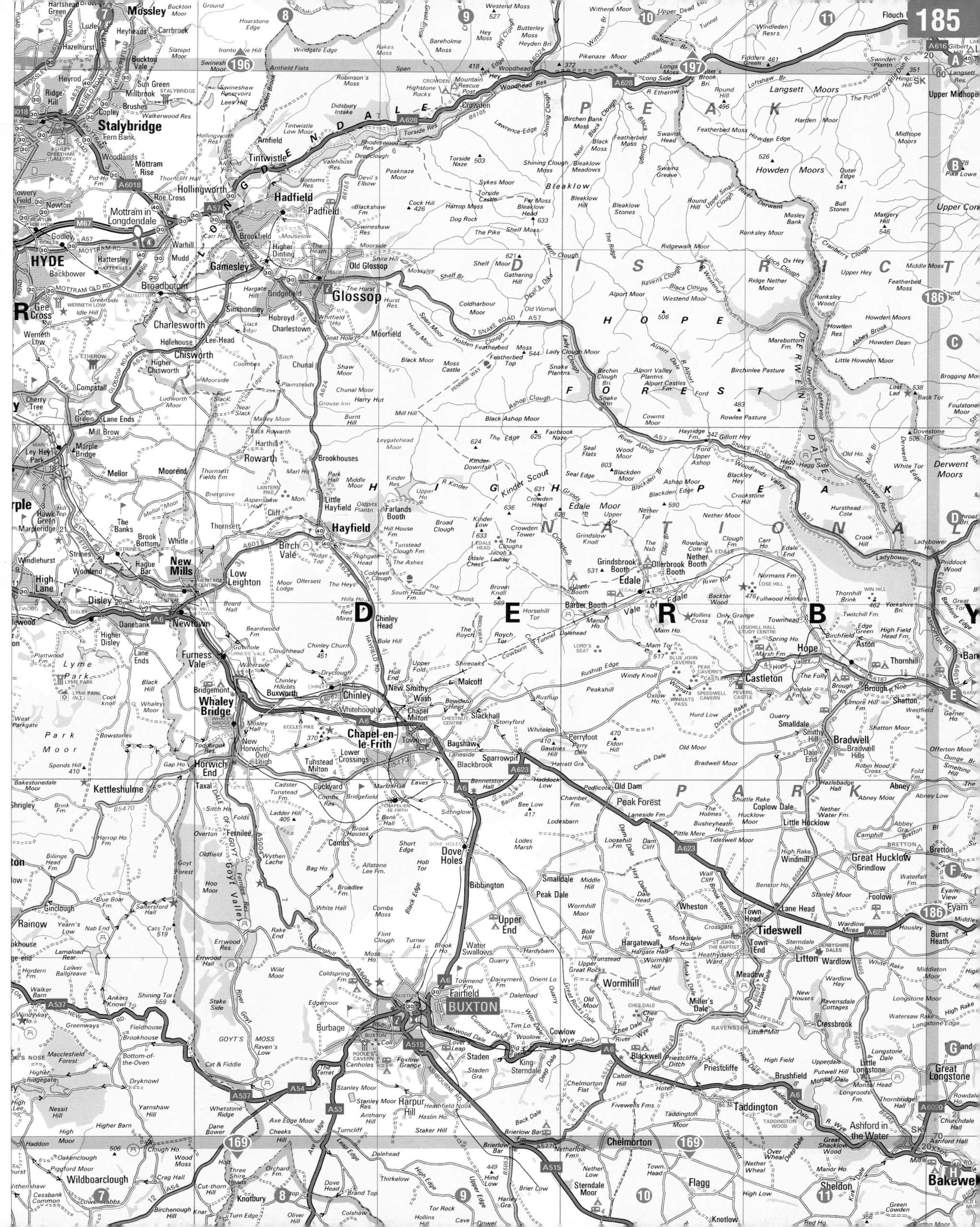

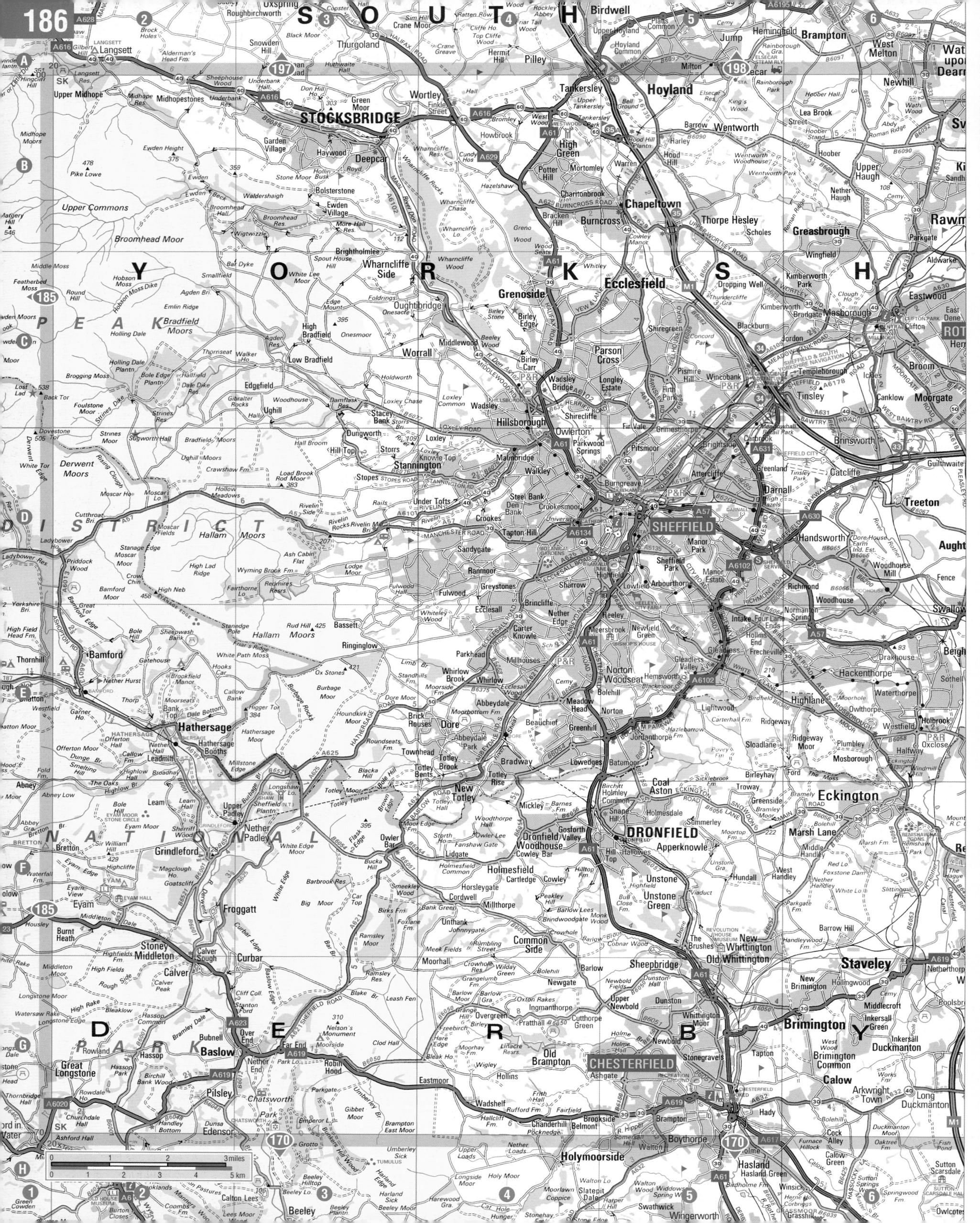

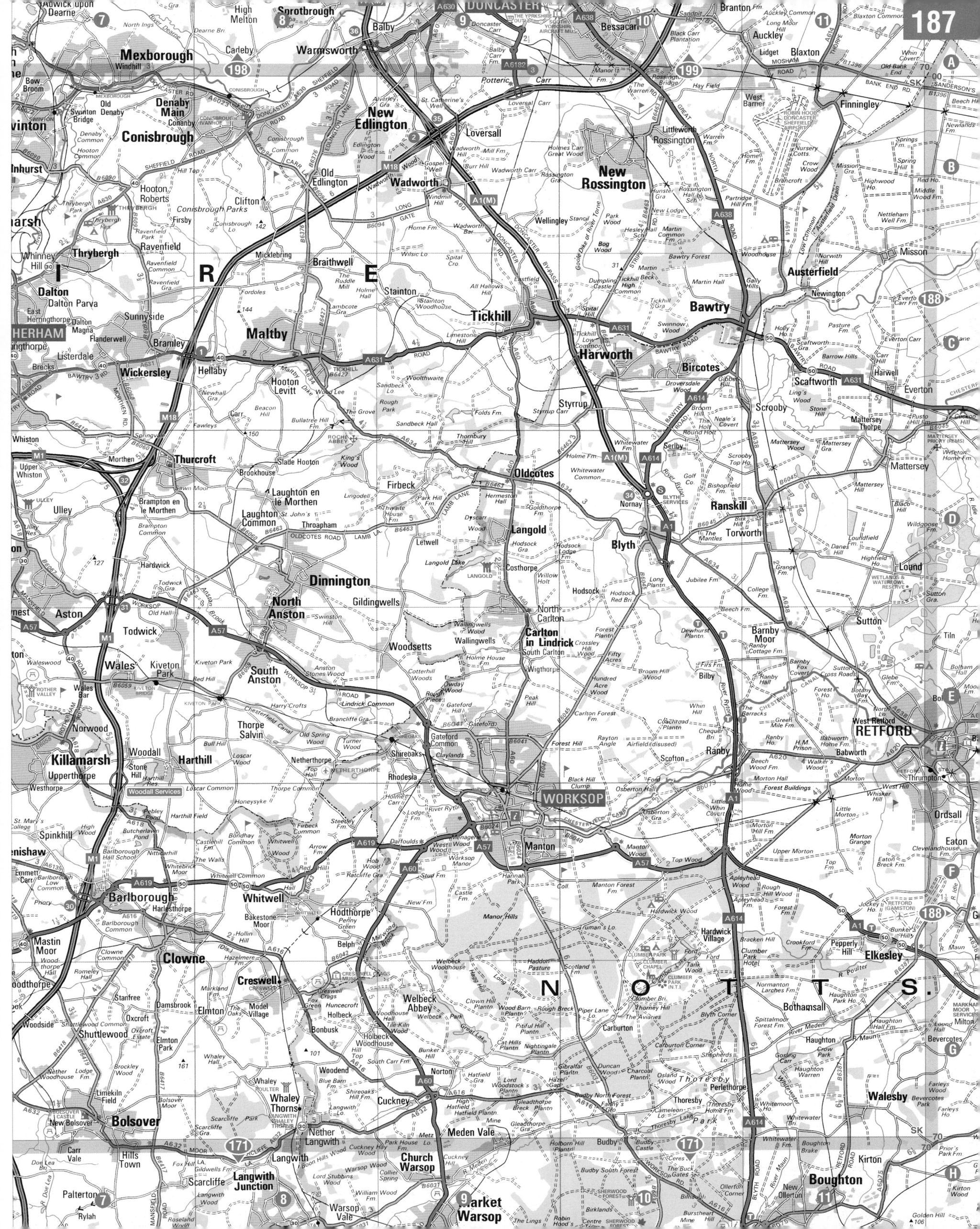

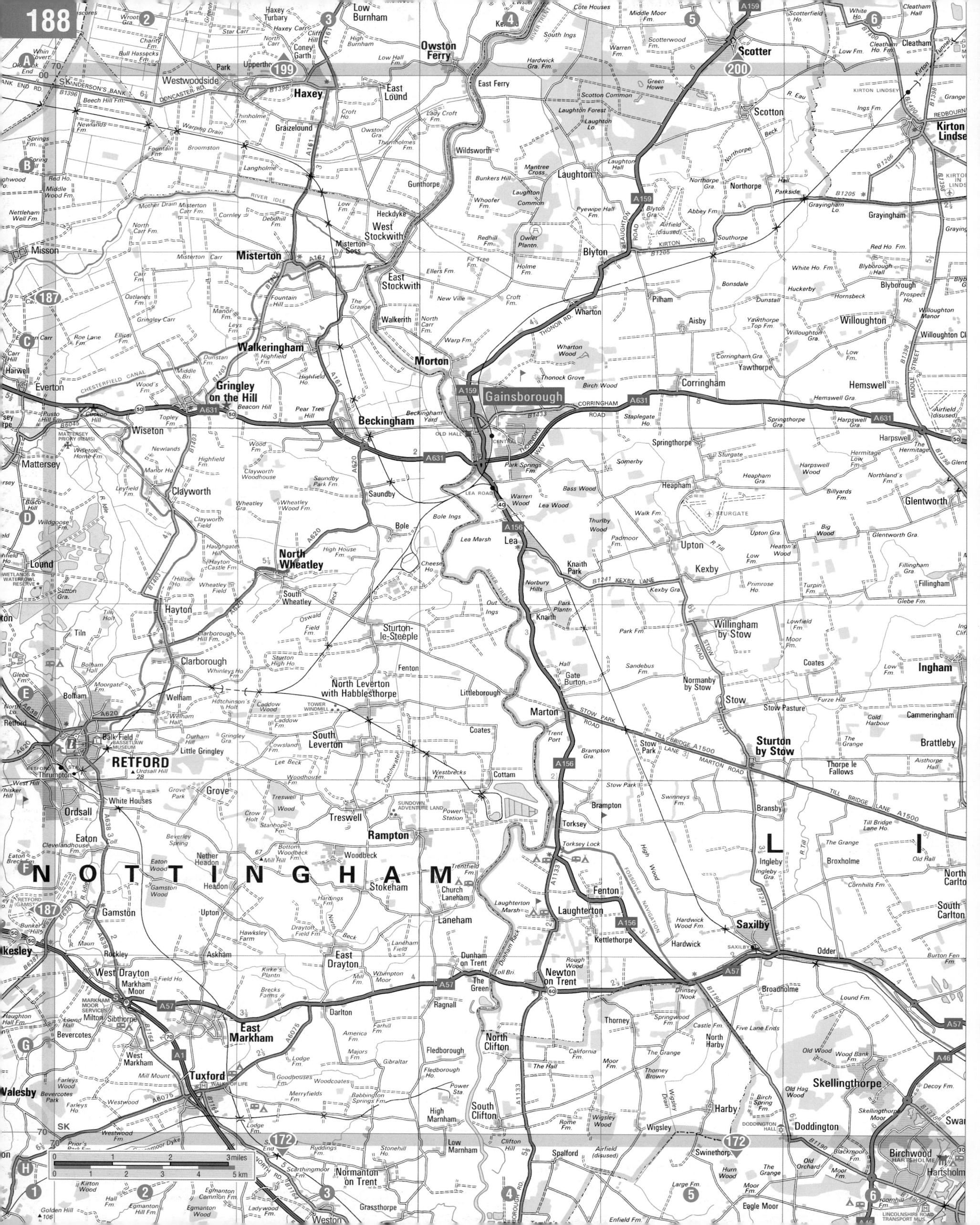

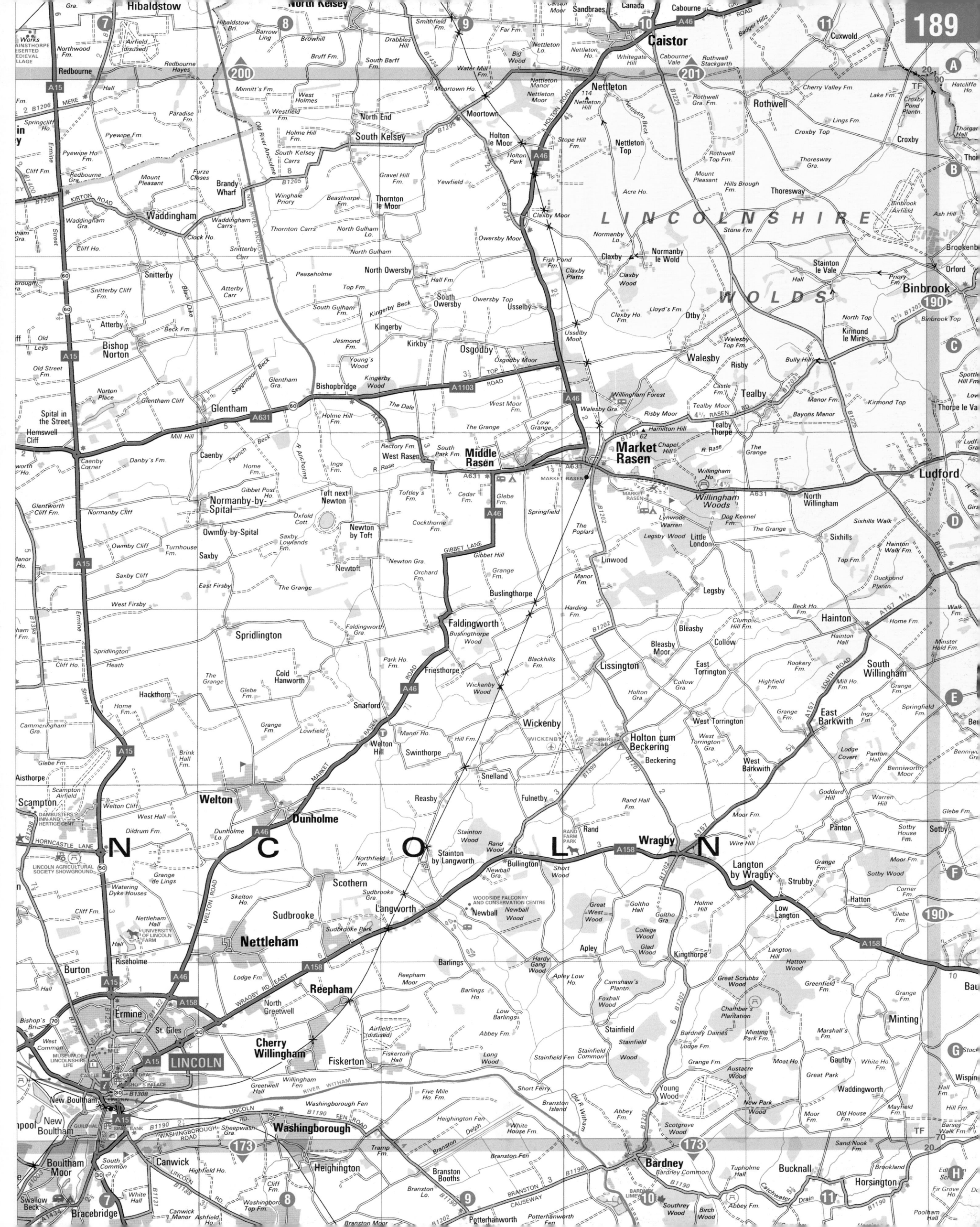

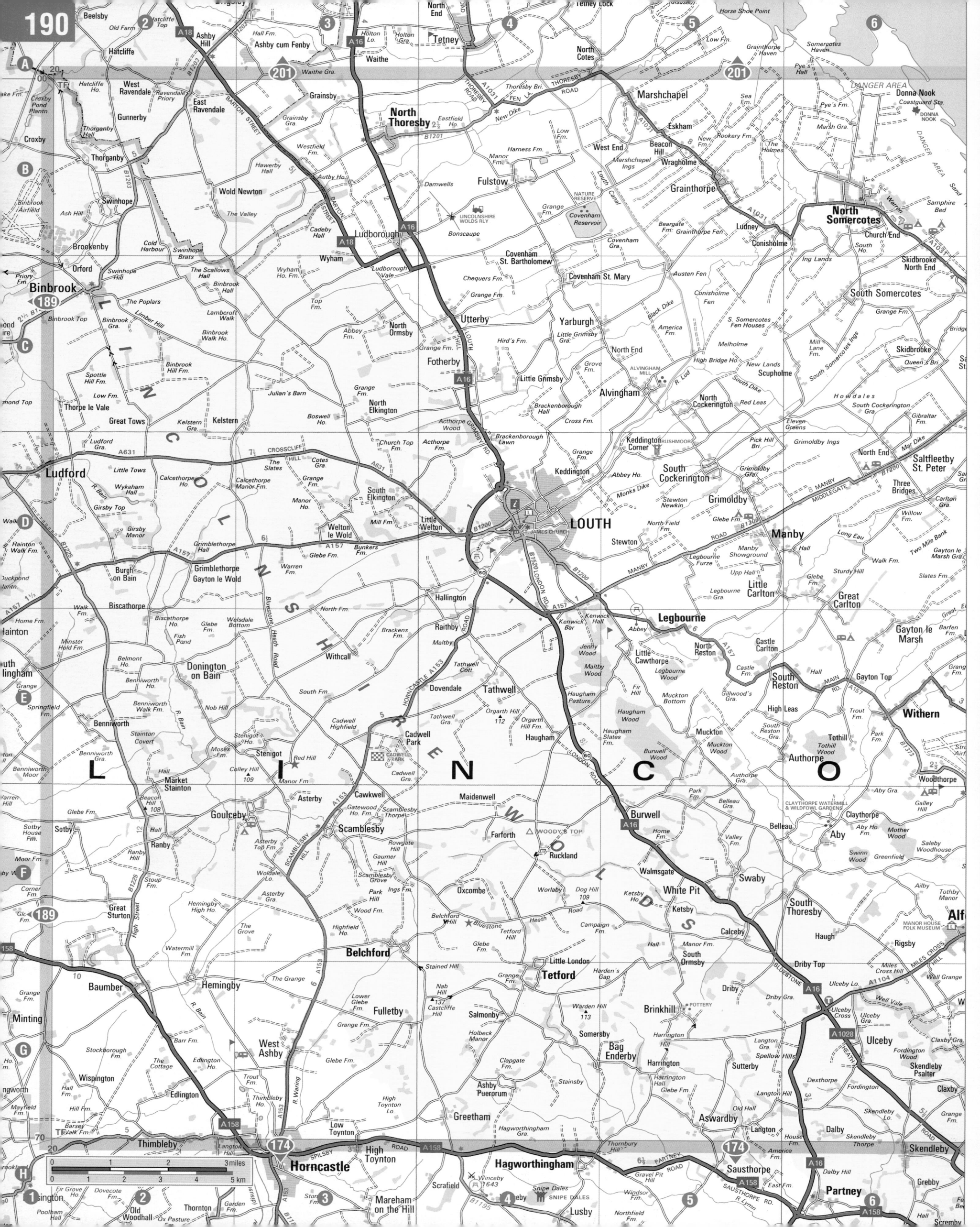

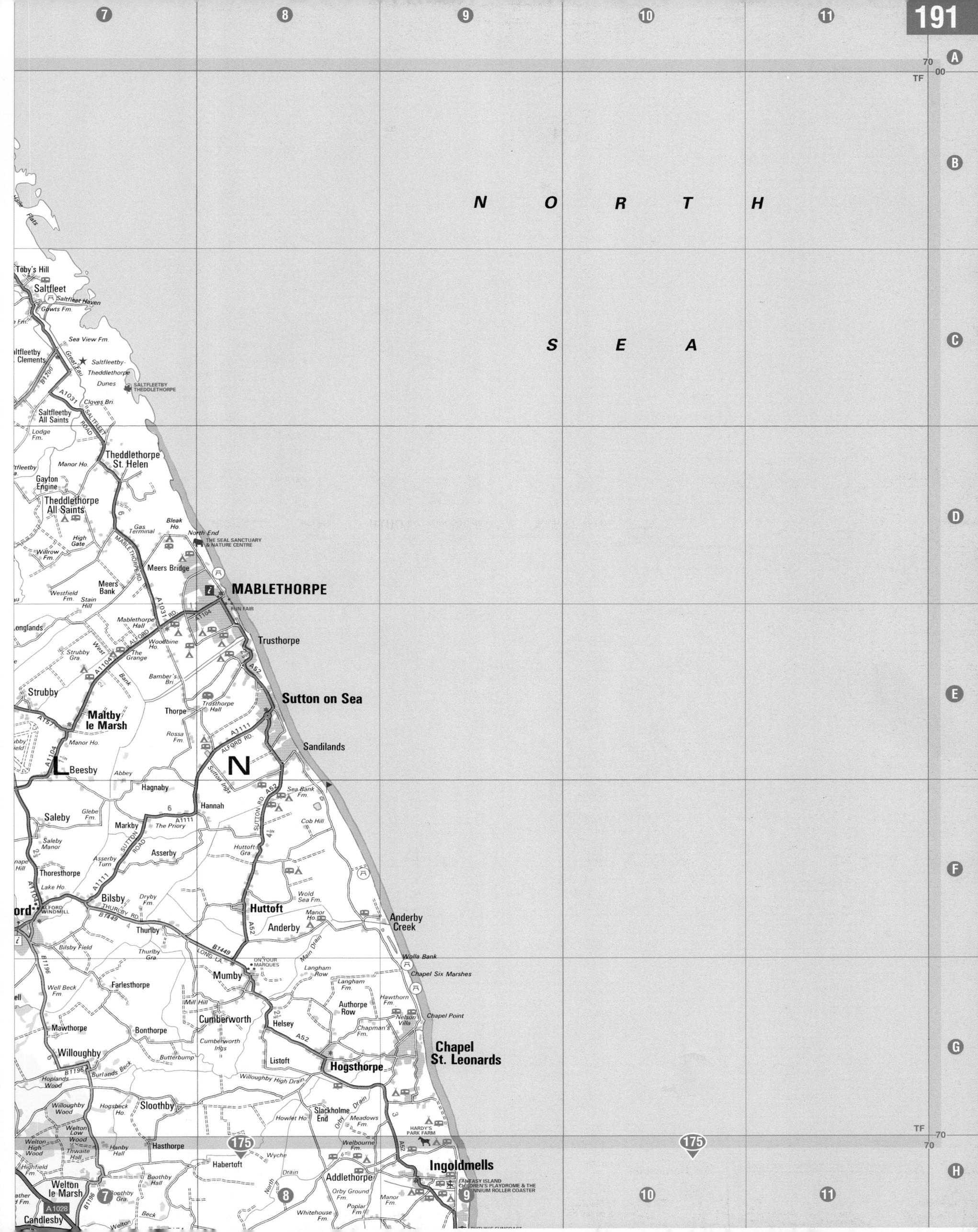

N O R T H

S E A

Toby's Hill
Saltfleet
Saltfleet Haven
Gowts Fm.
Sea View Fm.
Saltfleetby
Clements
Saltfleetby-
Theddlethorpe
Dunes
SALTFLEETBY
THEDDLETHORPE
Cloves Bri.
Saltfleetby
All Saints
Lodge
Fm.
Saltfleetby
Gayton
Engine
Manor Ho.
Theddlethorpe
St. Helen
Theddlethorpe
All Saints
Bleak
Ho.
High
Gate
Gas
Terminal
North End
THE SEAL SANCTUARY
& NATURE CENTRE
Willrow
Fm.
Westfield
Fm.
Meers
Bank
Meers Bridge
Stain
Hill
MABLETHORPE
FUN FAIR
Longlands
Mablethorpe
Hall
Woodbine
Ho.
Trusthorpe
Strubby
Gra.
The
Grange
West
Bamber's
Bri.
Strubby
Thorpe
Trusthorpe
Hall
Sutton on Sea
Maltby
le Marsh
Manor Ho.
Rossa
Fm.
Sandilands
Beesby
Abbey
Hagnaby
Saleby
Glebe
Fm.
Markby
The Priory
Hannah
Cob Hill
Sea Bank
Fm.
Saleby
Manor
Asserby
Turn
Asserby
Huttoft
Gra.
Thoresthorpe
Lake Ho.
Wold
Sea Fm.
Bilsby
Dryby
Fm.
Huttoft
Manor
Ho.
Anderby
Creek
Thurlby
Anderby
Bilsby Field
Thurlby
Gra.
Wolla Bank
Mumby
ON YOUR
MARQUES
Langham
Row
Chapel Six Marshes
Farlesthorpe
Well Beck
Fm.
Langham
Fm.
Hawthorn
Fm.
Mill Hill
Authorpe
Row
Nelson
Villa
Chapel Point
Cumberworth
Helsey
Chapman's
Fm.
Mawthorpe
Bonthorpe
Cumberworth
Ings
Chapel
St. Leonards
Willoughby
Listoft
Butterbump
Hogsthorpe
Hoplands
Wood
Willoughby High Drain
Willoughby
Wood
Hogsbeck
Ho.
Sloothby
Slackholme
End
Howlet Ho.
Orby
Meadows
Fm.
HARDY'S
PARK FARM
Welton
Low
Wood
Welton
High
Wood
Hanby
Hall
Thwaite
Hall
Wyche
Welbourne
Fm.
Ingoldmells
FANTASY ISLAND
CHILDREN'S PLAYDROME & THE
MILLENNIUM ROLLER COASTER
Highfield
Wood
Boothby
Hall
Habertoft
Addlethorpe
Orby Ground
Manor
Fm.
Welton
le Marsh
Boothby
Gra.
Poplar
Fm.
Whitehouse
Fm.
Candlesby

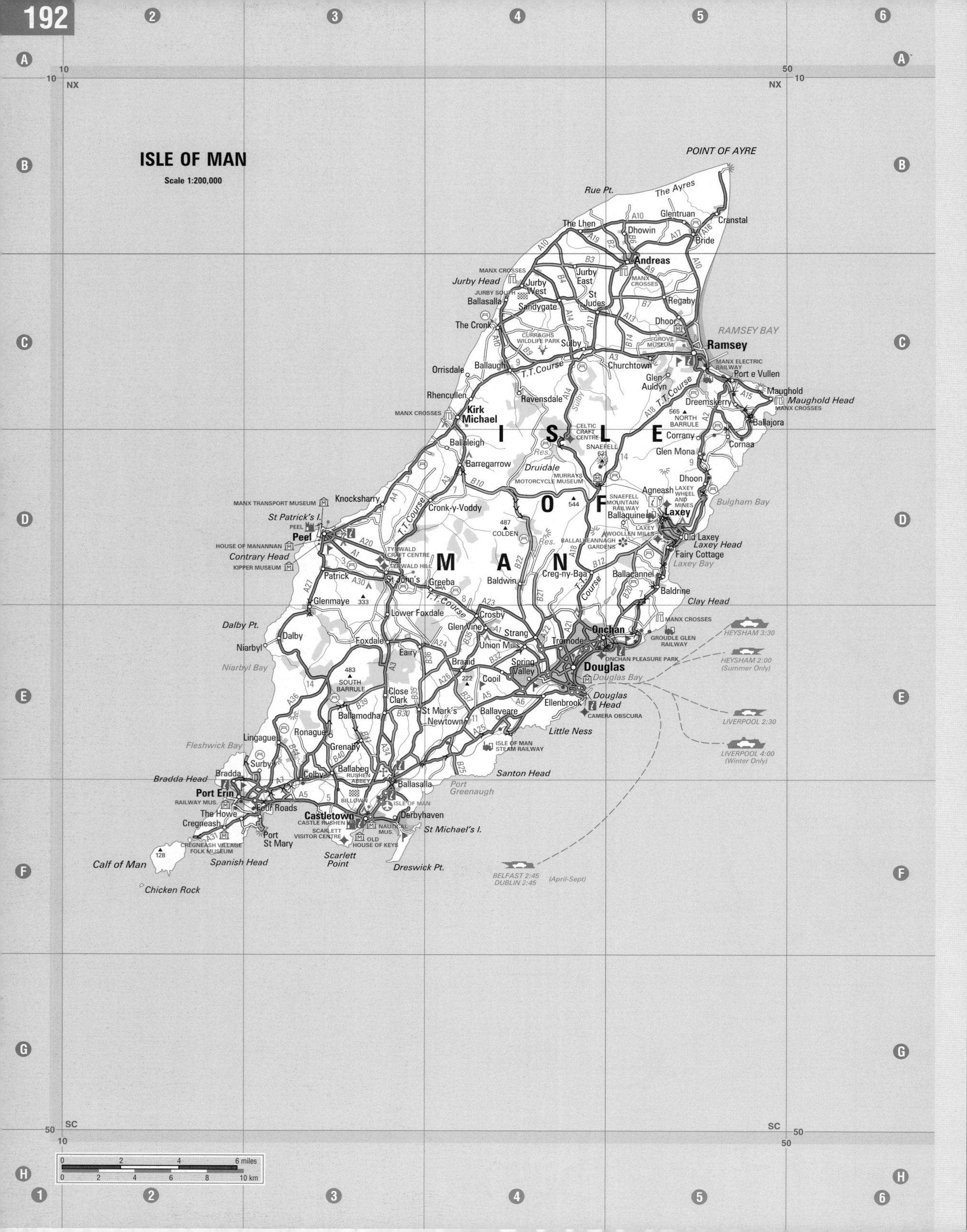

ISLE OF MAN

Scale 1:200,000

POINT OF AYRE

Rue Pt.   The Ayres

The Lhen   Glentruan   Cranstal
Dhowin   Bride

Andreas

MANX CROSSES   Jurby   A9   Regaby
Jurby Head   Jurby   East
Jurby   St   MANX CROSSES
West   Judes
JURBY SOUTH   Dhoor
Ballasalla   Sandygate
Dhoon

The Cronk   RAMSEY BAY

CURRAGHS   Sulby   GROVE   Ramsey
WILDLIFE PARK   MUSEUM   MANX ELECTRIC
Orrisdale   Ballaugh   Churchtown   RAILWAY
9   Glen   Port e Vullen
T.T. Course   Auldyn   Maughold
Rhencullen   Ravensdale   Dreemskerry   Maughold Head
MANX CROSSES   Kirk   565   MANX CROSSES
Michael   NORTH   Ballajora
BARRULE   Corrany
ISLE   Cornaa
Ballaleigh   CELTIC   Glen Mona
CRAFT   9
Barregarrow   CENTRE   Dhoon
SNAEFELL   Agneash   LAXEY
Druidale   621   WHEEL
Res.   MURRAYS   SNAEFELL   AND MINES
MOTORCYCLE MUSEUM   MOUNTAIN   Laxey
MANX TRANSPORT MUSEUM   14   RAILWAY
Knocksharry   Cronk-y-Voddy   544   Ballaquine   LAXEY
St Patrick's I.   OF   WOOLLEN   Old Laxey
PEEL   487   Ballaugh   MILLS   Laxey Head
HOUSE OF MANANNAN   COLDEN   BALLALHEANNAGH   Fairy Cottage
Peel   TYNWALD   Res.   GARDENS   Laxey Bay
Contrary Head   CRAFT CENTRE   MAN   Creg-ny-Baa   Ballacannel
KIPPER MUSEUM   TYNWALD HILL   Baldwin   Baldrine
Patrick   St John's   Greeba   Clay Head
Glenmaye   333   T.T. Course   A23   Crosby
Dalby Pt.   Lower Foxdale   Glen Vine   Strang
Dalby   Foxdale   Eairy   Union Mills   Tromode   Onchan
Niarbyl   Braaid   Spring   GROUDLE GLEN
Niarbyl Bay   483   Valley   Douglas   RAILWAY   HEYSHAM 3:30
SOUTH   222   Cooil   MANX CROSSES
BARRULE   Close   Douglas Bay   HEYSHAM 2:00
Clark   St Mark's   Ballaveare   Douglas   (Summer Only)
Lingague   Ballamodha   Newtown   Head
Ronague   Ellenbrook   CAMERA OBSCURA   LIVERPOOL 2:30
Fleshwick Bay   Grenaby   Little Ness
Surby   Ballabeg   Santon Head   LIVERPOOL 4:00
Bradda Head   Colby   RUSHEN   ISLE OF MAN   (Winter Only)
Bradda   ABBEY   Ballasalla   STEAM RAILWAY
Port Erin   5   Port
RAILWAY MUS.   Four Roads   BILLOWN   Greenaugh
The Howe   Castletown   Derbyhaven
Cregneash   CASTLE RUSHEN   NAUTICAL
A31   SCARLETT   MUS.
Port   VISITOR CENTRE   OLD   St Michael's I.
CREGNEASH VILLAGE   St Mary   HOUSE OF KEYS
FOLK MUSEUM   Scarlett
128   Point   BELFAST 2:45
Calf of Man   Spanish Head   Dreswick Pt.   DUBLIN 2:45   (April-Sept)

Chicken Rock

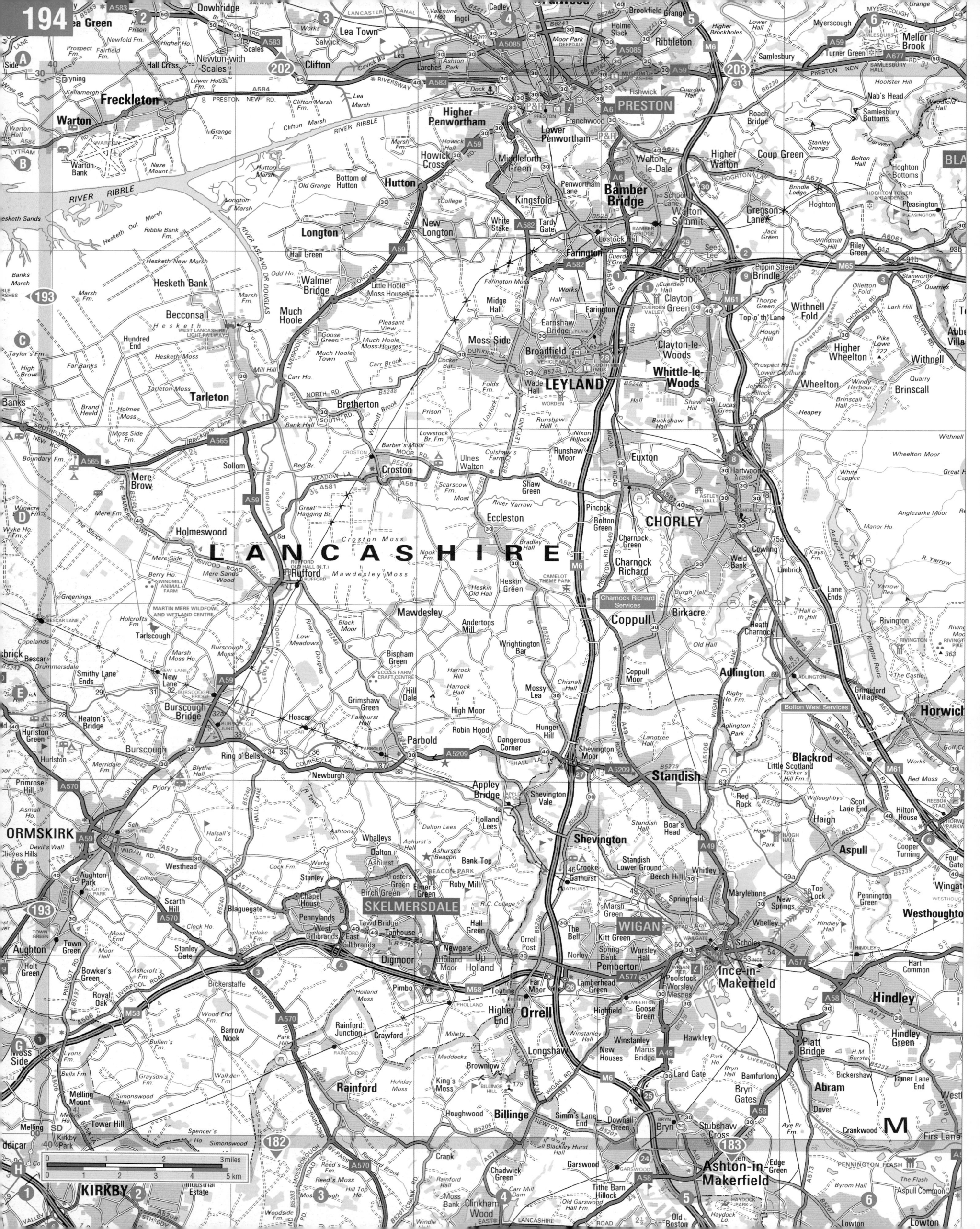

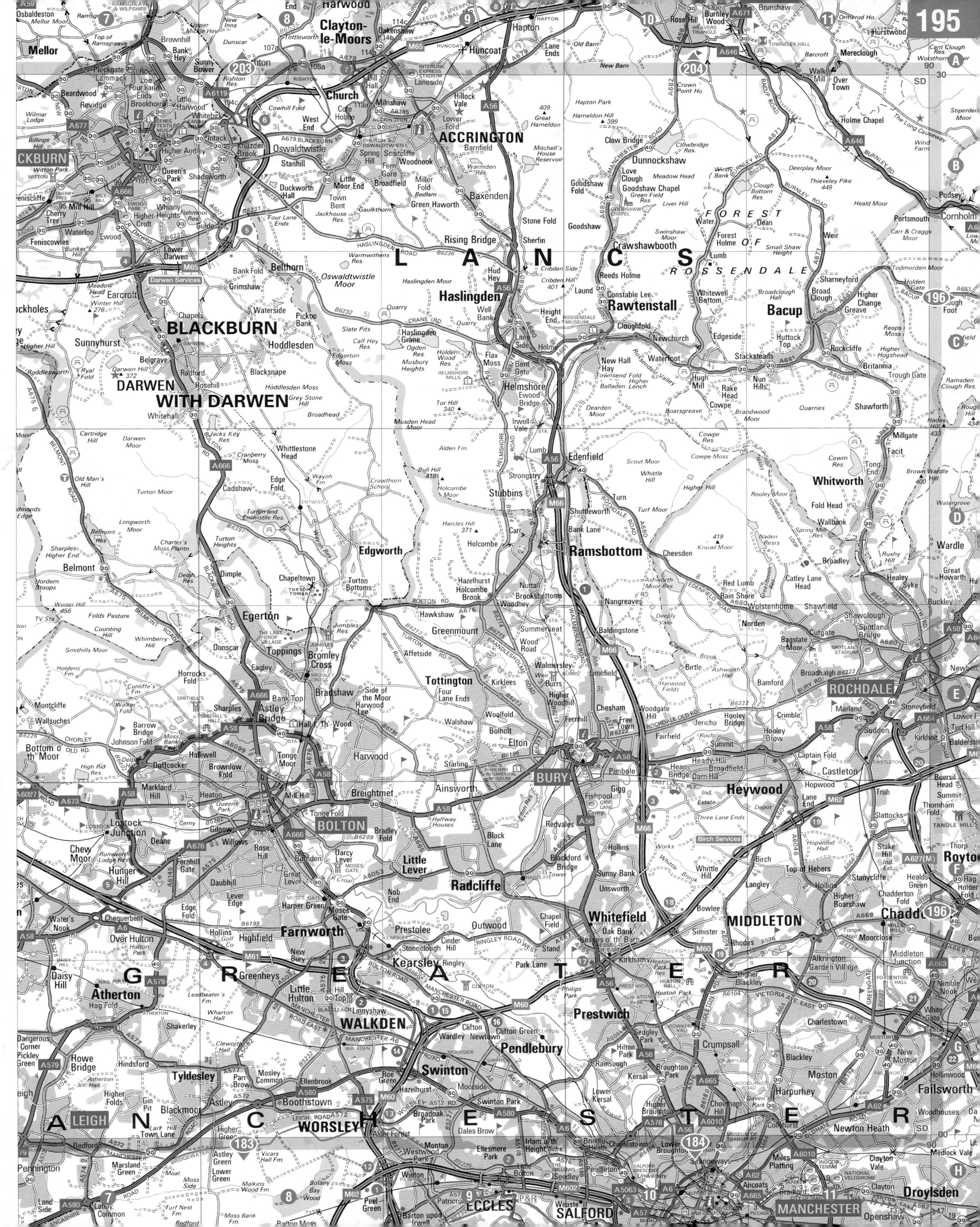

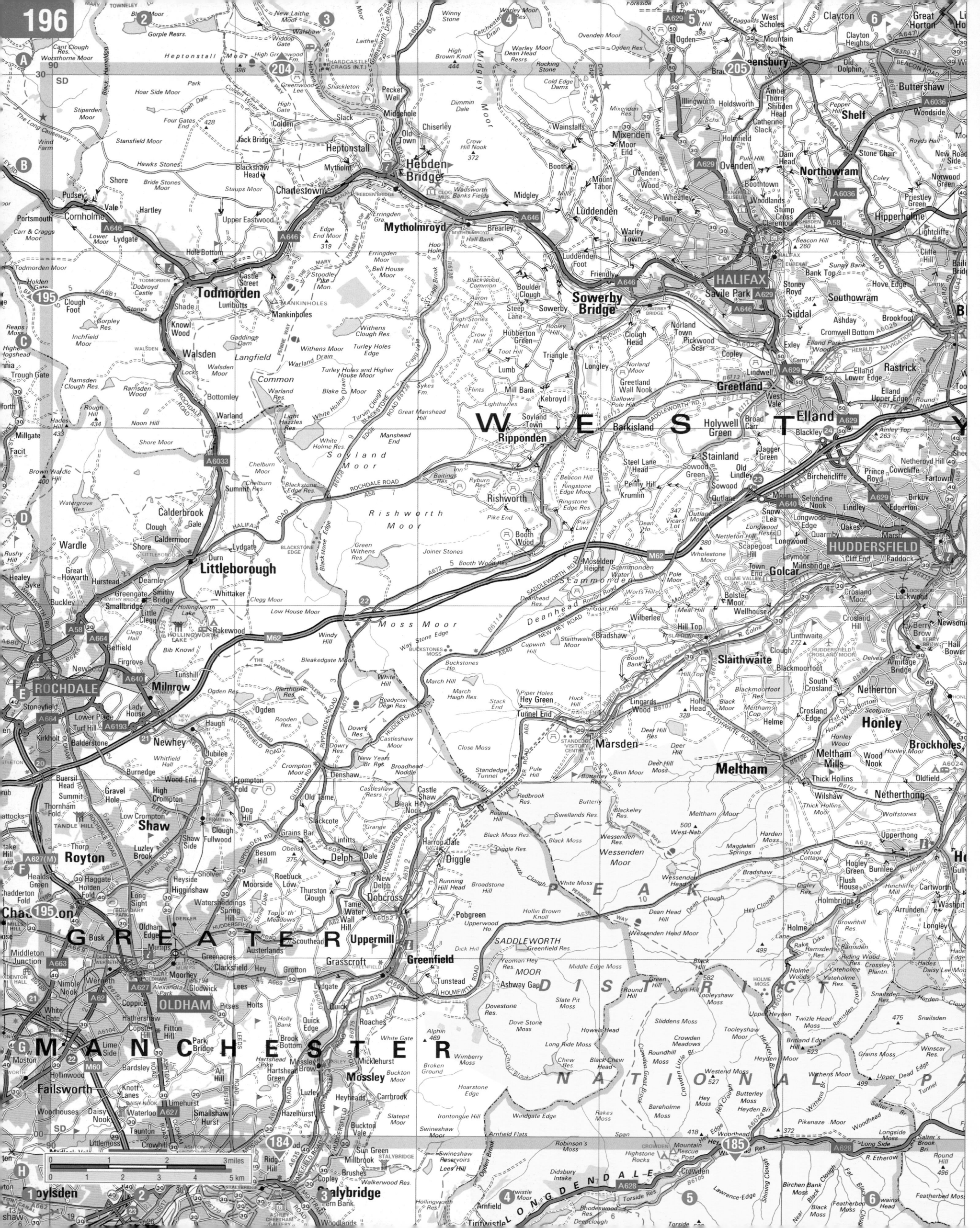

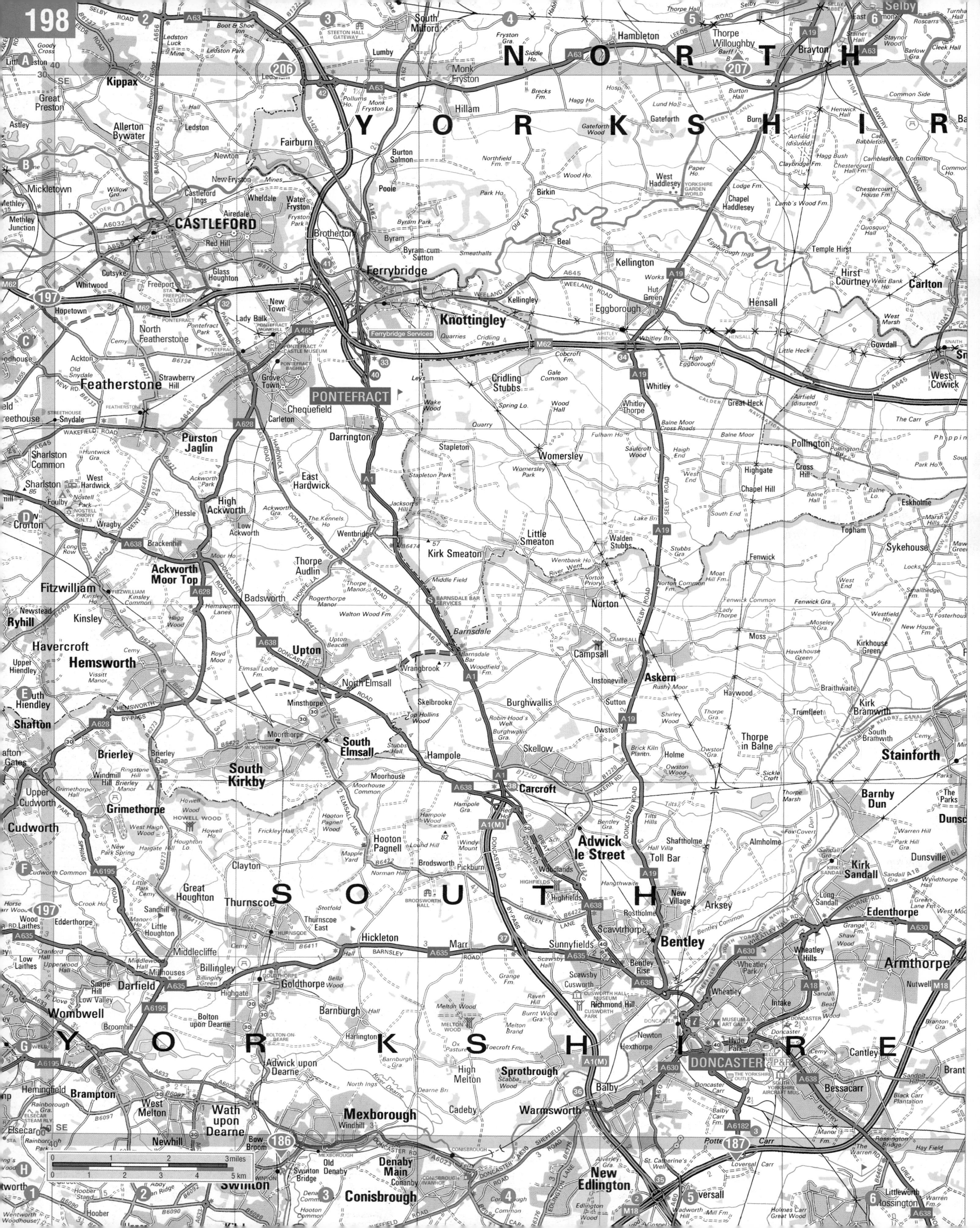

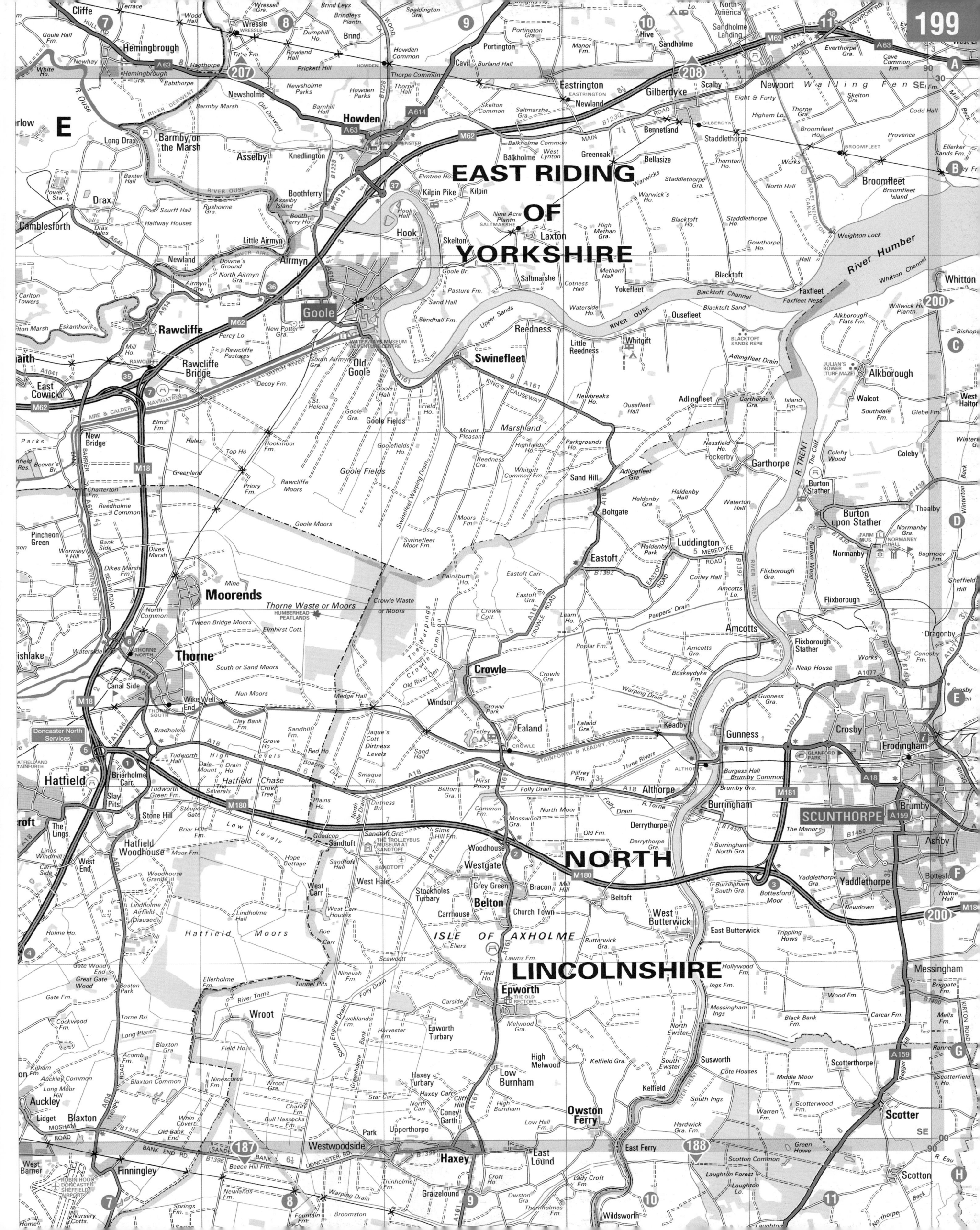

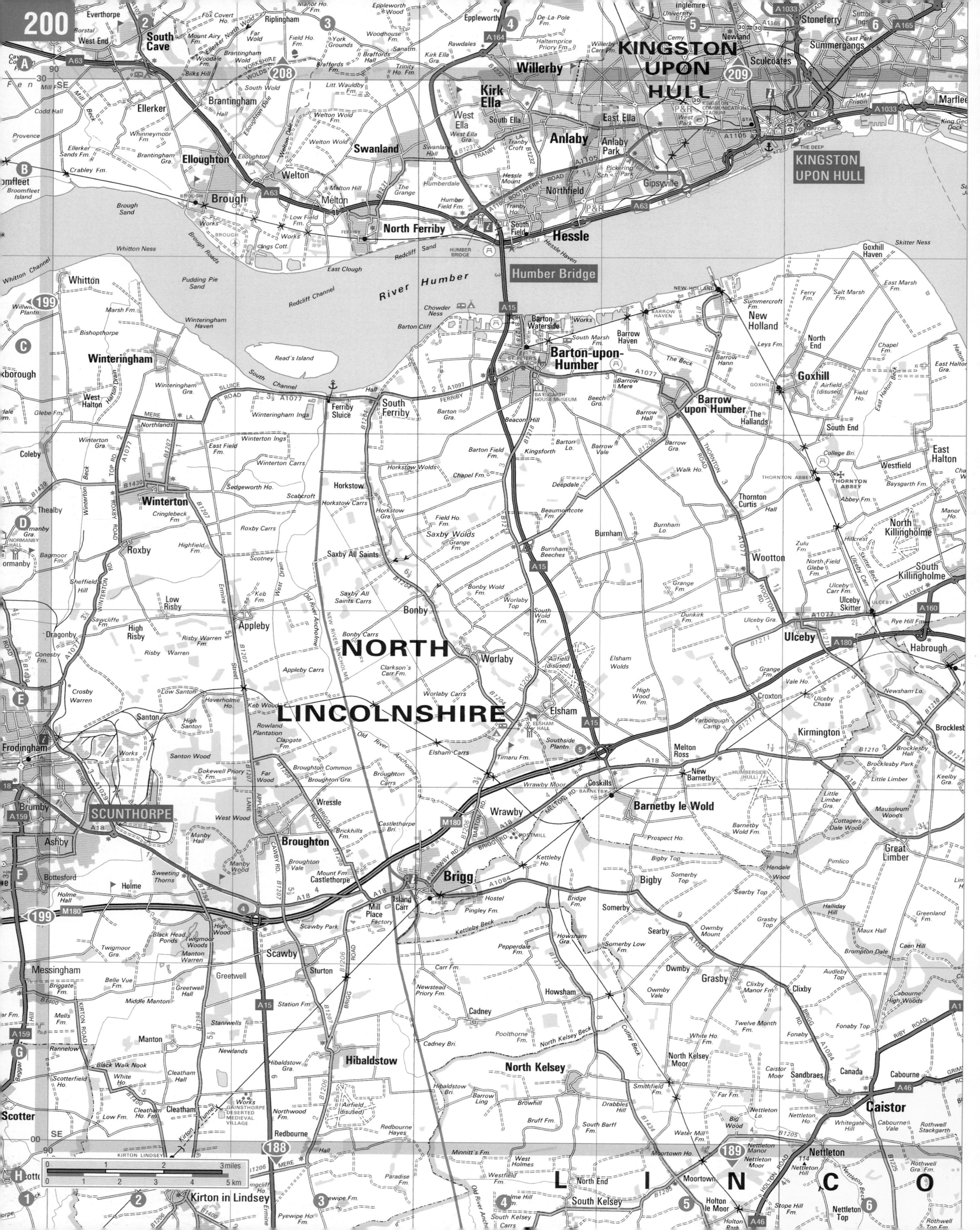

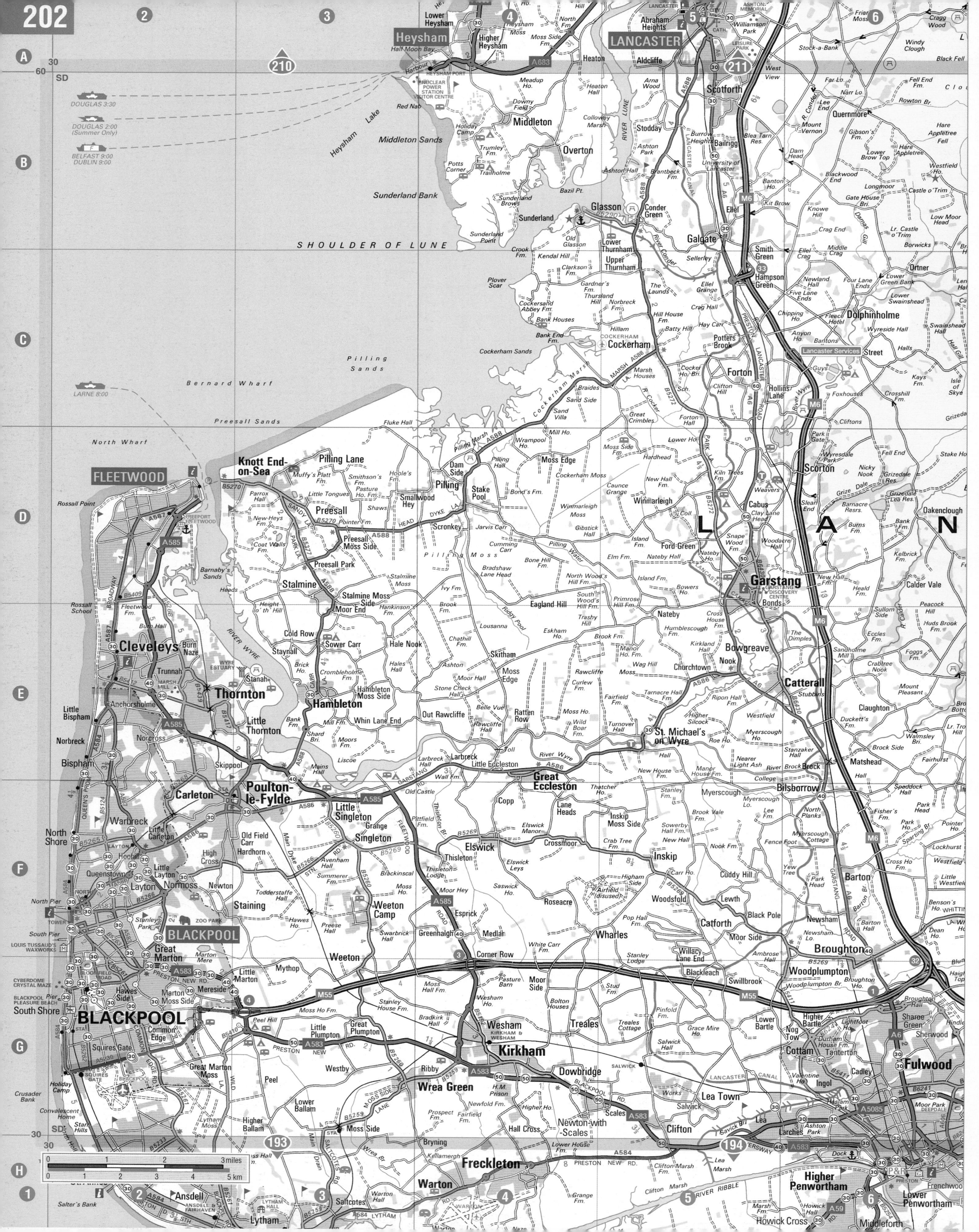

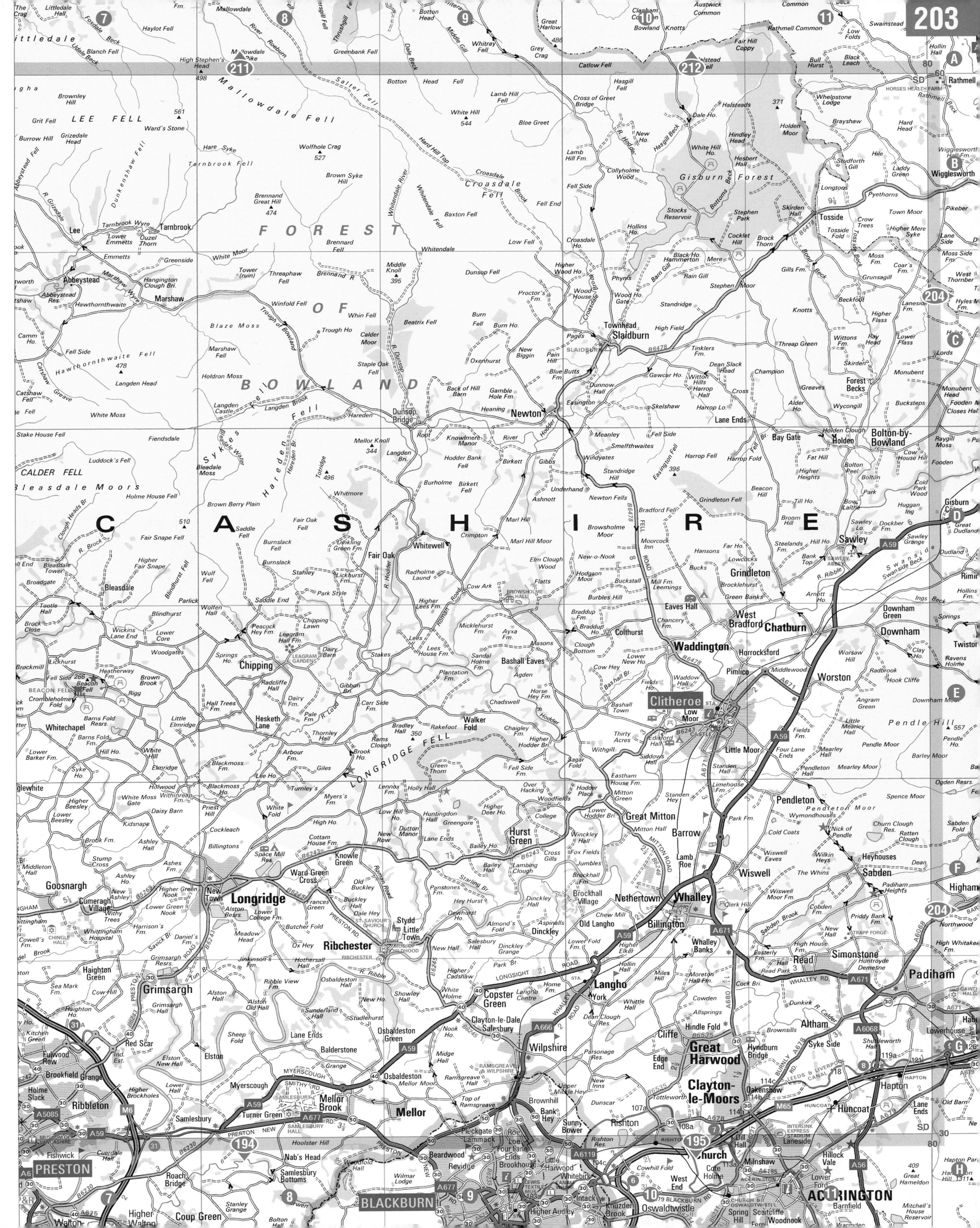

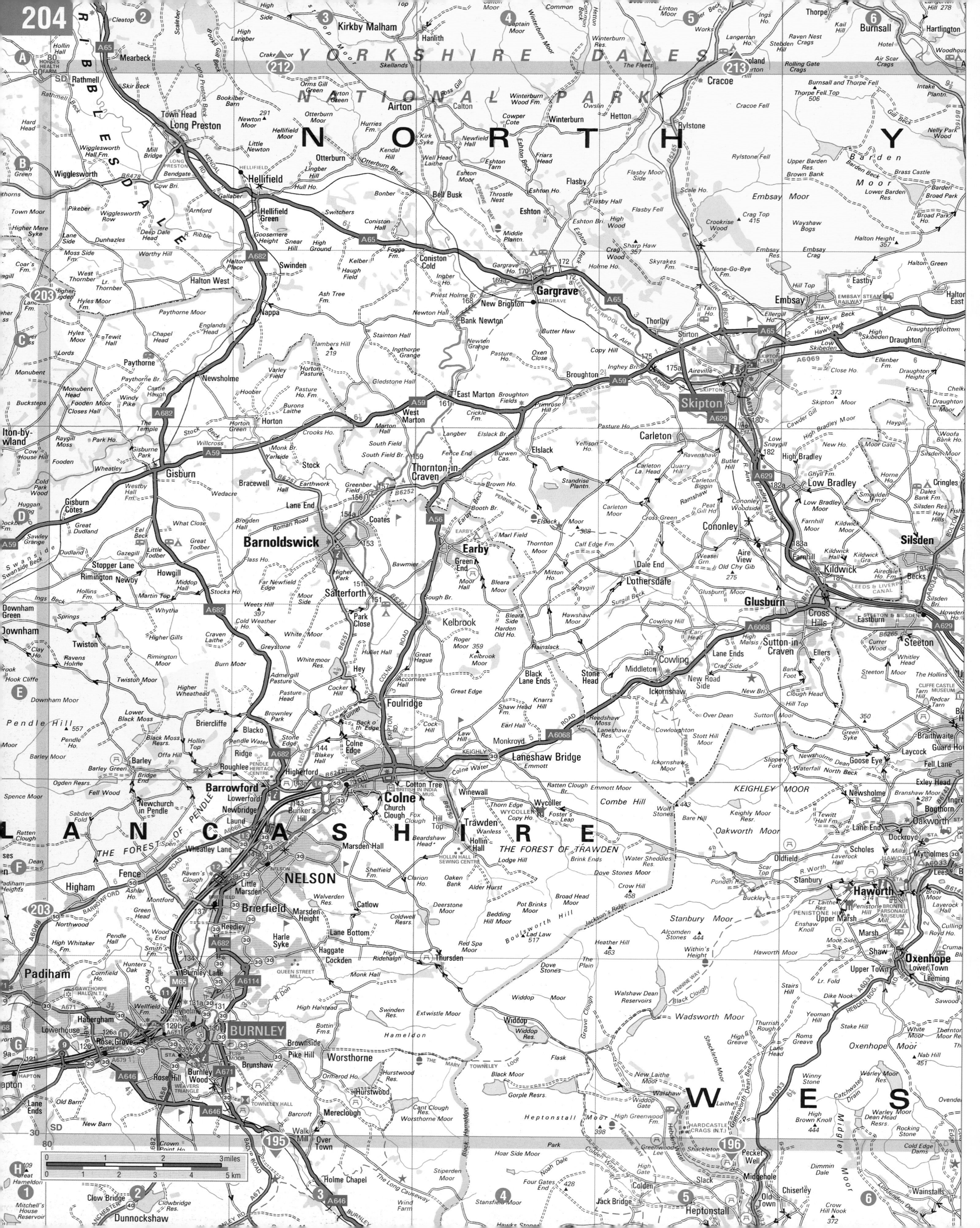

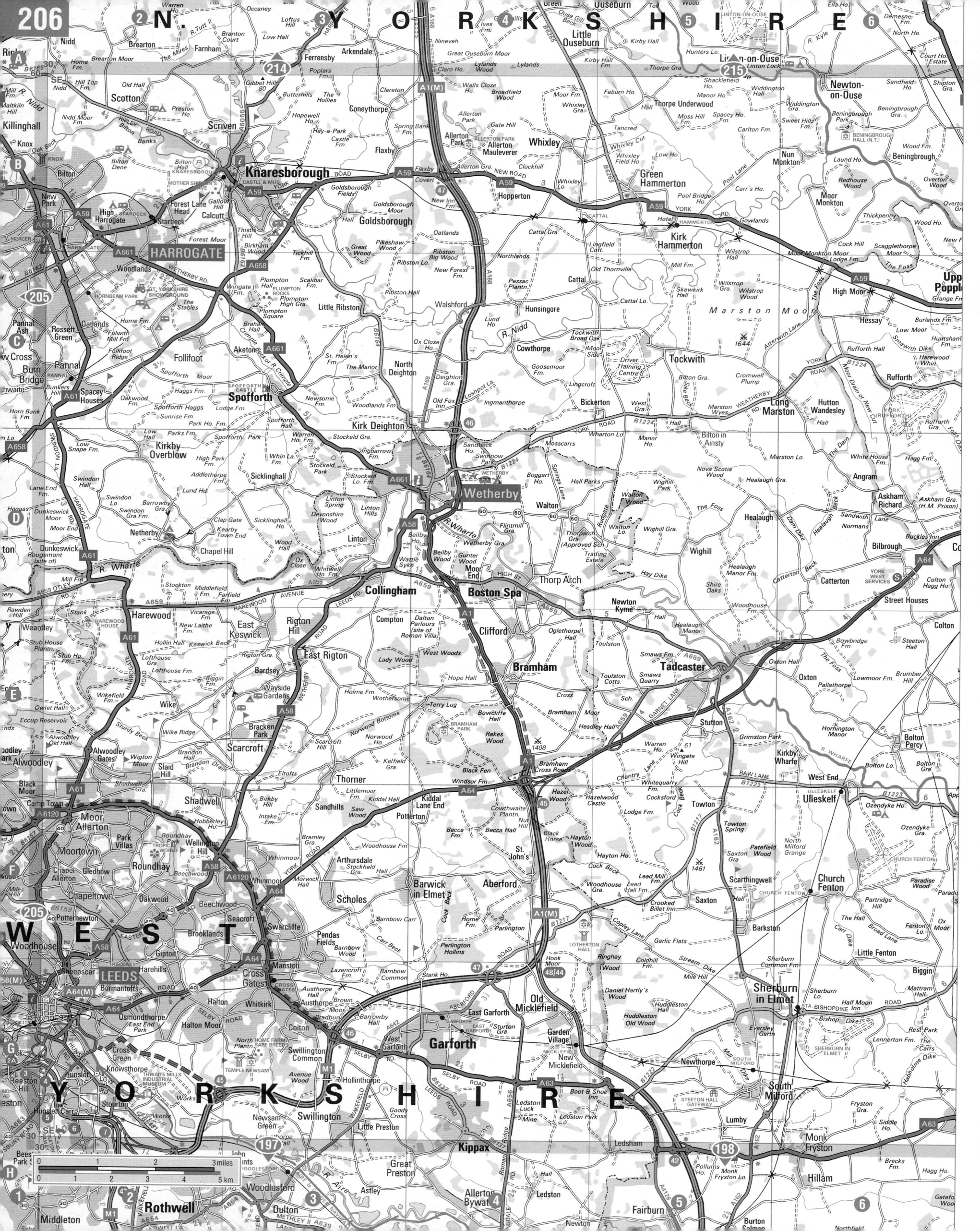

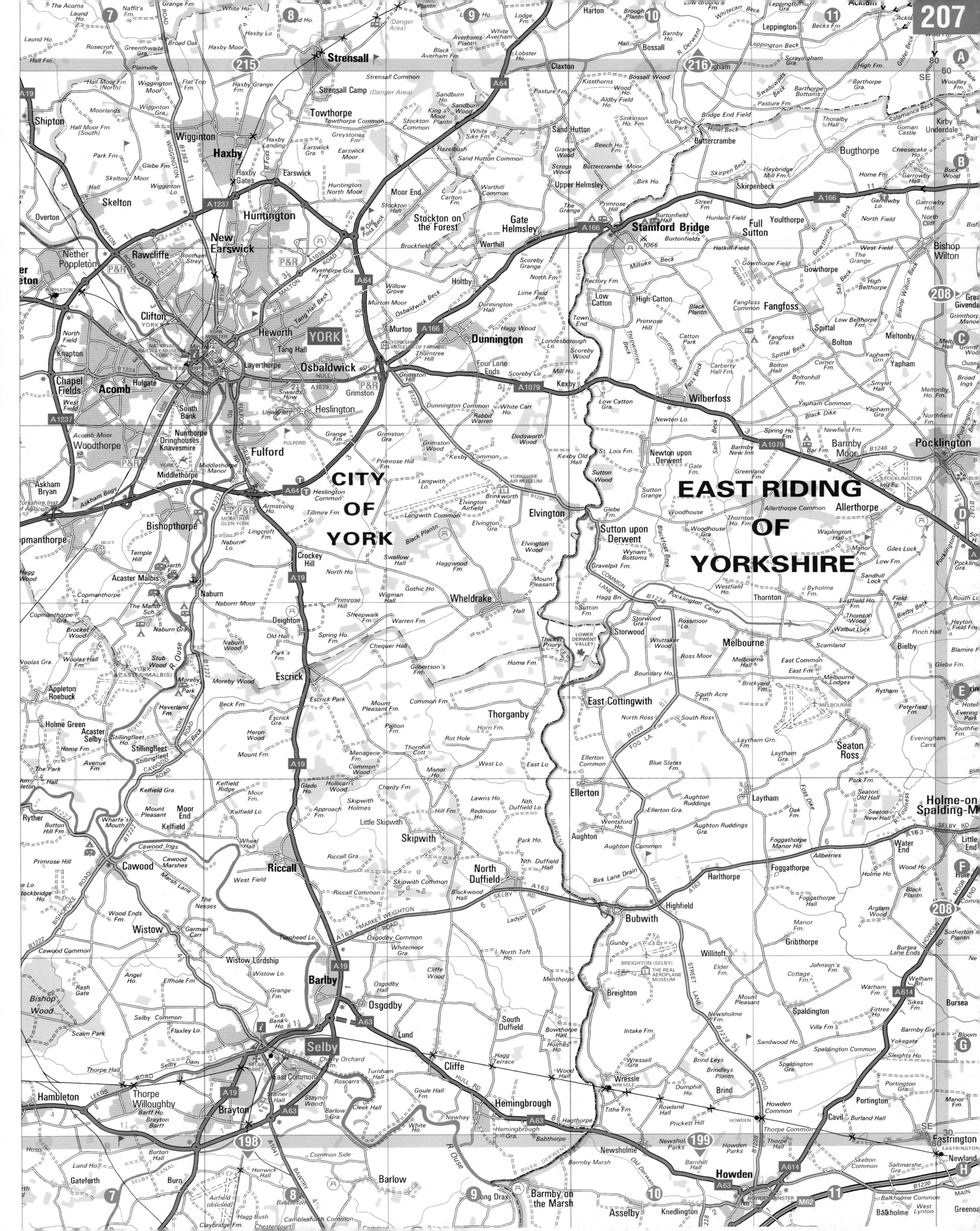

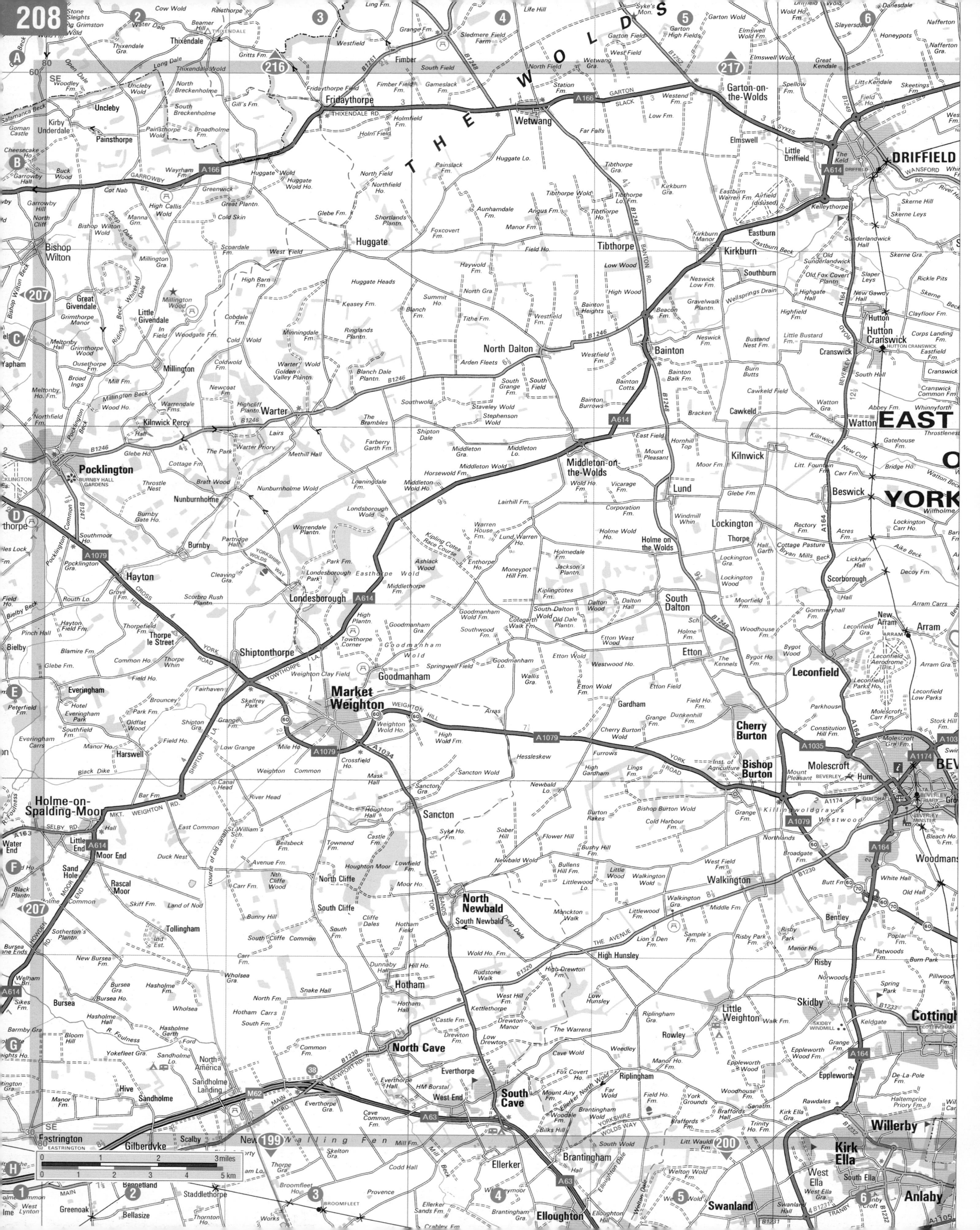

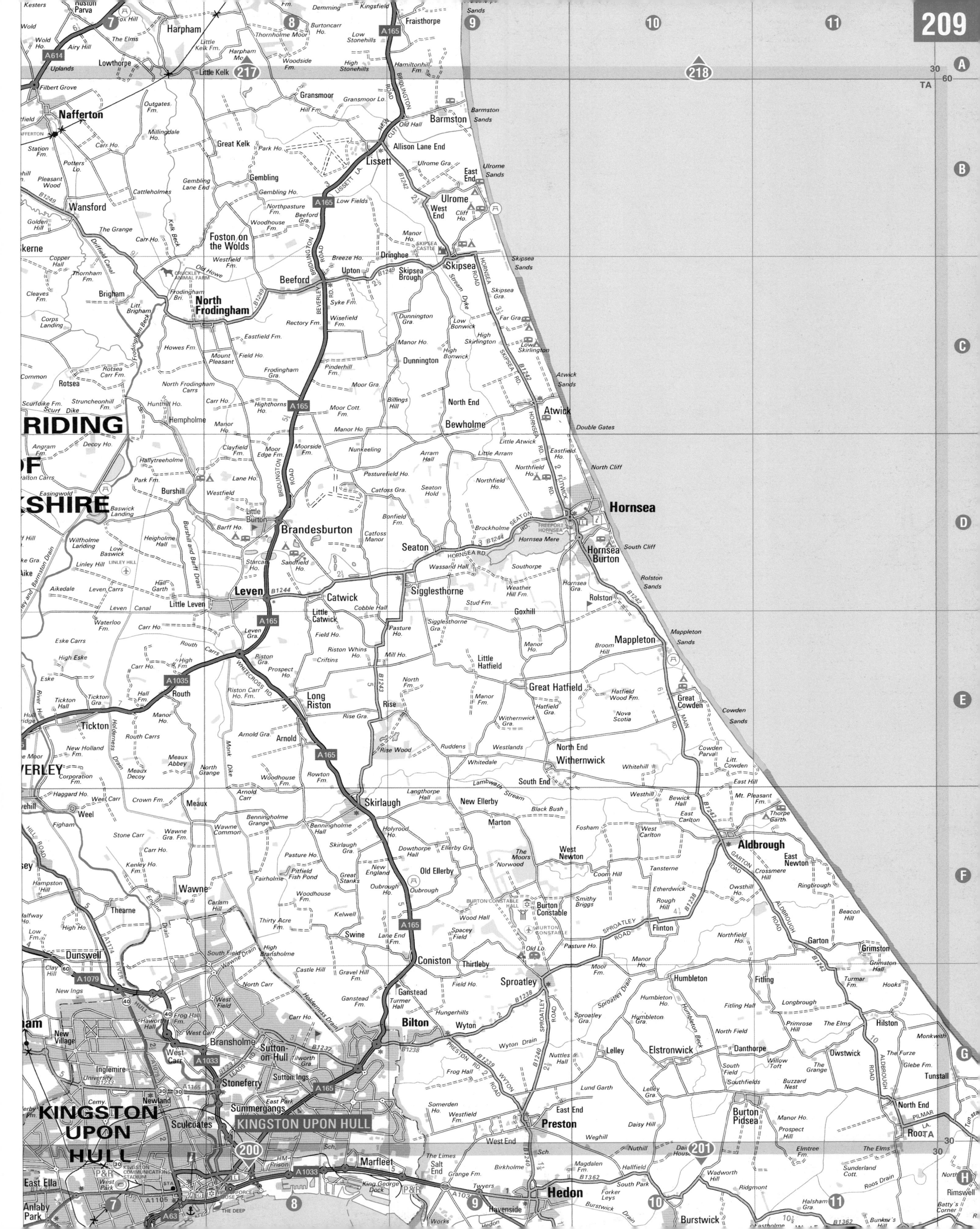

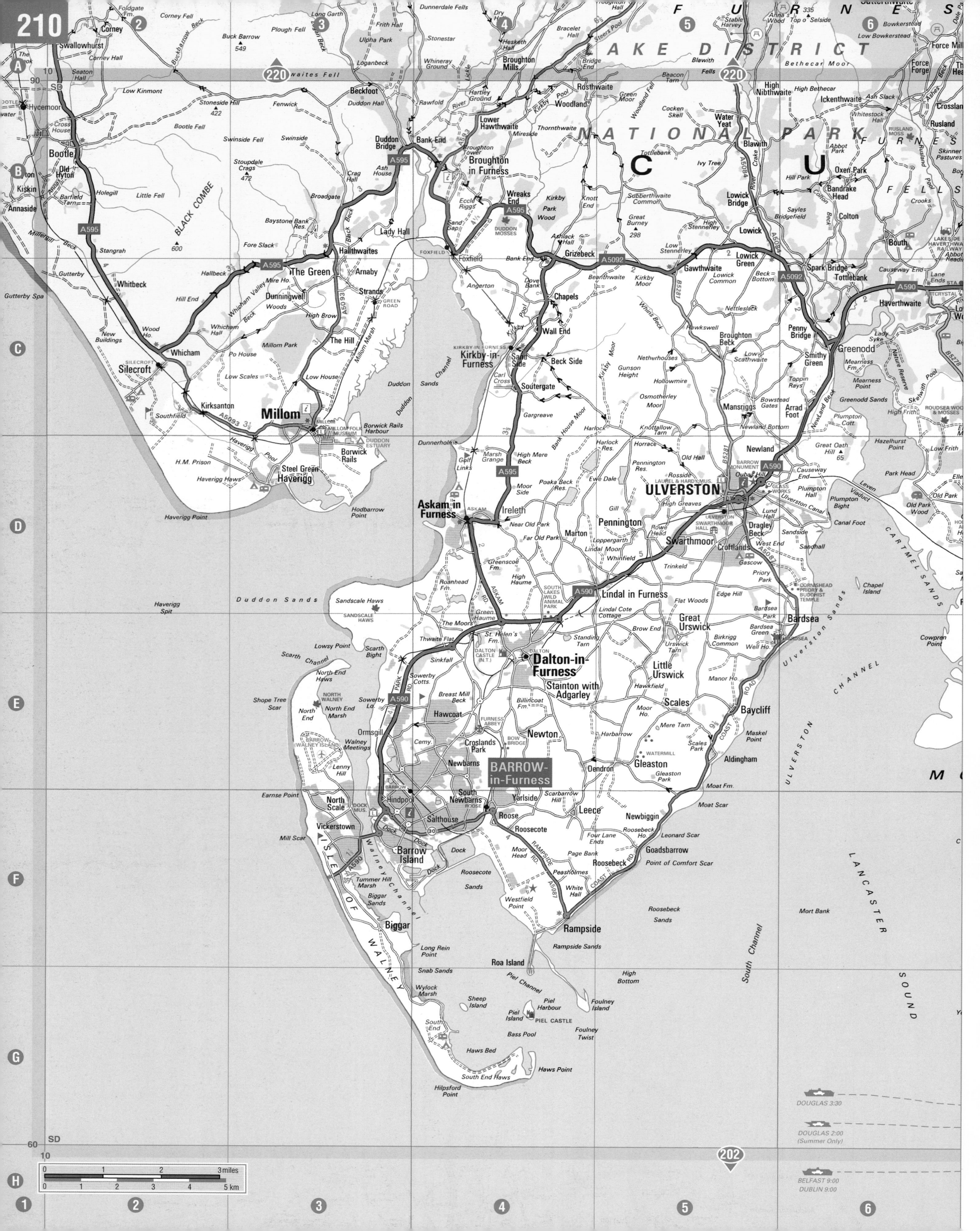

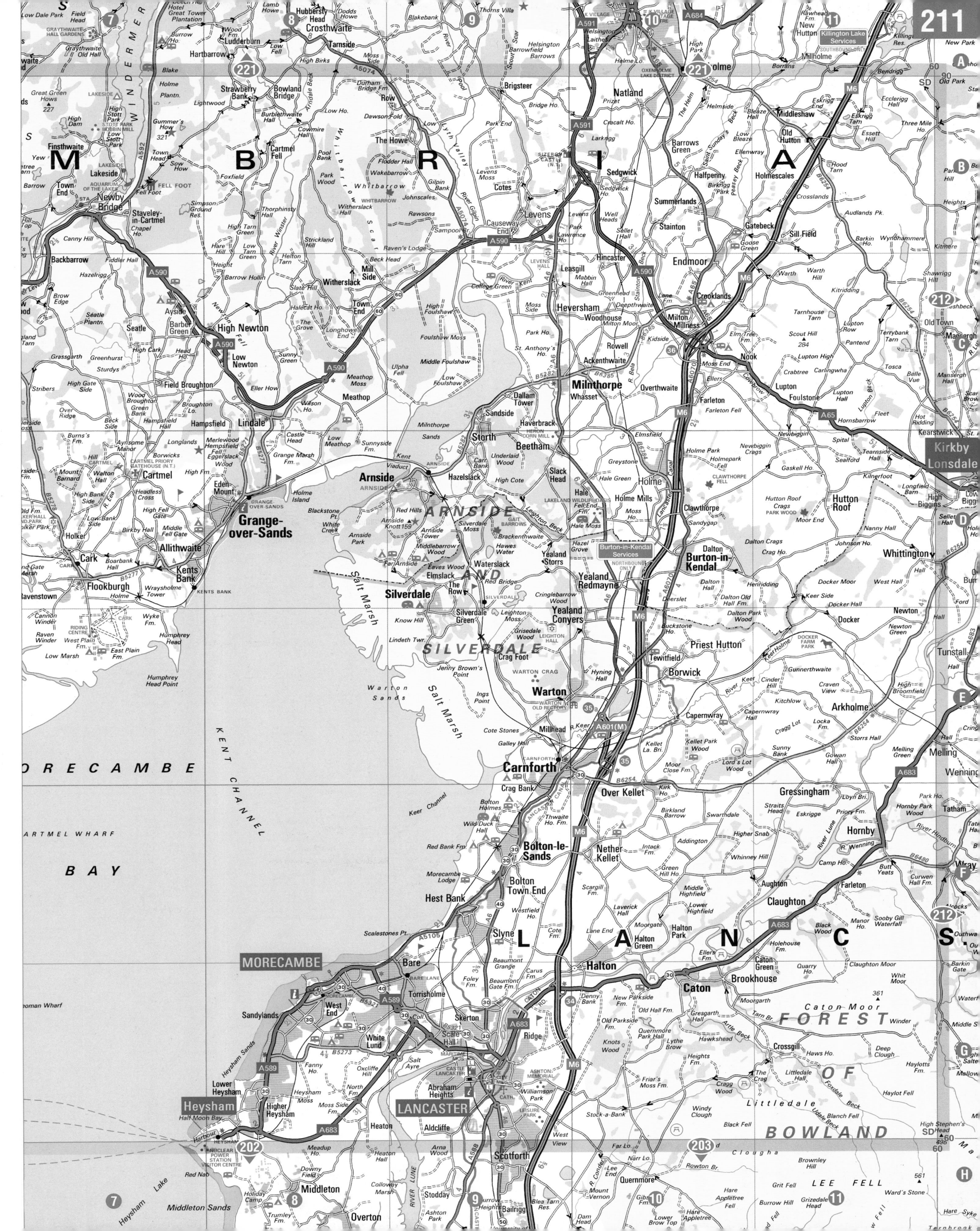

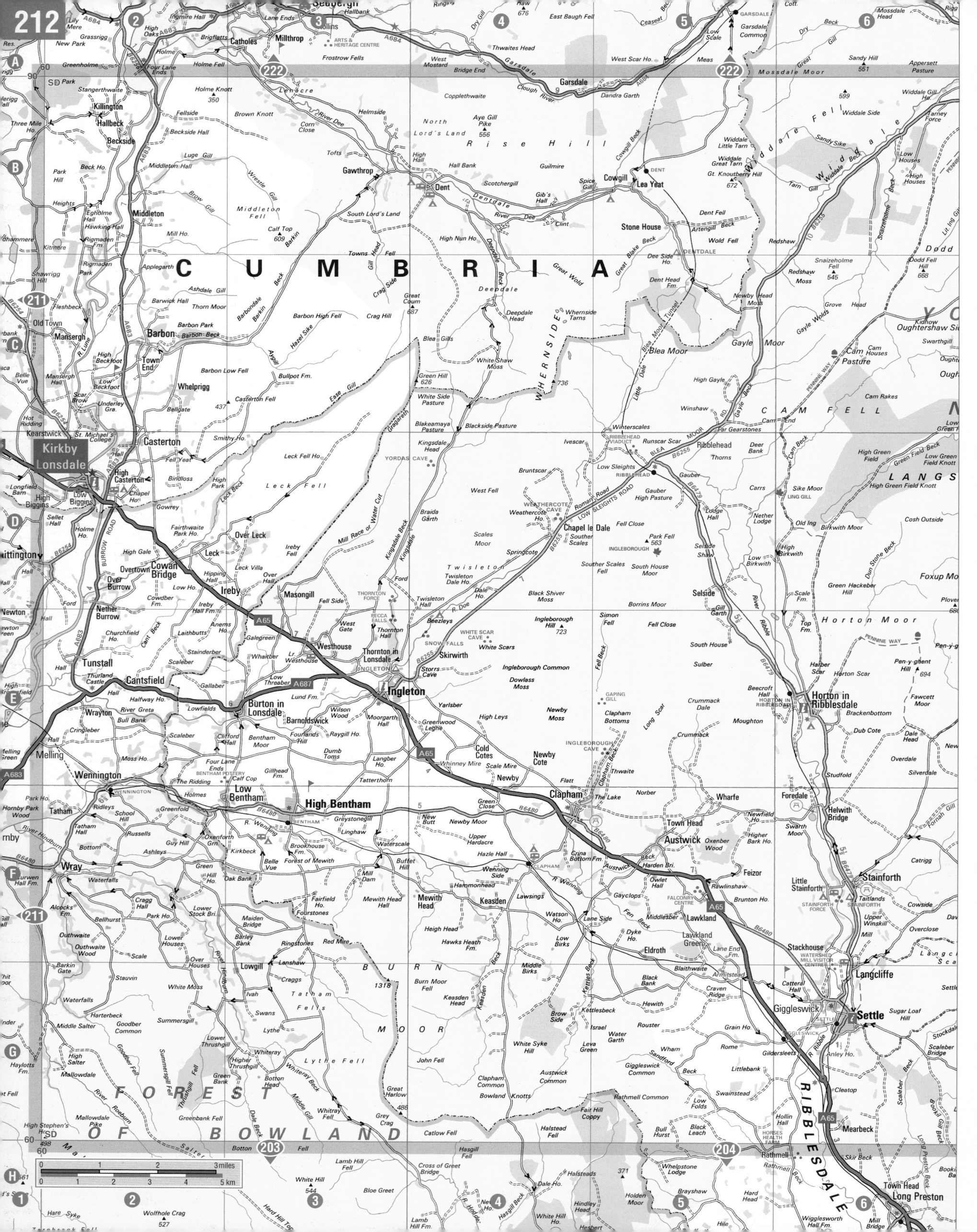

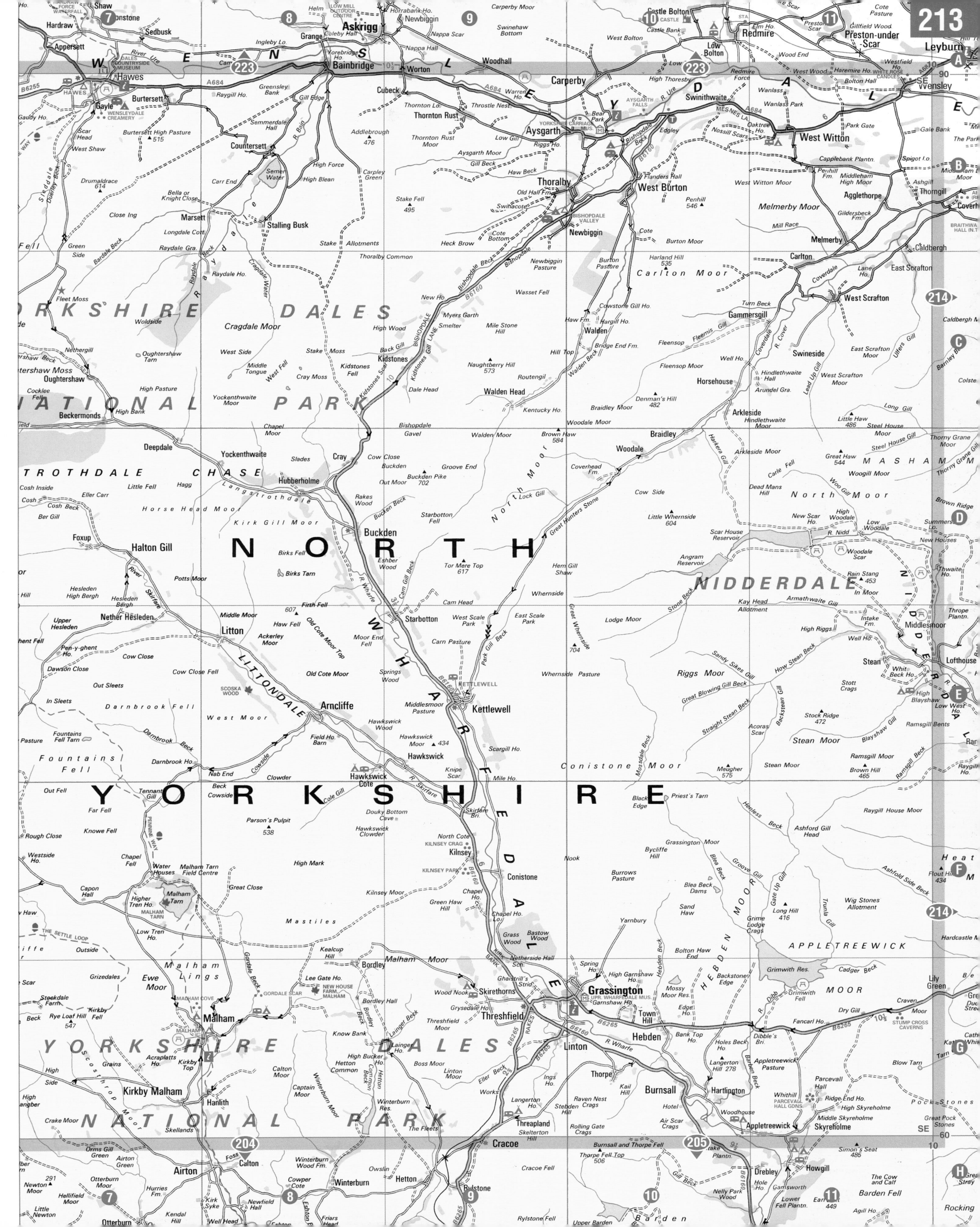

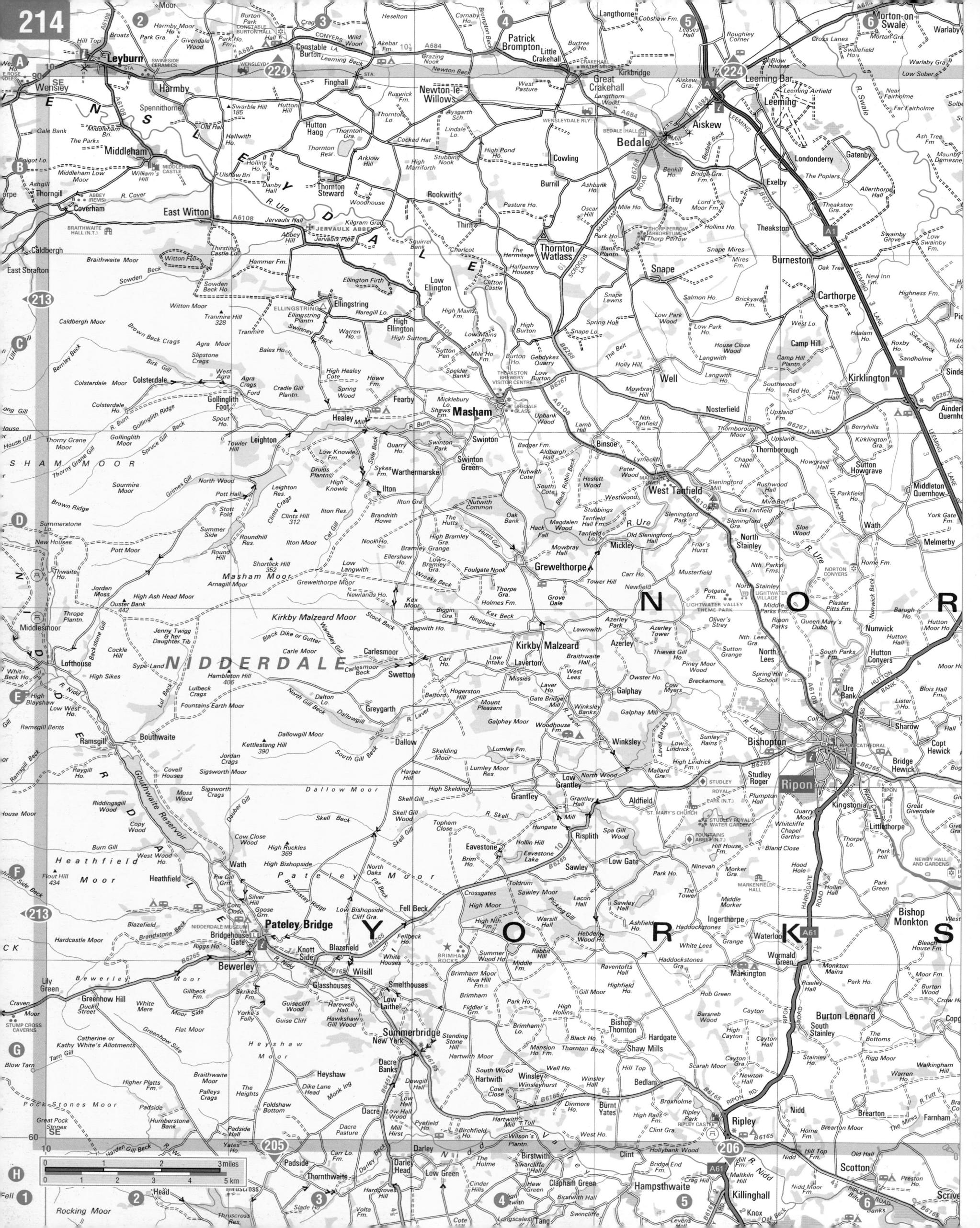

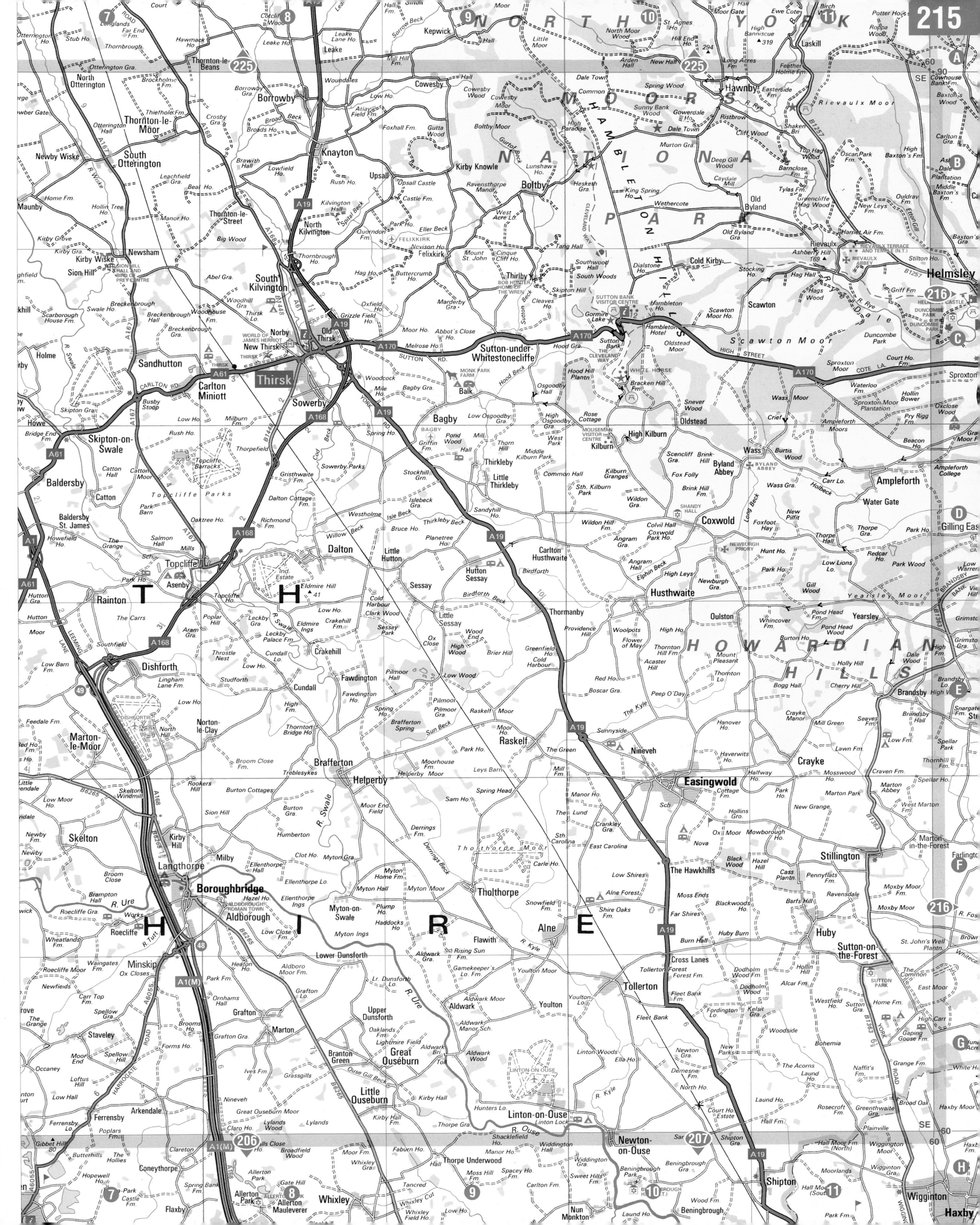

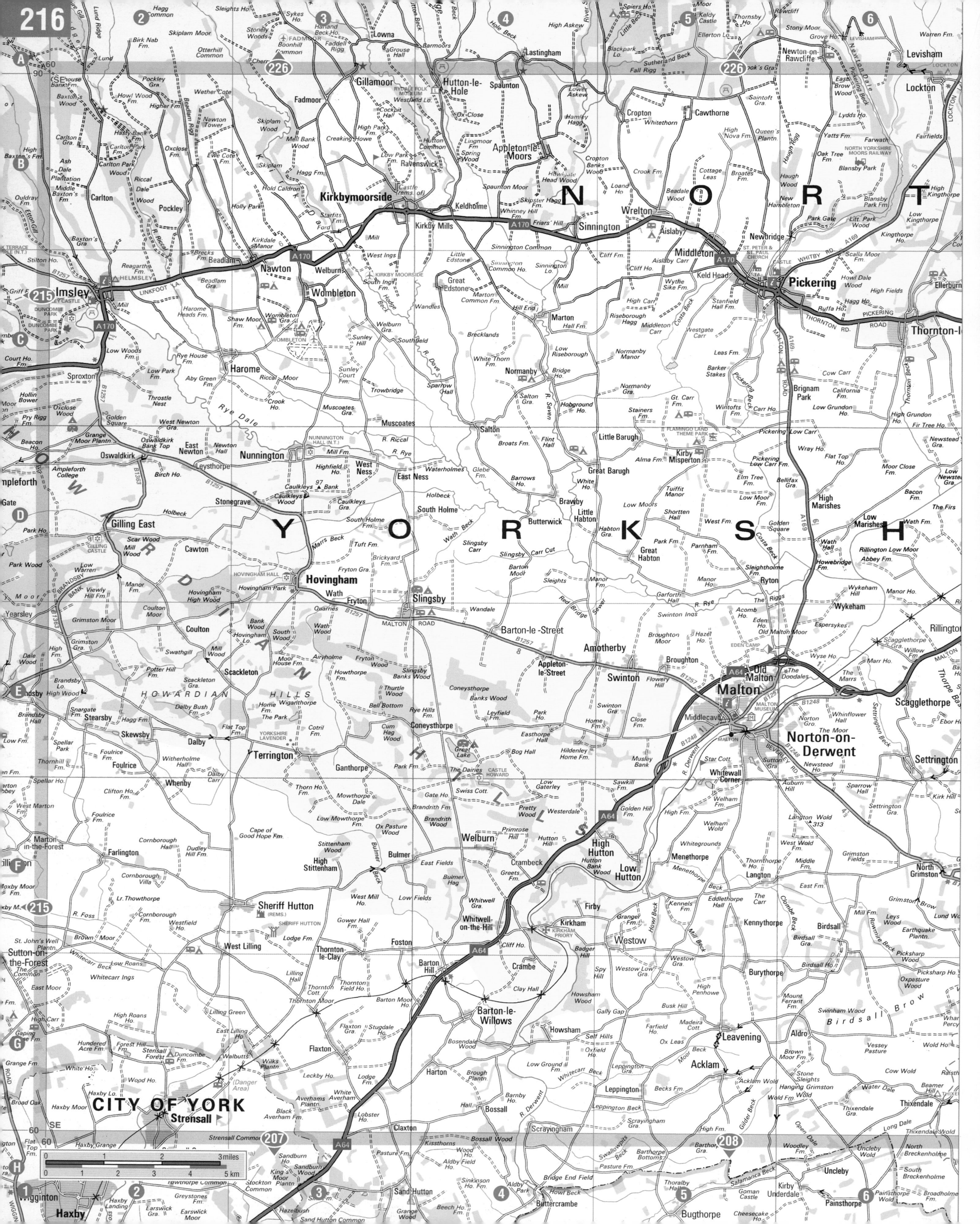

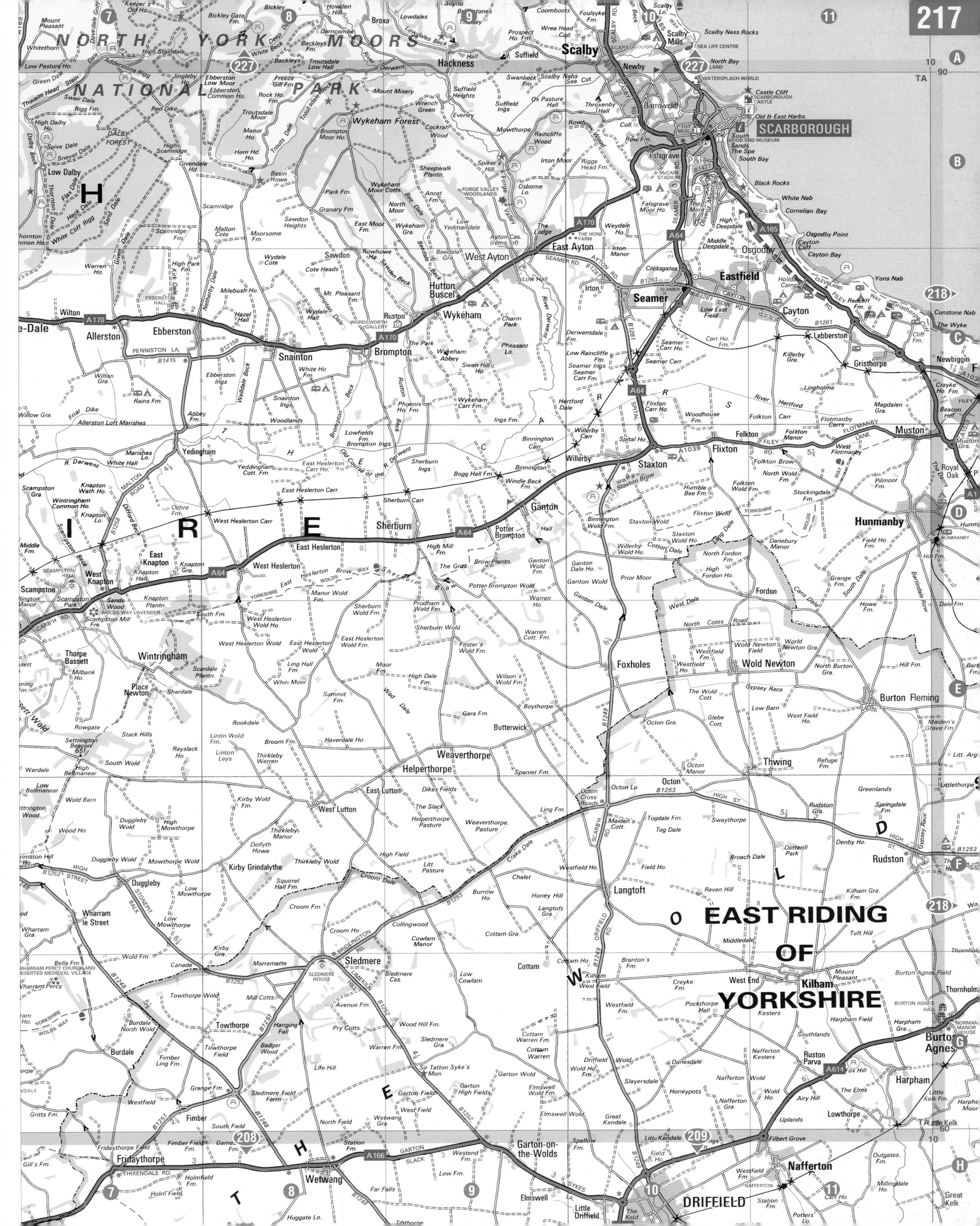

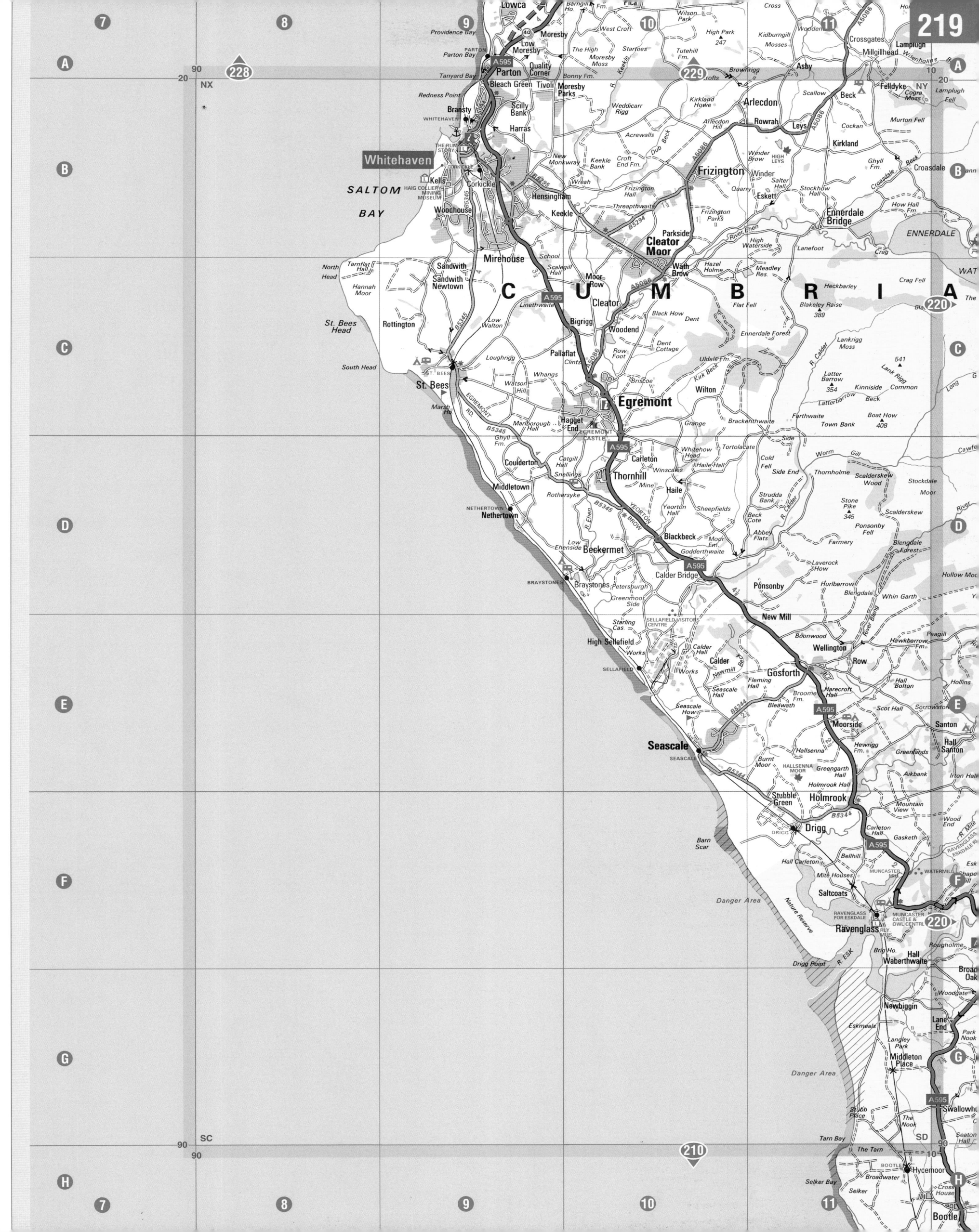

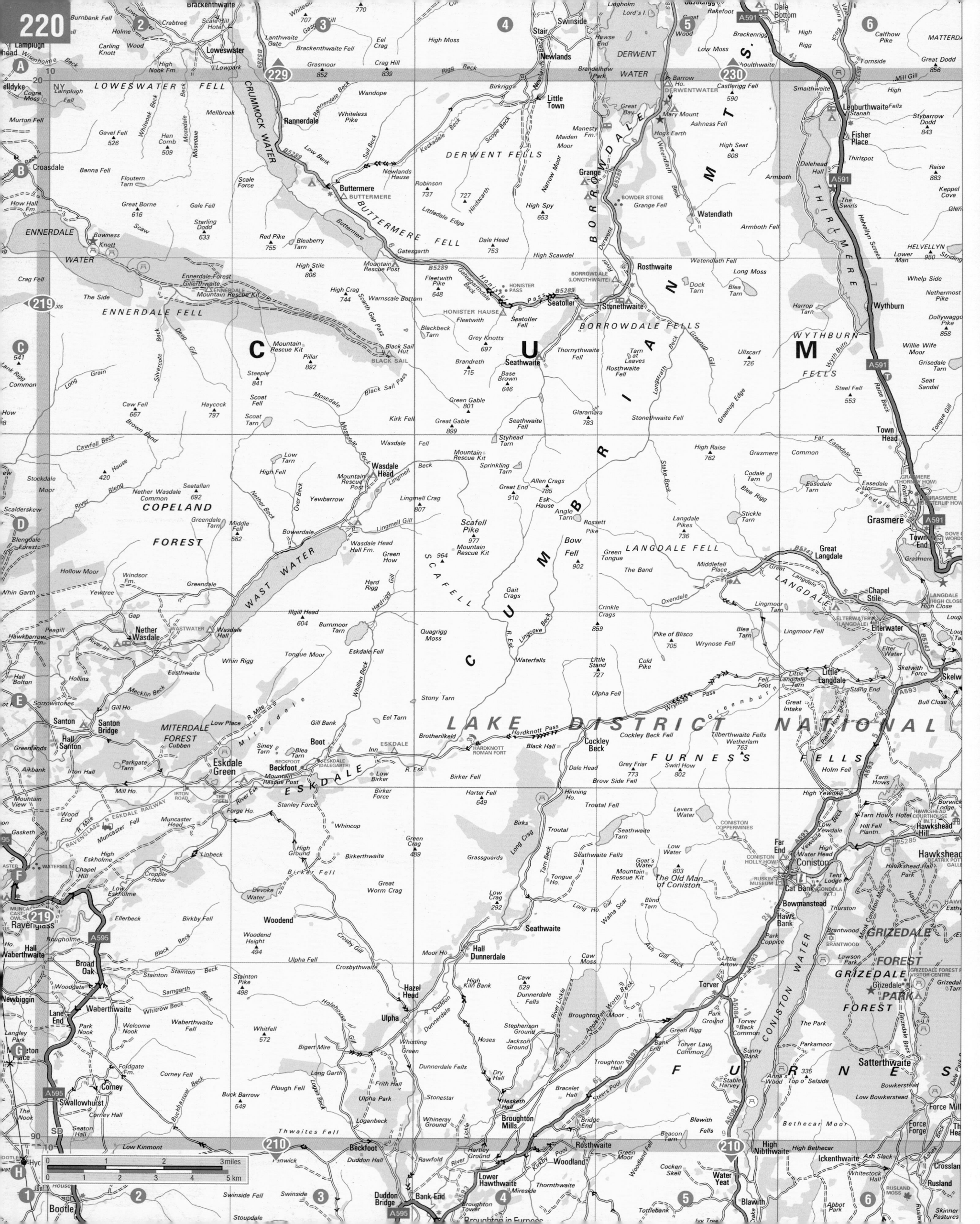

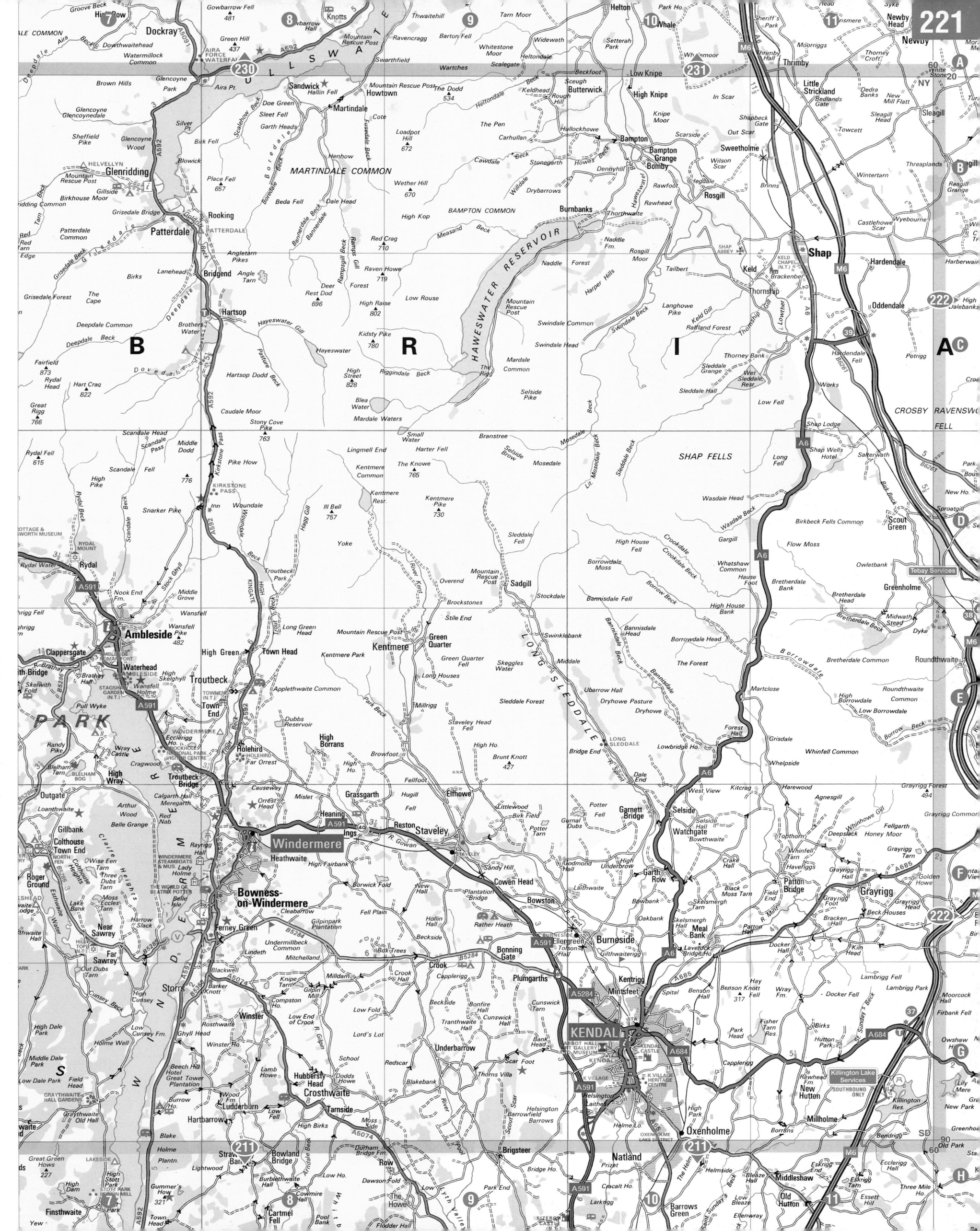

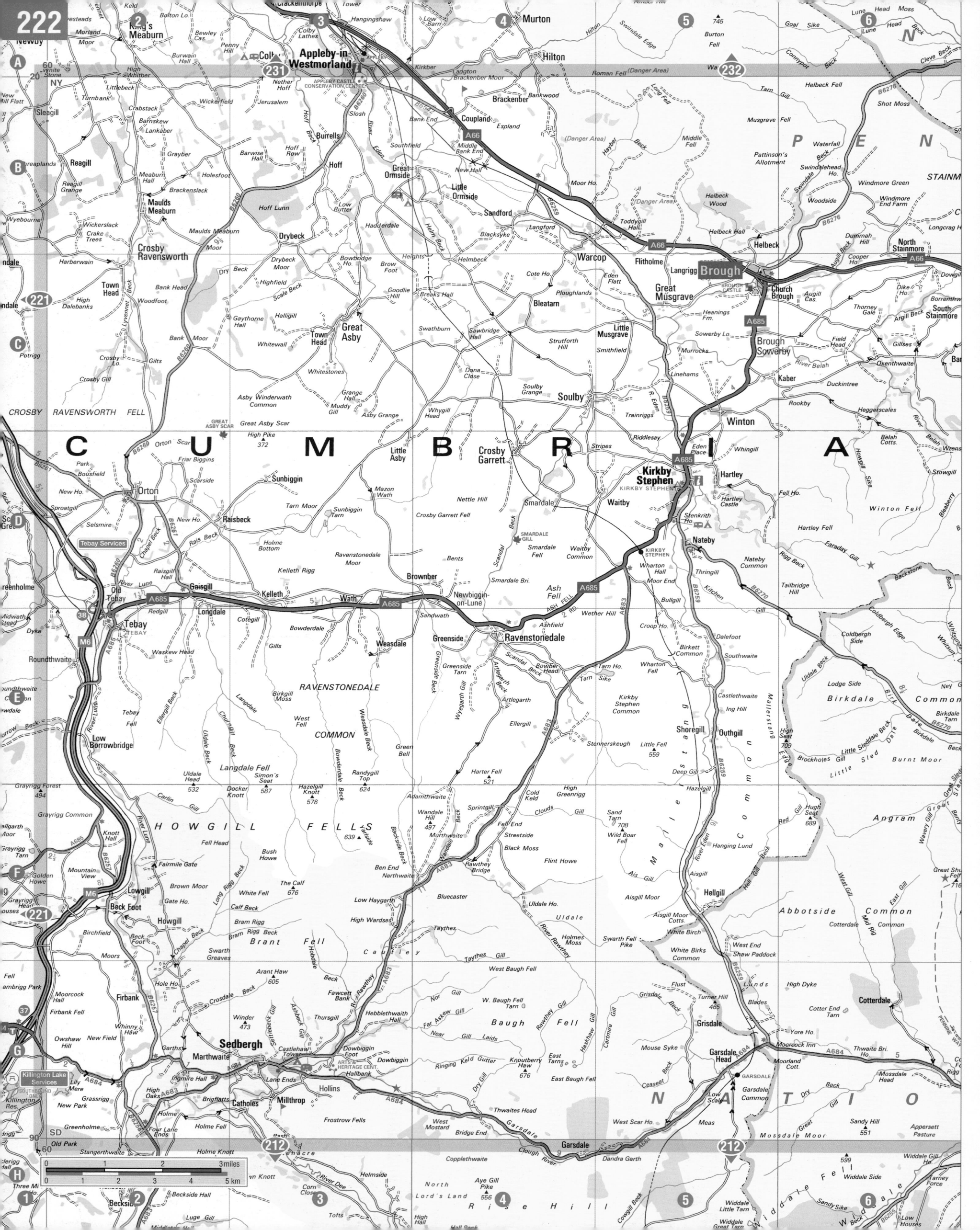

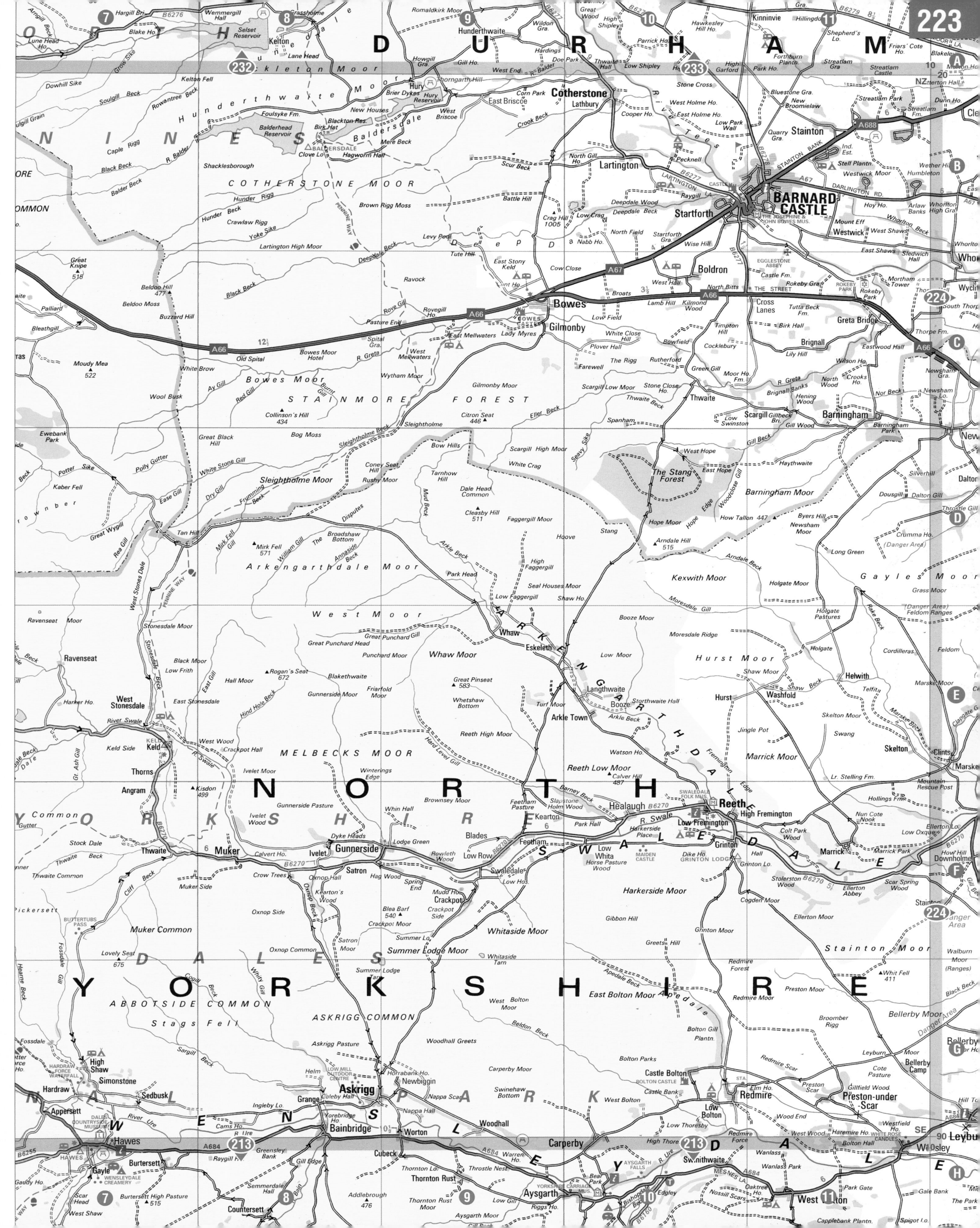

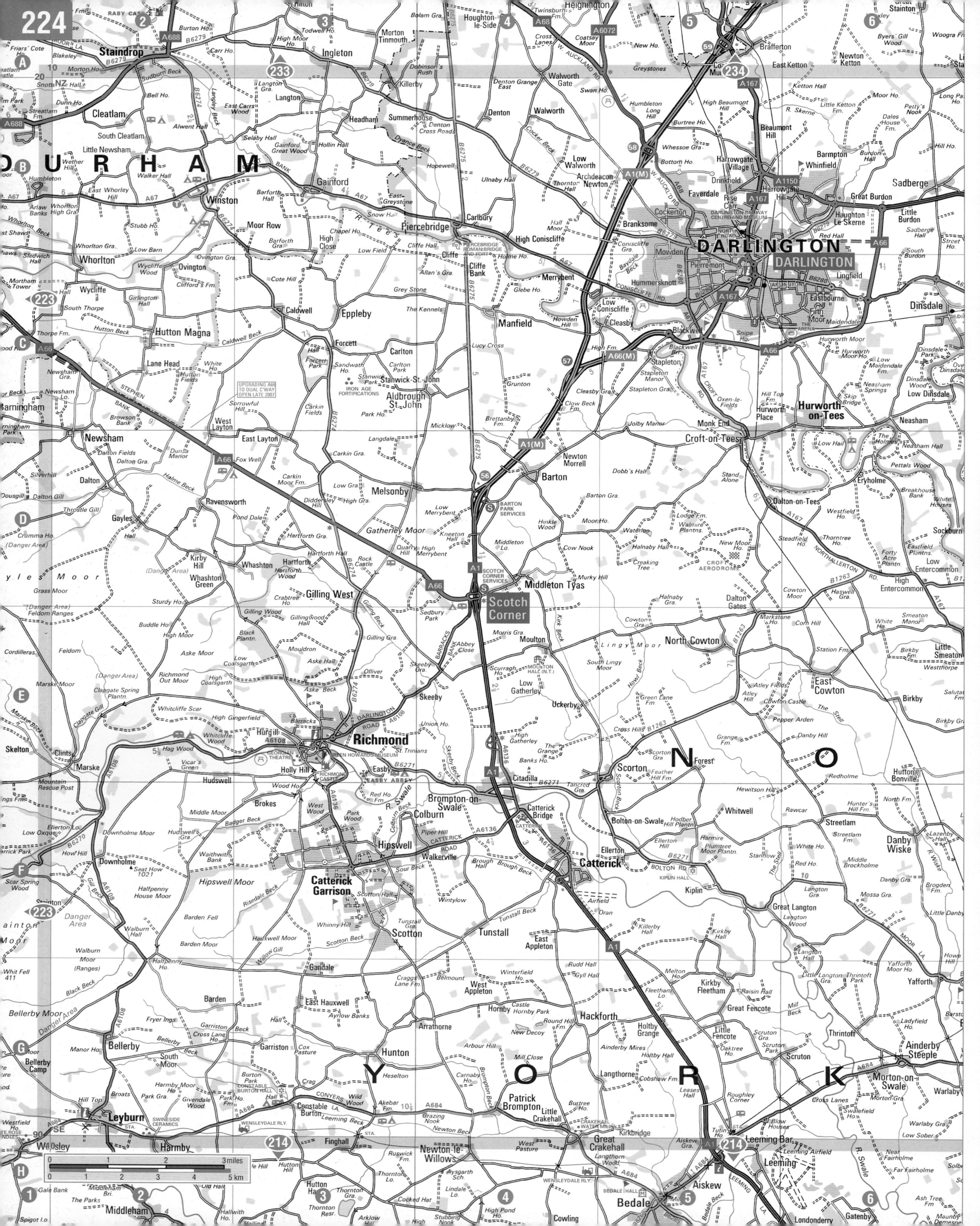

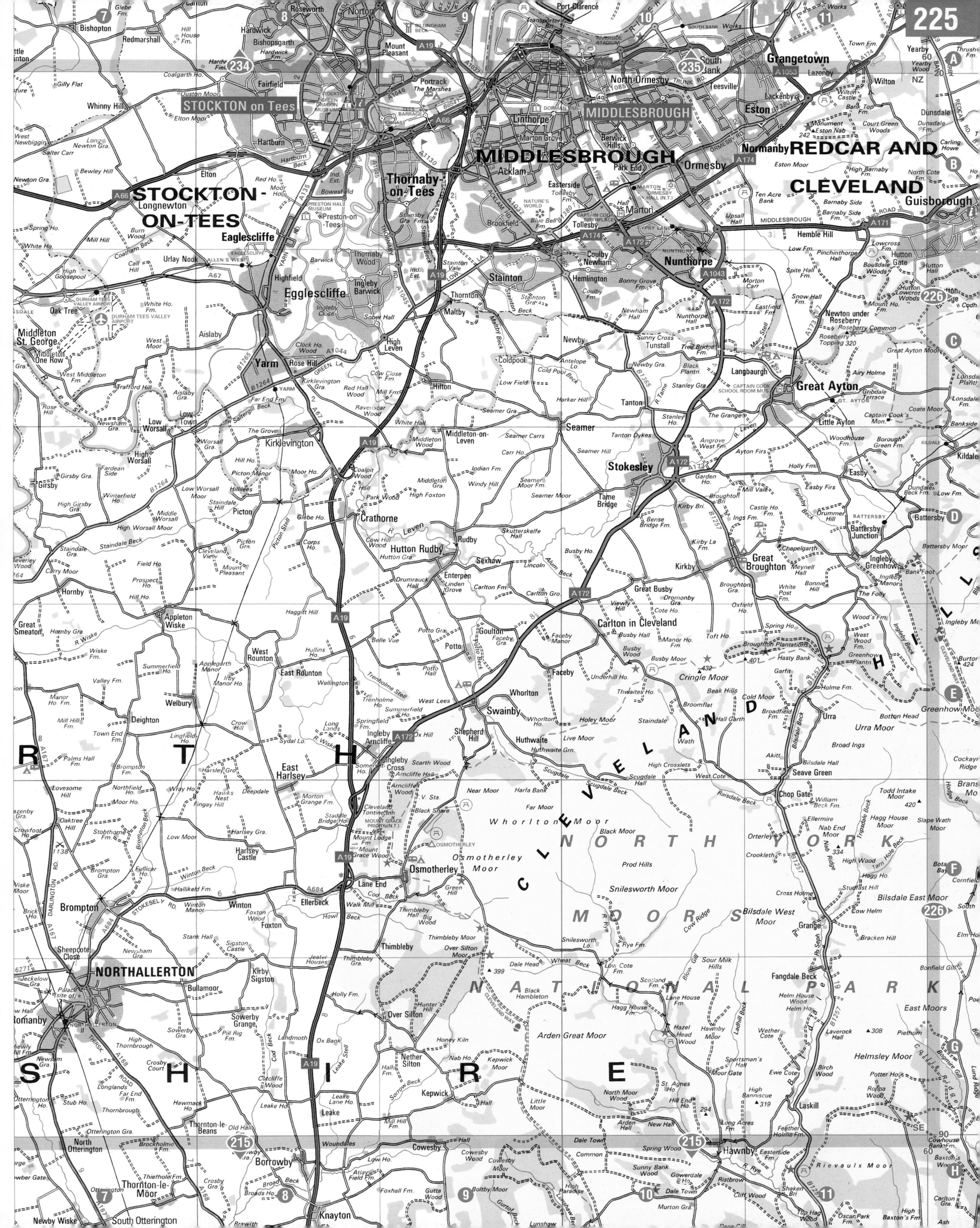

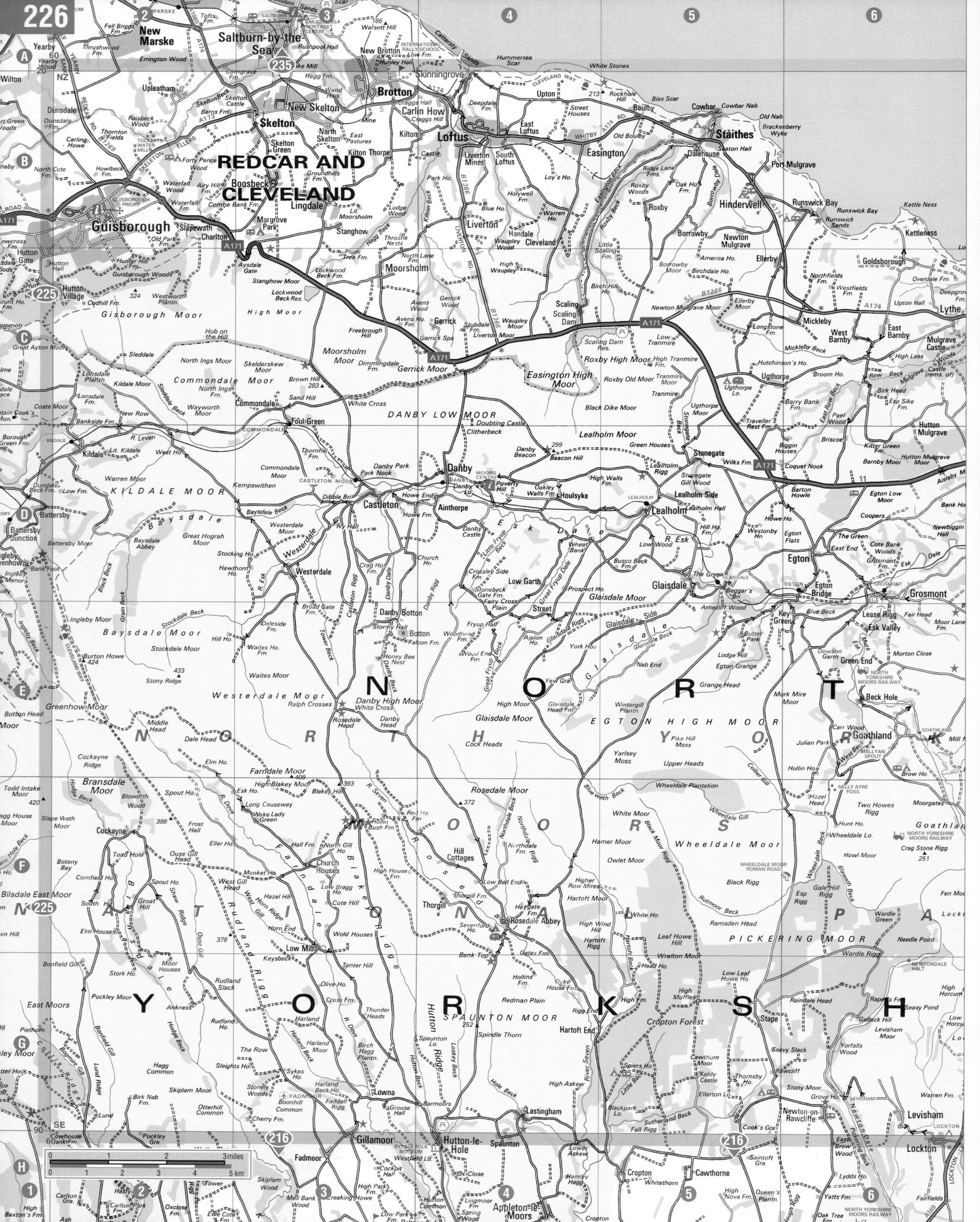

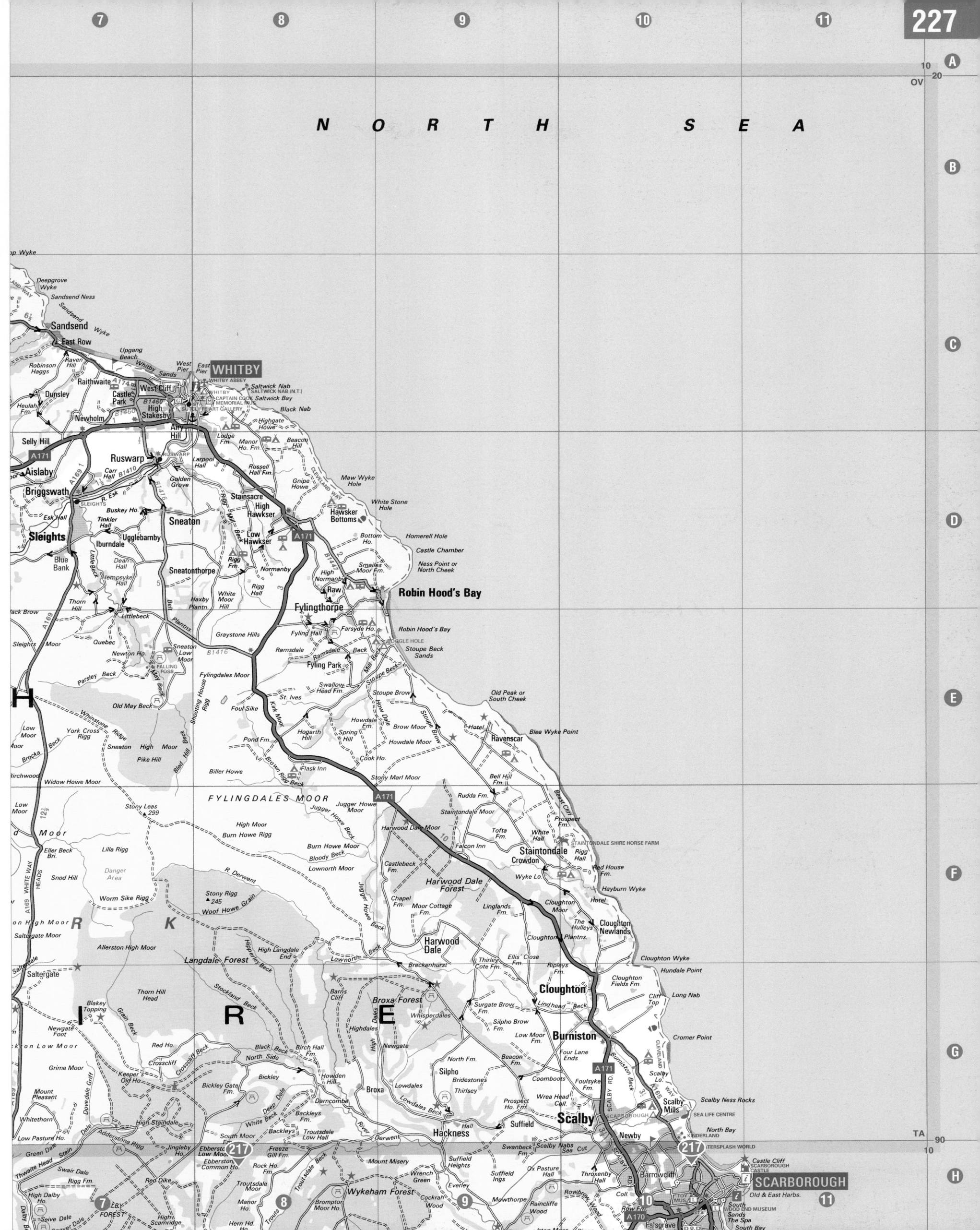

NORTH SEA

WHITBY

Sandsend
East Row
Upgang Beach
Robinson Haggs
Raven Hill
Raithwaite
Dunsley
Heulah Fm.
Newholm
Selly Hill
Aislaby
Briggswath
Ruswarp
Carr Hall
Golden Grove
Larpool Hall
Russell Hall Fm.
Gnipe Howe
Maw Wyke Hole
White Stone Hole
Sneaton
High Hawsker
Stainsacre
Hawsker Bottoms
Sleights
Buskey Ho.
Tinkler Hall
Esk Hall
Ugglebarnby
Iburndale
Low Hawsker
Blue Bank
Dean Hall
Hempsyke Hall
Rigg Fm.
Normanby
Bottom Ho.
Homerell Hole
Castle Chamber
Sneatonthorpe
Haxby Plantn.
White Moor Hill
Rigg Hall
High Normanby
Smailes Moor Fm.
Ness Point or North Cheek
Raw
Robin Hood's Bay
Thorn Hill
Littlebeck
Fylingthorpe
Robin Hood's Bay
Sleights Moor
Quebec
Newton Ho.
Sneaton Low Moor
Graystone Hills
Fyling Hall
Farsyde Ho.
Boggle Hole
Parsley Beck
Falling Foss
Old May Beck
Ramsdale
Ramsdale Beck
Stoupe Beck Sands
Fyling Park
Fylingdales Moor
Swallow Head Fm.
Stoupe Brow
Old Peak or South Cheek
St. Ives
Foul Sike
Howdale Fm.
How Dale
Whinstone Ridge
Low Moor
York Cross Rigg
Hogarth Hill
Spring Hill
Brow Moor Fm.
Hotel
Blea Wyke Point
Sneaton High Moor
Pike Hill
Howdale Moor
Ravenscar
Birchwood
Widow Howe Moor
Biller Howe
Flask Inn
Cook Ho.
Bell Hill Fm.
Low Moor
FYLINGDALES MOOR
Stony Marl Moor
Stony Leas 299
Jugger Howe Moor
Rudda Fm.
Staintondale Moor
Prospect
Moor
High Moor
Burn Howe Rigg
Tofta Fm.
White Hall
Falcon Inn
Eller Beck Bri.
Lilla Rigg
Burn Howe Moor
Bloody Beck
Castlebeck Fm.
Staintondale
Crowdon
Staintondale Shire Horse Farm
Rigg Hall
Red House Fm.
Snod Hill
Lownorth Moor
Wyke Lo.
Danger Area
Worm Sike Rigg
R. Derwent
Hayburn Wyke
Harwood Dale Forest
Chapel Fm.
Moor Cottage Fm.
Cloughton Moor
Hotel
Stony Rigg 245
Woof Howe Grain
Linglands Fm.
The Hulleys
Cloughton Newlands
Allerston High Moor
High Langdale End
Harwood Dale
Cloughton Plantns.
Saltergate Moor
Langdale Forest
Lownorth
Thirley Cote Fm.
Ellis' Close Fm.
Cloughton Wyke
Breckenhurst
Ripleys Fm.
Hundale Point
Blakey Topping
Barns Cliff
Broxa Forest
Surgate Brow Fm.
Lindhead
Cloughton Fields Fm.
Cliff Top
Long Nab
Salterfate
Whisperdales
Cloughton
Thorn Hill Head
Stockland Beck
Highdales
Silpho Brow
Low Moor Fm.
Cromer Point
Newgate Foot
Red Ho.
Black Beck
Birch Hill
Newgate
Burniston
Beacon Fm.
Mount Pleasant
Crosscliff
Keeper's Old Ho.
Bickley Gate Fm.
Howden Hill
North Fm.
Four Lane Ends
Cloughton Beck
Whitethorn
Grime Moor
Crosscliff Beck
North Side
Silpho
Bridestones
Wrea Head Coll.
Foulsyke
Scalby Lo.
Scalby Ness Rocks
Low Pasture Ho.
High Staindale
White Beck
Backleys Fm.
Lowdales
Thirlsey
Prospect Ho. Fm.
Scalby Mills
Sea Life Centre
Green Dale
Jingleby Moor
Troutsdale Low Moor
Broxa
Lowdales Beck
Hall Fm.
Suffield
Scalby
Newby
North Bay
Kinderland
Thwaite Head
Swair Dale
Rigg Fm.
Freeze Gill Fm.
Suffield Heights
Swanbeck
Scalby Nabs Sea Cut
Waterspash World
High Dalby Ho.
Ebberston Low Moor
Ebberston Common Ho.
Rock Ho.
Mount Misery
Suffield Ings
Throxenby Hall
Barrowcliff
Castle Cliff
SCARBOROUGH
Scarborough Castle
Old & East Harbs.
Seive Dale
L.BY. FOREST
Manor Ho.
Brompton Moor Ho.
Wykeham Forest
Cockrah Wood
Mowthorpe
Raincliffe Wood
Rowbrow Wood
Toy Mus.
Woodland Museum
South Sands
The Spa
South Bay
High Scamridge
Hern Hd.
Troutsdale
Everley
Falsgrave

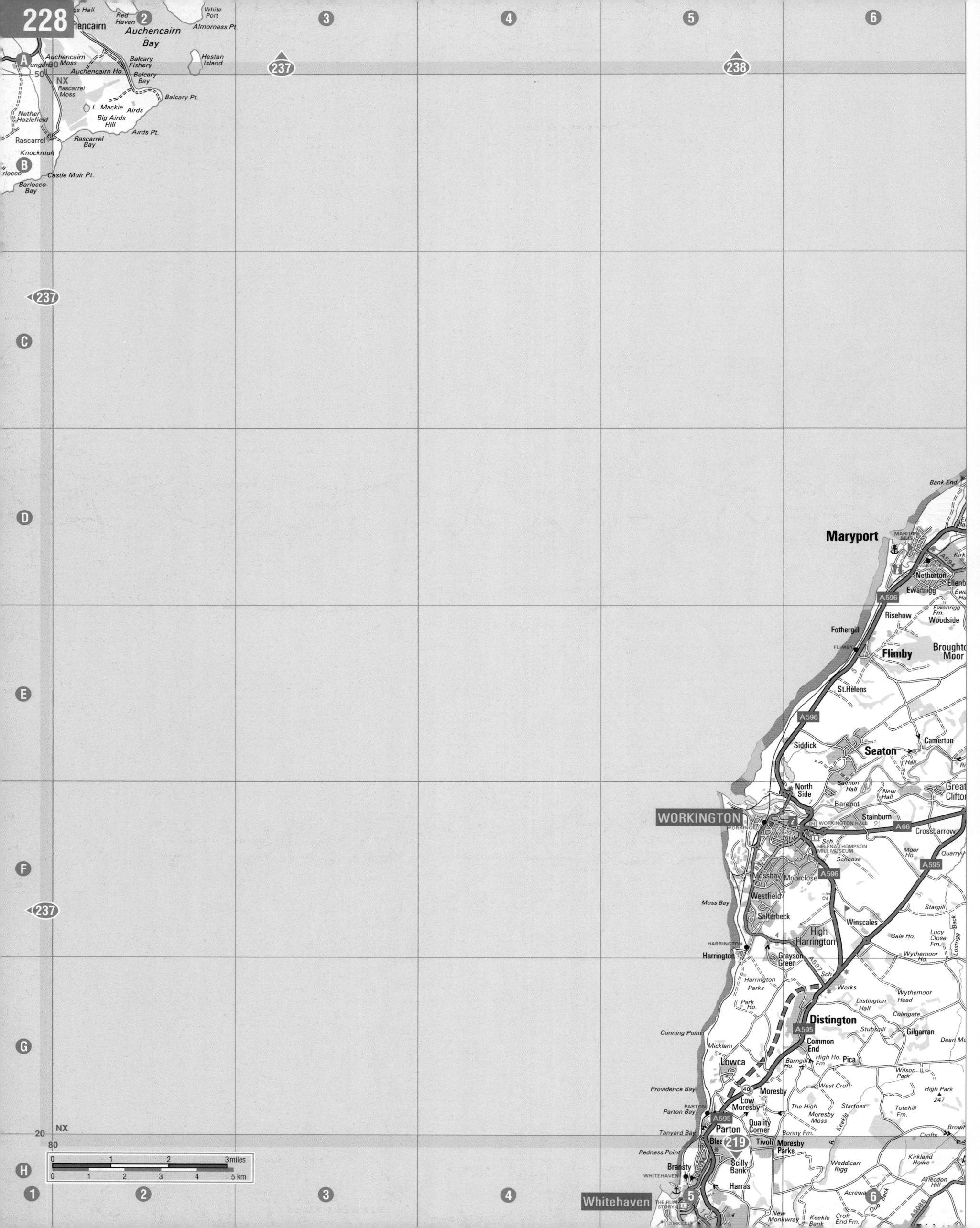

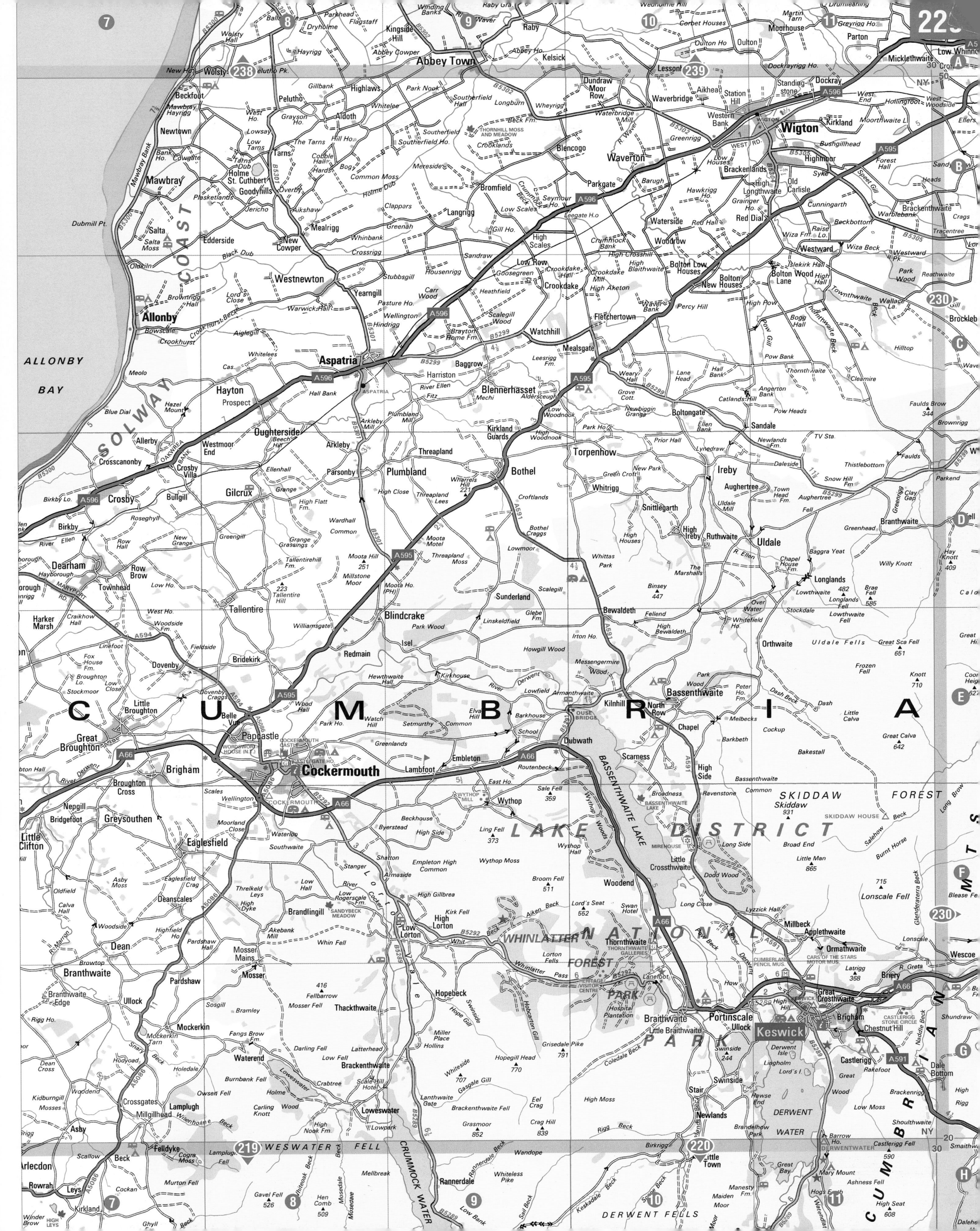

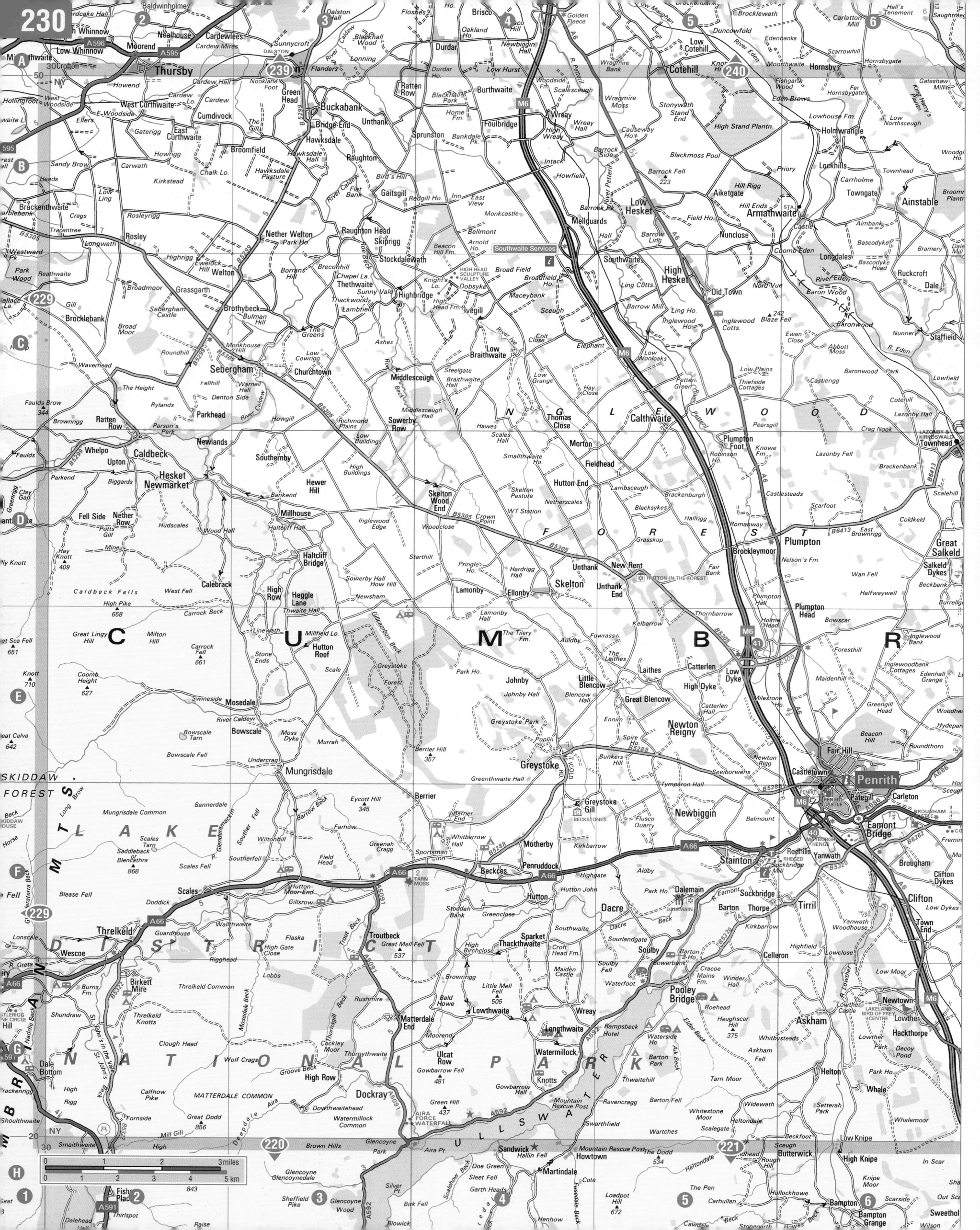

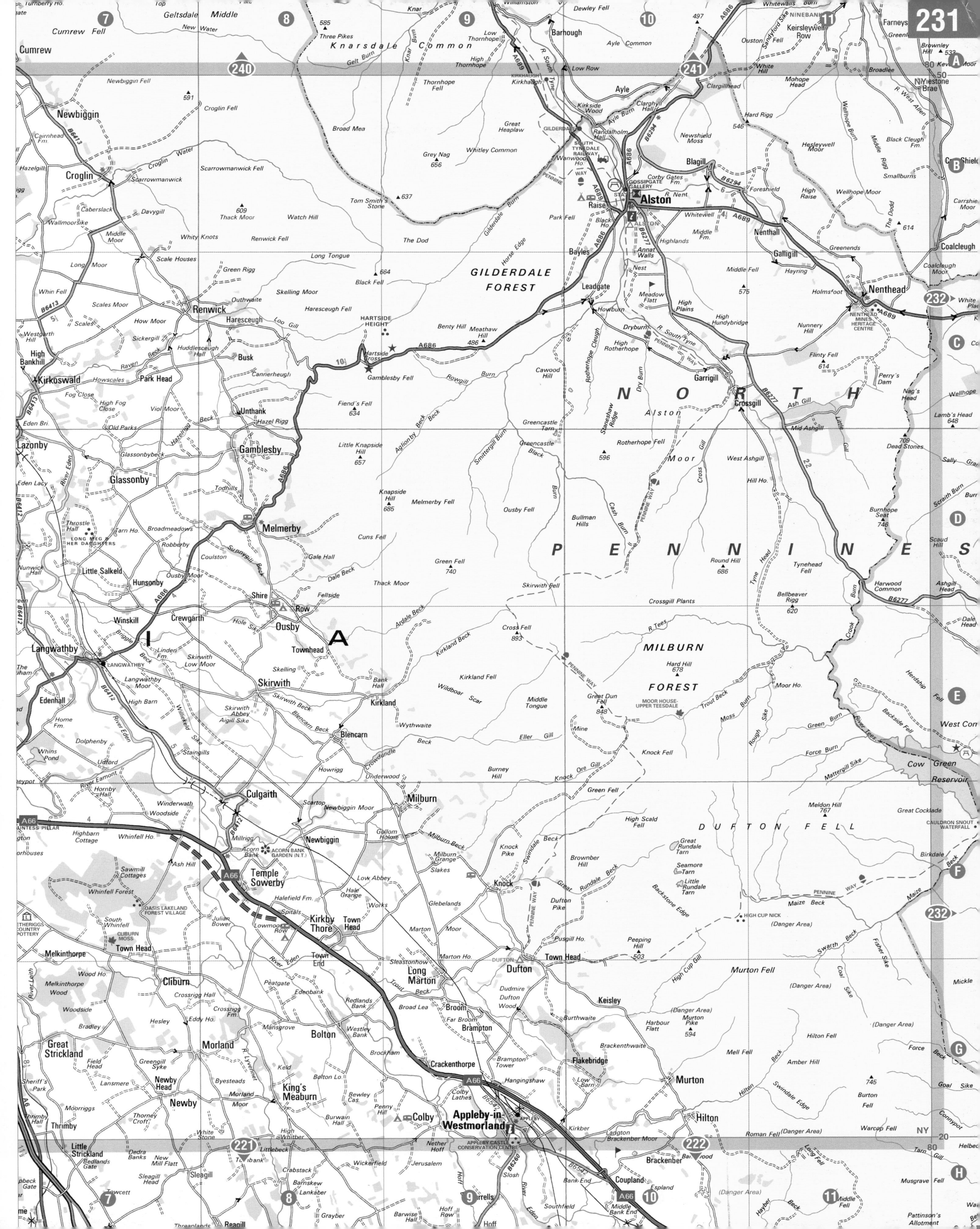

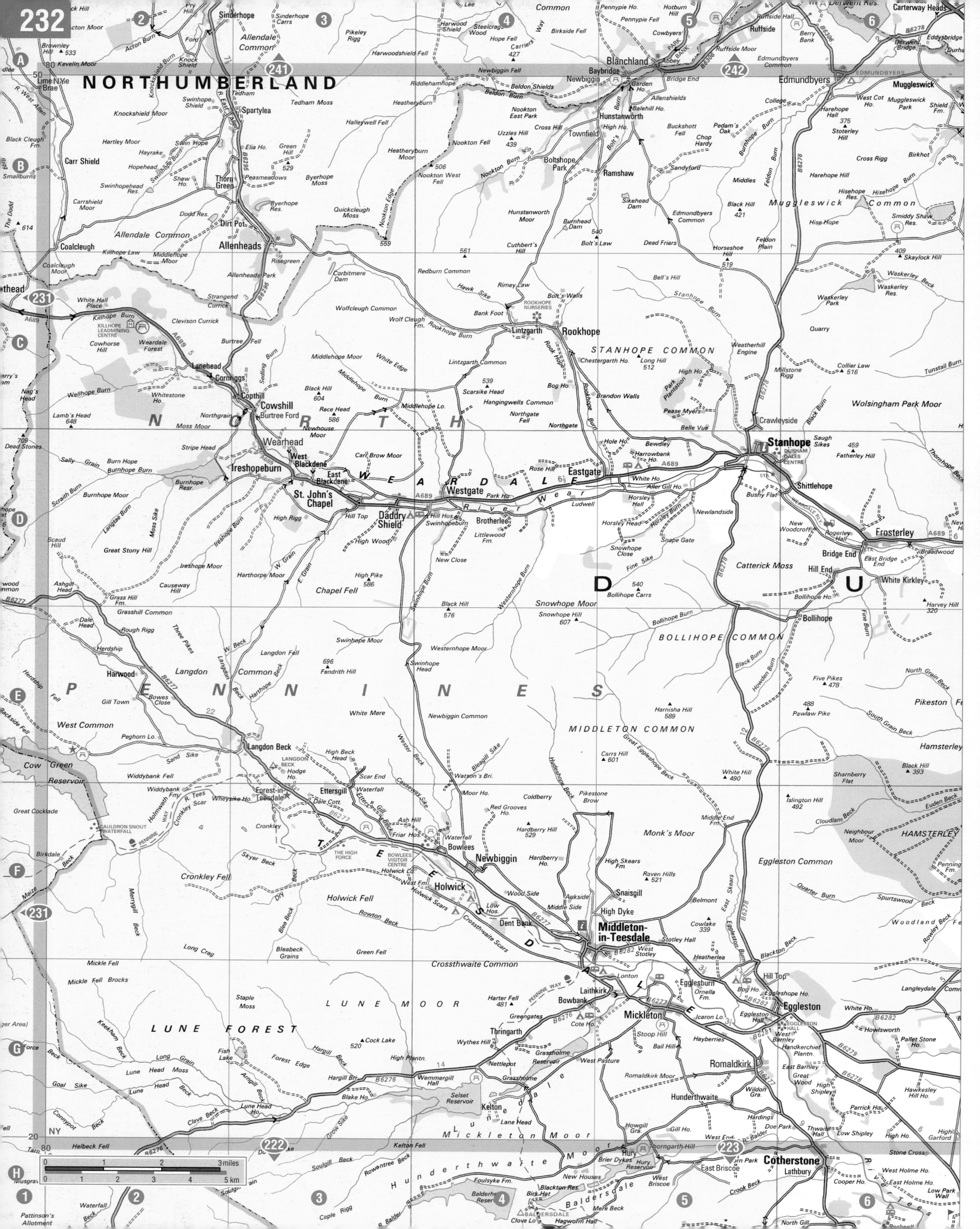

A 80 50 NZ

B

C

D

E

F

G

NZ 20 80

H

7 8 9 10 11

N O R T H

S E A

EES BAY

ROTTERDAM 16:00
ZEEBRUGGE 16:30

South Gare
Breakwater

Bran
Sands

Coatham Sands

Salt Scar

Coatham
Rocks

Redcar Rocks

Works

Coatham

REDCAR

Warrenby

REDCAR
CENTRAL

Redcar
Sands

BRITISH STEEL
REDCAR

Coatham Marsh

Westfield

Redcar
Sands

REDCAR EAST

Dormanstown

REDCAR RACECOURSE

COAST ROAD

**Marske-by-the
-Sea**

**REDCAR
AND
CLEVELAND**

Steel
Works

Chemical
Works

Manor
Fm.

Hall

LONGBECK

Marske Sands

**Saltburn-by-the
-Sea**

Pier

Saltburn
Scar

Kirkleatham
HALL MUSEUM

MARSKE

SALTBURN

Saltburn
Sands

SMUGGLERS
HERITAGE
CENTRE

Walsett Hill

Canterary Sands

Grangetown

Lazenby

Town Fm.

Fell Briggs
Fm.

Tofts
Fm.

New Brotton

INTERNATIONAL
RALLY SCHOOL

Low Fm.

Hummersea
Scar

White Stones

Wilton

Yearby

Yearby
Wood

Thrushwood
Fm.

**New
Marske**

Errington Wood

Rushpool Hall

Marske Mill

Hagg Fm.

Hunley Hall

Skinningrove

Deepdale
Fm.

Street
Houses

213

Rockhole
Hill

Bias Scar

Cowbar Cowbar Nab

Wilton Castle

Bank Top
Fm.

Dunsdale

Dunsdale
Fm.

Carling Howe

Raisbeck
Fm.

Thornton
Fields

Upleatham

Cotngrave
Fm.

Wand
Hills

Craggs Hall

Brotton

Up on

**East
Loftus**

Boulby

Old Boulby

Old Nab

Brackenberry
Wyke

Staithes

Eston

Normanby

242

Monument

Court Green
Woods

Bank
Fm.

Skelton
Castle

SKELTON
CASTLE

Barns Fm.

Kilton
Castle

Carlin How
Craggs Hill

Kilton

Loftus

Skelton

New Skelton

Skelton
Green

Kilton Thorpe

Liverton
Mines

South
Loftus

Easington

WHITBY

Old Boulby

Saaton Hall

Dalehouse

225 226

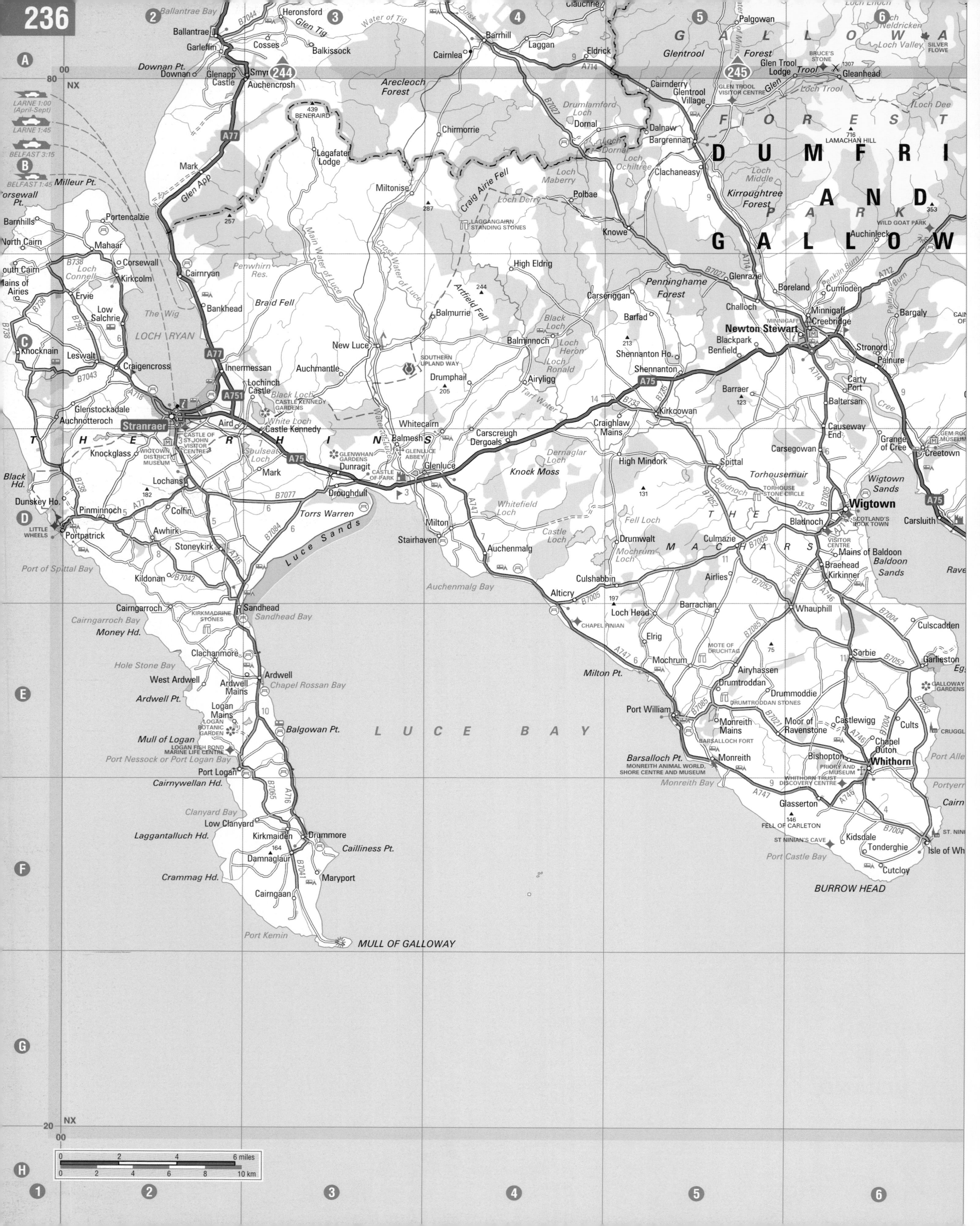

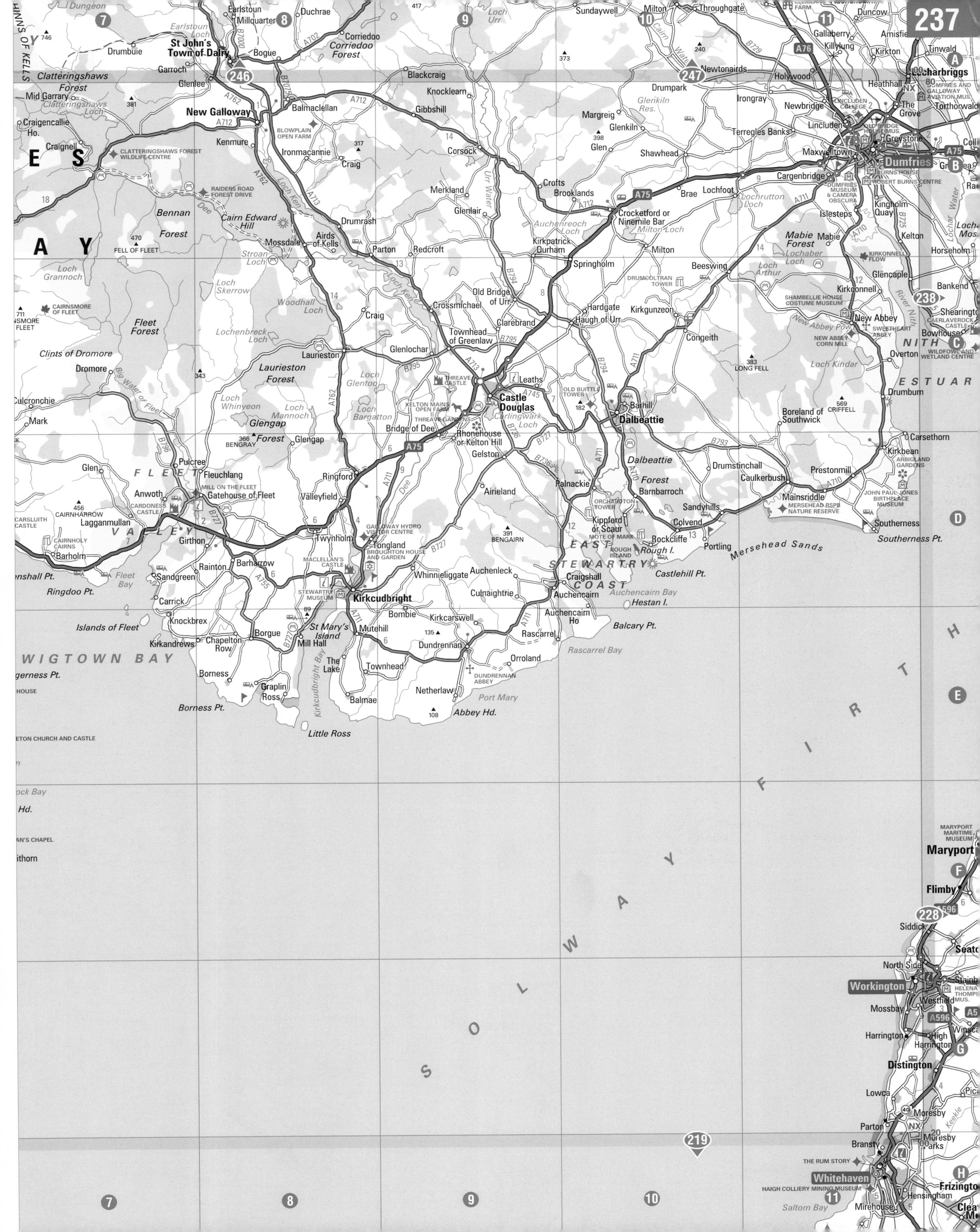

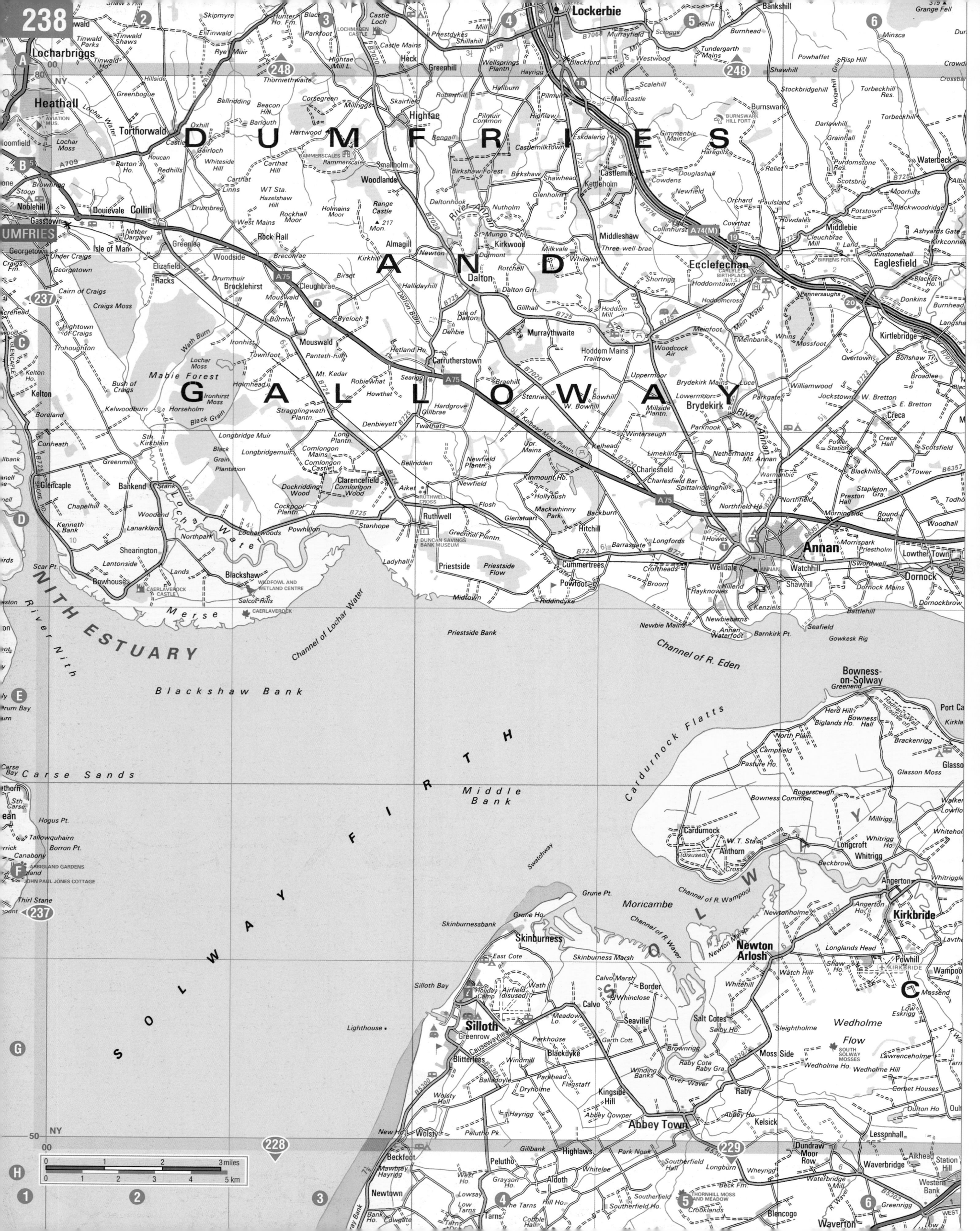

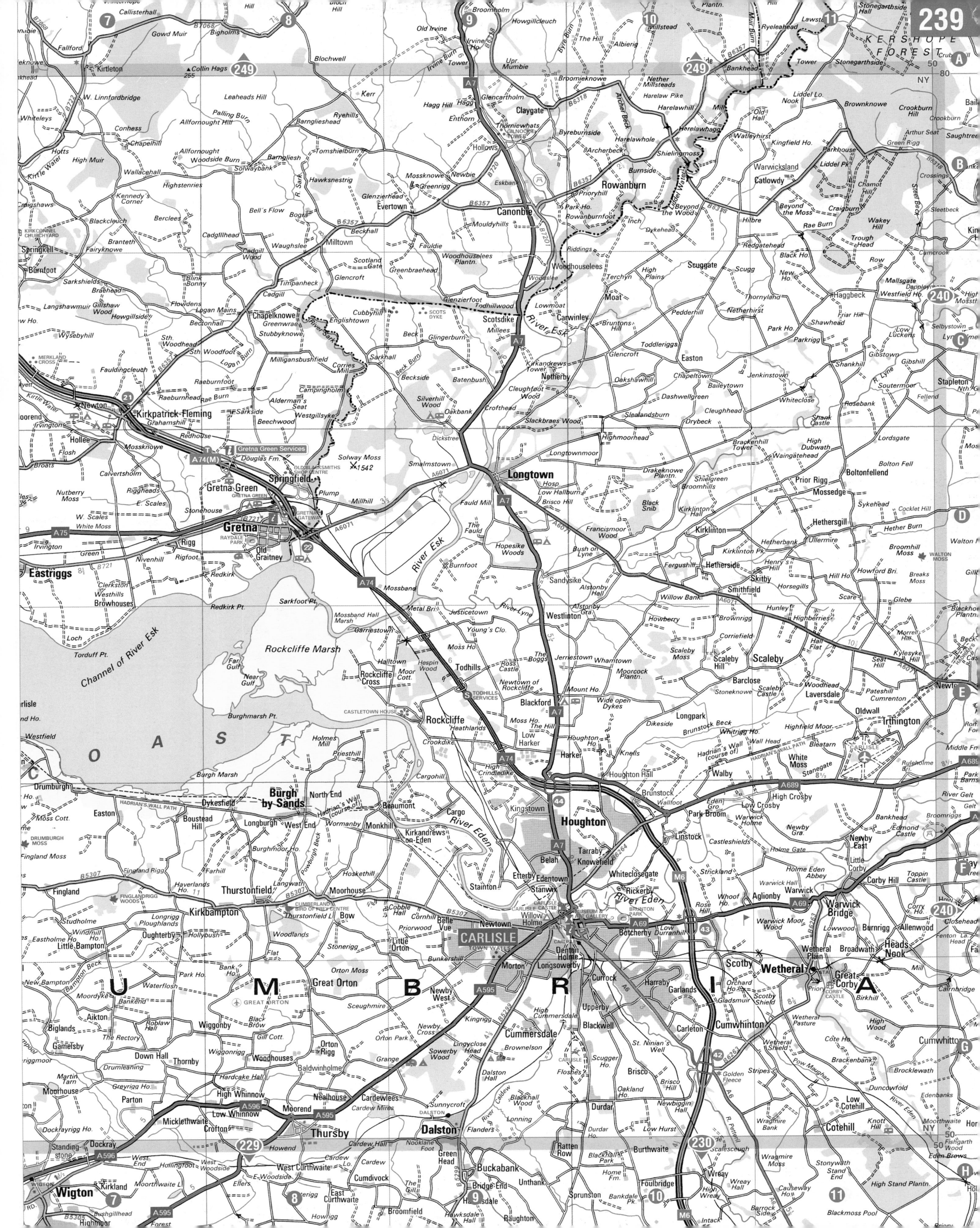

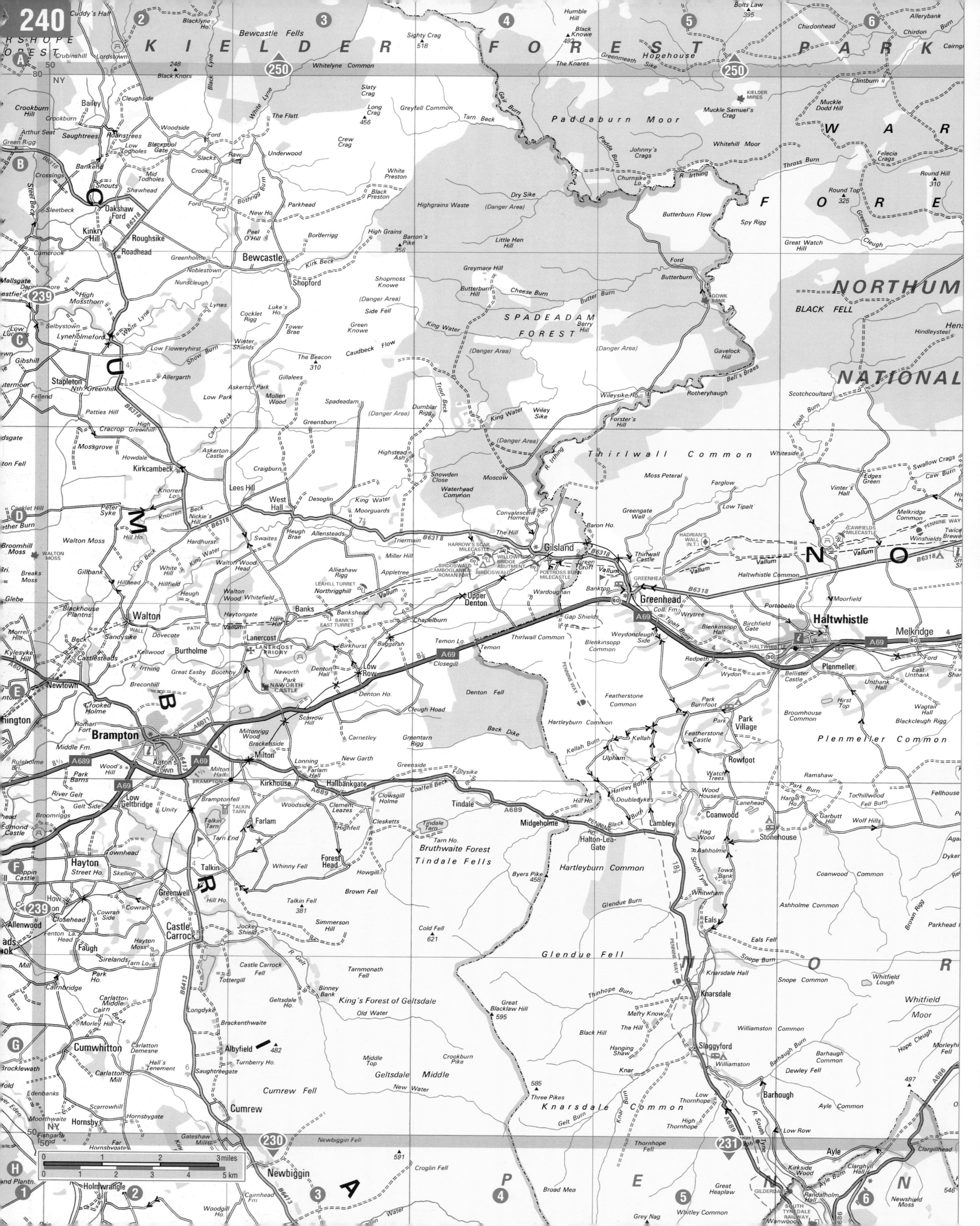

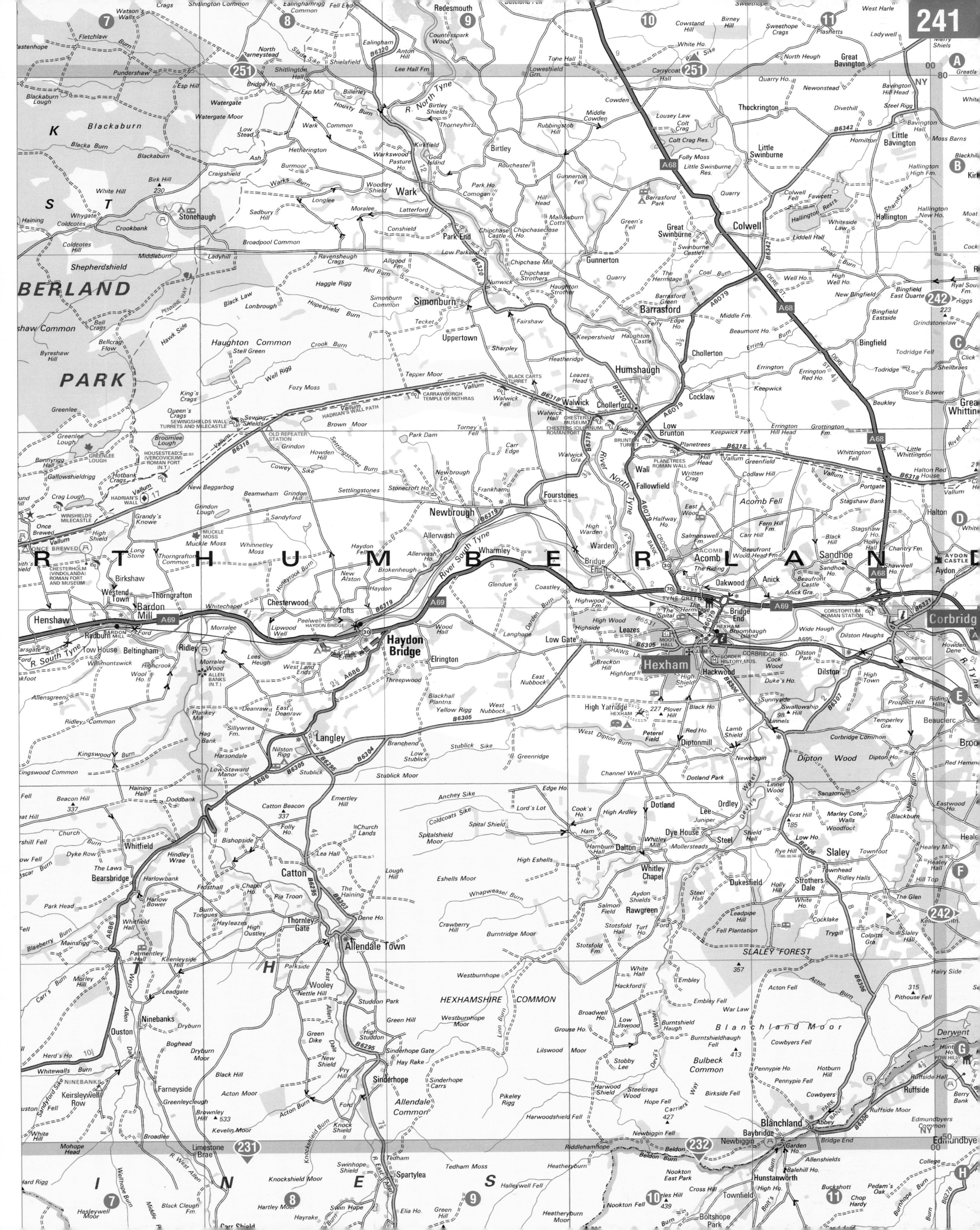

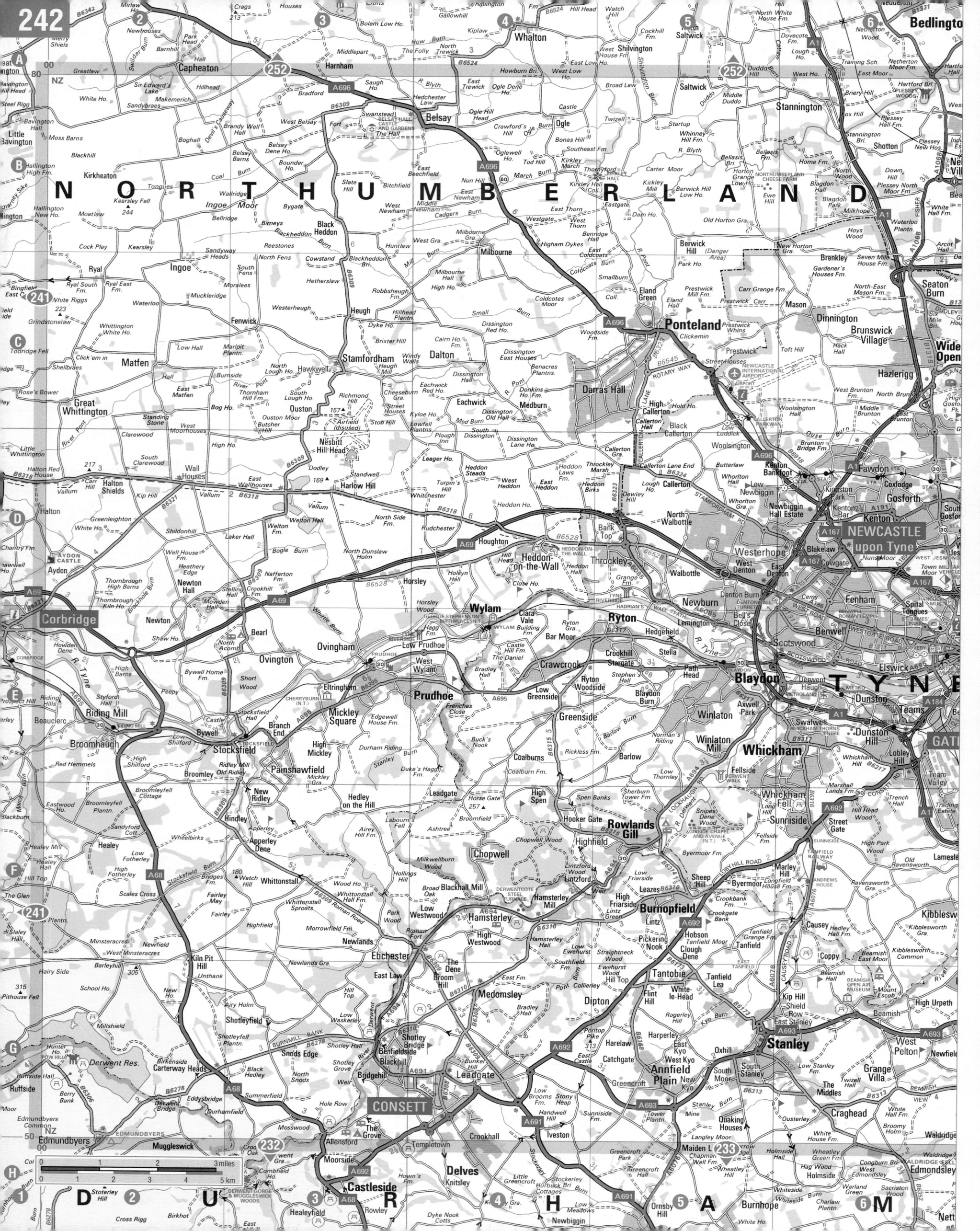

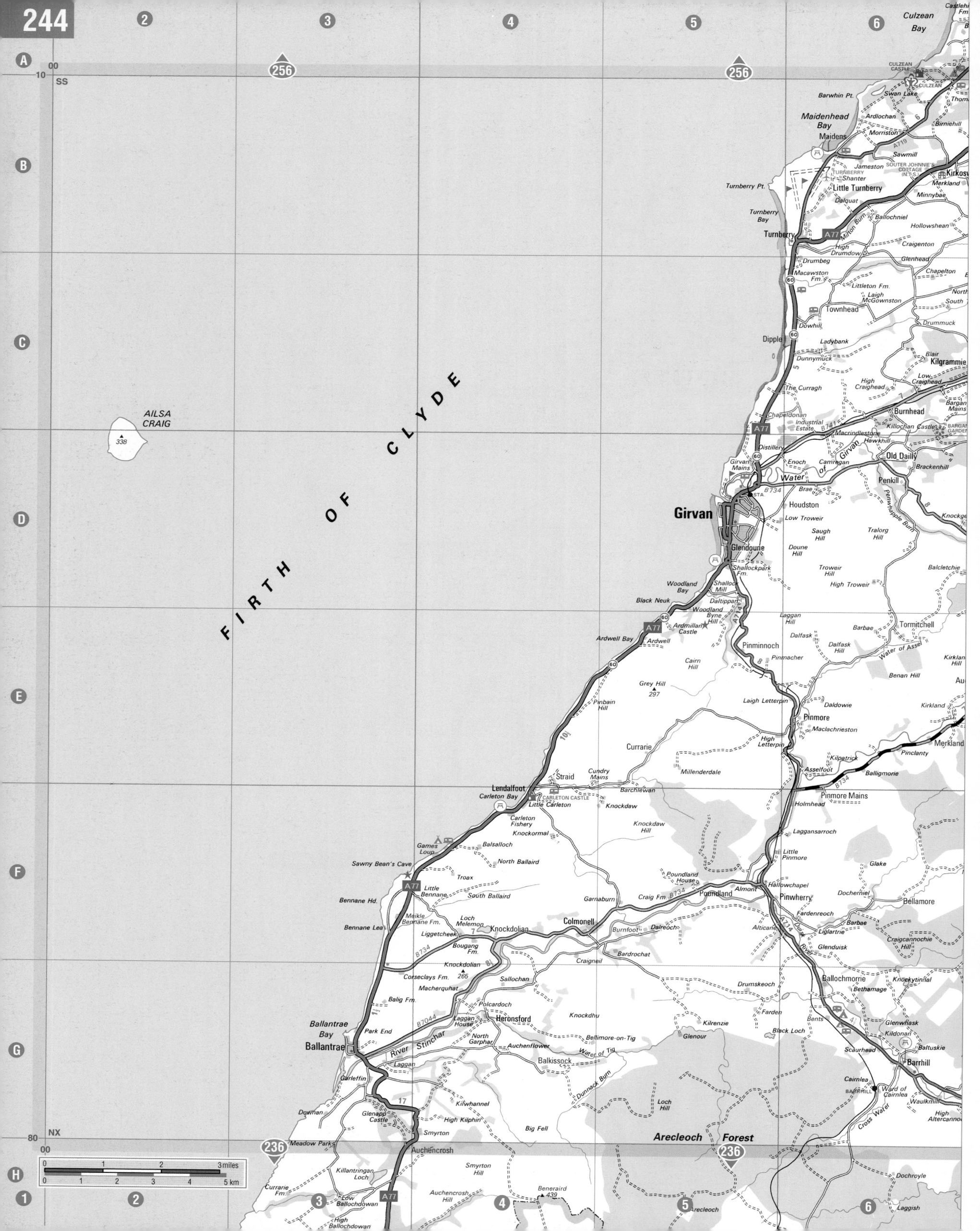

FIRTH OF CLYDE

AILSA CRAIG
▲338

Culzean Bay
Castlehill Fm.
CULZEAN CASTLE
Barwhin Pt.
Swan Lake
Thom
Maidenhead Bay
Ardlochan
Birniehill
Maidens
Morriston
A719
SOUTER JOHNNIE'S COTTAGE IN T.S.S.
Jameston
Shanter
Kirkosw
Merkland
TURNBERRY
Little Turnberry
Minnybae
Turnberry Pt.
Dalquat
Turnberry Bay
A77
Milton Burn
Ballochniel
Hollowshean
Turnberry
High Drumdow
Craigenton
Glenhead
Chapelton
Drumbeg
Macawston Fm.
Littleton Fm.
Laigh McGownston
North
South
Townhead
Drummuck
Dowhill
Dipple
Ladybank
Blair
Dunnymuck
Low Craighead
Kilgrammie
The Curragh
High Craighead
Bargan Mains
Chapeldonan
Industrial Estate
B741
Killochan Castle
BARGANY GARDEN
A77
Macrindlestone
Hawkhill
Burnhead
Distillery
Enoch
Camregan
Old Daily
Girvan Mains
of
Brackenhill
Girvan
Water
Penkill
B734
Brae
Houdston
GIRVAN
Low Troweir
Tralorg Hill
Knockge
Saugh Hill
Glendoune
Doune Hill
Shallockpark Fm.
Troweir Hill
Balcletchie
Woodland Bay
Shalloch Mill
High Troweir
Black Neuk
Daltippan
Woodland
Byne Hill
Laggan Hill
Barbae
Tormitchell
Ardmillan Castle
Dalfask
Ardwell Bay
Ardwell
Pinminnoch
Dalfask Hill
Water of Assel
Cairn Hill
Pinmacher
Kirklan Hill
Ardwell
Benan Hill
Grey Hill
▲297
Pinbain Hill
Laigh Letterpin
Daldowie
Kirkland
Au
Currarie
High Letterpin
Pinmore
Maclachrieston
Merkland
Kilpatrick
Pinclanty
Straid
Cundry Mains
Millenderdale
Asselfoot
Balligmore
B734
Lendalfoot
Barchlewan
Pinmore Mains
Carleton Bay
CARLETON CASTLE
Knockdaw
Holmhead
Little Carleton
Laggansarroch
Carleton Fishery
Knockdaw Hill
Knockormal
Little Pinmore
Glake
Games Loup
Balsalloch
Poundland House
Sawny Bean's Cave
North Ballaird
Hallowchapel
Docherniel
Bellamore
Troax
Garnaburn
Craig Fm.
B734
Poundland
Almont
Pinwherry
Little Bennane
A77
South Ballaird
Fardenreoch
Barbae
Bennane Hd.
Meikle Bennane Fm.
Loch Melemon
Knockdolian
Colmonell
Burnfoot
Dalreoch
Alticane
Liglartrie
Bennane Lea
Liggetcheek
Glenduisk
Craigcannochie Hill
Bougang Fm.
Bardrochat
Knockdolian
▲265
Craigneil
Drumskeoch
Ballochmorrie
Knockytinnal
Corseclays Fm.
Sallochan
Bethamage
Macherquhat
Balig Fm.
Polcardoch
Knockdhu
Kilrenzie
Farden
Bents
Glenwhisk
Ballantrae Bay
Park End
Laggan House
Heronsford
Black Loch
Kildonan
Ballantrae
River Stinchar
North Garphar
Auchenflower
Glenour
Scaurhead
Baltuskie
Laggan
Water of Tig
Balkissock
Barrhill
Garleffin
Cairnlea
Ward of Cairnlea
Downan
Kilwhannel
BARRHILL
Waulkmil
Glenapp Castle
High Kilphin
Loch Hill
High Altercannon
Smyrton
Big Fell
Arecleoch Forest
Cross Water
Meadow Parks
Auchencrosh
Dochroyle
Currarie Fm.
Killantringan Loch
Smyrton Hill
Beneraird
▲439
Auchencrosh Hill
Arecleoch
Laggish
Low Ballochdown
A77
High Ballochdown

Scale:
0   1   2   3 miles
0   1   2   3   4   5 km

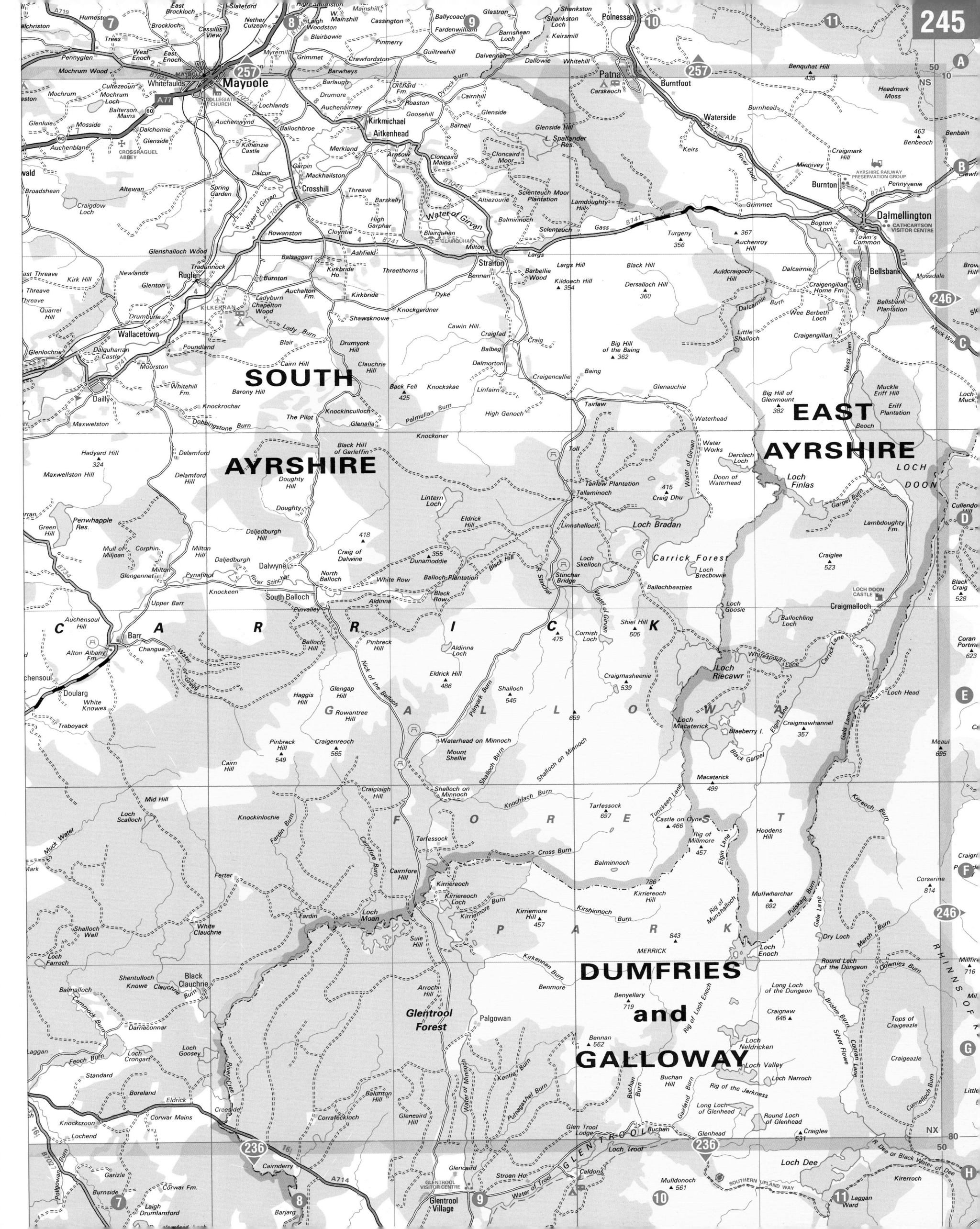

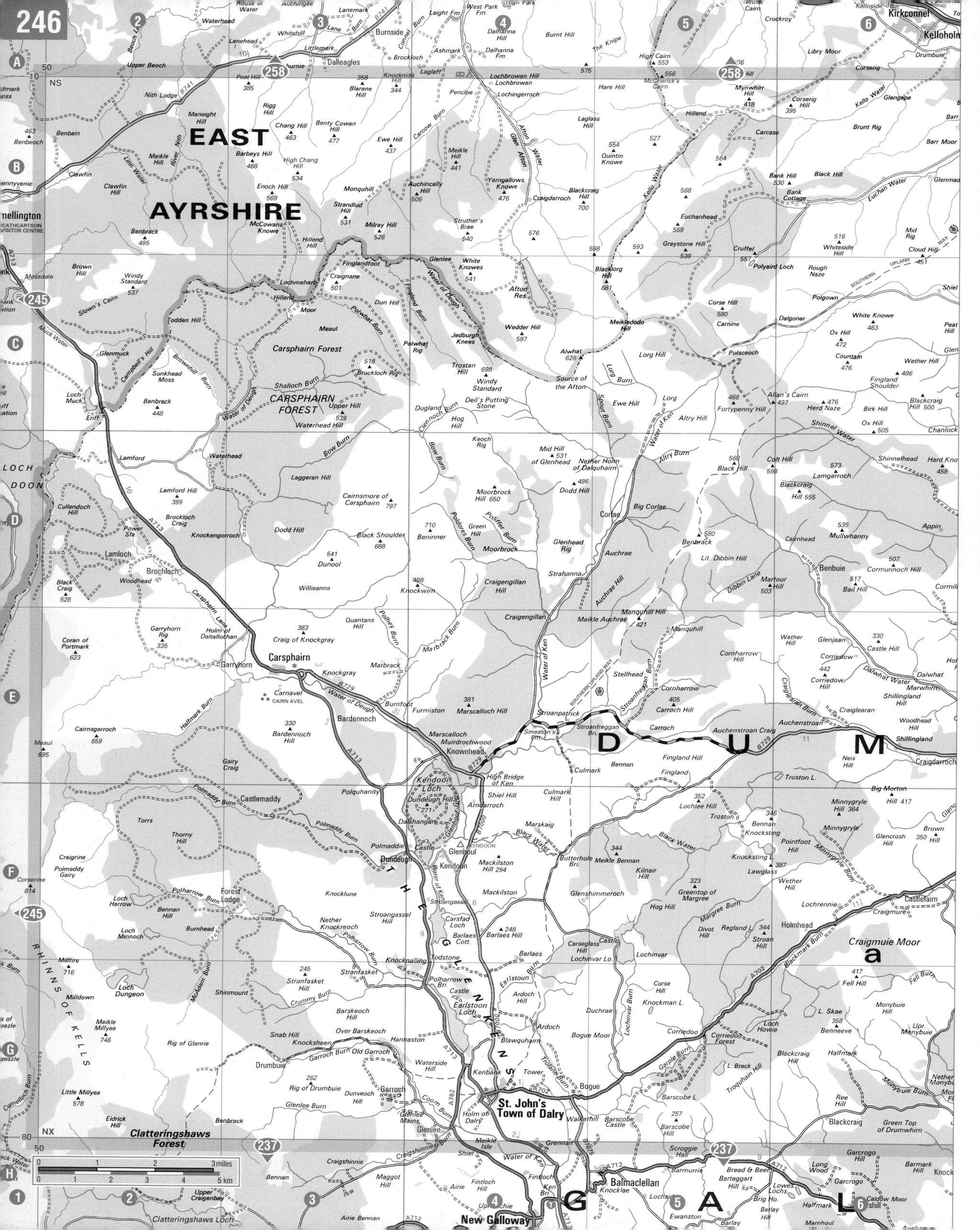

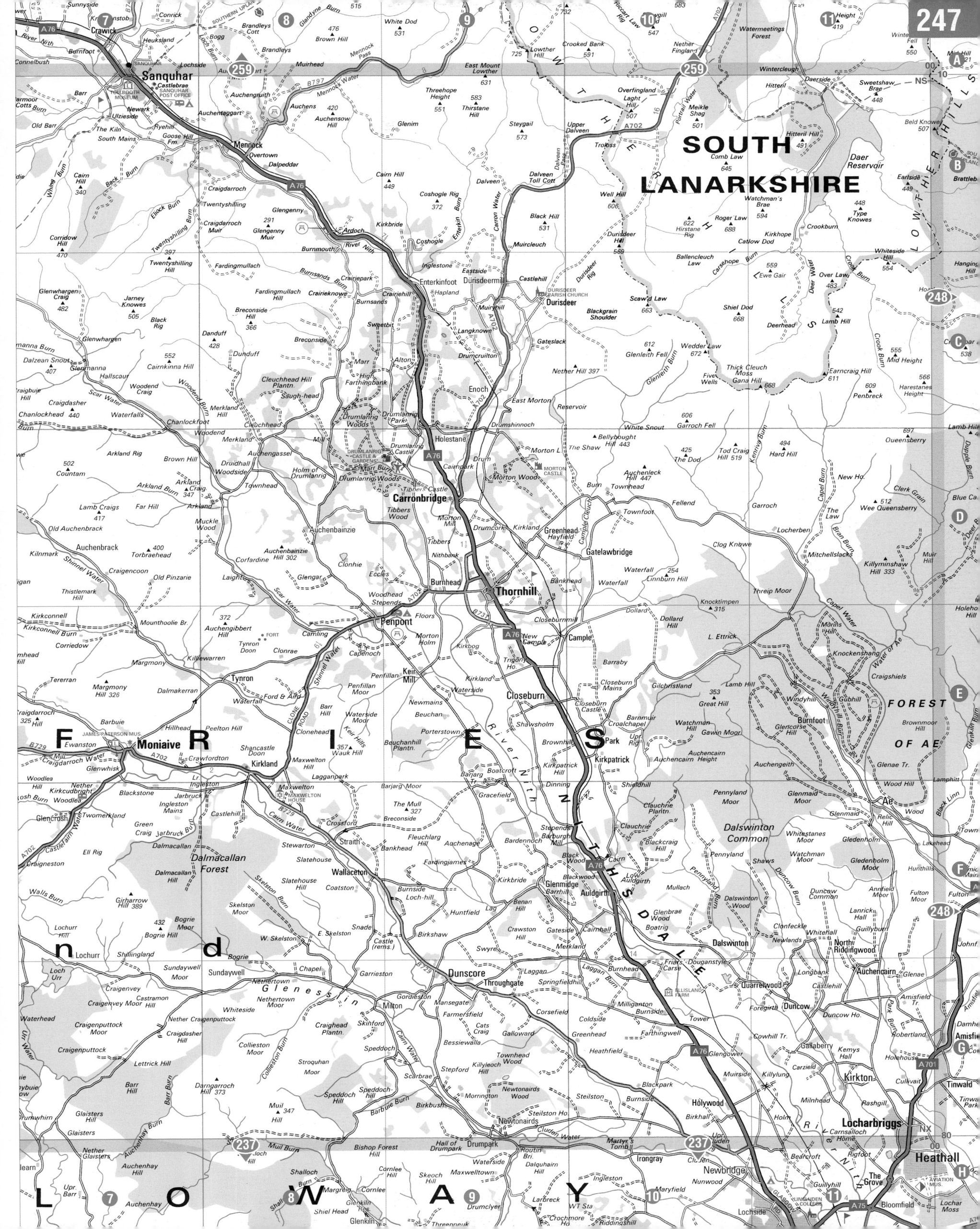

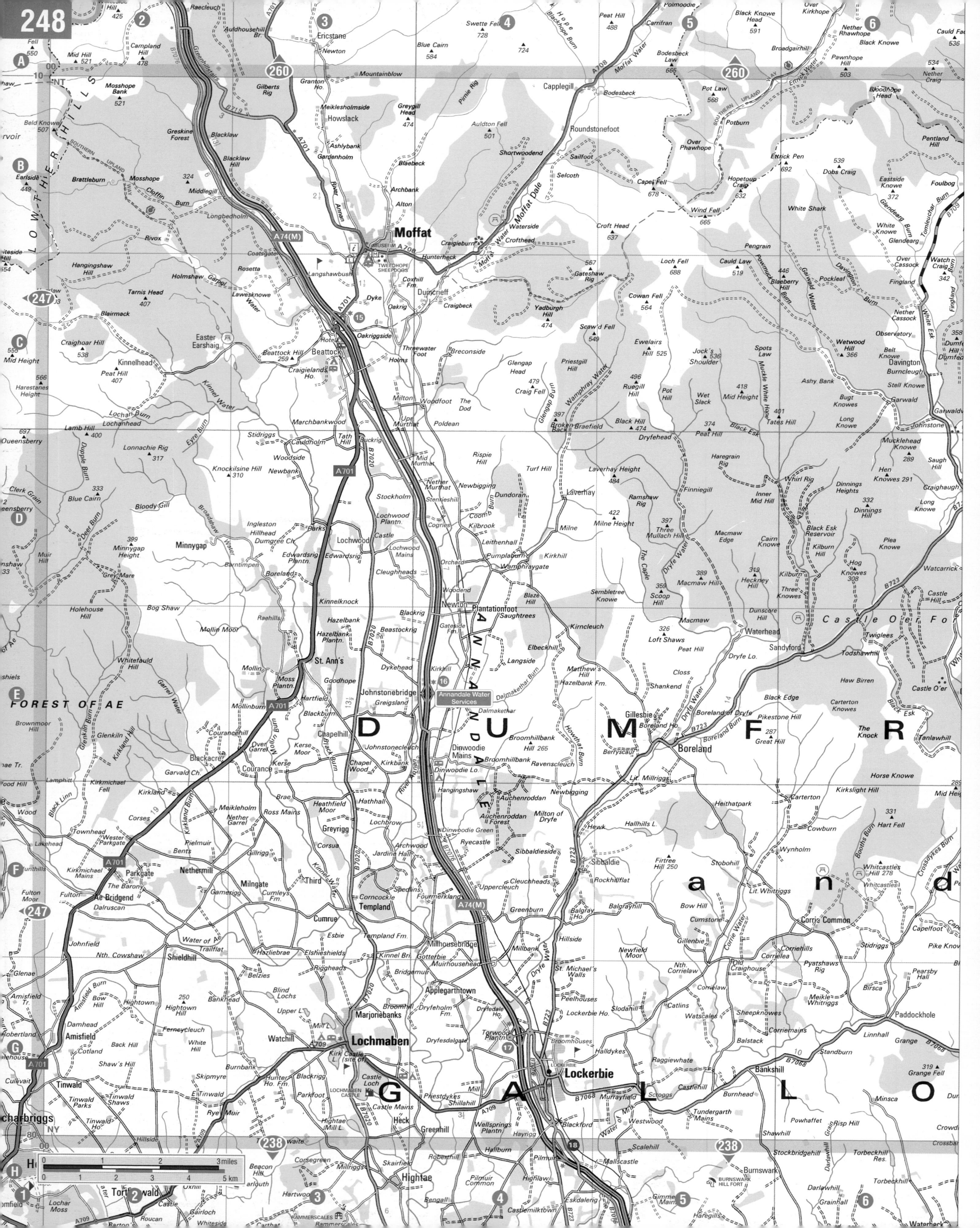

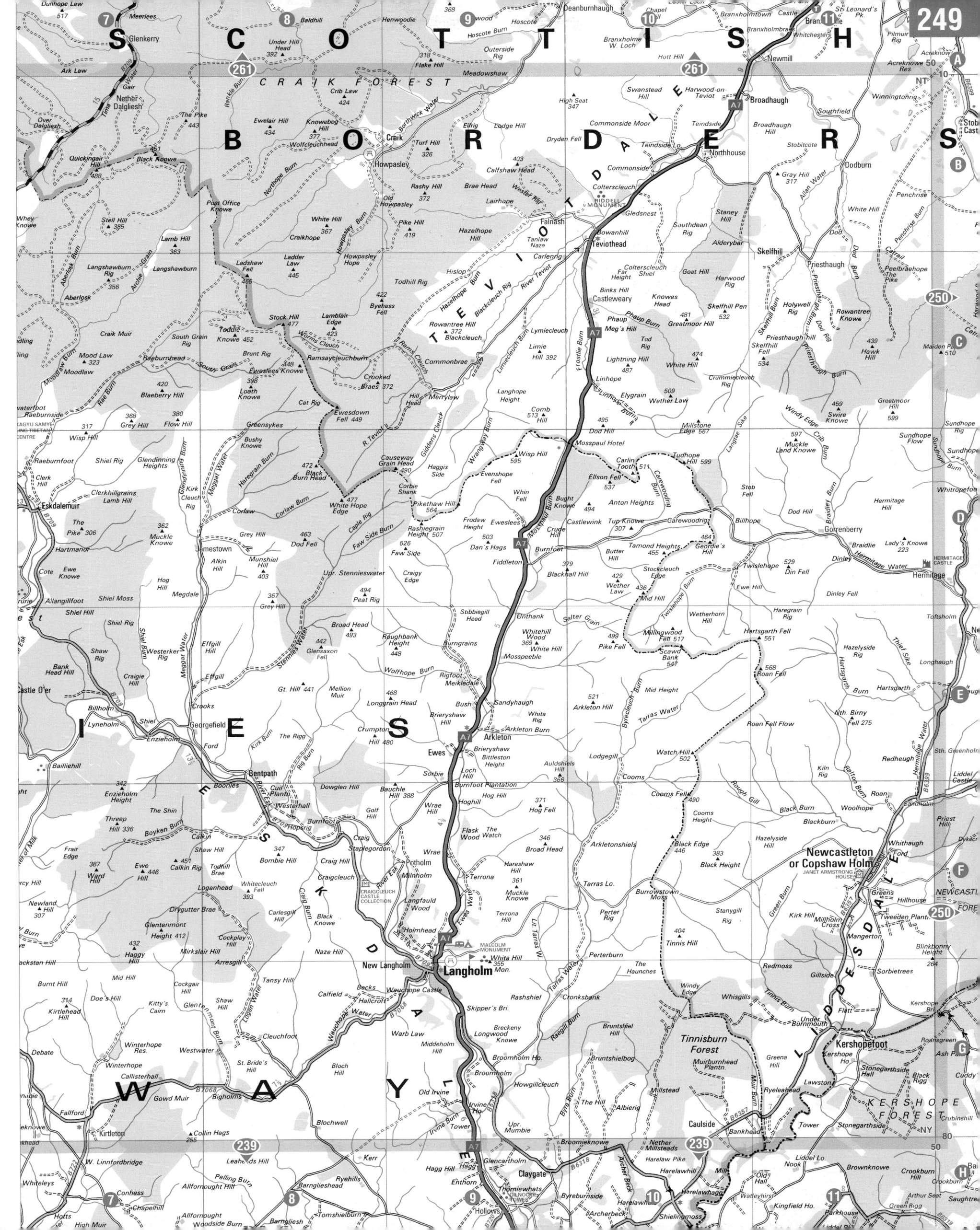

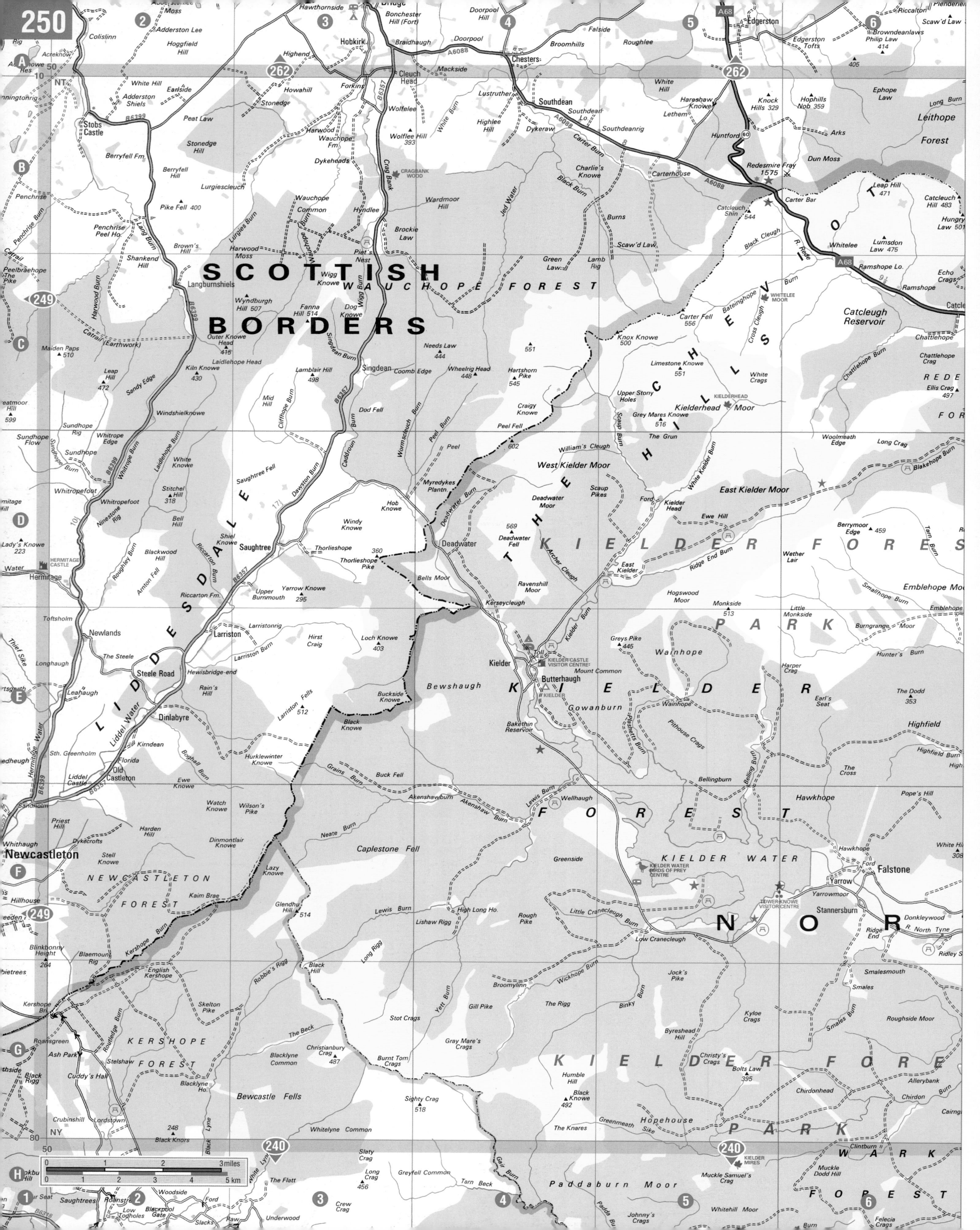

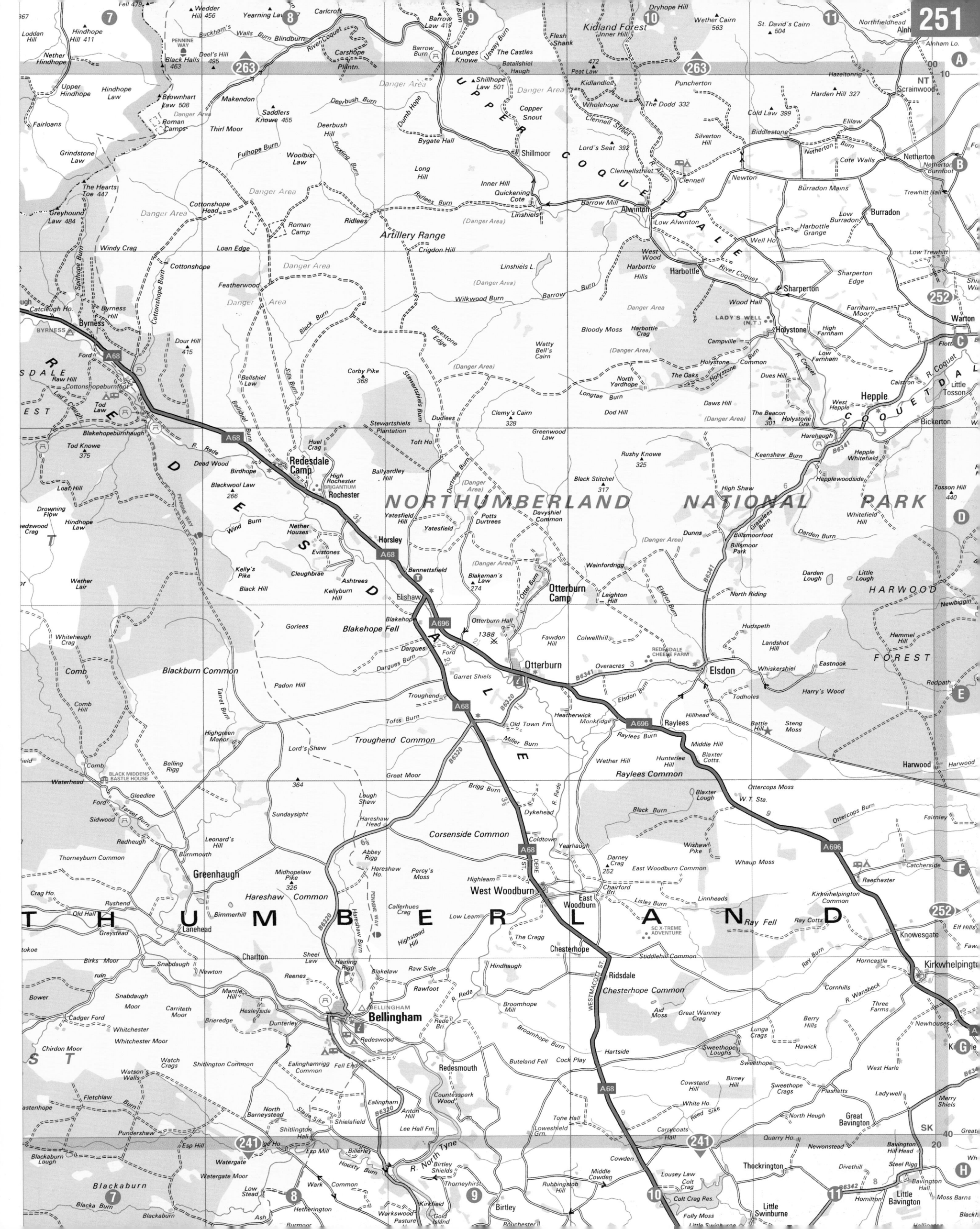

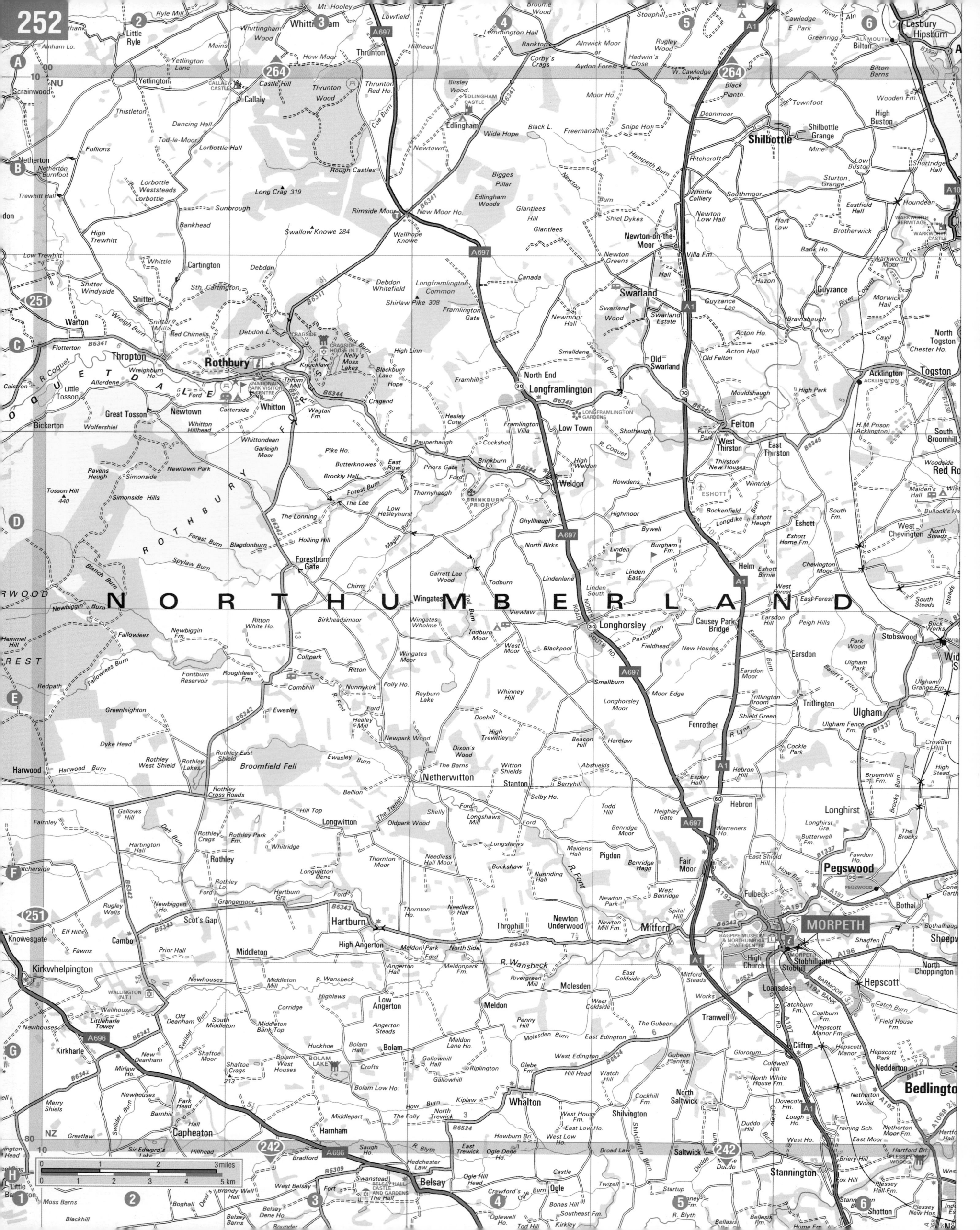

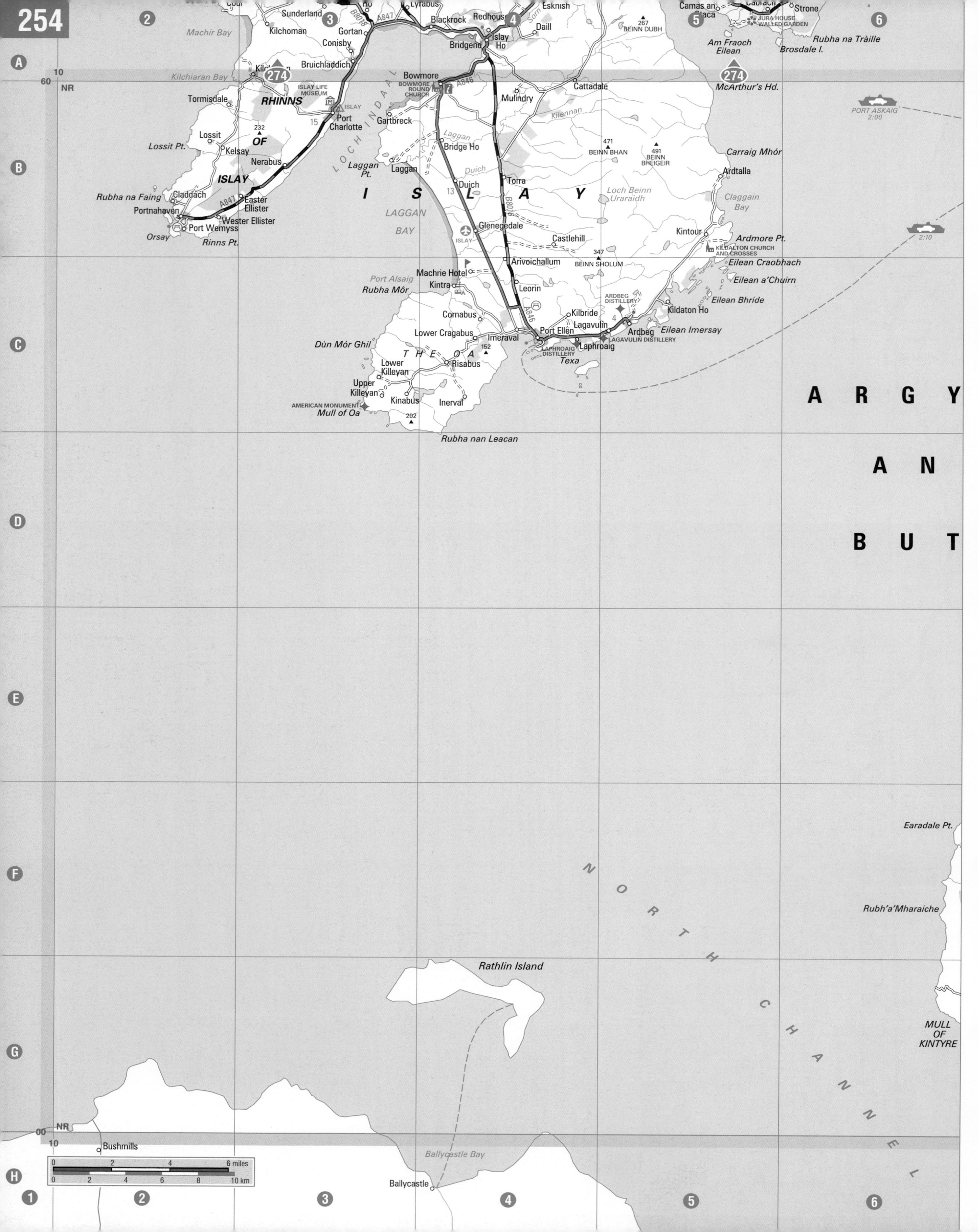

A R G Y

A N

B U T

Machir Bay
Sunderland
Kilchoman
Gortan
Conisby
Blackrock
Redhous
Esknish
BEINN DUBH
267
Camas an
Staca
Stone
JURA HOUSE
WALLED GARDEN
Am Fraoch
Eilean
Rubha na Tràille
Brosdale I.
Daill
Islay
Ho
Bruichladdich
Bridgend
Kilchiaran Bay
274
Bowmore
BOWMORE
ROUND
CHURCH
A846
McArthur's Hd.
274
Tormisdale
RHINNS
ISLAY LIFE
MUSEUM
Mulindry
Cattadale
PORT ASKAIG
2:00
Port
Charlotte
ISLAY
Gartbreck
Kilennan
232
OF
15
Loch Beinn
Uraraidh
Carraig Mhór
Lossit Pt.
Lossit
Kelsay
Nerabus
Laggan
Pt.
Bridge Ho
BEINN
BHAN
1052
471
491
BEINN
BHEIGEIR
Ardtalla
Rubha na Faing
Claddach
ISLAY
Duich
Laggan
13
Torra
Claggain
Bay
Portnahaven
A841
Easter
Ellister
Wester Ellister
Port Wemyss
LAGGAN
BAY
B8016
2:10
Orsay
Rinns Pt.
ISLAY
Glenegedale
Castlehill
Kintour
Ardmore Pt.
Arivoichallum
347
BEINN SHOLUM
KILDALTON CHURCH
AND CROSSES
Eilean Craobhach
Machrie Hotel
Port Alsaig
Kintra
Leorin
ARDBEG
DISTILLERY
Eilean a'Chuirn
Rubha Mór
A846
Eilean Bhride
Cornabus
Kilbride
Kildaton Ho
Lower Cragabus
Imeraval
Lagavulin
Ardbeg
Eilean Imersay
Dùn Mór Ghil
THE OA
152
Port Ellen
LAGAVULIN DISTILLERY
4
Risabus
LAPHROAIG
DISTILLERY
Laphroaig
Lower
Killeyan
Texa
Upper
Killeyan
Kinabus
Inerval
AMERICAN MONUMENT
Mull of Oa
202
Rubha nan Leacan

N O R T H

C H A N N E L

Earadale Pt.

Rubh'a'Mharaiche

Rathlin Island

MULL
OF
KINTYRE

Bushmills

Ballycastle Bay

Ballycastle

0   2   4   6 miles
0   2   4   6   8   10 km

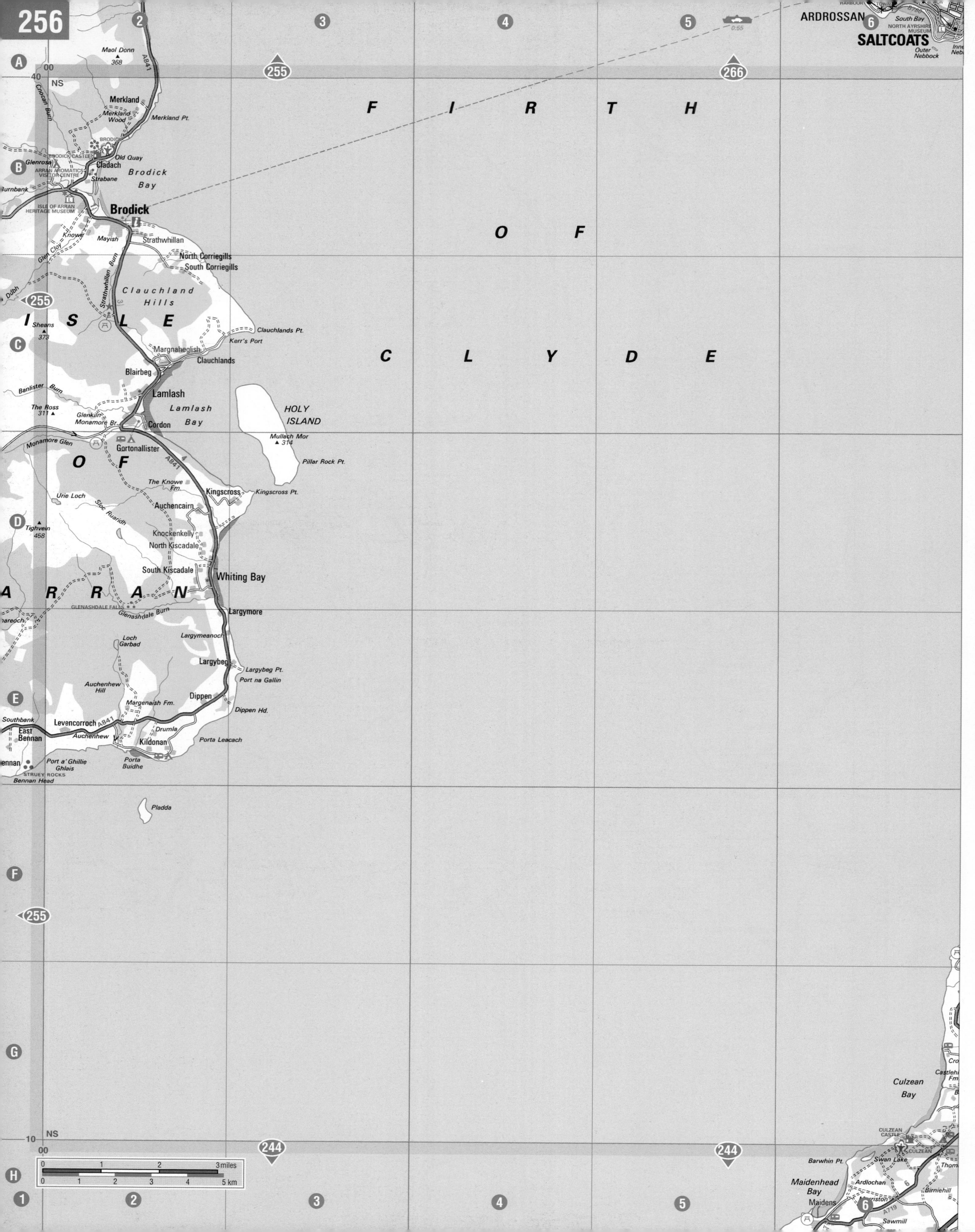

ARDROSSAN

SALTCOATS

FIRTH

OF

ISLE

OF

ARRAN

CLYDE

Maol Donn
368

Merkland
Merkland
Wood
Merkland Pt.

BRODICK
Glenrosa
Old Quay
Cladach
Strabane
Brodick
Bay
Burnbank
ISLE OF ARRAN
HERITAGE MUSEUM

Brodick

Knowe
Mayish
Strathwhillan

North Corriegills
South Corriegills

Clauchland
Hills

Sheans
373

Clauchlands Pt.

Kerr's Port

Margnaheglish
Clauchlands

Blairbeg

Banlister Burn

The Ross
311

Lamlash
Lamlash
Bay

HOLY
ISLAND

Glenkiln
Monamore Br.
Cordon

Monamore Glen
Gortonallister

Mullach Mor
314

Pillar Rock Pt.

The Knowe
Fm.

Urie Loch

Kingscross
Kingscross Pt.

Auchencairn

Sloc Ruaridh

Tighvein
458

Knockenkelly
North Kiscadale

South Kiscadale

Whiting Bay

ARRAN

GLENASHDALE FALLS
Glenashdale Burn

Largymore

Loch
Garbad

Largymeanoch

Largybeg

Largybeg Pt.
Port na Gallin

Auchenhew
Hill

Margenaish Fm.

Dippen

Dippen Hd.

Southbank
East
Bennan

Levencorroch
Auchenhew
Drumla

Kildonan

Porta Leacach

Bennan
Port a' Ghillie
Ghlais
STRUEY ROCKS
Bennan Head

Porta
Buidhe

Pladda

Culzean
Bay

CULZEAN
CASTLE

Barwhin Pt.
Swan Lake

Maidenhead
Bay
Ardlochan
Maidens

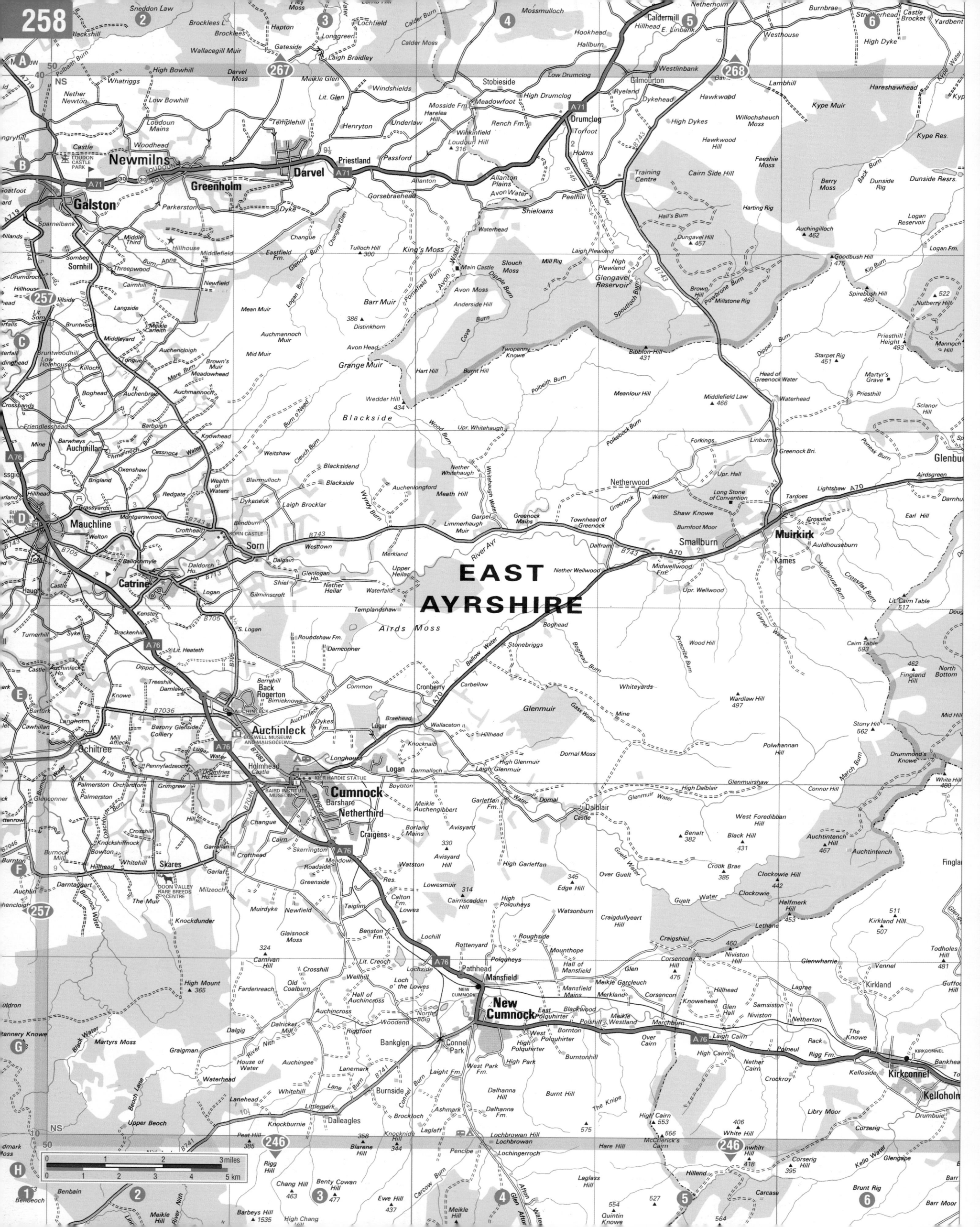

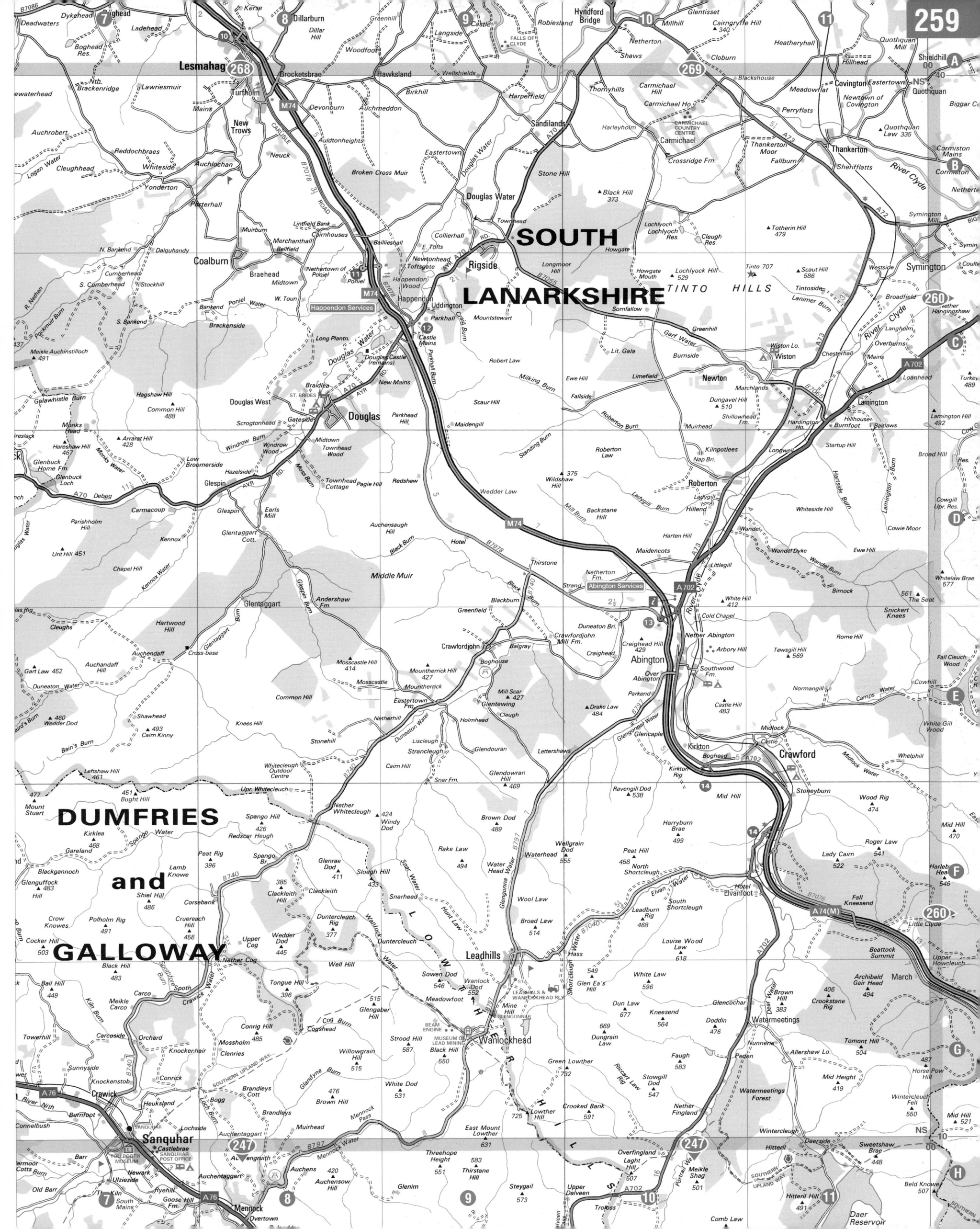

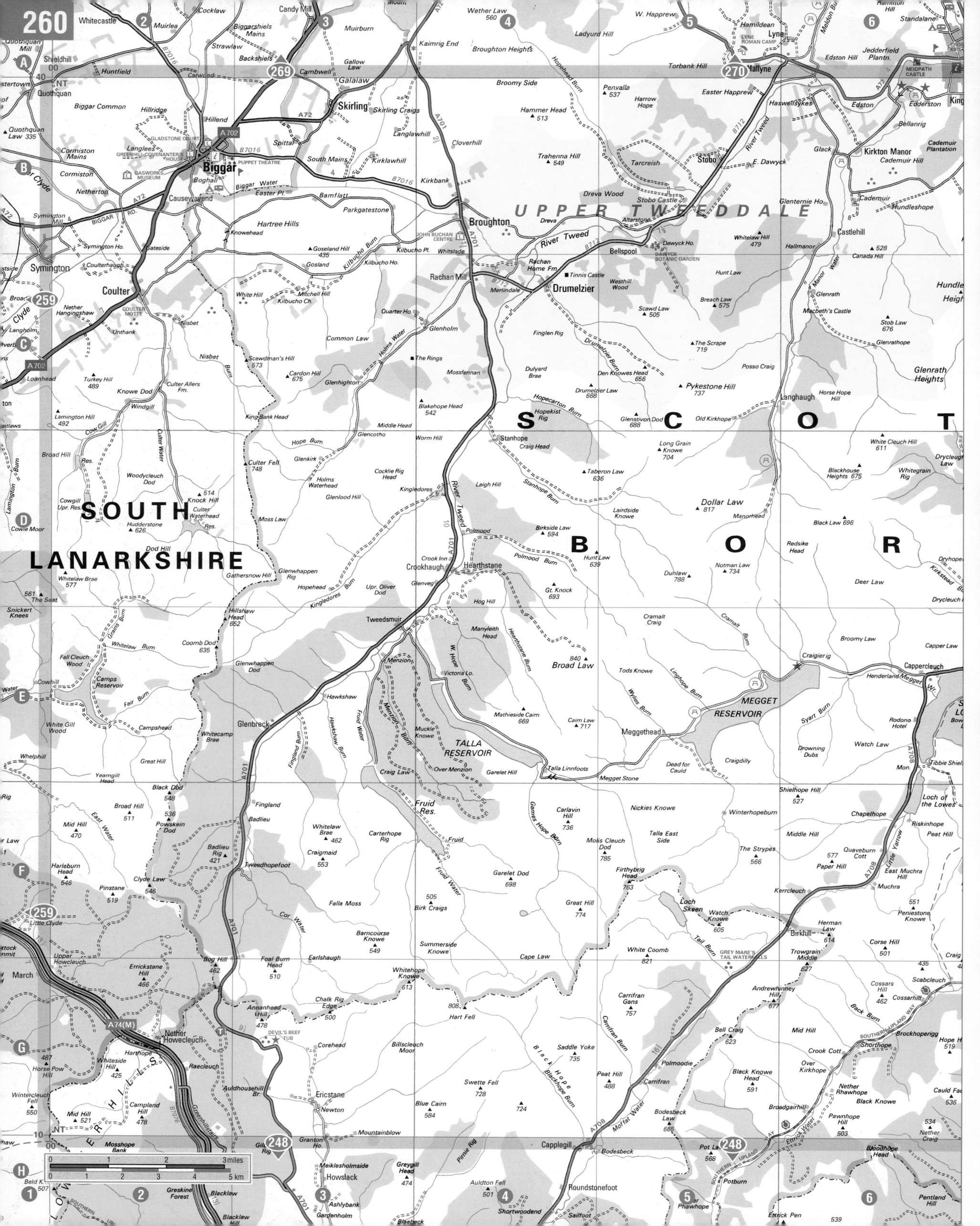

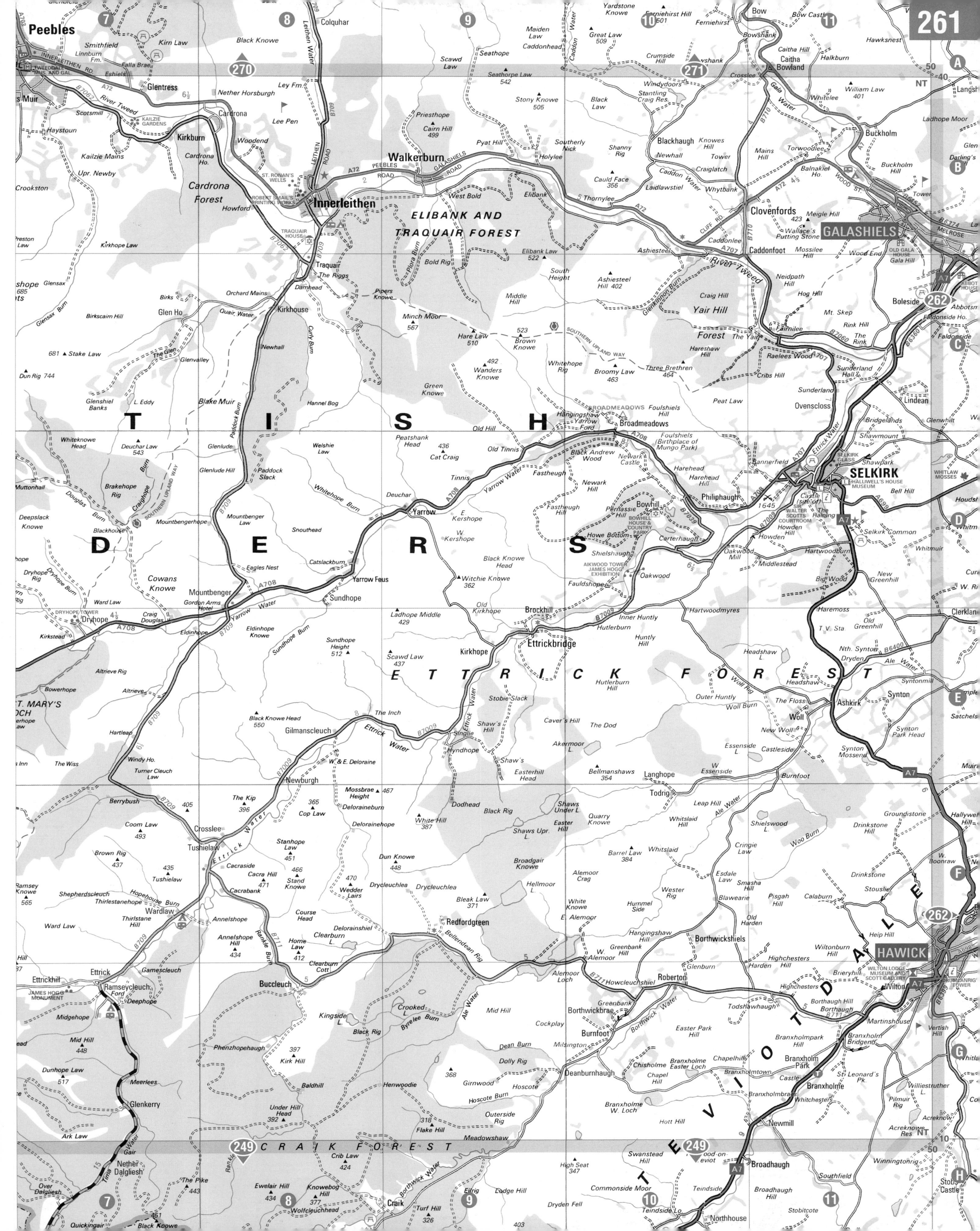

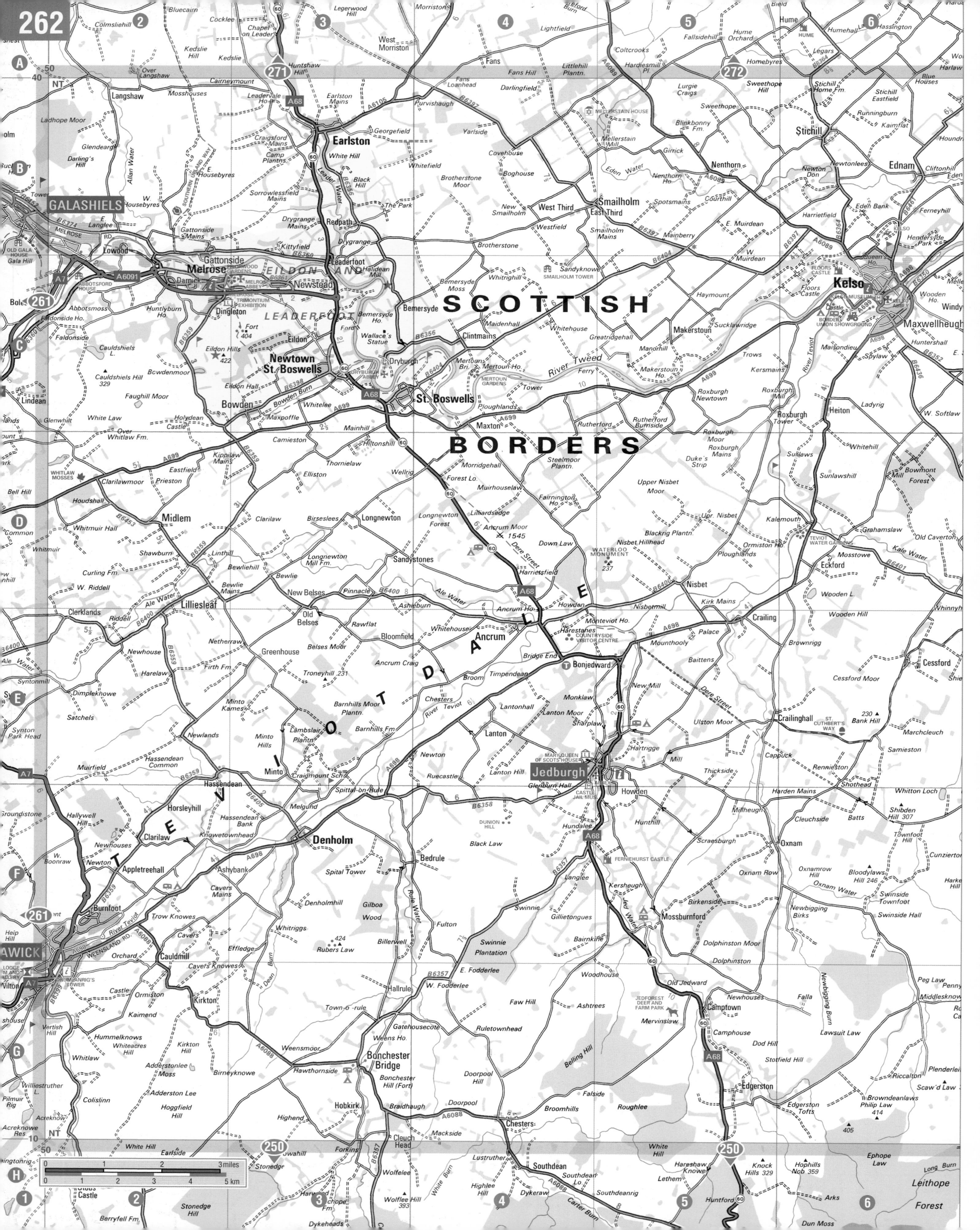

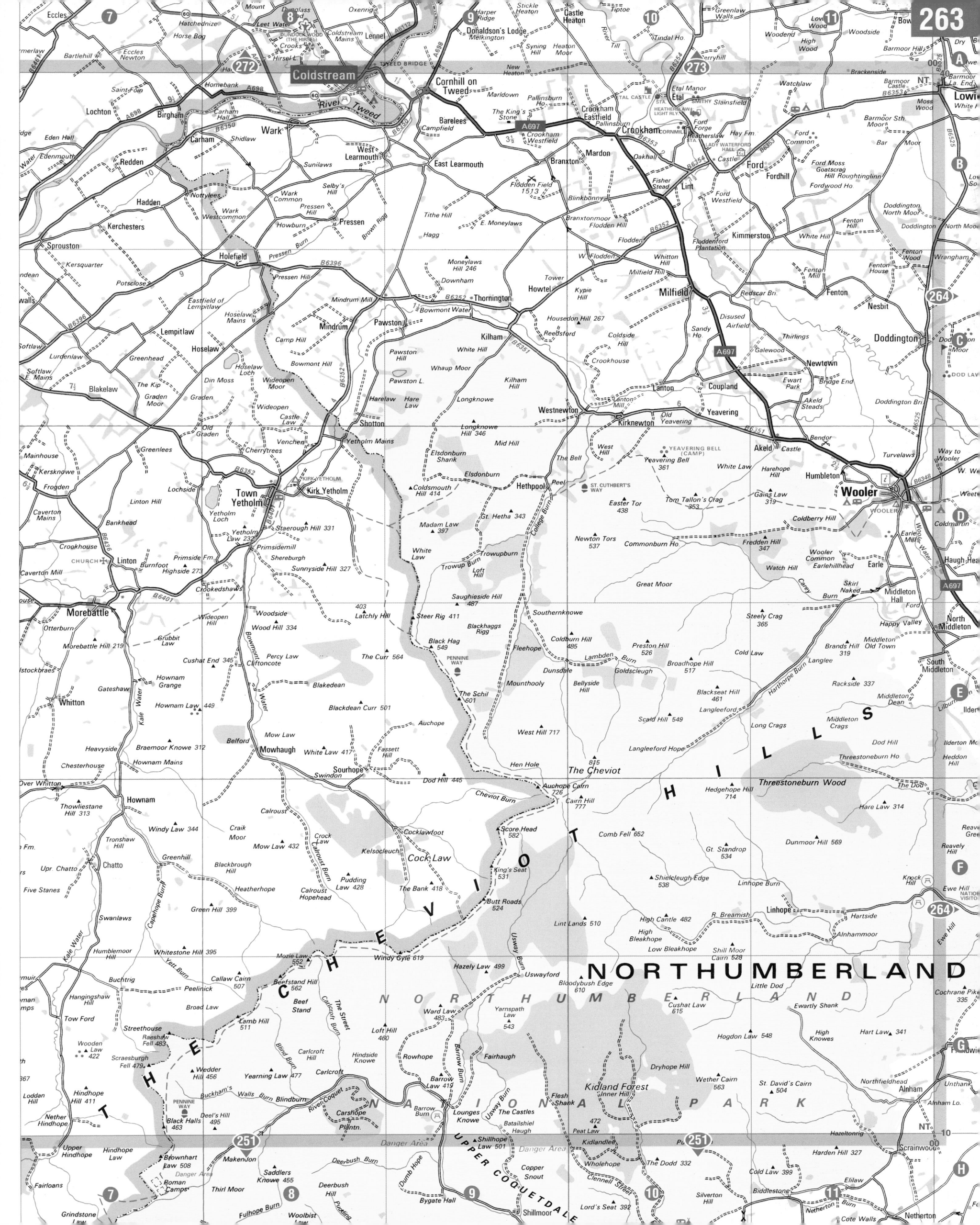

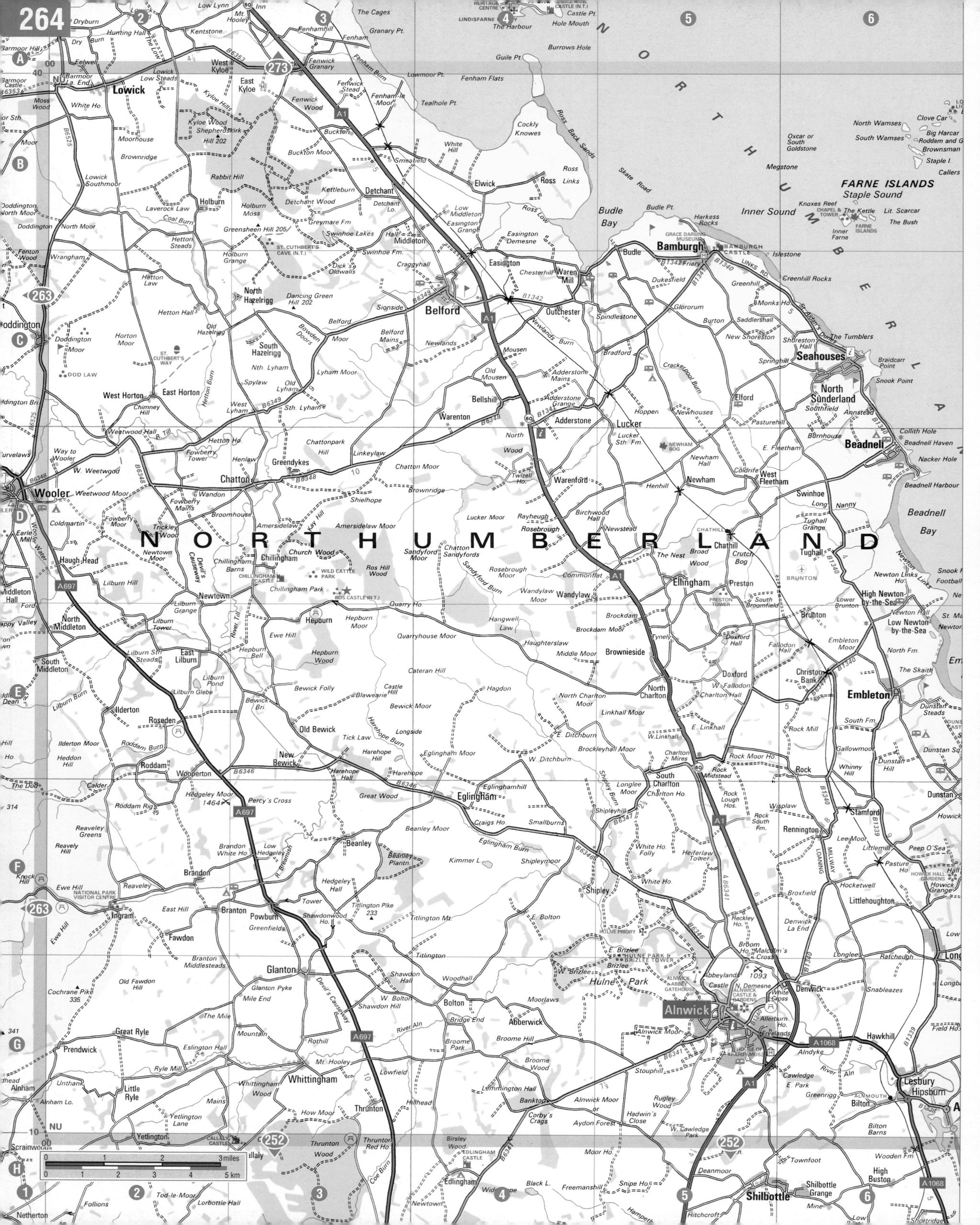

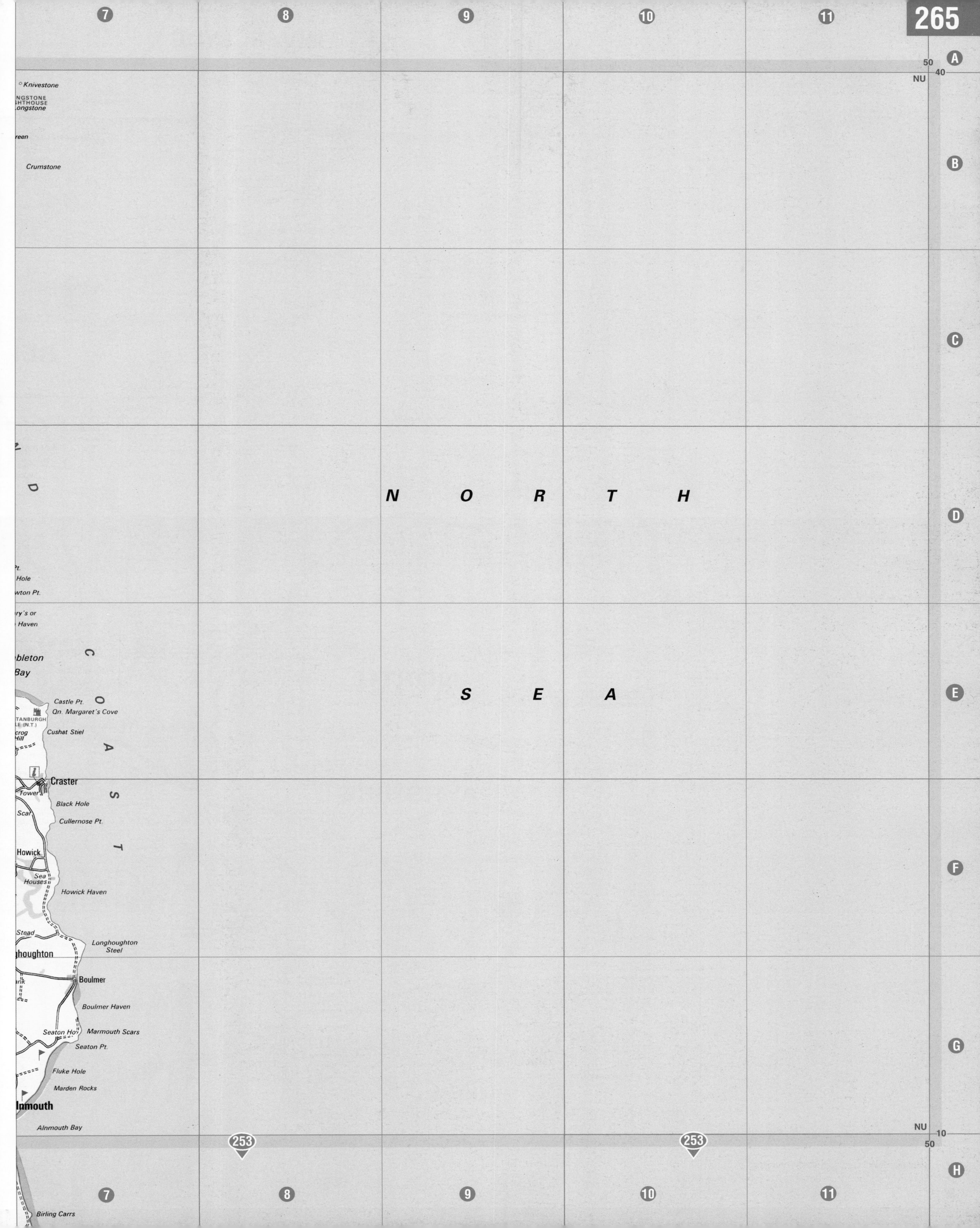

Knivestone

NGSTONE
HTHOUSE
ongstone

reen

Crumstone

N O R T H

Pt.
Hole
wton Pt.

ry's or
Haven

C
O
A
S
T

bleton
Bay

Castle Pt.
Qn. Margaret's Cove

TANBURGH
E (N.T.)
crog
Hill
Cushat Stiel

S E A

Craster
Tower
Black Hole
Scar
Cullernose Pt.

Howick

Sea
Houses
Howick Haven

Stead
Longhoughton
Steel
hhoughton

Boulmer

Boulmer Haven

Seaton Ho *Marmouth Scars*
Seaton Pt.

Fluke Hole
Marden Rocks

lnmouth

Alnmouth Bay

253

253

Birling Carrs

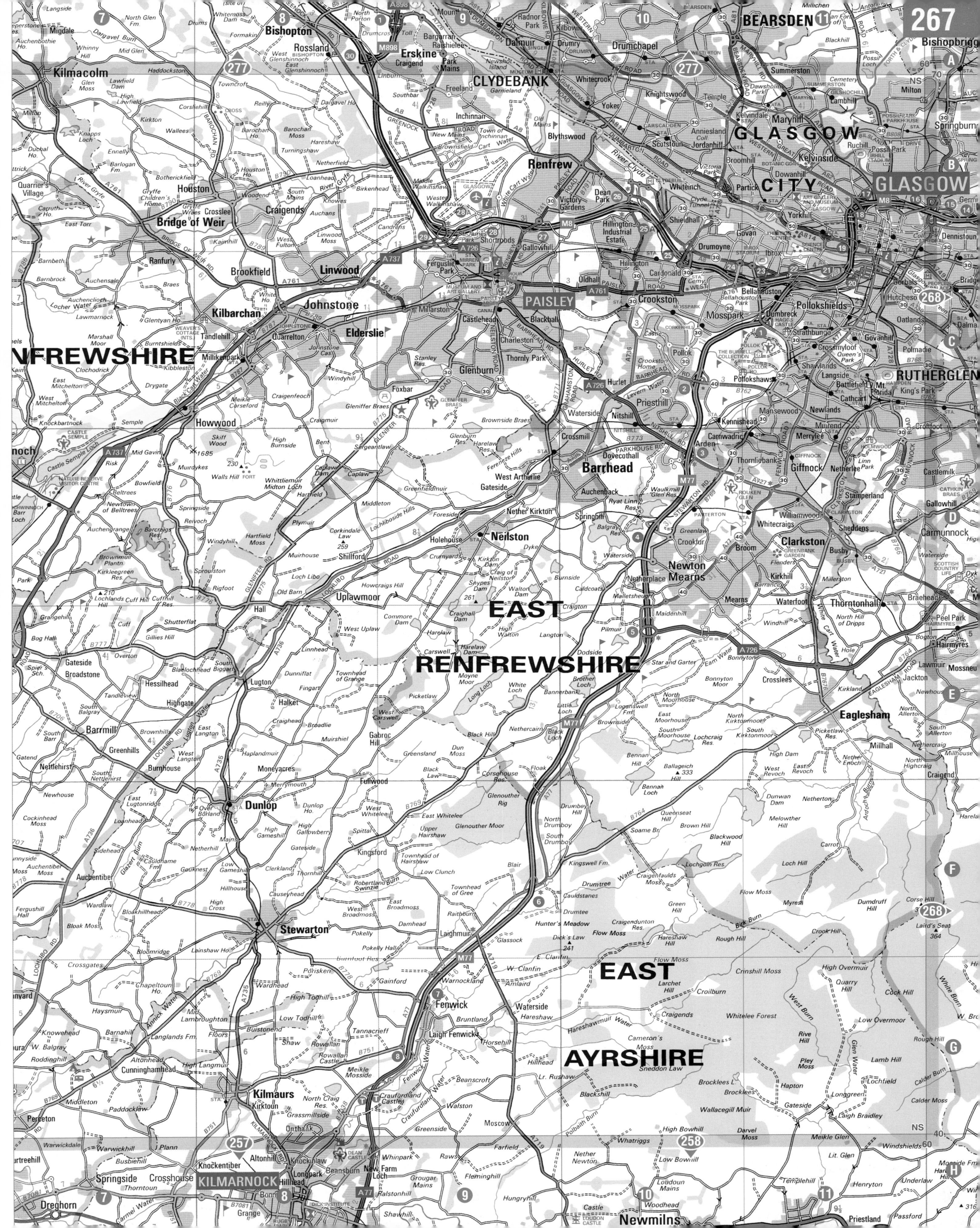

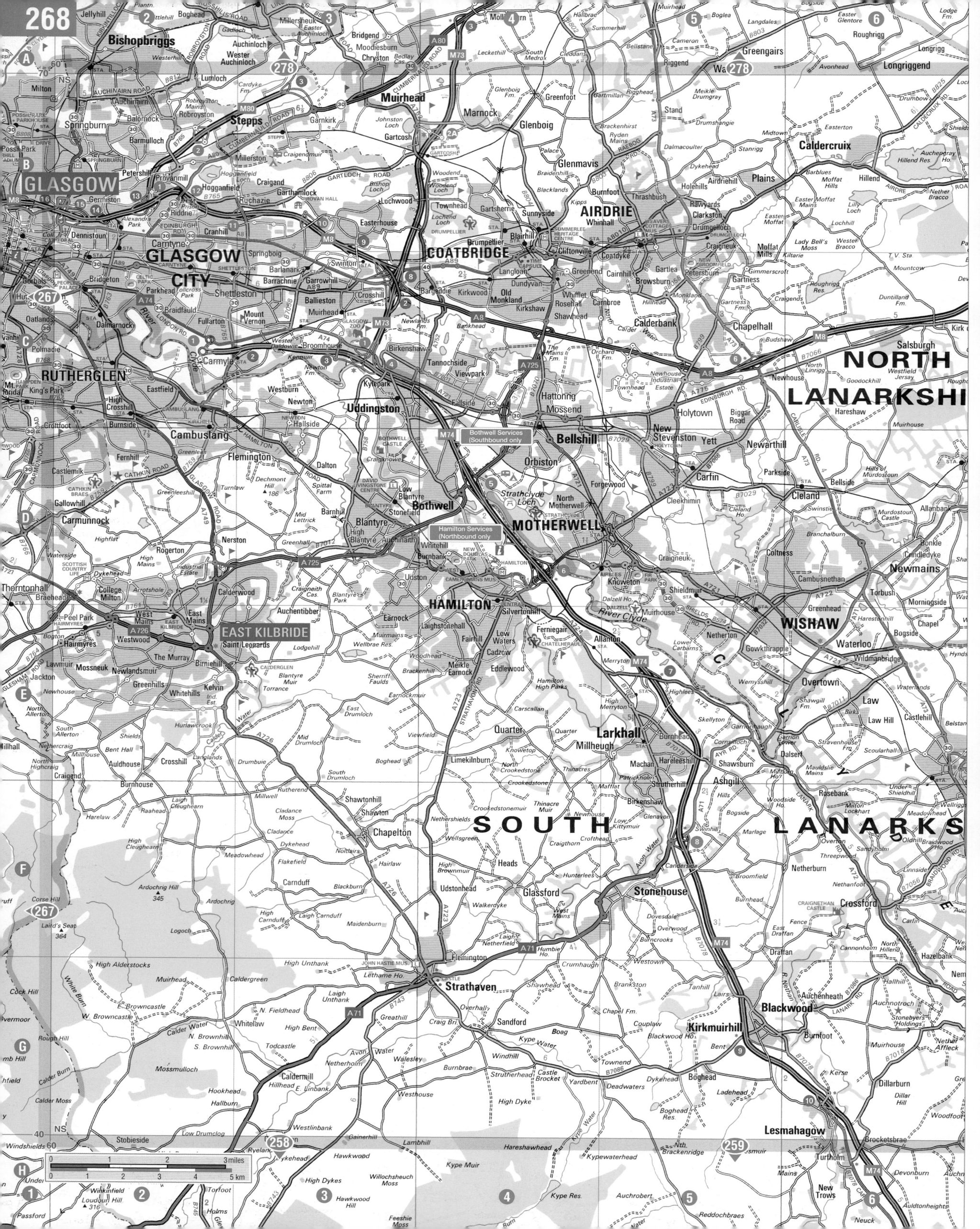

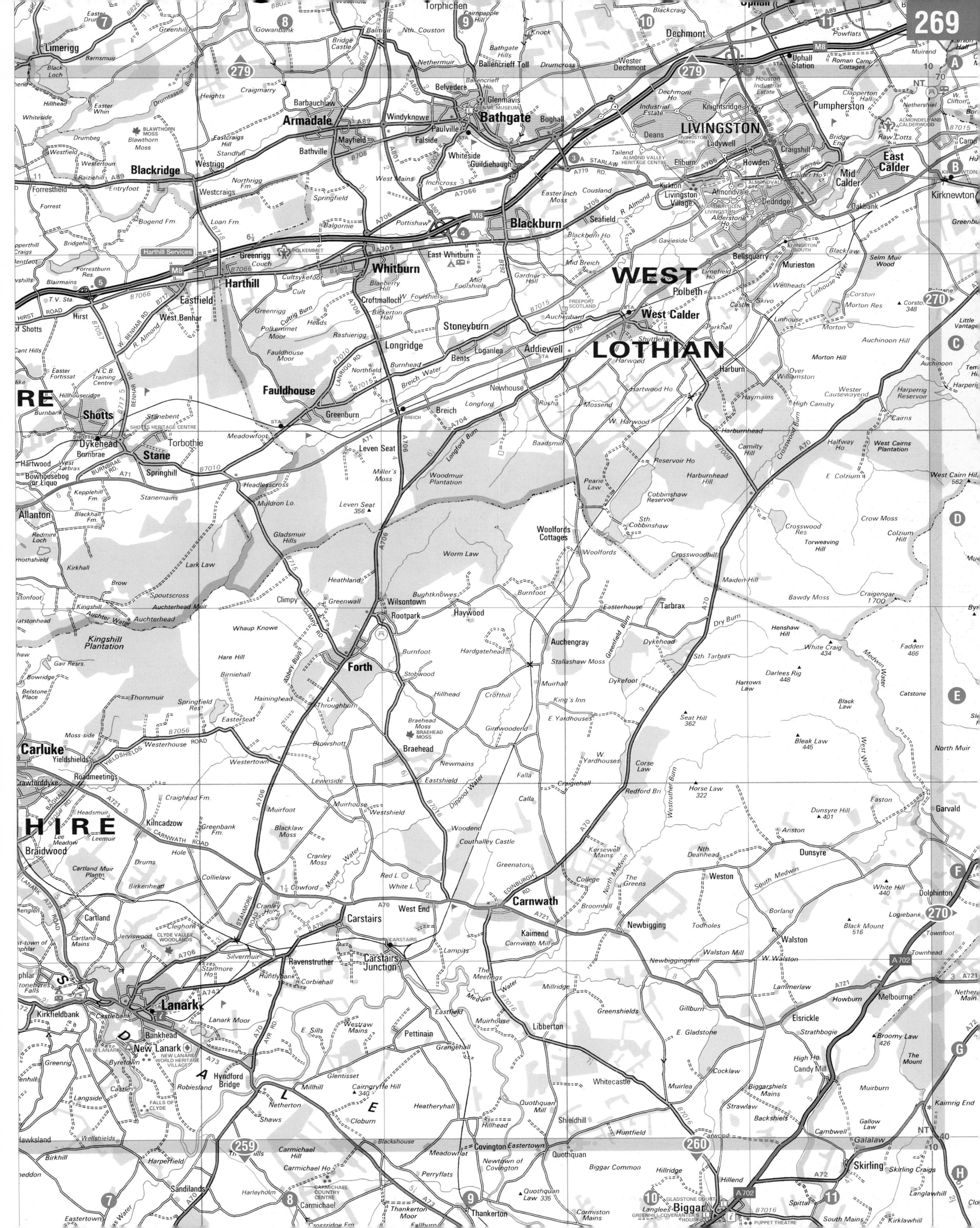

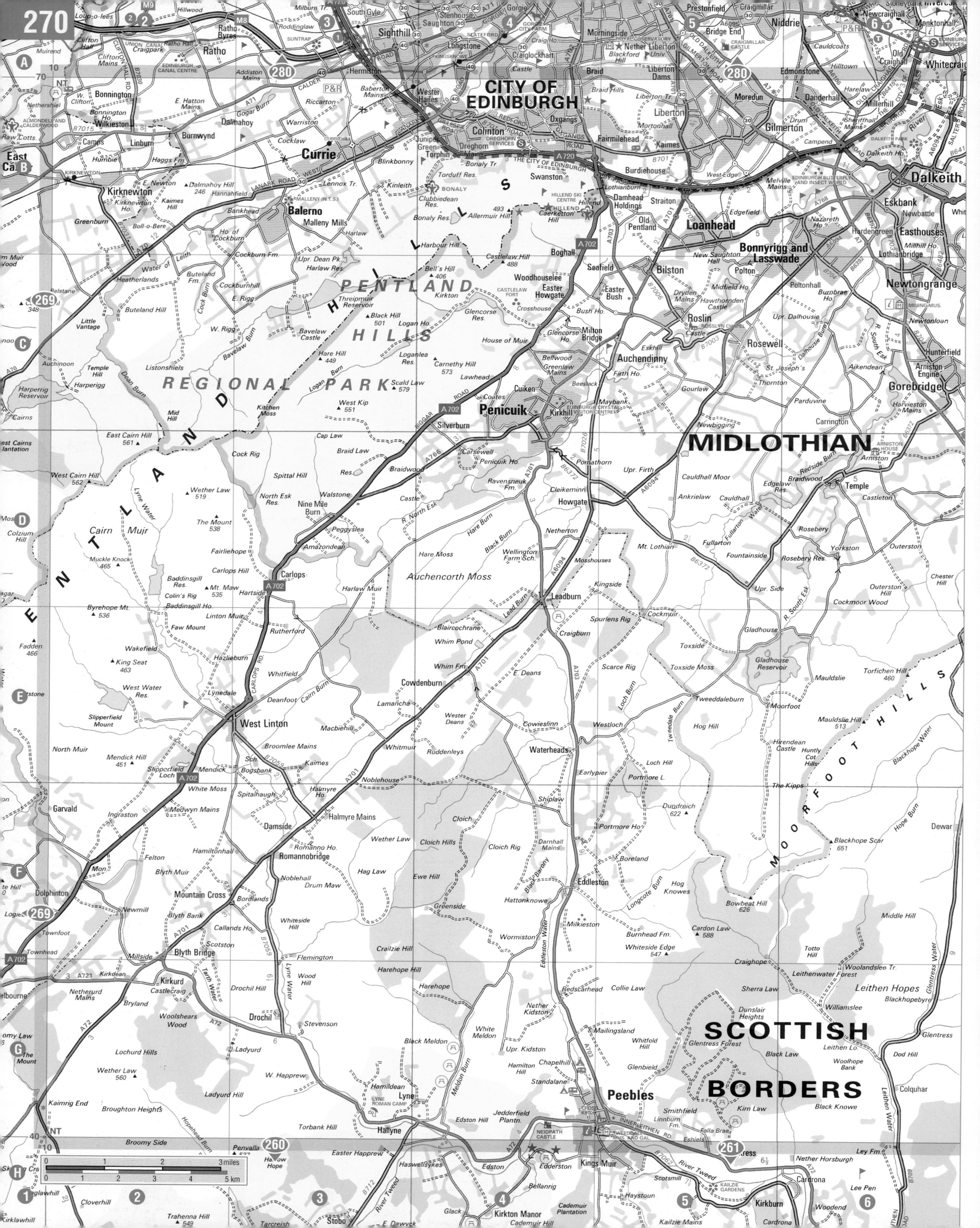

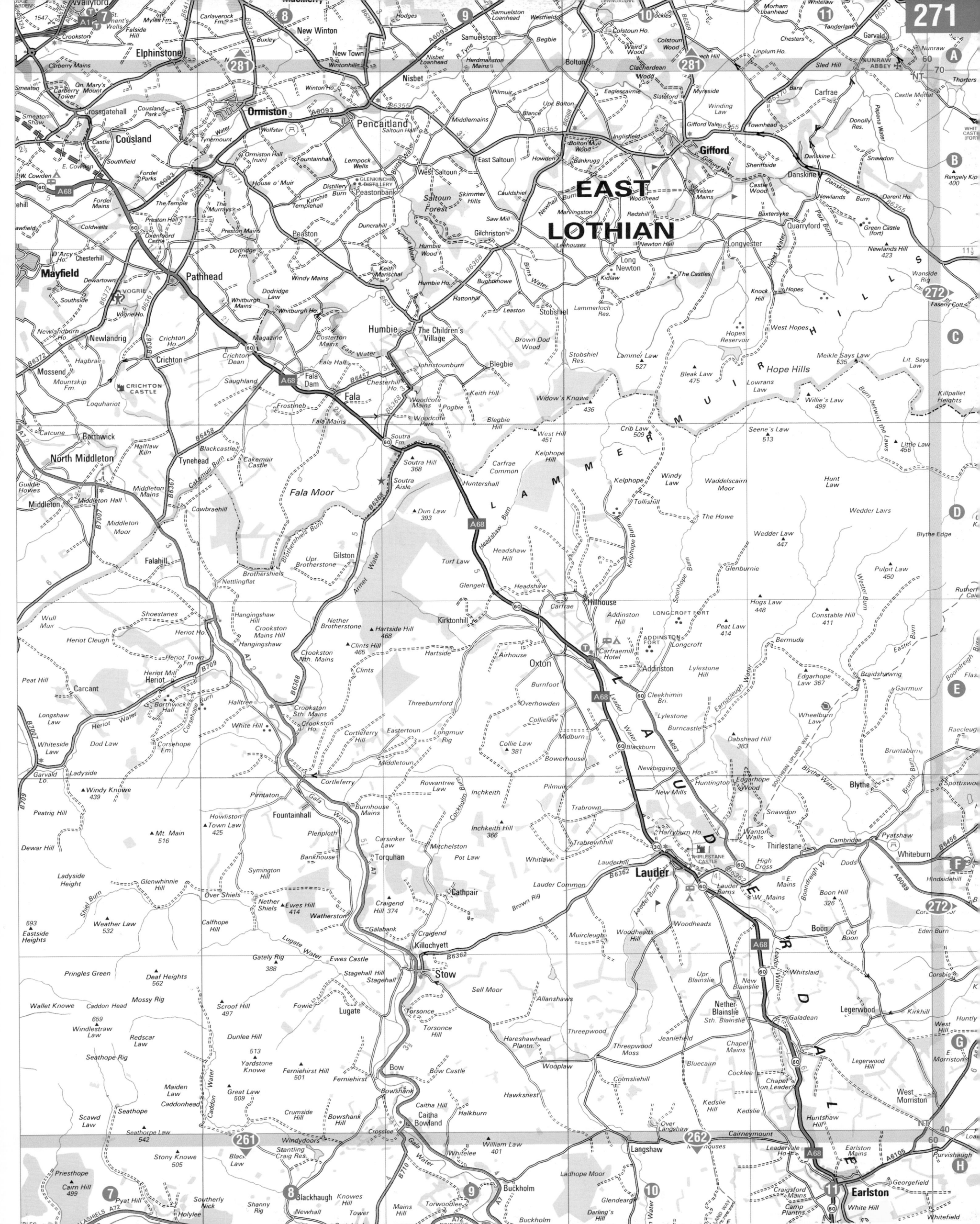

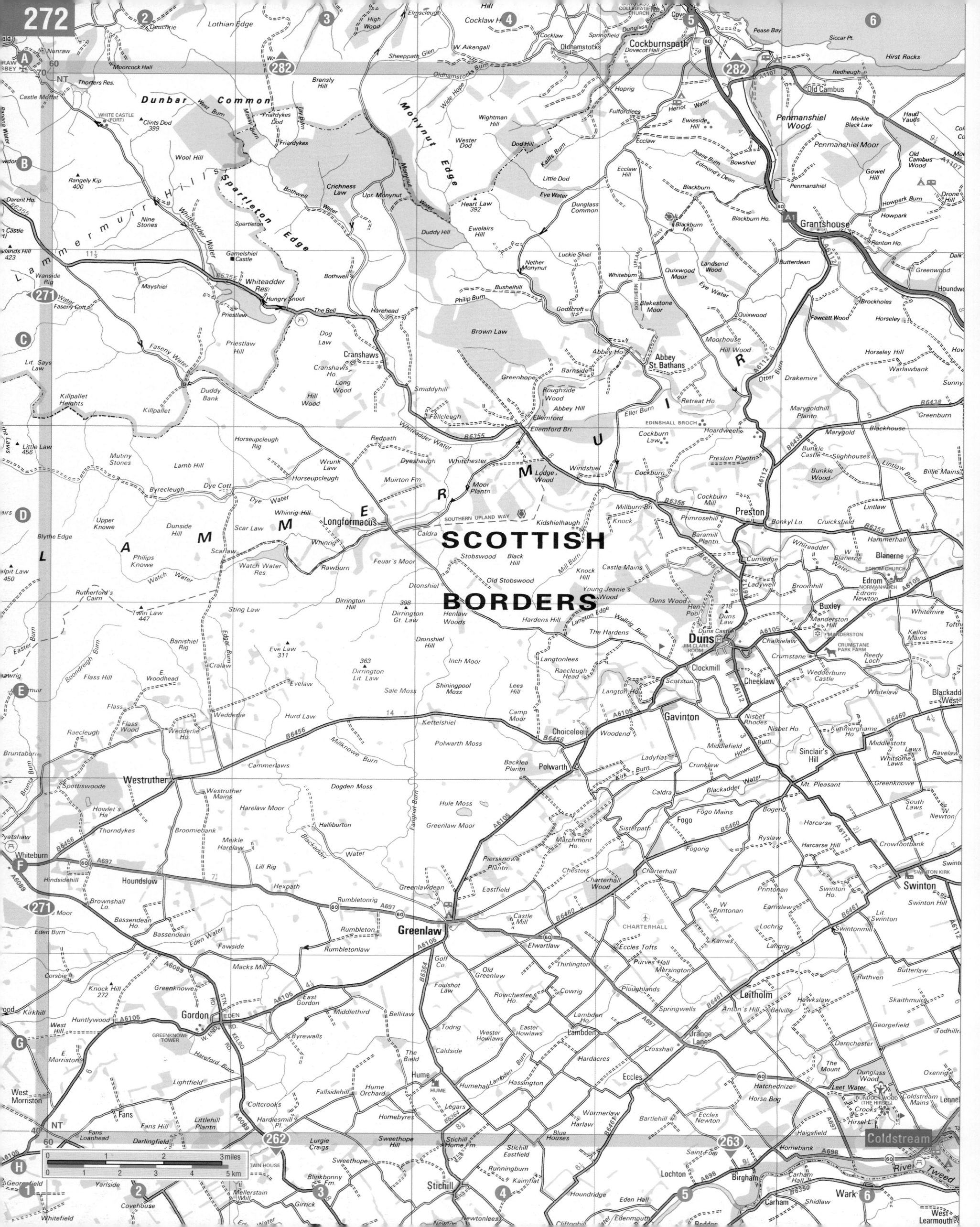

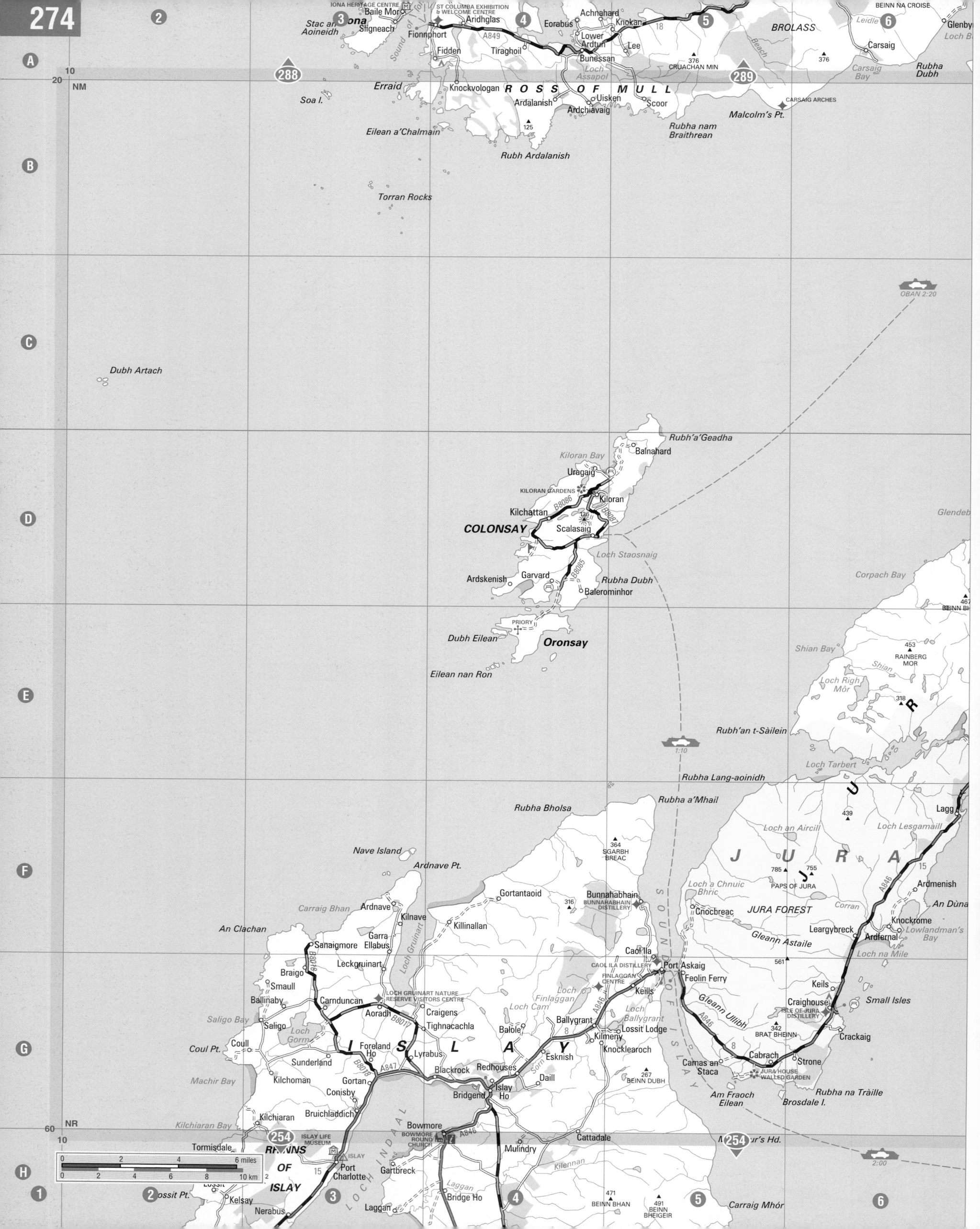

BEINN NA CROISE

Leidle

Glenby

Loch Ba

IONA HERITAGE CENTRE
Baile Mor

Achnahard

ST COLUMBA EXHIBITION
& WELCOME CENTRE

Stac an
Aoineidh

Iona
Sligneach

Aridhglas

Eorabus

Knokan

18

BROLASS

Fionnphort

A849

Lower
Ardtun

Carsaig

Fidden

Tiraghoil

Lee

376
CRUACHAN MIN

376

Erraid

A
10
20
NM

288

Bunessan

Loch
Assapol

Knockvologan

289

Carsaig
Bay

Rubha
Dubh

Soa I.

Ardalanish

ROSS OF MULL

Uisken

Scoor

CARSAIG ARCHES

Malcolm's Pt.

Eilean a'Chalmain

Ardchiavaig

125

Rubha nam
Braithrean

Rubh Ardalanish

B

Torran Rocks

OBAN 2:20

C

Dubh Artach

Rubh'a'Geadha

Kiloran Bay

Balnahard

Uragaig

KILORAN GARDENS

Kiloran

Kilchattan

126

D

Kilchattan

COLONSAY

Scalasaig

Glendeb

Loch Staosnaig

Corpach Bay

Ardskenish

Garvard

Rubha Dubh

467
BEINN BH

Balerominhor

453
RAINBERG
MOR

PRIORY

Shian Bay

Shian

Dubh Eilean

Oronsay

Loch Righ
Mòr

Eilean nan Ron

318
R

Loch Tarbert

E

Rubh'an t-Sàilein

1:10

Rubha Lang-aoinidh

Rubha Bholsa

Rubha a'Mhail

Lagg

439

Loch Lesgamaill

15

Nave Island

Ardnave Pt.

364
SGARBH
BREAC

J U R A

Loch an Aircill

A846

Ardmenish

F

Carraig Bhan

Ardnave

Kilnave

Gortantaoid

316

Bunnahabhain

BUNNAHABHAIN
DISTILLERY

785
755

PAPS OF JURA

An Dùna

An Clachan

Sanaigmore

Garra
Ellabus

Killinallan

Loch a Chnuic
Bhric

Cnocbreac

JURA FOREST

Corran

Knockrome

Braigo

Leckgruinart

Loch Gruinart

Caol Ila

Gleann Astaile

561

Leargybreck

Ardfernal

Lowlandman's
Bay

Smaull

LOCH GRUINART NATURE
RESERVE VISITORS CENTRE

CAOL ILA DISTILLERY

Port Askaig

Loch na Mile

Ballinaby

Carnduncan

Craigens

FINLAGGAN
CENTRE

Feolin Ferry

Gleann Ullibh

Keils

Small Isles

Aoradh

Tighnacachla

Loch
Finlaggan

Keills

Craighouse

Saligo Bay

Saligo

Loch
Gorm

ISLAY

Lyrabus

Balole

Ballygrant

Loch Cam

Loch
Ballygrant

8

Kilmeny

ISLE OF JURA
DISTILLERY

342
BRAT BHEINN

G

Coul Pt.

Coull

Foreland
Ho

Redhouses

Esknish

Knocklearoch

8

Cabrach

Camas an
Staca

JURA HOUSE
WALLED GARDEN

Strone

Crackaig

Sunderland

Blackrock

Daill

267
BEINN DUBH

Kilchoman

Gortan

Bridgend

Islay
Ho

Sorn

Am Fraoch
Eilean

Rubha na Tràille

Brosdale I.

Conisby

ISLAY LIFE
MUSEUM

H
NR
60
10

Kilchiaran Bay

254

Bowmore

A846

Cattadale

254

Arthur's Hd.

2:00

RHINNS
OF
ISLAY

Tormisdale

ISLAY

Port
Charlotte

15

BOWMORE
ROUND CHURCH

Mulindry

Kilnennan

Kilchiaran

Bruichladdich

Gartbreck

Laggan

Nerabus

1

ossit Pt.

2

ossit Pt.

Lossit

Kelsay

3

Port
Charlotte

Bridge Ho

Laggan

4

471
BEINN BHAN

491
BEINN
BHEIGEIR

5

Carraig Mhór

6

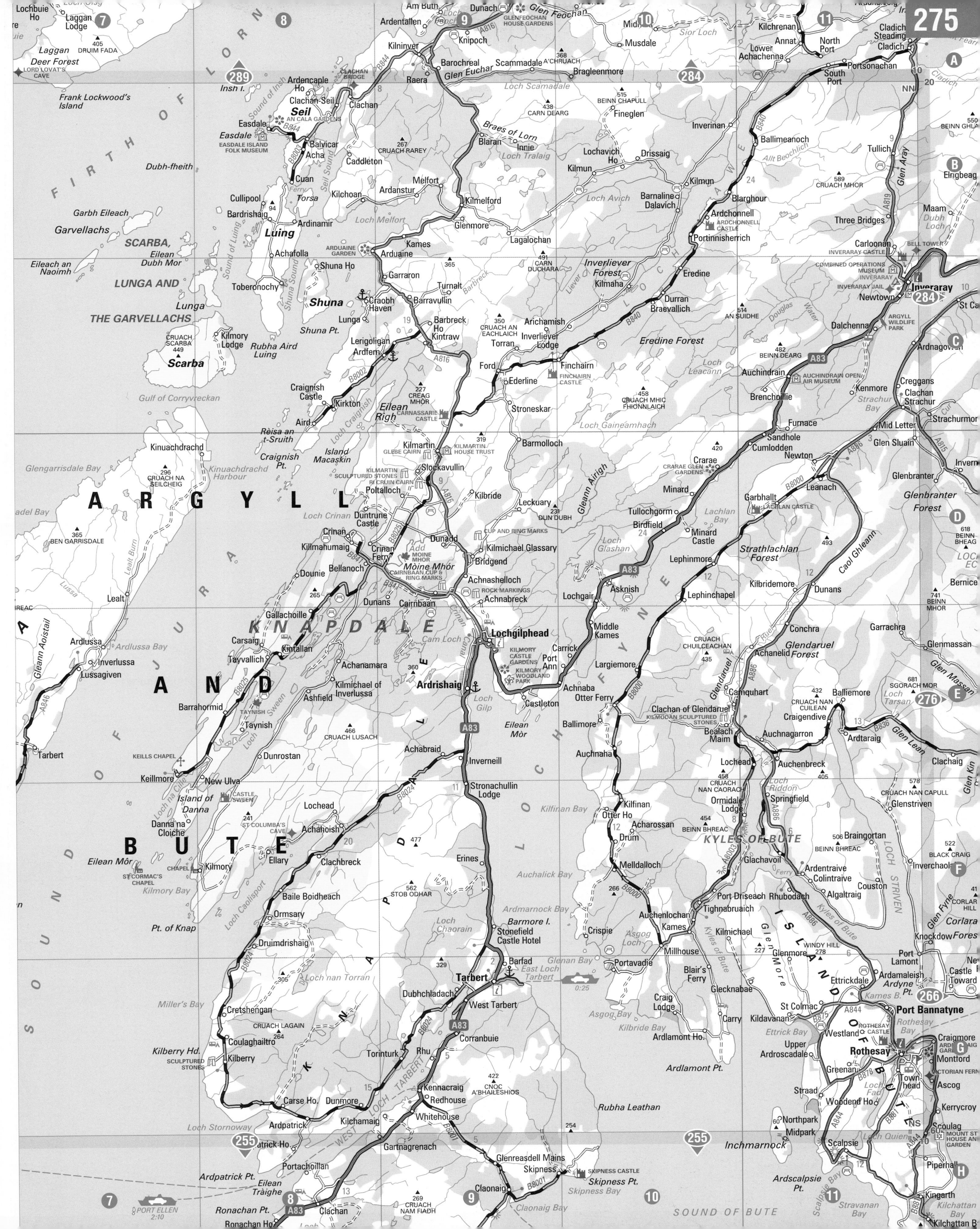

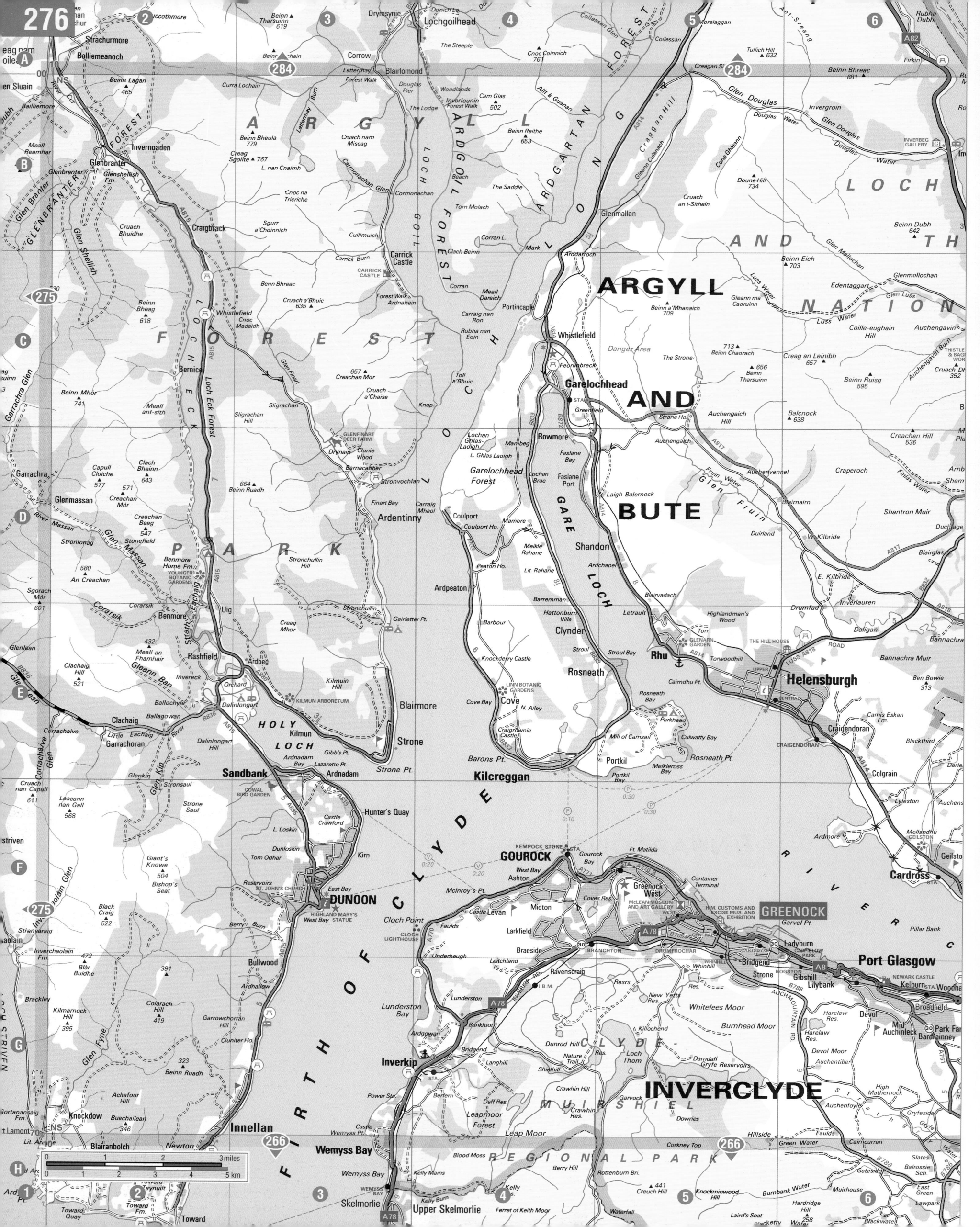

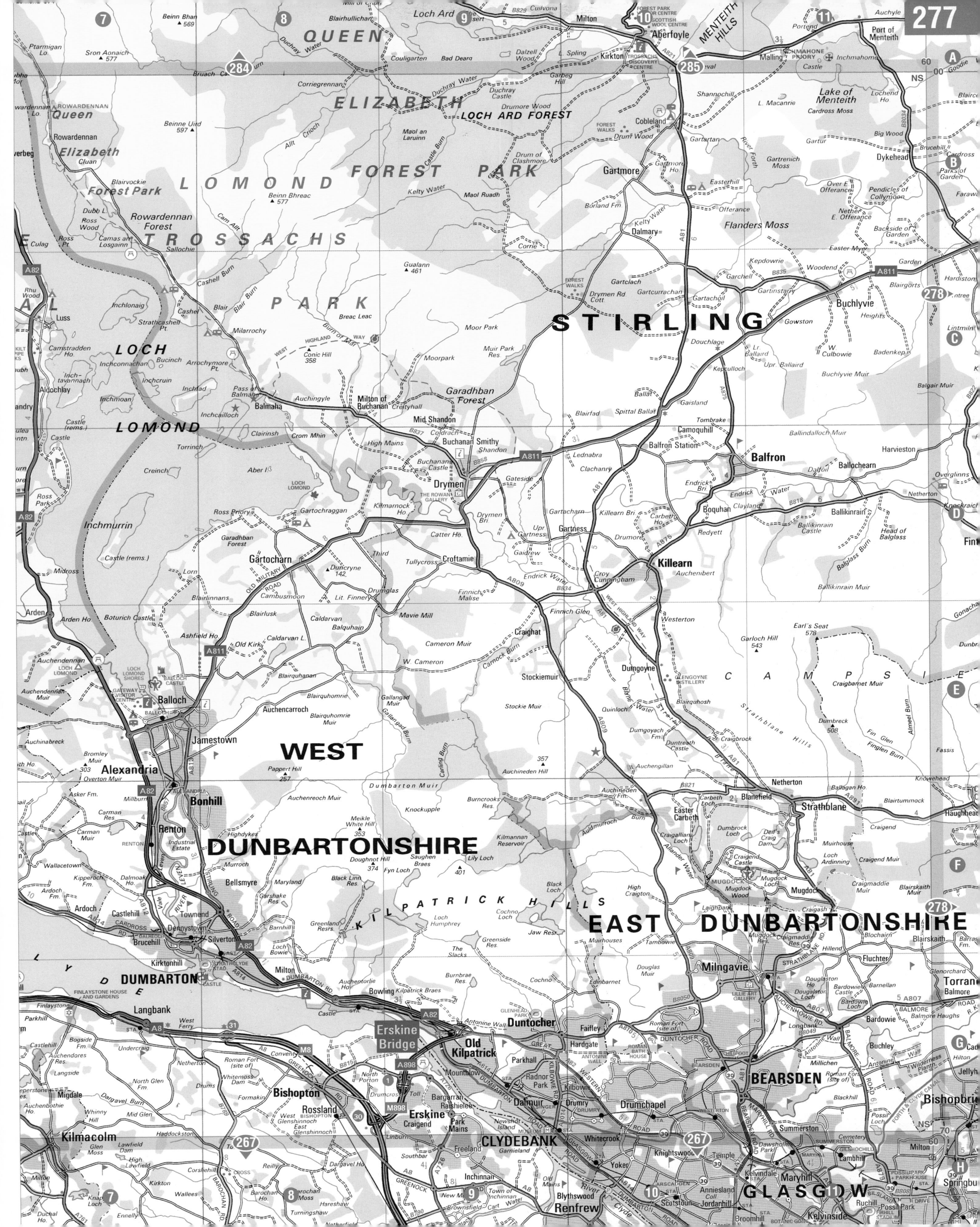

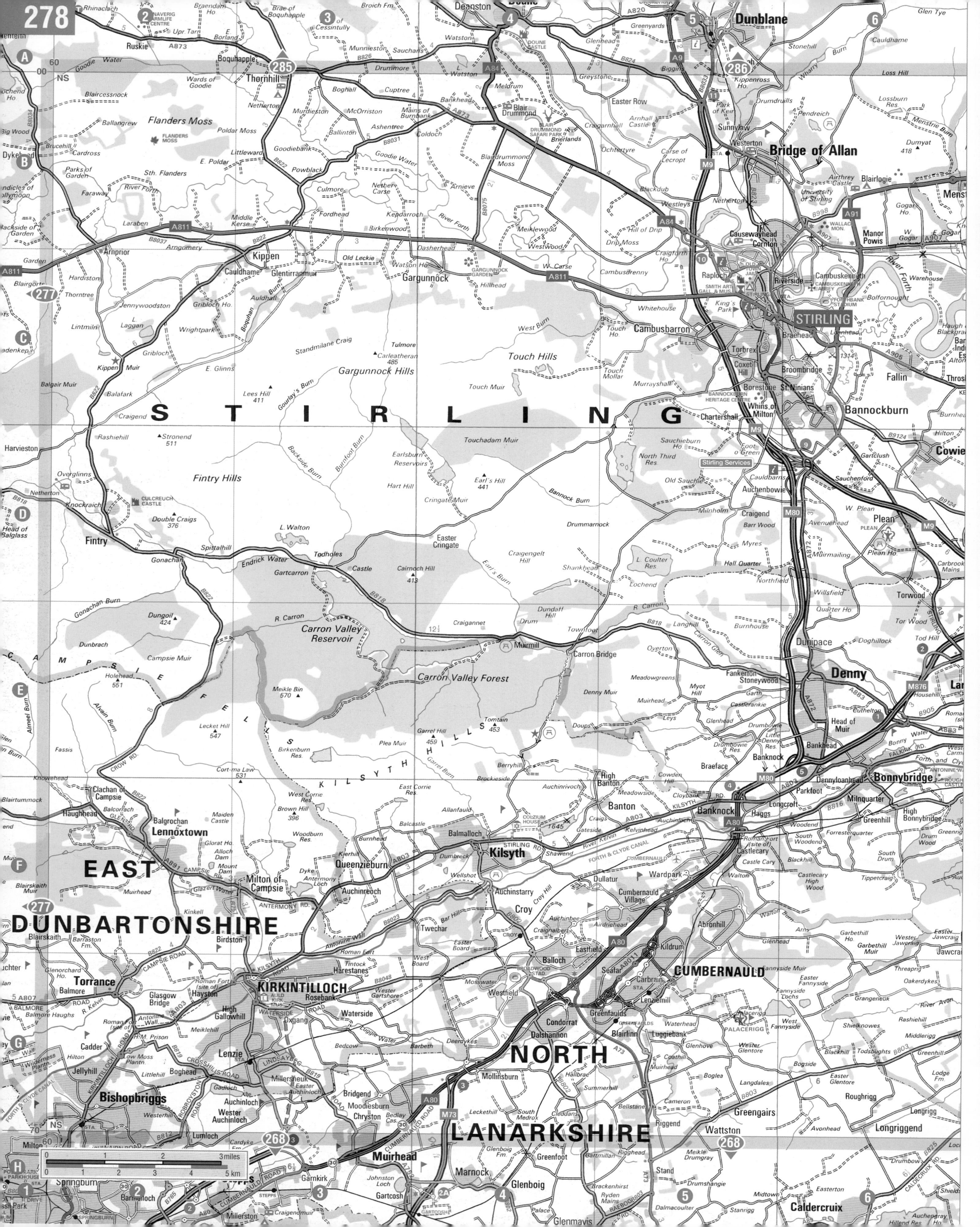

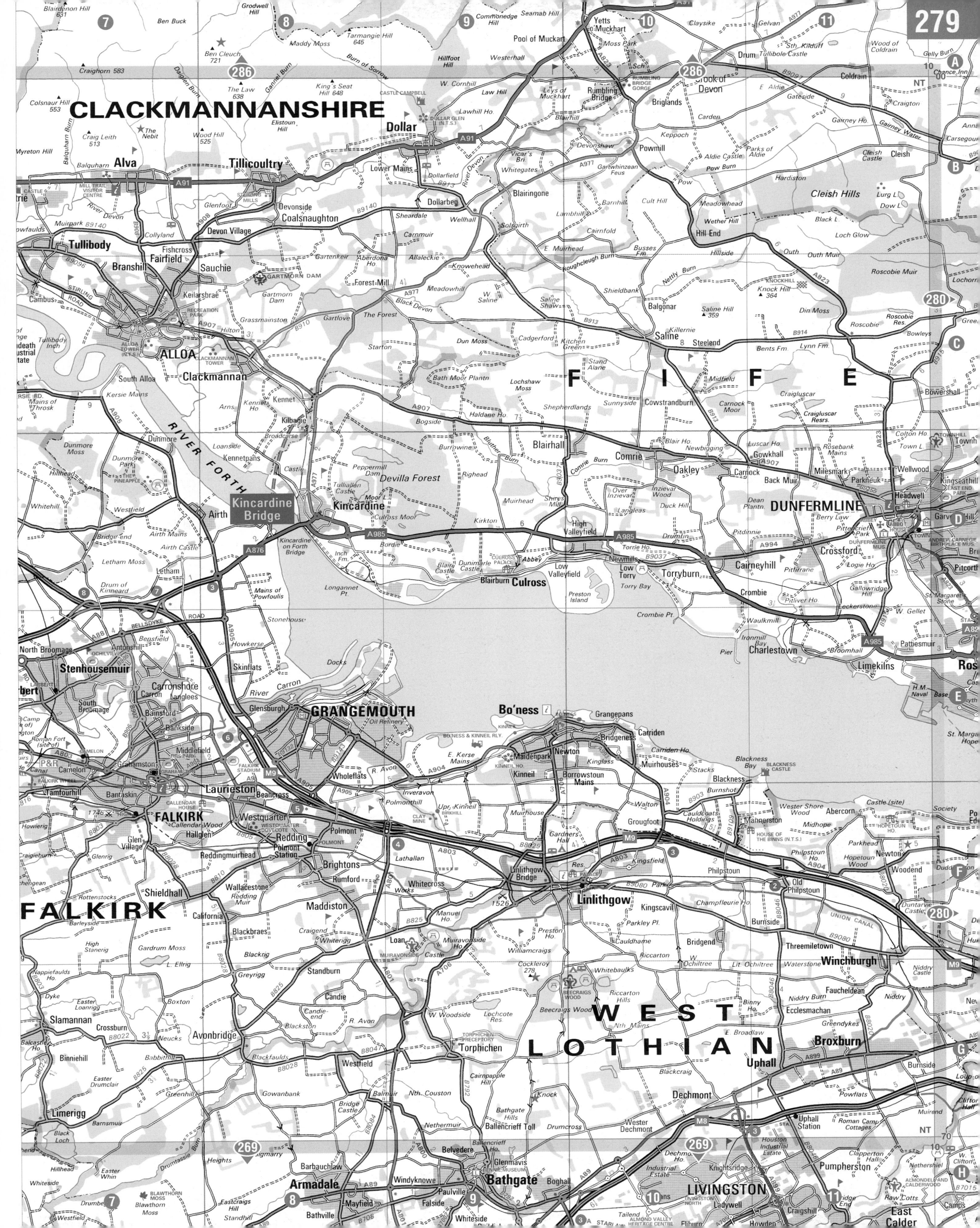

2   3   4   5   6

A
60
00
NT

287

Isle of May

ISLE OF
MAY

B

281

C

N   O

D

Bass Rock

Gin Head
TANTALLON
CASTLE
Auldhame
Car Rocks
Seacliff
Scoughall
Gleghornie   New Mains   Peffer
Sands
E   Ravensheugh
Sands
Whitekirk   Lochhouses
St. Baldred's
Cradle
Tyninghame
Links
Binning
Wood
Tyninghame Ho.
Tyninghame   JOHN MUIR   Belhaven
Hedderwick   Bay
Hill
Belhaven   Dunbar
West Barns   JOHN MUIR
BIRTHPLACE
STA
Broxmouth   White Sands   Barns Ness
Howmuir   Hedderwick   Broxburn
E. Broomhouse
281   S. Belton
Traprain   Beesknowe   Biel Water   East
Barns
Biel Grange   W.   Lit. Pinkerton   Chapel Pt.
Biel   Broomhouse   296   Torness Pt.
Grangemuir   Pitcox   Pleasants   Spott Burn   Doon Hill   Meikle   Power Sta.
Luggate   Lit. Spott   Spott   Pinkerton   Skateraw
E. Pinkerton
Luggate   Spott Ho.   Pinkerton   Dry Burn
Burn   Brunt Hill   Hill   Thorntonloch
Meiklerig   Crowhill
Stenton   Pressmennan
Tower   Pressmennan   Spott Dod   Innerwick   Thornton
Papple   Wood
Overfield   Forest Trail   Pathhead   Halls   Woodhall Burn   Thurston Mains   Thurston   Lawfield   Bilsdean
Deuchrie Dod   Branxton   DUNGLASS   Reed Pt.
EAST   Birnieknowes   COLLEGIATE
Blackcastle   CHURCH
Deuchrie   Lothian Edge   Hill   Cove
LOTHIAN   High   Elmscleugh   Cockburnspath
Nunraw   Wood   Cocklaw Hill   Cocklaw   Springfield   Dovecot Hall   Pease Bay   Siccar Pt.
Moorcock Hall   W. Aikengall   Oldhamstocks   Hirst Rocks
Thorters Res.   Watch   Bransly   Oldhamstocks Burn   Hoprig   Old Cambus
NT   Law   Hill   272   Redheugh
60   272   A1107
Castle M   on   Heriot   Water   Penmanshiel
0   1   2   3 miles   Wood   Meikle
0   1   2   3   4   5 km   Friardykes   Wightman   Fulfordlees   Black Law
Dod   Hill   Haud
Cliffs Dod   Wester   Ewieside   Yards
999   Friardykes   Dod   Dod Hill   Hill   Penmanshiel Moor
Wool Hill   Ecclaw   Pease Burn   A1107
Monynut   Bowshiel

1   2   3   4   5   6

A
10
NT 00

B

C

D

R T H   S E A

E

F

G

Fast Castle Head
FAST
CASTLE
Dowlaw

NT
70
10

Mawcarr Stells

273   Abb's Head   273

Dowlaw Burn

Oatlee Hill

Lumsdaine
Moor   Lumsdaine   Westerside   ST ABB'S HEAD

dingham
mmon   7   Coldingham L.   8   Mire L. The Buddy   9   Horsecastle Bay   10   Starney Bay   11

West Loch

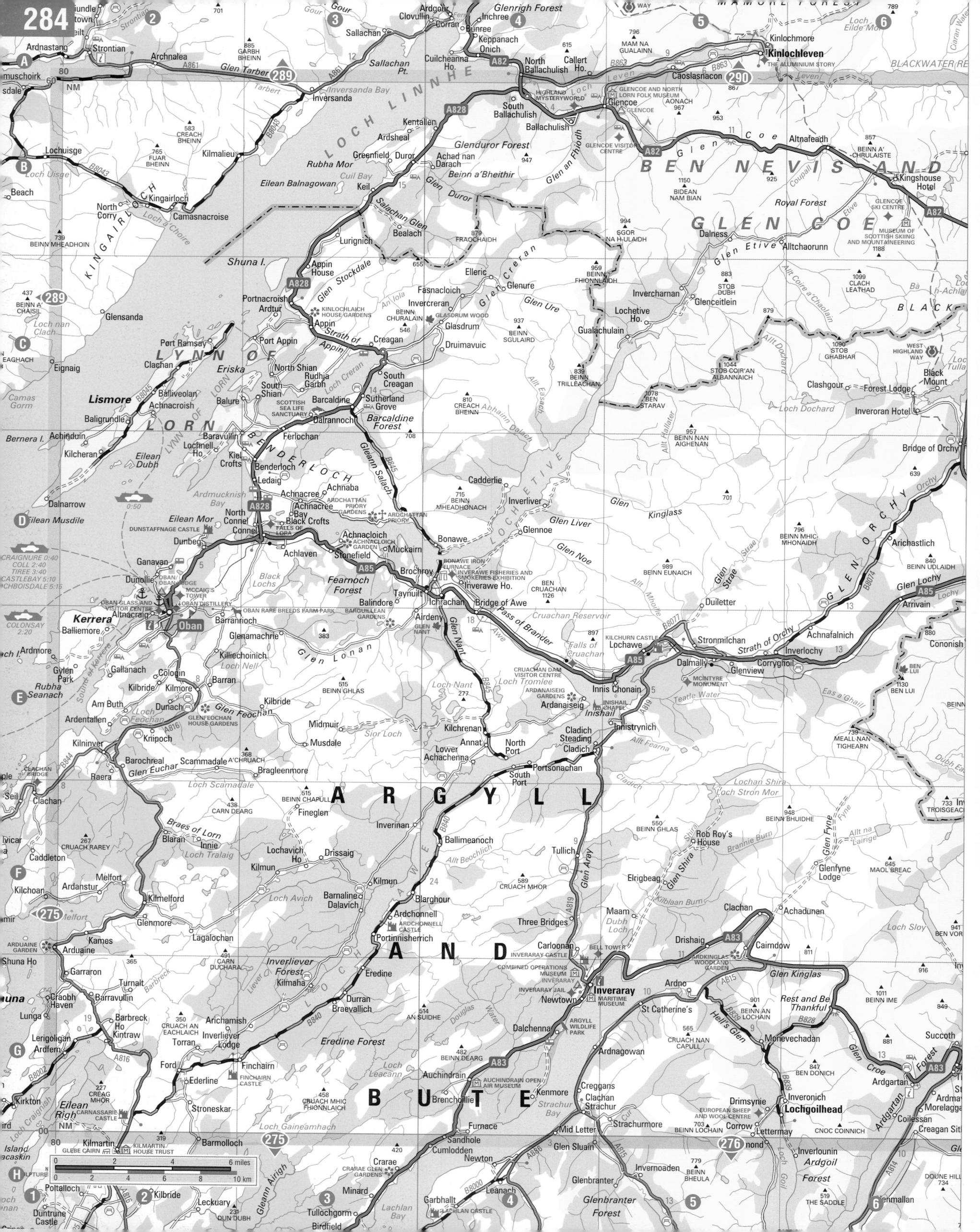

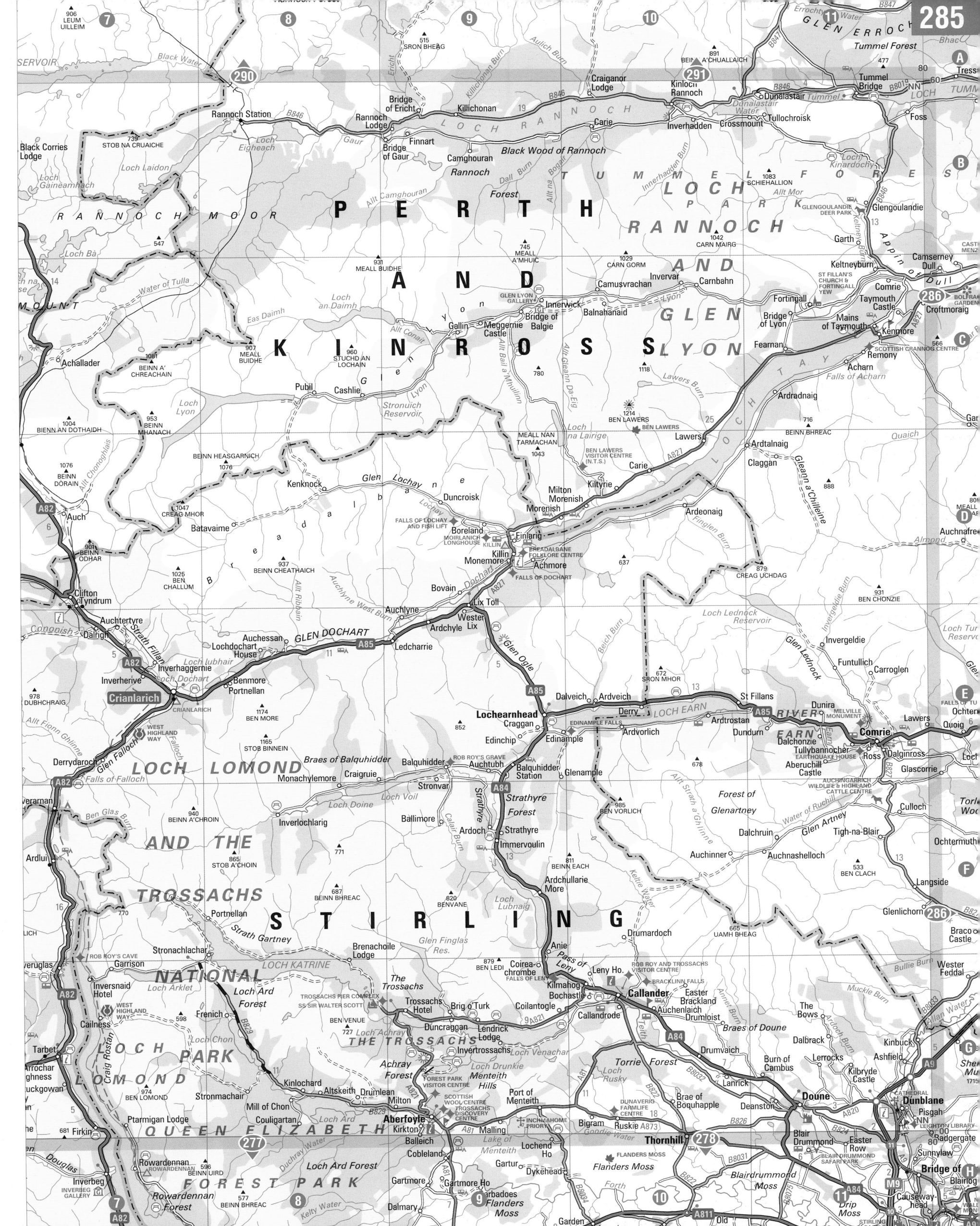

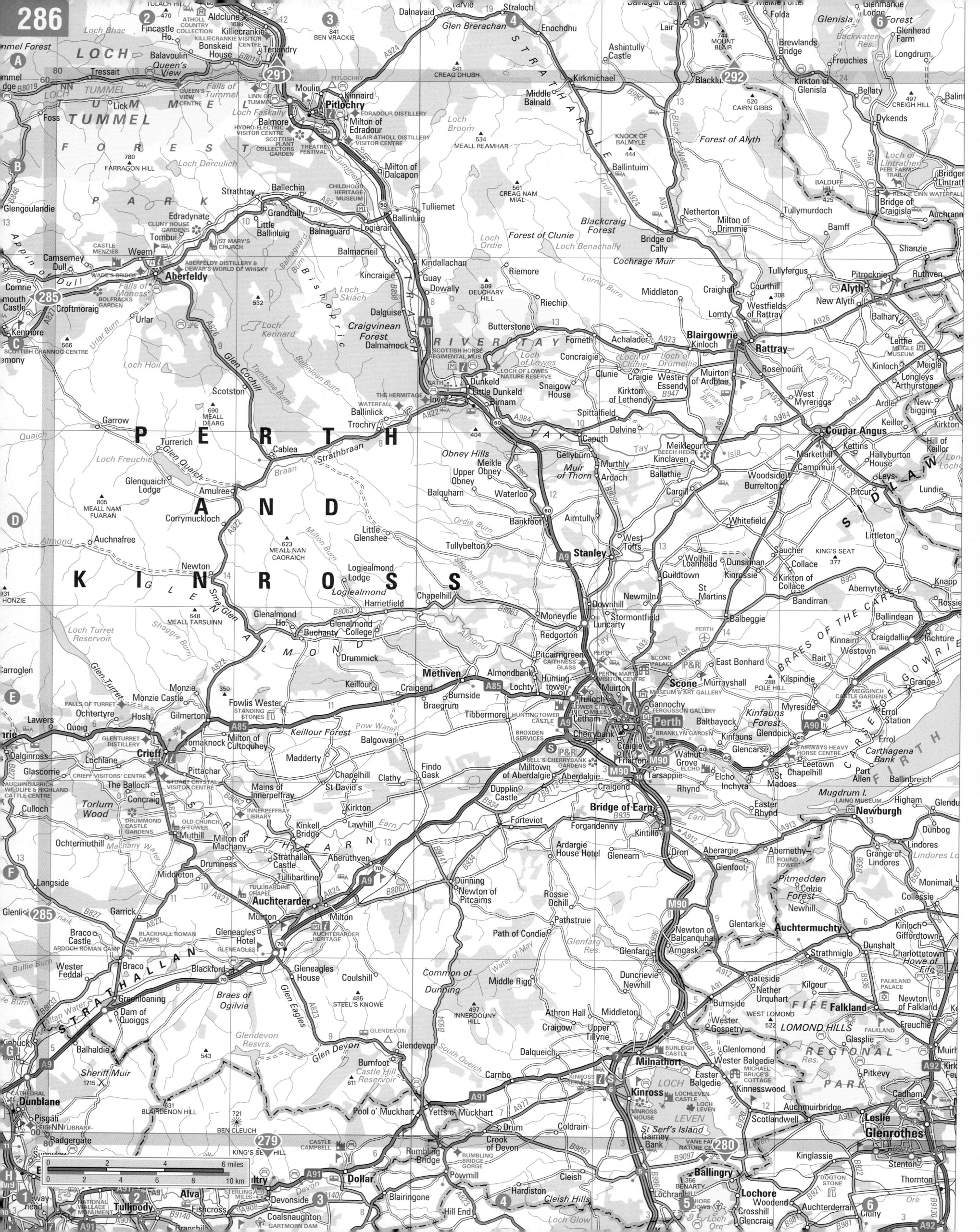

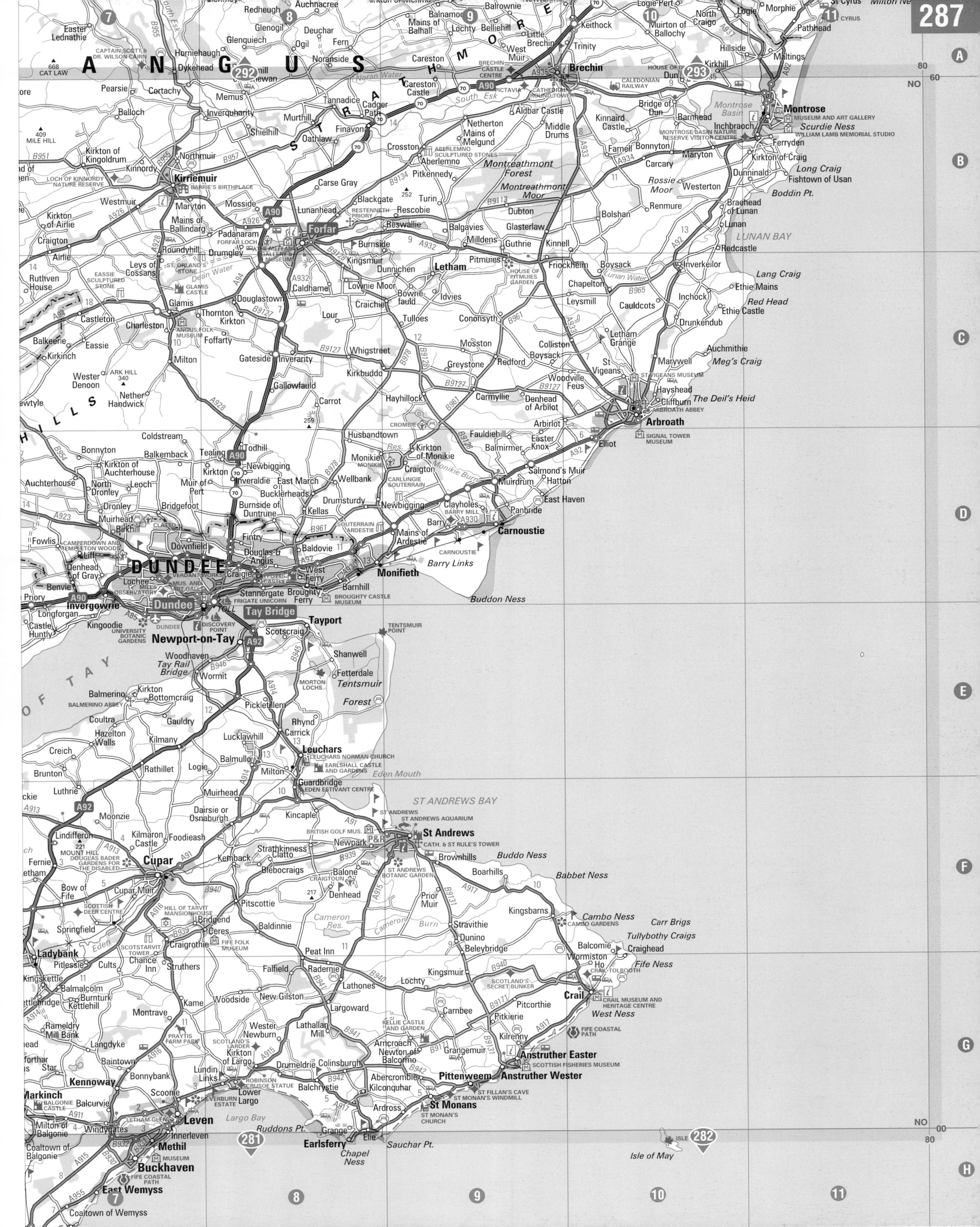

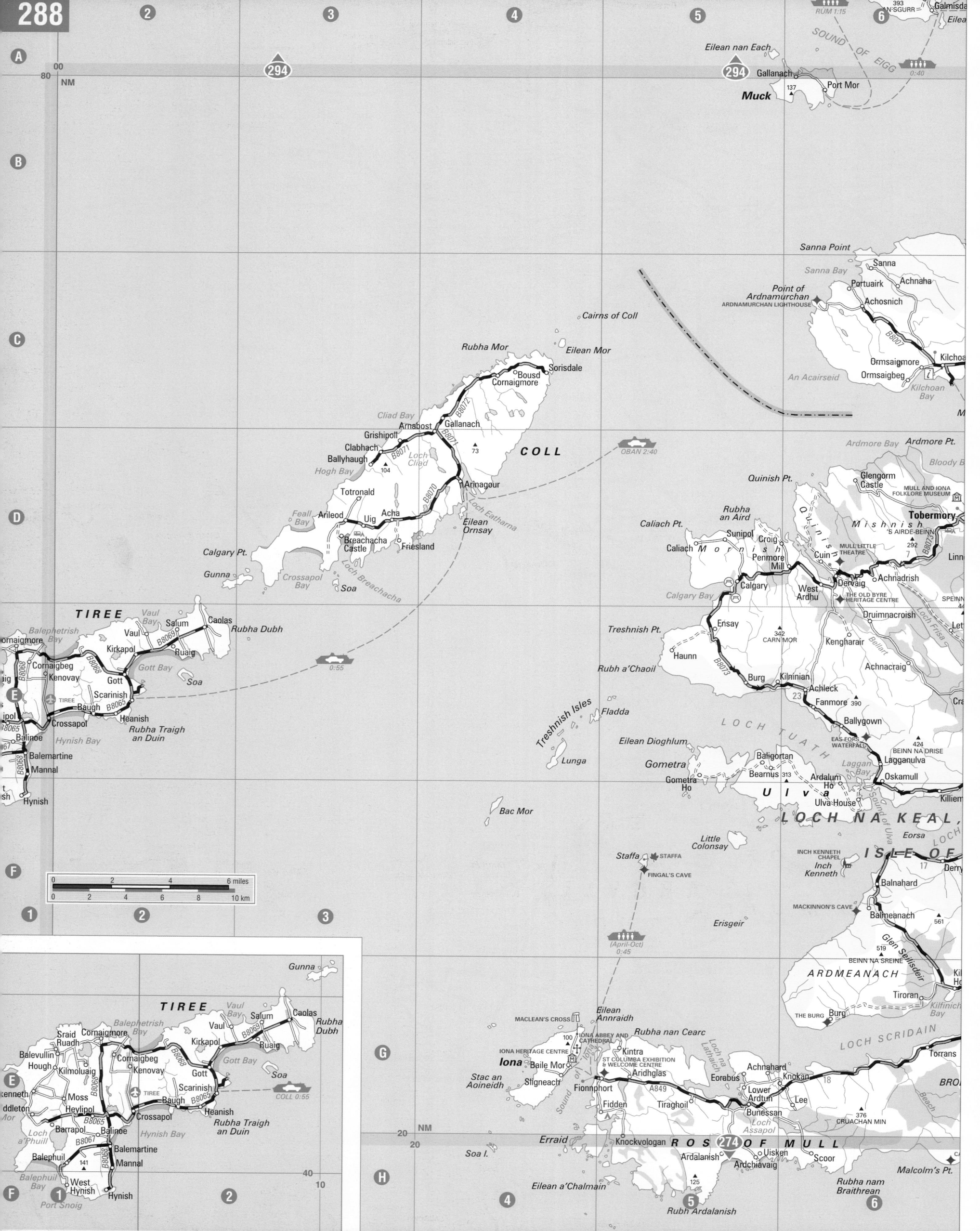

A

B

C

D

E

F

G

H

1 2 3 4 5 6

Muck

SOUND OF EIGG

RÙM 1:15

N-SGURR Galmisda

Eilean nan Each

Gallanach

Port Mor

137

0:40

Sanna Point

Sanna Bay

Sanna

Portuairk

Achnaha

Achosnich

Point of
Ardnamurchan

ARDNAMURCHAN LIGHTHOUSE

B8007

393

Cairns of Coll

Eilean Mor

Rubha Mor

Sorisdale

Bousd

Cornaigmore

Kilchoan

Ormsaigmore

An Acairseid

Ormsaigbeg

Kilchoan
Bay

i

Cliad Bay

Arnabost

Gallanach

Grishipoll

B8071

B8072

Clabhach

Loch
Cliad

B8071

Ballyhaugh

104

73

73

COLL

QBAN 2:40

Ardmore Bay

Ardmore Pt.

Bloody B

Hogh Bay

Totronald

Loch Etharna

B8070

Arinagour

Quinish Pt.

Glengorm
Castle

MULL AND IONA
FOLKLORE MUSEUM

M

Feall
Bay

Arileod

Uig

Acha

Eilean Ornsay

Rubha
an Aird

Caliach Pt.

Sunipol

Croig

Tobermory

'S AIRDE-BEINN

Mishnish

Breachacha
Castle

Friesland

Caliach

Mornish

Penmore
Mill

Cuin

292

B8073

Linn

Calgary Pt.

Gunna

Crossapol
Bay

Soa

Calgary

West
Ardhu

Dervaig

MULL LITTLE
THEATRE

Achnadrish

SPEINN

Calgary Bay

THE OLD BYRE
HERITAGE CENTRE

Druimnacroish

Let

TIREE

Balephetrish
Bay

Vaul
Bay

Salum

Caolas

Ensay

342
CARN MOR

Kengharair

Loch Frisa

Bellart

Achnacraig

Vaul

B8069

Rubha Dubh

Cornaigmore

Kirkapol

B8068

Ruaig

Treshnish Pt.

Haunn

B8073

Burg

Kilninian

Loch Tuath

ornaigmore

Cornaigbeg

Gott Bay

Rubh a'Chaoil

Achleck

Fanmore

390

Kenovay

Soa

23

B8068

Gott

Scarinish

Treshnish Isles

Fladda

Ballygown

EAS FORS
WATERFALL

424

BEINN NA DRISE

aig

Kenneth

Balinoe

B8065

TIREE

Baugh

Heanish

Eilean Dioghlum

Lunga

Gometra

Baligortan

Laggan
Bay

Lagganulva

B8068

Crossapol

Rubha Traigh
an Duin

Gometra
Ho

Bearnus

313

Ardalum

Oskamull

Balemartine

Hynish Bay

Ulva
House

U l v a

Killiem

67

Mannal

Bac Mor

LOCH NA KEAL,

Eorsa

Loch

ch

t

Hynish

Little
Colonsay

INCH KENNETH
CHAPEL

ISLE OF

Staffa

STAFFA

Inch
Kenneth

FINGAL'S CAVE

Balnahard

Erisgeir

MACKINNON'S CAVE

Balmeanach

17

Derry

519

BEINN NA SREINE

561

0 2 4 6 miles

0 2 4 6 8 10 km

ARDMEANACH

Glen Seilisder

Kil

Ho

1 2 3

Tiroran

THE BURG

Burg

Kilfinichen
Bay

MACLEAN'S CROSS

Eilean
Annraidh

Rubha nan Cearc

Loch Scridain

TIREE

Vaul
Bay

Salum

Caolas

Gunna

IONA ABBEY AND
CATHEDRAL

100

M

Loch na Lathaich

Sraid
Ruadh

Cornaigmore

Vaul

Kirkapol

Ruaig

Rubha
Dubh

IONA HERITAGE CENTRE

Kintra

Achnahard

Knokan

Torrans

18

Balevullin

Hough

Cornaigbeg

Gott Bay

Stac an
Aoineidh

Iona

Baile Mor

ST COLUMBA EXHIBITION
& WELCOME CENTRE

Eorabus

Lower
Ardtun

Lee

Kilmoluaig

Kenovay

Soa

Aridhglas

A849

Loch
Assapol

BRO

Moss

Gott

Scarinish

COLL 0:55

Sligneach

Fionnphort

Bunessan

376

CRUACHAN MIN

kenneth

Heylipol

TIREE

Baugh

B8065

Fidden

Tiraghoil

ddleton

Crossapol

Heanish

Knockvologan

Usken

125

Scoor

Barrapol

Balinoe

Rubha Traigh
an Duin

ROS OF MULL

A274

Loch
a'Phuill

B8067

Balemartine

Hynish Bay

Erraid

Soa I.

Ardalanish

Ardchiavaig

Malcolm's Pt.

Balephuil

141

Mannal

Eilean a'Chalmain

Rubh Ardalanish

Rubha nam
Braithrean

Balephuil
Bay

West
Hynish

Hynish

Port Snoig

NM

80

00

NM

20

20

40

10

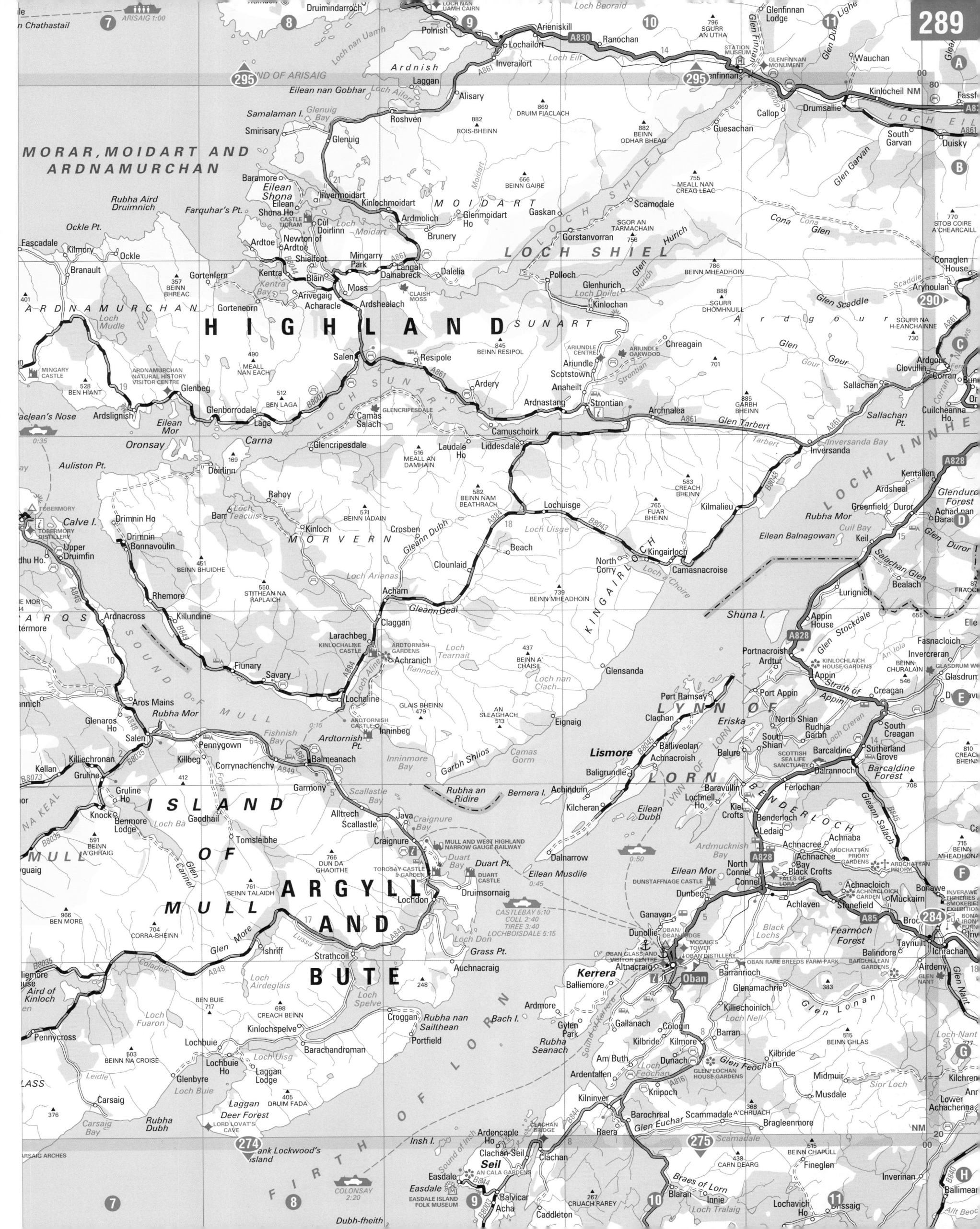

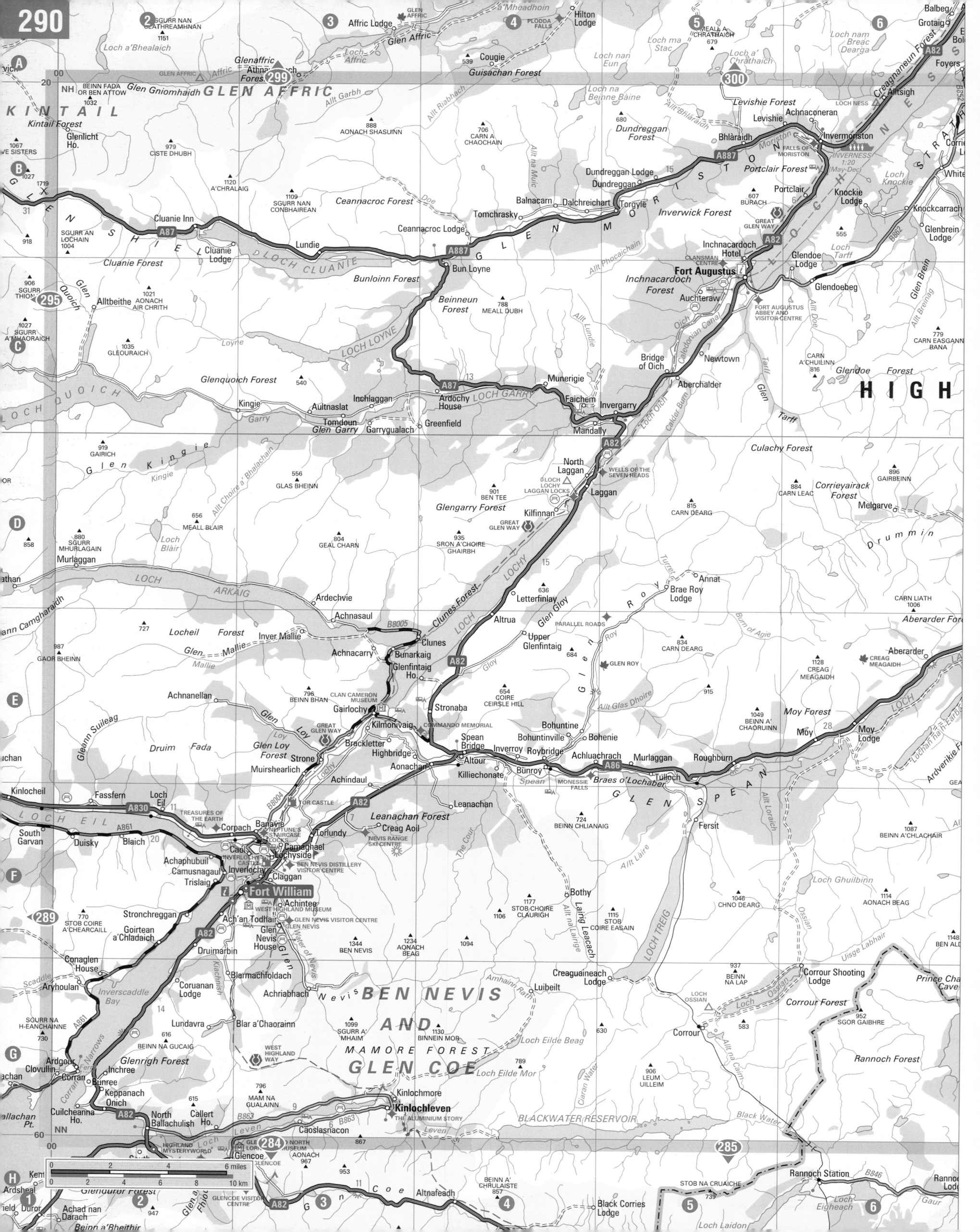

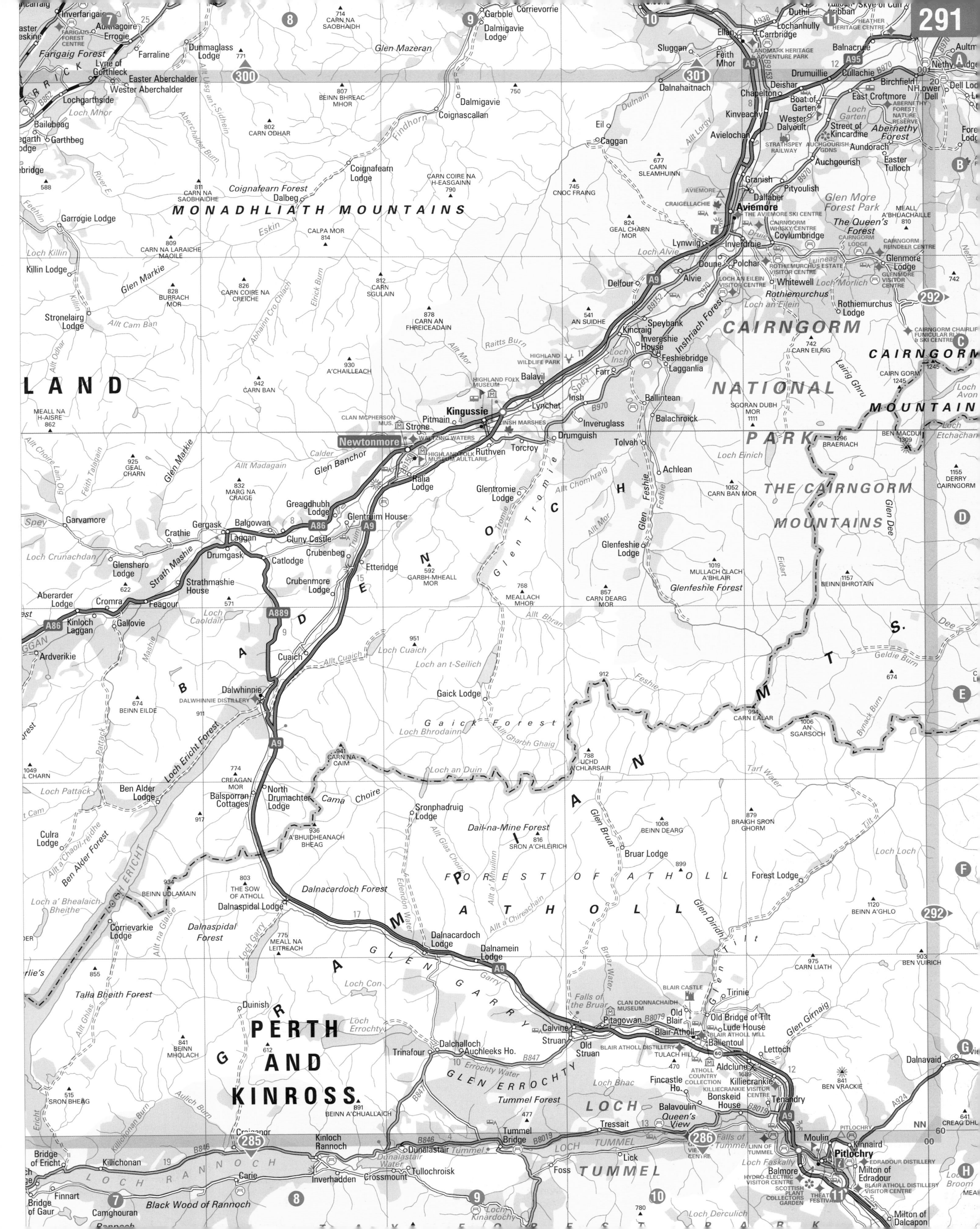

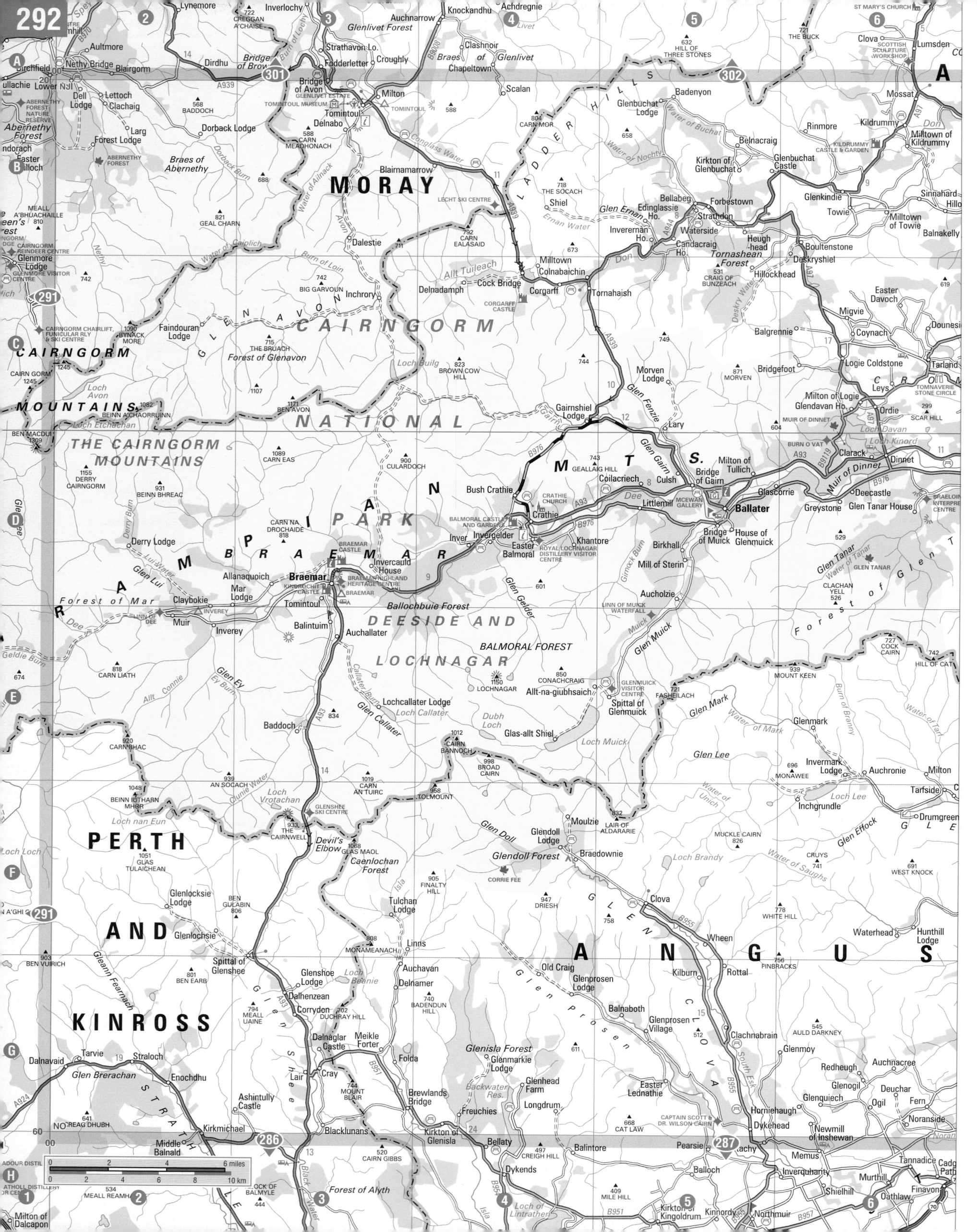

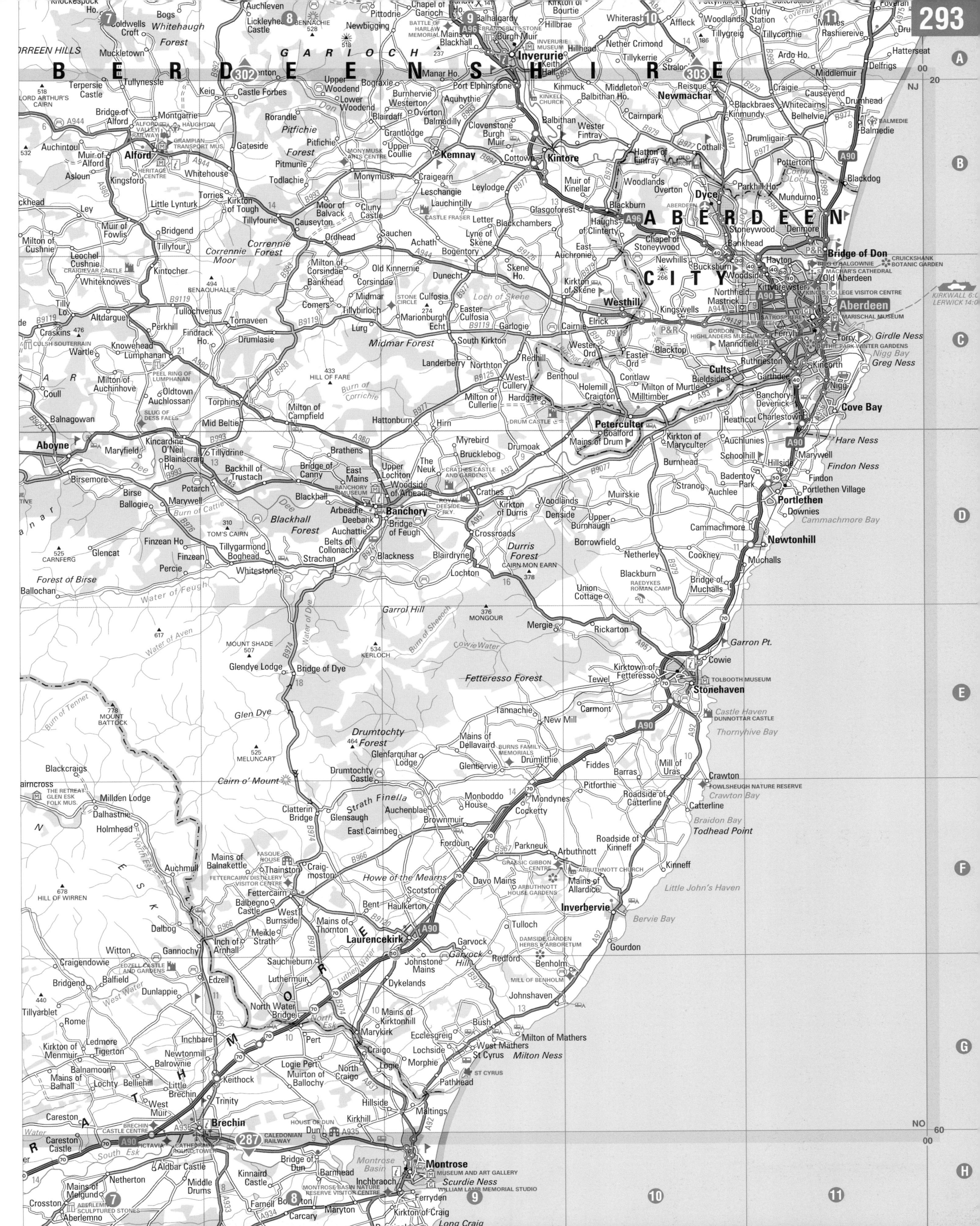

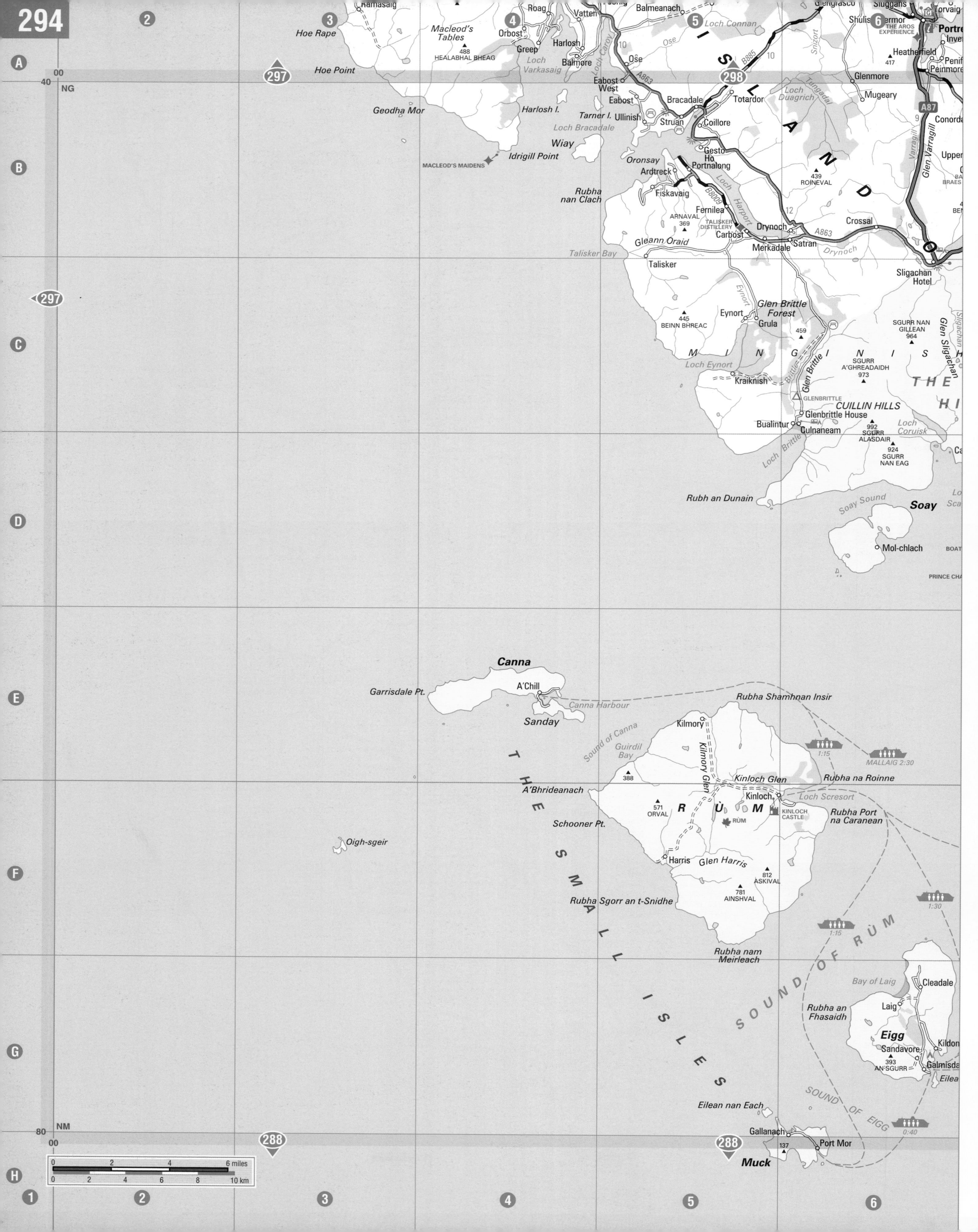

Ramasaig
Balmeanach
Glengrasco
Sluggans
Torvaig
Roag
Vatten
Loch Connan
Shulis
ermor
Portre
Hoe Rape
Orbost
THE AROS EXPERIENCE
Macleod's Tables
Greep
Harlosh
Ose
Ose
B885
Inver
488
HEALABHAL BHEAG
Harlosh
Heatherfield
Hoe Point
297
Balmore
417
Glenmore
Penit
Eabost West
A863
298
Peinmore
Geodha Mor
Bracadale
Totardor
Loch Duagrich
Mugeary
A87
Harlosh I.
Eabost
9
Loch Bracadale
Tarner I. Ullinish
Struan
Coillore
Conorda
Wiay
Gesto Ho
439
ROINEVAL
Upper
MACLEOD'S MAIDENS
Idrigill Point
Oronsay
Portnalong
Ardtreck
BRAES
Fiskavaig
Ferinlea
12
Rubha nan Clach
ARNAVAL
369
TALISKER DISTILLERY
Drynoch
Crossal
Gleann Oraid
Carbost
A863
Talisker Bay
Merkadale
Satran
Drynoch
Talisker
Sligachan Hotel
445
BEINN BHREAC
Eynort
Glen Brittle Forest
Grula
SGURR NAN GILLEAN
964
297
Loch Eynort
459
SGURR A'GHREADAIDH
973
THE
Kraiknish
CUILLIN HILLS
HI
GLENBRITTLE
Glenbrittle House
Loch Coruisk
Bualintur
Culnaneam
992
SGURR ALASDAIR
924
SGURR NAN EAG
Rubh an Dunain
Soay Sound
Soay
Lo
Sca
Mol-chlach
BOAT
PRINCE CHA

Canna
A'Chill
Rubha Shamhnan Insir
Garrisdale Pt.
Canna Harbour
Sanday
Kilmory
Guirdil Bay
Sound of Canna
1:15
MALLAIG 2:30
Kilmory Glen
388
Kinloch Glen
Rubha na Roinne
A'Bhrideanach
571
ORVAL
R Ü M
Kinloch
Loch Scresort
RÜM
KINLOCH CASTLE
Rubha Port na Caranean
Schooner Pt.
Oigh-sgeir
Harris
Glen Harris
812
ASKIVAL
Rubha Sgorr an t-Snidhe
781
AINSHVAL
1:30
1:15
SOUND OF RÜM
Rubha nam Meirleach
Bay of Laig
Cleadale
Rubha an Fhasaidh
Laig
Eigg
Eilean nan Each
393
AN SGURR
Galmisda
Sandavore
Eilea
SOUND OF EIGG
80 NM
00
288
288
0:40
Gallanach
137
Port Mor
Muck

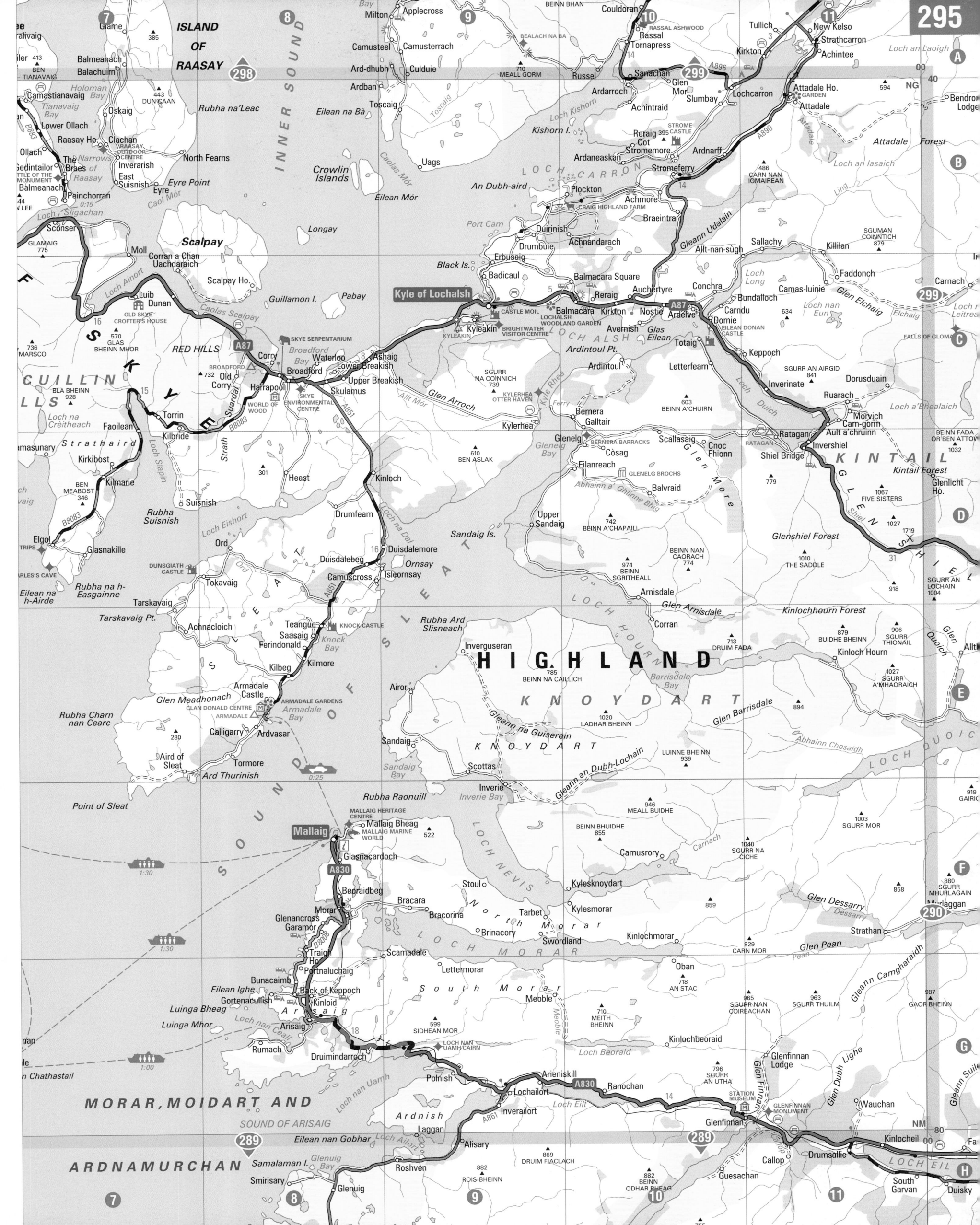

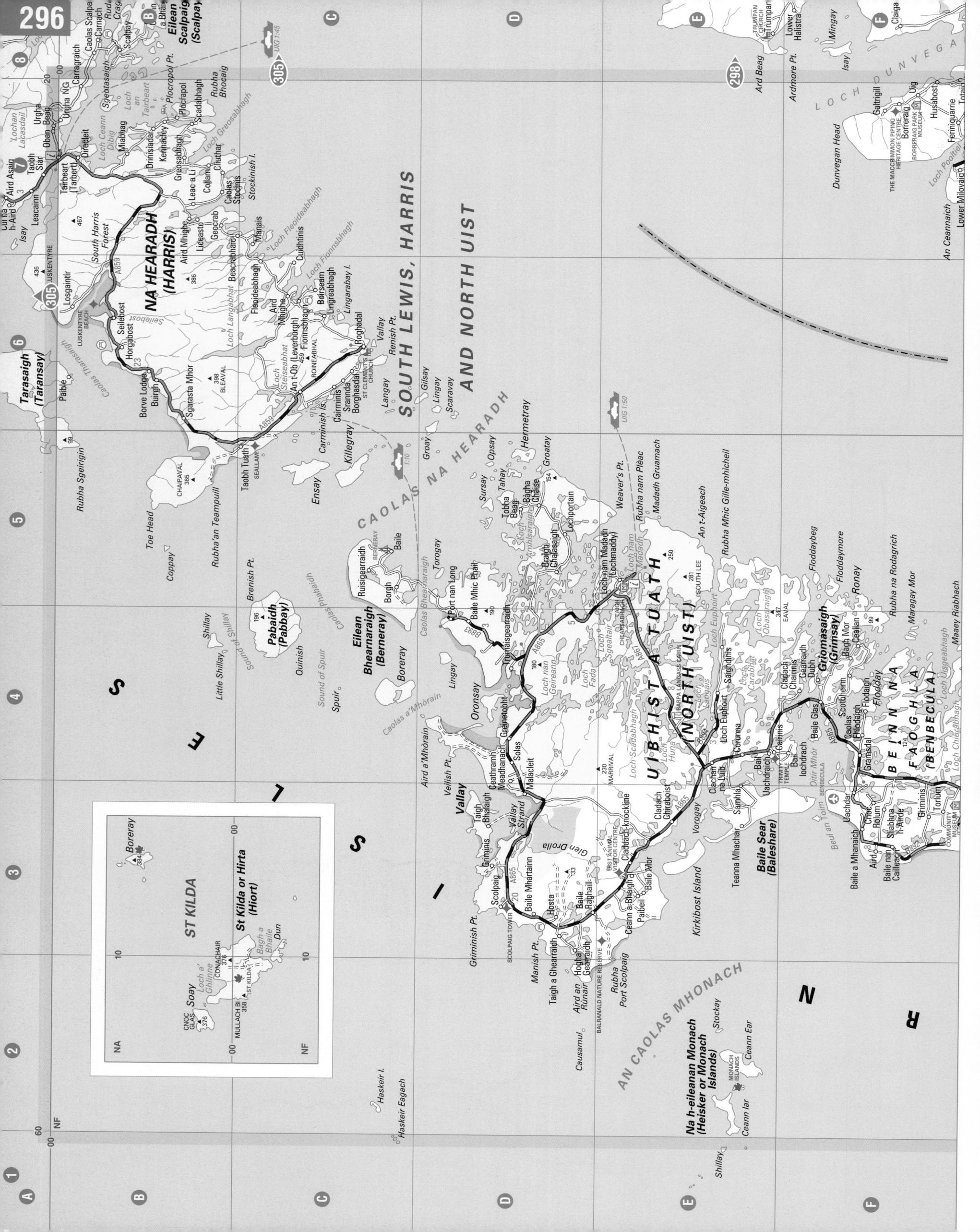

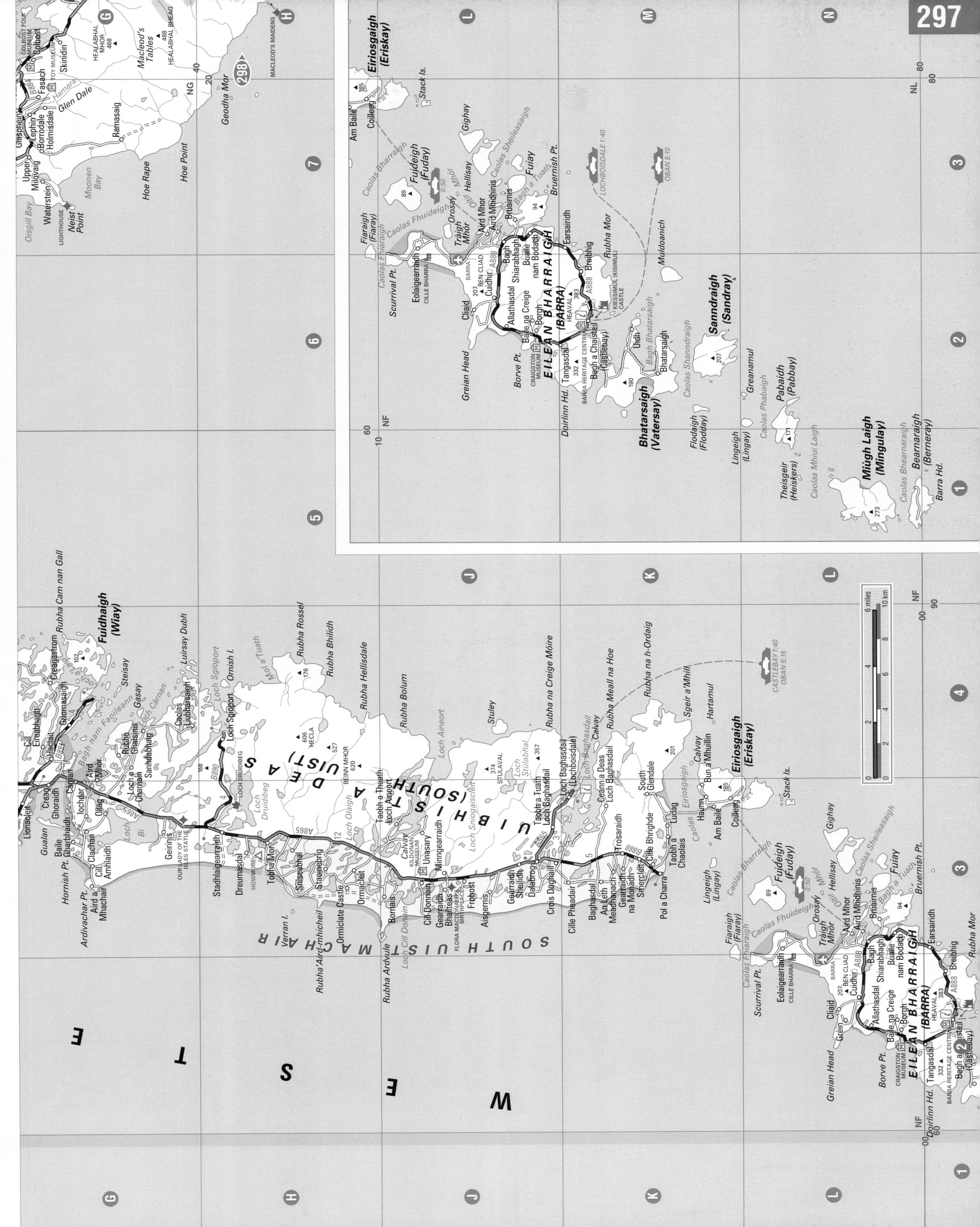

Top inset map (Barra area)

COLBOST FOUR
MUSEUM
Colbost
TOY MUSEUM
Fasach
Skinidin
G
464
Glasphein
Upper
Milovaig
Lephin
Borrodale
Holmisdale
Ramasaig
Glen Dale
Hamara
HEALABHAL
MHOR 468
Macleod's
Tables
HEALABHAL
BHEAG 488
Waterstein
Oisgill Bay
Moonen
Bay
LIGHTHOUSE
Neist
Point
Hoe Rape
Hoe Point
Waterhouse
Macleod's Maidens
Geodha Mor
NG 20
40
298
H
7

Eiriosgaigh
(Eriskay)
Am Baile
Colleck
185
Stack Is.
Fiaraigh
(Fiaray)
Caolas Bharralgh
Fuideigh
(Fuday)
0.50
Mhor
Gighay
Orosay
Oitir Hellisay
89
Caolas Fhuideigh
Traigh
Mhor
Aird Mhor
Aird Mhidhinis
Caolas Shelleasaigh
Bruaimis
Bagh a Tuath
94
Bruernish Pt.
Scurrival Pt.
Caolas Fhiaraigh
Eolaigearraidh
CILLE BHARRA
Cliaid
BARRA
BEN CLIAD
Cuidhir
207
A888
Bagh
Shiarabhagh
Buaile
nam Bodach
Earsairidh
Rubha Mor
LOCHBOISDALE 1:40
OBAN 5:10
L
6
M
EILEAN BHARRAIGH
(BARRA)
HEAVAL
383
A888
KIESSIMUL (KISIMUL)
CASTLE
Breibhig
Muldoanich
Greian Head
Borve Pt.
Allathasdal
Baile na Creige
Borgh
CRAIGSTON
MUSEUM
BARRA HERITAGE CENTRE
Tangasdal
332
Bagh a Chaistell
(Castlebay)
Udh
190
Bhatarsaigh
Bagh Bhatarsaigh
Sanndraigh
(Sandray)
207
5
Doirlinn Hd.
60
NF
10
Bhatarsaigh
(Vatersay)
Flodaigh
(Flodday)
Lingeigh
(Lingay)
Caolas Phabaigh
Greanamul
Pabaidh
(Pabbay)
171
Caolas Mhiui Laigh
Miugh Laigh
(Mingulay)
Caolas Bhearnaraigh
Bearnaraigh
(Berneray)
Barra Hd.
Theisgeir
(Heisters)
273
1

Main map (South Uist / Barra)

Rubha Cam nan Gall
Creagastrom
Fuidhaigh
(Wiay)
102
Steisay
Luirsay Dubh
Rubha Rossel
Rubha Bhilidh
Rubha Hellisdale
Cil
Eireabhagh
Griomasaigh
Gasay
Caolas
Luibharsaigh
Ormish I.
Rubha Bolum
Loch Aineort
Stuley
Rubha na Creige Mòire
Rubha na h-Ordaig
Cill a Ghoraidh
Sandabhaig
168
B890
LOCH DRUIDIBEG
Loch Druidbeg
606
HECLA
527
Mol a Tuath
176
BEINN MHOR
620
374
STULAVAL
357
Loch Stulabhal
Loch Baghasdail
(Lochboisdale)
Rubha Meall na Hoe
Sgeir a Mhill
Hartamul
Eiriosgaigh
(Eriskay)
CASTLEBAY 1:40
OBAN 5:15
L
4
NF
90
00
Lionacleit
Gualan
Baile
Ghoraidh
Clachan
Iochdar
Ollag
A865
Loch a
Charnain
Loch
Bi
Loch Olaigh
UIBHIST A DEAS
A865
Loch Sniogaisclett
Loch Baghasdail
Ceann a Deas
South
Glendale
201
Calvay
Bun a'Mhuilin
185
Stack Is.
Gighay
Hornish Pt.
Aird a
Mhachair
Creag
Ghoraidh
OUR LADY OF
THE ISLES STATUE
Geirinis
HOWMORE
Loch
Druidibeg
Stadhlaigearraidh
Tobha Mor
Staoinebrig
4
12
Taobh a Tuath
Loch Aineort
SOUTH (UIST)
Loch
Stulabhal
Taobh a Tuath
Loch Baghasdail
Ludag
Haun
Am Baile
Colleck
3
Ardivachar Pt.
Rubha 'Aird-mhicheil
Loch
Cill Donain
Verran I.
Dreumasdal
Sniseabhal
Staoinebrig
Borhais
Ormiclate Castle
KILDONAN
MUSEUM
Uachdar
FLORA MACDONALD'S
BIRTHPLACE
FLORA MACDONALD
MEMORIAL
Cill Donain
Bhaltreas
Gearraidh
Bhaileteas
Frobost
A865
Dalabrog
Crois Dughaill
Cille Pheadair
Pol a Charra
Baghasdal
An Leth
Meadhanach
Gearraidh
na Monadh
Smercleit
Cille Brighde
Taobh a
Chaolais
Caolas Eiriosgaigh
Lingeigh
(Lingay)
Caolas Bharralgh
Fuideigh
(Fuday)
89
0.50
Mhor
Orosay
Oitir Hellisay
Aird Mhor
Caolas Shelleasaigh
SOUTH UIST MACHAIR
E
S
T
W
E
S
T
W
E
Rubha Ardvule
Fiaraigh
(Fiaray)
Caolas Fhuideigh
Traigh
Mhor
Aird Mhidhinis
Bruaimis
Bagh a Tuath
94
Bruernish Pt.
Scurrival Pt.
Eolaigearraidh
CILLE BHARRA
Cliaid
BARRA
BEN CLIAD
Cuidhir
207
A888
Bagh
Shiarabhagh
Buaile
nam Bodach
Earsairidh
EILEAN BHARRAIGH
(BARRA)
HEAVAL
383
A888
Breibhig
Greian Head
Borve Pt.
Allathasdal
Baile na Creige
Borgh
CRAIGSTON
MUSEUM
BARRA HERITAGE CENTRE
Tangasdal
332
Bagh a Chaistell
(Castlebay)
Doirlinn Hd.
NF

Scale bar
6 miles
10 km
0   2   4   6   8
0   2   4   6   8

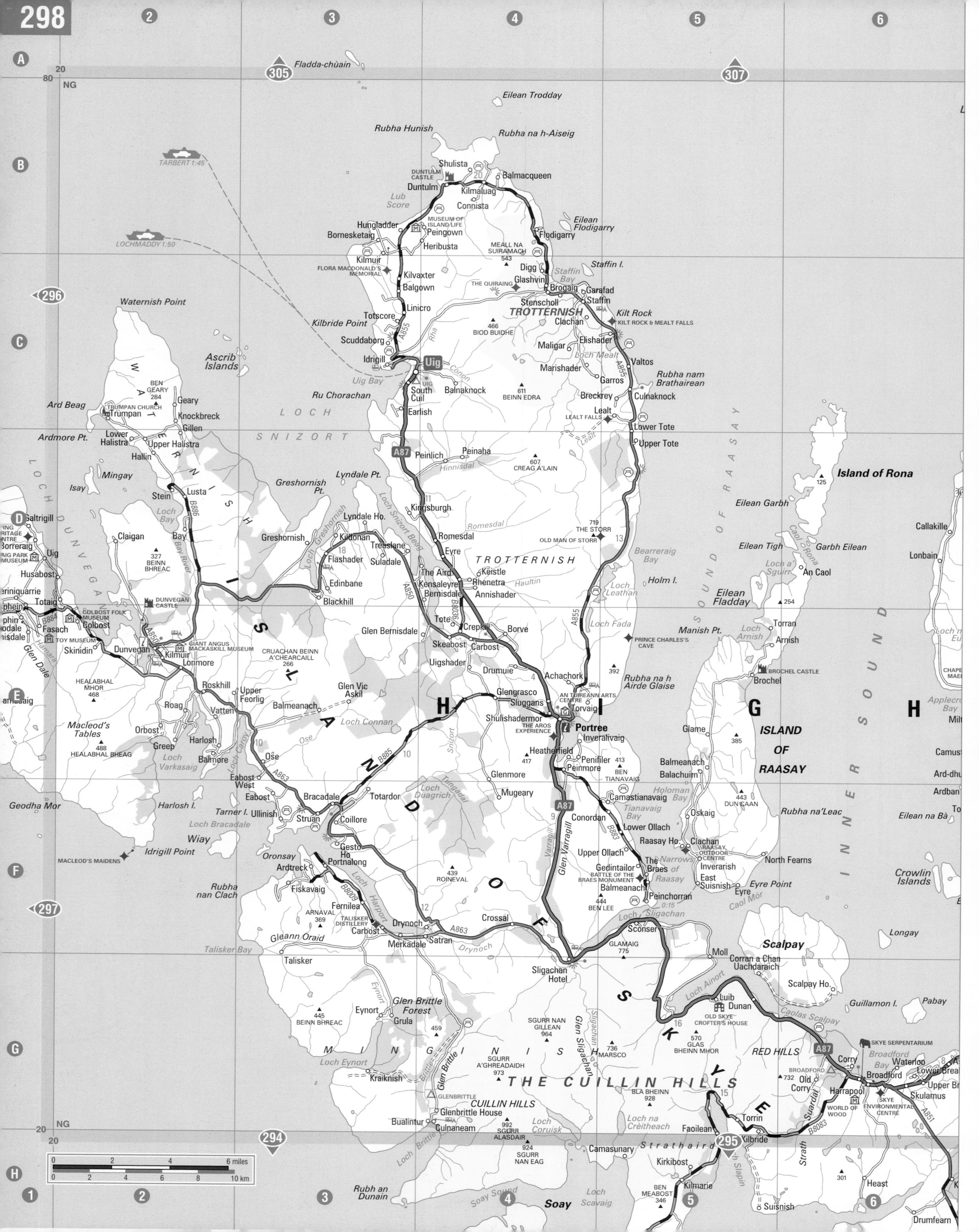

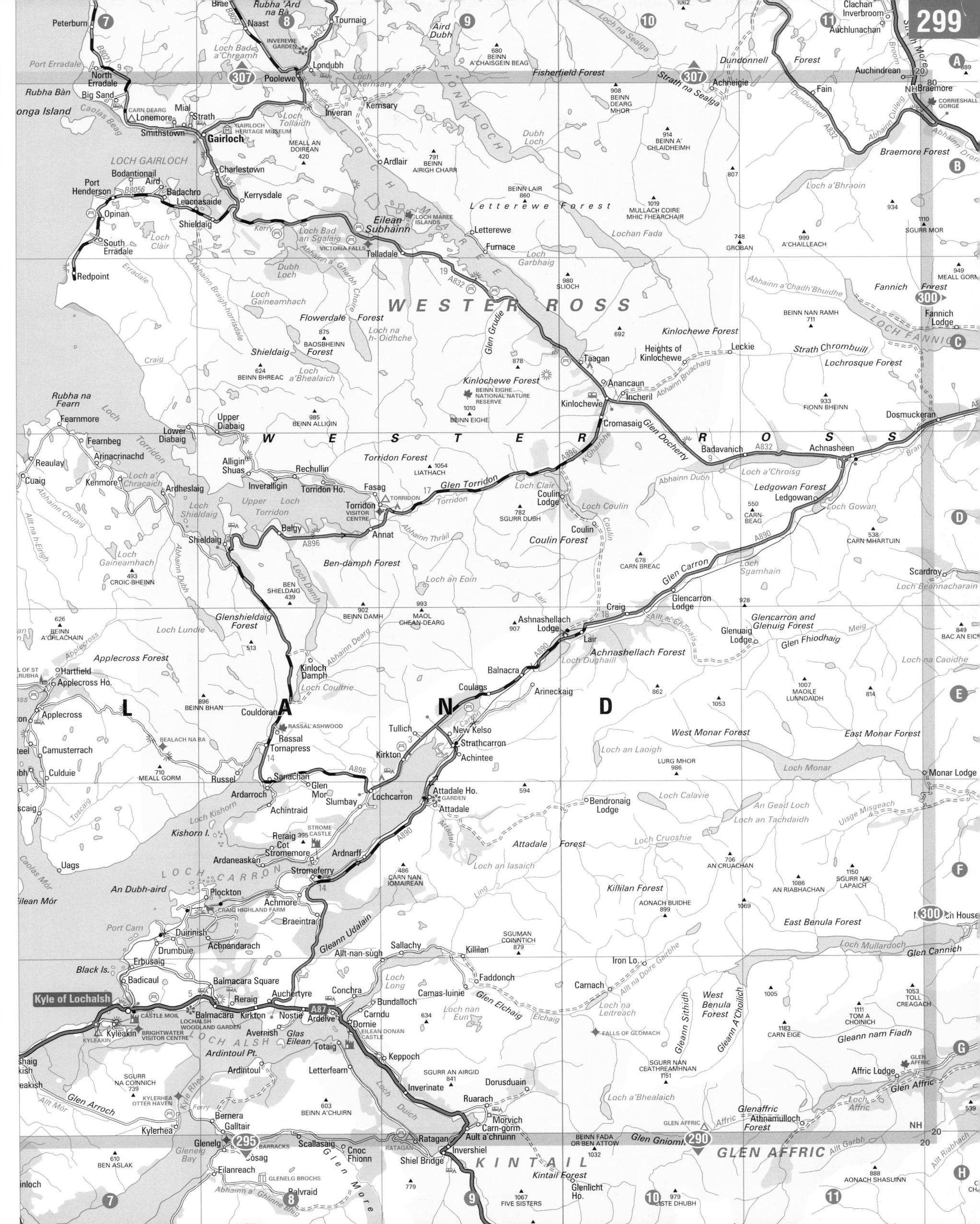

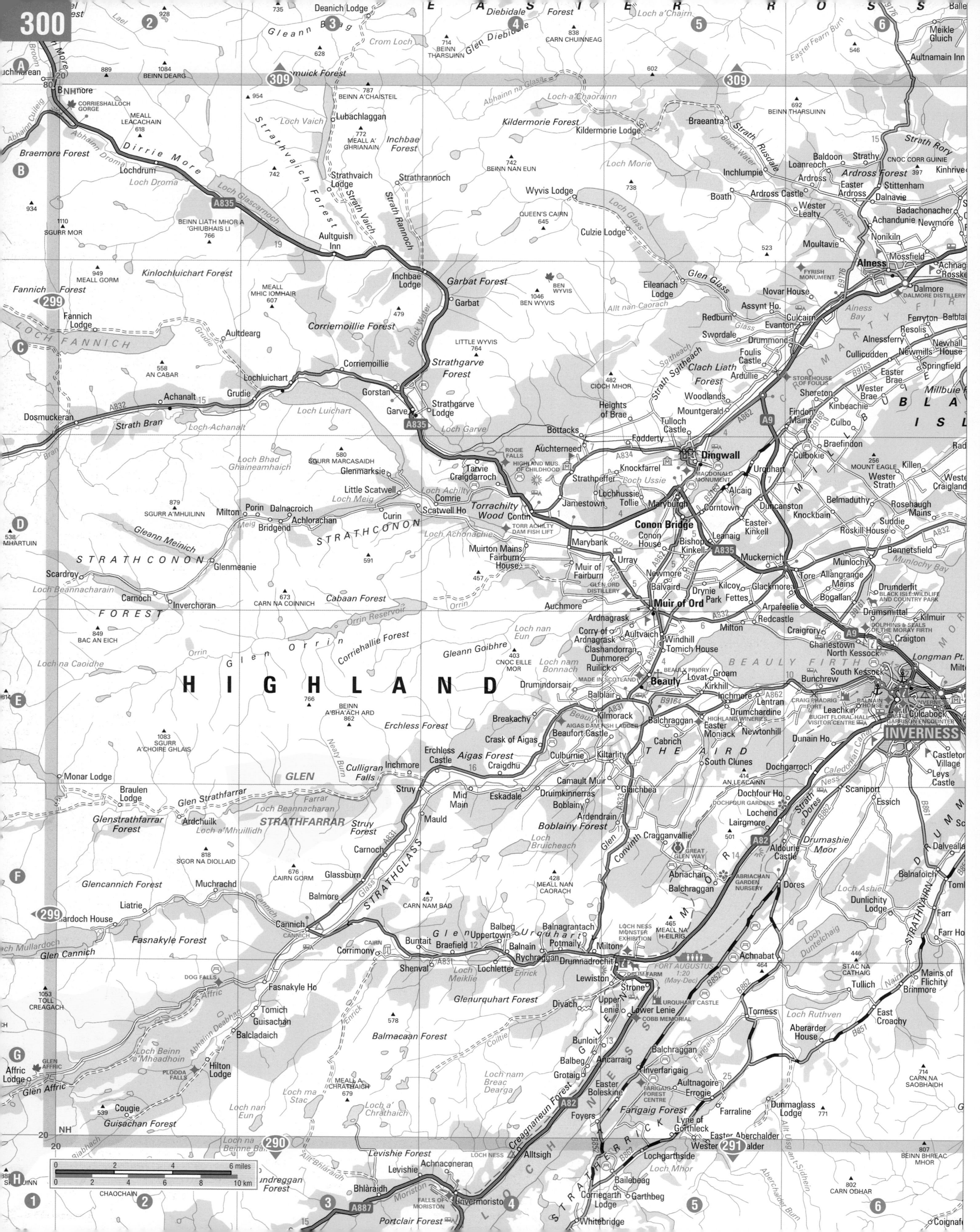

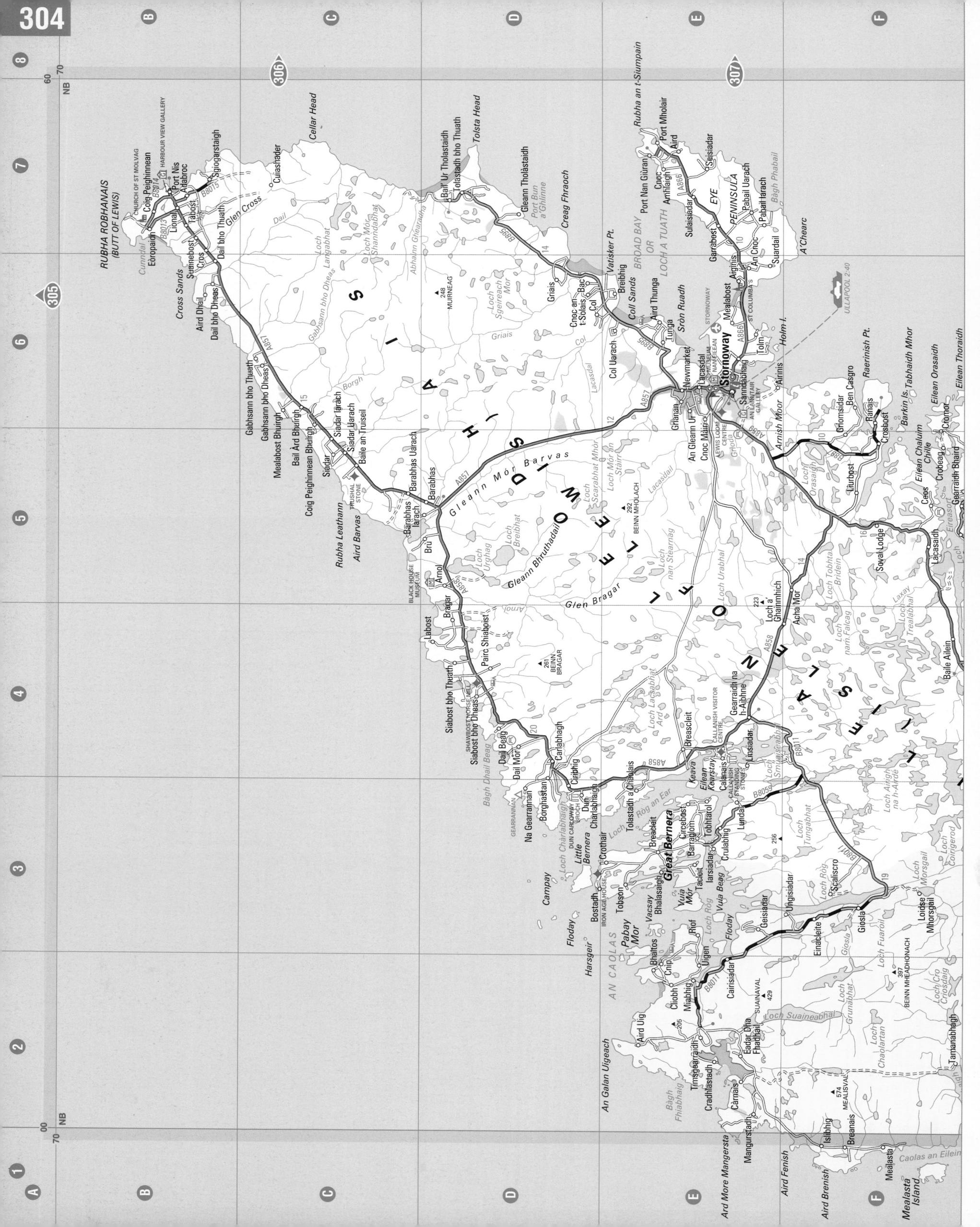

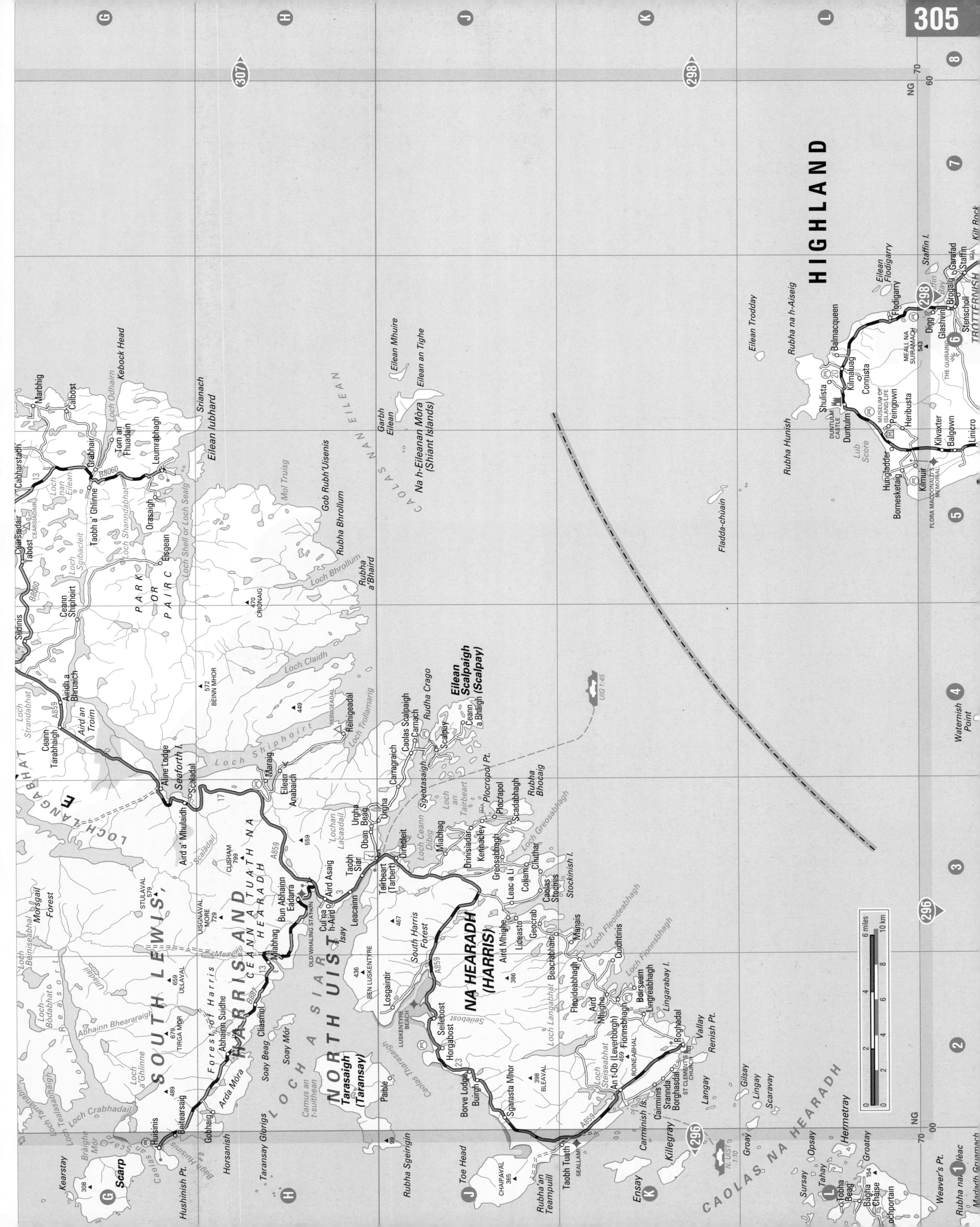

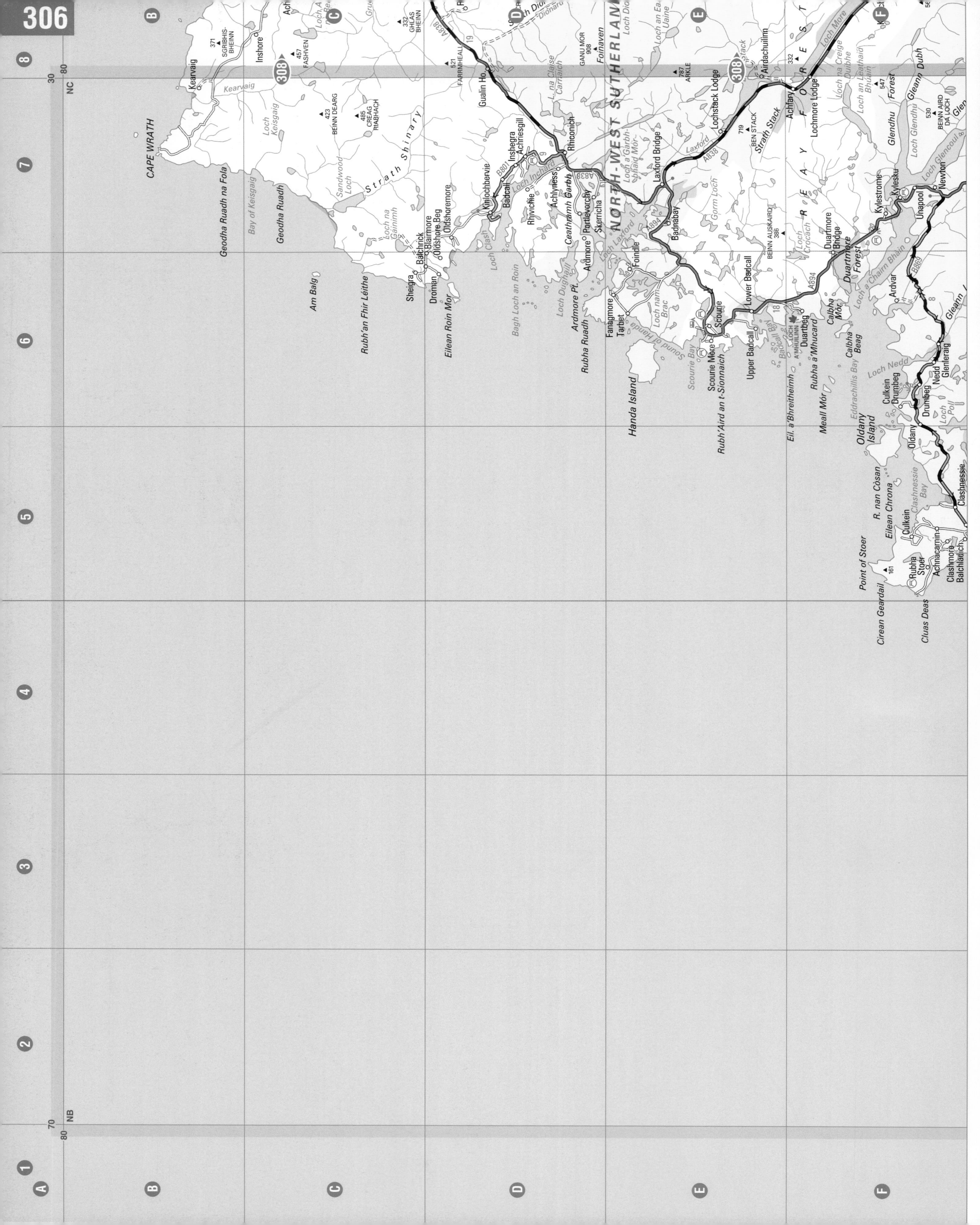

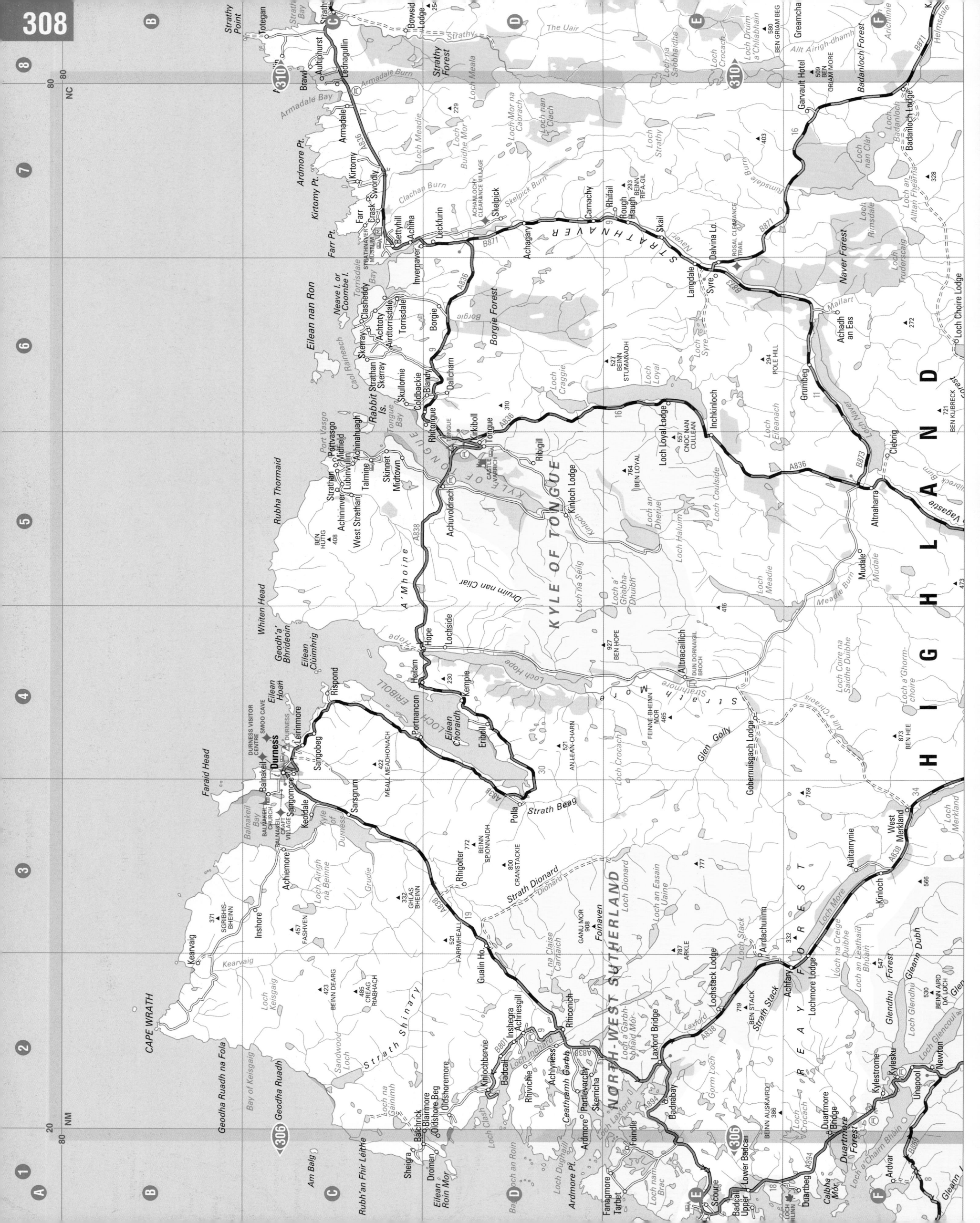

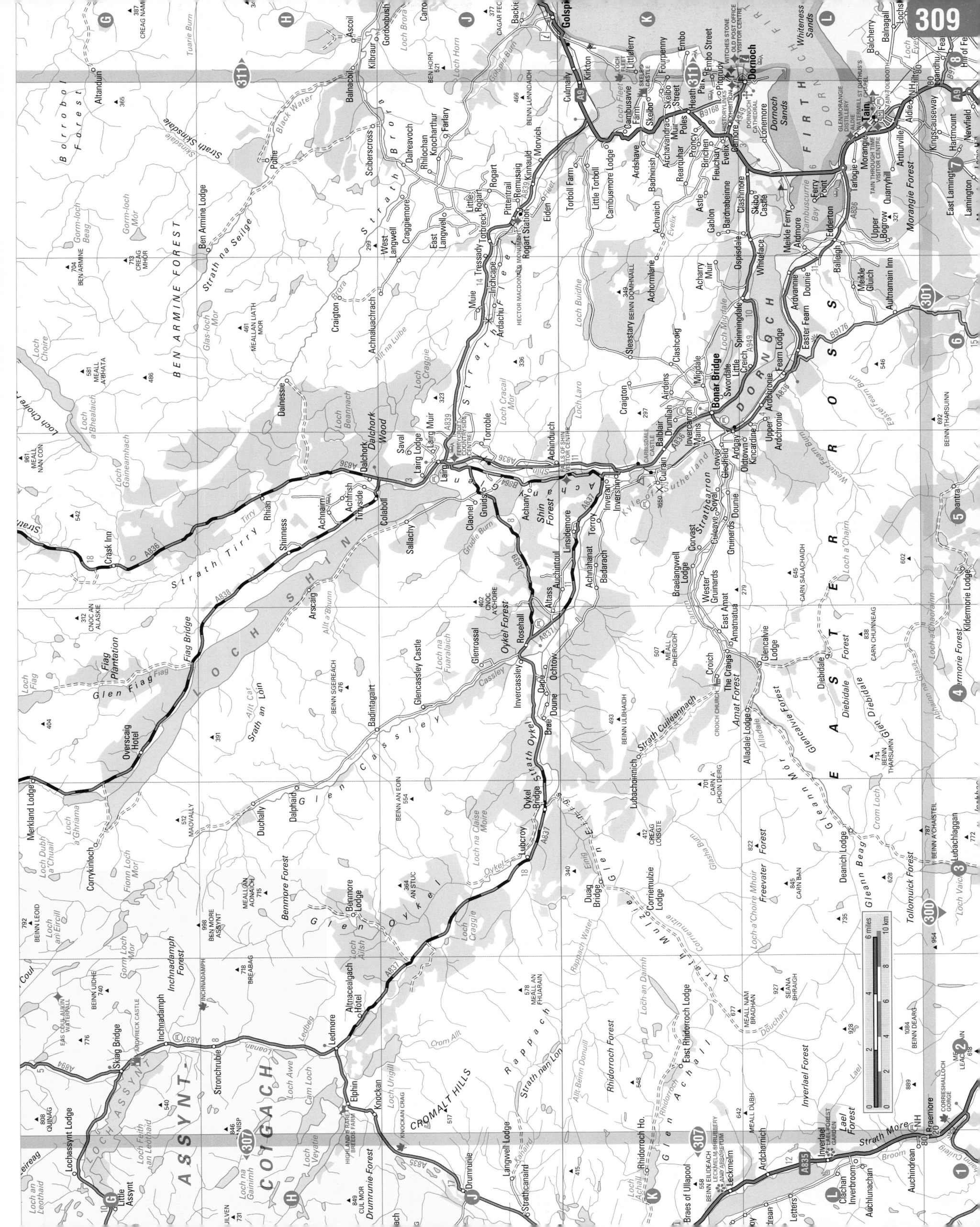

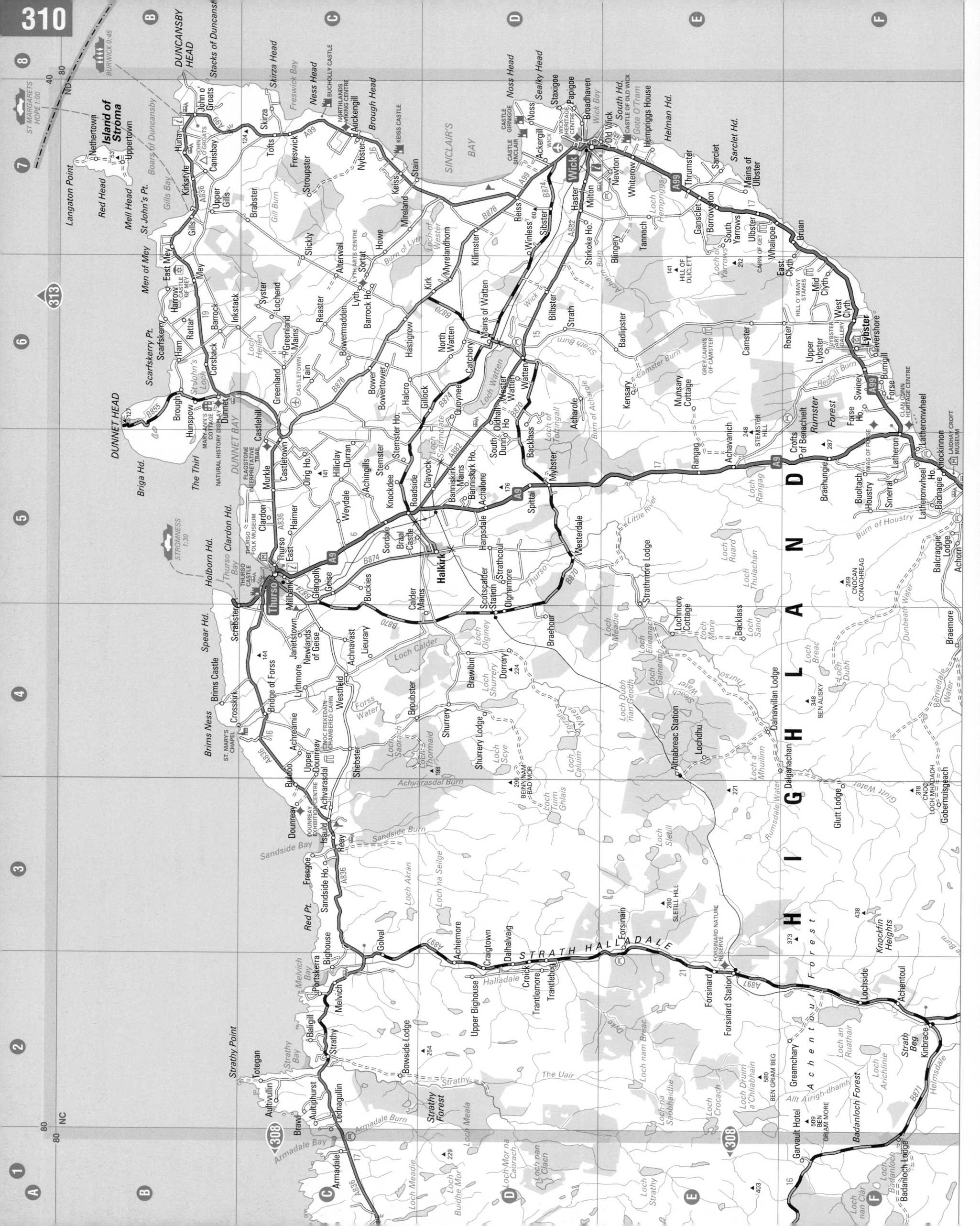

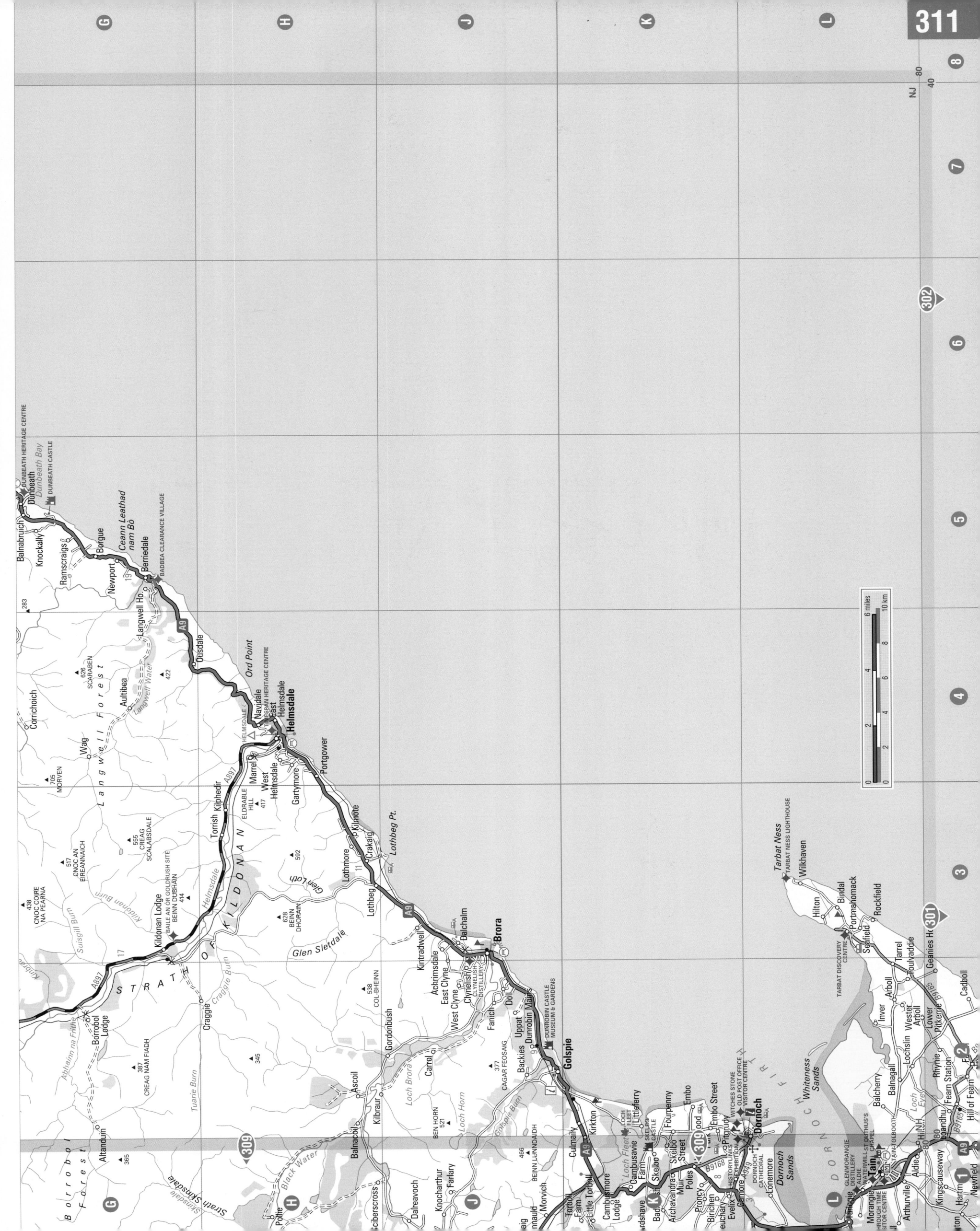

G H J K L

NJ 80 40

8
7
6
5
4
3

302

301

Dunbeath Heritage Centre
Dunbeath
Dunbeath Bay
Dunbeath Castle
Balnabruaich
Knockally
Ramscraigs
Borgue
Newport
Berriedale
Ceann Leathad nam Bò
Badbea Clearance Village
Langwell Ho.
Corrichoich
Langwell Forest
Wag
Aultibea
Ousdale
Ord Point
283
626 Scaraben
422
705 Morven
STRATH OF KILDONAN
Navidale
Helmsdale East
Helmsdale
West Helmsdale
Marrel
Portgower
Gartymore
Timespan Heritage Centre
Eldrable Hill 417
Torrish Kilphedir
Craig Scalabsdale
555 Craig Scalabsdale
517 Cnoc an Eireannaich
Baile an Or Goldrush Site
Beinn Dubhàin 414
438 Cnoc Coire na Pearna
Kildonan Lodge
Susgill Burn
Kildonan
592
628 Beinn Dhoraim
Lothmore
Kilmore
Crakaig
Lothbeg
Lothbeg Pt.
Glen Loth
Gartymore
17
Borrobol Lodge
387 Creag nam Fiadh
Abhainn na Frithe
Altanduin
365
Kinbrace
Dalreavoch
Kinbrace
Suath Skinsdale
Borrobol Forest
Glen Sletdale
Kintradwell
Achrimsdale
East Clyne
West Clyne
Clynelish Clynelish Distillery
Balchalm
Brora
Doll
Fanich
Dunrobin Mains
Dunrobin Castle Museum & Gardens
Golspie
Uppat
Backies
Craggie
Craggie Burn
Gordonbush
538 Col-Bheinn
Carrol
377 Cagar Feosaig
Ascoil
Kilbraur
Ben Horn 521
Loch Horn
Loch Brora
Balnacoil
Knocharthur
Farlary
Tuarie Burn
Black Water
466 Beinn Lunndaidh
Morvich
Polfe
Sciberscross
Dalchaird
Kinbrace
Culmaily
Kirkton
Loch Fleet
Loch
Skelbo Castle
Skelbo
Little Torboll
Torboll Farm
Cambusmore Lodge
Cambusavie
Skelbo Muir
Skelbo Street
Fourpenny
Embo
Embo Street
Littleferry
Poles
Proncy
Birichen
Evelix
Aichavandra
Witches Stone
Old Post Office
Dornoch Cathedral
Dornoch
Pitgrudy
Balvraid
Dornoch Sands
Whiteness Sands
DORNOCH FIRTH
Tarbat Ness
Tarbat Ness Lighthouse
Wilkhaven
Portmahomack
Tarbat Discovery Centre
Seafield
Rockfield
Hilton
Balintore
Shandwick
Nigg
Inver
Arboll
Lower Arboll
Wester Arboll
Loch Eye
Lochslin
Tarrel
Toulvaddie
Cadboll
Geanies Ho.
Hill of Fearn
Balnagall
Balcherry
Rhynie
Loch Evelix
Newton
Aldie
Meikle Ferry
Fearn Station
Kingscauseway
Edderton
Glenmorangie Distillery
Tain
Morangie
Tain Through Time Exhibition
Tarlogie
Arthurville
Cambuscurrie

6 miles
10 km

309

A9
A897

309
A9

301
302

THE ORKNEY ISLANDS

Scale 1:250,000

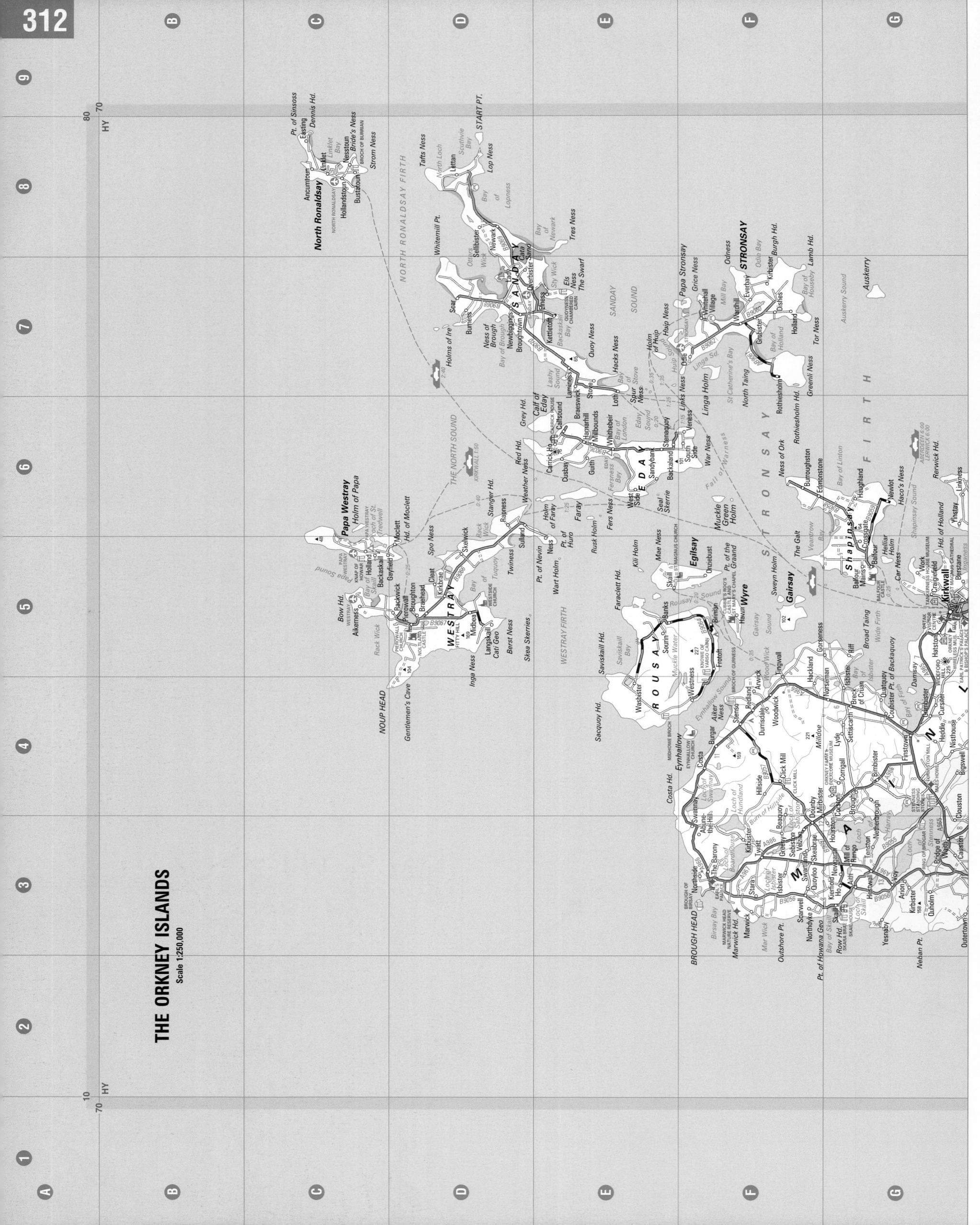

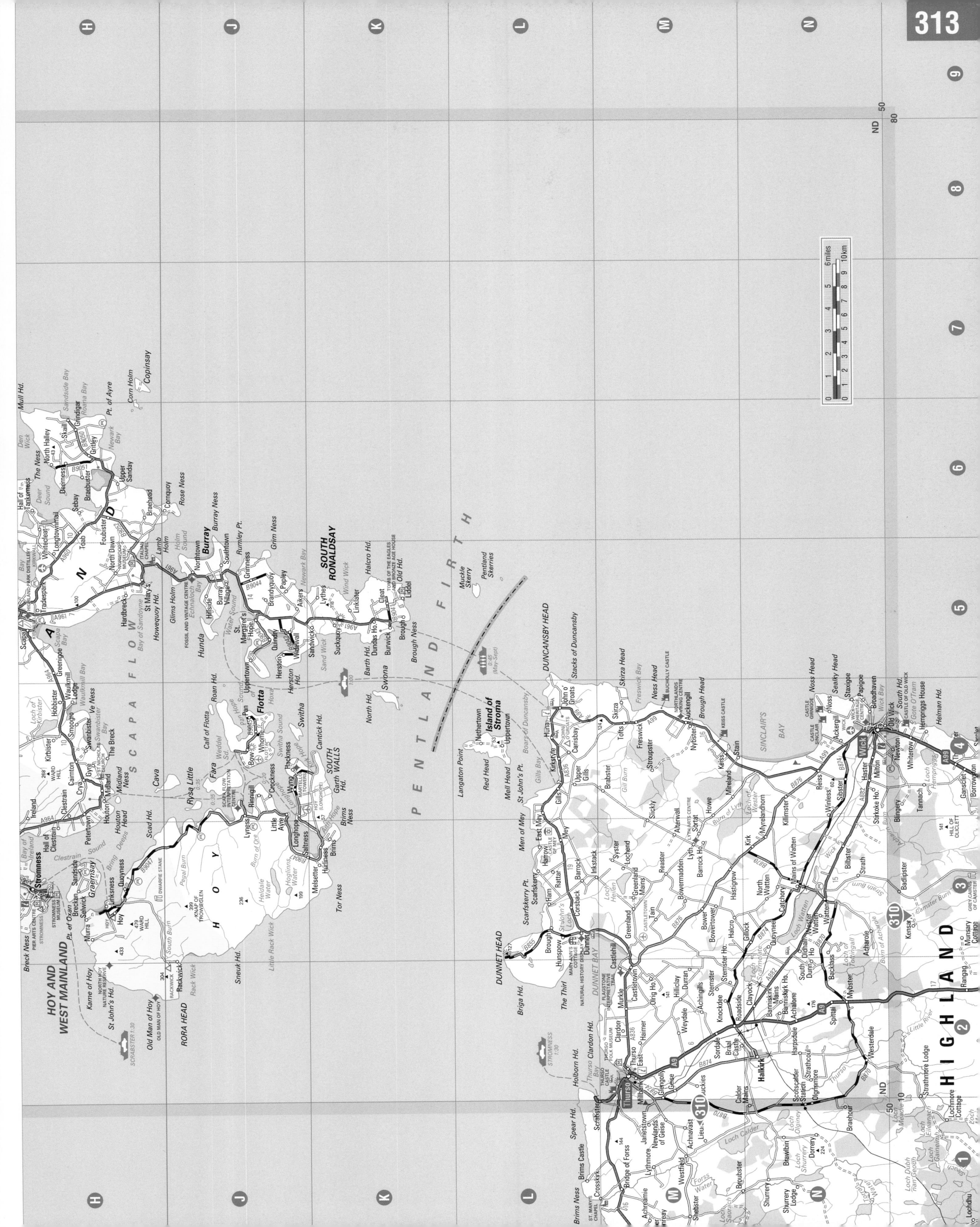

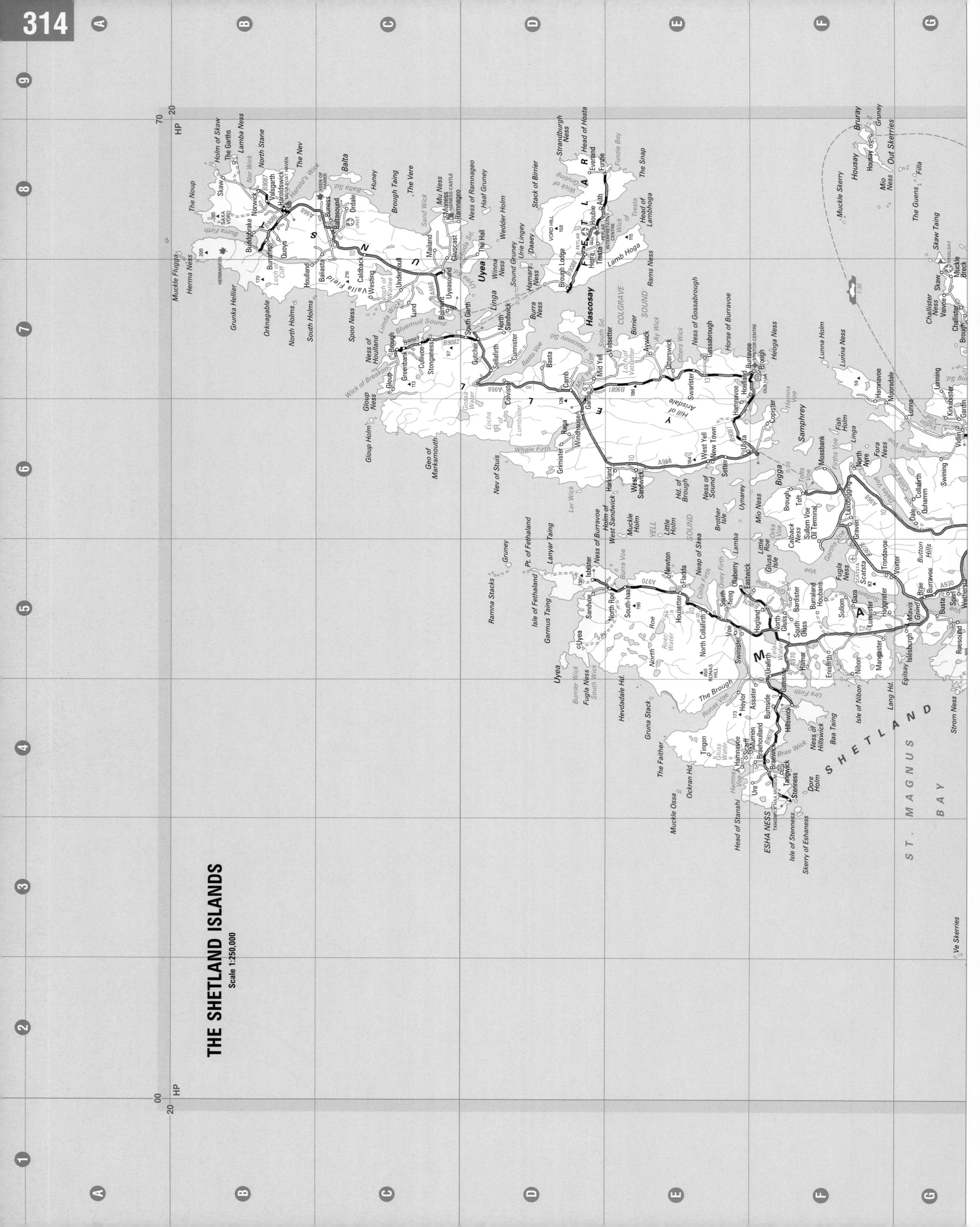

THE SHETLAND ISLANDS

Scale 1:250,000

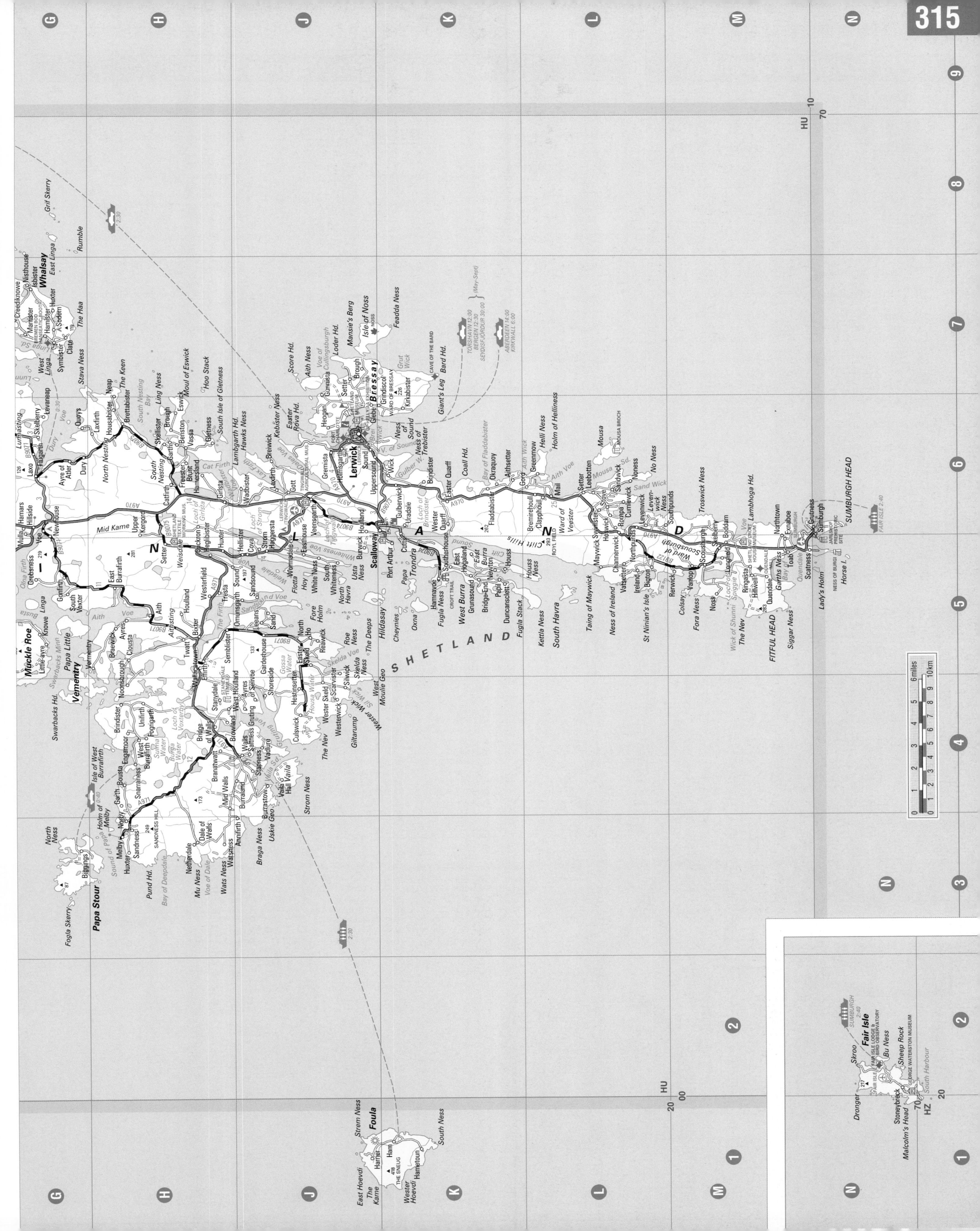

Key to Town Plan Symbols

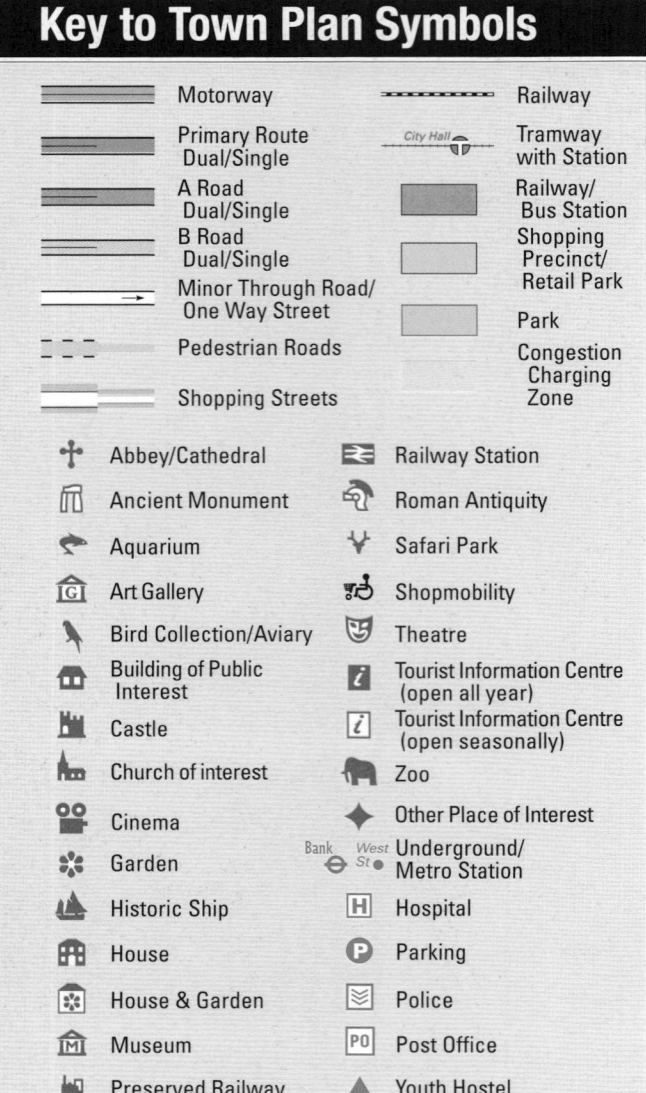

══════	Motorway	┄┄┄┄┄	Railway
═════	Primary Route Dual/Single	City Hall	Tramway with Station
════	A Road Dual/Single		Railway/ Bus Station
════	B Road Dual/Single		Shopping Precinct/ Retail Park
──→	Minor Through Road/ One Way Street		Park
┄┄┄	Pedestrian Roads		Congestion Charging Zone
────	Shopping Streets		

- ✝ Abbey/Cathedral
- 🏛 Ancient Monument
- Aquarium
- Art Gallery
- Bird Collection/Aviary
- Building of Public Interest
- Castle
- Church of interest
- Cinema
- Garden
- Historic Ship
- House
- House & Garden
- Museum
- Preserved Railway
- Railway Station
- Roman Antiquity
- Safari Park
- Shopmobility
- Theatre
- i Tourist Information Centre (open all year)
- i Tourist Information Centre (open seasonally)
- Zoo
- ◆ Other Place of Interest
- Bank West St ● Underground/ Metro Station
- H Hospital
- P Parking
- Police
- PO Post Office
- ▲ Youth Hostel

Key to Approach Mapping Symbols

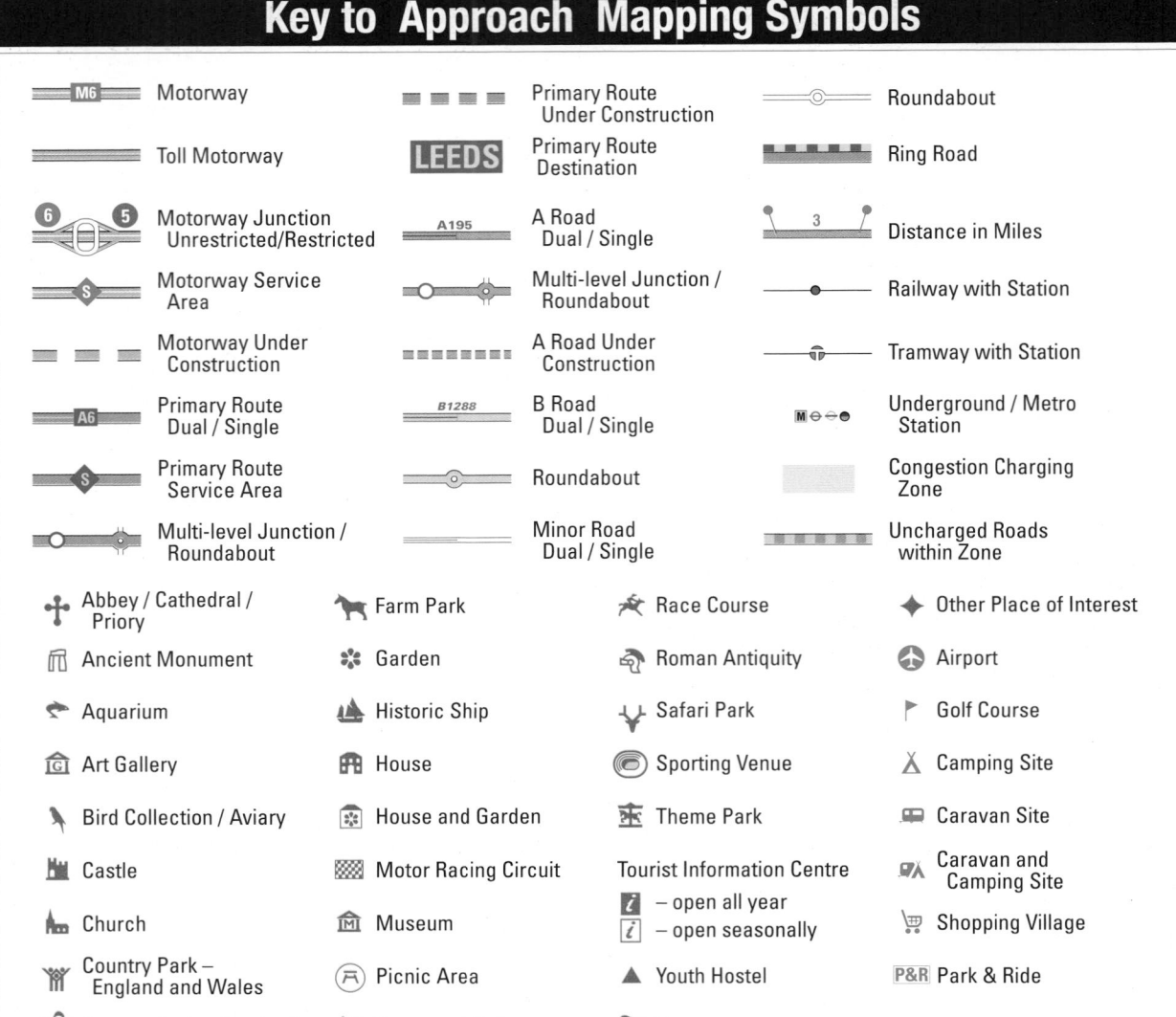

- M6 Motorway
- Toll Motorway
- 6 5 Motorway Junction Unrestricted/Restricted
- Motorway Service Area
- Motorway Under Construction
- A6 Primary Route Dual / Single
- S Primary Route Service Area
- Multi-level Junction / Roundabout
- ▭▭▭▭ Primary Route Under Construction
- LEEDS Primary Route Destination
- A195 A Road Dual / Single
- Multi-level Junction / Roundabout
- A Road Under Construction
- B1288 B Road Dual / Single
- Roundabout
- Minor Road Dual / Single
- ⊙ Roundabout
- Ring Road
- 3 Distance in Miles
- Railway with Station
- Tramway with Station
- M Underground / Metro Station
- Congestion Charging Zone
- Uncharged Roads within Zone

- ✝ Abbey / Cathedral / Priory
- 🏛 Ancient Monument
- Aquarium
- Art Gallery
- Bird Collection / Aviary
- Castle
- Church
- Country Park – England and Wales
- Country Park – Scotland
- Farm Park
- Garden
- Historic Ship
- House
- House and Garden
- Motor Racing Circuit
- Museum
- Picnic Area
- Preserved Railway
- Race Course
- Roman Antiquity
- Safari Park
- Sporting Venue
- Theme Park
- Tourist Information Centre
  - i – open all year
  - i – open seasonally
- Youth Hostel
- Zoo
- ◆ Other Place of Interest
- Airport
- ⚐ Golf Course
- Camping Site
- Caravan Site
- Caravan and Camping Site
- Shopping Village
- P&R Park & Ride

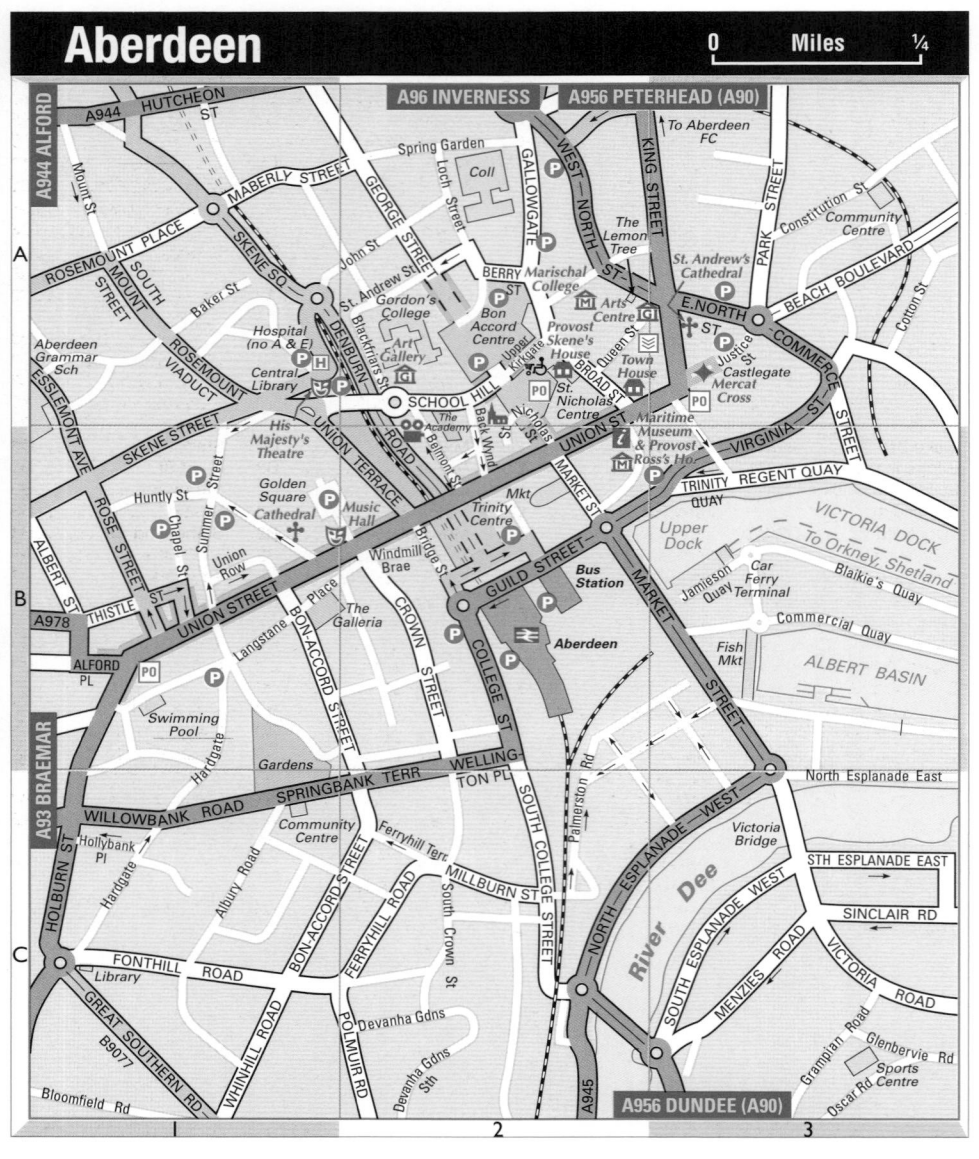

Aberdeen

0 — Miles — ¼

Aberystwyth

0 Miles ¼

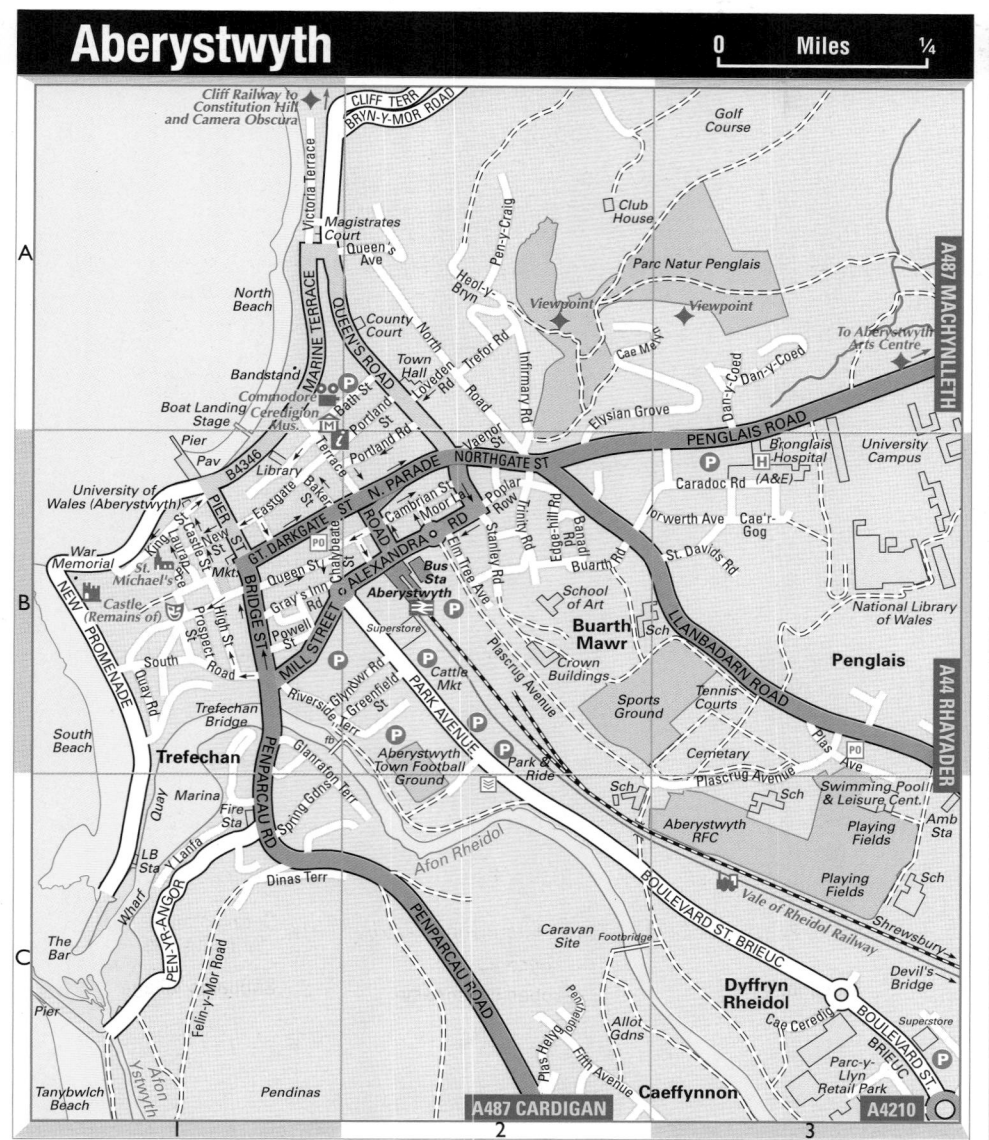

Barrow-in-Furness

0 Miles ¼

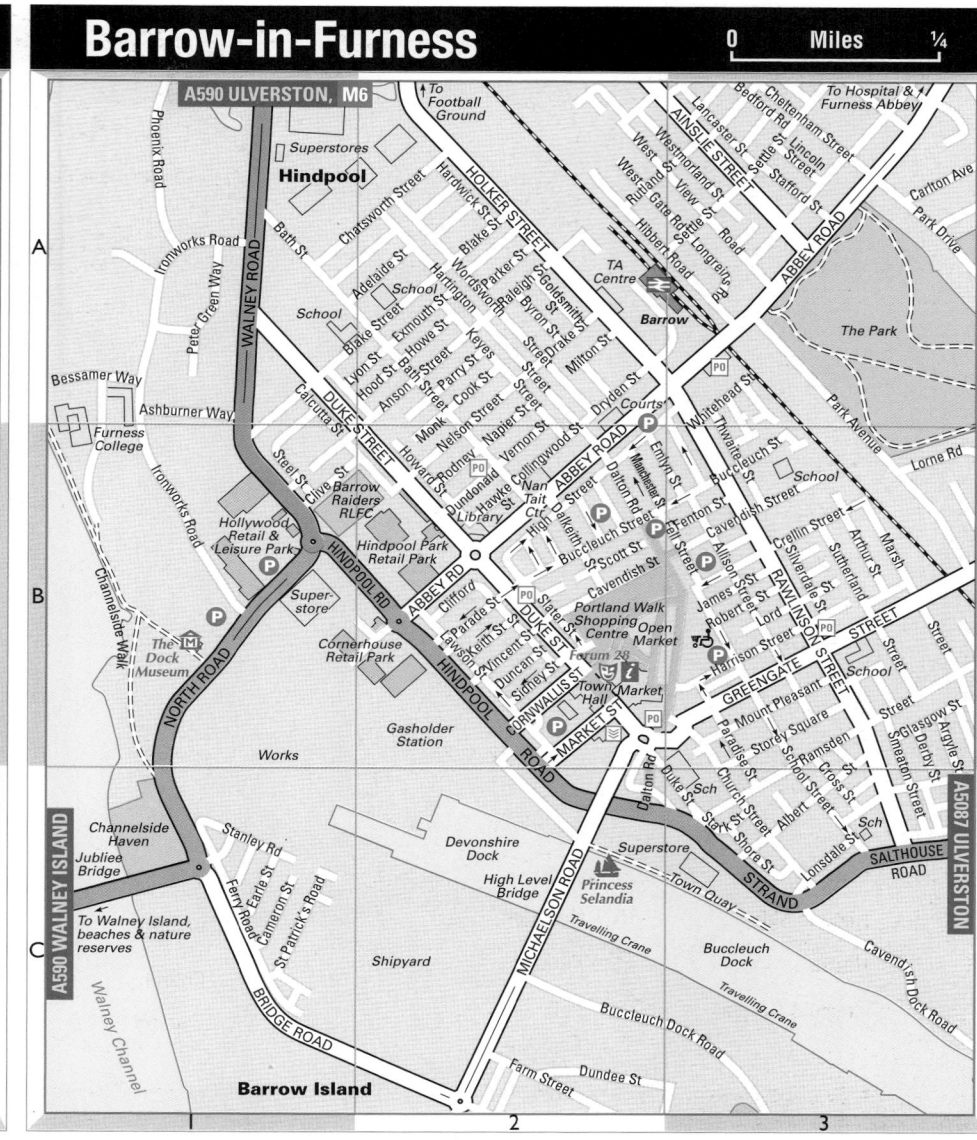

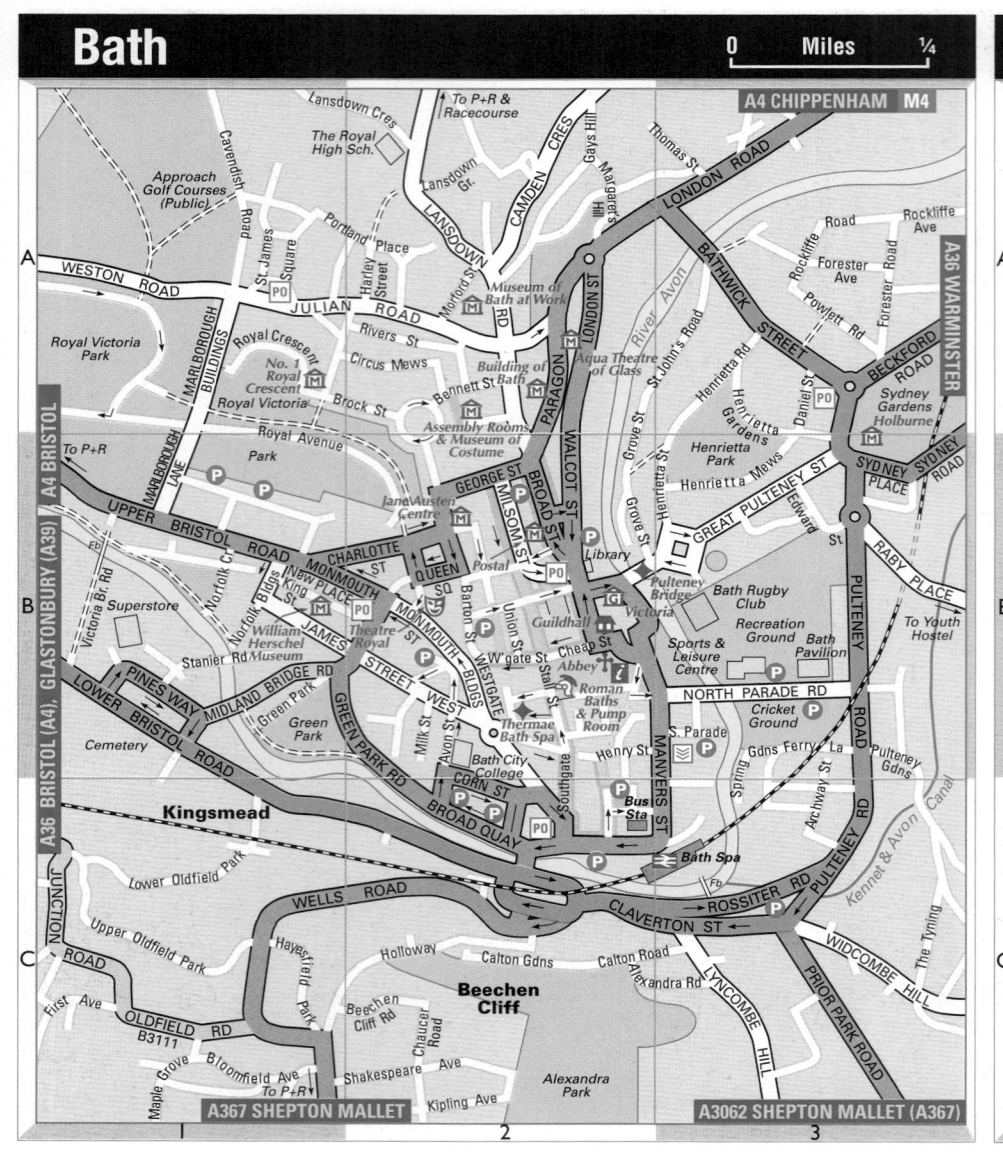

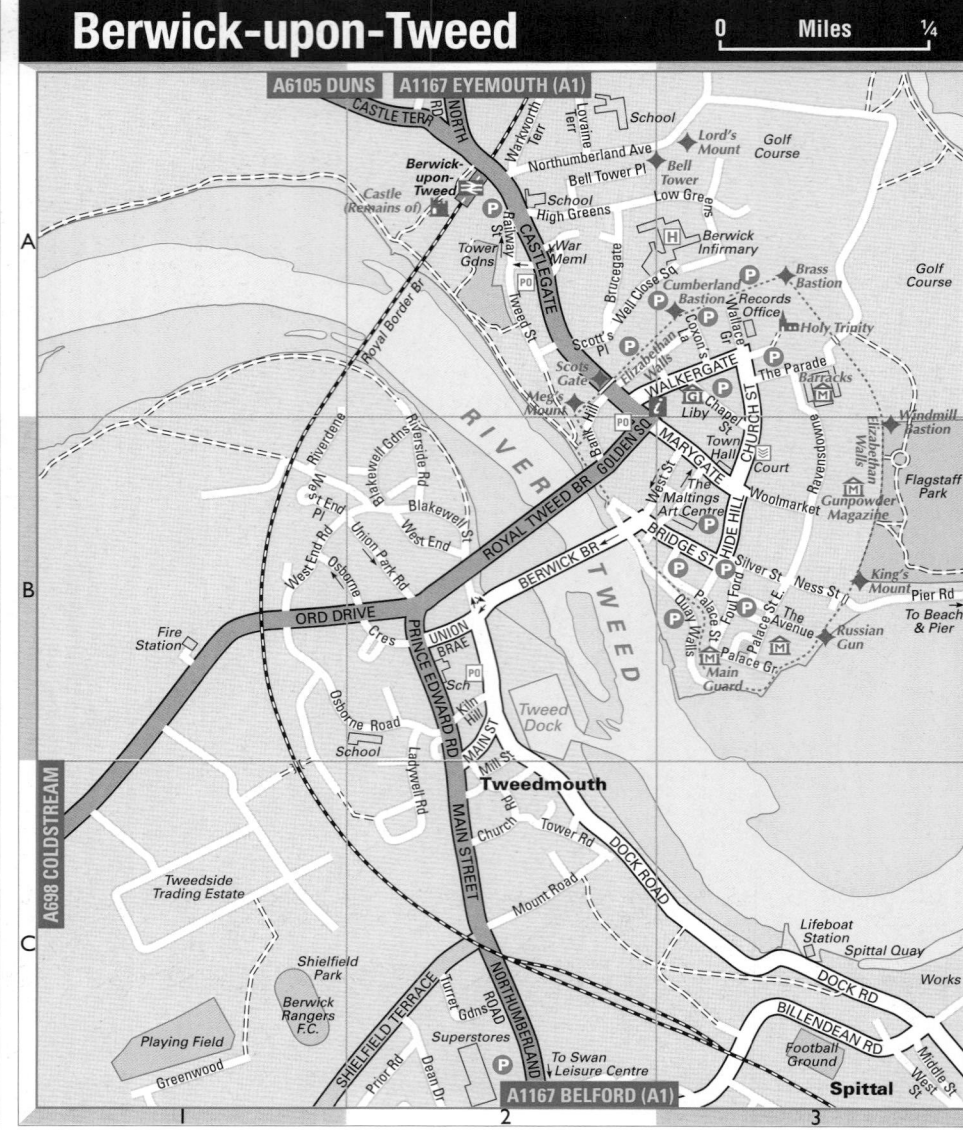

Bath

Alexandra Park......C2	
Alexandra Rd.......C2	
Approach Golf	
Courses (Public)....A1	
Aqua Theatre	
of Glass 🏛.......A2	
Archway St.......C3	
Assembly Rooms	
& Museum of	
Costume 🏛.......A2	
Avon St.........B2	
Barton St........B2	
Bath Abbey †......B2	
Bath City College....B2	
Bath Pavilion......B3	
Bath Rugby Club....B3	
Bath Spa Station 🚉.C3	
Bathwick St.......A3	
Beechen Cliff Rd....C2	
Bennett St........A2	
Bloomfield Ave.....C1	
Broad Quay.......C2	
Broad St.........B2	
Brock St.........A1	
Building of Bath	
Museum 🏛......A2	
Bus Station.......C2	
Calton Gdns......C2	
Calton Rd........C2	
Camden Cr.......A2	
Cavendish Rd......A1	
Cemetery........B1	
Charlotte St.......B2	
Chaucer Rd.......C2	
Cheap St.........B2	
Circus Mews......A2	
Claverton St......C2	

Corn St.........C2	
Cricket Ground.....B3	
Daniel St........A3	
Edward St........A3	
Ferry La.........B3	
First Ave........C1	
Forester Ave......A3	
Forester Rd.......A3	
Gays Hill........A2	
George St........B3	
Great Pulteney St...B3	
Green Park.......B1	
Green Park Rd.....B2	
Grove St.........B2	
Guildhall 🏛......B2	
Harley St........A2	
Hayesfield Park....C1	
Henrietta Gdns.....A3	
Henrietta Mews....B3	
Henrietta Park.....B3	
Henrietta Rd......A3	
Henrietta St......B3	
Henry St.........B2	
Holburne Museum 🏛.B3	
Holloway........C2	
Information Ctr 🅸....B2	
James St West...B1/B2	
Jane Austen	
Centre 🏛.......B2	
Julian Rd........A1	
Junction Rd......C1	
Kipling Ave.......C2	
Lansdown Cr......A1	
Lansdown Gr......A2	
Lansdown Rd......A2	
Library..........B2	
London Rd.......A3	
London St........A2	
Lower Bristol Rd....B1	

Lower Oldfield Park..C1	
Lyncombe Hill.....C3	
Manvers St.......B3	
Maple Gr........C1	
Margaret's Hill.....A2	
Marlborough	
Buildings........A1	
Marlborough La....B1	
Midland Bridge Rd...B1	
Milk St..........B2	
Milsom St........B2	
Monmouth St......B2	
Morford St........A2	
Museum of Bath	
at Work 🏛.......A2	
New King St......B1	
No. 1 Royal	
Crescent 🏛......A1	
Norfolk Bldgs......A1	
Norfolk Cr.......B1	
North Parade Rd....B3	
Oldfield Rd.......C1	
Paragon.........A2	
Pines Way........A1	
Police Station 🅿....B3	
Portland Pl.......A2	
Post Office 🏤	
......A1/A3/B2/C2	
Postal Museum 🏛...B2	
Powlett Rd.......A3	
Prior Park Rd......C3	
Pulteney Bridge ◆..B2	
Pulteney Gdns.....B3	
Pulteney Rd.......B3	
Queen Sq........B2	
Raby Pl.........B3	
Recreation Ground...B3	
Rivers St........A2	
Rockliffe Ave......A3	

Rockliffe Rd.......A3	
Roman Baths &	
Pump Room ♨...B2	
Rossiter Rd.......C3	
Royal Ave........A1	
Royal Cr.........A1	
Royal High	
School, The......A1	
Royal Victoria Park..A1	
St James Sq......A1	
St John's Rd......B2	
Shakespeare Ave...C2	
Southgate........C2	
South Pde.......B3	
Sports & Leisure	
Centre.........B3	
Spring Gdns......B2	
Stall St..........B2	
Stanier Rd.......A1	
Sydney Gdns......B3	
Sydney Pl........B3	
Theatre Royal 🎭...B2	
Thermae	
Bath Spa ◆......B2	
The Tyning.......C3	
Thomas St.......A3	
Union St.........B2	
Upper Bristol Rd....B1	
Upper Oldfield Park..C1	
Victoria Art	
Gallery 🏛.......B2	
Victoria Bridge Rd..B1	
Walcot St........B2	
Wells Rd.........C1	
Westgate St......B2	
Weston Rd.......A1	
Widcombe Hill.....C3	
William Herschel	
Museum 🏛......B1	

Berwick-upon-Tweed

Bank Hill........B2	
Barracks 🏛......A3	
Bell Tower ◆......A3	
Bell Tower Pl......A2	
Berwick Br.......B2	
Berwick Infirmary 🏥.A3	
Berwick	
Rangers F.C.....C1	
Berwick-upon-	
Tweed 🚉.......A2	
Billendean Rd......C3	
Blakewell Gdns....B2	
Blakewell St......B2	
Brass Bastion ◆...A3	
Bridge St........B3	
Brucegate St......A2	
Castle	
(Remains of) 🏛...A2	
Castle Terr.......A2	
Castlegate........A2	
Chapel St........A3	
Church Rd........C2	
Church St........B3	
Court...........B3	
Coxon's La.......A3	
Cumberland	
Bastion ◆.......A3	

Dean Dr.........C2	
Dock Rd......C2/C3	
Elizabethan Walls..A2/B3	
Fire Station.......B1	
Flagstaff Park.....B3	
Football Ground....C3	
Foul Ford........B3	
Gallery..........A2	
Golden Sq.......B2	
Golf Course.......A3	
Greenwood.......C1	
Gunpowder	
Magazine 🏛.....B3	
Hide Hill.........B3	
High Greens......A2	
Holy Trinity 🏛.....A3	
Information Ctr 🅸....B2	
Kiln Hill.........B2	
King's Mount ◆....B3	
Ladywell Rd......B2	
Library..........A3	
Lifeboat Station....C3	
Lord's Mount ◆....A3	
Lovaine Terr......A2	
Low Greens......A3	
Main Guard 🏛....B3	
Main St.......B2/C2	
Maltings Art	
Centre, The......B3	
Marygate........B3	
Meg's Mount ◆....A2	

Middle St........C3	
Mill St..........C2	
Mount Rd........C2	
Museum 🏛......B3	
Ness St.........B3	
North Rd........C2	
Northumberland Ave.A2	
Northumberland Rd..C2	
Ord Dr..........B1	
Osborne Cr.......B2	
Osborne Rd......B1	
Palace Gr........B3	
Palace St........B3	
Palace St East.....B3	
Pier Rd.........B3	
Playing Field......C1	
Police Station 🅿....B3	
Post Office 🏤.A2/B2/B2	
Prince Edward Rd..B2	
Prior Rd.........C2	
Quay Walls.......B3	
Railway St.......A2	
Ravensdowne.....B3	
Records Office.....A3	
Riverdene........B1	
Riverside Rd......B2	
Royal Border Br....A2	
Royal Tweed Br....B2	
Russian Gun ◆....B3	
Scots Gate ◆.....A2	
Scott's Pl........A2	

Shielfield Park.....C1	
Shielfield Terr.....C2	
Silver St........B3	
Spittal Quay......C3	
Superstores......C2	
The Avenue......B3	
The Parade.......A3	
Tower Gdns......A2	
Tower Rd........C2	
Town Hall.......B3	
Turret Gdns......C2	
Tweed Dock......B2	
Tweed St........A2	
Tweedside Trading	
Estate.........C1	
Union Brae.......B2	
Union Park Rd.....B2	
Walkergate.......A3	
Wallace Gr.......A3	
War Meml.......A2	
Warkworth Terr....A2	
Well Close Sq.....A2	
West End........B2	
West End Pl......B1	
West End Rd......B1	
West St.........B3	
West St.........C3	
Windmill Bastion ◆..B3	
Woolmarket......B3	
Works..........C3	

Birmingham

Abbey St.........A2	
Aberdeen St......A1	
Acorn Gr........B2	
Adams St........A5	
Adderley St......C5	
Albert St......B4/B5	
Albion St........B2	
Alcester St.......C5	
Aldgate Gr.......C5	
Alexandra Theatre 🎭.C3	
All Saint's St......A2	
All Saints Rd.....A2	

Allcock St.......C5	
Allesley St.......A4	
Allison St........C4	
Alma Cr.........B6	
Alston Rd........C1	
Arcadian Centre...C4	
Arthur St.........C6	
Assay Office 🏛....B3	
Aston Expressway...A5	
Aston Science Park..A5	
Aston St.........B4	
Avenue Rd.......A5	
Bacchus Rd......A1	

Bagot St.........B4	
Banbury St.......B5	
Barford Rd.......B1	
Barford St.......C4	
Barn St.........C5	
Barnwell Rd......C6	
Barr St..........A3	
Barrack St.......B5	
Barrack St.......B5	
Bartholomew St....C4	
Barwick St.......B4	
Bath Row........C3	
Beaufort Rd......C1	
Belmont Row.....B5	
Benson Rd.......A1	

Berkley St.......C3	
Bexhill Gr.......C3	
Birchall St.......C4	
Birmingham City F.C.	
(St Andrew's)....C6	
Birmingham City	
Hospital (A&E) 🏥..A1	
Bishopsgate St....C3	
Blews St.........A4	
Bloomsbury St....A6	
Blucher St.......C3	
Bordesley St......C4	
Bowyer St.......C5	
Bradburne Way...A5	

Bradford St.......C5	
Branston St......A3	
Brearley St......A4	
Brewery St.......A4	
Bridge St........A3	
Bridge St........C3	
Bridge St West....B3	
Brindley Dr.......B3	
Broad St........C2	
Broad St UGC 🎬...C2	
Broadway Plaza ◆..C2	
Bromley St.......C5	
Bromsgrove St....C4	
Brookfield Rd.....A2	

Browning St......C2	
Bryant St........A1	
Buckingham St....A3	
Bullring..........C4	
Bull St..........B4	
Cambridge St.....B3	
Camden Dr......B3	
Camden St.......B2	
Cannon St.......B4	
Cardigan St......B5	
Carlisle St.......A1	
Carlyle Rd.......B1	
Caroline St.......B3	
Carver St........B2	

Cato St.........A6	
Cato St North.....A6	
Cattell Rd........C6	
Cattells Gr.......A6	
Cawdor Cr.......C1	
Cecil St.........B4	
Cemetery.....A2/B2	
Cemetery La......A2	
Centre Link	
Industrial Estate...A6	
Charlotte St......B3	
Cheapside.......C4	
Chester St.......A5	
Children's Hospital 🏥.B4	

Church St........B4	
Claremont Rd.....A2	
Clarendon Rd.....C1	
Clark St.........C1	
Clement St.......B3	
Clissold St.......B2	
Cliveland St......B4	
Coach Station....C5	
College St.......B2	
Colmore Circus....B4	
Colmore Row.....B4	
Commercial St....C3	
Constitution Hill...B3	
Convention Centre..C3	

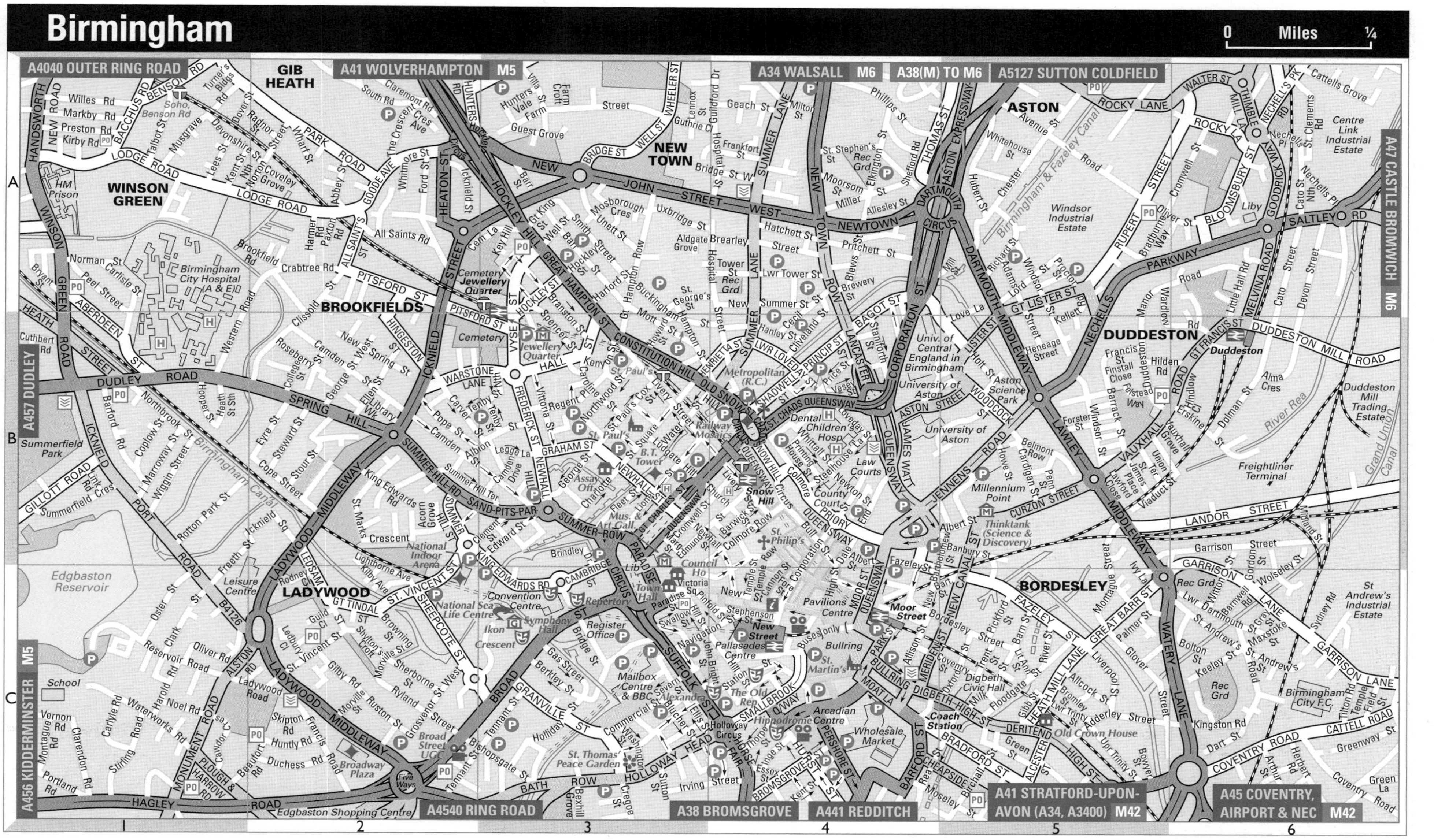

Birmingham continued

Cope St B2
Coplow St B1
Corporation St B4
Council House B3
County Court B4
Coveley Gr A2
Coventry Rd C6
Coventry St C5
Cox St B3
Crabtree Rd A2
Cregoe St C3
Crescent Ave A2
Crescent Theatre C3
Cromwell St A6
Cromwell St B3
Curzon St B5
Cuthbert Rd B1
Dale End B4
Dart St C6
Dartmouth Circus A4
Dartmouth Middleway A5
Dental Hospital B4
Deritend C5
Devon St A6
Devonshire St A1
Digbeth Civic Hall C5
Digbeth High St C4
Dolman St B6
Dover St A1
Duchess Rd C2
Duddeston B6
Duddeston Manor Rd B5
Duddeston Mill Rd B6
Duddeston Mill Trading Estate B6
Dudley Rd B1
Edgbaston Shopping Centre C2
Edmund St B3
Edward St B3
Elkington St A4
Ellen St B2
Ellis St C3
Erskine St B6
Essex St C4
Eyre St B2
Farm Croft A3
Farm St A3
Fazeley St B4
Felstead Way B5
Finstall Cl B5
Five Ways C2
Fleet St B3
Floodgate St C5
Ford St A2
Fore St C4
Forster St B5
Francis Rd C2
Francis St B5
Frankfort St A4
Frederick St B3
Freeth St C1
Freightliner Terminal B6
Garrison La C6
Garrison St B6
Gas St C3
Geach St A4
George St B3
George St West B2
Gibb St C5
Gilby Rd C2
Gillott Rd B1
Glover St C5
Goode Ave A2
Goodrick Way A6
Gordon St B6
Graham St B3
Granville St C3
Gray St C6
Great Barr St C5
Great Charles St B3
Great Francis St B6
Great Hampton Row A3
Great Hampton St A3
Great King St A3
Great Lister St A5
Great Tindal St C2
Green La C6
Green St C5
Greenway St C6
Grosvenor St West C2
Guest Gr A3
Guild Cl C2
Guildford Dr A4
Guthrie Cl A3
Hagley Rd C1
Hall St B3
Hampton St A3
Handsworth New Rd A1
Hanley St B4
Harford St A3
Harmer Rd A2
Harold Rd C1
Hatchett St A4
Heath Mill La C5
Heath St B1
Heath St South B1
Heaton St A2
Heneage St B5
Henrietta St B4
Herbert Rd C6
High St C4
High St C5
Hilden Rd B5
Hill St C3
Hindlow Cl B6
Hingeston St B2
Hippodrome Theatre C4
HM Prison A1
Hockley Circus A2
Hockley Hill A3
Hockley St A3
Holliday St C3
Holloway Circus C4
Holloway Head C3
Holt St B5
Hooper St B1
Horse Fair C4
Hospital St A4
Howard St B3
Howe St B5
Hubert St A5
Hunters Rd A2
Hunters Vale A3
Huntly Rd C2
Hurst St C4
Icknield Port Rd B1
Icknield Sq B2
Icknield St A2
Ikon Gallery C3
Information Ctr C4
Inge St C4
Irving St C3
Ivy La C5
James Watt Queensway B4
Jennens Rd B5
Jewellery Quarter A3
Jewellery Quarter Museum B3
John Bright St C4
Keeley St C6
Kellett Rd B5
Kent St C4
Kent St North A1
Kenyon St B3
Key Hill A3
Kilby Ave C2
King Edwards Rd B2
King Edwards Rd C3
Kingston Rd C6
Kirby Rd A1
Ladywood Middleway C2
Ladywood Rd C1
Lancaster St B4
Landor St B6
Law Courts B4
Lawford Cl B5
Lawley Middleway B5
Ledbury Cl C2
Ledsam St B2
Lees St A1
Legge La B3
Lennox St A3
Library A6/C3
Library Walk B2
Lighthorne Ave B2
Link Rd B1
Lionel St B3
Lister St B5
Little Ann St C5
Little Hall Rd A6
Liverpool St C5
Livery St B3
Lodge Rd A1
Lord St A5
Love La A5
Loveday St B4
Lower Dartmouth St C6
Lower Loveday St B4
Lower Tower St A4
Lower Trinty St C5
Ludgate Hill B3
Mailbox Centre & BBC C3
Margaret St B3
Markby Rd A1
Marroway St B1
Maxstoke St C6
Melvina Rd A6
Meriden St C4
Metropolitan (R.C.) B4
Midland St B6
Milk St C5
Mill St A5
Millennium Point B5
Miller St A4
Milton St A4
Moat La C4
Montague Rd C1
Montague St C5
Monument Rd C1
Moor Street C4
Moor St Queensway C4
Moorsom St A4
Morville St C2
Mosborough Cr A3
Moseley St C4
Mott St B3
Museum & Art Gallery B3
Musgrave Rd A1
National Indoor Arena B2
National Sea Life Centre C3
Navigation St C3
Nechell's Park Rd A6
Nechells Parkway A5
Nechells Pl A6
New Bartholomew St C4
New Canal St C5
New John St West A3
New Spring St B2
New St C4
New Street C4
New Summer St A4
New Town Row A4
Newhall Hill B3
Newhall St B3
Newton St B4
Newtown A4
Noel Rd C1
Norman St A1
Northbrook St B1
Northwood St B3
Norton St A2
Old Crown House C5
Old Rep Theatre, The C4
Old Snow Hill B4
Oliver Rd C1
Oliver St A5
Osler St C1
Oxford St C5
Pallasades Centre C4
Palmer St C5
Paradise Circus C3
Paradise St C3
Park Rd A2
Park St C4
Pavilions Centre C4
Paxton Rd A2
Peel St A1
Penn St B5
Pershore St C4
Phillips St A4
Pickford St C5
Pinfold St C4
Pitsford St A2
Plough & Harrow Rd C1
Police Station A4/B1/B4/C2/C4
Pope St B2
Portland Rd C1
Post Office A1/A3/A5/B1/B5/C1/C2/C3/C5
Preston Rd A1
Price St B4
Princip St B4
Printing House St B4
Priory Queensway B4
Pritchett St A4
Proctor St A5
Queensway B3
Radnor St A2
Railway Mosaics B4
Rea St C4
Regent Pl B3
Register Office C3
Repertory Theatre C3
Reservoir Rd C1
Richard St A5
River St C5
Rocky La A5
Rodney Cl C2
Roseberry St B2
Rotton Park St B1
Rupert St A5
Ruston St C2
Ryland St C2
St Andrew's Industrial Estate C6
St Andrew's Rd C6
St Andrew's St C6
St Bolton St C6
St Chads Circus B4
St Chads Queensway B4
St Clements Rd A6
St George's St A3
St James Pl B5
St Marks Cr B2
St Martin's C4
St Paul's B3
St Paul's (Metro) B3
St Paul's Sq B3
St Philip's B4
St Stephen's St A4
St Thomas' Peace Garden C3
St Vincent St C2
Saltley Rd A6
Sand Pits Pde B3
Severn St C3
Shadwell St B4
Sheepcote St C2
Shefford Rd A4
Sherborne St C2
Shylton's Croft C2
Skipton Rd C2
Smallbrook Queensway C4
Smith St A3
Snow Hill B4
Snow Hill Queensway B4
Soho, Benson Rd (Metro) A1
South Rd A2
Spencer St B3
Spring Hill B2
Staniforth St B4
Station St C4
Steelhouse La B4
Stephenson St C4
Steward St B2
Stirling Rd C1
Stour St B2
Suffolk St C3
Summer Hill Rd B2
Summer Hill St B2
Summer Hill Terr B2
Summer La A4
Summer Row B3
Summerfield Cr B1
Summerfield Park B1
Sutton St C3
Swallow St C3
Sydney Rd C6
Symphony Hall C3
Talbot St A1
Temple Row C4
Temple St C4
Templefield St C6
Tenby St B3
Tenby St North B2
Tennant St C2
The Crescent A2
Thimble Mill La A6
Thinktank (Science & Discovery) B5
Thomas St A4
Thorpe St C4
Tilton Rd C6
Tower St A4
Town Hall C3
Trent St C5
Turner's Buildings A1
Unett St A3
Union Terr B5
University of Central England in Birmingham B4
University of Aston B4/B5
Upper Trinity St C5
Uxbridge St A3
Vauxhall Gr B5
Vauxhall Rd B5
Vernon Rd C1
Vesey St B4
Viaduct St B5
Victoria Sq C3
Villa St A3
Vittoria St B3
Vyse St B3
Walter St A6
Wardlow Rd A5
Warstone La B2
Washington St C3
Water St B3
Waterworks Rd C1
Watery La C5
Well St A3
Western Rd B1
Wharf St A2
Wheeler St A3
Whitehouse St A5
Whitmore St A2
Whittall St B4
Wholesale Market C4
Wiggin St B1
Willes Rd A1
Windsor Industrial Estate A5
Windsor St A5
Windsor St B5
Winson Green Rd A1
Witton St C6
Wolseley St C6
Woodcock St B5

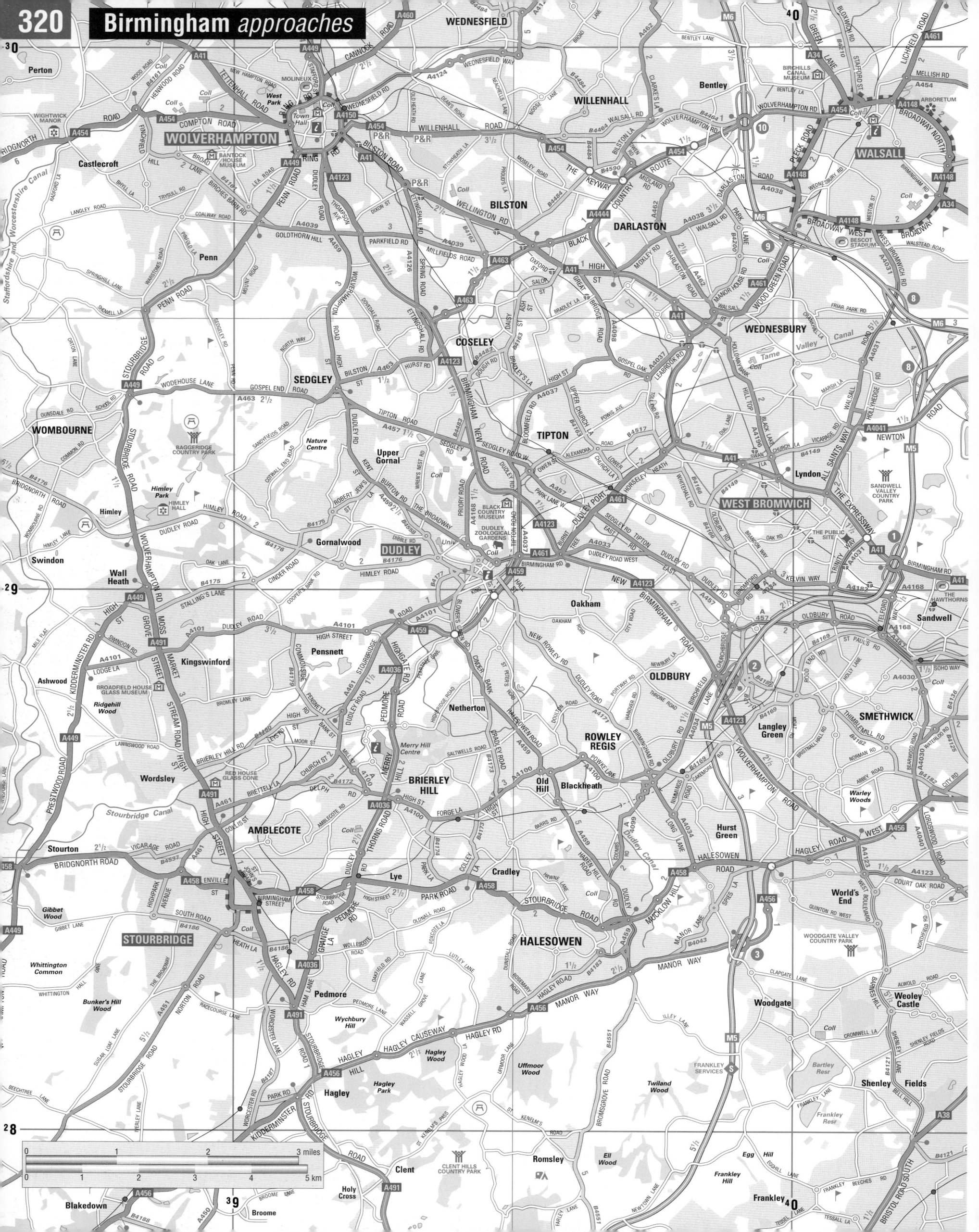

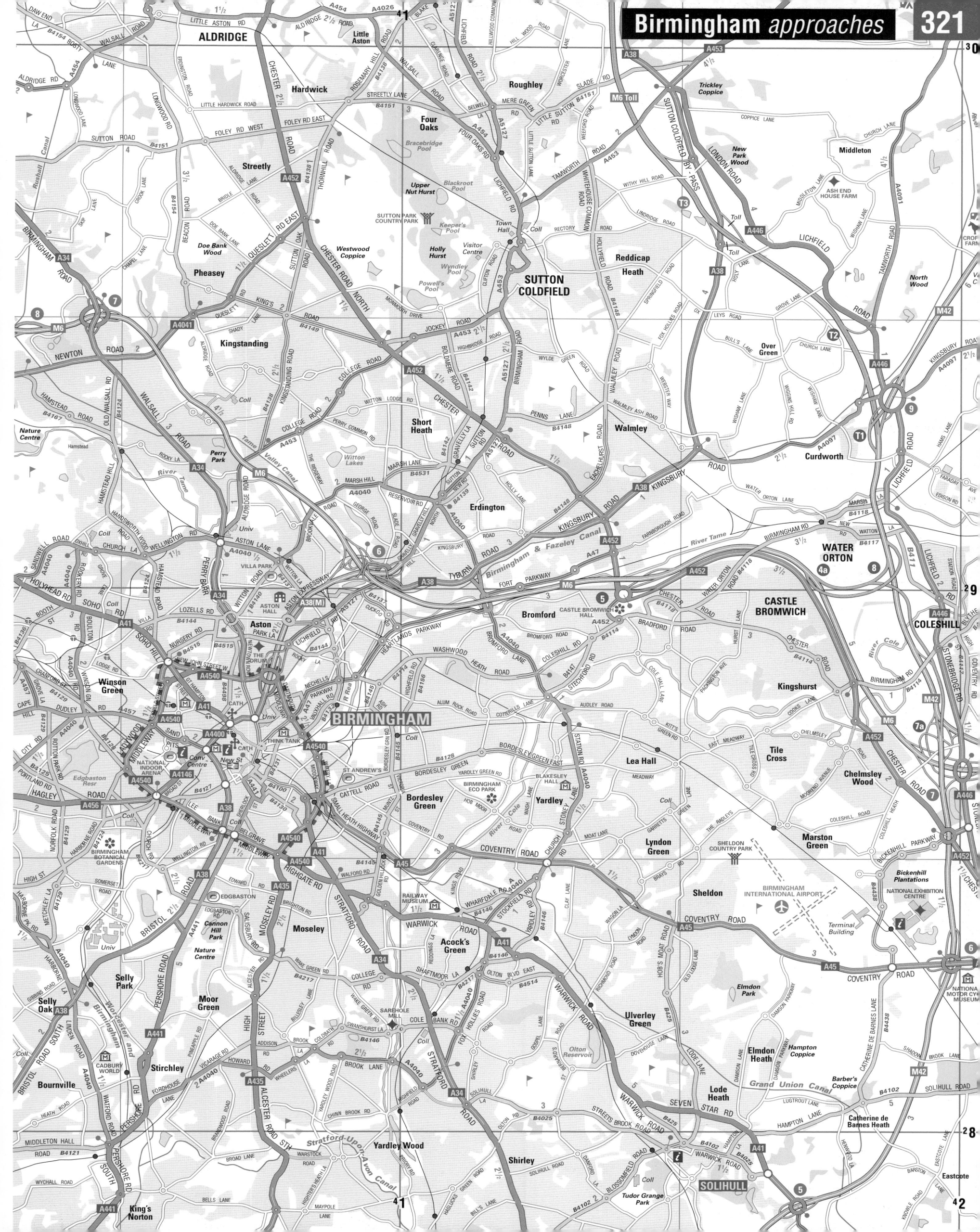

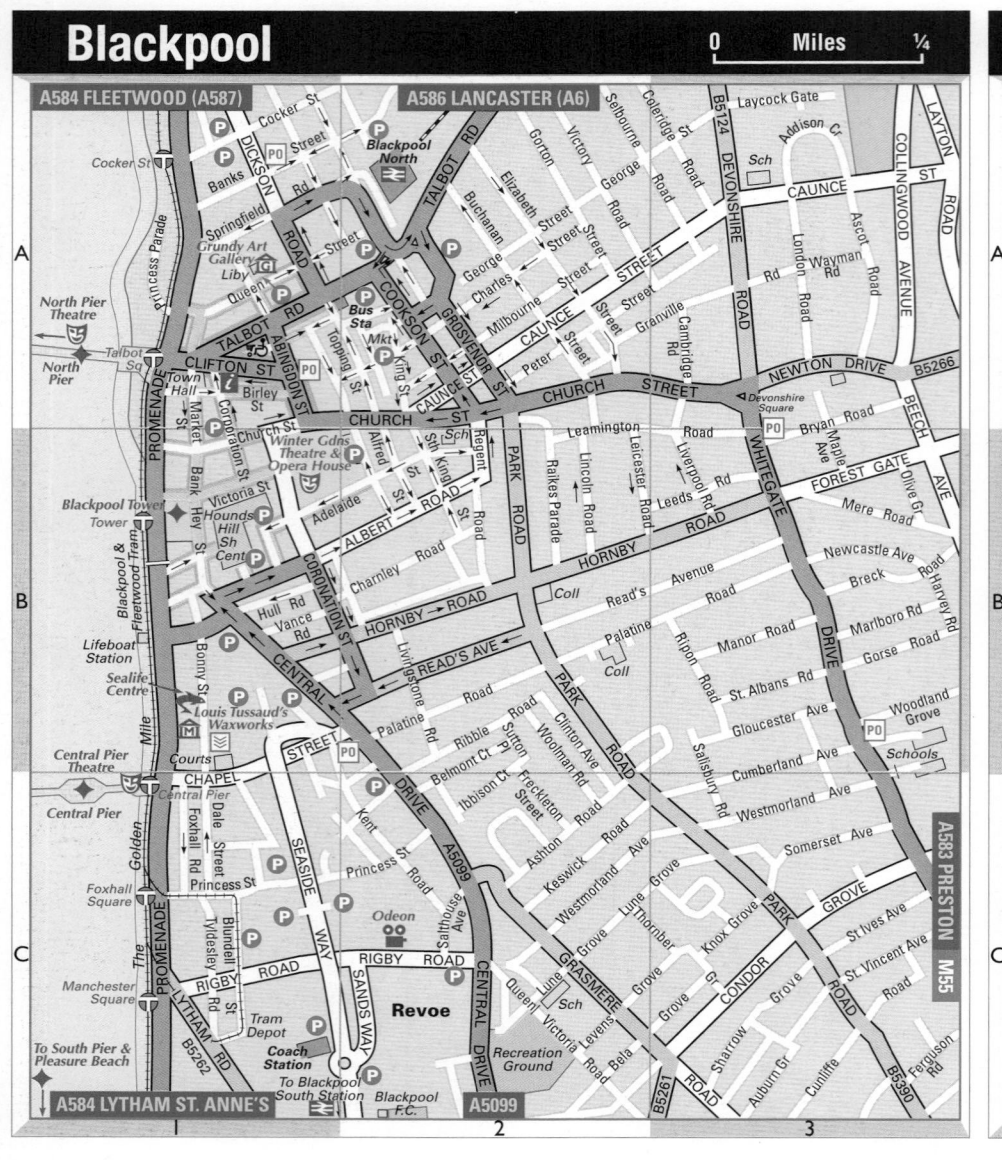

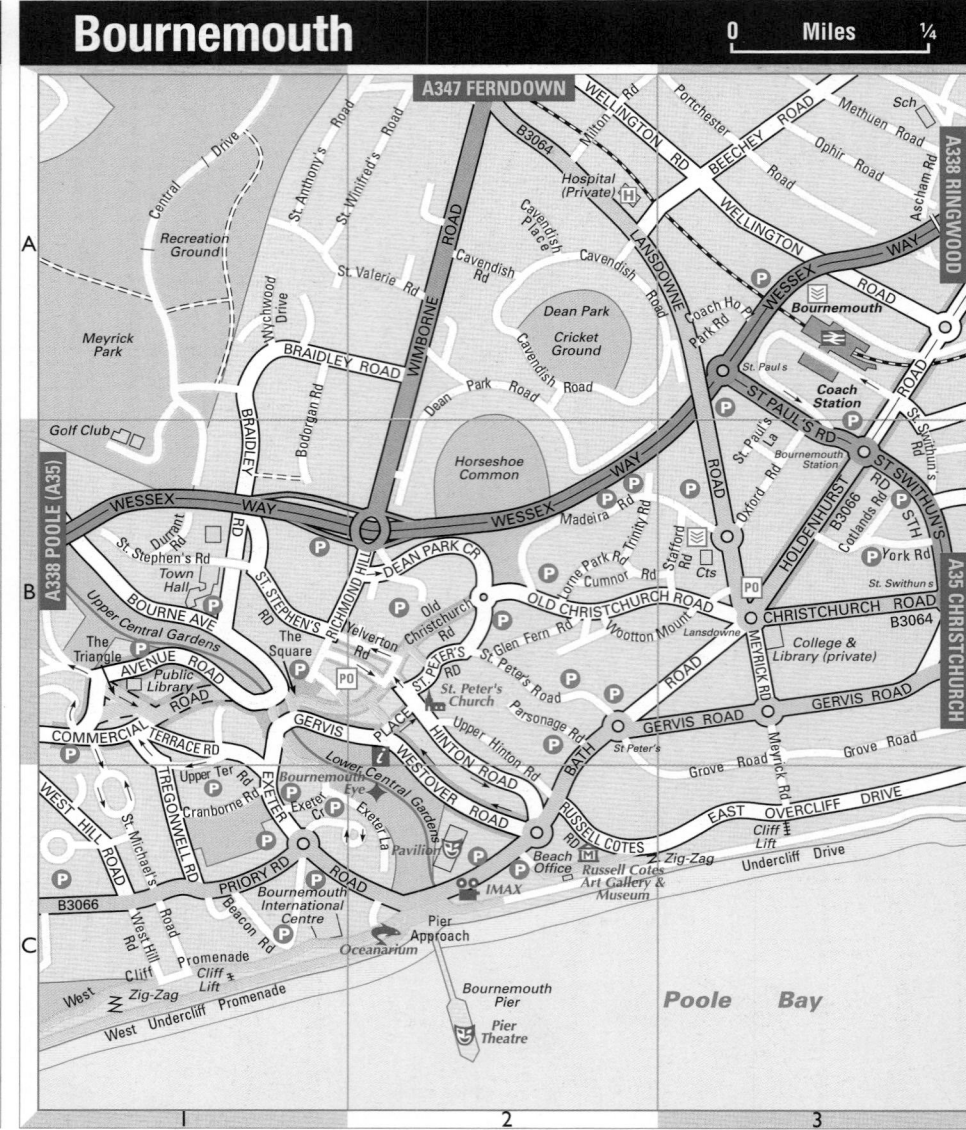

Blackpool

Abingdon St A1	Cocker St A1	King St A2	Queen Victoria Rd . . . C2
Addison Cr A3	Cocker St	Knox Gr C3	Raikes Pde B2
Adelaide St B1	(Tram stop) A1	Laycock Gate A3	Read's Ave B2
Albert Rd B2	Coleridge Rd A3	Layton Rd A3	Regent Rd B2
Alfred St B2	Collingwood Ave . . . A3	Leamington Rd B2	Ribble Rd B3
Ascot Rd A3	Condor Gr C3	Leeds Rd B3	Rigby Rd C1
Ashton Rd C2	Cookson St A2	Leicester Rd B2	Ripon Rd B3
Auburn Gr C3	Coronation St B1	Levens Gr C2	St Albans Rd B3
Bank Hey St B1	Corporation St A1	Library A1	St Ives Ave C3
Banks St A1	Courts B1	Lifeboat Station B1	St Vincent Ave C3
Beech Ave B3	Cumberland Ave. . . . B3	Lincoln Rd B2	Salisbury Rd B3
Bela Gr C2	Cunliffe Rd B3	Liverpool Rd B3	Salthouse Ave C2
Belmont Ct B2	Dale St C1	Livingstone Rd B2	Sands Way C2
Birley St A1	Devonshire Rd A3	London Rd A3	Sealife Centre ☞ . . . B1
Blackpool &	Devonshire Sq A3	Louis Tussaud's	Seaside Way C1
Fleetwood Tram . . . B1	Dickson Rd A1	Waxworks 🏛 B1	Selbourne Rd A2/A3
Blackpool F.C. C2	Elizabeth St A2	Lune Gr C2	Selbourne Rd A2/A3
Blackpool North ⇻ . . A2	Ferguson Rd C3	Lytham Rd C1	Sharrow Gr C3
Blackpool Tower ✦ . . B1	Forest Gate B3	Manchester Sq	Somerset Ave C3
Blundell St C1	Foxhall Rd C1	(Tram stop) C1	Springfield Rd A1
Bonny St B1	Foxhall Sq	Manor Rd B3	South King St B2
Breck Rd B3	(Tram stop) C1	Maple Ave B3	Sutton Pl. B2
Bryan Rd A3	Freckleton St C1	Market A2	Talbot Rd A1
Buchanan St. A2	George St A2	Market St A1	Talbot Sq
Bus Station. A2	Gloucester Ave. B3	Marlbro Rd B3	(Tram stop) A1
Cambridge Rd A3	Golden Mile, The . . . C1	Mere Rd B3	Thornber Gr C2
Caunce St A2	Gorse Rd B3	Milbourne St. A2	Topping St A1
Central Dr B1	Gorton St A2	Newcastle Ave B3	Town Hall A1
Central Pier ✦ C1	Granville Rd A2	Newton Dr A3	Tram Depot. C1
Central Pier	Grasmere Rd C2	North Pier ✦ A1	Tyldesley Rd C1
(Tram stop) C1	Grosvenor St A2	North Pier Theatre 🎭 . A1	Vance Rd B1
Central Pier	Grundy Art	Odeon 🎬 C2	Victoria St B1
Theatre 🎭 C1	Gallery 🏛 A1	Olive Gr B3	Victory Rd A2
Chapel St C1	Harvey Rd B3	Palatine Rd B2	Wayman Rd A3
Charles St A2	Hornby Rd B2	Park Rd B2	Westmorland Ave . . . C2
Charnley Rd B2	Hounds Hill Shopping	Peter St A2	Whitegate Dr B3
Church St A1	Centre B1	Police Station 🚓 . . . B1	Winter Gardens Theatre
Clifton St A1	Hull Rd B1	Post Office 🏤 . . A1/B2/B3	& Opera House 🎭 . . B1
Clinton Ave B2	Ibbison Ct C2	Princess Pde A1	Woodland Gr B3
Coach Station C1	Information Ctr ℹ . . . A1	Princess St C1/C2	Woolman Rd B2
	Kent Rd C2	Promenade A1/C1	
	Keswick Rd C2	Queen St A1	

Bournemouth

Ascham Rd A3	Cranborne Rd. C1	Milton Rd A2	St Swithun's Rd A3
Avenue Rd B1	Cricket Ground A2	Oceanarium ☞ C2	St Swithun's
Bath Rd C2	Cumnor Rd B2	Old Christchurch Rd. . B2	Rd South B3
Beacon Rd C1	Dean Park A2	Ophir Rd A3	St Valerie Rd A2
Beechey Rd A3	Dean Park Cr B2	Oxford Rd B2	St Winifred's Rd A2
Bodorgan Rd B1	Dean Park Rd A2	Park Rd A3	Stafford Rd B3
Bourne Ave B1	Durrant Rd B1	Parsonage Rd. B2	Terrace Rd B1
Bournemouth Eye ✦ . C2	East Overcliff Dr C3	Pavilion 🎭 C2	The Square B1
Bournemouth	Exeter Cr C1	Pier Approach C2	The Triangle B1
International Ctr . . . C1	Exeter La C2	Pier Theatre 🎭 C2	Town Hall B1
Bournemouth Pier . . C2	Exeter Rd C1	Police Station 🚓 . . A3/B3	Tregonwell Rd. C1
Bournemouth	Gervis Place B1	Portchester Rd A3	Trinity Rd B2
Station ⇻ A3	Gervis Rd B3	Post Office 🏤 B1/B3	Undercliff Drive. C3
Bournemouth Station	Glen Fern Rd B2	Priory Rd C1	Upper Central Gdns . . B1
(r'about) B3	Golf Club A1	Recreation Ground . . A1	Upper Hinton Rd B2
Braidley Rd. A1	Grove Rd B3	Richmond Hill Rd . . . B1	Upper Terr Rd C1
Cavendish Place . . . A2	Hinton Rd C2	Russell Cotes Art Gallery	Wellington Rd. A3
Cavendish Rd A2	Holdenhurst Rd B3	& Museum 🏛 C2	Wessex Way B2
Central Drive. A1	Horseshoe Common . B2	Russell Cotes Rd . . . C2	West Cliff
Christchurch Rd B2	Hospital (Private) 🏥 . A2	St Anthony's Rd A1	Promenade. C1
Cliff Lift C1/C3	IMAX 🎬 C2	St Michael's Rd C1	West Hill Rd C1
Coach House La . . . A3	Information Ctr ℹ . . . B2	St Paul's (r'about) . . . B3	West Undercliff
Coach Station A3	Lansdowne (r'about) . B2	St Paul's La B3	Promenade. C1
College & Library . . . A3	Lansdowne Rd B3	St Paul's Rd A3	Westover Rd B2
Commercial Rd B1	Lorne Park Rd B2	St Peter's ⛪ B2	Wimborne Rd A2
Cotlands Rd B3	Lower Central Gdns . . B2	St Peter's (r'about) . . B2	Wootton Mount B2
Courts B3	Madeira Rd B2	St Peter's Rd B2	Wychwood Dr. A1
	Methuen Rd A3	St Stephen's Rd B1	Yelverton Rd B2
	Meyrick Park A1	St Swithun's	York Rd B3
	Meyrick Rd B3	(r'about) B3	Zig-Zag Walks C1/C3

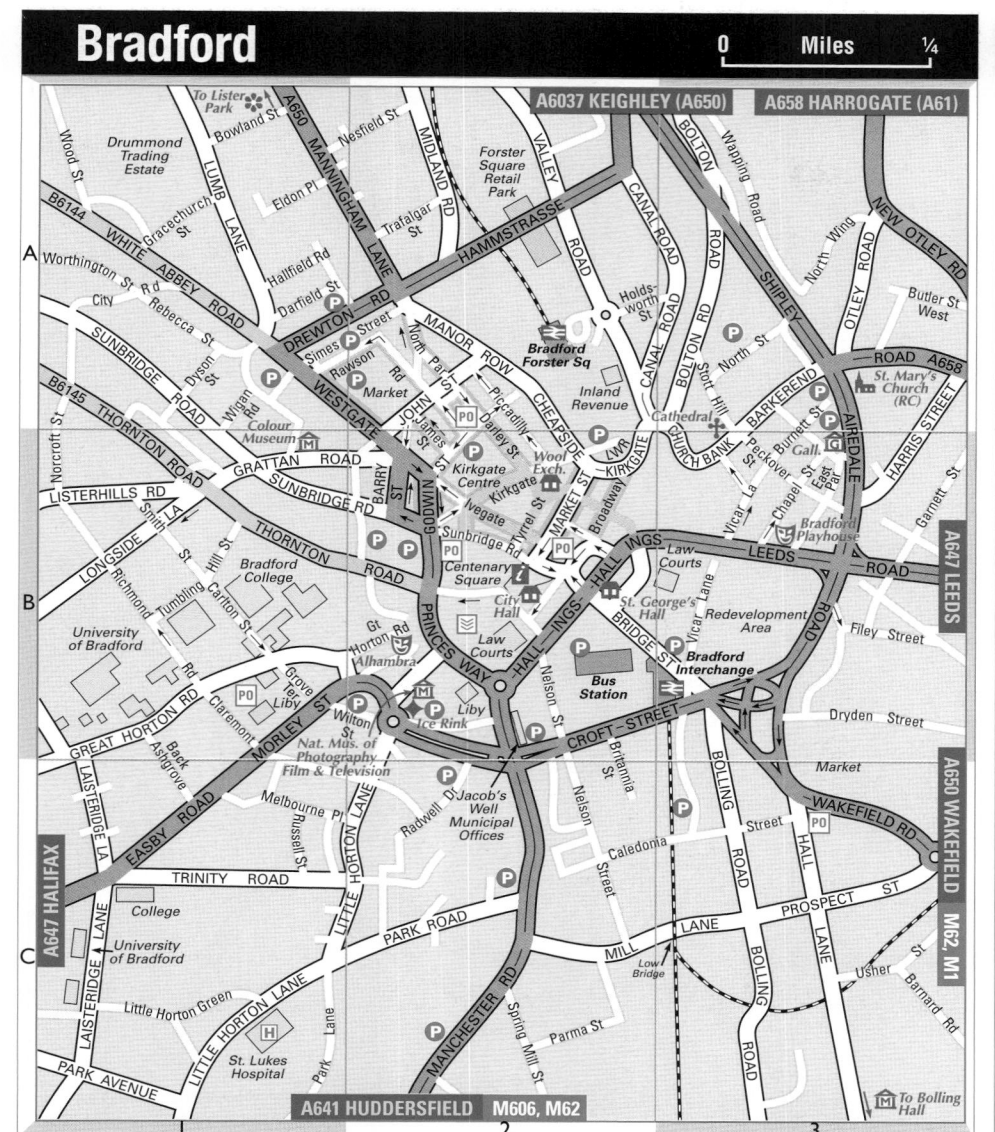

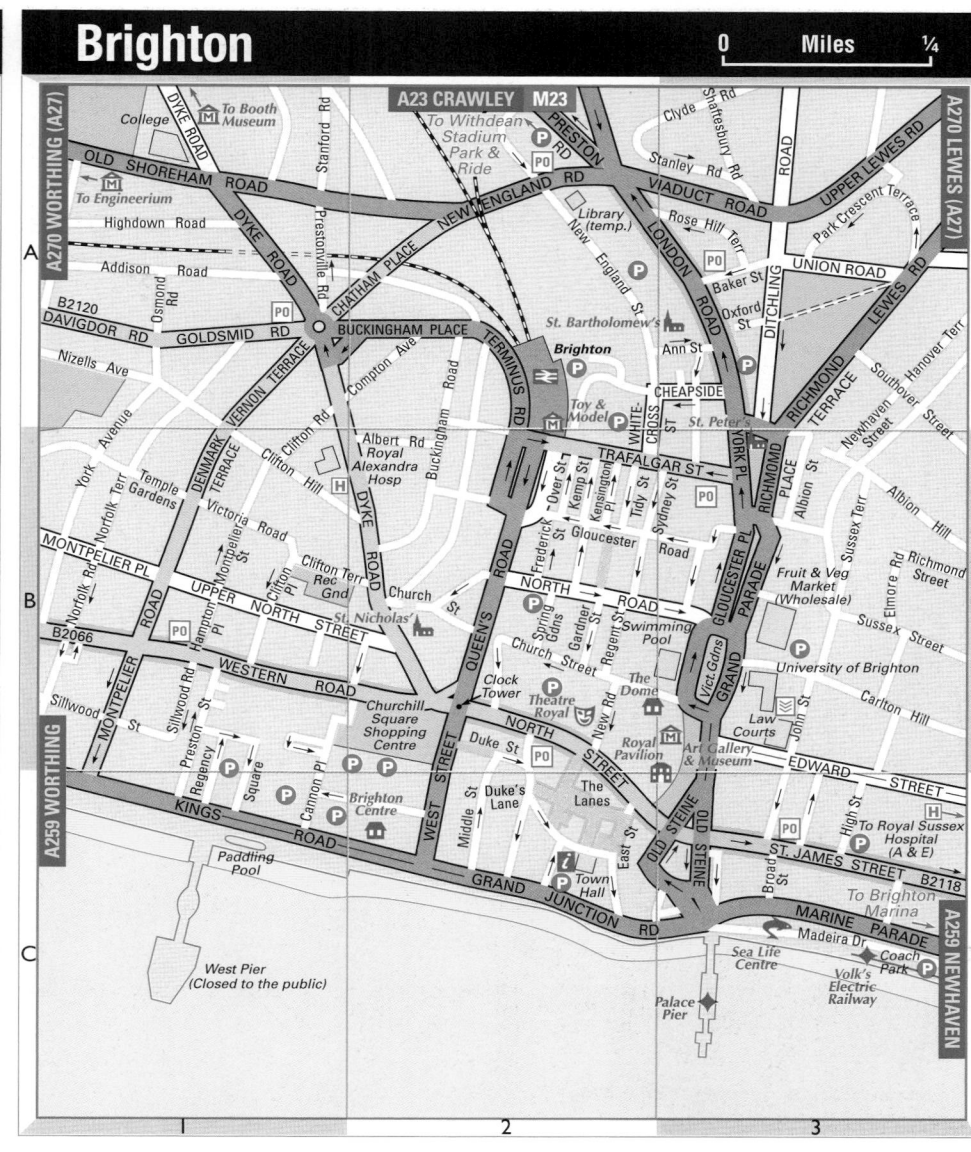

Bradford

Alhambra ♕ B2
Back Ashgrove B1
Barkerend Rd A3
Barnard Rd C3
Barry St B2
Bolling Rd B3
Bolton Rd A3
Bowland St A1
Bradford College B1
Bradford
 Forster Sq ₹ A2
Bradford
 Interchange ₹ B3
Bradford
 Playhouse ♕ B3
Bridge St B2
Britannia St B2
Broadway B2
Burnett St B3
Bus Station B2
Butler St West B1
Caledonia St C2
Canal Rd A2
Carlton St B2
Cathedral † A3
Centenary Sq B2
Chapel St B2
Cheapside A2
Church Bank B3
City Hall ⌂ B2
City Rd A1
Claremont B1
Colour Museum ⌂ . . . B1
Croft St B2

Darfield St A1
Darley St A2
Drewton Rd A1
Drummond Trading
 Estate A1
Dryden St B3
Dyson St A1
Easby Rd C1
East Parade B3
Eldon Pl A1
Filey St B3
Forster Square
 Retail Park A2
Garnett St B3
Godwin St B2
Gracechurch St A1
Grattan Rd B1
Great Horton Rd B1
Grove Terr B1
Hall Ings B2
Hall La C3
Hallfield Rd A1
Hammstrasse A2
Harris St B3
Holdsworth St A3
Ice Rink ♦ B2
Information Ctr ⓘ . . . B2
Ivegate B2
James St B2
John St A2
Kirkgate B2
Kirkgate Centre B2
Laisteridge La C1
Law Courts B3
Leeds Rd B3

Library B1/B2
Listerhills Rd B1
Little Horton La. C1
Little Horton Gn C1
Longside La B1
Lower Kirkgate B2
Lumb La A1
Manchester Rd C2
Manningham La A1
Manor Row A2
Market A2/C3
Market St B2
Melbourne Place C1
Midland Rd A1
Mill La. C2
Morley St B1
Nat. Museum of
 Photography, Film
 & Television ⌂ B2
Nelson St B2
Nesfield St A2
New Otley Rd A3
Norcroft St B1
North Parade A2
North St A3
North Wing A3
Otley Rd A3
Park Ave C1
Park La C1
Park Rd C2
Parma St C2
Peckover St B3
Piccadilly A2
Police Station ▣ . . . B2
Post Office ⓟ
 . . . . A2/B1/B2/C3

Princes Way B2
Prospect St C3
Radwell Drive C2
Rawson Rd A1
Rebecca St A1
Richmond Rd B1
Russell St C1
St George's Hall ⌂ . . . B2
St Lukes Hospital Ⓗ . . C1
St Mary's ♖ A3
Shipley
 Airedale Rd. . . . A3/B3
Simes St A1
Smith St B1
Spring Mill St C1
Stott Hill A3
Sunbridge Rd A1
Thornton Rd B1
Trafalgar St A2
Trinity Rd C1
Tumbling Hill St B1
Tyrrel St B2
University of
 Bradford B1/C1
Usher St C3
Valley Rd A2
Vicar La B3
Wakefield Rd C3
Wapping Rd A3
Westgate A1
White Abbey Rd A1
Wigan Rd A1
Wilton St B1
Wood St A1
Wool Exchange ⌂ . . . B2
Worthington St A1

Brighton

Addison Rd A1
Albert Rd B2
Albion Hill B3
Albion St B3
Ann St A3
Art Gallery &
 Museum ⌂ B3
Baker St A3
Brighton ₹ A2
Brighton Centre ⌂ . . . C2
Broad St C3
Buckingham Pl A2
Buckingham Rd B2
Cannon Pl C1
Carlton Hill B3
Chatham Pl A1
Cheapside A3
Church St B2
Churchill Square
 Shopping Centre . . . B2
Clifton Hill B1
Clifton Pl B1
Clifton Rd B1
Clifton Terr B1
Clock Tower B2
Clyde Rd A3
Coach Park C3
Compton Ave A2
Davigdor Rd A1
Denmark Terr B1
Ditchling Rd A3
Dome, The ⌂ B2
Duke St B2
Duke's La C2

Dyke Rd A1
East St C2
Edward St B3
Elmore Rd B3
Frederick St B2
Fruit & Veg Market
 (wholesale) B3
Gardner St B2
Gloucester Pl B2
Gloucester Rd B2
Goldsmid Rd A1
Grand Junction Rd. . . . C2
Grand Pde B3
Hampton Pl B1
Hanover Terr A3
High St C3
Highdown Rd A1
Information Ctr ⓘ . . . C2
John St B3
Kemp St B2
Kensington Pl B2
Kings Rd C1
Law Courts B3
Lewes Rd A3
Library (temp) A2
London Rd A3
Madeira Dr C3
Marine Pde C3
Middle St C2
Montpelier Pl B1
Montpelier Rd B1
Montpelier St B1
New England Rd A2
New England St A2
New Rd B2
Newhaven St A3

Nizells Ave A1
Norfolk Rd B1
Norfolk Terr. B1
North Rd B2
North St B2
Old Shoreham Rd. . . . A1
Old Steine C3
Osmond Rd A1
Over St B2
Oxford St A3
Paddling Pool C1
Palace Pier ♦ C3
Park Crescent Terr . . . A3
Police Station ▣ B3
Post Office ⓟ . . . A1/A2/
 . . . . A3/B1/B2/B3/C3
Preston Rd A2
Preston St B1
Prestonville Rd A1
Queen's Rd B2
Regency Sq C1
Regent St B2
Richmond Pl B3
Richmond St B3
Richmond Terr A3
Rose Hill Terr A3
Royal Alexandra
 Hospital Ⓗ B2
Royal Pavilion ⌂ B2
St Bartholomew's ♖. . . A2
St James' St C3
St Nicholas' ♖. B2
St Peter's ♖ A3
Sea Life Centre ← . . . C3
Shaftesbury Rd A3
Sillwood Rd B1

Sillwood St B1
Southover St A3
Spring Gdns B2
Stanford Rd A1
Stanley Rd A3
Sussex St B3
Sussex Terr. B3
Swimming Pool B3
Sydney St B3
Temple Gdns B1
Terminus Rd A2
The Lanes C2
Theatre Royal ♕ B2
Tidy St B2
Town Hall C2
Toy & Model
 Museum ⌂ A1
Trafalgar St B2
Union Rd A3
University of
 Brighton B3
Upper Lewes Rd A3
Upper North St B1
Vernon Terr A1
Viaduct Rd A3
Victoria Gdns B3
Victoria Rd B1
Volk's Electric
 Railway ♦ C3
West Pier (Closed
 to the Public) C1
West St C2
Western Rd B1
Whitecross St B2
York Ave B1
York Pl B3

Bristol

0   Miles   ¼

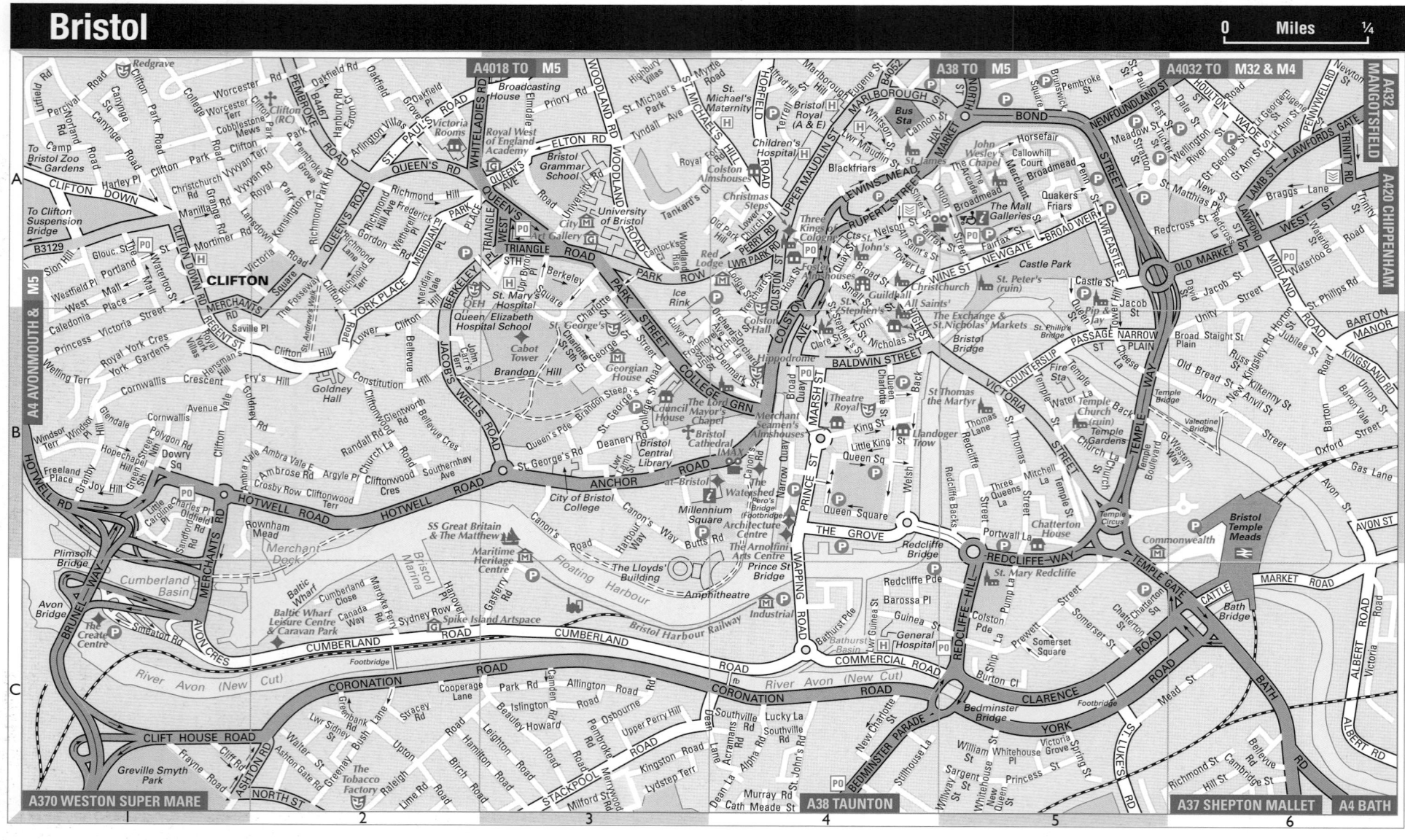

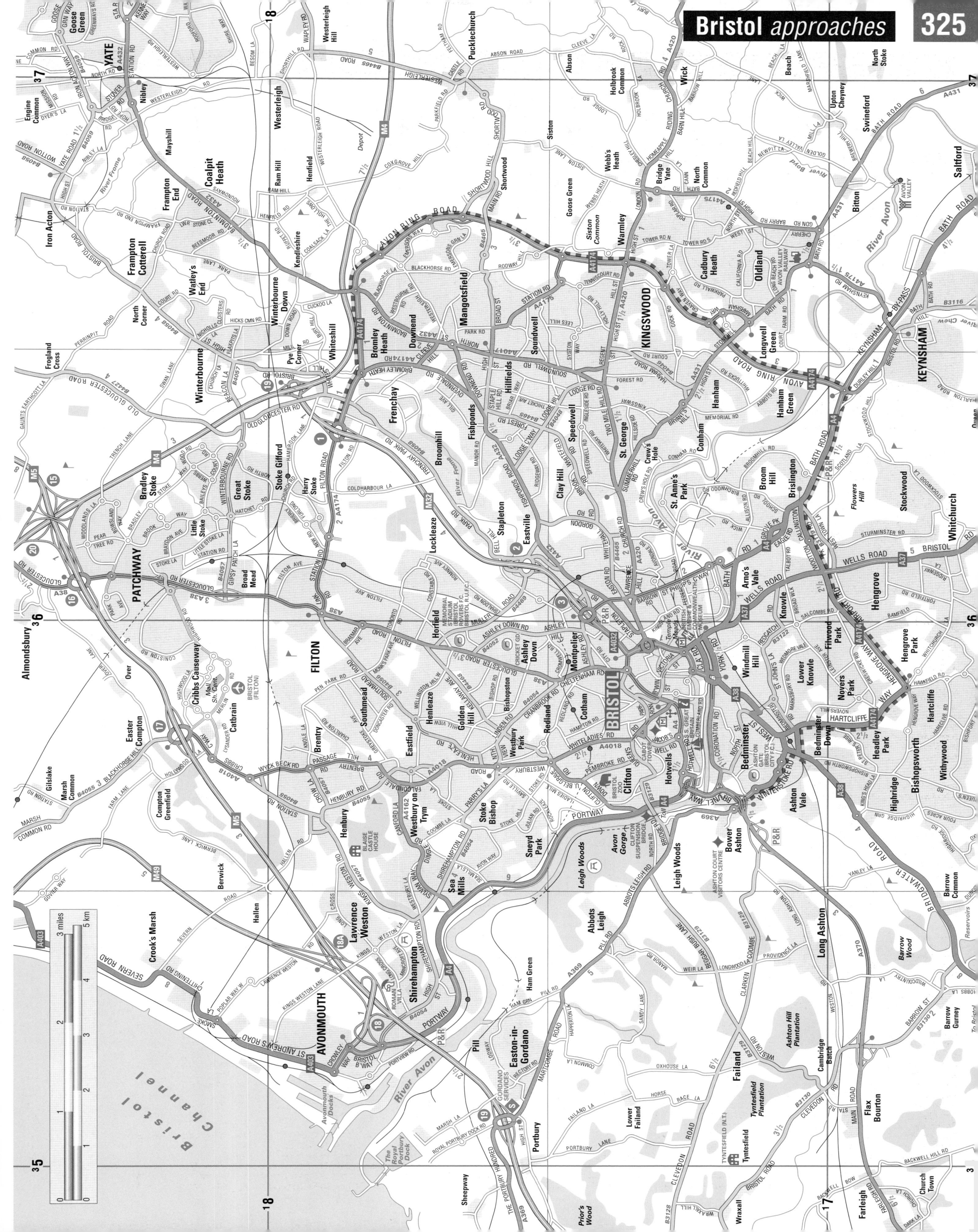

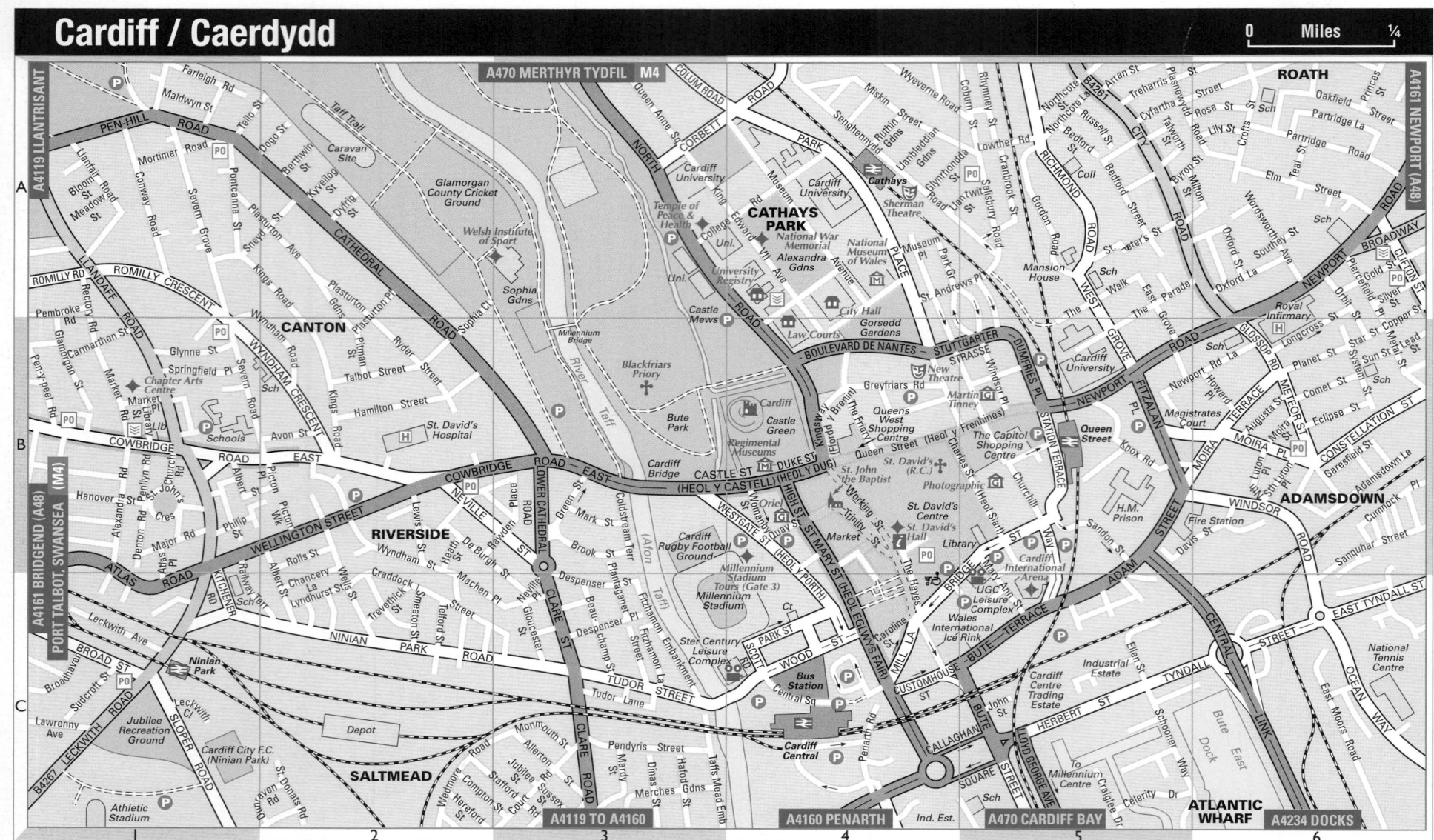

Cardiff / Caerdydd

0   Miles   ¼

Cardiff/Caerdydd

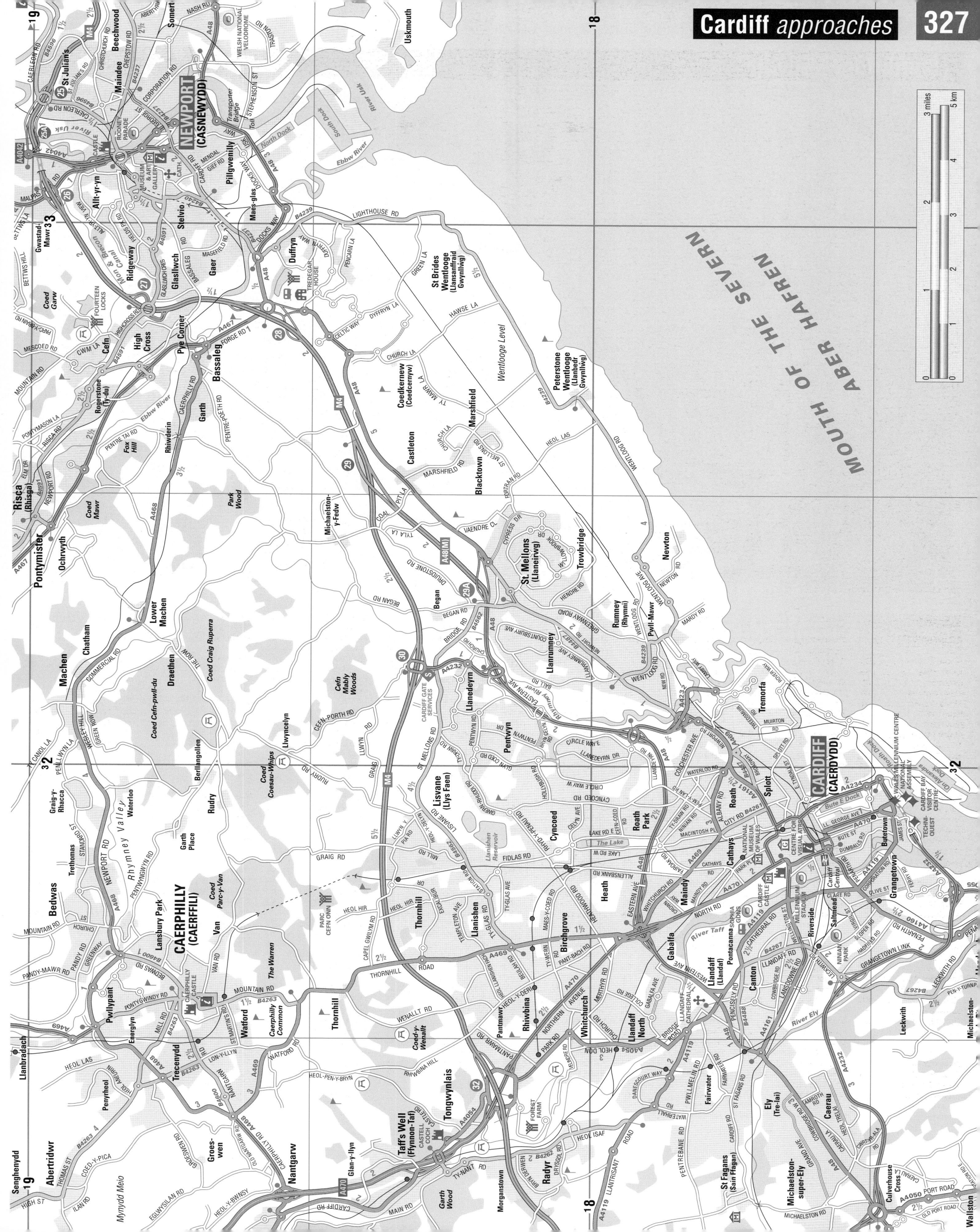

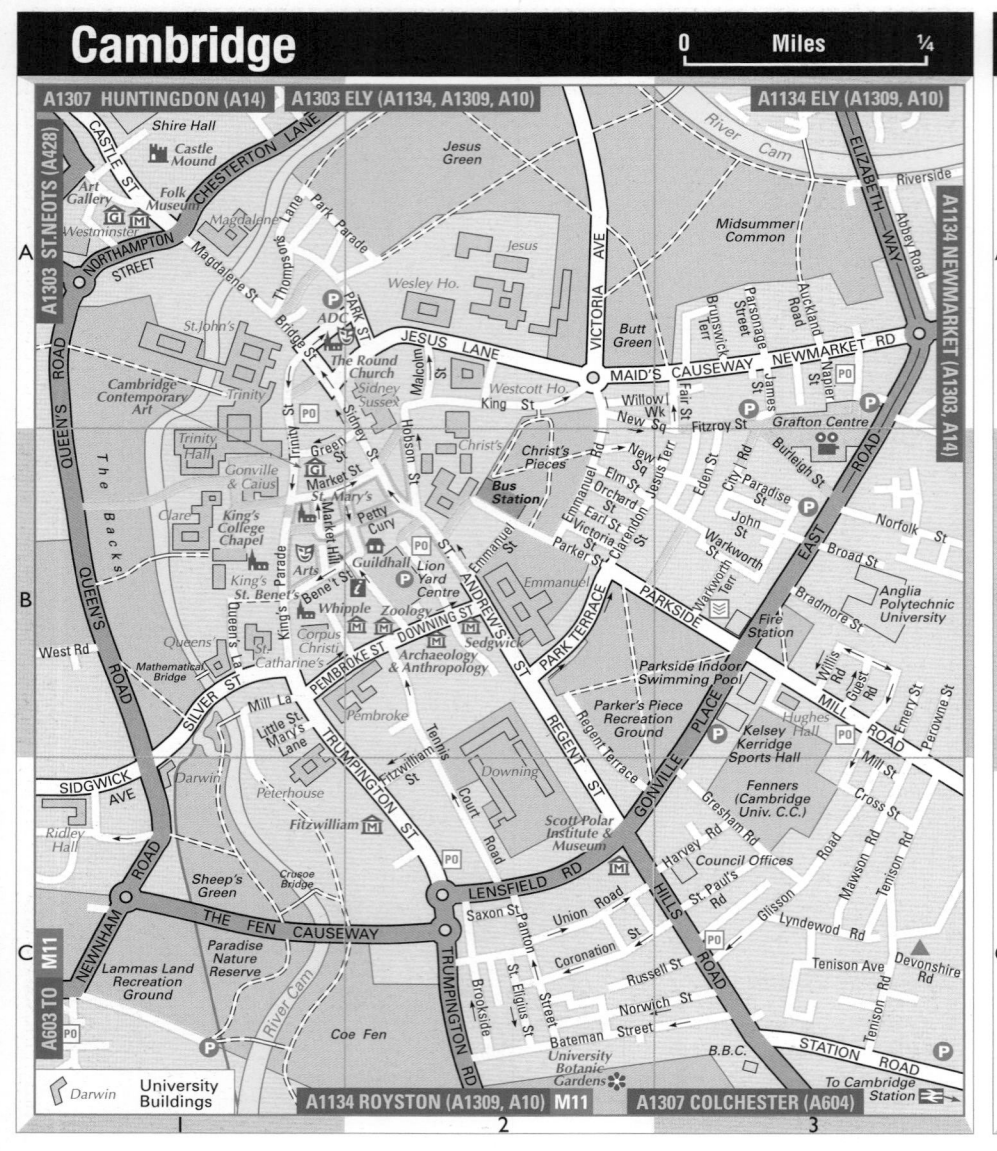

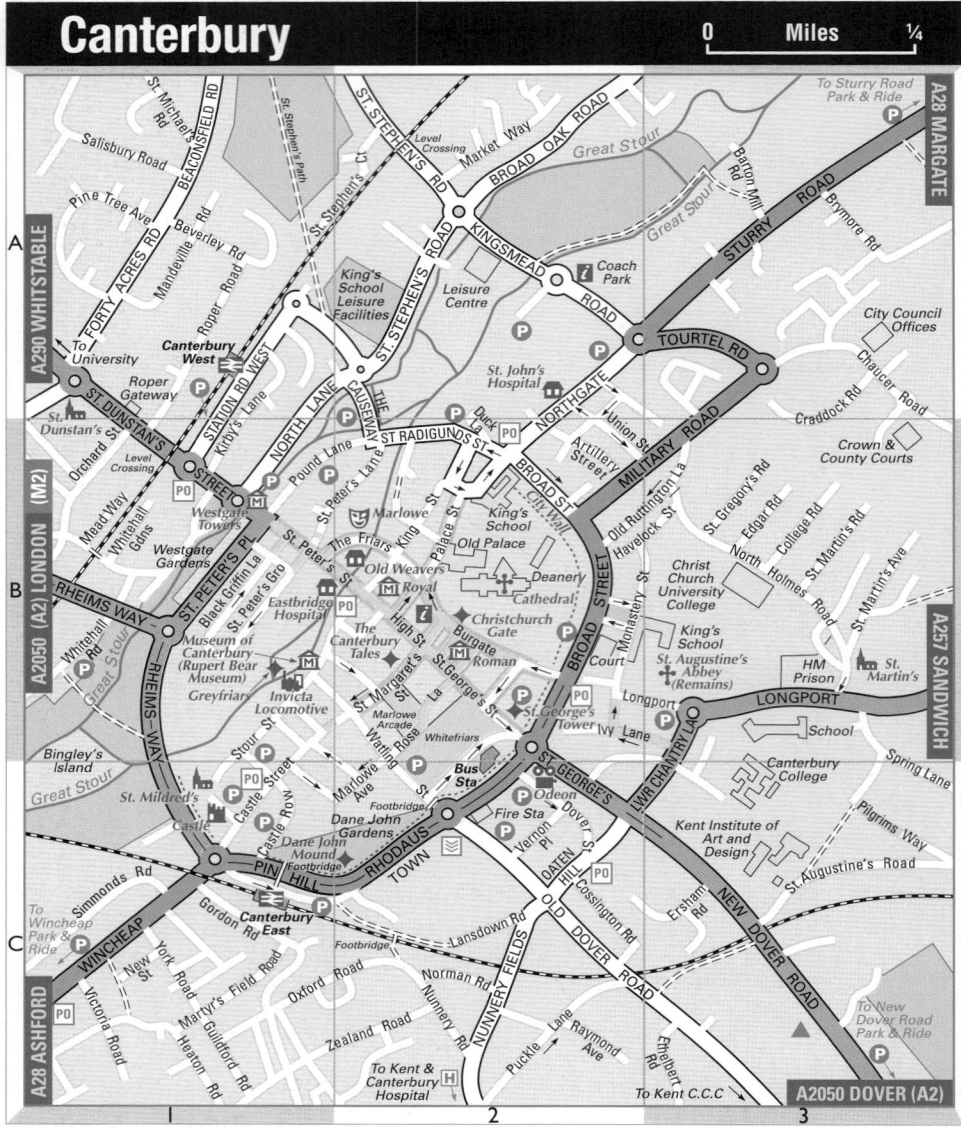

Cambridge

Abbey Rd	A3
ADC	A2
Anglia Polytechnic University	B3
Archaeology & Anthropology	B2
Art Gallery	A1
Arts Theatre	B1
Auckland Rd	A3
Bateman St	C2
B.B.C.	C3
Bene't St	B1
Bradmore St	B3
Bridge St	A1
Broad St	B3
Brookside	C2
Brunswick Terr	A3
Burleigh St	B3
Bus Station	B2
Butt Green	A2
Cambridge Contemporary Art Gallery	B1
Castle Mound	A1
Castle St	A1
Chesterton La	A1
Christ's (Coll)	B2
Christ's Pieces	B2
City Rd	B3
Clare (Coll)	B1
Clarendon St	B2
Coe Fen	C2
Coronation St	C3
Corpus Christi (Coll)	B1
Council Offices	C3
Cross St	C3
Crusoe Bridge	C1
Darwin (Coll)	C1
Devonshire Rd	C3
Downing (Coll)	B2
Downing St	B2
Earl St	B3
East Rd	B3
Eden St	B3
Elizabeth Way	A3
Elm St	B2

Emery St	B3
Emmanuel (Coll)	B2
Emmanuel Rd	B2
Emmanuel St	B2
Fair St	A3
Fenners (Cambridge Univ. C. C.)	C3
Fire Station	B3
Fitzroy St	A3
Fitzwilliam Museum	C1
Fitzwilliam St	C1
Folk Museum	A1
Glisson Rd	C3
Gonville & Caius (Coll)	B1
Gonville Place	B3
Grafton Centre	A3
Gresham Rd	C3
Green St	B1
Guest Rd	B3
Guildhall	B2
Harvey Rd	C3
Hills Rd	C3
Hobson St	B2
Hughes Hall (Coll)	B3
Information Ctr	B2
James St	A3
Jesus (Coll)	A2
Jesus Green	A2
Jesus La	A2
Jesus Terr	B3
John St	B3
Kelsey Kerridge Sports Hall	B3
King St	A2
King's (Coll)	B1
King's College Chapel	B1
King's Parade	B1
Lensfield Rd	C2
Lion Yard Centre	B2
Little St Mary's La	B1
Lyndewod Rd	C3
Magdalene (Coll)	A1
Magdalene St	A1
Maid's Causeway	A3
Malcolm St	A2

Market Hill	B1
Market St	B1
Mathematical Bridge	B1
Mawson Rd	C3
Midsummer Common	A3
Mill La	B1
Mill Rd	B3
Napier St	A3
New Square	A2
Newmarket Rd	A3
Newnham Rd	C1
Norfolk St	B3
Northampton St	A1
Norwich St	C2
Orchard St	B2
Panton St	C2
Paradise Nature Reserve	C1
Paradise St	B3
Park Parade	A1
Park St	A2
Park Terr	B2
Parker St	B2
Parker's Piece	B2
Parkside	B2
Parkside Swimming Pool	B3
Parsonage St	A3
Pembroke (Coll)	B1
Pembroke St	B1
Perowne St	B3
Peterhouse (Coll)	C1
Petty Cury	B2
Police Station	B2
Post Office	A1/A3/B2/B3/C1/C3
Queens' (Coll)	B1
Queen's La	B1
Queen's Rd	B1
Regent St	B2
Regent Terr	B2
Ridley Hall (Coll)	C1
Riverside	A3
Round Church, The	A1
Russell St	C2
St Andrew's St	B2

St Benet's	B1
St Catharine's (Coll)	B1
St Eligius St	C2
St John's (Coll)	A1
St Mary's	B1
St Paul's Rd	C3
Saxon St	C2
Scott Polar Institute & Museum	C2
Sedgwick Museum	B2
Sheep's Green	C1
Shelly Row	A1
Shire Hall	A1
Sidgwick Ave	C1
Sidney St	A1
Sidney Sussex (Coll)	A1
Silver St	B1
Station Rd	C3
Tenison Ave	C3
Tenison Rd	C3
Tennis Court Rd	B2
The Backs	B1
The Fen Causeway	C1
Thompson's La	A1
Trinity (Coll)	B1
Trinity Hall (Coll)	B1
Trinity St	B1
Trumpington Rd	C2
Trumpington St	C2
Union Rd	C2
University Botanic Gardens	C2
Victoria Ave	A2
Victoria St	B2
Warkworth St	B3
Warkworth Terr	B3
Wesley House (Coll)	A2
West Rd	B1
Westcott House (Coll)	A2
Westminster (Coll)	A1
Whipple	B2
Willis Rd	B3
Willow Walk	A2
Zoology	B2

Canterbury

Artillery St	B2
Barton Mill Rd	A3
Beaconsfield Rd	A1
Beverley Rd	A1
Bingley's Island	B1
Black Griffin La.	B1
Broad Oak Rd	A2
Broad St	B2
Brymore Rd	A3
Burgate	B2
Bus Station	C2
Canterbury College	C3
Canterbury East	C1
Canterbury Tales, The	B2
Canterbury West	A1
Castle	C1
Castle Row	C1
Castle St	C1
Cathedral	B2
Chaucer Rd	A3
Christ Church University College	B3
Christchurch Gate	B2
City Council Offices	A3
City Wall	B2
Coach Park	A2
College Rd	B3
Cossington Rd	C2
Court	B2
Craddock Rd	A3
Crown & County Courts	B3
Dane John Gdns	C2
Dane John Mound	C2
Deanery	B2
Dover St	C2
Duck La	B2

Eastbridge Hospital	B1
Edgar Rd	B3
Ersham Rd	C3
Ethelbert Rd	C3
Fire Station	C2
Forty Acres Rd	A1
Gordon Rd	C1
Greyfriars	B1
Guildford Rd	C1
Havelock St	B2
Heaton Rd	C1
High St	B2
HM Prison	B3
Information Ctr	A2/B2
Invicta Locomotive	B1
Ivy La	B2
Kent Institute of Art and Design	C3
King St	B2
King's School	B3
Kingsmead Rd	A2
Kirby's La	B1
Lansdown Rd	C2
Leisure Centre	A2
Longport	B3
Lower Chantry La	C3
Mandeville Rd	A1
Market Way	A2
Marlowe Arcade	B2
Marlowe Ave	C1
Marlowe Theatre	B2
Martyr's Field Rd	C1
Mead Way	B1
Military Rd	B2
Monastery St	B2
Museum of Canterbury (Rupert Bear Museum)	B1
New Dover Rd	C3

New St	C1
Norman Rd	C2
North Holmes Rd	B3
North La	B1
Northgate	A2
Nunnery Fields	C2
Nunnery Rd	C2
Oaten Hill	C2
Odeon Cinema	C1
Old Dover Rd	C2
Old Palace	B2
Old Ruttington La.	B2
Old Weavers	B2
Orchard St	B1
Oxford Rd	C1
Palace St	B2
Pilgrims Way	C3
Pin Hill	C1
Pine Tree Ave	A1
Police Station	C2
Post Office	B1/B2/C1/C2
Pound La	B1
Puckle La	C2
Raymond Ave	C2
Rheims Way	B1
Rhodaus Town	C2
Roman Museum	B2
Roper Gateway	A1
Roper Rd	A1
Rose La	B2
Royal Museum	B2
St Augustine's Abbey (remains)	B3
St Augustine's Rd.	C3
St Dunstan's	A1
St Dunstan's St	A1
St George's Pl	C2
St.George's St	B2
St.George's Tower	B2

St Gregory's Rd	B3
St John's Hospital	A2
St Margaret's St	B2
St Martin's	B3
St Martin's Ave	B3
St Martin's Rd	B3
St Michael's Rd	A1
St Mildred's	C1
St Peter's Gr	B1
St Peter's La	B2
St Peter's Pl	B1
St Peter's St	B1
St Radigunds St	B2
St Stephen's Ct	A1
St Stephen's Path	A1
St Stephen's Rd	A2
Salisbury Rd	A1
Simmonds Rd	C1
Spring La	C3
Station Rd West	B1
Stour St	B1
Sturry Rd	A3
The Causeway	A2
The Friars	B2
Tourtel Rd	A3
Union St	B2
Vernon Pl	C2
Victoria Rd	C1
Watling St	B2
Westgate Towers	B1
Westgate Gdns	B1
Whitefriars	B2
Whitehall Gdns	B1
Whitehall Rd	B1
Wincheap	C1
York Rd	C1
Zealand Rd	C2

Carlisle

0 Miles ¼

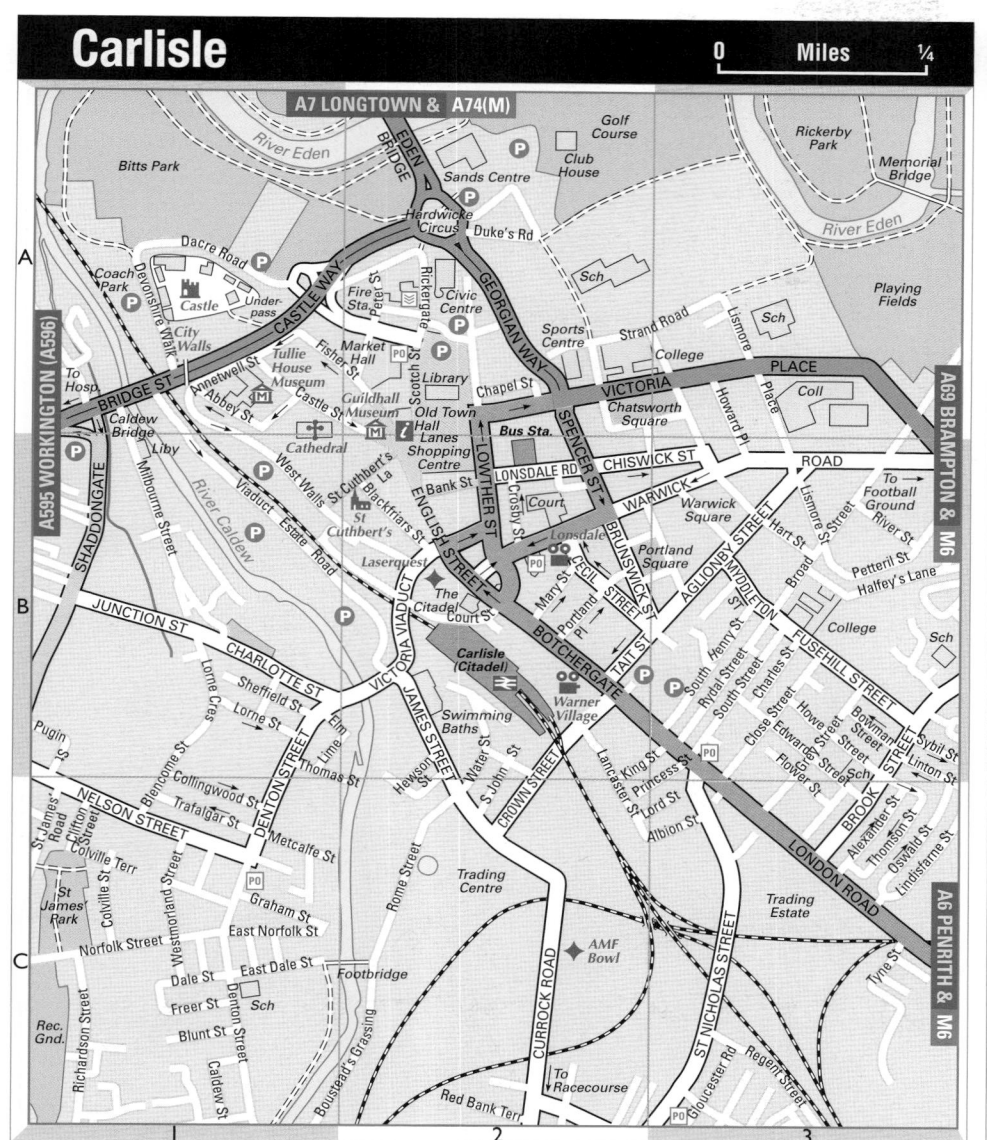

Cheltenham

0 Miles ¼

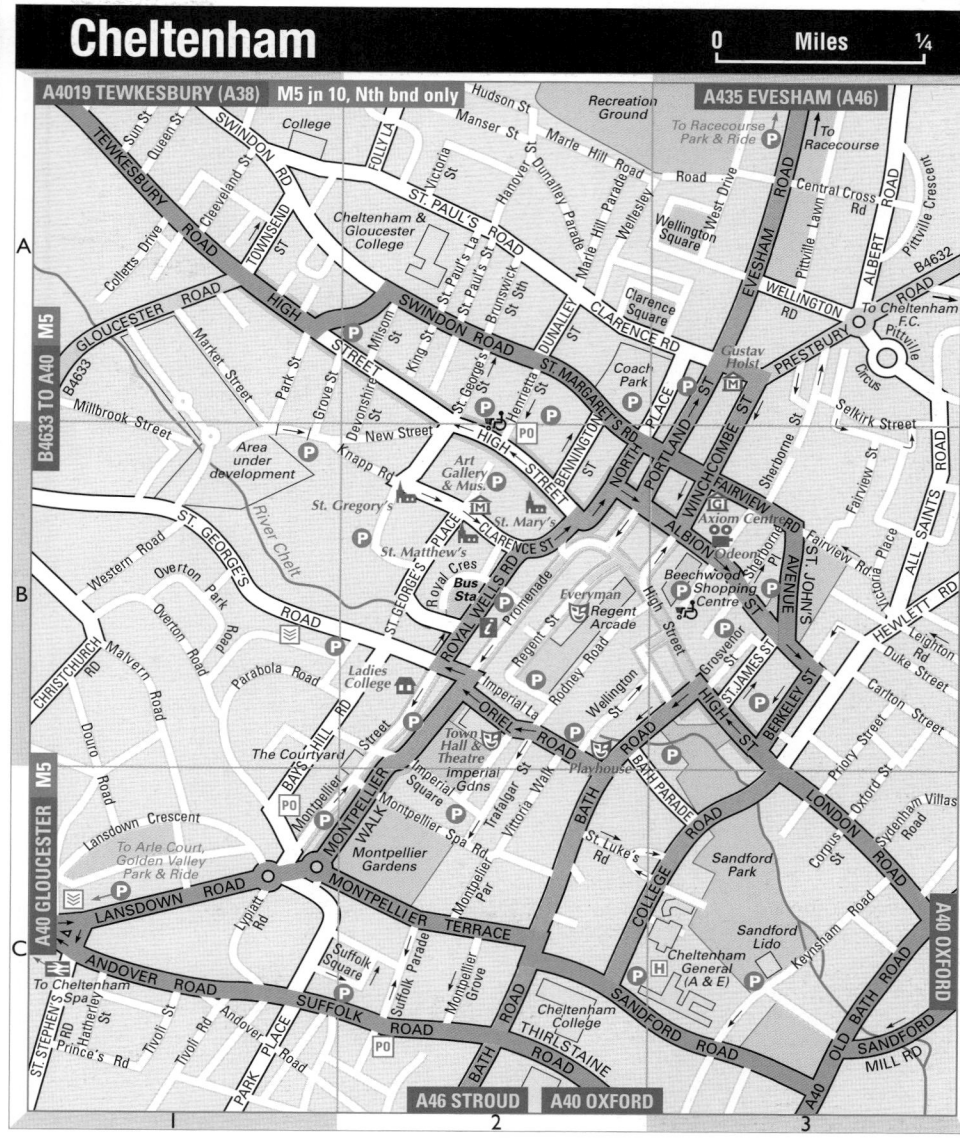

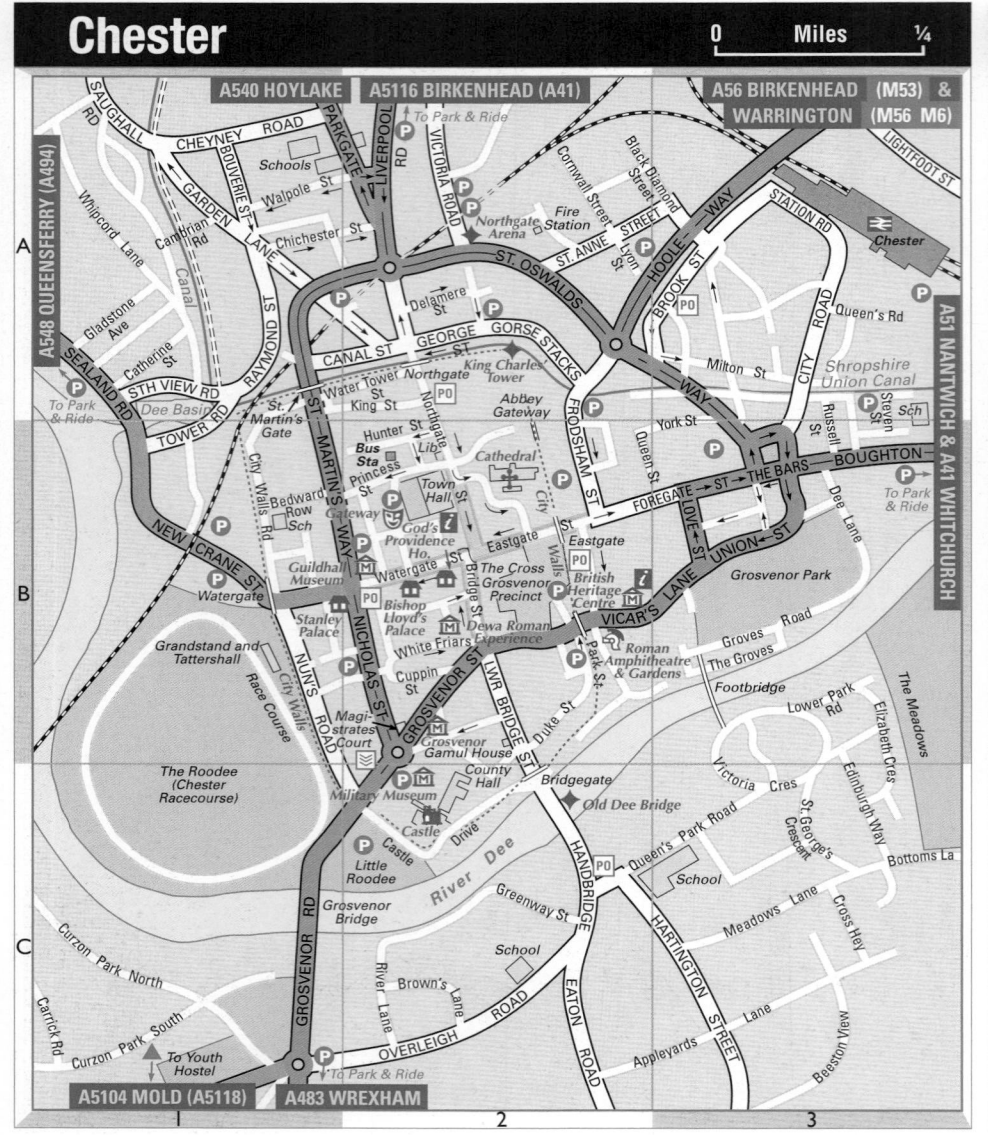

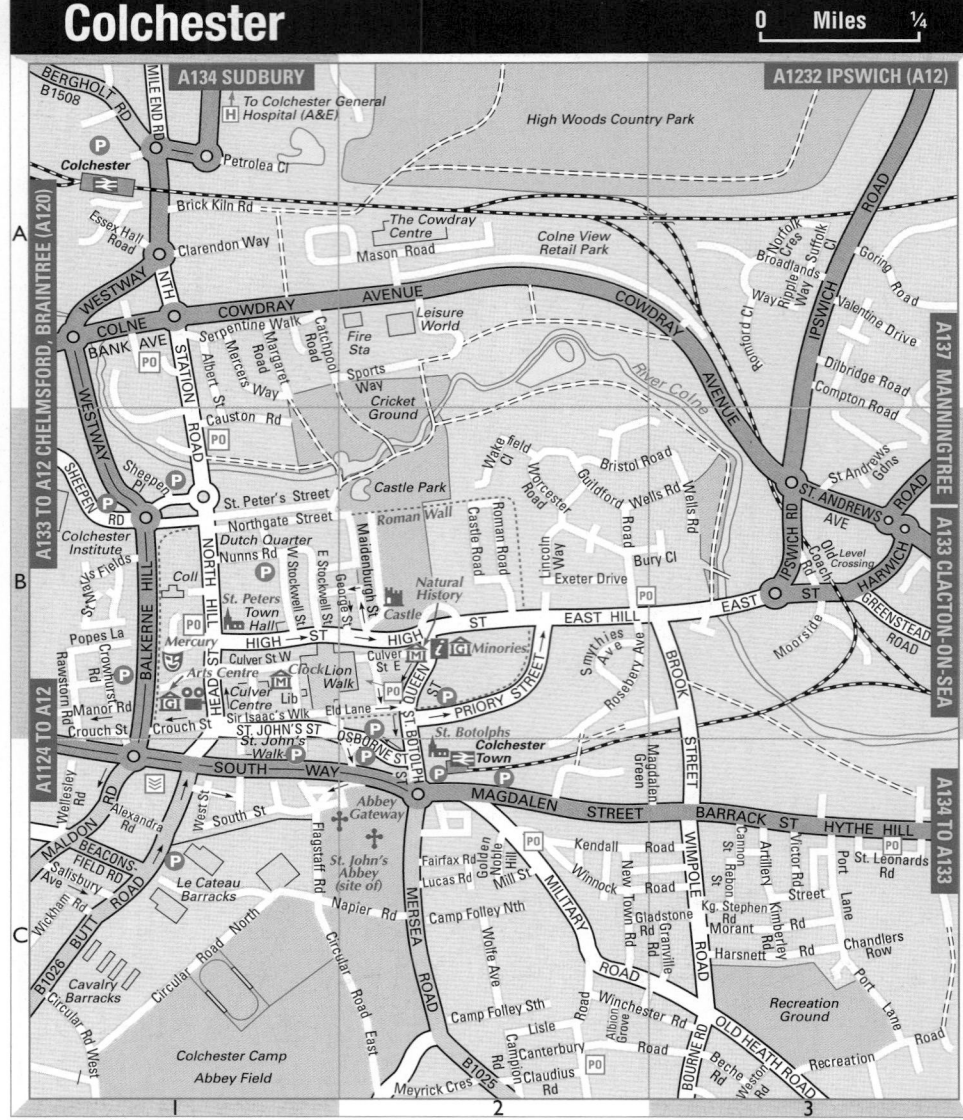

Chester

Abbey Gateway A2	
Appleyards La C3	
Bedward Row B1	
Beeston View C3	
Bishop Lloyd's	
Palace ⌂ B2	
Black Diamond St . . . A2	
Bottoms La. C3	
Boughton B3	
Bouverie St. A1	
Bridge St B2	
Bridgegate C2	
British Heritage	
Centre ⌂ B2	
Brook St A3	
Brown's La. C2	
Bus Station. B2	
Cambrian Rd A1	
Canal St A2	
Carrick Rd C1	
Castle ⌂ C2	
Castle Dr C2	
Cathedral † B2	
Catherine St A1	
Chester ⊒ A3	
Cheyney Rd A1	
Chichester St A1	
City Rd A3	
City Walls B1/B2	
City Walls Rd B1	
Cornwall St. A2	
County Hall. C2	
Cross Hey C3	
Cuppin St B2	

Curzon Park North . . . C1	
Curzon Park South. . . C1	
Dee Basin. A1	
Dee La B3	
Delamere St A2	
Dewa Roman	
Experience ⌂ B2	
Duke St. B2	
Eastgate B2	
Eastgate St. B2	
Eaton Rd A3	
Egerton St A3	
Elizabeth Cr B3	
Fire Station. A2	
Foregate St. B2	
Frodsham St. B2	
Gamul House C2	
Garden La. A1	
Gateway Theatre ☺ . B2	
George St A2	
Gladstone Ave A1	
God's Providence	
House ⌂ B2	
Gorse Stacks A2	
Greenway St. C2	
Grosvenor Bridge . . . C1	
Grosvenor	
Museum ⌂ B2	
Grosvenor Park B3	
Grosvenor Precinct . . B2	
Grosvenor Rd. C1	
Grosvenor St B2	
Groves Rd B3	
Guildhall Museum ⌂ . B1	
Handbridge. C2	
Hartington St C3	

Hoole Way A2	
Hunter St B2	
Information Ctr ⊡ . . . B2	
King Charles'	
Tower ♦ A2	
King St B2	
Library B2	
Lightfoot St. A3	
Little Roodee C2	
Liverpool Rd A2	
Love St B3	
Lower Bridge St B2	
Lower Park Rd B3	
Lyon St A2	
Magistrates Court. . . . B2	
Meadows La. C3	
Military Museum ⌂ . . C2	
Milton St A3	
New Crane St. B1	
Nicholas St B2	
Northgate A2	
Northgate Arena ♦ . . A2	
Northgate St. B2	
Nun's Rd B1	
Old Dee Bridge ♦ . . . C2	
Overleigh Rd. C1	
Park St B2	
Police Station ⊠ B2	
Post Office ⊡	
. . . . A2/A3/B2/C2	
Princess St. B2	
Queen St B2	
Queen's Park Rd C3	
Queen's Rd. A3	
Raymond St A1	
River La C2	

Roman Amphitheatre	
& Gardens ⌂ B2	
Roodee, The (Chester	
Racecourse). B1	
Russell St A3	
St Anne St A2	
St George's Cr C3	
St Martin's Gate A1	
St Martin's Way B1	
St Oswalds Way. A2	
Saughall Rd A1	
Sealand Rd. A1	
South View Rd A1	
Stanley Palace ⌂ . . . B1	
Station Rd A3	
Steven St A3	
The Bars B3	
The Cross B2	
The Groves B3	
The Meadows. B3	
Tower Rd B1	
Town Hall B2	
Union St B3	
Vicar's La B2	
Victoria Cr. A3	
Victoria Rd. A2	
Walpole St A1	
Water Tower St A1	
Watergate B1	
Watergate St. B2	
Whipcord La. A1	
White Friars B2	
York St B3	

Colchester

Abbey Gateway † . . C2	
Albert St A1	
Albion Grove. C1	
Alexandra Rd C1	
Artillery St. C3	
Arts Centre ⌂ B1	
Balkerne Hill B1	
Barrack St C3	
Barrington Rd C1	
Beaconsfield Rd. C1	
Beche Rd C3	
Bergholt Rd A1	
Bourne Rd C3	
Brick Kiln Rd A1	
Bristol Rd A3	
Broadlands Way A3	
Brook St B3	
Bury Cl B1	
Butt Rd C1	
Camp Folley North . . C2	
Camp Folley South. . . C2	
Campion Rd C3	
Cannon St C3	
Canterbury Rd C2	
Castle ⌂ B2	
Castle Rd B2	
Catchpool Rd A1	
Causton Rd B1	
Cavalry Barracks C1	
Chandlers Row C3	
Circular Rd East C2	
Circular Rd North C1	
Circular Rd West C1	
Clarendon Way. A1	
Claudius Rd C2	
Clock ⌂ B1	
Colchester Institute . . B1	
Colchester ⊒ A1	
Colchester Town ⊒ . C2	
Colne Bank Ave A1	
Colne View	
Retail Park A2	

Compton Rd. A3	
Cowdray Ave A1/A3	
Cowdray Centre,	
The A2	
Crouch St B1	
Crowhurst Rd. C1	
Culver Centre B1	
Culver St East B2	
Culver St West B1	
Dilbridge Rd A3	
East Hill B2	
East St B3	
East Stockwell St B1	
Eld La B1	
Essex Hall Rd A1	
Exeter Dr B2	
Fairfax Rd C2	
Fire Station A2	
Flagstaff Rd C1	
George St B2	
Gladstone Rd C2	
Golden Noble Hill C2	
Goring Rd. A3	
Granville Rd C3	
Greenstead Rd. B3	
Guildford Rd B2	
Harsnett Rd C3	
Harwich Rd. B3	
Head St B1	
High St B1	
Hythe Hill C3	
Information Ctr ⊡ . . . B2	
Ipswich Rd A3	
Kendall Rd C2	
Kimberley Rd C3	
King Stephen Rd C3	
Le Cateau Barracks . . C1	
Leisure World A2	
Library B1	
Lincoln Way B2	
Lion Walk Shopping	
Centre B1	
Lisle Rd C2	
Lucas Rd C2	

Magdalen Green. C3	
Magdalen St. C2	
Maidenburgh St B2	
Maldon Rd C1	
Manor Rd B1	
Margaret Rd A1	
Mason Rd A2	
Mercers Way A1	
Mercury ☺ B1	
Mersea Rd C2	
Meyrick Cr C2	
Mile End Rd A1	
Military Rd C2	
Mill St C2	
Minories ⌂ B2	
Moorside B3	
Morant Rd C2	
Napier Rd C2	
Natural History ⌂ . . . B2	
New Town Rd C2	
Norfolk Cr A3	
North Hill B1	
North Station Rd A1	
Northgate St. B1	
Nunns Rd B1	
Odeon ⌂ B1	
Old Coach Rd. B3	
Old Heath Rd C3	
Osborne St B2	
Petrolea Cl A1	
Police Station ⊠ C1	
Popes La B1	
Port La C3	
Post Office ⊡	
. . . . A1/B1/B2/C2/C3	
Priory St B2	
Queen St B2	
Rawstorn Rd B1	
Rebon St C3	
Recreation Rd C3	
Ripple Way A3	
Roman Rd B2	
Roman Wall B2	
Romford Cl. A3	

Rosebery Ave B2	
St Andrews Ave B3	
St Andrews Gdns B3	
St Botolph St B2	
St Botolphs ⛪ B2	
St John's Abbey	
(site of) † C2	
St John's St B1	
St John's Walk Shopping	
Centre B1	
St Leonards Rd C3	
St Marys Fields B1	
St Peters ⛪ B1	
St Peter's St B1	
Salisbury Ave C1	
Serpentine Walk A1	
Sheepen Pl B1	
Sheepen Rd B1	
Sir Isaac's Walk B1	
Smythies Ave B2	
South St C1	
South Way C1	
Sports Way A2	
Suffolk Cl A3	
Town Hall B1	
Turner Rd A1	
Valentine Dr A3	
Victor Rd. C3	
Wakefield Cl B2	
Wellesley Rd C1	
Wells Rd B2	
West St C1	
West Stockwell St . . . B1	
Weston Rd C3	
Westway A1	
Wickham Rd. C1	
Wimpole Rd C3	
Winchester Rd C2	
Winnock Rd C2	
Wolfe Ave C2	
Worcester Rd B2	

Coventry

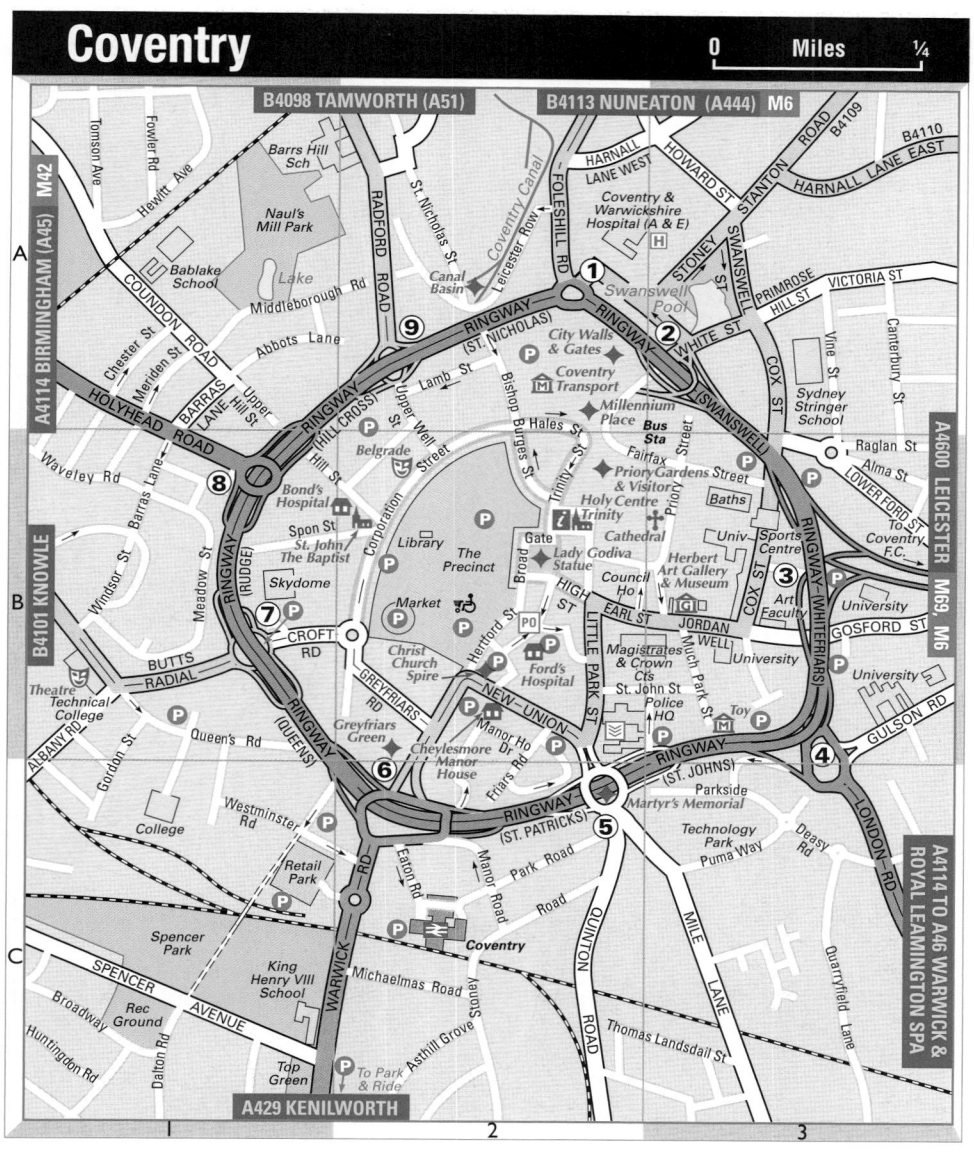

0 Miles ¼

B4098 TAMWORTH (A51) • B4113 NUNEATON (A444) M6

Derby

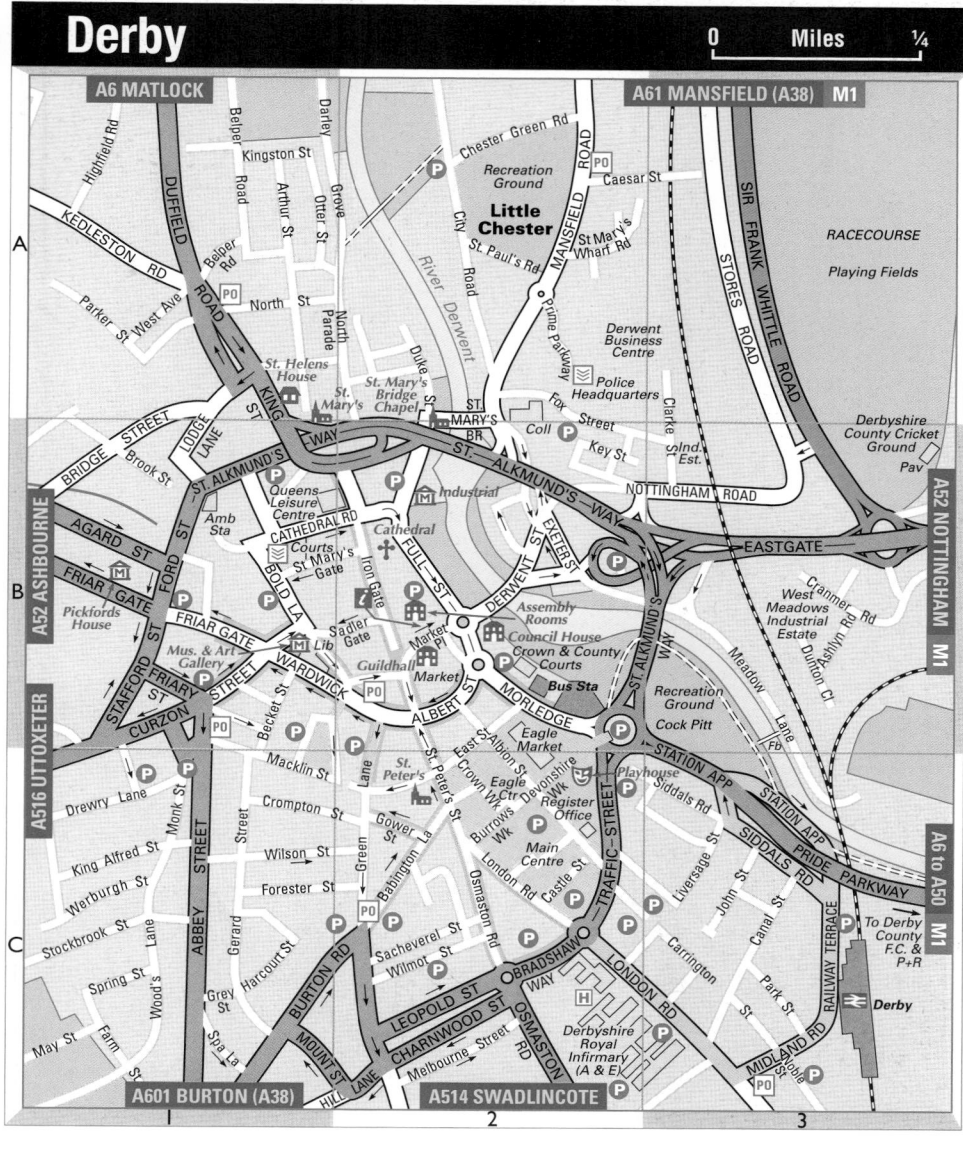

0 Miles ¼

A6 MATLOCK • A61 MANSFIELD (A38) M1

Coventry

Abbots La. A1
Albany Rd B1
Alma St. B3
Art Faculty B3
Asthill Grove C2
Bablake School A1
Barras La A1
Barrs Hill School. . . . A1
Belgrade ☺ B2
Bishop Burges St B2
Bond's Hospital ⌂ . . . B1
Broadgate B2
Broadway C1
Bus Station A3
Butts Radial B1
Canal Basin ✦ A2
Canterbury St A3
Cathedral † B3
Chester St A1
Cheylesmore Manor
  House ⌂ B2
Christ Church
  Spire ✦ B2
City Walls
  & Gates ✦ A2
Coach Park A3
Corporation St B2
Council House B2
Coundon Rd A1
Coventry & Warwickshire
  Hospital (A&E) Ⓗ . . A2
Coventry Station ⇌ . C2
Coventry Transport
  Museum ⌂ A2
Cox St A3
Croft Rd B1

Deasy Rd C3
Earl St. B2
Eaton Rd C2
Fairfax St B3
Foleshill Rd A2
Ford's Hospital ⌂ . . . B2
Fowler Rd A1
Friars Rd C2
Gordon St. C1
Gosford St B3
Greyfriars Green B2
Greyfriars Rd B2
Gulson Rd B3
Hales St A2
Harnall Lane East . . . A3
Harnall Lane West . . . A2
Herbert Art Gallery &
  Museum ⌂ B3
Hertford St B2
Hewitt Ave A1
High St B2
Hill St B1
Holy Trinity ♠ B2
Holyhead Rd ♠ A1
Howard St A3
Huntingdon Rd C1
Information Ctr ℹ . . . B2
Jordan Well B3
King Henry VIII
  School C1
Lady Godiva
  Statue ✦ B2
Lamb St A2
Leicester Row A2
Library B2
Little Park St B2
London Rd C3
Lower Ford St B3

Magistrates & Crown
  Courts B2
Manor House Drive . . B2
Manor Rd C2
Market B2
Martyr's Memorial ✦ . C2
Meadow St B1
Meriden St A1
Michaelmas Rd C2
Middleborough Rd . . . A1
Mile La C3
Millennium Place A2
Much Park St B3
Naul's Mill Park. A1
New Union B2
Park Rd C2
Parkside C3
Police HQ ▣ B3
Post Office ℙ B2
Primrose Hill St A3
Priory Gardens &
  Visitor Centre B2
Priory St. B2
Puma Way C3
Quarryfield La. C3
Queen's Rd B1
Quinton Rd C2
Radford Rd A2
Raglan St A3
Retail Park C1
Ringway (Hill Cross). . A1
Ringway (Queens) . . . B1
Ringway (Rudge) B1
Ringway (St Johns) . . B3
Ringway
  (St Nicholas). A2
Ringway
  (St Patricks) C2

Ringway (Swanswell) . A2
Ringway (Whitefriars). B3
St John St B2
St John
  The Baptist ♠ B2
St Nicholas St A2
Skydome B1
Spencer Ave C1
Spencer Park C1
Spencer Rd C1
Spon St B1
Sports Centre B3
Stoney Rd. C2
Stoney Stanton Rd. . . A3
Swanswell Pool A3
Swanswell St A3
Sydney Stringer
  School A3
Technical College . . . B1
Technology Park C3
The Precinct B2
Theatre ☺ B1
Thomas
  Landsdail St C2
Tomson Ave A1
Top Green. C1
Toy Museum ⌂ B3
Trinity St B2
University B3
Upper Hill St A1
Upper Well St A2
Victoria St. A3
Vine St A3
Warwick Rd C2
Waveley Rd B1
Westminster Rd C1
White St A3
Windsor St B1

Derby

Abbey St C1
Agard St B1
Albert St B2
Albion St. B2
Ambulance Station. . . B1
Arthur St A1
Ashlyn Rd A3
Assembly Rooms ⌂ . . B2
Babington La C2
Becket St B1
Belper Rd A1
Bold La. B1
Bradshaw Way C2
Bridge St B1
Brook St B1
Burrows Walk C2
Burton Rd C1
Bus Station B2
Caesar St A2
Canal St C3
Carrington St C3
Castle St C2
Cathedral † B2
Cathedral Rd B1
Charnwood St C2
Chester Green Rd . . . A2
City Rd A2
Clarke St A3
Cock Pitt. B3
Council House ⌂ B2
Cranmer Rd B3
Crompton St. C1
Crown & County
  Courts B2
Crown Walk C2
Curzon St B1

Darley Grove. A1
Derby ⇌ C3
Derbyshire County
  Cricket Ground. . . . B3
Derbyshire Royal
  Infirmary (A&E) Ⓗ . . C2
Derwent Business
  Centre A2
Derwent St B2
Devonshire Walk. . . . C2
Drewry La. C1
Duffield Rd A1
Duke St A2
Dunton Cl B3
Eagle Market B2
Eastgate B3
East St B2
Exeter St B2
Farm St C1
Ford St B1
Forester St C1
Fox St A2
Friar Gate B1
Friary St B1
Full St B2
Gerard St C1
Gower St C2
Green La. C2
Grey St C1
Guildhall ⌂ B2
Harcourt St C1
Highfield Rd A1
Hill La C1
Industrial ⌂ B2
Information Ctr ℹ . . . B2
Iron Gate B2
John St C3
Kedleston Rd A1

Key St B2
King Alfred St C1
King St A1
Kingston St A1
Leopold St C2
Library B1
Liversage St C3
Lodge La B1
London Rd C2
Macklin St C1
Main Centre C2
Mansfield Rd A2
Market B2
Market Pl B2
May St C1
Meadow La B3
Melbourne St C2
Midland Rd C3
Monk St C1
Morledge B2
Mount St C1
Museum & Art
  Gallery ⌂ B1
Noble St C3
North Parade A1
North St A1
Nottingham Rd B3
Osmaston Rd C2
Otter St. A1
Park St C3
Parker St A1
Pickfords House ⌂ . . B1
Playhouse ☺ C2
Police HQ ▣ A2
Police Station B1
Post Office ℙ
  . . . A1/A2/B1/B2/C2/C3
Pride Parkway C3

Prime Parkway A2
Queens Leisure
  Centre B1
Racecourse A3
Railway Terr C3
Register Office C2
Sacheverel St C2
Sadler Gate B1
St Alkmund's
  Way B1/B2
St Helens House ✦ . . A1
St Mary's ♠ A2
St Mary's Bridge. . . . A2
St Mary's Bridge
  Chapel ♠ A2
St Mary's Gate B1
St Paul's Rd A2
St Peter's ♠ C2
St Peter's St C2
Siddals Rd C3
Sir Frank Whittle Rd . . A3
Spa La C1
Spring St C1
Stafford St B1
Station Approach C3
Stockbrook St C1
Stores Rd A3
Traffic St C2
Wardwick B1
Werburgh St C1
West Ave A1
West Meadows
  Industrial Est B3
Wharf Rd A2
Wilmot St C2
Wilson St C1
Wood's La. C1

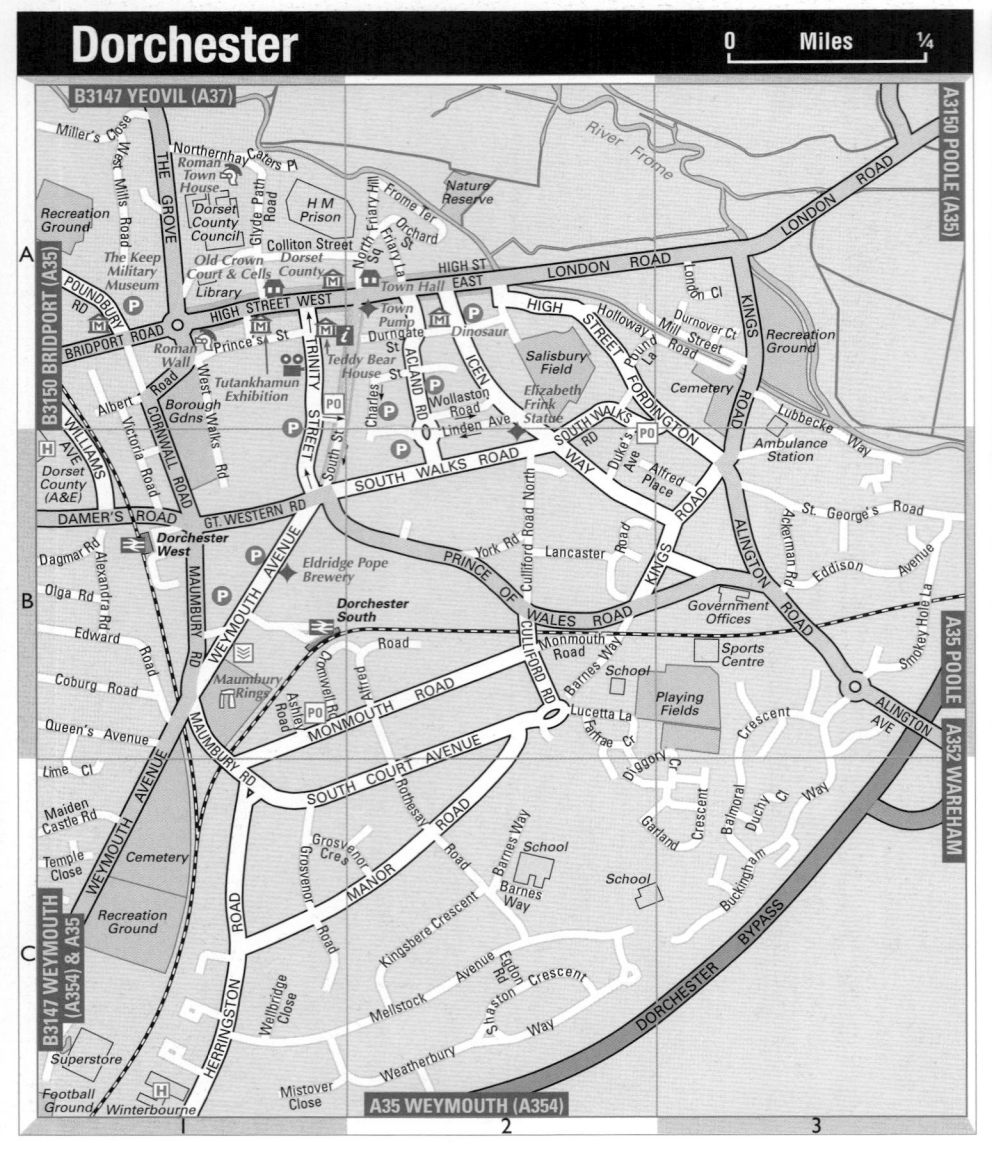

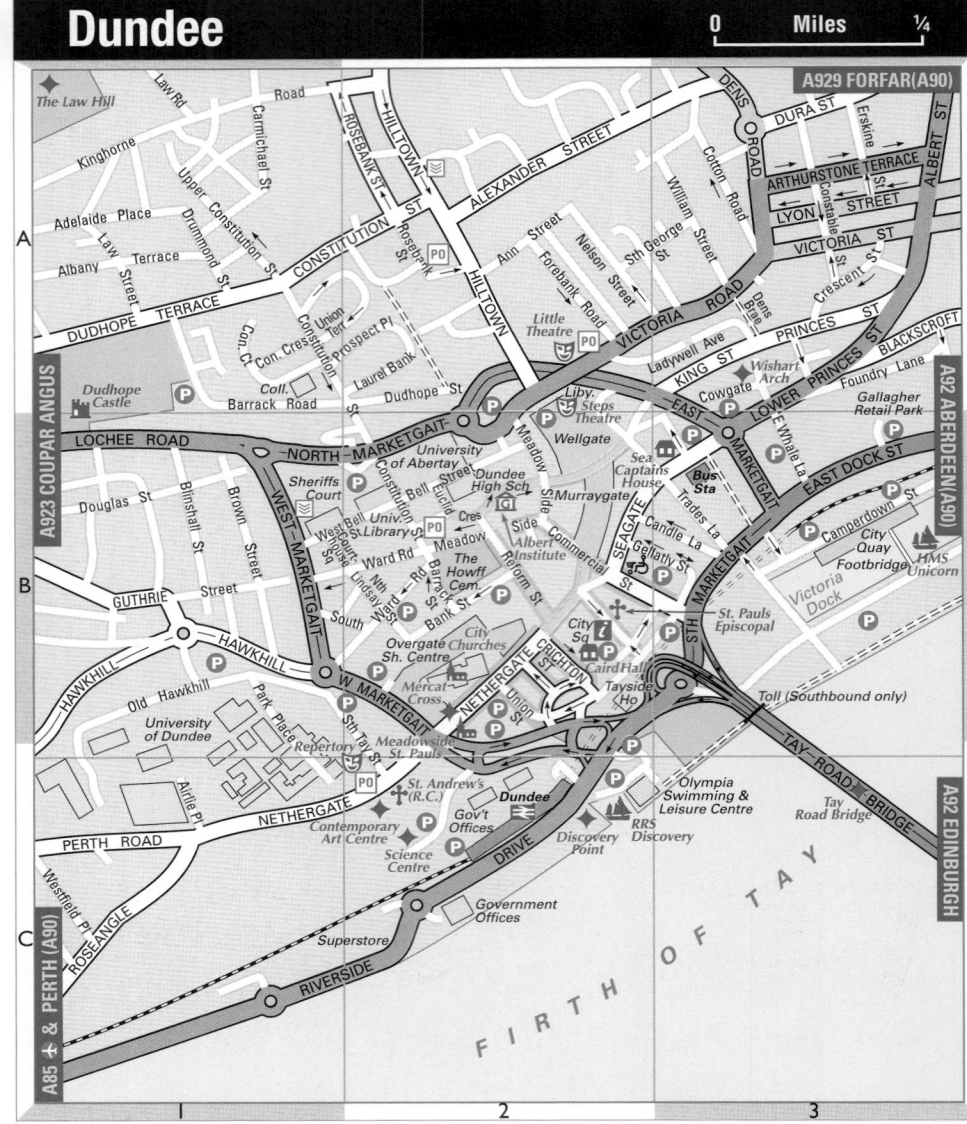

Dorchester

Ackerman Rd B3	Dorset County	Keep Military	Roman Town
Acland Rd A2	Council Offices A1	Museum, The 🏛 . . . A1	House 🏛 A1
Albert Rd A1	Dorset County	Kings Rd A3/B3	Roman Wall 🏛 A1
Alexandra Rd B1	(A+E) 🏥 B1	Kingsbere Cres C2	Rothesay Rd C2
Alfred Place B3	Dorset County	Lancaster Rd B2	St George's Rd B3
Alfred Rd B2	Museum 🏛 A1	Library A1	Salisbury Field A2
Alington Ave B3	Duchy Close C3	Lime Cl B1	Shaston Cres C2
Alington Rd B3	Duke's Ave B2	Linden Ave B2	Smokey Hole La B3
Ambulance Station . . B3	Durngate St A2	London Cl A3	South Court Ave C1
Ashley Rd B1	Durnover Court A3	London Rd A3	South St B1
Balmoral Cres C3	Eddison Ave B3	Lubbecke Way A3	South Walks Rd B2
Barnes Way B2/C2	Edward Rd B1	Lucetta La B2	Teddy Bear
Borough Gdns A1	Egdon Rd C2	Maiden Castle Rd . . . C1	House 🏛 A1
Bridport Rd A1	Eldridge Pope	Manor Rd C2	Temple Cl C1
Buckingham Way C3	Brewery ✦ B1	Maumbury Rd B1	The Grove A1
Caters Place A1	Elizabeth Frink	Maumbury Rings 🏛 . . B1	Town Hall 🏛 A2
Charles St A2	Statue ✦ B2	Mellstock Ave C2	Town Pump ✦ A2
Coburg Rd B1	Farfrae Cres B2	Mill St A3	Trinity St A1
Colliton St A2	Friary Hill A2	Miller's Cl A1	Tutankhamun
Cornwall Rd A1	Friary Lane A2	Mistover Cl C1	Exhibition 🏛 A1
Cromwell Rd B1	Frome Terr A2	Monmouth Rd B1	Victoria Rd B1
Culliford Rd B2	Garland Cres C3	North Sq A2	Weatherbury Way . . . C2
Culliford Rd North . . . B2	Glyde Path Rd A1	Northernhay A1	Wellbridge Cl C1
Dagmar Rd B1	Grosvenor Cres C1	Old Crown Court	West Mills Rd A1
Damer's Rd B1	Grosvenor Rd C1	& Cells 🏛 A1	West Walks Rd A1
Diggory Cres B2	H M Prison A1	Olga Rd B1	Weymouth Ave C1
Dinosaur Museum 🏛 . A2	Herrington Rd C1	Orchard St A2	Williams Ave B1
Dorchester Bypass . . . C3	High St East A2	Police Station 🔲 B1	Winterbourne
Dorchester South	High Street	Post Office ▣ . . . A1/B1/B2	Hospital 🏥 C1
Station ≠ B1	Fordington A2	Pound Lane A1	Wollaston Rd A2
Dorchester West	High Street West A1	Poundbury Rd A1	York Rd B2
Station ≠ B1	Holloway Rd A1	Prince of Wales Rd . . B2	
	Icen Way A2	Prince's St A1	
		Queen's Ave B1	

Dundee

Adelaide Pl A1	Courthouse Sq B1	Laurel Bank A2	RRS Discovery ⚓ . . . C2
Airlie Pl C1	Cowgate A3	Law Hill, The ✦ A1	St Andrew's ✝ C2
Albany Terr A1	Crescent St A3	Law Rd A1	St Pauls
Albert Institute 🏛 . . . B2	Crichton St B2	Law St A1	Episcopal ✝ B3
Albert St A3	Dens Brae A3	Library A2	Science Centre ✦ . . . C2
Alexander St B1	Dens Rd A3	Little Theatre 🎭 A2	Sea Captains
Ann St A2	Discovery Point ✦ . . C2	Lochee Rd B1	House 🏛 B3
Arthurstone Terr A3	Douglas St B1	Lower Princes St A3	Sheriffs Court B1
Bank St B2	Drummond St A1	Lyon St A3	South Ward Rd B2
Barrack Rd A1	Dudhope Castle 🏛 . . A1	Meadow Side B2	South George St A2
Barrack St B2	Dudhope St A2	Meadowside St	South Marketgait . . . B3
Bell St B2	Dudhope Terr A1	Pauls 🏛 B2	South Tay St B2
Blackscroft A3	Dundee ≠ C2	Mercat Cross ✦ B2	Steps 🎭 A2
Blinshall St B1	Dundee High School . B2	Murraygate B2	Tay Road Bridge ✦ . . C3
Brown St B1	Dura St A3	Nelson St A2	Tayside House B2
Bus Station B3	East Dock St B3	Nethergate B2/C1	Trades La B3
Caird Hall B2	East Whale La B3	North Marketgait . . . B2	Union St B2
Camperdown St B3	East Marketgait B3	North Lindsay St B2	Union Terr A1
Candle La B3	Erskine St A3	Old Hawkhill B1	University Library B1
Carmichael St A1	Euclid Cr B2	Olympia Swimming	University of Abertay . B2
Carnegie St B1	Forebank Rd A2	& Leisure Centre . . . C3	University of Dundee . B1
City Churches 🏛 B2	Foundry La A3	Overgate Shopping	Upper
City Quay B3	Gallagher Retail Park . B3	Centre B2	Constitution St A1
City Sq B2	Gellatly St B3	Park Pl B1	Victoria Rd A2
Commercial St B2	Government Offices . . C2	Perth Rd C1	Victoria St A3
Constable St A3	Guthrie St B1	Police Station 🔲 . . A2/B1	West Marketgait . . B1/B2
Constitution Ct A1	Hawkhill B1	Post Office ▣ . . A2/B2/C2	West Bell St B1
Constitution Cres A1	Hilltown A2	Princes St A3	Westfield Pl C1
Constitution St . . . A1/B2	Howff Cemetery, The . B2	Prospect Pl A2	William St A3
Contemporary	Information Ctr 🅾 B2	Reform St B2	Wishart Arch ✦ A3
Art Centre ✦ C2	King St A3	Repertory 🎭 C1	
Cotton Rd A3	Kinghorne Rd A1	Riverside Dr C2	
	Ladywell Ave A3	Roseangle C1	
		Rosebank St A2	

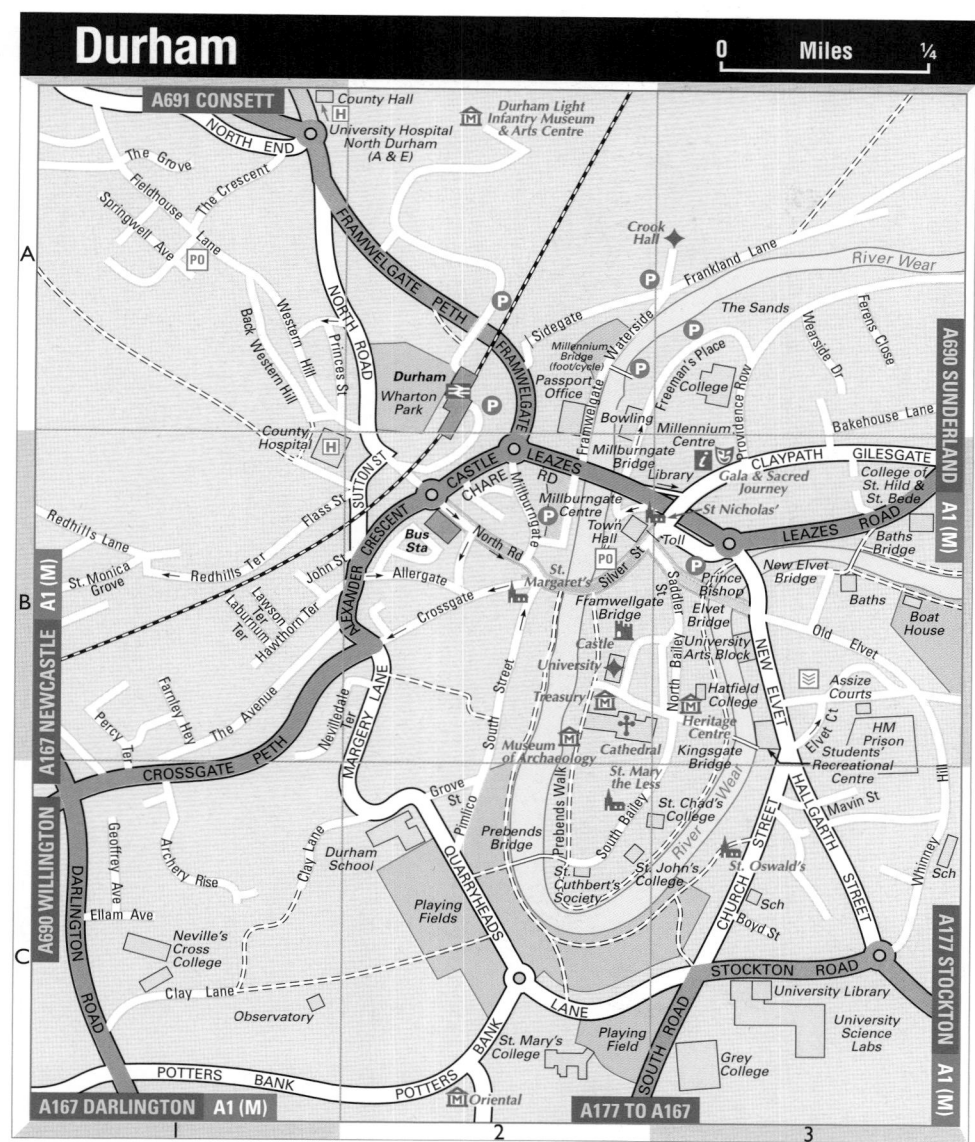

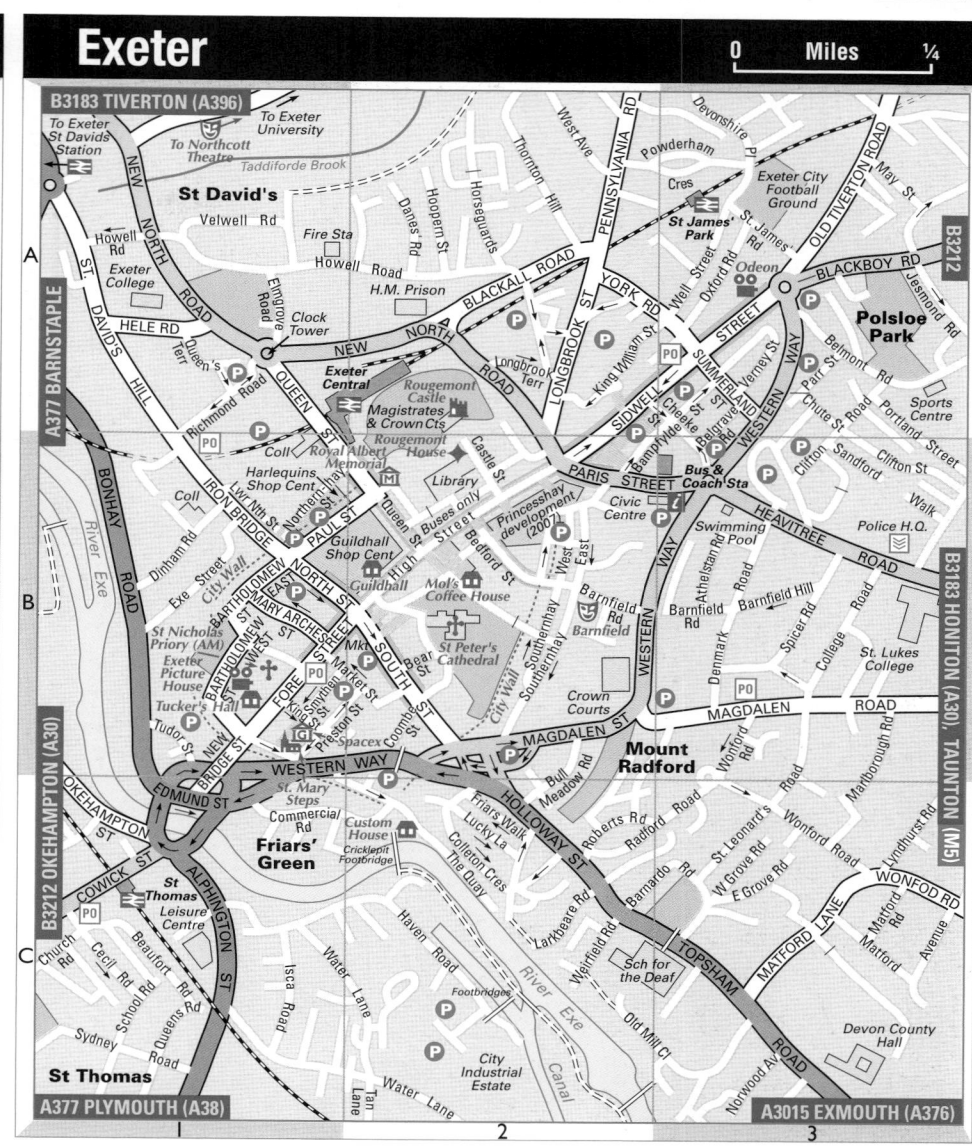

Durham

Exeter

Edinburgh

0   Miles   ¼

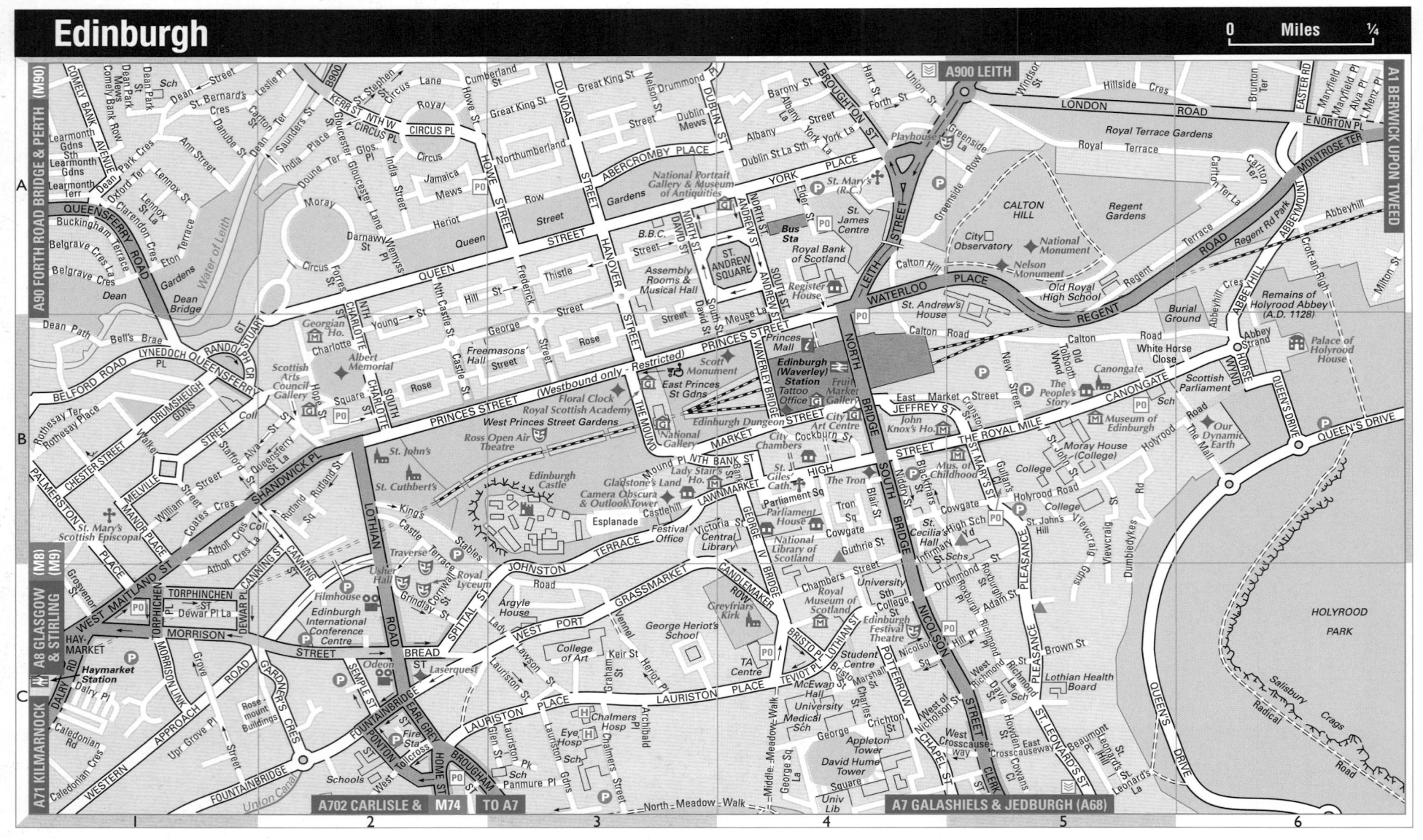

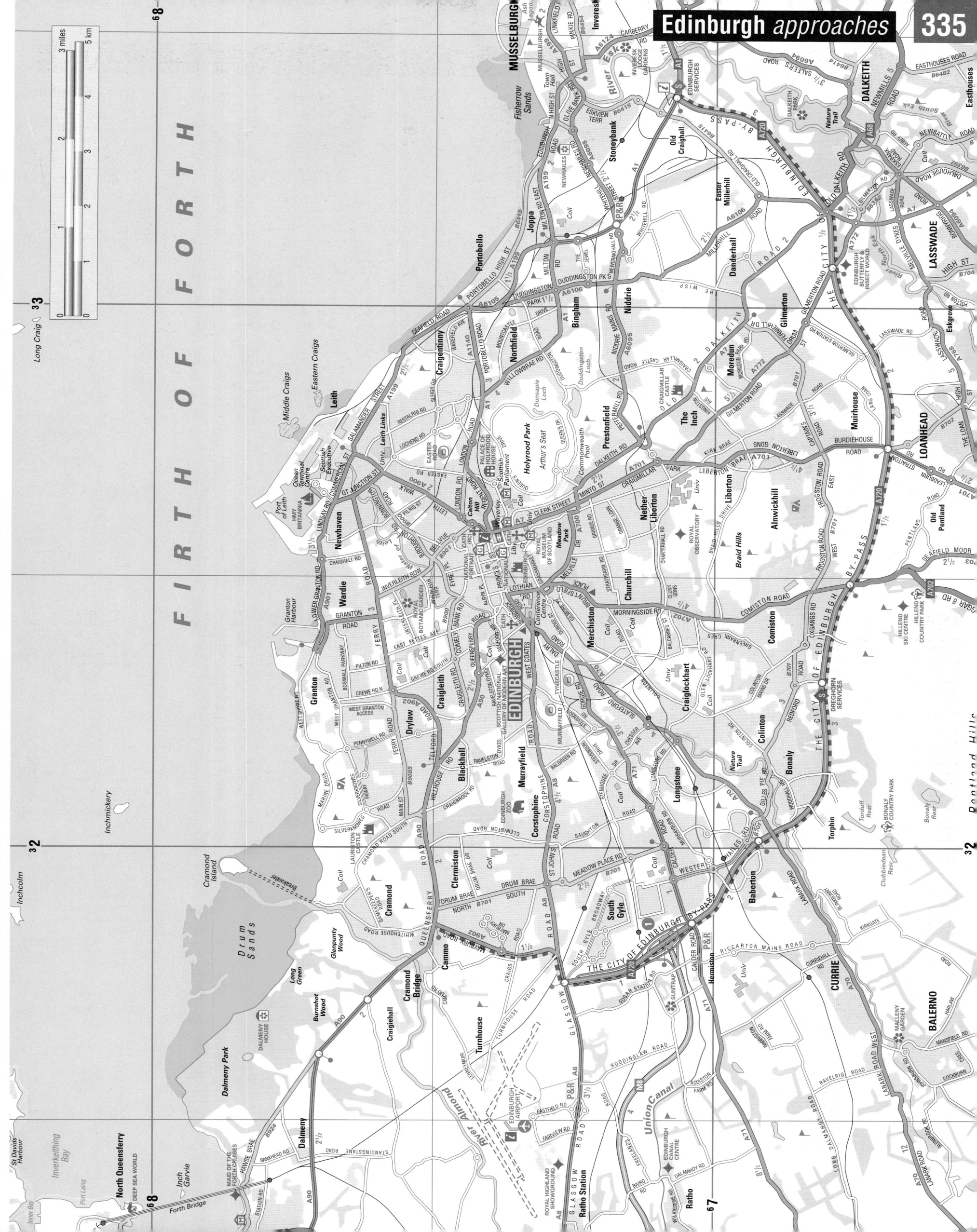

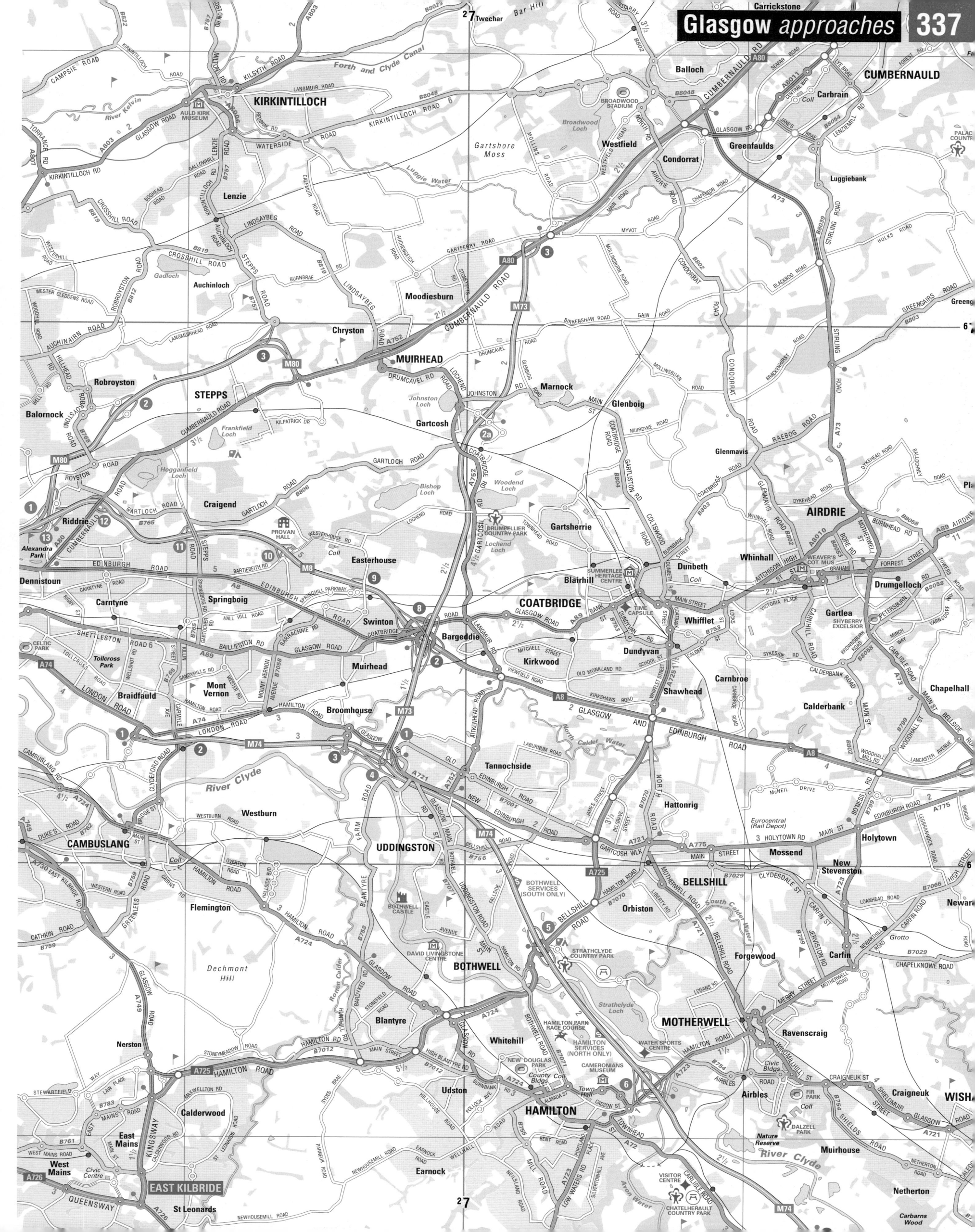

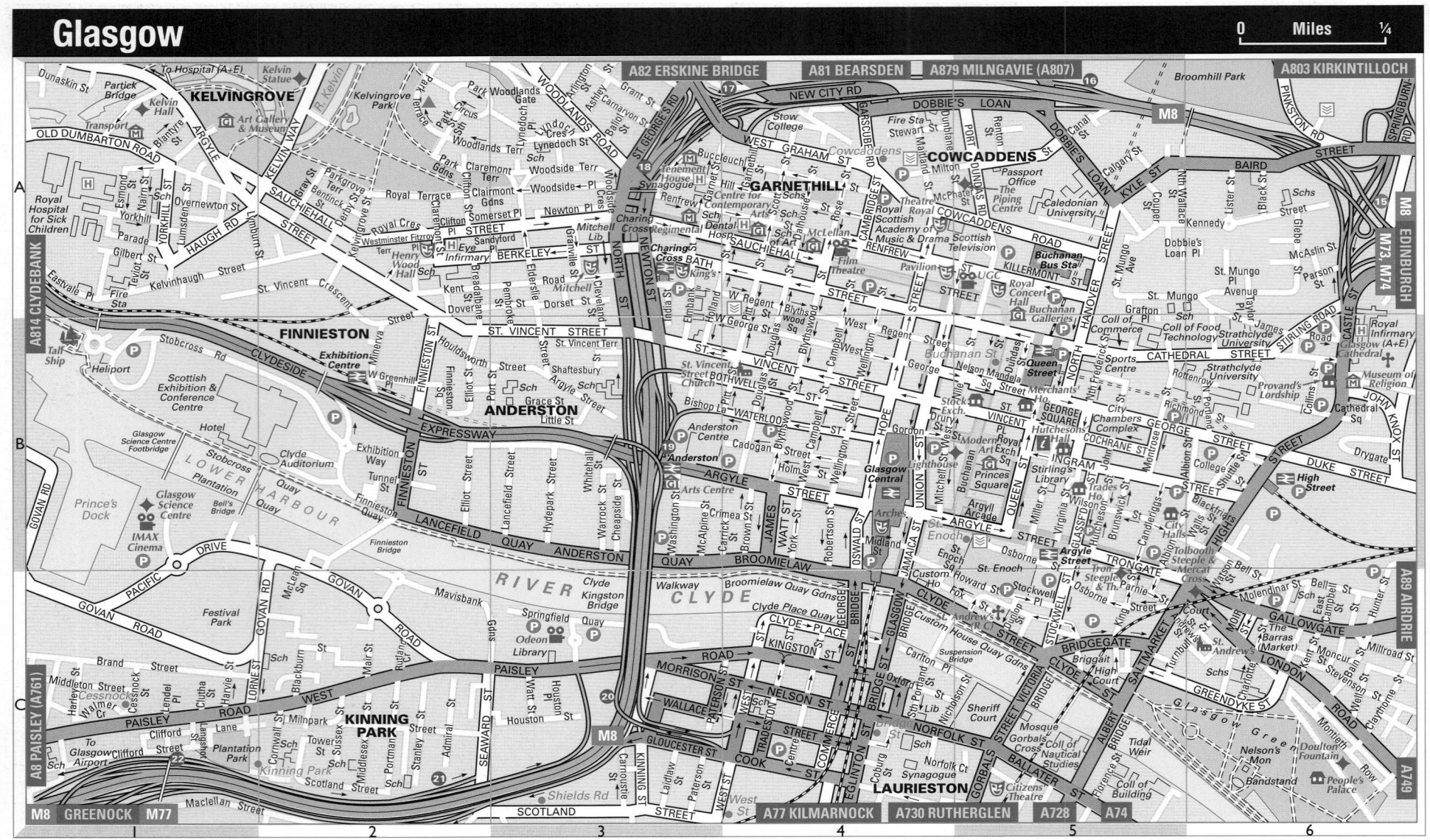

Glasgow

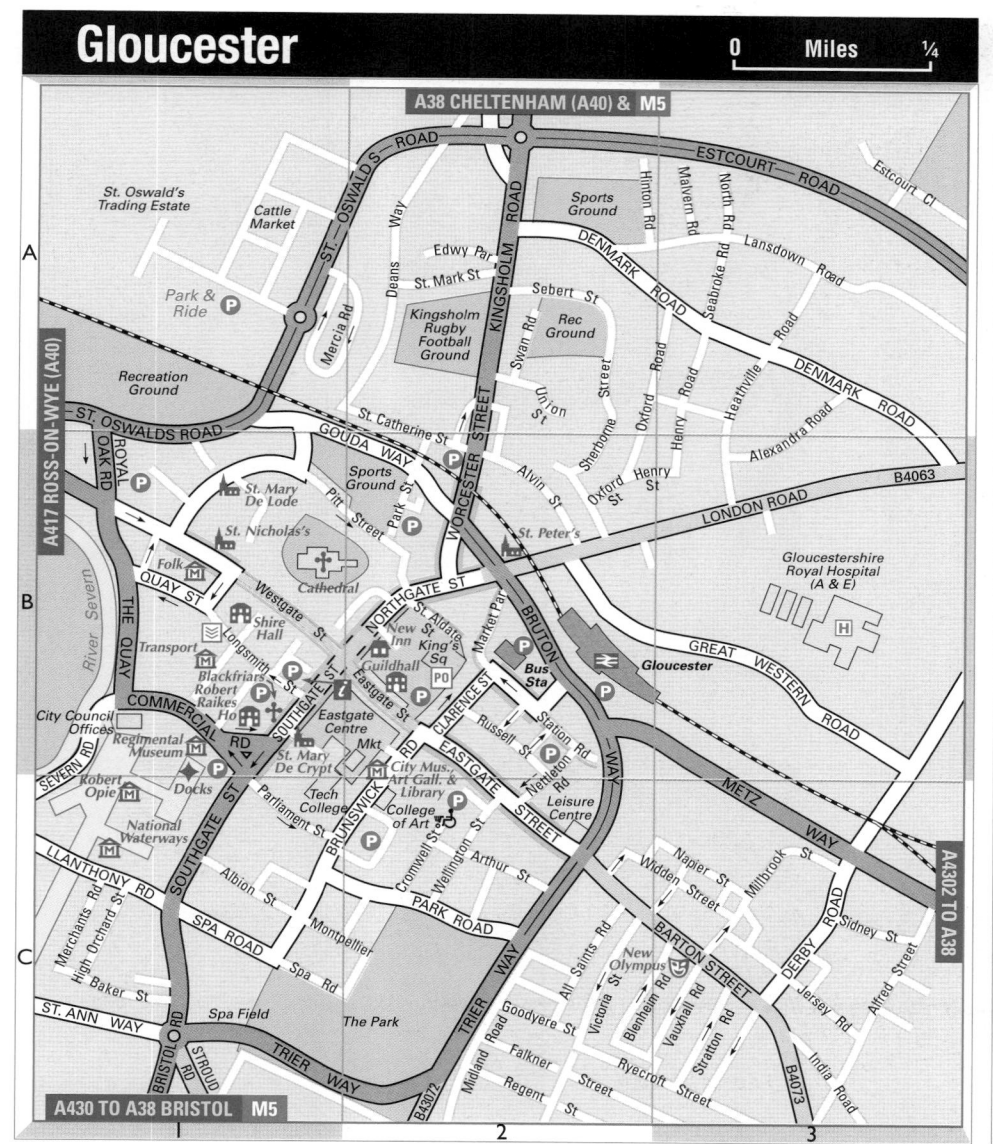

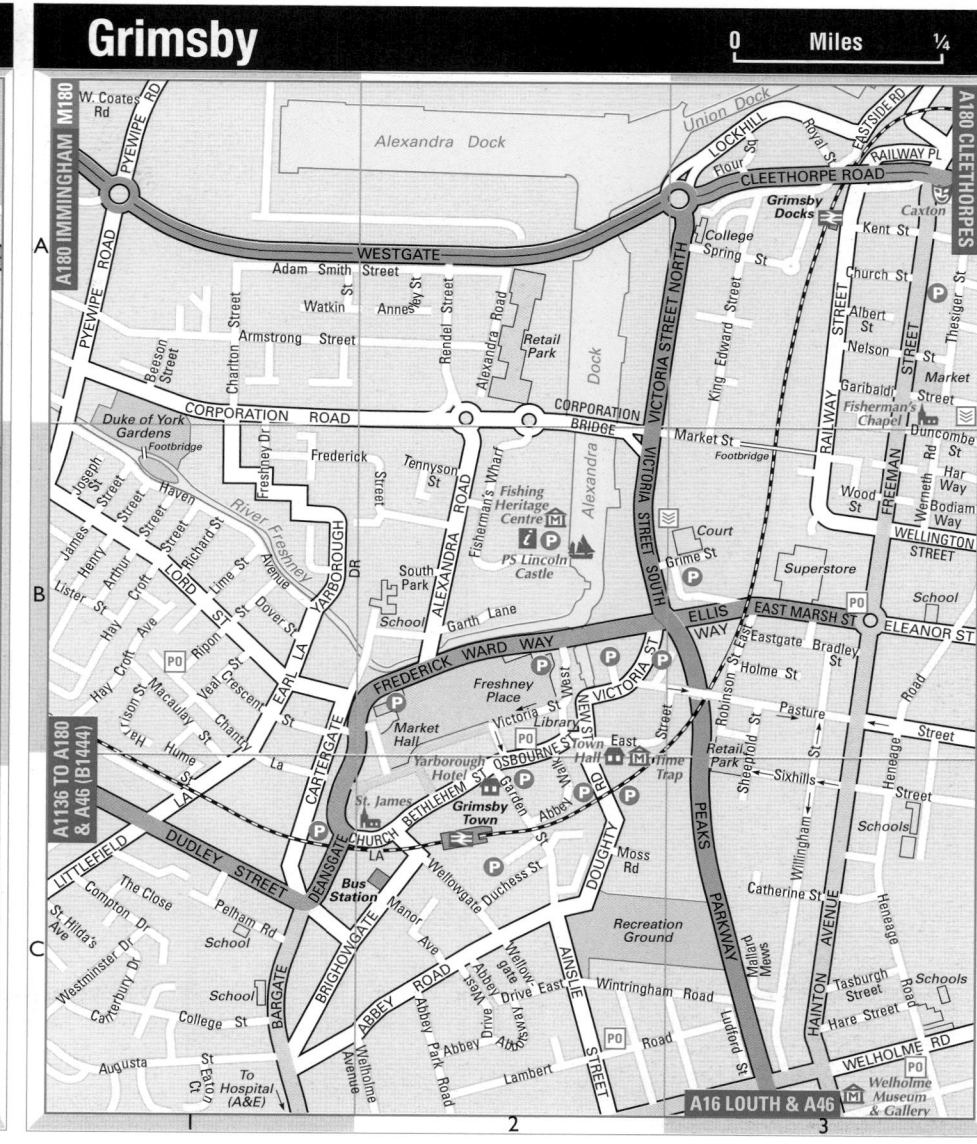

Gloucester

Albion St. C1
Alexandra Rd B3
Alfred St C3
All Saints Rd. C2
Alvin St B2
Arthur St C2
Baker St C1
Barton St B2
Blackfriars † B1
Blenheim Rd C2
Bristol Rd C1
Brunswick Rd C2
Bruton Way. B2
Bus Station. B2
Cattle Market A1
City Council Offices . B1
City Mus., Art Gall. &
   Library 🏛 B2
Clarence St. B2
College of Art B2
Commercial Rd B1
Cromwell St C2
Deans Way. A2
Denmark Rd A3
Derby Rd C3
Docks ✦. C1
Eastgate Centre B2
Eastgate St. B2
Edwy Pde A2
Estcourt Cl A3
Estcourt Rd A3
Falkner St C2

Folk Museum 🏛 B1
Gloucester
   Cathedral † B1
Gloucester
   Station ≥ B2
Gloucestershire Royal
   Hospital (A & E) 🇭 . B3
Nettleton Rd C2
New Inn 🏛 B2
New Olympus 🎭 C3
North Rd. A3
Northgate St. B2
Oxford Rd A2
Oxford St B2
Park & Ride
   Gloucester A1
Park Rd C2
Park St B2
Parliament St C1
Pitt St B1
Police Station 🏛 B1
Post Office 🄿 B2
Quay St B1
Recreation Gd . . . A1/A2
Regent St C2
Regimental 🏛 B1
Robert Opie 🏛 C1
Robert Raikes
   House 🏛 B1
Royal Oak Rd B1
Russell St B2
Ryecroft St C2
St Aldate St B2
St Ann Way C1
St Catherine St A2

Millbrook St C3
Market B2
Montpellier C1
Napier St C3
National
   Waterways 🏛 C1
St Mark St A2
St Mary De Crypt 🏛 . B1
St Mary De Lode 🏛 . B1
St Nicholas's 🏛 B1
St Oswald's Rd A1
St Oswald's Trading
   Estate A1
Seabroke Rd A3
Sebert St A2
Severn Rd C1
Sherborne St B2
Shire Hall 🏛 B1
Sidney St C3
Southgate St B1/C1
Spa Field C1
Spa Rd C1
Sports Ground . . . A2/B2
Station Rd B2
Stratton Rd C3
Stroud Rd C1
Swan Rd A2
Technical College . . . C1
The Park C2
The Quay B1
Transport 🏛 B1
Trier Way C1/C2
Union St A1
Vauxhall Rd C2
Victoria St C2
Wellington St B2
Westgate St B1
Widden St C2
Worcester St B2

Albion St C1
Alexandra Rd B3
Clarence St B2
High Orchard St C1
Hinton Rd A2
India Rd C3
Information Ctr 🄸 B1
Jersey Rd C3
King's Sq B2
Kingsholm Rd A2
Kingsholm Rugby
   Football Ground . . . A2
Lansdown Rd A3
Leisure Centre C2
Llanthony Rd C1
London Rd B3
Longsmith St B1
Malvern Rd A3
Market Pde B2
Merchants Rd C1
Mercia Rd A1
Metz Way C3
Midland Rd C2

Grimsby

Abbey Drive East C2
Abbey Drive West C2
Abbey Park Rd C2
Abbey Rd C2
Abbey Walk C2
Abbotsway C2
Adam Smith St . . . A1/A2
Ainslie St C2
Albert St B1
Alexandra Rd A2/B2
Annesley St A2
Armstrong St A1
Arthur St B1
Augusta St C1
Bargate C1
Beeson St A1
Bethlehem St C2
Bodiam Way B3
Bradley St B3
Brighowgate C1/C2
Bus Station. B2
Canterbury Dr C1
Cartergate B1/C1
Catherine St C3
Caxton 🎭 A3
Chantry La B1
Charlton La A1
Church La C2
Church St A3
Cleethorpe Rd A3
College A3
College St C1
Compton Dr C1
Corporation Bridge . . . A2
Corporation Rd A1
Court B3
Crescent St B1
Deansgate C1

Doughty Rd C2
Dover St B1
Duchess St B3
Dudley St C1
Duke of York
   Gardens B1
Duncombe St B3
Earl La B1
East Marsh St B3
East St B2
Eastgate B3
Eastside Rd A3
Eaton Ct C1
Eleanor St B1
Ellis Way B3
Fisherman's
   Chapel 🏛 A3
Fisherman's Wharf . . . B2
Fishing Heritage
   Centre 🏛 B2
Flour Sq A3
Frederick St B1
Frederick Ward Way . . B2
Freeman St A3/B3
Freshney Dr B1
Freshney Pl. B2
Garden St C2
Garibaldi St A3
Garth La B2
Grime St B3
Grimsby Docks
   Station ≥ A3
Grimsby Town
   Station ≥ C2
Hainton Ave C3
Har Way B3
Hare St C3
Harrison St B1
Haven Ave B1
Hay Croft Ave B1

Hay Croft St B1
Heneage Rd B3/C3
Henry St B1
Holme St B3
Hume St C1
Information Ctr 🄸 B2
James St B1
Joseph St B1
Kent St A3
King Edward St A3
Lambert Rd C2
Library B2
Lime St B1
Lister St B1
Littlefield La C1
Lockhill A3
Lord St B1
Ludford St C3
Macaulay St B1
Mallard Mews C3
Manor Ave C2
Market A3
Market Hall B2
Market St B3
Moss Rd C2
Nelson St A3
New St B2
Osbourne St B2
Pasture St B2
Peaks Parkway C3
Pelham Rd C1
Police Station 🏛 . . A3/B2
Post Office 🄿 . . . .
   . . . . . B1/B2/B3/C2/C3
PS Lincoln Castle ⚓ . B2
Pyewipe Rd A1
Railway Pl A3
Railway St A3
Rendel St B1
Retail Park A2

Retail Park B3
Richard St B1
Ripon St B3
Robinson St East B3
Royal St A3
St. Hilda's Ave C1
St. James 🏛 C2
Sheepfold St B3/C3
Sixhills St C3
South Park B2
Spring St A3
Superstore B3
Tasburgh St C3
Tennyson St B2
The Close C1
Thesiger St A3
Time Trap 🏛 C2
Town Hall 🏛 B2
Veal St B1
Victoria St North A2
Victoria St South B2
Victoria St West B2
W. Coates Rd A1
Watkin St A1
Welholme Ave C2
Welholme Museum &
   Gallery 🏛 C3
Welholme Rd C3
Wellington St B3
Wellowgate C2
Werneth Rd B3
Westgate A2
Westminster Dr C1
Willingham St C3
Wintringham Rd C2
Wood St B3
Yarborough Dr B1
Yarborough Hotel 🏨 . C2

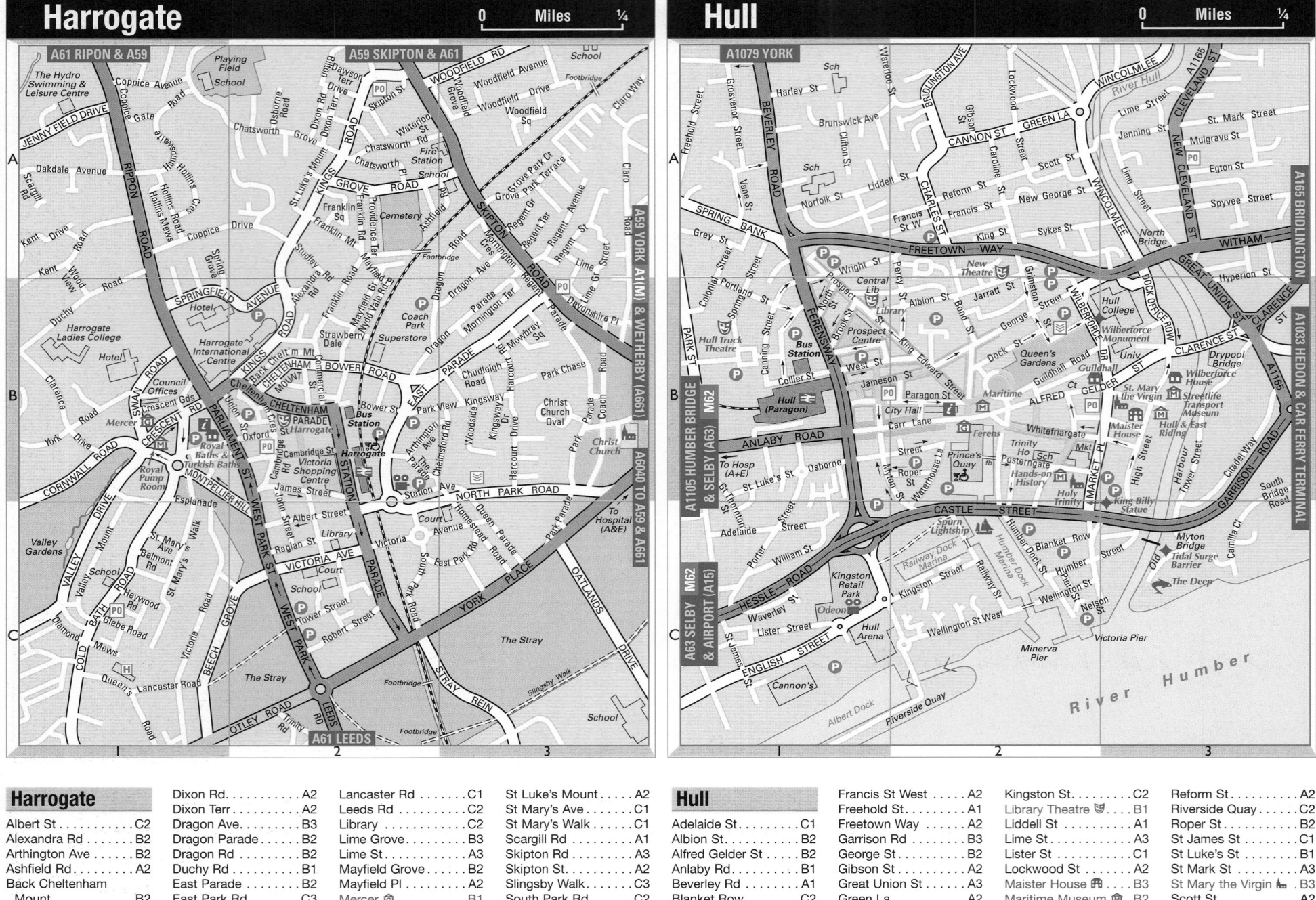

Harrogate

0   Miles   ¼

Hull

0   Miles   ¼

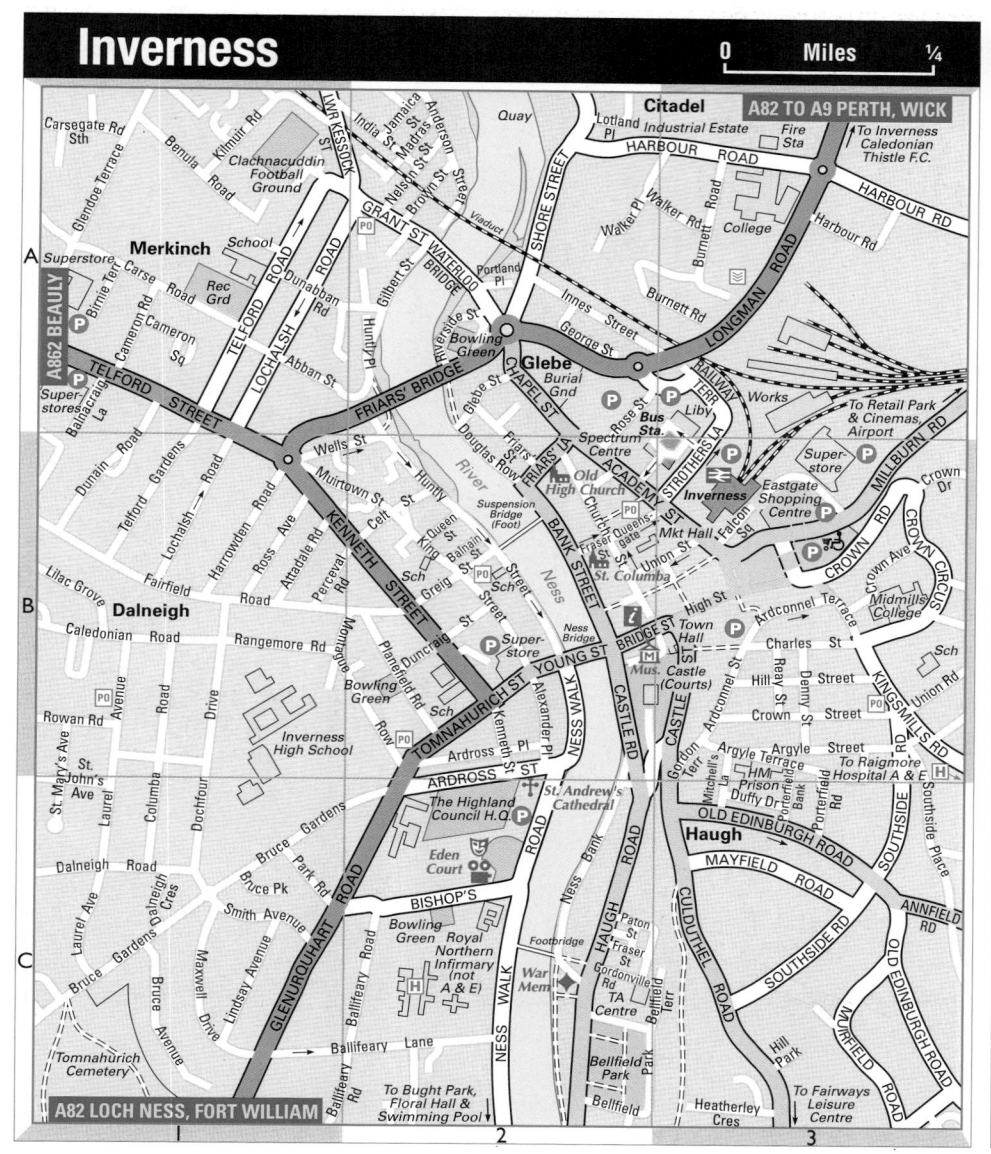
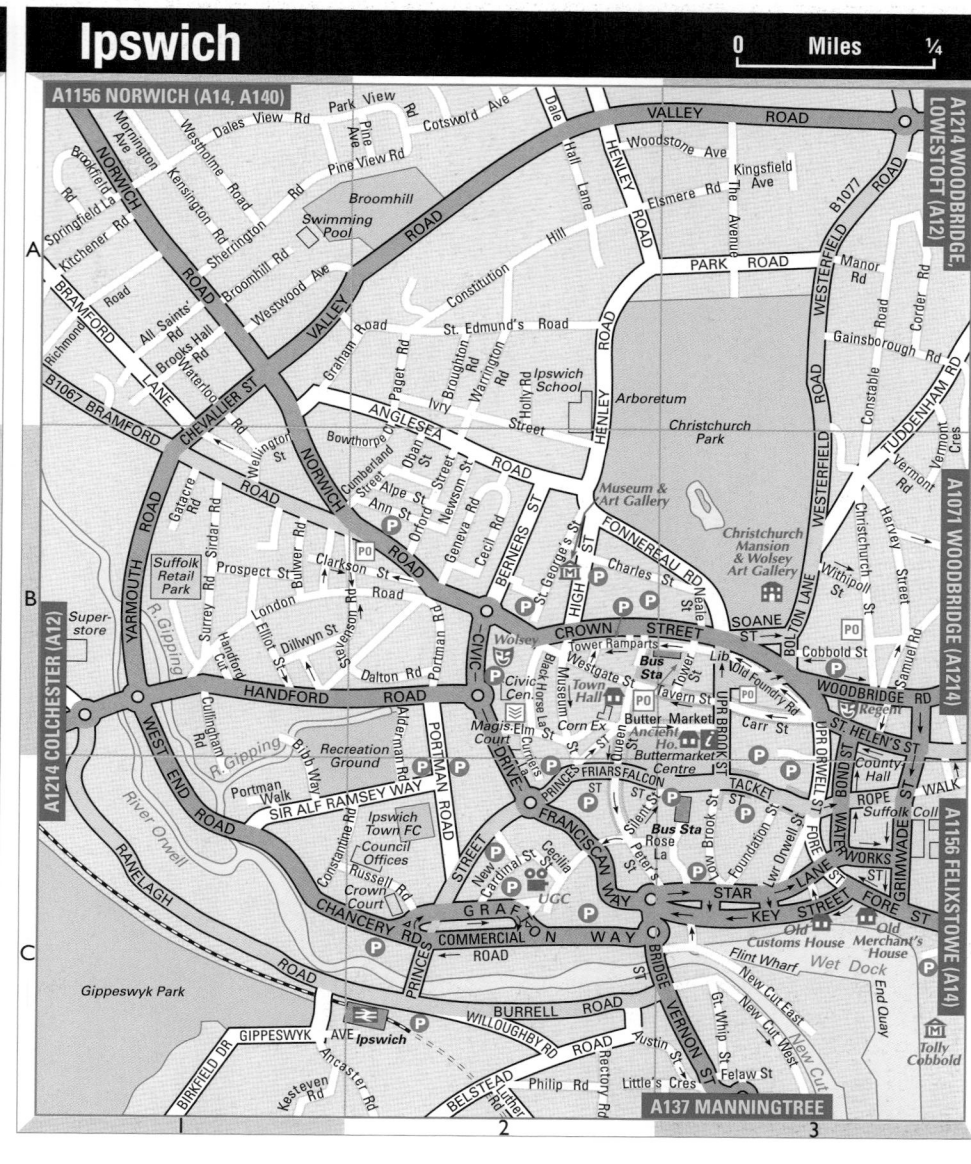

Inverness

Abban St A1
Academy St B2
Alexander Pl B2
Anderson St A2
Annfield Rd C3
Ardconnel St B3
Ardconnel Terr B3
Ardross Pl B2
Ardross St B2
Argyle St B3
Argyle Terr B3
Attadale Rd B1
Ballifeary La C2
Ballifeary Rd C1/C2
Balnacraig La A1
Balnain St B2
Bank St B2
Bellfield Park C2
Bellfield Terr C3
Benula Rd A1
Birnie Terr A1
Bishop's Rd C2
Bowling Green A2
Bowling Green B2
Bowling Green C2
Bridge St B2
Brown St A2
Bruce Ave C1
Bruce Gdns C1
Bruce Pk C1
Burial Ground A2
Burnett Rd A3
Bus Station B3
Caledonian Rd A1
Cameron Rd A1
Cameron Sq A1
Carse Rd A1
Carsegate Rd South . . A1
Castle (Courts) B3
Castle St B3
Castle St B3
Celt St B2
Chapel St A2
Charles St B3

Church St B2
Clachnacuddin Football
  Ground A1
College A3
Columba Rd B1/C1
Crown Ave B3
Crown Circus B3
Crown Dr B3
Crown Rd B3
Crown St B3
Culduthel Rd C3
Dalneigh Cres C1
Dalneigh Rd C1
Denny St B3
Dochfour Dr B1/C1
Douglas Row B2
Duffy Dr C3
Dunabban Rd A1
Dunain Rd B1
Duncraig St B2
Eastgate Shopping
  Centre B3
Eden Court C2
Fairfield Rd B1
Falcon Sq B3
Fire Station A3
Fraser St B2
Fraser St C2
Friars' Bridge A2
Friars' La B2
Friars' St A2
George St A2
Gilbert St A2
Glebe St A2
Glendoe Terr A1
Glenurquhart Rd C1
Gordon Terr B3
Gordonville Rd C2
Grant St A2
Greig St B2
H.M. Prison B3
Harbour Rd A2
Harrowden Rd B1
Haugh Rd C2
Heatherley Cres C3
High St B3

Highland Council
  H.Q., The C2
Hill Park C3
Hill St B3
Huntly Pl A2
Huntly St B2
India St A2
Industrial Estate A3
Information Ctr A3
Innes St A2
Inverness High
  School B1
Inverness B3
Jamaica St A2
Kenneth St B2
Kilmuir Rd A1
Kingsmills Rd B3
Laurel Ave B1/C1
Library A3
Lilac Gr B1
Lindsay Ave C1
Lochalsh Rd A1/B1
Longman Rd A3
Lotland Pl A2
Lower Kessock St . . . A1
Madras St A2
Market Hall B3
Maxwell Dr C1
Mayfield Rd C3
Midmills College B3
Millburn Rd B3
Mitchell's La C3
Montague Row B2
Muirfield Rd C3
Muirtown St B1
Museum B2
Nelson St A2
Ness Bank C2
Ness Bridge B2
Ness Walk B2/C2
Old Edinburgh Rd . . . C3
Old High Church B2
Park Rd C1
Paton St C2
Perceval Rd B1

Planefield Rd B2
Police Station A3
Porterfield Bank C3
Porterfield Rd C3
Portland Pl A2
Post Office
  . . . . . . A2/B1/B2/B3
Queen St B2
Queensgate B2
Railway Terr A3
Rangemore Rd B1
Reay St B3
Riverside St A2
Rose St A2
Ross Ave B1
Rowan Rd B1
Royal Northern
  Infirmary C2
St. Andrew's
  Cathedral C2
St. Columba B2
St. John's Ave C1
St. Mary's Ave C1
Shore St A2
Smith Ave C1
Southside Pl C3
Southside Rd C3
Spectrum Centre B2
Strothers La B2
TA Centre C2
Telford Gdns B1
Telford Rd A1
Telford St A1
Tomnahurich
  Cemetery C1
Tomnahurich St B2
Town Hall B3
Union Rd B3
Union St B3
Walker Pl A2
Walker Rd A2
War Memorial C2
Waterloo Bridge A2
Wells St B2
Young St B2

Ipswich

Alderman Rd B2
All Saints' Rd A1
Alpe St B2
Ancaster Rd C1
Ancient House B3
Anglesea Rd B2
Ann St B2
Austin St C2
Belstead Rd C2
Berners St B2
Bibb Way B1
Birkfield Dr B1
Black Horse La B2
Bolton La B3
Bond St C3
Bowthorpe Cl B2
Bramford La A1
Bramford Rd A1
Bridge St C2
Brookfield Rd A1
Brooks Hall Rd A1
Broomhill Rd A1
Broughton Rd A2
Bulwer Rd B1
Burrell Rd C2
Bus Station B2/C3
Butter Market B3
Butter Market Centre . B3
Carr St B3
Cecil Rd B2
Cecilia St C2
Chancery Rd C2
Charles St B2
Chevallier St A1
Christchurch Mansion
  & Wolsey Art
  Gallery B3
Christchurch Park . . . A3
Christchurch St B3
Civic Centre B2
Civic Dr B2
Clarkson St B1
Cobbold St B3
Commercial Rd C2
Constable Rd A3
Constantine Rd C1
Constitution Hill A2

Corder Rd A3
Corn Exchange B2
Cotswold Ave A2
Council Offices C2
County Hall B3
Crown Court B2
Crown St B2
Cullingham Rd B1
Cumberland St B2
Curriers La B2
Dale Hall La A2
Dales View Rd A1
Dalton Rd B2
Dillwyn St B1
Elliot St B2
Elm St B2
Elsmere Rd A3
End Quay C3
Falcon St B2
Felaw St C3
Flint Wharf C3
Fonnereau Rd B2
Fore St C3
Foundation St C3
Franciscan Way C2
Friars St C2
Gainsborough Rd . . . A3
Gatacre Rd B1
Geneva Rd B2
Gippeswyk Ave C1
Gippeswyk Park C1
Grafton Way C2
Graham Rd A1
Grimwade St C3
Great Whip St C3
Handford Cut B1
Handford Rd B1
Henley Rd A2
Hervey St B3
High St B2
Holly Rd A2
Information Ctr B3
Ipswich School A2
Ipswich Station C2
Ipswich Town FC
  (Portman Road) . . . C2
Ivry St A2
Kensington Rd A1
Kesteven Rd C1

Key St C3
Kingsfield Ave A3
Kitchener Rd A1
Little's Cr C2
London Rd B1
Low Brook St C3
Lower Orwell St C3
Luther Rd C2
Manor Rd A3
Mornington Ave A1
Museum & Art
  Gallery B2
Museum St B2
Neale St B3
New Cardinal St C2
New Cut East C3
New Cut West C3
Newson St B2
Norwich Rd A1/B1
Oban St B2
Old Customs
  House C3
Old Foundry Rd B3
Old Merchant's
  House C3
Orford St B2
Paget Rd A2
Park Rd A3
Park View Rd A2
Peter's St C2
Philip Rd C2
Pine Ave A3
Pine View Rd A2
Police Station B2
Portman Rd C2
Portman Walk C1
Post Office B2/B3
Princes St B2
Prospect St B1
Queen St B2
Ranelagh Rd C1
Rectory Rd C2
Regent Theatre B3
Richmond Rd A1
Rope Walk C3
Rose La C2
Russell Rd C2
St Edmund's Rd A2

St George's St B2
St Helen's St B3
Samuel Rd B3
Sherrington Rd A1
Silent St C2
Sir Alf Ramsey Way . . C1
Sirdar Rd B1
Soane St B3
Springfield La A1
Star La C3
Stevenson Rd B1
Suffolk College C3
Suffolk Retail Park . . . B1
Superstore B1
Surrey Rd B1
Swimming Pool A1
Tacket St C3
Tavern St B3
The Avenue A3
Tolly Cobbold
  Museum C3
Tower Ramparts B2
Tower St B3
Town Hall B2
Tuddenham Rd A3
UGC C2
Upper Brook St B3
Upper Orwell St B3
Valley Rd A2
Vermont Cr B3
Vermont Rd B3
Vernon St C2
Warrington Rd A2
Waterloo Rd A1
Waterworks St C3
Wellington St B1
West End Rd B1
Westerfield Rd A3
Westgate St B2
Westholme Rd A1
Westwood Ave A1
Willoughby Rd C2
Withipoll St B3
Wolsey Theatre B2
Woodbridge Rd B3
Woodstone Ave A3
Yarmouth Rd B1

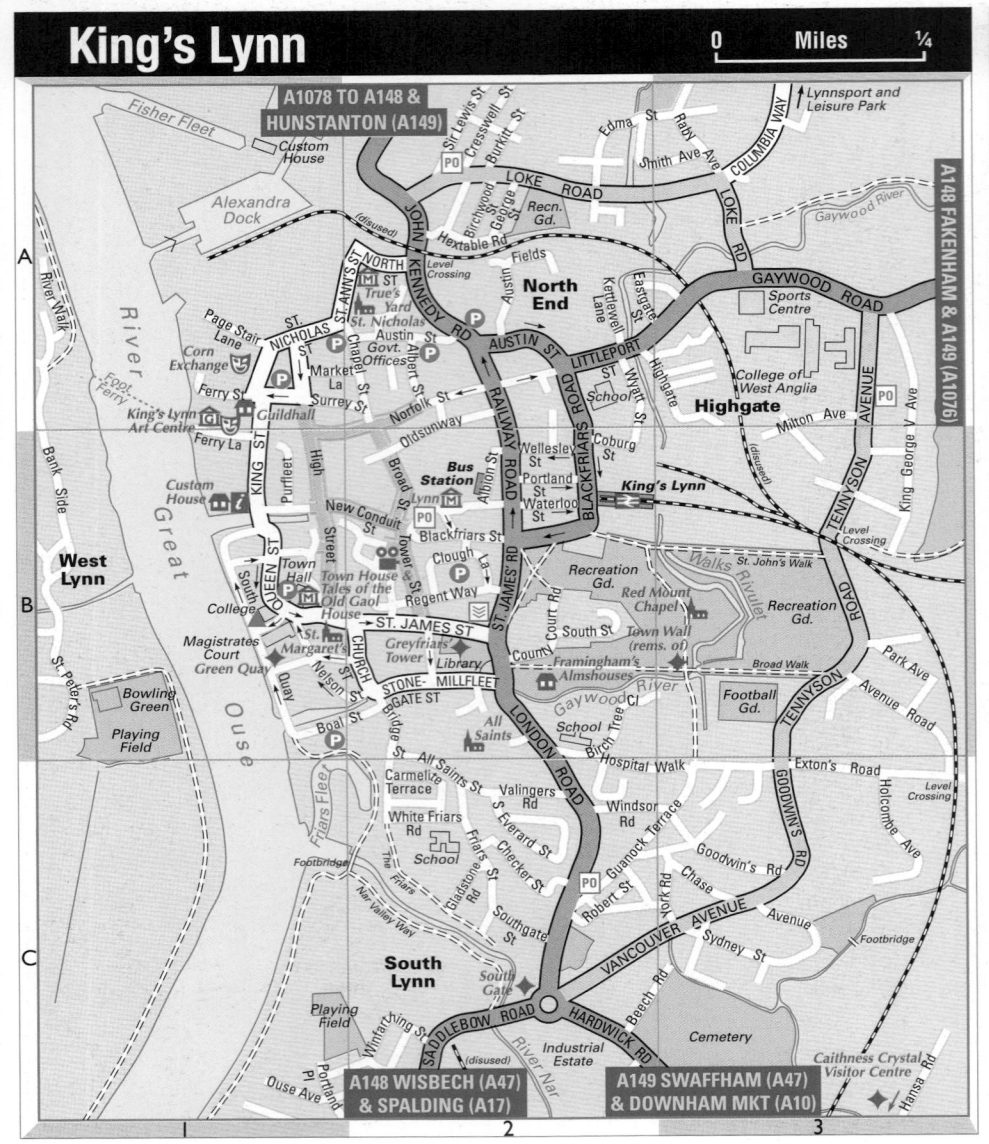

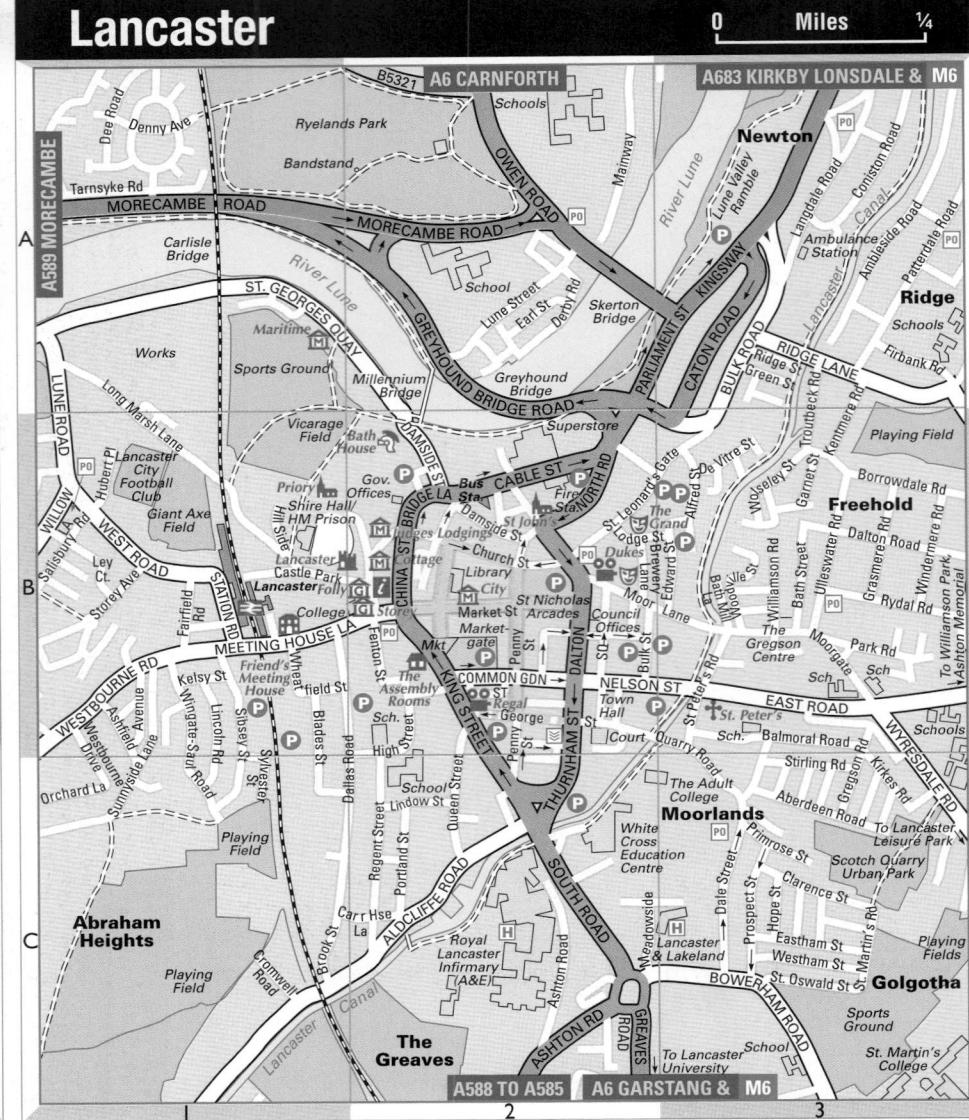

King's Lynn

Albert St	A2	Eastgate St	A2	Lynn Museum	B2
Albion St	B2	Edma St	A2	Majestic	B2
All Saints	B2	Exton's Rd	C2	Magistrates Court	B1
All Saints St	B2	Ferry La	B1	Market La	A1
Austin Fields	A2	Ferry St	A1	Millfleet	B2
Austin St	A2	Framingham's		Milton Ave	A3
Avenue Rd	B3	Almshouses	B2	Nar Valley Walk	C2
Bank Side	B1	Friars St	C2	Nelson St	B1
Beech Rd	C2	Gaywood Rd	A3	New Conduit St	B2
Birch Tree Cl	B2	George St	A2	Norfolk St	A2
Birchwood St	A2	Gladstone Rd	C2	North St	A2
Blackfriars Rd	B2	Goodwin's Rd	C2	Oldsunway	B2
Blackfriars St	B2	Green Quay	B1	Ouse Ave	C1
Boal St	B1	Greyfriars' Tower	B2	Page Stair Lane	A1
Bridge St	B2	Guanock Terr	C2	Park Ave	B3
Broad St	B2	Guildhall	A1	Police Station	B2
Broad Walk	B3	Hansa Rd	C3	Portland Pl	C1
Burkitt St	A2	Hardwick Rd	C2	Portland St	B2
Bus Station	B2	Hextable Rd	A2	Post Office	A3/B2/C2
Carmelite Terr	C2	High St	B1	Purfleet	B1
Chapel St	A2	Holcombe Ave	C3	Queen St	B1
Chase Ave	C3	Hospital Walk	C2	Raby Ave	A3
Checker St	C2	Information Ctr	B1	Railway Rd	A2
Church St	B2	John Kennedy Rd	A2	Red Mount	
Clough La	B2	Kettlewell Lane	A2	Chapel	B3
Coburg St	B2	King George V Ave	B3	Regent Way	B2
College of		King's Lynn Art		River Walk	A1
West Anglia	A3	Centre	A1	Robert St	C2
Columbia Way	A3	King's Lynn		Saddlebow Rd	C2
Corn Exchange	A1	Station	B2	St Ann's St	A1
County Court Rd	B2	King St	B1	St James' Rd	B2
Cresswell St	A2	Library	B2	St James St	B2
Custom House	A1	Littleport St	A2	St John's Walk	B3
		Loke Rd	A2	St Margaret's	B1
		London Rd	B2	St Nicholas	A2

St Nicholas St	A1	South Gate	C2
St Peter's Rd	B1	Southgate St	C2
S Everard St	C2	South Quay	B1
Sir Lewis St	A2	South St	B2
Smith Ave	A3	Stonegate St	B2
South Gate	C2	Surrey St	A1
		Sydney St	C3
		Tennyson Ave	B3
		Tennyson Rd	B3
		The Friars	C2
		Tower St	B2
		Town Hall	B1
		Town House & Tales	
		of The Old Gaol	
		House	B1
		Town Wall	
		(Remains)	B3
		True's Yard	
		Museum	A2
		Valingers Rd	C2
		Vancouver Ave	C2
		Waterloo St	B2
		Wellesley St	B2
		White Friars Rd	C2
		Windsor Rd	C2
		Winfarthing St	C2
		Wyatt St	C2
		York Rd	C3

Lancaster

Aberdeen Rd	C3	De Vitre St	B3
Adult College, The	C3	Dee Rd	A1
Aldcliffe Rd	C2	Denny Ave	A1
Alfred St	B2	Derby Rd	A2
Ambleside Rd	A3	Dukes	B2
Ambulance Sta	A3	Earl St	A1
Ashfield Ave	B1	East Rd	B3
Ashton Rd	C2	Eastham St	C3
Assembly Rooms,		Edward St	B3
The	B2	Fairfield Rd	B1
Balmoral Rd	B3	Fenton St	B2
Bath House	B2	Firbank Rd	A3
Bath Mill La	B3	Fire Station	B2
Bath St	B3	Folly Gallery	B2
Blades St	B1	Friend's Meeting	
Borrowdale Rd	A3	House	B1
Bowerham Rd	C3	Garnet St	B3
Brewery La	B2	George St	B2
Bridge La	B2	Giant Axe Field	B1
Brook St	C1	Gov. Offices	B2
Bulk Rd	A3	Grand, The	B2
Bulk St	B2	Grasmere Rd	B3
Bus Station	B2	Greaves Rd	C2
Cable St	B2	Green St	A3
Carlisle Bridge	A1	Gregson Centre, The	B3
Carr House La	C2	Gregson Rd	C2
Castle	B1	Greyhound Bridge	A2
Castle Park	B1	Greyhound	
Caton Rd	A3	Bridge Rd	A2
China St	B2	High St	B2
Church St	B2	Hill Side	B1
City Museum	B2	Hope St	C3
Clarence St	C3	Hubert Pl	B1
Common Gdn St	B2	Information Ctr	B2
Coniston Rd	A3	Judges	
Cottage Museum	B2	Lodgings	B2
Council Offices	B2	Kelsy St	B1
Court	B2	Kentmere Rd	B3
Cromwell Rd	C1	King St	B2
Dale St	C3	Kingsway	A3
Dallas Rd	B1/C1	Kirkes Rd	C3
Dalton Rd	B3	Lancaster	B1
Dalton Sq	B2	Lancaster &	
Damside St	B2	Lakeland	C2
		Lancaster City	
		Football Club	B1

Langdale Rd	A3	St. John's	B2
Ley Ct	B1	St. Nicholas Arcades	
Library	B2	Shopping Centre	B2
Lincoln Rd	C2	St. Peter's Rd	B3
Lindow St	C2	St. Georges Quay	A1
Lodge St	B2	St. Leonard's Gate	B2
Long Marsh La	B1	St. Martin's College	C3
Lune Rd	A2	St. Martin's Rd	C3
Lune St	A2	St. Oswald St	C3
Lune Valley Ramble	A3	St. Peter's	B3
Mainway	A2	Salisbury Rd	B1
Maritime Museum	A1	Scotch Quarry	
Market St	B2	Urban Park	C3
Marketgate Shopping		Shire Hall/HM Prison	B1
Centre	B2	Sibsey St	B1
Meadowside	C2	Skerton Bridge	A2
Meeting House La	B1	South Rd	C2
Millennium Bridge	A2	Station Rd	B1
Moor La	B2	Stirling Rd	C3
Moorgate	B2	Storey Ave	B1
Morecambe Rd	A1/A2	Storey Gallery	B2
Nelson St	B2	Sunnyside La	C1
North Rd	B2	Sylvester St	C1
Orchard La	C1	Tarnsyke Rd	A1
Owen Rd	A2	Thurnham St	C2
Park Rd	B2	Town Hall	B2
Parliament St	A3	Troutbeck Rd	B3
Patterdale Rd	A3	Ulleswater Rd	B3
Penny St	B2	Vicarage Field	B1
Police Station	B2	West Rd	B1
Portland St	C2	Westbourne Dr	C1
Post Office		Westbourne Rd	B1
A2/A3/B1/B2/B3/C3		Westham St	C3
Primrose St	C3	Wheatfield St	B1
Priory	B1	White Cross Education	
Prospect St	C3	Centre	C2
Quarry Rd	B3	Williamson Rd	B3
Queen St	C2	Willow La	B1
Regal	B2	Windermere Rd	B3
Regent St	C2	Wingate-Saul Rd	B1
Ridge La	A3	Wolseley St	B3
Ridge Rd	A3	Woodville St	B3
Royal Lancaster		Wyresdale Rd	C3
Infirmary (A&E)	C2		
Rydal Rd	B3		
Ryelands Park	A1		

Leeds

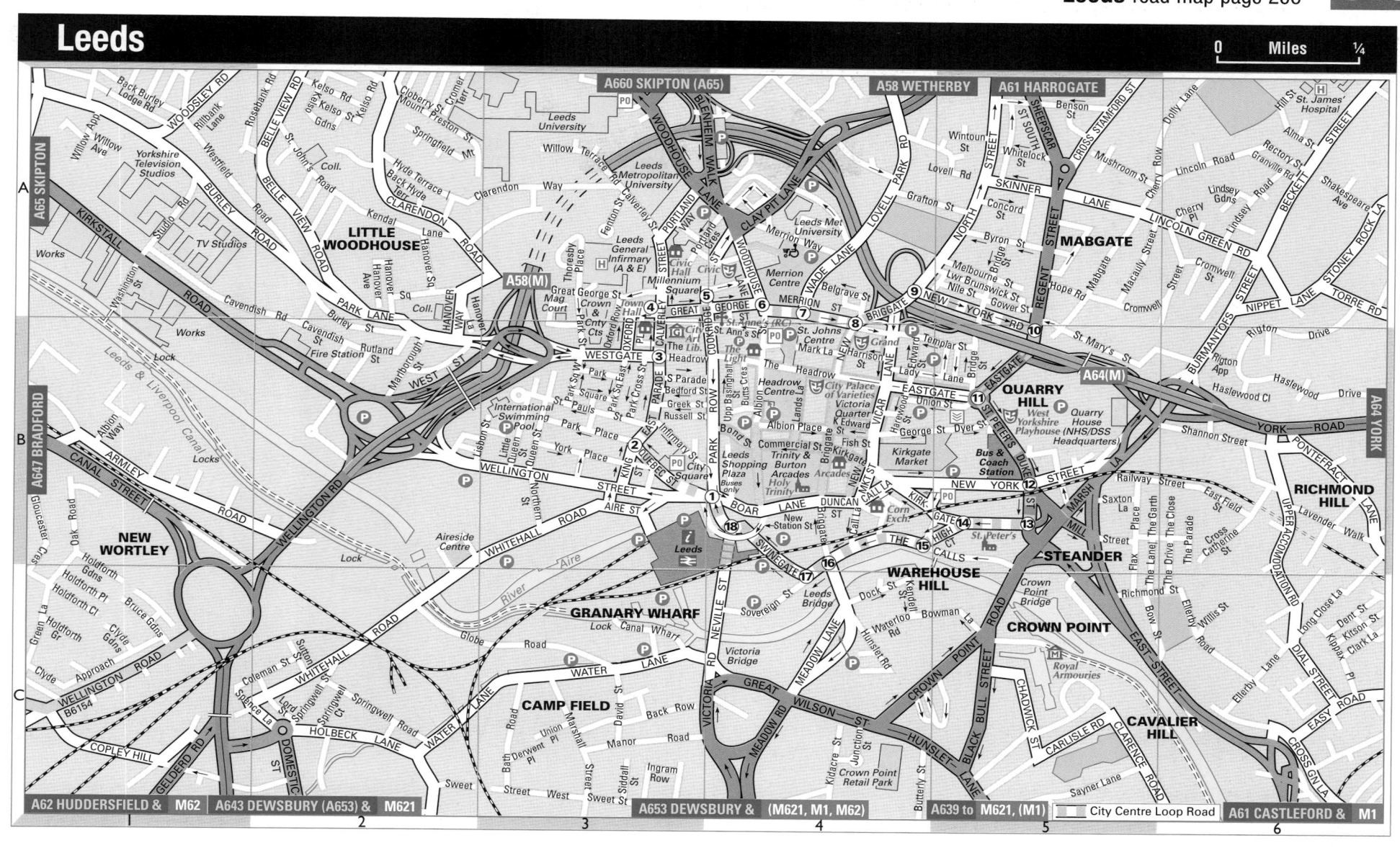

0   Miles   ¼

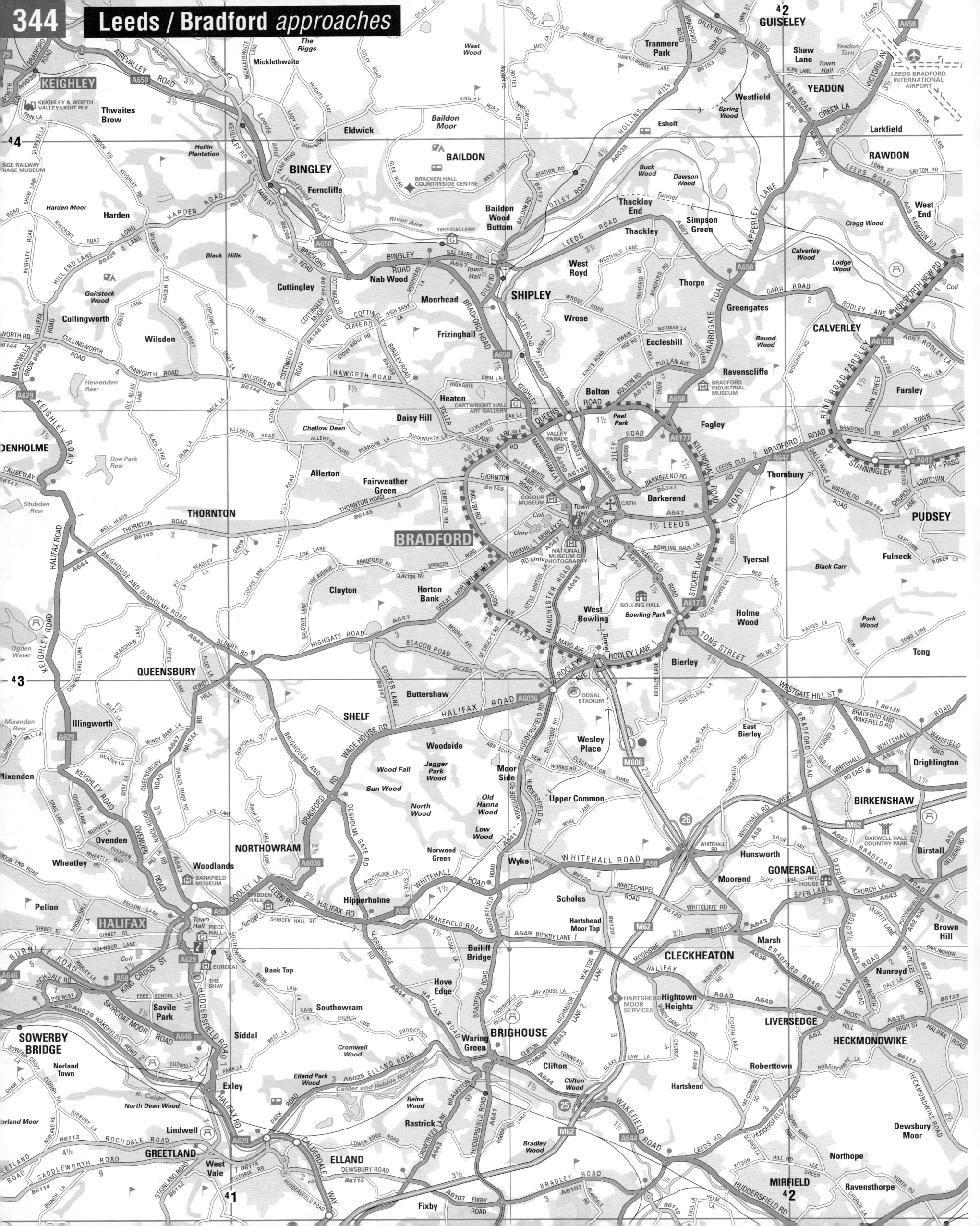

Liverpool

0   Miles   ¼

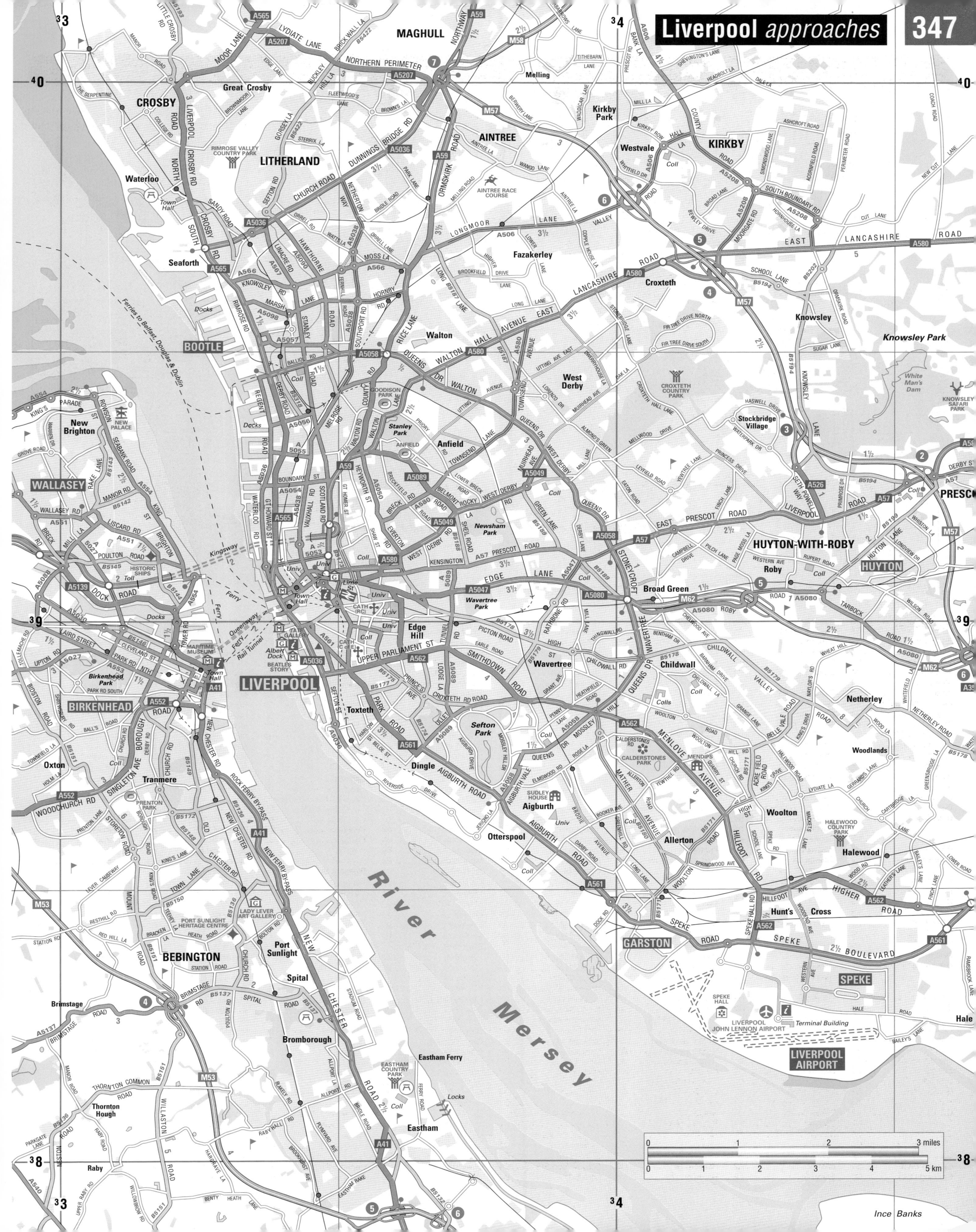

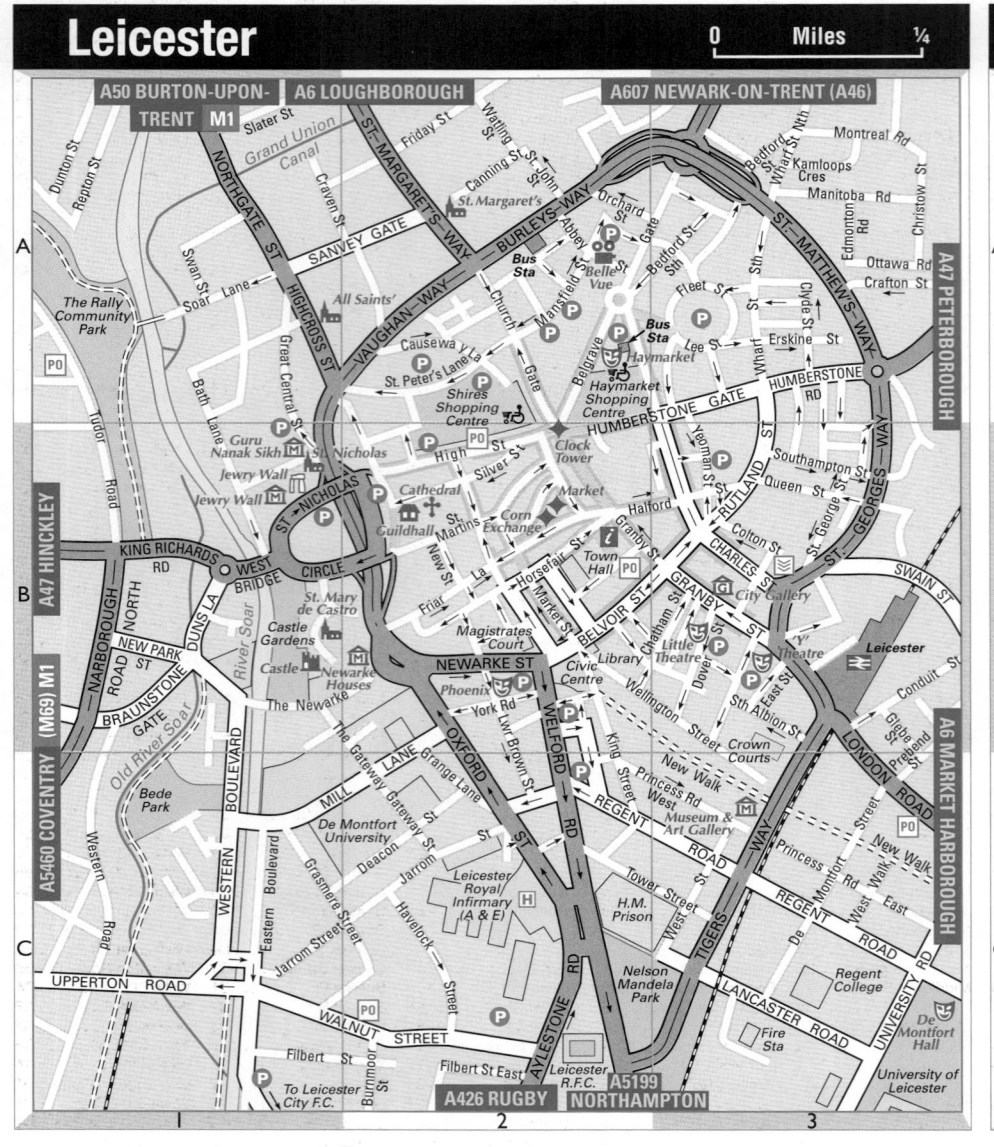

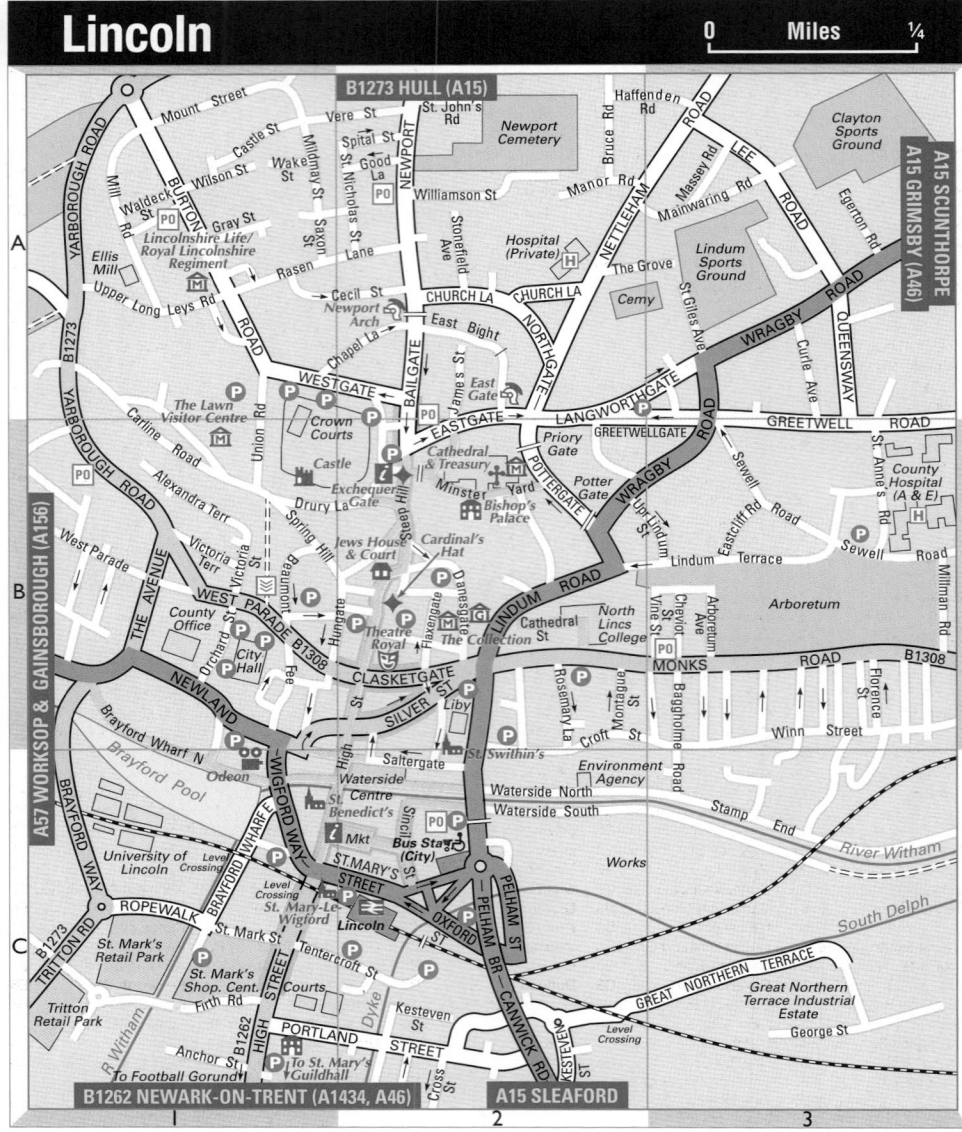

Leicester

Abbey St. A2	East St B3	Little Theatre 🎭 . . . B3	St Mary de Castro ⛪ . . B1
All Saints' ⛪ A1	Eastern Boulevard . . . C1	London Rd C3	St Matthew's Way . . . A3
Aylestone Rd C2	Edmonton Rd A3	Lower Brown St B2	St Nicholas ⛪ B1
Bath La A1	Erskine St A3	Magistrates Court. . . . B2	St Nicholas Circle . . . B1
Bede Park. C1	Filbert St C1	Manitoba Rd. A3	St Peter's La. A2
Bedford St A3	Filbert St East. C1	Mansfield St A2	Sanvey Gate. A2
Bedford St South A3	Fire Station C3	Market ✦ B2	Shires Shopping
Belgrave Gate A2	Fleet St A3	Market St B2	Centre A2
Belle Vue 🎭 A2	Friar La B2	Mill La C2	Silver St B2
Belvoir St B2	Friday St A2	Montreal Rd A3	Slater St A1
Braunstone Gate B1	Gateway St C2	Museum & Art	Soar La A1
Burleys Way A2	Glebe St B2	Gallery C3	South Albion St B3
Burnmoor St C2	Granby St B3	Narborough Rd	Southampton St B3
Bus Station. A2	Grange La. C2	North B1	Swain St B3
Canning St A2	Grasmere St C1	Nelson Mandela	Swan St A1
Castle 🏰 B1	Great Central St A1	Park C2	The Gateway C2
Castle Gardens. B1	Guildhall 🏛 B2	New St B2	The Newarke B1
Cathedral † B2	Guru Nanak Sikh	New Walk C3	The Rally Community
Causeway La A2	Museum 🏛 B1	New Park St B1	Park A2
Charles St B3	Halford St B2	Newarke Houses 🏛 . . . B2	Tigers Way C3
Chatham St B2	Havelock St C2	Newarke St B2	Tower St C3
Christow St A3	Haymarket 🎭 A2	Northgate St A1	Town Hall B2
Church Gate A2	Haymarket Shopping	Orchard St A2	Tudor Rd. B1
City Gallery 🏛 B3	Centre A2	Ottawa Rd A3	University of
Civic Centre B2	High St A2	Oxford St C2	Leicester. C3
Clock Tower ✦ B2	Highcross St. A1	Phoenix 🎭 B2	University Rd C3
Clyde St A3	H.M. Prison C2	Police Station 🏢 B3	Upperton Rd. C1
Colton St B3	Horsefair St B2	Post Office 🏤	Vaughan Way A2
Conduit St B3	Humberstone Gate. . . . B2	. . . . A1/B2/C2/C3	Walnut St C2
Corn Exchange ✦ B2	Humberstone Rd B2	Prebend St C3	Watling St A2
Crafton St A3	Information Ctr ℹ B2	Princess Rd East C3	Welford Rd B2
Craven St A1	Jarrom St C2	Princess Rd West C3	Wellington St B2
Crown Courts B3	Jewry Wall 🏛 🏛 B1	Queen St B3	West Bridge B1
Deacon St C2	Kamloops Cr A3	Regent College. C3	West St C3
De Montfort Hall 🎭 . . . C3	King Richards Rd B1	Regent Rd C2/C3	West Walk C3
De Montfort St C3	King St B2	Repton St A1	Western Boulevard. . . C1
De Montfort	Lancaster Rd C2	Rutland St B3	Western Rd C1
University C1	Lee St A3	St George St B3	Wharf St North A3
Dover St B3	Leicester Station ⚟ . . B3	St Georges Way B3	Wharf St South A3
Duns La B1	Leicester R.F.C. C2	St John St A2	'Y' Theatre 🎭 B3
Dunton St A1	Leicester Royal	St Margaret's St A2	Yeoman St A3
	Infirmary (A & E) 🏥 . . C2	St Margaret's Way . . . A2	York Rd B2
	Library B2	St Martins B2	

Lincoln

Alexandra Terr B1	Danesgate B2	Lindum Terr B3	St Mary-Le-
Anchor St C1	Drury La B1	Mainwaring Rd A3	Wigford ⛪ C1
Arboretum. B3	East Bight. A2	Manor Rd A2	St Mary's St C2
Arboretum Ave B3	East Gate 🏛 A2	Massey Rd A3	St Nicholas St A2
Baggholme Rd B3	Eastcliff Rd B3	Mildmay St A1	St Swithin's ⛪ B2
Bailgate A2	Eastgate B2	Mill Rd A1	Saltergate B2
Beaumont Fee B1	Egerton Rd A3	Millman Rd B3	Saxon St A1
Bishop's Palace 🏛 . . . B2	Ellis Mill A1	Minster Yard B2	Sewell Rd B3
Brayford Way C1	Environment Agency . . C2	Market C2	Silver St B2
Brayford Wharf East. . . C1	Exchequer Gate ✦ . . . B2	Monks Rd B3	Sincil St C2
Brayford Wharf	Firth Rd C1	Montague St B2	Spital St A2
North B1	Flaxengate B2	Mount St A1	Spring Hill B1
Bruce Rd A2	Florence St B3	Nettleham Rd A2	Stamp End C3
Burton Rd A1	George St C3	Newland B1	Steep Hill B2
Bus Station (City) C2	Good La A2	Newport A2	Stonefield Ave A2
Canwick Rd C2	Gray St A1	Newport Arch 🏛 A2	Tentercroft St C1
Cardinal's Hat ✦ B2	Great Northern Terr . . . C3	Newport Cemetery . . . A2	The Avenue B1
Carline Rd B1	Great Northern Terrace	North Lincs College . . B2	The Grove A3
Castle 🏰 A1	Industrial Estate . . . C3	Northgate A2	Theatre Royal 🎭 B2
Castle St. A1	Greetwell Rd B3	Odeon C1	Tritton Retail Park. . . . C1
Cathedral &	Greetwellgate B3	Orchard St B1	Tritton Rd C1
Treasury † 🏛 B2	Haffenden Rd A2	Oxford St C2	Union Rd B1
Cathedral St B2	High St B2/C1	Pelham Bridge C2	University of Lincoln. . C1
Cecil St A2	Hospital (Private) 🏥 . . A2	Pelham St C2	Upper Lindum St . . . B3
Chapel La A2	Hungate B2	Police Station 🏢 B1	Upper Long Leys Rd . A1
Cheviot St B3	Information Ctr ℹ B2	Portland St C2	Vere St A2
Church La A2	James St A2	Post Office 🏤	Victoria St. B1
City Hall B1	Jews House &	. . . . A1/A2/B1/B3/C2	Victoria Terr B1
Clasketgate B2	Court B2	Potter Gate. B2	Vine St B3
Clayton Sports	Kesteven St C2	Priory Gate. B2	Wake St A1
Ground A3	Langworthgate A2	Queensway A3	Waldeck St A1
Collection, The 🏛 B2	Lee Rd A3	Rasen La A1	Waterside Centre . . . C2
County Hospital	Lawn Visitor	Ropewalk C1	Waterside North C2
(A & E) 🏥 B3	Centre, The 🏛 B1	Rosemary La B2	Waterside South. . . . C2
County Office B1	Library B2	St Anne's Rd B3	West Pde B1
Courts. C1	Lincoln Station ⚟ . . . C2	St Benedict's ⛪ C1	Westgate A2
Croft St C2	Lincolnshire Life/Royal	St Giles Ave A3	Wigford Way C1
Cross St C2	Lincolnshire Regiment	St John's Rd A2	Williamson St A1
Crown Courts B1	Museum 🏛 A1	St Mark St C1	Wilson St A1
Curle Ave A3	Lindum Rd B2	St Mark's Retail Park . C1	Winn St B3
	Lindum Sports	St Mark's Shopping	Wragby Rd A3
	Ground A3	Centre C1	Yarborough Rd A1

London

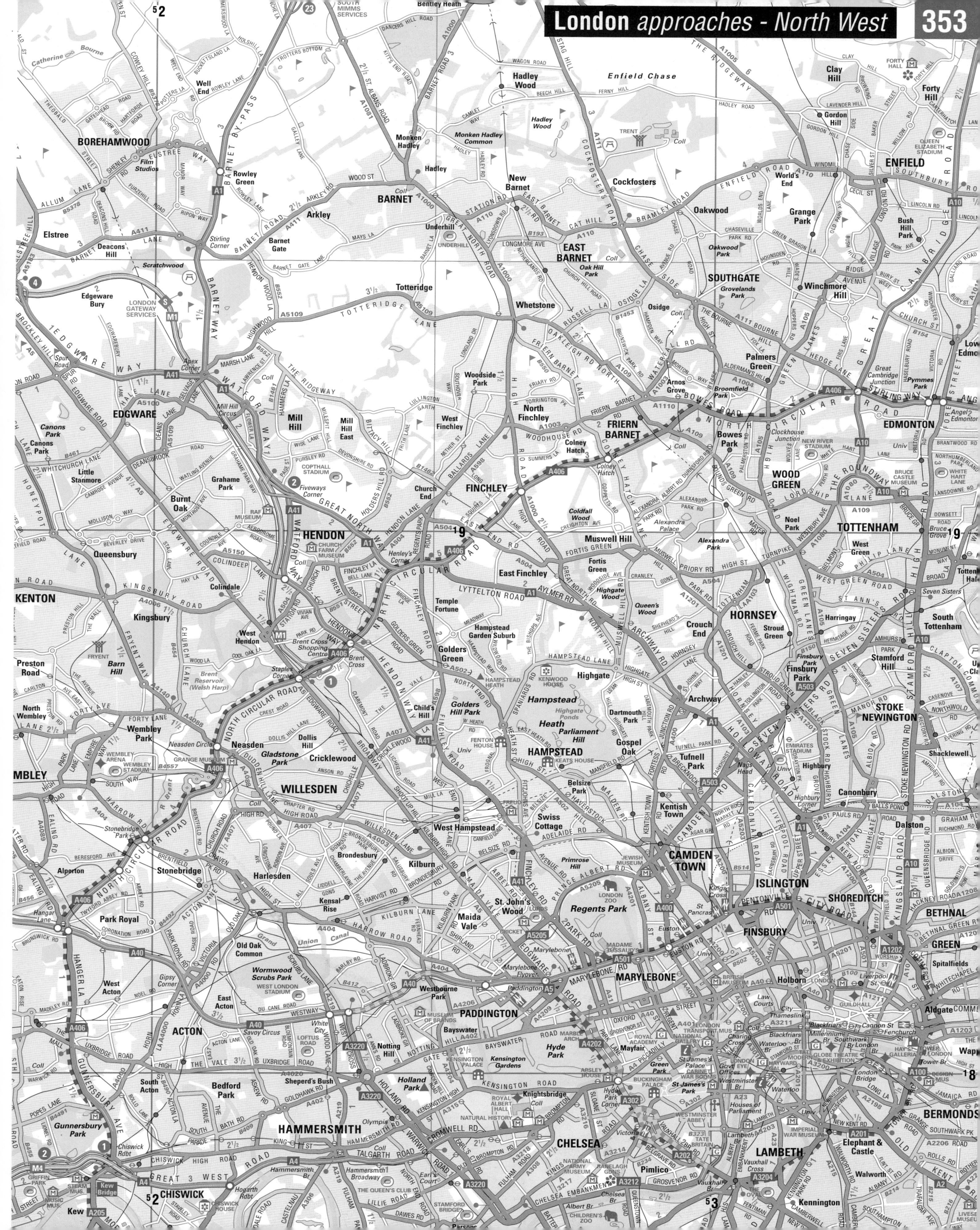

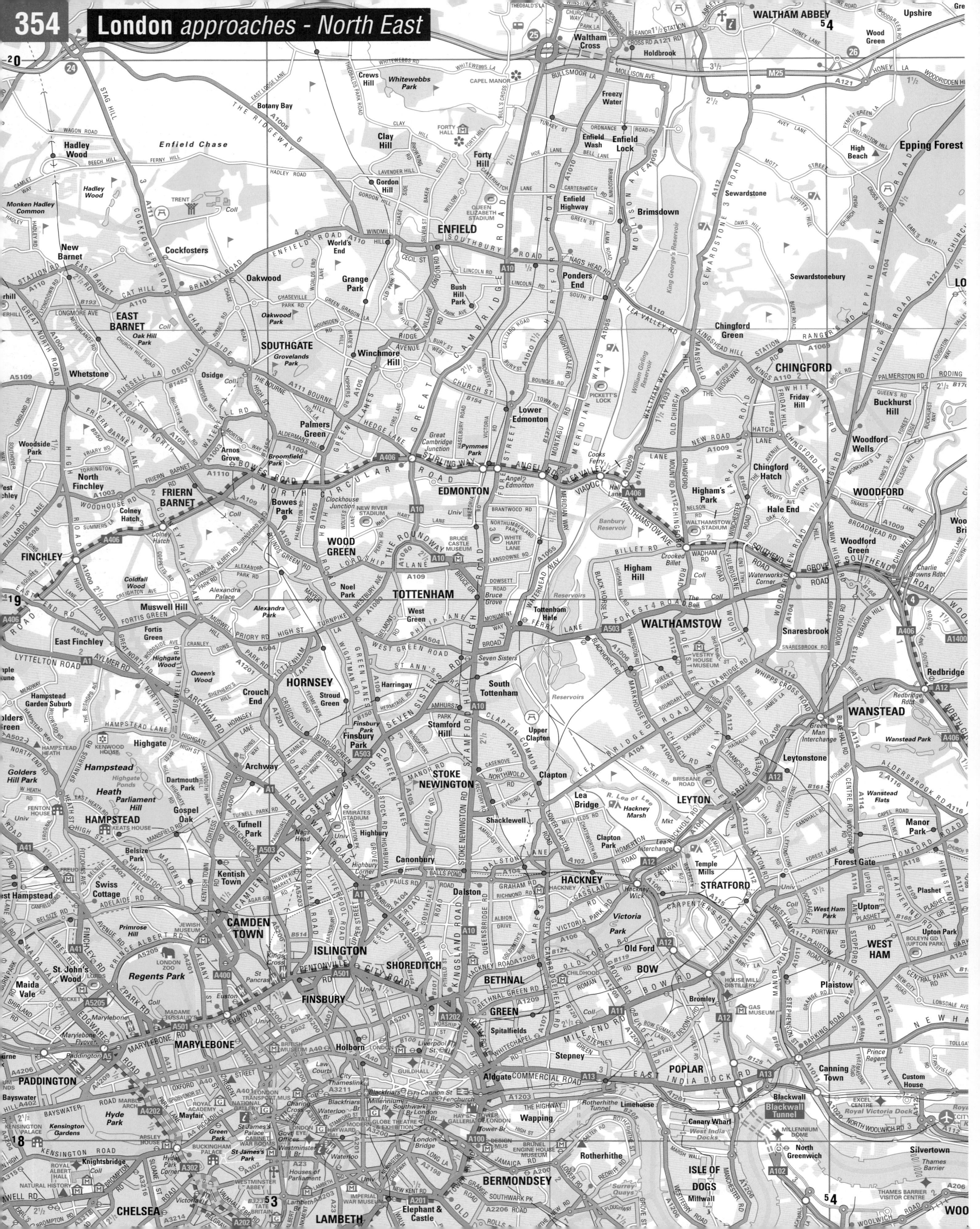

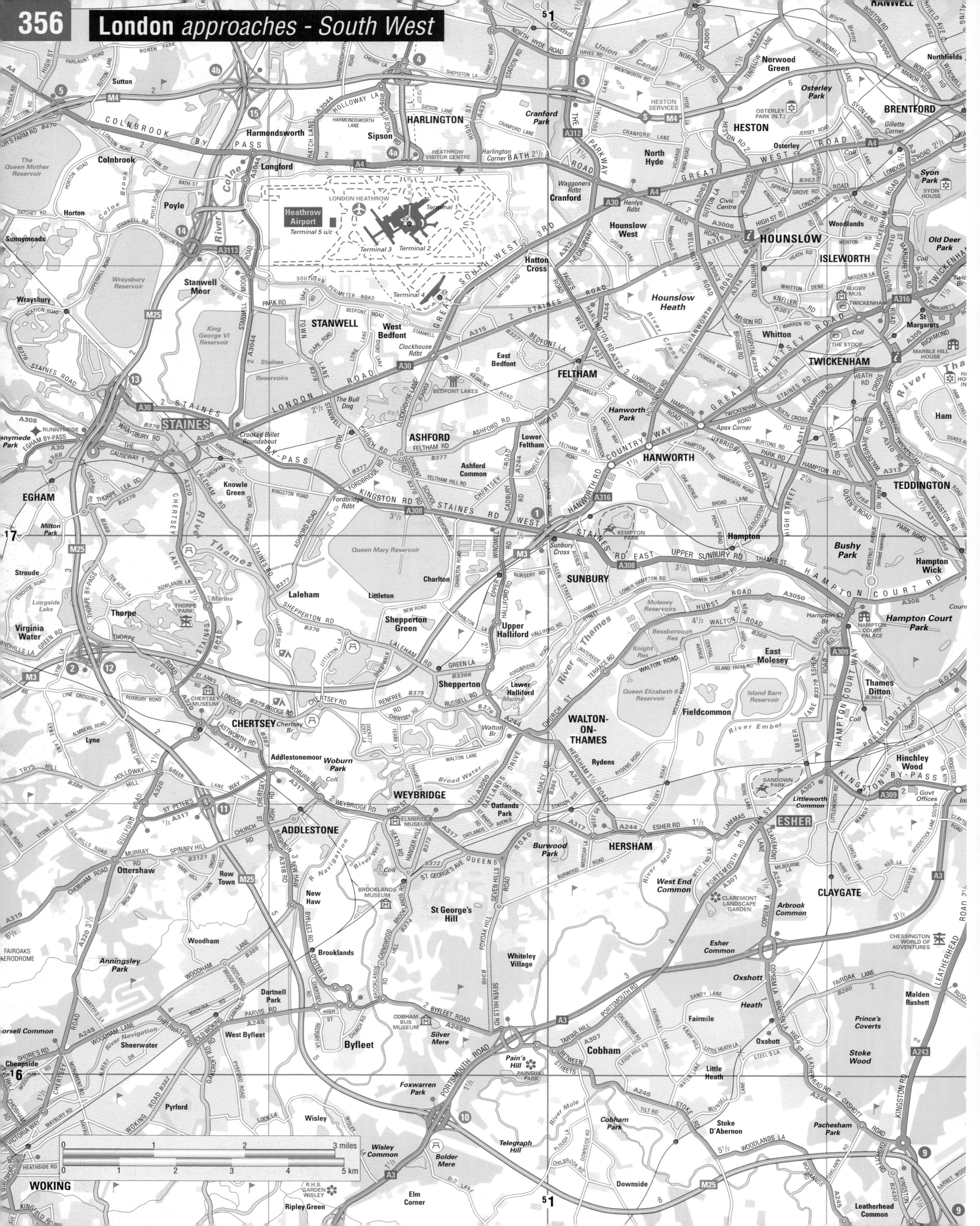

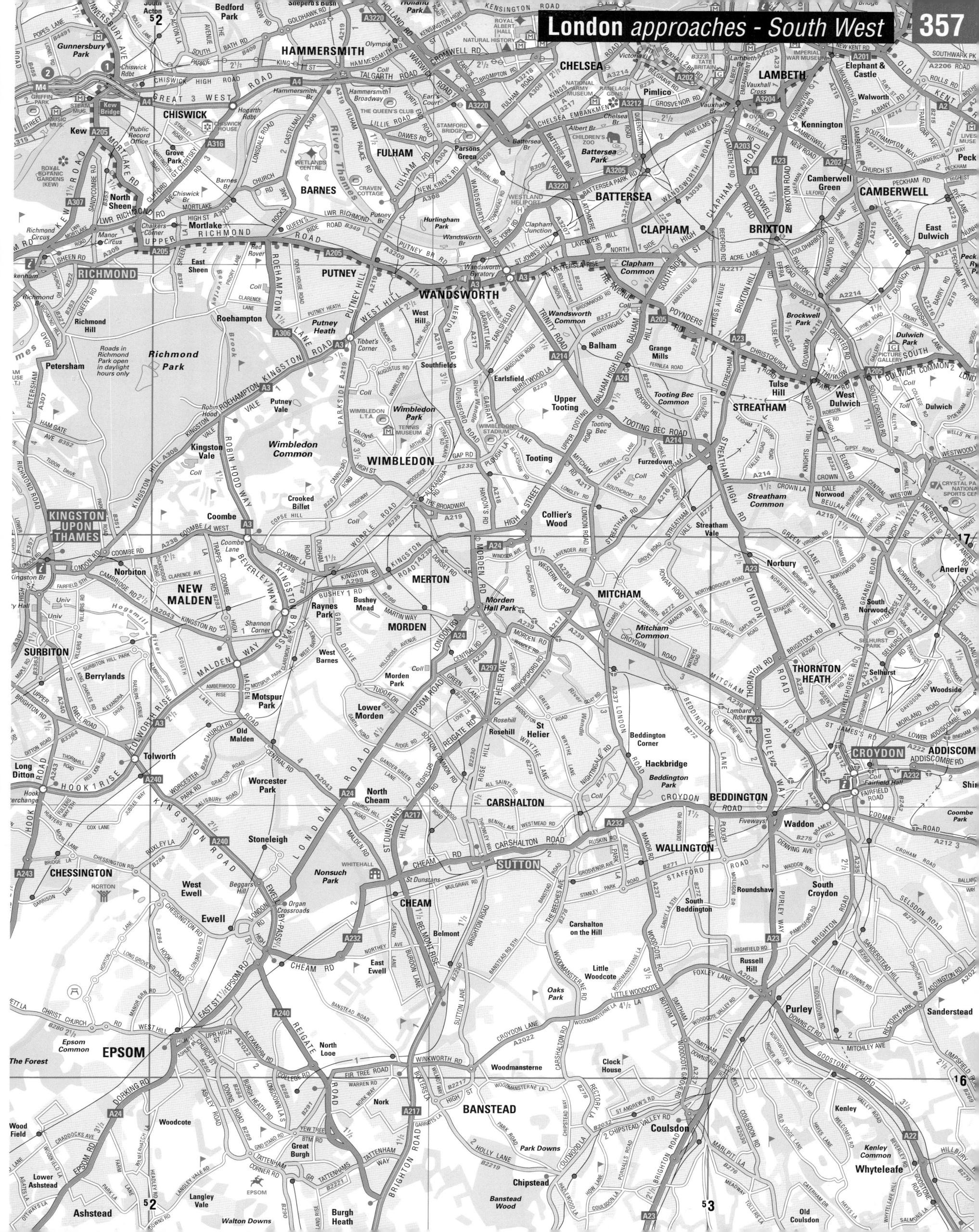

Manchester

0 Miles ¼

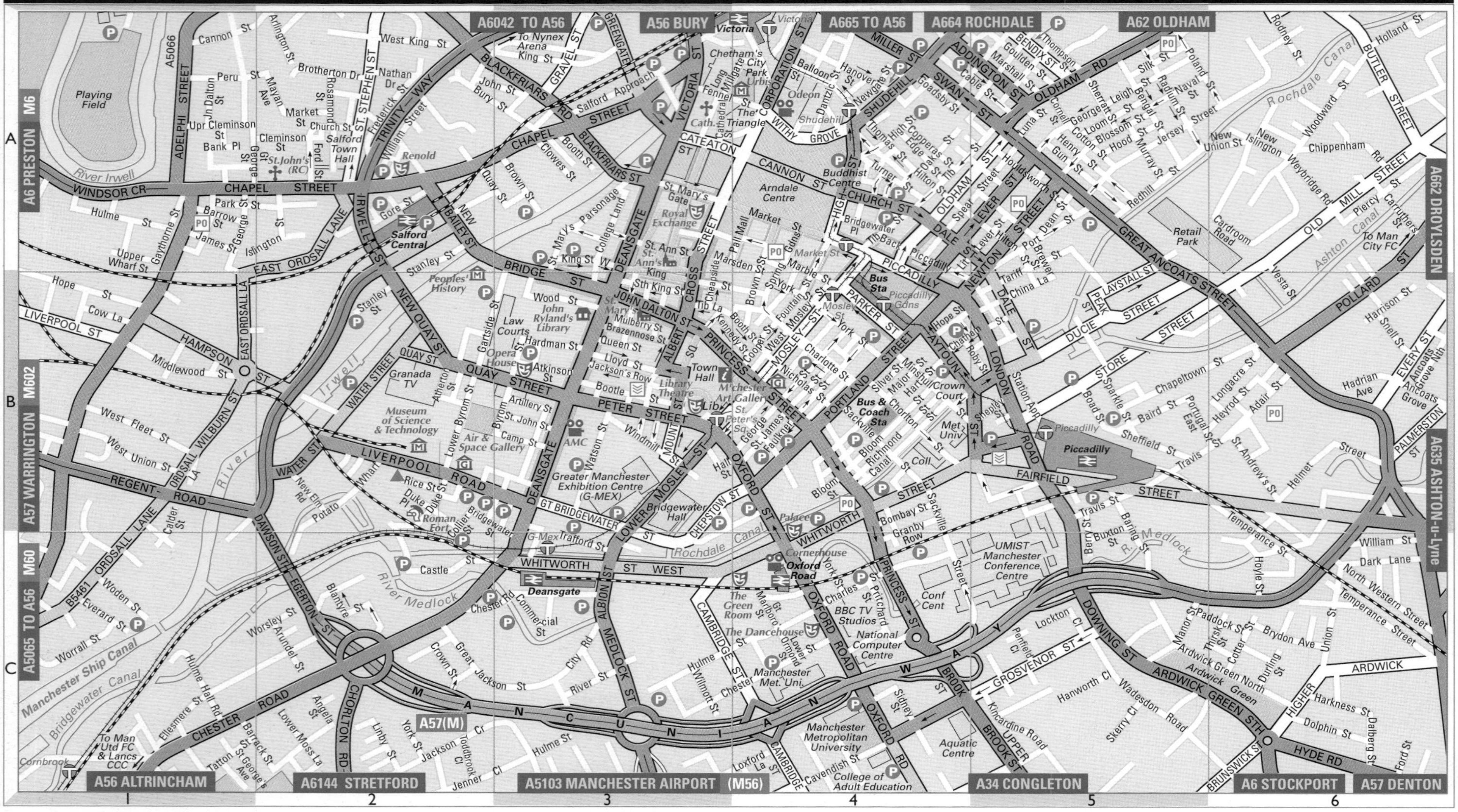
A6042 TO A56
A56 BURY
A665 TO A56
A664 ROCHDALE
A62 OLDHAM
A662 DROYLSDEN
A635 ASHTON-u-Lyne
A57 DENTON
A6 STOCKPORT
A34 CONGLETON
A5103 MANCHESTER AIRPORT (M56)
A6144 STRETFORD
A56 ALTRINCHAM
A5065 TO A56
M60
A57 WARRINGTON
M602
A6 PRESTON
M6
A57(M)
MANCUNIAN WAY
Piccadilly
Victoria
Salford Central
Deansgate
Oxford Road
Arndale Centre
Town Hall
Bus & Coach Sta
Chetham's City Park
Urbis
The Triangle
Royal Exchange
Greater Manchester Exhibition Centre (G-MEX)
Bridgewater Hall
Museum of Science & Technology
Granada TV
UMIST Manchester Conference Centre
Manchester Metropolitan University
Aquatic Centre
Retail Park
Playing Field
River Irwell
River Medlock
Rochdale Canal
Ashton Canal
Bridgewater Canal
Manchester Ship Canal
To Man City FC
To Man Utd FC & Lancs CCC
A
B
C
1
2
3
4
5
6

Manchester

Adair St. B6
Addington St A5
Adelphi St. A1
Air & Space Gallery B2
Albert Sq B3
Albion St. C3
AMC Great Northern B3
Ancoats Gr B6
Ancoats Gr North B6
Angela St C2
Aquatic Centre C4
Ardwick Green C5
Ardwick Green North C5
Ardwick Green South C5
Arlington St. A2
Arndale Centre A4
Artillery St. B3
Arundel St. C2
Atherton St. B2
Atkinson St. B3
Aytoun St B4
Back Piccadilly A4
Baird St B5
Balloon St. A4
Bank Pl. A1
Baring St B5
Barrack St C1
Barrow St. A1
BBC TV Studios C4
Bendix St A5
Bengal St A5
Berry St C5
Blackfriars Rd. A3
Blackfriars St A3
Blantyre St C2
Bloom St B4
Blossom St. A5
Boad St B5
Bombay St B4
Booth St A3
Booth St B4
Bootle St B3
Brazennose St B3
Brewer St A5
Bridge St A3
Bridgewater Hall B3
Bridgewater Pl A4
Bridgewater St B2
Brook St C4
Brotherton Dr A2
Brown St. A3
Brown St. B4
Brunswick St C6
Brydon Ave. C6
Buddhist Centre A4
Bury St A2
Bus & Coach Station B4
Bus Station B4
Butler St A6
Buxton St C5
Byrom St B3
Cable St A5
Calder St B1
Cambridge St C3/C4
Camp St B3
Canal St B4
Cannon St A1
Cannon St A4
Cardroom Rd A6
Carruthers St A6
Castle St. C2
Cateaton St A3
Cathedral A3
Cathedral St A3
Cavendish St C4
Chapel St A1/A3
Chapeltown St B5
Charles St. C4
Charlotte St B4
Chatham St B4
Cheapside A3
Chepstow St. B3
Chester Rd. C1/C2
Chester St C4
Chetham's (Dept Store) A3
China La B5
Chippenham Rd A6
Chorlton Rd C2
Chorlton St. B4
Church St A2
Church St A4
City Park A4
City Rd C3
Cleminson St A2
Clowes St. A3
College Land A3
College of Adult Education C4
Collier St. B2
Commercial St C3
Conference Centre C4
Cooper St. B4
Copperas St A4
Cornbrook (Metro) C1
Cornell St A5
Cornerhouse C4
Corporation St A4
Cotter St. C6
Cotton St A5
Cow La B1
Cross St B3
Crown Court B4
Crown St C2
Dalberg St C6
Dale St A4/B5
Dancehouse, The C4
Dantzic St A4
Dark La C6
Dawson St C2
Dean St. A5
Deansgate A3/B3
Deansgate C3
Dolphin St. C6
Downing St. C5
Ducie St B5
Duke Pl. B2
Duke St. B2
Durling St C6
East Ordsall La A2/B1
Edge St. A4
Egerton St C2
Ellesmere St C1
Everard St. C1
Every St B6
Fairfield St B5
Faulkner St. B4
Fennel St A3
Ford St A2
Ford St C6
Fountain St. B4
Frederick St A2
Gartside St. B2
Gaythorne St A1
George Leigh St A5
George St A1
George St B4
G-Mex (Metro) C3
Goadsby St A4
Gore St. A2
Goulden St A5
Granada TV Studios B2
Granby Row B4
Gravel St. A3
Great Ancoats St A5
Great Bridgewater St B3
Great George St A1
Great Jackson St C2
Great Marlborough St C4
Greater Manchester Exhibition Centre (G-Mex) B3
Greengate A3
Green Room, The C4
Grosvenor St C5
Gun St A5
Hadrian Ave B6
Hall St. B3
Hampson St B1
Hanover St A4
Hanworth Cl C5
Hardman St B3
Harkness St C6
Harrison St B6
Hart St B4
Helmet St B6
Henry St A5
Heyrod St B6
High St A4
Higher Ardwick C6
Hilton St A4/A5
Holland St A6
Hood St A5
Hope St B1
Hope St B4
Houldsworth St A5
Hoyle St C6
Hulme Hall Rd C1
Hulme St. A1
Hulme St. C3
Hyde Rd C6
Information Ctr B3
Irwell St. A2
Islington St A2
Jackson Cr C2
Jackson's Row B3
James St A1
Jenner Cl C2
Jersey St A5
John Dalton St A1
John Dalton St B3
John Ryland's Library B3
John St. A2
Kennedy St. B3
Kincardine Rd. C4
King St A3
King St West A3
Law Courts B3
Laystall St. B5
Lever St A5
Library B3
Library Theatre B3
Linby St C2
Little Lever St A4
Liverpool Rd B2
Liverpool St B1
Lloyd St B3
Lockton Cl C5
London Rd B5
Long Millgate A3
Longacre St B6
Loom St A5
Lower Byrom St B2
Lower Mosley St B3
Lower Moss La. C2
Lower Ormond St. C4
Loxford La C4
Luna St. A5
Major St B4
Manchester Art Gallery B4
Manchester Metropolitan University B4/C4
Mancunian Way C3
Manor St. C5
Marble St A4
Market St A2
Market St A4
Market St (Metro) A4
Marsden St. A3
Marshall St A5
Mayan Ave A2
Medlock St. C3
Middlewood St B1
Miller St A4
Minshull St B4
Mosley St A4
Mosley St (Metro) B4
Mount St. B3
Mulberry St. B3
Murray St A5
Museum of Science & Technology B2
Nathan Dr A2
National Computer Centre C4
Naval St A5
New Bailey St. A2
New Elm Rd B2
New Islington A6
New Quay St B2
New Union St A6
Newgate St. A4
Newton St A5
Nicholas St. B4
North George St A1
North Western St C6
Oak St A4
Odeon A4
Old Mill St. A6
Oldfield Rd A1/C1
Oldham Rd A5
Oldham St A4
Opera House B3
Ordsall La C1
Oxford Rd. C4
Oxford Road C4
Oxford St B4
Paddock St. C6
Palace Theatre B4
Pall Mall A3
Palmerston St. B6
Park St A1
Parker St B4
Peak St. B5
Penfield Cl C5
Peoples' History Museum B2
Peru St A1
Peter St B3
Piccadilly A4
Piccadilly B5
Piccadilly (Metro) B5
Piccadilly Gdns (Metro) B4
Piercy St. A6
Poland St A5
Police Station B3/B5
Pollard St B6
Port St A5
Portland St B4
Portugal St East B5
Post Office A1/A4/A5/B4/B6
Potato Wharf B2
Princess St B3/C4
Pritchard St C4
Quay St A2
Quay St B2
Queen St B3
Radium St. A5
Redhill St A5
Regent Rd B1
Renold Theatre A2
Retail Park A5
Rice St B2
Richmond St B4
River St. C3
Roby St B5
Rodney St. A6
Roman Fort B2
Rosamond St A2
Royal Exchange A3
Sackville St. B4
St Andrew's St B6
St Ann St A3
St Ann's A3
St George's Ave C1
St James St B4
St John St B3
St John's Cathedral (RC) A2
St Mary's B3
St Mary's Gate A3
St Mary's Parsonage A3
St Peter's Sq (Metro) B3
St Stephen St A2
Salford Approach A3
Salford Central A2
Sheffield St. B5
Shepley St B5
Sherratt St A5
Shudehill A4
Shudehill (Metro) A4
Sidney St C4
Silk St. A5
Silver St B4
Skerry Cl. C5
Snell St. B6
South King St B3
Sparkle St. B5
Spear St A4
Spring Gdns A4
Stanley St A2/B2
Station Approach B5
Store St B5
Swan St A4
Tariff St B5
Tatton St. C1
Temperance St B6/C6
The Triangle A4
Thirsk St. C6
Thomas St A4
Thompson St A5
Tib La B3
Tib St A4
Toddbrook Cl C2
Town Hall (Manchester) B3
Town Hall (Salford) A2
Trafford St. C3
Travis St B5
Trinity Way A2
Turner St. A4
UMIST Manchester Conference Centre C5
Union St C6
Upper Brook St C5
Upper Cleminson St A1
Upper Wharf St A1
Urbis Museum A4
Vesta St B6
Victoria (Metro) A4
Victoria A4
Victoria St. A3
Wadesdon Rd. C5
Water St B2
Watson St. B3
Wellington St A2
West Fleet St B1
West King St. A2
West Mosley St B4
West Union St B1
Weybridge Rd. A6
Whitworth St B4
Whitworth St West C3
Wilburn St. B1
William St A2
William St C6
Wilmott St. C3
Windmill St B3
Windsor Cr A1
Withy Gr A4
Woden St C1
Wood St B3
Woodward St A6
Worrall St C1
Worsley St C2
York St B4
York St C2
York St C4

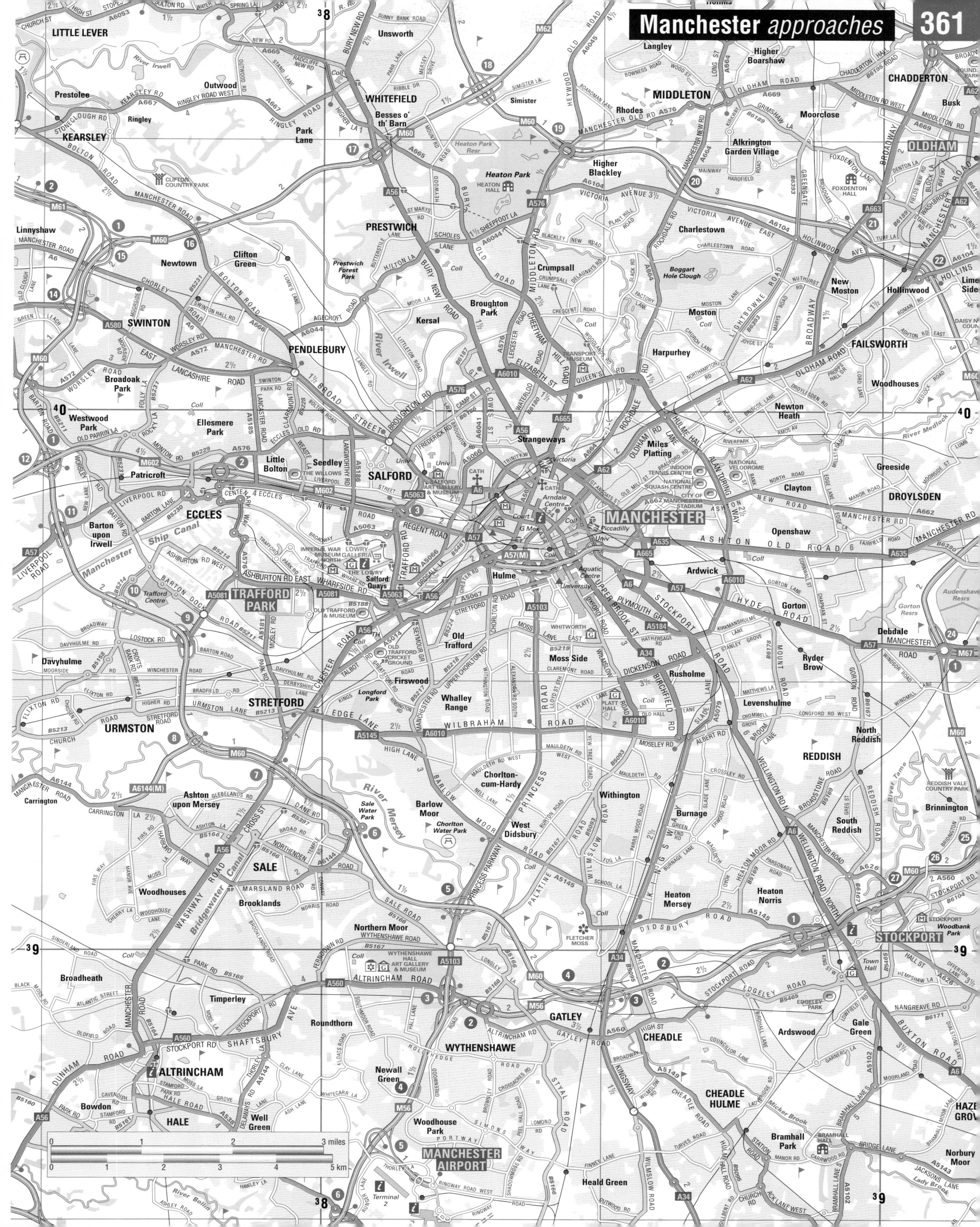

Middlesbrough

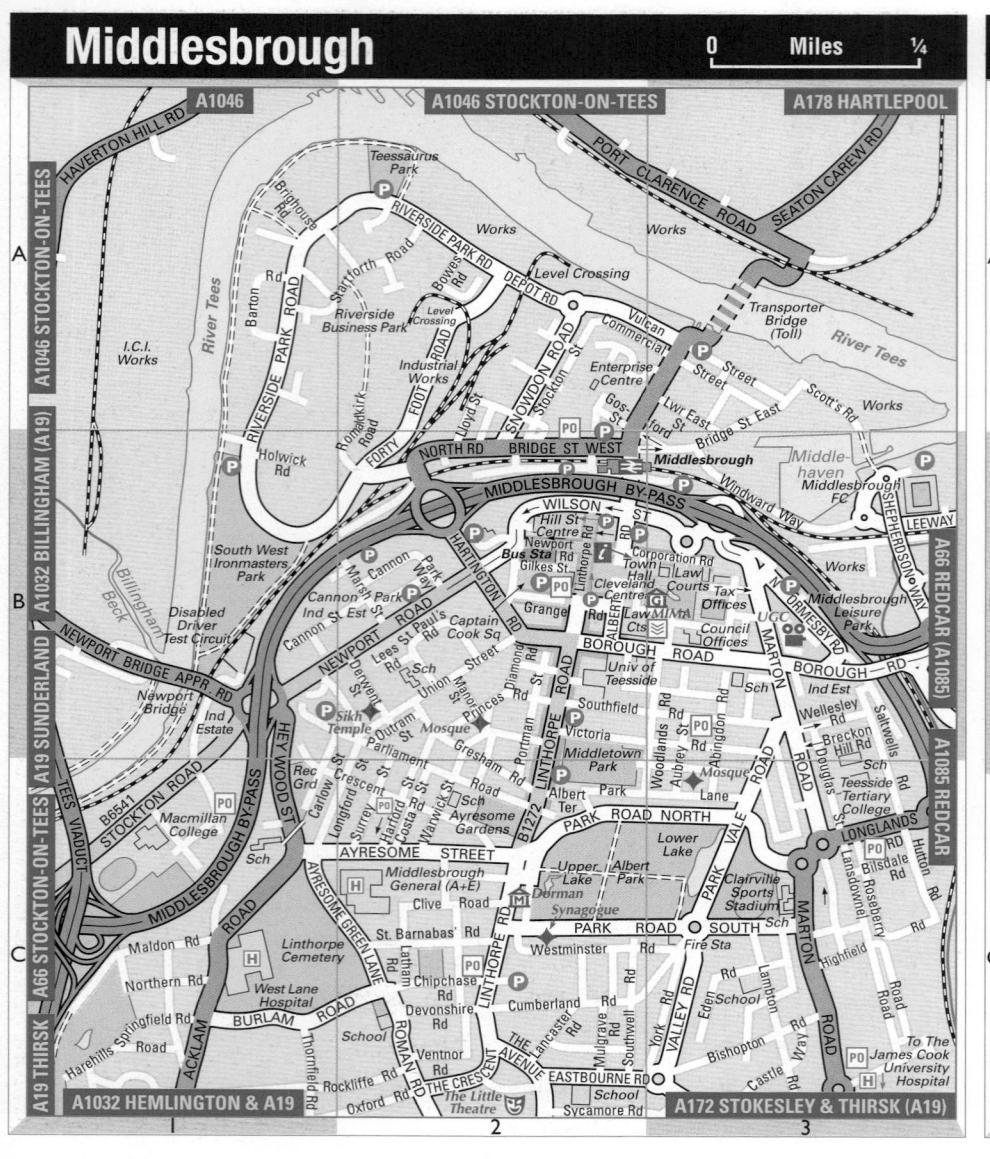

Milton Keynes

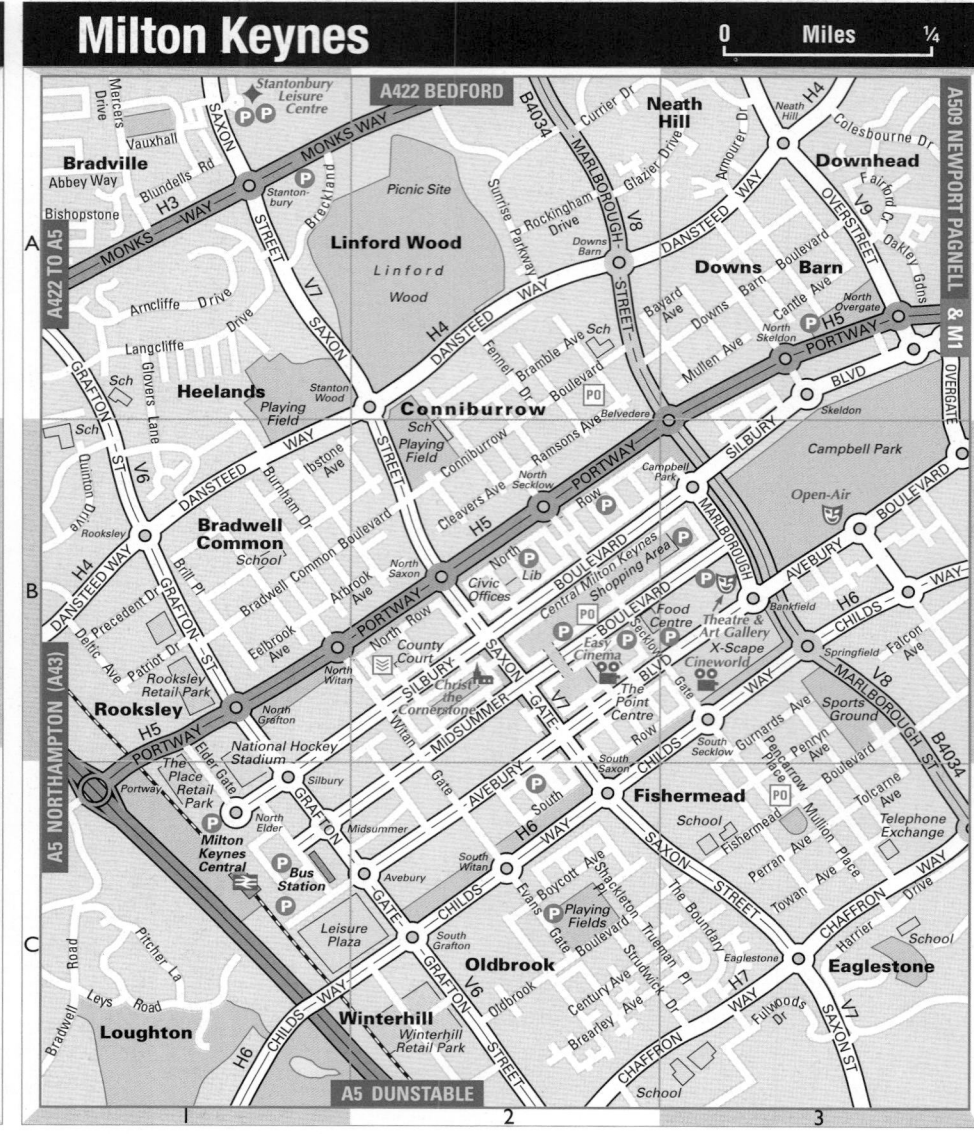

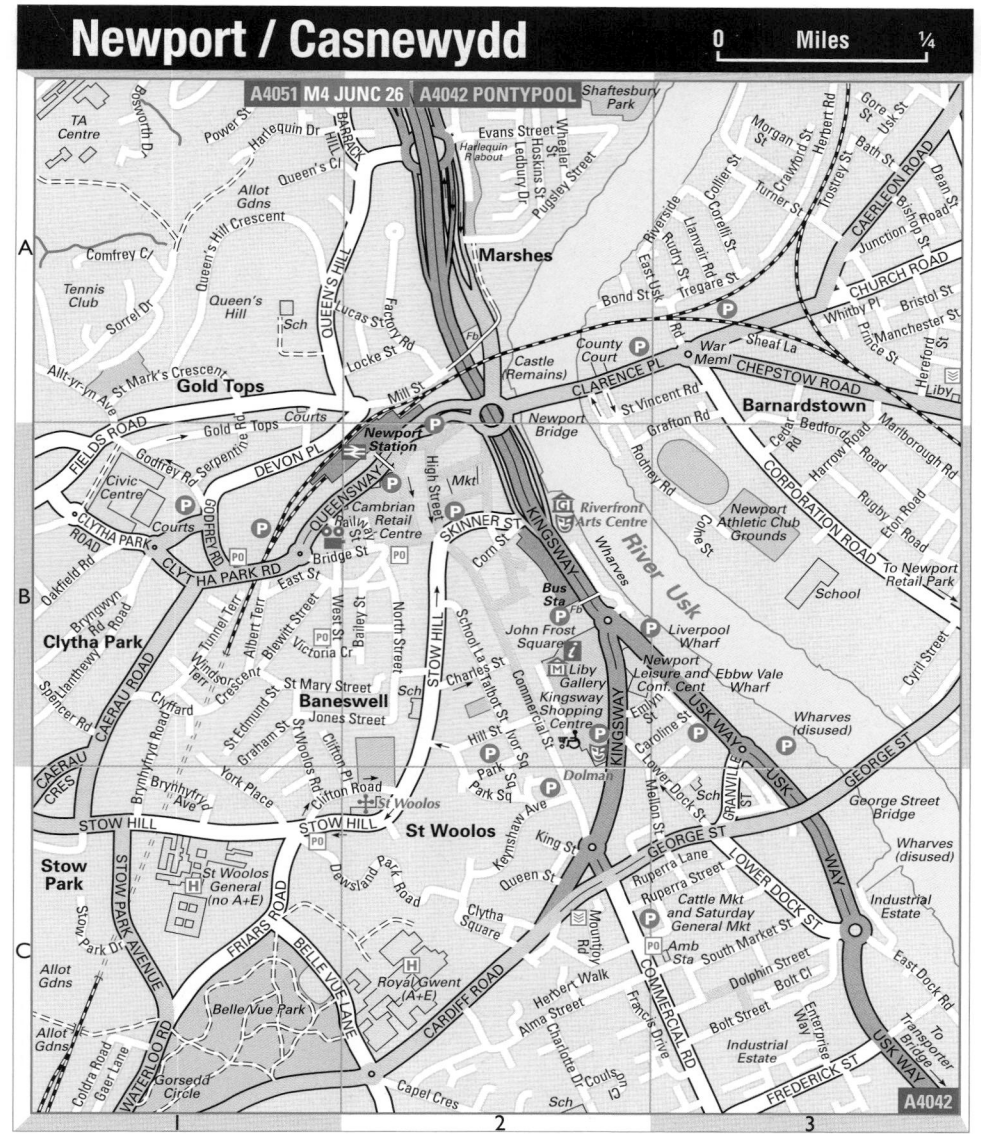

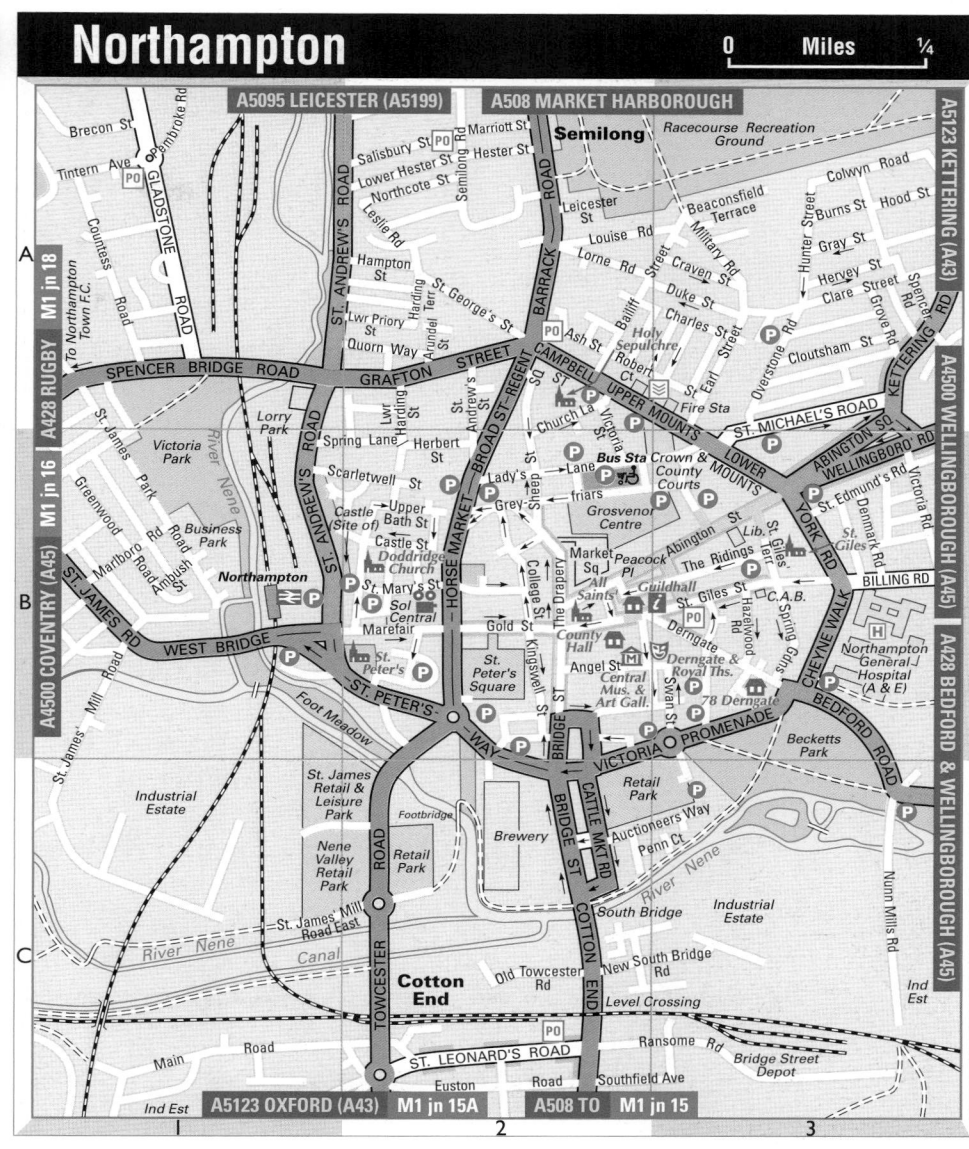

Newport / Casnewydd

Albert Terr.	B1
Allt-yr-Yn Ave	A1
Alma St.	C2
Ambulance Station	C3
Bailey St.	B2
Barrack Hill	A2
Bath St.	A3
Bedford Rd.	B3
Belle Vue La.	C1
Belle Vue Park	C1
Bishop St.	A3
Blewitt St.	B1
Bolt Cl.	C3
Bolt St.	C3
Bond St.	A2
Bosworth Dr.	A1
Bridge St.	B1
Bristol St.	A3
Bryngwyn Rd.	B1
Brynhyfryd Ave	C1
Brynhyfryd Rd	C1
Bus Station	B2
Caerau Cres	C1
Caerau Rd	B1
Caerleon Rd.	A3
Cambrian Retail Centre	B2
Capel Cres	C2
Cardiff Rd.	C2
Caroline St	B3
Castle (Remains)	A2
Cattle Market and Saturday General Market	C3
Cedar Rd	B3
Charles St.	B2
Charlotte Dr	C2
Chepstow Rd	A3
Church Rd	A3
City Cinema	B1
Civic Centre	B1
Clarence Pl.	B2
Clifton Pl.	B1
Clifton Rd.	C1
Clyffard Cres	B1
Clytha Park Rd	B1

Clytha Sq	C2
Coldra Rd.	C1
Collier St.	A3
Colne St.	B3
Comfrey Cl.	A1
Commercial Rd.	C3
Commercial St.	B2
Corelli St.	A3
Corn St.	B2
Corporation Rd.	B3
Coulson Cl.	C2
County Court	A2
Courts	A1
Courts	B1
Crawford St.	A3
Cyril St	B3
Dean St.	A3
Devon Pl.	B1
Dewsland Park Rd	C2
Dolman	B2
Dolphin St.	C3
East Dock Rd	C3
East St	B1
East Usk Rd.	A3
Ebbw Vale Wharf	B3
Emlyn St	B2
Enterprise Way	C3
Eton Rd	B3
Evans St.	A2
Factory Rd	A2
Fields Rd	B1
Francis Dr.	C2
Frederick St.	C3
Friars Rd.	C2
Gaer La.	C1
George St	C3
George Street Bridge	C3
Godfrey Rd.	B1
Gold Tops	B1
Gore St	A3
Gorsedd Circle	C1
Grafton Rd.	A3
Graham St	B1
Granville St.	C3
Harlequin Dr.	A2
Harrow Rd	B3
Herbert Rd.	A3
Herbert Walk	C2
Hereford St.	A3

High St	B2
Hill St	C2
Hoskins St	A2
Information Ctr	B2
Ivor Sq	A3
John Frost Sq.	B2
Jones St.	B1
Junction Rd	A3
Keynshaw Ave	C2
King St	C2
Kingsway	B2
Kingsway Shopping Centre	B2
Ledbury Dr	A1
Library	A3
Library, Museum & Art Gallery	B2
Liverpool Wharf	B3
Llanthewy Rd.	B1
Llanvair Rd.	A3
Locke St.	A2
Lower Dock St	C3
Lucas St.	A2
Manchester St.	A3
Market	B2
Marlborough Rd.	B3
Mellon St.	C3
Mill St.	B2/C1/C2
Morgan St.	A3
Mountjoy Rd.	C2
Newport Athletic Club Grounds	B3
Newport Bridge	A2
Newport Leisure and Conference Ctr.	B2
Newport Station	B2
North St	B1
Oakfield Rd.	B1
Park Sq.	C2
Police Station	A3/C2
Post Office	B1/B2/C1/C3
Power St.	A1
Prince St.	A3
Pugsley St.	A2
Queen St	A1
Queen's Cl.	A1
Queen's Hill	A1
Queen's Hill Cres	A1
Queensway.	B2

Railway St	B2
Riverfront Arts Centre	B2
Riverside.	A3
Rodney Rd.	B2
Royal Gwent (A+E)	C2
Rudry St.	A3
Rugby Rd.	B3
Ruperra La.	C3
Ruperra St.	C3
St. Edmund St	B1
St. Mark's Cres.	A1
St. Mary St.	B1
St. Vincent Rd	A3
St. Woolos	C2
St. Woolos General (no A+E)	C1
St. Woolos Rd.	B1
School La.	B2
Serpentine Rd.	B1
Shaftesbury Park	A2
Sheaf La.	A3
Skinner St.	B2
Sorrel Dr.	A1
South Market St.	C3
Spencer Rd.	B1
Stow Hill	B2/C1/C2
Stow Park Ave	C1
Stow Park Dr.	C1
TA Centre	A1
Talbot St.	B2
Tennis Club.	A1
Tregare St.	A3
Trostrey St.	A3
Tunnel Terr.	B1
Turner St.	A3
Usk St.	A3
Usk Way	B3/C3
Victoria Cr.	B1
War Memorial	A3
Waterloo Rd.	C1
West St.	B1
Wharves	B2
Wheeler St.	A2
Whitby Pl	A3
Windsor Terr.	B1
York Pl	C1

Northampton

78 Derngate	B3
Abington Sq	B3
Abington St.	B3
All Saints'	B2
Ambush St.	B1
Angel St	B2
Arundel St.	A2
Ash St.	A2
Auctioneers Way	C2
Bailiff St.	A3
Barrack Rd	A3
Beaconsfield Terr.	A3
Becketts Park.	C3
Bedford Rd.	B3
Billing Rd.	B3
Brecon St.	A1
Brewery	B2
Bridge St	C2
Bridge St Depot.	C3
Broad St.	A2
Burns St.	A3
Bus Station.	B2
Campbell St.	A2
Castle (Site of)	B2
Castle St.	B2
Cattle Market Rd.	C2
Central Museum & Art Gallery	B2
Charles St.	A3
Cheyne Walk	B3
Church La.	A2
Clare St.	A3
Cloutsham St.	A3
College St.	B2
Colwyn Rd.	A3
Cotton End.	C2
Countess Rd.	A1
County Hall	B2
Court.	A2

Craven St.	A3
Crown & County Courts	B2
Denmark Rd.	B3
Derngate.	B3
Derngate & Royal Theatres	B3
Doddridge Church	B2
Duke St.	A3
Earl St.	A3
Euston Rd.	C2
Fire Station	A3
Foot Meadow	B2
Gladstone Rd.	A1
Gold St.	B2
Grafton St.	A2
Gray St.	A3
Greenwood Rd.	B1
Greyfriars	B2
Grosvenor Centre.	B2
Grove Rd	A3
Guildhall	B2
Hampton St.	A2
Harding Terr.	A2
Hazelwood Rd.	B3
Herbert St.	A2
Hervey St.	A3
Hester St.	A2
Holy Sepulchre	A2
Hood St.	A3
Horse Market	B2
Hunter St.	A3
Information Ctr	B1
Kettering Rd.	A3
Kingswell St.	B2
Lady's La.	B2
Leicester St.	A2
Leslie Rd.	A2
Library.	B3
Lorne Rd.	A2

Lorry Park.	A1
Louise Rd.	A2
Lower Harding St.	A2
Lower Hester St.	A2
Lower Mounts.	B3
Lower Priory St.	A2
Main Rd	C1
Marefair	B2
Market Sq.	B2
Marlboro Rd.	B1
Marriott St.	A3
Military Rd.	A3
Nene Valley Retail Park	C1
New South Bridge Rd.	C2
Northampton General Hospital (A & E)	B3
Northampton Station	B1
Northcote St.	A2
Nunn Mills Rd.	C3
Old Towcester Rd.	C2
Overstone Rd.	A3
Peacock Pl.	B2
Pembroke Rd.	A1
Penn Court.	C2
Police Station	B3
Post Office	A1/A2/B3/C2
Quorn Way.	A2
Ransome Rd.	C3
Regent Sq.	A2
Retail Park.	C2
Robert St.	A2
St Andrew's Rd	B1
St Andrew's St.	A2
St Edmund's Rd.	B3
St George's St.	A2
St Giles	B3
St Giles St.	B3

St Giles' Terr.	B3
St James' Mill Rd.	B1
St James' Mill Rd East	C1
St James Park Rd	B1
St James Retail & Leisure Park	C1
St James Rd.	B1
St Leonard's Rd.	C2
St Mary's St.	B2
St Michael's Rd	A3
St Peter's	B2
St Peter's Square Shopping Precinct	B2
St Peter's Way.	B2
Salisbury St.	A2
Scarletwell St.	A2
Semilong Rd.	A2
Sheep St.	B2
Sol Central (Leisure Centre).	B2
South Bridge.	C2
Southfield Ave.	C2
Spencer Bridge Rd.	A1
Spencer Rd.	A3
Spring Gdns	B2
Spring La.	B2
Swan St.	B2
The Drapery.	B2
The Ridings.	B3
Tintern Ave.	A1
Towcester Rd.	C2
Upper Bath St.	B2
Upper Mounts.	A2
Victoria Park.	A1
Victoria Promenade	B2
Victoria Rd.	B3
Victoria St.	A2
Wellingborough Rd.	B3
West Bridge	B1
York Rd.	B3

Newcastle upon Tyne

0   Miles   ¼

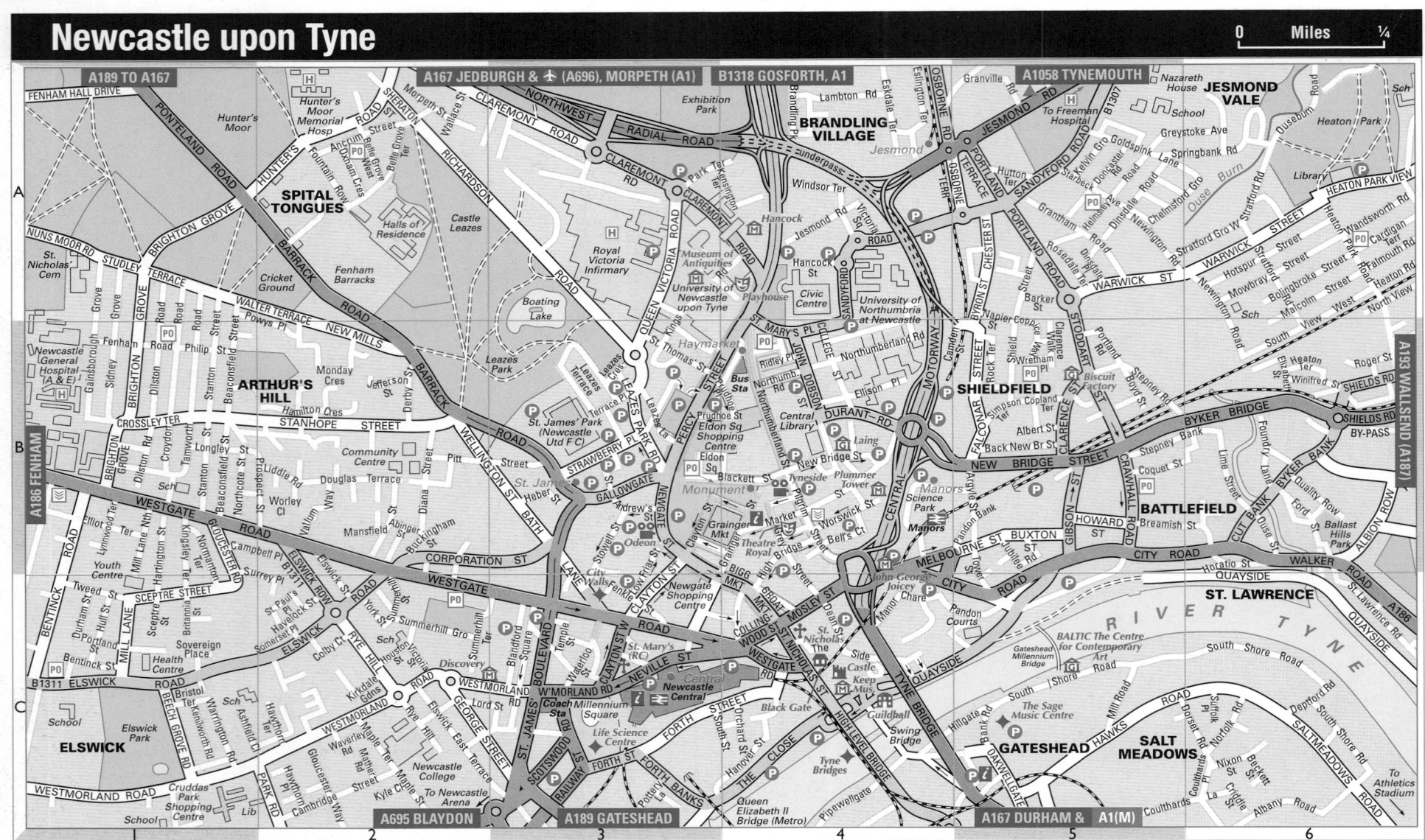

Newcastle upon Tyne

Abinger St B2
Albany Rd C6
Albert St B5
Albion Row B6
Ancrum St A2
Argyle St B5
Ashfield Cl C1
Athletics Stadium C6
Back New Bridge St . . B5
Ballast Hills Park B6
BALTIC The Centre
  for Contemporary
  Art C5
Bank Rd C5
Barker St B5
Barrack Rd A2/B2
Bath La B3
Beaconsfield St B1
Beckett St C6
Beech Grove Rd C1
Belle Grove Terr A2
Belle Grove West . . . A2
Bell's Court B4
Bentinck Rd C1
Bentinck St C1
Bigg Market C4
Biscuit Factory B5
Black Gate C4
Blackett St B4
Blandford St C3
Boating Lake A3
Bolingbroke St A6
Boyd St B5
Brandling Park A4
Breamish St B5
Brighton Gr A1/B1
Bristol Terr C1
Britannia St C1
Buckingham St B2
Bus Station B4
Buxton St B5
Byker Bank B6
Byker Bridge B6
Byron St A5
Cambridge St C2

Camden St B4
Campbell Pl B1
Cardigan Terr A6
Castle C4
Castle Leazes A2
Central (metro) C3
Central Library B4
Central Motorway . . . C4
Chelmsford Gr A5
Chester St A5
City Rd B5/C5
City Walls C3
Civic Centre A4
Claremont Rd A3
Clarence St B5
Clarence Walk A4
Clayton St B3
Clayton St West C3
Coach Station B4
Colby Court C2
College St B4
Collingwood St C4
Community Centre . . . B2
Copland Terr B5
Coppice Way B5
Coquet St B5
Corporation St B2
Coulthards La C5
Coulthards Pl C6
Courts C5
Crawhall Rd B5
Cricket Ground A2
Criddle St C6
Croydon Rd B1
Cruddas Park
  Shopping Centre . . . C1
Cut Bank B6
Dean St C4
Deptford Rd C6
Derby St B2
Diana St B2
Dilston Rd B1
Dinsdale Pl A5
Dinsdale Rd A5
Discovery
  Museum C2
Doncaster Rd A5
Dorset Rd C6

Douglas Terr B2
Durant Rd B4
Durham St C1
Eldon Sq. B3
Eldon Sq Shopping
  Centre B3
Elizabeth St B6
Elliot Terr B1
Ellison Pl B4
Elswick East Terr . . . C2
Elswick Park C2
Elswick Rd C1/C2
Elswick Row B2
Elswick St B2
Eskdale Terr A4
Eslington Terr A4
Exhibition Park A4
Falconar St B5
Falmouth Rd A6
Fenham Barracks . . . A2
Fenham Hall Dr A1
Fenham Rd B1
Fenkle St C3
Ford St B6
Forth Banks C3
Forth La C3
Forth St C3
Foundry La B6
Fountain Row A2
Gainsborough Gr . . . B1
Gallowgate B3
Gateshead Millennium
  Bridge C5
George St C2
Gibson St B5
Gloucester Rd B1
Gloucester Way C2
Goldspink La A5
Grainger Market B4
Grainger St B4
Grantham Rd A5
Granville Rd A5
Grey St B4
Greystoke Ave A5
Groat Market C4
Guildhall C4
Halls of Residence . . . A2
Hamilton Cr A2
Hancock
  Museum A4

Hanover St C4
Hartington St B1
Havelock St C2
Hawks Rd C5
Hawthorn Pl C2
Hawthorn Terr C2
Health Centre C1
Heaton Park A6
Heaton Park Rd A6
Heaton Park View . . . A6
Heaton Rd A6
Heaton Terr B6
Heber St B3
Helmsley Rd A5
High Bridge B4
High Level Bridge . . . C4
Hillgate C5
Horatio St B6
Hotspur St A6
Houston St C2
Howard St B5
Hull St C1
Hunter's Moor A1
Hunter's Moor Memorial
  Hospital A2
Hunter's Rd A2
Hutton Terr A5
Information Ctr . . . . .
  . . . . B3/B4/C3
Jefferson St B2
Jesmond (metro) A4
Jesmond Rd A4/A5
John Dobson St B4
John George Joicey
  Museum C4
Jubilee Rd B5
Kelvin Gr A5
Kenilworth Rd C1
Kensington Terr A4
Kings Rd B3
Kingsley Terr B1
Kirkdale Gdns C2
Kyle Cl C2
Laing Gallery B4
Lambton Rd A4
Leazes Cr B3
Leazes La B3

Leazes Park B3
Leazes Park Rd B3
Leazes Terr B3
Library A6/C1
Life Science
  Centre C3
Lime St B6
Longley St B1
Lord St C2
Low Friar St B3
Lynnwood Terr B1
Malcolm St A6
Manor Chare C4
Manors (metro) B4
Manors B4
Mansfield St B2
Maple St C2
Maple Terr C2
Market St B4
Mather Rd C2
Melbourne St B4
Mill La C1
Mill La North B1
Mill Rd C5
Millennium Sq. C3
Monday Cr B2
Monument (metro) . . . B4
Morpeth St A2
Mosley St C4
Mowbray St A6
Museum of
  Antiquities A3
Napier St C2
Nazareth House A5
Neville St C3
New Bridge St B4/B5
New Mills A3
Newcastle
  Central C3
Newcastle College . . . C2
Newcastle General
  Hospital (A&E) B1
Newgate Shopping
  Centre C3
Newgate St C3
Newington Rd A5/A6
Nixon St C6
Norfolk Rd C6

Normanton Terr B1
North View A6
Northcote St B1
Northumberland Rd . . B4
Northumberland St . . . B4
Northwest Radial Rd . . A3
Nuns Moor Rd A1
Oakwellgate C5
Odeon B3
Orchard St C4
Osborne Rd A4
Osborne Terr A4
Ouse Burn A6
Ouse St B6
Ouseburn Rd A6
Oxnam Cr A2
Pandon C5
Pandon Bank B5
Park Rd C2
Park Terr A3
Percy St B3
Philip St B1
Pilgrim St B4
Pipewellgate C4
Pitt St B3
Playhouse
  Theatre A4
Plummer Tower B4
Police Station . . . . .
  . . . . B1/B4/C4
Ponteland Rd A1
Portland Rd A5/B5
Portland St C1
Portland Terr C1
Post Office A2/A5/A6
  . .B1/B3/B4/B5/C1/C2
Pottery La C3
Powys Pl A1
Prospect St B2
Prudhoe Pl B3
Prudhoe St B3
Quality Row B6
Quayside C4/C6
Queen Elizabeth II
  Bridge C4
Queen Victoria Rd . . . A3
Railway St C3
Richardson Rd A3
Ridley Pl B4

Rock Terr B5
Roger St B6
Rosedale Terr A5
Royal Victoria
  Infirmary A3
Rye Hill C2
Sage Music Centre,
  The C5
St Andrew's St B3
St James (metro) B3
St James' Blvd C3
St James' Park
  (Newcastle Utd FC) . B3
St Lawrence Rd C6
St Mary's Place B4
St Mary's (RC) C3
St Nicholas C4
St Nicholas' Cem . . . A1
Saltmeadows Rd C6
Sandyford Rd A4/A5
Sceptre St C1
Science Park B4
Scotswood Rd C3
Sheraton St A2
Shield St B5
Shieldfield B5
Shields Rd B6
Shields Rd By-Pass . . B6
Sidney Gr B1
Simpson Terr B5
Somerset Pl C2
South Shore Rd C5
South St C3
South View West B6
Sovereign Pl C1
Springbank Rd A6
Stanhope St B2
Stanton St B1
Starbeck Ave A5
Stepney Bank B5
Stepney Rd B5
Stoddart St B5
Stowell St B3
Stratford Gr West . . . A6
Stratford Rd A6
Strawberry Pl B3

Studley Terr A1
Suffolk Pl C6
Summerhill Gr C2
Summerhill St C2
Summerhill Terr C2
Surrey Pl B1
Swing Bridge C4
Tamworth Rd B1
Temple St C3
Terrace Pl B3
The Close C4
The Side C4
Theatre Royal B4
Tower St C1
Tweed St C1
Tyne Bridge C4
Tyne Bridges C4
Tyneside B4
University of Newcastle
  upon Tyne A3
University of
  Northumbria at
  Newcastle A4
Vallum Way B2
Victoria Sq A4
Victoria St C3
Walker Rd B6
Wallace St B5
Walter Terr A1
Wandsworth Rd A6
Warrington Rd C1
Warwick St A5/A6
Waterloo St C3
Waverley Rd B1
Wellington St B2
Westgate Rd . B1/C2/C4
Westmorland Rd.
  . . . . C1/C2/C3
Windsor Terr A4
Winifred St B6
Worley Cl B1
Worswick St B4
Wretham Pl B5
York St C3
Youth Centre C1

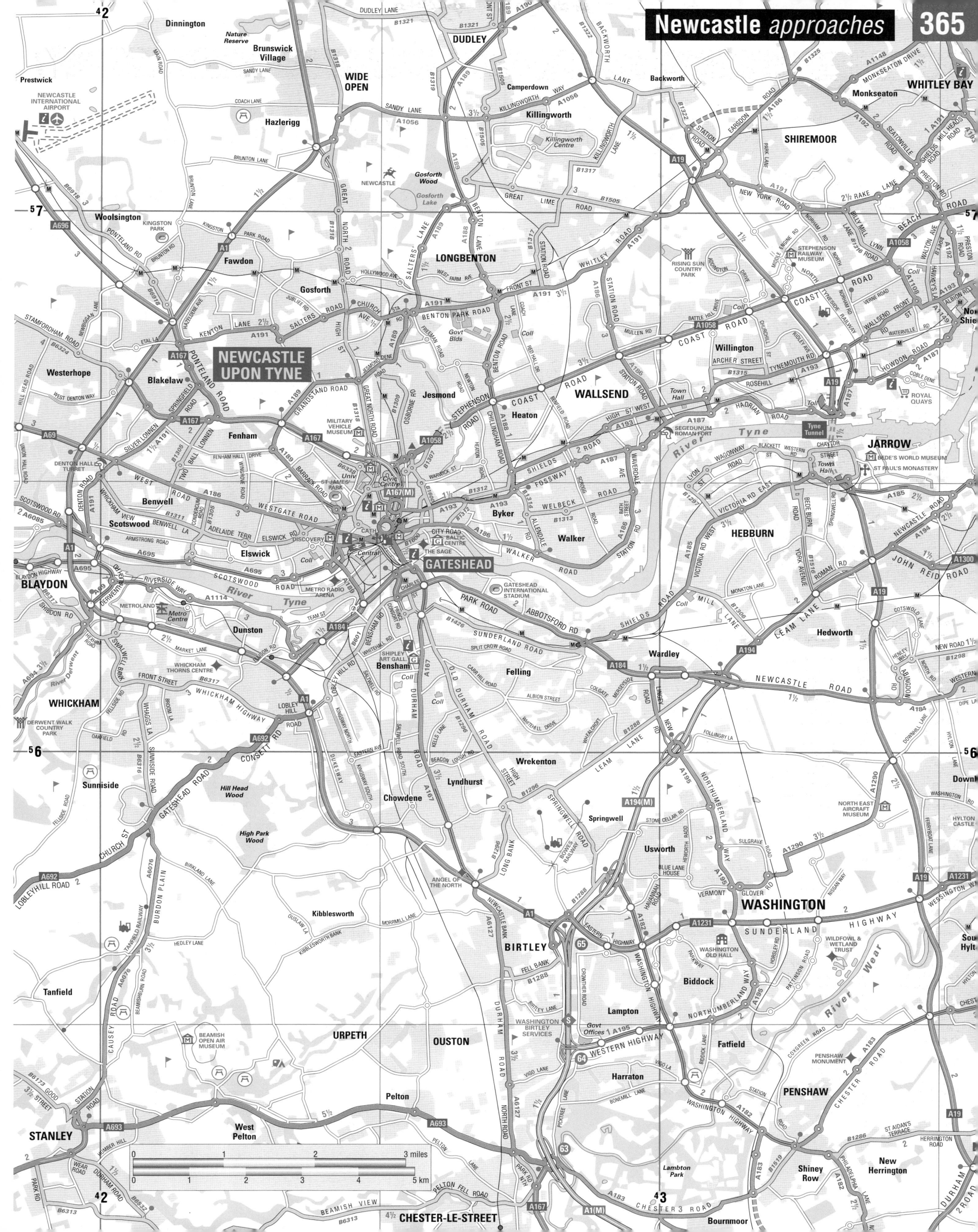

Norwich

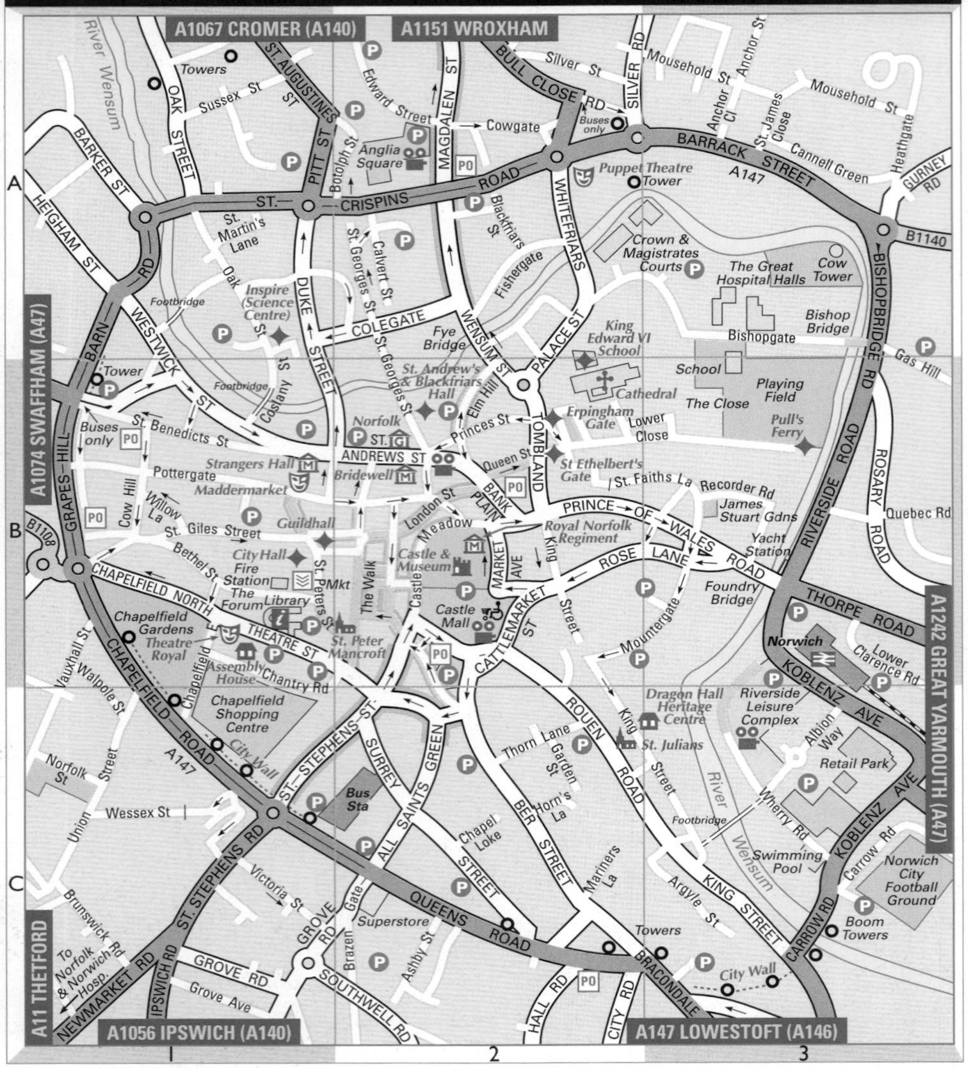

0 Miles ¼
A1067 CROMER (A140)
A1151 WROXHAM
A1074 SWAFFHAM (A47)
A1242 GREAT YARMOUTH (A47)
A11 THETFORD
A1056 IPSWICH (A140)
A147 LOWESTOFT (A146)

Nottingham

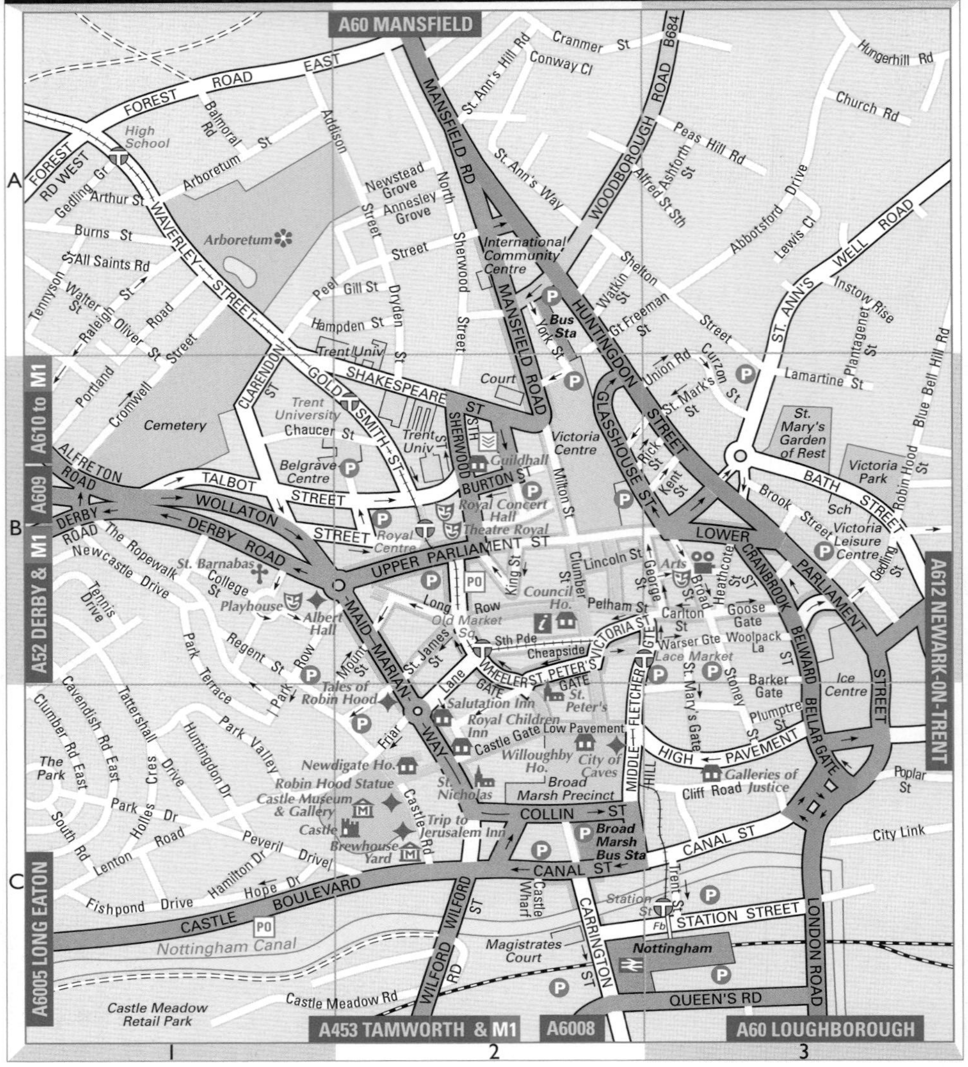

0 Miles ¼
A60 MANSFIELD
A609 | A610 to M1
A52 DERBY & M1
A6005 LONG EATON
A612 NEWARK-ON-TRENT
A453 TAMWORTH & M1
A6008
A60 LOUGHBOROUGH

Norwich

Albion Way C3
All Saints Green C2
Anchor Cl A3
Anchor St A3
Anglia Sq B2
Argyle St C3
Ashby St C2
Assembly House B1
Bank Plain B2
Barker St A1
Barn Rd A1
Barrack St A3
Ber St C2
Bethel St B1
Bishop Bridge A3
Bishopbridge Rd A3
Bishopgate A3
Blackfriars St A2
Botolph St A2
Bracondale C3
Brazen Gate C2
Bridewell B2
Brunswick Rd C1
Bull Close Rd A2
Bus Station C2
Calvert St A2
Cannell Green A3
Carrow Rd C3
Castle Mall B2
Castle Meadow B2
Castle & Museum B1
Cathedral ✝ B2
Cattlemarket St B2
Chantry Rd B1
Chapel Loke C2
Chapelfield East B1
Chapelfield Gdns B1
Chapelfield North B1
Chapelfield Rd B1
Chapelfield Shopping Centre C1
City Hall ✦ B1
City Rd C2
City Wall C1/C3
Colegate A2
Coslany St B1
Cow Hill B1
Cow Tower A3
Cowgate A2
Crown & Magistrates Courts B2
Dragon Hall Heritage Centre C3
Duke St A1
Edward St A2
Elm Hill B2
Erpingham Gate ✦ B2
Fire Station B1
Fishergate A2
Foundry Bridge B3
Fye Bridge A2
Garden St C2
Gas Hill B3
Grapes Hill B1
Great Hospital Halls, The A3
Grove Ave C1
Grove Rd C1
Guildhall ✦ B1
Gurney Rd A3
Hall Rd C2
Heathgate A3
Heigham St A1
Horn's La C2
Information Ctr B1
Inspire (Science Centre) ✦ A1
Ipswich Rd C1
James Stewart Gdns B3
King Edward VI School ✦ B2
King St B2
King St C3
Koblenz Ave C3
Library B1
London St B2
Lower Clarence Rd B3
Lower Cl B3
Maddermarket B1
Magdalen St A2
Mariners La C2
Market B2
Market Ave B2
Mountergate B3
Mousehold St A3
Newmarket Rd C1
Norfolk Gallery B2
Norfolk St C1
Norwich City FC C3
Norwich Station B3
Oak St A1
Palace St A2
Pitt St A1
Police Station B1
Post Office A2/B1/B2/C2
Pottergate B1
Prince of Wales Rd B2
Princes St B2
Pull's Ferry ✦ B3
Puppet Theatre A2
Quebec Rd B3
Queen St B2
Queens Rd C2
Recorder Rd B3
Retail Park C3
Riverside Leisure Complex C3
Riverside Rd B3
Rosary Rd B3
Rose La B2
Rouen Rd C2
Royal Norfolk Regiment Museum B2
St Andrew's & Blackfriars Hall ✦ B2
St Andrews St B2
St Augustines St A1
St Benedicts St B1
St Crispins Rd A1
St Ethelbert's Gate ✦ B2
St Faiths La B3
St Georges St A2
St Giles St B1
St James Cl A3
St Julians C2
St Martin's La A1
St Peter Mancroft B2
St Peters St B1
St Stephens Rd C1
St Stephens St C1
Silver Rd A2
Silver St A2
Southwell Rd C2
Strangers Hall B1
Superstore C2
Surrey St C2
Sussex St A1
Swimming Pool B3
The Close B3
The Forum B1
The Walk B2
Theatre Royal B1
Theatre St B1
Thorn La C2
Thorpe Rd B3
Tombland B2
Union St C1
Vauxhall St B1
Victoria St C1
Walpole St B1
Wensum St A2
Wessex St C1
Westwick St A1
Wherry Rd C3
Whitefriars A2
Willow La B1
Yacht Station B3

Nottingham

Abbotsford Dr A3
Addison St A1
Albert Hall ✦ B1
Alfred St South A3
Alfreton Rd B1
All Saints Rd A1
Annesley Gr A2
Arboretum ✽ A1
Arboretum St A1
Arthur St A1
Arts Theatre B3
Ashforth St A3
Balmoral Rd A1
Barker Gate B3
Bath St B3
Belgrave Centre B1
Bellar Gate B3
Belward St B3
Blue Bell Hill Rd B3
Brewhouse Yard C2
Broad Marsh Bus Station C2
Broad Marsh Precinct C2
Broad St B3
Brook St B3
Burns St A1
Burton St B2
Bus Station A2
Canal St C2
Carlton St B3
Carrington St C2
Castle Blvd C1
Castle C2
Castle Gate C2
Castle Meadow Retail Park C1
Castle Meadow Rd C2
Castle Museum & Gallery C2
Castle Rd C2
Castle Wharf C2
Cavendish Rd East C1
Cemetery B1
Chaucer St B1
Cheapside B2
Church Rd A3
City Link C3
City of Caves ✦ C2
Clarendon St B1
Cliff Rd C3
Clumber Rd East C1
Clumber St B2
College St B1
Collin St C2
Conway Cl A2
Council House B2
Court B2
Cranbrook St B3
Cranmer St A2
Cromwell St B1
Curzon St B3
Derby Rd B1
Dryden St A2
Fishpond Dr C1
Fletcher Gate B3
Forest Rd East A1
Forest Rd West A1
Friar La C2
Galleries of Justice C3
Gedling Gr A1
Gedling St B3
George St B3
Gill St A2
Glasshouse St B2
Goldsmith St B2
Goose Gate B3
Great Freeman St A2
Guildhall B2
Hamilton Dr C1
Hampden St A1
Heathcote St B3
High Pavement C3
High School (tram stop) A1
Holles Cr C1
Hope Dr C1
Hungerhill Rd A3
Huntingdon Dr C1
Huntingdon St A2
Ice Centre C3
Information Ctr B2
Instow Rise A3
International Community Centre A2
Kent St B3
King St B2
Lace Market (tram stop) B3
Lamartine St B3
Lenton Rd C1
Lewis Cl A3
Lincoln St B2
London Rd C3
Long Row B2
Low Pavement C2
Lower Parliament St B3
Magistrates Court C2
Maid Marian Way B2
Mansfield Rd A2/B2
Middle Hill C2
Milton St B2
Mount St B2
Newcastle Dr B1
Newdigate House C2
Newstead Gr A2
North Sherwood St A2
Nottingham Station C3
Old Market Square (tram stop) B2
Oliver St A1
Park Dr C1
Park Row C1
Park Terr B1
Park Valley C1
Peas Hill Rd A3
Peel St A1
Pelham St B2
Peveril Dr C1
Plantagenet St A3
Playhouse Theatre B1
Plumptre St C3
Police Station B2
Poplar St C3
Portland Rd B1
Post Office B2/C1
Queen's Rd C3
Raleigh St A1
Regent St B1
Rick St B3
Robin Hood Statue ✦ C2
Robin Hood St B3
Royal Centre (tram stop) B2
Royal Children Inn C2
Royal Concert Hall B2
St Ann's Hill Rd A2
St Ann's Way A2
St Ann's Well Rd A3
St Barnabas ✝ B1
St James' St B2
St Mark's St B3
St Mary's Garden of Rest B3
St Mary's Gate B3
St Nicholas C2
St Peter's C2
St Peter's Gate B2
Salutation Inn C2
Shakespeare St B2
Shelton St A2
South Pde B2
South Rd C1
South Sherwood St B2
Station St C3
Station Street (tram stop) C3
Stoney St B3
Talbot St B1
Tales of Robin Hood ✦ C2
Tattershall Dr C1
Tennis Dr B1
Tennyson St A1
The Park C1
The Ropewalk B1
Theatre Royal B2
Trent St C3
Trent University A2/B2
Trent University (tram stop) B2
Trip To Jerusalem Inn ✦ C2
Union Rd B3
Upper Parliament St B2
Victoria Centre B2
Victoria Leisure Centre B3
Victoria Park B3
Victoria St B2
Walter St A1
Warser Gate B3
Watkin St A2
Waverley St A1
Wheeler Gate B2
Wilford Rd C2
Wilford St C2
Willoughby House C2
Wollaton St B1
Woodborough Rd A2
Woolpack La B3
York St A2

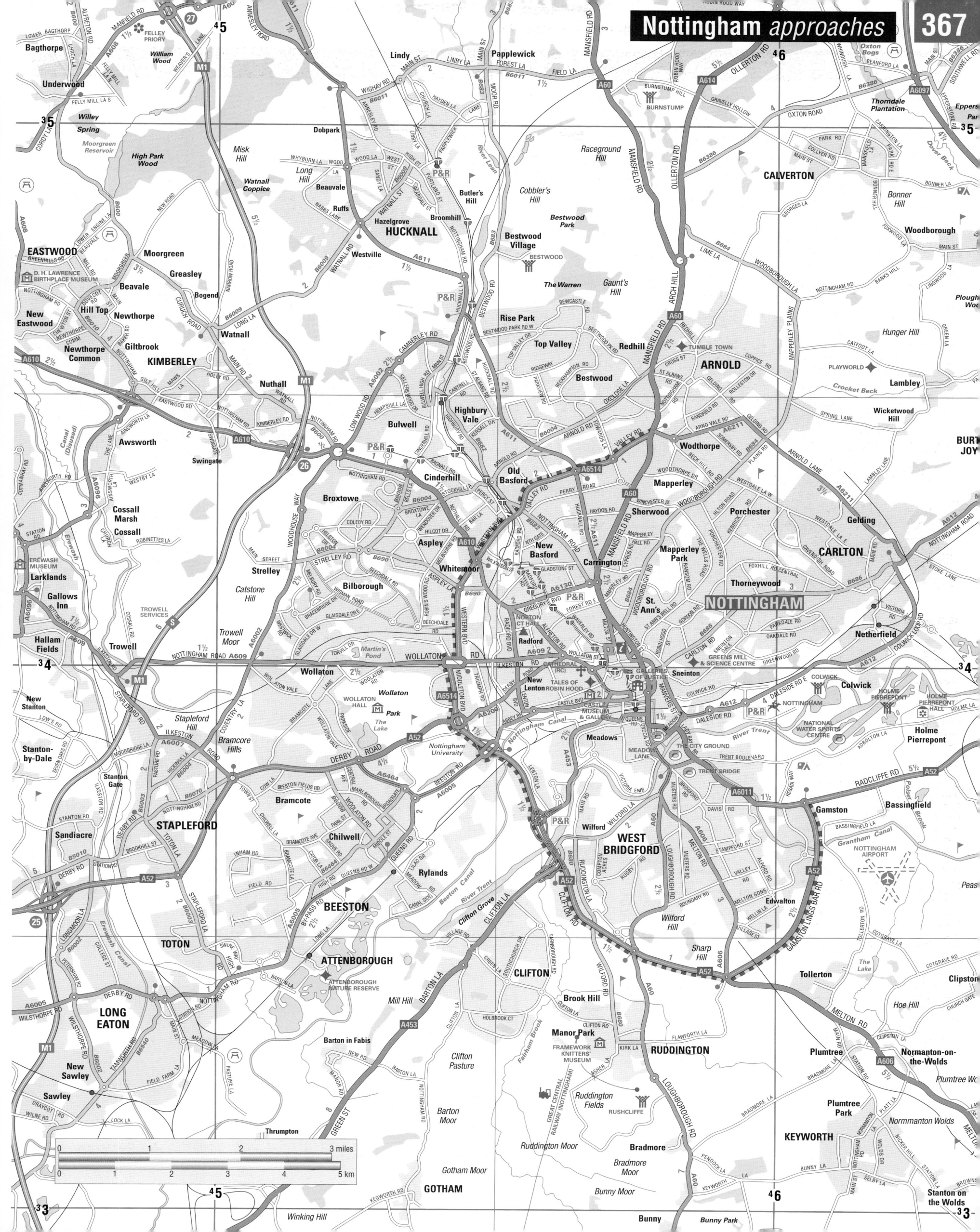

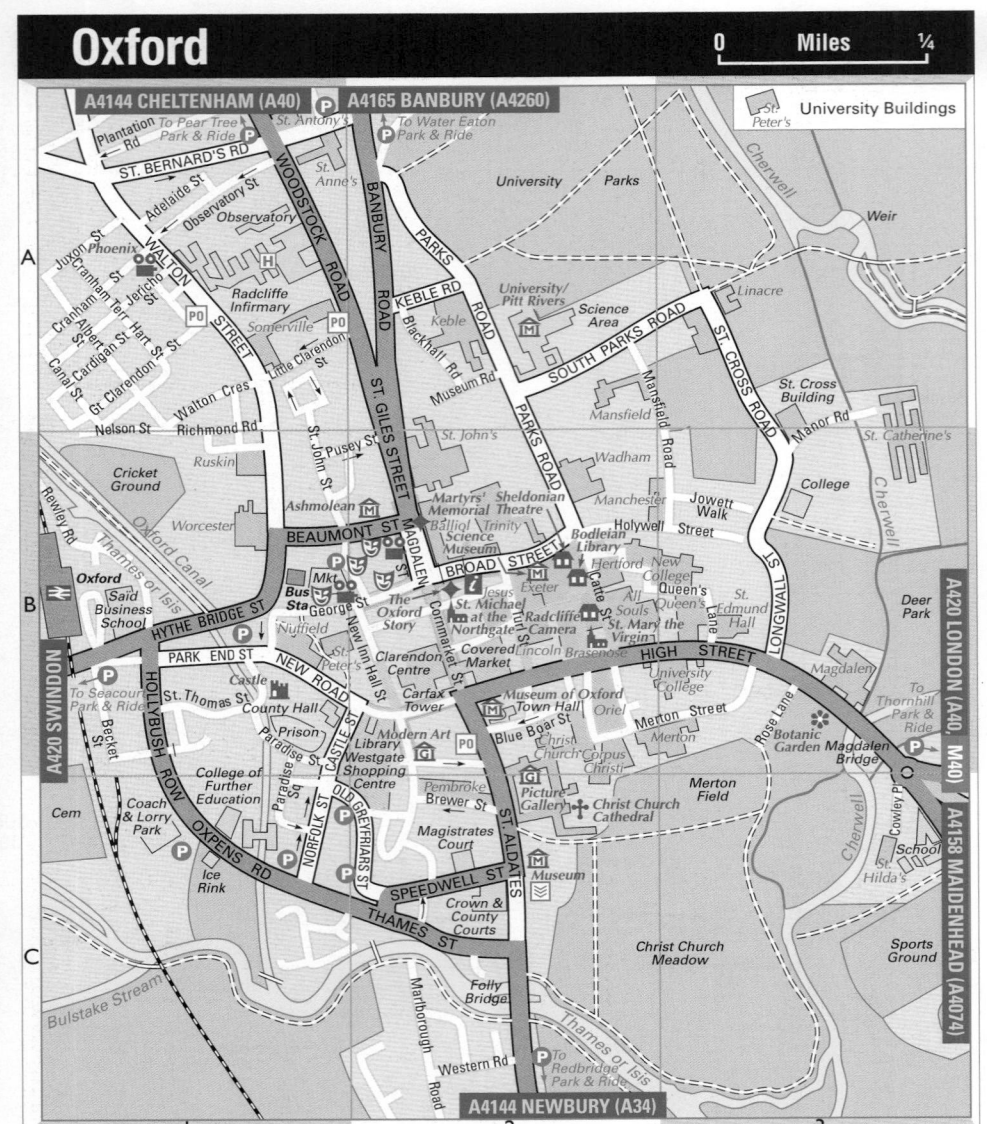

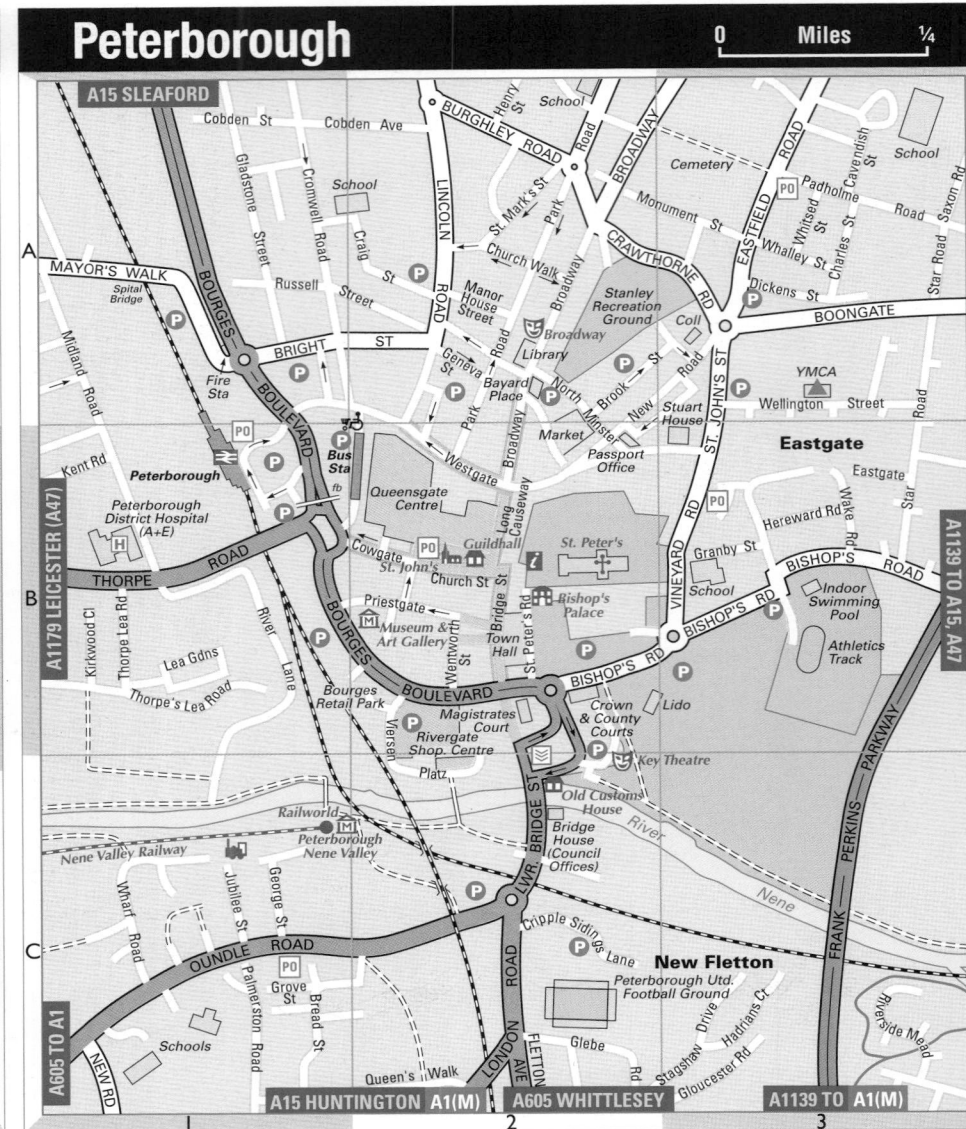

Oxford

Adelaide St A1	Cranham Terr A1	Museum of	St Antony's (Coll) A1
Albert St A1	Cricket Ground B1	Modern Art 🏛 B2	St Bernard's Rd A1
All Souls (Coll) B2	Crown & County	Museum of	St Catherine's (Coll) . B3
Ashmolean	Courts C2	Oxford 🏛 B2	St Cross Building A3
Museum 🏛 B2	Deer Park B3	Museum Rd A2	St Cross Rd A3
Balliol (Coll) B2	Exeter (Coll) B2	New College (Coll) . . . B2	St Edmund Hall
Banbury Rd A2	Folly Bridge C2	New Inn Hall St B2	(Coll) B3
Beaumont St B1	George St B1	New Rd B1	St Giles St A2
Becket St B1	Great Clarendon St . . A1	New Theatre 🎭 B1	St Hilda's (Coll) C3
Blackhall Rd A2	Hart St A1	Norfolk St C1	St John St B2
Blue Boar St B2	Hertford (Coll) B2	Nuffield (Coll) B1	St John's (Coll) B2
Bodleian Library 🏛 . . B2	High St B3	Observatory A1	St Mary the Virgin 🏛 . B2
Botanic Garden ❀ . . . B3	HM Prison B1	Observatory St A1	St Michael at the
Brasenose (Coll) B2	Hollybush Row B1	Odeon 🎬 B1/B2	Northgate 🏛 B2
Brewer St C2	Holywell St B2	Old Fire Station 🎭 . . B1	St Peter's (Coll) B1
Broad St B2	Hythe Bridge St B1	Old Greyfriars St . . . C2	St Thomas St B1
Burton-Taylor	Ice Rink C1	Oriel (Coll) B2	Science Area A2
Theatre 🎭 B2	Information Ctr ℹ . . . B2	Oxford 🚆 B1	Science Museum 🏛 . . B2
Bus Station B1	Jericho St A1	Oxford Story, The ♦ . B2	Sheldonian
Canal St A1	Jesus (Coll) B2	Oxpens Rd C1	Theatre 🏛 B2
Cardigan St A1	Jowett Walk B3	Paradise Sq C1	Somerville (Coll) A1
Carfax Tower B2	Juxon St A1	Paradise St B1	South Parks Rd A2
Castle B1	Keble (Coll) A2	Park End St B1	Speedwell St C2
Castle St B1	Keble Rd A2	Parks Rd A2/B2	Sports Ground C3
Catte St B2	Library B2	Pembroke (Coll) B2	Thames St C2
Cemetery C1	Linacre (Coll) A3	Phoenix 🎬 A1	Town Hall B2
Christ Church (Coll) . . B2	Lincoln (Coll) B2	Picture Gallery 🏛 . . . C2	Trinity (Coll) B2
Christ Church	Little Clarendon St . . A1	Plantation Rd A1	Turl St B2
Cathedral † C2	Longwall St B3	Playhouse 🎭 B2	University College
Christ Church	Magdalen (Coll) B3	Police Station 🏛 C2	(Coll) B3
Meadow C2	Magdalen Bridge . . . B3	Post Office 🏤 . . . A1/B2	University Museum & Pitt
Clarendon Centre . . . B2	Magdalen Rd B2	Pusey St B1	Rivers Museum A2
Coach & Lorry Park . . C1	Magistrates Court . . . C2	Queen's La B3	University Parks A2
College B3	Manchester (Coll) . . . B2	Queen's (Coll) B2	Wadham (Coll) B2
College of Further	Manor Rd B3	Radcliffe Camera 🏛 . B2	Walton Cr A1
Education C1	Mansfield (Coll) A2	Radcliffe Infirmary 🏥 . A1	Walton St A1
Cornmarket St B2	Mansfield Rd A3	Rewley Rd B1	Western Rd C2
Corpus Christi (Coll) . B2	Market B1	Richmond Rd B1	Westgate Shopping
County Hall B1	Marlborough Rd C2	Rose La B3	Centre B2
Covered Market B2	Martyrs' Memorial ♦ . B2	Ruskin B1	Woodstock Rd A1
Cowley Pl C3	Merton Field B3	Saïd Business	Worcester (Coll) B1
Cranham St A1	Merton (Coll) B3	School B1	
	Merton St B2	St Aldates C2	
	Museum 🏛 C2	St Anne's (Coll) A1	

Peterborough

Bishop's Palace 🏛 . . B2	Eastfield Rd A3	Mayor's Walk A1	Queensgate Centre . . B2
Bishop's Rd B2/B3	Eastgate B3	Midland Rd A1	Railworld 🏛 C1
Boongate A3	Fire Station A1	Monument St A2	River La B1
Bourges Boulevard . . A1	Fletton Ave C2	Museum & Art	Rivergate Shopping
Bread St C1	Frank Perkins	Gallery 🏛 B2	Centre B2
Bourges Retail	Parkway C3	Nene Valley	Riverside Mead C3
Park B1/B2	Geneva St A2	Railway 🚆 C1	Russell St A1
Bridge House	George St C1	New Rd A2	St John's 🏛 B2
(Council Offices) . . . C2	Gladstone St A1	New Rd C1	St John's St B2
Bridge St B2	Glebe Rd C2	North Minster A2	St Mark's St A2
Bright St A1	Gloucester Rd C3	Old Customs	St Peter's † B2
Broadway A2	Granby St B3	House 🏛 C2	St Peter's Rd B2
Broadway 🎭 A2	Grove St C1	Oundle Rd C1	Saxon Rd A3
Brook St A2	Guildhall 🏛 B2	Padholme Rd A3	Spital Bridge A1
Burghley Rd A1	Hadrians Ct C3	Palmerston Rd C1	Stagshaw Dr C3
Bus Station B2	Henry St A2	Park Rd A2	Star Rd B3
Cavendish St A3	Hereward Rd B3	Passport Office B2	Thorpe Lea Rd B1
Charles St A3	Information Ctr ℹ . . . B2	Peterborough District	Thorpe Rd B1
Church St B2	Jubilee St C1	Hospital (A+E) 🏥 . . B1	Thorpe's Lea Rd B1
Church Walk A2	Key Theatre 🎭 C2	Peterborough	Town Hall B2
Cobden Ave A1	Kent Rd B1	Station 🚆 B1	Viersen Platz B2
Cobden St A1	Kirkwood Cl B1	Peterborough Nene	Vineyard Rd B3
Cowgate B2	Lea Gdns B1	Valley Station 🚆 . . . C1	Wake Rd B3
Craig St A2	Library A2	Peterborough	Wellington St A3
Crawthorne Rd A2	Lincoln Rd A2	United FC C2	Wentworth St B2
Cripple Sidings La . . . C2	London Rd C2	Police Station 🏛 B2	Westgate B2
Cromwell Rd A1	Long Causeway B2	Post Office 🏤	Whalley St A3
Dickens St A3	Lower Bridge St C2	. . . . . A3/B1/B2/B3/C1	Wharf Rd C1
	Magistrates Court . . . B2	Priestgate B2	Whitsed St A3
	Manor House St A2	Queen's Walk C2	YMCA A3

Plymouth

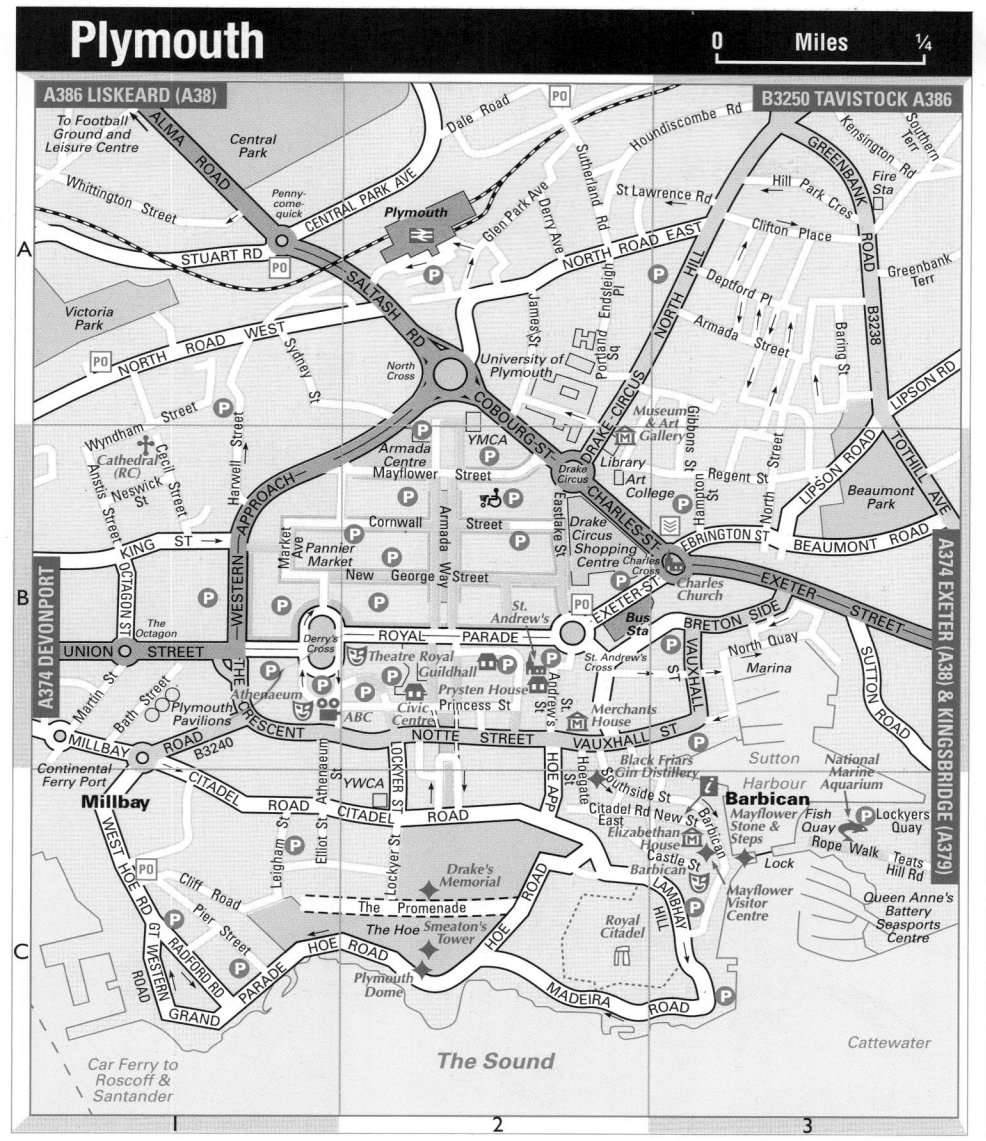

Poole

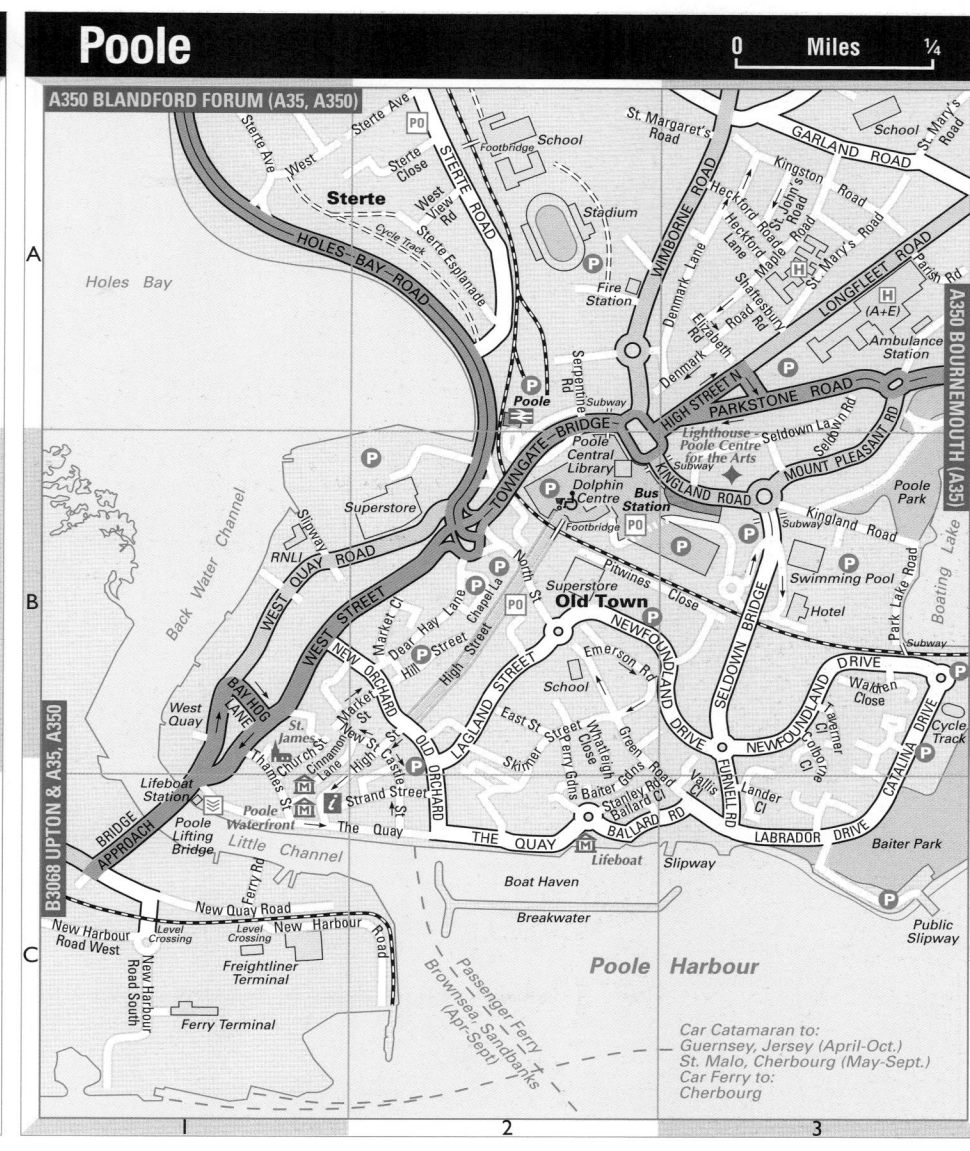

Portsmouth

0 Miles ¼

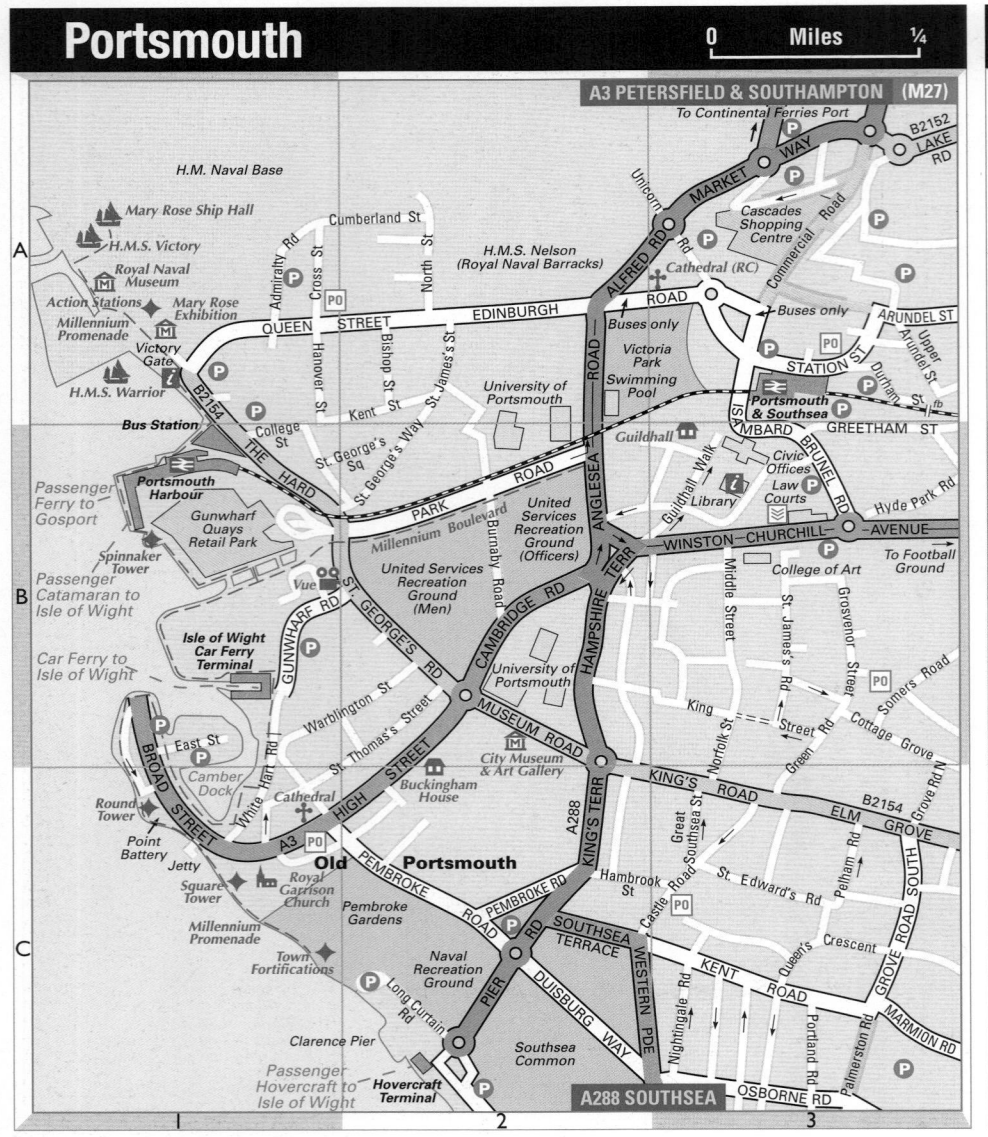

Preston

0 Miles ¼

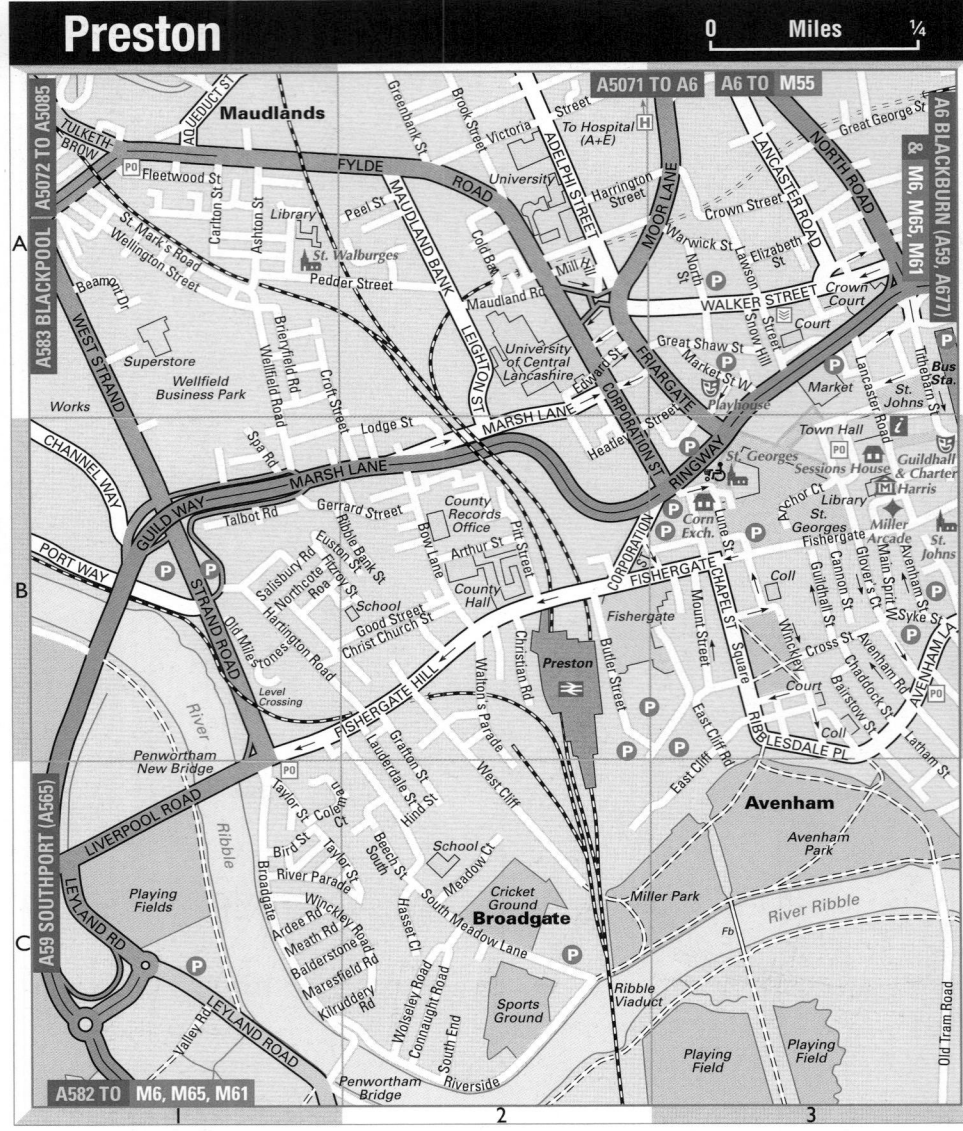

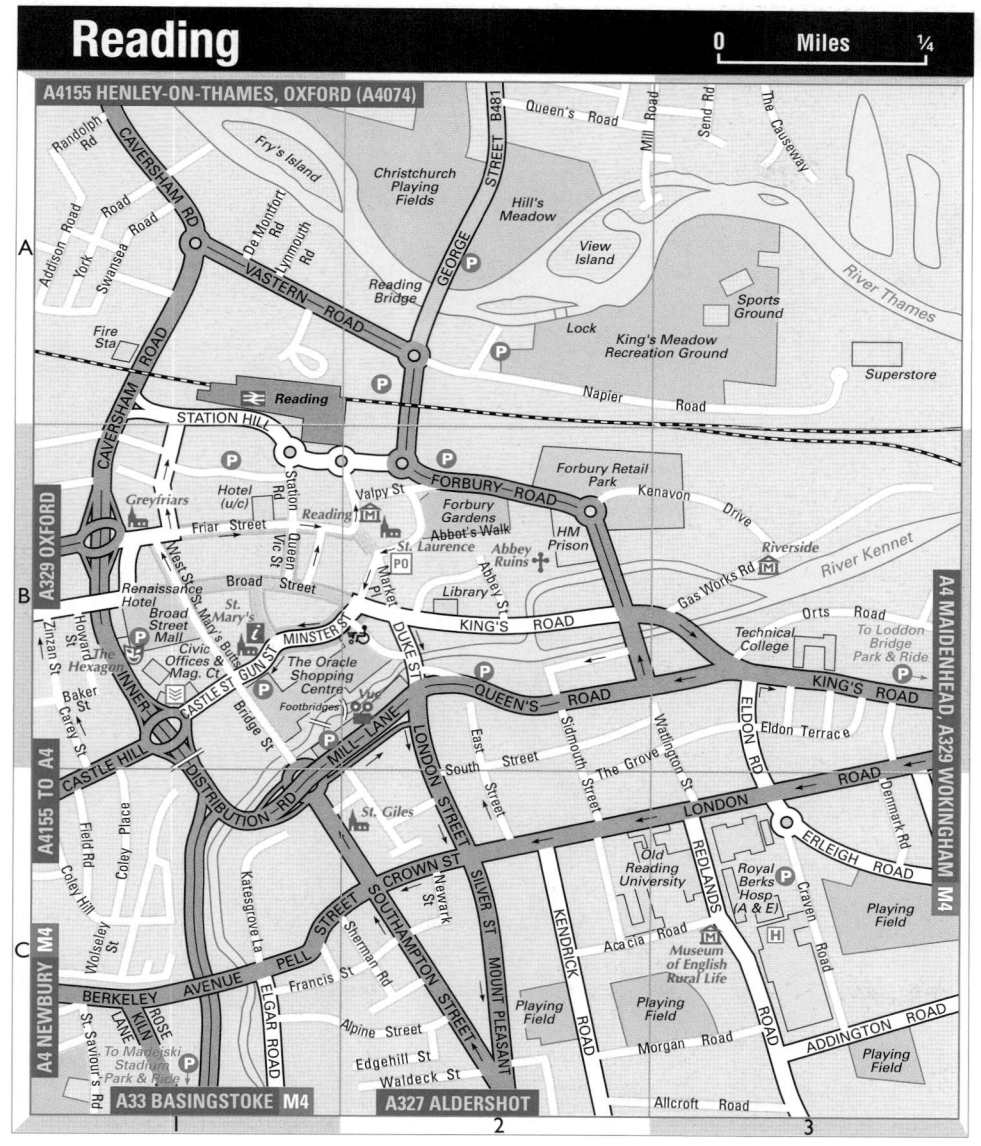

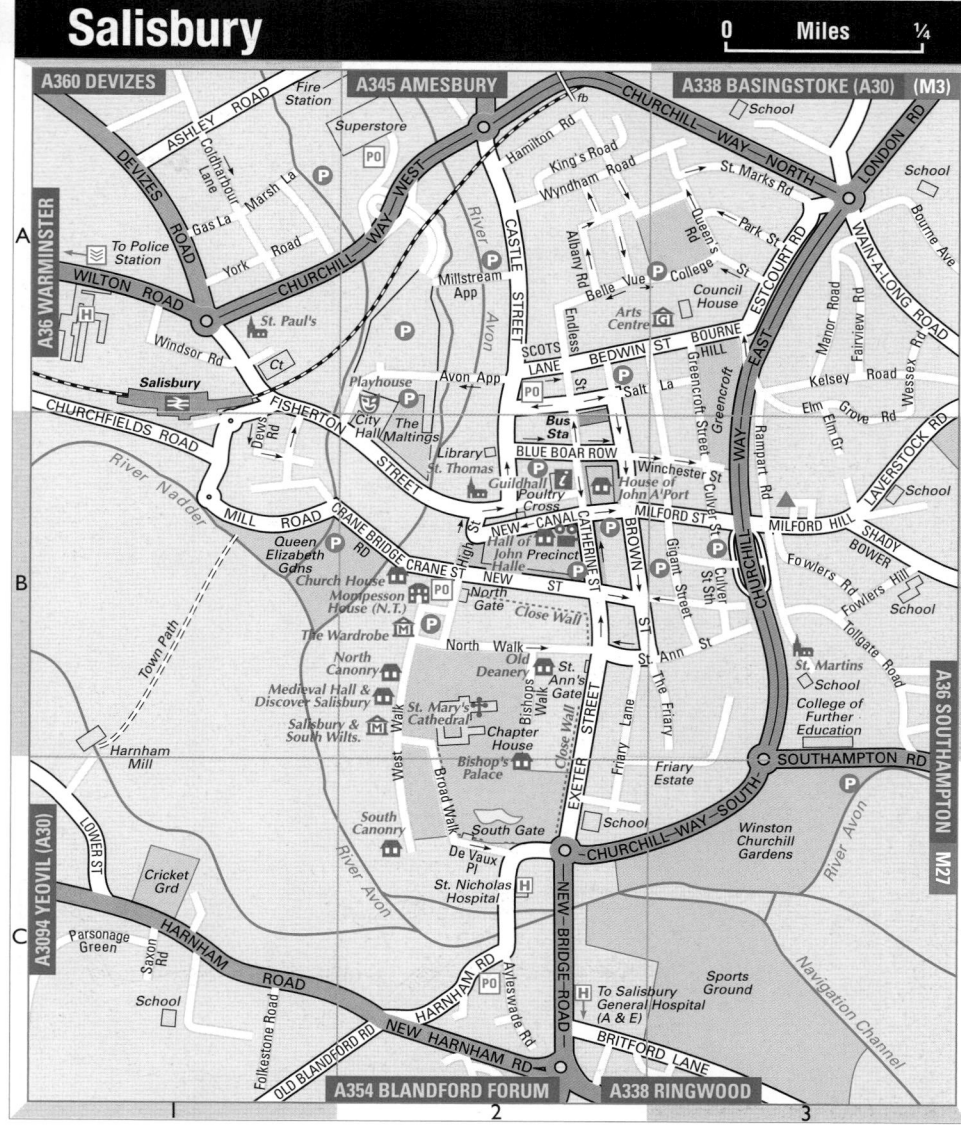

Reading

Abbey Ruins † B2
Abbey St B2
Abbot's Walk B2
Acacia Rd C2
Addington Rd C3
Addison Rd A1
Allcroft Rd C3
Alpine St C2
Baker St B1
Berkeley Ave C1
Bridge St B1
Broad St B1
Broad Street Mall . . . B1
Carey St B1
Castle Hill C1
Castle St B1
Caversham Rd A1
Christchurch
  Playing Fields A2
Civic Offices &
  Magistrate's Court . . B1
Coley Hill C1
Coley Pl C1
Craven Rd C3
Crown St C2
De Montfort Rd A1
Denmark Rd C3
Duke St B2
East St B2

Edgehill St C2
Eldon Rd B3
Eldon Terr B3
Elgar Rd C1
Erleigh Rd C3
Field Rd C1
Fire Station A1
Forbury Gdns B2
Forbury Retail Park . . B2
Forbury Rd B2
Francis St C1
Friar St B1
Gas Works Rd B3
George St A2
Greyfriars ♜ B1
Gun St B1
Hexagon Theatre,
  The ♖ B1
Hill's Meadow A2
HM Prison B2
Howard St B1
Information Ctr ⓘ . . . B1
Inner Distribution Rd . B1
Katesgrove La C1
Kenavon Dr B2
Kendrick Rd C2
King's Meadow
  Rec Ground A2
King's Rd B2
Library B2
London Rd C3

London St B2
Lynmouth Rd A1
Market Pl B1
Mill La B2
Mill Rd A2
Minster St B1
Morgan Rd C3
Mount Pleasant C2
Museum of English
  Rural Life ♜ C3
Napier Rd A2
Newark St C2
Old Reading
  University C3
Oracle Shopping
  Centre, The B1
Orts Rd B3
Pell St C1
Queen Victoria St . . . B1
Queen's Rd B1
Queen's Rd B2
Randolph Rd A1
Reading Bridge A2
Reading Station ⌖ . . . B1
Redlands Rd C3
Renaissance Hotel . . . B1
Riverside
  Museum ♜ B3
Rose Kiln La C1

Royal Berks Hospital
  (A & E) Ⓗ C3
St Giles ♜ C2
St Laurence ♜ B2
St Mary's ♜ B1
St Mary's Butts B1
St Saviour's Rd C1
Send Rd A3
Sherman Rd C2
Sidmouth St B2
Silver St C2
South St B2
Southampton St C2
Station Hill A1
Station Rd B1
Superstore A3
Swansea Rd A1
Technical College . . . B3
The Causeway A3
The Grove B2
Valpy St B2
Vastern Rd A1
Vue ♖ B2
Waldeck St C2
Watlington St B3
West St B1
Wolseley St C1
York Rd A1
Zinzan St B1

Salisbury

Albany Rd A2
Arts Centre ♜ A3
Ashley Rd A1
Avon Approach A2
Ayleswade Rd C2
Bedwin St A2
Belle Vue A2
Bishop's Palace ♜ . . C2
Bishops Rd B2
Blue Boar Row B2
Bourne Ave A3
Bourne Hill A3
Britford La C2
Broad Walk C2
Brown St B2
Bus Station B2
Castle St A2
Catherine St B2
Chapter House B2
Church House ♜ . . . B2
Churchfields Rd B1
Churchill Way East . . B3
Churchill Way North . . A3
Churchill Way South . . C2
Churchill Way West . . A1
City Hall B2
Close Wall B2
Coldharbour La A1
College of Further
  Education B3
College St A3
Council House A3
Court A1
Crane Bridge Rd . . . B2
Crane St B2

Cricket Ground C1
Culver St South B3
De Vaux Pl C2
Devizes Rd A1
Dews Rd B1
Elm Grove A3
Elm Grove Rd A3
Endless St A2
Estcourt Rd A3
Exeter St C2
Fairview Rd A3
Fire Station A1
Fisherton St A1
Folkestone Rd C1
Fowlers Hill B3
Fowlers Rd B3
Friary Estate C3
Friary La B2
Gas La A1
Gigant St B2
Greencroft B3
Greencroft St A3
Guildhall B2
Hall of John Halle ♜ . B2
Hamilton Rd A2
Harnham Mill C1
Harnham Rd C1/C2
High St B2
Hospital Ⓗ A1
House of John
  A'Port ♜ B2
Information Ctr ⓘ . . . B2
Kelsey Rd A3
King's Rd A2
Laverstock Rd B3
Library B2
London Rd A3

Lower St C1
Maltings, The B2
Manor Rd A3
Marsh La A1
Medieval Hall & Discover
  Salisbury ♜ B2
Milford Hill B3
Milford St B3
Mill Rd B1
Millstream
  Approach A2
Mompesson
  House (N.T.) ♜ . . . B2
New Bridge Rd C2
New Canal B2
New Harnham Rd . . . C2
New St B2
North Canonry ♜ . . . B2
North Gate B2
North Walk B2
Old Blandford Rd . . . C1
Old Deanery ♜ B2
Park St A3
Parsonage Green . . . C1
Playhouse
  Theatre ♖ A2
Post Office ⊠ A2/B2/C2
Poultry Cross B2
Precinct B2
Queen Elizabeth
  Gdns B1
Queen's Rd A3
Rampart Rd B3
St Ann's Gate B2
St Ann St B2
St Marks Rd A3
St Martins ♜ B3

St Mary's
  Cathedral † B2
St Nicholas
  Hospital Ⓗ C2
St Paul's ♜ A1
St Thomas ♜ B2
Salisbury &
  South Wiltshire
  Museum ♜ B2
Salisbury General
  Hospital (A & E) Ⓗ . C2
Salisbury Station ⌖ . . A1
Salt La A3
Saxon Rd C1
Scots La A2
Shady Bower B3
South Canonry ♜ . . . B2
South Gate C2
Southampton Rd . . . B2
Sports Ground C3
The Friary B3
Tollgate Rd B3
Town Path B1
Wain-a-Long Rd . . . A3
Wardrobe, The ♜ . . . B2
Wessex Rd A3
West Walk C2
Wilton Rd A1
Winchester St B3
Windsor Rd A1
Winston Churchill
  Gdns C3
Wyndham Rd A2
YHA ▲ B3
York Rd A1

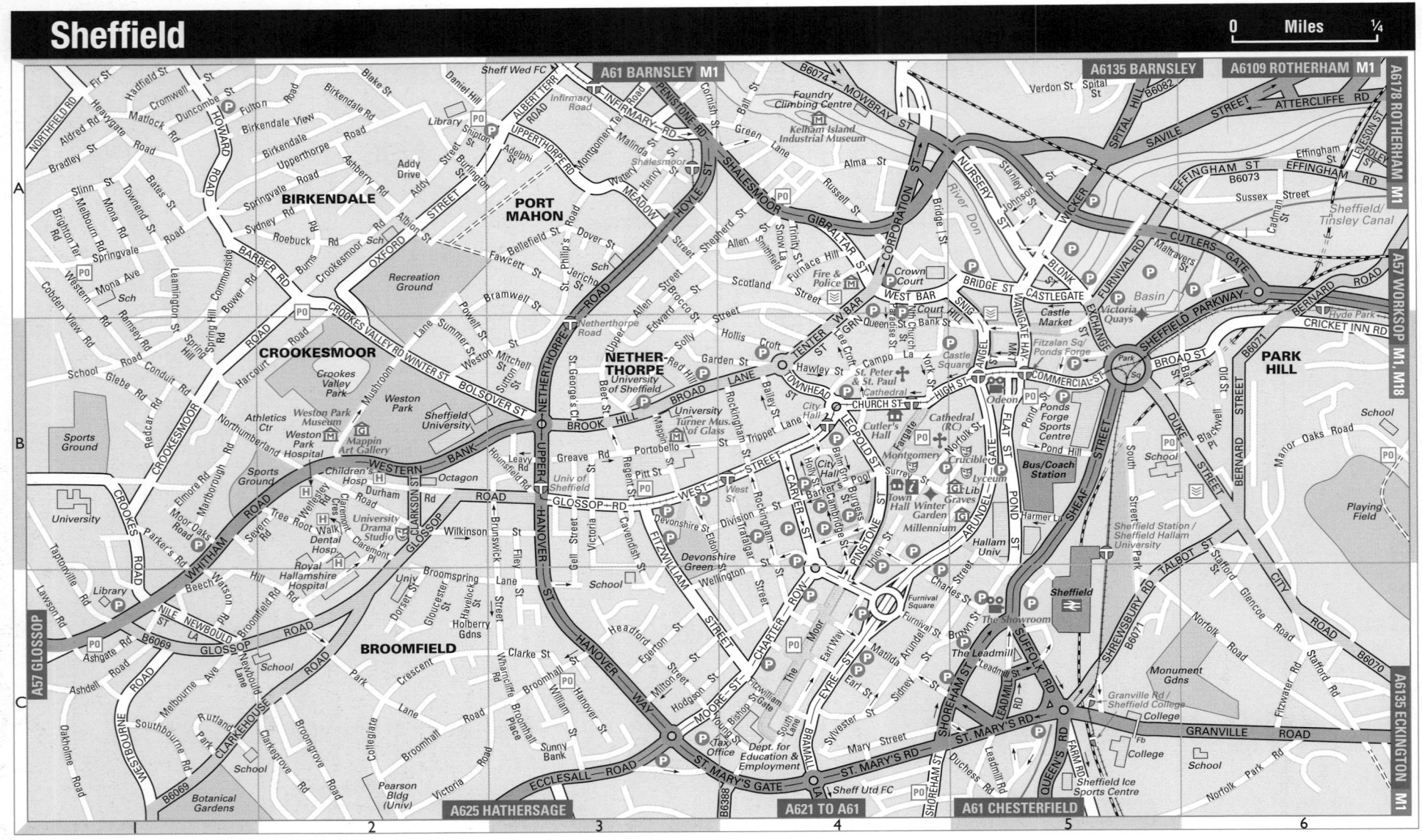

Sheffield

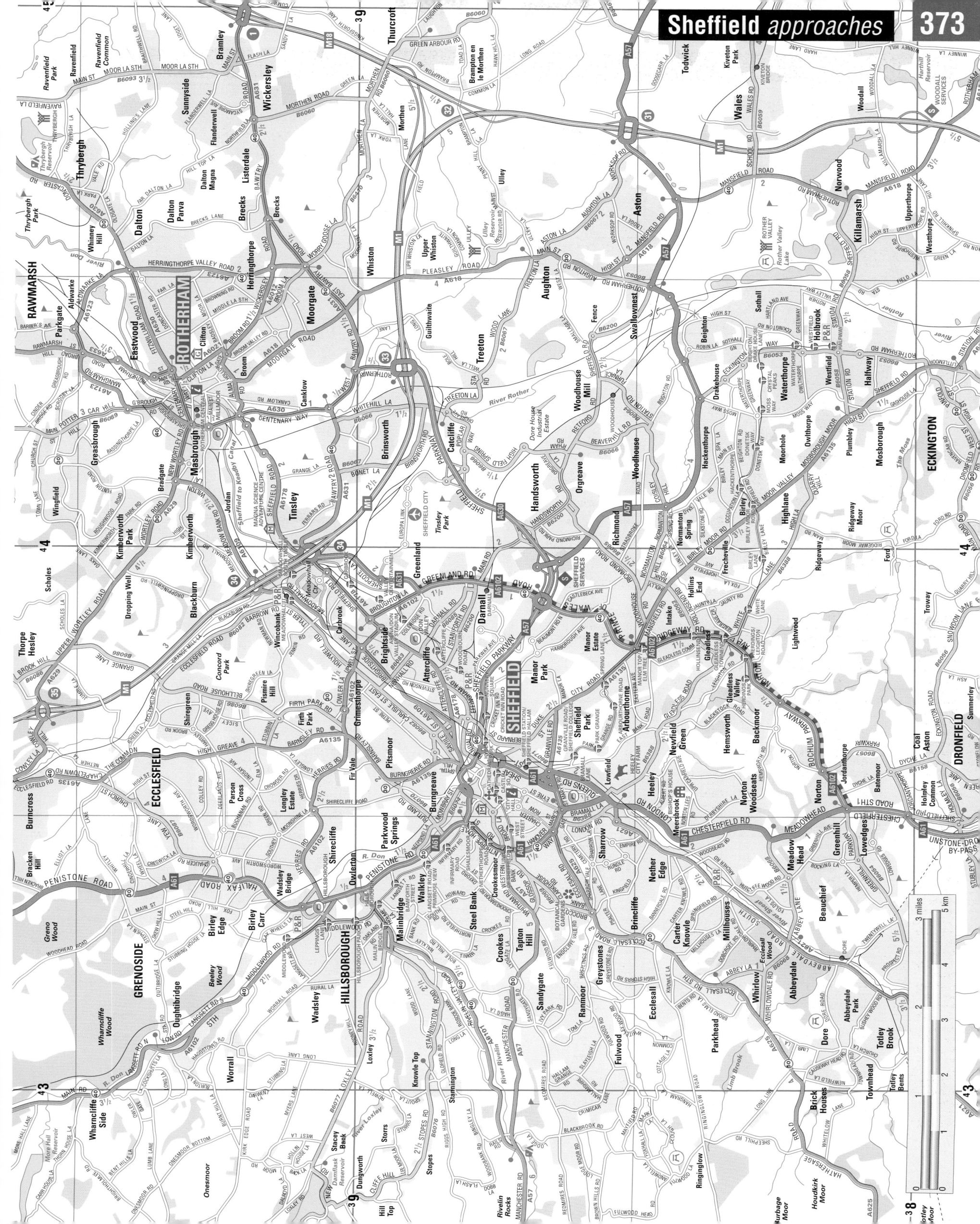

Scarborough

0 — Miles — ¼

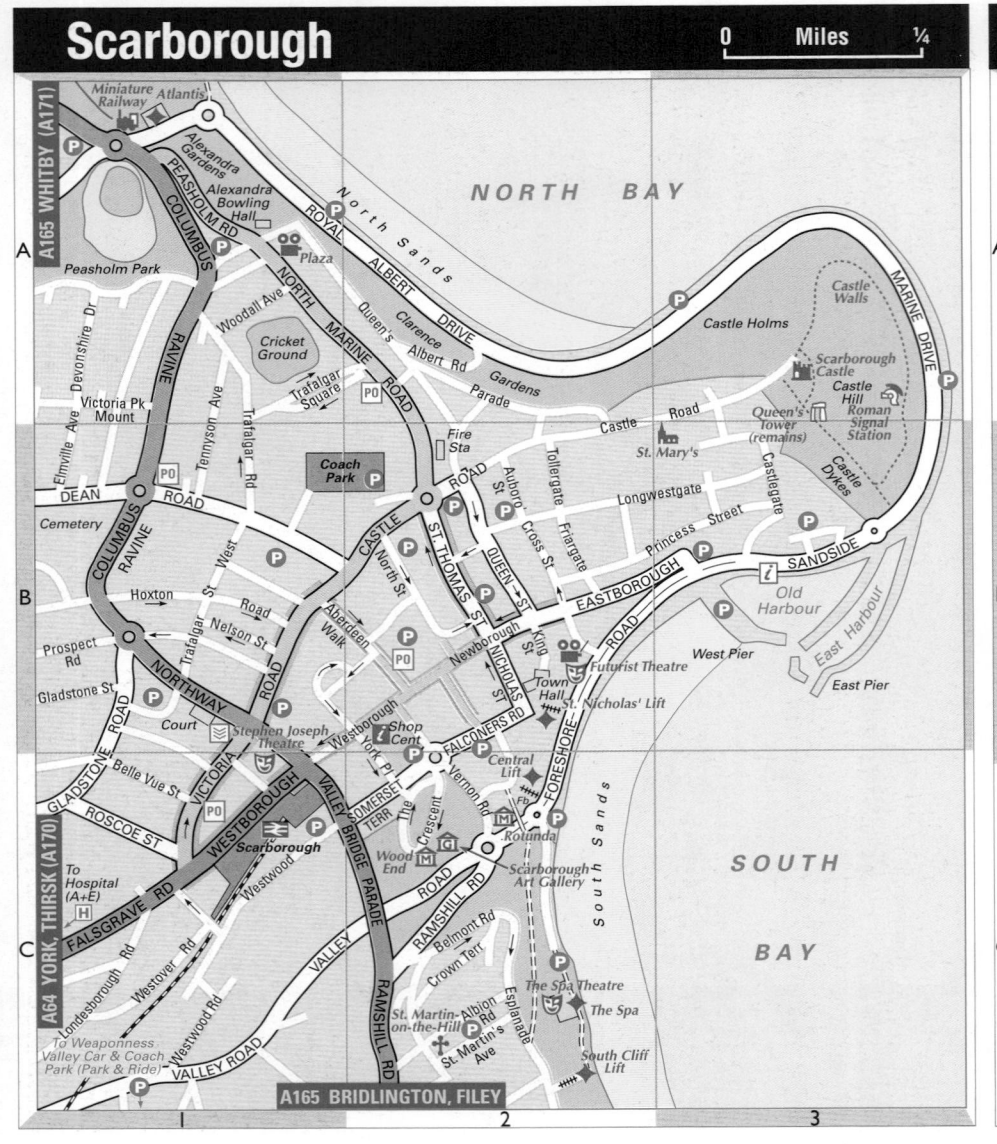

Shrewsbury

0 — Miles — ¼

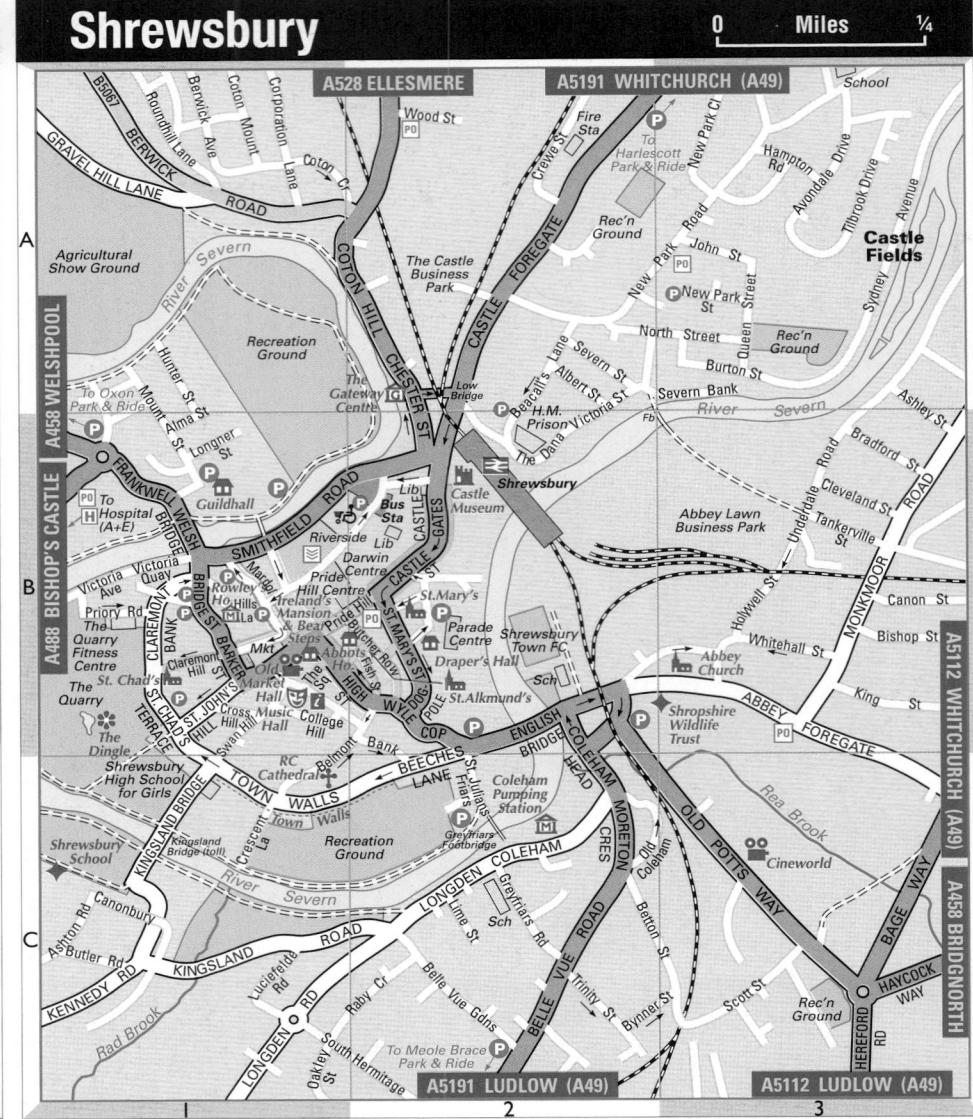

Southampton

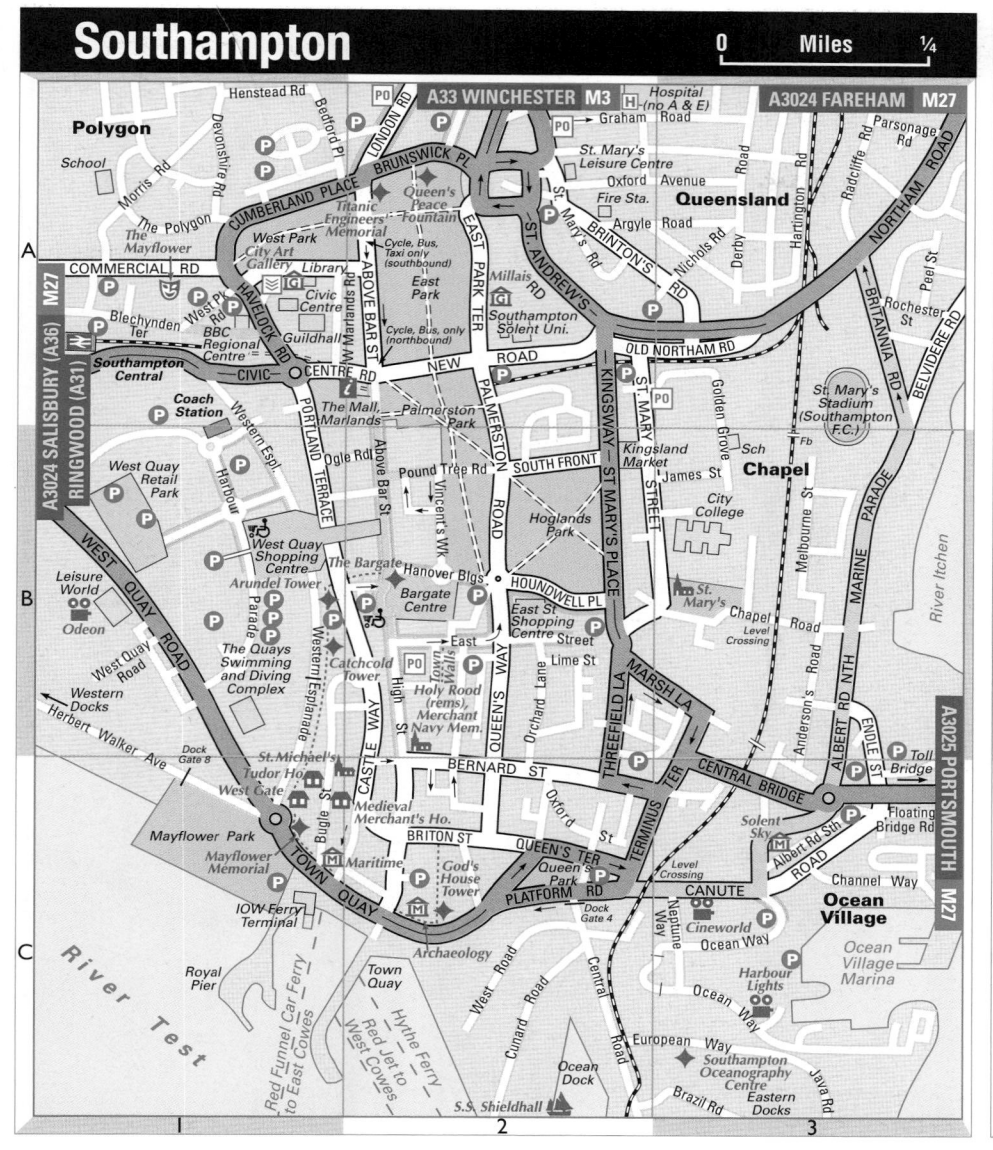

Stoke-on-Trent (Hanley)

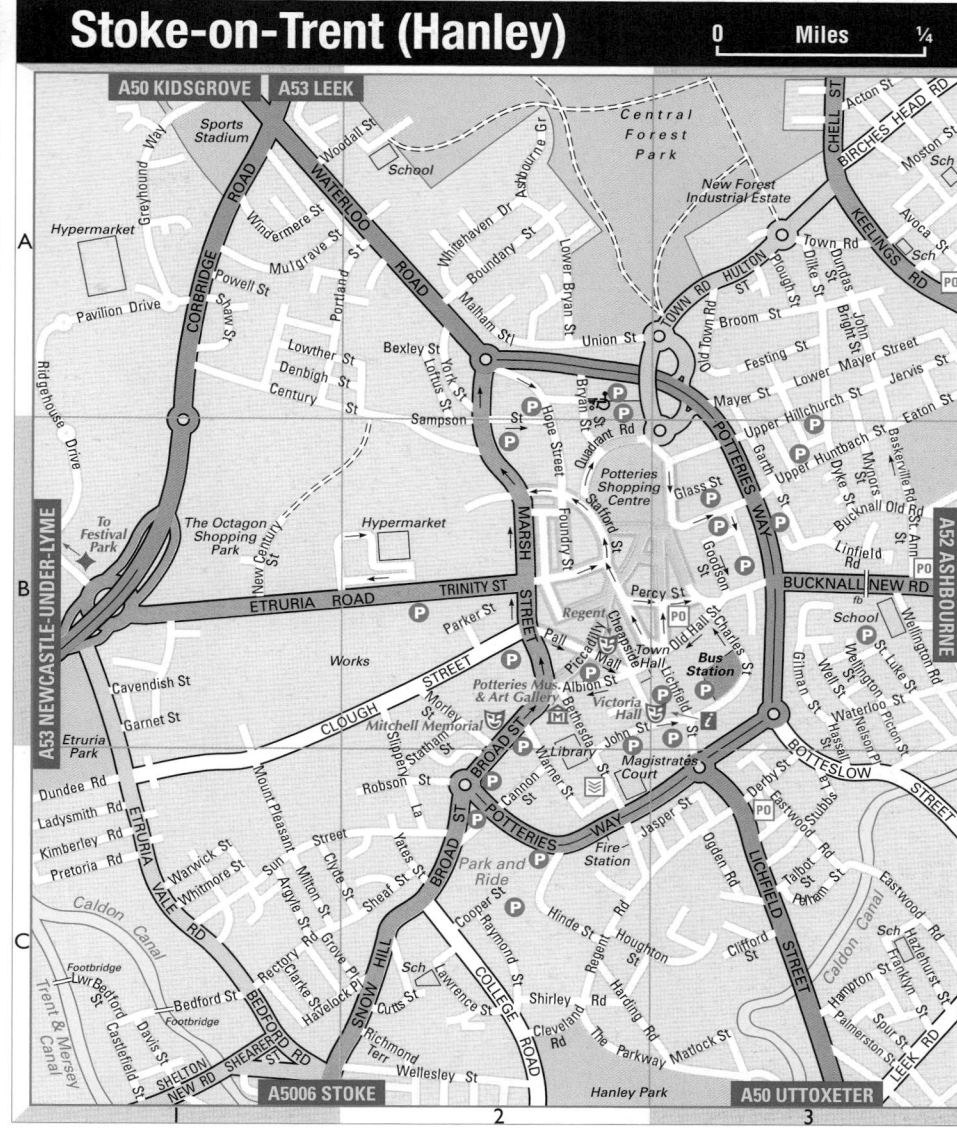

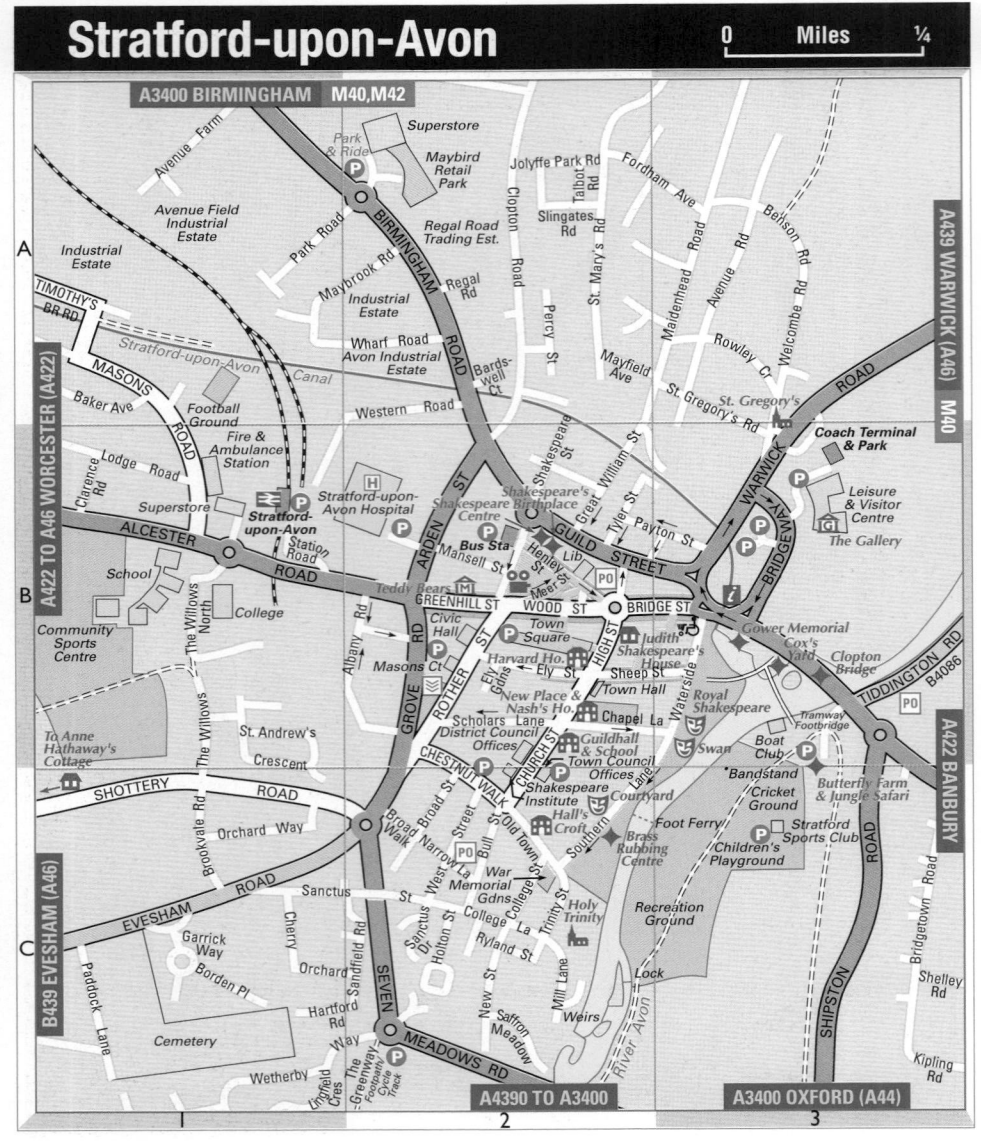

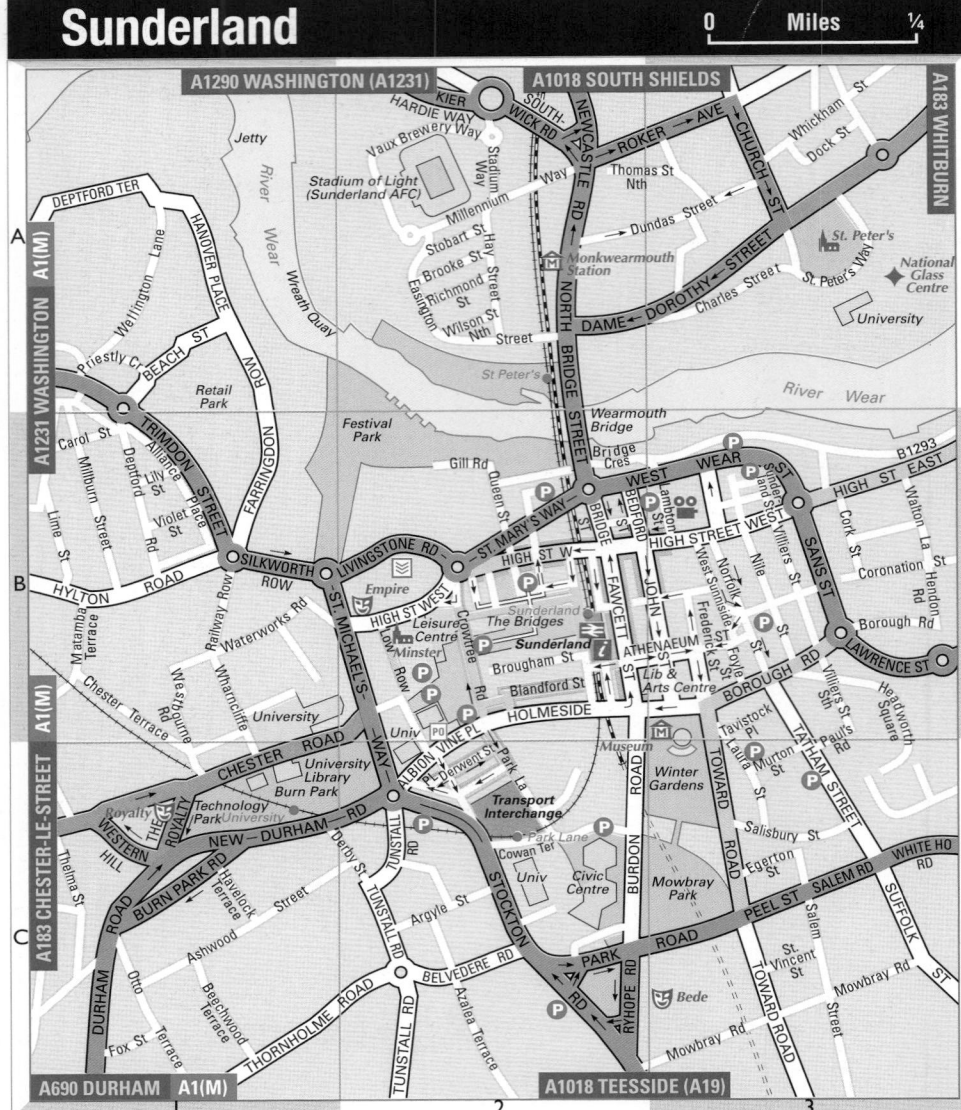

Stratford-upon-Avon

Sunderland

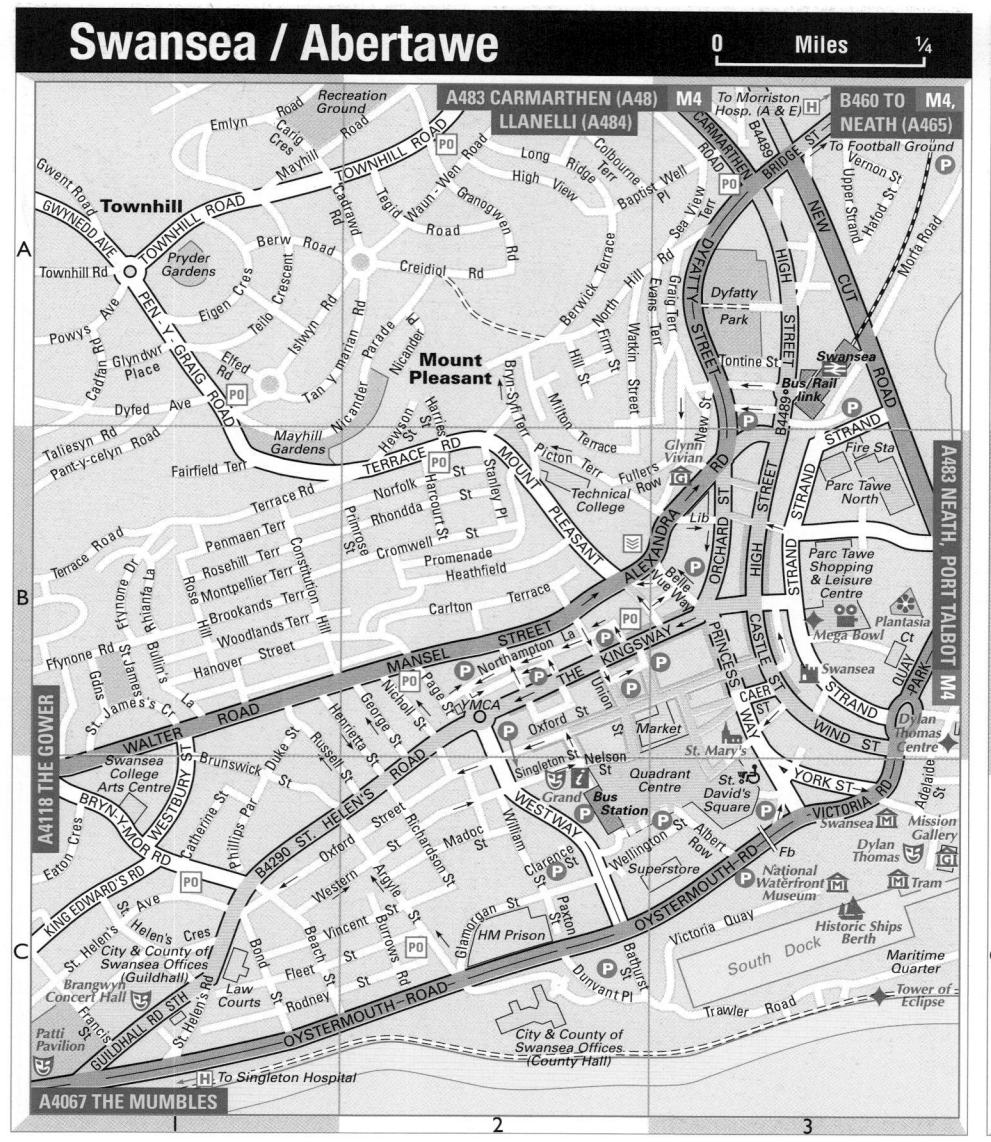

Swansea / Abertawe

0 Miles ¼

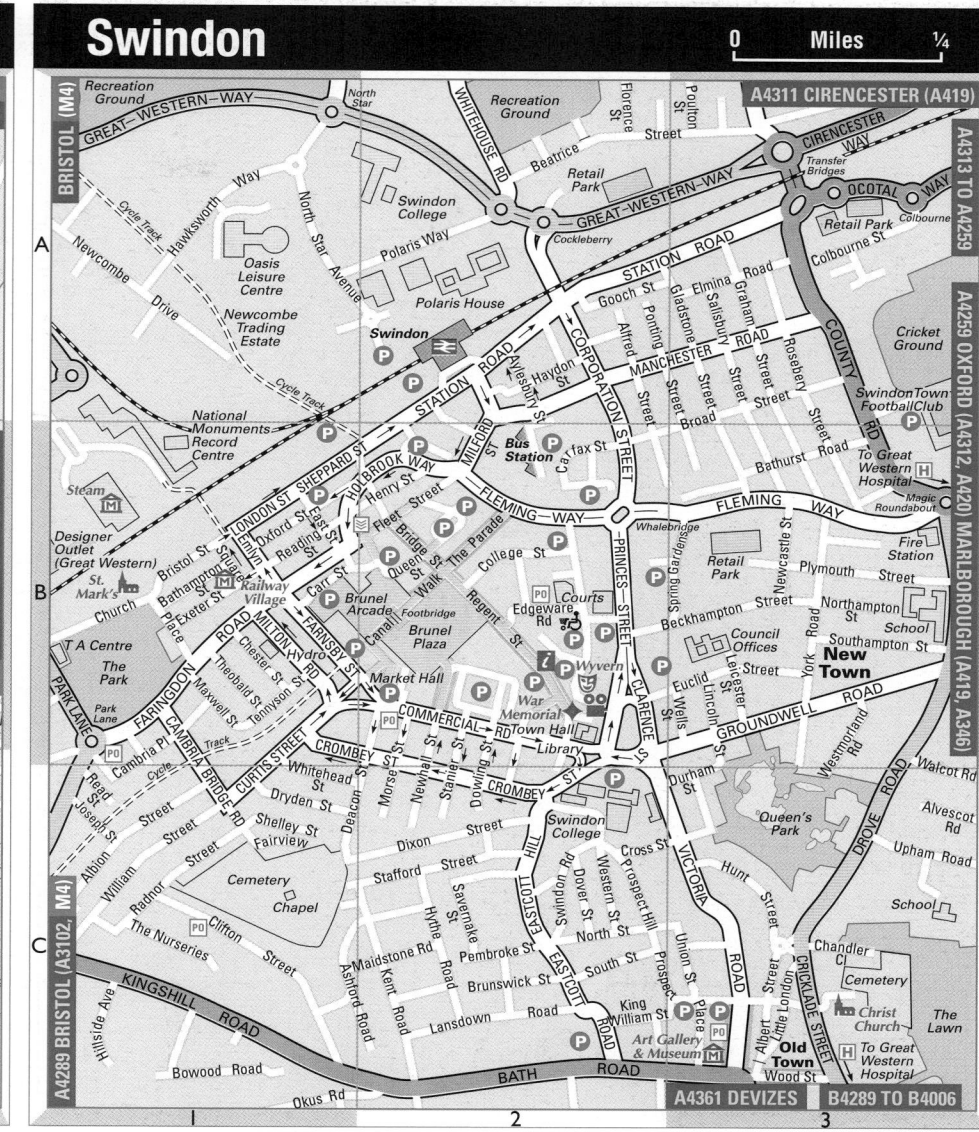

Swindon

0 Miles ¼

Telford

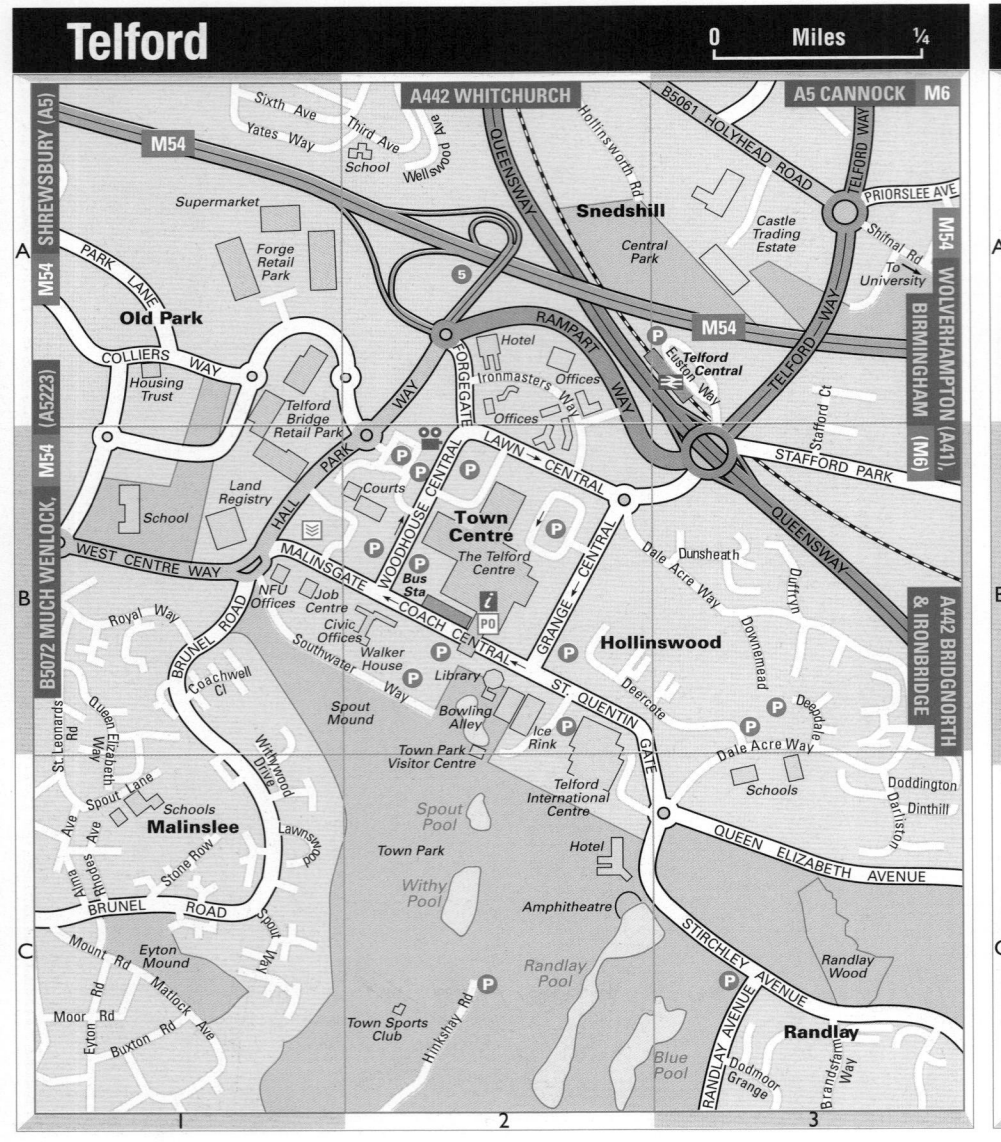

Torquay

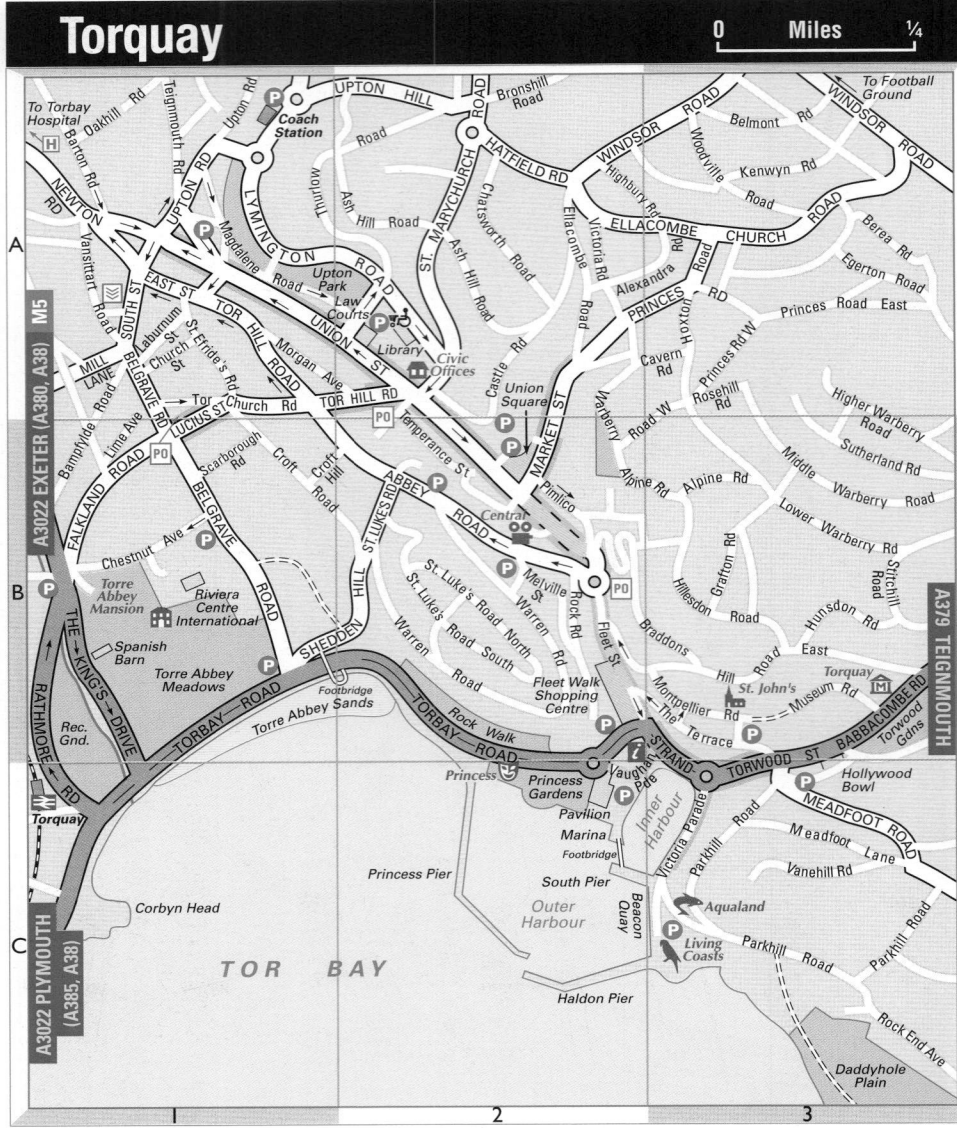

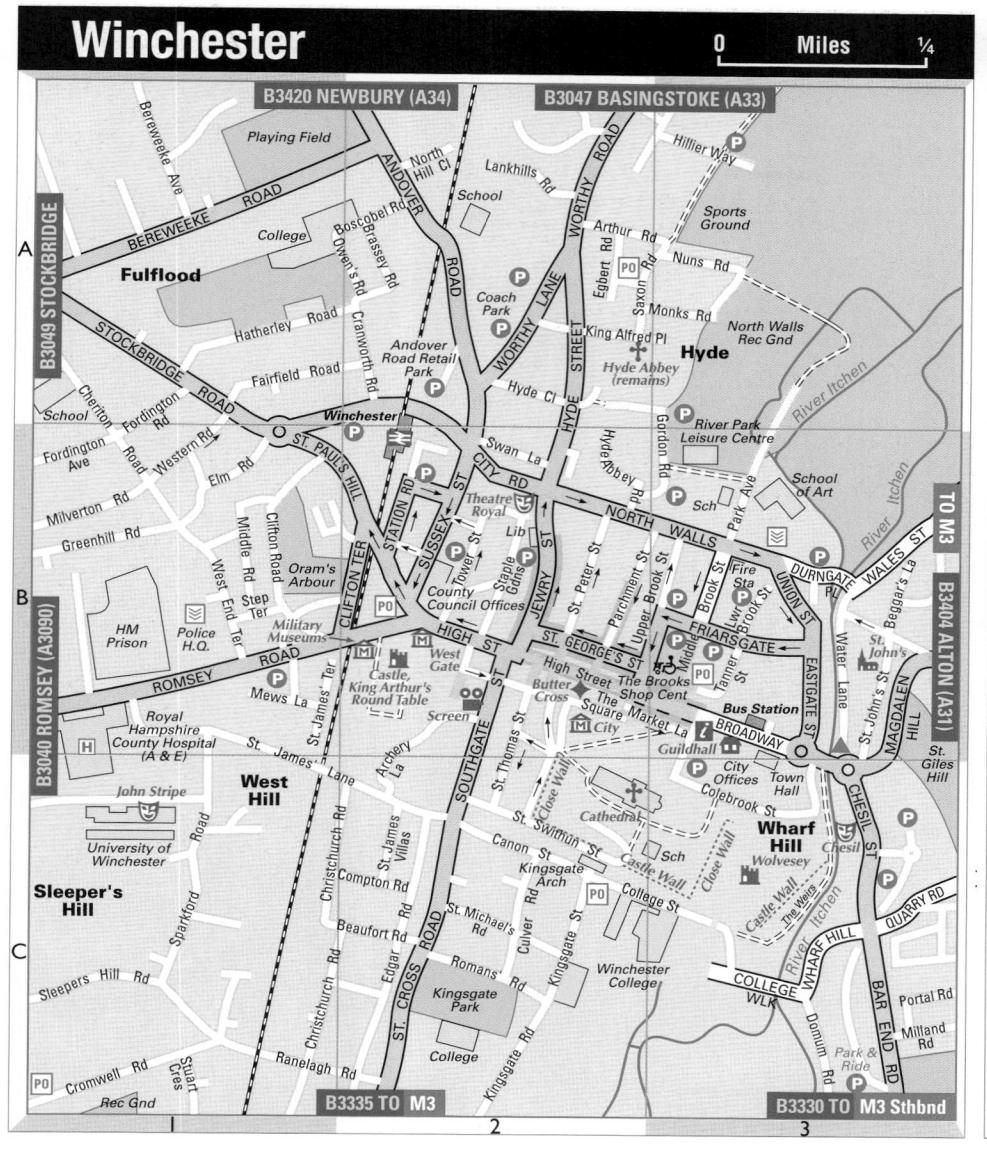

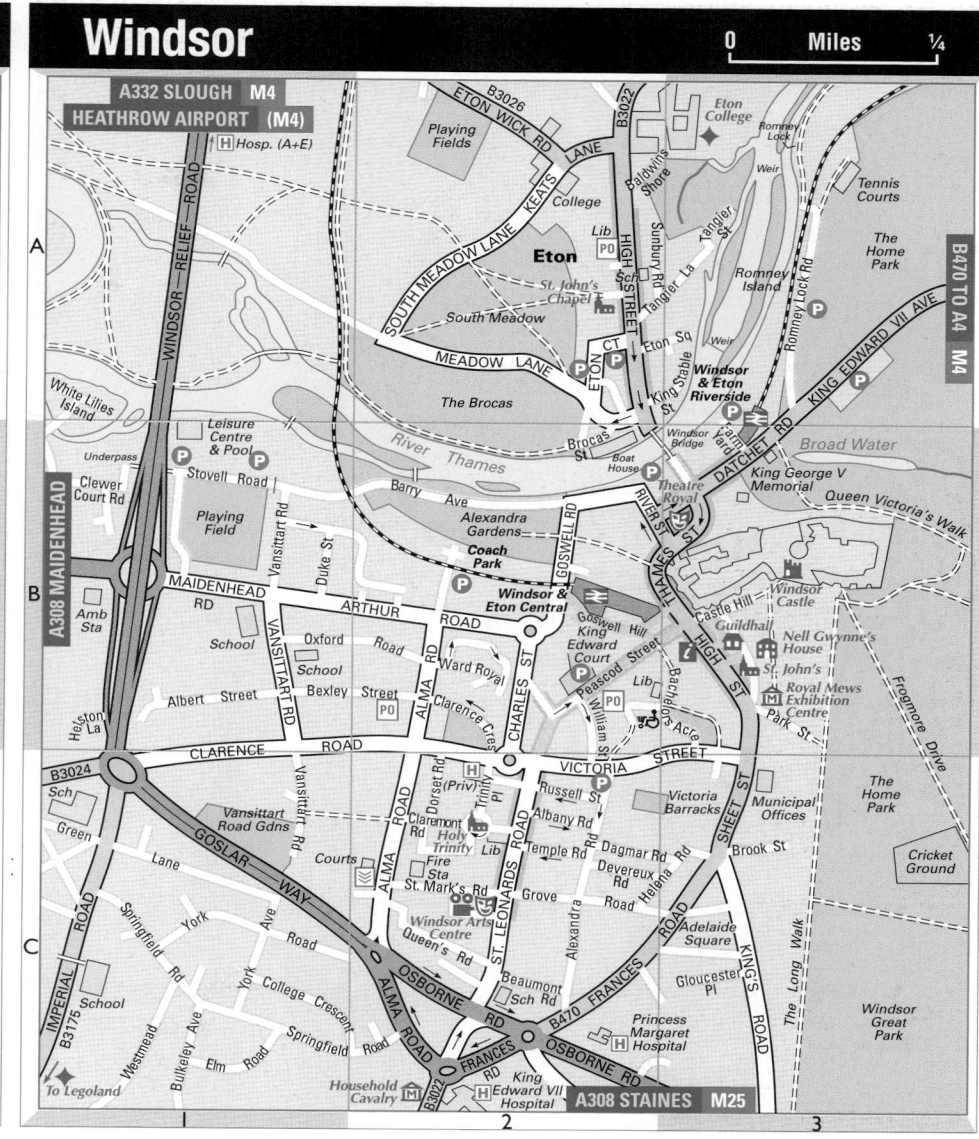

Winchester

Andover Rd A2	Cranworth Rd A2	Mews La B1	St Paul's Hill B1
Andover Road	Cromwell Rd. C1	Middle Brook St B3	St Peter St B2
Retail Park A2	Culver Rd C2	Middle Rd. B1	St Swithun St C2
Archery La C2	Domum Rd C3	Milford Rd. C3	St Thomas St C2
Arthur Rd A2	Durngate Pl B3	Milton Rd. B1	Saxon Rd A2
Bar End Rd. C3	Eastgate St. B3	Monks Rd A3	School of Art B3
Beaufort Rd C2	Edgar Rd C2	North Hill Cl A2	Screen 🎥 B2
Beggar's La B3	Egbert St A2	North Walls B2	Sleepers Hill Rd C1
Bereweeke Ave. A1	Elm Rd B1	North Walls	Southgate St C2
Bereweeke Rd A1	Fairfield Rd. A1	Rec Gnd A3	Sparkford Rd C1
Boscobel Rd. A2	Fire Station B3	Nuns Rd A3	Staple Gdns B2
Brassey Rd. A1	Fordington Ave. B1	Oram's Arbour B1	Station Rd B2
Broadway B3	Fordington Rd A1	Owen's Rd A2	Step Terr. B1
Brooks Shopping	Friarsgate B3	Parchment St B2	Stockbridge Rd A1
Centre, The B3	Gordon Rd B3	Park & Ride C3	Stuart Cres C2
Bus Station. B3	Greenhill Rd B1	Park Ave B3	Sussex St B2
Butter Cross ✦ B2	Guildhall 🏛 B3	Playing Field. A1	Swan Lane B2
Canon St C2	HM Prison B1	Police H.Q. 📠 B1	Tanner St B3
Castle Wall C2/C3	Hatherley Rd A1	Police Station 📠 B2	The Square. B2
Castle, King Arthur's	High St B2	Portal Rd C3	The Weirs C3
Round Table B2	Hillier Way A3	Post Office 📮	Theatre Royal 🎭 B2
Cathedral † C2	Hyde Abbey	. . . . . . A2/B2/B3/C1/C2	Tower St B2
Cheriton Rd A1	(Remains) † A2	Quarry Rd C3	Town Hall B2
Chesil St. C3	Hyde Abbey Rd B2	Ranelagh Rd. C1	Union St B3
Chesil Theatre 🎭 C3	Hyde Cl. A2	River Park Leisure	University of
Christchurch Rd C1	Hyde St A2	Centre B3	Winchester C1
City Museum 🏛 B2	Information Ctr 🛈 . . . B3	Romans' Rd C2	Upper Brook St B2
City Offices. C3	Jewry St B2	Romsey Rd. B1	Wales St B3
City Rd B2	John Stripe	Royal Hampshire County	Water Lane B3
Clifton Rd B1	Theatre 🎭 C1	Hospital (A & E) 🄷 . . B1	West End Terr B1
Clifton Terr B2	King Alfred Pl A2	St Cross Rd C2	West Gate 🏛 B2
Close Wall C2/C3	Kingsgate Arch. C2	St George's St B2	Western Rd. B1
Coach Park. B2	Kingsgate Park C2	St Giles Hill C3	Wharf Hill C3
Colebrook St C3	Kingsgate Rd C2	St James' La C1	Winchester College . . . C2
College St. C2	Kingsgate St. C2	St James' Terr B1	Winchester ₪ A2
College Walk C3	Lankhills Rd A2	St James Villas C2	Wolvesey Castle 🏰 . . . C3
Compton Rd C2	Library B2	St John's 🕍 B3	Worthy Lane A2
County Council. B2	Lower Brook St B3	St John's St B3	Worthy Rd A2
	Magdalen Hill B3	St Michael's Rd C2	
	Market La B2		

Windsor

Adelaide Sq C3	Elm Rd C1	King Stable St A2	South Meadow La . . . A2
Albany Rd C2	Eton College ✦ A3	Leisure Centre	Springfield Rd. C1
Albert St B1	Eton Ct A2	& Pool. B1	Stovell Rd. B1
Alexandra Gdns B2	Eton Sq. A2	Library C2	Sunbury Rd A2
Alexandra Rd C2	Eton Wick Rd A2	Maidenhead Rd B1	Tangier La A2
Alma Rd B2	Fire Station B1	Meadow La. A2	Tangier St A3
Ambulance Station. . . B1	Farm Yard. B3	Municipal Offices C3	Temple Rd C2
Arthur Rd B2	Frances Rd. C2	Nell Gwynne's	Thames St B3
Bachelors Acre B3	Frogmore Dr C3	House 🏠 B3	The Brocas A2
Barry Ave B2	Gloucester Pl C3	Osborne Rd C2	The Home Park . . A3/C3
Beaumont Rd C2	Goslar Way C1	Oxford Rd. B1	The Long Walk C3
Bexley St B1	Goswell Hill. B2	Park St B3	Theatre Royal 🎭 B3
Boat House B2	Goswell Rd. B2	Peascod St. B2	Trinity Pl C2
Brocas St B2	Green La. C1	Police Station 📠 B2	Vansittart Rd B1/C1
Brook St C3	Grove Rd C2	Post Office 📮 A2/B2	Vansittart Rd Gdns . . . C1
Bulkeley Ave C1	Guildhall 🏛 B3	Princess Margaret	Victoria Barracks C2
Castle Hill B3	Helena Rd. C2	Hospital 🄷 C2	Victoria St. C2
Charles St B2	Helston La B1	Queen Victoria's	Ward Royal B2
Claremont Rd C2	High St A2/B3	Walk B3	Westmead C1
Clarence Cr B2	Holy Trinity 🕍 C2	Queen's Rd C2	White Lilies Island . . . A1
Clarence Rd B1	Hospital (Private) 🄷 . . C2	River St. B2	William St B2
Clewer Court Rd B1	Household	Romney Island A3	Windsor Arts
Coach Park. B2	Cavalry C2	Romney Lock A3	Centre 🎭 C2
College Cr C1	Imperial Rd. C1	Romney Lock Rd A3	Windsor Castle 🏰 . . . B3
Courts. C2	Information Ctr 🛈 . . . B3	Royal Mews Exhibition	Windsor & Eton
Cricket Ground. C3	Keats La A2	Centre 🏛 B3	Central ₪ B2
Dagmar Rd C2	King Edward Ct B2	Russell St B2	Windsor & Eton
Datchet Rd B3	King Edward VII Ave . . A3	St John's 🕍 B3	Riverside ₪ A3
Devereux Rd C2	King Edward VII	St John's Chapel 🕍 . . A2	Windsor Bridge B3
Dorset Rd C2	Hospital 🄷 C2	St Leonards Rd C2	Windsor Great Park . . . C3
Duke St B1	King George V	St Mark's Rd. C2	Windsor Relief Rd . . . A1
	Memorial B3	Sheet St C3	York Ave C1
	King's Rd C3	South Meadow A2	York Rd C1

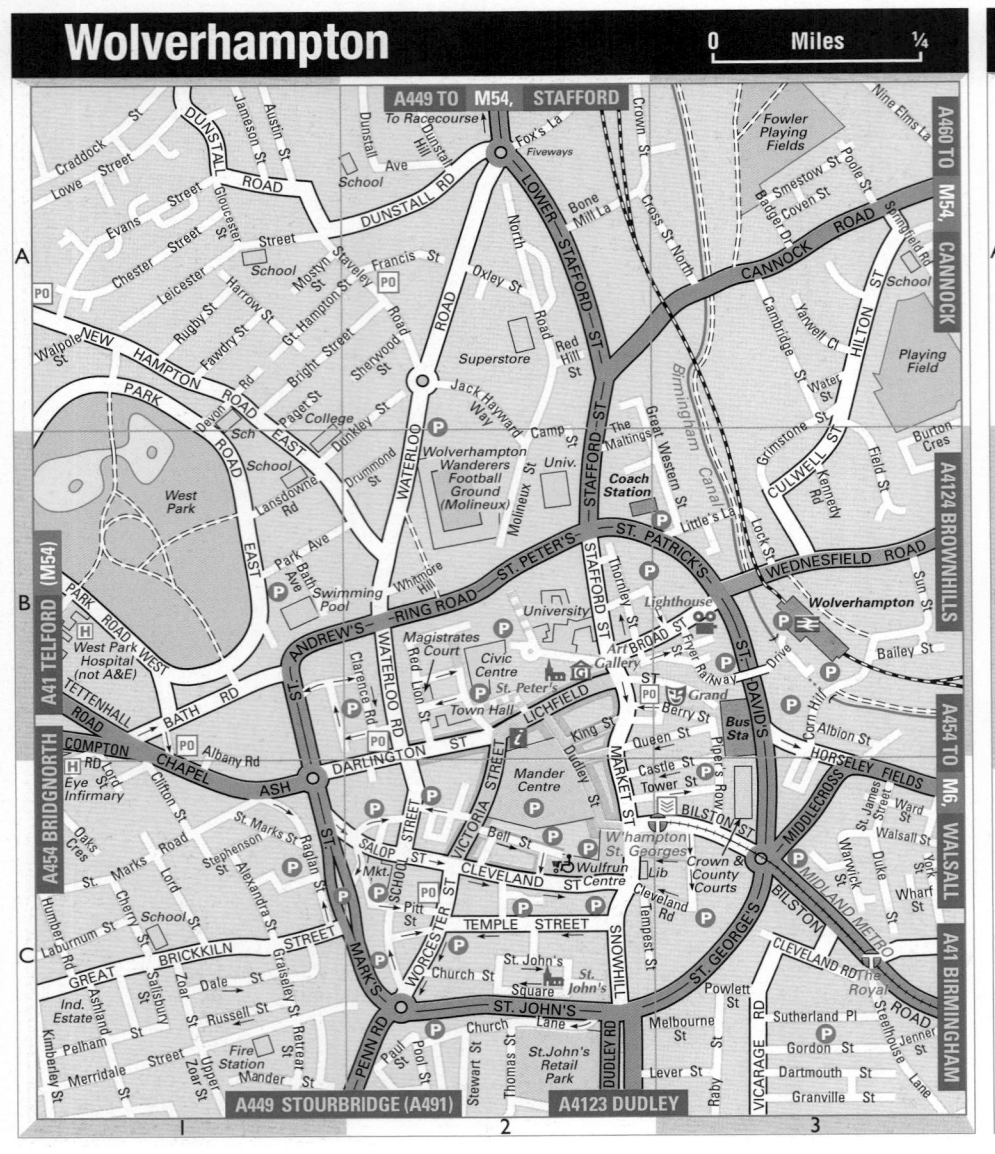

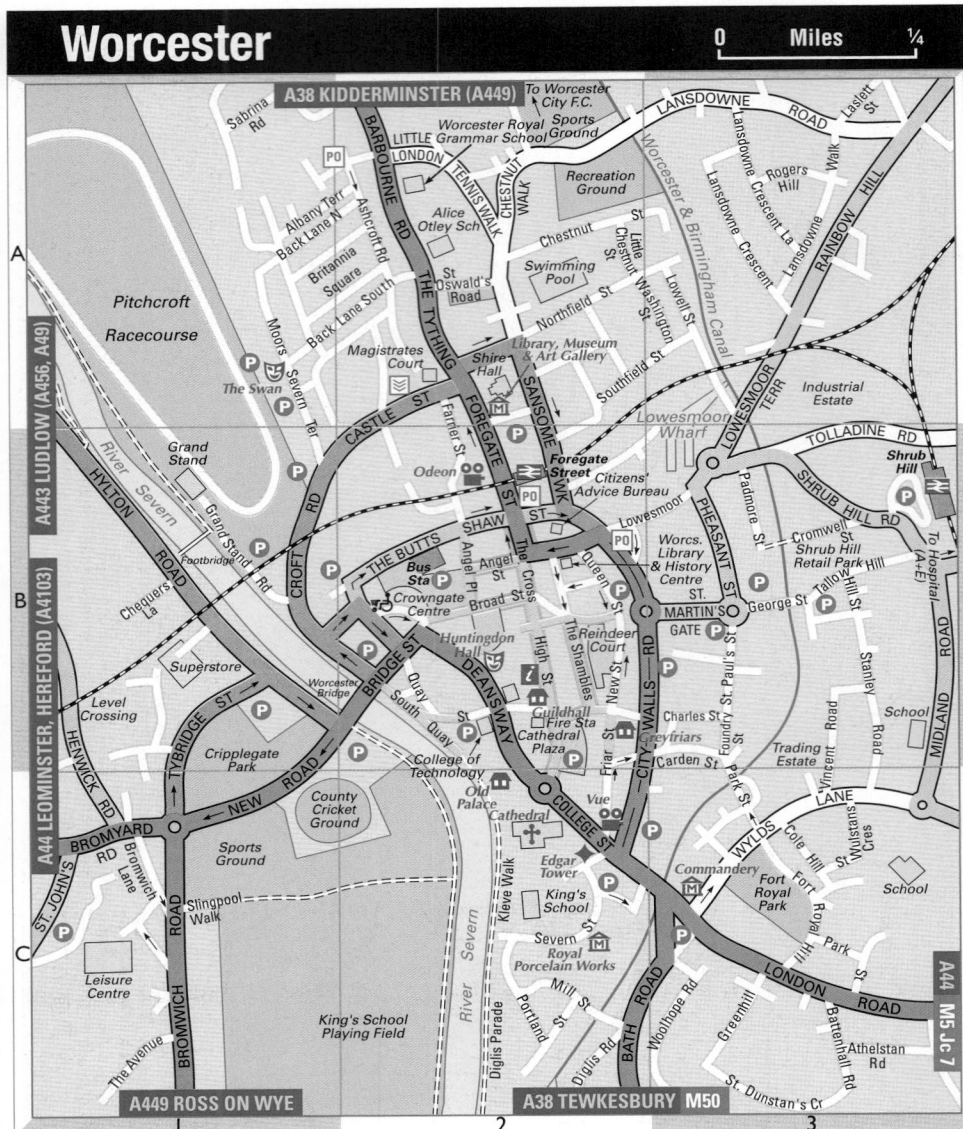

Wolverhampton

Albany Rd. B1	Duke St. C3	Melbourne St C3	Salop St C2
Albion St. B3	Dunkley St B1	Merridale St C1	School St C2
Alexandra St. C1	Dunstall Ave A2	Middlecross C3	Sherwood St A2
Gallery ⌂ B2	Dunstall Hill A2	Molineux St B2	Smestow St A3
Ashland St C1	Dunstall Rd. A1/A2	Mostyn St A1	Snowhill C2
Austin St. A3	Evans St A1	New Hampton	Springfield Rd. A3
Badger Dr. A3	Eye Infirmary Ⓗ . . . C1	Rd East A1	Stafford St B2
Bailey St. B3	Fawdry St. A1	Nine Elms La A3	Staveley Rd A1
Bath Ave. B1	Field St. B3	North Rd. A2	Steelhouse La. C3
Bath Rd B1	Fire Station C1	Oaks Cres. C1	Stephenson St C1
Bell St. C2	Fiveways (r'about) . . A2	Oxley St A2	Stewart St. C2
Berry St B3	Fowler Playing	Paget St A1	Sun St. B3
Bilston Rd. C3	Fields A3	Park Ave B1	Sutherland Pl C3
Bilston St C3	Fox's La A2	Park Rd East A1	Tempest St C2
Birmingham Canal . . . A3	Francis St A2	Park Road West B1	Temple St C2
Bone Mill La. A2	Fryer St B3	Paul St C2	Tettenhall Rd B1
Bright St A1	Gloucester St A1	Pelham St C1	The Maltings. B3
Burton Cres A3	Gordon St. C3	Penn Rd C2	The Royal (Metro) C3
Bus Station B3	Graiseley St C1	Piper's Row B3	Thomas St C2
Cambridge St A3	Grand ⌂ B3	Pitt St C2	Thornley St B2
Camp St. C2	Granville St. B3	Police Station ▣ C3	Tower St C2
Cannock Rd. A3	Great Western St . . . A2	Pool St C2	Town Hall B2
Castle St. C2	Great Brickkiln St . . . C1	Poole St. A3	University B2
Chapel Ash C1	Grimstone St B3	Post Office ▣	Upper Zoar St C1
Cherry St C1	Gt. Hampton St A1	. . . . . A1/A2/B2/B2/C2	Vicarage Rd C3
Chester St A1	Harrow St A1	Powlett St. C3	Victoria St. C2
Church La. C2	Hilton St C1	Queen St B2	Walpole St A1
Church St C2	Horseley Fields. . . . C3	Raby St. C3	Walsall St C3
Civic Centre B2	Humber Rd. C1	Raglan St C1	Ward St C2
Clarence Rd B2	Jack Hayward Way. . . B2	Railway Dr B3	Warwick St C3
Cleveland Rd C2	Jameson St A1	Red Hill St A2	Water St A3
Cleveland St C2	Jenner St C3	Red Lion St B2	Waterloo Rd B2
Clifton St C1	Kennedy Rd B3	Retreat St C1	Wednesfield Rd B3
Coach Station B2	Kimberley St C1	Ring Rd B2	West Park
Compton Rd. B1	King St B2	Rugby St A1	(not A&E) Ⓗ B1
Corn Hill C3	Laburnum St. C1	Russell St C1	West Park Swimming
Coven St. A3	Lansdowne Rd B1	St. Andrew's B1	Pool B1
Craddock St A1	Leicester St A1	St. David's B3	Wolverhampton
Cross St North A2	Lever St C3	St. George's C3	St. Georges (Metro) . C2
Crown & County	Library C3	St. James St. C3	Wharf St C3
Courts C3	Lichfield St B2	St. John's C2	Whitmore Hill B2
Crown St A2	Lighthouse 🎦 B3	St. John's ♣ C2	Wolverhampton ≋ . . B3
Culwell St B3	Little's La B3	St. John's Retail	Wolverhampton
Dale St C1	Lock St B3	Park C2	Wanderers Football
Darlington St C1	Lord St C1	St. John's Square . . . C2	Gnd. (Molineux) . . . B2
Dartmouth St C3	Lowe St A1	St. Mark's C1	Worcester St. C2
Devon Rd A1	Lower Stafford St. . . A2	St. Marks Rd C1	Wulfrun Centre C2
Drummond St B2	Magistrates Court. . . B2	St. Marks St C1	Yarwell Cl A3
Dudley Rd. C2	Mander Centre C2	St. Patrick's B2	York St C3
Dudley St B2	Mander St C1	St. Peter's B2	Zoar St C1
	Market St B2	St. Peter's ♣ B2	
	Market C2	Salisbury St C1	

Worcester

Albany Terr A1	Cripplegate Park B1	Little Chestnut St . . . A2	St Wulstans Cr C3
Alice Otley School . . . A2	Croft Rd B1	Little London A2	Sansome Walk A2
Angel Pl B2	Cromwell St B3	London Rd C3	Severn St C2
Angel St B2	Crowngate Centre . . . B2	Lowell St. A3	Shaw St B2
Ashcroft Rd A2	Deansway B2	Lowesmoor. B2	Shire Hall A2
Athelstan Rd. C3	Diglis Pde C2	Lowesmoor Terr. B2	Shrub Hill ≋ B3
Back Lane North A1	Diglis Rd C2	Lowesmoor Wharf . . . A3	Shrub Hill Retail Park B3
Back Lane South . . . A1	Edgar Tower ♣ C2	Magistrates Court. . . . A2	Shrub Hill Rd B3
Barbourne Rd. A2	Farrier St A2	Midland Rd. B3	Slingpool Walk C1
Bath Rd C2	Fire Station B2	Mill St C2	South Quay B2
Battenhall Rd C3	Foregate St. B2	Moors Severn Terr . . . A1	Southfield St A2
Bridge St B2	Foregate Street ≋ . . . B2	New Rd. B2	Sports Ground . . . A2/C1
Britannia Sq A1	Fort Royal Hill. C3	New St B2	Stanley Rd B3
Broad St B2	Fort Royal Park C3	Northfield St A2	Swimming Pool A2
Bromwich La C1	Foundry St B3	Odeon B2	Swan, The 🎦 A1
Bromwich Rd C1	Friar St C2	Old Palace ⌂ B2	Tallow Hill B3
Bromyard Rd C1	George St. B3	Padmore St B3	Tennis Walk A2
Broad St B2	Grand Stand Rd B1	Park St C2	The Avenue C1
Bus Station B2	Greenhill C3	Pheasant St B3	The Butts B2
Carden St B3	Greyfriars ⌂ B2	Pitchcroft	The Cross B2
Castle St. A2	Guildhall ⌂ B2	Racecourse A1	The Shambles B2
Cathedral ✝ C2	Henwick Rd B1	Police Station ▣ A2	The Tything A2
Cathedral Plaza B2	High St. B2	Portland St C2	Tolladine Rd B3
Charles St. B3	Hill St B3	Post Office ▣ . . A1/A2/B2	Tybridge St B1
Chequers La. B1	Huntingdon Hall ⌂ . . . B2	Quay St B2	Vincent Rd B3
Chestnut St A2	Hylton Rd B1	Queen St B2	Vue 🎦 C2
Chestnut Walk A2	Information Ctr ℹ B2	Rainbow Hill A3	Washington St A3
Citizens' Advice	King's School C2	Recreation Ground . . . A2	Woolhope Rd C3
Bureau B2	King's School	Reindeer Court B2	Worcester Bridge . . . B2
City Walls Rd B2	Playing Field. C2	Rogers Hill A3	Worcester Library &
Cole Hill C3	Kleve Walk C2	Royal Porcelain	History Centre B3
College of	Lansdowne Cr A3	Works C2	Worcester Royal
Technology. B2	Lansdowne Rd A3	Sabrina Rd A1	Grammar School . . . A2
College St. C2	Lansdowne Walk A3	St Dunstan's Cr C3	Wylds La. C3
Commandery ⌂ C3	Laslett St A3	St John's C1	
County Cricket	Leisure Centre A3	St Martin's Gate B3	
Ground C1	Library, Museum &	St Oswald's Rd. A2	
	Art Gallery ⌂ A2	St Paul's St B3	

Wrexham / Wrecsam

0 Miles ¼

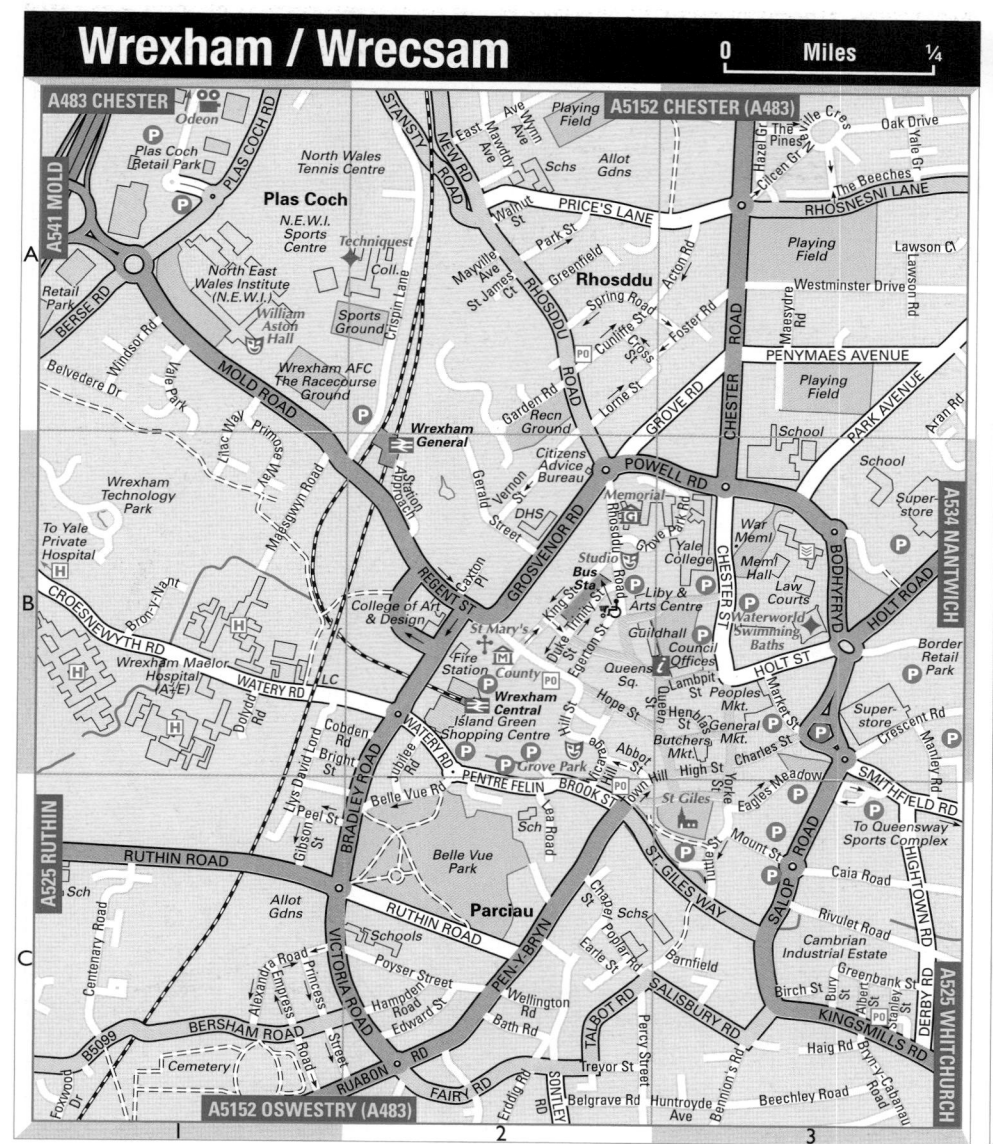

York

0 Miles ¼

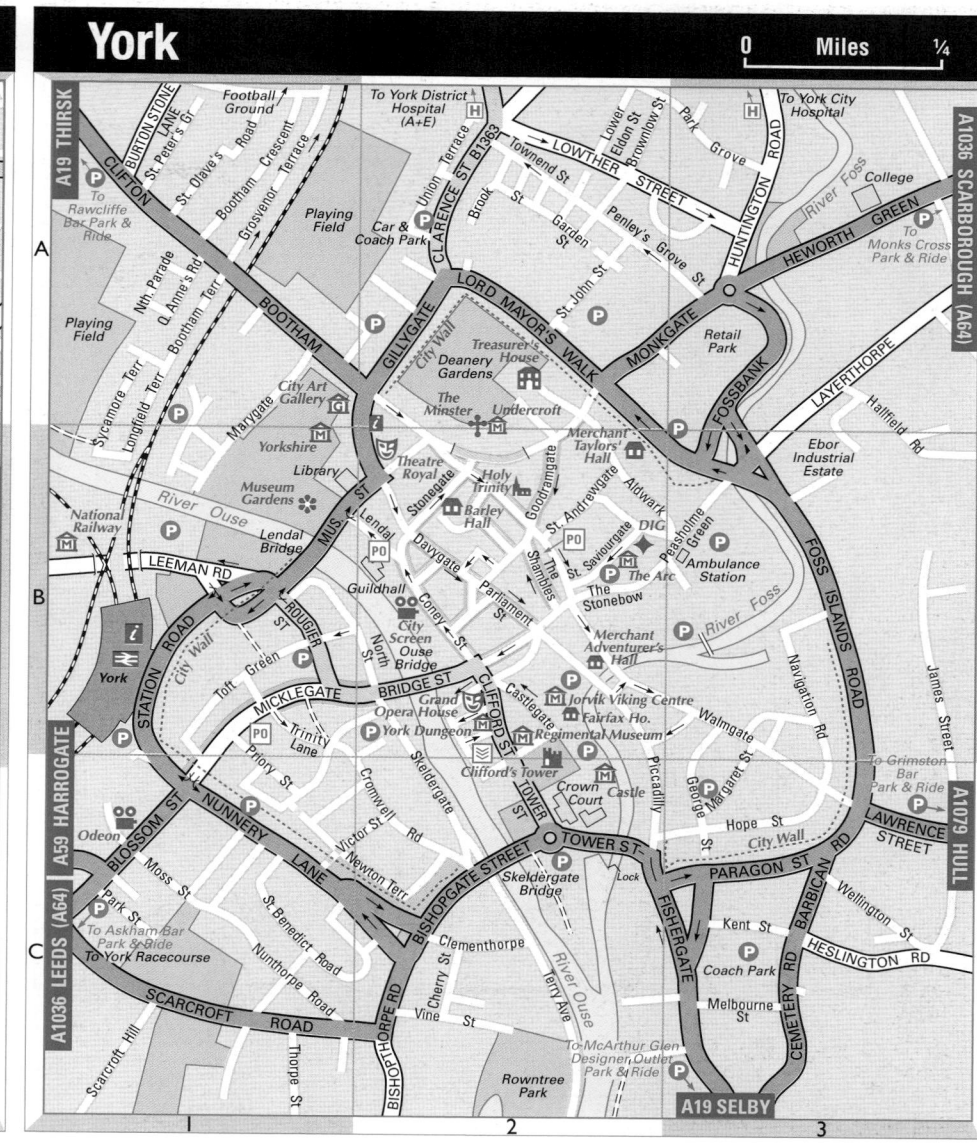

Wrexham / Wrecsam

Abbot St B2
Acton Rd A3
Albert St C3
Alexandra Rd C1
Aran Rd A3
Barnfield C3
Bath Rd C3
Beechley Rd C3
Belgrave Rd C2
Belle Vue Park C2
Belle Vue Rd C2
Belvedere Dr. A1
Bennion's Rd C2
Berse Rd A1
Bersham Rd C1
Birch St. C2
Bodhyfryd B3
Border Retail Park B3
Bradley Rd C2
Bright St B1
Bron-y-Nant B1
Brook St C2
Bryn-y-Cabanau Rd . . . C3
Bury St C3
Bus Station B2
Butchers Market B3
Citizens Advice
  Bureau B2
Caia Rd C3
Cambrian Industrial
  Estate C3
Caxton Pl B2
Cemetery C1
Centenary Rd C1
Chapel St C2
Charles St B3
Chester Rd A3
Chester St B3
Cilcen Gr A3
Cobden Rd B1
College of Art
  & Design B2
Council Offices B2
County B2
Crescent Rd B3
Crispin La A2

Croesnewyth Rd B1
Cross St A2
Cunliffe St A2
Derby Rd C3
DHS B2
Dolydd Rd B1
Duke St. B2
Eagles Meadow C3
Earle St C2
East Ave A2
Edward St C2
Egerton St B2
Empress Rd C1
Erddig Rd C2
Fairy Rd C2
Fire Station B2
Foster Rd A3
Foxwood Dr C1
Garden Rd A2
General Market B3
Gerald St B2
Gibson St C1
Greenbank St C3
Greenfield A2
Grosvenor Rd B2
Grove Park Rd B3
Grove Park B2
Grove Rd A3
Guildhall B2
Haig Rd C3
Hampden Rd C2
Hazel Gr A3
Henblas St B3
High St. B3
Hightown Rd C3
Hill St B2
Holt Rd B3
Holt St B3
Hope St B2
Huntroyde Ave C3
Information Ctr B2
Island Green Shopping
  Centre B2
Jubilee Rd B2
King St B2
Kingsmills Rd C3
Lambpit St B2
Law Courts B3
Lawson Cl A3
Lawson Rd A3

Lea Rd C2
Library & Arts Centre . B2
Lilac Way B1
Llys David Lord B1
Lorne St A2
Maesgwyn Rd B1
Maesydre Rd A3
Manley Rd B3
Market St B3
Mawddy Ave A2
Mayville Ave A2
Memorial Gallery B2
Memorial Hall B3
Mold Rd A1
Mount St. C3
North East Wales
  Institute (N.E.W.I.) . . . A1
N.E.W.I. Sports
  Centre A1
Neville Cres A3
New Rd A2
North Wales
  Tennis Centre A1
Oak Dr A3
Park Ave A3
Park St B2
Peel St C1
Pentre Felin C2
Pen-y-Bryn C2
Penymaes Ave A3
Peoples Market B3
Percy St C2
Plas Coch Retail
  Park A1
Plas Coch Rd A1
Police Station B3
Poplar Rd C2
Post Office . . . .
  . . . . A2/B2/C2/C3
Powell Rd B3
Poyser St C2
Price's La A2
Primose Way B1
Princess St C1
Queen St B3
Queens Sq B2
Regent St B2
Rhosddu Rd A2/B2
Rhosnesni La A3
Rivulet Rd C3

Ruabon Rd C2
Ruthin Rd C1/C2
St Giles C3
St James Ct A2
St Mary's B2
St. Giles Way C3
Salisbury Rd C3
Salop Rd C3
Smithfield Rd C3
Sontley Rd C3
Spring Rd A2
Stanley St B2
Stansty Rd A2
Station Approach B2
Studio A2
Talbot Rd C2
Techniquest A2
The Beeches A2
The Pines A3
Town Hill C2
Trevor St C2
Trinity St B2
Tuttle St C2
Vale Park A1
Vernon St B2
Vicarage Hill B2
Victoria Rd C2
Walnut St A2
War Memorial B2
Waterworld Swimming
  Baths B3
Watery Rd B1/B2
Wellington Rd C2
Westminster Dr. A3
William Aston Hall . . . A1
Windsor Rd A1
Wrexham AFC A1
Wrexham
  Central B2
Wrexham
  General B2
Wrexham Maelor
  Hospital (A+E) . . . B1
Wrexham Technology
  Park B1
Wynn Ave A2
Yale College B3
Yale Gr A3
Yorke St C3

York

Aldwark. B2
Ambulance Station. . . B3
Arc Museum, The . . . B2
Barbican Rd C3
Bishopgate St. C2
Bishopthorpe Rd C2
Blossom St C1
Bootham A1
Bootham Cr A1
Bootham Terr A1
Bridge St B2
Brook St A2
Brownlow St. A2
Burton Stone La A1
Castle Museum C2
Castlegate B2
Cemetery Rd C3
Cherry St C2
City Art Gallery A1
City Screen B2
City Wall A2/B1/C3
Clarence St. A2
Clementhorpe. C2
Clifford St B2
Clifford's Tower B2
Clifton A1
Coach park. A2/C3
Coney St B2
Cromwell Rd C2
Crown Court. C2
Davygate B2
Deaner Gdns A2
DIG B2

Ebor Industrial
  Estate B3
Fairfax House B2
Fishergate. C3
Foss Islands Rd B3
Fossbank A3
Garden St A2
George St C3
Gillygate A2
Goodramgate B2
Grand Opera
  House B2
Grosvenor Terr A1
Guildhall B2
Hallfield Rd B3
Heslington Rd C3
Heworth Green A3
Holy Trinity B2
Hope St C3
Huntington Rd A3
Information Ctr A2
James St B3
Jorvik Viking
  Centre B2
Kent St C3
Lawrence St B2
Layerthorpe A3
Leeman Rd B1
Lendal. B2
Lendal Bridge B1
Library B1
Longfield Terr A1
Lord Mayor's Walk . . . A1
Lower Eldon St. A2
Lowther St A2
Margaret St. C3

Marygate A1
Melbourne St C3
Merchant Adventurer's
  Hall B2
Merchant Taylors'
  Hall B2
Micklegate B1
Minster, The A2
Monkgate A2
Moss St C1
Museum Gdns B1
Museum St B2
National Railway
  Museum B1
Navigation Rd B3
Newton Terr C2
North Pde A1
North St B2
Nunnery La C1
Nunthorpe Rd C1
Odeon C1
Ouse Bridge B2
Paragon St C3
Park Gr A3
Park St C1
Parliament St B2
Peasholme Green . . . B3
Penley's Grove St. . . . A2
Piccadilly B2
Police Station B2
Post Office B1/B2
Priory St B1
Queen Anne's Rd A1
Regimental
  Museum B2
Rowntree Park C2

St Andrewgate B2
St Benedict Rd C1
St John St A2
St Olave's Rd A1
St Peter's Gr A1
St Saviourgate B2
Scarcroft Hill C1
Scarcroft Rd C1
Skeldergate C2
Skeldergate Bridge. . . C2
Station Rd B1
Stonegate B2
Sycamore Terr A1
Terry Ave. C2
The Shambles B2
The Stonebow B2
Theatre Royal B2
Thorpe St C1
Toft Green B1
Tower St C2
Townend St A2
Treasurer's House . . . A2
Trinity La B1
Undercroft
  Museum A2
Union Terr. A2
Victor St C2
Vine St C2
Walmgate B3
Wellington St C3
York Dungeon B2
York Station B1
Yorkshire
  Museum B1

Heathrow Airport (London)

0 Miles ¼

A4 SLOUGH
River Colne
Bath Road
A3044
COLNBROOK BY-PASS
A3044
Sheraton Heathrow
Abbey Bus. Cent.
McDonalds
Petrol
PO
Thistle Heathrow Park
Longford
National Car Hire
Staff
Hertz Car Hire
Europcar Car Hire
Pink Elephant Long Stay
Long Stay
Newbury Rd
Northern Perimeter Rd (W)
Staff
Fire Station
West Ramp
BATH ROAD
A4
Holiday Inn Hotel
JUNC. 4A
M4
Le Meridien Hotel
A408
Heathrow Express to Paddington
Petrol
McDonalds
Radisson Edwardian Hotel
Marriott Hotel
Sheraton Skyline Hotel
A437
Posthouse Hotel
Airport Bowl
Ibis Hotel
A4 LONDON
Pub
Custom House
Renaissance Hotel
World Business Centre
Newall Rd
Avis Car Hire
East Ramp
Concorde Replica
Long Stay
Heathrow Visitor Centre
Northern Perimeter Rd
Budget Car Hire
Parking Express
Eastern Perimeter Rd
NORTHERN RUNWAY
M25
Terminal 5 (under construction)
Fire Station
Pier 5
Pier 4
Pier 3
Terminal 1
Maintenance Area
M25
Stanwell Moor Rd
Western Perimeter Rd
Heathrow Express Station
Petrol
Heathrow Terminals 1, 2, 3
Bus Sta
Europier
Eastchurch Rd
A3044
TO M25 JUNC. 14
Terminal 3
Control Tower
Queen's Building
Piccadilly Line
CROSSWIND RUNWAY
A30 LONDON
Pier 2
Pier 7
All parking in central area is Short Stay
Pier 6
Terminal 2 (spectator area above)
Pier 1
Fire Station
Piccadilly Line
Hatton Cross
Bus Sta
A3113
AIRPORT WAY
SOUTHERN RUNWAY
Cargo Tunnel (permitted vehicles only)
Southern Perimeter Rd
Piccadilly Line
GREAT SOUTH-WEST RD
A30
HATTON ROAD
A1 LONDON
Terminal 4
Cargo Terminal
Heathrow Terminal 4
Short Stay
Walkway
Heathrow Hilton
Bedfont
Heathrow Express Station
Sch.
A3044
B378
PARK ROAD
P
PO
Stanwell
Southern Perimeter Rd
Heathrow Express Tunnel
RSPCA
Park & Fly
A30 STAINES
Duke of Northumberland's River

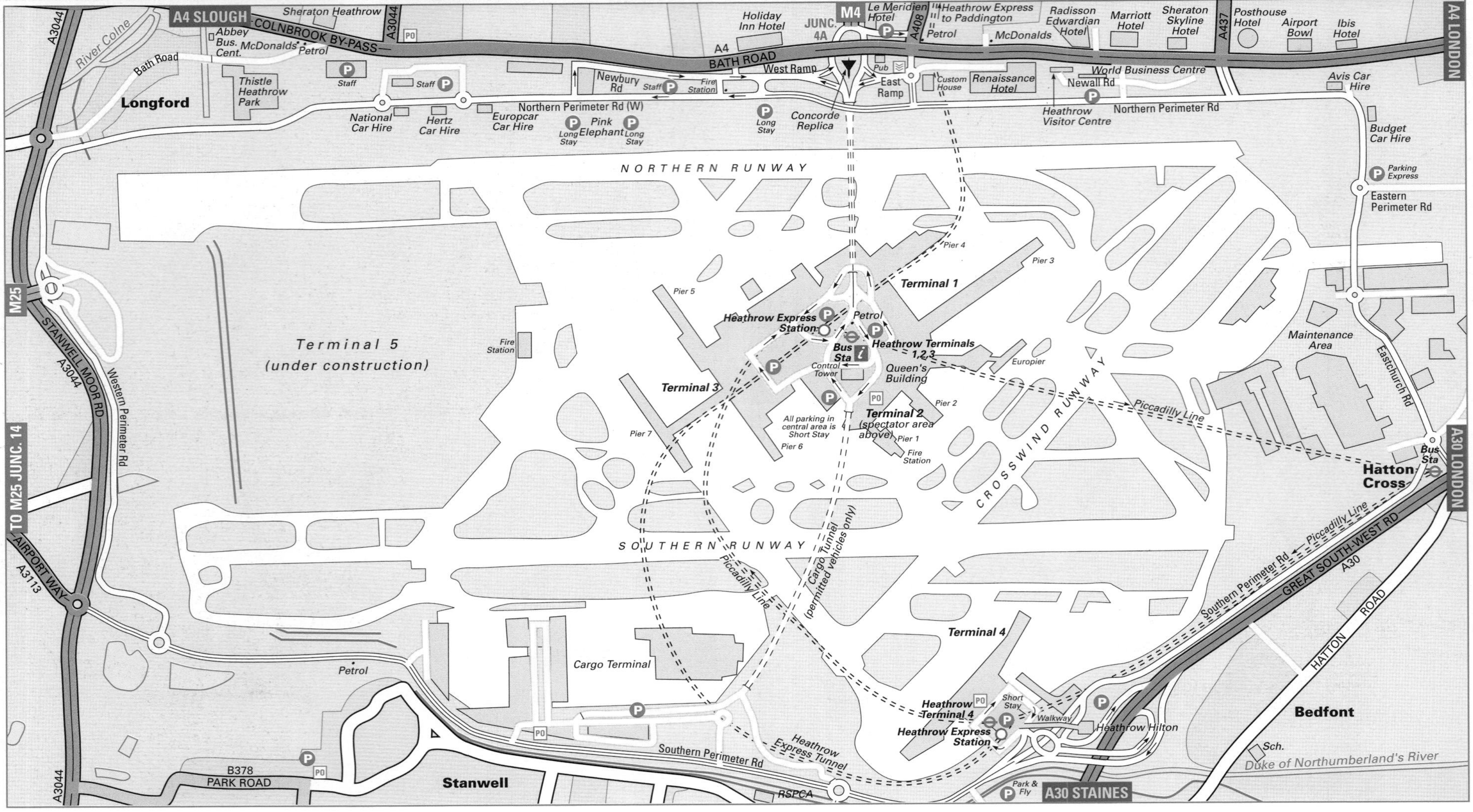

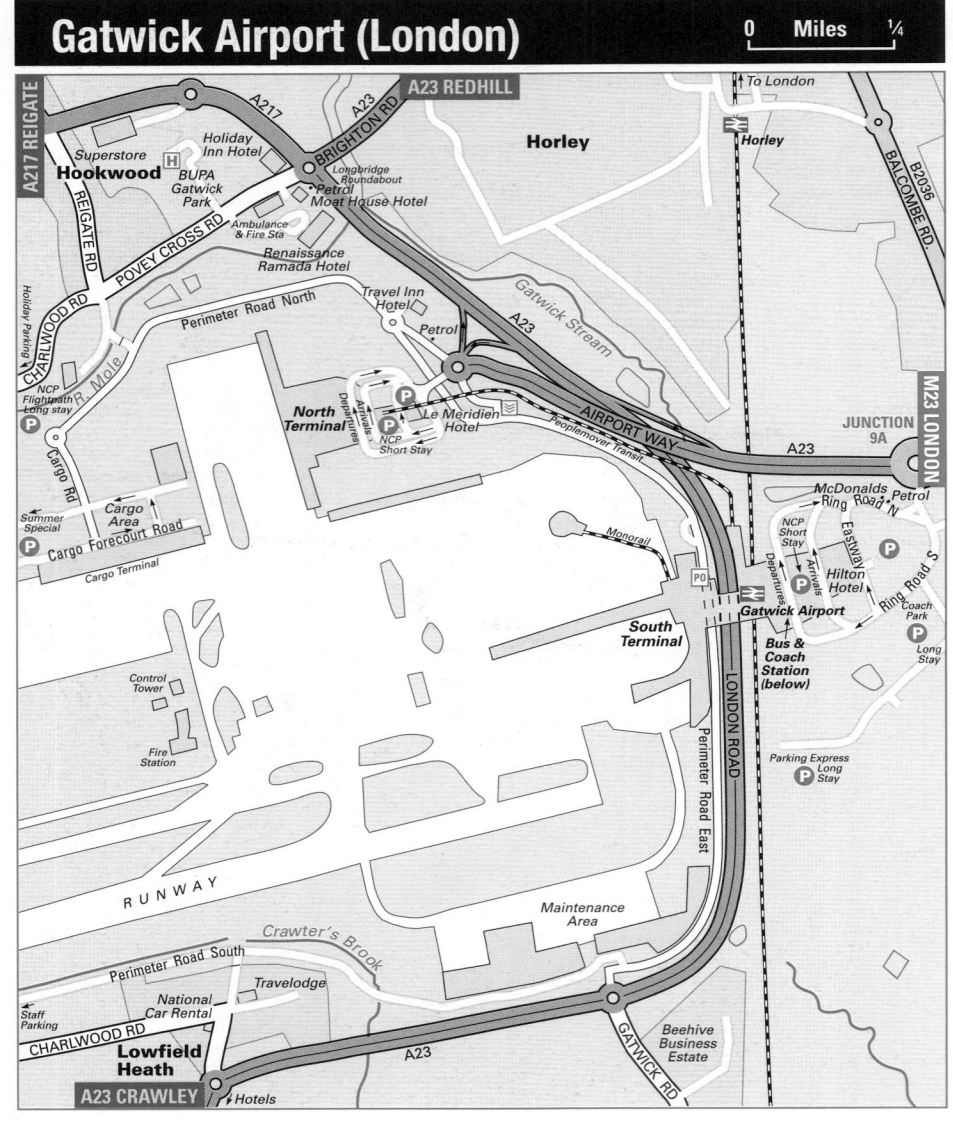

Gatwick Airport (London)

0 Miles ¼

A217 REIGATE
A217
Superstore
Hookwood
REIGATE RD
Holiday Inn Hotel
BUPA Gatwick Park
Ambulance & Fire Sta
Renaissance Ramada Hotel
Petrol
Moat House Hotel
Longbridge Roundabout
A23
BRIGHTON RD
A23 REDHILL
Horley
B2036
BALCOMBE RD
To London
Horley
CHARLWOOD RD
POVEY CROSS RD
Travel Inn Hotel
Perimeter Road North
Petrol
A23
Gatwick Stream
River Mole
CHARLWOOD RD
NCP Flighthatch Long stay
Cargo Rd
North Terminal
Le Meridien Hotel
NCP Short Stay
AIRPORT WAY
Peoplemover Transit
JUNCTION 9A
A23
M23 LONDON
Summer Special
Cargo Area
Cargo Forecourt Road
Cargo Terminal
Monorail
McDonalds
Ring Road N
NCP Short Stay
Eastway
Arrivals
Hilton Hotel
Departures
PO
Ring Road S
Petrol
Gatwick Airport
Car Park
Long Stay
Control Tower
South Terminal
Bus & Coach Station (below)
Fire Station
Maintenance Area
RUNWAY
Crawter's Brook
Perimeter Road South
Perimeter Road East
LONDON ROAD
Parking Express Long Stay
National Car Rental
Travelodge
Beehive Business Estate
Staff Parking
CHARLWOOD RD
Lowfield Heath
A23
A23 CRAWLEY
Hotels
GATWICK RD

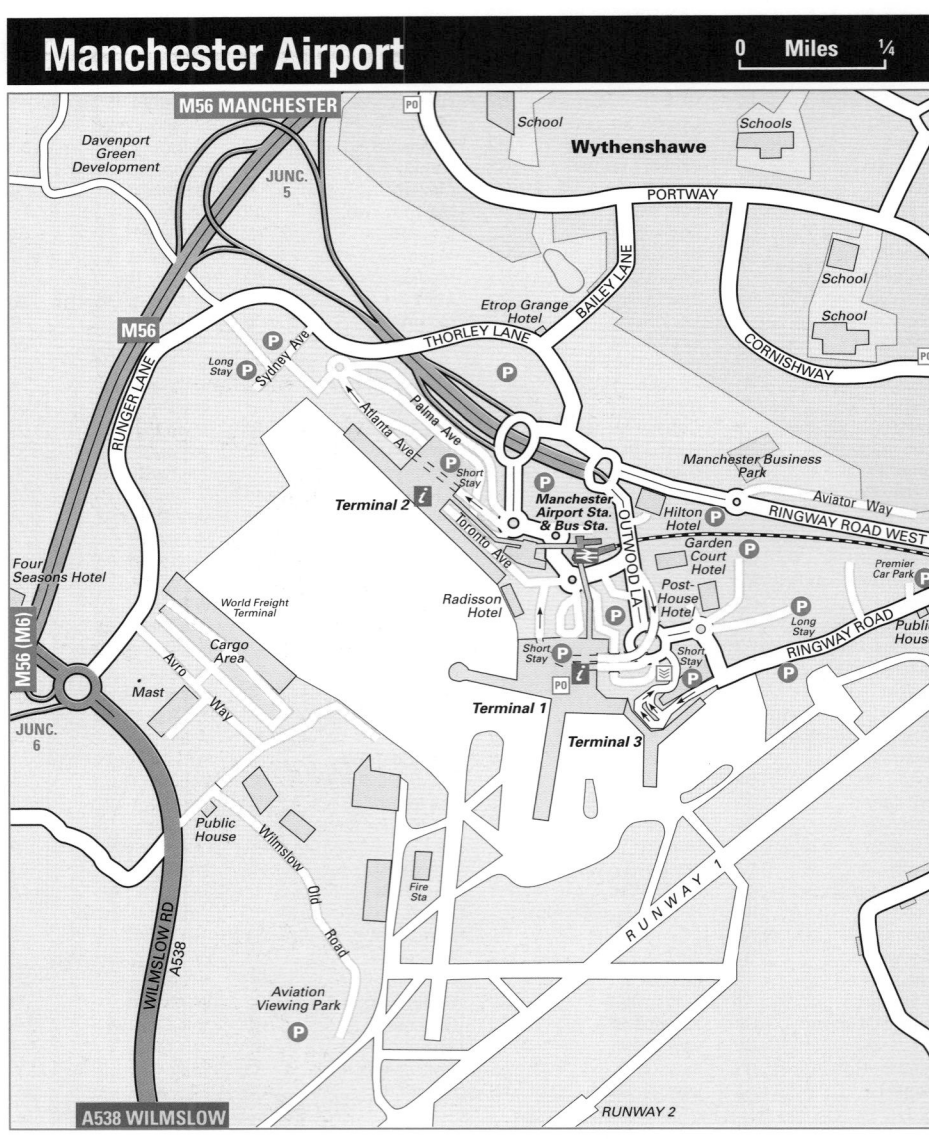

Manchester Airport

0 Miles ¼

M56 MANCHESTER
PO
Davenport Green Development
School
Wythenshawe
Schools
RUNGER LANE
JUNC. 5
PORTWAY
M56
Etrop Grange Hotel
BAILEY LANE
THORLEY LANE
School
CORNISHWAY
Long Stay
Sydney Ave
Palma Ave
Short Stay
Atlanta Ave
Terminal 2
Manchester Business Park
School
M56 (M6)
Manchester Airport Sta. & Bus Sta.
Aviator Way
RINGWAY ROAD WEST
Four Seasons Hotel
Toronto Ave
Hilton Hotel
Garden Court Hotel
Premier Car Park
World Freight Terminal
Post-House Hotel
Public House
Cargo Area
Radisson Hotel
Short Stay
Short Stay
Long Stay
RINGWAY ROAD
JUNC. 6
Avro Way
Mast
Terminal 1
Terminal 3
Public House
WILMSLOW RD
A538
Wilmslow Old Road
Fire Sta
RUNWAY
Aviation Viewing Park
A538 WILMSLOW
RUNWAY 2

Port of Dover

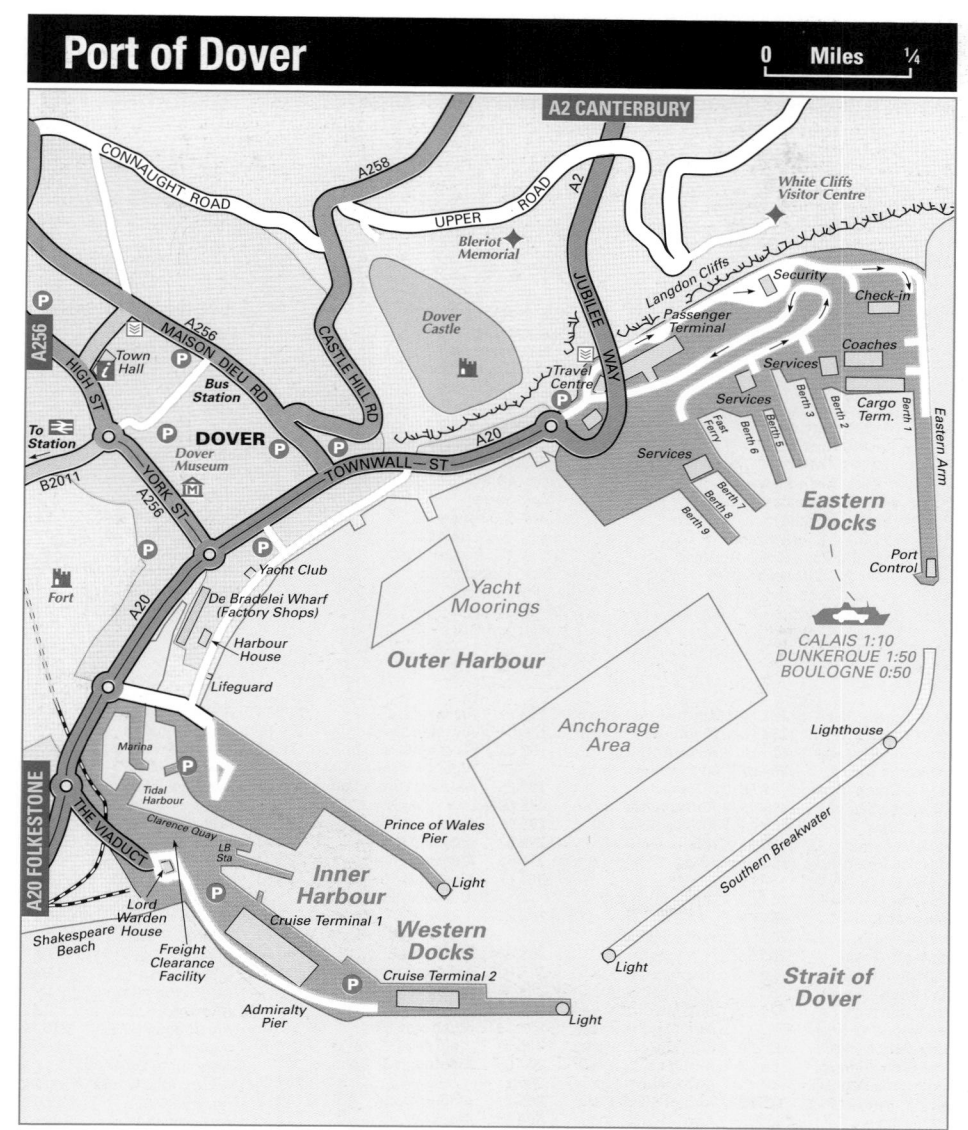

Port of Felixstowe

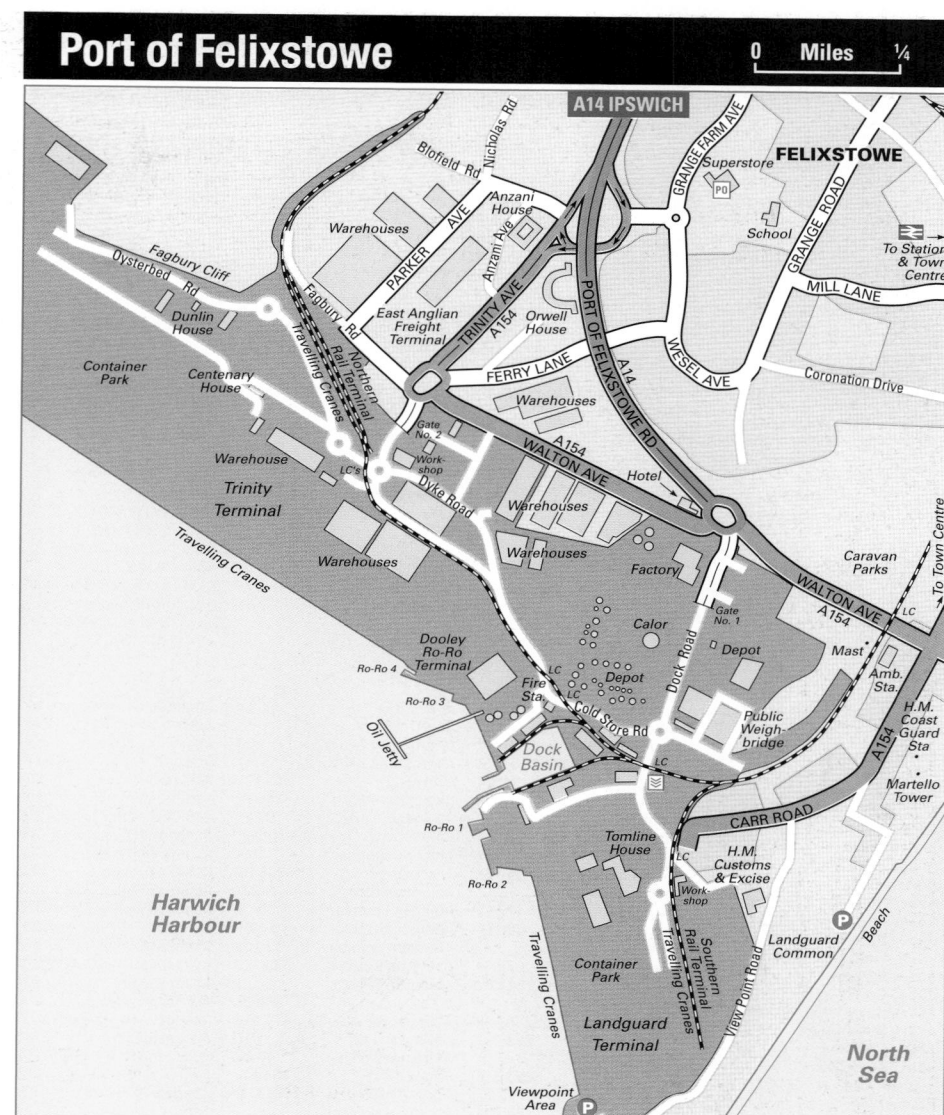

Portsmouth-Continental Ferry Port

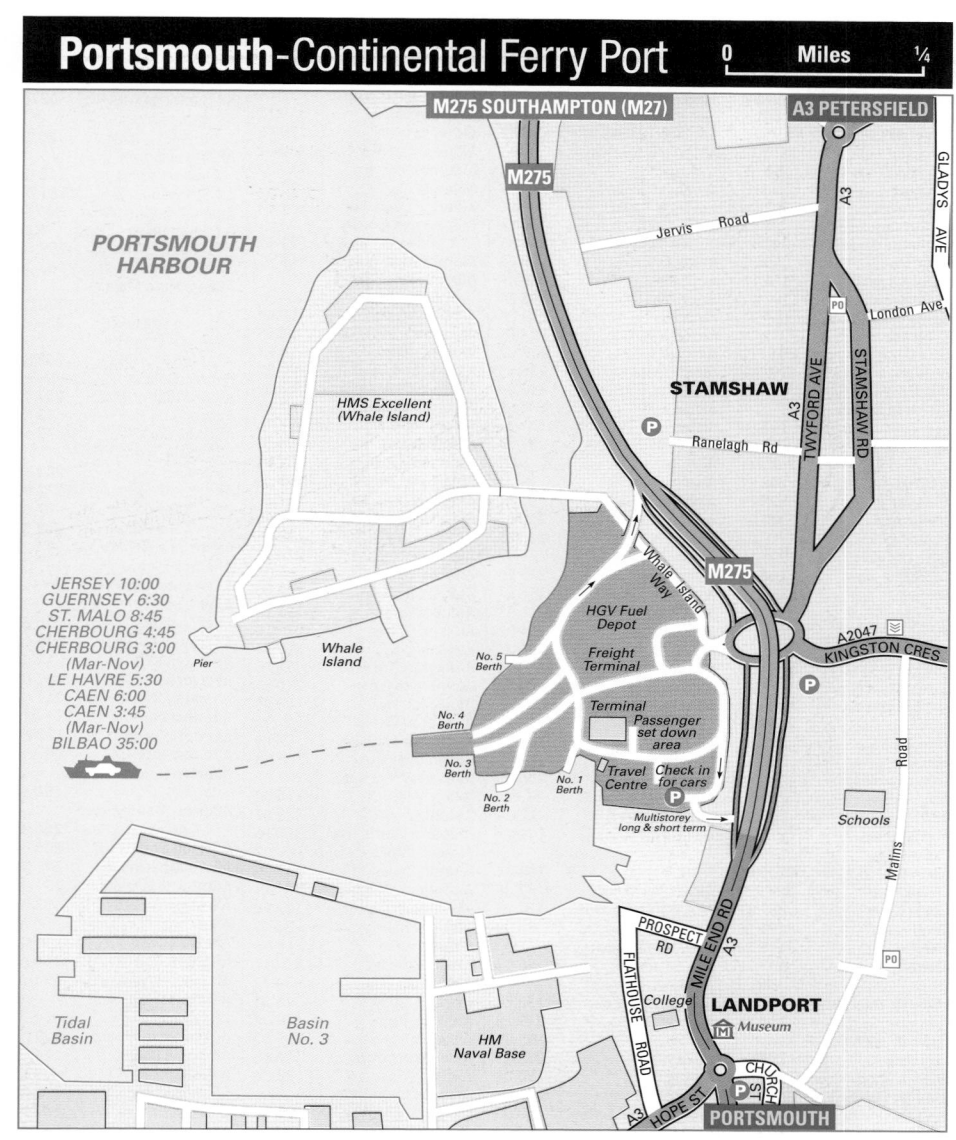

Port of Southampton

Index to road maps of Britain

Abbreviations used in the index

Aberdeen **Aberdeen City**
Aberds **Aberdeenshire**
Ald **Alderney**
Anglesey **Isle of Anglesey**
Angus **Angus**
Argyll **Argyll and Bute**
Bath **Bath and North East Somerset**
Beds **Bedfordshire**
Bl Gwent **Blaenau Gwent**
Blkburn **Blackburn with Darwen**
Blkpool **Blackpool**
Bmouth **Bournemouth**
Borders **Scottish Borders**
Brack **Bracknell**
Bridgend **Bridgend**
Brighton **City of Brighton and Hove**
Bristol **City and County of Bristol**
Bucks **Buckinghamshire**
Caerph **Caerphilly**
Cambs **Cambridgeshire**
Cardiff **Cardiff**
Carms **Carmarthenshire**
Ceredig **Ceredigion**
Ches **Cheshire**

Clack **Clackmannanshire**
Conwy **Conwy**
Corn **Cornwall**
Cumb **Cumbria**
Darl **Darlington**
Denb **Denbighshire**
Derby **City of Derby**
Derbys **Derbyshire**
Devon **Devon**
Dorset **Dorset**
Dumfries **Dumfries and Galloway**
Dundee **Dundee City**
Durham **Durham**
E Ayrs **East Ayrshire**
E Dunb **East Dunbartonshire**
E Loth **East Lothian**
E Renf **East Renfrewshire**
E Sus **East Sussex**
E Yorks **East Riding of Yorkshire**
Edin **City of Edinburgh**
Essex **Essex**
Falk **Falkirk**
Fife **Fife**
Flint **Flintshire**
Glasgow **City of Glasgow**
Glos **Gloucestershire**
Gtr Man **Greater Manchester**

Guern **Guernsey**
Gwyn **Gwynedd**
Halton **Halton**
Hants **Hampshire**
Hereford **Herefordshire**
Herts **Hertfordshire**
Highld **Highland**
Hrtlpl **Hartlepool**
Hull **Hull**
I o M **Isle of Man**
I o W **Isle of Wight**
Invclyd **Inverclyde**
Jersey **Jersey**
Kent **Kent**
Lancs **Lancashire**
Leicester **City of Leicester**
Leics **Leicestershire**
Lincs **Lincolnshire**
London **Greater London**
Luton **Luton**
M Keynes **Milton Keynes**
M Tydf **Merthyr Tydfil**
M'bro **Middlesbrough**
Medway **Medway**
Mers **Merseyside**
Midloth **Midlothian**
Mon **Monmouthshire**
Moray **Moray**
N Ayrs **North Ayrshire**
N Lincs **North Lincolnshire**
N Lnrk **North Lanarkshire**

N Som **North Somerset**
N Yorks **North Yorkshire**
NE Lincs **North East Lincolnshire**
Neath **Neath Port Talbot**
Newport **City and County of Newport**
Norf **Norfolk**
Northants **Northamptonshire**
Northumb **Northumberland**
Nottingham **City of Nottingham**
Notts **Nottinghamshire**
Orkney **Orkney**
Oxon **Oxfordshire**
P'boro **Peterborough**
Pembs **Pembrokeshire**
Perth **Perth and Kinross**
Plym **Plymouth**
Poole **Poole**
Powys **Powys**
Ptsmth **Portsmouth**
Reading **Reading**
Redcar **Redcar and Cleveland**
Renfs **Renfrewshire**
Rhondda **Rhondda Cynon Taff**
Rutland **Rutland**
S Ayrs **South Ayrshire**
S Glos **South Gloucestershire**
S Lnrk **South Lanarkshire**
S Yorks **South Yorkshire**
Scilly **Scilly**
Shetland **Shetland**

Shrops **Shropshire**
Slough **Slough**
Som **Somerset**
Soton **Southampton**
Staffs **Staffordshire**
Sthend **Southend-on-Sea**
Stirl **Stirling**
Stockton **Stockton-on-Tees**
Stoke **Stoke-on-Trent**
Suff **Suffolk**
Sur **Surrey**
Swansea **Swansea**
T & W **Tyne and Wear**
Telford **Telford and Wrekin**
Thamesdown **Thamesdown**
Thurrock **Thurrock**
Torbay **Torbay**
Torf **Torfaen**

V Glam **The Vale of Glamorgan**
W Berks **West Berkshire**
W Dunb **West Dunbartonshire**
W Isles **Western Isles**
W Loth **West Lothian**
W Mid **West Midlands**
W Sus **West Sussex**
W Yorks **West Yorkshire**
Warks **Warwickshire**
Warr **Warrington**
Wilts **Wiltshire**
Windsor **Windsor and Maidenhead**
Wokingham **Wokingham**
Worcs **Worcestershire**
Wrex **Wrexham**
York **City of York**

How to use the index

Example

Muddlebridge Devon   40   G4
- grid square
- page number
- county or unitary authority

Places of special interest are highlighted in magenta

Allison Lane End ER Yorks 209 B9
Allithwaite Cumb 211 D7
Allmore Green Staffs 151 F7
Alloa Clack 279 C7
Allonby Cumb 229 C7
Allostock Ches 184 G2
Alloway S Ayrs 257 F8
Allowenshay Som'set 28 E5
Allscott Telford 150 G2
Allt Carms 75 E9
Allt na h-Airbhe H'land 307 K6
Alltami Flints 166 B3
Alltbeithe H'land 290 C2
Alltchaorunn H'land 284 B5
Alltmawr Powys 95 B11
Alltnacaillich H'land 308 E4
Allt-na-giubhsaich Aberds 292 E4
Allt-nan-sùgh H'land 295 C11
Alltrech Arg/Bute 289 F8
Alltsigh H'land 290 B6
Alltwalis Carms 93 E8
Alltwen Neath P Talb 76 E2
Alltyblaca Ceredig'n 93 B10
Allt-yr-yn Newp 59 B9
Allweston Dorset 29 E11
Allwood Green Suffolk 125 C10
Alma Park Estate Lincs 155 B8
Almagill Dumf/Gal 238 B3
Almeley Heref'd 114 G6
Almeley Wooton Heref'd 114 G6
Almer Dorset 18 B4
Almholme S Yorks 198 F5
Almshouse Green Essex 106 E5
Almington Staffs 150 C4
Alminstone Cross Devon 24 C5
Almodington W Sussex 22 D4
Almondbank Perth/Kinr 286 E4
Almondbury W Yorks 197 D7
Almondsbury S Glos 60 C6
Almondvale W Loth 269 B10
Alne N Yorks 215 F9
Alne End Warwick 118 F2
Alness H'land 300 C6
Alnessferry H'land 300 C6
Alney Island Glos 80 B4
Alnham Northum 263 G11
Alnmouth Northum 264 G6
Alnwick Northum 264 G5
Alperton London 67 C7
Alphamstone Essex 107 D7
Alpheton Suffolk 125 G7
Alphington Devon 14 D4
Alpington Norfolk 142 C5
Alport Derby 170 C2
Alpraham Ches 167 D9
Alresford Essex 107 G11
Alrewas Staffs 152 F3
Alsager Ches 168 E4
Alsagers Bank Staffs 168 F4
Alsop en le Dale Derby 169 D11
Alston Cumb 231 B10
Alston Devon 28 G4
Alston Sutton Som'set 44 C2
Alstone Glos 99 E8
Alstone Glos 99 E9
Alstone Som'set 43 D10
Alstonefield Staffs 169 D10
Alswear Devon 26 C2
Alt Hill Gtr Man 196 G2
Altandhu H'land 307 H4
Altanduin H'land 311 G2
Altarnun Cornw'l 11 E10
Altass H'land 309 J4
Altdargue Aberds 293 C7
Alterwall H'land 310 C6
Altham Lancs 203 G11
Althorne Essex 88 F6
Althorp House, Great Brington Northants 120 D3
Althorpe N Lincs 199 F10
Alticry Dumf/Gal 236 D4
Altnabreac Station H'land 310 E4
Altnacealgach Hotel H'land 307 H7
Altnacraig Arg/Bute 289 G10
Altnafeadh H'land 284 B6
Altnaharra H'land 308 F5
Altofts W Yorks 197 C11
Alton Derby 170 C5
Alton Hants 49 F8
Alton Staffs 169 G9
Alton Barnes Wilts 62 G6
Alton Pancras Dorset 29 G11
Alton Priors Wilts 62 G6
Alton Towers Staffs 169 G9
Altonhill E Ayrs 257 B10
Altonside Moray 302 D2
Altour H'land 290 E4
Altrincham Gtr Man 184 D3
Altrua H'land 290 E4
Altskeith Stirl 285 G8
Altyre Ho. Moray 301 D10
Alum Rock W Midlands 134 F2
Alva Clack 279 B7
Alvanley Ches 183 G7
Alvaston Derby C 153 C7
Alvechurch Worcs 117 C10
Alvecote Warwick 134 C4
Alvediston Wilts 31 C7
Alveley Shrops 132 G5
Alverdiscott Devon 25 B8
Alverstoke Hants 21 B8
Alverstone I/Wight 21 D7
Alverthorpe W Yorks 197 C10
Alverton Notts 172 G3
Alves Moray 301 C11
Alvescot Oxon 82 E3
Alveston S Glos 60 B6
Alveston Warwick 118 F4
Alveston Down S Glos 60 B6
Alvie H'land 291 C10
Alvingham Lincs 190 C5
Alvington Devon 24 C6
Alvington Glos 79 E10
Alwalton Peterbro 138 D2
Alway Newp 59 B10
Alwinton Northum 251 B10
Alwoodley W Yorks 205 E11
Alwoodley Gates W Yorks 206 E2
Alwoodley Park W Yorks 205 E11
Alwyn Lawn Bucks 84 C3
Alyth Perth/Kinr 286 C6
Am Baile W Isles 297 K3
Am Buth Arg/Bute 289 G10
Amatnatua H'land 309 K4
Ambaston Derby 153 C8
Amber Hill Lincs 174 F2
Ambergate Derby 170 E5
Amberley Glos 80 E5
Amberley W Sussex 35 E8
Amble Northum 253 C7
Amblecote Worcs 133 F7
Ambler Thorn W Yorks 196 B5
Ambleside Cumb 221 E7
Ambleston Pembs 91 F10
Ambrosden Oxon 83 B10
Amcotts N Lincs 199 E11
Amen Corner Brackn'l 65 F10
American Adventure, Ilkeston Derby 170 G6
American Air Museum, Duxford Cambs 105 B9
Amersham Bucks 85 F7
Amersham Common Bucks 85 F7
Amersham Old Town Bucks 85 F7
Amersham on the Hill Bucks 85 F7
Amerton Staffs 151 D9
Amerton Working Farm, Stowe-by-Chartley Staffs 151 D9
Amesbury Wilts 47 E7
Ameysford Dorset 31 G9
Amington Staffs 134 C4
Amisfield Dumf/Gal 248 G2
Amlwch Angl 178 C6
Amlwch Port Angl 179 C7
Ammanford = Rhydaman Carms 75 C10
Amod Arg/Bute 255 D8
Amotherby N Yorks 216 E5
Ampfield Hants 32 C6
Ampleforth N Yorks 215 D11
Ampney Crucis Glos 81 E9
Ampney St. Mary Glos 81 E9
Ampney St. Peter Glos 81 E9
Amport Hants 47 E9
Ampthill Beds 103 D10
Ampton Suffolk 125 C7
Amroth Pembs 73 D11
Amulree Perth/Kinr 286 D2
Amwell Herts 85 C11
An Caol H'land 298 D6
An Cnoc W Isles 304 E6
An Gleann Ur W Isles 304 E6
An Leth Meadhanach W Isles 297 K3
An t-Ob = Leverburgh W Isles 296 C6
Anagach H'land 301 G10
Anaheilt H'land 289 C10
Anancaun H'land 299 C10
Ancarraig H'land 300 G4
Ancaster Lincs 173 G7
Anchor Shrops 130 G3
Anchor Corner Norfolk 141 D10
Anchor Street Norfolk 160 E6
Anchorsholme Blackp'l 202 E2
Ancoats Gtr Man 184 B5
Ancroft Northum 273 F10
Ancrum Scot Borders 262 E4
Ancton W Sussex 35 G7
Ancumtoun Orkney 312 C8
Anderby Lincs 191 F8
Anderby Creek Lincs 191 F8
Andersea Som'set 43 G10
Andersfield Som'set 43 G8
Anderson Dorset 18 B3
Anderton Ches 183 F10
Anderton Cornw'l 7 E8
Anderton's Mill Lancs 194 E4
Andover Hants 47 D11
Andover Down Hants 47 D11
Andoversford Glos 81 B8
Andreas I/Man 192 C5
Anerley London 67 F10
Anfield Mersey 182 C5
Angarrack Cornw'l 2 B3
Angarrick Cornw'l 3 B7
Angelbank Shrops 115 B11
Angersleigh Som'set 27 D11
Angerton Cumb 238 F6
Angle Pembs 72 E5
Anglesey Sea Zoo Angl 163 B7
Angmering W Sussex 35 G9
Angram N Yorks 206 D6
Angram N Yorks 223 F7
Anick Northum 241 D11
Anie Stirl 285 F9
Ankerbold Derby 170 B5
Ankerville H'land 301 B8
Anlaby ER Yorks 200 B4
Anlaby Park Kingston/Hull 200 B5
Anmer Norfolk 158 D4
Anmore Hants 33 E11
Anna Valley Hants 47 E10
Annan Dumf/Gal 238 D5
Annaside Cumb 210 B1
Annat Arg/Bute 284 E4
Annat H'land 290 D5
Annat H'land 299 D8
Annbank S Ayrs 257 E10
Anne Hathaway's Cottage, Stratford-upon-Avon Warwick 118 G3
Annesley Notts 171 E8
Annesley Woodhouse Notts 171 E7
Annfield Plain Durham 242 G5
Anniesland Glasg C 267 B10
Annifirth Shetl'd 315 J3
Annis Hill Suffolk 143 F7
Annishader H'land 298 D4
Annitsford Tyne/Wear 243 C7
Ann's Hill Hants 33 G9
Annscroft Shrops 131 B9
Ansdell Lancs 193 B10
Ansdore Kent 54 D6
Ansells End Herts 85 B11
Ansford Som'set 44 G6
Ansley Warwick 134 E5
Ansley Common Warwick 134 E6
Anslow Staffs 152 D4
Anslow Gate Staffs 152 E3
Ansteadbrook Surrey 50 G2
Anstey Hants 49 E8
Anstey Herts 105 E8
Anstey Leics C 135 B11
Anstruther Easter Fife 287 G9
Anstruther Wester Fife 287 G9
Ansty Warwick 135 G7
Ansty Wilts 31 B7
Ansty W Sussex 36 C3
Ansty Coombe Wilts 30 B6
Ansty Cross Dorset 30 G3
Anthill Common Hants 33 E10
Anthony's Surrey 66 G4
Anthorn Cumb 238 F5
Antingham Norfolk 160 C5
Anton's Gowt Lincs 174 F3
Antonshill Falk 279 E7
Antony Cornw'l 7 E7
Antrobus Ches 183 F10
Antron Cornw'l 2 D4
Anvil Green Kent 54 D6
Anwick Lincs 173 E11
Anwoth Dumf/Gal 237 D7
Aonachan H'land 290 E4
Aoradh Arg/Bute 274 G3
Apes Dale Worcs 117 C9
Apethorpe Northants 137 D10
Apeton Staffs 151 F7
Apley Lincs 189 F10
Apperknowle Derby 186 F5
Apperley Glos 99 F7
Apperley Bridge W Yorks 205 F9
Apperley Dene Northum 242 F3
Appersett N Yorks 223 G7
Appin Arg/Bute 289 E11
Appin House Arg/Bute 289 E11
Appleby N Lincs 200 E3
Appleby Magna Leics 134 B6
Appleby Parva Leics 134 B6
Appleby-in-Westmorland Cumb 231 G9
Applecross H'land 299 E7
Applecross Ho. H'land 299 E7
Appledore Devon 27 E9
Appledore Devon 40 G3
Appledore Kent 39 B7
Appledore Heath Kent 54 G2
Appleford Oxon 83 G8
Applegarthtown Dumf/Gal 248 G4
Applehaigh W Yorks 197 E10
Applehouse Hill Windsor 65 C10
Applemore Hants 32 F5
Appleshaw Hants 47 D10
Applethwaite Cumb 229 F11
Appleton Halton 183 D8
Appleton Oxon 82 E6
Appleton Park Warrington 183 E10
Appleton Roebuck N Yorks 207 E7
Appleton Thorn Warrington 183 E10
Appleton Wiske N Yorks 225 E7
Appleton-le-Moors N Yorks 216 B4
Appleton-le-Street N Yorks 216 E4
Appletree Northants 101 B9
Appletreehall Scot Borders 262 F2
Appletreewick N Yorks 213 G11
Appley I/Wight 21 C8
Appley Som'set 27 C9
Appley Bridge Lancs 194 F4
Apse Hill I/Wight 21 E7
Apsey Green Suffolk 126 E5
Apsley Herts 85 E9
Apsley End Beds 104 E2
Apuldram W Sussex 34 G4
Aquhythie Aberds 293 B9
Arabella H'land 301 B8
Arbeadie Aberds 293 D8
Arbeia Roman Fort and Museum Tyne/Wear 243 D9
Arberth = Narberth Pembs 73 C10
Arbirlot Angus 287 C10
Arboll H'land 311 L2
Arborfield Wokingham 65 F9
Arborfield Cross Wokingham 65 F9
Arborfield Garrison Wokingham 65 G9
Arbourthorne S Yorks 186 D5
Arbroath Angus 287 C10
Arbury Cambs 123 E9
Arbuthnott Aberds 293 F9
Archavandra Muir H'land 309 K7
Archdeacon Newton D'lington 224 B5
Archiestown Moray 302 E2
Archnalea H'land 289 C10
Ardachu H'land 309 J6
Ardailly Arg/Bute 255 B7
Ardalanish Arg/Bute 288 H5
Ardallie Aberds 303 F10
Ardalum Ho Arg/Bute 288 F6
Ardamaleish Arg/Bute 275 G11
Ardanaiseig Arg/Bute 284 E4
Ardaneaskan H'land 295 B10
Ardanstur Arg/Bute 275 B9
Ardargie House Hotel Perth/Kinr 286 F4
Ardarroch H'land 295 B10
Ardban H'land 295 B9
Ardbeg Arg/Bute 254 C5
Ardbeg Arg/Bute 266 B1
Ardbeg Arg/Bute 276 E3
Ardbeg Distillery, Port Ellen Arg/Bute 254 C5
Ardcharnich H'land 307 L6
Ardchiavaig Arg/Bute 288 H5
Ardchonnell Arg/Bute 275 B10
Ardchronie H'land 309 L6
Ardchuilk H'land 300 F2
Ardchullarie More Stirl 285 F9
Ardchyle Stirl 285 E9
Ardclach H'land 301 E9
Ard-dhubh H'land 299 E7
Arddleen Powys 148 F5
Ardechvie H'land 290 D3
Ardeley Herts 104 F6
Ardelve H'land 295 C10
Arden Arg/Bute 277 E7
Arden Glasg C 267 D10
Ardencaple Ho Arg/Bute 275 B8
Ardendrain H'land 300 F5
Ardens Grafton Warwick 118 G2
Ardentallen Arg/Bute 289 G10
Ardentinny Arg/Bute 276 D3
Ardentraive Arg/Bute 275 F11
Ardeonaig Stirl 285 D10
Ardersier H'land 301 D7
Ardery H'land 289 C9
Ardessie H'land 307 L5
Ardfern Arg/Bute 275 C9
Ardfernal Arg/Bute 274 F6
Ardgartan Arg/Bute 284 G6
Ardgay H'land 309 K5
Ardglassie Aberds 303 C10
Ardgour H'land 290 G2
Ardgye Moray 301 C11
Ardheslaig H'land 299 D7
Ardiecow Moray 302 C5
Ardinamir Arg/Bute 275 B8
Ardindrean H'land 307 L6
Ardingly W Sussex 36 B4
Ardington Oxon 64 B2
Ardintoul H'land 295 C10
Ardlair Aberds 302 G5
Ardlair H'land 299 B9
Ardlamey Arg/Bute 255 C7
Ardlamont Ho. Arg/Bute 275 G10
Ardlawhill Aberds 303 C8
Ardleigh Essex 107 F10
Ardleigh Green London 68 B4
Ardleigh Heath Essex 107 E10
Ardler Perth/Kinr 286 C6
Ardley Oxon 101 F10
Ardlui Arg/Bute 285 F7
Ardlussa Arg/Bute 275 E7
Ardmair H'land 307 K6
Ardmay Arg/Bute 284 G6
Ardmenish Arg/Bute 274 F6
Ardminish Arg/Bute 255 C7
Ardmolich H'land 289 B9
Ardmore Arg/Bute 289 G9
Ardmore H'land 306 D7
Ardmore H'land 309 L7
Ardnacross Arg/Bute 289 E7
Ardnadam Arg/Bute 276 E3
Ardnagowan Arg/Bute 284 G4
Ardnagrask H'land 300 E5
Ardnarff H'land 295 B10
Ardnastang H'land 289 C10
Ardnave Arg/Bute 274 F3
Ardno Arg/Bute 284 G5
Ardo Aberds 303 F8
Ardo Ho. Aberds 303 G9
Ardoch Arg/Bute 277 F7
Ardoch Perth/Kinr 286 D4
Ardoch Stirl 285 F9
Ardochy House H'land 290 C4
Ardoyne Aberds 302 G6
Ardpatrick Arg/Bute 275 G8
Ardpatrick Ho. Arg/Bute 255 B8
Ardpeaton Arg/Bute 276 D4
Ardradnaig Perth/Kinr 285 C11
Ardrishaig Arg/Bute 275 E9
Ardross Fife 287 G9
Ardross H'land 300 B6
Ardross Castle H'land 300 B6
Ardrossan N Ayrs 266 G4
Ardshave H'land 309 K7
Ardsheal H'land 289 D11
Ardshealach H'land 289 C8
Ardskenish Arg/Bute 274 D4
Ardsley S Yorks 197 F11
Ardslignish H'land 289 C7
Ardtalla Arg/Bute 254 B5
Ardtalnaig Perth/Kinr 285 D11
Ardtaraig Arg/Bute 275 E11
Ardtoe H'land 289 B8
Ardtreck H'land 294 B5
Ardtrostan Perth/Kinr 285 E10
Ardtur Arg/Bute 289 E11
Arduaine Arg/Bute 275 B8
Ardullie H'land 300 C5
Ardvannie H'land 309 L6
Ardvar H'land 306 F6
Ardvasar H'land 295 E8
Ardveich Stirl 285 E10
Ardverikie H'land 291 E7
Ardvorlich Perth/Kinr 285 E10
Ardwell Dumf/Gal 236 E3
Ardwell Moray 302 F3
Ardwell Mains Dumf/Gal 236 E3
Ardwick Gtr Man 184 B5
Areley Kings Worcs 116 C6
Arford Hants 49 F10
Argoed Caerph 77 F11
Argoed Powys 113 E9
Argyll & Sutherland Highlanders Museum (See Stirling Castle) Stirl 278 C5
Arichamish Arg/Bute 275 C10
Arichastlich Arg/Bute 284 D6
Aridhglas Arg/Bute 288 G5
Arienskill H'land 295 G9
Arileod Arg/Bute 288 D3
Arinacrinachd H'land 299 D7
Arinagour Arg/Bute 288 D4
Arineckaig H'land 299 E9
Arion Orkney 312 G3
Arisaig H'land 295 G8
Ariundle H'land 289 C10
Arivegaig H'land 289 C8
Arivoichallum Arg/Bute 254 C4
Arkendale N Yorks 215 G7
Arkesden Essex 105 E9
Arkholme Lancs 211 E11
Arkle Town N Yorks 223 E10
Arkleby Cumb 229 D8
Arkleside N Yorks 213 C10
Arkleton Dumf/Gal 249 E9
Arkley London 86 F2
Arksey S Yorks 198 F5
Arkwright Town Derby 186 G6
Arle Glos 99 G8
Arlecdon Cumb 219 B10
Arlescote Warwick 101 B7
Arlesey Beds 104 D3
Arleston Telford 150 G3
Arley Ches 183 E11
Arley Green Ches 183 E11
Arlingham Glos 80 C2
Arlington Devon 40 E6
Arlington E Sussex 23 D8
Arlington Glos 81 D10
Arlington Becott Devon 40 E6
Arlington Court Devon 40 E6
Armadale H'land 308 C7
Armadale W Loth 269 B8
Armadale Castle H'land 295 E8
Armathwaite Cumb 230 B6
Arminghall Norfolk 142 C4
Armitage Staffs 151 F11
Armitage Bridge W Yorks 196 E6
Armley W Yorks 205 G11
Armscote Warwick 100 C4
Armshead Staffs 168 F6
Armston Northants 137 F11
Armthorpe S Yorks 198 G6
Arnabost Arg/Bute 288 D4
Arnaby Cumb 210 C3
Arncliffe N Yorks 213 E8
Arncroach Fife 287 G9
Arndilly Ho. Moray 302 E2
Arne Dorset 18 D5
Arnesby Leics 136 E2
Arnfield Derby 185 B8
Arngask Perth/Kinr 286 F5
Arnisdale H'land 295 D10
Arnish H'land 298 E5
Arniston Engine Midloth 270 C6
Arnol W Isles 304 D5
Arnold ER Yorks 209 E8
Arnold Notts 171 F9
Arnolfini Gallery Bristol 60 E5
Arno's Vale Bristol 60 E6
Arnprior Stirl 278 B2
Arnside Cumb 211 D9
Aros Mains Arg/Bute 289 E7
Arowry Wrex 149 B9
Arpafeelie H'land 300 D6
Arpinge Kent 55 F7
Arpinge Kent 55 F8
Arrad Foot Cumb 210 C6
Arram ER Yorks 208 E6
Arrathorne N Yorks 224 G4
Arreton I/Wight 20 D6
Arrington Cambs 122 G6
Arrivain Arg/Bute 284 D6
Arrochar Arg/Bute 284 G6
Arrow Warwick 117 F11
Arrowe Hill Mersey 182 D3
Arrowfield Top Worcs 117 C10
Arrunden W Yorks 196 F6
Arscaig H'land 309 H5
Arscott Shrops 131 B8
Arthill Ches 184 D2
Arthington W Yorks 205 E11
Arthingworth Northants 136 G5
Arthog Gwyn 146 G2
Arthrath Aberds 303 F9
Arthursdale W Yorks 206 F3
Arthurstone Perth/Kinr 286 C6
Arthurville H'land 309 L7
Artrochie Aberds 303 F10
Arundel W Sussex 35 F8
Arundel Castle W Sussex 35 F8
Arwick Orkney 312 F4
Aryhoulan H'land 290 G2
Asby Cumb 229 G7
Ascog Arg/Bute 266 C2
Ascoil H'land 311 H2
Ascot Windsor 66 F2
Ascot Racecourse Windsor 66 F2
Ascott Warwick 100 E6
Ascott d'Oyley Oxon 82 B4
Ascott Earl Oxon 82 B3
Ascott under Wychwood Oxon 82 B4
Asenby N Yorks 215 D7
Asfordby Leics 154 F4
Asfordby Hill Leics 154 F4
Asgarby Lincs 174 B4
Asgarby Lincs 173 F10
Ash Dorset 30 E5
Ash Devon 8 F6
Ash Kent 55 B9
Ash Kent 68 G5
Ash Som'set 28 C3
Ash Som'set 29 C7
Ash Surrey 49 C11
Ash Bank Staffs 168 F6
Ash Corner Suffolk 126 F6
Ash Green Surrey 50 C3
Ash Green Warwick 134 G6
Ash Hill Devon 14 G4
Ash Magna Shrops 149 B11
Ash Mill Devon 26 C3
Ash Parva Shrops 149 B11
Ash Priors Som'set 27 B11
Ash Street Suffolk 107 B10
Ash Thomas Devon 27 E8
Ash Vale Bl Gwent 77 C10
Ash Vale Surrey 49 C11
Ash Wharf Surrey 49 C11
Ashaig H'land 295 C8
Ashampstead W Berks 64 D5
Ashampstead Green W Berks 64 D5
Ashbank Ches 167 D11
Ashbank Ches 183 G10
Ashbocking Suffolk 126 G3
Ashbourne Derby 169 F11
Ashbrittle Som'set 27 C8
Ashbrook Herts 104 F4
Ashbrook Shrops 131 E9
Ashbrooke Tyne/Wear 243 F9
Ashburton Devon 8 B5
Ashbury Devon 12 B6
Ashbury Oxon 63 B9
Ashby N Lincs 200 F2
Ashby by Partney Lincs 174 B6
Ashby cum Fenby NE Lincs 201 G9
Ashby de la Launde Lincs 173 D9
Ashby de la Zouch Leics 153 F7
Ashby Folville Leics 154 G4
Ashby Hill NE Lincs 201 G8
Ashby Magna Leics 135 E11
Ashby Parva Leics 135 G10
Ashby Puerorum Lincs 190 G4
Ashby St. Ledgers Northants 119 D11
Ashby St. Mary Norfolk 142 B6
Ashchurch Glos 99 E8
Ashcombe Devon 14 F4
Ashcott Som'set 44 F2
Ashcott Corner Som'set 44 F3
Ashday W Yorks 196 C6
Ashdon Essex 105 C11
Ashe Hants 48 C4
Asheldham Essex 89 E7
Ashen Essex 106 C4
Ashendon Bucks 84 C2
Ashey I/Wight 21 D7
Ashfield Arg/Bute 275 E8
Ashfield Carms 94 F3
Ashfield Heref'd 97 G11
Ashfield Suffolk 126 E4
Ashfield Stirl 285 G11
Ashfield Green Suffolk 126 C5
Ashfield Green Suffolk 124 F5
Ashfold Crossways W Sussex 36 B2
Ashford Devon 8 F3
Ashford Devon 40 F4
Ashford Kent 54 E4
Ashford Surrey 66 E5
Ashford Bowdler Shrops 115 C10
Ashford Carbonell Shrops 115 C10
Ashford Common Surrey 66 F5
Ashford Hill Hants 64 G5
Ashford in the water Derby 169 B11
Ashgate Derby 186 G5
Ashgill S Lanarks 268 E5
Ashgrove Bath/NE Som'set 45 B8
Ashill Devon 27 E9
Ashill Norfolk 141 C7
Ashill Som'set 28 D4
Ashingdon Essex 88 G5
Ashington Northum 253 F7
Ashington Som'set 29 C9
Ashington W Sussex 35 D10
Ashington End Lincs 175 B8
Ashintully Castle Perth/Kinr 292 G3
Ashkirk Scot Borders 261 E11
Ashlett Hants 33 G7
Ashleworth Glos 98 F6
Ashleworth Quay Glos 98 F6
Ashley Cambs 124 E3
Ashley Ches 184 E3
Ashley Dorset 31 G10
Ashley Glos 80 G6
Ashley Hants 47 G11
Ashley Hants 19 C11
Ashley Kent 55 D10
Ashley Northants 136 E5
Ashley Staffs 150 B5
Ashley Wilts 61 F10
Ashley Dale Staffs 150 B5
Ashley Down Bristol 60 D5
Ashley Green Bucks 85 D7
Ashley Heath Dorset 31 G10
Ashley Heath Gtr Man 184 D3
Ashley Heath Staffs 150 B4
Ashley Park Surrey 66 F6
Ashmanhaugh Norfolk 160 E6
Ashmansworth Hants 48 B2
Ashmansworthy Devon 24 D4
Ashmead Green Glos 80 F3
Ashmill Devon 12 B3
Ashmore Dorset 30 D6
Ashmore Green W Berks 64 F4
Ashmore Lake W Midlands 133 D9
Ashmore Park W Midlands 133 C9
Ashnashellach Lodge H'land 299 E10
Ashorne Warwick 118 F6
Ashover Derby 170 C5
Ashow Warwick 118 C6
Ashperton Heref'd 98 C2
Ashprington Devon 8 D6
Ashreigney Devon 25 E10
Ashstead Surrey 51 B7
Ashton Ches 167 B8
Ashton Cornw'l 2 D4
Ashton Hants 33 D8
Ashton Inverc'l 276 F4
Ashton Northants 137 F11
Ashton Northants 102 B5
Ashton Peterbro 138 B2
Ashton Som'set 44 D2
Ashton Common Wilts 45 B10
Ashton Hill Wilts 46 B3
Ashton Keynes Wilts 81 G9
Ashton under Hill Worcs 99 D9
Ashton upon Mersey Gtr Man 184 C3
Ashton Vale Bristol 60 E5
Ashton-in-Makerfield Gtr Man 183 B9
Ashton's Green Mersey 183 B8
Ashton-under-Lyne Gtr Man 184 B6
Ashurst Hants 32 E4
Ashurst Kent 52 F4
Ashurst Mersey 194 F3
Ashurst W Sussex 35 D11
Ashurst Bridge Hants 32 E4
Ashurstwood W Sussex 52 F2
Ashwater Devon 12 B3
Ashway Gap Gtr Man 196 G4
Ashwell Herts 104 D5
Ashwell Rutl'd 155 G7
Ashwell Som'set 28 D5
Ashwell End Herts 104 C5
Ashwellthorpe Norfolk 142 D2
Ashwick Som'set 44 D6
Ashwicken Norfolk 158 F4
Ashwood Staffs 133 F7
Ashybank Scot Borders 262 F2
Askern S Yorks 198 E5
Askerswell Dorset 16 C6
Askett Bucks 84 D4
Askham Cumb 230 G6
Askham Notts 188 G2
Askham Bryan C/York 207 D7
Askham in Furness Cumb 210 D4
Askham Richard C/York 206 D6
Asknish Arg/Bute 275 D10
Askrigg N Yorks 223 G8
Askwith N Yorks 205 D9
Aslackby Lincs 155 C11
Aslacton Norfolk 142 E3
Aslockton Notts 172 G2
Asloun Aberds 293 B7
Asney Som'set 44 F3
Aspall Suffolk 126 D3
Aspatria Cumb 229 C8
Aspenden Herts 105 F7
Asperton Lincs 156 B5
Aspey Green Suffolk 126 E5
Aspley Nott'ham 171 G8
Aspley Guise Beds 103 D8
Aspley Heath Beds 103 E8
Aspley Heath Warwick 118 C2
Aspull Gtr Man 194 F6
Aspull Common Gtr Man 183 B10
Assater Shetl'd 314 F4
Asselby ER Yorks 199 B8
Asserby Lincs 191 F7
Assington Suffolk 107 D8
Assington Green Suffolk 124 F5
Assynt Ho. H'land 300 C5
Astbury Ches 168 C4
Astcote Northants 120 G3
Asterby Lincs 190 F3
Asterley Shrops 131 B7
Asterton Shrops 131 E7
Asthall Oxon 82 C3
Asthall Leigh Oxon 82 C4
Astle H'land 309 K7
Astley Gtr Man 195 G8
Astley Shrops 149 F10
Astley Warwick 134 F6
Astley Worcs 116 D5
Astley W Yorks 197 B11
Astley Abbotts Shrops 132 D4
Astley Bridge Gtr Man 195 E8
Astley Cross Worcs 116 D6
Astley Green Gtr Man 184 B2
Astmoor Halton 183 E8
Aston Ches 167 F10
Aston Ches 183 F9
Aston Derby 152 C3
Aston Derby 185 E11
Aston Flints 166 B4
Aston Heref'd 115 E9
Aston Heref'd 115 G9
Aston Herts 104 G5
Aston Oxon 82 E4
Aston Shrops 132 E6
Aston Shrops 149 D10
Aston Staffs 168 G3
Aston S Yorks 187 E7
Aston Telford 132 B2
Aston W Midlands 133 F11
Aston Wokingham 65 C9
Aston Abbotts Bucks 102 G6
Aston Botterell Shrops 132 G2
Aston Cantlow Warwick 118 F2
Aston Clinton Bucks 84 C5
Aston Crews Heref'd 98 G3
Aston Cross Glos 99 E8
Aston End Herts 104 G5
Aston Eyre Shrops 132 E3
Aston Fields Worcs 117 D9
Aston Flamville Leics 135 E9
Aston Ingham Heref'd 98 G3
Aston Juxta Mondrum Ches 167 D10
Aston le Walls Northants 119 G9
Aston Magna Glos 100 D3
Aston Munslow Shrops 131 F10
Aston on Carrant Glos 99 E8
Aston on Clun Shrops 131 G7
Aston Pigott Shrops 130 B6
Aston Rogers Shrops 130 B6
Aston Rowant Oxon 84 F2
Aston Sandford Bucks 84 D3
Aston Somerville Worcs 99 D10
Aston Square Shrops 148 D6
Aston Subedge Glos 100 C2
Aston Tirrold Oxon 64 B5
Aston Upthorpe Oxon 64 B5
Aston-By-Stone Staffs 151 C8
Aston-on-Trent Derby 153 D8
Astrop Northants 101 D10
Astrope Herts 84 C5
Astwick Beds 104 D4
Astwith Derby 170 C6
Astwood M/Keynes 103 B9
Astwood Worcs 117 F7
Astwood Bank Worcs 117 E10
Aswarby Lincs 155 B11
Aswardby Lincs 190 G5
Atch Lench Worcs 117 G10
Atcham Shrops 131 B10
Athelhampton Dorset 17 C11
Athelington Suffolk 126 C4
Athelstaneford E Loth 281 F10
Atherfield Green I/Wight 20 F5
Atherington Devon 25 C9
Athersley North S Yorks 197 F10
Athersley South S Yorks 197 F11
Atherstone Som'set 28 D5
Atherstone Warwick 134 D6
Atherstone on Stour Warwick 118 G4
Atherton Gtr Man 195 G7
Athnamulloch H'land 299 G11
Athron Hall Perth/Kinr 286 G4
Atlow Derby 170 F2
Atrim Dorset 16 B5
Attadale H'land 295 B11
Attadale Ho. H'land 295 B11
Attenborough Notts 153 C10
Atterby Lincs 189 C7
Attercliffe S Yorks 186 D5
Atterton Leics 134 D6
Attleborough Norfolk 141 D10
Attleborough Warwick 135 E7
Attlebridge Norfolk 160 F2
Attleton Green Suffolk 124 G4
Atwick ER Yorks 209 C9
Atworth Wilts 61 F11
Auberrow Heref'd 97 B9
Aubourn Lincs 172 C6
Auch Arg/Bute 285 D7
Auchagallon N Ayrs 255 D9
Auchallater Aberds 292 E3
Aucharnie Aberds 302 E6
Auchattie Aberds 293 D8
Auchavan Angus 292 G3
Auchbreck Moray 302 G2
Auchenback E Renf 267 D10
Auchenbainzie Dumf/Gal 247 D8
Auchenblae Aberds 293 F9
Auchenbowie Stirl 278 D5
Auchenbrack Dumf/Gal 247 D7
Auchenbreck Arg/Bute 255 C8
Auchenbreck Arg/Bute 275 E11
Auchencairn Dumf/Gal 237 D9
Auchencairn Dumf/Gal 247 G11
Auchencairn N Ayrs 256 D2
Auchencairn Ho Dumf/Gal 237 D10
Auchencar N Ayrs 255 D9
Auchencarroch W Dunb 277 E8
Auchencrosh S Ayrs 236 B3
Auchendinny Midloth 270 C5
Auchengray S Lanarks 269 E9
Auchenhalrig Moray 302 C3
Auchenharvie N Ayrs 266 G5
Auchenheath S Lanarks 268 G6
Auchenlaich Stirl 285 G10
Auchenleck Dumf/Gal 237 D9
Auchenlochan Arg/Bute 275 F10
Auchenmalg Dumf/Gal 236 D4
Auchensoul S Ayrs 245 E7
Auchentibber S Lanarks 268 E3
Auchentiber N Ayrs 267 F7
Auchertyre H'land 295 C10
Auchessan Stirl 285 E8
Auchgourish H'land 291 B11
Auchinairn Glasg C 268 B2
Auchindrain Arg/Bute 284 G4
Auchindrean H'land 307 L6
Auchininna Aberds 302 E6
Auchinleck Dumf/Gal 236 B6
Auchinleck E Ayrs 258 E3
Auchinloch N Lanarks 278 G3
Auchinner Perth/Kinr 285 F10
Auchinraith S Lanarks 268 D3
Auchinroath Moray 302 D2
Auchinstarry N Lanarks 278 F4
Auchintoul Aberds 293 B7
Auchintoul H'land 309 K5
Auchiries Aberds 303 F10
Auchlee Aberds 293 D10
Auchleeks Ho. Perth/Kinr 291 G9
Auchleven Aberds 302 G6
Auchlinn Aberds 303 D7
Auchlossan Aberds 293 C7
Auchlunachan H'land 307 L6
Auchlunies Aberds 293 D10

Auchlyne Stirl 285 E9
Auchmacoy Aberds 303 F9
Auchmair Moray 302 G3
Auchmantle Dumf/Gal 236 C3
Auchmenzie Aberds 302 G5
Auchmillan E Ayrs 258 D2
Auchmithie Angus 287 C10
Auchmore H'land 300 D4
Auchmuirbridge Fife 286 G6
Auchmull Angus 293 F7
Auchmuty Fife 280 A5
Auchnacraig Arg/Bute 289 G9
Auchnacree Angus 292 G6
Auchnafree Perth/Kinr 286 D2
Auchnagallin H'land 301 F10
Auchnagarron Arg/Bute 275 E11
Auchnagatt Aberds 303 E9
Auchnaha Arg/Bute 275 E10
Auchnahillin H'land 301 F7
Auchnarrow Moray 302 G2
Auchnashelloch Perth/Kinr 285 F11
Auchnotteroch Dumf/Gal 236 C1
Aucholzie Aberds 292 D5
Auchrannie Angus 286 B6
Auchroisk H'land 301 G10
Auchronie Angus 292 E6
Auchterarder Perth/Kinr 286 F3
Auchteraw H'land 290 C5
Auchterderran Fife 280 B4
Auchterhouse Angus 287 D7
Auchtermuchty Fife 286 F6
Auchterneed H'land 300 D4
Auchtertool Fife 280 C4
Auchtertyre Moray 301 D11
Auchtertyre Stirl 285 E7
Auchtubh Stirl 285 E9
Auckengill H'land 310 C7
Auckland Park Durham 233 F10
Auckley S Yorks 199 G7
Audenshaw Gtr Man 184 B6
Audlem Ches 167 G11
Audley Staffs 168 E3
Audley End Essex 105 D10
Audley End Essex 106 D6
Audley End Suffolk 125 G7
Audley End House Essex 105 D10
Audmore Staffs 150 E6
Audnam W Midlands 133 F7
Auds Aberds 302 C6
Aughertree Cumb 229 D11
Aughton ER Yorks 207 F10
Aughton Lancs 211 F11
Aughton Lancs 193 F11
Aughton S Yorks 187 D7
Aughton Wilts 47 B8
Aughton Park Lancs 194 F2
Auldearn H'land 301 D9
Aulden Heref'd 115 G9
Auldgirth Dumf/Gal 247 F10
Auldhame E Loth 281 E11
Auldhouse S Lanarks 268 E2
Auldtown of Carnoustie Aberds 302 E6
Ault a'chruinn H'land 295 C11
Ault Hucknall Derby 171 B7
Aultanrynie H'land 308 F3
Aultbea H'land 307 L3
Aultdearg H'land 300 C2
Aultgrishan H'land 307 L2
Aultguish Inn H'land 300 B3
Aultibea H'land 311 G4
Aultiphurst H'land 310 C2
Aultivullin H'land 310 C2
Aultmore H'land 301 G10
Aultmore Moray 302 D4
Aultnagoire H'land 300 G5
Aultnamain Inn H'land 309 L6
Aultnaslat H'land 290 C3
Aulton Aberds 302 G6
Aulton of Atherb Aberds 303 E9
Aultvaich H'land 300 E5
Aunby Lincs 155 G10
Aundorach H'land 291 B11
Aunk Devon 27 G8
Aunsby Lincs 155 B10
Auquhorthies Aberds 303 G8
Aust S Glos 60 B5
Austerfield Notts 187 C11
Austerlands Gtr Man 196 F3
Austhorpe W Yorks 206 G3
Austrey Warwick 134 B5
Austwick N Yorks 212 F5
Authorpe Lincs 190 E6
Authorpe Row Lincs 191 G8
Avebury Wilts 62 F6
Avebury Trusloe Wilts 62 F5
Aveley Thurr'k 68 C5
Avening Glos 80 F5
Avening Green S Glos 80 G2
Averham Notts 172 E3
Averham Park Notts 172 D2
Avernish H'land 295 C10
Avery Hill London 68 E2
Aveton Gifford Devon 8 F3
Avielochan H'land 291 B11
Aviemore H'land 291 B10
Avington Hants 48 G4
Avington W Berks 63 F11
Avoch H'land 301 D7
Avon Wilts 62 D3
Avon Dassett Warwick 119 G8
Avonbridge Falk 279 G8
Avoncliffe Wilts 45 B10
Avonmouth Bristol 60 D4
Avonwick Devon 8 D4
Awbridge Hants 32 C4
Awhirk Dumf/Gal 236 D2
Awkley S Glos 60 B5
Awliscombe Devon 27 G10
Awre Glos 80 D2
Awsworth Notts 171 G7
Axbridge Som'set 44 C2
Axford Hants 48 E6
Axford Wilts 63 E8
Axminster Devon 15 B11
Axmouth Devon 15 C11
Axton Flints 181 E10
Axtown Devon 7 B10
Axwell Park Tyne/Wear 242 E5
Axworthy Devon 12 D5
Aycliff Kent 55 E10
Aycliffe Village Durham 233 G11
Aydon Northum 242 D2
Aykley Heads Durham 233 C11
Aylburton Glos 79 E10
Ayle Northum 231 B10
Aylesbeare Devon 14 C6
Aylesbury Bucks 84 C4
Aylesby NE Lincs 201 F8
Aylesford Kent 53 B8
Aylesham Kent 55 C8
Aylestone Leics C 135 C11
Aylestone Hill Heref'd 97 C10
Aylestone Park Leics C 135 C11
Aylmerton Norfolk 160 B3
Aylsham Norfolk 160 D3
Aylton Heref'd 98 D3
Aymestrey Heref'd 115 D8
Aynho Northants 101 E10
Ayot Green Herts 86 C2
Ayot St. Lawrence Herts 85 B11
Ayot St. Peter Herts 86 B2
Ayr S Ayrs 257 E8
Ayr Racecourse S Ayrs 257 E9
Ayre of Atler Shetl'd 315 G6
Ayres Shetl'd 315 H5
Ayres of Selivoe Shetl'd 315 J4
Ayreville Torbay 8 C6
Aysgarth N Yorks 213 B10
Ayshford Devon 27 D8
Ayside Cumb 211 C7
Ayston Rutl'd 137 C7
Aythorpe Roding Essex 87 B9
Ayton Scot Borders 273 C8
Ayton Tyne/Wear 243 F7
Aywick Shetl'd 314 E7
Azerley N Yorks 214 E5

B

Babbacombe Torbay 9 B8
Babbinswood Shrops 148 C6
Babb's Green Herts 86 B5
Babcary Som'set 29 B9
Babel Carms 94 D6
Babel Green Suffolk 106 B4
Babell Flints 181 G11
Babingley Norfolk 158 D3
Babraham Cambs 123 G10
Babworth Notts 187 E11
Babylon Flints 166 C4
Bac W Isles 304 D6
Bacchus Glos 80 C4
Bachau Angl 178 E6
Bacheldre Powys 130 E4
Back Muir Fife 279 D11
Back o' th' Brook Staffs 169 E9
Back of Keppoch H'land 295 G8
Back Rogerton E Ayrs 258 E3
Back Street Suffolk 124 F4
Backaland Orkney 312 E6
Backaskaill Orkney 312 C5
Backbarrow Cumb 211 C7
Backbower Gtr Man 185 C7
Backe Carms 74 B3
Backfolds Aberds 303 D10
Backford Ches 182 G6
Backford Cross Ches 182 G5
Backhill Aberds 303 F10
Backhill Aberds 303 F7
Backhill of Clackriach Aberds 303 E9
Backhill of Fortree Aberds 303 E9
Backhill of Trustach Aberds 293 D8
Backies H'land 311 J2
Backlass H'land 310 D6
Backlass H'land 310 E4
Backney Heref'd 97 F11
Back's Green Suffolk 143 G7
Backwell N Som'set 60 F3
Backwell Green N Som'set 60 F4
Backwell Hill N Som'set 60 F3
Backworth Tyne/Wear 243 C8
Bacon End Essex 87 B10
Baconend Green Essex 87 B10
Bacon's End W Midlands 134 F3
Baconsthorpe Norfolk 160 B2
Bacton Heref'd 97 E7
Bacton Norfolk 160 C6
Bacton Suffolk 125 D11
Bacton Green Norfolk 160 C6
Bacton Green Suffolk 125 D11
Bacup Lancs 195 C11
Badachonacher H'land 300 B6
Badachro H'land 299 B7
Badanloch Lodge H'land 308 F7
Badarach H'land 309 K5
Badavanich H'land 299 D11
Badbea H'land 307 K5
Badbury Swindon 63 C7
Badbury Wick Swindon 63 C7
Badby Northants 119 F11
Badcall H'land 306 D7
Badcaul H'land 307 K5
Baddeley Green Stoke 168 E6
Baddesley Clinton Warwick 118 C4
Baddesley Clinton Warwick 118 C4
Baddesley Ensor Warwick 134 D5
Baddidarach H'land 307 G5
Baddoch Aberds 292 E3
Baddock H'land 301 D7
Badeach Moray 302 F2
Badenscallie H'land 307 J5
Badenscoth Aberds 303 F7
Badentoy Park Aberds 293 D11
Badenyon Aberds 292 B5
Badgall Cornw'l 11 D10
Badgeney Cambs 139 D8
Badger Shrops 132 D5
Badger Street Som'set 28 D3
Badgergate Stirl 285 H11
Badger's Mount Kent 68 G3
Badgeworth Glos 80 B6
Badgworth Som'set 43 C11
Badharlick Cornw'l 11 D11
Badicaul H'land 295 C9
Badingham Suffolk 126 D6
Badintagairt H'land 309 H4
Badlesmere Kent 54 C4
Badlipster H'land 310 E6
Badluarach H'land 307 K4
Badminton S Glos 61 C10
Badnaban H'land 307 G5
Badnabay H'land 306 E7
Badnagie H'land 310 F5
Badninish H'land 309 K7
Badrallach H'land 307 K5
Badsey Worcs 99 C11
Badshot Lea Surrey 49 D11
Badsworth W Yorks 198 D3
Badwell Ash Suffolk 125 D9
Badwell Green Suffolk 125 D10
Bae Cinmel = Kinmel Bay Conwy 181 E7
Bae Colwyn = Colwyn Bay Conwy 180 F5
Bae Penrhyn = Penrhyn Bay Conwy 180 E4
Baffins Hants 33 G11
Bag Enderby Lincs 190 G5
Bagber Dorset 30 E3
Bagby N Yorks 215 C9
Bagendon Glos 81 D8
Bàgha Chàise W Isles 296 D5
Baggrow Cumb 229 C9
Bagh a Chaisteil = Castlebay W Isles 297 M2
Bagh Mor W Isles 296 F4
Bagh Shiarabhagh W Isles 297 L3
Bagham Kent 54 C5
Baghasdal W Isles 297 K3
Bagillt Flints 182 F2
Baginton Warwick 118 C6
Baglan Rh Cyn Taff 76 G2
Bagley Shrops 149 D8
Bagley Som'set 44 D3
Bagley W Yorks 205 F10
Bagley Green Som'set 27 D10
Bagmore Hants 49 E7
Bagnall Staffs 168 E6
Bagnor W Berks 64 F2
Bagpath Glos 80 G4
Bagpath Glos 80 E5
Bagshaw Derby 185 E9
Bagshot Surrey 66 G2
Bagshot Wilts 63 F10
Bagslate Moor Gtr Man 195 E11
Bagstone S Glos 61 B7
Bagthorpe Norfolk 158 C5
Bagthorpe Notts 171 E7
Baguley Gtr Man 184 D4
Bagworth Leics 135 B8
Bagwyllydiart Heref'd 97 F8
Bail Àrd Bhuirgh W Isles 304 C6
Bail Uachdraich W Isles 296 E4
Bailbrook Bath/NE Som'set 61 F9
Baildon W Yorks 205 F9
Baildon Green W Yorks 205 F8
Baile W Isles 296 C5
Baile a Mhanaich W Isles 296 F3
Baile Ailein W Isles 304 F4
Baile an Truiseil W Isles 304 C5
Baile Boidheach Arg/Bute 275 F8
Baile Gharbhaidh W Isles 297 G3
Baile Glas W Isles 296 F4
Baile Mhartainn W Isles 296 D3
Baile Mhic Phail W Isles 296 D4
Baile Mor Arg/Bute 288 G4
Baile Mor W Isles 296 E3
Baile na Creige W Isles 297 L2
Baile nan Cailleach W Isles 296 F3
Baile Raghaill W Isles 296 D3
Bailebeag H'land 291 B7
Bailey Cumb 240 B2
Bailey Green Hants 33 B11
Bailey Hill Essex 106 D4
Bailiesward Aberds 302 F4
Bailiff Bridge W Yorks 196 C6
Baillieston Glasg C 268 C3
Bail'lochdrach W Isles 296 F4
Bailrigg Lancs 202 B5
Bail'Ur Tholastaidh W Isles 304 D7
Bainbridge N Yorks 223 G8
Bainsford Falk 279 E7
Bainshole Aberds 302 F6
Bainton ER Yorks 208 C5
Bainton Oxon 101 F11
Bainton Peterbro 137 B11
Baintown Fife 287 G7
Baker Street Thurr'k 68 C6
Baker's End Herts 86 B5
Baker's Hill Glos 79 C9
Baker's Wood Bucks 66 B4
Bakestone Moor Derby 187 F8
Bakewell Derby 170 B2
Bala = Y Bala Gwyn 147 B8
Balachroick H'land 291 C10
Balachuirn H'land 298 E5
Balavil H'land 291 C9
Balavoulin Perth/Kinr 291 G10
Balbeg H'land 300 F4
Balbeg H'land 300 G4
Balbeggie Perth/Kinr 286 E5
Balbegno Castle Aberds 293 F8
Balbithan Aberds 293 B9
Balbithan Ho. Aberds 293 B10
Balblair H'land 300 E5
Balblair H'land 301 C7
Balblair H'land 309 K5
Balby S Yorks 198 G5
Balcherry H'land 311 L2
Balchladich H'land 306 F5
Balchraggan H'land 300 E5
Balchraggan H'land 300 F5
Balchraggan H'land 300 G5
Balchrick H'land 306 D6
Balchrystie Fife 287 G8
Balcladaich H'land 300 G2
Balcombe W Sussex 51 G10
Balcombe Lane W Sussex 51 G10
Balcomie Fife 287 F10
Balcraggie Lodge H'land 310 F5
Balcurvie Fife 287 G7
Balderfield Notts 172 F4
Baldersby N Yorks 215 D7
Baldersby St. James N Yorks 215 D7
Balderstone Gtr Man 196 E2
Balderstone Lancs 203 G8
Balderton Ches 166 C5
Balderton Notts 172 E4
Baldhu Cornw'l 4 G5
Baldingstone Gtr Man 195 E10
Baldinnie Fife 287 F8
Baldock Herts 104 E5
Baldon Row Oxon 83 E9
Baldoon H'land 300 B6
Baldovie Dundee C 287 D8
Baldrine I/Man 192 D5
Baldslow E Sussex 38 E4
Baldwin I/Man 192 D4
Baldwinholme Cumb 239 G8
Baldwin's Gate Staffs 150 B5
Baldwins Hill Surrey 51 F11
Bale Norfolk 159 B10
Balearn Aberds 303 D10
Balemartine Arg/Bute 288 E1
Balephuil Arg/Bute 288 E1
Balerno C/Edinb 270 B3
Balerominhor Arg/Bute 274 D4
Balevullin Arg/Bute 288 E1
Balfield Angus 293 G7
Balfour Orkney 312 G5
Balfour Mains Orkney 312 G5
Balfron Stirl 277 D10
Balfron Station Stirl 277 D10
Balgaveny Aberds 302 E6
Balgavies Angus 287 B9
Balgonar Fife 279 C10
Balgove Aberds 303 F8
Balgowan H'land 291 D8
Balgowan Perth/Kinr 286 E3
Balgown H'land 298 C3
Balgrennie Aberds 292 C6
Balgrochan E Dunb 278 F2
Balgy H'land 299 D8
Balhaldie Stirl 286 G2
Balhalgardy Aberds 303 G7
Balham London 67 E9
Balhary Perth/Kinr 286 C6
Baliasta Shetl'd 314 C8
Baligill H'land 310 C2
Baligortan Arg/Bute 288 E5
Baligrundle Arg/Bute 289 E10
Balindore Arg/Bute 289 F11
Balingham Hill Heref'd 97 E11
Balinoe Arg/Bute 288 E1
Balintore Angus 286 B6
Balintore H'land 301 B8
Balintraid H'land 301 B7
Balintuim Aberds 292 E3
Balk N Yorks 215 C9
Balk Field Notts 188 E2
Balkeerie Angus 287 C7
Balkemback Angus 287 D7
Balkholme ER Yorks 199 B9
Balkissock S Ayrs 244 G4
Ball Shrops 148 D6
Ball Green Stoke 168 E5
Ball Haye Green Staffs 169 D7
Ball Hill Hants 64 G2
Ball o' Ditton Halton 183 D8
Ballabeg I/Man 192 E3
Ballacannel I/Man 192 D5
Ballachraggan Moray 301 E11
Ballachrochin H'land 301 F8
Ballachulish H'land 284 B4
Ballajora I/Man 192 C5
Ballaleigh I/Man 192 D4
Ballamodha I/Man 192 E3
Ballantrae S Ayrs 244 G3
Ballaquine I/Man 192 D5
Ballard's Gore Essex 88 G6
Ballard's Green Warwick 134 E5
Ballasalla I/Man 192 C4
Ballasalla I/Man 192 E3
Ballater Aberds 292 D5
Ballathie Perth/Kinr 286 D5
Ballaugh I/Man 192 C4
Ballaveare I/Man 192 E4
Ballcorach Moray 301 G11
Ballechin Perth/Kinr 286 B3
Balleich Stirl 285 H9
Balleigh H'land 309 L7
Ballencrieff E Loth 281 F9
Ballencrieff Toll W Loth 279 G9
Ballentoul Perth/Kinr 291 G10
Ballhill Devon 24 C3
Ballidon Derby 170 E2
Balliekine N Ayrs 255 D9
Balliemeanoch Arg/Bute 276 A2
Balliemore Arg/Bute 275 E11
Balliemore Arg/Bute 289 G10
Ballikinrain Stirl 277 D11
Ballimeanoch Arg/Bute 284 F4
Ballimore Arg/Bute 275 E10
Ballimore Stirl 285 F9
Ballinaby Arg/Bute 274 G3
Ballinbreich Fife 286 E6
Ballindean Perth/Kinr 286 E6
Ballingdon Suffolk 107 C7
Ballinger Common Bucks 84 E6
Ballingham Heref'd 97 E11
Ballingry Fife 280 B3
Ballinlick Perth/Kinr 286 C3
Ballinluig Perth/Kinr 286 B3
Ballintean H'land 291 C10
Ballintuim Perth/Kinr 286 B5
Ballivoelan Arg/Bute 289 E10
Balloch Angus 287 B7
Balloch H'land 301 E7
Balloch N Lanarks 278 G4
Balloch W Dunb 277 E7
Ballochan Aberds 293 D7
Ballochearn Stirl 277 D11
Ballochford Moray 302 F3
Ballochmorrie S Ayrs 244 G6
Ballogie Aberds 293 D7
Balls Cross W Sussex 35 B7
Balls Green E Sussex 52 F3
Ball's Green Essex 107 G11
Ball's Green Glos 80 F5
Balls Hill W Midlands 133 E9
Ballygown Arg/Bute 288 E6
Ballygrant Arg/Bute 274 G4
Ballygroggan Arg/Bute 255 F7
Ballyhaugh Arg/Bute 288 D3
Balmacara H'land 295 C10
Balmacara Square H'land 295 C10
Balmaclellan Dumf/Gal 237 B8
Balmacneil Perth/Kinr 286 B3
Balmacqueen H'land 298 B4
Balmae Dumf/Gal 237 E8
Balmaha Stirl 277 C8
Balmalcolm Fife 287 G7
Balmalloch N Lanarks 278 F4
Balmeanach Arg/Bute 288 F6
Balmeanach Arg/Bute 289 E8
Balmeanach H'land 295 B7
Balmeanach H'land 298 E3
Balmeanach H'land 298 E5
Balmedie Aberds 293 B11
Balmer Heath Shrops 149 C8
Balmerino Fife 287 E7
Balmerlawn Hants 32 G4
Balmesh Dumf/Gal 236 D3
Balmichael N Ayrs 255 D10
Balminnoch Dumf/Gal 236 C4
Balmirmer Angus 287 D9
Balmoral Castle and Gardens Aberds 292 D4
Balmore E Dunb 278 G2
Balmore H'land 298 E2
Balmore H'land 300 F3
Balmore H'land 301 E8
Balmore Perth/Kinr 286 B3
Balmule Fife 280 D4
Balmullo Fife 287 E8
Balmungie H'land 301 D7
Balmurrie Dumf/Gal 236 C4
Balnaboth Angus 292 G5
Balnabreich Moray 302 D3
Balnabruaich H'land 301 C7
Balnabruich H'land 311 G5
Balnacarn H'land 290 B4
Balnacoil H'land 311 H2
Balnacra H'land 299 E9
Balnacruie H'land 301 G9
Balnafoich H'land 300 F6
Balnagall H'land 311 L2
Balnagowan Aberds 293 C7
Balnagrantach H'land 300 F4
Balnaguard Perth/Kinr 286 B3
Balnahanaid Perth/Kinr 285 C10
Balnahard Arg/Bute 274 D5
Balnahard Arg/Bute 288 F6
Balnain H'land 300 F4
Balnakeil H'land 308 C3
Balnakelly Aberds 293 B7
Balnaknock H'land 298 C4
Balnamoon Aberds 303 D9
Balnamoon Angus 293 G7
Balnapaling H'land 301 C7
Balochroy Arg/Bute 255 B8
Balole Arg/Bute 274 G4
Balone Fife 287 F8
Balornock Glasg C 268 B2
Balquharn Perth/Kinr 286 D4
Balquhidder Stirl 285 E9
Balquhidder Station Stirl 285 E9
Balquhindachy Aberds 303 E8
Balrownie Angus 293 G7
Balsall W Midlands 118 B4
Balsall Common W Midlands 118 B4
Balsall Heath W Midlands 133 G11
Balsall Street W Midlands 118 B4
Balscote Oxon 101 C7
Balsham Cambs 123 G11
Balsporran Cottages H'land 291 F8
Balstonia Thurr'k 69 C7
Baltasound Shetl'd 314 C8
Balterley Staffs 168 E3
Balterley Heath Staffs 168 E2
Baltersan Dumf/Gal 236 C6
Balthangie Aberds 303 D8
Balthayock Perth/Kinr 286 E5
Baltonsborough Som'set 44 G4
Balure Arg/Bute 289 E11
Balvaird H'land 300 D5
Balvenie Moray 302 E3
Balvicar Arg/Bute 275 B8
Balvraid H'land 295 D10
Balvraid H'land 301 F8
Balwest Cornw'l 2 C3
Bamber Bridge Lancs 194 B5
Bamber's Green Essex 105 G11
Bamburgh Northum 264 B5
Bamburgh Castle Northum 264 B5
Bamff Perth/Kinr 286 B6
Bamford Derby 186 E2
Bamford Gtr Man 195 E11
Bamfurlong Glos 99 G8
Bamfurlong Gtr Man 194 G5
Bampton Cumb 221 B10
Bampton Devon 27 C7
Bampton Oxon 82 E4
Bampton Grange Cumb 221 B10
Banavie H'land 290 F3
Banbury Oxon 101 C9
Banburylane Northants 120 F3
Bancffosfelen Carms 75 C7
Banchor H'land 301 E9
Banchory Aberds 293 D8
Banchory-Devenick Aberds 293 C11
Bancroft M/Keynes 102 C6
Bancycapel Carms 74 B6
Bancyfelin Carms 74 B4
Bandeath Industrial Estate Stirl 278 C6
Bandirran Perth/Kinr 286 D6
Bandon Hill London 67 G10
Bandrake Head Cumb 210 B6
Bandry Arg/Bute 277 C7
Banff Aberds 302 C6
Bangor Gwyn 179 G9
Bangor on Dee Racecourse Wrex 166 G5
Bangor Teifi Ceredig'n 93 C7
Bangor-is-y-coed Wrex 166 F4
Bangors Cornw'l 11 B10
Bangor's Green Lancs 193 F11
Bangrove Suffolk 125 C8
Banham Norfolk 141 F11
Banham Zoo, Diss Norfolk 141 F11
Bank Hants 32 F3
Bank End Cumb 210 B4
Bank Fold Blackb'n 195 C8
Bank Hey Blackb'n 203 G9
Bank Lane Gtr Man 195 D10
Bank Newton N Yorks 204 C4
Bank Street Worcs 116 E2
Bank Top Derby 186 E2
Bank Top Gtr Man 195 E8
Bank Top Lancs 194 F4
Bank Top Tyne/Wear 242 D5
Bank Top W Yorks 196 C6
Bank Top W Yorks 205 F9
Bankend Dumf/Gal 238 D2
Bankfoot Perth/Kinr 286 D4
Bankglen E Ayrs 258 G3
Bankhead Aberds 293 C8
Bankhead Aberd C 293 B10
Bankhead Dumf/Gal 236 C2
Bankhead Falk 278 E6
Bankhead S Lanarks 269 G7
Bankland Som'set 28 B5
Banklands Norfolk 157 E11
Banknock Falk 278 E5
Banknock Falk 278 F5
Banks Cumb 240 E3
Banks Lancs 193 C11
Banks Orkney 312 E5
Bankshill Dumf/Gal 248 G5
Bankside Falk 279 E7
Banners Gate W Midlands 133 D11
Banningham Norfolk 160 D4
Banniskirk Ho. H'land 310 D5
Banniskirk Mains H'land 310 D5
Bannister Green Essex 106 G3
Bannockburn Stirl 278 C6
Banstead Surrey 51 B9
Bantam Grove W Yorks 197 B9
Bantaskin Falk 279 F7
Bantham Devon 8 G3
Banton N Lanarks 278 F5
Banwell N Som'set 44 B2
Banwen Pyrddin Neath P Talb 76 D5
Banyard's Green Suffolk 126 C6
Bapchild Kent 70 G2
Baptist End W Midlands 133 F8
Bapton Wilts 46 F3
Bar End Hants 33 B7
Bar Hill Cambs 123 E7
Bar Moor Tyne/Wear 242 E4
Barabhas W Isles 304 D5
Barabhas Iarach W Isles 304 D5
Barabhas Uarach W Isles 304 C5
Barachandroman Arg/Bute 289 G8
Baramore H'land 289 B8
Barassie S Ayrs 257 C8
Baravullin Arg/Bute 289 F10
Barbaraville H'land 301 B7
Barbauchlaw W Loth 269 B8
Barber Booth Derby 185 E10
Barber Green Cumb 211 C7
Barbican Plym'th 7 E9
Barbieston S Ayrs 257 F10
Barbon Cumb 212 C2
Barbreck Ho Arg/Bute 275 C9
Barbridge Ches 167 D10
Barbrook Devon 41 D8
Barby Northants 119 C10
Barby Nortoft Northants 119 C11
Barcaldine Arg/Bute 289 E11
Barcheston Warwick 100 D5
Barclose Cumb 239 E10
Barcombe E Sussex 36 E6
Barcombe Cross E Sussex 36 D6
Barcroft W Yorks 204 F6
Barden N Yorks 205 B7
Barden N Yorks 224 G2
Barden Park Kent 52 D5
Bardennoch Dumf/Gal 246 E3
Bardfield End Green Essex 106 E2
Bardfield Saling Essex 106 F3
Bardister Shetl'd 314 F5
Bardnabeinne H'land 309 K7
Bardney Lincs 173 B10
Bardon Leics 153 G8
Bardon Mill Northum 241 E7
Bardowie E Dunb 277 G11
Bardown E Sussex 37 B11
Bardrainney Inverc'l 276 G6
Bardrishaig Arg/Bute 275 B8
Bardsea Cumb 210 E6
Bardsey W Yorks 206 E3
Bardsley Gtr Man 196 G2
Bardwell Suffolk 125 C8
Bare Lancs 211 G9
Barelees Northum 263 B9
Barepot Cumb 228 F6
Bareppa Cornw'l 3 D7
Barfad Arg/Bute 275 G9
Barfad Dumf/Gal 236 C5
Barford Hants 49 F10
Barford Norfolk 142 B2
Barford Warwick 118 E5
Barford St. John Oxon 101 E8
Barford St. Martin Wilts 46 G5
Barford St. Michael Oxon 101 E8
Barfrestone Kent 55 C9
Bargaly Dumf/Gal 236 C6
Bargarran Renf 277 G9
Bargeddie N Lanarks 268 C4
Bargod = Bargoed Caerph 77 F10
Bargoed = Bargod Caerph 77 F10
Bargrennan Dumf/Gal 236 B5
Barham Cambs 122 B2
Barham Kent 55 C8
Barham Suffolk 126 G2
Barharrow Dumf/Gal 237 D8
Barhill Dumf/Gal 237 C10
Barholm Dumf/Gal 237 D7
Barholm Lincs 155 G11
Barhough Northum 240 G5
Barkby Leics 136 B2
Barkby Thorpe Leics 136 B2
Barkers Green Shrops 149 D10
Barkestone-le-Vale Leics 154 C5
Barkham Wokingham 65 G9
Barkham Common Wokingham 65 G9
Barking London 68 C2
Barking Suffolk 125 G11
Barking Tye Suffolk 125 G11
Barkingside London 68 B2
Barkisland W Yorks 196 D5
Barkla Shop Cornw'l 4 E4
Barklye E Sussex 37 C10
Barkston Lincs 172 G6
Barkston N Yorks 206 F5
Barkway Herts 105 D7
Barlanark Glasg C 268 C3
Barlaston Staffs 151 B7
Barlavington W Sussex 35 D7
Barlborough Derby 187 F7
Barlby N Yorks 207 G8
Barlestone Leics 135 B8
Barley Herts 105 D8
Barley Lancs 204 E2
Barley Green Suffolk 126 C4
Barley Mow Tyne/Wear 243 G7
Barleycroft End Herts 105 F8
Barleythorpe Rutl'd 137 B6
Barling Essex 70 B2
Barlings Lincs 189 G9
Barlow Derby 186 G4
Barlow N Yorks 198 B6
Barlow Tyne/Wear 242 E5
Barlow Moor Gtr Man 184 C4
Barmby Moor ER Yorks 207 D11
Barmby on the Marsh ER Yorks 199 B7
Barmer Norfolk 158 C6
Barming Heath Kent 53 B8
Barmolloch Arg/Bute 275 D9
Barmouth = Abermaw Gwyn 146 F2
Barmpton D'lington 224 B6
Barmston ER Yorks 209 B9
Barmston Tyne/Wear 243 F8
Barmulloch Glasg C 268 B2
Barn Hill Worcs 117 B11
Barnaby Green Suffolk 127 B9
Barnack Peterbro 137 C11
Barnacle Warwick 135 G7
Barnaline Arg/Bute 275 B10
Barnard Castle Durham 223 B11
Barnard Gate Oxon 82 C6
Barnardiston Suffolk 106 B4
Barnard's Green Worcs 98 B5
Barnbarroch Dumf/Gal 237 D10
Barnburgh S Yorks 198 G3
Barnby Suffolk 143 F9
Barnby Dun S Yorks 198 F6
Barnby in the Willows Notts 172 E5
Barnby Moor Notts 187 E11
Barne Barton Plym'th 7 D8
Barnehurst London 68 D4
Barnes London 67 D8
Barnes Street Kent 52 D6
Barnet London 86 F2
Barnet Gate London 86 F2
Barnetby-le-Wold N Lincs 200 F5
Barnettbrook Worcs 117 B7
Barney Norfolk 159 C9
Barnfield Lancs 195 B9
Barnfields Staffs 169 D7
Barnham Suffolk 125 B7
Barnham W Sussex 35 G7
Barnham Broom Norfolk 141 B11
Barnhead Angus 287 B10
Barnhill Dundee C 287 D8
Barnhill Moray 301 D11
Barnhill S Lanarks 268 D3
Barnhills Dumf/Gal 236 B1
Barningham Durham 223 C11
Barningham Suffolk 125 B9
Barningham Green Norfolk 160 C2
Barnmoor Green Warwick 118 D3
Barnoldby le Beck NE Lincs 201 G8
Barnoldswick Lancs 204 D3
Barnoldswick N Yorks 212 E3
Barns Green W Sussex 35 B10
Barnsbury London 67 C10
Barnsden E Sussex 37 B7
Barnsley Glos 81 D9
Barnsley Shrops 132 E5
Barnsley S Yorks 197 F11
Barnsole Kent 55 B9
Barnstaple Devon 40 G5
Barnston Essex 87 B10
Barnston Mersey 182 E3
Barnstone Notts 154 B4
Barnt Green Worcs 117 C10
Barnton C/Edinb 280 F3
Barnton Ches 183 F10
Barnwell Cambs 123 F9
Barnwell Northants 137 G10
Barnwood Glos 80 B5
Barnyards Fife 281 A9
Barochreal Arg/Bute 289 G10
Barons Cross Heref'd 115 F9
Barr H'land 289 D8
Barr S Ayrs 245 E7
Barr Som'set 27 C11
Barr Common W Midlands 133 D11
Barra Airport W Isles 297 L2
Barra Castle Aberds 303 G7
Barrachan Dumf/Gal 236 E5
Barrachnie Glasg C 268 C3
Barrack Aberds 303 E8
Barrack Hill Newp 59 B10
Barraer Dumf/Gal 236 C5
Barraglom W Isles 304 E3
Barrahormid Arg/Bute 275 E8
Barran Arg/Bute 289 G10
Barranrioch Arg/Bute 289 G10
Barrapol Arg/Bute 288 E1
Barras Aberds 293 E10
Barras Cumb 222 C6
Barrasford Northum 241 C10
Barravullin Arg/Bute 275 C9
Barregarrow I/Man 192 D4
Barrhead E Renf 267 D10
Barrhill S Ayrs 244 G6
Barrington Cambs 105 B7
Barrington Som'set 28 D5
Barripper Cornw'l 2 B4
Barrmill N Ayrs 267 E7
Barrock H'land 310 B6
Barrock Ho. H'land 310 C6
Barrow Glos 99 G7
Barrow Lancs 203 F10
Barrow Rutl'd 155 F7
Barrow Shrops 132 C3
Barrow Suffolk 124 E5
Barrow Som'set 44 E5
Barrow S Yorks 186 B5
Barrow Bridge Gtr Man 195 E7
Barrow Common N Som'set 60 F4
Barrow Green Kent 70 G3
Barrow Gurney N Som'set 60 F4
Barrow Haven N Lincs 200 C5
Barrow Hill Derby 186 F6
Barrow Hill Dorset 18 B5
Barrow Hill Hants 32 D4
Barrow Hill Suffolk 107 B7
Barrow Island Cumb 210 F3
Barrow Nook Lancs 194 G2
Barrow Street Wilts 45 G10
Barrow upon Humber N Lincs 200 C5
Barrow upon Soar Leics 153 F11
Barrow upon Trent Derby 152 D6
Barrow Vale Bath/NE Som'set 60 G6
Barroway Drove Norfolk 139 C11
Barrowby Lincs 155 B7
Barrowcliff N Yorks 217 B10
Barrowden Rutl'd 137 C8
Barrowford Lancs 204 F3
Barrowhill Kent 54 F6
Barrow-in-Furness Cumb 210 E4
Barrows Green Ches 167 D11
Barrows Green Cumb 211 B10
Barrow's Green Halton 183 D8
Barrows Green Notts 170 E6
Barry Angus 287 D9
Barry V/Glam 58 F6
Barry Docks V/Glam 58 F6
Barry Island V/Glam 58 F6

Barsby Leics 154 G3
Barsham Suffolk 143 F7
Barshare E Ayrs 258 F3
Barstable Essex 69 B8
Barston W Midlands 118 B4
Bartestree Heref'd 97 C11
Barthol Chapel Aberds 303 F8
Bartholomew Green Essex 106 G4
Barthomley Ches 168 E3
Bartley Hants 32 E4
Bartley Green W Midlands 133 G10
Bartlow Cambs 105 B11
Barton Cambs 123 F8
Barton Ches 166 E6
Barton Cumb 230 F5
Barton Glos 100 F2
Barton I/Wight 20 D6
Barton Lancs 202 F6
Barton Lancs 193 F11
Barton N Som'set 43 B11
Barton N Yorks 224 D4
Barton Oxon 83 D9
Barton Torbay 9 B8
Barton Warwick 118 G2
Barton Bendish Norfolk 140 B4
Barton End Glos 80 F5
Barton Gate Devon 41 E7
Barton Gate Staffs 152 F3
Barton Green Staffs 152 F3
Barton Hartshorn Bucks 102 E2
Barton Hill N Yorks 216 G4
Barton in Fabis Notts 153 C10
Barton in the Beans Leics 135 B7
Barton Mills Suffolk 124 C4
Barton Moss Gtr Man 184 B2
Barton on Sea Hants 19 C10
Barton on the Heath Warwick 100 E5
Barton St. David Som'set 44 G4
Barton Seagrave Northants 121 B7
Barton Stacey Hants 48 E2
Barton Town Devon 41 E7
Barton Turf Norfolk 160 E7
Barton Turn Staffs 152 F4
Barton upon Irwell Gtr Man 184 B3
Barton Waterside N Lincs 200 C4
Bartongate Oxon 101 F8
Barton-le-Clay Beds 103 E11
Barton-le-Street N Yorks 216 E4
Barton-le-Willows N Yorks 216 G4
Bartonsham Heref'd 97 D10
Barton-under-Needwood Staffs 152 F3
Barton-upon-Humber N Lincs 200 C4
Barugh S Yorks 197 F10
Barugh Green S Yorks 197 F10
Barway Cambs 123 B10
Barwell Leics 135 D8
Barwick Hants 86 B5
Barwick Som'set 29 E9
Barwick in Elmet W Yorks 206 F4
Baschurch Shrops 149 E8
Bascote Warwick 119 E8
Bascote Heath Warwick 119 E7
Base Green Suffolk 125 E10
Basford Staffs 168 F5
Bashall Eaves Lancs 203 E9
Bashley Hants 19 B10
Basildon Essex 69 B8
Basildon W Berks 64 D6
Basingstoke Hants 48 C6
Baslow Derby 186 G2
Bason Bridge Som'set 43 D10
Bassaleg Newp 59 B9
Bassenthwaite Cumb 229 E10
Bassett S'thampton 32 D6
Bassett Green S'thampton 32 D6
Bassingbourn Cambs 104 B6
Bassingfield Notts 154 B2
Bassingham Lincs 172 C6
Bassingthorpe Lincs 155 D9
Bassus Green Herts 104 F6
Basta Shetl'd 314 D7
Basted Kent 52 B6
Baston Lincs 156 G2
Bastonford Worcs 116 G6
Bastwick Norfolk 161 F8
Baswich Staffs 151 E8
Batavaine Stirl 285 D8
Batch Som'set 43 B10
Batchley Worcs 117 D10
Batchworth Herts 85 G9
Batchworth Heath Herts 85 G9
Batcombe Dorset 29 G10
Batcombe Som'set 45 F7
Bate Heath Ches 183 F11
Bateman's, Burwash E Sussex 37 C11
Bateman's Green Worcs 117 B11
Batemoor S Yorks 186 E5
Batford Herts 85 B10
Bath Bath/NE Som'set 61 F9
Bath Abbey Bath/NE Som'set 61 G9
Bath Racecourse Bath/NE Som'set 61 F9
Bath Side Essex 108 E5
Bathampton Bath/NE Som'set 61 F9
Bathealton Som'set 27 C9
Batheaston Bath/NE Som'set 61 F9
Bathford Bath/NE Som'set 61 F9
Bathgate W Loth 269 B9
Bathley Notts 172 D3

Bathpool Cornw'l 11 G11
Bathpool Som'set 28 B3
Bathville W Loth 269 B8
Bathway Som'set 44 C5
Batley W Yorks 197 C8
Batley Carr W Yorks 197 C8
Batsford Glos 100 E3
Batson Devon 9 G9
Batsworthy Devon 26 D4
Battersby N Yorks 225 D11
Battersby Junction N Yorks 225 D11
Battersea London 67 D9
Battisborough Cross
Battisford Suffolk 125 G11
Battisford Tye Suffolk 125 G10
Battle E Sussex 38 D3
Battle Powys 95 G10
Battle Abbey E Sussex 38 D2
Battle Hill E Sussex 38 D2
Battleborough Som'set 43 C10
Battledown Glos 99 G9
Battlefield Glasg C 267 C11
Battlefield Shrops 149 F10
Battlesbridge Essex 88 G3
Battlesden Beds 103 F9
Battlesea Green Suffolk 126 B4
Battleton Som'set 26 B6
Battlies Green Suffolk 125 E7
Battram Leics 135 B8
Battramsley Hants 20 B2
Batt's Corner Surrey 49 E10
Battyeford W Yorks 197 C7
Bauds of Cullen Moray 302 C4
Baugh Arg/Bute 288 E2
Baughton Worcs 99 C7
Baughurst Hants 64 G5
Baulking Oxon 82 G4
Baumber Lincs 190 G2
Baunton Glos 81 E8
Baverstock Wilts 46 G4
Bawburgh Norfolk 142 B2
Bawdeswell Norfolk 159 G10
Bawdrip Som'set 43 F10
Bawdsey Suffolk 108 C6
Bawdsey Manor Suffolk 108 D6
Bawsey Norfolk 158 F3
Bawtry S Yorks 187 C11
Baxenden Lancs 195 B9
Baxterley Warwick 134 D5
Baxter's Green Suffolk 124 F5
Bay Dorset 30 B4
Bay H'land 298 D2
Bay Gate Lancs 203 D11
Baycliff Cumb 210 E5
Baycliff Cumb 210 E5
Baydon Wilts 63 D9
Bayford Herts 86 D4
Bayford Som'set 30 B2
Bayles Cumb 231 B10
Bayley's Hill Kent 52 C4
Baylham Suffolk 126 G2
Baylis Green Worcs 117 C11
Baylisden Kent 54 E2
Baynard's Green Oxon 101 F11
Baysham Heref'd 97 F11
Bayston Hill Shrops 131 B9
Bayswater London 67 C9
Baythorn End Essex 106 C4
Baythorpe Lincs 174 G2
Bayton Worcs 116 C3
Bayton Common Worcs 116 C4
Bayworth Oxon 83 E8
Beach Heref'd 289 D9
Beach S Glos 61 E8
Beachamp Roding Essex 87 D9
Beachampton Bucks 102 D5
Beachamwell Norfolk 140 B5
Beachans Moray 301 E10
Beacharr Arg/Bute 255 C7
Beachley Glos 79 G9
Beacon Devon 27 F11
Beacon Devon 28 F2
Beacon End Essex 107 G9
Beacon Hill Bath/NE Som'set 61 F8
Beacon Hill Bucks 84 G6
Beacon Hill Dorset 18 C5
Beacon Hill Essex 88 C5
Beacon Hill Kent 53 G10
Beacon Hill Lincs 190 B5
Beacon Hill Notts 172 E4
Beacon Hill Suffolk 108 B4
Beacon Hill Surrey 49 F11
Beacon Lough Tyne/Wear 243 F7
Beaconhill Northum 243 B7
Beacon's Bottom Bucks 84 F3
Beaconsfield Bucks 84 G6
Beaconside Staffs 151 E8
Beacrabhaic W Isles 305 J3
Beadlam N Yorks 216 C3
Beadlow Beds 104 D2
Beadnell Northum 264 D6
Beaford Devon 25 E9
Beal Northum 273 G11
Beal N Yorks 198 B4
Bealach H'land 289 D11
Bealach Maim Arg/Bute 275 G10
Bealbury Cornw'l 7 B7
Beale Park, Goring W Berks 64 D6
Bealeys Devon 25 D8
Bealsmill Cornw'l 12 F3
Beam Hill Staffs 152 D4
Beamhurst Staffs 151 B11
Beaminster Dorset 29 G7
Beamish Durham 242 G6
Beamish Open Air Museum, Stanley Durham 242 G6
Beamond End Bucks 84 F6
Beamsley N Yorks 205 C7
Bean Kent 68 E5
Beanacre Wilts 62 F2

Beancross Falk 279 F8
Beanhill M/Keynes 103 D7
Beanley Northum 264 F3
Beansburn E Ayrs 257 B10
Beaquoy Orkney 312 F4
Bear Cross Bournem'th 19 B7
Beardwood Blackb'n 195 B7
Beare Devon 27 G7
Beare Green Surrey 51 E7
Bearley Warwick 118 E3
Bearnus Arg/Bute 288 E5
Bearpark Durham 233 C10
Bearsbridge Northum 241 F7
Bearsden E Dunb 277 G10
Bearsted Kent 53 B10
Bearstone Shrops 150 B4
Bearwood Bournem'th 19 B7
Bearwood Heref'd 115 F7
Bearwood W Midlands 133 G10
Beattock Dumf/Gal 248 C3
Beau Vale Notts 171 E8
Beauchamp Roding Essex 87 D9
Beauchief S Yorks 186 E4
Beauclerc Northum 242 E2
Beaudesert Warwick 118 D3
Beaufort Bl Gwent 77 C11
Beaufort Castle H'land 300 E5
Beaulieu Hants 32 G5
Beauly H'land 300 E5
Beaumaris Angl 179 F10
Beaumaris Castle Angl 179 F10
Beaumont Cumb 239 F8
Beaumont Essex 108 F3
Beaumont Hill D'lington 224 B5
Beaumont Leys Leics C 135 B11
Beausale Warwick 118 C4
Beauvale Notts 171 F7
Beauworth Hants 33 B9
Beaworthy Devon 12 B5
Beazley End Essex 106 F4
Bebington Mersey 182 E4
Bebside Northum 253 G7
Beccles Suffolk 143 E8
Becconsall Lancs 194 C2
Beck Cumb 219 B11
Beck Bottom W Yorks 197 C9
Beck Foot Cumb 222 F2
Beck Hole N Yorks 226 E6
Beck Row Suffolk 124 B3
Beck Side Cumb 210 C4
Beckbury Shrops 132 C5
Beckenham London 67 F11
Beckering Lincs 189 E10
Beckermet Cumb 219 D10
Beckermonds N Yorks 213 C7
Beckery Som'set 44 F3
Beckett End Norfolk 140 D5
Beckfoot Cumb 210 B3
Beckfoot Cumb 220 E3
Beckfoot Cumb 229 B7
Beckford Worcs 99 D9
Beckhampton Wilts 62 F5
Beckhithe Norfolk 142 B3
Beckingham Lincs 172 E5
Beckingham Notts 188 C3
Beckington Som'set 45 C10
Beckley E Sussex 38 C4
Beckley Hants 19 B10
Beckley Oxon 83 C9
Beckoes Cumb 230 F4
Becks W Yorks 204 D6
Beckside Cumb 212 B2
Beckton London 68 C2
Beckwithshaw N Yorks 205 C11
Becontree London 68 B3
Bedale N Yorks 214 B5
Bedburn Durham 233 E8
Bedchester Dorset 30 D5
Beddau Rh Cyn Taff 58 B5
Beddgelert Gwyn 163 F9
Beddingham E Sussex 36 F6
Beddington London 67 F9
Beddington Corner London 67 F9
Bedfield Suffolk 126 D4
Bedford Beds 103 B11
Bedford Gtr Man 183 B11
Bedgebury Cross Kent 53 G8
Bedgrove Bucks 84 C4
Bedham W Sussex 35 C8
Bedhampton Hants 34 F2
Bedingfield Suffolk 126 D3
Bedingfield Green Suffolk 126 D3
Bedingham Green Norfolk 142 E5
Bedlam N Yorks 205 C11
Bedlar's Green Essex 105 G10
Bedlington Northum 253 G7
Bedlington Station Northum 253 G7
Bedlinog Merth Tyd 77 E9
Bedminster Bristol 60 E5
Bedminster Down Bristol 60 F5
Bedmond Herts 85 E9
Bednall Staffs 151 F9
Bedrule Scot Borders 262 F4
Bedstone Shrops 115 B7
Bedwas Caerph 59 B7
Bedwell Plash Herts 104 G4
Bedwellty Caerph 77 E11
Bedwellty Pits Bl Gwent 77 D11
Bedworth Warwick 135 F7
Bedworth Heath Warwick 134 F6
Bedworth Woodlands Warwick 134 F6
Beeby Leics 136 B3
Beech Hants 49 F7
Beech Staffs 151 B7
Beech Hill Gtr Man 194 F5
Beech Hill Reading 65 G8

Beech Lanes W Midlands 133 F10
Beechen Cliff Bath/NE Som'set 61 G9
Beechingstoke Wilts 46 B5
Beechwood Halton 183 E8
Beechwood Newp 59 B10
Beechwood W Midlands 118 B5
Beechwood W Yorks 206 F2
Beedon W Berks 64 D3
Beedon Manor W Berks 64 D3
Beeford ER Yorks 209 C8
Beeley Derby 170 B3
Beelsby NE Lincs 201 G8
Beenham W Berks 64 F5
Beenham Stocks W Berks 64 F5
Beenham's Heath Windsor 65 D10
Beeny Cornw'l 11 C8
Beer Devon 15 D10
Beer Som'set 44 G2
Beer Crocombe Som'set 28 C4
Beer Hackett Dorset 29 E9
Beesands Devon 8 G6
Beesby Lincs 191 E7
Beeson Devon 8 G6
Beeston Beds 104 B3
Beeston Ches 167 D8
Beeston Norfolk 159 F8
Beeston Notts 153 B10
Beeston W Yorks 205 G11
Beeston Hill W Yorks 205 G11
Beeston Park Side W Yorks 197 B9
Beeston Regis Norfolk 177 E11
Beeston St. Lawrence Norfolk 160 E6
Beeswing Dumf/Gal 237 C10
Beetham Cumb 211 D9
Beetham Som'set 28 E3
Beetley Norfolk 159 F9
Beffcote Staffs 150 F6
Began Card 59 C8
Begbroke Oxon 83 C7
Begdale Cambs 139 B9
Begelly Pembs 73 D10
Beggarington Hill W Yorks 197 C9
Beggar's Bush Powys 114 E5
Beggars Pound V/Glam 58 F4
Beggearn Huish Som'set 42 F4
Beggor Hill Essex 87 E10
Beggshill Aberds 302 F5
Beguildy Powys 114 B3
Beighton Norfolk 143 B7
Beighton S Yorks 186 E6
Beitearsaig W Isles 305 G1
Beith N Ayrs 266 E6
Bekesbourne Kent 55 B7
Bekesbourne Hill Kent 55 B7
Bekonscot Model Village, Beaconsfield Bucks 84 G6
Belah Dumf/Gal 239 F9
Bel-Air Essex 89 C10
Belaugh Norfolk 160 F5
Belbroughton Worcs 117 B8
Belchamp Otten Essex 106 C6
Belchamp St. Paul Essex 106 C5
Belchamp Walter Essex 106 C6
Belchawell Dorset 30 F3
Belchawell Street Dorset 30 F3
Belchford Lincs 190 F3
Beleybridge Fife 287 F9
Belfield Gtr Man 196 E2
Belford Northum 264 C4
Belgrano Conwy 181 F7
Belgrave Blackb'n 195 C7
Belgrave Leics C 135 B11
Belgrave Staffs 134 C4
Belgravia London 67 D9
Belhaven E Loth 282 F3
Belhelvie Aberds 293 B11
Belhinnie Aberds 302 G4
Bell Bar Herts 86 D2
Bell Busk N Yorks 204 B4
Bell End Worcs 117 B8
Bell Heath Worcs 117 B9
Bell Hill Hants 34 C2
Bell o'th'Hill Ches 167 F8
Bellabeg Aberds 292 B5
Bellahouston Glasg C 267 C11
Bellamore S Ayrs 244 F6
Bellanoch Arg/Bute 275 D8
Bellasize ER Yorks 199 B10
Bellaty Angus 286 B6
Belle Isle W Yorks 197 B10
Belle Vale Mersey 182 D6
Belle Vale W Midlands 133 G9
Belle Vue Cumb 229 E8
Belle Vue Cumb 239 F9
Belle Vue Gtr Man 184 B5
Belle Vue Shrops 149 G9
Belle Vue W Yorks 197 D10
Belleau Lincs 190 F6
Bellehiglash Moray 301 F11
Bellerby N Yorks 224 G2
Bellerby Camp N Yorks 223 G11
Bellever Devon 13 F9
Bellfield E Ayrs 257 B10
Bellfields Surrey 50 C3
Belliehill Angus 293 G7
Bellingham London 67 E11
Bellingham Northum 251 G8
Belloch Arg/Bute 255 D7
Bellochantuy Arg/Bute 255 D7
Bell's Close Tyne/Wear 242 E5
Bell's Corner Suffolk 107 D9
Bell's Cross Suffolk 126 G3
Bells Yew Green E Sussex 52 F6
Bellsbank E Ayrs 245 C11
Bellshill N Lanarks 268 C5
Bellshill Northum 264 C4

Bellside N Lanarks 268 D6
Bellsmyre W Dunb 277 F8
Bellspool Scot Borders 260 B5
Bellsquarry W Loth 269 C11
Belluton Bath/NE Som'set 60 G6
Belmaduthy H'land 300 D6
Belmesthorpe Leics 155 G10
Belmont Blackb'n 195 D7
Belmont Derby 186 G4
Belmont Durham 234 C2
Belmont London 67 G9
Belmont London 85 G11
Belmont Oxon 63 B11
Belmont S Ayrs 257 E8
Belmont Shetl'd 314 C7
Belnacraig Aberds 292 B5
Belnagarrow Moray 302 E3
Belnie Lincs 156 C5
Belowda Cornw'l 5 C9
Belper Derby 170 F5
Belper Lane End Derby 170 F4
Belph Derby 187 F8
Belsay Northum 242 B4
Belses Scot Borders 262 D3
Belsize Herts 85 E8
Belstead Suffolk 108 C2
Belston S Ayrs 257 E9
Belstone Devon 13 C8
Belstone Corner Devon 13 B8
Belthorn Lancs 195 C8
Beltinge Kent 71 F7
Beltingham Northum 241 E7
Beltoft N Lincs 199 F10
Belton Leics 153 E8
Belton Lincs 155 B8
Belton Norfolk 143 C9
Belton N Lincs 199 F9
Belton House, Grantham Lincs 155 B8
Belton-in-Rutland Rutl'd 136 C6
Beltring Kent 53 D7
Belts of Collonach Aberds 293 D8
Belvedere London 68 D3
Belvedere W Loth 269 B9
Belvoir Leics 154 C6
Belvoir Castle Leics 154 C6
Bembridge I/Wight 21 D9
Bemersyde Scot Borders 262 C3
Bemerton Wilts 46 G6
Bempton ER Yorks 218 E3
Ben Alder Lodge H'land 291 F7
Ben Armine Lodge H'land 309 H7
Ben Casgro W Isles 304 F6
Ben Rhydding W Yorks 205 D8
Benacre Suffolk 143 G10
Benbecula Airport W Isles 296 F3
Benbuie Dumf/Gal 246 D6
Benchill Gtr Man 184 D4
Benderloch Arg/Bute 289 F11
Bendish Herts 104 G3
Bendronaig Lodge H'land 299 F10
Beneknowle Devon 8 D4
Benenden Kent 53 G10
Benfield Dumf/Gal 236 C5
Benfieldside Durham 242 G3
Bengate Norfolk 160 D6
Bengeworth Worcs 99 C10
Benhall Green Suffolk 127 E7
Benhall Street Suffolk 127 E7
Benham Burslot W Berks 64 E2
Benholm Aberds 293 G10
Beningbrough N Yorks 206 B6
Beningbrough Hall N Yorks 206 B6
Benington Herts 104 G6
Benington Lincs 174 F5
Benington Sea End Lincs 174 F6
Benllech Angl 179 E8
Benmore Arg/Bute 276 E2
Benmore Stirl 285 E8
Benmore Lodge Arg/Bute 289 F7
Benmore Lodge H'land 309 H3
Bennacott Cornw'l 11 C11
Bennah Devon 14 E2
Bennan N Ayrs 255 E10
Bennetland ER Yorks 199 B10
Bennettsfield H'land 300 D6
Bennett's End Bucks 84 F3
Bennetts End Herts 85 D9
Benniworth Lincs 190 E2
Benoak Cornw'l 6 C4
Benover Kent 53 D8
Bensham Tyne/Wear 243 E7
Benslie N Ayrs 266 G6
Benson Oxon 83 G10
Benston Shetl'd 315 H6
Bent Aberds 293 F8
Bent Gate Lancs 195 C9
Benthall Shrops 132 C3
Bentham Glos 80 B6
Benthoul Aberd C 293 C10
Bentilee Stoke 168 F6
Bentlawnt Shrops 130 C6
Bentley Essex 87 F9
Bentley ER Yorks 208 F6
Bentley Hants 49 E9
Bentley S Yorks 198 F5
Bentley Suffolk 108 D2
Bentley Warwick 134 E5
Bentley W Midlands 133 D9
Bentley Common Warwick 134 D6
Bentley Heath Herts 86 F2
Bentley Heath W Midlands 118 B3
Bentley Rise S Yorks 198 G5
Benton Square Tyne/Wear 243 D7
Bentpath Dumf/Gal 249 E8

Bents W Loth 269 C9
Bentwichen Devon 41 G8
Bentworth Hants 49 E7
Benvie Dundee C 287 D7
Benville Lane Dorset 29 G8
Benwell Tyne/Wear 242 E6
Benwick Cambs 138 E6
Beoley Worcs 117 D11
Beoraidbeg H'land 295 F8
Bepton W Sussex 34 D5
Berden Essex 105 G9
Bere Alston Devon 7 B8
Bere Ferrers Devon 7 C9
Bere Regis Dorset 18 B2
Berefold Aberds 303 F9
Berepper Cornw'l 2 E5
Bergh Apton Norfolk 142 C6
Berhill Som'set 44 F2
Berinsfield Oxon 83 F9
Berkeley Glos 79 F11
Berkeley Heath Glos 79 F11
Berkeley Road Glos 80 F2
Berkeley Towers Ches 167 E11
Berkhamsted Herts 85 D8
Berkley Som'set 45 D10
Berkley Marsh Som'set 45 D10
Berkswell W Midlands 118 B4
Bermondsey London 67 D10
Bernards Heath Herts 85 D11
Bernera H'land 295 C10
Berner's Hill E Sussex 53 G8
Berners Roding Essex 87 D10
Bernice Arg/Bute 276 C2
Bernisdale H'land 298 D4
Berrick Prior Oxon 83 G10
Berrick Salome Oxon 83 G10
Berrier Cumb 230 F3
Berriew Powys 130 C3
Berringtonbridge Cornw'l 11 F11
Berrington Shrops 131 B10
Berrington Worcs 115 D11
Berrington Green Worcs 115 D11
Berriowbridge Cornw'l 11 F11
Berrow Som'set 43 C9
Berrow Worcs 98 E5
Berrow Green Worcs 116 F4
Berry Brow W Yorks 196 E6
Berry Cross Devon 25 E7
Berry Hill Glos 79 C9
Berry Hill Stoke 168 F5
Berry Hill Worcs 117 F7
Berry Pomeroy Devon 8 C6
Berryfield Wilts 61 G11
Berryhillock Moray 302 C5
Berrylands London 67 F7
Berrynarbor Devon 40 D5
Berry's Green London 52 B2
Bersham Wrex 166 F4
Berstane Orkney 312 G5
Berthengam Flints 181 F10
Berthlwyd Swan 75 F9
Berwick E Sussex 23 D8
Berwick Kent 54 F6
Berwick S Glos 60 C5
Berwick Bassett Wilts 62 E5
Berwick Hill Northum 242 B5
Berwick Hills Middlesbro 225 B10
Berwick St. James Wilts 46 F5
Berwick St. John Wilts 30 C6
Berwick St. Leonard Wilts 46 G2
Berwick-upon-Tweed Northum 273 E10
Berwyn Denbs 165 G11
Bescaby Leics 154 D6
Bescar Lancs 193 E11
Bescot W Midlands 133 D10
Besford Worcs 99 C8
Besom Hill Gtr Man 196 F3
Bessacarr S Yorks 198 G6
Bessels Green Kent 52 B4
Bessels Leigh Oxon 83 E7
Besses o'th' Barn Gtr Man 195 F10
Bessingby ER Yorks 218 F3
Bessingham Norfolk 160 B3
Best Beech Hill E Sussex 52 F6
Besthorpe Norfolk 141 D11
Besthorpe Notts 188 G3
Bestwood Nott'ham 171 F9
Bestwood Village Notts 171 F9
Beswick ER Yorks 208 D6
Betchworth Surrey 51 D8
Beth Shalom Holocaust Centre, Laxton Notts 172 B2
Bethania Ceredig'n 111 E11
Bethania Gwyn 164 F2
Bethania Gwyn 163 E10
Bethel Angl 178 G5
Bethel Cornw'l 5 E10
Bethel Gwyn 147 B9
Bethel Gwyn 163 B8
Bethel Row Kent 54 C4
Bethelnie Aberds 303 F7
Bethersden Kent 54 E3
Bethesda Gwyn 163 B10
Bethesda Pembs 73 B9
Bethlehem Carms 94 F3
Bethnal Green London 67 C10
Betley Staffs 168 F3
Betsham Kent 68 E6
Betteshanger Kent 55 C10
Bettiscombe Dorset 16 B4
Bettisfield Wrex 149 B9
Betton Shrops 150 B3
Betton Abbots Shrops 131 B10
Betton Strange Shrops 131 B10
Bettws Bridg 57 D11
Bettws Monmouths 78 G3
Bettws Newp 78 G3
Bettws Cedewain Powys 130 D3
Bettws Gwerfil Goch Denbs 165 F8
Bettws Newydd Monmouths 78 D5

Bettyhill H'land 308 C7
Betws Carms 75 C10
Betws Bledrws Ceredig'n 111 G11
Betws Garmon Gwyn 163 D8
Betws-Ifan Ceredig'n 92 B6
Betws-y-Coed Conwy 164 D3
Betws-yn-Rhos Conwy 180 G6
Beulah Ceredig'n 92 B5
Beulah Powys 113 G8
Bevendean Brighton/Hove 36 F4
Bevercotes Notts 187 G11
Bevere Worcs 116 F6
Beverley ER Yorks 208 E6
Beverley Minster ER Yorks 208 E6
Beverley Racecourse ER Yorks 208 E6
Beverston Glos 80 G5
Bevington Glos 79 F11
Bewaldeth Cumb 229 E10
Bewbush W Sussex 51 F8
Bewcastle Cumb 240 C3
Bewdley Worcs 116 C5
Bewerley N Yorks 214 G3
Bewholme ER Yorks 209 C9
Bewley Common Wilts 62 F2
Bewsey Warrington 183 D9
Bexfield Norfolk 159 D10
Bexhill E Sussex 38 F2
Bexhill Down E Sussex 38 F2
Bexley London 68 E3
Bexleyheath London 68 D3
Bexleyhill W Sussex 34 B6
Bexwell Norfolk 140 C2
Beyton Suffolk 125 E8
Beyton Green Suffolk 125 E8
Bhalasaigh W Isles 304 E3
Bhaltos W Isles 304 E2
Bhatarsaigh W Isles 297 M2
Bhlàraidh H'land 290 B5
Bibury Glos 81 D10
Bicester Oxon 101 G11
Bickenhall Som'set 28 D3
Bickenhill W Midlands 134 G3
Bicker Lincs 156 B4
Bicker Bar Lincs 156 B4
Bicker Gauntlet Lincs 156 B4
Bickershaw Gtr Man 194 G6
Bickerstaffe Lancs 194 G2
Bickerton Ches 167 E8
Bickerton Devon 8 G6
Bickerton Northum 251 C11
Bickerton N Yorks 206 C5
Bickington Devon 13 G11
Bickington Devon 7 C11
Bickleigh Devon 26 E6
Bickleigh Devon 7 C11
Bickleton Devon 40 G4
Bickley London 68 F2
Bickley Worcs 116 C2
Bickley Moss Ches 167 F8
Bickley Town Ches 167 F8
Bicknacre Essex 88 E3
Bicknoller Som'set 42 F6
Bicknor Kent 53 B11
Bickton Hants 31 E10
Bicton Heref'd 115 E9
Bicton Shrops 130 G5
Bicton Shrops 149 F8
Bicton Heath Shrops 149 G9
Bicton Park Gardens Devon 15 D7
Bidborough Kent 52 E5
Biddenden Kent 53 F10
Biddenden Green Kent 53 E11
Biddenham Beds 121 G10
Biddestone Wilts 61 E11
Biddick Tyne/Wear 243 F8
Biddick Hall Tyne/Wear 243 E9
Biddisham Som'set 43 C11
Biddlesden Northants 102 C2
Biddlestone Northum 251 C9
Biddulph Staffs 168 D5
Biddulph Moor Staffs 168 D6
Bideford Devon 24 B6
Bidford on Avon Warwick 118 G2
Bidlake Devon 12 D5
Bidston Mersey 182 C3
Bidwell Beds 103 G10
Bielby ER Yorks 207 E11
Bieldside Aberd C 293 C10
Bierley I/Wight 20 F6
Bierley W Yorks 205 G9
Bierton Bucks 84 B4
Big Mancot Flints 166 B4
Big Pit National Mining Museum, Blaenavon Torf 78 D2
Big Sand H'land 299 B7
Bigbury Devon 8 F3
Bigbury-on-Sea Devon 8 G3
Bigby Lincs 200 F5
Bigfrith Windsor 65 C11
Biggar Cumb 210 F3
Biggar S Lanarks 260 B2
Biggar Road N Lanarks 268 C5
Biggin Derby 169 D11
Biggin Derby 170 F3
Biggin N Yorks 206 G6
Biggin Hill London 52 B2
Biggings Shetl'd 315 G3
Biggleswade Beds 104 C3
Bighouse H'land 310 C2
Bighton Hants 48 G6
Biglands Cumb 239 G7
Bignor W Sussex 35 F7
Bigod's Hill Norfolk 143 G7
Bigram Stirl 285 G10
Bigrigg Cumb 219 C10
Bigsby's Corner Suffolk 127 E7
Bigswell Orkney 312 G4
Bigton Shetl'd 315 L5
Bilberry Cornw'l 5 D10
Bilborough Nott'ham 171 G8
Bilbrook Som'set 42 E4
Bilbrook Staffs 133 C7

Bilbrough N Yorks 206 D1
Bilbster H'land 310 D6
Bilby Notts 187 E10
Bildershaw Durham 233 G9
Bildeston Suffolk 107 B9
Bill Quay Tyne/Wear 243 E7
Billacombe Plym'th 7 E10
Billacott Cornw'l 11 C11
Billericay Essex 87 G11
Billesdon Leics 136 C4
Billesley Warwick 118 F2
Billesley W Midlands 133 G11
Billingborough Lincs 156 C2
Billinge Mersey 194 G4
Billingford Norfolk 126 B3
Billingford Norfolk 159 D10
Billingham Stockton 234 G5
Billinghay Lincs 173 E11
Billingley S Yorks 198 G2
Billingshurst W Sussex 35 B9
Billingsley Shrops 132 F4
Billington Beds 103 G8
Billington Lancs 203 F10
Billington Staffs 151 E7
Billockby Norfolk 161 G8
Billown Motor Racing Circuit I/Man 192 F3
Billy Mill Tyne/Wear 243 D8
Billy Row Durham 233 D9
Bilsborrow Lancs 202 F6
Bilsby Lincs 191 F7
Bilsdean E Loth 282 G5
Bilsham W Sussex 35 G7
Bilsington Kent 54 G4
Bilson Green Glos 79 C10
Bilsthorpe Notts 171 C10
Bilsthorpe Moor Notts 171 D11
Bilston Midloth 270 C5
Bilston W Midlands 133 D9
Bilstone Leics 135 B7
Bilting Kent 54 D5
Bilton ER Yorks 209 G9
Bilton Northum 264 G6
Bilton N Yorks 206 B2
Bilton Warwick 119 C9
Bilton in Ainsty N Yorks 206 D5
Bimbister Orkney 312 G4
Binbrook Lincs 190 C2
Binchester Blocks Durham 233 E10
Bincombe Dorset 17 E9
Bindal H'land 311 L3
Bindon Som'set 27 C10
Binegar Som'set 44 D6
Bines Green W Sussex 35 D11
Binfield Brack'l 65 E10
Binfield Heath Oxon 65 D8
Bingfield Northum 241 C11
Bingham C/Edinb 280 G5
Bingham Notts 154 B4
Bingham's Melcombe Dorset 30 G3
Bingley W Yorks 205 F8
Bings Heath Shrops 149 G10
Binham Norfolk 159 B9
Binley Hants 48 C2
Binley W Midlands 119 B7
Binley Woods Warwick 119 B7
Binnegar Dorset 18 D3
Binniehill Falk 279 G7
Binsoe N Yorks 214 D4
Binstead I/Wight 21 C7
Binsted Hants 49 E9
Binsted W Sussex 35 F7
Binton Warwick 118 G2
Bintree Norfolk 159 E10
Binweston Shrops 130 C6
Birch Essex 107 G9
Birch Gtr Man 195 F11
Birch Cross Staffs 152 C2
Birch Green Essex 88 B6
Birch Green Herts 86 C3
Birch Green Lancs 194 F3
Birch Green Worcs 99 B7
Birch Heath Ches 167 C8
Birch Hill Ches 183 G8
Birch Vale Derby 185 D8
Birch Wood Som'set 28 E2
Birchall Staffs 169 E7
Birchall Corner Essex 107 E10
Bircham Newton Norfolk 158 C5
Bircham Tofts Norfolk 158 C5
Birchanger Essex 105 G10
Birchburn N Ayrs 255 E10
Birchen Coppice Worcs 116 C6
Birchencliffe W Yorks 196 C6
Birchend Heref'd 98 C3
Bircher Heref'd 115 D9
Bircher Common Heref'd 115 D9
Birches Green W Midlands 134 E2
Birchett's Green E Sussex 53 G7
Birchfield H'land 301 G9
Birchfield W Midlands 133 E11
Birchgrove Card 59 C7
Birchgrove Swan 76 F2
Birchgrove W Sussex 36 B5
Birchill Devon 28 G4
Birchington Kent 71 F10
Birchley Heath Warwick 134 E5
Birchmoor Warwick 134 C5
Birchmoor Green Beds 103 E8
Bircholt Forstal Kent 54 E5
Birchover Derby 170 C2
Birchwood Lincs 172 B6
Birchwood Warrington 183 C11
Birdham W Sussex 34 G4
Birdholme Derby 170 B5

Birdingbury Warwick 119 D8
Birdland Park, Bourton-on-the-Water Glos 100 G3
Birdlip Glos 80 C6
Birds Edge W Yorks 197 F8
Birds Green Essex 87 D9
Birdsall N Yorks 216 F6
Birdsend Glos 98 G5
Birdsgreen Shrops 132 G5
Birdsmoor Gate Dorset 28 G5
Birdston E Dunb 278 F3
Birdwell S Yorks 197 G10
Birdwood Glos 80 B2
Birdworld and Underwaterworld, Farnham Hants 49 E10
Birgham Scot Borders 263 B7
Birichen H'land 309 K7
Birkacre Lancs 194 E5
Birkby Cumb 229 D7
Birkby N Yorks 224 E6
Birkby W Yorks 196 D6
Birkdale Mersey 193 E10
Birkenbog Aberds 302 C5
Birkenhead Mersey 182 D4
Birkenhills Aberds 303 E7
Birkenshaw S Lanarks 268 C3
Birkenshaw S Lanarks 268 F5
Birkenshaw W Yorks 197 B8
Birkett Mire Cumb 230 G2
Birkhall Aberds 292 D5
Birkhill Angus 287 D7
Birkhill Dumf/Gal 260 F6
Birkholme Lincs 155 E9
Birkin N Yorks 198 B4
Birks W Yorks 197 B9
Birkshaw Northum 241 D7
Birley Heref'd 115 G9
Birley Carr S Yorks 186 C4
Birley Edge S Yorks 186 C4
Birleyhay Derby 186 E5
Birling Kent 69 G7
Birling Northum 253 B7
Birling Gap E Sussex 23 F9
Birlingham Worcs 99 C8
Birmingham W Midlands 133 F10
Birmingham Botanical Gardens W Midlands 133 F10
Birmingham International Airport W Midlands 134 G3
Birmingham Museum and Art Gallery W Midlands 133 F11
Birmingham Museum of Science and Technology W Midlands 133 F11
Birnam Perth/Kinr 286 C4
Birniehill S Lanarks 268 E2
Birse Aberds 293 D7
Birsemore Aberds 293 D7
Birstall Leics 135 B11
Birstall W Yorks 197 B8
Birstall Smithies W Yorks 197 B8
Birstwith N Yorks 205 B10
Birthorpe Lincs 156 C2
Birtle Gtr Man 195 E10
Birtley Heref'd 115 D7
Birtley Northum 241 B9
Birtley Tyne/Wear 243 F7
Birts Street Worcs 98 D5
Birtsmorton Worcs 98 D6
Bisbrooke Rutl'd 137 D7
Biscathorpe Lincs 190 E2
Biscombe Som'set 27 E11
Biscot Luton 103 G11
Biscovey Cornw'l 5 E11
Bish Mill Devon 26 B2
Bisham Windsor 65 C10
Bishampton Worcs 117 G9
Bishop Auckland Durham 233 F9
Bishop Burton ER Yorks 208 E5
Bishop Kinkell H'land 300 D5
Bishop Middleham Durham 234 E2
Bishop Monkton N Yorks 214 F6
Bishop Norton Lincs 189 C7
Bishop Sutton Bath/NE Som'set 44 B5
Bishop Thornton N Yorks 214 G5
Bishop Wilton ER Yorks 207 B11
Bishopbridge Lincs 189 C8
Bishopbriggs E Dunb 278 G2
Bishopdown Wilts 47 G7
Bishopmill Moray 302 C2
Bishops Cannings Wilts 62 G4
Bishop's Castle Shrops 130 F6
Bishop's Caundle Dorset 29 E11
Bishop's Cleeve Glos 99 F8
Bishops Frome Heref'd 98 B3
Bishops Gate Surrey 66 E3
Bishop's Green Essex 87 B10
Bishop's Green Hants 64 G3
Bishop's Hull Som'set 28 C2
Bishop's Itchington Warwick 119 F7
Bishops Lydeard Som'set 27 B11
Bishop's Norton Glos 98 G6
Bishop's Nympton Devon 26 C3
Bishop's Offley Staffs 150 D5
Bishop's Stortford Herts 105 G9
Bishops Sutton Hants 48 G6
Bishop's Tachbrook Warwick 118 E6
Bishop's Tawton Devon 25 B9
Bishop's Waltham Hants 33 D8
Bishop's Wood Staffs 132 B6
Bishopsbourne Kent 55 C7
Bishopsgarth Stockton 234 G4
Bishopsteignton Devon 14 G4
Bishopstoke Hants 33 D7
Bishopston Bristol 60 D5
Bishopston Swan 56 D5
Bishopstone Bucks 84 C4
Bishopstone E Sussex 37 G7
Bishopstone Heref'd 97 C8
Bishopstone Kent 71 F8
Bishopstone Swindon 63 C8
Bishopstone Wilts 31 B9
Bishopstrow Wilts 45 E11
Bishopswood Som'set 28 E3
Bishopsworth Bristol 60 F5
Bishopthorpe C/York 207 D7
Bishopton D'lington 234 G3
Bishopton Dumf/Gal 236 E6
Bishopton N Yorks 214 E5
Bishopton Renf 277 G8
Bishopton Warwick 118 F3
Bishopwearmouth Tyne/Wear 243 F9
Bishpool Newp 59 B10
Bishton Newp 59 B11
Bishton Staffs 151 E10
Bisley Glos 80 D6
Bisley Surrey 50 B3
Bisley Camp Surrey 50 B2
Bispham Blackp'l 202 E2
Bispham Green Lancs 194 E3
Bissoe Cornw'l 4 G5
Bisterne Hants 31 G10
Bisterne Close Hants 32 G2
Bitchet Green Kent 52 C5
Bitchfield Lincs 155 D9
Bittadon Devon 40 E4
Bittaford Devon 8 D3
Bitterley Shrops 115 B11
Bitterne S'thampton 32 E6
Bitterne Park S'thampton 32 E6
Bitterscote Staffs 134 C4
Bitteswell Leics 135 G10
Bittles Green Dorset 30 B5
Bitton S Glos 61 F7
Bix Oxon 65 B8
Bixter Shetl'd 315 H5
Blaby Leics 135 D11
Black Bank Cambs 139 F10
Black Bank Warwick 135 F7
Black Barn Lincs 157 D8
Black Bourton Oxon 82 E3
Black Bridge Pembs 72 D6
Black Callerton Tyne/Wear 242 D5
Black Carr Norfolk 141 D11
Black Clauchrie S Ayrs 245 G7
Black Corner W Sussex 51 E9
Black Corries Lodge H'land 284 B6
Black Crofts Arg/Bute 289 F11
Black Cross Cornw'l 5 C8
Black Dog Devon 26 F4
Black Heddon Northum 242 B3
Black Hill W Yorks 205 E7
Black Lane Gtr Man 195 F9
Black Lane Ends Lancs 204 E3
Black Moor W Yorks 205 F11
Black Mount Arg/Bute 284 C6
Black Notley Essex 106 G5
Black Pill Swan 75 G10
Black Pole Lancs 202 E5
Black Rock Brighton/Hove 36 G4
Black Rock Monmouths 60 B4
Black Street Suffolk 143 F10
Black Tar Pembs 73 D7
Black Torrington Devon 25 F7
Black Vein Caerph 78 G2
Blackacre Dumf/Gal 248 E2
Blackadder West Scot Borders 272 E6
Blackawton Devon 8 E6
Blackbeck Cumb 219 D10
Blackborough Devon 27 G9
Blackborough Norfolk 158 G3
Blackborough End Norfolk 158 G3
Blackboys E Sussex 37 C8
Blackbraes Aberds 293 B10
Blackbraes Falk 279 F8
Blackbrook Derby 170 F4
Blackbrook Derby 185 E9
Blackbrook Mersey 183 B8
Blackbrook Surrey 51 D7
Blackbrook Staffs 150 B5
Blackburn Aberds 293 B10
Blackburn Aberds 293 D10
Blackburn Aberds 302 F5
Blackburn Blackb'n 195 B7
Blackburn S Yorks 186 C5
Blackburn W Loth 269 B9
Blackchambers Aberds 293 B9
Blackcraig Dumf/Gal 246 G6
Blackcraigs Angus 293 E7
Blackden Heath Ches 184 G3
Blackditch Oxon 82 D6
Blackdog Aberds 293 B11
Blackdown Dorset 28 G5
Blackdyke Cumb 238 G4
Blackenhall Ches 168 F2
Blackenhall W Midlands 133 D8
Blacker S Yorks 197 F10
Blacker Hill S Yorks 197 G11
Blackfell Tyne/Wear 243 F7
Blackfen London 68 E3
Blackfield Hants 32 G6
Blackford Cumb 239 E9
Blackford Perth/Kinr 286 G2
Blackford Som'set 44 D2
Blackford Som'set 29 B11
Blackford Bridge Gtr Man 195 F9
Blackfordby Leics 152 F6
Blackgang I/Wight 20 F5
Blackgang Chine Fantasy Park I/Wight 20 F5
Blackgate Angus 287 B8
Blackhall Aberds 293 D8
Blackhall C/Edinb 280 G4
Blackhall Herts 105 E8
Blackhall Renf 267 C9
Blackhall Colliery Durham 234 D4
Blackhall Mill Tyne/Wear 242 F4
Blackhall Rocks Durham 234 D5
Blackham E Sussex 52 F3
Blackhaugh Scot Borders 261 B10
Blackheath Essex 107 G10
Blackheath London 67 D11
Blackheath Suffolk 127 B8
Blackheath W Midlands 133 F9
Blackhill Aberds 303 D10
Blackhill Aberds 303 E10
Blackhill Aberds 303 F10
Blackhill Durham 242 G3
Blackhill H'land 298 D3
Blackhillock Moray 302 E4
Blackhills H'land 301 D9
Blackhills Moray 302 D2
Blackhills Swan 75 G9
Blackhorse Devon 14 C5
Blackhorse S Glos 61 D7
Blackjack Lincs 156 B5
Blackland Som'set 41 F10
Blackland Wilts 62 F4
Blacklaw Aberds 302 D6
Blackleach Lancs 202 G5
Blackley Gtr Man 195 G11
Blackley W Yorks 196 D6
Blacklunans Perth/Kinr 292 G3
Blackmanston Dorset 18 E4
Blackmarstone Heref'd 97 D10
Blackmill Bridg 58 B2
Blackmoor Gtr Man 195 G7
Blackmoor Hants 49 G9
Blackmoor N Som'set 60 G3
Blackmoor Som'set 27 D11
Blackmoorfoot W Yorks 196 E6
Blackmore Essex 87 E10
Blackmore Shrops 130 B6
Blackmore End Essex 106 E4
Blackmore End Herts 85 B11
Blackmore End Worcs 98 C6
Blackness Aberds 293 D8
Blackness E Sussex 37 B8
Blackness Falk 279 E10
Blacknest Hants 49 E9
Blacknest Windsor 66 F3
Blackney Dorset 16 B4
Blacknoll Dorset 18 D2
Blacko Lancs 204 E3
Blackpark Dumf/Gal 236 C5
Blackpole Worcs 117 F7
Blackpool Blackp'l 202 F2
Blackpool Devon 9 F7
Blackpool Devon 14 G2
Blackpool Pembs 73 C9
Blackpool Airport Lancs 202 G2
Blackpool Corner Devon 16 B2
Blackpool Pleasure Beach Blackp'l 202 G2
Blackpool Sea Life Centre Blackp'l 202 F2
Blackpool Tower Blackp'l 202 F2
Blackpool Zoo Park Blackp'l 202 F2
Blackridge W Loth 269 B7
Blackrock Arg/Bute 274 G4
Blackrock Monmouths 78 C2
Blackrod Gtr Man 194 E6
Blackshaw Dumf/Gal 238 D3
Blackshaw Head W Yorks 196 C2
Blacksmith's Corner Suffolk 108 C2
Blacksmith's Green Suffolk 126 D2
Blacksnape Blackb'n 195 C8
Blackstone W Sussex 36 D2
Blackthorn Oxon 83 B10
Blackthorpe Suffolk 125 E8
Blacktoft ER Yorks 199 C10
Blacktop Aberd C 293 C10
Blacktown Newp 59 C9
Blackwall London 67 C11
Blackwall Tunnel London 67 C11
Blackwater Cornw'l 4 F4
Blackwater Dorset 19 B8
Blackwater Hants 49 B10
Blackwater I/Wight 20 D6
Blackwater Norfolk 159 E11
Blackwater Som'set 28 D3
Blackwater Lodge Moray 302 G3
Blackwaterfoot N Ayrs 255 E9
Blackwell Cumb 239 G10
Blackwell D'lington 224 C5
Blackwell Derby 170 D6
Blackwell Derby 185 G10
Blackwell Som'set 27 B8
Blackwell Warwick 100 C4
Blackwell Worcs 117 C9
Blackwell W Sussex 51 F11
Blackwell's End Green Glos 98 F5
Blackwood = Coed Duon Caerph 77 F11
Blackwood S Lanarks 268 G5
Blackwood Warrington 183 C10
Blackwood Hill Staffs 168 D6
Blacky Moor Northants 120 F5
Blacon Ches 166 B5
Bladbean Kent 55 D7
Blades N Yorks 223 F9
Bladnoch Dumf/Gal 236 D6
Bladon Oxon 82 C6
Blaen Clydach Rh Cyn Taff 77 G7
Blaenannerch Ceredig'n 92 B4
Blaenau Bl Gwent 78 E2
Blaenau Dolwyddelan Conwy 164 E2
Blaenau Ffestiniog Gwyn 164 F2
Blaenau Uchaf Wrex 166 G3
Blaenavon Torf 78 D3
Blaencaerau Bridg 76 F5
Blaencarno Caerph 77 D9
Blaencelyn Ceredig'n 111 G7
Blaencwm Rh Cyn Taff 76 F6
Blaendulais = Seven Sisters Neath P Talb 76 D4
Blaendyryn Powys 95 D8
Blaenffos Pembs 92 D3
Blaengarw Bridg 76 G6
Blaengavenny Monmouths 78 B4
Blaen-geuffordd Ceredig'n 128 G2
Blaengwawr Rh Cyn Taff 77 E8
Blaengwrach Neath P Talb 76 D5
Blaengwynfi Neath P Talb 76 F5
Blaenllechau Rh Cyn Taff 77 F8
Blaenpennal Ceredig'n 112 E2
Blaenplwyf Ceredig'n 111 B11
Blaenporth Ceredig'n 92 B5
Blaenrhondda Rh Cyn Taff 76 F6
Blaenwaun Carms 92 F4
Blaen-y-Coed Carms 92 F6
Blaen-y-cwm Bl Gwent 77 C10
Blaenycwm Ceredig'n 112 B6
Blaen-y-cwm Torf 78 E3
Blagdon N Som'set 44 B4
Blagdon Torbay 9 C7
Blagdon Hill Som'set 28 D2
Blagill Cumb 231 B10
Blaguegate Lancs 194 F3
Blaich H'land 290 F2
Blain H'land 289 C8
Blaina Bl Gwent 78 D2
Blainacraig Ho Aberds 293 D8
Blair Atholl Perth/Kinr 291 G10
Blair Castle, Blair Atholl Perth/Kinr 291 G10
Blair Drummond Stirl 278 B4
Blair Drummond Safari Park, Dunblane Stirl 278 B4
Blairanbolch Arg/Bute 266 B2
Blairbeg N Ayrs 256 C2
Blairburn Fife 279 D9
Blairdaff Aberds 293 B8
Blairdryne Aberds 293 D9
Blairgorm H'land 301 G10
Blairgowrie Perth/Kinr 286 C5
Blairhall Fife 279 D10
Blairhill N Lanarks 268 B4
Blairingone Perth/Kinr 279 B9
Blairland N Ayrs 266 F6
Blairlinn N Lanarks 278 G5
Blairlogie Stirl 278 B6
Blairlomond Arg/Bute 276 B3
Blairmore Arg/Bute 276 E3
Blairmore H'land 306 D6
Blairnamarrow Moray 292 B4
Blair's Ferry Arg/Bute 275 G10
Blairskaith E Dunb 277 F11
Blaisdon Glos 80 C2
Blaise Hamlet Bristol 60 D5
Blaize Bailey Glos 79 C11
Blake End Essex 106 G4
Blakebrook Worcs 116 B6
Blakedown Worcs 117 B7
Blakelands M/Keynes 103 C7
Blakelaw Scot Borders 263 C7
Blakelaw Tyne/Wear 242 D6
Blakeley Staffs 133 E7
Blakeley Lane Staffs 169 F7
Blakelow Ches 167 E11
Blakemere Heref'd 97 C7
Blakenall Heath W Midlands 133 C10
Blakeney Glos 79 D11
Blakeney Norfolk 177 E8
Blakeney Hill Glos 79 D11
Blakeney Point NNR Norfolk 177 D8
Blakeshall Worcs 132 G6
Blakesley Northants 120 G2
Blanchland Northum 241 G11
Bland Hill N Yorks 205 C10
Blandford Camp Dorset 30 F6
Blandford Forum Dorset 30 F5
Blandford St. Mary Dorset 30 F5
Blandy H'land 308 D6
Blanefield Stirl 277 F11
Blanerne Scot Borders 272 D6
Blankney Lincs 173 C9
Blantyre S Lanarks 268 D3
Blar a'Chaorainn H'land 290 G3
Blaran Arg/Bute 275 B9
Blarghour Arg/Bute 275 B10
Blarmachfoldach H'land 290 G2
Blarnalearoch H'land 307 K6
Blasford Hill Essex 88 C2
Blashford Hants 31 F10
Blaston Leics 136 D6
Blatherwycke Northants 137 D9
Blawith Cumb 210 C4
Blaxhall Suffolk 127 F7
Blaxton S Yorks 199 G7
Blaydon Tyne/Wear 242 E5
Blaydon Burn Tyne/Wear 242 E5
Blazefield N Yorks 214 F3
Bleach Green Cumb 219 B9
Bleach Green Suffolk 126 B4
Bleadney Som'set 44 D3
Bleadon N Som'set 43 B10
Bleak Hey Nook Gtr Man 196 F4
Bleak Hill Hants 31 E10
Bleak Street Som'set 45 G9
Blean Kent 70 G6
Bleasby Lincs 189 E10
Bleasby Notts 172 F2
Bleasby Moor Lincs 189 E10
Bleasdale Lancs 203 D7
Bleatarn Cumb 222 C4
Blebocraigs Fife 287 F8
Bleddfa Powys 114 D4
Bledington Glos 100 G4
Bledlow Bucks 84 E3
Bledlow Ridge Bucks 84 F3
Bleet Wilts 45 B10
Blegbie E Loth 271 C9
Blencarn Cumb 231 E8
Blencogo Cumb 229 B9
Blendworth Hants 34 E2
Blenheim Palace, Woodstock Oxon 82 B6
Blenheim Park Norfolk 158 C6
Blennerhasset Cumb 229 C9
Blervie Castle Moray 301 D10
Bletchingdon Oxon 83 B8
Bletchingley Surrey 51 C10
Bletchley M/Keynes 103 E7
Bletchley Shrops 150 C2
Bletherston Pembs 91 G11
Bletsoe Beds 121 F10
Blewbury Oxon 64 B4
Blickling Norfolk 160 D3
Blickling Hall, Aylsham Norfolk 160 D3
Blidworth Notts 171 D9
Blidworth Bottoms Notts 171 E9
Blindcrake Cumb 229 E9
Blindley Heath Surrey 51 D11
Blindmore Som'set 28 E3
Blingery H'land 310 E7
Blisland Cornw'l 11 G7
Bliss Gate Worcs 116 C4
Blissford Hants 31 E11
Blisworth Northants 120 G4
Blithbury Staffs 151 E11
Blitterlees Cumb 238 G4
Blo' Norton Norfolk 125 B10
Blockley Glos 100 E3
Blofield Norfolk 142 B6
Blofield Corner Norfolk 160 G6
Blofield Heath Norfolk 160 G6
Bloodman's Corner Suffolk 143 D10
Bloomfield Scot Borders 262 E3
Bloomfield Dumf/Gal 238 B1
Bloomfield W Midlands 133 E9
Bloomsbury London 67 C10
Blore Staffs 169 F10
Blossomfield W Midlands 118 B2
Blount's Green Staffs 151 C11
Blowick Mersey 193 D11
Bloxham Oxon 101 D8
Bloxholm Lincs 173 E9
Bloxwich W Midlands 133 C9
Bloxworth Dorset 18 C3
Blubberhouses N Yorks 205 B9
Blue Anchor Cornw'l 5 D8
Blue Anchor Som'set 42 E4
Blue Anchor Swan 75 F8
Blue Bank N Yorks 227 D7
Blue Bell Hill Kent 69 G8
Blue Bridge M/Keynes 102 C6
Blue Planet Aquarium Ches 182 G6
Blue Reef Aquarium, Newquay Cornw'l 4 C6
Blue Reef Aquarium, Portsmouth Portsm'th 33 H10
Blue Reef Aquarium, Tynemouth Tyne/Wear 243 C9
Blue Row Essex 89 C8
Blue Town Kent 70 D2
Blue Vein Wilts 61 F10
Bluetown Kent 54 B2
Blughasary H'land 307 J6
Blundell's Hill Mersey 183 C7
Blundellsands Mersey 182 B4
Blundeston Suffolk 143 D10
Blunham Beds 122 G3
Blunsdon St. Andrew Swindon 62 B6
Bluntington Worcs 117 C7
Bluntisham Cambs 123 C7
Blunt's Cornw'l 6 C6
Blunt's Green Warwick 118 D2
Blurton Stoke 168 G5
Blyborough Lincs 188 C6
Blyford Suffolk 127 B8
Blymhill Staffs 150 G6
Blymhill Common Staffs 150 G5
Blymhill Lawn Staffs 150 G6
Blyth Notts 187 D10
Blyth Northum 253 G8
Blyth Bridge Scot Borders 270 F2
Blyth End Warwick 134 E4
Blythburgh Suffolk 127 B9
Blythe Bridge Staffs 169 G7
Blythe Marsh Staffs 169 G7
Blythswood Renf 267 B10
Blyton Lincs 188 C5
Boarhills Fife 287 F9
Boarhunt Hants 33 F10
Boar's Head Gtr Man 194 F5
Boars Hill Oxon 83 E7
Boarshead E Sussex 52 G4
Boarstall Bucks 83 C10
Boasley Cross Devon 12 C6
Boat of Garten H'land 291 B11
Boath H'land 300 B5
Bobbing Kent 69 F11
Bobbington Staffs 132 E6
Bobbingworth Essex 87 D8
Bobby Hill Suffolk 125 C10
Boblainy H'land 300 F4
Bocaddon Cornw'l 6 D3
Bochastle Stirl 285 G10
Bocking Essex 106 G5
Bocking Churchstreet Essex 106 F5
Bockings Elm Essex 89 B11
Bockleton Worcs 115 E11
Bockmer End Bucks 65 B10
Bodantionail H'land 299 B7
Boddam Aberds 303 E11
Boddam Shetl'd 315 M5
Bodden Som'set 44 E6
Boddington Glos 99 G7
Bodedern Angl 178 E4
Bodelwyddan Denbs 181 F8
Bodenham Heref'd 115 G10
Bodenham Arboretum and Earth Centre Worcs 132 G6
Bodenham Bank Heref'd 98 E3
Bodenham Moor Heref'd 115 G10
Bodenham Wilts 31 B11
Bodewryd Angl 178 C5
Bodfari Denbs 181 G9
Bodffordd Angl 178 F6
Bodham Norfolk 177 E10
Bodiam E Sussex 38 B3
Bodiam Castle E Sussex 38 B3
Bodicote Oxon 101 D9
Bodiechell Aberds 303 E7
Bodieve Cornw'l 10 G5
Bodilly Cornw'l 2 C5
Bodiniel Cornw'l 5 B11
Bodinnick Cornw'l 6 E2
Bodle Street Green E Sussex 37 E11
Bodley Devon 41 D7
Bodlith Powys 148 D4
Bodlondeb Conwy 180 G4
Bodmin Cornw'l 5 B11
Bodnant Conwy 180 G4
Bodnant Garden, Colwyn Bay Conwy 180 G3
Bodney Norfolk 140 D6
Bodrane Cornw'l 6 C4
Bodsham Kent 54 D6
Boduan Gwyn 144 B6
Boduel Cornw'l 6 C4
Bodwen Cornw'l 5 C10
Bodymoor Heath Warwick 134 D3
Bofarnel Cornw'l 6 C2
Bogallan H'land 300 D6
Bogbrae Aberds 303 F10
Bogend Notts 171 F7
Bogend S Ayrs 257 C9
Bogentory Aberds 293 C9
Boghall Midloth 270 B4
Boghall W Loth 269 B9
Boghead Aberds 293 D8
Boghead E Dunb 278 G2
Boghead S Lanarks 268 G5
Bogmarsh Heref'd 97 D10
Bogmoor Moray 302 C3
Bogniebrae Aberds 302 E5
Bogniebrae Aberds 302 E6
Bognor Regis W Sussex 22 D6
Bograxie Aberds 293 B9
Bogs Aberds 302 G5
Bogside N Lanarks 268 E6
Bogthorn W Yorks 204 F6
Bogton Aberds 302 D6
Bogtown Aberds 302 C5
Bogtown Devon 12 B5
Bogue Dumf/Gal 246 G4
Bohemia E Sussex 38 F4
Bohemia Wilts 32 D2
Bohenie H'land 290 E4
Bohetherick Cornw'l 7 B8
Boholt Gtr Man 195 E9
Bohortha Cornw'l 3 C9
Bohuntine H'land 290 E4
Bohuntinville H'land 290 E4
Boirseam W Isles 296 C6
Bojewyan Cornw'l 1 C3
Bokiddick Cornw'l 5 C10
Bolam Durham 233 G9
Bolam Northum 252 G3
Bolberry Devon 8 H3
Bold Heath Mersey 183 D8
Boldmere W Midlands 134 E2
Boldon Colliery Tyne/Wear 243 E8
Boldre Hants 20 B2
Boldron Durham 223 C10
Bole Notts 188 D3
Bolehall Staffs 134 C4
Bolehill Derby 170 D3
Bolehill S Yorks 186 E5
Bolenowe Cornw'l 2 B5
Boleside Scot Borders 261 C11
Bolham Devon 27 E7
Bolham Notts 188 E2
Bolham Water Devon 27 E11
Bolingey Cornw'l 4 E5
Bollihope Durham 232 E6
Bollington Ches 184 F6
Bollington Cross Ches 184 F6
Bollow Glos 80 C2
Bolney W Sussex 36 C3
Bolnhurst Beds 121 F11
Bolshan Angus 287 B10
Bolsover Derby 187 G7
Bolster Moor W Yorks 196 D5
Bolsterstone S Yorks 186 B3
Bolstone Heref'd 97 E10
Boltby N Yorks 215 B9
Bolter End Bucks 84 G3
Boltgate N Lincs 199 D10
Bolton Cumb 231 G9
Bolton E Loth 281 G10
Bolton ER Yorks 207 C11
Bolton Gtr Man 195 F8
Bolton Northum 264 G4
Bolton W Yorks 205 F9
Bolton Abbey N Yorks 205 C7
Bolton Abbey, Skipton N Yorks 205 C7
Bolton Bridge N Yorks 205 C7
Bolton by Bowland Lancs 203 D11
Bolton Castle, Leyburn N Yorks 223 G10
Bolton Green Lancs 194 D5
Bolton Low Houses Cumb 229 C10
Bolton New Houses Cumb 229 C10
Bolton Percy N Yorks 206 E6
Bolton Town End Lancs 211 F9
Bolton upon Dearne S Yorks 198 G2
Bolton Wood Lane Cumb 229 C11
Bolton Woods W Yorks 205 F9
Boltonfellend Cumb 239 D11
Boltongate Cumb 229 C10
Bolton-le-Sands Lancs 211 F9
Bolton-on-Swale N Yorks 224 F5
Boltshope Park Durham 232 B4
Bolventor Cornw'l 11 F9
Bomarsund Northum 253 G7
Bombie Dumf/Gal 237 D9
Bomby Cumb 221 B10
Bomere Heath Shrops 149 F9
Bonar Bridge H'land 309 K6
Bonawe Arg/Bute 284 D4
Bonbusk Notts 187 G8
Bonby N Lincs 200 D4
Bonc Wrex 148 B3
Boncath Pembs 92 D4
Bonchester Bridge Scot Borders 262 G3
Bonchurch I/Wight 21 F7
Bond End Staffs 152 F2
Bondend Glos 80 B5
Bondleigh Devon 25 G10
Bonds Lancs 202 D5
Bonehayne Devon 15 C10
Bonehill Devon 13 F10
Bonehill Staffs 134 C3
Bo'ness Falk 279 E9
Boney Hay Staffs 151 G11
Bonhill W Dunb 277 F7
Boningdale Shrops 132 C6
Bonjedward Scot Borders 262 E5
Bonkle N Lanarks 268 D6
Bonnavoulin H'land 289 D7
Bonning Gate Cumb 221 F9
Bonnington C/Edinb 270 B2
Bonnington Kent 54 F5
Bonnybank Fife 287 G7
Bonnybridge Falk 278 E6
Bonnykelly Aberds 303 D8
Bonnyrigg Midloth 270 B6
Bonnyton Aberds 302 F6
Bonnyton Angus 287 B10
Bonnyton Angus 287 D7
Bonnyton E Ayrs 257 B10
Bonsall Derby 170 D3
Bonskeid House Perth/Kinr 291 G10
Bonson Som'set 43 E8
Bont Monmouths 78 B5
Bont Dolgadfan Powys 129 C7
Bont Newydd Gwyn 164 G2
Bontddu Gwyn 146 F3
Bont-goch = Elerch Ceredig'n 128 F3
Bonthorpe Lincs 191 G7
Bont-newydd Conwy 181 G8
Bontnewydd Ceredig'n 112 D2
Bontnewydd Gwyn 163 D7
Bontuchel Denbs 165 D9
Bonvilston V/Glam 58 E5
Bonwm Denbs 165 G10
Bon-y-maen Swan 75 F11
Boode Devon 40 F4
Booker Bucks 84 G4
Boomer Som'set 43 G9
Boon Scot Borders 271 F11
Boon Hill Staffs 168 E4
Boorley Green Hants 33 E8
Boosbeck Redcar/Clevel'd 226 B3
Boose's Green Essex 106 E6
Boot Cumb 220 E3
Boot Street Suffolk 108 B4
Booth W Yorks 196 B4
Booth Bank Ches 184 D2
Booth Green Ches 184 E6
Booth Wood W Yorks 196 D4
Boothby Graffoe Lincs 173 D7
Boothby Pagnell Lincs 155 C9
Boothen Stoke 168 G5
Boothferry ER Yorks 199 B8
Boothroyd W Yorks 197 C8
Booth's Hill Warrington 183 D11
Boothsdale Ches 167 B8
Boothstown Gtr Man 195 G8
Boothtown W Yorks 196 B5
Boothville Northants 120 E5
Bootle Cumb 210 B2
Bootle Mersey 182 C4
Booton Norfolk 160 E2
Boots Green Ches 184 G3
Booze N Yorks 223 E10
Boquhan Stirl 277 D10
Boquhapple Stirl 278 A3
Boraston Shrops 116 D2
Borden Kent 69 G11
Borden W Sussex 34 C4
Border Cumb 238 G5
Bordesley Green W Midlands 134 F2
Bordley N Yorks 213 G8
Bordon Hants 49 F10
Bordon Camp Hants 49 F9
Boreham Essex 88 D3
Boreham Wilts 45 E11
Boreham Street E Sussex 37 E11
Borehamwood Herts 85 F11
Boreland Dumf/Gal 236 C5
Boreland Dumf/Gal 248 E5
Boreland Fife 280 C6
Boreland Stirl 285 D9
Boreland of Southwick Dumf/Gal 237 C11
Borestone Stirl 278 C5
Borgh W Isles 296 C5
Borgh W Isles 297 L2
Borghasdal W Isles 296 C6
Borghastan W Isles 304 D4
Borgie H'land 308 D6
Borgue Dumf/Gal 237 E8
Borgue H'land 311 G5
Borley Essex 106 C6
Borley Green Essex 106 C6
Borley Green Suffolk 125 E9
Bornais W Isles 297 J3
Borneskeitaig H'land 298 B3
Borness Dumf/Gal 237 E8
Borough Green Kent 52 B6
Boroughbridge N Yorks 215 F7
Borras Wrex 166 E4
Borreraig H'land 296 F7
Borrobol Lodge H'land 311 G2
Borrodale H'land 297 G7
Borrohill Aberds 303 D9
Borrowash Derby 153 C8
Borrowby N Yorks 215 B8
Borrowby N Yorks 226 B5
Borrowcop Hill Staffs 134 B2
Borrowfield Aberds 293 D10
Borrowston H'land 310 E7
Borrowstoun Mains Falk 279 E10
Borstal Medway 69 F8
Borth = Y Borth Ceredig'n 128 E2
Borthwick Midloth 271 D7
Borthwickbrae Scot Borders 261 G10
Borthwickshiels Scot Borders 261 F10
Borthwnog Gwyn 146 F3
Borth-y-Gest Gwyn 145 B11
Borve H'land 298 E4
Borve Lodge W Isles 305 J2
Borwick Lancs 211 E10
Borwick Rails Cumb 210 D3
Bosavern Cornw'l 1 C3
Bosbury Heref'd 98 C3
Boscarne Cornw'l 5 B10
Boscastle Cornw'l 11 C7
Boscombe Bournem'th 19 C8
Boscombe Wilts 47 F8
Boscomoor Staffs 151 G8
Boscoppa Cornw'l 5 E10
Boscreege Cornw'l 2 C3
Bosham W Sussex 34 G4
Bosherston Pembs 73 G7
Boskenna Cornw'l 1 E4
Bosleake Cornw'l 4 G3
Bosley Ches 168 B6
Bossall N Yorks 216 G4
Bossiney Cornw'l 11 D7
Bossingham Kent 55 D7
Bossington Hants 47 G10
Bossington Kent 55 B8
Bossington Som'set 41 D11
Bostadh W Isles 304 D3
Bostock Green Ches 167 B11
Boston Lincs 174 G4
Boston Long Hedges Lincs 174 F4
Boston Spa W Yorks 206 D4
Boswarthen Cornw'l 1 C4
Boswinger Cornw'l 5 G9
Botallack Cornw'l 1 C3
Botany Bay Bristol 60 D5
Botany Bay London 86 F3
Botany Bay Monmouths 79 E8
Botcherby Cumb 239 F10
Botcheston Leics 135 B9
Botley Oxon 83 D7
Botesdale Suffolk 125 B10
Bothal Northum 252 F6
Bothampstead W Berks 64 D4
Bothamsall Notts 187 G11
Bothel Cumb 229 D9
Bothenhampton Dorset 16 C5
Bothwell S Lanarks 268 D4
Bothy H'land 290 F4
Botley Bucks 85 E7
Botley Hants 33 E8
Botloe's Green Glos 98 F4
Botolph Bridge Peterboro 138 D3
Botolph Claydon Bucks 102 G4
Botolphs W Sussex 35 F11
Botolph's Bridge Kent 54 G6
Bottacks H'land 300 C4
Botternell Cornw'l 11 G11
Bottesford Leics 154 B6
Bottesford N Lincs 200 F2
Bottisham Cambs 123 E10
Bottlesford Wilts 46 B6
Bottom Boat W Yorks 197 C11
Bottom House Staffs 169 E8
Bottom of Hutton Lancs 194 B3
Bottom o'th'Moor Gtr Man 195 E7
Bottomcraig Fife 287 E7
Bottomley W Yorks 196 C2
Bottoms Cornw'l 1 E3
Botton N Yorks 226 E3
Botusfleming Cornw'l 7 C8
Botwnnog Gwyn 144 C5
Bough Beech Kent 52 D3
Boughrood Powys 96 D2
Boughrood Brest Powys 96 D2
Boughspring Glos 79 F9
Boughton Norfolk 140 C4
Boughton Northants 120 D5

Boughton Notts 171 B11
Boughton Aluph Kent 54 D4
Boughton Corner Kent 54 D4
Boughton End Beds 103 D9
Boughton Green Kent 53 C9
Boughton Heath Ches 166 B6
Boughton Hill Kent 54 B5
Boughton Lees Kent 54 D4
Boughton Malherbe Kent 53 D11
Boughton Monchelsea Kent 53 C9
Boughton Street Kent 54 B5
Boulby Redcar/Clevel'd 226 B5
Boulder Clough W Yorks 196 C4
Bouldnor I/Wight 20 D3
Bouldon Shrops 131 F10
Boulge Suffolk 126 G5
Boulmer Northum 265 G7
Boulsdon Glos 98 G4
Boultenstone Aberds 292 B6
Boultham Moor Lincs 173 B7
Boulton Derby C 153 C7
Boundary Derby 152 F6
Boundary Staffs 169 G7
Boundstone Surrey 49 E10
Bourn Cambs 122 F6
Bournbrook W Midlands 133 G10
Bourne Lincs 155 E11
Bourne End Beds 103 C9
Bourne End Beds 85 D8
Bourne End Beds 121 E10
Bourne End Bucks 65 B11
Bournemouth Bournem'th 19 C7
Bournemouth International Airport Dorset 19 B8
Bournes Green Glos 80 E6
Bournes Green Southend 70 B2
Bournheath Worcs 117 C8
Bournmoor Durham 243 G8
Bournside Glos 99 G8
Bournstream Glos 80 G3
Bournville W Midlands 133 G10
Bourton Bucks 102 E4
Bourton Dorset 45 G9
Bourton N Som'set 59 G11
Bourton Oxon 63 B8
Bourton Shrops 131 D11
Bourton Wilts 62 G4
Bourton on Dunsmore Warwick 119 C8
Bourton on the Hill Glos 100 E3
Bourton-on-the-Water Glos 100 G3
Bourtreehill N Ayrs 257 B8
Bousd Arg/Bute 288 C4
Bousta Shetl'd 315 H4
Boustead Hill Cumb 239 F7
Bouth Cumb 210 B6
Bouthwaite N Yorks 214 E2
Bouts Worcs 117 F10
Bovain Stirl 285 D9
Boveney Bucks 66 D2
Boveridge Dorset 31 E9
Boverton V/Glam 58 F3
Bovey Tracey Devon 14 F2
Bovingdon Herts 85 E8
Bovingdon Green Bucks 65 B10
Bovingdon Green Herts 85 E8
Bovinger Essex 87 D8
Bovington Camp Dorset 18 D2
Bow Scot Borders 271 G9
Bow Cumb 239 F8
Bow Devon 26 G2
Bow London 67 C11
Bow Orkney 313 J4
Bow Oxon 82 G4
Bow Brickhill M/Keynes 103 E8
Bow Broom S Yorks 187 B7
Bow of Fife Fife 287 F7
Bow Street Ceredig'n 128 G2
Bow Street Norfolk 141 D10
Bowbank Durham 232 G4
Bowbeck Suffolk 125 B8
Bowbridge Glos 80 E5
Bowbrook Shrops 149 G9
Bowburn Durham 234 D2
Bowcombe I/Wight 20 D5
Bowd Devon 15 C8
Bowden Scot Borders 262 C3
Bowden Devon 8 F6
Bowden Derra Cornw'l 11 E11
Bowden Hill Wilts 62 F2
Bowdon Gtr Man 184 D3
Bower H'land 310 C6
Bower Ashton Bristol 60 E5
Bower Hinton Som'set 29 D7
Bower House Tye Suffolk 107 C9
Bowerchalke Wilts 31 C8
Bowerhill Wilts 62 G2
Bowermadden H'land 310 C6
Bowers Staffs 150 B6
Bowers Gifford Essex 69 B9
Bowershall Fife 279 C11
Bowertower H'land 310 C6
Bowes Durham 223 C9
Bowe's Gate Ches 167 D9
Bowes Park London 86 G4
Bowgreave Lancs 202 E5
Bowgreen Gtr Man 184 D3
Bowhill Scot Borders 261 D10
Bowhill Fife 280 B4
Bowhouse Dumf/Gal 238 D2
Bowhousebog N Lanarks 269 D7
Bowithick Cornw'l 11 E9
Bowker's Green Lancs 194 G2
Bowland Bridge Cumb 211 B8
Bowlee Gtr Man 195 F10
Bowlees Durham 232 F4
Bowley Heref'd 115 G10
Bowley Town Heref'd 115 G10
Bowlhead Green Surrey 50 F2
Bowling W Dunb 277 G8
Bowling W Yorks 205 G9
Bowling Alley Hants 49 D9
Bowling Bank Wrex 166 F6
Bowling Green Cornw'l 12 G3
Bowling Green Worcs 116 G6
Bowlish Som'set 44 E6
Bowmanstead Cumb 220 F6
Bowmore Arg/Bute 254 B4
Bowness-on-Solway Cumb 238 E6
Bowness-on-Windermere Cumb 221 F8
Bowood House and Gardens, Calne Wilts 62 E3
Bowrie-fauld Angus 287 C9
Bowring Park Mersey 182 D6
Bowscale Cumb 230 E3
Bowsden Northum 273 G9
Bowside Lodge H'land 310 C2
Bowston Cumb 221 F9
Bowthorpe Norfolk 142 B3
Box Glos 80 E5
Box Wilts 61 F10
Box End Beds 103 B10
Box Hill Surrey 51 C7
Box Hill Wilts 61 F10
Boxbush Glos 98 G3
Boxbush Glos 80 C2
Boxford Suffolk 107 C9
Boxford W Berks 64 E2
Boxgrove W Sussex 34 F6
Boxley Kent 53 B9
Boxmoor Herts 85 D8
Box's Shop Cornw'l 24 G2
Boxted Essex 107 E9
Boxted Essex 107 E10
Boxted Suffolk 124 G6
Boxted Cross Essex 107 E10
Boxwell Glos 80 G4
Boxworth Cambs 122 E6
Boxworth End Cambs 123 D7
Boyden End Suffolk 124 F4
Boyden Gate Kent 71 F8
Boyland Common Norfolk 141 G11
Boylestone Derby 152 B3
Boyndie Aberds 302 C6
Boynton ER Yorks 218 F2
Boys Hill Dorset 29 E11
Boys Village V/Glam 58 F4
Boysack Angus 287 C10
Boysack Angus 287 C9
Boythorpe Derby 170 B5
Boyton Cornw'l 12 C2
Boyton Suffolk 109 B7
Boyton Wilts 46 F3
Boyton Cross Essex 87 D11
Boyton End Essex 106 E2
Boyton End Suffolk 106 C4
Bozeat Northants 121 F8
Braaid I/Man 192 E4
Braal Castle H'land 310 C5
Brabling Green Suffolk 126 E5
Brabourne Kent 54 E6
Brabourne Lees Kent 54 E5
Brabster H'land 310 C7
Bracadale H'land 294 B5
Bracara H'land 295 F9
Braceborough Lincs 155 G11
Bracebridge Lincs 173 B7
Bracebridge Heath Lincs 173 B7
Braceby Lincs 155 B10
Bracewell Lancs 204 D3
Bracken Hall W Yorks 197 D7
Bracken Hill W Yorks 197 C7
Bracken Park W Yorks 206 E3
Brackenber Cumb 222 B4
Brackenfield Derby 170 D5
Brackenhill W Yorks 198 D2
Brackenlands Cumb 229 B11
Brackenthwaite Cumb 229 G9
Brackenthwaite Cumb 229 B11
Brackenthwaite N Yorks 205 C11
Bracklamore Aberds 303 D8
Bracklesham W Sussex 22 D4
Brackletter H'land 290 E3
Brackley Arg/Bute 255 C8
Brackley Northants 101 D11
Brackley Hatch Northants 102 C3
Brackloch H'land 307 G6
Bracknell Brackn'l 65 F11
Braco Perth/Kinr 286 G2
Braco Castle Perth/Kinr 286 F2
Braco Park Aberds 303 C9
Bracobrae Moray 302 D5
Bracon N Lincs 199 F9
Bracon Ash Norfolk 142 D3
Bracorina H'land 295 F9
Bradbourne Derby 170 E2
Bradbury Durham 234 F2
Bradda I/Man 192 F2
Bradden Northants 102 B2
Braddock Cornw'l 6 C3
Braddocks Hay Staffs 168 D5
Bradeley Stoke 168 E5
Bradenham Bucks 84 F4
Bradenham Norfolk 141 B8
Bradenstoke Wilts 62 D4
Brades Village W Midlands 133 E9
Bradfield Devon 27 F9
Bradfield Essex 108 E2
Bradfield Norfolk 160 C5
Bradfield W Berks 64 E5
Bradfield Combust Suffolk 125 F7
Bradfield Green Ches 167 D11
Bradfield Heath Essex 108 F2
Bradfield St. Clare Suffolk 125 F8
Bradfield St. George Suffolk 125 F8
Bradford Cornw'l 11 F8
Bradford Devon 24 F6
Bradford Gtr Man 184 B5
Bradford W Yorks 205 G9
Bradford Abbas Dorset 29 E9
Bradford Cathedral W Yorks 205 G9
Bradford Industrial Museum W Yorks 205 F9
Bradford Leigh Wilts 61 G10
Bradford on Avon Wilts 61 G10
Bradford on Tone Som'set 27 C11
Bradford Peverell Dorset 17 C9
Bradgate S Yorks 186 C6
Bradiford Devon 40 G5
Brading I/Wight 21 D8
Bradley Ches 183 F8
Bradley Derby 170 F2
Bradley Glos 80 G2
Bradley Hants 48 E6
Bradley NE Lincs 201 F8
Bradley Staffs 151 F7
Bradley W Midlands 133 D9
Bradley Wrex 166 E4
Bradley W Yorks 197 C7
Bradley Cross Som'set 44 C3
Bradley Fold Gtr Man 195 F9
Bradley Green Ches 167 F8
Bradley Green Som'set 43 F9
Bradley Green Warwick 134 C5
Bradley Green Worcs 117 E9
Bradley in the Moors Staffs 169 G9
Bradley Mills W Yorks 197 D7
Bradley Mount Ches 184 F6
Bradley Stoke S Glos 60 C6
Bradlow Heref'd 98 D4
Bradmore Notts 153 C11
Bradmore W Midlands 133 D7
Bradney Som'set 43 F10
Bradninch Devon 27 G7
Bradnop Staffs 169 D8
Bradpole Dorset 16 C5
Bradshaw Gtr Man 195 E8
Bradshaw W Yorks 196 E5
Bradshaw W Yorks 205 G7
Bradstone Devon 12 E3
Bradville M/Keynes 102 C6
Bradwall Green Ches 168 C3
Bradway S Yorks 186 E4
Bradwell Derby 185 E11
Bradwell Devon 40 E3
Bradwell Essex 106 G6
Bradwell M/Keynes 102 D6
Bradwell Norfolk 143 C10
Bradwell Staffs 168 F4
Bradwell Hills Derby 185 E11
Bradwell on Sea Essex 89 D8
Bradwell Waterside Essex 89 D7
Bradworthy Devon 24 E4
Brae Dumf/Gal 237 B10
Brae H'land 307 L3
Brae H'land 309 J4
Brae Shetl'd 314 G5
Brae of Achnahaird H'land 307 H5
Brae of Boquhapple Stirl 285 G10
Brae Roy Lodge H'land 290 D5
Braeantra H'land 300 B5
Braebuster Orkney 313 H6
Braedownie Angus 292 F4
Braeface Falk 278 E5
Braefield H'land 300 F4
Braefindon H'land 300 D6
Braegrum Perth/Kinr 286 E4
Braehead Dumf/Gal 236 D6
Braehead Orkney 312 D5
Braehead Orkney 313 H6
Braehead S Ayrs 257 E8
Braehead Stirl 278 C6
Braehead S Lanarks 259 C8
Braehead S Lanarks 269 E9
Braehead of Lunan Angus 287 B10
Braehoulland Shetl'd 314 F4
Braehour H'land 310 D4
Braehungie H'land 310 F5
Braeintra H'land 295 B10
Braelangwell Lodge H'land 309 K5
Braemar Aberds 292 D3
Braemore H'land 299 B11
Braemore H'land 310 F4
Braepark C/Edinb 280 F3
Braes of Enzie Moray 302 D3
Braes of Ullapool H'land 307 K6
Braeside Inverci 276 F4
Braeswick Orkney 312 E7
Braevallich Arg/Bute 275 C10
Braewick Shetl'd 314 F4
Braewick Shetl'd 315 H5
Brafferton D'lington 233 G11
Brafferton N Yorks 215 E8
Brafield-on-the-Green Northants 120 F6
Bragar W Isles 304 D4
Bragbury End Herts 104 G5
Bragleenmore Arg/Bute 289 G11
Braichmelyn Gwyn 163 B10
Braid C/Edinb 280 G4
Braidfauld Glasg C 268 C2
Braidley N Yorks 213 D10
Braids Arg/Bute 255 C8
Braidwood S Lanarks 269 F7
Braigh Chalasaigh W Isles 296 D5
Braigo Arg/Bute 274 G3
Brailsford Derby 170 G3
Brailsford Green Derby 170 G2
Braingortan Arg/Bute 275 F11
Brain's Green Glos 79 D11
Braintree Essex 106 G5
Braiseworth Suffolk 126 C2
Braishfield Hants 32 B5
Braithwaite Cumb 229 G10
Braithwaite S Yorks 198 E6
Braithwaite W Yorks 204 E6
Braithwell S Yorks 187 B8
Brakefield Green Norfolk 141 B10
Bramber W Sussex 35 E11
Brambledown Kent 70 E3
Brambridge Hants 33 C7
Bramcote Notts 153 B10
Bramcote Camp Warwick 135 F8
Bramdean Hants 33 B10
Bramelane N Yorks 205 C10
Bramerton Norfolk 142 C5
Bramfield Herts 86 B3
Bramfield Suffolk 127 C8
Bramford Suffolk 108 B2
Bramford W Midlands 133 E8
Bramhall Gtr Man 184 D5
Bramhall Moor Gtr Man 184 D6
Bramhall Park Gtr Man 184 D5
Bramham W Yorks 206 E4
Bramhope W Yorks 205 E11
Bramley Hants 48 B6
Bramley Surrey 50 D4
Bramley S Yorks 187 C7
Bramley W Yorks 205 G10
Bramley Corner Hants 48 B6
Bramley Green Hants 49 B7
Bramley Head N Yorks 205 B9
Bramley Vale Derby 171 B7
Bramling Kent 55 B8
Brampford Speke Devon 14 B4
Brampton Cambs 122 C4
Brampton Cumb 231 G9
Brampton Cumb 240 E2
Brampton Derby 186 F5
Brampton Heref'd 97 D8
Brampton Lincs 188 F4
Brampton Norfolk 160 E4
Brampton Suffolk 143 G8
Brampton S Yorks 198 G2
Brampton Abbotts Heref'd 98 F2
Brampton Ash Northants 136 F5
Brampton Bryan Heref'd 115 C7
Brampton en le Morthen S Yorks 187 D7
Brampton Park Cambs 122 C4
Brampton Park Cambs 122 D4
Brampton Street Suffolk 143 G8
Bramshall Staffs 151 C11
Bramshaw Hants 32 D3
Bramshill Hants 65 G8
Bramshott Hants 49 G10
Bramshott Vale Hants 49 G10
Bramwell Som'set 28 B6
Bran End Essex 106 F3
Branatwatt Shetl'd 315 H4
Branault H'land 289 C7
Branbridges Kent 53 D7
Brancaster Norfolk 176 E3
Brancaster Staithe Norfolk 176 E3
Brancepeth Durham 233 D10
Branch End Northum 242 E3
Branchill Moray 301 D10
Brand End Lincs 174 F5
Brand Green Glos 98 F4
Brand Green Heref'd 98 C5
Branderburgh Moray 302 B2
Brandesburton ER Yorks 209 D8
Brandeston Suffolk 126 E5
Brandhill Shrops 115 B8
Brandingill Cumb 229 F8
Brandis Corner Devon 24 G6
Brandish Street Som'set 42 D2
Brandiston Norfolk 160 E2
Brandon Durham 233 C10
Brandon Lincs 172 F6
Brandon Northum 264 F2
Brandon Suffolk 140 F5
Brandon Warwick 119 B8
Brandon Bank Norfolk 140 F2
Brandon Creek Norfolk 140 E2
Brandon Parva Norfolk 141 B11
Brands Hatch Motor Racing Circuit Kent 68 G5
Brands Hill Slough 66 D4
Brandsby N Yorks 215 E11
Brandwood End W Midlands 117 B11
Brandy Wharf Lincs 189 B8
Brandyquoy Orkney 313 J5
Brane Cornw'l 1 D4
Branksome D'lington 224 B5
Branksome Poole 19 C7
Branksome Park Poole 19 C7
Bransbury Hants 48 E2
Bransby Lincs 188 F5
Branscombe Devon 15 D9
Bransford Worcs 116 G5
Bransgore Hants 19 B9
Branshill Clack 279 C7
Bransholme Kingston/Hull 209 G8
Bransley Shrops 116 B3
Branson's Cross Worcs 117 C11
Branston Leics 154 D6
Branston Lincs 173 B8
Branston Staffs 152 E4
Branston Booths Lincs 173 B9
Branstone I/Wight 21 E7
Bransty Cumb 219 B9
Brant Broughton Lincs 172 E6
Brantham Suffolk 108 D2
Branthwaite Cumb 229 G7
Branthwaite Cumb 229 D11
Branthwaite Edge Cumb 229 G7
Brantingham ER Yorks 200 B2
Branton Northum 264 F2
Branton S Yorks 198 G6
Branton Green N Yorks 215 G8
Branxholm Park Scot Borders 261 G11
Branxholme Scot Borders 261 G11
Branxton Northum 263 B9
Brascote Leics 135 C8
Brassey Green Ches 167 C8
Brasside Durham 233 B11
Brassington Derby 170 E2
Brassknocker Bath/NE Som'set 61 G9
Brasted Kent 52 C3
Brasted Chart Kent 52 C3
Brathens Aberds 293 D8
Bratoft Lincs 175 B7
Bratoft Corner Lincs 175 C7
Brattle Kent 54 G2
Brattleby Lincs 188 E6
Bratton Som'set 42 D2
Bratton Wilts 46 C2
Bratton Clovelly Devon 12 C5
Bratton Fleming Devon 40 F6
Bratton Seymour Som'set 29 B11
Braughing Herts 105 F7
Braughing Friars Herts 105 G8
Braulen Lodge H'land 300 F2
Brauncewell Lincs 173 E8
Braunston Northants 119 D10
Braunstone Town Leics 135 C11
Braunston-in-Rutland Rutl'd 136 B6
Braunton Devon 40 F3
Brawby N Yorks 216 D4
Brawl H'land 310 C2
Brawlbin H'land 310 D4
Bray Windsor 66 D2
Bray Shop Cornw'l 12 G2
Bray Wick Windsor 65 D11
Braybrooke Northants 136 G5
Braydon Side Wilts 62 B4
Brayford Devon 41 G7
Brayfordhill Devon 41 G7
Brays Grove Essex 87 D7
Bray's Hill E Sussex 37 E11
Braystones Cumb 219 D10
Braythorn N Yorks 205 D10
Brayton N Yorks 207 G8
Braytown Dorset 18 D2
Braywoodside Windsor 65 D11
Brazacott Cornw'l 11 C11
Brea Cornw'l 4 G3
Breach Kent 55 D7
Breach Kent 69 F10
Breach W Sussex 34 F3
Breach Hill Bath/NE Som'set 44 B4
Breachacha Castle Arg/Bute 288 D3
Breachwood Green Herts 104 G2
Breacleit W Isles 304 E3
Bread Street Glos 80 D4
Breaden Heath Shrops 149 B8
Breadsall Derby 153 B7
Breadsall Hilltop Derby C 153 B7
Breadstone Glos 80 E2
Breage Cornw'l 2 D4
Breakachy H'land 300 E4
Bream Glos 79 D10
Breamore Hants 31 D11
Bream's Meend Glos 79 D9
Brean Som'set 43 B9
Breanais W Isles 304 F1
Brearley W Yorks 196 B4
Brearton N Yorks 214 G6
Breascleit W Isles 304 E4
Breaston Derby 153 C9
Brechfa Carms 93 E10
Brechin Angus 293 G7
Breck of Cruan Orkney 312 G4
Breckan Orkney 313 H3
Breckles Norfolk 141 E9
Breckrey H'land 298 C5
Brecks S Yorks 187 C7
Brecon = Aberhonddu Powys 95 F10
Brecon Beacons Mountain Centre Powys 95 F9
Bredbury Gtr Man 184 C6
Bredbury Green Gtr Man 184 C6
Brede E Sussex 38 D4
Bredenbury Heref'd 116 F2
Bredfield Suffolk 126 G5
Bredgar Kent 69 G11
Bredhurst Kent 69 G9
Bredicot Worcs 117 G8
Bredon Worcs 99 D8
Bredon's Hardick Worcs 99 D8
Bredon's Norton Worcs 99 D8
Bredwardine Heref'd 96 B6
Breedon on the Hill Leics 153 E8
Breibhig W Isles 297 M2
Breibhig W Isles 304 E6
Breich W Loth 269 C9
Breightmet Gtr Man 195 F8
Breighton ER Yorks 207 G10
Breinton Common Heref'd 97 D9
Breiwick Shetl'd 315 J6
Brelston Green Heref'd 97 G11
Bremhill Wilts 62 E3
Bremhill Wick Wilts 62 E3
Bremirehoull Shetl'd 315 L6
Brenachoile Lodge Stirl 285 G8
Brenchley Kent 53 E7
Brenchoillie Arg/Bute 284 G4
Brendon Devon 24 E5
Brendon Devon 41 D9
Brenkley Tyne/Wear 242 B6
Brent Cross London 67 B8
Brent Eleigh Suffolk 107 B8
Brent Knoll Som'set 43 C10
Brent Mill Devon 8 D3
Brent Pelham Herts 105 E8
Brentford London 67 D7
Brentingby Leics 154 F5
Brentry Bristol 60 D5
Brentwood Essex 87 G10
Brenzett Kent 39 B7
Brenzett Green Kent 39 B8
Brereton Staffs 151 F11
Brereton Cross Staffs 151 F11
Brereton Green Ches 168 C3
Brereton Heath Ches 168 C4
Breretonhill Staffs 151 F11
Bressingham Norfolk 141 G11
Bressingham Common Norfolk 141 G11
Bretby Derby 152 E5
Bretford Warwick 119 B8
Bretforton Worcs 99 C11
Bretherton Lancs 194 C3
Brettabister Shetl'd 315 H6
Brettenham Norfolk 141 G8
Brettenham Suffolk 125 G9
Bretton Derby 186 F2
Bretton Flints 166 C5
Bretton Peterbro 138 C3
Brewer Street Surrey 51 C10
Brewer's End Essex 105 G11
Brewers Green Norfolk 142 G2
Brewlands Bridge Angus 292 G3
Brewood Staffs 133 B7
Briach Moray 301 D10
Briantspuddle Dorset 18 C2
Brick End Essex 105 F11
Brick Houses S Yorks 186 E4
Brickendon Herts 86 D4
Bricket Wood Herts 85 E10
Brickfields Worcs 117 F7
Brickhill Beds 121 G11
Brickkiln Green Essex 106 E4
Bricklehampton Worcs 99 C9
Bride I/Man 192 B5
Bridekirk Cumb 229 E8
Bridell Pembs 92 C3
Bridestowe Devon 12 D6
Brideswell Aberds 302 F5
Bridford Devon 14 D2
Bridfordmills Devon 14 D2
Bridge Cornw'l 4 G3
Bridge Dorset 30 E3
Bridge Kent 55 B7
Bridge End C/Edinb 280 G5
Bridge End Cumb 230 B3
Bridge End Durham 232 D6
Bridge End Devon 8 F3
Bridge End Devon 15 D7
Bridge End Essex 106 E3
Bridge End Flints 166 D4
Bridge End Heref'd 98 B2
Bridge End Lincs 156 B2
Bridge End Northum 241 E10
Bridge End Northum 241 D10
Bridge End Oxon 83 G9
Bridge End Surrey 50 B5
Bridge End Warwick 118 E5
Bridge End Worcs 98 E6
Bridge Green Essex 105 D9
Bridge Green Norfolk 142 G2
Bridge Hewick N Yorks 214 E6
Bridge Ho Arg/Bute 254 B4
Bridge of Alford Aberds 293 B7
Bridge of Allan Stirl 278 B5
Bridge of Avon Moray 301 F11
Bridge of Avon Moray 301 G11
Bridge of Awe Arg/Bute 284 E4
Bridge of Balgie Perth/Kinr 285 C9
Bridge of Cally Perth/Kinr 286 B5
Bridge of Canny Aberds 293 D8
Bridge of Craigisla Angus 286 B6
Bridge of Dee Dumf/Gal 237 D9
Bridge of Don Aberd C 293 B11
Bridge of Dun Angus 287 B10
Bridge of Dye Aberds 293 E8
Bridge of Earn Perth/Kinr 286 F5
Bridge of Ericht Perth/Kinr 285 B9
Bridge of Feugh Aberds 293 D9
Bridge of Forss H'land 310 C4
Bridge of Gairn Aberds 292 D5
Bridge of Gaur Perth/Kinr 285 B9
Bridge of Lyon Perth/Kinr 285 C11
Bridge of Muchalls Aberds 293 D10
Bridge of Muick Aberds 292 D5
Bridge of Oich H'land 290 C5
Bridge of Orchy Arg/Bute 284 D6
Bridge of Waith Orkney 312 G3
Bridge of Walls Shetl'd 315 H4
Bridge of Weir Renf 267 B7
Bridge Reeve Devon 25 E11
Bridge Sollars Heref'd 97 C8
Bridge Street Suffolk 107 B7
Bridge Trafford Ches 183 G7
Bridge-End Shetl'd 315 K5
Bridgefield Derby 185 C8
Bridgefoot Aberds 292 C6
Bridgefoot Angus 287 D7
Bridgefoot Cumb 229 F7
Bridgehampton Som'set 29 C9
Bridgehill Durham 242 G3
Bridgehouse Gate N Yorks 214 F3
Bridgemary Hants 33 G9
Bridgemont Derby 185 E8
Bridgend Aberds 293 B7
Bridgend Aberds 302 F5
Bridgend Angus 293 G7
Bridgend Arg/Bute 255 D8
Bridgend Arg/Bute 274 G4
Bridgend Arg/Bute 275 D9
Bridgend Bridg 58 D2
Bridgend Cumb 221 C8
Bridgend Cornw'l 6 D2
Bridgend Devon 7 F11
Bridgend Fife 287 F7
Bridgend Glos 80 E4
Bridgend H'land 300 D3
Bridgend Inverci 276 F5
Bridgend Moray 302 F3
Bridgend N Lanarks 278 G3
Bridgend Pembs 92 B3
Bridgend W Loth 279 F10
Bridgend of Lintrathen Angus 286 B6
Bridgeness Falk 279 E10
Bridgerule Devon 24 G3
Bridges Cornw'l 5 D10
Bridges Shrops 131 D7
Bridgeton Glasg C 268 C2
Bridgetown Cornw'l 12 D2
Bridgetown Devon 8 C6
Bridgetown Som'set 42 G2
Bridgeyate S Glos 61 E7
Bridgham Norfolk 141 F9
Bridgnorth Shrops 132 E4
Bridgnorth Cliff Railway Shrops 132 E4
Bridgtown Staffs 133 B9
Bridgwater Som'set 43 F9
Bridlington ER Yorks 218 F3
Bridport Dorset 16 C5
Bridstow Heref'd 97 G11
Briercliffe Lancs 204 E2
Brierfield Lancs 204 F3
Brierholme Carr S Yorks 199 E7
Brierley Glos 79 B10
Brierley S Yorks 198 E2
Brierley Gap S Yorks 198 E2
Brierley Hill W Midlands 133 F8
Brierton Hartlep'l 234 F5
Briery Cumb 229 G11
Briery Hill Bl Gwent 77 D11
Briestfield W Yorks 197 D8
Brig o'Turk Stirl 285 G9
Brigg N Lincs 200 F4
Briggate Norfolk 160 D6
Briggswath N Yorks 227 D7
Brigham Cumb 229 E7
Brigham Cumb 229 G11
Brigham ER Yorks 209 C7
Brighouse W Yorks 196 C6
Brighstone I/Wight 20 E4
Brightgate Derby 170 D3
Brighthampton Oxon 82 E5
Brightholmlee S Yorks 186 C3
Brightley Devon 13 B7
Brightling E Sussex 37 C11
Brightlingsea Essex 89 B9
Brighton Brighton/Hove 36 G4
Brighton Cornw'l 5 E8
Brighton Hill Hants 48 D6
Brighton le Sands Mersey 182 B4
Brighton Museum and Art Gallery Brighton/Hove 36 G4
Brighton Racecourse Brighton/Hove 36 F4
Brighton Sea Life Centre Brighton/Hove 36 G4
Brightons Falk 279 F8
Brightor Cornw'l 7 C7
Brightside S Yorks 186 D5
Brightwalton W Berks 64 D2
Brightwalton Green W Berks 64 D2
Brightwalton Holt W Berks 64 D2
Brightwell Suffolk 108 C4
Brightwell Baldwin Oxon 83 G11
Brightwell-cum-Sotwell Oxon 83 G9
Briglands Perth/Kinr 279 B10
Brigmarston Wilts 47 D7
Brignall Durham 223 C11
Brignam Park N Yorks 216 C6
Brigsley NE Lincs 201 G9
Brigsteer Cumb 211 B9
Brigstock Northants 137 F8
Brill Bucks 83 C11
Brill Cornw'l 2 D6
Brilley Heref'd 96 B5
Brimaston Pembs 91 F8
Brimfield Heref'd 115 D10
Brimington Derby 186 G6
Brimington Common Derby 186 G6
Brimley Devon 13 F11
Brimpsfield Glos 80 C6
Brimpton W Berks 64 G5
Brimpton Common W Berks 64 G5
Brims Orkney 313 K3
Brims Castle H'land 310 B4
Brimscombe Glos 80 E5
Brimsdown London 86 F5
Brimstage Mersey 182 E4
Brinacory H'land 295 F9
Brincliffe S Yorks 186 D4
Brind ER Yorks 207 G10
Brindister Shetl'd 315 H4
Brindister Shetl'd 315 K6
Brindle Lancs 194 C5
Brindle Heath Gtr Man 184 B4
Brindley Ches 167 E9
Brindley Ford Stoke 168 E5
Brineton Staffs 150 G6
Bringhurst Leics 136 E6
Brington Cambs 121 B11
Brinian Orkney 312 F5
Briningham Norfolk 159 C10
Brinkhill Lincs 190 G5
Brinkley Cambs 124 F2
Brinkley Notts 172 E2
Brinkley Hill Heref'd 97 E11
Brinklow M/Keynes 103 D8
Brinklow Warwick 119 B8
Brinkworth Wilts 62 C4
Brinmore H'land 300 G6
Brinnington Gtr Man 184 C6
Brinscall Lancs 194 C6
Brinscombe Som'set 44 C2
Brinsea N Som'set 60 G2
Brinsley Notts 171 F7
Brinsop Heref'd 97 C8
Brinsworth S Yorks 186 D6
Brinton Norfolk 159 B10
Brisco Cumb 239 G10
Brisley Norfolk 159 E9
Brislington Bristol 60 E6
Brissenden Green Kent 54 F2
Brister End Dorset 29 E9
Bristnall Fields W Midlands 133 F9
Bristol Bristol 60 E6
Bristol City Museum and Art Gallery Bristol 60 E5
Bristol International Airport N Som'set 60 G4
Bristol Zoo Bristol 60 E5
Briston Norfolk 159 C11
Briston Common Norfolk 159 C11
Britannia Lancs 195 C11
Britford Wilts 31 B11
Brithdir Caerph 77 E11
Brithdir Ceredig'n 92 B6
Brithdir Denbs 146 F5
Brithem Bottom Devon 27 E8
British Museum London 67 C9
Briton Ferry = Llansawel Rh Cyn Taff 76 G2
Britwell Salome Oxon 83 G11
Brixham Torbay 9 D8
Brixton Devon 7 E11
Brixton London 67 D10
Brixton Deverill Wilts 45 F11
Brixworth Northants 120 C4
Brize Norton Oxon 82 D4
Broad Alley Worcs 117 D7
Broad Blunsdon Swindon 81 G11
Broad Campden Glos 100 D3
Broad Carr W Yorks 196 D5
Broad Chalke Wilts 31 B8
Broad Clough Lancs 195 C11
Broad Colney Herts 85 E11
Broad Ford Kent 53 F8
Broad Green Beds 103 C9
Broad Green Cambs 124 F3
Broad Green Essex 105 D8
Broad Green Essex 107 G7
Broad Green Mersey 182 D6
Broad Green Suffolk 124 F5
Broad Green Suffolk 125 F11
Broad Green Suffolk 126 E2
Broad Green Worcs 116 F5
Broad Green Worcs 117 C9
Broad Haven = Aberllydan Pembs 72 C5
Broad Heath Worcs 116 E3
Broad Hill Cambs 123 B11
Broad Hinton Wilts 62 D6
Broad Laying Hants 64 G2
Broad Marston Worcs 100 B2
Broad Mead S Glos 60 C6
Broad Meadow Staffs 168 F4
Broad Oak Carms 93 G11
Broad Oak Cumb 220 G2
Broad Oak Dorset 30 E3
Broad Oak Devon 15 C7
Broad Oak E Sussex 38 C4
Broad Oak E Sussex 37 C10
Broad Oak Hants 49 C9
Broad Oak Hants 33 E7
Broad Oak Heref'd 97 G9
Broad Oak Kent 71 G7
Broad Oak Mersey 183 B8
Broad Parkham Devon 24 C5
Broad Street E Sussex 38 D5
Broad Street Kent 54 E6
Broad Street Kent 55 E7
Broad Street Kent 53 B10
Broad Street Medway 69 E9
Broad Street Suffolk 107 C9
Broad Street Wilts 46 B6
Broad Street Green Essex 88 D5
Broad Town Wilts 62 D5
Broadbottom Gtr Man 185 C7
Broadbridge W Sussex 34 F4
Broadbridge Heath W Sussex 50 G6
Broadbush Swindon 81 G11
Broadclyst Devon 14 B5
Broadfield Gtr Man 195 E10
Broadfield Inverci 276 G6
Broadfield Lancs 194 C4
Broadfield Lancs 195 B8
Broadfield Pembs 73 E10
Broadfield W Sussex 51 G9
Broadford H'land 295 C8
Broadford Surrey 50 D3
Broadford Bridge W Sussex 35 C9
Broadgrass Green Suffolk 125 E9
Broadhalgh Gtr Man 195 E11
Broadham Green Surrey 51 C11
Broadhaugh Scot Borders 249 B10
Broadhaven H'land 310 D7

390 Bro – Bur

Broadheath Gtr Man 184 D3
Broadhembury Devon 27 G9
Broadhempston Devon 8 B6
Broadholm Derby 170 F5
Broadholme Notts 188 G5
Broadland Row E Sussex 38 D4
Broadlands Devon 14 G2
Broadlane Cornw'l 4 G3
Broadlay Carms 74 D5
Broadley Gtr Man 195 D11
Broadley Moray 302 C3
Broadley Common Essex 86 D6
Broadleys Aberds 303 C8
Broadmayne Dorset 17 D10
Broadmeadows Scot Borders 261 C10
Broadmere Hants 48 D6
Broadmoor Glos 79 B10
Broadmoor Pembs 72 C4
Broadmoor Pembs 73 D9
Broadoak Dorset 16 B4
Broadoak Glos 79 C11
Broadoak Kent 70 G2
Broadoak End Herts 86 C4
Broadoak Park Gtr Man 195 G9
Broadrashes Moray 302 D4
Broadrock Glos 79 F8
Broad's Green Essex 87 C11
Broad's Green Wilts 62 F3
Broadsands Torbay 9 D7
Broadsea Aberds 303 C9
Broadshard Som'set 28 E6
Broadstairs Kent 71 F11
Broadstone Kent 53 D11
Broadstone Monmouths 79 E8
Broadstone N Ayrs 267 E7
Broadstone Poole 18 B6
Broadstone Shrops 131 F10
Broadstreet Common Newp 59 B11
Broadview Gardens, Hadlow Kent 52 D6
Broadwas Worcs 116 F5
Broadwater Herts 104 G5
Broadwater W Sussex 35 G11
Broadwater Down Kent 52 F5
Broadwaters Worcs 116 B6
Broadwath Cumb 239 F11
Broadway Carms 74 C3
Broadway Oxon 64 B3
Broadway Pembs 72 C5
Broadway Suffolk 127 B7
Broadway Som'set 28 D4
Broadway Som'set 44 C6
Broadway Worcs 99 D11
Broadway Pound Som'set 28 D4
Broadwell Glos 100 F4
Broadwell Glos 79 C9
Broadwell Oxon 82 E3
Broadwell Warwick 119 D9
Broadwey Dorset 17 E9
Broadwindsor Dorset 28 G6
Broadwood Kelly Devon 25 F10
Broadwoodwidger Devon 12 D4
Brobury Heref'd 96 C6
Brochel H'land 298 E5
Brochloch Dumf/Gal 246 D2
Brochroy Arg/Bute 284 D4
Brock Lancs 202 E6
Brockamin Worcs 116 G5
Brockbridge Hants 33 D10
Brockdish Norfolk 126 B4
Brockencote Worcs 117 C7
Brockenhurst Hants 32 G4
Brockford Green Suffolk 126 D2
Brockford Street Suffolk 126 D2
Brockhall Northants 120 E2
Brockhall Village Lancs 203 F10
Brockham Surrey 51 D7
Brockham End Bath/NE Som'set 61 F8
Brockhampton Glos 99 F8
Brockhampton Glos 99 G10
Brockhampton Hants 34 F2
Brockhampton Heref'd 116 F3
Brockhampton Heref'd 97 E11
Brockhampton Green Dorset 30 F2
Brockhill Scot Borders 261 E9
Brockhole -National Park Visitor Centre, Windermere Cumb 221 E7
Brockholes W Yorks 196 E6
Brockhollands Glos 79 D10
Brockhurst Derby 170 C4
Brockhurst Portsm'th 33 G10
Brockhurst Warwick 135 G9
Brocklebank Cumb 230 C2
Brocklehirst Dumf/Gal 238 C2
Brocklesby Lincs 200 E6
Brockley London 67 E11
Brockley N Som'set 60 F3
Brockley Suffolk 124 C6
Brockley Green Suffolk 106 B4
Brockley Green Suffolk 124 G6
Brockleymoor Cumb 230 D5
Brockmoor W Midlands 133 F8
Brock's Green Hants 64 G4
Brockscombe Devon 12 C5
Brockton Shrops 130 F6
Brockton Shrops 131 E11
Brockton Shrops 130 C6
Brockton Shrops 132 C4
Brockton Staffs 150 C6
Brockton Telford 150 F4
Brockweir Glos 79 E8
Brockworth Glos 80 B5
Brocton Cornw'l 5 B10
Brocton Staffs 151 F9
Brodick N Ayrs 256 B2
Brodick Castle N Ayrs 255 D11
Brodie Moray 301 D9
Brodiesord Aberds 302 C5
Brodley NE Lincs 201 F8
Brodsworth S Yorks 198 F4
Brogaig H'land 298 C4
Brogborough Beds 103 D9
Broken Cross Ches 183 G11
Broken Cross Ches 184 F5
Brokenborough Wilts 62 B2
Brokerswood Wilts 45 C10
Brokes N Yorks 224 F3
Brombil Neath P Talb 57 D9
Bromborough Mersey 182 E5
Brome Suffolk 126 B2
Brome Street Suffolk 126 B3
Bromeswell Suffolk 126 G6
Bromfield Cumb 229 B9
Bromfield Shrops 115 B9
Bromford W Midlands 134 F2
Bromham Beds 121 G10
Bromham Wilts 62 F3
Bromley Herts 105 G8
Bromley London 68 F2
Bromley London 67 C11
Bromley Shrops 132 D4
Bromley W Midlands 133 F8
Bromley Common London 68 F2
Bromley Cross Essex 107 F11
Bromley Cross Gtr Man 195 E8
Bromley Green Kent 54 F3
Bromley Heath S Glos 61 D7
Bromley Wood Staffs 152 E2
Bromlow Shrops 130 C6
Brompton Medway 69 F9
Brompton N Yorks 225 F7
Brompton N Yorks 217 C8
Brompton Shrops 131 B10
Brompton Ralph Som'set 42 G5
Brompton Regis Som'set 42 G3
Brompton-on-Swale N Yorks 224 F4
Bromsash Heref'd 98 G2
Bromsberrow Glos 98 E4
Bromsberrow Heath Glos 98 E4
Bromsgrove Worcs 117 C9
Bromstead Heath Staffs 150 F5
Bromstone Kent 71 F11
Bromyard Heref'd 116 G3
Bronaber Gwyn 146 C4
Brondesbury London 67 C8
Brondwydd Arms Carms 93 G8
Broneirion Powys 129 F10
Brongest Ceredig'n 92 B6
Brongwyn Ceredig'n 92 C5
Bronington Wrex 149 B9
Bronllys Powys 96 D2
Bronnant Ceredig'n 112 D2
Bronte Parsonage Museum, Keighley W Yorks 204 F6
Bronwydd Ceredig'n 93 C7
Bronydd Powys 96 B4
Bronygarth Shrops 148 B5
Bron-y-main Powys 148 G3
Brook Carms 74 D3
Brook Devon 12 G5
Brook Hants 32 B4
Brook Hants 32 E3
Brook I/Wight 20 E3
Brook Kent 54 E5
Brook Surrey 50 F2
Brook Surrey 50 D5
Brook Wilts 45 C11
Brook Bottom Derby 185 D7
Brook Bottom Gtr Man 196 G3
Brook End Beds 121 E11
Brook End Beds 104 B3
Brook End Cambs 121 C11
Brook End Herts 104 F6
Brook End M/Keynes 103 C8
Brook End Wilts 61 C10
Brook End Worcs 99 B7
Brook Hill Notts 153 C11
Brook Street Essex 87 G9
Brook Street Kent 54 G2
Brook Street Kent 52 D5
Brook Street W Sussex 36 B4
Brookbottoms Gtr Man 195 D9
Brooke Norfolk 142 D5
Brooke Rutl'd 136 B6
Brookeador Devon 9 B7
Brookenby Lincs 190 B2
Brookend Essex 88 D2
Brookend Glos 79 F9
Brookend Oxon 100 G6
Brookend S Glos 79 G11
Brookfield Derby 185 B8
Brookfield Glos 99 G7
Brookfield Lancs 203 G7
Brookfield Middlesbro 225 C9
Brookfield Renf 267 C8
Brookfoot W Yorks 196 C6
Brookgreen I/Wight 20 E3
Brookhampton Oxon 83 F10
Brookhampton Som'set 29 B10
Brookhill Hants 32 E3
Brookhouse Blackb'n 195 B7
Brookhouse Ches 184 F6
Brookhouse Lancs 211 G10
Brookhouse S Yorks 187 D8
Brookhouse Green Ches 168 C4
Brookhouses Derby 185 D8
Brookhouses Staffs 169 G7
Brookhurst Mersey 182 E4
Brookland Kent 39 B7
Brooklands Dumf/Gal 237 B10
Brooklands Gtr Man 184 C3
Brooklands Shrops 167 G8
Brooklands W Yorks 206 F2
Brookmans Park Herts 86 E2
Brooks Powys 130 D2
Brooks End Kent 71 F9
Brooks Green W Sussex 35 B10
Brooksby Leics 154 F3
Brookside Derby 186 G4
Brookside Telford 132 B4
Brookthorpe Glos 80 C4
Brookvale Halton 183 E8
Brookville Norfolk 140 D4
Brookwood Surrey 50 B3
Broom Beds 104 C3
Broom Cumb 231 G9
Broom E Renf 267 D10
Broom Fife 281 A7
Broom Pembs 73 D10
Broom S Yorks 186 C6
Broom Warwick 117 G11
Broom Court Warwick 117 G11
Broom Green Norfolk 159 E9
Broom Hill Bristol 60 E6
Broom Hill Dorset 31 G8
Broom Hill Durham 242 G4
Broom Hill London 68 F3
Broom Hill Medway 69 E8
Broom Hill Tyne/Wear 234 B3
Broom Hill Worcs 117 B8
Broom Street Kent 70 G4
Broombridge Stirl 278 C6
Broome Norfolk 143 E7
Broome Shrops 131 G8
Broome Worcs 117 B8
Broomedge Warrington 184 D2
Broomer's Corner W Sussex 35 C10
Broomershill W Sussex 35 D9
Broomfield Aberds 303 F9
Broomfield Cumb 230 B2
Broomfield Essex 88 C2
Broomfield Kent 71 F8
Broomfield Kent 53 C10
Broomfield Som'set 43 G8
Broomfields Shrops 149 F8
Broomfleet ER Yorks 199 B11
Broomhall Surrey 66 F3
Broomhaugh Northum 242 E2
Broomhill Bristol 60 D6
Broomhill Glasg C 267 B10
Broomhill H'land 301 G9
Broomhill Kent 55 B8
Broomhill Norfolk 140 C2
Broomhill Notts 171 F8
Broomhill Northum 253 C7
Broomhill S Yorks 198 G2
Broomholm Norfolk 160 C6
Broomhouse Glasg C 268 C3
Broomlands N Ayrs 257 C8
Broomley Northum 242 E2
Broompark Durham 233 C10
Broom's Green Heref'd 98 E4
Broomton H'land 301 B8
Broomy Hill Heref'd 97 D10
Brora H'land 311 J3
Broseley Shrops 132 C3
Broseley Wood Shrops 132 C3
Brotherhouse Bar Lincs 156 G5
Brotheridge Green Worcs 98 C6
Brotherlee Durham 232 D5
Brothertoft Lincs 174 F3
Brotherton W Yorks 198 B3
Brothybeck Cumb 230 C3
Brotton Redcar/Clevel'd 226 B3
Broubster H'land 310 C4
Brough Cumb 222 C5
Brough Derby 185 E11
Brough ER Yorks 200 B2
Brough H'land 310 B6
Brough Notts 172 D4
Brough Orkney 312 G4
Brough Orkney 313 K5
Brough Shetl'd 314 C7
Brough Shetl'd 314 F6
Brough Shetl'd 314 F7
Brough Shetl'd 314 G7
Brough Shetl'd 315 H6
Brough Shetl'd 315 J7
Brough Lodge Shetl'd 314 D7
Brough Sowerby Cumb 222 C5
Broughall Shrops 167 G9
Brougham Cumb 230 F6
Broughton Scot Borders 260 B4
Broughton Cambs 122 B5
Broughton Flints 166 C4
Broughton Hants 47 G10
Broughton Lancs 202 F6
Broughton M/Keynes 103 D7
Broughton Northants 120 B6
Broughton N Lincs 200 F3
Broughton N Yorks 204 C4
Broughton N Yorks 216 E5
Broughton Orkney 312 D5
Broughton Oxon 101 D8
Broughton V/Glam 58 E2
Broughton Astley Leics 135 E10
Broughton Beck Cumb 210 C5
Broughton Common Wilts 61 G11
Broughton Cross Cumb 229 E7
Broughton Gifford Wilts 61 G11
Broughton Green Worcs 117 E9
Broughton Hackett Worcs 117 G8
Broughton in Furness Cumb 210 B4
Broughton Mills Cumb 220 G4
Broughton Moor Cumb 229 E7
Broughton Park Gtr Man 195 G10
Broughton Poggs Oxon 82 E2
Broughtown Orkney 312 D7
Broughty Ferry Dundee C 287 D8
Browhouses Dumf/Gal 239 E7
Browland Shetl'd 315 H4
Brown Candover Hants 48 F5
Brown Edge Lancs 193 E11
Brown Edge Mersey 183 C7
Brown Edge Staffs 168 E6
Brown Heath Ches 167 C7
Brown Heath Hants 33 D8
Brown Knowl Ches 167 E7
Brown Lees Staffs 168 D5
Brown Street Suffolk 125 E11
Brownber Cumb 222 D4
Brownbread Street E Sussex 37 D11
Brownheath Shrops 149 D9
Brownhill Aberds 302 E6
Brownhill Aberds 303 E8
Brownhill Blackb'n 203 G9
Brownhill Shrops 149 E8
Brownhills Fife 287 F9
Brownhills W Midlands 133 B10
Brownieside Northum 264 E5
Browninghill Green Hants 48 B5
Brownlow Gtr Man 194 G4
Brownlow Fold Gtr Man 195 E8
Brownmuir Aberds 293 F9
Brown's Bank Ches 167 G10
Brown's Green W Midlands 133 E10
Browns Wood M/Keynes 103 D8
Brownshill Glos 80 E5
Brownshill Green W Midlands 134 G6
Brownside Lancs 204 G3
Brownsover Warwick 119 B10
Brownston Devon 8 E3
Brownstone Devon 26 F3
Browsburn N Lanarks 268 C5
Browston Green Norfolk 143 C9
Broxa N Yorks 227 G9
Broxbourne Herts 86 D5
Broxburn E Loth 282 F3
Broxburn W Loth 279 G11
Broxholme Lincs 188 F6
Broxstowe Nott'ham 171 G8
Broxted Essex 105 F11
Broxton Ches 167 E7
Broyle Side E Sussex 37 E7
Bruairnis W Isles 297 L3
Bruan H'land 310 F7
Bruar Lodge Perth/Kinr 291 F10
Brucefield Fife 280 D2
Brucehill W Dunb 277 F7
Bruchag Arg/Bute 266 D2
Bruche Warrington 183 D10
Brucklebog Aberds 293 D9
Bruera Ches 166 C6
Brù W Isles 304 D5
Bruichladdich Arg/Bute 274 G3
Bruisyard Suffolk 126 D6
Brumby N Lincs 199 F11
Brundall Norfolk 142 B6
Brundish Norfolk 143 D7
Brundish Suffolk 126 D5
Brundish Street Suffolk 126 C5
Brundon Suffolk 107 C7
Brunery H'land 289 B9
Brune's Purlieu Hants 31 D11
Brunshaw Lancs 204 G3
Brunstock Cumb 239 F10
Brunswick Park London 86 G3
Brunswick Village Tyne/Wear 242 C6
Brunt Hamersland Shetl'd 315 H6
Bruntcliffe W Yorks 197 B8
Brunthwaite W Yorks 205 D7
Bruntingthorpe Leics 136 F2
Brunton Fife 287 E7
Brunton Northum 264 E6
Brunton Wilts 47 B8
Brushes Gtr Man 185 B7
Brushfield Derby 185 G11
Brushford Som'set 25 F11
Brushford Som'set 26 B6
Bruton Som'set 45 G7
Bryan's Green Worcs 117 D7
Bryanston Dorset 30 F5
Bryant's Bottom Bucks 84 F5
Brycethin Bridg 58 C2
Brydekirk Dumf/Gal 238 C5
Brymbo Conwy 180 G4
Brymbo Wrex 166 E3
Brympton D'Evercy Som'set 29 D8
Bryn Caerph 77 F11
Bryn Ches 183 G10
Bryn Gtr Man 194 G5
Bryn Gwyn 179 G9
Bryn Heref'd 96 F6
Bryn Neath P Talb 76 G4
Bryn Rh Cyn Taff 76 D6
Bryn Shrops 130 F5
Bryn Bwbach Gwyn 146 B2
Bryn Du Angl 178 G4
Bryn Eden Gwyn 146 D4
Bryn Eglwys Gwyn 163 B10
Bryn Eisteddfod Conwy 180 F4
Bryn Gates Gtr Man 194 G5
Bryn Golau Rh Cyn Taff 58 B4
Bryn Gwynant Gwyn 163 E10
Bryn Iwan Carms 92 E6
Bryn Mawr Powys 148 F5
Bryn Rhyd-yr-Arian Conwy 164 B6
Bryn Saith Marchon Denbs 165 E9
Brynafan Ceredig'n 112 C4
Brynamman Carms 76 C2
Brynawel Caerph 77 G11
Brynberian Pembs 92 D2
Brynbryddan Rh Cyn Taff 76 G3
Bryncae Rh Cyn Taff 58 C3
Bryn-celyn Flints 181 F11
Bryn-celyn Gwyn 144 D6
Bryncir Gwyn 163 G7
Bryncoch Bridg 58 C2
Bryn-coch Rh Cyn Taff 76 F2
Bryncroes Gwyn 144 C4
Bryncrug Gwyn 128 C2
Bryndrinog Shrops 130 G5
Bryneglwys Denbs 165 F10
Brynford Flints 181 G11
Brynglas Newp 78 G4
Bryngwran Angl 178 F5
Bryngwyn Ceredig'n 128 F2
Bryngwyn Ceredig'n 92 B5
Bryngwyn Monmouths 78 D5
Bryngwyn Powys 96 B3
Bryn-henllan Pembs 91 D10
Brynhoffnant Ceredig'n 110 G6
Bryniau Denbs 181 E9
Bryning Lancs 194 B2
Brynithel Bl Gwent 78 E2
Brynmawr Bl Gwent 77 C11
Bryn-mawr Gwyn 144 C5
Brynmenyn Bridg 57 E11
Brynmill Swan 75 G10
Brynna Rh Cyn Taff 58 C3
Bryn-nantllech Conwy 164 B6
Bryn-newydd Denbs 165 G11
Bryn-Offa Wrex 166 F4
Brynowen Ceredig'n 128 F2
Bryn-penarth Powys 130 C2
Bryn-Pen-y-lan Wrex 166 G4
Bryn-Perthy Powys 148 F5
Brynrefail Gwyn 163 C9
Brynrefail Angl 179 D7
Bryn-rhys Conwy 180 F4
Brynrodyn Ceredig'n 128 F2
Brynsadler Rh Cyn Taff 58 C4
Brynsiencyn Angl 163 B7
Bryn-Tanat Powys 148 E4
Brynteg Ceredig'n 93 C9
Brynteg Angl 179 E7
Brynteg Rh Cyn Taff 58 C5
Brynteg Wrex 166 E4
Bryntirion Bridg 57 E11
Bryn-Vyrnwy Powys 148 E4
Bryn-y-cochin Shrops 149 B7
Brynygwenin Monmouths 78 B4
Bryn-y-gwin Denbs 146 F4
Bryn-y-maen Conwy 180 F4
Buaile nam Bodach W Isles 297 L3
Bualintur H'land 294 C6
Bualnaluib H'land 307 K3
Bubbenhall Warwick 119 C7
Bubnell Derby 186 G2
Bubwith ER Yorks 207 F10
Buccleuch Scot Borders 261 G8
Buchanan Smithy Stirl 277 D9
Buchanhaven Aberds 303 E11
Buchanty Perth/Kinr 286 E3
Buchley E Dunb 277 G11
Buchlyvie Stirl 277 C11
Buck Hill Wilts 62 E3
Buckabank Cumb 230 B3
Buckcastle Hill Heref'd 97 F11
Buckden Cambs 122 D3
Buckden N Yorks 213 D8
Buckenham Norfolk 143 B7
Buckerell Devon 27 G10
Buckfast Devon 8 B4
Buckfast Abbey, Buckfastleigh Devon 8 B4
Buckfastleigh Devon 8 B4
Buckhaven Fife 281 B7
Buckholm Scot Borders 261 B11
Buckholt Heref'd 79 B8
Buckhorn Devon 12 B3
Buckhorn Weston Dorset 30 C3
Buckhurst Hill Essex 86 G6
Buckie Moray 302 C4
Buckies H'land 310 C5
Buckingham Bucks 102 E3
Buckingham Palace London 67 D9
Buckland Bucks 84 C5
Buckland Devon 8 G3
Buckland Devon 14 G3
Buckland Glos 99 D11
Buckland Hants 20 B2
Buckland Herts 105 E7
Buckland Kent 55 E10
Buckland Oxon 82 F4
Buckland Surrey 51 C8
Buckland Abbey Devon 7 B9
Buckland Brewer Devon 24 C6
Buckland Common Bucks 84 D6
Buckland Dinham Som'set 45 C9
Buckland End W Midlands 134 F2
Buckland Filleigh Devon 25 F7
Buckland in the Moor Devon 13 G10
Buckland Manachorum Devon 7 B9
Buckland Newton Dorset 29 F11
Buckland Ripers Dorset 17 E8
Buckland St. Mary Som'set 28 E3
Buckland Valley Kent 55 E10
Buckland-tout-Saints Devon 8 F5
Bucklandwharf Bucks 84 C6
Bucklebury W Berks 64 E5
Bucklebury Alley W Berks 64 E4
Bucklegate Lincs 156 B6
Buckleigh Devon 24 B6
Bucklerheads Angus 287 D8
Bucklers Hard Hants 32 G6
Bucklesham Suffolk 108 C5
Buckley = Bwcle Flints 166 C3
Buckley Gtr Man 196 D2
Buckley Green Warwick 118 D3
Buckley Hill Mersey 182 B5
Bucklow Hill Ches 184 E2
Buckminster Leics 155 E7
Bucknall Lincs 173 B11
Bucknall Stoke 168 F6
Bucknell Oxon 101 F11
Bucknell Shrops 115 C7
Buckpool Moray 302 C4
Buckpool W Midlands 133 F7
Buckridge Worcs 116 C4
Buck's Cross Devon 24 C4
Bucks Green W Sussex 50 G5
Bucks Hill Herts 85 E9
Bucks Horn Oak Hants 49 E10
Buck's Mills Devon 24 C5
Bucksburn Aberd C 293 C10
Buckshead Cornw'l 4 F6
Buckskin Hants 48 C6
Buckton ER Yorks 218 E3
Buckton Heref'd 115 C7
Buckton Vale Gtr Man 196 G3
Buckworth Cambs 122 B2
Budbrooke Warwick 118 D5
Budby Notts 171 B10
Buddgbrake Shetl'd 314 B8
Buddileigh Staffs 168 F2
Budds Kent 52 C5
Bude Cornw'l 24 F2
Budge's Shop Cornw'l 6 D6
Budlake Devon 27 G7
Budle Northum 264 B5
Budleigh Salterton Devon 15 E7
Budlett's Common E Sussex 37 C7
Budna Beds 104 B2
Budock Water Cornw'l 3 C7
Budworth Heath Ches 183 F11
Buersil Head Gtr Man 196 E2
Buerton Ches 167 G11
Buffler's Holt Bucks 102 E3
Bugbrooke Northants 120 F3
Bugford Devon 40 E6
Bughtlin C/Edinb 280 G3
Buglawton Ches 168 C5
Bugle Cornw'l 5 D10
Bugley Wilts 45 E11
Bugthorpe ER Yorks 207 B11
Building End Essex 105 D8
Buildwas Shrops 132 C2
Builth Road Powys 113 G10
Builth Wells = Llanfair-ym-Muallt Powys 113 G10
Buirgh W Isles 305 J2
Bulbourne Herts 84 C6
Bulbridge Wilts 46 G5
Bulby Lincs 155 D11
Bulcote Notts 171 G11
Buldoo H'land 310 C3
Bulford Wilts 47 E7
Bulford Camp Wilts 47 E7
Bulkeley Ches 167 E8
Bulkington Warwick 135 F7
Bulkington Wilts 46 B2
Bulkworthy Devon 24 E5
Bull Bay = Porthllechog Angl 178 C6
Bull Farm Notts 171 C8
Bull Hill Hants 20 B2
Bullamoor N Yorks 225 G7
Bullbridge Derby 170 E5
Bullbrook Brackn'l 65 F11
Bullen's Bank Heref'd 96 C5
Bullen's Green Herts 86 D2
Bulley Glos 80 B3
Bullgill Cumb 229 D7
Bullinghope Heref'd 97 D10
Bullingstone Kent 52 E4
Bullington Lincs 189 F9
Bullockstone Kent 71 F7
Bull's Cross London 86 F4
Bull's Green Herts 86 B3
Bull's Green Norfolk 143 E8
Bulls Green Som'set 45 D8
Bullwood Arg/Bute 276 G3
Bullyhole Bottom Monmouths 79 F7
Bulmer Essex 106 C6
Bulmer N Yorks 216 F3
Bulmer Tye Essex 106 D6
Bulmore Newp 78 G5
Bulphan Thurr'k 68 B6
Bulstrode Herts 85 E8
Bulthy Shrops 148 G6
Bulverhythe E Sussex 38 F3
Bulverton Devon 15 D8
Bulwark Aberds 303 E9
Bulwell Nott'ham 171 G8
Bulwick Northants 137 E9
Bulworthy Devon 25 B8
Bumble's Green Essex 86 D6
Bun Abhainn Eadarra W Isles 305 H3
Bun a'Mhuillin W Isles 297 K3
Bun Loyne H'land 290 C4
Bunacaimb H'land 295 G8
Bunarkaig H'land 290 E3
Bunbury Ches 167 D9
Bunbury Heath Ches 167 D9
Bunce Common Surrey 51 D8
Bunchrew H'land 300 E6
Bundalloch H'land 295 C10
Buness Shetl'd 314 C8
Bunessan Arg/Bute 288 G5
Bungay Suffolk 142 F6
Bunker Hill Norfolk 142 B3
Bunker's Hill Cambs 139 B8
Bunkers Hill Gtr Man 184 D6
Bunkers Hill Hants 33 E10
Bunkers Hill Lancs 204 F3
Bunker's Hill Lincs 174 E3
Bunker's Hill Norfolk 143 C10
Bunloit H'land 300 G5
Bunnahabhain Arg/Bute 274 F5
Bunny Notts 153 D11
Bunree H'land 290 G2
Bunroy H'land 290 E4
Buntait H'land 300 F3
Buntingford Herts 105 F7
Bunting's Green Essex 106 E6
Bunwell Norfolk 142 E2
Bunwell Bottom Norfolk 142 D2
Bunwell Hill Norfolk 142 E2
Buoltach H'land 310 F5
Burbage Derby 185 G8
Burbage Leics 135 E8
Burbage Wilts 63 G8
Burchett's Green Windsor 65 C10
Burcombe Wilts 46 G5
Burcot Oxon 83 F9
Burcot Worcs 117 C9
Burcott Bucks 84 B4
Burcott Bucks 103 G7
Burcott Som'set 44 D4
Burdale N Yorks 217 G7
Burdiehouse C/Edinb 270 B5
Burdon Tyne/Wear 243 G9
Burdrop Oxon 101 D7
Bures Suffolk 107 E8
Bures Green Suffolk 107 D8
Burford Ches 167 E10
Burford Devon 24 C4
Burford Oxon 82 C3
Burford Shrops 115 D11
Burford Som'set 44 E5
Burg Arg/Bute 288 E5
Burg Arg/Bute 288 G6
Burgar Orkney 312 F4
Burgate Suffolk 125 B11
Burgates Hants 34 B3
Burge End Herts 104 E2
Burgedin Powys 148 G4
Burgess Hill W Sussex 36 D4
Burgh Suffolk 126 G4
Burgh by Sands Cumb 239 F8
Burgh Castle Norfolk 143 C9
Burgh Heath Surrey 51 B8
Burgh Hill E Sussex 38 B2
Burgh le Marsh Lincs 175 B7
Burgh Muir Aberds 293 B9
Burgh Muir Aberds 303 G7
Burgh next Aylsham Norfolk 160 D4
Burgh on Bain Lincs 190 D2
Burgh St. Margaret = Fleggburgh Norfolk 161 G8
Burgh St. Peter Norfolk 143 E9
Burghclere Hants 64 G3
Burghead Moray 301 C11
Burghfield W Berks 65 F7
Burghfield Common W Berks 64 F6
Burghfield Hill W Berks 65 F7
Burghill Heref'd 97 C9
Burghope Heref'd 115 G10
Burghwallis S Yorks 198 E4
Burham Kent 69 G8
Buriton Hants 34 C2
Burland Ches 167 E10
Burlawn Cornw'l 10 G5
Burleigh Brackn'l 66 E2
Burleigh Glos 80 E5
Burlescombe Devon 27 D9
Burleston Dorset 17 C11
Burlestone Devon 8 F6
Burley Hants 32 G2
Burley Rutl'd 155 G7
Burley W Yorks 205 G11
Burley Gate Heref'd 97 B11
Burley in Wharfdale W Yorks 205 D9
Burley Lawn Hants 32 G2
Burley Street Hants 32 G2
Burley Woodhead W Yorks 205 E9
Burleydam Ches 167 G10
Burlingham Green Norfolk 161 G7
Burlingjobb Powys 114 F5
Burlish Park Worcs 116 C6
Burlow E Sussex 37 D9
Burlton Shrops 149 D9
Burmantofts W Yorks 206 G2
Burmarsh Kent 54 G5
Burmarsh Kent 54 G6
Burmington Warwick 100 D5
Burn N Yorks 198 B5
Burn Bridge N Yorks 205 C11
Burn Naze Lancs 202 E2
Burn of Cambus Stirl 285 G11
Burnage Gtr Man 184 C5
Burnaston Derby 152 C5
Burnbank S Lanarks 268 D4
Burnbanks Cumb 221 B10
Burnbrae N Lanarks 269 D7
Burnby ER Yorks 208 D2
Burncross S Yorks 186 B4
Burndell W Sussex 35 G7
Burnden Gtr Man 195 F8
Burnedge Gtr Man 196 E2
Burnend Aberds 303 E8
Burneside Cumb 221 F10
Burness Orkney 312 D7
Burneston N Yorks 214 C6
Burnett Bath/NE Som'set 61 F7
Burnfoot Scot Borders 261 G10
Burnfoot Scot Borders 262 F2
Burnfoot Dumf/Gal 247 E11
Burnfoot Dumf/Gal 239 C7
Burnfoot E Ayrs 245 B10
Burnfoot N Lanarks 268 B4
Burnfoot Perth/Kinr 286 G3
Burnfoot S Lanarks 268 G6
Burngreave S Yorks 186 D5
Burnham Bucks 66 C2
Burnham N Lincs 200 D5
Burnham Deepdale Norfolk 176 E4
Burnham Green Herts 86 B3
Burnham Market Norfolk 176 E4
Burnham Norton Norfolk 176 E4
Burnham on Sea Som'set 43 D10
Burnham Overy Norfolk 176 E4
Burnham Overy Staithe Norfolk 176 E4
Burnham Thorpe Norfolk 176 E5
Burnham-on-Crouch Essex 89 F7
Burnhead Aberds 293 D10
Burnhead Dumf/Gal 247 D9
Burnhead S Ayrs 244 C6
Burnhead S Lanarks 268 E5
Burnhervie Aberds 293 B9
Burnhill Green Staffs 132 C5
Burnhope Durham 233 B9
Burnhouse N Ayrs 267 E7
Burnhouse S Lanarks 268 E2
Burniestrype Moray 302 C3
Burniston N Yorks 227 G10
Burnlee W Yorks 196 F6
Burnley Lancs 204 G2
Burnley Lane Lancs 204 G2
Burnley Wood Lancs 204 G2
Burnmouth Scot Borders 273 C9
Burnopfield Durham 242 F5
Burnrigg Cumb 239 F11
Burn's Green Herts 104 G6
Burnsall N Yorks 213 G10
Burnside Aberds 303 E8
Burnside Angus 287 B9
Burnside E Ayrs 258 G3
Burnside Fife 286 G5
Burnside Perth/Kinr 286 E4
Burnside Shetl'd 314 F4
Burnside S Lanarks 268 C2
Burnside Tyne/Wear 243 G8
Burnside W Loth 279 G11
Burnside W Loth 279 F11
Burnside of Duntrune Angus 287 D8
Burnswark Dumf/Gal 238 B4
Burnt Heath Derby 186 F2
Burnt Heath Essex 107 F11
Burnt Hill W Berks 64 E5
Burnt Houses Durham 233 G8
Burnt Oak E Sussex 37 B8
Burnt Oak London 86 G2
Burnt Tree W Midlands 133 E9
Burnt Yates N Yorks 214 G5
Burntcommon Surrey 50 B4
Burntheath Derby 152 C4
Burnthouse Cornw'l 3 B7
Burntisland Fife 280 D4
Burnton E Ayrs 245 B11
Burnturk Fife 287 G7
Burntwood Staffs 133 B11
Burntwood Green Staffs 133 B11
Burnworthy Som'set 27 D11
Burnwynd C/Edinb 270 B2
Burpham Surrey 50 C4
Burpham W Sussex 35 F8
Burradon Northum 251 B11
Burradon Tyne/Wear 243 C7
Burrafirth Shetl'd 314 B8
Burraland Shetl'd 314 F5
Burraland Shetl'd 315 J4
Burras Cornw'l 2 C5
Burrastow Shetl'd 315 J4
Burraton Cornw'l 7 D8
Burraton Coombe Cornw'l 7 D8
Burravoe Shetl'd 314 F7
Burravoe Shetl'd 314 G5
Burray Village Orkney 313 J5
Burreldales Aberds 303 F7
Burrells Cumb 222 B3
Burrelton Perth/Kinr 286 D6
Burridge Devon 26 E2
Burridge Devon 28 F4
Burridge Devon 40 F5
Burridge Hants 33 E8
Burrigill H'land 310 F6
Burrill N Yorks 214 B4
Burringham N Lincs 199 F10
Burrington Devon 25 D10
Burrington Heref'd 115 C8
Burrington N Som'set 44 B3
Burrough End Cambs 124 G2
Burrough Green Cambs 124 F2
Burrough on the Hill Leics 154 G5
Burroughs Grove Bucks 65 B11
Burroughston Orkney 312 F6
Burrow Devon 15 D7
Burrow Devon 14 B5
Burrow Som'set 42 E2
Burrow Som'set 28 C6
Burrow Bridge Som'set 28 B5
Burrowhill Surrey 66 G3
Burrows Cross Surrey 50 D5
Burrs Gtr Man 195 E9
Burrsville Park Essex 89 B11
Burry Swan 75 G7
Burry Green Swan 75 G7
Burry Port = Porth Tywyn Carms 74 E6
Burscough Lancs 194 E2
Burscough Bridge Lancs 194 E2
Bursea ER Yorks 208 G2
Burshill ER Yorks 209 D7
Bursledon Hants 33 F7
Burslem Stoke 168 F5
Burstall Suffolk 107 C11
Burstock Dorset 28 G6
Burston Devon 26 G2
Burston Norfolk 142 G2
Burston Staffs 151 C8
Burstow Surrey 51 E10
Burstwick ER Yorks 201 B8
Burtersett N Yorks 213 B7
Burtholme Cumb 240 E2
Burthorpe Suffolk 124 E5
Burthwaite Cumb 230 B4
Burtle Som'set 44 E2
Burtle Hill Som'set 43 E11
Burtoft Lincs 156 B5
Burton Ches 182 G4
Burton Ches 167 C8
Burton Dorset 17 C9
Burton Dorset 19 C9
Burton Lincs 189 G7
Burton Pembs 73 D7

Burton Som'set 29 E8
Burton Som'set 43 E7
Burton Wilts 45 G10
Burton Wilts 61 D10
Burton Wrex 166 D5
Burton Agnes ER Yorks 218 G2
Burton Bradstock Dorset 16 D5
Burton Constable ER Yorks 209 F9
Burton Corner Lincs 174 F4
Burton Dassett Warwick 119 G7
Burton End Essex 105 G10
Burton Ferry Pembs 73 D7
Burton Fleming ER Yorks 217 E11
Burton Green W Midlands 118 B5
Burton Green Wrex 166 D4
Burton Hastings Warwick 135 F8
Burton in Lonsdale N Yorks 212 E3
Burton Joyce Notts 171 G10
Burton Latimer Northants 121 C8
Burton Lazars Leics 154 F5
Burton Leonard N Yorks 214 G6
Burton on the Wolds Leics 153 E11
Burton Overy Leics 136 D3
Burton Pedwardine Lincs 173 G10
Burton Pidsea ER Yorks 209 G10
Burton Salmon N Yorks 198 B3
Burton Stather N Lincs 199 D11
Burton upon Trent Staffs 152 E5
Burton-in-Kendal Cumb 211 D10
Burton-le-Coggles Lincs 155 D9
Burton's Green Essex 106 F6
Burton-upon-Stather N Lincs 199 D11
Burtonwood Warrington 183 C9
Burtree Ford Durham 232 C3
Burwardsley Ches 167 D8
Burwarton Shrops 132 G2
Burwash E Sussex 37 C11
Burwash Common E Sussex 37 C10
Burwash Weald E Sussex 37 C10
Burwell Cambs 123 D11
Burwell Lincs 190 F5
Burwen Angl 178 C6
Burwick Orkney 313 K5
Burwick Shetl'd 315 J5
Burwood Park Surrey 66 G5
Bury Cambs 138 G5
Bury Gtr Man 195 E9
Bury Som'set 26 B6
Bury W Sussex 35 E8
Bury End Beds 104 D2
Bury End Beds 121 G9
Bury End Worcs 99 D11
Bury Green Herts 86 E4
Bury Green Herts 105 G9
Bury Hill S Glos 61 B8
Bury St. Edmunds Suffolk 124 E7
Burys Bank W Berks 64 F3
Burythorpe N Yorks 216 G5
Busbridge Surrey 50 E3
Busby E Renf 267 D11
Buscot Oxon 82 F2
Buscott Som'set 44 F2
Bush Aberds 293 G9
Bush Cornw'l 24 F2
Bush Som'set 43 F8
Bush Bank Heref'd 115 G8
Bush Crathie Aberds 292 D4
Bush Green Norfolk 141 D10
Bush Green Norfolk 142 F4
Bush Green Suffolk 125 F8
Bush Hill London 86 F4
Bush Hill Park London 86 F4
Bushbury Surrey 51 D7
Bushbury W Midlands 133 C8
Bushby Leics 136 C3
Bushey Dorset 18 E5
Bushey Herts 85 F10
Bushey Heath Herts 85 G11
Bushley Worcs 99 E7
Bushley Green Worcs 99 E7
Bushmead Beds 122 E2
Bushton Wilts 62 D5
Bushy Common Norfolk 159 G9
Bushy Hill Surrey 50 C4
Busk Cumb 231 C8
Busk Gtr Man 196 F2
Buslingthorpe Lincs 189 D9
Bussage Glos 80 E5
Bussex Som'set 43 F11
Buss's Green E Sussex 52 F6
Busta Shetl'd 314 G5
Bustard Green Essex 106 F2
Bustard's Green Norfolk 142 E3
Bustatoun Orkney 312 C8
Busveal Cornw'l 4 G4
Butcher's Common Norfolk 160 E6
Butcher's Cross E Sussex 37 B9
Butcher's Row W Sussex 35 C11
Butcombe N Som'set 60 G4
Bute Town Caerph 77 D10
Butetown Card 59 D7
Butleigh Som'set 44 G4
Butleigh Wootton Som'set 44 G4
Butler's Cross Bucks 84 D4
Butler's Hill Notts 171 F8
Butlers Marston Warwick 118 G6
Butley Suffolk 127 G7
Butley Corner Suffolk 109 B7
Butley Town Ches 184 F6
Butlocks Heath Hants 33 F7
Butt Green Ches 167 E11
Butt Green Glos 80 C5
Butt Lane Staffs 168 E4
Buttercrambe N Yorks 207 B10
Butterfield Green Beds 104 F2
Butterhaugh Northum 250 E4
Butterknowle Durham 233 F8
Butterleigh Devon 27 F7
Butterley Derby 170 E6
Butterley Grange Derby 170 E6
Buttermere Cumb 220 B3
Buttermere Wilts 63 G10
Butterow Glos 80 E5
Butters Green Staffs 168 E4
Buttershaw W Yorks 196 B6
Butterstone Perth/Kinr 286 C4
Butterton Staffs 168 G4
Butterton Staffs 169 D9
Butterwick Cumb 221 B10
Butterwick Durham 234 F3
Butterwick Lincs 174 F5
Butterwick N Yorks 216 D4
Butterwick N Yorks 217 D9
Buttington Powys 130 B5
Button Haugh Green Suffolk 125 D9
Buttonbridge Shrops 116 B4
Buttonoak Shrops 116 B4
Butts Devon 14 D2
Butt's Close Herts 104 F3
Butt's Green Essex 88 E3
Butt's Green Hants 32 B4
Butt's Knap Dorset 30 C5
Buttsash Hants 32 F6
Buttsole Kent 55 C10
Buxhall Suffolk 125 F10
Buxhall Fen Street Suffolk 125 F10
Buxley Scot Borders 272 D6
Buxted E Sussex 37 C7
Buxton Derby 185 G9
Buxton Norfolk 160 E4
Buxworth Derby 185 E8
Bwcle = Buckley Flints 166 C3
Bwlch Powys 96 G2
Bwlch Shrops 148 D5
Bwlch y Garreg Powys 129 D10
Bwlch-derwin Gwyn 163 F7
Bwlchgwyn Wrex 166 E3
Bwlch-Llan Ceredig'n 111 F11
Bwlchnewydd Carms 93 G7
Bwlchtocyn Gwyn 144 D6
Bwlch-y-cibau Powys 148 F3
Bwlchyddar Powys 148 E3
Bwlch-y-fadfa Ceredig'n 93 B8
Bwlch-y-ffridd Powys 129 D11
Bwlch-y-groes Ceredig'n 93 B7
Bwlchygroes Pembs 92 D4
Bwlch-y-haiarn Conwy 164 D3
Bwlchyllyn Gwyn 163 D8
Bwlchymynydd Swan 75 F9
Bwlch-y-sarnau Powys 113 C10
Bybrook Kent 54 E4
Bye Green Bucks 84 C5
Byeastwood Bridg 58 C2
Byebush Aberds 303 F7
Byermoor Tyne/Wear 242 F5
Byers Green Durham 233 E10
Byfield Northants 119 G10
Byfleet Surrey 66 G5
Byford Heref'd 97 C7
Byford Common Heref'd 97 C7
Bygrave Herts 104 D5
Byker Tyne/Wear 243 E7
Byland Abbey N Yorks 215 D10
Byley Ches 168 B2
Bynea Carms 75 F8
Byram N Yorks 198 B3
Byram-cum-Sutton N Yorks 198 C3
Byrness Northum 251 C7
Bystock Devon 14 E6
Bythorn Cambs 121 B11
Byton Heref'd 115 E7
Bywell Northum 242 E2
Byworth W Sussex 35 C7

C

Cabharstadh W Isles 304 F5
Cablea Perth/Kinr 286 D3
Cabourne Lincs 200 G6
Cabrach Arg/Bute 274 G5
Cabrach Moray 302 G3
Cabrich H'land 300 E5
Cabus Lancs 202 D5
Cackle Hill Lincs 157 D7
Cackle Street E Sussex 37 B7
Cackle Street E Sussex 38 D4
Cad Green Som'set 28 D4
Cadboll H'land 301 B8
Cadbury Devon 26 G6
Cadbury Heath S Glos 61 E7
Cadbury World, Bournville W Midlands 133 G10
Cadder E Dunb 278 G2
Cadderlie Arg/Bute 284 D4
Caddington Beds 85 B9
Caddleton Arg/Bute 275 B8
Caddonfoot Scot Borders 261 B11
Cade Street E Sussex 37 C10
Cadeby Leics 135 C8
Cadeby S Yorks 198 G4
Cadeleigh Devon 26 F6
Cadger Path Angus 287 B8
Cadgwith Cornw'l 2 G6
Cadham Fife 286 G6
Cadishead Gtr Man 184 C2
Cadle Swan 75 F10
Cadley Lancs 202 G6
Cadley Wilts 47 B8
Cadley Wilts 63 F8
Cadmore End Bucks 84 G3
Cadnam Hants 32 E3
Cadney N Lincs 200 G4
Cadole Flints 166 C2
Cadoxton V/Glam 58 F6
Cadoxton-Juxta-Neath Rh Cyn Taff 76 F3
Cadshaw Blackb'n 195 D8
Cadwell Herts 104 E3
Cadwell Park Lincs 190 E3
Cadwell Park Motor Racing Circuit Lincs 190 E3
Cadwin Cornw'l 5 C10
Cadwst Denbs 147 B10
Cadzow S Lanarks 268 E4
Caeathro Gwyn 163 C8
Caehopkin Powys 76 C4
Caenby Lincs 189 D8
Caerau Bridg 76 G5
Caerau Card 58 D6
Cae'r-bont Powys 76 C4
Cae'r-bryn Carms 75 C9
Caerdeon Gwyn 146 F3
Cae'r-dynyn Gwyn 146 E6
Caerfarchell Pembs 90 F5
Caerfyrddin = Carmarthen Carms 93 G8
Caergeiliog Angl 178 F4
Caergwrle Flints 166 D4
Caergybi = Holyhead Angl 178 E3
Caerhendy Rh Cyn Taff 76 G3
Caerhun Gwyn 163 B9
Cae'r-Lan Powys 76 C4
Caerleon Newp 78 G4
Caernarfon Gwyn 163 C7
Caernarfon Castle Gwyn 163 C7
Caerphilly Caerph 59 B7
Caersws Powys 129 E10
Caerwedros Ceredig'n 111 F7
Caerwent Monmouths 79 G7
Caerwent Brook Monmouths 60 B3
Caerwys Flints 181 G10
Caethiwed Conwy 180 F4
Cafn-coed-y-cymmer Merth Tyd 77 D8
Cage Green Kent 52 D5
Caggan H'land 291 B10
Caggle Street Monmouths 78 B5
Càrnais W Isles 304 E2
Càrnan W Isles 297 G3
Cailness Stirl 285 G7
Caim Angl 179 E10
Cainscross Glos 80 E4
Caio Carms 94 D3
Cairinis W Isles 296 E4
Cairisiadar W Isles 304 E2
Cairminis W Isles 296 C6
Cairnbaan Arg/Bute 275 D9
Cairnbanno Ho. Aberds 303 E8
Cairnborrow Aberds 302 E4
Cairnbrogie Aberds 303 G8
Cairnbulg Castle Aberds 303 C10
Cairncross Angus 292 F6
Cairncross Scot Borders 273 C7
Cairnderry Dumf/Gal 236 B5
Cairndow Arg/Bute 284 F5
Cairness Aberds 303 C10
Cairneyhill Fife 279 D10
Cairnfield Ho. Moray 302 C4
Cairngaan Dumf/Gal 236 F3
Cairngarroch Dumf/Gal 236 E2
Cairnhill Aberds 302 F6
Cairnhill Aberds 303 D7
Cairnhill N Lanarks 268 C5
Cairnie Aberds 293 C10
Cairnie Aberds 302 E4
Cairnleith Crofts Aberds 303 F9
Cairnmuir Aberds 303 C9
Cairnorrie Aberds 303 E8
Cairnpark Aberds 293 B10
Cairnryan Dumf/Gal 236 C2
Cairnton Orkney 313 H4
Cairston Orkney 312 G3
Caister-on-Sea Norfolk 161 G10
Caistor Lincs 200 G6
Caistor St. Edmund Norfolk 142 C4
Caitha Bowland Scot Borders 271 G9
Caithness Glass, Perth Perth/Kinr 286 E4
Cakebole Worcs 117 C7
Calais Street Suffolk 107 D9
Calamansack Cornw'l 2 D6
Calanais W Isles 304 E4
Calbost W Isles 305 G6
Calbourne I/Wight 20 D4
Calceby Lincs 190 F5
Calcoed Flints 181 G11
Calcot Glos 81 C9
Calcot W Berks 65 E7
Calcott Kent 71 G7
Calcott Shrops 149 G9
Calcott's Green Glos 80 B3
Calcutt N Yorks 206 B2
Calcutt Wilts 81 G10
Caldback Shetl'd 314 C8
Caldbeck Cumb 230 D2
Caldbergh N Yorks 213 B11
Caldecote Cambs 138 F2
Caldecote Cambs 122 F4
Caldecote Cambs 122 F6
Caldecote Herts 104 D4
Caldecote M/Keynes 103 C7
Caldecote Northants 120 G3
Caldecote Warwick 135 E7
Caldecott Northants 121 D9
Caldecott Oxon 83 F7
Caldecott Rutl'd 137 E7
Caldecotte M/Keynes 103 D7
Calder Cumb 219 E10
Calder Bridge Cumb 219 D10
Calder Grove W Yorks 197 D9
Calder Mains H'land 310 D4
Calder Vale Lancs 202 D6
Calderbank N Lanarks 268 C5
Calderbrook Gtr Man 196 D2
Caldercruix N Lanarks 268 B6
Caldermill S Lanarks 268 G2
Caldermoor Gtr Man 196 D2
Calderstones Mersey 182 D6
Calderwood S Lanarks 268 D2
Caldhame Angus 287 C8
Caldicot Monmouths 60 B3
Caldwell N Yorks 224 C3
Caldwell Staffs 152 F5
Caldy Mersey 182 D2
Calebrack Cumb 230 D2
Calenick Cornw'l 4 G6
Calf Bridge Lincs 156 C3
Calford Green Suffolk 106 B3
Calfsound Orkney 312 E6
Calgary Arg/Bute 288 D5
Caliach Arg/Bute 288 D5
Califer Moray 301 D10
California Cambs 139 G10
California Falk 279 F8
California Norfolk 161 G10
California W Midlands 133 G10
Calke Derby 153 E7
Callakille H'land 298 D6
Callaly Northum 252 B3
Callander Stirl 285 G10
Callandrode Stirl 285 G10
Callands Warrington 183 C9
Callaughton Shrops 132 D2
Callert Ho. H'land 290 G2
Callerton Tyne/Wear 242 D5
Callestick Cornw'l 4 E5
Calligarry H'land 295 E8
Callington Cornw'l 7 B7
Callingwood Staffs 152 E3
Callop H'land 289 B11
Callow Heref'd 97 E9
Callow End Worcs 98 B6
Callow Hill Som'set 44 B2
Callow Hill Surrey 66 F3
Callow Hill Wilts 62 C4
Callow Hill Worcs 117 E10
Callow Hill Worcs 116 C4
Callowell Glos 80 D4
Callow's Grave Worcs 115 D11
Calmore Hants 32 E4
Calmsden Glos 81 D8
Calne Wilts 62 E4
Calne Marsh Wilts 62 E4
Calow Derby 186 G6
Calow Green Derby 170 B6
Calshot Hants 33 G7
Calstock Cornw'l 7 B8
Calstone Wellington Wilts 62 F4
Calthorpe Norfolk 160 C3
Calthorpe Oxon 101 D9
Calthorpe Street Norfolk 161 D8
Calthwaite Cumb 230 C5
Calton N Yorks 204 B4
Calton Staffs 169 E10
Calton Lees Derby 170 B3
Calveley Ches 167 D9
Calver Derby 186 G2
Calver Hill Heref'd 97 B7
Calver Sough Derby 186 F2
Calverhall Shrops 150 B2
Calverleigh Devon 26 E6
Calverley W Yorks 205 F10
Calvert Bucks 102 G3
Calverton M/Keynes 102 D5
Calverton Notts 171 F10
Calvine Perth/Kinr 291 G10
Calvo Cumb 238 G4
Cam Glos 80 F3
Camaghael H'land 290 F3
Camas an Staca Arg/Bute 274 G5
Camas Salach H'land 289 C8
Camas-luinie H'land 295 C11
Camasnacroise H'land 289 D10
Camastianavaig H'land 295 B7
Camasunary H'land 295 D7
Camault Muir H'land 300 E5
Camb Shetl'd 314 D7
Camber E Sussex 39 D7
Camberley Surrey 65 G11
Camberwell London 67 D10
Camblesforth N Yorks 199 B7
Cambo Northum 252 F2
Cambois Northum 253 G8
Camborne Cornw'l 4 G3
Cambourne Cambs 122 F6
Cambridge Cambs 123 F9
Cambridge Glos 80 E2
Cambridge W Yorks 205 D10
Cambridge Airport Cambs 123 F9
Cambridge Batch N Som'set 60 E4
Cambridge Town Southend 70 B2
Cambrose Cornw'l 4 F3
Cambus Clack 279 C7
Cambusavie Farm H'land 309 K7
Cambusbarron Stirl 278 C5
Cambuskenneth Stirl 278 C6
Cambuslang S Lanarks 268 D2
Cambusmore Lodge H'land 309 K7
Cambusnethan N Lanarks 268 D6
Camden Town London 67 C9
Camel Hill Som'set 29 B9
Cameley Bath/NE Som'set 44 B6
Camelford Cornw'l 11 E8
Camelon Falk 279 E7
Camelot Theme Park, Chorley Lancs 194 D4
Camelsdale W Sussex 49 G11
Camer Kent 69 F7
Camerory H'land 301 F10
Camer's Green Worcs 98 E5
Camerton Bath/NE Som'set 45 B7
Camerton Cumb 228 E6
Camerton ER Yorks 201 B8
Camghouran Perth/Kinr 285 B9
Cammachmore Aberds 293 D11
Cammeringham Lincs 188 E6
Camoquhill Stirl 277 D10
Camore H'land 309 K7
Camp Hill N Yorks 214 C6
Camp Hill Warwick 134 E6
Camp Town W Yorks 206 F2
Campbeltown Arg/Bute 255 E8
Campbeltown Airport Arg/Bute 255 E7
Camperdown Tyne/Wear 243 C7
Campion Hills Warwick 118 D6
Cample Dumf/Gal 247 E10
Campmuir Perth/Kinr 286 D6
Camps W Loth 270 B2
Camps End Cambs 106 C2
Camps Heath Suffolk 143 E10
Campsall S Yorks 198 E4
Campsey Ash Suffolk 126 F6
Campsfield Oxon 83 B7
Campton Beds 104 D2
Camptoun E Loth 281 F10
Camptown Scot Borders 262 G5
Camquhart Arg/Bute 275 E10
Camrose Pembs 72 B6
Camserney Perth/Kinr 286 C2
Camster H'land 310 E6
Camuschoirk H'land 289 C9
Camuscross H'land 295 D8
Camusnagaul H'land 290 F2
Camusnagaul H'land 307 L5
Camusrory H'land 295 F10
Camusteel H'land 299 E7
Camusterrach H'land 299 E7
Camusvrachan Perth/Kinr 285 C10
Canada Hants 32 D3
Canada Lincs 200 G6
Canada Common Hants 32 D3
Canadia E Sussex 38 D2
Canal Side S Yorks 199 E7
Canary Wharf London 67 C11
Canaston Bridge Pembs 73 C9
Candacraig Ho. Aberds 292 B5
Candie Falk 279 G8
Candle Street Suffolk 125 C10
Candlesby Lincs 175 B7
Candy Mill S Lanarks 269 G11
Cane End Oxon 65 D7
Canewdon Essex 88 G5
Canfield End Essex 105 G11
Canford Cliffs Dorset 19 D7
Canford Magna Poole 18 B6
Canham's Green Suffolk 125 D11
Canisbay H'land 310 B7
Canklow S Yorks 186 C6
Canley W Midlands 118 B6
Cann Dorset 30 C5
Cann Common Dorset 30 C5
Cannard's Grave Som'set 44 E6
Cannich H'land 300 F3
Canning Town London 67 C11
Cannington Som'set 43 F9
Cannock Staffs 151 G9
Cannock Wood Staffs 151 G10
Cannon Hill London 67 F8
Cannon's Green Essex 87 D9
Cannop Glos 79 C10
Canon Bridge Heref'd 97 B9
Canon Frome Heref'd 98 C3
Canon Pyon Heref'd 97 B9
Canonbie Dumf/Gal 239 B9
Canonbury London 67 C10
Canons Ashby Northants 119 G11
Canons Park London 85 G11
Canonstown Cornw'l 2 B2
Canterbury Kent 55 B7
Canterbury Cathedral Kent 55 B7
Canterbury Tales Kent 54 B6
Cantley Norfolk 143 C7
Cantley S Yorks 198 G6
Cantlop Shrops 131 B10
Canton Card 59 D7
Cantraybruich H'land 301 E7
Cantraydoune H'land 301 E7
Cantraywood H'land 301 E7
Cantsfield Lancs 212 E2
Canvey Island Essex 69 C9
Canwick Lincs 173 B7
Canworthy Cornw'l 11 C10
Canworthy Water Cornw'l 11 C10
Caol H'land 290 F3
Caol Ila Arg/Bute 274 F5
Caolas Arg/Bute 288 E2
Caolas W Isles 297 M2
Caolas Fhlodaigh W Isles 296 F4
Caolas Liubharsaigh W Isles 297 G4
Caolas Scalpaigh W Isles 305 J4
Caolas Stocinis W Isles 305 J3
Caoslasnacon H'land 290 G3
Capel Carms 75 E8
Capel Kent 52 E6
Capel Surrey 51 E7
Capel Bangor Ceredig'n 128 G3
Capel Betws Lleucu Ceredig'n 112 F2
Capel Carmel Gwyn 144 D3
Capel Coch Angl 179 E7
Capel Curig Conwy 164 D2
Capel Cynon Ceredig'n 93 B7
Capel Dewi Carms 93 G9
Capel Dewi Ceredig'n 128 G2
Capel Dewi Ceredig'n 93 C9
Capel Garmon Conwy 164 D4
Capel Green Suffolk 109 B7
Capel Gwyn Carms 93 G9
Capel Gwyn Angl 178 F4
Capel Gwynfe Carms 94 G4
Capel Hendre Carms 75 C9
Capel Isaac Carms 93 F11
Capel Iwan Carms 92 D5
Capel le Ferne Kent 55 F8
Capel Mawr Angl 178 G6
Capel St. Andrew Suffolk 109 B7
Capel St. Mary Suffolk 107 D11
Capel Seion Ceredig'n 112 B2
Capel Tygwydd Ceredig'n 92 C5
Capel Uchaf Gwyn 162 F6
Capelulo Conwy 180 F2
Capel-y-ffin Powys 96 E5
Capel-y-graig Gwyn 163 B8
Capenhurst Ches 182 G5
Capernwray Lancs 211 E10
Capheaton Northum 252 G2
Capon's Green Suffolk 126 D5
Cappercleuch Scot Borders 260 E6
Capplegill Dumf/Gal 248 B4
Caprington E Ayrs 257 B10
Capstone Medway 69 G9
Captain Fold Gtr Man 195 E11
Capton Devon 8 E6
Capton Som'set 42 F5
Caputh Perth/Kinr 286 D4
Car Colston Notts 172 F2
Caradon Town Cornw'l 11 G11
Carbis Cornw'l 5 D10
Carbis Bay Cornw'l 2 B2
Carbost H'land 294 B5
Carbost H'land 298 E4
Carbrain N Lanarks 278 G5
Carbrook S Yorks 186 D5
Carbrooke Norfolk 141 C9
Carburton Notts 187 G10
Carcant Scot Borders 271 E7
Carcary Angus 287 B10
Carclaze Cornw'l 5 E10
Carcroft S Yorks 198 E4
Cardenden Fife 280 B4
Cardeston Shrops 149 G7
Cardewlees Cumb 239 G8
Cardiff Card 59 D7
Cardiff Bay Barrage Card 59 E7
Cardiff Castle Card 59 D7
Cardiff International Airport V/Glam 58 F5
Cardigan = Aberteifi Ceredig'n 92 B3
Cardinal's Green Cambs 106 B2
Cardington Beds 103 B11
Cardington Shrops 131 D10
Cardinham Cornw'l 6 B2
Cardonald Glasg C 267 C10
Cardow Moray 301 E11
Cardrona Scot Borders 261 B8
Cardross Inverc'l 276 F6
Cardurnock Cumb 238 F5
Careby Lincs 155 F10
Careston Angus 293 G7
Careston Castle Angus 287 B9
Carew Pembs 73 E8
Carew Cheriton Pembs 73 E8
Carew Newton Pembs 73 E8
Carey Heref'd 97 E11
Carey Park Cornw'l 6 E4
Carfin N Lanarks 268 D5
Carfrae E Loth 271 B11
Carfury Cornw'l 1 C4
Cargate Suffolk 125 F8
Cargate Common Norfolk 142 E2
Cargate Green Norfolk 161 G7
Cargenbridge Dumf/Gal 237 B11
Cargill Perth/Kinr 286 D5
Cargo Cumb 239 F9
Cargreen Cornw'l 7 C8
Carham Scot Borders 263 B7
Carhampton Som'set 42 E4
Carharrack Cornw'l 4 G4
Carie Perth/Kinr 285 B10
Carie Perth/Kinr 285 D10
Caring Kent 53 C10
Carisbrooke I/Wight 20 D5
Carisbrooke Castle I/Wight 20 D5
Cark Cumb 211 D7
Carkeel Cornw'l 7 C8
Carlabhagh W Isles 304 D4
Carlbury D'lington 224 B4
Carlby Lincs 155 G10
Carlecotes S Yorks 197 G7
Carleen Cornw'l 2 C4
Carlesmoor N Yorks 214 E3
Carleton Blackp'l 202 F2
Carleton Cumb 219 D10
Carleton Cumb 230 F6
Carleton Cumb 239 G10
Carleton N Yorks 204 D5
Carleton W Yorks 198 C3
Carleton Forehoe Norfolk 141 B11
Carleton Rode Norfolk 142 E2
Carleton St. Peter Norfolk 142 C6
Carley Hill Tyne/Wear 243 F9
Carlidnack Cornw'l 3 D7
Carlin How Redcar/Clevel'd 226 B4
Carlincraig Aberds 302 E6
Carlingcott Bath/NE Som'set 45 B7
Carlisle Cumb 239 F9
Carlisle Airport Cumb 239 E11
Carlisle Cathedral Cumb 239 F9
Carlisle Racecourse Cumb 239 G10
Carloggas Cornw'l 5 B7
Carloonan Arg/Bute 284 F4
Carlops Scot Borders 270 D3
Carlton Beds 121 F9
Carlton Cambs 124 G2
Carlton Leics 135 B7
Carlton Notts 171 G10
Carlton N Yorks 198 C6
Carlton N Yorks 213 C11
Carlton N Yorks 216 B2
Carlton N Yorks 224 C3
Carlton Suffolk 127 E7
Carlton Stockton 234 G3
Carlton S Yorks 197 E11
Carlton W Yorks 197 B10
Carlton Colville Suffolk 143 E10
Carlton Curlieu Leics 136 D3
Carlton Green Cambs 124 G2
Carlton Husthwaite N Yorks 215 D9
Carlton in Cleveland N Yorks 225 E11
Carlton in Lindrick Notts 187 D9
Carlton Miniott N Yorks 215 C8
Carlton Scroop Lincs 172 F6
Carlton-le-Moorland Lincs 172 D6
Carlton-on-Trent Notts 172 C3
Carluke S Lanarks 269 E6
Carmarthen = Caerfyrddin Carms 93 G8
Carmel Carms 75 B9
Carmel Flints 181 F11
Carmel Gwyn 163 D7
Carmel Angl 178 E5
Carmichael S Lanarks 259 B10
Carmont Aberds 293 E10
Carmunnock Glasg C 268 D2
Carmyle Glasg C 268 C2
Carmyllie Angus 287 C9
Carn Brea Cornw'l 4 G3
Carn Towan Cornw'l 1 D3
Carnaby ER Yorks 218 F2
Carnach H'land 299 G10
Carnach H'land 307 K5
Carnach W Isles 305 J4
Carnachy H'land 308 D7
Carnbahn Perth/Kinr 285 C10
Carnbee Fife 287 G9
Carnbo Perth/Kinr 286 G4
Carnbroe N Lanarks 268 C4
Carndu H'land 295 C10
Carnduff S Lanarks 268 F3
Carnduncan Arg/Bute 274 G3
Carne Cornw'l 3 B10
Carne Cornw'l 5 D9
Carnebone Cornw'l 2 C6
Carnetown Rh Cyn Taff 77 G9
Carnforth Lancs 211 E9
Carnglas Swan 75 G10
Carn-gorm H'land 295 C11
Carnhedryn Pembs 90 F6
Carnhell Green Cornw'l 2 B4
Carnhot Cornw'l 4 F4
Carnkie Cornw'l 2 B5
Carnkie Cornw'l 2 C6
Carnkief Cornw'l 4 E5
Carno Powys 129 D9
Carnoch H'land 300 D2
Carnoch H'land 300 F3
Carnock Fife 279 D10
Carnon Downs Cornw'l 4 G5
Carnousie Aberds 302 D6
Carnoustie Angus 287 D9
Carntyne Glasg C 268 B2
Carnwadric Glasg C 267 D10
Carnwath S Lanarks 269 F9
Carnyorth Cornw'l 1 C3
Carol Green W Midlands 118 B5
Carpalla Cornw'l 5 E9
Carperby N Yorks 213 B10
Carr Gtr Man 195 D9
Carr Cross Lancs 193 E11
Carr Gate W Yorks 197 C10
Carr Green Gtr Man 184 D2
Carr Hill Tyne/Wear 243 E7
Carr Houses Mersey 193 G10
Carr Shield Northum 232 B2
Carr Vale Derby 171 B7
Carradale Arg/Bute 255 D9
Carragraich W Isles 305 J3
Carrbridge H'land 301 G9
Carrbrook Gtr Man 196 G3
Carreglefn Angl 178 D5
Carregwen Pembs 92 C4
Carreg-y-Garth Gwyn 163 B9
Carrhouse N Lincs 199 F9
Carrick Arg/Bute 275 E10
Carrick Dumf/Gal 237 D7
Carrick Fife 287 E8
Carrick Castle Arg/Bute 276 C3
Carrick Ho. Orkney 312 E6
Carriden Falk 279 E10
Carrington Nott'ham 171 G9
Carrington Gtr Man 184 C2
Carrington Lincs 174 D4
Carrington Midloth 270 C6
Carrog Conwy 164 F3
Carrog Denbs 165 G10
Carroglen Perth/Kinr 285 E11
Carrol H'land 311 J2
Carron Falk 279 E7
Carron Moray 302 E2
Carron Bridge Stirl 278 E4
Carronbridge Dumf/Gal 247 D9
Carronshore Falk 279 E7
Carrot Angus 287 C8
Carrow Hill Monmouths 78 G6
Carrutherstown Dumf/Gal 238 C4
Carrville Durham 234 C2
Carry Arg/Bute 275 G10
Carsaig Arg/Bute 275 E8
Carsaig Arg/Bute 289 G7
Carscreugh Dumf/Gal 236 D4
Carse Gray Angus 287 B8
Carse Ho. Arg/Bute 275 G8
Carsegowan Dumf/Gal 236 D6
Carseriggan Dumf/Gal 236 C5
Carsethorn Dumf/Gal 237 D11
Carshalton London 67 F9
Carshalton Beeches London 67 G9
Carshalton on the Hill London 67 G9
Carsington Derby 170 E2
Carskiey Arg/Bute 255 G7
Carsluith Dumf/Gal 236 D6
Carsphairn Dumf/Gal 246 E3
Carstairs S Lanarks 269 F8
Carstairs Junction S Lanarks 269 F9
Cartbridge Surrey 50 B4
Carter Knowle S Yorks 186 E4
Carter's Clay Hants 32 C4
Carter's Green Essex 87 C8
Carterton Oxon 82 D3
Carterway Heads Northum 242 G2
Carthew Cornw'l 5 D10
Carthorpe N Yorks 214 C6
Cartington Northum 252 C2
Cartland S Lanarks 269 F7
Cartledge Derby 186 F4
Cartmel Cumb 211 D7
Cartmel Fell Cumb 211 B8
Cartmel Racecourse Cumb 211 D7
Cartworth W Yorks 196 F6
Carty Port Dumf/Gal 236 C6
Carway Carms 75 D7
Carwinley Cumb 239 C10
Cary Fitzpaine Som'set 29 B8
Cascob Powys 114 D4
Cashes Green Glos 80 D4
Cashlie Perth/Kinr 285 C8
Cashmere Visitor Centre, Elgin Moray 302 C2
Cashmoor Dorset 31 E7
Caskieberran Fife 280 A5
Cassey Compton Glos 81 B8
Cassington Oxon 83 C7
Cassop Durham 234 D2
Casswell's Bridge Lincs 156 D3
Castallack Cornw'l 1 D5
Castell Conwy 164 B3
Castell Coch Card 58 C6
Castell Howell Ceredig'n 93 B8
Castell Newydd Emlyn = Newcastle Emlyn Carms 92 C6
Castell-nedd = Neath Rh Cyn Taff 76 F3
Casterton Cumb 212 D2
Castle Acre Norfolk 158 F6
Castle Ashby Northants 121 F7
Castle Bolton N Yorks 223 G10
Castle Bromwich W Midlands 134 F3
Castle Bytham Lincs 155 F9
Castle Caereinion Powys 130 B3
Castle Camps Cambs 106 C2
Castle Carlton Lincs 190 E5
Castle Carrock Cumb 240 F2
Castle Cary Som'set 44 G6
Castle Combe Wilts 61 D10
Castle Combe Motor Racing Circuit Wilts 61 D11
Castle Donington Leics 153 D8
Castle Douglas Dumf/Gal 237 C9
Castle Drogo, Exeter Devon 13 C10
Castle Eaton Swindon 81 F10
Castle Eden Durham 234 D4
Castle End Peterbro 138 B2
Castle End Warwick 118 C5
Castle Field Som'set 43 F10
Castle Forbes Aberds 293 B8
Castle Frome Heref'd 98 B3
Castle Gate Cornw'l 1 C5
Castle Goring W Sussex 35 F10
Castle Green Surrey 66 G3
Castle Green S Yorks 197 G9
Castle Gresley Derby 152 F5
Castle Heaton Northum 273 G8
Castle Hedingham Essex 106 D5
Castle Hill E Sussex 37 B8
Castle Hill Gtr Man 184 C6
Castle Hill Kent 53 E7
Castle Hill Suffolk 108 B2
Castle Hill Wilts 46 G6
Castle Howard, Malton N Yorks 216 E4
Castle Huntly Perth/Kinr 287 E7
Castle Kennedy Dumf/Gal 236 D3
Castle Mill Wrex 148 B5
Castle O'er Dumf/Gal 249 E6
Castle Park N Yorks 227 C7
Castle Rising Norfolk 158 E3
Castle Shaw Gtr Man 196 F4
Castle Street W Yorks 196 C3
Castle Stuart H'land 301 E7
Castle Toward Arg/Bute 275 A12
Castle Town W Sussex 36 F2
Castle Vale W Midlands 134 E2
Castlebay = Bagh a Chaisteil W Isles 297 M2
Castlebythe Pembs 91 F10
Castlecary Falk 278 F5
Castlecraig H'land 301 C8
Castlecroft W Midlands 133 D7
Castlefairn Dumf/Gal 246 F6

Castlefields Halton 183 E8
Castleford W Yorks 198 B2
Castleford Ings W Yorks 198 B2
Castlehead Renf 267 C9
Castlehill Arg/Bute 254 B4
Castlehill Scot Borders 260 B6
Castlehill H'land 310 C5
Castlehill S Ayrs 257 E9
Castlehill S Lanarks 268 E6
Castlehill W Dunb 277 F7
Castlemaddy Dumf/Gal 246 F3
Castlemartin Pembs 72 F6
Castlemilk Glasg C 268 D2
Castlemilk Dumf/Gal 238 B5
Castlemorris Pembs 91 E8
Castlemorton Worcs 98 D5
Castlerigg Cumb 229 G11
Castleside Durham 233 B7
Castlethorpe M/Keynes 102 C6
Castlethorpe N Lincs 200 F3
Castleton Angus 287 C7
Castleton Arg/Bute 275 E9
Castleton Derby 185 E11
Castleton Gtr Man 195 E11
Castleton Moray 301 G11
Castleton Newp 59 C9
Castleton N Yorks 226 D3
Castletown Ches 166 E6
Castletown Cumb 230 E6
Castletown Dorset 17 G9
Castletown H'land 301 E7
Castletown H'land 310 C5
Castletown I/Man 192 F3
Castletown Staffs 151 E8
Castletown Tyne/Wear 243 F9
Castleweary Scot Borders 249 C10
Castlewigg Dumf/Gal 236 E6
Castley W Yorks 205 D11
Castling's Heath Suffolk 107 C9
Caston Norfolk 141 D9
Castor Peterbro 138 D2
Caswell Swan 56 D5
Cat Bank Cumb 220 F6
Catacol N Ayrs 255 C10
Catbrain S Glos 60 C5
Catbrook Monmouths 79 E8
Catchall Cornw'l 1 D4
Catchems Corner W Midlands 118 B5
Catchems End Worcs 116 B5
Catchgate Durham 242 G5
Catchory H'land 310 D6
Catcleugh Northum 250 C6
Catcliffe S Yorks 186 D6
Catcomb Wilts 62 D4
Catcott Som'set 43 F11
Caterham Surrey 51 C10
Catfield Norfolk 161 E7
Catfirth Shetl'd 315 H6
Catford London 67 E11
Catforth Lancs 202 F5
Cathays Card 59 D7
Cathays Park Card 59 D7
Cathcart Glasg C 267 C11
Cathedine Powys 96 F2
Catherine de Barnes Heath W Midlands 134 G3
Catherine Slack W Yorks 196 B5
Catherington Hants 33 E11
Catherston Leweston Dorset 16 C3
Cathiron Warwick 119 B9
Catholes Cumb 222 G3
Cathpair Scot Borders 271 F9
Catisfield Hants 33 F9
Catley Lane Head Gtr Man 195 D11
Catley Southfield Heref'd 98 C3
Catlodge H'land 291 D8
Catlow Lancs 204 F3
Catlowdy Cumb 239 B11
Catmere End Essex 105 D9
Catmore W Berks 64 C2
Caton Devon 13 G11
Caton Lancs 211 F11
Caton Green Lancs 211 F11
Catrine E Ayrs 258 D2
Cat's Ash Newp 78 G5
Catsfield E Sussex 38 E2
Catsfield Stream E Sussex 38 E2
Catsgore Som'set 29 B8
Catsham Som'set 44 G5
Catshill W Midlands 133 C11
Catshill Worcs 117 C9
Cattadale Arg/Bute 274 G4
Cattal N Yorks 206 C5
Cattawade Suffolk 108 E2
Cattedown Plym'th 7 E9
Catterall Lancs 202 E5
Catteralslane Shrops 167 G9
Catterick N Yorks 224 F4
Catterick Bridge N Yorks 224 F4
Catterick Garrison N Yorks 224 F3
Catterick Racecourse N Yorks 224 F4
Catterlen Cumb 230 E5
Catterline Aberds 293 F10
Catterton N Yorks 206 D6
Catteshall Surrey 50 E3
Catthorpe Leics 119 B10
Cattistock Dorset 17 B7
Cattle End Northants 102 C3
Catton Northum 241 F8
Catton N Yorks 215 D7
Catwick ER Yorks 209 D8
Catworth Cambs 121 C11
Caudle Green Glos 80 C6
Caudlesprings Norfolk 141 C8
Caudwell's Mill, Matlock Derby 170 B2
Caudworthy Park Cornw'l 11 C11
Caulcott Beds 103 C10
Caulcott Oxon 101 G10
Cauldcots Angus 287 C10
Cauldham Kent 55 F8
Cauldhame Stirl 278 C2
Cauldmill Scot Borders 262 F2
Cauldon Staffs 169 F9
Cauldon Lowe Staffs 169 F9
Cauldwell Derby 152 F5
Cauldwell Tyne/Wear 243 D9
Cauldwells Aberds 303 D7
Caulkerbush Dumf/Gal 237 D11
Caulside Dumf/Gal 249 G10
Caundle Marsh Dorset 29 E11
Caundle Wake Dorset 29 E11
Caunsall Worcs 133 G7
Caunton Notts 172 C2
Causeway Hants 34 C2
Causeway Hants 33 E11
Causeway End Cumb 211 B9
Causeway End Dumf/Gal 236 C6
Causeway End Essex 87 B11
Causeway Foot W Yorks 197 E7
Causeway Green W Midlands 133 F9
Causewayend S Lanarks 260 B2
Causewayhead Stirl 278 B5
Causey Tyne/Wear 242 F6
Causey Park Bridge Northum 252 E5
Causeyend Aberds 293 B11
Causeyton Aberds 293 B8
Caute Devon 24 E6
Cavendish Suffolk 106 B6
Cavenham Suffolk 124 C5
Caversfield Oxon 101 F11
Caversham Reading 65 E8
Caversham Heights Reading 65 D8
Caverswall Staffs 169 G7
Cavil ER Yorks 207 G11
Cawdor H'land 301 D8
Cawdor Castle and Gardens H'land 301 E8
Cawkeld ER Yorks 208 C5
Cawkwell Lincs 190 F3
Cawood N Yorks 207 F7
Cawsand Cornw'l 7 E8
Cawston Norfolk 160 E2
Cawston Warwick 119 C9
Cawthorne N Yorks 216 B5
Cawthorne S Yorks 197 F9
Cawthorpe Lincs 155 E11
Cawton N Yorks 216 D2
Caxton Cambs 122 F6
Cay Hill Suffolk 125 E11
Caynham Shrops 115 C10
Caythorpe Lincs 172 F6
Caythorpe Notts 171 F11
Cayton N Yorks 217 C11
Ceallan W Isles 296 F4
Ceann a Bhàigh W Isles 305 J4
Ceann a Bhaigh W Isles 296 E3
Ceann a Deas Loch Baghasdail W Isles 297 K3
Ceann Shiphoirt W Isles 305 G4
Ceann Tarabhaigh W Isles 305 G4
Ceannacroc Lodge H'land 290 B4
Cearsiadair W Isles 304 F5
Ceathramh Meadhanach W Isles 296 D4
Cefn Newp 59 B9
Cefn Powys 148 G5
Cefn Berain Conwy 165 B7
Cefn Canol Powys 148 C4
Cefn Coch Powys 129 C10
Cefn Côch Powys 148 D2
Cefn Cribwr Bridg 57 E11
Cefn Cross Bridg 57 E11
Cefn Einion Shrops 130 F5
Cefn Fforest Caerph 77 F11
Cefn Glas Bridg 57 E11
Cefn Golau Bl Gwent 77 D10
Cefn Hengoed Caerph 77 F10
Cefn Rhigos Rh Cyn Taff 76 D6
Cefn-brith Conwy 164 E6
Cefn-bryn-brain Carms 76 C2
Cefn-bychan Flints 165 C11
Cefnbychan Swan 75 F8
Cefn-bychan Wrex 166 G3
Cefn-Byrle Powys 76 C4
Cefncaeau Carms 75 F8
Cefn-coch Conwy 164 B5
Cefn-crib Torf 78 F2
Cefn-ddwysarn Gwyn 147 B9
Cefneithin Carms 75 C9
Cefngorwydd Powys 95 B8
Cefn-hengoed Swan 75 F11
Cefn-llwyd Ceredig'n 128 G3
Cefn-mawr Wrex 166 G3
Cefnpennar Rh Cyn Taff 77 E8
Cefn-Rhouniarth Powys 148 G4
Cefn-y-Bedd Flints 166 D4
Cefn-y-garth Swan 76 E2
Cefn-y-pant Carms 92 F3
Cegidfa = Guilsfield Powys 148 G4
Cegidfa Powys 148 G4
Cei-bach Ceredig'n 111 F8
Ceinewydd = New Quay Ceredig'n 111 E7
Cellan Ceredig'n 94 B2
Cellarhead Staffs 169 F7
Cellerton Cumb 230 F5
Celyn-Mali Flints 165 B11
Cemaes Angl 178 C5
Cemmaes Powys 128 B6
Cemmaes Road Powys 128 C6
Cenarth Ceredig'n 92 C5
Ceos W Isles 304 F5
Ceres Fife 287 F8
Cerne Abbas Dorset 29 G11
Cerney Wick Glos 81 F9
Cerrigceinwen Angl 178 G6
Cerrigydrudion Conwy 165 F7
Cess Norfolk 161 F8
Cessford Scot Borders 262 E6
Ceunant Gwyn 163 C8
Chaceley Glos 99 E7
Chacewater Cornw'l 4 G4
Chackmore Bucks 102 D3
Chacombe Northants 101 C9
Chad Valley W Midlands 133 F10
Chadderton Gtr Man 196 F2
Chadderton Fold Gtr Man 195 F11
Chaddesden Derby C 153 B7
Chaddesden Common Derby C 153 B7
Chaddesley Corbett Worcs 117 C7
Chaddlehanger Devon 12 F5
Chaddlewood Plym'th 7 D11
Chaddleworth W Berks 64 D2
Chadlington Oxon 100 G6
Chadshunt Warwick 118 G6
Chadstone Northants 120 F6
Chadwell Leics 154 E5
Chadwell Shrops 150 G5
Chadwell End Beds 121 D11
Chadwell Heath London 68 B3
Chadwell St. Mary Thurr'k 68 E6
Chadwick Worcs 116 D6
Chadwick End W Midlands 118 C4
Chadwick Green Mersey 183 B8
Chaffcombe Som'set 28 E5
Chagford Devon 13 D10
Chailey E Sussex 36 D5
Chain Bridge Lincs 174 G4
Chainbridge Cambs 139 D8
Chainhurst Kent 53 D8
Chalbury Dorset 31 F8
Chalbury Common Dorset 31 F8
Chaldon Surrey 51 B10
Chaldon Herring Dorset 17 E11
Chale I/Wight 20 F5
Chale Green I/Wight 20 F5
Chalfont Common Bucks 85 G8
Chalfont St. Giles Bucks 85 G7
Chalfont St. Peter Bucks 85 G8
Chalford Glos 80 E6
Chalford Wilts 45 C11
Chalgrave Beds 103 F10
Chalgrove Oxon 83 F10
Chalk Kent 69 E7
Chalk End Essex 87 C10
Chalk Hill Beds 103 G10
Chalk Hill Glos 100 G3
Chalkhouse Green Oxon 65 D8
Chalkshire Bucks 84 D4
Chalksole Kent 55 E8
Chalkway Som'set 28 F5
Chalkwell Kent 69 G11
Chalkwell Southend 69 B11
Challaborough Devon 8 F2
Challacombe Devon 41 E7
Challister Shetl'd 314 G7
Challoch Dumf/Gal 236 C5
Challock Kent 54 C4
Chalmington Dorset 29 G9
Chalton Beds 103 F10
Chalton Beds 122 G2
Chalton Hants 34 D2
Chalvey Slough 66 D3
Chalvington E Sussex 23 D8
Chambercombe Devon 40 D4
Chamber's Green Kent 54 E2
Chambers Wall Kent 71 F9
Chance Inn Fife 287 F7
Chancery Ceredig'n 111 B11
Chanderhill Derby 186 G4
Chandler's Cross Herts 85 F9
Chandler's Cross Worcs 98 D5
Chandler's Ford Hants 32 C6
Channel's End Beds 122 F2
Channerwick Shetl'd 315 L6
Chantry Suffolk 108 C2
Chantry Som'set 45 D8
Chapel Cumb 229 E10
Chapel Fife 280 C5
Chapel N Lanarks 268 E6
Chapel Allerton Som'set 44 C2
Chapel Allerton W Yorks 205 F11
Chapel Amble Cornw'l 10 F5
Chapel Brampton Northants 120 D4
Chapel Chorlton Staffs 150 B6
Chapel Cleeve Som'set 42 E4
Chapel Cross E Sussex 37 C10
Chapel End Beds 103 B11
Chapel End Ches 167 G11
Chapel End Essex 105 F11
Chapel End Northants 138 F2
Chapel End Warwick 134 E6
Chapel Field Gtr Man 195 F9
Chapel Field Norfolk 161 E7
Chapel Fields C/York 207 C7
Chapel Fields W Midlands 118 B6
Chapel Green Herts 104 D6
Chapel Green Warwick 119 E9
Chapel Green Warwick 134 F5
Chapel Green Wokingham 65 F10
Chapel Haddlesey N Yorks 198 B5
Chapel Hill Aberds 303 F10
Chapel Hill Glos 79 E10
Chapel Hill Lincs 174 E2
Chapel Hill Monmouths 79 F8
Chapel Hill N Yorks 198 D5
Chapel Hill N Yorks 206 D2
Chapel House Lancs 194 F3
Chapel Houses Medway 69 G7
Chapel Lawn Shrops 114 B6
Chapel Leigh Som'set 27 B10
Chapel Milton Derby 185 E9
Chapel of Ease Caerph 78 F2
Chapel of Garioch Aberds 303 G7
Chapel of Stoneywood Aberd C 293 B10
Chapel Outon Dumf/Gal 236 E6
Chapel Plaister Wilts 61 F10
Chapel Row E Sussex 37 E10
Chapel Row Essex 88 E3
Chapel Row W Berks 64 F5
Chapel St. Leonards Lincs 191 G9
Chapel Stile Cumb 220 D6
Chapel Town Cornw'l 5 D7
Chapelbridge Cambs 138 E5
Chapel-en-le-Frith Derby 185 E9
Chapelgate Lincs 157 E8
Chapelhall N Lanarks 268 C5
Chapelhill Dumf/Gal 248 E3
Chapelhill H'land 301 B8
Chapelhill N Ayrs 266 G4
Chapelhill Perth/Kinr 286 D4
Chapelhill Perth/Kinr 286 E3
Chapelhill Perth/Kinr 286 E6
Chapelknowe Dumf/Gal 239 C8
Chapel-le-Dale N Yorks 212 D4
Chapels Blackb'n 195 C7
Chapels Cumb 210 C4
Chapelthorpe W Yorks 197 D10
Chapelton Angus 287 C10
Chapelton Devon 25 B9
Chapelton H'land 291 B11
Chapelton S Lanarks 268 F3
Chapelton Row Dumf/Gal 237 E8
Chapeltown Blackb'n 195 D8
Chapeltown Moray 302 G2
Chapeltown S Yorks 186 B5
Chapeltown W Yorks 206 F2
Chapman's Town E Sussex 37 D10
Chapmans Well Devon 12 C3
Chapmanslade Wilts 45 D10
Chapmore End Herts 86 B4
Chappel Essex 107 F7
Charaton Cornw'l 6 B6
Charcott Kent 52 D4
Chard Som'set 28 F4
Chard Junction Dorset 28 G4
Chardleigh Green Som'set 28 E4
Chardstock Devon 28 G4
Charfield S Glos 80 G2
Charford Worcs 117 D9
Chargrove Glos 80 B6
Chargy Hill Glos 98 G6
Charing Kent 54 D3
Charing Cross Dorset 31 E10
Charing Heath Kent 54 D2
Charing Hill Kent 54 C3
Charingworth Glos 100 D4
Charltonbrook S Yorks 186 B4
Charlacott Devon 25 B8
Charlbury Oxon 82 B5
Charlcombe Bath/NE Som'set 61 F9
Charlcutt Wilts 62 D3
Charlecote Warwick 118 F5
Charlecote Park, Wellesbourne Warwick 118 F5
Charles Devon 41 G7
Charles Bottom Devon 41 G7
Charles Manning's Amusement Park, Felixstowe Suffolk 108 E5
Charles Tye Suffolk 125 G10
Charlesfield Dumf/Gal 238 D5
Charleshill Surrey 49 E11
Charleston Angus 287 C7
Charleston Renf 267 C9
Charlestown Aberd C 293 C11
Charlestown Cornw'l 5 E10
Charlestown Derby 185 C8
Charlestown Dorset 17 F9
Charlestown Fife 279 E11
Charlestown Gtr Man 184 B4
Charlestown Gtr Man 195 G11
Charlestown H'land 299 B8
Charlestown H'land 300 E6
Charlestown W Yorks 196 B3
Charlestown W Yorks 205 G8
Charlestown of Aberlour Moray 302 E2
Charlesworth Derby 185 C7
Charlinch Som'set 43 F8
Charlottetown Fife 286 F6
Charlton Hants 47 D11
Charlton Herts 104 F3
Charlton London 68 D2
Charlton Northants 101 D10
Charlton Northum 251 F8
Charlton Oxon 64 B2
Charlton Redcar/Clevel'd 226 B2
Charlton Som'set 28 B3
Charlton Som'set 44 E6
Charlton Som'set 45 C7
Charlton Surrey 66 F5
Charlton Telford 149 G11
Charlton Wilts 30 C6
Charlton Wilts 46 B6
Charlton Wilts 62 B3
Charlton Worcs 99 B10
Charlton Worcs 116 C6
Charlton W Sussex 34 E5
Charlton Abbots Glos 99 G10
Charlton Adam Som'set 29 B8
Charlton All Saints Wilts 31 C11
Charlton Down Dorset 17 C9
Charlton Horethorne Som'set 29 C10
Charlton Kings Glos 99 G9
Charlton Mackrell Som'set 29 B8
Charlton Marshall Dorset 30 G6
Charlton Musgrove Som'set 45 G8
Charlton on Otmoor Oxon 83 B9
Charlton on the Hill Dorset 30 G5
Charlwood E Sussex 51 G11
Charlwood Hants 49 G7
Charlwood Surrey 51 E8
Charminster Bournem'th 19 C8
Charminster Dorset 17 C9
Charmouth Dorset 16 C3
Charndon Bucks 102 G3
Charney Bassett Oxon 82 G5
Charnock Green Lancs 194 D5
Charnock Richard Lancs 194 D5
Charsfield Suffolk 126 F4
Chart Corner Kent 53 C9
Chart Hill Kent 53 D9
Chart Sutton Kent 53 D10
Charter Alley Hants 48 B5
Charterhouse Som'set 44 B4
Chartershall Stirl 278 C5
Chartham Kent 54 C6
Chartham Hatch Kent 54 B6
Chartridge Bucks 84 E6
Chartwell, Westerham Kent 52 C3
Charvil Wokingham 65 D9
Charwelton Northants 119 F10
Chase Cross London 87 G8
Chase End Street Worcs 98 D5
Chase Hill Glos 61 B8
Chase Terrace Staffs 133 B10
Chaselbourne Dorset 17 B11
Chasetown Staffs 133 B11
Chastleton Oxon 100 F4
Chasty Devon 24 G4
Chatburn Lancs 203 E11
Chatcull Staffs 150 C5
Chatham Caerph 59 B8
Chatham Medway 69 F8
Chatham Green Essex 88 B2
Chathill Northum 264 D5
Chatley Worcs 117 E7
Chatsworth, Bakewell Derby 186 G3
Chattenden Medway 69 E9
Chatter End Essex 105 G9
Chatteris Cambs 139 F7
Chattern Hill Surrey 66 E5
Chattisham Suffolk 107 C11
Chatto Scot Borders 263 F7
Chatton Northum 264 D3
Chaul End Beds 103 G11
Chaulden Herts 85 D8
Chavel Shrops 149 G8
Chavenage Green Glos 80 F5
Chavey Down Brackn'l 65 F11
Chawleigh Devon 26 E2
Chawley Oxon 83 E7
Chawson Worcs 117 E7
Chawston Beds 122 F3
Chawton Hants 49 F8
Chaxhill Glos 80 C2
Chazey Heath Oxon 65 D7
Cheadle Gtr Man 184 D5
Cheadle Staffs 169 G8
Cheadle Heath Gtr Man 184 D5
Cheadle Hulme Gtr Man 184 D5
Cheadle Park Staffs 169 G8
Cheam London 67 G8
Cheapside Herts 105 E8
Cheapside Surrey 66 G4
Cheapside Windsor 66 F2
Cheapside Worcs 100 B2
Chearsley Bucks 84 C2
Chebsey Staffs 151 D7
Checkendon Oxon 65 C7
Checkley Heref'd 97 D11
Checkley Staffs 151 B10
Checkleybank Staffs 151 B10
Chedburgh Suffolk 124 F5
Cheddar Som'set 44 C3
Cheddar Gorge Caves Som'set 44 C3
Cheddington Bucks 84 B6
Cheddleton Staffs 169 E7
Cheddon Fitzpaine Som'set 28 B2
Chedglow Wilts 80 G6
Chedgrave Norfolk 143 D7
Chedington Dorset 29 F7
Chediston Suffolk 127 B7
Chediston Green Suffolk 127 B7
Chedworth Glos 81 C9
Chedworth Laines Glos 81 C8
Chedworth Roman Villa Glos 81 C9
Chedzoy Som'set 43 F10
Cheeklaw Scot Borders 272 E5
Cheesden Gtr Man 195 D10
Cheeseman's Green Kent 54 F4
Cheetham Hill Gtr Man 195 G10
Cheglinch Devon 40 E4
Cheldon Devon 26 E2
Chelford Ches 184 F4
Chell Heath Stoke 168 E5
Chellaston Derby C 153 C7
Chellington Beds 121 F9
Chells Herts 104 F5
Chelmarsh Shrops 132 F4
Chelmondiston Suffolk 108 D4
Chelmorton Derby 169 B10
Chelmsford Essex 88 D2
Chelmsine Som'set 27 D11
Chelmsley Wood W Midlands 134 F3
Chelsea London 67 D9
Chelsfield London 68 G3
Chelsham Surrey 51 B11
Chelston Som'set 27 C10
Chelston Heathfield Som'set 27 C11
Chelsworth Suffolk 107 B9
Chelsworth Common Suffolk 107 B9
Cheltenham Glos 99 G8
Cheltenham Racecourse Glos 99 G9
Chelveston Northants 121 D9
Chelvey N Som'set 60 F3
Chelwood Bath/NE Som'set 60 G6
Chelwood Common E Sussex 36 B6
Chelwood Gate E Sussex 36 B6
Chelworth Wilts 81 G7
Chelworth Lower Green Wilts 81 G9
Chelworth Upper Green Wilts 81 G9
Chelynch Som'set 45 E7
Chemistry Shrops 167 G8
Cheney Longville Shrops 131 G8
Chenies Bucks 85 F8
Chepstow Monmouths 79 G8
Chepstow Racecourse Monmouths 79 F8
Chequerbent Gtr Man 195 F7
Chequerfield W Yorks 198 C3
Chequers Corner Norfolk 139 B9
Cherhill Wilts 62 E4
Cherington Glos 80 F6
Cherington Warwick 100 D5
Cheriton Carms 75 G7
Cheriton Devon 41 D8
Cheriton Hants 33 B9
Cheriton Kent 55 F8
Cheriton Pembs 73 F7
Cheriton Barton Devon 26 F5
Cheriton Bishop Devon 13 C11
Cheriton Cross Devon 13 C11
Cheriton Fitzpaine Devon 26 F5
Cherrington Telford 150 F3
Cherry Burton ER Yorks 208 E5
Cherry Green Essex 105 F11
Cherry Green Herts 105 F7
Cherry Hinton Cambs 123 F9
Cherry Orchard Shrops 149 G9
Cherry Orchard Worcs 117 G7
Cherry Tree Blackb'n 195 B7
Cherry Tree Gtr Man 185 C7
Cherry Willingham Lincs 189 G8
Cherrybank Perth/Kinr 286 E5
Cherrytree Hill Derby C 153 B7
Chertsey Surrey 66 F5
Chesham Bucks 85 E7
Chesham Gtr Man 195 E10
Chesham Bois Bucks 85 F7
Cheshire Candle Workshops, Burwardsley Ches 167 D8
Cheshunt Herts 86 E5
Chesil Dorset 17 G9
Cheslyn Hay Staffs 133 B9
Chesnut Hill Cumb 229 G11
Chessett's Wood Warwick 118 C3
Chessington London 67 G7
Chessington World of Adventures London 67 G7
Chessmount Bucks 85 E7
Chestall Staffs 151 G11
Chester Ches 166 B5
Chester Cathedral Ches 166 B6
Chester Moor Durham 233 B11
Chester Racecourse Ches 166 B6
Chester Zoo Ches 166 A6
Chesterblade Som'set 45 E7
Chesterfield Derby 186 G5
Chesterfield Staffs 134 B2
Chesterhill Midloth 271 C7
Chesterhope Northum 251 F9
Chester-le-Street Durham 243 G7
Chesters Scot Borders 262 G4
Chesterton Cambs 138 D2
Chesterton Cambs 123 F9
Chesterton Glos 81 E8
Chesterton Oxon 101 G11
Chesterton Shrops 132 D5
Chesterton Staffs 168 F4
Chesterton Warwick 119 F7
Chesterton Green Warwick 118 F6
Chesterwood Northum 241 D8
Chestfield Kent 70 F6
Chestnut Street Kent 69 G11
Cheston Devon 8 D3
Cheswardine Shrops 150 D4
Cheswell Telford 150 F4
Cheswick Northum 273 F10
Cheswick Green W Midlands 118 B2
Chetnole Dorset 29 F10
Chetterwood Dorset 31 F7
Chettiscombe Devon 27 E7
Chettisham Cambs 139 G10
Chettle Dorset 31 E7
Chetton Shrops 132 E3
Chetwode Bucks 102 F2
Chetwynd Aston Telford 150 F5
Cheveley Cambs 124 E3
Cheveney Kent 53 D8
Chevening Kent 52 B3
Cheverell's Green Herts 85 B9
Chevin End W Yorks 205 E9
Chevington Suffolk 124 F5
Chevithorne Devon 27 D7
Chew Magna Bath/NE Som'set 60 G5
Chew Moor Gtr Man 195 F7
Chew Stoke Bath/NE Som'set 60 G5
Chewton Keynsham Bath/NE Som'set 61 F7
Chewton Mendip Som'set 44 C5
Chewton Place Bath/NE Som'set 61 F7
Cheylesmore W Midlands 118 B6
Chichacott Devon 13 B8
Chicheley M/Keynes 103 B8
Chichester W Sussex 34 F5
Chichester Cathedral W Sussex 34 G5
Chickenley W Yorks 197 C9
Chickerell Dorset 17 E8
Chickering Suffolk 126 B4
Chicklade Wilts 46 G2
Chickney Essex 105 F11
Chicksands Beds 104 D2
Chickward Heref'd 114 G5
Chidden Hants 33 D11
Chiddingfold Surrey 50 F3
Chiddingly E Sussex 37 E8
Chiddingstone Kent 52 E3
Chiddingstone Causeway Kent 52 D4
Chiddingstone Hoath Kent 52 E3
Chideock Dorset 16 C4
Chidham W Sussex 34 G3
Chidswell W Yorks 197 C9
Chieveley W Berks 64 E3
Chignall St. James Essex 87 D11
Chignall Smealy Essex 87 C11
Chigwell Essex 86 G6
Chigwell Row Essex 87 G7
Chilbolton Hants 47 F11
Chilcomb Hants 33 B8
Chilcombe Dorset 16 C6
Chilcompton Som'set 44 C6
Chilcote Leics 152 G5
Child Okeford Dorset 30 E4
Childer Thornton Ches 182 F5
Childerditch Essex 68 B6
Childrey Oxon 63 B11
Child's Ercall Shrops 150 E3
Child's Hill London 67 B8
Childsbridge Kent 52 B4
Childswickham Worcs 99 D11
Childwall Mersey 182 D6
Childwick Green Herts 85 C10
Chilfrome Dorset 17 B7
Chilgrove W Sussex 34 E4
Chilham Kent 54 C5
Chilhampton Wilts 46 G5
Chilla Devon 24 G6
Chilland Hants 48 G4
Chillaton Devon 12 E4
Chillenden Kent 55 C9
Chillerton I/Wight 20 E5
Chillesford Suffolk 127 G7
Chillingham Northum 264 D3
Chillington Devon 8 G5
Chillington Som'set 28 E5
Chillmill Kent 53 E7
Chilmark Wilts 46 G3
Chilmington Green Kent 54 E3
Chilson Oxon 82 B4
Chilsworthy Cornw'l 12 G4
Chilsworthy Devon 24 F4
Chiltern Green Beds 85 B10
Chilthorne Domer Som'set 29 D8
Chiltington E Sussex 36 D5
Chilton Bucks 83 C11
Chilton Durham 233 F11
Chilton Devon 26 G5
Chilton Kent 71 G11
Chilton Oxon 64 B3
Chilton Suffolk 107 C7
Chilton Candover Hants 48 E5
Chilton Cantelo Som'set 29 C9
Chilton Foliat Wilts 63 E10
Chilton Lane Durham 234 E2
Chilton Polden Som'set 43 F11
Chilton Street Suffolk 106 B5
Chilton Trinity Som'set 43 F9
Chilvers Coton Warwick 135 E7
Chilverton Elms Kent 55 E9
Chilwell Notts 153 B10
Chilworth Hants 32 D6
Chimney Oxon 82 E5
Chimney Street Suffolk 106 B4
Chineham Hants 49 C7
Chingford London 86 G5
Chingford Green London 86 G5
Chingford Hatch London 86 G5
Chinley Derby 185 E8
Chinley Head Derby 185 E8
Chinnor Oxon 84 E3
Chipley Som'set 27 C10
Chipnall Shrops 150 C4
Chippenhall Green Suffolk 126 B5
Chippenham Cambs 124 D3
Chippenham Wilts 62 E2
Chipperfield Herts 85 E8
Chipping Herts 105 E7
Chipping Lancs 203 E8
Chipping Barnet London 86 F2
Chipping Campden Glos 100 D3
Chipping Hill Essex 88 B4
Chipping Norton Oxon 100 F6
Chipping Ongar Essex 87 E9
Chipping Sodbury S Glos 61 C8
Chipping Warden Northants 101 B10
Chipstable Som'set 27 B8
Chipstead Kent 52 B4
Chipstead Surrey 51 B9
Chirbury Shrops 130 D5
Chirk = Y Waun Wrex 148 B5
Chirk Bank Shrops 148 B5
Chirk Castle Wrex 148 B5
Chirk Green Wrex 148 B5
Chirmorrie S Ayrs 236 B4
Chirnside Scot Borders 273 D7
Chirnsidebridge Scot Borders 273 D7
Chirton Tyne/Wear 243 D8
Chirton Wilts 46 B5
Chisbury Wilts 63 F9
Chisel Hill Norfolk 160 F4
Chiselborough Som'set 29 D7
Chiseldon Swindon 63 D7
Chiserley W Yorks 196 B4
Chislehampton Oxon 83 F9
Chislehurst London 68 F2
Chislet Kent 71 G8
Chislet Forstal Kent 71 G8
Chiswell Green Herts 85 E10
Chiswick London 67 D8
Chiswick End Cambs 105 B7
Chisworth Derby 185 C7
Chithurst W Sussex 34 C4
Chittering Cambs 123 C9
Chitterley Devon 26 G6
Chitterne Wilts 46 E3
Chittlehamholt Devon 25 C10
Chittlehampton Devon 25 B10
Chittoe Wilts 62 F3
Chitty Kent 71 G8
Chivelstone Devon 9 G10
Chivenor Devon 40 G4
Chiworth Surrey 50 D4
Chobham Surrey 66 G3
Choicelee Scot Borders 272 E4
Cholderton Wilts 47 E8
Cholesbury Bucks 84 D6
Chollerford Northum 241 C10
Chollerton Northum 241 C10
Cholsey Oxon 64 B5
Cholwell Bath/NE Som'set 44 B6
Choon Cornw'l 4 F5
Chop Gate N Yorks 225 F11
Choppington Northum 253 G7
Chopwell Tyne/Wear 242 F4
Chorley Ches 167 E9
Chorley Lancs 194 D5
Chorley Shrops 132 G3
Chorley Staffs 151 G11
Chorley Green Ches 167 E9
Chorleywood Herts 85 F8
Chorleywood Bottom Herts 85 F8
Chorleywood West Herts 85 F8
Chorlton Ches 168 E2
Chorlton cum Hardy Gtr Man 184 C4
Chorlton Lane Ches 167 F7
Choulton Shrops 131 F7
Chowdene Tyne/Wear 243 F7
Chreagain H'land 289 C10
Chrishall Essex 105 D8
Christ Church Oxford Oxon 83 D8
Christchurch Cambs 139 D9
Christchurch Dorset 19 C9
Christchurch Glos 79 C9
Christchurch Newp 59 B10
Christchurch Priory Dorset 19 C9
Christian Malford Wilts 62 D3
Christleton Ches 166 B6
Christmas Common Oxon 84 G2
Christon N Som'set 43 B11
Christon Bank Northum 264 E6
Christow Devon 14 E2
Chryston N Lanarks 278 G3
Chuck Hatch E Sussex 52 G3
Chudleigh Devon 14 F3
Chudleigh Knighton Devon 14 F2
Chulmleigh Devon 25 E11
Chunal Derby 185 C8
Church Lancs 195 B8
Church Aston Telford 150 F4
Church Brampton Northants 120 D4
Church Brough Cumb 222 C5
Church Broughton Derby 152 C4
Church Charwelton Northants 119 F10
Church Clough Lancs 204 F3
Church Cove Cornw'l 2 G6
Church Crookham Hants 49 C10
Church Eaton Staffs 151 F7
Church End Beds 121 F11
Church End Beds 103 G9
Church End Beds 103 E9
Church End Beds 104 D3
Church End Beds 122 F2
Church End Bucks 84 D2
Church End Bucks 84 B6
Church End Cambs 121 C11
Church End Cambs 123 C7
Church End Cambs 138 G4
Church End Cambs 139 B7
Church End Cambs 123 D7
Church End Cambs 123 F9
Church End Essex 105 F11
Church End Essex 88 B2
Church End Essex 106 F4
Church End Essex 105 C11
Church End Glos 99 D7
Church End Glos 80 D2
Church End Hants 49 B7
Church End Herts 85 F8
Church End Herts 85 C10

Church End Herts 104 E5
Church End Herts 105 G8
Church End Lincs 156 C4
Church End Lincs 190 B6
Church End London 67 C8
Church End London 86 G2
Church End Norfolk 157 F10
Church End Suffolk 108 D4
Church End Surrey 50 B5
Church End Warwick 134 E4
Church End Warwick 134 E5
Church End Wilts 62 D4
Church Enstone Oxon 101 F7
Church Fenton N Yorks 206 F6
Church Green Devon 15 B9
Church Green Norfolk 141 E11
Church Green Warrington 183 D11
Church Gresley Derby 152 F5
Church Grounds Dorset 16 B5
Church Hanborough Oxon 82 C6
Church Hill Ches 167 B10
Church Hill Derby 170 C6
Church Hill Pembs 73 C7
Church Hill Staffs 151 G10
Church Hill Worcs 117 D11
Church Hougham Kent 55 E9
Church Houses N Yorks 226 F3
Church Knowle Dorset 18 E4
Church Laneham Notts 188 F4
Church Langley Essex 87 D7
Church Langton Leics 136 E4
Church Lawford Warwick 119 B9
Church Lawton Ches 168 D4
Church Leigh Staffs 151 B10
Church Lench Worcs 117 G10
Church Mayfield Staffs 169 G11
Church Minshull Ches 167 C11
Church Norton W Sussex 22 D5
Church Oakley Hants 48 C5
Church Preen Shrops 131 D10
Church Pulverbatch Shrops 131 C8
Church Stoke Powys 130 E5
Church Stowe Northants 120 F2
Church Street Essex 106 C5
Church Street Kent 69 E8
Church Stretton Shrops 131 E9
Church Town Cornw'l 4 G3
Church Town Leics 153 F7
Church Town Surrey 51 C11
Church Village Rh Cyn Taff 58 B5
Church Warsop Notts 171 B9
Church Whitfield Kent 55 D10
Church Wilne Derby 153 C9
Churcham Glos 80 B3
Churchbridge Cornw'l 6 D4
Churchbridge Staffs 133 B9
Churchdown Devon 24 G3
Churchdown Glos 80 B5
Churchend Essex 89 G8
Churchend Essex 106 G2
Churchend Glos 80 D3
Churchend Reading 65 E7
Churchend S Glos 80 G2
Churchfield W Midlands 133 E10
Churchgate Herts 86 E4
Churchgate Street Essex 87 C7
Churchill Devon 28 G3
Churchill Devon 40 E5
Churchill N Som'set 44 B2
Churchill Oxon 100 G5
Churchill Worcs 117 G8
Churchill Worcs 117 B7
Churchill Green N Som'set 60 G2
Churchinford Som'set 28 E2
Churchover Warwick 135 G10
Churchstanton Som'set 27 E11
Churchstanton Hill Som'set 28 E2
Churchstow Devon 8 F4
Churchtown Cumb 230 C3
Churchtown Cornw'l 11 F7
Churchtown Devon 41 E7
Churchtown I/Man 192 C5
Churchtown Lancs 202 E5
Churchtown Mersey 193 D11
Churchtown N Lincs 199 F9
Churchtown Shrops 130 F5
Churchwood W Sussex 35 D8
Churscombe Torbay 9 C7
Churston Ferrers Torbay 9 D8
Churt Surrey 49 F11
Churt Common Surrey 49 F11
Churton Ches 166 D6
Churwell W Yorks 197 B9
Chute Cadley Wilts 47 C10
Chute Standen Wilts 47 C10
Chwilog Gwyn 145 B8
Chyandour Cornw'l 1 C5
Cicelyford Monmouths 79 E8
Cilau Pembs 91 D8
Cilcain Flints 165 C11
Cilcennin Ceredig'n 111 E10
Cilcewydd Powys 130 C4
Cilfrew Neath P Talb 76 E3
Cilfynydd Rh Cyn Taff 77 F9
Cilgerran Pembs 92 C3
Cil-Gwrgan Powys 130 E2
Cilgwyn Carms 94 F4
Cilgwyn Gwyn 163 E7
Cilgwyn Pembs 91 D11
Ciliau Aeron Ceredig'n 111 F10
Cill Amhlaidh W Isles 297 G3
Cill Donnain W Isles 297 J3
Cill Eireabhagh W Isles 297 G4
Cille Bhrighde W Isles 297 K3
Cille Pheadair W Isles 297 K3
Cilmaengwyn Neath P Talb 76 D2
Cilmery Powys 113 G10
Cilrhedyn Pembs 92 E5
Cilsan Carms 93 G11
Ciltwrch Powys 96 C3
Cilybebyll Neath P Talb 76 E2
Cilycwm Carms 94 C5
Cimla Rh Cyn Taff 76 F3
Cinder Hill Gtr Man 195 F9
Cinder Hill W Midlands 133 E8
Cinder Hill W Sussex 36 B5
Cinderford Glos 79 C11
Cinderhill Nott'ham 171 G8
Cinnamon Brow Warrington 183 C10
Cippenham Slough 66 C2
Cippyn Pembs 92 B2
Circebost W Isles 304 E3
Cirencester Glos 81 E8
Ciribhig W Isles 304 D3
Citadilla N Yorks 224 E4
City Powys 130 F4
City V/Glam 58 D3
City Dulas Angl 179 D7
Clabhach Arg/Bute 288 D3
Clachaig Arg/Bute 276 E2
Clachaig H'land 292 B2
Clachaig N Ayrs 255 E10
Clachan Arg/Bute 255 B8
Clachan Arg/Bute 275 B8
Clachan Arg/Bute 284 F5
Clachan Arg/Bute 289 E10
Clachan H'land 295 B7
Clachan H'land 298 C4
Clachan H'land 299 E3
Clachan H'land 307 L6
Clachan W Isles 297 G3
Clachan na Luib W Isles 296 E4
Clachan of Campsie E Dunb 278 F2
Clachan of Glendaruel Arg/Bute 275 E10
Clachan Strachur Arg/Bute 284 G4
Clachaneasy Dumf/Gal 236 B5
Clachanmore Dumf/Gal 236 E2
Clachan-Seil Arg/Bute 275 B8
Clachbreck Arg/Bute 275 F8
Clachnabrain Angus 292 G5
Clachtoll H'land 307 G5
Clackmannan Clack 279 C8
Clackmarras Moray 302 D2
Clacton-on-Sea Essex 89 C11
Cladach N Ayrs 256 B2
Cladach Chairinis W Isles 296 F4
Cladach Chireboist W Isles 296 E3
Claddach Arg/Bute 254 B2
Claddach-knockline W Isles 296 E3
Cladich Arg/Bute 284 E4
Cladich Steading Arg/Bute 284 E4
Cladswell Worcs 117 F10
Claggan H'land 289 E8
Claggan H'land 290 F3
Claggan Perth/Kinr 285 D11
Claigan H'land 298 D2
Claines Worcs 116 F6
Clandown Bath/NE Som'set 45 B7
Clanfield Hants 34 D2
Clanfield Oxon 82 E3
Clanking Bucks 84 D4
Clanville Hants 47 D10
Clanville Som'set 44 G6
Claonaig Arg/Bute 255 B9
Claonel H'land 309 J5
Clap Hill Kent 54 F5
Clapgate Dorset 31 G8
Clapgate Herts 105 F8
Clapham Beds 121 G10
Clapham Devon 14 D3
Clapham London 67 D9
Clapham N Yorks 212 F4
Clapham W Sussex 35 F9
Clapham Green Beds 121 G10
Clapham Green N Yorks 205 B10
Clapham Hill Kent 70 G6
Clapham Park London 67 E9
Clapper Hill Kent 53 F11
Clappers Scot Borders 273 D8
Clappersgate Cumb 221 E7
Clapphoull Shetl'd 315 L6
Clapton Som'set 28 F6
Clapton Som'set 44 C6
Clapton Wick N Som'set 60 E2
Clapton-in-Gordano N Som'set 60 E3
Clapton-on-the-Hill Glos 81 B11
Clapworthy Devon 25 C11
Clara Vale Tyne/Wear 242 E4
Clarach Ceredig'n 128 G2
Clarack Aberds 292 D6
Clarbeston Pembs 91 G10
Clarbeston Road Pembs 91 G10
Clarborough Notts 188 E2
Clardon H'land 310 C5
Clare Suffolk 106 B5
Clarebrand Dumf/Gal 237 C9
Claregate W Midlands 133 C7
Claremont Landscape Garden, Esher Surrey 66 G6
Claremont Park Surrey 66 G6
Claremount W Yorks 196 B5
Clarence Park N Som'set 59 G10
Clarencefield Dumf/Gal 238 D3
Clarendon Park Leics C 135 C11
Clareston Pembs 73 C7
Clarilaw Scot Borders 262 F3
Clark Green Ches 184 F6
Clarken Green Hants 48 C5
Clark's Green Worcs 99 C10
Clark's Green Surrey 51 F7
Clark's Hill Lincs 157 E7
Clarksfield Gtr Man 196 G2
Clarkston E Renf 267 D11
Clarkston N Lanarks 268 B5
Clase Swan 75 F11
Clashandorran H'land 300 E5
Clashcoig H'land 309 K6
Clasheddy H'land 308 C6
Clashgour Arg/Bute 284 C6
Clashindarroch Aberds 302 F4
Clashmore H'land 306 F5
Clashmore H'land 309 L7
Clashnessie H'land 306 F5
Clashnoir Moray 302 G2
Clate Shetl'd 315 G7
Clatford Wilts 63 F7
Clatford Oakcuts Hants 47 F10
Clathy Perth/Kinr 286 F3
Clatt Aberds 302 G5
Clatter Powys 129 E9
Clatterford I/Wight 20 D5
Clatterford End Essex 87 C10
Clatterford End Essex 87 E8
Clatterford End Essex 87 D9
Clatterin Bridge Aberds 293 F8
Clatto Fife 287 F8
Clatworthy Som'set 42 G5
Clauchlands N Ayrs 256 C2
Claughton Lancs 202 E6
Claughton Lancs 211 F11
Claughton Mersey 182 D4
Clavelshay Som'set 43 G9
Claverdon Warwick 118 E3
Claverham N Som'set 60 F2
Clavering Essex 105 E9
Claverley Shrops 132 E5
Claverton Bath/NE Som'set 61 G9
Claverton Wilts 62 B3
Claverton Down Bath/NE Som'set 61 G9
Clawdd Poncen Denbs 165 G9
Clawddcoch V/Glam 58 D5
Clawdd-llesg Powys 148 G3
Clawdd-newydd Denbs 165 E9
Clawthorpe Cumb 211 D10
Clawton Devon 12 B3
Claxby Lincs 190 G6
Claxby Lincs 189 B10
Claxby Pluckacre Lincs 174 B4
Claxton Norfolk 142 B6
Claxton N Yorks 216 G3
Clay Common Suffolk 143 G9
Clay Coton Northants 119 B11
Clay Cross Derby 170 C5
Clay End Herts 104 F6
Clay Hill Bristol 60 E6
Clay Hill London 86 F4
Clay Hill W Berks 64 F3
Clay Hill W Berks 64 E5
Clay Lake Lincs 156 E4
Clay Mills Derby 152 D5
Claybokie Aberds 292 D2
Claybrooke Magna Leics 135 F9
Claybrooke Parva Leics 135 F9
Claydon Oxon 101 B9
Claydon Suffolk 126 G2
Claygate Dumf/Gal 239 B9
Claygate Kent 52 C6
Claygate Kent 53 E8
Claygate Surrey 67 G7
Claygate Cross Kent 52 B6
Clayhall Hants 21 B8
Clayhall London 68 B2
Clayhanger Devon 27 C8
Clayhanger Som'set 28 E4
Clayhanger W Midlands 133 C10
Clayhidon Devon 27 D11
Clayhill E Sussex 38 C4
Clayhill Hants 32 F4
Clayhithe Cambs 123 E10
Clayholes Angus 287 D9
Claylock H'land 310 D5
Claypit Hill Cambs 123 G7
Claypits Glos 80 D3
Claypole Lincs 172 F5
Clays End Bath/NE Som'set 61 G8
Claythorpe Lincs 190 F6
Clayton Gtr Man 184 B5
Clayton Staffs 168 G4
Clayton S Yorks 198 F3
Clayton W Sussex 36 E4
Clayton W Yorks 205 G8
Clayton Brook Lancs 194 C5
Clayton Green Lancs 194 C5
Clayton Heights W Yorks 205 G8
Clayton Vale Gtr Man 184 B5
Clayton West W Yorks 197 E9
Clayton-le-Dale Lancs 203 G9
Clayton-le-Moors Lancs 203 G10
Clayton-le-Woods Lancs 194 C5
Clayworth Notts 188 D2
Cleadale H'land 294 G6
Cleadon Tyne/Wear 243 E9
Cleadon Park Tyne/Wear 243 E9
Clearbrook Devon 7 B10
Clearwell Glos 79 D9
Clearwell Meend Glos 79 D9
Clearwood Wilts 45 D10
Cleasby N Yorks 224 C5
Cleat Orkney 312 D5
Cleat Orkney 313 K5
Cleat Hill Beds 121 G11
Cleatham N Lincs 200 G2
Cleatlam Durham 224 B2
Cleator Cumb 219 C10
Cleator Moor Cumb 219 B10
Cleave Devon 28 G2
Clebrig H'land 308 F5
Cleckheaton W Yorks 197 B7
Clee St. Margaret Shrops 131 G11
Cleedownton Shrops 131 G11
Cleehill Shrops 115 B11
Cleekhimin N Lanarks 268 D5
Cleers Cornw'l 5 D9
Cleestanton Shrops 115 B11
Cleethorpes NE Lincs 201 F10
Cleeton St. Mary Shrops 116 B2
Cleeve Glos 80 C2
Cleeve N Som'set 60 F3
Cleeve Oxon 64 C6
Cleeve Hill Glos 99 F9
Cleeve Prior Worcs 99 B11
Clegyrnant Powys 129 B8
Clehonger Heref'd 97 D8
Cleish Perth/Kinr 279 B11
Cleland N Lanarks 268 D6
Clement Street London 68 E4
Clement's End Beds 85 C8
Clench Wilts 63 G7
Clench Common Wilts 63 F7
Clenchwarton Norfolk 157 E11
Clent Worcs 117 B8
Cleobury Mortimer Shrops 116 B3
Cleobury North Shrops 132 F2
Cleongart Arg/Bute 255 D7
Clephanton H'land 301 D8
Clerk Green W Yorks 197 C8
Clerkenwell London 67 C10
Clerklands Scot Borders 262 E2
Clermiston C/Edinb 280 G3
Clestrain Orkney 313 H4
Cleuch Head Scot Borders 262 G3
Cleughbrae Dumf/Gal 238 C3
Clevancy Wilts 62 D4
Clevedon N Som'set 60 E2
Cleveland N Yorks 226 B4
Cleverley Oxon 101 G7
Cleveleys Lancs 202 E2
Clevelode Worcs 98 B6
Clewer Som'set 44 C2
Clewer Windsor 66 D3
Clewer Green Windsor 66 D2
Clewer New Town Windsor 66 D3
Clewers Hill Hants 33 D9
Cley next the Sea Norfolk 177 E9
Cliaid W Isles 297 L2
Cliasmol W Isles 305 H2
Cliburn Cumb 231 G7
Click Mill Orkney 312 F4
Cliddesden Hants 48 D6
Clieves Hills Lancs 193 F11
Cliff Cornw'l 6 D2
Cliff Derby 185 D8
Cliff Warwick 134 D4
Cliff End E Sussex 38 E5
Cliff End W Yorks 196 D6
Cliffburn Angus 287 C10
Cliffe Lancs 203 G10
Cliffe Medway 69 D8
Cliffe N Yorks 207 G9
Cliffe N Yorks 224 C4
Cliffe Bank N Yorks 224 C4
Cliffe Hill W Yorks 196 C6
Cliffe Woods Medway 69 E8
Clifford Heref'd 96 B4
Clifford W Yorks 206 E4
Clifford Chambers Warwick 118 G3
Clifford's Mesne Glos 98 G3
Cliffs End Kent 71 G10
Clifftown Southend 69 B11
Clifton Beds 104 D3
Clifton Bristol 60 E5
Clifton Nott'ham 153 C11
Clifton Cumb 230 F6
Clifton C/York 207 C7
Clifton Derby 169 G11
Clifton Devon 40 E6
Clifton Lancs 202 G5
Clifton Northum 252 G6
Clifton N Yorks 205 D9
Clifton Oxon 101 E9
Clifton Stirl 285 D7
Clifton S Yorks 186 C6
Clifton S Yorks 187 B8
Clifton Worcs 98 B6
Clifton W Yorks 197 C7
Clifton Campville Staffs 152 G5
Clifton Dykes Cumb 230 F6
Clifton Green Gtr Man 195 G9
Clifton Hampden Oxon 83 F8
Clifton Hill Worcs 116 E4
Clifton Maybank Dorset 29 E9
Clifton Reynes M/Keynes 121 G8
Clifton upon Dunsmore Warwick 119 C10
Clifton upon Teme Worcs 116 E4
Clifton Wood W Yorks 197 C7
Cliftonville Kent 71 E11
Cliftonville Norfolk 160 B6
Cliftonville N Lanarks 268 B4
Climping W Sussex 35 G8
Climpy S Lanarks 269 D8
Clink Som'set 45 D9
Clinkham Wood Mersey 183 B8
Clint N Yorks 205 B11
Clint Green Norfolk 159 G10
Clintmains Scot Borders 262 C4
Clints N Yorks 224 E2
Cliobh W Isles 304 E2
Clippesby Norfolk 161 G8
Clippings Green Norfolk 159 G10
Clipsham Rutl'd 155 F9
Clipston Northants 136 G4
Clipston Notts 154 C2
Clipstone Notts 171 C9
Clitheroe Lancs 203 E10
Cliuthar W Isles 305 J3
Clive Ches 167 B11
Clive Shrops 149 E10
Clive Vale E Sussex 38 E4
Clivocast Shetl'd 314 C8
Clixby Lincs 200 G6
Cloatley Wilts 81 G7
Cloatley End Wilts 81 G7
Clocaenog Denbs 165 E9
Clochan Aberds 303 E9
Clochan Moray 302 C4
Clock Face Mersey 183 C8
Clockmill Scot Borders 272 E5
Cloddiau Powys 130 B4
Cloddymoss Moray 301 D9
Clodock Heref'd 96 F6
Cloford Som'set 45 E8
Clogwyn Melyn Gwyn 163 E7
Cloigyn Carms 74 C6
Clola Aberds 303 E10
Clophill Beds 103 D11
Clopton Northants 137 G11
Clopton Corner Suffolk 126 G4
Clopton Green Suffolk 126 G4
Clopton Green Suffolk 124 G5
Clopton Green Suffolk 125 E9
Close Clark I/Man 192 E3
Close House Durham 233 F10
Closeburn Dumf/Gal 247 E9
Closworth Som'set 29 E9
Clothall Herts 104 E5
Clotton Ches 167 C8
Clough Gtr Man 196 F2
Clough Gtr Man 196 D2
Clough W Yorks 196 E5
Clough Dene Durham 242 F5
Clough Fold Lancs 195 C10
Clough Foot W Yorks 196 C2
Clough Hall Staffs 168 E4
Clough Head W Yorks 196 C5
Cloughton N Yorks 227 G10
Cloughton Newlands N Yorks 227 F10
Clounlaid H'land 289 D9
Clousta Shetl'd 315 H5
Clouston Orkney 312 G3
Clova Aberds 302 G4
Clova Angus 292 F5
Clovelly Devon 24 C4
Clovelly Village Devon 24 C4
Clovenfords Scot Borders 261 B11
Clovenstone Aberds 293 B9
Cloves Moray 301 C11
Clovullin H'land 290 G2
Clow Bridge Lancs 195 B10
Clown Hills Leics C 136 C2
Clowne Derby 187 F7
Clows Top Worcs 116 C4
Cloy Wrex 166 G5
Cluanie Inn H'land 290 B2
Cluanie Lodge H'land 290 B2
Clubmoor Mersey 182 C5
Cluddley Telford 150 G2
Clun Shrops 130 F6
Clunbury Shrops 131 G7
Clunderwen Pembs 73 B10
Clune H'land 301 D9
Clune H'land 301 G7
Clunes H'land 290 E4
Clungunford Shrops 115 B8
Clunie Aberds 302 D6
Clunie Perth/Kinr 286 C5
Clunton Shrops 130 G6
Cluny Fife 280 B4
Cluny Castle Aberds 293 B8
Cluny Castle H'land 291 D8
Clutton Bath/NE Som'set 44 B6
Clutton Ches 167 E7
Clutton Hill Bath/NE Som'set 44 B6
Clwt-grugoer Conwy 165 C7
Clwt-y-bont Gwyn 163 C9
Clydach Monmouths 78 C2
Clydach Swan 75 E11
Clydach Terrace Bl Gwent 77 C11
Clydach Vale Rh Cyn Taff 77 G7
Clydebank Renf 267 B9
Clydey Pembs 92 D5
Clyffe Pypard Wilts 62 D5
Clynder Arg/Bute 276 E4
Clyne Neath P Talb 76 E4
Clynelish H'land 311 J2
Clyn-mil Merth Tyd 77 F9
Clynnog-fawr Gwyn 162 F6
Clyro Powys 96 C4
Clyst Honiton Devon 14 C5
Clyst Hydon Devon 27 G8
Clyst St. George Devon 14 D5
Clyst St. Lawrence Devon 27 G8
Clyst St. Mary Devon 14 C5
Cnip W Isles 304 E2
Cnoc Amhlaigh W Isles 304 E7
Cnoc an t-Solais W Isles 304 D6
Cnoc Fhionn H'land 295 D10
Cnoc Màiri W Isles 304 E6
Cnoc Rolum W Isles 296 F3
Cnocbreac Arg/Bute 274 F5
Cnwch Coch Ceredig'n 112 C3
Coachford Aberds 302 E4
Coad's Green Cornw'l 11 F11
Coal Aston Derby 186 F5
Coal Pool W Midlands 133 C10
Coalbournbrook W Midlands 133 F7
Coalbrook Swan 75 E9
Coalbrookdale Telford 132 C3
Coalbrookvale Bl Gwent 77 D11
Coalburn S Lanarks 259 C8
Coalburns Tyne/Wear 242 E4
Coalcleugh Northum 232 B2
Coaley Glos 80 E3
Coaley Peak Glos 80 E3
Coalford Aberds 293 D10
Coalhall E Ayrs 257 F10
Coalhill Essex 88 F3
Coalpit Field Warwick 135 F7
Coalpit Heath S Glos 61 C7
Coalpit Hill Staffs 168 E4
Coalport Telford 132 C3
Coalsnaughton Clack 279 B8
Coaltown of Balgonie Fife 280 B6
Coaltown of Wemyss Fife 280 B6
Coalville Leics 153 G8
Coalway Glos 79 C9
Coanwood Northum 240 F5
Coat Som'set 29 C7
Coatbridge N Lanarks 268 C4
Coatdyke N Lanarks 268 C5
Coate Swindon 63 C7
Coate Wilts 62 G4
Coates Cambs 138 D6
Coates Glos 81 E7
Coates Lancs 204 D3
Coates Lincs 188 E6
Coates Notts 188 E4
Coates W Sussex 35 D7
Coatham Redcar/Clevel'd 235 F7
Coatham Mundeville D'lington 233 G11
Cobairdy Aberds 302 E5
Cobb Dorset 16 C2
Cobbaton Devon 25 B10
Cobbler's Green Norfolk 142 E5
Cobbler's Plain Monmouths 79 E7
Cobbs Warrington 183 D10
Coberley Glos 81 B7
Cobhall Common Heref'd 97 D9
Cobham Kent 69 F7
Cobham Surrey 66 G6
Cobholm Island Norfolk 143 B10
Cobleland Stirl 277 B10
Cobler's Green Essex 87 B11
Cobnash Heref'd 115 E9
Cobridge Stoke 168 F5
Coburg Devon 14 F3
Coburty Aberds 303 C9
Cock Alley Derby 170 B6
Cock and End Suffolk 124 G4
Cock Bank Wrex 166 F5
Cock Bridge Aberds 292 C4
Cock Clarks Essex 88 E4
Cock Gate Heref'd 115 D9
Cock Green Essex 87 B11
Cock Marling E Sussex 38 D5
Cock Street Kent 53 C9
Cockayne N Yorks 226 F2
Cockayne Hatley Beds 104 B5
Cockburnspath Scot Borders 282 G5
Cockden Lancs 204 G3
Cockenzie & Port Seton E Loth 281 F7
Cockerham Lancs 202 C5
Cockermouth Cumb 229 E8
Cockernhoe Herts 104 G2
Cockersdale W Yorks 197 B8
Cockerton D'lington 224 B5
Cockett Swan 75 G10
Cockett Hill Dorset 18 B4
Cocketty Aberds 293 F9
Cockfield Durham 233 G8
Cockfield Suffolk 125 G8
Cockfosters London 86 F3
Cockhill Som'set 44 G6
Cocking W Sussex 34 D5
Cocking Causeway W Sussex 34 D5
Cockington Torbay 9 C7
Cocklake Som'set 44 D2
Cocklaw Northum 241 C10
Cockley Beck Cumb 220 E4
Cockley Cley Norfolk 140 C5
Cockpole Green Windsor 65 C9
Cocks Cornw'l 4 E5
Cocks Green Suffolk 125 F7
Cockshead Ceredig'n 112 F2
Cockshoot Hill Beds 104 D2
Cockshutford Shrops 131 F11
Cockshutt Shrops 132 G4
Cockshutt Shrops 149 D8
Cockthorpe Norfolk 177 E7
Cockwood Devon 14 E5
Cockwood Som'set 43 E8
Cockyard Derby 185 F8
Cockyard Heref'd 97 E8
Coddenham Suffolk 126 G2
Coddenham Green Suffolk 126 F2
Coddington Ches 167 D7
Coddington Heref'd 98 C5
Coddington Notts 172 E4
Codford St. Mary Wilts 46 F3
Codford St. Peter Wilts 46 E3
Codicote Herts 86 B2
Codmore Hill W Sussex 35 C9
Codnor Derby 170 F6
Codnor Breach Derby 170 F6
Codnor Gate Derby 170 E6
Codrington S Glos 61 D8
Codsall Staffs 133 C7
Codsall Wood Staffs 132 C6
Codsend Som'set 41 F11
Coed Duon = Blackwood Caerph 77 F11
Coed Eva Torf 78 G3
Coed Mawr Gwyn 179 G9
Coed Morgan Monmouths 78 C5
Coed Ystumgwern Gwyn 145 E11
Coedcae Bl Gwent 78 D2
Coedcae Torf 78 D3
Coed-Cwnwr Monmouths 78 F6
Coedely Rh Cyn Taff 58 B4
Coedkernew Newp 59 C9
Coedpoeth Wrex 166 E3
Coed-Talon Flints 166 D3
Coedway Powys 148 G6
Coed-y-bryn Ceredig'n 93 B7
Coed-y-caerau Newp 78 G5
Coed-y-go Shrops 148 D5
Coed-y-maen Powys 148 G3
Coed-y-paen Monmouths 78 F4
Coed-y-parc Gwyn 163 B10
Coed-yr-ynys Powys 96 G3
Coelbren Powys 76 C4
Coffinswell Devon 9 B7
Cofton Devon 14 E5
Cofton Common W Midlands 117 B10
Cofton Hackett Worcs 117 B10
Cogan V/Glam 59 E7
Cogenhoe Northants 120 E6
Cogges Oxon 82 D5
Coggeshall Essex 107 G7
Coggeshall Hamlet Essex 106 G6
Coggins Mill E Sussex 37 B9
Còsag H'land 295 D10
Coham Devon 25 F7
Coig Peighinnean W Isles 304 B7
Coig Peighinnean Bhuirgh W Isles 304 C6
Coignafearn Lodge H'land 291 B8
Coignascallan H'land 291 B9
Coilacriech Aberds 292 D5
Coilantogle Stirl 285 G9
Coilessan Arg/Bute 284 G6
Coilleag W Isles 297 K3
Coillemore H'land 300 B6
Coillore H'land 294 B5
Coirea-chrombe Stirl 285 G9
Coity Bridg 58 C2
Cokenach Herts 105 D7
Cokhay Green Derby 152 D5
Col W Isles 304 D6
Col Uarach W Isles 304 E6
Colaboll H'land 309 H5
Colan Cornw'l 5 C7
Colaton Raleigh Devon 15 D7
Colbost H'land 298 E2
Colbrooke Devon 26 G3
Colburn N Yorks 224 F4
Colbury Hants 32 E5
Colby Cumb 231 G9
Colby I/Man 192 E3
Colby Norfolk 160 C4
Colchester Essex 107 G10
Colchester Green Suffolk 125 F8
Colchester Zoo Essex 107 G9
Colcot V/Glam 58 F6
Cold Ash W Berks 64 F4
Cold Ashby Northants 120 B3
Cold Ashton S Glos 61 E8
Cold Aston Glos 81 B10
Cold Brayfield M/Keynes 121 G8
Cold Cotes N Yorks 212 E4
Cold Green Heref'd 98 C3
Cold Hanworth Lincs 189 E8
Cold Harbour Herts 85 B10
Cold Harbour Oxon 64 D6
Cold Harbour Wilts 45 D11
Cold Hatton Telford 150 E2
Cold Hatton Heath Telford 150 E2
Cold Hesledon Durham 234 B4
Cold Hiendley W Yorks 197 E11
Cold Higham Northants 120 G3
Cold Inn Pembs 73 D10
Cold Kirby N Yorks 215 C10
Cold Northcott Cornw'l 11 D10
Cold Norton Essex 88 E4
Cold Overton Leics 154 G6
Cold Row Lancs 202 E3
Coldbackie H'land 308 D6
Coldblow London 68 E4
Coldbrook Powys 96 D3
Coldean Brighton/Hove 36 F4
Coldeast Devon 14 G2
Colden W Yorks 196 B3
Colden Common Hants 33 C7
Coldham Cambs 139 C8
Coldharbour Cornw'l 4 F5
Coldharbour Dorset 17 E8
Coldharbour Devon 27 E9
Coldharbour Glos 79 E9
Coldharbour Kent 52 C5
Coldharbour London 68 D4
Coldingham Scot Borders 273 B8
Coldmeece Staffs 151 C7
Coldpool N Yorks 225 C9
Coldrain Perth/Kinr 286 G4
Coldred Kent 55 D9
Coldridge Devon 25 F11
Coldstream Angus 287 D7
Coldstream Scot Borders 263 B8
Coldvreath Cornw'l 5 D9
Coldwaltham W Sussex 35 D8
Coldwells Aberds 303 E11
Coldwells Croft Aberds 302 G5
Cole Som'set 45 G7
Cole End Essex 105 D11
Cole End Warwick 134 F4
Cole Green Herts 86 C3
Cole Green Herts 105 E8
Cole Henley Hants 48 C3
Colebatch Shrops 130 F6
Colebrook Devon 27 F8
Coleburn Moray 302 D2
Coleby Lincs 173 C7
Coleby N Lincs 199 D11
Coleford Devon 26 G3
Coleford Glos 79 C9
Coleford Som'set 45 D7
Coleford Water Som'set 42 G6
Colegate End Norfolk 142 F3
Colehill Dorset 31 G8
Coleman Green Herts 85 C11
Coleman's Hatch E Sussex 52 G2
Colemere Shrops 149 C8
Colemore Hants 49 G8
Colemore Green Shrops 132 D4
Coleorton Leics 153 F8
Coleorton Moor Leics 153 F8
Colerne Wilts 61 E10
Cole's Common Norfolk 142 F4
Cole's Cross Dorset 28 G5
Coles Green Suffolk 107 C11
Coles Green Worcs 116 G5
Coles Meads Surrey 51 C9
Colesbourne Glos 81 C7
Colesbrook Dorset 30 B4
Colesden Beds 122 F2
Coleshill Bucks 84 F6
Coleshill Oxon 82 G2
Coleshill Warwick 134 F4
Colestocks Devon 27 G9
Coley Bath/NE Som'set 44 B5
Coley Wokingham 65 E8
Colfin Dumf/Gal 236 D2
Colgate W Sussex 51 G8
Colgrain Arg/Bute 276 E6
Colham Green London 66 C5
Colindale London 67 B8
Colinsburgh Fife 287 G8
Colinton C/Edinb 270 B4
Colintraive Arg/Bute 275 F11
Colkirk Norfolk 159 D8
Collace Perth/Kinr 286 D6
Collafirth Shetl'd 314 G6
Collam W Isles 305 J3
Collaton Devon 9 G9
Collaton St. Mary Torbay 9 D7
College Milton S Lanarks 268 D2
College of Roseisle Moray 301 C11
College Town Brackn'l 65 G11
Collennan S Ayrs 257 C8
Collessie Fife 286 F6
Collett's Bridge Norfolk 139 B9
Collett's Green Worcs 116 G6
Collfryn Powys 148 F4
Collier Row London 87 G8
Collier Street Kent 53 D8
Collier's End Herts 105 G7
Collier's Green E Sussex 38 C3
Colliers Green Kent 53 F9
Colliers Hatch Essex 87 E8
Colliery Row Tyne/Wear 234 B2
Collieston Aberds 303 G10
Collin Dumf/Gal 238 B2
Collingbourne Ducis Wilts 47 B8
Collingbourne Kingston Wilts 47 B8
Collingham Notts 172 C4
Collingham W Yorks 206 D3
Collington Heref'd 116 E3
Collingtree Northants 120 F5
Collingwood Northum 243 B7
Collins End Oxon 65 D7
Collins Green Worcs 116 F4
Collins Green Warrington 183 C9
Colliston Angus 287 C10
Collow Lincs 189 E10
Collum Green Bucks 66 B3
Collycroft Warwick 135 F7
Collyhurst Gtr Man 195 G11
Collynie Aberds 303 F8
Collyweston Northants 137 C9
Colmonell S Ayrs 244 F4
Colmworth Beds 122 F2
Coln Rogers Glos 81 D9
Coln St. Aldwyn Glos 81 D10
Coln St. Dennis Glos 81 C9
Colnabaichin Aberds 292 C4
Colnbrook Slough 66 D4
Colne Cambs 123 B7
Colne Lancs 204 E3
Colne Bridge W Yorks 197 D7
Colne Edge Lancs 204 E3
Colne Engaine Essex 107 E7
Colney Norfolk 142 B3
Colney Hatch London 86 G3
Colney Heath Herts 86 D2
Colney Street Herts 85 E11
Cologin Arg/Bute 289 G10
Colpy Aberds 302 F6
Colquhar Scot Borders 270 G6
Colscott Devon 24 E5
Colsden Beds 122 F2
Colsterdale N Yorks 214 C2
Colsterworth Lincs 155 E8
Colston Pembs 91 F9
Colston Bassett Notts 154 C3
Colt Hill Hants 49 C8
Coltfield Moray 301 C11
Colthouse Cumb 221 F7
Colthurst Lancs 203 E10
Coltishall Norfolk 160 F5
Coltness N Lanarks 268 D5
Colton Cumb 210 B6
Colton Norfolk 142 B2
Colton N Yorks 206 E6
Colton Staffs 151 E11
Colton W Yorks 206 G3
Colt's Green S Glos 61 C8
Colt's Hill Kent 52 E6
Colts Hill Swan 56 D6
Columbia Tyne/Wear 243 F8
Columbjohn Devon 14 B5
Colva Powys 114 G4
Colvend Dumf/Gal 237 D10
Colvister Shetl'd 314 D7
Colwall Heref'd 98 C4
Colwall Green Heref'd 98 C5
Colwall Stone Heref'd 98 C5
Colwell Northum 241 B11
Colwich Staffs 151 E10

Colwick Notts 154 B2
Colwinston V/Glam 58 D2
Colworth W Sussex 34 G6
Colwyn Bay = Bae
Colwyn Conwy 180 F5
Colyford Devon 15 C11
Colyton Devon 15 C10
Colzie Fife 286 F6
Combe Devon 7 E10
Combe Devon 8 B4
Combe Heref'd 115 E6
Combe Oxon 82 B6
Combe Som'set 28 B6
Combe W Berks 63 G11
Combe Almer Dorset 18 B4
Combe Common Surrey 50 F3
Combe Down
 Bath/NE Som'set 61 G9
Combe Fishacre Devon 8 B6
Combe Florey Som'set 42 G6
Combe Hay
 Bath/NE Som'set 45 B8
Combe Martin Devon 40 D5
Combe Moor Heref'd 115 E8
Combe Pafford Torbay 9 B8
Combe Raleigh Devon 27 G11
Combe St. Nicholas
 Som'set 28 E4
Combe Throop Som'set 30 C2
Combebow Devon 12 D5
Combeinteignhead
 Devon 14 G4
Comberbach Ches 183 F10
Comberford Staffs 134 B3
Comberton Cambs 123 F7
Comberton Heref'd 115 D10
Combpyne Devon 15 C11
Combridge Staffs 151 B11
Combrook Warwick 118 G6
Combs Derby 185 F8
Combs Suffolk 125 F10
Combs W Yorks 197 D8
Combs Ford Suffolk 125 F10
Combwich Som'set 43 E9
Comely Bank C/Edinb 280 G4
Comers Aberds 293 C8
Come-to-Good Cornw'l 4 G6
Comeytrowe Som'set 28 C2
Comford Cornw'l 2 B6
Comhampton Worcs 116 D6
Comins Coch Ceredig'n 128 G2
Commercial End
 Cambs 123 E11
Commins Capel Betws
 Ceredig'n 112 F2
Commins Coch Powys 128 C6
Common Edge Blackp'l 202 G2
Common End Cumb 228 G6
Common End Derby 170 C6
Common End Norfolk 159 D8
Common Gate Dorset 18 C5
Common Hill Heref'd 97 E11
Common Moor Cornw'l 6 B4
Common Platt Wilts 62 B6
Common Side Derby 167 B9
Common Side Derby 170 F6
Commondale N Yorks 226 C3
Commonside Ches 183 G8
Commonside Derby 170 G2
Commonwood Herts 85 E8
Common-y-Coed
 Monmouths 60 B2
Comp Kent 52 B6
Compass Som'set 43 G10
Compstall Gtr Man 185 C7
Compton Devon 9 C7
Compton Hants 32 B4
Compton Hants 33 B7
Compton Plym'th 7 D9
Compton Surrey 49 D11
Compton Surrey 50 D3
Compton Staffs 132 G6
Compton W Berks 64 D4
Compton Wilts 46 C6
Compton W Midlands 133 D7
Compton W Sussex 34 E3
Compton Wilts 206 E3
Compton Abbas Dorset 30 D5
Compton Abdale Glos 81 B9
Compton Acres Poole 19 D7
Compton Bassett Wilts 62 E4
Compton Beauchamp
 Oxon 63 C10
Compton Bishop Som'set 44 B2
Compton
 Chamberlayne Wilts 31 B8
Compton Common
 Bath/NE Som'set 60 G6
Compton Common
 Surrey 50 D3
Compton Dando
 Bath/NE Som'set 60 G6
Compton Dundon
 Som'set 44 G3
Compton Durville
 Som'set 28 D6
Compton End Hants 33 B7
Compton Green Glos 98 F4
Compton Greenfield
 S Glos 60 C5
Compton Martin
 Bath/NE Som'set 44 B4
Compton Pauncefoot
 Som'set 29 B10
Compton Valance
 Dorset 17 C7
Compton Verney
 Warwick 118 G6
Comrie Fife 279 D10
Comrie H'land 300 D4
Comrie Perth/Kinr 285 C11
Comrie Perth/Kinr 285 E11
Conaglen House H'land 290 C4

Conanby S Yorks 187 B8
Conchra Arg/Bute 275 E11
Conchra H'land 295 C10
Concord Tyne/Wear 243 F8
Concraig Perth/Kinr 286 F2
Concraigie Perth/Kinr 286 C5
Conderton Worcs 99 D9
Condicote Glos 100 F2
Condorrat N Lanarks 278 G4
Condover Shrops 131 B9
Coney Garth N Lincs 199 G9
Coney Green Notts 172 C4
Coney Hill Glos 80 B5
Coneygar Hill Dorset 16 C5
Coneyhurst W Sussex 35 C10
Coneysthorpe N Yorks 216 E4
Coneythorpe N Yorks 206 B3
Coney-Weston Suffolk 125 B9
Conford Hants 49 G10
Congash H'land 301 G10
Congdon's Shop
 Cornw'l 11 F11
Congeith Dumf/Gal 237 C10
Congelow Kent 53 D7
Congerstone Leics 135 B7
Congham Norfolk 158 E4
Congleton Ches 168 C5
Congl-y-wal Gwyn 164 G2
Congresbury N Som'set 60 G2
Conham S Glos 60 E6
Conicavel Moray 301 D9
Coningsby Lincs 174 D2
Coningsby Moor Lincs 174 D2
Conington Cambs 138 F3
Conington Cambs 122 D6
Conisbrough S Yorks 187 B8
Conisby Arg/Bute 274 G3
Conisholme Lincs 190 B5
Coniston Cumb 220 F6
Coniston E R Yorks 209 F9
Coniston Cold N Yorks 204 C4
Conistone N Yorks 213 F9
Conkwell Wilts 61 G9
Connage Moray 302 C4
Connah's Quay Flints 166 B3
Connaught Park Kent 55 E10
Connel Arg/Bute 289 F11
Connel Park E Ayrs 258 G4
Conniburrow M/Keynes 103 D7
Connista Arg/Bute 298 B4
Connor Downs Cornw'l 2 B3
Conock Wilts 46 B5
Conon Bridge H'land 300 D5
Conon House H'land 300 D5
Cononish Stirl 285 E7
Cononley N Yorks 204 D5
Cononsyth Angus 287 C9
Conordan H'land 295 B7
Consall Staffs 169 F7
Consett Durham 242 G4
Constable Burton
 N Yorks 214 B3
Constable Lee Lancs 195 C10
Constantine Cornw'l 2 D6
Constantine Bay Cornw'l 10 G3
Contin H'land 300 D4
Contlaw Aberd C 293 C10
Conwy Conwy 180 F3
Conwy Castle Conwy 180 F3
Conyer Kent 70 G3
Conyers Green Suffolk 125 D7
Cooden E Sussex 38 F2
Cookbury Devon 24 F6
Cookbury Wick Devon 24 F5
Cookham Windsor 65 B11
Cookham Dean
 Windsor 65 C11
Cookham Rise Windsor 65 C11
Cookhill Worcs 117 F11
Cookley Suffolk 126 B6
Cookley Worcs 132 G6
Cookley Green Oxon 84 G2
Cookley Green Suffolk 126 B6
Cookney Aberds 293 D10
Cookridge W Yorks 205 E10
Cook's Green Essex 89 B11
Cook's Green Suffolk 125 G9
Cooksbridge E Sussex 36 E6
Cooksey Green Worcs 117 D8
Cookshill Staffs 168 G6
Cooksmill Green Essex 87 D10
Coolham W Sussex 35 C10
Cooling Medway 69 D9
Cooling Street Medway 69 E8
Coolinge Kent 55 F8
Coombe Bucks 84 D4
Coombe Cornw'l 24 E2
Coombe Cornw'l 4 G6
Coombe Cornw'l 5 E9
Coombe Devon 14 G4
Coombe Devon 15 C8
Coombe Glos 80 G3
Coombe Hants 33 C11
Coombe Kent 55 B9
Coombe London 67 E8
Coombe Som'set 28 F6
Coombe Wilts 30 C5
Coombe Wilts 46 C6
Coombe Bissett Wilts 31 B10
Coombe End Som'set 27 B8
Coombe Green Wilts 62 B2
Coombe Hill Glos 99 F7
Coombe Keynes Dorset 18 E2
Coombe Street Som'set 45 G9
Coombelake Devon 15 B7
Coombes W Sussex 35 F11
Coombes End S Glos 61 C9
Coombeswood
 W Midlands 133 F9
Coombs Pembs 72 D6
Cooper Street Kent 55 B10
Cooper Turning
 Gtr Man 194 F6
Cooper's Corner Kent 52 D3
Cooper's Green E Sussex 37 C7
Cooper's Hill Beds 103 D10

Coopersale Common
 Essex 87 E7
Coopersale Street Essex 87 E7
Cootham W Sussex 35 E9
Cop Street Kent 55 B9
Copalder Corner
 Cambs 139 E7
Copdock Suffolk 108 C2
Copford Essex 107 G8
Copford Green Essex 107 G8
Copgrove N Yorks 214 G6
Copister Shetl'd 314 F6
Cople Beds 104 B2
Copley Durham 233 F7
Copley Gtr Man 185 B7
Copley W Yorks 196 C5
Copley Hill W Yorks 197 B8
Coplow Dale Derby 185 F11
Copmanthorpe C/York 207 D7
Copmere End Staffs 150 D6
Copnor Portsm'th 33 G11
Copp Lancs 202 F4
Copp Hill S Glos 61 C8
Coppathorne Cornw'l 24 G2
Coppenhall Staffs 151 F8
Coppenhall Moss Ches 168 D2
Copperhouse Cornw'l 2 B3
Coppermills Cornw'l 54 F1
Coppice Gtr Man 196 G2
Coppicegate Shrops 132 G4
Coppingford Cambs 138 G3
Coppins Corner Kent 54 D2
Copplerdige Dorset 30 B4
Copplestone Devon 26 G3
Coppull Lancs 194 E5
Coppull Moor Lancs 194 E5
Coppy Durham 242 F6
Copsale W Sussex 35 B11
Copshaw Holm =
 Newcastleton
 Scot Borders 249 F11
Copster Green Lancs 203 G9
Copster Hill Gtr Man 196 G2
Copston Magna
 Warwick 135 F9
Copt Green Warwick 118 D3
Copt Heath W Midlands 118 B3
Copt Hewick N Yorks 214 E6
Copt Oak Leics 153 G9
Copthall Green Essex 86 E6
Copthill Durham 232 C3
Copthorne Ches 167 G10
Copthorne Cornw'l 11 C11
Copthorne Shrops 149 G9
Copthorne W Sussex 51 F10
Copthorne Common
 W Sussex 51 F10
Copy's Green Norfolk 159 B8
Copythorne Hants 32 E4
Corbets Tey London 68 B5
Corbridge Northum 241 E11
Corby Northants 137 F8
Corby Glen Lincs 155 D9
Corby Hill Cumb 239 F11
Cordon N Ayrs 256 C2
Cordwell Derby 186 F4
Cordwell Norfolk 142 E2
Coreley Shrops 116 C2
Cores End Bucks 66 B2
Corfe Som'set 28 D2
Corfe Castle Dorset 18 E5
Corfe Castle Dorset 18 E5
Corfe Mullen Dorset 18 B5
Corfton Shrops 131 G10
Corgarff Aberds 292 C4
Corhampton Hants 33 C10
Corkickle Cumb 219 B9
Corlae Dumf/Gal 246 D5
Corlannau Rh Cyn Taff 76 G3
Corley Warwick 134 F5
Corley Ash Warwick 134 F5
Corley Moor Warwick 134 F5
Cornaa I/Man 192 D5
Cornabus Arg/Bute 254 C4
Cornaigbeg Arg/Bute 288 E1
Cornaigmore Arg/Bute 288 C4
Cornaigmore Arg/Bute 288 E1
Cornard Tye Suffolk 107 C8
Corncatterach Aberds 302 F5
Corndon Devon 13 D9
Corner Row Lancs 202 F4
Cornets End
 W Midlands 134 G4
Corney Cumb 220 G2
Cornforth Durham 234 E2
Cornhill Aberds 302 D5
Cornhill Staffs 168 E5
Cornhill on Tweed
 Northum 263 B9
Cornholme W Yorks 196 B2
Cornish Cyder Farm,
 Truro Cornw'l 4 E5
Cornish Hall End Essex 106 E2
Cornmeadow Green
 Worcs 117 F7
Cornquoy Orkney 313 J4
Cornriggs Durham 232 C2
Cornsay Durham 233 C8
Cornsay Colliery
 Durham 233 C9
Cornton Stirl 278 B5
Corntown H'land 300 D5
Corntown V/Glam 58 D2
Cornwal Conwy 164 C6
Cornwell Oxon 100 F5
Cornwood Devon 8 D2
Cornworthy Devon 8 D2
Corpach H'land 290 F2
Corpusty Norfolk 160 D2
Corran H'land 290 G2
Corran H'land 295 E10
Corran a Chan
 Uachdaraich H'land 295 C11
Corranbuie Arg/Bute 275 G9
Corrany I/Man 192 D5
Corrichoich H'land 311 G4
Corrie N Ayrs 255 C11
Corrie Common
 Dumf/Gal 248 F6

Corriecravie N Ayrs 255 E10
Corriecravie Moor
 N Ayrs 255 E10
Corriegarth Lodge
 H'land 291 B7
Corriemoillie H'land 300 C3
Corriemulzie Lodge
 H'land 309 K3
Corrievarkie Lodge
 Perth/Kinr 291 F7
Corrievorrie H'land 301 G7
Corrigall Orkney 312 G4
Corrimony H'land 300 F3
Corringham Lincs 188 C5
Corringham Thurr'k 69 C8
Corris Gwyn 128 B5
Corris Uchaf Gwyn 128 B4
Corrour Shooting
 Lodge H'land 290 C5
Corrow Arg/Bute 284 G5
Corry H'land 295 C8
Corry of Ardnagrask
 H'land 300 E5
Corrybrough H'land 301 E8
Corrydon Perth/Kinr 292 G3
Corryghoil Arg/Bute 284 E5
Corrykinloch H'land 309 E10
Corrylach Arg/Bute 255 D8
Corrymuckloch
 Perth/Kinr 286 D2
Corrynachenchy
 Arg/Bute 289 E8
Corsback H'land 310 B6
Corscombe Dorset 29 F8
Corse Aberds 302 E6
Corse Glos 98 F5
Corse Covert
 Warrington 183 C11
Corse Lawn Glos 98 E6
Corse of Kinnoir
 Aberds 302 E5
Corsewall Dumf/Gal 236 C2
Corsham Wilts 61 E11
Corsindae Aberds 293 C8
Corsley Heath Wilts 45 D10
Corsock Dumf/Gal 237 B9
Corston Bath/NE Som'set 61 F7
Corston Orkney 312 G4
Corston Wilts 62 C2
Corstorphine C/Edinb 280 G3
Cors-y-Gedol Gwyn 146 E2
Cortachy Angus 287 B7
Corton Suffolk 143 D10
Corton Wilts 46 E2
Corton Denham
 Som'set 29 C10
Coruanan Lodge H'land 290 G2
Corunna W Isles 296 E4
Corvast H'land 309 K5
Corwen Denbs 165 G9
Coryates Dorset 17 D8
Coryton Devon 12 E5
Coryton Thurr'k 69 C8
Cosby Leics 135 D10
Coscote Oxon 64 B4
Coseley W Midlands 133 E9
Cosford Warwick 119 B10
Cosgrove Northants 102 C5
Cosham Portsm'th 33 G11
Cosheston Pembs 73 E8
Coskills N Lincs 200 E5
Cossall Notts 171 F7
Cossall Marsh Notts 171 G7
Cossington Leics 154 G2
Cossington Som'set 43 E11
Costa Orkney 312 F4
Costessey Norfolk 160 G3
Costhorpe Notts 187 D9
Costock Notts 153 D11
Coston Leics 155 E7
Coston Norfolk 141 B11
Cote Oxon 82 E5
Cote Som'set 43 E10
Cote W Sussex 35 F10
Cote Green Gtr Man 185 C7
Cote Holme Lancs 195 B8
Cotebrook Ches 167 B9
Cotehele House Cornw'l 7 B8
Cotehill Cumb 239 G11
Cotes Cumb 211 B9
Cotes Leics 153 E11
Cotes Staffs 150 C6
Cotes Park Derby 170 E6
Cotesbach Leics 135 G10
Cotford Devon 15 C8
Cotford St. Luke
 Som'set 27 B11
Cotgrave Notts 154 B2
Cothall Aberds 293 B10
Cotham Bristol 60 E5
Cotham Notts 172 F3
Cotmanhay Derby 171 G7
Cotmaton Devon 15 D8
Coton Cambs 123 F8
Coton Northants 120 C3
Coton Shrops 149 C10
Coton Staffs 150 C6
Coton Staffs 134 B3
Coton Staffs 151 C9
Coton Hill Shrops 149 G9
Coton in the Clay
 Staffs 152 D3
Coton in the Elms
 Derby 152 F4
Coton Park Derby 152 F5
Cotonwood Shrops 149 B10

Cotonwood Staffs 150 E6
Cotswold Community
 Glos 81 F8
Cotswold Wild Life
 Park, Burford Oxon 82 D2
Cott Devon 8 C5
Cottage End Hants 48 E2
Cottagers Plot NE Lincs 201 F8
Cottam E R Yorks 217 G9
Cottam Lancs 202 G6
Cottam Notts 188 E4
Cottartown H'land 301 F10
Cottenham Cambs 123 D9
Cottenham Park London 67 F8
Cotterdale N Yorks 222 G6
Cottered Herts 104 F6
Cotteridge W Midlands 133 G10
Cotterstock Northants 137 E11
Cottesbrooke Northants 120 C4
Cottesmore Rutl'd 155 G8
Cotteylands Devon 26 E6
Cottingham E R Yorks 208 G6
Cottingham Northants 136 E6
Cottingley W Yorks 205 F8
Cottisford Oxon 101 E11
Cotton Suffolk 125 D11
Cotton Staffs 169 F9
Cotton End Beds 103 B11
Cotton End Northants 120 F4
Cotton Tree Lancs 204 F4
Cottonworth Hants 47 F11
Cottown Aberds 293 B9
Cottown Aberds 302 G5
Cottown Aberds 303 E8
Cotwall Telford 150 F2
Cotwalton Staffs 151 C8
Coubister Orkney 312 G4
Coughton Heref'd 97 G11
Coughton Warwick 117 E11
Cougie H'land 300 F2
Coulaghailtro Arg/Bute 275 G8
Coulags H'land 299 E9
Coulby Newham
 Middlesbro 225 C10
Coulderton Cumb 219 D9
Couldoran H'land 299 D9
Couligartan Stirl 285 G8
Coulin H'land 299 D10
Coulin Lodge H'land 299 D10
Coull Aberds 293 C7
Coull Arg/Bute 274 G3
Coulmony Ho H'land 301 E9
Coulport Arg/Bute 276 D4
Coulsdon London 67 G9
Coulshill Perth/Kinr 286 G3
Coulston Wilts 46 D2
Coulter S Lanarks 260 C2
Coultings Som'set 43 E8
Coulton N Yorks 216 E2
Coultra Fife 287 E7
Cound Shrops 131 C11
Coundlane Shrops 131 B11
Coundmoor Shrops 131 C11
Coundon Durham 233 F10
Coundon W Midlands 134 G6
Coundon Grange
 Durham 233 F10
Coundongate Durham 233 F10
Countersett N Yorks 213 B8
Countess Wilts 47 E7
Countess Cross Essex 107 E7
Countess Wear Devon 14 C4
Countesthorpe Leics 135 D11
Countisbury Devon 41 D8
County Oak W Sussex 51 F9
Coup Green Lancs 194 B5
Coupar Angus
 Perth/Kinr 286 C6
Coupland Cumb 222 B4
Coupland Northum 263 D10
Cour Arg/Bute 255 C9
Courance Dumf/Gal 248 E3
Court Colman Bridg 57 E11
Court Corner Hants 48 B6
Court Henry Carms 93 G11
Court Herbert Rh Cyn Taff 76 E2
Court Hey Mersey 182 D6
Court House Green
 W Midlands 135 G7
Court-at-Street Kent 54 F5
Courteenhall Northants 120 G5
Courthill Perth/Kinr 286 C5
Courtsend Essex 89 G8
Courtway Som'set 43 G8
Cousland Midloth 271 B7
Cousley Wood E Sussex 53 G7
Couston Arg/Bute 275 F11
Cova Shetl'd 315 J5
Cove Arg/Bute 276 E4
Cove Scot Borders 282 G5
Cove Devon 27 D7
Cove Hants 49 B10
Cove H'land 307 K3
Cove Bay Aberd C 293 C11
Cove Bottom Suffolk 127 B9
Covehithe Suffolk 143 G10
Coven Staffs 133 B8
Coven Heath Staffs 133 C8
Coveney Cambs 139 G9
Covenham St.
 Bartholomew Lincs 190 B4
Covenham St. Mary
 Lincs 190 B4
Coventry W Midlands 119 B7
Coventry Airport
 Warwick 119 C7
Coventry Cathedral
 W Midlands 118 B6
Coverack Cornw'l 3 F7
Coverack Bridges Cornw'l 2 C5
Coverham N Yorks 214 B2
Covesea Moray 301 B11
Covingham Swindon 63 C7
Covington Cambs 121 C11
Covington S Lanarks 259 B11
Cow Green Suffolk 125 D11
Cowan Bridge Lancs 212 D1

Cowbar Redcar/Clevel'd 226 B5
Cowbeech E Sussex 37 E10
Cowbeech Hill E Sussex 37 E10
Cowbit Lincs 156 F5
Cowbog Aberds 303 D8
Cowbridge Lincs 174 F4
Cowbridge Som'set 42 E3
Cowbridge V/Glam 58 E3
Cowcliffe W Yorks 196 D6
Cowden Kent 52 E3
Cowden Pound Kent 52 E3
Cowdenbeath Fife 280 C3
Cowdenburn
 Scot Borders 270 E4
Cowdenend Fife 280 D3
Cowen Head Cumb 221 F9
Cowers Lane Derby 170 F4
Cowes I/Wight 20 B5
Cowesby N Yorks 215 B9
Cowesfield Green Wilts 32 C3
Cowey Green Essex 107 F11
Cowfold W Sussex 36 C2
Cowgate Tyne/Wear 242 D6
Cowgill Cumb 212 B5
Cowgrove Dorset 18 B5
Cowhill Derby 170 F5
Cowhill S Glos 79 G10
Cowie Aberds 293 D10
Cowie Stirl 278 D6
Cowlands Cornw'l 4 G6
Cowley Derby 186 F4
Cowley Devon 14 B4
Cowley Glos 81 C7
Cowley London 66 C5
Cowley Oxon 83 E8
Cowley Staffs 150 F6
Cowley Bar Derby 186 F4
Cowley Peachey London 66 C5
Cowleymoor Devon 27 E7
Cowling Lancs 194 D5
Cowling N Yorks 204 E5
Cowling N Yorks 214 B4
Cowlinge Suffolk 124 G4
Cowlow Derby 185 G9
Cowmes W Yorks 197 D7
Cowpe Lancs 195 C10
Cowpen Northum 253 G7
Cowpen Bewley
 Stockton 234 G5
Cowplain Hants 33 E11
Cowsden Worcs 117 G8
Cowshill Durham 232 C3
Cowslip Green N Som'set 60 G3
Cowstrandburn Fife 279 C10
Cowthorpe N Yorks 206 C5
Cox Common Suffolk 143 G8
Cox Green Essex 88 F2
Cox Green Surrey 50 G5
Cox Green Tyne/Wear 243 F8
Cox Green Windsor 65 D11
Cox Hill Beds 104 B3
Cox Moor Notts 171 D8
Coxbank Ches 167 G11
Coxbench Derby 170 G5
Coxbridge Som'set 44 F4
Coxet Hill Stirl 278 C5
Coxford Norfolk 158 D6
Coxford S'thampton 32 E5
Coxheath Kent 53 C8
Coxhoe Durham 234 D2
Coxley Som'set 44 E4
Coxley Wick Som'set 44 E4
Coxlodge Tyne/Wear 242 D6
Coxpark Cornw'l 12 G4
Coxtie Green Essex 87 F9
Coxwold N Yorks 215 D10
Coychurch Bridg 58 D2
Coylton S Ayrs 257 F10
Coylumbridge H'land 291 B11
Coynach Aberds 292 C6
Coynachie Aberds 302 F4
Coytrahen Bridg 57 D11
Crab Orchard Dorset 31 F9
Crabble Kent 55 E9
Crabbs Cross Worcs 117 E10
Crabgate Norfolk 159 D11
Crabtree Plym'th 7 D10
Crabtree W Sussex 36 B2
Crabtree Green Wrex 166 G4
Crackaig Arg/Bute 274 G6
Crackenedge W Yorks 197 C8
Crackenthorpe Cumb 231 G9
Crackington Haven
 Cornw'l 11 B8
Crackley Staffs 168 E4
Crackleybank Shrops 150 G5
Crackpot N Yorks 223 F9
Cracoe N Yorks 204 B5
Craddock Devon 27 E9
Cradhlastadh W Isles 304 E2
Cradle End Herts 105 G9
Cradley Heref'd 98 B4
Cradley W Midlands 133 G8
Cradley Heath Worcs 133 G8
Cradoc Powys 95 E10
Crafthole Cornw'l 7 E9
Crag Bank Lancs 211 F9
Crag Foot Lancs 211 E9
Cragg Hill W Yorks 205 F10
Craggan H'land 301 G10
Craggan Moray 301 F11
Craggan Stirl 285 E9
Cragganvallie H'land 300 F5
Craggenmore Moray 301 F11
Craghead Durham 242 G6
Crai Powys 95 G7
Craibstone Moray 302 D4
Craichie Angus 287 C9
Craig Dumf/Gal 237 B8
Craig Dumf/Gal 237 D10
Craig H'land 299 E10
Craig Berthlwyd
 Merth Tyd 77 F9

Craig Castle Aberds 302 G4
Craig Gellinudd
 Neath P Talb 76 E2
Craig Llangiwg
 Neath P Talb 76 E2
Craig Lodge Arg/Bute 275 G10
Craig-moston Aberds 293 B9
Craig Trebanos
 Neath P Talb 76 E2
Craiganor Lodge
 Perth/Kinr 285 B10
Craigbrack Arg/Bute 276 B2
Craig-cefn-parc Swan 75 E11
Craigdallie Perth/Kinr 286 E6
Craigdam Aberds 303 F8
Craigdarroch Dumf/Gal 246 E6
Craigdarroch H'land 300 D4
Craigdhu H'land 300 E4
Craigearn Aberds 293 B9
Craigellachie Moray 302 E2
Craigencallie Ho.
 Dumf/Gal 237 B7
Craigencross Dumf/Gal 236 C2
Craigend Glasg C 268 B3
Craigend Perth/Kinr 286 E5
Craigend Perth/Kinr 286 C5
Craigend Renf 277 G9
Craigend Stirl 278 B5
Craigend S Lanarks 268 E2
Craigendoran Arg/Bute 276 E6
Craigends Renf 267 B8
Craigens Arg/Bute 274 G3
Craigens E Ayrs 258 F3
Craigentinny C/Edinb 280 G5
Craighall Perth/Kinr 286 C5
Craighat Stirl 277 E9
Craighead Fife 287 G10
Craighead H'land 301 C7
Craighill Aberds 303 E7
Craighlaw Mains
 Dumf/Gal 236 C5
Craighouse Arg/Bute 274 G6
Craigie Aberds 293 B11
Craigie Dundee C 287 D8
Craigie Perth/Kinr 286 C5
Craigie Perth/Kinr 286 E5
Craigie S Ayrs 257 E8
Craigiefield Orkney 312 G5
Craigiehall C/Edinb 280 F3
Craigielaw E Loth 281 F9
Craigleith C/Edinb 280 G4
Craig-llwyn Shrops 148 D4
Craiglockhart C/Edinb 280 G4
Craigmalloch E Ayrs 245 E11
Craigmaud Aberds 303 D9
Craigmillar C/Edinb 280 G5
Craigmore Arg/Bute 266 B2
Craignant Shrops 148 C5
Craigneuk N Lanarks 268 D5
Craigneuk N Lanarks 268 D5
Craignish Castle
 Arg/Bute 275 C8
Craignure Arg/Bute 289 F9
Craigo Angus 293 G8
Craigow Perth/Kinr 286 G4
Craigrory H'land 300 E6
Craigrothie Fife 287 F7
Craigroy Moray 301 D11
Craigruie Stirl 285 E8
Craig's End Essex 106 E4
Craigshall Dumf/Gal 237 D10
Craigshill W Loth 269 B11
Craigston Castle
 Aberds 303 D7
Craigton Aberd C 293 C10
Craigton Angus 287 B7
Craigton Angus 287 D9
Craigton H'land 300 E5
Craigton H'land 309 H6
Craigton H'land 309 K6
Craigtown H'land 310 D2
Craig-y-don Conwy 180 E3
Craig-y-Duke
 Neath P Talb 76 E2
Craig-y-nos Powys 76 C3
Craig-y-pal Swan 76 E2
Craik Scot Borders 249 E8
Crail Fife 287 G10
Crailing Scot Borders 262 E5
Crailinghall
 Scot Borders 262 E5
Crakaig H'land 311 H3
Crakehill N Yorks 215 E8
Crakemarsh Staffs 151 B11
Crambe N Yorks 216 G4
Crambeck N Yorks 216 F4
Cramlington Northum 243 B7
Cramond C/Edinb 280 F3
Cramond Bridge
 C/Edinb 280 F3
Crampmoor Hants 32 C5
Cranage Ches 168 B3
Cranberry Staffs 150 B6
Cranborne Dorset 31 E8
Cranbourne Brackn'l 66 E2
Cranbourne Hants 48 C6
Cranbrook London 68 B2
Cranbrook Common
 Kent 53 F9
Crane Moor S Yorks 197 G10
Cranes Essex 88 G2
Crane's Corner Norfolk 159 G8
Cranfield Beds 103 C9
Cranford Devon 24 C4
Cranford London 66 D6
Cranford St. Andrew
 Northants 121 B8
Cranford St. John
 Northants 121 B8
Cranham Glos 80 C5
Cranham London 68 B5
Cranhill Warwick 118 F2
Crank Mersey 183 B8
Crankwood Gtr Man 194 G6
Cranleigh Surrey 50 F5

Cranley Suffolk 126 C3
Cranley Gardens
 London 67 B9
Cranmer Green
 Suffolk 125 C10
Cranmore I/Wight 20 C3
Cranmore Som'set 45 E7
Cranna Aberds 302 D6
Crannich Arg/Bute 289 E7
Crannoch Moray 302 D4
Cranoe Leics 136 D5
Cransford Suffolk 126 E6
Cranshaws Scot Borders 272 C3
Cranstal I/Man 192 B5
Crantock Cornw'l 4 C5
Cranwell Lincs 173 E8
Cranwich Norfolk 140 D5
Cranworth Norfolk 141 C9
Craobh Haven Arg/Bute 275 C8
Crapstone Devon 7 B10
Crarae Arg/Bute 275 D10
Crask H'land 308 C7
Crask Inn H'land 309 G5
Crask of Aigas H'land 300 E4
Craskins Aberds 293 C7
Craster Northum 265 F7
Craswall Heref'd 96 E5
Cratfield Suffolk 126 B6
Crathes Aberds 293 D9
Crathes Castle and
 Gardens Aberds 293 D9
Crathie Aberds 292 D4
Crathie H'land 291 D7
Crathorne N Yorks 225 D8
Craven Arms Shrops 131 G8
Crawcrook Tyne/Wear 242 E4
Crawford Lancs 194 G3
Crawford S Lanarks 259 E11
Crawforddyke S Lanarks 269 E7
Crawfordjohn S Lanarks 259 E8
Crawick Dumf/Gal 259 G7
Crawley Devon 28 F3
Crawley Glos 80 F3
Crawley Hants 48 G2
Crawley Oxon 82 C4
Crawley W Sussex 51 F9
Crawley Down
 W Sussex 51 F10
Crawley End Essex 105 C8
Crawley Hill Surrey 65 G11
Crawleyside Durham 232 C5
Crawshawbooth Lancs 195 B10
Crawton Aberds 293 F10
Cray N Yorks 213 D8
Cray Perth/Kinr 292 G3
Crayford London 68 D4
Crayke N Yorks 215 E11
Craymere Beck
 Norfolk 159 C11
Crays Hill Essex 88 G2
Cray's Pond Oxon 64 C6
Crazies Hill Wokingham 65 C9
Creacombe Devon 26 D4
Creag Aoil H'land 290 F3
Creag Ghoraidh
 W Isles 297 G3
Creagan Arg/Bute 289 E11
Creagan Sithe Arg/Bute 284 G5
Creagastrom W Isles 297 G4
Creaguaineach Lodge
 H'land 290 G5
Creamore Bank
 Shrops 149 C10
Creaton Northants 120 C4
Creca Dumf/Gal 238 B6
Credenhill Heref'd 97 C8
Crediton Devon 26 G4
Creebridge Dumf/Gal 236 C6
Creech Dorset 18 E4
Creech Heathfield
 Som'set 28 B3
Creech St. Michael
 Som'set 28 B3
Creed Cornw'l 5 F8
Creediknowe Shetl'd 314 G7
Creegbrawse Cornw'l 4 G4
Creekmouth London 68 C3
Creephole Glos 61 B10
Creeting Bottoms
 Suffolk 126 F2
Creeting St. Mary
 Suffolk 125 F11
Creeting St. Peter
 Suffolk 125 F11
Creeton Lincs 155 F10
Creetown Dumf/Gal 236 D6
Creggans Arg/Bute 284 G4
Cregneash I/Man 192 F2
Creg-ny-Baa I/Man 192 D4
Cregrina Powys 114 G2
Creich Fife 287 E7
Creigau Card 58 C5
Creigau Monmouths 79 F7
Creighton Staffs 151 B11
Cremyll Cornw'l 7 E9
Crendell Dorset 31 E8
Crepkill H'land 298 E4
Creslow Bucks 102 G6
Cressage Shrops 131 C11
Cressbrook Derby 185 G11
Cresselly Pembs 73 D9
Cressex Bucks 84 G5
Cressing Essex 106 G5
Cresswell Northum 253 E7
Cresswell Staffs 151 B9
Cresswell Quay Pembs 73 D9
Creswell Derby 187 G8
Creswell Staffs 151 C8
Creswell Green Staffs 151 G11
Cretingham Suffolk 126 F4
Cretshengan Arg/Bute 275 G8
Creunant = Crynant
 Neath P Talb 76 E3
Crewe Ches 166 D4
Crewe Ches 168 D2

Dudley Wood W Midlands 133 F8
Dudley Zoological Gardens W Midlands 133 E8
Dudlow's Green Warrington 183 E10
Dudsbury Dorset 19 B7
Dudswell Herts 85 D7
Dudwells Pembs 91 G8
Duffield Derby 170 G4
Duffryn Neath P Talb 76 F4
Duffryn Newp 59 B9
Duffryn Shrops 130 G4
Dufftown Moray 302 F3
Duffus Moray 301 C11
Dufton Cumb 231 F9
Duggleby N Yorks 217 F7
Duich Arg/Bute 254 B4
Duiletter Arg/Bute 284 D5
Duinish Perth/Kinr 291 G8
Duirinish H'land 295 B9
Duisdalebeg H'land 295 D8
Duisdalemore H'land 295 D9
Duisky H'land 290 F2
Duke End Warwick 134 F4
Duke Street Suffolk 107 C11
Dukesfield Northum 241 F10
Dukestown Bl Gwent 77 C10
Dukinfield Gtr Man 184 B6
Dulas Angl 179 D7
Dulcote Som'set 44 E5
Dulford Devon 27 G9
Dull Perth/Kinr 286 C2
Dullatur N Lanarks 278 F4
Dullingham Cambs 124 F2
Dullingham Ley Cambs 124 F2
Dulnain Bridge H'land 301 G9
Duloch Fife 280 D2
Duloe Beds 122 E3
Duloe Cornw'l 6 D4
Dulsie H'land 301 E9
Dulverton Som'set 26 B6
Dulwich Village London 67 E10
Dumbarton W Dunb 277 F7
Dumbleton Glos 99 D10
Dumbreck Glasg C 267 C11
Dumcrieff Dumf/Gal 248 C4
Dumfries Dumf/Gal 237 B11
Dumgoyne Stirl 277 E10
Dummer Hants 48 D5
Dumpford W Sussex 34 C4
Dumpling Green Norfolk 159 G10
Dumplington Gtr Man 184 B3
Dumpton Kent 71 F11
Dun Angus 287 B10
Dun Charlabhaigh W Isles 304 D3
Dunach Arg/Bute 289 G10
Dunadd Arg/Bute 275 D9
Dunain Ho. H'land 300 E6
Dunalastair Perth/Kinr 285 B11
Dunan H'land 295 C7
Dunans Arg/Bute 275 D11
Dunans Arg/Bute 275 D9
Dunball Som'set 43 E10
Dunbar E Loth 282 F3
Dunbeath H'land 311 G5
Dunbeg Arg/Bute 289 F10
Dunblane Stirl 285 G11
Dunbog Fife 286 F6
Dunbridge Hants 32 B4
Dunburgh Norfolk 143 E8
Duncan Down Kent 70 F6
Duncansclett Shetl'd 315 K5
Duncanston Aberds 302 G5
Duncanston H'land 300 D5
Dunchurch Warwick 119 C9
Duncote Northants 120 G3
Duncow Dumf/Gal 247 G11
Duncraggan Stirl 285 G9
Duncrievie Perth/Kinr 286 G5
Duncroisk Stirl 285 D9
Duncton W Sussex 35 D7
Dundas Ho. Orkney 313 K5
Dundee Dundee C 287 D8
Dundee Airport Dundee C 287 E7
Dundeugh Dumf/Gal 246 F4
Dundon Som'set 44 G3
Dundon Hayes Som'set 44 G3
Dundonald Fife 280 C4
Dundonald S Ayrs 257 C9
Dundonald Camp N Ayrs 257 C8
Dundonnell H'land 307 L5
Dundonnell Hotel H'land 307 L5
Dundonnell House H'land 307 L6
Dundraw Cumb 229 B10
Dundreggan H'land 290 B5
Dundreggan Lodge H'land 290 B5
Dundrennan Dumf/Gal 237 E9
Dundridge Hants 33 D9
Dundry N Som'set 60 F5
Dunduirn Perth/Kinr 285 E11
Dundyvan N Lanarks 268 C4
Dunecht Aberds 293 C9
Dunfermline Fife 279 D11
Dunfield Glos 81 F10
Dungate Kent 54 B2
Dunge Wilts 45 C11
Dungeness Kent 39 D9
Dungworth S Yorks 186 D3
Dunham Massey Gtr Man 184 D2
Dunham on Trent Notts 188 G4
Dunham Town Gtr Man 184 D2
Dunham Woodhouses Gtr Man 184 D2
Dunham-on-the-Hill Ches 183 G7
Dunhampton Worcs 117 D7
Dunholme Lincs 189 F8
Dunino Fife 287 F9
Dunipace Falk 278 E6
Dunira Perth/Kinr 285 E11
Dunkeld Perth/Kinr 286 C4
Dunkerton Bath/NE Som'set 45 B8
Dunkeswell Devon 27 F10
Dunkeswick W Yorks 206 D2
Dunkirk Cambs 139 F10
Dunkirk Ches 182 G5
Dunkirk Kent 54 B5
Dunkirk Norfolk 160 D4
Dunkirk S Glos 61 B9
Dunkirk Wilts 62 G3
Dunk's Green Kent 52 C6
Dunlappie Angus 293 G7
Dunley Hants 48 C3
Dunley Worcs 116 D5
Dunlichity Lodge H'land 300 F6
Dunlop E Ayrs 267 F8
Dunmaglass Lodge H'land 300 G5
Dunmere Cornw'l 5 B10
Dunmore Arg/Bute 275 G8
Dunmore Falk 279 D7
Dunmore H'land 300 E5
Dunn Street Kent 54 D3
Dunn Street Kent 69 G9
Dunnet H'land 310 B6
Dunnichen Angus 287 C9
Dunnikier Fife 280 C5
Dunninald Angus 287 B11
Dunning Perth/Kinr 286 F4
Dunnington C/York 207 C9
Dunnington ER Yorks 209 C9
Dunnington Warwick 117 G11
Dunningwell Cumb 210 C3
Dunnockshaw Lancs 195 B10
Dunollie Arg/Bute 289 F10
Dunoon Arg/Bute 276 F3
Dunragit Dumf/Gal 236 D3
Dunrobin Castle Museum & Gardens H'land 311 J2
Dunrobin Mains H'land 311 J2
Dunrostan Arg/Bute 275 E8
Duns Scot Borders 272 E5
Duns Tew Oxon 101 F9
Dunsby Lincs 156 D2
Dunscar Gtr Man 195 E8
Dunscore Dumf/Gal 247 G9
Dunscroft S Yorks 199 F7
Dunsdale Redcar/Clevel'd 226 B2
Dunsden Green Oxon 65 D8
Dunsfold Surrey 50 F4
Dunsfold Green Surrey 50 F4
Dunsford Devon 14 D2
Dunshalt Fife 286 F6
Dunshill Notts 171 C7
Dunshill Worcs 98 E6
Dunshillock Aberds 303 E9
Dunsinnan Perth/Kinr 286 D5
Dunskey Ho. Dumf/Gal 236 D2
Dunsley N Yorks 227 C7
Dunsley Staffs 133 G7
Dunsmore Bucks 84 D5
Dunsop Bridge Lancs 203 D8
Dunstable Beds 103 G10
Dunstall Staffs 152 E3
Dunstall Green Suffolk 124 E4
Dunstall Hill W Midlands 133 D8
Dunstall Hill W Midlands 133 C8
Dunstan Northum 264 F6
Dunstan Staffs 151 F8
Dunster Som'set 42 E3
Dunster Beach Som'set 42 E4
Dunster Castle, Minehead Som'set 42 E3
Dunston Derby 186 G5
Dunston Lincs 173 C9
Dunston Norfolk 142 C4
Dunston Tyne/Wear 242 E6
Dunston Hill Tyne/Wear 242 E6
Dunstone Devon 7 E11
Dunstone Devon 13 F10
Dunsville S Yorks 198 F6
Dunswell ER Yorks 209 F7
Dunsyre S Lanarks 269 F11
Dunterton Devon 12 F3
Dunthrop Oxon 101 F7
Duntisborne Abbots Glos 81 D7
Duntisbourne Leer Glos 81 D7
Duntisbourne Rouse Glos 81 D7
Duntish Dorset 29 F11
Duntocher W Dunb 277 G9
Dunton Beds 104 C4
Dunton Bucks 102 G6
Dunton Norfolk 159 C7
Dunton Bassett Leics 135 E10
Dunton Green Kent 52 B4
Dunton Patch Norfolk 159 C7
Dunton Wayletts Essex 87 G11
Duntrune Castle Arg/Bute 275 D8
Duntulm H'land 298 B4
Dunure S Ayrs 257 F7
Dunvant = Dynfant Swan 75 G9
Dunvegan H'land 298 E2
Dunvegan Castle H'land 298 E2
Dunwear Som'set 43 F10
Dunwich Suffolk 127 C9
Duporth Cornw'l 5 E10
Dupplin Castle Perth/Kinr 286 F4
Durdar Cumb 239 G10
Durgan Cornw'l 3 D7
Durgates E Sussex 52 G6
Durham Durham 233 C11
Durham Cathedral Durham 233 C11
Durham Tees Valley Airport Stockton 225 C7
Durisdeer Dumf/Gal 247 C9
Durisdeermill Dumf/Gal 247 C9
Durkar W Yorks 197 D10
Durleigh Som'set 43 F9
Durley Hants 33 D8
Durley Wilts 63 G8
Durley Hill Bath/NE Som'set 60 F6
Durlock Kent 71 G10
Durlock Kent 55 B9
Durlow Common Heref'd 98 D2
Durn Gtr Man 196 D2
Durnamuck H'land 307 K5
Durness H'land 308 C4
Durno Aberds 303 G7
Durns Town Hants 19 B11
Durns Town Hants 19 B11
Duror H'land 289 D11
Durran Arg/Bute 275 C10
Durran H'land 310 C5
Durrant Green Kent 53 F11
Durrants Hants 34 F2
Durrington Wilts 47 E7
Durrington W Sussex 35 G10
Durrisdale Orkney 312 F4
Dursley Glos 80 F3
Dursley Cross Glos 79 B11
Durston Som'set 28 B3
Durweston Dorset 30 F5
Dury Shetl'd 315 G6
Duston Northants 120 E4
Duthil H'land 301 G9
Dutlas Powys 114 B4
Duton Hill Essex 106 F2
Dutson Cornw'l 12 D2
Dutton Warrington 183 F9
Dutwoods Derby 152 E4
Duxford Cambs 105 B9
Duxford Oxon 82 F5
Duxford Airfield (Imperial War Museum), Sawston Cambs 105 B9
Duxmoor Shrops 115 B8
Dwygyfylchi Conwy 180 F2
Dwyran Angl 162 B6
Dyce Aberd C 293 B10
Dye House Northum 241 F10
Dyer's Common S Glos 60 C5
Dyfatty Carms 75 E7
Dyffryn Bridg 76 G5
Dyffryn Carms 92 G6
Dyffryn Pembs 91 D8
Dyffryn Powys 148 G2
Dyffryn Powys 96 G5
Dyffryn V/Glam 58 E5
Dyffryn Ardudwy Gwyn 145 E11
Dyffryn Castell Ceredig'n 128 G5
Dyffryn Cellwen Neath P Talb 76 D5
Dyke Devon 24 C4
Dyke Lincs 156 E2
Dyke Moray 301 D9
Dykehead Angus 292 G5
Dykehead N Lanarks 269 D7
Dykehead Stirl 277 B11
Dykelands Aberds 293 G9
Dykends Angus 286 B6
Dykesfield Cumb 239 F8
Dykeside Aberds 303 E7
Dykesmains N Ayrs 266 G4
Dylife Powys 129 E7
Dymchurch Kent 39 B10
Dymock Glos 98 E3
Dynfant = Dunvant Swan 75 G9
Dyrham S Glos 61 D8
Dyrham Park S Glos 61 D8
Dysart Fife 280 C6
Dyserth Denbs 181 F9

E

Eabost H'land 294 B5
Eabost West H'land 298 E3
Each End Kent 55 B10
Eachway Worcs 117 B9
Eachwick Northum 242 C4
Eadar Dha Fhadhail W Isles 304 E2
Eagland Hill Lancs 202 D4
Eagle Lincs 172 B5
Eagle Barnsdale Lincs 172 B5
Eagle Hall Lincs 172 B5
Eagle Moor Lincs 172 B5
Eaglescliffe Stockton 225 B8
Eaglesfield Cumb 229 F7
Eaglesfield Dumf/Gal 238 C6
Eaglesham E Renf 267 E11
Eaglestone M/Keynes 103 D7
Eaglethorpe Northants 137 E11
Eagley Gtr Man 195 E8
Eairy I/Man 192 E3
Eakley M/Keynes 120 G6
Eakring Notts 171 C11
Ealand N Lincs 199 E9
Ealing London 67 C7
Ealing Common London 67 C7
Eals Northum 240 F5
Eamont Bridge Cumb 230 F6
Earby Lancs 204 D4
Earcroft Blackb'n 195 C7
Eardington Shrops 132 E4
Eardisland Heref'd 115 F8
Eardisley Heref'd 96 B6
Eardiston Shrops 149 E7
Eardiston Worcs 116 D3
Earith Cambs 123 B7
Earl Shilton Leics 135 D9
Earl Soham Suffolk 126 E4
Earl Sterndale Derby 169 B9
Earl Stonham Suffolk 126 F2
Earle Northum 263 D11
Earlesfield Lincs 155 B7
Earlestown Mersey 183 B9
Earley Wokingham 65 E9
Earlham Norfolk 142 B3
Earlish H'land 298 C3
Earls Barton Northants 121 E7
Earls Colne Essex 107 F7
Earl's Common Worcs 117 F9
Earl's Court London 67 D9
Earl's Croome Worcs 99 C7
Earl's Down E Sussex 37 D11
Earl's Green Suffolk 125 D10
Earlsdon W Midlands 118 B6
Earlsferry Fife 281 B9
Earlsfield London 67 E9
Earlsford Aberds 303 F8
Earlsheaton W Yorks 197 C9
Earlsmill Moray 301 D9
Earlston Scot Borders 262 B3
Earlston E Ayrs 257 B10
Earlswood Monmouths 79 F7
Earlswood Surrey 51 D9
Earlswood Warwick 118 C2
Earnley W Sussex 22 D4
Earnock S Lanarks 268 E3
Earnshaw Bridge Lancs 194 C4
Earsairidh W Isles 297 M3
Earsdon Northum 252 E6
Earsdon Tyne/Wear 243 C8
Earsham Norfolk 142 F6
Earsham Street Suffolk 126 B4
Earswick C/York 207 B8
Eartham W Sussex 34 F6
Earthcott Green S Glos 61 B7
Easby N Yorks 224 E3
Easby N Yorks 225 D11
Easdale Arg/Bute 275 B8
Easebourne W Sussex 34 C5
Easenhall Warwick 119 B9
Eashing Surrey 50 E2
Easington Bucks 83 C11
Easington Durham 234 C4
Easington ER Yorks 201 D11
Easington Northum 264 C4
Easington Oxon 83 F11
Easington Oxon 101 D9
Easington Redcar/Clevel'd 226 B4
Easington Colliery Durham 234 C4
Easington Lane Tyne/Wear 234 B3
Easingwold N Yorks 215 F10
Easole Street Kent 55 C9
Eassie Angus 287 C7
East Aberthaw V/Glam 58 F4
East Acton London 67 C8
East Adderbury Oxon 101 D9
East Allington Devon 8 F5
East Amat H'land 309 K4
East Anstey Devon 26 B5
East Anton Hants 47 D11
East Appleton N Yorks 224 F4
East Ardsley W Yorks 197 B9
East Ashling W Sussex 34 F4
East Ashton Hants 48 D2
East Auchronie Aberds 293 C10
East Ayton N Yorks 217 B9
East Bank Bl Gwent 78 D2
East Barkwith Lincs 189 E11
East Barming Kent 53 C8
East Barnby N Yorks 226 C6
East Barnet London 86 F3
East Barns E Loth 282 F4
East Barsham Norfolk 159 C8
East Barton Suffolk 125 D8
East Beach W Sussex 22 E5
East Beckham Norfolk 177 E11
East Bedfont London 66 E5
East Bergholt Suffolk 107 D11
East Bierley W Yorks 197 B7
East Bilney Norfolk 159 F9
East Blackdene Durham 232 D3
East Blackdene Durham 232 D3
East Blatchington E Sussex 37 G7
East Bloxworth Dorset 18 C3
East Boldon Tyne/Wear 243 E9
East Boldre Hants 32 G5
East Bonhard Perth/Kinr 286 E5
East Bower Som'set 43 F10
East Brent Som'set 43 C10
East Bridgeford Notts 171 G11
East Briscoe Durham 223 B9
East Buckland Devon 41 G7
East Budleigh Devon 15 E7
East Burnham Bucks 66 C3
East Burrafirth Shetl'd 315 H5
East Burton Dorset 18 D2
East Butsfield Durham 233 B8
East Butterleigh Devon 27 F7
East Butterwick N Lincs 199 F10
East Cairnbeg Aberds 293 F9
East Calder W Loth 269 B11
East Carleton Norfolk 142 C3
East Carlton Northants 136 F6
East Carlton W Yorks 205 E10
East Chaldon Dorset 17 E11
East Challow Oxon 63 B11
East Charleton Devon 8 G5
East Chelborough Dorset 29 F9
East Chiltington E Sussex 36 E5
East Chinnock Som'set 29 E7
East Chisenbury Wilts 46 C6
East Cholderton Hants 47 D9
East Clandon Surrey 50 C5
East Claydon Bucks 102 F4
East Clevedon N Som'set 60 E2
East Clyne H'land 311 J3
East Clyth H'land 310 F7
East Coker Som'set 29 E8
East Combe Som'set 43 G7
East Common N Yorks 207 G8
East Compton Dorset 30 D5
East Compton Som'set 44 E6
East Cornworthy Devon 8 D6
East Cottingwith ER Yorks 207 E10
East Coulston Wilts 46 C3
East Cowes I/Wight 20 B6
East Cowick ER Yorks 199 C7
East Cowton N Yorks 224 E6
East Cramlington Northum 243 B7
East Cranmore Som'set 45 E7
East Creech Dorset 18 E4
East Croachy H'land 300 G6
East Croftmore H'land 291 B11
East Curthwaite Cumb 230 B2
East Dean E Sussex 23 F9
East Dean Glos 98 G3
East Dean Hants 32 B3
East Dean W Sussex 34 E6
East Dene S Yorks 186 C6
East Denton Tyne/Wear 242 D6
East Didsbury Gtr Man 184 D5
East Down Devon 40 E6
East Drayton Notts 188 F3
East Dulwich London 67 E10
East Dundry N Som'set 60 F5
East Ella Kingston/Hull 200 B5
East End Beds 103 C9
East End Beds 122 F2
East End Bucks 84 B4
East End Cambs 124 C3
East End Dorset 18 B5
East End Essex 89 D8
East End ER Yorks 201 B9
East End ER Yorks 209 G9
East End ER Yorks 209 B9
East End Glos 81 E11
East End Hants 33 C11
East End Hants 64 G2
East End Hants 20 B3
East End Herts 105 G9
East End Kent 53 F10
East End Kent 70 E3
East End M/Keynes 103 C8
East End N Som'set 60 E3
East End Oxon 82 C5
East End Oxon 101 E7
East End Oxon 82 B6
East End Oxon 101 D9
East End Suffolk 107 D11
East End Suffolk 126 F3
East End S Glos 61 E9
East End Som'set 45 D7
East End Som'set 44 C5
East End Green Herts 86 C3
East Everleigh Wilts 47 C6
East Ewell Surrey 67 G8
East Farleigh Kent 53 C8
East Farndon Northants 136 F4
East Ferry Lincs 188 B4
East Finchley London 67 B9
East Flexford Surrey 50 D2
East Fortune E Loth 281 F10
East Garforth W Yorks 206 G4
East Garston W Berks 63 D11
East Garston Woodlands W Berks 63 E11
East Gateshead Tyne/Wear 243 E7
East Gillibrands Lancs 194 F3
East Ginge Oxon 64 B2
East Gores Essex 107 G7
East Goscote Leics 154 G2
East Grafton Wilts 63 G9
East Grange Moray 301 C10
East Green Hants 49 E10
East Green Suffolk 127 D8
East Green Suffolk 124 G3
East Grimstead Wilts 32 B2
East Grinstead W Sussex 51 F11
East Guldeford E Sussex 38 B6
East Haddon Northants 120 D3
East Hagbourne Oxon 64 B4
East Halton N Lincs 200 D6
East Ham London 68 C2
East Hampnett W Sussex 34 F6
East Hanney Oxon 82 G6
East Hanningfield Essex 88 E3
East Hardwick W Yorks 198 D3
East Harling Norfolk 141 F9
East Harlsey N Yorks 225 F8
East Harnham Wilts 31 B10
East Harptree Bath/NE Som'set 44 B5
East Hartford Northum 243 B7
East Harting W Sussex 34 D3
East Hatch Wilts 30 B6
East Hatley Cambs 122 G5
East Hauxwell N Yorks 224 G3
East Haven Angus 287 D9
East Heckington Lincs 173 G11
East Hedleyhope Durham 233 C9
East Helmsdale H'land 311 H4
East Hendred Oxon 64 B3
East Herringthorpe S Yorks 187 C7
East Herrington Tyne/Wear 243 G9
East Heslerton N Yorks 217 D8
East Hewish N Som'set 59 G11
East Hill Hants 34 B3
East Hill Kent 68 G5
East Hoathly E Sussex 37 D8
East Hogaland Shetl'd 315 K5
East Holme Dorset 18 D3
East Holywell Northum 243 C8
East Horrington Som'set 44 D5
East Horsley Surrey 50 C5
East Horton Northum 264 C2
East Howdon Tyne/Wear 243 D8
East Howe Bournem'th 19 B7
East Huntspill Som'set 43 E10
East Hyde Beds 85 B10
East Ilsley W Berks 64 C3
East Keal Lincs 174 C5
East Kennett Wilts 62 F6
East Keswick W Yorks 206 E2
East Ketton D'lington 234 G2
East Kilbride S Lanarks 268 E2
East Kingston W Sussex 35 G9
East Kirkby Lincs 174 C4
East Knapton N Yorks 217 D7
East Knighton Dorset 18 D2
East Knowstone Devon 26 C4
East Knoyle Wilts 45 G11
East Kyloe Northum 264 B3
East Kyo Durham 242 G5
East Lambrook Som'set 28 D6
East Lamington H'land 301 B7
East Langdon Kent 55 D10
East Langton Leics 136 E4
East Langwell H'land 309 J7
East Lavant W Sussex 34 F5
East Lavington W Sussex 34 D6
East Law Durham 242 G3
East Layton N Yorks 224 D3
East Leake Notts 153 D11
East Learmouth Northum 263 B9
East Leigh Devon 8 E3
East Leigh Devon 25 F11
East Lenham Kent 54 C2
East Lexham Norfolk 159 F7
East Lilburn Northum 264 E2
East Linton E Loth 281 F11
East Liss Hants 34 B3
East Lockinge Oxon 64 B2
East Loftus Redcar/Clevel'd 226 B4
East Looe Cornw'l 6 E5
East Lound N Lincs 188 B3
East Lulworth Dorset 18 E3
East Lutton N Yorks 217 F8
East Lydford Som'set 44 G5
East Lynch Som'set 42 D2
East Lyng Som'set 28 B4
East Mains Aberds 293 D8
East Mains S Lanarks 268 E2
East Malling Kent 53 B8
East Malling Heath Kent 53 B7
East March Angus 287 D8
East Marden W Sussex 34 E4
East Markham Notts 188 G2
East Marsh NE Lincs 201 F9
East Martin Hants 31 D9
East Marton N Yorks 204 C4
East Meon Hants 33 C11
East Mere Devon 27 D7
East Mersea Essex 89 C9
East Mey H'land 310 B7
East Molesey Surrey 66 F6
East Moor W Yorks 197 C10
East Morden Dorset 18 C4
East Morton W Yorks 205 E8
East Ness N Yorks 216 D3
East Newton ER Yorks 209 F11
East Newton N Yorks 216 D2
East Norton Leics 136 C5
East Nynehead Som'set 27 C11
East Oakley Hants 48 D5
East Ogwell Devon 14 G2
East Orchard Dorset 30 D4
East Ord Northum 273 E9
East Parley Dorset 19 B8
East Peckham Kent 53 D7
East Pennard Som'set 44 F5
East Perry Cambs 122 D3
East Portlemouth Devon 9 G9
East Prawle Devon 9 G10
East Preston W Sussex 35 G9
East Pulham Dorset 30 F2
East Putford Devon 24 D5
East Quantoxhead Som'set 42 E6
East Rainton Tyne/Wear 234 B2
East Ravendale NE Lincs 190 B2
East Raynham Norfolk 159 D7
East Rhidorroch Lodge H'land 307 K7
East Rigton W Yorks 206 E2
East Rolstone N Som'set 59 G11
East Rounton N Yorks 225 E8
East Row N Yorks 227 C7
East Rudham Norfolk 158 D6
East Runton Norfolk 177 E11
East Ruston Norfolk 160 D6
East Saltoun E Loth 271 B9
East Scrafton N Yorks 213 C11
East Sheen London 67 D8
East Shefford W Berks 63 D11
East Sleekburn Northum 253 G7
East Somerton Norfolk 161 F9
East Stanley Durham 242 G6
East Stockwith Lincs 188 C3
East Stoke Dorset 18 D3
East Stoke Notts 172 F3
East Stoke Som'set 29 D7
East Stour Dorset 30 C3
East Stourmouth Kent 71 G9
East Stowford Devon 25 B10
East Stratton Hants 48 F4
East Street Kent 55 B10
East Street Som'set 44 F4
East Studdal Kent 55 D10
East Suisnish H'land 295 B7
East Taphouse Cornw'l 6 C3
East Third Scot Borders 262 B4
East Thirston Northum 252 D5
East Tilbury Thurr'k 69 D7
East Tisted Hants 49 G8
East Torrington Lincs 189 E10
East Town Som'set 42 G6
East Town Som'set 44 E6
East Tuddenham Norfolk 159 G11
East Tytherley Hants 32 B3
East Tytherton Wilts 62 D3
East Village Devon 26 F4
East Village V/Glam 58 E3
East Wall Shrops 131 E10
East Walton Norfolk 158 F4
East Water Som'set 44 C4
East Week Devon 13 C9
East Wellow Hants 32 C4
East Wemyss Fife 280 B6
East Whitburn W Loth 269 B9
East Wickham London 68 D3
East Williamston Pembs 73 E9
East Winch Norfolk 158 F3
East Winterslow Wilts 47 G8
East Wittering W Sussex 22 D4
East Witton N Yorks 214 B2
East Woodburn Northum 251 F10
East Woodhay Hants 64 G2
East Woodlands Som'set 45 E9
East Worldham Hants 49 F8
East Worlington Devon 26 E3
East Worthing W Sussex 35 G11
Eastacombe Devon 25 B8
Eastbourne D'lington 224 C6
Eastbourne E Sussex 23 F10
Eastbridge Suffolk 127 D8
Eastbrook Som'set 28 C2
Eastbrook V/Glam 59 E7
Eastburn ER Yorks 208 B5
Eastburn W Yorks 204 E6
Eastbury Herts 85 G9
Eastbury W Berks 63 D10
Eastby N Yorks 204 C6
Eastchurch Kent 70 E3
Eastcombe Glos 80 E5
Eastcote London 66 B6
Eastcote Northants 120 G3
Eastcote W Midlands 118 B3
Eastcote Village London 66 B6
Eastcott Cornw'l 24 D3
Eastcott Devon 12 E5
Eastcott Wilts 46 B4
Eastcotts Beds 103 B11
Eastcourt Wilts 63 G8
Eastcourt Wilts 81 G7
Eastend Essex 86 C6
Eastend Green Essex 89 B9
Easter Aberchalder H'land 291 B7
Easter Ardross H'land 300 B6
Easter Balgedie Perth/Kinr 286 G5
Easter Balmoral Aberds 292 D4
Easter Boleskine H'land 300 G5
Easter Brackland Stirl 285 G10
Easter Brae H'land 300 C6
Easter Bush Midloth 270 C5
Easter Carbeth Stirl 277 F10
Easter Cardno Aberds 303 C9
Easter Compton S Glos 60 C5
Easter Cringate Stirl 278 D4
Easter Culfosie Aberds 293 C9
Easter Davoch Aberds 292 C6
Easter Earshaig Dumf/Gal 248 C2
Easter Ellister Arg/Bute 254 B3
Easter Fearn H'land 309 L6
Easter Galcantray H'land 301 E8
Easter Howgate Midloth 270 C4
Easter Kinkell H'land 300 D5
Easter Knox Angus 287 D9
Easter Lednathie Angus 292 G5
Easter Milton H'land 301 D9
Easter Moniack H'land 300 E5
Easter Ord Aberds 293 C10
Easter Quarff Shetl'd 315 K6
Easter Rhynd Perth/Kinr 286 F5
Easter Row Stirl 278 B5
Easter Silverford Aberds 303 C7
Easter Skeld Shetl'd 315 J5
Easter Tulloch H'land 291 B11
Easter Whyntie Aberds 302 C6
Eastergate W Sussex 35 F7
Easterhouse Glasg C 268 B3
Easterside Middlesbro 225 B10
Easterton Wilts 46 B4
Easterton of Lenabo Aberds 303 E10
Easterton Sands Wilts 46 B4
Eastertown Som'set 43 C10
Eastertown of Auchleuchries Aberds 303 F10
Eastfield Bristol 60 D5
Eastfield N Lanarks 269 C7
Eastfield N Lanarks 278 F4
Eastfield Northum 243 B7
Eastfield N Yorks 217 C10
Eastfield Peterbro 138 D4
Eastfield S Lanarks 268 C2
Eastfield S Yorks 197 G9
Eastfield S Yorks 187 C9
Eastgate Durham 232 D5
Eastgate Norfolk 160 E2
Easthall Herts 104 G4
Eastham Mersey 182 E5
Eastham Worcs 116 D3
Eastham Ferry Mersey 182 E5
Easthampstead Brackn'l 65 F11
Easthampton Heref'd 115 E8
Easthaugh Norfolk 159 F11
Eastheath Wokingham 65 F10
Easthope Shrops 131 D11
Easthorpe Essex 107 G9
Easthorpe ER Yorks 208 D3
Easthorpe Leics 154 B6
Easthorpe Notts 172 E2
Easthouse Shetl'd 315 J5
Easthouses Midloth 270 B6
Easting Orkney 312 C8
Eastington Devon 26 F2
Eastington Glos 80 D3
Eastington Glos 81 C10
Eastlands Dumf/Gal 237 B10
Eastleach Martin Glos 82 D2
Eastleach Turville Glos 81 D11
Eastleaze Swindon 62 C6
Eastleigh Devon 25 B7
Eastleigh Hants 33 D7
Eastling Kent 54 B3
Eastly End Surrey 66 F4
Eastmoor Derby 186 G4
Eastmoor Norfolk 140 C4
Eastney Portsm'th 21 B9
Eastnor Heref'd 98 D4
Eastoft N Lincs 199 D10
Eastoke Hants 22 D2
Easton Cambs 122 C2
Easton Cumb 239 F7
Easton Cumb 239 C10
Easton Dorset 17 G9
Easton Devon 13 D10
Easton Hants 48 G4
Easton I/Wight 20 D2
Easton Lincs 155 D8
Easton Norfolk 160 G2
Easton Suffolk 126 F5
Easton Som'set 44 D4
Easton W Berks 64 E2
Easton Wilts 61 E11
Easton Grey Wilts 61 B11
Easton Maudit Northants 121 F7
Easton on the Hill Northants 137 B10
Easton Royal Wilts 63 G8
Easton Town Som'set 44 G6
Easton Town Wilts 61 B11
Easton-in-Gordano N Som'set 60 D4
Eastrea Cambs 138 D5
Eastriggs Dumf/Gal 238 D6
Eastrington ER Yorks 199 B9
Eastrip Wilts 61 E10
Eastrop Wilts 82 G2
Eastry Kent 55 C10
East-the-Water Devon 25 B7
Eastville Bristol 60 D6
Eastville Lincs 174 D6
Eastwell Leics 154 D5
Eastwick Herts 86 C6
Eastwick Shetl'd 314 F5
Eastwood Notts 171 F7
Eastwood Southend 69 B11
Eastwood S Yorks 186 C6
Eastwood End Cambs 139 E8
Eastwood Park S Glos 79 G11
Eathorpe Warwick 119 D7
Eaton Ches 167 C9
Eaton Ches 168 B5
Eaton Heref'd 115 F10
Eaton Leics 154 D5
Eaton Norfolk 142 B4
Eaton Norfolk 158 B3
Eaton Notts 188 F2
Eaton Oxon 82 E6
Eaton Shrops 131 F7
Eaton Bishop Heref'd 97 D8
Eaton Bray Beds 103 G9
Eaton Constantine Shrops 131 B11
Eaton Green Beds 103 G9
Eaton Hastings Oxon 82 F3
Eaton Socon Cambs 122 F3
Eaton upon Tern Shrops 150 E3
Eau Brink Norfolk 157 F11
Eau Well Lincs 156 E2
Eau Withington Heref'd 97 C10
Eaves Green W Midlands 134 G5
Eaves Hall Lancs 203 E10
Eavestone N Yorks 214 F4
Ebberston N Yorks 217 C7
Ebbesbourne Wake Wilts 31 C7
Ebblake Dorset 31 F10
Ebbw Vale = Glyn Ebwy Bl Gwent 77 D11
Ebchester Durham 242 F4
Ebdon N Som'set 59 G11
Ebford Devon 14 D5
Ebley Glos 80 E4
Ebnal Ches 167 F7
Ebreywood Shrops 149 F10
Ebrington Glos 100 C3
Ecchinswell Hants 48 B4
Ecclefechan Dumf/Gal 238 C5
Eccles Scot Borders 272 G5
Eccles Gtr Man 184 B3
Eccles Kent 69 G8
Eccles Green Heref'd 97 B7
Eccles on Sea Norfolk 161 D8
Eccles Road Norfolk 141 E10
Ecclesall S Yorks 186 E4
Ecclesfield S Yorks 186 C5
Ecclesgreig Aberds 293 G9
Eccleshall Staffs 150 D6
Eccleshill W Yorks 205 F9
Ecclesmachan W Loth 279 G11
Eccleston Ches 166 C6
Eccleston Lancs 194 D4
Eccleston Mersey 183 B7
Eccleston Park Mersey 183 C7
Eccliffe Dorset 30 B4
Eccup W Yorks 205 E11
Echt Aberds 293 C9
Eckford Scot Borders 262 D6
Eckington Derby 186 F6
Eckington Worcs 99 C8
Ecton Northants 120 E6
Ecton Brook Northants 120 E6
Edale Derby 185 D10
Edbrook Som'set 43 E8
Edbrooke Som'set 42 G2
Edburton W Sussex 36 E2
Edderside Cumb 229 B8
Edderthorpe S Yorks 198 F2
Edderton H'land 309 L7
Eddington Kent 71 F7
Eddington W Berks 63 F10
Eddleston Scot Borders 270 F4
Eddlewood S Lanarks 268 E4
Eden Camp, Malton N Yorks 216 E5

Eden Mount Cumb 211 D8
Eden Vale Durham 234 D4
Eden Vale Wilts 45 C11
Edenbridge Kent 52 D2
Edenfield Lancs 195 D10
Edenhall Cumb 231 E7
Edenham Lincs 155 E11
Edensor Derby 186 G2
Edenthorpe S Yorks 198 F6
Edentown Cumb 239 F9
Ederline Arg/Bute 275 C9
Edern Gwyn 144 B5
Edford Som'set 45 D7
Edgarley Som'set 44 F4
Edgbaston W Midlands 133 G11
Edgcote Northants 101 B10
Edgcott Bucks 102 G3
Edgcott Som'set 41 F10
Edgcumbe Cornw'l 2 C6
Edge Glos 80 D4
Edge Shrops 131 B7
Edge End Glos 79 C9
Edge End Lancs 203 G10
Edge Fold Blackb'n 195 D8
Edge Fold Gtr Man 195 F7
Edge Green Norfolk 141 G10
Edge Green Warrington 183 B10
Edge Hill Mersey 182 D5
Edge Hill Warwick 134 D4
Edgebolton Shrops 149 E11
Edgefield Norfolk 159 C11
Edgefield S Yorks 186 B3
Edgefield Street Norfolk 159 C11
Edgehill Derby 170 G5
Edgeley Gtr Man 184 D5
Edgerston Scot Borders 262 G5
Edgerton W Yorks 196 D6
Edgeside Lancs 195 C10
Edgeworth Glos 80 D6
Edginswell Devon 9 B7
Edgiock Worcs 117 E10
Edgmond Telford 150 F4
Edgmond Marsh Telford 150 E4
Edgton Shrops 131 G7
Edgware London 85 G11
Edgworth Blackb'n 195 D8
Edinample Stirl 285 E9
Edinbane H'land 298 D3
Edinburgh C/Edinb 280 G4
Edinburgh Airport C/Edinb 280 G2
Edinburgh Castle C/Edinb 280 G5
Edinburgh Crystal Visitor Centre, Penicuik Midloth 270 C4
Edinburgh Hill Kent 55 E10
Edinburgh Zoo C/Edinb 280 G4
Edinchip Stirl 285 E9
Edingale Staffs 152 G4
Edingight Ho. Moray 302 D5
Edinglassie Ho. Aberds 292 B5
Edingley Notts 171 D11
Edingthorpe Norfolk 160 C6
Edingthorpe Green Norfolk 160 C6
Edington Som'set 43 F11
Edington Wilts 46 C2
Edingworth Som'set 43 C11
Edintore Moray 302 E4
Edistone Devon 24 C2
Edith Weston Rutl'd 137 B8
Edithmead Som'set 43 D10
Edlaston Derby 169 G11
Edlesborough Bucks 85 B7
Edlingham Northum 252 B4
Edlington Lincs 190 G2
Edmondsham Dorset 31 E9
Edmondsley Durham 233 B10
Edmondstown Rh Cyn Taff 77 G8
Edmondthorpe Leics 155 F7
Edmonstone C/Edinb 280 G6
Edmonstone Orkney 312 F6
Edmonstown Rh Cyn Taff 77 G8
Edmonton Cornw'l 10 G5
Edmonton London 86 G4
Edmund Hill Som'set 44 F4
Edmundbyers Durham 232 B6
Ednam Scot Borders 262 B6
Ednaston Derby 170 G2
Edney Common Essex 87 E11
Edradynate Perth/Kinr 286 B2
Edrom Scot Borders 272 D6
Edstaston Shrops 149 C10
Edvin Loach Heref'd 116 F3
Edwalton Notts 153 B11
Edwardstone Suffolk 107 C8
Edwardsville Merth Tyd 77 F9
Edwinstowe Notts 171 B10
Edworth Beds 104 C4
Edwyn Ralph Heref'd 116 F2
Edzell Angus 293 G7
Efail Isaf Rh Cyn Taff 58 C5
Efail-fach Rh Cyn Taff 76 F3
Efailnewydd Gwyn 145 B7
Efail-rhyd Powys 148 D3
Efailwen Carms 92 F2
Efenechtyd Denbs 165 D10
Effingham Surrey 50 C6
Effirth Shetl'd 315 H5
Efflinch Staffs 152 F3
Efford Plym'th 7 D10
Egbury Hants 48 C2
Egde Green Ches 167 E7
Egdean W Sussex 35 C7
Egdon Worcs 117 G8
Egerton Gtr Man 195 E8
Egerton Kent 54 D2
Egerton Forstal Kent 53 D11
Egerton Green Ches 167 E8
Eggborough N Yorks 198 C5
Eggbuckland Plym'th 7 D9
Eggington Beds 103 G9
Egginton Derby 152 D5
Egglesburn Durham 232 G5
Egglescliffe Stockton 225 C8
Eggleston Durham 232 G6
Egham Surrey 66 E4
Egham Wick Surrey 66 E3
Egleton Rutl'd 137 B7
Eglingham Northum 264 F4
Egloshayle Cornw'l 10 G6
Egloskerry Cornw'l 11 D11
Eglwys Cross Wrex 167 G7
Eglwys Fach Ceredig'n 128 D3
Eglwysbach Conwy 180 G4
Eglwys-Brewis V/Glam 58 F4
Eglwyswen Pembs 92 D3
Eglwyswrw Pembs 92 D2
Egmanton Notts 172 B2
Egremont Cumb 219 C10
Egremont Mersey 182 C4
Egton N Yorks 226 D6
Egton Bridge N Yorks 226 D6
Egypt Hants 48 F3
Eiden H'land 309 J7
Eight Ash Green Essex 107 F8
Eighton Banks Tyne/Wear 243 F7
Eign Hill Heref'd 97 D10
Eignaig H'land 289 E9
Eil H'land 291 B10
Eilanreach H'land 295 D10
Eildon Scot Borders 262 C3
Eilean Anabaich W Isles 305 H4
Eilean Darach H'land 307 L6
Eilean Shona Ho H'land 289 B8
Eileanach Lodge H'land 300 C5
Einacleite W Isles 304 F3
Eisgean W Isles 305 G5
Eisingrug Gwyn 146 C2
Elan Village Powys 113 D8
Eland Green Northum 242 C5
Elberton S Glos 60 B6
Elborough N Som'set 43 B11
Elburton Plym'th 7 E10
Elcho Perth/Kinr 286 E5
Elcombe Glos 80 F3
Elcombe Swindon 62 C6
Elcot W Berks 63 F11
Eldene Swindon 63 C7
Elder Street Essex 105 E11
Eldernell Cambs 138 D6
Eldersfield Worcs 98 E6
Elderslie Renf 267 C8
Eldon Durham 233 F10
Eldon Lane Durham 233 F10
Eldroth N Yorks 212 F5
Eldwick W Yorks 205 E8
Elemore Vale Tyne/Wear 234 B3
Elerch = Bont-goch Ceredig'n 128 F3
Elerch Ceredig'n 128 F3
Elfhowe Cumb 221 F9
Elford Northum 264 C5
Elford Staffs 152 G3
Elford Closes Cambs 123 C10
Elgin Moray 302 C2
Elgol H'land 295 D7
Elham Kent 55 E7
Eliburn W Loth 269 B10
Elie Fife 287 G8
Elim Angl 178 E5
Eling Hants 32 E5
Eling W Berks 64 D4
Elishader H'land 298 C5
Elishaw Northum 251 D9
Elizafield Dumf/Gal 238 C2
Elkesley Notts 187 F11
Elkington Northants 120 B2
Elkins Green Essex 87 E10
Elkstone Glos 81 C7
Ellacombe Torbay 9 C8
Ellan H'land 301 G8
Ellanbrook Gtr Man 195 G8
Elland W Yorks 196 C6
Elland Lower Edge W Yorks 196 C6
Elland Upper Edge W Yorks 196 C6
Ellary Arg/Bute 275 F8
Ellastone Staffs 169 G10
Ellbridge Cornw'l 7 C8
Ellel Lancs 202 B5
Ellenborough Cumb 228 D6
Ellenbrook Herts 86 D2
Ellenbrook I/Man 192 E4
Ellenglaze Cornw'l 4 D5
Ellenhall Staffs 150 D6
Ellen's Green Surrey 50 F5
Ellerbeck N Yorks 225 F8
Ellerburn N Yorks 216 C6
Ellerby N Yorks 226 C5
Ellerdine Telford 150 E2
Ellerdine Heath Telford 150 E2
Ellergreen Cumb 221 F10
Ellerhayes Devon 27 G7
Elleric Arg/Bute 284 C4
Ellerker ER Yorks 200 B2
Ellers N Yorks 204 E6
Ellerton ER Yorks 207 F10
Ellerton N Yorks 224 F5
Ellesborough Bucks 84 D4
Ellesmere Shrops 149 C7
Ellesmere Park Gtr Man 184 B3
Ellesmere Port Ches 182 F6
Ellicombe Som'set 42 E3
Ellinge Kent 55 E8
Ellingham Hants 31 F10
Ellingham Norfolk 143 E7
Ellingham Northum 264 D5
Ellingstring N Yorks 214 C3
Ellington Cambs 122 C3
Ellington Northum 253 E7
Ellington Thorpe Cambs 122 C3
Elliot Angus 287 D10
Elliots Green Som'set 45 D9
Ellisfield Hants 48 D6
Ellistown Leics 153 G8
Ellon Aberds 303 F9
Ellonby Cumb 230 D4
Ellough Suffolk 143 F8
Ellough Moor Suffolk 143 F8
Elloughton ER Yorks 200 B2
Ellwood Glos 79 D9
Elm Cambs 139 B9
Elm Corner Surrey 50 B5
Elm Park London 68 B4
Elmbridge Glos 80 B5
Elmbridge Worcs 117 D8
Elmdon Essex 105 D9
Elmdon W Midlands 134 G3
Elmdon Heath W Midlands 134 G3
Elmer W Sussex 35 G7
Elmers End London 67 F11
Elmer's Green Lancs 194 F4
Elmesthorpe Leics 135 D9
Elmfield I/Wight 21 C8
Elmhurst Bucks 84 B4
Elmhurst Staffs 152 G2
Elmley Castle Worcs 99 C9
Elmley Lovett Worcs 117 D7
Elmore Glos 80 B3
Elmore Back Glos 80 B3
Elms Farm Beds 121 G11
Elmscott Devon 24 C2
Elmsett Suffolk 107 B11
Elmslack Lancs 211 D9
Elmstead Essex 107 F11
Elmstead Kent 54 D6
Elmstead London 68 E2
Elmstead Heath Essex 107 G11
Elmstead Market Essex 107 G11
Elmstone Kent 71 G9
Elmstone Hardwicke Glos 99 F8
Elmswell ER Yorks 208 B5
Elmswell Suffolk 125 E9
Elmton Derby 187 G8
Elmton Park Derby 187 G7
Elness Orkney 312 E7
Elphin H'land 307 H7
Elphinstone E Loth 281 G7
Elrick Aberds 293 C10
Elrig Dumf/Gal 236 E5
Elrigbeag Arg/Bute 284 F5
Elrington Northum 241 E9
Elsdon Heref'd 114 G6
Elsdon Northum 251 E10
Elsecar S Yorks 197 G11
Elsenham Essex 105 F10
Elsfield Oxon 83 D8
Elsham N Lincs 200 E4
Elsing Norfolk 159 F11
Elslack N Yorks 204 D4
Elson Portsm'th 33 G10
Elson Shrops 149 B7
Elsrickle S Lanarks 269 G11
Elstead Surrey 50 E2
Elsted W Sussex 34 D4
Elsted Marsh W Sussex 34 C4
Elsthorpe Lincs 155 E11
Elstob Durham 234 G2
Elston Lancs 203 G8
Elston Notts 172 F3
Elston Wilts 46 E5
Elstone Devon 25 D11
Elstow Beds 103 B11
Elstree Herts 85 F11
Elstronwick ER Yorks 209 G10
Elswick Lancs 202 F4
Elswick Tyne/Wear 242 E6
Elsworth Cambs 122 E6
Elterwater Cumb 220 E6
Eltham London 68 E2
Eltisley Cambs 122 F5
Elton Cambs 137 E11
Elton Ches 183 F7
Elton Derby 170 C2
Elton Glos 79 C11
Elton Gtr Man 195 E9
Elton Heref'd 115 C9
Elton Notts 154 B5
Elton Stockton 225 B8
Elton Green Ches 183 G7
Elton's Marsh Heref'd 97 C9
Eltringham Northum 242 E3
Elvanfoot S Lanarks 259 F10
Elvaston Derby 153 C8
Elveden Suffolk 140 G6
Elverland Kent 54 B3
Elvingston E Loth 281 G9
Elvington C/York 207 D9
Elvington Kent 55 C9
Elwell Dorset 17 D9
Elwick Hartlep'l 234 E5
Elwick Northum 264 B4
Elworth Ches 168 C2
Elworthy Som'set 42 G5
Ely Cambs 139 G10
Ely Card 58 D6
Ely Cathedral and Museum Cambs 139 G10
Emberton M/Keynes 103 B7
Embleton Cumb 229 E9
Embleton Durham 234 F4
Embleton Northum 264 E6
Embo H'land 311 K2
Embo Street H'land 311 K2
Emborough Som'set 44 C6
Embsay N Yorks 204 C6
Emerson Park London 68 B4
Emery Down Hants 32 F3
Emley W Yorks 197 E8
Emmbrook Wokingham 65 F10
Emmer Green Wokingham 65 D8
Emmets Nest Brackn'l 65 E10
Emmett Carr Derby 187 F7
Emmington Oxon 84 E2
Emneth Norfolk 139 B9
Emneth Hungate Norfolk 139 B10
Emorsgate Norfolk 157 E10
Empingham Rutl'd 137 B9
Empshott Hants 49 G9
Empshott Green Hants 49 G8
Emstrey Shrops 149 G10
Emsworth Hants 34 F2
Enborne W Berks 64 F2
Enborne Row W Berks 64 G2
Enchmarsh Shrops 131 D10
Enderby Leics 135 D10
Endmoor Cumb 211 C10
Endon Staffs 168 E6
Endon Bank Staffs 168 E6
Energlyn Caerph 59 B7
Enfield London 86 F4
Enfield Worcs 117 D10
Enfield Highway London 86 F5
Enfield Island Village Essex 86 F5
Enfield Lock London 86 F5
Enfield Town London 86 F4
Enfield Wash London 86 F5
Enford Wilts 46 C6
Engamoor Shetl'd 315 H4
Engedi Angl 178 F5
Engine Common S Glos 61 C7
Englefield W Berks 64 E6
Englefield Green Surrey 66 E3
Englemere Brackn'l 66 F2
Engleseabrook Ches 168 E3
English Bicknor Glos 79 B9
English Frankton Shrops 149 D9
Englishcombe Bath/NE Som'set 61 G8
Engollen Cornw'l 5 B7
Enham-Alamein Hants 47 D11
Enisfirth Shetl'd 314 F5
Enmore Som'set 43 F8
Enmore Green Dorset 30 C5
Ennerdale Bridge Cumb 219 B11
Enniscaven Cornw'l 5 D9
Enoch Dumf/Gal 247 C9
Enochdhu Perth/Kinr 292 G2
Ensay Arg/Bute 288 E5
Ensbury Bournem'th 19 B7
Ensbury Park Dorset 19 C7
Ensdon Shrops 149 F8
Ensis Devon 25 B9
Enslow Oxon 83 B7
Enson Staffs 151 D8
Enstone Oxon 101 G7
Enterkinfoot Dumf/Gal 247 C9
Enterpen N Yorks 225 D9
Enton Green Surrey 50 E3
Enville Staffs 132 F6
Eòropaidh W Isles 304 B7
Eolaigearraidh W Isles 297 L3
Eorabus Arg/Bute 288 G5
Epney Glos 80 C3
Eppelby N Yorks 224 C3
Epperstone Notts 171 F11
Epping Essex 87 E7
Epping Green Essex 86 D6
Epping Green Herts 86 D3
Epping Upland Essex 86 E6
Eppleworth ER Yorks 208 G6
Epsom Surrey 67 G8
Epsom Racecourse Surrey 67 H8
Epwell Oxon 101 C7
Epworth N Lincs 199 G9
Epworth Turbary N Lincs 199 G9
Erbistock Wrex 166 G5
Erbusaig H'land 295 C9
Erchless Castle H'land 300 E4
Erddig Wrex 166 F4
Erdington W Midlands 134 E2
Eredine Arg/Bute 275 C10
Eriboll H'land 308 D4
Ericstane Dumf/Gal 260 G3
Eridge Green E Sussex 52 F5
Erines Arg/Bute 275 F9
Eriswell Suffolk 124 B4
Erith London 68 D4
Erlestoke Wilts 46 C3
Ermine Lincs 189 G7
Ermington Devon 8 E2
Ernesettle Plym'th 7 D8
Erpingham Norfolk 160 C3
Erriottwood Kent 54 B2
Errogie H'land 300 G5
Errol Perth/Kinr 286 E6
Errol Station Perth/Kinr 286 E6
Erskine Renf 277 G9
Erskine Bridge Renf 277 G9
Ervie Dumf/Gal 236 C2
Erwarton Suffolk 108 D4
Erwood Powys 95 C11
Eryholme N Yorks 224 D6
Eryrys Denbs 166 D2
Escalls Cornw'l 1 D3
Escomb Durham 233 E9
Escott Som'set 42 F5
Escrick N Yorks 207 E8
Esgair Carms 93 F7
Esgairgeiliog Powys 128 B5
Esgyryn Conwy 180 F4
Esh Durham 233 C9
Esh Winning Durham 233 C9
Esher Surrey 66 G6
Esholt W Yorks 205 E9
Eshott Northum 252 D6
Eshton N Yorks 204 B4
Esk Valley N Yorks 226 E6
Eskadale H'land 300 F4
Eskbank Midloth 270 B6
Eskdale Green Cumb 220 E2
Eskdalemuir Dumf/Gal 249 D7
Eskeleth N Yorks 223 E9
Eskett Cumb 219 B11
Eskham Lincs 190 B5
Eskholme S Yorks 198 D6
Esknish Arg/Bute 274 G4
Esperley Lane Ends Durham 233 G8
Esprick Lancs 202 F4
Essendine Rutl'd 155 G10
Essendon Herts 86 D3
Essich H'land 300 F6
Essington Staffs 133 C9
Esslemont Aberds 303 G9
Eston Redcar/Clevel'd 225 B11
Estover Plym'th 7 D10
Eswick Shetl'd 315 H6
Etal Northum 263 B10
Etchilhampton Wilts 62 G4
Etchingham E Sussex 38 B2
Etchinghill Kent 55 F7
Etchinghill Staffs 151 F10
Etchingwood E Sussex 37 C8
Etherley Dene Durham 233 F9
Etherley Grange Durham 233 F9
Ethie Castle Angus 287 C10
Ethie Mains Angus 287 C10
Etling Green Norfolk 159 G10
Etloe Glos 79 D11
Eton Windsor 66 D3
Eton Wick Windsor 66 D2
Etrop Green Gtr Man 184 D4
Etruria Stoke 168 F5
Etterby Cumb 239 F9
Etteridge H'land 291 D8
Ettersgill Durham 232 F3
Ettiley Heath Ches 168 C2
Ettingshall W Midlands 133 D8
Ettingshall Park W Midlands 133 D8
Ettington Warwick 100 B5
Etton ER Yorks 208 E5
Etton Peterbro 138 B2
Ettrick Scot Borders 261 G7
Ettrickbridge Scot Borders 261 E9
Ettrickdale Arg/Bute 275 G11
Ettrickhill Scot Borders 261 G7
Etwall Derby 152 C5
Eudon George Shrops 132 F3
Eureka!, Halifax W Yorks 196 C5
Euston Suffolk 125 B7
Euximoor Drove Cambs 139 D9
Euxton Lancs 194 D5
Evancoyd Powys 114 E5
Evanstown Bridg 58 B3
Evanton H'land 300 C6
Eve Hill W Midlands 133 E8
Evedon Lincs 173 F9
Evelix H'land 309 K7
Even Swindon Swindon 62 B6
Evendine Heref'd 98 C5
Evenjobb Powys 114 E5
Evenley Northants 101 D11
Evenlode Glos 100 F4
Evenwood Durham 233 F9
Evenwood Gate Durham 233 G9
Ever Green Suffolk 124 G3
Everbay Orkney 312 F7
Evercreech Som'set 44 G6
Everdon Northants 119 F11
Everingham ER Yorks 208 E2
Everland Shetl'd 314 D8
Everleigh Wilts 47 C8
Eversholt Beds 103 E9
Evershot Dorset 29 G9
Eversley Hants 65 G9
Eversley Cross Hants 65 G9
Everthorpe ER Yorks 208 G4
Everton Beds 122 G4
Everton Hants 19 C11
Everton Mersey 182 C5
Everton Notts 187 C11
Evertown Dumf/Gal 239 B9
Eves Corner Essex 88 D2
Eves Corner Essex 88 F6
Evesbatch Heref'd 98 B3
Evesham Worcs 99 C10
Evington Leics C 136 C2
Ewanrigg Cumb 228 D6
Ewden Village S Yorks 186 B3
Ewell Surrey 67 G8
Ewell Minnis Kent 55 E9
Ewelme Oxon 83 G10
Ewen Glos 81 F8
Ewenny V/Glam 58 D2
Ewerby Lincs 173 F10
Ewerby thorpe Lincs 173 F10
Ewes Dumf/Gal 249 E9
Ewesley Northum 252 E3
Ewhurst Surrey 50 E5
Ewhurst Green E Sussex 38 C3
Ewhurst Green Surrey 50 F5
Ewloe Flints 166 B4
Ewloe Green Flints 166 C3
Ewood Blackb'n 195 B7
Ewood Bridge Lancs 195 C9
Eworthy Devon 12 B4
Ewshot Hants 49 D10
Ewyas Harold Heref'd 97 F7
Exbourne Devon 25 G10
Exbury Hants 32 G6
Exbury Gardens, Fawley Hants 32 G6
Exebridge Som'set 26 C6
Exelby N Yorks 214 B5
Exeter Devon 14 C4
Exeter Cathedral Devon 14 C4
Exeter International Airport Devon 14 C6
Exford Som'set 41 F11
Exfords Green Shrops 131 B9
Exhall Warwick 118 F2
Exhall Warwick 134 F6
Exlade Street Oxon 65 C7
Exley W Yorks 196 C5
Exley Head W Yorks 204 E6
Exminster Devon 14 D4
Exmouth Devon 14 E6
Exnaboe Shetl'd 315 M5
Exning Suffolk 124 D2
Explosion, Gosport Hants 33 G10
Exted Kent 55 E7
Exton Devon 14 D5
Exton Hants 33 C10
Exton Rutl'd 155 G8
Exton Som'set 42 G2
Exwick Devon 14 C4
Eyam Derby 186 F2
Eydon Northants 119 G10
Eye Heref'd 115 E9
Eye Peterbro 138 C4
Eye Suffolk 126 C2
Eye Green Peterbro 138 C4
Eye Kettleby Leics 154 F4
Eyemouth Scot Borders 273 C8
Eyeworth Beds 104 B5
Eyhorne Street Kent 53 C10
Eyke Suffolk 126 G6
Eynesbury Cambs 122 F2
Eynort H'land 294 C5
Eynsford Kent 68 F4
Eynsham Oxon 82 D6
Eype Dorset 16 C5
Eyre H'land 295 B7
Eyre H'land 298 D4
Eyres Monsell Leics 135 D11
Eythorne Kent 55 D9
Eyton Heref'd 115 E9
Eyton Shrops 131 F7
Eyton Shrops 149 G7
Eyton Wrex 166 G5
Eyton on Severn Shrops 131 B11
Eyton upon the Weald Moors Telford 150 G3

F

Faberstown Hants 47 C9
Faccombe Hants 47 B11
Faceby N Yorks 225 E9
Fachwen Gwyn 163 C9
Facit Lancs 195 D11
Faddiley Ches 167 E9
Faddonch H'land 295 C11
Fadmoor N Yorks 216 B3
Faerdre Swan 75 E11
Fagley W Yorks 205 F9
Fagwyr Swan 75 E11
Faichem H'land 290 C4
Faifley W Dunb 277 G10
Fail S Ayrs 257 D10
Failand N Som'set 60 E4
Failford S Ayrs 257 D11
Failsworth Gtr Man 196 G2
Fain H'land 299 B11
Faindouran Lodge Moray 292 C2
Fair Cross W Berks 65 G7
Fair Green Norfolk 158 F3
Fair Hill Cumb 230 E6
Fair Moor Northum 252 F5
Fair Oak Hants 64 G5
Fair Oak Hants 33 D7
Fair Oak Lancs 203 D9
Fair Oak Green Hants 65 G7
Fairbourne Gwyn 146 G2
Fairbourne Heath Kent 53 C11
Fairburn N Yorks 198 B3
Fairburn House H'land 300 D4
Fairfield Clack 279 C7
Fairfield Derby 185 G9
Fairfield Gtr Man 195 E10
Fairfield Gtr Man 184 B6
Fairfield Kent 39 B7
Fairfield Mersey 182 C5
Fairfield Stockton 225 B8
Fairfield Worcs 99 C10
Fairfield Worcs 117 B9
Fairfield Park Bath/NE Som'set 61 F9
Fairford Glos 81 E11
Fairhaven Lancs 193 B10
Fairhaven N Ayrs 255 C10
Fairhill S Lanarks 268 E4
Fairlands Surrey 50 C3
Fairlie N Ayrs 266 D4
Fairlight E Sussex 38 E5
Fairlight Cove E Sussex 38 E5
Fairlop London 87 G7
Fairmile Devon 15 B7
Fairmile Surrey 66 G6
Fairmile Common Surrey 66 G6
Fairmilehead C/Edinb 270 B4
Fairoak Caerph 77 F11
Fairoak Staffs 150 C5
Fairseat Kent 68 G6
Fairstead Essex 88 B3
Fairstead Norfolk 158 F2
Fairwarp E Sussex 37 B7
Fairwater Card 58 D6
Fairwater Torf 78 G3
Fairy Cottage I/Man 192 D5
Fairy Cross Cornw'l 6 C2
Fairy Cross Devon 24 C6
Fakenham Norfolk 159 C8
Fakenham Magna Suffolk 125 B8
Fakenham Racecourse Norfolk 159 D8
Fala Midloth 271 C8
Fala Dam Midloth 271 C8
Falahill Scot Borders 271 D7
Falcon Heref'd 98 E2
Falcon Lodge W Midlands 134 D2
Falconwood London 68 D3
Faldingworth Lincs 189 E9
Falfield Fife 287 G8
Falfield S Glos 79 G11
Falkenham Suffolk 108 D5
Falkirk Falk 279 F7
Falkland Fife 286 G6
Falkland Palace Fife 286 G6
Fallin Stirl 278 C6
Fallings Heath W Midlands 133 D9
Fallowfield Gtr Man 184 C5
Fallowfield Northum 241 D10
Fallside N Lanarks 268 C4
Falmer E Sussex 36 F5
Falmouth Cornw'l 3 C8
Falnash Scot Borders 249 B9
Falsgrave N Yorks 217 B10
Falside W Loth 269 B9
Falstone Northum 250 F6
Fanagmore H'land 306 E6
Fancott Beds 103 F10
Fangdale Beck N Yorks 225 G11
Fangfoss ER Yorks 207 C11
Fanich H'land 311 J2
Fankerton Falk 278 E5
Fanmore Arg/Bute 288 E6
Fanner's Green Essex 87 C11
Fannich Lodge H'land 300 C2
Fans Scot Borders 272 G2
Fanshawe Ches 184 F5
Fant Kent 53 C8
Faoilean H'land 295 C7
Far Bletchley M/Keynes 102 E6
Far Cotton Northants 120 F4
Far End Cumb 220 F6
Far End Derby 186 G3
Far Forest Worcs 116 B4
Far Green Glos 80 E3
Far Hoarcross Staffs 152 E2
Far Moor Gtr Man 194 G4
Far Oakridge Glos 80 E6
Far Royds W Yorks 205 G11
Far Sawrey Cumb 221 F7
Farcet Cambs 138 E4
Farden Shrops 115 B11
Fareham Hants 33 F9
Farewell Staffs 151 G11
Farforth Lincs 190 F4
Faringdon Oxon 82 F3
Farington Lancs 194 C5
Farlam Cumb 240 F3
Farlands Booth Derby 185 D9
Farlary H'land 309 J7
Farleigh N Som'set 60 F3
Farleigh Surrey 67 G11
Farleigh Green Kent 53 C8
Farleigh Hungerford Som'set 45 B10
Farleigh Wallop Hants 48 D6
Farleigh Wick Wilts 61 G10
Farlesthorpe Lincs 191 G7
Farleton Cumb 211 C10
Farleton Lancs 211 F11
Farley N Som'set 60 E2
Farley Shrops 131 B7
Farley Staffs 169 G9
Farley Wilts 32 B2
Farley Common Kent 52 C2
Farley Green Suffolk 124 G4
Farley Green Surrey 50 D5
Farley Hill Luton 103 G11
Farley Hill Wokingham 65 G9
Farlington N Yorks 216 F2
Farlington Portsm'th 33 F11
Farlow Shrops 132 G2
Farm Town Leics 153 F7
Farmborough Bath/NE Som'set 61 G7
Farmbridge End Essex 87 C10
Farmcote Glos 99 F11
Farmington Glos 81 B10
Farmoor Oxon 83 D7
Farms Common Cornw'l 2 C5
Farmtown Moray 302 D5
Farnborough Hants 49 C11
Farnborough London 68 G2
Farnborough Warwick 101 B8
Farnborough W Berks 64 C2
Farnborough Green Herts 49 B11
Farnborough Park Hants 49 B11
Farncombe Surrey 50 D3
Farndish Beds 121 E8
Farndon Ches 166 E6
Farndon Notts 172 E3
Farnell Angus 287 B10
Farneyside Northum 241 G7
Farnham Dorset 31 D7
Farnham Essex 105 G9
Farnham N Yorks 214 G6
Farnham Suffolk 127 E7
Farnham Surrey 49 D10
Farnham Common Bucks 66 B3
Farnham Green Essex 105 G9
Farnham Royal Bucks 66 C3
Farnhill N Yorks 204 D6
Farningham Kent 68 F4
Farnley N Yorks 205 D10
Farnley W Yorks 205 G11
Farnley Tyas W Yorks 197 E7
Farnsfield Notts 171 D11
Farnworth Gtr Man 195 F8
Farnworth Halton 183 D8
Farr H'land 291 C10
Farr H'land 300 F6
Farr H'land 308 C7
Farr House H'land 300 F6
Farraline H'land 300 G5
Farringdon Devon 14 C6
Farringdon Tyne/Wear 243 G9
Farringdon Cross Devon 14 C6
Farrington Gurney Bath/NE Som'set 44 B6
Farsley W Yorks 205 F10
Farsley Beck Bottom W Yorks 205 F10
Farther Howegreen Essex 88 E4
Farthing Common Kent 54 E6
Farthing Corner Medway 69 G10
Farthing Green Kent 53 D10
Farthinghoe Northants 101 D10
Farthingloe Kent 55 E9
Farthingstone Northants 120 G2
Fartown W Yorks 196 D6
Farway Devon 15 B9
Fasach H'land 297 G7
Fasag H'land 299 D8
Fascadale H'land 289 B7
Faslane Port Arg/Bute 276 D4
Fasnacloich Arg/Bute 284 C4
Fasnakyle Ho H'land 300 G3
Fassfern H'land 290 F2
Fatfield Tyne/Wear 243 G8
Fattahead Aberds 302 D6
Faucheldean W Loth 279 G11
Faugh Cumb 240 F2
Fauld Staffs 152 D3
Fauldhouse W Loth 269 C8
Fauldiehill Angus 287 D9
Faulkbourne Essex 88 B3
Faulkland Som'set 45 B9
Fauls Shrops 149 C11
Faulston Wilts 31 B9
Faverdale D'lington 224 B5
Faversham Kent 70 G4
Favillar Moray 302 F2
Fawdington N Yorks 215 E8
Fawdon Northum 264 F2
Fawdon Tyne/Wear 242 D6
Fawfieldhead Staffs 169 C9
Fawkham Kent 68 F5
Fawler Oxon 63 B10
Fawler Oxon 82 B5
Fawley Bucks 65 B9
Fawley Hants 33 G7
Fawley W Berks 63 C11
Fawley Bottom Bucks 65 B8
Fawley Chapel Heref'd 97 F11
Fawton Cornw'l 6 B3
Faxfleet ER Yorks 199 C11
Faxton Northants 120 B5
Faygate W Sussex 51 G8
Fazakerley Mersey 182 B5
Fazeley Staffs 134 C4
Feagour H'land 291 D7
Fearby N Yorks 214 C3
Fearn H'land 301 B8
Fearn Lodge H'land 309 L6
Fearn Station H'land 301 B8
Fearnan Perth/Kinr 285 C11
Fearnbeg H'land 299 D7
Fearnhead Warrington 183 C10
Fearnmore H'land 299 C7
Featherstone Staffs 133 C8
Featherstone W Yorks 198 C2
Feckenham Worcs 117 E10
Fedw Monmouths 79 F8
Feering Essex 107 G7
Feetham N Yorks 223 F9
Fegg Hayes Stoke 168 E5
Fèith Mhor H'land 301 G8
Feizor N Yorks 212 F5
Felbridge Surrey 51 F11
Felbrigg Norfolk 160 B4
Felcourt Surrey 51 E11
Felday Surrey 50 E6
Felden Herts 85 E8
Felderland Kent 55 B10
Felhampton Shrops 131 F8
Felin-Crai Powys 95 G7
Felindre Bridg 58 C3
Felindre Carms 93 G11
Felindre Carms 92 D6
Felindre Carms 94 E3
Felindre Carms 94 F4
Felindre Ceredig'n 111 F11
Felindre Powys 130 C3
Felindre Powys 130 G3
Felindre Powys 96 G3
Felindre Swan 75 E10
Felindre Farchog Pembs 92 D2
Felinfach Ceredig'n 111 F10
Felinfach Powys 95 E11
Felinfoel Carms 75 E8
Felingwmisaf Carms 93 G10
Felingwmuchaf Carms 93 G10
Felin-Wnda Ceredig'n 92 B6
Felinwynt Ceredig'n 110 G4
Felixkirk N Yorks 215 C9
Felixstowe Suffolk 108 D5
Felixstowe Ferry Suffolk 108 D6
Felkington Northum 273 G8
Felkirk W Yorks 197 E11
Fell Beck N Yorks 214 F4
Fell Lane W Yorks 204 E6
Fell Side Cumb 230 D2
Felldyke Cumb 219 B11
Fellgate Tyne/Wear 243 E8
Felling Tyne/Wear 243 E7
Felling Shore Tyne/Wear 243 E7
Fellside Tyne/Wear 242 E5
Felmersham Beds 121 F9
Felmingham Norfolk 160 D4
Felpham W Sussex 35 H7
Felsham Suffolk 125 F8
Felsted Essex 106 G3
Feltham London 66 E6
Feltham Som'set 28 D2
Felthamhill London 66 E6
Felthorpe Norfolk 160 F3
Felton Heref'd 97 B11
Felton N Som'set 60 F4
Felton Northum 252 C5
Felton Butler Shrops 149 F7
Feltwell Norfolk 140 E4
Fen Ditton Cambs 123 E9
Fen Drayton Cambs 122 D6
Fen End Lincs 156 E4
Fen End W Midlands 118 B4
Fen Side Cambs 123 C11
Fen Side Lincs 174 D4
Fen Street Norfolk 141 G11
Fen Street Suffolk 125 B9
Fen Street Suffolk 125 B11
Fenay Bridge W Yorks 197 D7
Fence Lancs 204 F2
Fence S Yorks 186 D6
Fence Houses Tyne/Wear 243 G8
Fencott Oxon 83 B9

Fengate Norfolk 140 F5
Fengate Norfolk 160 E3
Fengate Peterbro 138 D4
Fenham Tyne/Wear 242 D6
Fenhouses Lincs 174 G3
Feniscliffe Blackb'n 195 B7
Feniscowles Blackb'n 195 B7
Feniton Devon 15 B7
Fenlake Beds 103 B11
Fenn Green Shrops 132 G5
Fenn Street Medway 69 D10
Fennifach Powys 95 F10
Fennington Som'set 27 B11
Fenny Bentley Derby 169 E11
Fenny Bridges Devon 15 B8
Fenny Compton Warwick 119 G8
Fenny Drayton Leics 134 D6
Fenny Stratford M/Keynes 103 E7
Fenrother Northum 252 E5
Fenstanton Cambs 122 D6
Fenstead End Suffolk 124 G6
Fenton Cambs 122 B6
Fenton Cumb 240 F2
Fenton Lincs 172 E5
Fenton Lincs 188 F4
Fenton Notts 188 E3
Fenton Northum 263 C11
Fenton Stoke 168 G6
Fenton Barns E Loth 281 E10
Fenwick E Ayrs 267 G9
Fenwick Northum 242 C3
Fenwick Northum 273 G11
Fenwick S Yorks 198 D5
Feochaig Arg/Bute 255 F8
Feock Cornw'l 3 B8
Feolin Ferry Arg/Bute 274 G5
Ferens Art Gallery, Hull Kingston/Hull 200 B5
Ferguslie Park Renf 267 C9
Ferindonald H'land 295 E8
Feriniquarrie H'land 296 F7
Ferlochan Arg/Bute 289 E11
Fern Angus 292 G6
Fern Bank Gtr Man 185 B7
Fern Gore Lancs 195 B9
Ferndale Rh Cyn Taff 77 F7
Ferndown Dorset 31 G9
Ferness H'land 301 E9
Ferney Green Cumb 221 F8
Fernham Oxon 82 G3
Fernhill Gtr Man 195 E10
Fernhill S Lanarks 268 D2
Fernhill W Sussex 51 E10
Fernhill Gate Gtr Man 195 F7
Fernhill Heath Worcs 117 F7
Fernhurst W Sussex 34 C5
Fernie Fife 287 F7
Ferniebrae Aberds 303 D9
Ferniegair S Lanarks 268 E4
Fernilea H'land 294 B5
Fernilee Derby 185 F8
Fernsplatt Cornw'l 4 G5
Ferrensby N Yorks 215 G7
Ferriby Sluice N Lincs 200 C3
Ferring W Sussex 35 G9
Ferry Hill Cambs 139 G7
Ferry Point H'land 309 L7
Ferrybridge W Yorks 198 C3
Ferryden Angus 287 B11
Ferryhill Aberd C 293 C11
Ferryhill Durham 233 E11
Ferryhill Station Durham 234 E2
Ferryside = Glan-y-Fferi Carms 74 D5
Ferryton H'land 300 C6
Fersfield Norfolk 141 G11
Fersfield Common Norfolk 141 G11
Fersit H'land 290 F5
Ferwig Ceredig'n 92 B3
Feshiebridge H'land 291 C10
Festival Park Visitor Centre, Ebbw Vale Bl Gwent 77 D11
Fetcham Surrey 50 B6
Fetlar Airport Shetl'd 314 D8
Fetterangus Aberds 303 D10
Fettercairn Aberds 293 F8
Fetterdale Fife 287 E8
Fettes H'land 300 D5
Fewcott Oxon 101 F10
Fewston N Yorks 205 C9
Ffair Rhos Ceredig'n 112 D4
Ffairfach Carms 94 G2
Ffaldy-brenin Carms 94 B2
Ffarmers Carms 94 C3
Ffawyddog Powys 78 B2
Ffestiniog Railway, Porthmadog Gwyn 145 B11
Ffinnant Powys 148 E4
Ffordd las Denbs 165 C10
Fforddlas Powys 96 D4
Fforest Carms 75 E9
Fforest Gôch Neath P Talb 76 E2
Fforest-fach Swan 75 F10
Ffos y ffin Merth Tyd 77 D9
Ffostrasol Ceredig'n 93 B7
Ffos-y-ffin Ceredig'n 111 E9
Ffridd Powys 130 D3
Ffrith Flints 166 D3
Ffrwd Gwyn 163 D7
Ffynnon Gynydd Powys 96 C3
Ffynnongroyw Flints 181 E10
Ffynnon-oer Ceredig'n 111 G10
Ffynone Pembs 92 D4
Fickleshole Surrey 67 G11
Fidden Arg/Bute 288 G5
Fidder's Green Norfolk 158 F6
Fiddes Aberds 293 E10
Fiddington Glos 99 E8
Fiddington Som'set 43 E8
Fiddington Sands Wilts 46 C4
Fiddleford Dorset 30 E4
Fiddler's Ferry Warrington 183 D9
Fiddler's Green Cornw'l 4 E6
Fiddler's Green Glos 99 G8
Fiddler's Green Heref'd 97 D11
Fiddler's Green Norfolk 141 D10
Fiddlers Hamlet Essex 87 E7
Field Som'set 44 E6
Field Staffs 151 C10
Field Assarts Oxon 82 C4
Field Broughton Cumb 211 C7
Field Common Surrey 66 F6
Field Dalling Norfolk 159 B10
Field Green Kent 38 B3
Field Head Leics 135 B9
Fieldhead Cumb 230 D5
Fields End Herts 85 D8
Fife Keith Moray 302 D4
Fifehead Magdalen Dorset 30 C3
Fifehead Neville Dorset 30 E3
Fifehead St. Quintin Dorset 30 E3
Fifield Oxon 82 B2
Fifield Wilts 46 C6
Fifield Windsor 66 D2
Fifield Bavant Wilts 31 B8
Figheldean Wilts 47 D7
Filands Wilts 62 B2
Filby Norfolk 161 G9
Filey N Yorks 218 C2
Filford Dorset 16 B4
Filgrave M/Keynes 103 B7
Filham Devon 8 D3
Filkins Oxon 82 E2
Filleigh Devon 25 B11
Fillingham Lincs 188 D6
Fillongley Warwick 134 F5
Filmore Hill Hants 33 B11
Filton S Glos 60 D5
Filwood Park Bristol 60 F5
Fimber ER Yorks 217 G7
Finavon Angus 287 B8
Fincastle Ho. Perth/Kinr 291 G10
Finchairn Arg/Bute 275 C10
Fincham Mersey 182 C6
Fincham Norfolk 140 B3
Finchampstead Wokingham 65 G10
Finchdean Hants 34 E2
Finchingfield Essex 106 E3
Finchley London 86 G3
Findern Derby 152 C6
Findhorn Moray 301 C10
Findhorn Bridge H'land 301 G8
Findo Gask Perth/Kinr 286 E4
Findochty Moray 302 C4
Findon Aberds 293 D11
Findon W Sussex 35 F10
Findon Mains H'land 300 C6
Findon Valley W Sussex 35 F10
Findrack Ho. Aberds 293 C8
Finedon Northants 121 C8
Fineglen Arg/Bute 275 B10
Fingal Street Suffolk 126 D4
Fingask Aberds 303 G7
Fingerpost Worcs 116 C4
Fingest Bucks 84 G3
Finghall N Yorks 214 B3
Fingland Cumb 239 F7
Fingland Dumf/Gal 259 F7
Finglesham Kent 55 C10
Fingringhoe Essex 107 G10
Finham W Midlands 118 B6
Finkle Green Essex 106 C4
Finkle Street S Yorks 186 B4
Finlarig Stirl 285 D9
Finmere Oxon 102 E2
Finnart Perth/Kinr 285 B9
Finney Green Ches 184 E5
Finney Hill Leics 153 F9
Finningham Suffolk 125 D11
Finningley S Yorks 187 B11
Finnygaud Aberds 302 D5
Finsbury London 67 C10
Finstall Worcs 117 C9
Finsthwaite Cumb 211 B7
Finstock Oxon 82 B5
Finstown Orkney 312 G4
Fintry Aberds 303 D7
Fintry Dundee C 287 D8
Fintry Stirl 278 D2
Finwood Warwick 118 D3
Finzean Aberds 293 D8
Finzean Ho Aberds 293 D7
Fionnphort Arg/Bute 288 G5
Fionnsbhagh W Isles 296 C6
Fir Tree Durham 233 E8
Fir Vale S Yorks 186 C5
Firbank Cumb 222 G2
Firbeck S Yorks 187 D9
Firby N Yorks 216 F4
Firby N Yorks 214 B5
Firemore H'land 307 L3
Firepool Som'set 28 B2
Firgrove Gtr Man 196 E2
Firkin Arg/Bute 285 G7
Firs Lane Gtr Man 194 G6
Firs Road Wilts 47 G8
Firsby Lincs 175 C7
Firsby S Yorks 187 B7
First Coast H'land 307 K4
Firswood Gtr Man 184 B4
Firth Moor D'lington 224 C6
Firth Park S Yorks 186 C5
Fishbourne I/Wight 21 C7
Fishbourne W Sussex 34 G4
Fishbourne Palace W Sussex 34 G4
Fishburn Durham 234 E3
Fishcross Clack 279 B7
Fisher W Sussex 34 G5
Fisher Place Cumb 220 B6
Fisherford Aberds 302 F6
Fishermead M/Keynes 103 D7
Fisherrow E Loth 280 G6
Fishers Green Essex 86 E5
Fisher's Green Herts 104 F4
Fisher's Pond Hants 33 C7
Fishersgate W Sussex 36 F2
Fisherstreet W Sussex 50 G3
Fisherton H'land 301 D7
Fisherton S Ayrs 257 F7
Fisherton de la Mere Wilts 46 F4
Fishery Estate Windsor 65 C11
Fishguard = Abergwaun Pembs 91 D9
Fishlake S Yorks 199 E7
Fishley Norfolk 161 G8
Fishmere End Lincs 156 B5
Fishpond Bottom Dorset 16 B3
Fishponds Bristol 60 D6
Fishpool Gtr Man 195 F10
Fishpool Heref'd 98 F3
Fishtoft Lincs 174 G5
Fishtoft Drove Lincs 174 F4
Fishtown of Usan Angus 287 B11
Fishwick Scot Borders 273 E8
Fishwick Lancs 194 B5
Fiskavaig H'land 294 B5
Fiskerton Lincs 189 G9
Fiskerton Notts 172 E2
Fitling ER Yorks 209 G11
Fittleton Wilts 46 D6
Fittleworth W Sussex 35 D8
Fitton End Cambs 157 G8
Fitton Hill Gtr Man 196 G2
Fitz Shrops 149 F8
Fitzhead Som'set 27 B10
Fitzroy Som'set 27 B11
Fitzwilliam W Yorks 198 D2
Fitzwilliam Museum, Cambridge Cambs 123 F8
Fiunary H'land 289 E8
Five Acres Glos 79 C9
Five Ash Down E Sussex 37 C7
Five Ashes E Sussex 37 B9
Five Bells Som'set 42 E5
Five Bridges Heref'd 98 B3
Five Chimneys E Sussex 37 C8
Five Houses I/Wight 20 D4
Five Lanes Monmouths 78 G6
Five Oak Green Kent 52 E6
Five Oaks W Sussex 35 B9
Five Roads Carms 75 D7
Five Ways Warwick 118 C4
Five Wents Kent 53 C10
Fivecrosses Ches 183 F8
Fivehead Som'set 28 C5
Fivelanes Cornw'l 11 E10
Flackley Ash E Sussex 38 C5
Flack's Green Essex 88 C3
Flackwell Heath Bucks 84 G5
Fladbury Worcs 99 B9
Fladbury Cross Worcs 99 B9
Fladda Shetl'd 314 E5
Fladdabister Shetl'd 315 K6
Flagg Derby 169 B10
Flakebridge Cumb 231 G10
Flambards Experience, Helston Cornw'l 2 D5
Flamborough ER Yorks 218 E4
Flamingo Land, Pickering N Yorks 216 D5
Flamstead Herts 85 C9
Flamstead End Herts 86 E4
Flanders Green Herts 104 F6
Flanderwell S Yorks 187 B7
Flansham W Sussex 35 G7
Flanshaw W Yorks 197 C10
Flappit Spring W Yorks 205 F7
Flasby N Yorks 204 B4
Flash Staffs 169 B8
Flashader H'land 298 D3
Flaunden Herts 85 E8
Flawborough Notts 172 G3
Flawith N Yorks 215 F9
Flax Bourton N Som'set 60 F4
Flax Moss Lancs 195 C9
Flaxby N Yorks 206 B3
Flaxholme Derby 170 G4
Flaxlands Norfolk 142 E2
Flaxley Glos 79 B11
Flaxpool Som'set 42 F6
Flaxton N Yorks 216 G3
Fleckney Leics 136 E2
Flecknoe Warwick 119 E10
Fledborough Notts 188 G4
Fleet Dorset 17 E8
Fleet Hants 34 G2
Fleet Hants 49 C10
Fleet Lincs 157 E7
Fleet Air Arm Museum, Yeovil Som'set 29 C9
Fleet Hargate Lincs 157 D7
Fleetend Hants 33 F8
Fleetlands Hants 33 G9
Fleetville Herts 85 D11
Fleetwood Lancs 202 D2
Fleggburgh = Burgh St. Margaret Norfolk 161 G8
Flemings Kent 55 B9
Flemingston V/Glam 58 E4
Flemington S Lanarks 268 D3
Flemington S Lanarks 268 F4
Flempton Suffolk 124 D6
Fleoideabhagh W Isles 296 C6
Fletcher's Green Kent 52 D4
Fletchersbridge Cornw'l 6 B2
Fletchertown Cumb 229 C10
Fletching E Sussex 36 C6
Fleuchary H'land 309 K7
Fleuchlang Dumf/Gal 237 D8
Fleur-de-lis Caerph 77 F11
Flexbury Cornw'l 24 F2
Flexford Hants 32 C6
Flexford Surrey 50 D2
Flimby Cumb 228 E6
Flimwell E Sussex 53 G8
Flint = Y Fflint Flints 182 G2
Flint Cross Cambs 105 C8
Flint Hill Durham 242 G5
Flint Mountain Flints 182 G2
Flintham Notts 172 F2
Flinton ER Yorks 209 F10
Flint's Green W Midlands 134 G5
Flishinghurst Kent 53 F9
Flitcham Norfolk 158 D4
Flitholme Cumb 222 C5
Flitton Beds 103 D11
Flitwick Beds 103 E10
Flixborough N Lincs 199 D11
Flixborough Stather N Lincs 199 E11
Flixton Gtr Man 184 C2
Flixton N Yorks 217 D10
Flixton Suffolk 142 F6
Flockton W Yorks 197 D8
Flockton Green W Yorks 197 D9
Flodaigh W Isles 296 F4
Flodigarry H'land 298 B4
Flood Street Hants 31 D10
Flood's Ferry Cambs 139 E7
Flookburgh Cumb 211 D7
Flordon Norfolk 142 D3
Flore Northants 120 F2
Florence Stoke 168 G6
Flouch Inn S Yorks 197 G7
Flowers Bottom Bucks 84 F4
Flowers Green E Sussex 37 E10
Flowery Field Gtr Man 184 B6
Flowton Suffolk 107 B11
Fluchter E Dunb 277 G11
Fluder Devon 9 B7
Flugarth Shetl'd 315 G6
Flush House W Yorks 196 F6
Flushdyke W Yorks 197 C9
Flushing Aberds 303 E10
Flushing Cornw'l 3 D7
Flushing Cornw'l 3 C8
Fluxton Devon 15 C7
Flyford Flavell Worcs 117 G9
Foals Green Suffolk 126 C5
Fobbing Thurr'k 69 C8
Fochabers Moray 302 D3
Fochriw Bl Gwent 77 D10
Fockerby N Lincs 199 D10
Fodderletter Moray 301 G11
Fodderty H'land 300 D5
Foddington Som'set 29 B9
Foel Powys 147 G9
Foelgastell Carms 75 C8
Foffarty Angus 287 C8
Foggathorpe ER Yorks 207 F11
Foggbrook Gtr Man 184 D6
Fogo Scot Borders 272 F5
Fogrigarth Shetl'd 315 H4
Fogwatt Moray 302 D2
Foindle H'land 306 E6
Fold Head Lancs 195 D11
Fold Hill Lincs 175 E7
Folda Angus 292 G3
Fole Staffs 151 B10
Foleshill W Midlands 135 G7
Foley Park Worcs 116 B6
Folke Dorset 29 E11
Folkestone Kent 55 F8
Folkestone Racecourse Kent 54 F6
Folkingham Lincs 155 C11
Folkington E Sussex 23 E9
Folksworth Cambs 138 F2
Folkton N Yorks 217 D11
Folla Rule Aberds 303 F7
Follifoot N Yorks 206 C2
Follingsby Tyne/Wear 243 E8
Folly Pembs 91 G8
Folly Gate Devon 13 B7
Fonmon V/Glam 58 F4
Fonston Cornw'l 11 C10
Fonthill Bishop Wilts 46 G2
Fonthill Gifford Wilts 46 G2
Fontmell Magna Dorset 30 D5
Fontmell Parva Dorset 30 E4
Fontwell W Sussex 35 F7
Fontwell Park Racecourse W Sussex 34 F6
Font-y-gary V/Glam 58 F5
Foodieash Fife 287 F7
Foolow Derby 185 F11
Footbridge Glos 99 F10
Footherley Staffs 134 C2
Foots Cray London 68 E3
Forbestown Aberds 292 B5
Force Forge Cumb 220 G6
Force Green Kent 52 B3
Force Mills Cumb 221 G7
Forcett N Yorks 224 C3
Ford Arg/Bute 275 C9
Ford Bucks 84 D3
Ford Derby 186 E6
Ford Devon 8 E2
Ford Devon 8 G5
Ford Devon 28 G2
Ford Devon 24 C3
Ford Devon 24 C6
Ford Glos 99 F11
Ford Kent 71 F8
Ford Mersey 182 B4
Ford Northum 263 B10
Ford Pembs 91 F9
Ford Plym'th 7 D9
Ford Shrops 149 G8
Ford Som'set 27 B9
Ford Som'set 44 C5
Ford Tyne/Wear 243 F9
Ford Wilts 61 D10
Ford W Sussex 35 G7
Ford End Essex 105 E9
Ford End Essex 87 B11
Ford Green Lancs 202 D5
Ford Heath Shrops 149 G8
Ford Street Som'set 27 D11
Forda Devon 12 C6
Forda Devon 40 F3
Fordbridge W Midlands 134 F3
Fordcombe Kent 52 E4
Fordell Fife 280 D3
Forden Powys 130 C4
Forder Cornw'l 7 D8
Forder Green Devon 8 B5
Fordgate Som'set 43 G10
Fordham Cambs 124 C2
Fordham Essex 107 F8
Fordham Norfolk 140 D2
Fordham Heath Essex 107 F8
Fordhill Northum 263 B11
Fordhouses W Midlands 133 C8
Fordingbridge Hants 31 E10
Fordon ER Yorks 217 D11
Fordoun Aberds 293 F9
Ford's Green E Sussex 36 B6
Ford's Green Suffolk 125 D11
Ford's Water Kent 54 E5
Fordstreet Essex 107 F8
Fordton Mill Devon 14 B2
Fordwells Oxon 82 C4
Fordwich Kent 55 B7
Fordyce Aberds 302 C5
Forebridge Staffs 151 E8
Foredale N Yorks 212 F6
Forehill S Ayrs 257 E8
Foreland Ho Arg/Bute 274 G3
Foremark Derby 152 D6
Forest N Yorks 224 E5
Forest Becks Lancs 203 C11
Forest Coal Pit Monmouths 96 G5
Forest Gate London 68 B2
Forest Green Glos 80 E4
Forest Green Surrey 50 E6
Forest Hall Tyne/Wear 243 D7
Forest Head Cumb 240 F3
Forest Hill London 67 E11
Forest Hill Oxon 83 D9
Forest Hill Wilts 63 F8
Forest Holme Lancs 195 B10
Forest Lane N Yorks 206 B2
Forest Lodge Arg/Bute 284 C6
Forest Lodge Dumf/Gal 246 F3
Forest Lodge H'land 292 B2
Forest Lodge Perth/Kinr 291 F11
Forest Mill Clack 279 C9
Forest Row E Sussex 52 F2
Forest Side I/Wight 20 D5
Forest Town Notts 171 C9
Forestburn Gate Northum 252 D3
Foresterseat Moray 301 D11
Forest-in-Teesdale Durham 232 F3
Forestside W Sussex 34 E3
Forfar Angus 287 B8
Forgandenny Perth/Kinr 286 F4
Forge Powys 128 D5
Forge Hammer Torf 78 F3
Forge Side Torf 78 D2
Forgewood N Lanarks 268 D4
Forgie Moray 302 D3
Forglen Ho. Aberds 302 D6
Forgue Aberds 302 E6
Formby Mersey 193 F9
Forncett End Norfolk 142 E2
Forncett St. Mary Norfolk 142 E3
Forncett St. Peter Norfolk 142 E3
Forneth Perth/Kinr 286 C4
Fornham All Saints Suffolk 124 D6
Fornham St. Martin Suffolk 124 D6
Fornighty H'land 301 D9
Forres Moray 301 D10
Forrestfield N Lanarks 269 B7
Forry's Green Essex 106 E5
Forsbrook Staffs 169 G7
Forse H'land 310 F6
Forse Ho. H'land 310 F6
Forsinain H'land 310 E3
Forsinard H'land 310 E2
Forsinard Station H'land 310 E2
Forstal Kent 53 B8
Forston Dorset 17 B9
Fort Augustus H'land 290 C5
Fort George H'land 301 D7
Fort William H'land 290 F3
Fortescue Devon 15 D8
Forteviot Perth/Kinr 286 F4
Forth S Lanarks 269 E8
Forth Road Bridge Fife 280 E2
Forthampton Glos 99 E7
Forthay Glos 80 F2
Fortingall Perth/Kinr 285 C11
Fortis Green London 67 B9
Forton Hants 48 E2
Forton Lancs 202 C5
Forton Shrops 149 F8
Forton Som'set 28 F4
Forton Staffs 150 E5
Fortrie Aberds 302 E6
Fortrie Aberds 303 D7
Fortrose H'land 301 D7
Fortune Green London 67 B8
Fortuneswell Dorset 17 G9
Forty Foot Bridge Norfolk 139 B10
Forty Green Bucks 84 G6
Forty Green Oxon 84 E3
Forty Hill London 86 F4
Forward Green Suffolk 125 F11
Forwood Glos 80 E5
Foryd Denbs 181 E7
Fosbury Wilts 47 B10
Foscot Glos 100 G4
Foscote Bucks 102 D4
Foscote Wilts 61 D11
Fosdyke Lincs 156 C6
Fosdyke Bridge Lincs 156 C6
Foss Perth/Kinr 285 B11
Foss Cross Glos 81 D9
Fossebridge Glos 81 C9
Fostall Kent 70 G5
Fosten Green Kent 53 F10
Foster Street Essex 87 D7
Fosters Green Lancs 194 F3
Foston Derby 152 C3
Foston Leics 136 E2
Foston Lincs 172 G5
Foston N Yorks 216 F3
Foston on the Wolds ER Yorks 209 B8
Fotherby Lincs 190 C4
Fothergill Cumb 228 E6
Fotheringhay Northants 137 E11
Foubister Orkney 313 H6
Foul Anchor Cambs 157 F9
Foul End Warwick 134 D4
Foul Green N Yorks 226 C3
Foul Mile E Sussex 37 D10
Foulbridge Cumb 230 B4
Foulby W Yorks 198 D2
Foulden Scot Borders 273 D8
Foulden Norfolk 140 D5
Foulis Castle H'land 300 C5
Foulrice N Yorks 216 E2
Foulridge Lancs 204 E3
Foulsham Norfolk 159 D10
Foulstone Cumb 211 C11
Fountainhall Scot Borders 271 F8
Fountains Abbey, Ripon N Yorks 214 F5
Four Ashes Suffolk 125 C10
Four Crosses Powys 148 F5
Four Crosses Staffs 133 B8
Four Crosses Wrex 166 E3
Four Elms Devon 28 F3
Four Elms Kent 52 D3
Four Foot Som'set 44 G5
Four Forks Som'set 43 F8
Four Gates Gtr Man 195 F7
Four Gotes Cambs 157 F8
Four Lane End S Yorks 197 G9
Four Lane Ends Blackb'n 195 B7
Four Lane Ends Ches 167 C9
Four Lane Ends C/York 207 C9
Four Lane Ends Gtr Man 195 E9
Four Lane Ends S Yorks 186 E5
Four Lane Ends W Yorks 205 G8
Four Lanes Cornw'l 2 B5
Four Lanes End Hants 49 C7
Four Marks Hants 49 G7
Four Mile Bridge Angl 178 F3
Four Mile Elm Glos 80 C4
Four Oaks E Sussex 38 C5
Four Oaks Glos 98 F3
Four Oaks W Midlands 134 D2
Four Oaks W Midlands 134 G4
Four Oaks Park W Midlands 134 D2
Four Points W Berks 64 D5
Four Pools Worcs 99 C10
Four Roads Carms 74 D6
Four Roads I/Man 192 F3
Four Sisters Suffolk 107 D11
Four Throws Kent 38 B3
Four Wents Kent 52 C6
Fourlane Ends Derby 170 D5
Fourlanes End Ches 168 D4
Fourpenny H'land 311 K2
Fourstones Northum 241 D9
Fovant Wilts 31 B8
Foveran Aberds 303 G9
Fowey Cornw'l 6 E2
Fowler's Plot Som'set 43 F10
Fowley Common Warrington 183 B11
Fowlis Angus 287 D7
Fowlis Wester Perth/Kinr 286 E3
Fowlmere Cambs 105 B8
Fownhope Heref'd 97 E11
Fox Corner Surrey 50 C3
Fox Hatch Essex 87 F9
Fox Hill Bath/NE Som'set 61 G9
Fox Lane Hants 49 B11
Fox Royal W Yorks 197 D8
Fox Street Essex 107 F10
Foxash Estate Essex 107 E11
Foxbar Renf 267 C9
Foxcombe Hill Oxon 83 E7
Foxcote Glos 81 B8
Foxcote Som'set 45 B8
Foxcotte Hants 47 D10
Foxdale I/Man 192 E3
Foxearth Essex 106 C6
Foxendown Kent 69 F7
Foxfield Cumb 210 B4
Foxford W Midlands 135 G7
Foxham Wilts 62 D3
Foxhills Hants 32 E4
Foxhole Cornw'l 5 E9
Foxhole Norfolk 142 D4
Foxholes N Yorks 217 E10
Foxholt Kent 55 E8
Foxhunt Green E Sussex 37 D8
Foxley Norfolk 159 E10
Foxley Wilts 61 B11
Foxlydiate Worcs 117 D10
Fox's Cross Kent 70 G5
Foxt Staffs 169 F8
Foxton Cambs 105 B8
Foxton Durham 234 G3
Foxton Leics 136 E4
Foxton N Yorks 225 F8
Foxton Canal Locks Leics 136 F3
Foxup N Yorks 213 D7
Foxwist Green Ches 167 B10
Foxwood Shrops 116 B2
Foy Heref'd 98 F2
Foyers H'land 300 G4
Foynesfield H'land 301 D8
Fraddam Cornw'l 2 C3
Fraddon Cornw'l 5 D8
Fradley Staffs 152 G3
Fradley South Staffs 152 G3
Fradswell Staffs 151 C9
Fraisthorpe ER Yorks 218 G3
Framfield E Sussex 37 C7
Framingham Earl Norfolk 142 C5
Framingham Pigot Norfolk 142 C5
Framlingham Suffolk 126 E5
Framlingham Castle Suffolk 126 E5
Frampton Dorset 17 B8
Frampton Lincs 156 B6
Frampton Cotterell S Glos 61 C7
Frampton End S Glos 61 C7
Frampton Mansell Glos 80 E6
Frampton on Severn Glos 80 D2
Frampton West End Lincs 174 G4
Framsden Suffolk 126 F3
Framwellgate Moor Durham 233 C11
France Lynch Glos 80 E6
Franche Worcs 116 B6
Frandley Ches 183 F10
Frankby Mersey 182 D2
Frankfort Norfolk 160 E6
Frankley Worcs 117 B9
Frankley Worcs 133 G9
Frank's Bridge Powys 114 F2
Frankton Warwick 119 C8
Frankwell Shrops 149 G9
Frant E Sussex 52 F5
Fraserburgh Aberds 303 C9
Frating Essex 107 G11
Frating Green Essex 107 G11
Fratton Portsm'th 33 G11
Freasley Warwick 134 D4
Freathy Cornw'l 7 E7
Frecheville S Yorks 186 E5
Freckenham Suffolk 124 C3
Freckleton Lancs 194 B2
Free Piece Hants 49 F9
Free Town Gtr Man 195 E10
Freeby Leics 155 E6
Freefolk Priors Hants 48 D3
Freehay Staffs 169 G8
Freeland Oxon 82 C6
Freeland Renf 267 B9
Freemantle S'thampton 32 E6
Freeport W Yorks 198 C2
Freeport Hornsea Outlet Village ER Yorks 209 D9
Freester Shetl'd 315 H6
Freethorpe Norfolk 143 B8
Freezing Hill S Glos 61 E8
Freezy Water London 86 F5
Freiston Lincs 174 G5
Freiston Shore Lincs 174 G5
Fremington Devon 40 G4
French Street Kent 52 C3
Frenchay S Glos 60 D6
Frenchbeer Devon 13 D9
Frenches Green Essex 106 G4
Frenchwood Lancs 194 B4
Frenich Stirl 285 G8
Frensham Surrey 49 E10
Frenze Norfolk 142 G2
Fresgoe H'land 310 C3
Freshbrook Swindon 62 C6
Freshfield Mersey 193 F9
Freshford Bath/NE Som'set 61 G9
Freshwater I/Wight 20 D2
Freshwater Bay I/Wight 20 D2
Freshwater East Pembs 73 F8
Fressingfield Suffolk 126 B5
Freston Suffolk 108 D3
Freswick H'land 310 C7
Fretherne Glos 80 D2
Frettenham Norfolk 160 F4
Freuchie Fife 286 G6
Freuchies Angus 292 G4
Freystrop Pembs 73 C7
Friar Park W Midlands 133 E10
Friar Waddon Dorset 17 D8
Friars Gate E Sussex 52 G3
Friarton Perth/Kinr 286 E5
Friday Bridge Cambs 139 C9
Friday Hill London 86 G5
Friday Street E Sussex 23 E10
Friday Street Suffolk 127 E7
Friday Street Suffolk 126 F4
Friday Street Suffolk 126 G6
Friday Street Surrey 50 D6
Fridaythorpe ER Yorks 208 B3
Friendly W Yorks 196 C5
Friern Barnet London 86 G3
Friesland Arg/Bute 288 D3
Friesthorpe Lincs 189 E9
Frieston Lincs 172 F6
Frieth Bucks 84 G3
Frieze Hill Som'set 28 B2
Friezeland Notts 171 E7
Friford Oxon 82 F6
Frilsham W Berks 64 E4
Frimley Surrey 49 B11
Frimley Green Surrey 49 B11
Frimley Ridge Surrey 49 B11
Frindsbury Medway 69 F8
Fring Norfolk 158 C4
Fringford Oxon 102 F2
Friningham Kent 53 B10
Frinsted Kent 53 B11
Frinton-on-Sea Essex 108 H4
Friockheim Angus 287 C9
Friog Gwyn 146 G2
Frisby on the Wreake Leics 154 F3
Friskney Lincs 175 D7
Friskney Eaudyke Lincs 175 D7
Friskney Tofts Lincs 175 E7
Friston E Sussex 23 F8
Friston Suffolk 127 E8
Fritchley Derby 170 E5
Frith Bank Lincs 174 F4
Frith Common Worcs 116 D3
Fritham Hants 32 E2
Frithelstock Devon 25 D7
Frithelstock Stone Devon 25 D7
Frithend Hants 49 F10
Frithsden Herts 85 D8
Frithville Lincs 174 E4
Frittenden Kent 53 E10
Frittiscombe Devon 8 G6
Fritton Norfolk 142 E4
Fritton Norfolk 143 C9
Fritton Norfolk 161 F8
Fritwell Oxon 101 F10
Frizinghall W Yorks 205 F8
Frizington Cumb 219 B10
Frizzeler's Green Suffolk 124 E5
Frobost W Isles 297 J3
Frocester Glos 80 E3
Frochas Powys 130 B3
Frodesley Shrops 131 C10
Frodingham N Lincs 199 E11
Frodsham Ches 183 F8
Frog End Cambs 123 G8
Frog End Cambs 123 F10
Frog Pool Worcs 116 D6
Frog Street Som'set 28 D4
Froggatt Derby 186 F2
Froghall Staffs 169 F8
Frogham Hants 31 E11
Frogham Kent 55 C9
Froghole Kent 52 C3
Frogholt Kent 55 F7
Frogland Cross S Glos 60 C6
Frogmore Devon 8 G5
Frogmore Hants 49 B10
Frogmore Herts 85 E11
Frognall Kent 55 B8
Frognall Lincs 156 G3
Frogpool Cornw'l 3 B7
Frogs Green Essex 105 D11
Frogshall Norfolk 160 B4
Frogwell Cornw'l 6 B6
Frogwell Devon 26 E6
Frogwell Wilts 62 E2
Frolesworth Leics 135 E10
Frome Som'set 45 D9
Frome St. Quintin Dorset 29 G9
Frome Whitfield Dorset 17 C9
Fromefield Som'set 45 D9
Fromes Hill Heref'd 98 B3
Fron Denbs 165 B9
Fron Flints 181 G11
Fron Gwyn 163 E8
Fron Powys 113 D11
Fron Powys 130 D3
Fron Powys 130 C4
Fron Isaf Wrex 166 G3
Fron Uchaf Wrex 166 G3
Froncysyllte Wrex 166 G3
Frongoch Gwyn 147 B8
Fron-las Powys 148 G3
Frost Devon 26 F3
Frost Row Norfolk 141 C10
Frost Street Som'set 28 D3
Frostenden Suffolk 143 G9
Frostenden Bottom Suffolk 143 G9
Frostenden Corner Suffolk 143 G9
Frosterley Durham 232 D6
Frotoft Orkney 312 F5
Froxfield Beds 103 E9
Froxfield Wilts 63 F9
Froxfield Green Hants 34 B2
Fryern Hill Hants 32 C6
Fryerning Essex 87 E10
Fryerns Essex 69 B8
Fryton N Yorks 216 E3
Fugglestone St. Peter Wilts 46 G6
Fulbeck Lincs 172 E6
Fulbeck Northum 252 F5
Fulbourn Cambs 123 F10
Fulbrook Oxon 82 C3
Fulflood Hants 33 B7
Fulford C/York 207 D8
Fulford Som'set 28 B2
Fulford Staffs 151 B9
Fulham London 67 D8
Fulking W Sussex 36 E2
Full Sutton ER Yorks 207 B10
Fullaford Devon 41 F7
Fullarton Glasg C 268 C2
Fullarton N Ayrs 257 B8
Fuller Street Essex 88 B2
Fuller's End Essex 105 F10
Fuller's Moor Ches 167 E7
Fullers Slade M/Keynes 102 D5
Fullerton Hants 47 F11
Fulletby Lincs 190 G3
Fullready Warwick 100 B5
Fullwood E Ayrs 267 E8
Fullwood Gtr Man 196 F2
Fulmer Bucks 66 B4
Fulmodestone Norfolk 159 C9
Fulneck W Yorks 205 G10
Fulnetby Lincs 189 F9
Fulney Lincs 156 E5
Fulshaw Park Ches 184 G4
Fulstone W Yorks 197 F7
Fulstow Lincs 190 B4
Fulwell Oxon 101 G7
Fulwell Tyne/Wear 243 F9
Fulwood Lancs 202 G6
Fulwood Notts 171 D7
Fulwood Som'set 28 C2
Fulwood S Yorks 186 D4
Fulwood Row Lancs 203 F7
Fundenhall Norfolk 142 D2
Fundenhall Street Norfolk 142 D2

Funtington W Sussex 34 F3
Funtley Hants 33 F9
Funtullich Perth/Kinr 285 E11
Funzie Shetl'd 314 D8
Furley Devon 28 G3
Furnace Arg/Bute 284 G4
Furnace Carms 75 E8
Furnace Ceredig'n 128 D3
Furnace H'land 299 B9
Furnace End Warwick 134 E4
Furnace Green W Sussex 51 F9
Furneaux Pelham Herts 105 F8
Furner's Green E Sussex 36 B6
Furness Vale Derby 185 E8
Furnham Som'set 28 F4
Further Ford End Essex 105 E8
Further Quarter Kent 53 F11
Furze Green Norfolk 142 G4
Furze Platt Windsor 65 C11
Furzebrook Dorset 18 E4
Furzehill Dorset 31 G8
Furzeley Corner Hants 33 E11
Furzley Hants 32 D3
Furzton M/Keynes 102 D6
Futho Northants 102 C5
Fyfett Som'set 28 E2
Fyfield Essex 87 D9
Fyfield Hants 47 D9
Fyfield Oxon 82 F6
Fyfield Wilts 63 G7
Fyfield Wick Oxon 82 F6
Fyling Park N Yorks 227 E8
Fylingthorpe N Yorks 227 E8
Fyning W Sussex 34 C4
Fyvie Aberds 303 F7

G

Gabalfa Card 59 D7
Gabhsann bho Dheas W Isles 304 C6
Gabhsann bho Thuath W Isles 304 C6
Gable Head Hants 22 D2
Gablon H'land 309 K7
Gabroc Hill E Ayrs 267 E9
Gadbrook Surrey 51 D8
Gaddesby Leics 154 G3
Gadebridge Herts 85 D8
Gadfa Angl 179 D7
Gadlas Shrops 149 B7
Gadlys Rh Cyn Taff 77 E7
Gadshill Kent 69 E8
Gaer Newp 59 B9
Gaer Powys 96 G3
Gaer-fawr Monmouths 78 F6
Gaerllwyd Monmouths 79 F6
Gaerwen Angl 179 G7
Gagingwell Oxon 101 F8
Gaick Lodge H'land 291 E9
Gailey Staffs 151 G8
Gain Hill Kent 53 D8
Gainford Durham 224 B3
Gainsborough Lincs 188 C4
Gainsborough Suffolk 108 C3
Gainsford End Essex 106 D4
Gairloch H'land 299 B8
Gairlochy H'land 290 E3
Gairney Bank Perth/Kinr 280 B2
Gairnshiel Lodge Aberds 292 C4
Gaisgill Cumb 222 D2
Gaitsgill Cumb 230 B3
Galashiels Scot Borders 261 B11
Gale Gtr Man 196 D2
Gale Green Gtr Man 184 D5
Galgate Lancs 202 B5
Galhampton Som'set 29 B10
Gallaberry Dumf/Gal 247 G11
Gallachoille Arg/Bute 275 E8
Gallanach Arg/Bute 288 C4
Gallanach Arg/Bute 289 G10
Gallanach H'land 294 G6
Gallantry Bank Ches 167 E8
Gallatown Fife 280 C5
Galley Common Warwick 134 E6
Galley Hill Cambs 122 D6
Galley Hill Lincs 173 F9
Galleyend Essex 88 E2
Galleywood Essex 88 E2
Galligill Cumb 231 C11
Gallin Perth/Kinr 285 C9
Gallovie H'land 291 E7
Gallowfauld Angus 287 C8
Gallowhill Glasg C 268 D2
Gallowhill Renf 267 B9
Gallowhills Aberds 303 D10
Gallows Green Essex 106 F2
Gallows Green Essex 107 F8
Gallows Green Staffs 169 G9
Gallows Inn Derby 171 G7
Gallowsgreen Torf 78 D3
Gallowstree Common Oxon 65 C7
Gallt Melyd = Meliden Denbs 181 E9
Galltair H'land 295 C10
Galltegfa Denbs 165 D10
Gallt-y-foel Gwyn 163 C9
Gallypot Street E Sussex 52 F3
Galmington Som'set 28 C2
Galmisdale H'land 294 G6
Galmpton Devon 8 G3
Galmpton Torbay 9 D7
Galmpton Warborough Torbay 9 D7
Galon Uchaf Merth Tyd 77 D9
Galphay N Yorks 214 E4
Galston E Ayrs 258 B2
Galton Dorset 17 D11
Galtrigill H'land 296 F7
Gamble Hill W Yorks 205 G11
Gamble's Green Essex 88 C3
Gamblesby Cumb 231 D8
Gamelsby Cumb 239 G7
Gamesley Derby 185 C8
Gamlingay Cambs 122 G4
Gamlingay Cinques Cambs 122 G4
Gamlingay Great Heath Cambs 122 G4
Gammersgill N Yorks 213 C11
Gamston Notts 154 B2
Gamston Notts 188 F2
Ganavan Arg/Bute 289 F10
Ganborough Glos 100 F3
Gandale N Yorks 224 G3
Gang Cornw'l 6 B6
Ganllwyd Gwyn 146 E4
Gannochy Angus 293 F7
Gannochy Perth/Kinr 286 E5
Gannow Hill Shrops 149 C7
Gansclet H'land 310 E7
Ganstead ER Yorks 209 G9
Ganthorpe N Yorks 216 E3
Ganton N Yorks 217 D9
Gants Hill London 68 B2
Ganwick Corner Herts 86 F3
Gaodhail Arg/Bute 289 F8
Gappah Devon 14 F3
Garafad H'land 298 C4
Garamor H'land 295 F8
Garaway Hill Heref'd 97 F8
Garazim Conwy 179 F11
Garbat H'land 300 C4
Garbhallt Arg/Bute 275 D11
Garboldisham Norfolk 141 G10
Garbole H'land 301 G7
Garden City Bl Gwent 77 D11
Garden City Flints 166 B4
Garden Village S Yorks 186 B3
Garden Village Swan 75 F9
Garden Village Wrex 166 E4
Garden Village W Yorks 206 G4
Gardener's Green Wokingham 65 F10
Gardenstown Aberds 303 C7
Garderhouse Shetl'd 315 J5
Gardham ER Yorks 208 E5
Gardie Shetl'd 314 D7
Gardin Shetl'd 314 G6
Gare Hill Som'set 45 E9
Garelochhead Arg/Bute 276 C4
Garford Oxon 82 F6
Garforth W Yorks 206 G4
Gargrave N Yorks 204 C4
Gargunnock Stirl 278 C4
Garker Cornw'l 5 E10
Garlandhayes Devon 27 D11
Garlands Cumb 239 G10
Garlic Street Norfolk 142 G4
Garlieston Dumf/Gal 236 E6
Garlinge Kent 71 F10
Garlinge Green Kent 54 C6
Garlogie Aberds 293 C9
Garmond Aberds 303 D8
Garmondsway Durham 234 E2
Garmony Arg/Bute 289 E8
Garmouth Moray 302 C3
Garmston Shrops 132 B2
Garnant Carms 75 C11
Garndiffaith Torf 78 E3
Garndolbenmaen Gwyn 163 G7
Garnett Bridge Cumb 221 F10
Garnfadryn Gwyn 144 C5
Garnkirk N Lanarks 268 B3
Garnlydan Bl Gwent 77 C11
Garnsgate Lincs 157 E8
Garnswilt Swan 75 D10
Garn-yr-erw Torf 78 C2
Garra Ellabus Arg/Bute 274 F3
Garrabost W Isles 304 E7
Garrachoran Arg/Bute 276 E2
Garrachra Arg/Bute 275 E11
Garralburn Moray 302 D4
Garraron Arg/Bute 275 C9
Garras Cornw'l 2 E6
Garreg Gwyn 163 G10
Garrett's Green W Midlands 134 F2
Garrick Perth/Kinr 286 F2
Garrigill Cumb 231 C10
Garrison Stirl 285 G7
Garriston N Yorks 224 G3
Garroch Dumf/Gal 246 G3
Garrogie Lodge H'land 291 B7
Garros H'land 298 C4
Garrow Perth/Kinr 286 C2
Garrowhill Glasg C 268 C3
Garrygualach H'land 290 C3
Garryhorn Dumf/Gal 246 E2
Garsdale Cumb 212 B4
Garsdale Head Cumb 222 G5
Garsdon Wilts 62 B3
Garshall Green Staffs 151 C9
Garsington Oxon 83 E9
Garstang Lancs 202 D5
Garston Herts 85 E10
Garston Mersey 182 E6
Garswood Mersey 183 B8
Gartbreck Arg/Bute 254 B3
Gartcosh N Lanarks 268 B3
Garth Bridg 76 G5
Garth Ceredig'n 128 G2
Garth Gwyn 179 G9
Garth Monmouths 78 G4
Garth Perth/Kinr 285 B11
Garth Powys 128 C5
Garth Powys 95 B9
Garth Powys 114 C5
Garth Shetl'd 315 H4
Garth Shetl'd 315 H6
Garth Wrex 166 G3
Garth Owen Powys 130 E2
Garth Place Caerph 59 B7
Garth Row Cumb 221 F10
Garth Trevor Wrex 166 G3
Garthamlock Glasg C 268 B3
Garthbeg H'land 291 B7
Garthbrengy Powys 95 E10
Garthdee Aberd C 293 C11
Gartheli Ceredig'n 111 F11
Garthmyl Powys 130 D3
Garthmyn Conwy 164 D4
Garthorpe Leics 154 E6
Garthorpe N Lincs 199 D10
Gartlea N Lanarks 268 C5
Gartly Aberds 302 F5
Gartmore Stirl 277 B10
Gartmore Ho. Stirl 285 H9
Gartnagrenach Arg/Bute 255 B8
Gartness N Lanarks 268 C5
Gartness Stirl 277 D10
Garton ER Yorks 209 F11
Garton-on-the-Wolds ER Yorks 208 B5
Gartsherrie N Lanarks 268 B4
Gartur Stirl 285 H9
Gartymore H'land 311 H4
Garvald Scot Borders 270 F2
Garvald E Loth 281 G11
Garvamore H'land 291 D7
Garvard Arg/Bute 274 D4
Garvault Hotel H'land 308 F7
Garve H'land 300 C3
Garvestone Norfolk 141 B10
Garvock Aberds 293 F9
Garvock Hill Fife 280 D2
Garway Heref'd 97 G9
Garway Common Heref'd 97 G9
Garwick Lincs 173 G11
Gas Terminal Aberds 303 D10
Gascote W Midlands 133 C10
Gaskan H'land 289 B9
Gasper Wilts 45 G9
Gasstown Dumf/Gal 238 B1
Gastard Wilts 61 F11
Gasthorpe Norfolk 141 G9
Gaston Green Essex 87 B7
Gatcombe I/Wight 20 E5
Gate Burton Lincs 188 E4
Gate Helmsley N Yorks 207 B9
Gateacre Mersey 182 D6
Gatebeck Cumb 211 B10
Gateford Common Notts 187 E9
Gateforth N Yorks 198 B5
Gatehead E Ayrs 257 B9
Gatehouse of Fleet Dumf/Gal 237 D8
Gatelawbridge Dumf/Gal 247 D10
Gateley Norfolk 159 E9
Gatenby N Yorks 214 B6
Gateshead Tyne/Wear 243 E7
Gateshead International Stadium Tyne/Wear 243 E7
Gatesheath Ches 167 C7
Gateside Aberds 293 B8
Gateside Angus 287 C8
Gateside E Renf 267 D9
Gateside Fife 286 G5
Gateside N Ayrs 267 E7
Gateside Shetl'd 314 F4
Gathurst Gtr Man 194 F4
Gatley Gtr Man 184 D4
Gatley End Cambs 104 C5
Gattonside Scot Borders 262 B2
Gatwick Glos 80 C2
Gatwick Airport W Sussex 51 E9
Gaufron Powys 113 D9
Gaulby Leics 136 C3
Gauldry Fife 287 E7
Gauntons Bank Ches 167 F9
Gaunt's Common Dorset 31 F8
Gaunt's Earthcott S Glos 60 C6
Gaunt's End Essex 105 F10
Gautby Lincs 189 G11
Gavinton Scot Borders 272 E5
Gawber S Yorks 197 F10
Gawcott Bucks 102 E3
Gawsworth Ches 168 B5
Gawthorpe W Yorks 197 D7
Gawthorpe W Yorks 197 C9
Gawthrop Cumb 212 B3
Gawthwaite Cumb 210 C5
Gay Bowers Essex 88 E3
Gay Street W Sussex 35 C9
Gaydon Warwick 119 G7
Gayfield Orkney 312 C5
Gayhurst M/Keynes 102 B6
Gayle N Yorks 213 B7
Gayles N Yorks 224 D2
Gayton Mersey 182 E3
Gayton Norfolk 158 F4
Gayton Northants 120 G4
Gayton Staffs 151 D9
Gayton Engine Lincs 191 D7
Gayton le Marsh Lincs 190 E6
Gayton le Wold Lincs 190 D2
Gayton Thorpe Norfolk 158 F4
Gayton Top Lincs 190 E6
Gaywood Norfolk 158 E2
Gaza Shetl'd 314 F5
Gazeley Suffolk 124 E4
Geàrraidh Sheilidh W Isles 297 J3
Geanies House H'land 301 B8
Gear Sands Cornw'l 4 D5
Gearraidh Bhailteas W Isles 297 J3
Gearraidh Bhaird W Isles 304 F5
Gearraidh Dubh W Isles 296 F4
Gearraidh na h-Aibhne W Isles 304 E4
Gearraidh na Monadh W Isles 297 K3
Geary H'land 298 C2
Geddes House H'land 301 D8
Gedding Suffolk 125 F8
Geddington Northants 137 F7
Gedintailor H'land 295 B7
Gedling Notts 171 G10
Gedney Lincs 157 E8
Gedney Broadgate Lincs 157 E8
Gedney Drove End Lincs 157 D9
Gedney Dyke Lincs 157 D8
Gedney Hill Lincs 156 G6
Gee Cross Gtr Man 185 C7
Geenmoor Hill Oxon 64 C6
Geeston Rutl'd 137 C9
Gefnan Gwyn 163 B10
Geilston Invercl 276 F6
Geirinis W Isles 297 G3
Geise H'land 310 C5
Geisiadar W Isles 304 E3
Geldeston Norfolk 143 E7
Gell Conwy 164 B5
Gelli Pembs 73 B9
Gelli Rh Cyn Taff 77 G7
Gellideg Merth Tyd 77 D8
Gellifor Denbs 165 C10
Gelligaer Caerph 77 F10
Gelligroes Caerph 77 F11
Gelli-haf Caerph 77 F11
Gellilydan Gwyn 146 B3
Gellinudd Neath P Talb 76 E2
Gellyburn Perth/Kinr 286 D4
Gellywen Carms 92 G5
Gelston Dumf/Gal 237 D9
Gelston Lincs 172 F6
Gembling ER Yorks 209 B8
Gendros Swan 75 F10
Genesis Green Suffolk 124 F5
Geneva Ceredig'n 111 F9
Gentleshaw Staffs 151 G11
Geocrab W Isles 305 J3
George Green Bucks 66 C4
George Nympton Devon 26 C2
Georgefield Dumf/Gal 249 E7
Georgeham Devon 40 F3
Georgetown Bl Gwent 77 D10
Georgetown Dumf/Gal 238 B1
Gergask H'land 291 D8
Gerlan Gwyn 163 B10
Germansweek Devon 12 C4
Germiston Glasg C 268 B2
Germoe Cornw'l 2 D3
Gerrans Cornw'l 3 B9
Gerrard's Cross Bucks 66 B3
Gerrick Redcar/Clevel'd 226 B4
Gestingthorpe Essex 106 D6
Gesto Ho H'land 294 B5
Geuffordd Powys 148 G4
Gib Heath W Midlands 133 F11
Gibb Hill Ches 183 F10
Gibbet Hill Som'set 45 D9
Gibbshill Dumf/Gal 237 B9
Gibraltar Beds 103 B10
Gibraltar Bucks 84 C3
Gibraltar Kent 55 F8
Gibraltar Oxon 83 B7
Gibraltar Suffolk 126 G3
Gibshill Invercl 276 G6
Giddeahall Wilts 61 E11
Giddy Green Dorset 18 D2
Gidea Park London 87 G8
Gidleigh Devon 13 D9
Giffnock E Renf 267 D11
Gifford E Loth 271 B10
Giffordland N Ayrs 266 F5
Giffordtown Fife 286 F6
Gigg Gtr Man 195 F10
Giggleswick N Yorks 212 G6
Giggshill Surrey 67 F7
Gignog Pembs 91 G7
Gilbent Gtr Man 184 E5
Gilberdyke ER Yorks 199 B10
Gilbert Street Hants 49 G7
Gilbert's Coombe Cornw'l 4 G3
Gilbert's End Worcs 98 C6
Gilbert's Green Warwick 118 C2
Gilbertstone W Midlands 134 G2
Gilchriston E Loth 271 B9
Gilcrux Cumb 229 D8
Gildersome W Yorks 197 B8
Gildersome Street W Yorks 197 B8
Gildingwells S Yorks 187 D9
Gilesgate Durham 233 C11
Gilesgate Moor Durham 233 C11
Gileston V/Glam 58 F4
Gilfach Caerph 77 F11
Gilfach Goch Rh Cyn Taff 58 B3
Gilfachrheda Ceredig'n 111 F8
Gilgarran Cumb 228 G6
Gill N Yorks 204 E5
Gillamoor N Yorks 216 B3
Gillan Cornw'l 3 D7
Gillar's Green Mersey 183 C7
Gillbank Cumb 221 F7
Gillen H'land 298 D2
Gillesbie Dumf/Gal 248 E5
Gillham Kent 53 E11
Gilling East N Yorks 216 D2
Gilling West N Yorks 224 D3
Gillingham Dorset 30 B4
Gillingham Medway 69 F9
Gillingham Norfolk 143 E8
Gillmoss Mersey 182 B6
Gillock H'land 310 D6
Gillow Heath Staffs 168 D5
Gills H'land 310 B7
Gill's Green Kent 53 G9
Gilmanscleuch Scot Borders 261 E8
Gilmerton C/Edinb 270 B5
Gilmerton Perth/Kinr 286 E2
Gilmonby Durham 223 C9
Gilmorton Leics 135 F11
Gilmourton S Lanarks 258 B3
Gilnow Gtr Man 195 F8
Gilridge Kent 52 E3
Gilroyd S Yorks 197 G10
Gilslake S Glos 60 C5
Gilsland Cumb 240 D4
Gilson Warwick 134 E3
Gilstead W Yorks 205 F8
Gilston Scot Borders 271 D8
Gilston Herts 87 C7
Giltbrook Notts 171 F7
Gilver's Lane Worcs 98 C6
Gilwern Monmouths 78 C2
Gimingham Norfolk 160 B5
Gin Pit Gtr Man 195 G7
Ginclough Ches 185 F7
Ginger's Green E Sussex 37 E10
Giosla W Isles 304 F3
Gippeswyk Park Suffolk 108 C2
Gipping Suffolk 125 E11
Gipsey Bridge Lincs 174 F3
Gipsy Row Suffolk 107 D11
Gipsyville Kingston/Hull 200 B5
Gipton W Yorks 206 F2
Girdle Toll N Ayrs 266 G6
Girlington W Yorks 205 G8
Girlsta Shetl'd 315 H6
Girsby N Yorks 225 D7
Girtford Beds 122 G2
Girthon Dumf/Gal 237 D8
Girton Cambs 123 E8
Girton Notts 172 B4
Girvan S Ayrs 244 D5
Gisburn Lancs 204 D2
Gisburn Cotes Lancs 204 D2
Gisleham Suffolk 143 F10
Gislingham Suffolk 125 C11
Gissing Norfolk 142 F2
Gissing Common Norfolk 142 F3
Gittisham Devon 15 B8
Givons Grove Surrey 51 C7
Glachavoil Arg/Bute 275 F11
Glack of Midthird Moray 302 E3
Glackmore H'land 300 D6
Gladestry Powys 114 F4
Gladsmuir E Loth 281 G9
Glaichbea H'land 300 F5
Glais Swan 76 E2
Glaisdale N Yorks 226 D5
Glaisdale Side N Yorks 226 E5
Glame H'land 298 E5
Glamis Angus 287 C7
Glamis Castle Angus 287 C7
Glan Duar Carms 93 C10
Glan Dwyfach Gwyn 163 G7
Glan yr afon Gwyn 145 B10
Glanaber Terrace Conwy 164 F3
Glan-Adda Gwyn 179 G9
Glanafon Pembs 73 B7
Glanaman Carms 75 C11
Glandford Norfolk 177 E8
Glandwr Bl Gwent 78 E2
Glandwr Pembs 92 F3
Glandy Cross Carms 92 F2
Glaneirw Ceredig'n 92 B5
Glangrwyney Monmouths 78 B2
Glanllynfi Bridg 76 G5
Glanmule Powys 130 E3
Glanpwllafon Pembs 92 C3
Glanrafon Ceredig'n 128 G2
Glan-rhyd Gwyn 163 D7
Glanrhyd Pembs 92 C2
Glan-rhyd Powys 76 D3
Glanton Northum 264 G3
Glanvilles Wootton Dorset 29 F11
Glanwern Ceredig'n 128 F2
Glan-wr-afon Denbs 165 G8
Glanwydden Conwy 180 E4
Glan-y-don Flints 181 F11
Glan-y-Fferi = Ferryside Carms 74 D5
Glan-y-llyn Rh Cyn Taff 58 C6
Glan-y-nant Caerph 77 F10
Glan-y-nant Powys 129 G8
Glan-yr-afon Gwyn 164 G6
Glan-yr-afon Angl 178 F5
Glan-yr-afon Angl 179 E10
Glanyrafon Powys 148 D4
Glan-y-wern Gwyn 146 C2
Glapthorn Northants 137 E10
Glapwell Derby 171 B7
Glas-allt Shiel Aberds 292 E4
Glasbury Powys 96 D3
Glaschoil H'land 301 F10
Glascoed Denbs 181 G7
Glascoed Monmouths 78 E4
Glascoed Powys 130 B2
Glascoed Powys 148 G2
Glascoed Wrex 166 E3
Glascorrie Aberds 292 D5
Glascorrie Perth/Kinr 286 E2
Glascote Staffs 134 C4
Glascote Heath Staffs 134 C4
Glascwm Powys 114 G3
Glasdrum Arg/Bute 284 C4
Glasfryn Conwy 164 E6
Glasgoforest Aberds 293 B10
Glasgow Glasg C 267 B11
Glasgow Airport Renf 267 B9
Glasgow Art Gallery & Museum Glasg C 267 B11
Glasgow Botanic Gardens Glasg C 267 B11
Glasgow Bridge E Dunb 278 G2
Glasgow Cathedral Glasg C 268 B2
Glasgow Prestwick International Airport S Ayrs 257 D9
Glashvin H'land 298 C4
Glasinfryn Gwyn 163 B9
Glasllwch Newp 59 B9
Glasnacardoch H'land 295 F8
Glasnakille H'land 295 D7
Glasphein H'land 297 G7
Glaspwll Powys 128 D4
Glass Houghton W Yorks 198 C2
Glassburn H'land 300 F3
Glassenbury Kent 53 F9
Glasserton Dumf/Gal 236 F6
Glassford S Lanarks 268 F4
Glassgreen Moray 302 C2
Glasshouse Glos 98 G4
Glasshouse Hill Glos 98 G4
Glasshouses N Yorks 214 G3
Glasslie Fife 286 G6
Glasson Cumb 239 D7
Glasson Lancs 202 B4
Glassonby Cumb 231 D7
Glasterlaw Angus 287 B9
Glaston Rutl'd 137 C7
Glastonbury Som'set 44 F4
Glastonbury Abbey Som'set 44 F4
Glatton Cambs 138 F3
Glazebrook Warrington 183 C11
Glazebury Warrington 183 B11
Glazeley Shrops 132 F4
Gleadless S Yorks 186 E5
Gleadless Valley S Yorks 186 E5
Gleadsmoss Ches 168 B4
Gleann Tholàstaidh W Isles 304 D7
Gleaston Cumb 210 E5
Glebe Shetl'd 315 J6
Glebe Tyne/Wear 243 F8
Glebe Cliff Cornw'l 10 D7
Glebe Farm W Midlands 134 F2
Glecknabae Arg/Bute 275 G11
Gledhow W Yorks 206 F2
Gleiniant Powys 129 E9
Glemsford Suffolk 106 B6
Glen Dumf/Gal 237 B10
Glen Dumf/Gal 237 D7
Glen Auldyn I/Man 192 C5
Glen Bernisdale H'land 298 E4
Glen Ho Scot Borders 261 C7
Glen Mona I/Man 192 D5
Glen Mor H'land 295 B10
Glen Nevis House H'land 290 F3
Glen of Newmill Moray 302 D4
Glen Parva Leics C 135 D11
Glen Sluain Arg/Bute 275 D11
Glen Tanar House Aberds 292 D6
Glen Vic Askil H'land 298 E3
Glen Village Falk 279 F7
Glen Vine I/Man 192 E4
Glenallachie Moray 302 E2
Glenalmond College Perth/Kinr 286 E3
Glenalmond Ho. Perth/Kinr 286 E3
Glenamachrie Arg/Bute 289 G11
Glenample Stirl 285 E9
Glenancross H'land 295 F8
Glenaros Ho Arg/Bute 289 E7
Glenbarr Arg/Bute 255 D7
Glenbeg H'land 289 C7
Glenbeg H'land 301 G10
Glenbervie Aberds 293 E9
Glenboig N Lanarks 268 B4
Glenborrodale H'land 289 C8
Glenbranter Arg/Bute 276 B2
Glenbreck Scot Borders 260 E3
Glenbrein Lodge H'land 290 B6
Glenbrittle House H'land 294 C6
Glenbuchat Castle Aberds 292 B5
Glenbuchat Lodge Aberds 292 B5
Glenbuck E Ayrs 259 D7
Glenburn Renf 267 C9
Glenbyre Arg/Bute 289 G7
Glencalvie Lodge H'land 309 L4
Glencanisp Lodge H'land 307 G6
Glencaple Dumf/Gal 237 C11
Glencarron Lodge H'land 299 D10
Glencarse Perth/Kinr 286 E5
Glencassley Castle H'land 309 J4
Glencat Aberds 293 D7
Glenceitlein H'land 284 C5
Glencoe H'land 284 B4
Glencraig Fife 280 C3
Glencripesdale H'land 289 D8
Glencrosh Dumf/Gal 247 F7
Glendavan Ho. Aberds 292 C6
Glendevon Perth/Kinr 286 G3
Glendoe Lodge H'land 290 C6
Glendoebeg H'land 290 C6
Glendoick Perth/Kinr 286 E6
Glendoll Lodge Angus 292 F4
Glendon Hall Northants 136 G6
Glendoune S Ayrs 244 D5
Glenduckie Fife 286 F6
Glendye Lodge Aberds 293 E8
Gleneagles Hotel Perth/Kinr 286 F3
Gleneagles House Perth/Kinr 286 G3
Glenearn Perth/Kinr 286 F5
Glenegedale Arg/Bute 254 B4
Glenelg H'land 295 D10
Glenernie Moray 301 E10
Glenfarg Perth/Kinr 286 F5
Glenfarquhar Lodge Aberds 293 E9
Glenferness House H'land 301 E9
Glenfeshie Lodge H'land 291 D10
Glenfiddich Distillery, Dufftown Moray 302 E3
Glenfiddich Lodge Moray 302 F3
Glenfield Leics 135 B10
Glenfinnan H'land 295 G10
Glenfinnan Lodge H'land 295 G11
Glenfintaig Ho. H'land 290 E4
Glenfoot Perth/Kinr 286 F5
Glenfyne Lodge Arg/Bute 284 F6
Glengap Dumf/Gal 237 D8
Glengarnock N Ayrs 266 E6
Glengolly H'land 310 C5
Glengorm Castle Arg/Bute 288 D6
Glengoulandie Perth/Kinr 285 B11
Glengrasco H'land 298 E4
Glenhead Farm Angus 292 G4
Glenholt Plym'th 7 C10
Glenhoul Dumf/Gal 246 F4
Glenhurich H'land 289 C10
Glenkerry Scot Borders 261 G7
Glenkiln Dumf/Gal 237 B10
Glenkindie Aberds 292 B6
Glenlair Dumf/Gal 237 B9
Glenlatterach Moray 301 D11
Glenlee Dumf/Gal 246 G4
Glenleraig H'land 306 F6
Glenlichorn Perth/Kinr 285 F11
Glenlicht Ho. H'land 290 B2
Glenlivet Moray 301 G11
Glenlochar Dumf/Gal 237 C9
Glenlochsie Perth/Kinr 292 F2
Glenlocksie Lodge Perth/Kinr 292 F2
Glenloig N Ayrs 255 D10
Glenlomond Perth/Kinr 286 G5
Glenluce Dumf/Gal 236 D4
Glenlussa Ho Arg/Bute 255 E8
Glenmallan Arg/Bute 276 B4
Glenmark Angus 292 E6
Glenmarkie Lodge Angus 292 G4
Glenmarksie H'land 300 D3
Glenmassan Arg/Bute 276 D2
Glenmavis N Lanarks 268 B5
Glenmavis W Loth 269 B9
Glenmaye I/Man 192 E3
Glenmeanie H'land 300 D2
Glenmidge Dumf/Gal 247 F9
Glenmoidart Ho H'land 289 B9
Glenmore Arg/Bute 275 B9
Glenmore Arg/Bute 275 G11
Glenmore H'land 298 E4
Glenmore Lodge H'land 291 C11
Glenmoy Angus 292 G6
Glennoe Arg/Bute 284 D4
Glenogil Angus 292 G6
Glenprosen Lodge Angus 292 G4
Glenprosen Village Angus 292 G5
Glenquaich Lodge Perth/Kinr 286 D2
Glenquiech Angus 292 G6
Glenquithlie Aberds 303 C8
Glenrazie Dumf/Gal 236 C5
Glenreasdell Mains Arg/Bute 255 B9
Glenree N Ayrs 255 E10
Glenridding Cumb 221 B7
Glenrosa N Ayrs 255 D10
Glenrossal H'land 309 J4
Glenrothes Fife 286 G6
Glensanda H'land 289 E10
Glensaugh Aberds 293 F8
Glensburgh Falk 279 E8
Glenshero Lodge H'land 291 D7
Glenshoe Lodge Perth/Kinr 292 G3
Glenstockadale Dumf/Gal 236 C2
Glenstriven Arg/Bute 275 F11
Glentaggart S Lanarks 259 D8
Glentarkie Perth/Kinr 286 F5
Glentham Lincs 189 C8
Glentirranmuir Stirl 278 C3
Glenton Aberds 302 G6
Glentress Scot Borders 261 B7
Glentromie Lodge H'land 291 D9
Glentrool Village Dumf/Gal 236 B5
Glentruan I/Man 192 B5
Glentruim House H'land 291 D8
Glenturret Distillery, Crieff Perth/Kinr 286 E2
Glentworth Lincs 188 D6
Glenuaig Lodge H'land 299 E11
Glenuig H'land 289 B8
Glenure Arg/Bute 284 C4
Glenurquhart H'land 301 C7
Glenview Arg/Bute 284 E5
Glespin S Lanarks 259 D8
Gletness Shetl'd 315 H6
Glewstone Heref'd 97 G11
Glinton Peterbro 138 B3
Glodwick Gtr Man 196 G2
Glogue Pembs 92 E4
Glooston Leics 136 D5
Glossop Derby 185 C8
Gloucester Glos 80 B4
Gloucester Cathedral Glos 80 B4
Gloucestershire Airport Glos 99 G7
Gloup Shetl'd 314 C7
Glover's Hawes Kent 52 E3
Gloweth Cornw'l 4 G5
Glusburn N Yorks 204 D6
Glutt Lodge H'land 310 F3
Glutton Bridge Derby 169 B9
Gluvian Cornw'l 5 C8
Glympton Oxon 101 G8
Glyn Ceiriog Wrex 148 B4
Glyn Ebwy = Ebbw Vale Bl Gwent 77 D11
Glynarthen Ceredig'n 92 B6
Glynbrochan Powys 129 G8
Glyncoch Rh Cyn Taff 77 G9
Glyncorrwg Neath P Talb 76 F5
Glynde E Sussex 37 F7
Glyndebourne E Sussex 37 E7
Glyndyfrdwy Denbs 165 G10
Glynedd = Glyn-neath Neath P Talb 76 D5
Glynmorlas Shrops 148 B6
Glyn-neath = Glynedd Neath P Talb 76 D5
Glynogwr Bridg 58 B3
Glyntaff Rh Cyn Taff 58 B5
Glyntawe Powys 76 B4
Gnosall Staffs 150 E6
Gnosall Heath Staffs 150 E6
Goadby Leics 136 D5
Goadby Marwood Leics 154 D5
Goadsbarrow Cumb 210 F5
Goat Lees Kent 54 D4
Goatacre Wilts 62 D4
Goatham Green E Sussex 38 D4
Goathill Dorset 29 D11
Goathland N Yorks 226 E6
Goathurst Som'set 43 G9
Goathurst Common Kent 52 C3
Gobernuisgach Lodge H'land 308 E4
Gobernuisgeach H'land 310 F3
Gobhaig W Isles 305 H2
Gobowen Shrops 148 C6
Godalming Surrey 50 E3
Goddard's Corner Suffolk 126 D5
Goddard's Green Kent 53 F9
Goddard's Green Kent 53 G10
Goddard's Green W Berks 65 F7
Goddard's Green W Sussex 36 C3
Godden Green Kent 52 B5
Goddington London 68 F3
Godford Cross Devon 27 G10
Godington Oxon 102 F2
Godley Gtr Man 185 B7
Godmanchester Cambs 122 C5
Godmanstone Dorset 17 B9
Godmersham Kent 54 C5
Godney Som'set 44 E3
Godolphin Cross Cornw'l 2 C4
Godre'r-graig Neath P Talb 76 D2
Godshill Hants 31 E11
Godshill I/Wight 20 E6
Godstone Surrey 51 C10
Godstone Staffs 151 C10
Godstone Farm Surrey 51 C11
Godsworthy Devon 12 F6
Godwell Devon 8 D2
Godwinscroft Hants 19 B9
Goetre Monmouths 78 D4
Goff's Oak Herts 86 E4
Gogar C/Edinb 280 G3
Gogarth Conwy 180 E3
Goginan Ceredig'n 128 G3
Goirtean a'Chladaich H'land 290 F2
Golan Gwyn 163 G8
Golant Cornw'l 6 E2
Golberdon Cornw'l 12 G2
Golborne Gtr Man 183 B10
Golcar W Yorks 196 D5
Gold Hill Cambs 139 E10
Gold Hill Dorset 30 E4
Goldcliff Newp 59 C11
Golden Cross E Sussex 37 E8
Golden Green Kent 52 D6
Golden Grove Carms 75 B9
Golden Hill Bristol 60 D5
Golden Hill Hants 19 B11
Golden Hill Pembs 73 E7
Golden Hill Pembs 91 G9
Golden Pot Hants 49 E8
Golden Square Devon 28 G2
Golden Valley Derby 170 E6
Golden Valley Glos 99 G8
Golden Valley Heref'd 98 B3
Golden Valley S Glos 61 E7
Goldenhill Stoke 168 E4
Golders Green London 67 B8
Goldfinch Bottom W Berks 64 G4
Goldhanger Essex 88 D6
Goldington Beds 121 G11
Golds Green W Midlands 133 E9
Goldsborough N Yorks 206 B3
Goldsborough N Yorks 226 C6
Goldsithney Cornw'l 2 C2
Goldstone Shrops 150 D4
Goldsworth Park Surrey 50 B3
Goldthorn Park W Midlands 133 D8
Goldthorpe S Yorks 198 G3
Goldwick Glos 80 F2
Goldworthy Devon 24 C5
Golfa Powys 148 D3
Golford Kent 53 F10
Golftyn Flints 166 B3
Golgotha Kent 55 D9
Gollanfield H'land 301 D8
Gollawater Cornw'l 4 E5
Gollinglith Foot N Yorks 214 C2
Golly Wrex 166 D4
Golsoncott Som'set 42 F4
Golspie H'land 311 J2
Golval H'land 310 C2
Golynus Torf 78 E3
Gomeldon Wilts 47 F7
Gomersal W Yorks 197 B8
Gometra Ho Arg/Bute 288 E5
Gomshall Surrey 50 D5
Gonalston Notts 171 F11
Gonamena Cornw'l 11 G11
Gonerby Hill Foot Lincs 155 B8

Gonfirth Shetl'd 315 G5
Good Easter Essex 87 C10
Gooderstone Norfolk 140 C5
Goodleigh Devon 40 G5
Goodmanhan ER Yorks 208 E3
Goodmayes London 68 B3
Goodnestone Kent 55 C9
Goodnestone Kent 70 G4
Goodrich Heref'd 79 B9
Goodrington Torbay 9 D7
Goodshaw Lancs 195 B10
Goodshaw Chapel Lancs 195 B10
Goodshaw Fold Lancs 195 B10
Goodstone Devon 13 G11
Goodwick = Wdig Pembs 91 D8
Goodwood Racecourse W Sussex 34 E5
Goodworth Clatford Hants 47 E11
Goodyers End Warwick 134 F6
Goodyhills Cumb 229 B8
Goole ER Yorks 199 C8
Goole Fields ER Yorks 199 C9
Goonabarn Cornw'l 5 E9
Goonbell Cornw'l 4 F4
Goonhavern Cornw'l 4 E5
Goonown Cornw'l 4 E4
Goonpiper Cornw'l 3 B8
Goonvrea Cornw'l 4 F4
Goose Eye W Yorks 204 E6
Goose Green Essex 108 F2
Goose Green Gtr Man 194 G5
Goose Green Hants 32 F4
Goose Green Herts 86 D5
Goose Green Kent 53 F10
Goose Green Kent 52 C6
Goose Green Norfolk 142 F2
Goose Green S Glos 61 E7
Goose Green S Glos 61 C8
Goose Green W Sussex 35 D10
Goose Pool Heref'd 97 D9
Gooseberry Green Essex 87 F11
Gooseham Cornw'l 24 D2
Goosehill W Yorks 197 C11
Goosemoor Devon 15 D7
Goosemoor Green Staffs 151 G11
Goosenford Som'set 28 B2
Goosewell Plym'th 7 E10
Goosey Oxon 82 G5
Goosnargh Lancs 203 G7
Goostrey Ches 184 G3
Gorbals Glasg C 267 C11
Gorcott Hill Worcs 117 D11
Gord Shetl'd 315 L6
Gorddinog Conwy 179 G11
Gordon Scot Borders 272 G2
Gordonbush H'land 311 J2
Gordonsburgh Moray 302 C4
Gordonstoun Moray 301 C11
Gordonstown Aberds 302 D5
Gordonstown Aberds 303 F7
Gore Kent 55 B10
Gore End Hants 64 G2
Gore Houses Mersey 193 G11
Gore Pit Essex 88 B5
Gore Street Kent 71 F9
Gorebridge Midloth 270 C6
Gorefield Cambs 157 G8
Gores Wilts 46 B6
Gorgie C/Edinb 280 G4
Goring Oxon 64 C6
Goring Heath Oxon 65 D7
Goring-by-Sea W Sussex 35 G10
Gorleston-on-Sea Norfolk 143 C10
Gornalwood W Midlands 133 E8
Gorrachie Aberds 303 D7
Gorran Churchtown Cornw'l 5 G9
Gorran Haven Cornw'l 5 G10
Gorran High Lanes Cornw'l 5 G9
Gorrenberry Scot Borders 249 D11
Gors Ceredig'n 112 B2
Gorse Covert Warrington 183 C11
Gorse Hill Gtr Man 184 B4
Gorse Hill Swindon 63 B7
Gorsedd Flints 181 F11
Gorseinon Swan 75 F9
Gorseness Orkney 312 G5
Gorsey Bank Shrops 150 G5
Gorseybank Derby 170 E3
Gorsgoch Ceredig'n 111 G9
Gorslas Carms 75 C9
Gorsley Glos 98 F3
Gorsley Common Heref'd 98 F3
Gorstage Ches 183 G10
Gorstan H'land 300 C3
Gorstanvorran H'land 289 B10
Gorstella Ches 166 C5
Gorsty Hill Staffs 152 D2
Gortan Arg/Bute 274 G3
Gortantaoid Arg/Bute 274 F4
Gortenacullish H'land 295 G8
Gorteneorn H'land 289 C8
Gortenfern H'land 289 C8
Gortinanane Arg/Bute 255 C8
Gortleigh Devon 25 F7
Gorton Gtr Man 184 B5
Gortonallister N Ayrs 256 D2
Gosbeck Suffolk 126 F3
Gosberton Lincs 156 C4
Gosberton Cheal Lincs 156 D4
Gosberton Clough Lincs 156 D3
Goseley Dale Derby 152 E6
Gosfield Essex 106 F5
Gosford Devon 15 B7
Gosford Heref'd 115 D10
Gosford Oxon 83 C8
Gosford Green W Midlands 118 B6
Gosforth Cumb 219 E11
Gosforth Tyne/Wear 242 D6
Gosforth Valley Derby 186 F4
Gosland Green Ches 167 D9
Gosland Green Suffolk 124 G5
Gosling Green Suffolk 107 C9
Gosmore Herts 104 F3
Gospel End Staffs 133 E7
Gospel Oak London 67 B9
Gosport Hants 32 C5
Gosport Hants 21 B8
Gossabrough Shetl'd 314 E7
Gossard's Green Beds 103 C9
Gossington Glos 80 E2
Gossops Green W Sussex 51 F8
Goswick Northum 273 F11
Gotham Dorset 31 E9
Gotham E Sussex 38 F2
Gotham Notts 153 C10
Gothelney Green Som'set 43 F9
Gotherington Glos 99 F9
Gothers Cornw'l 5 D9
Gott Arg/Bute 288 E2
Gott Shetl'd 315 J6
Gotton Som'set 28 B2
Goudhurst Kent 53 F8
Goukstone Moray 302 D4
Goulceby Lincs 190 F3
Goulton N Yorks 225 E9
Gourdas Aberds 303 E7
Gourdon Aberds 293 F10
Gourock Inverc'l 276 F4
Govan Glasg C 267 B11
Govanhill Glasg C 267 C11
Gover Valley Cornw'l 5 E9
Goverton Notts 172 E2
Goveton Devon 8 F5
Govilon Monmouths 78 C3
Gowanhill Aberds 303 C10
Gowanwell Aberds 303 E8
Gowdall ER Yorks 198 C6
Gowerton = Tre-Gwyr Swan 75 F9
Gowkhall Fife 279 D11
Gowkthrapple N Lanarks 268 E5
Gowthorpe ER Yorks 207 C11
Goxhill ER Yorks 209 E9
Goxhill N Lincs 200 C6
Goxhill Haven N Lincs 200 B6
Goytre Neath P Talb 57 D9
Gozzard's Ford Oxon 83 F7
Grabhair W Isles 305 G5
Graby Lincs 155 D11
Gracca Cornw'l 5 D10
Grade Cornw'l 2 G6
Gradeley Green Ches 167 E9
Graffham W Sussex 34 D6
Grafham Cambs 122 D3
Grafham Surrey 50 E4
Grafton Bucks 84 C5
Grafton Heref'd 97 D9
Grafton N Yorks 215 G8
Grafton Oxon 82 E3
Grafton Shrops 149 F8
Grafton Worcs 99 D9
Grafton Flyford Worcs 117 F9
Grafton Regis Northants 102 B5
Grafton Underwood Northants 137 G8
Grafty Green Kent 53 D11
Grahamston Falk 279 E7
Graianrhyd Denbs 166 D2
Graig Carms 74 E6
Graig Conwy 180 G4
Graig Denbs 181 G9
Graig Rh Cyn Taff 58 B5
Graig Shrops 114 B5
Graig Felen Swan 75 E11
Graig Penllyn V/Glam 58 D3
Graig Trewyddfa Swan 75 F11
Graig-Fawr Swan 75 E10
Graig-fechan Denbs 165 E10
Grain Medway 69 D11
Grains Bar Gtr Man 196 F3
Grainsby Lincs 190 B3
Grainthorpe Lincs 190 B5
Graizelound N Lincs 188 B3
Grampound Cornw'l 5 F8
Grampound Road Cornw'l 5 E8
Gramsdal W Isles 296 F4
Granborough Bucks 102 F5
Granby Notts 154 B5
Grandborough Warwick 119 D9
Grandpont Oxon 83 D8
Grandtully Perth/Kinr 286 B3
Grange Cumb 220 B5
Grange Dorset 31 G8
Grange E Ayrs 257 B10
Grange Fife 287 G8
Grange Halton 183 E8
Grange Lancs 202 F3
Grange Lancs 203 G7
Grange Mersey 182 D2
Grange Medway 69 F9
Grange NE Lincs 201 F9
Grange N Yorks 223 G8
Grange N Yorks 225 F11
Grange Perth/Kinr 286 E6
Grange Warrington 183 C10
Grange Crossroads Moray 302 D4
Grange Estate Dorset 31 G10
Grange Hall Moray 301 C10
Grange Hill Durham 233 F10
Grange Hill Essex 86 G6
Grange Moor W Yorks 197 D8
Grange of Cree Dumf/Gal 236 D6
Grange of Lindores Fife 286 F6
Grange Park London 86 F4
Grange Park Mersey 183 C7
Grange Park Swindon 62 C6
Grange Villa Durham 242 G6
Grangemill Derby 170 D2
Grangemouth Falk 279 E8
Grangemuir Fife 287 G9
Grange-over-Sands Cumb 211 D8
Grangepans Falk 279 E10
Grangetown Card 59 E7
Grangetown Redcar/Clevel'd 235 G7
Grangetown Tyne/Wear 243 G10
Granish H'land 291 B11
Gransmoor ER Yorks 209 B8
Gransmore Green Essex 106 G3
Granston = Treopert Pembs 91 E7
Grant Thorold NE Lincs 201 F9
Grantchester Cambs 123 F8
Grantham Lincs 155 B8
Granthouse Scot Borders 272 B6
Grantley N Yorks 214 F4
Grantlodge Aberds 293 B9
Granton C/Edinb 280 F4
Grantown Aberds 302 D5
Grantown-on-Spey H'land 301 G10
Graplin Dumf/Gal 237 E8
Grappenhall Warrington 183 D10
Grasby Lincs 200 G5
Grasmere Cumb 220 D6
Grass Green Essex 106 D4
Grasscroft Gtr Man 196 G3
Grassendale Mersey 182 D5
Grassgarth Cumb 221 F8
Grassgarth Cumb 230 C2
Grasshill Derby 170 B6
Grassington N Yorks 213 G10
Grassmoor Derby 170 B6
Grassthorpe Notts 172 B3
Grasswell Tyne/Wear 243 G8
Grateley Hants 47 E9
Gratton Devon 24 E5
Gratwich Staffs 151 C10
Gravel Castle Kent 55 D8
Gravel Hill Bucks 85 G8
Gravel Hole Gtr Man 196 F2
Graveley Cambs 122 E5
Graveley Herts 104 F4
Gravelly Hill W Midlands 134 E2
Gravelsbank Shrops 130 C6
Graven Shetl'd 314 F6
Graveney Kent 70 G5
Graveney Hill Kent 70 G5
Gravesend Herts 105 F8
Gravesend Kent 68 E6
Grayingham Lincs 188 B6
Grayrigg Cumb 221 F11
Grays Thurr'k 68 D6
Grayshott Hants 49 F11
Grayson Green Cumb 228 F5
Grayswood Surrey 50 G2
Graythorp Hartlep'l 234 F6
Graze Hill Beds 121 G11
Grazeley Wokingham 65 F7
Greagdhubh Lodge H'land 291 D8
Greamchary H'land 310 F2
Greasbrough S Yorks 186 B6
Greasby Mersey 182 D3
Greasley Notts 171 F7
Great Abington Cambs 105 B10
Great Addington Northants 121 B9
Great Alne Warwick 118 F2
Great Altcar Lancs 193 F10
Great Amwell Herts 86 C5
Great Asby Cumb 222 C3
Great Ashfield Suffolk 125 D9
Great Ayton N Yorks 225 C11
Great Baddow Essex 88 E2
Great Bardfield Essex 106 E3
Great Barford Beds 122 G2
Great Barr W Midlands 133 D10
Great Barrington Glos 82 C2
Great Barrow Ches 167 B7
Great Barton Suffolk 125 D7
Great Barugh N Yorks 216 D4
Great Bavington Northum 251 G11
Great Bealings Suffolk 108 B4
Great Bedwyn Wilts 63 G9
Great Bentley Essex 108 G2
Great Billing Northants 120 E6
Great Bircham Norfolk 158 C5
Great Blakenham Suffolk 126 G2
Great Blencow Cumb 230 E5
Great Bolas Telford 150 E3
Great Bookham Surrey 50 C6
Great Bourton Oxon 101 B9
Great Bowden Leics 136 F4
Great Bradley Suffolk 124 G3
Great Braxted Essex 88 C5
Great Bricett Suffolk 125 G10
Great Brickhill Bucks 103 E8
Great Bridge W Midlands 133 E9
Great Bridgeford Staffs 151 D7
Great Brington Northants 120 D3
Great Bromley Essex 107 F11
Great Broughton Cumb 229 E7
Great Broughton N Yorks 225 D11
Great Buckland Kent 69 G7
Great Budworth Ches 183 F11
Great Burdon D'lington 224 B6
Great Burgh Surrey 51 B8
Great Burstead Essex 87 G11
Great Busby N Yorks 225 D10
Great Cambourne Cambs 122 F6
Great Canfield Essex 87 B9
Great Carlton Lincs 190 D6
Great Casterton Rutl'd 137 B10
Great Chart Kent 54 E3
Great Chatfield Wilts 61 G11
Great Chatwell Staffs 150 G5
Great Chell Staffs 168 E5
Great Chesterford Essex 105 C10
Great Cheveney Kent 53 E8
Great Cheverell Wilts 46 C3
Great Chilton Durham 233 E11
Great Chishill Cambs 105 D8
Great Clacton Essex 89 B11
Great Cliff W Yorks 197 D10
Great Clifton Cumb 228 F6
Great Coates NE Lincs 201 E8
Great Comberton Worcs 99 C9
Great Common Suffolk 143 F7
Great Corby Cumb 239 F11
Great Cornard Suffolk 107 C7
Great Cowden ER Yorks 209 E10
Great Coxwell Oxon 82 G3
Great Crakehall N Yorks 214 B5
Great Cransley Northants 120 B6
Great Cressingham Norfolk 141 C7
Great Crosby Mersey 182 B4
Great Crosthwaite Cumb 229 G11
Great Cubley Derby 152 B3
Great Dalby Leics 154 G4
Great Doddington Northants 121 E7
Great Doward Heref'd 79 B9
Great Dunham Norfolk 159 G7
Great Dunmow Essex 106 G2
Great Durnford Wilts 46 F6
Great Easton Essex 106 F2
Great Easton Leics 137 E7
Great Eccleston Lancs 202 E4
Great Edstone N Yorks 216 C4
Great Ellingham Norfolk 141 D10
Great Elm Som'set 45 D8
Great Eppleton Tyne/Wear 234 B3
Great Eversden Cambs 123 G7
Great Fen Cambs 123 B11
Great Fencote N Yorks 224 G5
Great Finborough Suffolk 125 F10
Great Fransham Norfolk 159 G7
Great Gaddesden Herts 85 C8
Great Gidding Cambs 138 G2
Great Givendale ER Yorks 208 C2
Great Glemham Suffolk 126 E6
Great Glen Leics 136 D3
Great Gonerby Lincs 155 B7
Great Gransden Cambs 122 F5
Great Green Cambs 104 C5
Great Green Norfolk 142 F5
Great Green Suffolk 125 B11
Great Green Suffolk 126 B2
Great Green Suffolk 125 F8
Great Green Suffolk 125 D8
Great Habton N Yorks 216 D5
Great Hale Lincs 173 G10
Great Hallingbury Essex 87 B8
Great Hampden Bucks 84 E5
Great Harrowden Northants 121 C7
Great Harwood Lancs 203 G10
Great Haseley Oxon 83 E10
Great Hatfield ER Yorks 209 E9
Great Haywood Staffs 151 E9
Great Heath W Midlands 134 G6
Great Heck N Yorks 198 C5
Great Henny Essex 107 D7
Great Hinton Wilts 46 B2
Great Hivings Bucks 85 E7
Great Hockham Norfolk 141 E9
Great Holland Essex 108 H4
Great Hollands Brackn'l 65 F11
Great Holm M/Keynes 102 D6
Great Horkesley Essex 107 E9
Great Hormead Herts 105 F8
Great Horton W Yorks 205 G8
Great Horwood Bucks 102 E5
Great Houghton Northants 120 F5
Great Houghton S Yorks 198 F2
Great Howarth Gtr Man 196 D2
Great Hucklow Derby 185 F11
Great Job's Cross Kent 38 B4
Great Kelk ER Yorks 209 B8
Great Kimble Bucks 84 D4
Great Kingshill Bucks 84 F5
Great Langdale Cumb 220 D6
Great Langton N Yorks 224 F5
Great Lea Common Wokingham 65 F8
Great Leighs Essex 88 B2
Great Leighs Racecourse Essex 88 B2
Great Lever Gtr Man 195 F8
Great Limber Lincs 200 F6
Great Linford M/Keynes 103 C7
Great Livermere Suffolk 125 C7
Great Longstone Derby 186 G2
Great Lumley Durham 233 B11
Great Malvern Worcs 98 B5
Great Maplestead Essex 106 E6
Great Marton Blackp'l 202 F2
Great Marton Moss Lancs 202 G3
Great Massingham Norfolk 158 E5
Great Melton Norfolk 142 B2
Great Milton Oxon 83 E10
Great Missenden Bucks 84 E5
Great Mitton Lancs 203 F10
Great Mongeham Kent 55 C10
Great Moor Gtr Man 184 D6
Great Moulton Norfolk 142 E3
Great Munden Herts 105 G7
Great Musgrave Cumb 222 C5
Great Ness Shrops 149 F7
Great Norman Street Kent 52 C3
Great Notley Essex 106 G4
Great Oak Monmouths 78 D5
Great Oakley Essex 108 F3
Great Oakley Northants 137 F7
Great Offley Herts 104 F2
Great Orme Tramway, Llandudno Conwy 180 E3
Great Ormside Cumb 222 B3
Great Orton Cumb 239 G8
Great Ouseburn N Yorks 215 G8
Great Oxendon Northants 136 G4
Great Oxney Green Essex 87 D11
Great Parndon Essex 86 D6
Great Pattenden Kent 53 D8
Great Paxton Cambs 122 E4
Great Plumpton Lancs 202 G3
Great Plumstead Norfolk 160 G6
Great Ponton Lincs 155 C8
Great Preston W Yorks 198 B2
Great Purston Northants 101 D10
Great Raveley Cambs 138 G5
Great Rissington Glos 81 B11
Great Rollright Oxon 100 E6
Great Ryburgh Norfolk 159 D9
Great Ryle Northum 264 G2
Great Ryton Shrops 131 C9
Great Saling Essex 106 F4
Great Salkeld Cumb 230 D6
Great Sampford Essex 106 D2
Great Sankey Warrington 183 D9
Great Saredon Staffs 133 B9
Great Saxham Suffolk 124 E5
Great Shefford W Berks 63 D11
Great Shelford Cambs 123 G9
Great Smeaton N Yorks 225 E7
Great Snoring Norfolk 159 C8
Great Somerford Wilts 62 C3
Great Stainton D'lington 234 G2
Great Stambridge Essex 88 G6
Great Staughton Cambs 122 E2
Great Steeping Lincs 174 C6
Great Stoke S Glos 60 C6
Great Stonar Kent 55 B10
Great Strickland Cumb 231 G7
Great Stukeley Cambs 122 C4
Great Sturton Lincs 190 F2
Great Sutton Ches 182 F5
Great Sutton Shrops 131 G10
Great Swinburne Northum 241 B10
Great Tew Oxon 101 F7
Great Tey Essex 107 F7
Great Thorness I/Wight 20 C5
Great Thurlow Suffolk 124 G3
Great Torrington Devon 25 D7
Great Tosson Northum 252 C2
Great Totham Essex 88 C5
Great Tows Lincs 190 C2
Great Tree Cornw'l 6 D5
Great Urswick Cumb 210 E5
Great Wakering Essex 70 B2
Great Waldingfield Suffolk 107 C8
Great Walsingham Norfolk 159 B8
Great Waltham Essex 87 C11
Great Warley Essex 87 G9
Great Washbourne Glos 99 E9
Great Watersend Kent 55 E9
Great Weeke Devon 13 D10
Great Welnetham Suffolk 125 F7
Great Wenham Suffolk 107 D11
Great Whittington Northum 242 C2
Great Wigborough Essex 89 C7
Great Wilbraham Cambs 123 F10
Great Wilne Derby 153 C9
Great Wishford Wilts 46 F5
Great Witchingham Norfolk 160 F2
Great Witcombe Glos 80 C6
Great Witley Worcs 116 D5
Great Wolford Warwick 100 E5
Great Wratting Suffolk 106 B3
Great Wymondley Herts 104 F4
Great Wyrley Staffs 133 B9
Great Wytheford Shrops 149 F11
Great Yarmouth Norfolk 143 B10
Great Yarmouth Sea Life Centre Norfolk 143 B10
Great Yeldham Essex 106 D5
Greatfield Wilts 62 B5
Greatford Lincs 155 G11
Greatgap Bucks 84 B6
Greatgate Staffs 169 G9
Greatham Hants 49 G9
Greatham Hartlep'l 234 F5
Greatham W Sussex 35 D8
Greatness Kent 52 B4
Greatstone-on-Sea Kent 39 C9
Greatworth Northants 101 C11
Greave Gtr Man 184 C6
Greave Lancs 195 C11
Grebby Lincs 174 B6
Greeba I/Man 192 D4
Green Denbs 165 B9
Green Bottom Cornw'l 4 F5
Green Bottom Glos 79 B11
Green Cross Surrey 49 F11
Green End Beds 103 B10
Green End Beds 121 E11
Green End Beds 122 G2
Green End Beds 122 E2
Green End Bucks 103 E8
Green End Cambs 122 C4
Green End Cambs 123 D9
Green End Cambs 123 F7
Green End Herts 104 E5
Green End Herts 104 G6
Green End Herts 104 E6
Green End Lancs 204 D4
Green End N Yorks 226 E6
Green End Warwick 134 F5
Green Gate Devon 27 D8
Green Hailey Bucks 84 E4
Green Hammerton N Yorks 206 B5
Green Haworth Lancs 195 B9
Green Head Cumb 230 B3
Green Heath Staffs 151 G9
Green Hill Lincs 155 B8
Green Hill Wilts 62 B5
Green Hill Worcs 99 B10
Green Lane Devon 13 F11
Green Lane Heref'd 98 B2
Green Lane Powys 130 D3
Green Lane Worcs 117 E11
Green Moor S Yorks 186 B3
Green Ore Som'set 44 C5
Green Quarter Cumb 221 E9
Green Street E Sussex 38 E3
Green Street Essex 87 F10
Green Street Glos 80 E3
Green Street Glos 80 B5
Green Street Herts 105 G9
Green Street Worcs 99 B7
Green Street W Sussex 35 C10
Green Street Green Kent 68 E5
Green Street Green London 68 G3
Green Tye Herts 86 B6
Greenacres Gtr Man 196 F2
Greenan Arg/Bute 275 G11
Greenbank Shetl'd 314 C7
Greenburn W Loth 269 C8
Greencroft Durham 242 G5
Greencroft Norfolk 177 E8
Greendown Som'set 44 C5
Greendykes Northum 264 D3
Greenend Oxon 100 G6
Greenfaulds N Lanarks 278 G5
Greenfield Beds 103 E11
Greenfield Flints 181 F11
Greenfield Gtr Man 196 G3
Greenfield H'land 289 D11
Greenfield H'land 290 C4
Greenfield Oxon 84 G2
Greenfoot N Lanarks 268 B4
Greenford London 66 C6
Greengairs N Lanarks 278 G5
Greengate Gtr Man 196 D2
Greengate Norfolk 159 F10
Greengates W Yorks 205 F9
Greenhalgh Lancs 202 F4
Greenham Dorset 28 F6
Greenham Som'set 27 C9
Greenham W Berks 64 F3
Greenhaugh Northum 251 F7
Greenhead Dumf/Gal 247 D9
Greenhead N Lanarks 268 D6
Greenhead Northum 240 D5
Greenheyes Gtr Man 195 G8
Greenhill Dumf/Gal 248 G4
Greenhill Durham 234 B3
Greenhill Falk 278 F6
Greenhill Heref'd 98 B4
Greenhill Kent 71 F7
Greenhill Leics 153 F8
Greenhill London 67 B7
Greenhill S Glos 60 B6
Greenhill S Yorks 186 E4
Greenhill Worcs 116 B6
Greenhillocks Derby 170 F6
Greenhills N Ayrs 267 E7
Greenhithe Kent 68 D5
Greenholm E Ayrs 258 B2
Greenholme Cumb 221 D11
Greenhouse Scot Borders 262 E3
Greenhow Hill N Yorks 214 G2
Greenigoe Orkney 313 H5
Greenland H'land 310 C6
Greenland S Yorks 186 D5
Greenland Mains H'land 310 C6
Greenlands Worcs 117 D11
Greenlaw Aberds 302 D6
Greenlaw Scot Borders 272 F4
Greenlea Dumf/Gal 238 B2
Greenleys M/Keynes 102 C6
Greenloaning Perth/Kinr 286 G2
Greenmeadow Swindon 62 B6
Greenmeadow Torf 78 F3
Greenmeadow Community Farm, Pontnewydd Torf 78 F3
Greenmount Gtr Man 195 E9
Greenmow Shetl'd 315 L6
Greenoak ER Yorks 199 B10
Greenock Inverc'l 276 F5
Greenock West Inverc'l 276 F5
Greenodd Cumb 210 C6
Greenrigg W Loth 269 C8
Greenrow Cumb 238 G4
Greens Norton Northants 102 B3
Greensforge Staffs 133 F7
Greenshills S Lanarks 268 E2
Greenside Cumb 222 E4
Greenside Derby 186 F5
Greenside Tyne/Wear 242 E4
Greenside W Yorks 197 D7
Greenstead Essex 107 F10
Greenstead Green Essex 106 F6
Greensted Essex 87 E8
Greensted Green Essex 87 E8
Greensted Log Church, Chipping Ongar Essex 87 E8
Greenstreet Green Suffolk 125 G10
Greenway Glos 98 E4
Greenway Som'set 28 C4
Greenway V/Glam 58 E5
Greenway Worcs 116 C4
Greenways Som'set 27 B11
Greenwell Cumb 240 F2
Greenwich London 67 D11
Greenwich Wilts 46 G2
Greenwith Common Cornw'l 4 G5
Greeny Orkney 312 F3
Greep H'land 298 E2
Greet Glos 99 E10
Greete Shrops 115 C11
Greetham Lincs 190 G4
Greetham Rutl'd 155 G8
Greetland W Yorks 196 C5
Greetland Wall Nook W Yorks 196 C5
Greetwell N Lincs 200 G2
Grèin W Isles 297 L2
Gregson Lane Lancs 194 B5
Gregynog Powys 129 D11
Greinetobht W Isles 296 D4
Greinton Som'set 44 F2
Gremista Shetl'd 315 J6
Grenaby I/Man 192 E3
Grendon Northants 121 E7
Grendon Warwick 134 C5
Grendon Bishop Heref'd 115 F11
Grendon Common Warwick 134 D5
Grendon Underwood Bucks 102 G3
Grenend N Lanarks 268 C4
Grenofen Devon 12 G5
Grenoside S Yorks 186 C4
Greosabhagh W Isles 305 J3
Gresford Wrex 166 E5
Gresham Norfolk 160 B3
Greshornish H'land 298 D3
Gressenhall Norfolk 159 F9
Gressingham Lancs 211 F11
Greta Bridge Durham 223 C11
Gretna Dumf/Gal 239 D8
Gretna Green Dumf/Gal 239 D8
Gretton Glos 99 E10
Gretton Northants 137 E7
Gretton Shrops 131 D10
Gretton Field Glos 99 E10
Grewelthorpe N Yorks 214 D4
Grey Green N Lincs 199 F9
Greyfriars Surrey 50 D4
Greygarth N Yorks 214 E3
Greylake Som'set 43 G11
Greylake Fosse Som'set 44 F2
Greynor Carms 75 D9
Greyrigg Dumf/Gal 248 F3
Greys Green Oxon 65 C8
Greysouthern Cumb 229 F7
Greystoke Cumb 230 E4
Greystoke Gill Cumb 230 F4
Greystone Aberds 292 D6
Greystone Aberds 302 F6
Greystone Angus 287 C9
Greystone Dumf/Gal 237 B11
Greystones S Yorks 186 D4
Greytree Heref'd 97 F11
Greywell Hants 49 C8
Griais W Isles 304 D6
Grianan W Isles 304 E6
Grianllyn Conwy 180 F4
Gribb Dorset 28 G5
Gribbleford Bridge Devon 25 G8
Gribthorpe ER Yorks 207 F11
Griff Warwick 135 F7
Griff Hollow Warwick 135 F7
Griffithstown Torf 78 F3
Griffydam Leics 153 F8
Griggs Green Hants 49 G10
Grimbister Orkney 312 G4
Grimblethorpe Lincs 190 D2
Grimeford Village Lancs 194 E6
Grimesthorpe S Yorks 186 C5
Grimethorpe S Yorks 198 F2
Griminis W Isles 296 D3
Griminis W Isles 296 F3
Grimister Shetl'd 314 D6
Grimley Worcs 116 E6
Grimness Orkney 313 J5
Grimoldby Lincs 190 D5
Grimpo Shrops 149 D7
Grimsargh Lancs 203 G7
Grimsbury Oxon 101 C9
Grimsby NE Lincs 201 E9
Grimscote Northants 120 G2
Grimscott Cornw'l 24 F3
Grimshaw Blackb'n 195 C8
Grimshaw Green Lancs 194 E3
Grimsthorpe Lincs 155 E10
Grimston C/York 207 C8
Grimston ER Yorks 209 F11
Grimston Leics 154 E3
Grimston Norfolk 158 E4
Grimstone Dorset 17 C8
Grimstone End Suffolk 125 D8
Grindale ER Yorks 218 E2
Grindigar Orkney 313 H6
Grindiscol Shetl'd 315 K6
Grindle Shrops 132 C5
Grindleford Derby 186 F2
Grindleton Lancs 203 D11
Grindley Staffs 151 D10
Grindley Brook Shrops 167 G8
Grindlow Derby 185 F11
Grindon Northum 273 G8
Grindon Stockton 234 F3
Grindon Staffs 169 E9
Grindon Tyne/Wear 243 F9
Grindsbrook Booth Derby 185 D10
Gringley on the Hill Notts 188 C2
Grinnacombe Moor Devon 12 C4
Grinshill Shrops 149 E10
Grinton N Yorks 223 F10
Griomasaigh W Isles 297 G4
Griomsidar W Isles 304 F5
Grisdale Cumb 222 G5
Grishipoll Arg/Bute 288 D3
Grisling Common E Sussex 36 C6
Gristhorpe N Yorks 217 C11
Griston Norfolk 141 D8
Gritley Orkney 313 H6
Grittenham Wilts 62 C4
Grittlesend Heref'd 98 B4
Grittleton Wilts 61 C11
Grizebeck Cumb 210 B4
Grizedale Cumb 220 G6
Groam H'land 300 E5
Grobister Orkney 312 F7
Grobsness Shetl'd 315 G5
Groby Leics 135 B10
Groes Conwy 165 C8
Groes Neath P Talb 57 D9
Groes Efa Denbs 165 B10
Groesfaen Rh Cyn Taff 58 C5
Groesffordd Conwy 180 F3
Groesffordd Gwyn 144 B5
Groeslon Gwyn 163 C8
Groeslon Gwyn 163 D7
Groes-lwyd Powys 148 G4
Groespluan Powys 130 B4
Groes-wen Caerph 58 B6
Grogoth Wallas Cornw'l 5 G8
Grogport Arg/Bute 255 C9
Gronant Flints 181 E9
Groombridge E Sussex 52 F4
Groomford Suffolk 127 F7
Grosmont Monmouths 97 G8
Grosmont N Yorks 226 D6
Grosvenor Museum, Chester Ches 166 B6
Grotaig H'land 300 G4
Groton Suffolk 107 C9
Grotton Gtr Man 196 G3
Groudle Glen Railway I/Man 192 E5
Grougfoot Falk 279 F10
Grove Dorset 17 G9
Grove Kent 71 G8
Grove Notts 188 F2
Grove Oxon 82 G5
Grove Pembs 73 E7
Grove End Bucks 84 B2
Grove End Warwick 134 D3
Grove Green Kent 53 B9
Grove Park London 68 E2
Grove Town W Yorks 198 C3
Grove Vale W Midlands 133 E10
Grovehill ER Yorks 208 F6
Grovehill Herts 85 D9
Grovehurst Kent 53 E8
Groves Kent 55 B9
Grovesend S Glos 61 B7
Grovesend Swan 75 E9
Grub Street Kent 68 F5
Grudie H'land 300 C3
Gruids H'land 309 J5
Gruinard House H'land 307 K4
Gruinards H'land 309 K5
Grula H'land 294 C5
Gruline Arg/Bute 289 E7
Gruline Ho Arg/Bute 289 F7
Grumbeg H'land 308 F6
Grumbla Cornw'l 1 D4
Grunasound Shetl'd 315 K5
Grundisburgh Suffolk 126 G4
Gruting Shetl'd 315 J4
Grutness Shetl'd 315 N6
Gualachulain H'land 284 C5
Gualin Ho. H'land 308 D3
Guard House W Yorks 204 E6
Guardbridge Fife 287 F8
Guarlford Worcs 98 B6
Guay Perth/Kinr 286 C4
Gubbions Green Essex 88 B2
Gubblacote Herts 84 B6
Guesachan H'land 289 B10
Guestling Green E Sussex 38 E4
Guestling Thorn E Sussex 38 D5
Guestwick Norfolk 159 D11
Guestwick Green Norfolk 159 D11
Guide Blackb'n 195 B8
Guide Bridge Gtr Man 184 B6
Guide Post Northum 253 F7
Guilden Morden Cambs 104 C5
Guilden Sutton Ches 167 B7
Guildford Surrey 50 D4
Guildford Park Surrey 50 D3
Guildiehaugh W Loth 269 B9
Guildtown Perth/Kinr 286 D5
Guilford Pembs 73 D7
Guilsborough Northants 120 C3
Guilsfield = Cegidfa Powys 148 G4
Guilthwaite S Yorks 186 D6
Guilton Kent 55 B9
Guineaford Devon 40 F5
Guisachan H'land 300 G3
Guisborough Redcar/Clevel'd 226 B2
Guiseley W Yorks 205 E9
Guist Norfolk 159 D9
Guith Orkney 312 E6
Guiting Power Glos 99 G11
Gulberwick Shetl'd 315 K6
Gullane E Loth 281 E9
Guller's End Worcs 99 D7
Gulling Green Suffolk 124 F6
Gully W Yorks 196 F6
Gulpher Suffolk 108 D6
Gulval Cornw'l 1 C5

Gulworthy Devon 12 G5
Gumfreston Pembs 73 E10
Gumley Leics 136 E3
Gummow's Shop Cornw'l 5 D7
Gun Green Kent 53 G9
Gun Hill E Sussex 37 E9
Gun Hill Warwick 134 F5
Gunby Lincs 175 B7
Gunby Lincs 155 E8
Gundleton Hants 48 G6
Gunn Devon 41 G6
Gunnerby NE Lincs 190 B2
Gunnersbury London 67 D7
Gunnerside N Yorks 223 F8
Gunnerton Northum 241 B10
Gunness N Lincs 199 E10
Gunnislake Cornw'l 12 G4
Gunnista Shetl'd 315 J7
Guns Village W Midlands 133 E9
Gunthorpe Norfolk 159 C10
Gunthorpe N Lincs 188 B4
Gunthorpe Notts 171 G11
Gunthorpe Peterbro 138 C3
Gunthorpe Rutl'd 137 B7
Gunton Suffolk 143 D10
Gunville I/Wight 20 D5
Gunwalloe Cornw'l 2 E5
Gunwalloe Fishing Cove Cornw'l 2 E5
Gupworthy Som'set 42 G3
Gurnard I/Wight 20 B5
Gurnett Ches 184 G6
Gurney Slade Som'set 44 D6
Gurney Street Som'set 43 F10
Gurnos Merth Tyd 77 D8
Gurnos Powys 76 D3
Gushmere Kent 54 B5
Gussage All Saints Dorset 31 E8
Gussage St. Andrew Dorset 31 E7
Gussage St. Michael Dorset 31 E7
Guston Kent 55 E10
Gutcher Shetl'd 314 D7
Guthram Gowt Lincs 156 E3
Guthrie Angus 287 B9
Guyhirn Cambs 139 C8
Guyhirn Gull Cambs 139 C7
Guy's Marsh Dorset 30 C4
Guyzance Northum 252 C6
Gwaelod-y-garth Rh Cyn Taff 58 C6
Gwaenysgor Flints 181 E9
Gwaithla Powys 114 F4
Gwalchmai Angl 178 F5
Gwar-cwm Ceredig'n 128 E3
Gwarn-Leisian Neath P Talb 76 C2
Gwarthlow Shrops 130 D4
Gwastad Pembs 91 G10
Gwastadgoed Gwyn 128 A1
Gwastadnant Gwyn 163 D10
Gwaun Leisian Carms 76 C2
Gwaun Meisgyn Rh Cyn Taff 58 C5
Gwaun-Cae-Gurwen Neath P Talb 76 C2
Gwbert Ceredig'n 92 B3
Gweek Cornw'l 2 D6
Gwehelog Monmouths 78 E5
Gweithdy Angl 179 F8
Gwenddwr Powys 95 C11
Gwennap Cornw'l 4 G4
Gwent Bl Gwent 78 E2
Gwenter Cornw'l 2 F6
Gwernaffel Powys 114 C5
Gwernaffield Flints 166 C2
Gwernau Caerph 77 G11
Gwerneirin Powys 129 F10
Gwerneirin Powys 130 G3
Gwernesney Monmouths 78 E6
Gwern-Estyn Flints 166 D4
Gwernogle Carms 93 E10
Gwernymynydd Flints 166 C2
Gwern-y-Steeple V/Glam 58 D5
Gwersyllt Wrex 166 E4
Gwespyr Flints 181 E10
Gwindra Cornw'l 5 E9
Gwinear Cornw'l 2 B3
Gwithian Cornw'l 2 A3
Gwredog Angl 178 D6
Gwrhay Caerph 77 F11
Gwrhyd Mawr Pembs 90 F5
Gwyddelwern Denbs 165 F9
Gwyddgrug Carms 93 D9
Gwydir Gwyn 162 F5
Gwynfryn Wrex 166 E3
Gwystre Powys 113 D11
Gwytherin Conwy 164 C5
Gyfelia Wrex 166 F4
Gyffin Conwy 180 F3
Gylen Park Arg/Bute 289 G10
Gyre Orkney 313 H4
Gyrn Goch Gwyn 162 F6

H

Habberley Shrops 131 C8
Habberley Worcs 116 B6
Habergham Lancs 204 G2
Habertoft Lincs 175 B8
Habin W Sussex 34 C4
Habrough NE Lincs 200 E6
Haccombe Devon 14 G3
Hacconby Lincs 156 D2
Haceby Lincs 155 B10
Hacheston Suffolk 126 F6
Hackbridge London 67 F9
Hackenthorpe S Yorks 186 E6
Hackford Norfolk 141 C11
Hackforth N Yorks 224 G4
Hackland Orkney 312 F4
Hackleton Northants 120 F6
Hacklinge Kent 55 C10
Hackman's Gate Worcs 117 B7
Hackness N Yorks 227 G9
Hackness Orkney 313 J4
Hackness Som'set 43 D10
Hackney London 67 C10
Hackney Wick London 67 C11
Hackthorn Lincs 189 E7
Hackthorpe Cumb 230 G6
Hackwood Northum 241 E10
Haclait W Isles 297 G4
Hacton London 68 C5
Hadden Scot Borders 263 B7
Haddenham Bucks 84 D2
Haddenham Cambs 123 B9
Haddington E Loth 281 G10
Haddington Lincs 172 C6
Haddiscoe Norfolk 143 D8
Haddoch Aberds 302 E5
Haddon Cambs 138 E2
Haddon Hall Derby 170 B2
Hademore Staffs 134 B3
Haden Cross W Midlands 133 F9
Hadfield Derby 185 B8
Hadham Cross Herts 86 B6
Hadham Ford Herts 105 G8
Hadleigh Essex 69 B10
Hadleigh Suffolk 107 C10
Hadleigh Heath Suffolk 107 C9
Hadley London 86 F2
Hadley Telford 150 G3
Hadley Worcs 117 E7
Hadley Castle Telford 150 G3
Hadley End Staffs 152 E2
Hadley Wood London 86 F3
Hadlow Kent 52 D6
Hadlow Down E Sussex 37 C8
Hadlow Stair Kent 52 D6
Hadnall Shrops 149 E10
Hadspen Som'set 45 G7
Hadstock Essex 105 C11
Hadston Northum 253 D7
Hady Derby 186 G5
Hadzor Worcs 117 E8
Haffenden Quarter Kent 53 E11
Hafod Swan 75 G11
Hafod Dinbych Conwy 164 E5
Hafodrisclawdd Caerph 77 E11
Hafodyrynys Torf 78 F2
Hag Fold Gtr Man 195 G7
Hagg Hill Derby 170 B6
Haggate Gtr Man 196 F2
Haggate Lancs 204 F3
Haggbeck Cumb 239 C11
Haggersta Shetl'd 315 J5
Haggerston London 67 C10
Haggerston Northum 273 G10
Hagget End Cumb 219 C10
Haggington Hill Devon 40 D5
Haggrister Shetl'd 314 F5
Haggs Falk 278 F5
Hagley Heref'd 97 C11
Hagley Worcs 133 G8
Hagmore Green Suffolk 107 D8
Hagnaby Lincs 174 C4
Hagnaby Lincs 191 F7
Hague Bar Derby 185 D7
Hagworthingham Lincs 174 B4
Haigh Gtr Man 194 F6
Haigh S Yorks 197 E9
Haigh Moor W Yorks 197 C9
Haighton Green Lancs 203 G7
Hail Weston Cambs 122 E3
Haile Cumb 219 D10
Hailey Herts 86 C5
Hailey Oxon 64 B6
Hailey Oxon 82 C5
Hailsham E Sussex 23 D9
Haimer H'land 310 C5
Hainault London 87 G7
Haine Kent 71 F11
Haines Hill Som'set 28 C2
Hainford Norfolk 160 F4
Hainton Lincs 189 E11
Hainworth W Yorks 205 F7
Hairmyres S Lanarks 268 E2
Haisthorpe ER Yorks 218 G2
Hakin Pembs 72 D5
Halabezack Cornw'l 2 C6
Halam Notts 171 E11
Halamanning Cornw'l 2 C3
Halbeath Fife 280 D2
Halberton Devon 27 E8
Halcon Som'set 28 B2
Halcro H'land 310 C6
Haldens Herts 86 C2
Hale Cumb 211 D10
Hale Gtr Man 184 D3
Hale Hants 31 D11
Hale Halton 183 E7
Hale Kent 71 F9
Hale Medway 69 F9
Hale Som'set 30 B3
Hale Surrey 49 D10
Hale Bank Halton 183 E7
Hale End London 86 G5
Hale Green E Sussex 37 E9
Hale Mills Cornw'l 4 G5
Hale Nook Lancs 202 E3
Hale Street Kent 53 D7
Halebarns Gtr Man 184 D3
Halehird Cumb 221 E8
Hales Norfolk 143 D7
Hales Staffs 150 C4
Hales Green Derby 169 G11
Hales Park Worcs 116 B5
Hales Place Kent 54 B6
Hales Street Norfolk 142 F3
Halesfield Telford 132 C4
Halesgate Lincs 156 D6
Halesowen W Midlands 133 G9
Halesworth Suffolk 127 B7
Halewood Halton 183 D7
Halford Devon 14 G2
Halford Shrops 131 G8
Halford Warwick 100 B5
Halfpenny Furze Carms 74 C3
Halfpenny Green Staffs 132 E6
Halfway Carms 75 E8
Halfway Carms 94 E2
Halfway Carms 94 E6
Halfway S Yorks 186 E6
Halfway W Berks 64 F2
Halfway Bridge W Sussex 34 C6
Halfway House Shrops 148 G6
Halfway Houses Kent 70 E2
Halfway Houses Lincs 172 C5
Halfway Street Kent 55 D9
Halgabron Cornw'l 11 D7
Halifax W Yorks 196 C5
Halket E Ayrs 267 E8
Halkirk H'land 310 D5
Halkyn Flints 182 G2
Hall E Renf 267 D8
Hall Suffolk 125 G11
Hall Bower W Yorks 196 E6
Hall Common Norfolk 161 F7
Hall Cross Lancs 202 G4
Hall Dunnerdale Cumb 220 F4
Hall End Beds 103 D11
Hall End Beds 103 B9
Hall End Lincs 174 E6
Hall End S Glos 61 B8
Hall End Warwick 134 C5
Hall Green Ches 168 D4
Hall Green Essex 106 D5
Hall Green Lancs 194 C3
Hall Green Lancs 194 F4
Hall Green Norfolk 159 F8
Hall Green S Yorks 197 E10
Hall Green W Midlands 134 G2
Hall Green W Midlands 135 G7
Hall Green Wrex 167 G8
Hall Grove Herts 86 C3
Hall of Clestrain Orkney 313 H3
Hall of Tankerness Orkney 313 H6
Hall Stanton Cumb 220 E2
Hall Waberthwaite Cumb 219 F11
Hallam Fields Derby 171 G7
Halland E Sussex 37 D8
Hallaton Leics 136 D5
Hallatrow Bath/NE Som'set 44 B6
Hallbankgate Cumb 240 F3
Hallbeck Cumb 212 B2
Hallen S Glos 60 C4
Hallew Cornw'l 5 D10
Hallfield Gate Derby 170 D5
Hallgarth Durham 234 C2
Hallglen Falk 279 F7
Hallin H'land 298 D2
Halling Medway 69 G8
Hallingbury Street Essex 87 B8
Hallington Lincs 190 D4
Hallington Northum 241 B11
Halliwell Gtr Man 195 E8
Halloughton Notts 171 E11
Hallow Worcs 116 F6
Hallow Heath Worcs 116 F6
Hallowes Derby 186 F5
Hallrule Scot Borders 262 G3
Halls E Loth 282 G3
Halls Green Essex 86 D6
Hall's Green Herts 104 F5
Hall's Green Kent 52 D4
Hallsands Devon 9 G11
Hallside S Lanarks 268 C3
Hallspill Devon 25 C7
Hallthwaites Cumb 210 B3
Hallwood Green Heref'd 98 E3
Hallwood Park Halton 183 E8
Hallworthy Cornw'l 11 D9
Hallyburton House Perth/Kinr 286 D6
Hallyne Scot Borders 270 G3
Halmer End Staffs 168 F3
Halmond's Frome Heref'd 98 B3
Halmore S Glos 79 E11
Halmyre Mains Scot Borders 270 F3
Halnaker W Sussex 34 F6
Halpenny Cumb 211 B10
Halsall Lancs 193 E11
Halse Northants 101 C11
Halse Som'set 27 B10
Halsetown Cornw'l 2 B2
Halsfordwood Devon 14 C3
Halsham ER Yorks 201 B9
Halstead Essex 106 E6
Halstead Kent 68 G3
Halstead Leics 136 B5
Halstock Dorset 29 F8
Halsway Som'set 42 F6
Haltcliff Bridge Cumb 230 D3
Halterworth Hants 32 C5
Haltham Lincs 174 C2
Haltoft End Lincs 174 F5
Halton Bucks 84 C5
Halton Halton 183 E8
Halton Lancs 211 G10
Halton Northum 241 D11
Halton Wrex 148 B6
Halton W Yorks 206 G2
Halton Brook Halton 183 E8
Halton East N Yorks 204 C6
Halton Fenside Lincs 174 C6
Halton Gill N Yorks 213 D7
Halton Green Lancs 211 F10
Halton Holegate Lincs 174 B6
Halton Moor W Yorks 206 G2
Halton Park Lancs 211 F10
Halton Shields Northum 242 D2
Halton View Halton 183 D8
Halton West N Yorks 204 C2
Halton-Lea-Gate Northum 240 F5
Haltwhistle Northum 240 E6
Halvergate Norfolk 143 B8
Halwell Devon 8 E5
Halwill Devon 12 B4
Halwill Junction Devon 12 B4
Ham Devon 28 G2
Ham Glos 79 F11
Ham Glos 99 G9
Ham H'land 310 B6
Ham Kent 55 C10
Ham London 67 E7
Ham Plym'th 7 D9
Ham Shetl'd 315 K1
Ham Som'set 28 E3
Ham Som'set 27 C11
Ham Som'set 28 B3
Ham Som'set 45 D7
Ham Som'set 43 C10
Ham Wilts 63 G10
Ham Common Dorset 30 B4
Ham Green Bristol 60 D4
Ham Green Hants 48 G2
Ham Green Kent 38 B5
Ham Green Kent 69 F10
Ham Green Worcs 117 E10
Ham Hill Medway 69 G8
Ham Street Som'set 44 G5
Hamar Shetl'd 314 F5
Hamarhill Orkney 312 E6
Hamars Shetl'd 315 G6
Hambleden Bucks 65 B9
Hambledon Hants 33 D10
Hambledon Surrey 50 F3
Hamble-le-Rice Hants 33 F7
Hambleton Lancs 202 E3
Hambleton N Yorks 207 G7
Hambleton Moss Side Lancs 202 E3
Hambridge Som'set 28 C5
Hambrook S Glos 60 D6
Hambrook W Sussex 34 F3
Hameringham Lincs 174 B4
Hamerton Cambs 122 B2
Hametoun Shetl'd 315 K1
Hamilton Leics C 136 B2
Hamilton S Lanarks 268 D4
Hamilton Park Racecourse S Lanarks 268 D4
Hamister Shetl'd 315 G7
Hamlet Dorset 29 F9
Hamlet of Shell Ness Kent 70 F5
Hammer W Sussex 49 G11
Hammer Bottom Hants 49 G11
Hammerpot W Sussex 35 F9
Hammersmith Derby 170 E5
Hammersmith London 67 D8
Hammerwich Staffs 133 B11
Hammerwood E Sussex 52 F2
Hammill Kent 55 B9
Hammond Street Herts 86 E4
Hammond's Green Hants 32 E4
Hammoon Dorset 30 E4
Hamnavoe Shetl'd 314 E4
Hamnavoe Shetl'd 314 E6
Hamnavoe Shetl'd 314 F6
Hamnavoe Shetl'd 315 K5
Hamnish Clifford Heref'd 115 F10
Hamp Som'set 43 F10
Hampden National Stadium Glasg C 267 C11
Hampden Park E Sussex 23 E10
Hamperden End Essex 105 E11
Hampnett Glos 81 B10
Hampole S Yorks 198 E4
Hampreston Dorset 19 B7
Hampsfield Cumb 211 C8
Hampson Green Lancs 202 C5
Hampstead London 67 B9
Hampstead Garden Suburb London 67 B9
Hampstead Norreys W Berks 64 D4
Hampsthwaite N Yorks 205 B11
Hampt Cornw'l 12 G3
Hampton Devon 15 B11
Hampton Kent 71 F7
Hampton London 66 F6
Hampton Shrops 132 F4
Hampton Swindon 81 G11
Hampton Worcs 99 C10
Hampton Bishop Heref'd 97 D11
Hampton Court Palace, Teddington London 67 F7
Hampton Fields Glos 80 F5
Hampton Gay Oxon 83 B7
Hampton Green Ches 167 F8
Hampton Heath Ches 167 F8
Hampton Hill London 66 E6
Hampton in Arden W Midlands 134 G4
Hampton Loade Shrops 132 F5
Hampton Lovett Worcs 117 D7
Hampton Lucy Warwick 118 F5
Hampton Magna Warwick 118 D5
Hampton on the Hill Warwick 118 E5
Hampton Park S'thampton 32 D6
Hampton Park Wilts 47 G7
Hampton Poyle Oxon 83 B8
Hampton Wick London 67 F7
Hamptons Kent 52 C6
Hamptworth Wilts 32 D2
Hamrow Norfolk 159 E8
Hams Som'set 28 D6
Hamsey E Sussex 36 E6
Hamsey Green Surrey 51 B11
Hamshill Glos 80 E3
Hamstall Ridware Staffs 152 F2
Hamstead W Midlands 133 E10
Hamstead Marshall W Berks 64 F2
Hamsterley Durham 233 E8
Hamsterley Durham 242 F4
Hamsterley Mill Durham 242 F4
Hamstreet Kent 54 G4
Hamwood N Som'set 43 B11
Hamworthy Poole 18 C5
Hanbury Staffs 152 D3
Hanbury Worcs 117 E9
Hanbury Woodend Staffs 152 D3
Hanby Lincs 155 C10
Hanchet End Suffolk 106 B3
Hanchurch Staffs 168 G4
Hand and Pen Devon 14 B6
Hand Green Ches 167 C8
Handale Redcar/Clevel'd 226 B4
Handbridge Ches 166 B6
Handcross W Sussex 36 B3
Handforth Ches 184 E5
Handley Ches 167 D7
Handley Derby 170 C5
Handley Green Essex 87 E11
Handsacre Staffs 151 F11
Handside Herts 86 C2
Handsworth S Yorks 186 D6
Handsworth W Midlands 133 E10
Handy Cross Bucks 84 G4
Handy Cross Devon 24 B6
Hanford Dorset 30 E4
Hanford Stoke 168 G5
Hangersley Hants 31 F11
Hanging Bank Kent 52 C3
Hanging Heaton W Yorks 197 C9
Hanging Houghton Northants 120 C5
Hanging Langford Wilts 46 F4
Hangleton Brighton/Hove 36 F3
Hangleton W Sussex 35 G9
Hanham S Glos 60 E6
Hanham Green S Glos 60 E6
Hankelow Ches 167 F11
Hankerton Wilts 81 G7
Hankham E Sussex 23 D10
Hanley Stoke 168 F5
Hanley Castle Worcs 98 C6
Hanley Child Worcs 116 D3
Hanley Swan Worcs 98 C6
Hanley William Worcs 116 D3
Hanlith N Yorks 213 G8
Hanmer Wrex 149 B9
Hannaford Devon 25 B10
Hannafore Cornw'l 6 E5
Hannah Lincs 191 F8
Hanningfields Green Suffolk 125 G7
Hannington Hants 48 B4
Hannington Northants 120 C6
Hannington Swindon 81 G11
Hannington Wick Swindon 81 F11
Hanscombe End Beds 104 D2
Hansel Village S Ayrs 257 C9
Hanslope M/Keynes 102 B6
Hanthorpe Lincs 155 E11
Hanwell London 67 C7
Hanwell Oxon 101 C8
Hanwood Shrops 131 B8
Hanwood Bank Shrops 149 G9
Hanworth London 66 E6
Hanworth Norfolk 160 B3
Happendon S Lanarks 259 C9
Happisburgh Norfolk 161 C7
Happisburgh Common Norfolk 161 D7
Hapsford Ches 183 G7
Hapton Lancs 203 G11
Hapton Norfolk 142 D3
Harberton Devon 8 D5
Harbertonford Devon 8 D5
Harbledown Kent 54 B6
Harborne W Midlands 133 G10
Harborough Magna Warwick 119 B9
Harborough Parva Warwick 119 B9
Harbottle Northum 251 C10
Harbour Park, Littlehampton W Sussex 35 G8
Harbourland Kent 53 B9
Harbourneford Devon 8 C4
Harbours Hill Worcs 117 D9
Harbridge Hants 31 E10
Harbridge Green Hants 31 E10
Harburn W Loth 269 C10
Harbury Warwick 119 F7
Harby Leics 154 C4
Harby Notts 188 G5
Harcombe Devon 14 E3
Harcombe Devon 15 C9
Harcombe Bottom Devon 16 B2
Harcourt Cornw'l 3 B8
Hardbreck Orkney 313 H5
Harden W Midlands 133 C10
Harden W Yorks 205 F7
Harden Park Ches 184 G4
Hardendale Cumb 221 C11
Hardengreen Midloth 270 B6
Hardenhuish Wilts 62 E2
Hardgate Aberds 293 C9
Hardgate Dumf/Gal 237 C10
Hardgate N Yorks 214 G5
Hardgate W Dunb 277 G10
Hardham W Sussex 35 D8
Hardhorn Lancs 202 F3
Hardingham Norfolk 141 C10
Hardings Booth Staffs 169 C9
Hardings Wood Ches 168 E4
Hardingstone Northants 120 F5
Hardington Som'set 45 C8
Hardington Mandeville Som'set 29 E8
Hardington Marsh Som'set 29 F8
Hardington Moor Som'set 29 E8
Hardley Hants 32 G6
Hardley Street Norfolk 143 C7
Hardmead M/Keynes 103 B8
Hardraw N Yorks 223 G7
Hardstoft Derby 170 C6
Hardstoft Common Derby 170 C6
Hardway Portsm'th 33 G10
Hardway Som'set 45 G8
Hardwick Bucks 84 B4
Hardwick Cambs 123 F7
Hardwick Cambs 122 D3
Hardwick Lincs 188 F5
Hardwick Norfolk 142 E4
Hardwick Norfolk 158 F2
Hardwick Northants 121 D7
Hardwick Oxon 82 E5
Hardwick Oxon 101 C8
Hardwick Oxon 101 F11
Hardwick Stockton 234 G4
Hardwick S Yorks 187 D7
Hardwick W Midlands 133 D11
Hardwick Green Worcs 98 E6
Hardwick Hall Derby 171 C7
Hardwick Village Notts 187 G10
Hardwicke Glos 80 C3
Hardwicke Glos 99 F8
Hardwicke Heref'd 96 C5
Hardy's Green Essex 107 G9
Hare Green Essex 107 G11
Hare Hatch Wokingham 65 D10
Hare Street Essex 86 D6
Hare Street Herts 105 F7
Hareby Lincs 174 B4
Harecroft W Yorks 205 F7
Harefield London 85 G9
Harefield S'thampton 33 E7
Haregate Staffs 169 D7
Harehill Derby 152 B3
Harehills W Yorks 206 G2
Harelaw Durham 242 G5
Hareleeshill S Lanarks 268 E5
Hareplain Kent 53 F10
Hare's Down Devon 14 C3
Harescugh Cumb 231 C8
Harescombe Glos 80 C4
Haresfield Glos 80 C4
Haresfinch Mersey 183 B8
Hareshaw N Lanarks 268 C6
Harestanes E Dunb 278 G3
Harestock Hants 48 G3
Harewood Windsor 66 F3
Harewood W Yorks 206 E2
Harewood End Heref'd 97 F10
Harewood House, Wetherby W Yorks 206 E2
Harford Carms 94 C2
Harford Devon 8 D2
Hargate Norfolk 142 E2
Hargatewall Derby 185 F10
Hargrave Ches 167 C7
Hargrave Northants 121 C10
Hargrave Suffolk 124 F5
Harker Cumb 239 E9
Harker Marsh Cumb 229 E7
Harkland Shetl'd 314 E6
Harknett's Gate Essex 86 D6
Harkstead Suffolk 108 D3
Harlaston Staffs 152 G4
Harlaw Ho. Aberds 303 G7
Harlaxton Lincs 155 C7
Harle Syke Lancs 204 F3
Harlech Gwyn 145 C11
Harlech Castle Gwyn 145 C11
Harlequin Notts 154 B3
Harlescott Shrops 149 F10
Harlesden London 67 C8
Harlesthorpe Derby 187 F7
Harleston Devon 8 F5
Harleston Norfolk 142 G4
Harleston Suffolk 125 E10
Harleston Common Norfolk 142 G4
Harlestone Northants 120 E4
Harley Shrops 131 C11
Harley S Yorks 186 B5
Harley Shute E Sussex 38 F3
Harleywood Glos 80 F4
Harling Road Norfolk 141 F9
Harlington Beds 103 E10
Harlington London 66 D5
Harlington S Yorks 198 G3
Harlington Woodend Beds 103 E10
Harlosh H'land 298 E2
Harlow Essex 87 C7
Harlow Carr RHS Garden, Harrogate N Yorks 205 C11
Harlow Green Tyne/Wear 243 F7
Harlow Hill Northum 242 D3
Harlow Hill N Yorks 205 C11
Harlthorpe ER Yorks 207 F10
Harlton Cambs 123 G7
Harlyn Cornw'l 10 F3
Harman's Corner Kent 69 G11
Harman's Cross Dorset 18 E5
Harmans Water Brackn'l 65 F11
Harmby N Yorks 214 B2
Harmer Green Herts 86 B3
Harmer Hill Shrops 149 E9
Harmondsworth London 66 D5
Harmston Lincs 173 C7
Harnage Shrops 131 C11
Harnham Northum 252 G3
Harnham Wilts 31 B10
Harnhill Glos 81 E9
Harold Hill London 87 G8
Harold Park London 87 G9
Harold Wood London 87 G9
Haroldston West Pembs 72 B5
Haroldswick Shetl'd 314 B8
Harome N Yorks 216 C2
Harpenden Herts 85 C10
Harper Green Gtr Man 195 F8
Harperley Durham 242 G5
Harper's Hill Devon 8 C5
Harpford Devon 15 C7
Harpham ER Yorks 217 G11
Harpley Norfolk 158 D5
Harpley Worcs 116 E3
Harpole Northants 120 E3
Harpsdale H'land 310 D5
Harpsden Oxon 65 C9
Harpsden Bottom Oxon 65 C8
Harpswell Lincs 188 D6
Harpur Hill Derby 185 G9
Harpurhey Gtr Man 195 G11
Harraby Cumb 239 G10
Harracott Devon 25 B9
Harrapool H'land 295 C8
Harras Cumb 219 B9
Harraton Tyne/Wear 243 G7
Harrier Shetl'd 315 J1
Harrietfield Perth/Kinr 286 E3
Harrietsham Kent 53 C11
Harringay London 67 B10
Harrington Cumb 228 F5
Harrington Lincs 190 G5
Harrington Northants 120 B5
Harringworth Northants 137 D8
Harris H'land 294 F5
Harris Green Norfolk 142 F4
Harris Museum, Preston Lancs 194 B4
Harriseahead Staffs 168 D5
Harriston Cumb 229 C9
Harrogate N Yorks 206 B2
Harrold Beds 121 F8
Harrop Dale Gtr Man 196 F4
Harrow H'land 310 B6
Harrow London 66 B6
Harrow Green Suffolk 125 G7
Harrow Hill Glos 79 B10
Harrow on the Hill London 67 B7
Harrow Weald London 85 G10
Harrowbarrow Cornw'l 7 B7
Harrowbeer Devon 7 B10
Harrowden Beds 103 B11
Harrowgate Hill D'lington 224 B5
Harrowgate Village D'lington 224 B5
Harry Stoke S Glos 60 D6
Harsley Castle N Yorks 225 F8
Harston Cambs 123 G8
Harston Leics 154 C6
Harswell ER Yorks 208 E2
Hart Hartlep'l 234 E5
Hart Common Gtr Man 194 G6
Hart Hill Luton 104 G2
Hart Station Hartlep'l 234 D5
Hartbarrow Cumb 221 G8
Hartbarrow Cumb 221 G8
Hartburn Northum 252 F3
Hartburn Stockton 225 B8
Hartcliffe Bristol 60 F5
Hartest Suffolk 124 G6
Hartest Hill Suffolk 124 G6
Hartfield E Sussex 52 F3
Hartfield H'land 299 E7
Hartford Cambs 122 C4
Hartford Ches 183 G10
Hartford Som'set 27 B7
Hartford End Essex 87 B11
Hartfordbeach Ches 183 G10
Hartfordbridge Hants 49 B9
Hartforth N Yorks 224 D3
Hartgrove Dorset 30 D4
Harthill Ches 167 D8
Harthill Derby 185 D8
Harthill N Lanarks 269 C8
Harthill S Yorks 187 E7
Hartington Derby 169 C10
Hartland Devon 24 C3
Hartland Quay Devon 24 C2
Hartlands Hill Glos 80 B3
Hartle Worcs 117 B8
Hartlebury Worcs 116 C6
Hartlepool Hartlep'l 234 E6
Hartlepool's Maritime Experience Hartlep'l 234 E6
Hartley Cumb 222 D5
Hartley Kent 53 G9
Hartley Kent 68 F6
Hartley Northum 243 B8
Hartley Plym'th 7 D9
Hartley W Yorks 196 B2
Hartley Green Kent 68 F5
Hartley Green Staffs 151 D9
Hartley Mauditt Hants 49 F8
Hartley Wespall Hants 49 B8
Hartley Wintney Hants 49 B9
Hartlington N Yorks 213 G10
Hartlip Kent 69 G10
Hartlip Hill Kent 69 G10
Hartmount H'land 301 B7
Hartoft End N Yorks 226 G4
Harton N Yorks 216 G4
Harton Shrops 131 F9
Harton Tyne/Wear 243 E9
Hartpury Glos 98 G6
Hart's Green Suffolk 125 F7
Hartshead W Yorks 197 C7
Hartshead Green Gtr Man 196 G3
Hartshill Warwick 134 E6
Hartsholme Lincs 172 B6
Hartshorne Derby 152 E6
Hartsop Cumb 221 C8
Hartswell Som'set 27 B9
Hartwell Northants 120 G5
Hartwith N Yorks 214 G4
Hartwood Lancs 194 D5
Hartwood N Lanarks 269 D7
Harvel Kent 68 G6
Harvieston Stirl 277 D11
Harvington Worcs 99 B11
Harvington Worcs 117 C7
Harwell Notts 187 B10
Harwell Oxon 64 B3
Harwich Essex 108 E5
Harwood Durham 232 E2
Harwood Gtr Man 195 E8
Harwood Northum 251 E11
Harwood Dale N Yorks 227 F9
Harwood Lee Gtr Man 195 E8
Harworth Notts 187 B10
Hasbury W Midlands 133 G9
Hascombe Surrey 50 E3
Haselbech Northants 120 B4
Haselbury Plucknett Som'set 29 E7
Haseley Warwick 118 D4
Haseley Green Warwick 118 D4
Haseley Knob Warwick 118 C4
Haselor Warwick 118 F2
Hasendean Scot Borders 262 E2
Hasfield Glos 98 F6
Hasguard Pembs 72 D5
Hasguard Cross Pembs 72 C4
Haskayne Lancs 193 F11
Hasketon Suffolk 126 G5
Hasland Derby 170 B5
Hasland Green Derby 170 B5
Haslemere Surrey 49 G11
Haslesten Suffolk 125 E10
Haslingden Lancs 195 C9
Haslingden Grane Lancs 195 C9
Haslingfield Cambs 123 G8
Haslington Ches 168 D2
Hasluck's Green W Midlands 118 B2
Hassal Ches 168 D3
Hassal Green Ches 168 D3
Hassell Street Kent 54 D5
Hassingham Norfolk 143 B7
Hassocks W Sussex 36 D4
Hassop Derby 186 G2
Haster H'land 310 D7
Hasthorpe Lincs 175 B7
Hastigrow H'land 310 C6
Hasting Hill Tyne/Wear 243 G9
Hastingleigh Kent 54 E5
Hastings E Sussex 38 F4
Hastings Som'set 28 D4
Hastings Castle E Sussex 38 F4
Hastings Sea Life Centre E Sussex 38 F4
Hastingwood Essex 87 D7
Hastoe Herts 84 D6
Haswell Durham 234 C3
Haswell Moor Durham 234 C3
Haswell Plough Durham 234 C3
Hatch Beds 104 B3
Hatch Hants 49 C7
Hatch Beauchamp Som'set 28 C4
Hatch Bottom Hants 33 D7
Hatch End Beds 121 E11
Hatch End London 85 G10
Hatch Green Som'set 28 D4
Hatch Warren Hants 48 D6
Hatchet Gate Hants 32 G5
Hatchet Green Hants 31 D11
Hatching Green Herts 85 C10
Hatchmere Ches 183 G9
Hatcliffe NE Lincs 201 G8
Hatfield Heref'd 115 F11
Hatfield Herts 86 D2
Hatfield S Yorks 199 E7
Hatfield Worcs 117 G7
Hatfield Broad Oak Essex 87 B8
Hatfield Garden Village Herts 86 D2
Hatfield Heath Essex 87 C8
Hatfield House Herts 86 D2
Hatfield Hyde Herts 86 C2
Hatfield Peverel Essex 88 C3
Hatfield Woodhouse S Yorks 199 F7
Hatford Oxon 82 G4
Hatherden Hants 47 C10
Hatherleigh Devon 25 G8
Hatherley Glos 99 G8
Hathern Leics 153 E10
Hatherop Glos 81 D11
Hathersage Derby 186 E2
Hathersage Booths S Yorks 186 E2
Hathershaw Gtr Man 196 G2
Hatherton Ches 167 F11
Hatherton Staffs 151 G9
Hatley St. George Cambs 122 G5
Hatston Orkney 312 G5
Hatt Cornw'l 7 C7
Hatt Hill Hants 32 B4
Hatterseat Aberds 303 G9
Hattersley Gtr Man 185 C7
Hattingley Hants 48 F6
Hatton Aberds 303 F10
Hatton Angus 287 D9
Hatton Derby 152 C4
Hatton Lincs 189 F11
Hatton London 66 D6
Hatton Moray 301 D11
Hatton Shrops 131 E9
Hatton Warwick 118 D4
Hatton Warrington 183 E9
Hatton Castle Aberds 303 E7
Hatton Country World Warwick 118 D4
Hatton Heath Ches 167 C7
Hatton of Fintray Aberds 293 B10
Hattonburn Aberds 293 C9
Hattoncrook Aberds 303 G8
Hattonknowe N Lanarks 268 C4
Haugh E Ayrs 257 D11
Haugh Gtr Man 196 E2
Haugh Lincs 190 F6
Haugh Head Northum 264 D2
Haugh of Glass Moray 302 F4
Haugh of Kilnmaichlie Moray 301 F11
Haugh of Urr Dumf/Gal 237 C10

Haugham Lincs 190 E4
Haughhead E Dunb 278 F2
Haughland Orkney 312 G6
Haughley Suffolk 125 E10
Haughley Green Suffolk 125 E10
Haughley New Street Suffolk 125 E10
Haughs of Clinterty Aberd C 293 B10
Haughton Notts 187 G11
Haughton Powys 148 F6
Haughton Shrops 149 D7
Haughton Shrops 149 F11
Haughton Shrops 132 B4
Haughton Staffs 151 E7
Haughton Green Gtr Man 184 C6
Haughton Le Skerne D'lington 224 B6
Haughton Moss Ches 167 D9
Haulkerton Aberds 293 F9
Haultwick Herts 104 G6
Haunn Arg/Bute 288 E5
Haunn W Isles 297 K3
Haunton Staffs 152 G5
Hauxton Cambs 123 F8
Havannah Ches 168 C5
Havant Hants 34 F2
Haven Heref'd 115 G8
Haven Bank Lincs 174 E2
Havenside ER Yorks 201 B7
Havenstreet I/Wight 21 C7
Haverbrack Cumb 211 C9
Havercroft N Yorks 197 E11
Haverfordwest = Hwlffordd Pembs 72 B6
Haverhill Suffolk 106 B3
Haverholme Priory Lincs 173 F10
Haverigg Cumb 210 D3
Havering-atte-Bower London 87 G8
Haversham M/Keynes 102 C6
Haverthwaite Cumb 210 C6
Haverton Hill Stockton 234 G5
Haviker Street Kent 53 D8
Havyatt Som'set 44 F4
Havyatt Green N Som'set 60 G3
Hawarden = Penarlâg Flints 166 B4
Hawbridge Worcs 99 B8
Hawbush Green Essex 106 G5
Hawcoat Cumb 210 E4
Hawen Ceredig'n 92 B6
Hawes N Yorks 213 B7
Hawe's Green Norfolk 142 D4
Hawes Side Blackp'l 202 G2
Hawford Worcs 116 E6
Hawick Scot Borders 262 F2
Hawk Green Gtr Man 185 D7
Hawkchurch Devon 28 G4
Hawkcombe Som'set 41 D11
Hawkedon Suffolk 124 G6
Hawkenbury Kent 53 E10
Hawkenbury Kent 52 F6
Hawkeridge Wilts 45 C11
Hawkerland Devon 15 D7
Hawkes End W Midlands 134 G5
Hawkesbury S Glos 61 B9
Hawkesbury Warwick 135 G7
Hawkesbury Common S Glos 61 B9
Hawkesbury Upton S Glos 61 B9
Hawkhill N Ayrs 266 G5
Hawkhill Northum 264 G6
Hawkhurst Kent 53 G9
Hawkinge Kent 55 E8
Hawkley Gtr Man 194 G5
Hawkley Hants 34 B2
Hawkridge Som'set 41 G11
Hawks Green Staffs 151 G9
Hawks Hill Bucks 66 B2
Hawksdale Cumb 230 B3
Hawkshaw Gtr Man 195 E9
Hawkshead Cumb 220 F6
Hawkshead Hill Cumb 220 F6
Hawkshill Down Kent 55 D11
Hawksland S Lanarks 269 G6
Hawkspur Green Essex 106 E3
Hawkswick N Yorks 213 E9
Hawkswick Cote N Yorks 213 E8
Hawksworth Notts 172 G3
Hawksworth W Yorks 205 E9
Hawksworth W Yorks 205 F11
Hawkwell Essex 88 G5
Hawkwell Northum 242 C3
Hawley Hants 49 B11
Hawley Kent 68 E4
Hawley's Corner London 52 B2
Hawling Glos 99 G11
Hawn Orkney 312 F5
Hawnby N Yorks 215 B10
Haworth W Yorks 204 F6
Haws Bank Cumb 220 F6
Hawsker Bottoms N Yorks 227 D8
Hawstead Suffolk 125 F7
Hawstead Green Suffolk 125 F7
Hawthorn Durham 234 B4
Hawthorn Hants 49 G7
Hawthorn Rh Cyn Taff 58 B5
Hawthorn Wilts 61 F10
Hawthorn Corner Kent 71 F8
Hawthorn Hill Brackn'l 65 E11
Hawthorn Hill Lincs 174 D2
Hawthorpe Lincs 155 D10
Hawton Notts 172 E3
Haxby C/York 207 B8
Haxby Gates C/York 207 B8
Haxey N Lincs 188 B3
Haxey Turbary N Lincs 199 G9
Haxted Surrey 52 D2
Haxton Wilts 47 D6
Hay Green Essex 87 E10
Hay Green Herts 104 D6
Hay Green Norfolk 157 F10
Hay Mills W Midlands 134 G2
Hay on Wye = Y Gelli Gandryll Powys 96 C4
Hay Street Herts 105 F7
Haybridge Shrops 116 C2
Haybridge Som'set 44 D4
Haybridge Telford 150 G3
Hayden Glos 99 G8
Haydock Mersey 183 B9
Haydock Park Racecourse Mersey 183 B9
Haydon Bath/NE Som'set 45 C7
Haydon Dorset 29 D11
Haydon Devon 26 D6
Haydon Som'set 28 C3
Haydon Swindon 62 B6
Haydon Bridge Northum 241 E8
Haydon Wick Swindon 62 B6
Haye Cornw'l 12 G2
Hayes London 68 F2
Hayes London 66 C5
Hayes End London 66 C5
Hayes End Som'set 28 D6
Hayes Green Warwick 134 F6
Hayes Knoll Wilts 81 G10
Hayes Town London 66 C6
Hayfield Derby 185 D8
Hayfield Fife 280 C5
Haygate Telford 150 G2
Hayhill E Ayrs 257 F11
Hayhillock Angus 287 C9
Haylands I/Wight 21 C7
Hayle Cornw'l 2 B3
Hayley Green W Midlands 133 G9
Haymoor Bottom Poole 18 C6
Haymoor End Som'set 28 B4
Hayne Devon 26 F5
Hayne Devon 27 D7
Hayne Som'set 28 D2
Haynes Beds 103 C11
Haynes Church End Beds 103 C11
Haynes West End Beds 103 C11
Hayscastle Pembs 91 F7
Hayscastle Cross Pembs 91 F8
Haysden Kent 52 D5
Haysford Pembs 91 G8
Hayshead Angus 287 C10
Hayston E Dunb 278 G2
Haythorn Dorset 31 F8
Hayton Aberd C 293 C11
Hayton Cumb 229 C8
Hayton Cumb 240 F2
Hayton ER Yorks 208 D2
Hayton Notts 188 E2
Hayton's Bent Shrops 131 G10
Haytor Vale Devon 13 F11
Haytown Devon 24 E5
Haywards Heath W Sussex 36 C4
Haywood S Lanarks 269 E9
Haywood S Yorks 186 B3
Haywood S Yorks 198 E5
Hazard's Green E Sussex 37 E11
Hazel Grove Gtr Man 184 D6
Hazel Head Cumb 220 G3
Hazel Street Kent 53 F7
Hazel Stub Suffolk 106 B3
Hazelbank S Lanarks 268 F6
Hazelbeach Pembs 73 E6
Hazelbury Bryan Dorset 30 F2
Hazeleigh Essex 88 E4
Hazeley Hants 49 B8
Hazeley Heath Hants 49 B9
Hazelford Ferry Notts 172 F2
Hazelgrove Notts 171 F8
Hazelhead S Yorks 197 G7
Hazelhurst Gtr Man 195 G10
Hazelhurst Gtr Man 195 D9
Hazelhurst Gtr Man 196 G3
Hazelmere Bucks 84 G5
Hazelslack Cumb 211 D9
Hazelslade Staffs 151 G10
Hazelton Walls Fife 287 E7
Hazelwood Derby 170 F4
Hazelwood Devon 8 E4
Hazelwood London 68 G2
Hazler Shrops 131 E9
Hazlerigg Tyne/Wear 242 C6
Hazleton Glos 81 B9
Hazlewood N Yorks 205 C7
Heacham Norfolk 158 B3
Head of Muir Falk 278 E6
Headbourne Worthy Hants 48 G3
Headcorn Kent 53 E10
Headham Durham 224 B3
Headingley W Yorks 205 F11
Headington Oxon 83 D8
Headington Hill Oxon 83 D8
Headless Cross Worcs 117 D10
Headley Hants 49 F10
Headley Hants 64 G4
Headley Surrey 51 C8
Headley Down Hants 49 F10
Headley Heath Worcs 117 B11
Headley Park Bristol 60 F5
Headon Devon 24 G5
Headon Notts 188 F2
Heads S Lanarks 268 F4
Heads Nook Cumb 239 F11
Headstone London 66 B6
Headwell Fife 279 D11
Heady Hill Gtr Man 195 E10
Heage Derby 170 E5
Healaugh N Yorks 206 D5
Healaugh N Yorks 223 F10
Heald Green Gtr Man 184 D5
Healds Green Gtr Man 195 F11
Heale Devon 40 D6
Heale Som'set 28 B5
Heale Som'set 45 E7
Healey Lancs 195 D11
Healey Northum 242 F3
Healey N Yorks 214 C3
Healey W Yorks 197 D9
Healey W Yorks 197 C8
Healeyfield Durham 233 B7
Healing NE Lincs 201 E8
Heamoor Cornw'l 1 C5
Heaning Cumb 221 F8
Heanish Arg/Bute 288 E2
Heanor Derby 170 F6
Heanor Gate Derby 170 F6
Heap Bridge Gtr Man 195 E10
Heapham Lincs 188 D5
Hearn Hants 49 F10
Hearnden Green Kent 53 D10
Hearthstane Scot Borders 260 D4
Hearts Delight Kent 69 G11
Heasley Mill Devon 41 G8
Heast H'land 295 D8
Heath Card 59 D7
Heath Derby 170 B6
Heath W Yorks 197 C11
Heath and Reach Beds 103 F8
Heath Charnock Lancs 194 E5
Heath Common Devon 28 G3
Heath Common W Sussex 35 E10
Heath Cross Devon 13 B10
Heath End Bucks 84 F5
Heath End Bucks 85 D7
Heath End Hants 64 G2
Heath End Hants 64 G5
Heath End Leics 153 E7
Heath End S Glos 61 B7
Heath End Surrey 49 D10
Heath End Warwick 118 E4
Heath End W Midlands 133 C10
Heath End W Sussex 35 D7
Heath Green Hants 48 F6
Heath Green Worcs 117 C11
Heath Hayes Staffs 151 G10
Heath Hill Shrops 150 G5
Heath House Som'set 44 D2
Heath Park London 68 B4
Heath Town W Midlands 133 D8
Heathbrook Shrops 150 D2
Heathcot Aberds 293 C10
Heathcote Derby 169 C10
Heathcote Warwick 118 E6
Heathencote Northants 102 B4
Heather Leics 153 G7
Heather Row Hants 49 C8
Heatherfield H'land 298 E4
Heatherside Surrey 50 B2
Heatherwood Park H'land 311 K2
Heatherybanks Aberds 303 E7
Heathfield Devon 14 F2
Heathfield E Sussex 37 C9
Heathfield N Yorks 214 F2
Heathfield S Ayrs 257 E9
Heathfield Som'set 27 B11
Heathhall Dumf/Gal 237 B11
Heathlands Wokingham 65 F10
Heathrow Airport London 66 D5
Heathstock Devon 28 G2
Heathton Shrops 132 E6
Heathtop Derby 152 C4
Heathwaite Cumb 221 F8
Heathy Brow E Sussex 36 G6
Heatley Ches 184 D2
Heatley Staffs 151 D11
Heaton Gtr Man 195 F8
Heaton Lancs 211 G8
Heaton Staffs 169 C7
Heaton Tyne/Wear 243 D7
Heaton W Yorks 205 F8
Heaton Chapel Gtr Man 184 C5
Heaton Mersey Gtr Man 184 C5
Heaton Moor Gtr Man 184 C5
Heaton Norris Gtr Man 184 C5
Heaton Punchardon Devon 40 F4
Heaton's Bridge Lancs 194 E2
Heaverham Kent 52 B5
Heaviley Gtr Man 184 D6
Heavitree Devon 14 C4
Hebburn Tyne/Wear 243 E8
Hebburn Colliery Tyne/Wear 243 D8
Hebburn Hall Ponds Tyne/Wear 243 E8
Hebburn New Town Tyne/Wear 243 E8
Hebden N Yorks 213 G10
Hebden Bridge W Yorks 196 B3
Hebden Green Ches 167 B10
Hebing End Herts 104 G6
Hebron Carms 92 F3
Hebron Angl 179 E7
Hebron Northum 252 F5
Heck Dumf/Gal 248 G3
Heckdyke Notts 188 B3
Heckfield Hants 65 G8
Heckfield Green Suffolk 126 B3
Heckfordbridge Essex 107 G8
Heckingham Norfolk 143 D7
Heckington Lincs 173 G10
Heckmondwike W Yorks 197 C8
Heddington Wilts 62 F4
Heddington Wick Wilts 62 F3
Heddle Orkney 312 G4
Heddon Devon 25 B11
Heddon Oak Som'set 42 F6
Heddon-on-the-Wall Northum 242 D4
Hedenham Norfolk 142 E6
Hedge End Hants 33 E7
Hedgefield Tyne/Wear 242 E5
Hedgerley Bucks 66 B3
Hedgerley Green Bucks 66 B3
Hedging Som'set 28 B4
Hedley on the Hill Northum 242 F3
Hednesford Staffs 151 G9
Hedon ER Yorks 201 B7
Hedsor Bucks 66 B2
Hedworth Tyne/Wear 243 E8
Heelands M/Keynes 102 D6
Heeley S Yorks 186 E5
Heeley City Farm, Sheffield S Yorks 186 D5
Heggle Lane Cumb 230 D3
Heglibister Shetl'd 315 H5
Heighington D'lington 233 G10
Heighington Lincs 173 B8
Heightington Worcs 116 C5
Height End Lancs 195 C9
Heights of Brae H'land 300 C5
Heights of Kinlochewe H'land 299 C10
Heilam H'land 308 C4
Heiton Scot Borders 262 C6
Helbeck Cumb 222 B5
Hele Devon 13 G10
Hele Devon 12 C2
Hele Devon 27 G7
Hele Devon 40 D4
Hele Som'set 27 C10
Hele Torbay 9 B8
Hele Lane Devon 26 E3
Helebridge Cornw'l 24 G2
Helensburgh Arg/Bute 276 E6
Helentongate S Ayrs 257 C9
Helford Cornw'l 3 D7
Helford Passage Cornw'l 3 D7
Helham Green Herts 86 B6
Helhoughton Norfolk 159 D7
Helions Bumpstead Essex 106 C3
Hell Corner W Berks 63 G11
Hellaby S Yorks 187 C9
Helland Cornw'l 11 G7
Helland Som'set 28 C4
Hellandbridge Cornw'l 11 G7
Hellescott Cornw'l 11 D11
Hellesdon Norfolk 160 G4
Hellesveor Cornw'l 2 A2
Hellgill Cumb 222 F5
Hellidon Northants 119 F10
Hellifield N Yorks 204 B3
Hellifield Green N Yorks 204 B3
Hellingly E Sussex 37 E9
Hellington Norfolk 142 C6
Hellington Corner Norfolk 142 C6
Hellister Shetl'd 315 J5
Helm Northum 252 D5
Helmdon Northants 101 C11
Helme W Yorks 196 E5
Helmingham Suffolk 126 F3
Helmington Row Durham 233 D9
Helmsdale H'land 311 H4
Helmshore Lancs 195 C9
Helmsley N Yorks 216 C2
Helperby N Yorks 215 F8
Helperthorpe N Yorks 217 D9
Helpringham Lincs 173 G10
Helpston Peterbro 138 B2
Helsby Ches 183 F7
Helsey Lincs 191 G8
Helston Cornw'l 2 D5
Helston Water Cornw'l 4 G5
Helstone Cornw'l 11 E7
Helton Cumb 230 G6
Helwith N Yorks 223 E11
Helwith Bridge N Yorks 212 F6
Hem Powys 130 C4
Hem Heath Stoke 168 G5
Hemble Hill Redcar/Clevel'd 225 B11
Hemblington Norfolk 160 G6
Hemblington Corner Norfolk 160 G6
Hemel Hempstead Herts 85 D9
Hemerdon Devon 7 D11
Hemingbrough N Yorks 207 G9
Hemingby Lincs 190 F2
Hemingfield S Yorks 197 G11
Hemingford Abbots Cambs 122 C5
Hemingford Grey Cambs 122 C5
Hemingstone Suffolk 126 G2
Hemington Leics 153 D9
Hemington Northants 137 F11
Hemington Som'set 45 C8
Hemley Suffolk 108 C5
Hemlington Middlesbro 225 C10
Hemp Green Suffolk 127 D7
Hempholme ER Yorks 209 C7
Hempnall Norfolk 142 E4
Hempnall Green Norfolk 142 E4
Hempriggs House H'land 310 E7
Hemp's Green Essex 107 F8
Hempstead Essex 106 D2
Hempstead Medway 69 G9
Hempstead Norfolk 160 B2
Hempstead Norfolk 161 D8
Hempsted Glos 80 B4
Hempton Norfolk 159 D8
Hempton Oxon 101 E8
Hempton Wainhill Bucks 84 E3
Hemsby Norfolk 161 F9
Hemsted Kent 54 E6
Hemswell Lincs 188 C6
Hemswell Cliff Lincs 189 D7
Hemsworth Dorset 31 F7
Hemsworth S Yorks 186 E5
Hemsworth W Yorks 198 E2
Hemyock Devon 27 E10
Hen Bentref Llandegfan Angl 179 F9
Henbrook Worcs 117 D8
Henbury Bristol 60 D5
Henbury Ches 184 F5
Henbury Kent 55 E7
Hendomen Powys 130 D4
Hendon London 67 B8
Hendon Tyne/Wear 243 F10
Hendra Cornw'l 10 E6
Hendra Cornw'l 2 B6
Hendra Cornw'l 5 D9
Hendra Croft Cornw'l 4 D5
Hendrabridge Cornw'l 6 B5
Hendre Bridg 58 C2
Hendre Flints 165 B11
Hendre Heref'd 97 G10
Hendre-ddu Conwy 164 B5
Hendreforgan Rh Cyn Taff 58 B3
Hendre-hen Powys 148 G4
Hendy Carms 75 E9
Hendy-Gwyn = Whitland Carms 73 B11
Heneglwys Angl 178 F6
Henfield S Glos 61 D7
Henfield W Sussex 36 D2
Henford Devon 12 C3
Henfords Marsh Wilts 45 E11
Henghurst Kent 54 F3
Hengoed Caerph 77 F11
Hengoed Shrops 148 C5
Hengrave Suffolk 124 D6
Hengrove Bristol 60 F6
Hengrove Park Bristol 60 F5
Henham Essex 105 F10
Heniarth Powys 130 B2
Henlade Som'set 28 C3
Henley Dorset 29 G11
Henley Glos 80 B6
Henley Shrops 131 F9
Henley Suffolk 126 G3
Henley Som'set 28 F6
Henley Som'set 44 G2
Henley Wilts 61 F10
Henley W Sussex 34 B5
Henley Green W Midlands 135 G7
Henley in Arden Warwick 118 D2
Henley Park Surrey 50 C2
Henley Street Kent 69 F7
Henley-on-Thames Oxon 65 C9
Henley's Down E Sussex 38 E2
Henllan Ceredig'n 93 C7
Henllan Denbs 165 B8
Henllan Amgoed Carms 73 B11
Henllys Torf 78 G3
Henllys Vale Torf 78 G3
Henlow Beds 104 D3
Hennock Devon 14 E2
Henny Street Essex 107 D7
Henryd Conwy 180 G3
Henry's Moat Pembs 91 F10
Hensall N Yorks 198 C5
Henshaw Northum 241 E7
Henshaw W Yorks 205 E9
Hensingham Cumb 219 B9
Hensington Oxon 83 B7
Henstead Suffolk 143 F9
Hensting Hants 33 C7
Henstridge Som'set 30 D2
Henstridge Ash Som'set 30 C2
Henstridge Bowden Som'set 29 C11
Henstridge Marsh Som'set 30 C2
Henton Oxon 84 E3
Henton Som'set 44 D3
Henwood Cornw'l 11 G11
Henwood Oxon 83 E7
Henwood Green Kent 52 E6
Henzleaze Bristol 60 D5
Heogan Shetl'd 315 J6
Heol Senni Powys 95 G8
Heolgerrig Merth Tyd 77 D8
Heol-laethog Bridg 58 C2
Heol-las Bridg 58 C2
Heol-y-Cyw Bridg 58 C2
Hepburn Northum 264 E3
Hepple Northum 251 C11
Hepscott Northum 252 G6
Hepthorne Lane Derby 170 C6
Heptonstall W Yorks 196 B3
Hepworth Suffolk 125 C9
Hepworth W Yorks 197 F7
Herbrandston Pembs 72 D5
Hereford Heref'd 97 D10
Hereford Cathedral Heref'd 97 D10
Hereford Racecourse Heref'd 97 C10
Heribusta H'land 298 B4
Heriot Scot Borders 271 E7
Heritage Motor Centre, Gaydon Warwick 119 G7
Hermiston C/Edinb 280 G3
Hermit Hill S Yorks 197 G10
Hermitage Scot Borders 250 D2
Hermitage Dorset 29 F10
Hermitage W Berks 64 E4
Hermitage W Sussex 34 F3
Hermitage Green Warrington 183 C10
Hermon Carms 93 E7
Hermon Carms 94 F3
Hermon Angl 162 B5
Hermon Pembs 92 E4
Herne Kent 71 F7
Herne Bay Kent 71 F7
Herne Common Kent 71 G7
Herne Hill London 67 E10
Herne Pound Kent 53 C7
Hernhill Kent 70 G5
Hernston V/Glam 58 D2
Herodsfoot Cornw'l 6 C4
Heronden Kent 55 C9
Herongate Essex 87 G10
Heron's Ghyll E Sussex 37 B7
Heronsford S Ayrs 244 G4
Heronsgate Herts 85 G8
Herra Shetl'd 314 D8
Herriard Hants 49 D7
Herringfleet Suffolk 143 D9
Herring's Green Beds 103 C11
Herringswell Suffolk 124 D4
Herringthorpe S Yorks 187 C7
Hersden Kent 71 G8
Hersham Cornw'l 24 F3
Hersham Surrey 66 G6
Herstmonceux E Sussex 37 E10
Herston Dorset 18 F6
Herston Orkney 313 J5
Hertford Herts 86 C4
Hertford Heath Herts 86 C4
Hertingfordbury Herts 86 C4
Hesket Newmarket Cumb 230 D2
Hesketh Bank Lancs 194 C2
Hesketh Lane Lancs 203 E8
Heskin Green Lancs 194 D4
Hesleden Durham 234 D4
Heslington C/York 207 C8
Hessay C/York 206 C6
Hessenford Cornw'l 6 D6
Hessett Suffolk 125 E8
Hessilhead N Ayrs 267 E7
Hessle ER Yorks 200 B4
Hessle W Yorks 198 D2
Hest Bank Lancs 211 F9
Hester's Way Glos 99 G8
Hestinsetter Shetl'd 315 J4
Hestley Green Suffolk 126 D3
Heston London 66 D6
Hestwall Orkney 312 G3
Heswall Mersey 182 E3
Hethe Oxon 101 F11
Hethel Norfolk 142 C3
Hethelpit Cross Glos 98 F5
Hethersett Norfolk 142 C2
Hethersgill Cumb 239 D11
Hetherside Cumb 239 D10
Hetherson Green Ches 167 F8
Hethpool Northum 263 D9
Hett Durham 233 D11
Hetton N Yorks 204 B5
Hetton Downs Tyne/Wear 234 B3
Hetton le Hill Tyne/Wear 234 C3
Hetton-le-Hole Tyne/Wear 234 B3
Heugh Northum 242 C3
Heugh-head Aberds 292 B5
Heveningham Suffolk 126 C6
Hever Kent 52 E3
Hever Castle and Gardens Kent 52 D3
Heversham Cumb 211 C9
Hevingham Norfolk 160 E3
Hewas Cornw'l 5 E8
Hewas Water Cornw'l 5 F9
Hewelsfield Glos 79 E9
Hewelsfield Common Glos 79 E8
Hewer Hill Cumb 230 D3
Hewish Som'set 28 F6
Hewood Dorset 28 G5
Heworth C/York 207 C8
Heworth Tyne/Wear 243 E7
Hexham Northum 241 E10
Hexham Abbey Northum 241 E10
Hexham Racecourse Northum 241 E10
Hextable Kent 68 E4
Hexthorpe S Yorks 198 G5
Hexton Herts 104 E2
Hexworthy Devon 13 G9
Hey Gtr Man 196 G3
Hey Lancs 204 E3
Hey Green W Yorks 196 E4
Hey Houses Lancs 193 B10
Heybridge Essex 87 F10
Heybridge Essex 88 D5
Heybridge Basin Essex 88 D5
Heybrook Bay Devon 7 F9
Heydon Cambs 105 D8
Heydon Norfolk 160 D2
Heydour Lincs 155 B10
Heyhead Gtr Man 184 D4
Heyheads Gtr Man 196 G3
Heyhouses Lancs 203 F11
Heylipol Arg/Bute 288 E1
Heylor Shetl'd 314 E4
Heyop Powys 114 C4
Heyrod Gtr Man 185 B7
Heysham Lancs 211 G8
Heyshaw N Yorks 214 G3
Heyshott W Sussex 34 D5
Heyshott Green W Sussex 34 D5
Heyside Gtr Man 196 F2
Heytesbury Wilts 46 E2
Heythrop Oxon 101 F7
Heywood Gtr Man 195 F11
Heywood Wilts 45 C11
Hibaldstow N Lincs 200 G3
Hibb's Green Suffolk 125 G7
Hickford Hill Essex 106 C5
Hickleton S Yorks 198 F3
Hickling Norfolk 161 E8
Hickling Notts 154 D3
Hickling Green Norfolk 161 E8
Hickling Heath Norfolk 161 E8
Hickmans Green Kent 54 B5
Hicks Forstal Kent 71 G7
Hick's Mill Cornw'l 4 G5
Hickstead W Sussex 36 C3
Hidcote Bartrim Glos 100 C3
Hidcote Boyce Glos 100 C3
Hidcote Manor Garden, Moreton-in-Marsh Glos 100 C3
Higford Shrops 132 C5
Higginshaw Gtr Man 196 F2
High Ackworth W Yorks 198 D2
High Angerton Northum 252 F3
High Bankhill Cumb 231 C7
High Banton N Lanarks 278 E5
High Barnes Tyne/Wear 243 F9
High Barnet London 86 F2
High Beach Essex 86 F6
High Beechburn Durham 233 E9
High Bentham N Yorks 212 F3
High Bickington Devon 25 C9
High Biggins Cumb 212 D2
High Blantyre S Lanarks 268 D3
High Bonnybridge Falk 278 F6
High Borrans Cumb 221 E8
High Bradfield S Yorks 186 B3
High Bradley N Yorks 204 D6
High Bray Devon 41 G7
High Brooms Kent 52 E5
High Bullen Devon 25 C8
High Buston Northum 252 B6
High Callerton Northum 242 C5
High Casterton Cumb 212 D2
High Catton ER Yorks 207 C10
High Church Northum 252 F5
High Clarence Stockton 234 G5
High Close N Yorks 224 B3
High Cogges Oxon 82 D5
High Common Norfolk 141 B9
High Common Norfolk 142 G3
High Common Suffolk 143 F7
High Condurrow Cornw'l 2 B5
High Coniscliffe D'lington 224 B4
High Crompton Gtr Man 196 F2
High Crosby Cumb 239 F11
High Cross Cornw'l 2 D6
High Cross Hants 34 B2
High Cross Herts 85 F10
High Cross Herts 86 B5
High Cross Lancs 202 F2
High Cross Leics 135 F9
High Cross Newp 59 B9
High Cross Warwick 118 D3
High Cross W Sussex 36 D3
High Cross Bank Derby 152 F5
High Crosshill S Lanarks 268 C2
High Dubmire Tyne/Wear 234 B2
High Dyke Cumb 230 E5
High Dyke Durham 232 F5
High Easter Essex 87 C10
High Eldrig Dumf/Gal 236 C4
High Ellington N Yorks 214 C3
High Entercommon N Yorks 224 D6
High Ercall Telford 149 F11
High Etherley Durham 233 F9
High Ferry Lincs 174 F4
High Flatts W Yorks 197 F8
High Fremington N Yorks 223 F10
High Friarside Durham 242 F5
High Gallowhill E Dunb 278 G3
High Garrett Essex 106 F5
High Grange Durham 233 E9
High Green Cumb 221 E8
High Green Norfolk 141 B8
High Green Norfolk 142 B2
High Green Shrops 132 G4
High Green Suffolk 125 E7
High Green S Yorks 186 B4
High Green Worcs 99 B7
High Green W Yorks 197 E7
High Halden Kent 53 F11
High Halstow Medway 69 E9
High Ham Som'set 44 G2
High Harrington Cumb 228 F6
High Harrogate N Yorks 206 B2
High Haswell Durham 234 C3
High Hatton Shrops 150 E2
High Hauxley Northum 253 C7
High Hawsker N Yorks 227 D8
High Heath Shrops 150 D3
High Heath W Midlands 133 C10
High Hesket Cumb 230 C5
High Hesleden Durham 234 D5
High Hoyland S Yorks 197 E9
High Hunsley ER Yorks 208 F5
High Hurstwood E Sussex 37 B7
High Hutton N Yorks 216 F5
High Ireby Cumb 229 D10
High Kelling Norfolk 177 E10
High Kilburn N Yorks 215 D10
High Knipe Cumb 221 B10
High Lands Durham 233 F8
High Lane Derby 170 G6
High Lane Gtr Man 185 D7
High Lane Heref'd 116 E3
High Lanes Cornw'l 2 B3
High Laver Essex 87 D8
High Leas Lincs 190 E5
High Legh Ches 184 E2
High Leven Stockton 225 C9
High Littleton Bath/NE Som'set 44 B6
High Longthwaite Cumb 229 B11
High Lorton Cumb 229 F9
High Marishes N Yorks 216 D6
High Marnham Notts 188 G4
High Melton S Yorks 198 G4
High Melwood N Lincs 199 G9
High Mickley Northum 242 E3
High Mindork Dumf/Gal 236 D5
High Moor C/York 206 C6
High Moor Lancs 194 E4
High Moorland Visitor Centre, Princetown Devon 13 G7
High Moorsley Tyne/Wear 234 C2
High Nash Glos 79 C9
High Newport Tyne/Wear 243 G9
High Newton Cumb 211 C9
High Newton-by-the-Sea Northum 264 D6
High Nibthwaite Cumb 210 C4
High Offley Staffs 150 D5
High Ongar Essex 87 E9
High Onn Staffs 150 F6
High Orchard Glos 80 B4
High Park Mersey 193 D11
High Risby N Lincs 200 E2
High Rocks Kent 52 F4
High Roding Essex 87 B10
High Rougham Suffolk 125 E8
High Row Cumb 230 G3
High Row Cumb 230 D3
High Salvington W Sussex 35 F10
High Scales Cumb 229 B9
High Sellafield Cumb 219 E10
High Shaw N Yorks 223 G7
High Shields Tyne/Wear 243 D9
High Shincliffe Durham 234 D2
High Side Cumb 229 E10
High Southwick Tyne/Wear 243 F9
High Spen Tyne/Wear 242 F4
High Stakesby N Yorks 227 C7
High Stittenham N Yorks 216 F3
High Street Cornw'l 5 E9
High Street Kent 53 G8
High Street Suffolk 127 C8
High Street Suffolk 143 G7
High Street Suffolk 127 F8
High Street Suffolk 107 B7
High Street Green Suffolk 125 F10
High Throston Hartlep'l 234 E5
High Tirfergus Arg/Bute 255 F7
High Town Staffs 151 G9
High Toynton Lincs 174 B3
High Urpeth Durham 242 G6
High Valleyfield Fife 279 D10
High Westwood Durham 242 F4
High Whinnow Cumb 239 G8
High Woolaston Glos 79 F9
High Worsall N Yorks 225 D7
High Wray Cumb 221 E7
High Wych Herts 87 C7
High Wycombe Bucks 84 G5
High Yarridge Northum 241 E10
Higham Derby 170 D5
Higham Fife 286 F6
Higham Kent 69 E8
Higham Lancs 204 F2
Higham Suffolk 107 D10
Higham Suffolk 124 D4
Higham S Yorks 197 F10
Higham Common S Yorks 197 F10
Higham Cross M/Keynes 102 B5
Higham Ferrers Northants 121 D9
Higham Gobion Beds 104 E2
Higham Hill London 86 G5
Higham on the Hill Leics 135 D7
Higham Park Northants 121 E9
Higham Wood Kent 52 D6
Highams Park London 86 G5
Highbridge Cumb 230 C3
Highbridge Hants 33 C7
Highbridge H'land 290 E3
Highbridge Som'set 43 D10
Highbrook W Sussex 51 G11
Highburton W Yorks 197 E7
Highbury London 67 B10
Highbury Som'set 45 D7
Highbury Vale Nott'ham 171 G8
Highclere Hants 64 G2
Highcliffe Dorset 19 C10
Highcliffe Northum 273 E10
Higher Alham Som'set 45 E7
Higher Ansty Dorset 30 G3
Higher Ashton Devon 14 E3
Higher Audley Blackb'n 195 B7
Higher Bal Cornw'l 4 E4
Higher Ballam Lancs 202 G3
Higher Bartle Lancs 202 G6
Higher Bebington Mersey 182 D4
Higher Berry End Beds 103 E9
Higher Blackley Gtr Man 195 G10
Higher Boarshaw Gtr Man 195 F11
Higher Bockhampton Dorset 17 C10
Higher Boscaswell Cornw'l 1 C3
Higher Broughton Gtr Man 195 G10
Higher Burrow Som'set 28 C6
Higher Burwardsley Ches 167 D8
Higher Change Lancs 195 C11
Higher Cheriton Devon 27 G10
Higher Chisworth Derby 185 C7
Higher Crackington Cornw'l 11 B9
Higher Croft Blackb'n 195 B7
Higher Denham Bucks 66 B4
Higher Dinting Derby 185 C8
Higher Disley Ches 185 E7
Higher Downs Cornw'l 2 C3
Higher End Gtr Man 194 G4
Higher Folds Gtr Man 195 G7
Higher Gabwell Devon 9 B8
Higher Green Gtr Man 195 G8
Higher Halstock Leigh Dorset 29 F8
Higher Heysham Lancs 211 G8
Higher Holnest Dorset 29 F10
Higher Holton Som'set 29 B11

404 Hig – Hos

Higher Hurdsfield Ches 184 G6
Higher Kingcombe Dorset 29 G8
Higher Kinnerton Flints 166 C4
Higher Marsh Som'set 30 C2
Higher Marston Ches 183 F11
Higher Melcombe Dorset 30 G2
Higher Metcombe Devon 15 C7
Higher Muddiford Devon 40 F5
Higher Northcott Devon 12 C2
Higher Nyland Dorset 30 C2
Higher Penwortham Lancs 194 B4
Higher Porthpean Cornw'l 5 E10
Higher Poynton Ches 184 E6
Higher Priestacott Devon 12 B3
Higher Rocombe Barton Devon 9 B8
Higher Row Dorset 31 G8
Higher Runcorn Halton 183 E8
Higher Sandford Dorset 29 C10
Higher Shotton Flints 166 B4
Higher Shurlach Ches 183 G11
Higher Slade Devon 40 D4
Higher Stanbear Cornw'l 11 G11
Higher Street Som'set 42 E6
Higher Tale Devon 27 G9
Higher Town Cornw'l 5 C10
Higher Town I/Scilly 1 F4
Higher Town Som'set 42 D3
Higher Tremarcoombe Cornw'l 6 B5
Higher Vexford Som'set 42 F6
Higher Walton Lancs 194 B5
Higher Walton Warrington 183 D9
Higher Wambrook Som'set 28 F3
Higher Warcombe Devon 40 D3
Higher Waterston Dorset 17 B10
Higher Whatcombe Dorset 30 G4
Higher Wheelton Lancs 194 C6
Higher Whitley Ches 183 E10
Higher Wincham Ches 183 F11
Higher Woodhill Gtr Man 195 E9
Higher Wraxall Dorset 29 G9
Higher Wych Ches 167 G7
Higherfence Ches 184 G6
Higherford Lancs 204 E3
Highertown Cornw'l 11 E8
Highertown Cornw'l 4 G6
Highfield ER Yorks 207 F10
Highfield Gtr Man 195 F8
Highfield Gtr Man 194 G5
Highfield Herts 85 D9
Highfield N Ayrs 266 E6
Highfield Oxon 101 G11
Highfield S'thampton 32 E6
Highfield Stockton 225 C8
Highfield S Yorks 186 D5
Highfield Tyne/Wear 242 F5
Highfields Cambs 123 F7
Highfields Derby 170 B6
Highfields Northum 273 E9
Highfields Staffs 151 E8
Highfields S Yorks 198 F4
Highgate E Sussex 52 G2
Highgate Kent 53 G9
Highgate London 67 B9
Highgate N Ayrs 267 E7
Highgate N Yorks 198 D5
Highgate Powys 130 D2
Highgate S Yorks 198 G3
Highhampton Devon 25 G7
Highland Folk Museum, Aultlarie H'land 291 D9
Highland Folk Museum, Kingussie H'land 291 C9
Highlane Ches 168 B5
Highlane Derby 186 E6
Highlaws Cumb 229 B8
Highleadon Glos 98 G5
Highleigh W Sussex 22 D4
Highley Shrops 132 G4
Highmoor Cumb 229 B11
Highmoor Oxon 65 B7
Highmoor Cross Oxon 65 C8
Highmoor Hill Monmouths 60 B3
Highnam Glos 98 G5
Highnam Green Glos 98 F5
Highridge Bristol 60 F5
Highstead Kent 71 F8
Highsted Kent 70 G2
Highstreet Kent 70 G5
Highstreet Green Essex 106 E5
Highstreet Green Surrey 50 F3
Hightae Dumf/Gal 238 B3
Highters Heath W Midlands 117 B11
Hightown Ches 168 C5
Hightown Hants 31 G11
Hightown Mersey 193 G10
Hightown S'thampton 33 E7
Hightown Wrex 166 F4
Hightown W Yorks 197 C7
Hightown Green Suffolk 125 F9
Hightown Heights W Yorks 197 C7
Highway Cornw'l 4 G4
Highway Cornw'l 6 E2
Highway Heref'd 97 B9
Highway Wilts 62 E4
Highweek Devon 14 G2
Highwood Dorset 18 D3
Highwood Hants 31 F11
Highwood Staffs 151 C11
Highwood Worcs 116 D3
Highwood Hill London 86 G2
Highworth Swindon 81 G11
Hilborough Norfolk 140 C6
Hilcote Derby 171 D7
Hilcott Wilts 46 B6
Hilden Park Kent 52 D5
Hildenborough Kent 52 D5
Hildersham Cambs 105 B10
Hildersley Heref'd 98 G2
Hilderstone Staffs 151 C8
Hilderthorpe ER Yorks 218 F3
Hilgay Norfolk 140 D2
Hill Devon 25 B11
Hill S Glos 79 F10
Hill Warwick 119 D9
Hill Worcs 99 B9
Hill Bottom Oxon 64 D6
Hill Brow W Sussex 34 B3
Hill Chorlton Staffs 150 B5
Hill Common Norfolk 161 E8
Hill Cottages N Yorks 226 F4
Hill Crest Worcs 116 B6
Hill Croome Worcs 99 C7
Hill Dale Lancs 194 E3
Hill Deverill Wilts 45 E11
Hill End Durham 232 D6
Hill End Fife 279 B10
Hill End Glos 99 D8
Hill End London 85 G9
Hill End N Yorks 205 C7
Hill End Shrops 131 E10
Hill End Worcs 117 E8
Hill Gate Heref'd 97 F9
Hill Green Essex 105 E9
Hill Green Kent 69 G10
Hill Head Hants 33 G8
Hill Hoath Kent 52 E3
Hill Houses Derby 170 B5
Hill Houses Shrops 116 B2
Hill Mountain Pembs 73 D7
Hill of Beath Fife 280 C2
Hill of Fearn H'land 301 B8
Hill of Keillor Angus 286 C6
Hill of Mountblairy Aberds 302 D6
Hill of Overbrae Aberds 303 C8
Hill Park Kent 52 B2
Hill Ridware Staffs 151 F11
Hill Side Hants 34 B3
Hill Side Hants 49 C9
Hill Side S Yorks 197 G8
Hill Side W Yorks 197 D7
Hill Somersal Derby 152 C2
Hill Street Dorset 30 E2
Hill Street Kent 54 D6
Hill Top Derby 186 F5
Hill Top Durham 232 G5
Hill Top Durham 242 G5
Hill Top Durham 233 C10
Hill Top Gtr Man 195 G8
Hill Top Hants 32 G6
Hill Top Notts 171 F7
Hill Top S Yorks 197 F9
Hill Top S Yorks 186 D3
Hill Top W Midlands 133 E9
Hill Top W Yorks 196 E5
Hill Top W Yorks 197 D10
Hill Top W Yorks 205 G7
Hill Top W Yorks 205 G11
Hill Top, Sawrey Cumb 221 F7
Hill View Dorset 18 B5
Hill Wootton Warwick 118 D6
Hillam N Yorks 198 B4
Hillborough Kent 71 F8
Hillbourne Dorset 18 C6
Hillbrae Aberds 302 E6
Hillbrae Aberds 303 G7
Hillbutts Dorset 31 G7
Hillcliffe Warrington 183 D10
Hillcommon Som'set 27 B10
Hillcross Derby C 152 C6
Hilldyke Lincs 174 F4
Hillend Fife 280 E3
Hillend N Lanarks 268 B6
Hillend N Som'set 43 B11
Hillend Green Glos 98 F4
Hillersland Glos 79 C9
Hillerton Devon 13 B10
Hillesden Bucks 102 F3
Hillesley Glos 61 B9
Hillfarrance Som'set 27 C11
Hillfield Dorset 29 F10
Hillfield Devon 8 E6
Hillfields Bristol 60 D6
Hillfields W Berks 65 F7
Hillfoot Aberds 303 D9
Hillfoot W Yorks 205 G10
Hillfoot End Beds 104 D2
Hillgreen W Berks 64 D3
Hillgrove W Sussex 34 B6
Hillhampton Heref'd 97 B11
Hillhead Aberds 302 F5
Hillhead Aberds 303 G8
Hillhead Cornw'l 5 C11
Hillhead Devon 9 E8
Hillhead E Ayrs 257 B10
Hillhead S Ayrs 257 F10
Hillhead of Auchentumb Aberds 303 D9
Hillhead of Blairy Aberds 302 D6
Hillhead of Cocklaw Aberds 303 E10
Hillhouse Scot Borders 271 D10
Hilliard's Cross Staffs 152 G2
Hilliclay H'land 310 C5
Hillier Gardens and Arboretum Hants 32 C5
Hillingdon London 66 C5
Hillingdon Heath London 66 C5
Hillington Glasg C 267 C10
Hillington Norfolk 158 D4
Hillington Industrial Estate Glasg C 267 B10
Hillis Corner I/Wight 20 C5
Hillmorton Warwick 119 C10
Hillock Vale Lancs 195 B9
Hillockhead Aberds 292 B6
Hillockhead Aberds 292 C5
Hillpool Worcs 117 B7
Hill's End Beds 103 E9
Hills Town Derby 171 B7
Hillsborough S Yorks 186 C4
Hillside Aberds 293 D11
Hillside Angus 293 G9
Hillside Devon 8 C4
Hillside Orkney 312 F4
Hillside Orkney 313 J5
Hillside Shetl'd 315 G6
Hillside Wilts 81 G9
Hillside Worcs 116 E5
Hillstreet Hants 32 D4
Hillswick Shetl'd 314 F4
Hillview Tyne/Wear 243 F9
Hillway I/Wight 21 D8
Hillwell Shetl'd 315 M5
Hilmarton Wilts 62 D4
Hilperton Wilts 45 B10
Hilperton Marsh Wilts 61 G11
Hilsea Portsm'th 33 G11
Hilston ER Yorks 209 G11
Hiltingbury Hants 32 C6
Hilton Aberds 303 F9
Hilton Cambs 122 D5
Hilton Cumb 231 G10
Hilton Derby 152 C4
Hilton Dorset 30 G3
Hilton Durham 233 G9
Hilton H'land 309 L7
Hilton H'land 311 L3
Hilton Shrops 132 D5
Hilton Stockton 225 C9
Hilton Staffs 133 B11
Hilton House Gtr Man 194 F6
Hilton Lodge H'land 300 G2
Hilton of Cadboll H'land 301 B8
Hilton Park Gtr Man 195 G10
Himbleton Worcs 117 F8
Himley Staffs 133 D7
Hincaster Cumb 211 C10
Hinchley Wood Surrey 67 G7
Hinchwick Glos 100 E2
Hinckley Leics 135 E8
Hinderclay Suffolk 125 B10
Hinderton Ches 182 F4
Hinderwell N Yorks 226 B5
Hindford Shrops 148 C6
Hindhead Surrey 49 F11
Hindle Fold Lancs 203 G10
Hindley Gtr Man 194 G6
Hindley Northum 242 F3
Hindley Green Gtr Man 194 G6
Hindolveston Norfolk 159 D10
Hindon Wilts 46 G2
Hindringham Norfolk 159 B9
Hindsford Gtr Man 195 G7
Hingham Norfolk 141 C10
Hinlip Worcs 117 F7
Hinstock Shrops 150 D3
Hintlesham Suffolk 107 C11
Hinton Glos 79 E11
Hinton Hants 19 B10
Hinton Heref'd 96 D6
Hinton Northants 119 G10
Hinton Shrops 131 B8
Hinton S Glos 61 D8
Hinton Som'set 29 C9
Hinton Ampner Hants 33 B9
Hinton Blewett Bath/NE Som'set 44 B5
Hinton Charterhouse Bath/NE Som'set 45 B9
Hinton Green Worcs 99 C10
Hinton Martell Dorset 31 F8
Hinton on the Green Worcs 99 D10
Hinton Parva Dorset 31 G7
Hinton Parva Swindon 63 C8
Hinton St. George Som'set 28 E6
Hinton St. Mary Dorset 30 D3
Hinton Waldrist Oxon 82 F5
Hinton-in-the-Hedges Northants 101 D11
Hints Staffs 134 C3
Hinwick Beds 121 E8
Hinxhill Kent 54 E5
Hinxton Cambs 105 B9
Hinxworth Herts 104 C4
Hipperholme W Yorks 196 B6
Hipsburn Northum 264 G6
Hipswell N Yorks 224 F3
Hirael Gwyn 179 G9
Hiraeth Carms 92 G3
Hirn Aberds 293 C9
Hirnant Powys 147 E10
Hirst N Lanarks 269 C7
Hirst Northum 253 F7
Hirst Courtney N Yorks 198 C6
Hirwaen Denbs 165 C10
Hirwaun Rh Cyn Taff 77 D7
Hiscott Devon 25 B8
Histon Cambs 123 E8
Hitcham Suffolk 125 G9
Hitcham Causeway Suffolk 125 G9
Hitchill Dumf/Gal 238 D4
Hitchin Herts 104 F3
Hither Green London 67 E11
Hittisleigh Devon 13 C10
Hive ER Yorks 208 G2
Hixon Staffs 151 D10
HMS Victory Portsm'th 33 G10
HMY Britannia C/Edinb 280 F5
Hoaden Kent 55 B9
Hoar Cross Staffs 152 E2
Hoarwithy Heref'd 97 F10
Hoath Kent 71 G8
Hoath Corner Kent 52 E3
Hobarris Shrops 114 B6
Hobbister Orkney 313 H4
Hobbles Green Suffolk 124 G4
Hobbs Cross Essex 87 F7
Hobbs Cross Essex 87 C7
Hobbs Point Pembs 73 E7
Hobkirk Scot Borders 262 G3
Hobroyd Derby 185 C8
Hobson Durham 242 F5
Hoby Leics 154 F3
Hoccombe Som'set 27 B10
Hockenden London 68 F3
Hockerill Herts 105 G9
Hockering Norfolk 159 G11
Hockering Heath Norfolk 159 G11
Hockerton Notts 172 D2
Hockholler Som'set 27 C11
Hockleton Shrops 130 C5
Hockley Ches 184 E6
Hockley Derby 170 B5
Hockley Essex 88 G4
Hockley Kent 54 B3
Hockley Staffs 134 C4
Hockley W Midlands 118 B5
Hockley Heath W Midlands 118 C3
Hockliffe Beds 103 F9
Hockwold cum Wilton Norfolk 140 F4
Hockworthy Devon 27 D8
Hoddesdon Herts 86 D5
Hoddlesden Blackb'n 195 C8
Hoddom Mains Dumf/Gal 238 C5
Hodgefield Ches 168 B4
Hodgehill W Midlands 134 F2
Hodgeston Pembs 73 F8
Hodley Powys 130 E3
Hodnet Shrops 150 D2
Hodnetheath Shrops 150 D2
Hodsall Street Kent 68 G6
Hodsock Notts 187 E10
Hodson Swindon 63 C7
Hodthorpe Derby 187 F9
Hoe Hants 33 D9
Hoe Norfolk 159 F9
Hoe Benham W Berks 64 E2
Hoe Gate Hants 33 E10
Hoel-ddu Swan 75 F11
Hoff Cumb 222 B3
Hog Hatch Surrey 49 D10
Hog Hill E Sussex 38 D5
Hogbarn Kent 53 B11
Hogben's Hill Kent 54 B4
Hogganfield Glasg C 268 B2
Hoggard's Green Suffolk 125 F7
Hoggeston Bucks 102 F6
Hoggrill's End Warwick 134 E4
Hogha Gearraidh W Isles 296 D3
Hoghton Lancs 194 B6
Hoghton Bottoms Lancs 194 B6
Hogland Shetl'd 314 F5
Hogley Green W Yorks 196 F6
Hognaston Derby 170 E2
Hogspit Bottom Herts 85 E8
Hogsthorpe Lincs 191 G8
Holbeach Lincs 157 E7
Holbeach Bank Lincs 157 D7
Holbeach Clough Lincs 156 D6
Holbeach Drove Lincs 156 G6
Holbeach Hurn Lincs 157 D7
Holbeach St. Johns Lincs 156 F6
Holbeach St. Marks Lincs 157 C7
Holbeach St. Matthew Lincs 157 C8
Holbeache Worcs 116 B5
Holbeck Notts 187 G8
Holbeck W Yorks 205 G11
Holbeck Woodhouse Notts 187 G8
Holberrow Green Worcs 117 F10
Holbeton Devon 8 E2
Holborn London 67 C10
Holborough Kent 69 G7
Holbrook Derby 170 F5
Holbrook Suffolk 108 D3
Holbrook S Yorks 186 E6
Holbrook Common S Glos 61 E7
Holbrooks W Midlands 134 G6
Holburn Northum 264 B2
Holbury Hants 32 G6
Holbury Purlieu Hants 32 G6
Holcombe Devon 14 G5
Holcombe Devon 16 C2
Holcombe Gtr Man 195 D9
Holcombe Som'set 45 D7
Holcombe Brook Gtr Man 195 D9
Holcombe Burnell Barton Devon 14 C3
Holcombe Rogus Devon 27 D9
Holcot Northants 120 D5
Holden Lancs 203 D11
Holden Fold Gtr Man 196 F2
Holdenby Northants 120 D3
Holdenhurst Bournem'th 19 B8
Holder's Green Essex 106 F2
Holders Hill London 86 G2
Holdgate Shrops 131 F11
Holdingham Lincs 173 F9
Holditch Dorset 28 G4
Holdsworth W Yorks 196 B5
Hole Devon 27 E11
Hole Bottom W Yorks 196 C2
Hole in the Wall Heref'd 98 F2
Hole Street W Sussex 35 E10
Holefield Scot Borders 263 C8
Holehills N Lanarks 268 B5
Holehouse Derby 185 C7
Holehouse E Renf 267 D9
Holemill Aberd C 293 C10
Holemoor Devon 24 F6
Holestane Dumf/Gal 247 D9
Holford Som'set 43 E7
Holgate C/York 207 C7
Holincote Som'set 42 D2
Holker Cumb 211 D7
Holkham Norfolk 176 E5
Hollacombe Devon 24 G5
Holland Orkney 312 C5
Holland Orkney 312 F7
Holland Surrey 52 C2
Holland Fen Lincs 174 F2
Holland Lees Lancs 194 F4
Holland Moor Lancs 194 G4
Holland Park W Midlands 133 B10
Holland-on-Sea Essex 89 B12
Hollandstoun Orkney 312 C8
Hollee Dumf/Gal 239 D7
Hollesley Suffolk 109 C6
Hollicombe Torbay 9 C7
Hollin Green Ches 167 E9
Hollin Hall Lancs 204 F4
Hollinfare Warrington 183 C11
Hollingbourne Kent 53 B10
Hollingbury Brighton/Hove 36 F4
Hollingdon Bucks 103 F7
Hollingrove E Sussex 37 C11
Hollington Derby 152 B4
Hollington E Sussex 38 E3
Hollington Hants 64 G2
Hollington Staffs 151 B11
Hollington Grove Derby 152 B4
Hollingwood Derby 186 G6
Hollingworth Gtr Man 185 B8
Hollins Cumb 222 G3
Hollins Derby 186 G4
Hollins Gtr Man 195 F8
Hollins Gtr Man 195 F11
Hollins Gtr Man 195 F10
Hollins Staffs 168 E4
Hollins End S Yorks 186 E5
Hollins Green Warrington 183 C11
Hollins Lane Lancs 202 C5
Hollinsclough Staffs 169 B9
Hollinswood Telford 132 B4
Hollinthorpe W Yorks 206 G3
Hollinwood Gtr Man 196 G2
Hollinwood Shrops 149 B10
Hollis Head Devon 27 G7
Hollocombe Devon 25 E10
Hollocombe Town Devon 25 E10
Hollow Oak Dorset 18 C2
Hollow Street Kent 71 G8
Holloway Derby 170 D4
Holloway Wilts 45 G11
Holloway Windsor 65 C10
Holloway End W Midlands 133 G7
Holloway Hill Surrey 50 E3
Hollowell Northants 120 C3
Hollows Dumf/Gal 239 B9
Hollowsgate Ches 167 B8
Holly Bank W Midlands 133 C11
Holly Brook Som'set 44 D4
Holly Cross Wokingham 65 C10
Holly End Norfolk 139 B9
Holly Green Bucks 84 E3
Holly Green Worcs 99 C7
Holly Hill Norfolk 142 E6
Holly Hill N Yorks 224 E3
Hollybed Common Worcs 98 D5
Hollyberry End W Midlands 134 G5
Hollybush Caerph 77 E11
Hollybush E Ayrs 257 G9
Hollybush Stoke 168 G5
Hollybush Worcs 98 D5
Hollybush Corner Bucks 66 B3
Hollybush Corner Suffolk 125 F8
Hollybush Hill Essex 89 B10
Hollybushes Kent 54 B2
Hollym ER Yorks 201 B10
Hollywater Hants 49 G10
Hollywood Worcs 117 B11
Holman Clavel Som'set 28 D2
Holmbridge W Yorks 196 F6
Holmbury St. Mary Surrey 50 E6
Holmbush Cornw'l 5 E10
Holmcroft Staffs 151 D8
Holme Beds 104 C3
Holme Cambs 138 F3
Holme Cumb 211 D10
Holme Lancs 195 C9
Holme N Lincs 200 F2
Holme Notts 172 D4
Holme N Yorks 215 C7
Holme S Yorks 198 E5
Holme W Yorks 196 F6
Holme W Yorks 205 G9
Holme Bank Ches 167 B7
Holme Chapel Lancs 195 B11
Holme Green N Yorks 207 E7
Holme Green Wokingham 65 F10
Holme Hale Norfolk 141 B7
Holme Hill NE Lincs 201 F9
Holme Lacy Heref'd 97 D11
Holme Marsh Heref'd 114 G6
Holme Mills Cumb 211 D10
Holme next the Sea Norfolk 176 E2
Holme on the Wolds ER Yorks 208 D5
Holme Pierrepont Notts 154 B2
Holme St. Cuthbert Cumb 229 B8
Holme Slack Lancs 203 G7
Holme Wood W Yorks 205 G9
Holmebridge Dorset 18 D3
Holme-on-Spalding-Moor ER Yorks 208 F2
Holmer Heref'd 97 C9
Holmer Green Bucks 84 F6
Holmes Chapel Ches 168 B3
Holme's Hill E Sussex 37 E8
Holmescales Cumb 211 B11
Holmesdale Derby 186 F5
Holmesfield Derby 186 F4
Holmeswood Lancs 194 D2
Holmethorpe Surrey 51 C9
Holmewood Derby 170 B6
Holmfield W Yorks 196 B5
Holmfirth W Yorks 196 F6
Holmhead Angus 293 F7
Holmhead Dumf/Gal 246 F6
Holmhead E Ayrs 258 E3
Holmhurst St. Mary E Sussex 38 E4
Holmisdale H'land 297 G7
Holmley Common Derby 186 F5
Holmpton ER Yorks 201 C11
Holmrook Cumb 219 F11
Holmsgarth Shetl'd 315 J6
Holmside Durham 233 B10
Holmston S Ayrs 257 E9
Holmwood Corner Surrey 51 E7
Holmwrangle Cumb 230 B6
Holne Devon 8 B4
Holnest Dorset 29 E11
Holsworthy Devon 24 G4
Holsworthy Beacon Devon 24 F5
Holt Dorset 31 G8
Holt Hants 49 C8
Holt Mersey 183 C7
Holt Norfolk 159 B11
Holt Wilts 61 G11
Holt Worcs 116 E6
Holt Wrex 166 E6
Holt End Hants 49 F7
Holt End Worcs 117 D11
Holt Fleet Worcs 116 E6
Holt Green Lancs 193 G11
Holt Head W Yorks 196 E5
Holt Heath Dorset 31 G9
Holt Heath Worcs 116 E6
Holt Park W Yorks 205 E11
Holt Pound Hants 49 E10
Holt Street Kent 55 C9
Holt Wood Dorset 31 F8
Holtby C/York 207 C9
Holtby Grange N Yorks 224 G5
Holton Oxon 83 D10
Holton Suffolk 127 B8
Holton Som'set 29 B11
Holton cum Beckering Lincs 189 D10
Holton Heath Dorset 18 C5
Holton Hill E Sussex 37 B11
Holton le Clay NE Lincs 201 G9
Holton le Moor Lincs 189 B9
Holton St. Mary Suffolk 107 D11
Holts Gtr Man 196 G3
Holtsmere End Herts 85 C9
Holtwood W Berks 64 G2
Holtye E Sussex 52 F3
Holway Flints 181 F11
Holway Som'set 28 C2
Holwelbury Beds 104 D3
Holwell Dorset 30 E2
Holwell Herts 104 E3
Holwell Leics 154 E4
Holwell Oxon 82 D2
Holwell Som'set 45 D8
Holwick Durham 232 F4
Holwood Cornw'l 7 C7
Holy City Devon 28 G3
Holy Cross Tyne/Wear 243 D8
Holy Cross Worcs 117 B8
Holy Island Northum 273 B11
Holybourne Hants 49 E8
Holyfield Essex 86 E5
Holyhead = Caergybi Angl 178 E3
Holymoorside Derby 170 B4
Holyport Windsor 65 D11
Holystone Northum 251 C11
Holytown N Lanarks 268 C5
Holywell Beds 85 B8
Holywell Cambs 122 C6
Holywell Cornw'l 4 D5
Holywell Dorset 29 G9
Holywell Glos 80 G3
Holywell Northum 243 C8
Holywell = Treffynon Flints 181 F11
Holywell Warwick 118 D3
Holywell Bay Fun Park, Newquay Cornw'l 4 D5
Holywell Green W Yorks 196 D5
Holywell Lake Som'set 27 C10
Holywell Row Suffolk 124 B4
Holywood Dumf/Gal 247 G10
Hom Green Heref'd 97 G11
Home End Cambs 123 F10
Homer Shrops 132 C2
Homer Green Mersey 193 G10
Homersfield Suffolk 142 F5
Homerton London 67 C11
Homestead Hants 47 G10
Homington Wilts 31 B10
Honey Hill Kent 70 G6
Honey Street Wilts 62 G6
Honey Tye Suffolk 107 D9
Honeybourne Worcs 100 C2
Honeychurch Devon 25 G10
Honeydon Beds 122 G2
Honicknowle Plym'th 7 D9
Honiley Warwick 118 C4
Honing Norfolk 160 D6
Honingham Norfolk 160 G2
Honington Lincs 172 G6
Honington Suffolk 125 C8
Honington Warwick 100 C5
Honiton Devon 27 G10
Honkley Wrex 166 D4
Honley W Yorks 196 E6
Honor Oak London 67 E11
Hoo Suffolk 126 F5
Hoo End Herts 104 G3
Hoo Green Ches 184 E2
Hoo St. Werburgh Medway 69 E9
Hoober S Yorks 186 B6
Hoobrook Worcs 116 C6
Hood Green S Yorks 197 G10
Hood Hill S Yorks 186 B5
Hood Manor Warrington 183 D9
Hooe E Sussex 23 D11
Hooe Plym'th 7 E10
Hooe Common E Sussex 37 E11
Hoohill Blackp'l 202 F2
Hook Cambs 139 E8
Hook Devon 28 F4
Hook ER Yorks 199 B9
Hook Hants 49 C8
Hook Hants 33 F8
Hook London 67 G7
Hook Pembs 73 C7
Hook Wilts 62 C5
Hook Common Worcs 98 C6
Hook End Essex 87 F9
Hook End Oxon 65 C7
Hook Green Kent 53 F7
Hook Green Kent 68 E4
Hook Green Kent 68 F6
Hook Green Kent 68 E6
Hook Heath Surrey 50 B3
Hook Norton Oxon 101 E7
Hook Street Glos 79 F11
Hook Street Wilts 62 C5
Hook-a-gate Shrops 131 B9
Hooke Dorset 16 B6
Hooke Dorset 29 F8
Hooker Gate Tyne/Wear 242 F4
Hookgate Staffs 150 B4
Hookhills Torbay 9 D7
Hook's Cross Herts 104 G5
Hookway Devon 14 B3
Hookwood Surrey 51 E9
Hoole Ches 166 B6
Hooley London 51 B9
Hooley Bridge Gtr Man 195 E10
Hooley Brow Gtr Man 195 E11
Hooley Hill Gtr Man 184 B6
Hoop Monmouths 79 D8
Hooton Ches 182 F5
Hooton Levitt S Yorks 187 B8
Hooton Pagnell S Yorks 198 F3
Hooton Roberts S Yorks 187 B7
Hop Pole Lincs 156 G3
Hope Derby 185 E11
Hope H'land 308 D4
Hope Powys 130 B5
Hope Shrops 130 C6
Hope Staffs 169 D10
Hope = Yr Hôb Flints 166 D4
Hope Bagot Shrops 115 C11
Hope Bowdler Shrops 131 E9
Hope End Green Essex 105 G11
Hope Green Ches 184 E6
Hope Mansell Heref'd 79 B10
Hope under Dinmore Heref'd 115 G10
Hopebeck Cumb 229 G9
Hopeman Moray 301 C11
Hope's Green Essex 69 B9
Hope's Rough Heref'd 98 B2
Hopesay Shrops 131 G7
Hopetown W Yorks 198 C2
Hopkinstown Rh Cyn Taff 77 G9
Hoplands Hants 32 B5
Hopleys Staffs 134 C4
Hopley's Green Heref'd 114 G6
Hopperton N Yorks 206 B4
Hopsford Warwick 135 G8
Hopstone Shrops 132 E5
Hopton Derby 170 E3
Hopton Shrops 149 E7
Hopton Suffolk 125 B9
Hopton Staffs 151 D8
Hopton Cangeford Shrops 131 G10
Hopton Castle Shrops 115 B7
Hopton on Sea Norfolk 143 C10
Hopton Wafers Shrops 116 B2
Hoptonheath Shrops 115 B7
Hopwas Staffs 134 C3
Hopwood Gtr Man 195 F11
Hopwood Worcs 117 B10
Hopworthy Devon 24 G4
Horam E Sussex 37 D9
Horbling Lincs 156 B2
Horbury W Yorks 197 D9
Horbury Bridge W Yorks 197 D9
Horbury Junction W Yorks 197 D10
Horcott Glos 81 E10
Horden Durham 234 C4
Horderley Shrops 131 F8
Hordle Hants 19 B11
Hordley Shrops 149 C7
Horeb Carms 75 D7
Horeb Carms 93 F10
Horeb Ceredig'n 93 C7
Horeb Flints 166 D3
Horfield Bristol 60 D5
Horgabost W Isles 305 J2
Horham Suffolk 126 C4
Horingford I/Wight 20 D6
Horkesley Heath Essex 107 F9
Horkstow N Lincs 200 D3
Horley Oxon 101 C8
Horley Surrey 51 E9
Horn Som'set 28 F4
Horn Hill Bucks 85 G8
Horn Street Kent 55 F7
Horn Street Kent 69 G7
Hornblotton Som'set 44 G5
Hornblotton Green Som'set 44 G5
Hornby Lancs 211 F11
Hornby N Yorks 224 G4
Hornby N Yorks 225 D7
Horncastle Lincs 174 B3
Hornchurch London 68 B4
Horncliffe Northum 273 F8
Horndean Scot Borders 273 F7
Horndean Hants 33 E11
Horndon Devon 12 E6
Horndon on the Hill Thurr'k 69 C7
Horne Surrey 51 E10
Horne Row Essex 88 E3
Horner Devon 8 E5
Horner Som'set 41 D11
Horner's Green Suffolk 107 C9
Hornestreet Essex 107 E10
Horngrove Worcs 116 C6
Hornick Cornw'l 5 E9
Horniehaugh Angus 292 G6
Horning Norfolk 161 F6
Horninghold Leics 136 D6
Horninglow Staffs 152 E4
Horningsea Cambs 123 E9
Horningsham Wilts 45 D10
Horningtoft Norfolk 159 E8
Horningtops Cornw'l 6 C5
Horns Corner Kent 38 B2
Horns Cross Devon 24 C5
Horns Cross Kent 38 C4
Horns Cross Kent 68 E5
Horns Green London 52 B2
Hornsbury Som'set 28 E4
Hornsby Cumb 240 G2
Hornsea ER Yorks 209 D10
Hornsea Burton ER Yorks 209 D10
Hornsey London 67 B10
Hornton Oxon 101 C7
Horpit Swindon 63 C8
Horrabridge Devon 12 G7
Horringer Suffolk 124 D6
Horrocks Fold Gtr Man 195 E7
Horrocksford Lancs 203 E10
Horsebridge Devon 12 G4
Horsebridge Hants 47 G10
Horsebrook Devon 8 D4
Horsebrook Staffs 151 G7
Horsecastle N Som'set 60 F2
Horsedowns Cornw'l 2 C4
Horsehay Telford 132 B3
Horseheath Cambs 106 B2
Horsehill Dumf/Gal 237 B12
Horsehouse N Yorks 213 C10
Horselees Kent 54 B5
Horseley Heath W Midlands 133 E9
Horsell Surrey 50 B3
Horseman Side Essex 87 F8
Horseman's Green Wrex 166 G6
Horsemoor W Berks 64 E3
Horsenden Bucks 84 E3
Horseshoe Green Kent 52 E3
Horseway Cambs 139 F8
Horsey Norfolk 161 E9
Horsey Som'set 43 F10
Horsey Corner Norfolk 161 E9
Horsey Down Wilts 81 G9
Horsford Norfolk 160 F3
Horsforth W Yorks 205 F10
Horsforth Woodside W Yorks 205 F11
Horsham W Sussex 51 G7
Horsham St. Faith Norfolk 160 G4
Horsington Lincs 173 B11
Horsington Som'set 30 C2
Horsington Marsh Som'set 30 C2
Horsley Derby 170 G5
Horsley Glos 80 F4
Horsley Northum 242 D3
Horsley Northum 251 D8
Horsley Cross Essex 108 F2
Horsley Hill Tyne/Wear 243 D9
Horsley Woodhouse Derby 170 G5
Horsleycross Street Essex 108 F2
Horsleygate Derby 186 F4
Horsleyhill Scot Borders 262 F2
Horsleyhope Durham 233 B7
Horsleys Green Bucks 84 F3
Horsmonden Kent 53 E8
Horspath Oxon 83 E9
Horstead Norfolk 160 F5
Horsted Keynes W Sussex 36 B5
Horton Bucks 84 B6
Horton Dorset 31 F8
Horton Kent 54 B6
Horton Lancs 204 C3
Horton Northants 120 G6
Horton Shrops 149 C9
Horton S Glos 61 C9
Horton Som'set 28 E4
Horton Staffs 168 D6
Horton Swan 56 D3
Horton Telford 150 G3
Horton Wilts 62 G5
Horton Windsor 66 D4
Horton Cross Som'set 28 D4
Horton Green Ches 167 F7
Horton Heath Dorset 31 F9
Horton Heath Hants 33 D7
Horton in Ribblesdale N Yorks 212 E6
Horton Kirby Kent 68 F5
Horton-cum-Studley Oxon 83 C9
Hortonlane Shrops 149 G8
Hortonwood Telford 150 G3
Horwich Gtr Man 194 E6
Horwich End Derby 185 E8
Horwood Devon 25 B8
Hoscar Lancs 194 E3
Hose Leics 154 D4

Hoselaw Scot Borders 263 C8
Hosey Hill Kent 52 C3
Hosh Perth/Kinr 286 E2
Hosta W Isles 296 D3
Hoswick Shetl'd 315 L6
Hotham ER Yorks 208 G3
Hothfield Kent 54 E3
Hoton Leics 153 E11
Hotwells Bristol 60 E5
Houbans Shetl'd 314 F5
Houbie Shetl'd 314 D8
Houdston S Ayrs 244 D6
Hough Arg/Bute 288 E1
Hough Ches 168 E2
Hough Ches 184 G5
Hough End W Yorks 205 G10
Hough Green Halton 183 D7
Hough Side W Yorks 205 G10
Hougham Lincs 172 G5
Hough-on-the-Hill Lincs 172 F6
Houghton Cambs 122 C5
Houghton Cumb 239 F10
Houghton Hants 47 G10
Houghton Northum 242 D4
Houghton Pembs 73 D7
Houghton W Sussex 35 E8
Houghton Bank D'lington 233 G10
Houghton Conquest Beds 103 C11
Houghton Green E Sussex 38 C6
Houghton Green Warrington 183 C10
Houghton Hall Cumb 239 E10
Houghton Hill Cambs 122 C5
Houghton on the Hill Leics 136 C3
Houghton Regis Beds 103 G10
Houghton St. Giles Norfolk 159 B8
Houghton-le-Side D'lington 233 G10
Houghton-le-Spring Tyne/Wear 243 G8
Houghwood Mersey 194 G4
Houlland Shetl'd 314 B7
Houlland Shetl'd 315 G6
Houlland Shetl'd 315 H5
Houlland Shetl'd 315 J6
Houlsyke N Yorks 226 D4
Hound Hants 33 F7
Hound Green Hants 49 B8
Hound Hill Dorset 31 G7
Houndmills Hants 48 C6
Houndscroft Glos 80 E5
Houndslow Scot Borders 272 F2
Houndsmoor Som'set 27 B10
Houndstone Som'set 29 D8
Houndwood Scot Borders 272 C6
Hounsdown Hants 32 E5
Hounsley Batch N Som'set 60 G4
Hounslow London 66 D6
Hounslow Green Essex 87 B11
Hourston Orkney 312 G3
Housabister Shetl'd 315 H6
Housay Shetl'd 314 F8
House of Daviot H'land 301 E7
House of Glenmuick Aberds 292 D5
Househill H'land 301 D8
Houses Hill W Yorks 197 D8
Housesteads Roman Fort Northum 241 D7
Housetter Shetl'd 314 E5
Housham Lincs 172 C5
Housham Tye Essex 87 C8
Houss Shetl'd 315 K5
Houston Renf 267 B8
Houstry H'land 310 F5
Houton Orkney 313 H4
Hove Brighton/Hove 36 G3
Hove Edge W Yorks 196 C6
Hoveringham Notts 171 G10
Hoveton Norfolk 160 F6
Hovingham N Yorks 216 D3
How Cumb 240 F2
How Caple Heref'd 98 E2
How End Beds 103 C10
How Green Kent 52 D3
How Green Warwick 134 F6
How Hill Norfolk 161 F7
Howbrook S Yorks 186 B4
Howden Scot Borders 262 F5
Howden ER Yorks 199 B8
Howden W Loth 269 B11
Howden Clough W Yorks 197 B8
Howden-le-Wear Durham 233 E9
Howdon Tyne/Wear 243 D8
Howdon Pans Tyne/Wear 243 D8
Howe H'land 310 C7
Howe Norfolk 142 D5
Howe N Yorks 215 C7
Howe Bridge Gtr Man 195 G7
Howe Green Essex 88 E2
Howe Green Essex 87 B8
Howe of Teuchar Aberds 303 E7
Howe Street Essex 87 C11
Howe Street Essex 106 E3
Howegreen Essex 88 E4
Howell Lincs 173 F10
Howey Powys 113 F11
Howgate Midloth 270 D4
Howgill Cumb 222 F2
Howgill Lancs 204 D2
Howgill N Yorks 205 B7
Howick Northum 265 F7
Howick Cross Lancs 194 B4
Howle Telford 150 E3
Howle Hill Heref'd 98 G2
Howleigh Som'set 28 D3
Howlett End Essex 105 E11
Howley Glos 80 G2
Howley Som'set 28 F3
Howley Warrington 183 D10
Hownam Scot Borders 263 F7
Howpasley Scot Borders 249 B8
Howsen Worcs 116 G5
Howsham N Lincs 200 G4
Howsham N Yorks 216 G4
Howslack Dumf/Gal 248 B3
Howt Green Kent 69 F11
Howtel Northum 263 C9
Howtown Cumb 221 B8
Howwood Renf 267 C8
Hoxne Suffolk 126 B3
Hoxton London 67 C10
Hoy Orkney 313 H3
Hoylake Mersey 182 D2
Hoyland S Yorks 197 G11
Hoyland Common S Yorks 197 G11
Hoylandswaine S Yorks 197 G9
Hoyle W Sussex 34 D6
Hoyle Mill S Yorks 197 F11
Hubberholme N Yorks 213 D8
Hubberston Pembs 72 D6
Hubbersty Head Cumb 221 G8
Hubberton Green W Yorks 196 C4
Hubbert's Bridge Lincs 174 G3
Huby N Yorks 205 D11
Huby N Yorks 215 F11
Huccaby Devon 13 G9
Hucclecote Glos 80 B5
Hucclecote Green Glos 80 B5
Hucking Kent 53 B10
Hucknall Notts 171 F8
Hud Hey Lancs 195 C9
Huddersfield W Yorks 196 D6
Huddington Worcs 117 F8
Huddox Hill Bath/NE Som'set 45 B8
Hudnall Herts 85 C8
Hudnalls Glos 79 E8
Hudswell N Yorks 224 E2
Hudswell Wilts 61 F11
Huggate ER Yorks 208 B3
Hugglescote Leics 153 G8
Hugh Mill Lancs 195 C10
Hugh Town I/Scilly 1 G4
Hughenden Valley Bucks 84 F5
Hughley Shrops 131 D11
Hugus Cornw'l 4 G5
Huish Devon 25 E8
Huish Devon 25 B7
Huish Wilts 62 G6
Huish Champflower Som'set 27 B8
Huish Episcopi Som'set 28 B6
Huisinis W Isles 305 G1
Hulberry Kent 68 F4
Hulcote Northants 102 B4
Hulcott Bucks 84 B5
Hulham Devon 14 E6
Hulland Derby 170 F2
Hulland Ward Derby 170 F3
Hullavington Wilts 61 C11
Hullbridge Essex 88 F4
Hulme Gtr Man 184 B4
Hulme Staffs 168 F6
Hulme Warrington 183 C10
Hulme Walfield Ches 168 B4
Hulseheath Ches 184 E2
Hulver Street Suffolk 143 F9
Hulverstone I/Wight 20 E4
Humber Devon 14 F4
Humberside International Airport N Lincs 200 E5
Humberston NE Lincs 201 F10
Humberston Fitties NE Lincs 201 F10
Humberstone Leics C 136 B2
Humbie E Loth 271 C9
Humble Green Suffolk 107 B8
Humbledon Tyne/Wear 243 F9
Humbleton ER Yorks 209 G10
Humbleton Northum 263 D11
Humby Lincs 155 C10
Hume Scot Borders 272 G4
Hummer Dorset 29 D9
Hummersknott D'lington 224 C5
Humshaugh Northum 241 C10
Huna H'land 310 B7
Huncoat Lancs 203 G11
Huncote Leics 135 D10
Hundall Derby 186 F5
Hunderthwaite Durham 232 G5
Hunderton Heref'd 97 D9
Hundle Houses Lincs 174 E2
Hundleby Lincs 174 B5
Hundleton Pembs 73 E7
Hundon Suffolk 106 B4
Hundred Acres Hants 33 E9
Hundred End Lancs 194 C2
Hundred House Powys 114 G2
Hungarton Leics 136 B3
Hungate End M/Keynes 102 B5
Hunger Hill Gtr Man 195 F7
Hunger Hill Lancs 194 E4
Hungerdown Wilts 61 E11
Hungerford Hants 31 E11
Hungerford Shrops 131 F10
Hungerford Som'set 42 E4
Hungerford W Berks 63 F10
Hungerford Green W Berks 64 D5
Hungerford Newtown W Berks 63 E11
Hungershall Park Kent 52 F5
Hungerstone Heref'd 97 D8
Hungerton Lincs 155 C7
Hungladder H'land 298 B3
Hungryhatton Shrops 150 D3
Hunmanby N Yorks 217 D11
Hunningham Warwick 119 D7
Hunnington Worcs 133 G9
Hunny Hill I/Wight 20 D5
Hunsdon Herts 86 C6
Hunsdonbury Herts 86 C6
Hunsingore N Yorks 206 C4
Hunslet W Yorks 206 G2
Hunslet Carr W Yorks 206 G2
Hunsonby Cumb 231 D7
Hunspow H'land 310 B6
Hunstanton Norfolk 175 G11
Hunstanworth Durham 232 B5
Hunston Suffolk 125 D9
Hunston W Sussex 34 G5
Hunston Green Suffolk 125 D9
Hunstrete Bath/NE Som'set 60 G6
Hunsworth W Yorks 197 B7
Hunt End Worcs 117 E10
Hunt Hill Glos 80 C2
Huntenhull Green Wilts 45 D10
Huntercombe End Oxon 65 B7
Hunterfield Midloth 270 C6
Hunters Forstal Kent 71 F7
Hunter's Quay Arg/Bute 276 F3
Huntham Som'set 28 B4
Hunthill Lodge Angus 292 F6
Hunting-tower Perth/Kinr 286 E4
Huntingdon Cambs 122 C4
Huntingdon Racecourse Cambs 122 C4
Huntingfield Suffolk 126 C6
Huntingford Dorset 30 B4
Huntington Ches 166 C6
Huntington C/York 207 B8
Huntington E Loth 281 G9
Huntington Heref'd 114 G5
Huntington Heref'd 97 C9
Huntington Staffs 151 G9
Huntley Glos 80 B2
Huntley Staffs 169 G8
Huntly Aberds 302 F5
Hunton Hants 48 F3
Hunton Kent 53 D8
Hunton N Yorks 224 G3
Hunton Bridge Herts 85 E9
Hunt's Corner Norfolk 141 F11
Hunt's Cross Mersey 182 D6
Hunt's Green Bucks 84 E5
Hunts Green Warwick 134 D3
Hunt's Green W Berks 64 E2
Huntscott Som'set 42 E2
Huntsham Devon 27 C8
Huntspill Som'set 43 D10
Huntstile Som'set 43 G9
Huntworth Som'set 43 G10
Hunwick Durham 233 E9
Hunworth Norfolk 159 B11
Hurcott Som'set 28 D5
Hurcott Som'set 29 B8
Hurdcott Wilts 47 G7
Hurdley Powys 130 E5
Hurdsfield Ches 184 G6
Hurgill N Yorks 224 E3
Hurlet Glasg C 267 C10
Hurley Warwick 134 D4
Hurley Windsor 65 C10
Hurley Bottom Windsor 65 C10
Hurley Common Warwick 134 D4
Hurlford E Ayrs 257 B11
Hurliness Orkney 313 K3
Hurlston Lancs 194 E2
Hurlston Green Lancs 193 E11
Hurn Dorset 19 B8
Hurn ER Yorks 208 E6
Hursey Dorset 28 G6
Hursley Hants 32 B6
Hurst Gtr Man 196 G2
Hurst N Yorks 223 E10
Hurst Som'set 29 D7
Hurst Wokingham 65 E9
Hurst Green E Sussex 38 B2
Hurst Green Essex 89 B9
Hurst Green Lancs 203 F9
Hurst Green Surrey 51 C11
Hurst Green W Midlands 133 F9
Hurst Hill W Midlands 133 E8
Hurst Park Surrey 66 F6
Hurst Wickham W Sussex 36 D3
Hurstbourne Priors Hants 48 D2
Hurstbourne Tarrant Hants 47 C11
Hurstead Gtr Man 196 D2
Hurstley Heref'd 97 B7
Hurstpierpoint W Sussex 36 D3
Hurstwood Lancs 204 G3
Hurtmore Surrey 50 D3
Hurworth Place D'lington 224 C5
Hurworth-on-Tees D'lington 224 C6
Hury Durham 223 B9
Husabost H'land 298 D2
Husbands Bosworth Leics 136 G2
Husbandtown Angus 287 D8
Husborne Crawley Beds 103 D9
Husthwaite N Yorks 215 D10
Hut Green N Yorks 198 C5
Hutcherleigh Devon 8 E5
Hutchesontown Glasg C 267 C11
Huthwaite Notts 171 D7
Huthwaite N Yorks 225 E9
Huttock Top Lancs 195 C11
Huttoft Lincs 191 F8
Hutton Scot Borders 273 E8
Hutton Cumb 230 F4
Hutton Essex 87 F10
Hutton ER Yorks 208 C6
Hutton Lancs 194 B3
Hutton N Som'set 43 B11
Hutton Bonville N Yorks 224 E6
Hutton Buscel N Yorks 217 C9
Hutton Conyers N Yorks 214 E6
Hutton Cranswick ER Yorks 208 C6
Hutton End Cumb 230 D4
Hutton Gate Redcar/Clevel'd 225 C11
Hutton Hang N Yorks 214 B3
Hutton Henry Durham 234 D4
Hutton Magna Durham 224 C2
Hutton Mount Essex 87 G10
Hutton Mulgrave N Yorks 226 C6
Hutton Roof Cumb 211 D11
Hutton Roof Cumb 230 E3
Hutton Rudby N Yorks 225 D9
Hutton Sessay N Yorks 215 D9
Hutton Village Redcar/Clevel'd 226 C2
Hutton Wandesley N Yorks 206 C6
Hutton-le-Hole N Yorks 216 B4
Huxham Devon 14 B4
Huxham Green Som'set 44 F5
Huxley Ches 167 C8
Huxter Shetl'd 315 G7
Huxter Shetl'd 315 H8
Huxter Shetl'd 315 H5
Huxton Scot Borders 273 B7
Huyton Mersey 182 C6
Huyton Park Mersey 182 C6
Huyton Quarry Mersey 183 C7
Huyton-with-Roby Mersey 182 C6
Hwlffordd = Haverfordwest Pembs 72 B6
Hycemoor Cumb 210 B1
Hyde Glos 80 E5
Hyde Glos 99 F11
Hyde Gtr Man 185 C7
Hyde Hants 31 E11
Hyde End W Berks 64 G5
Hyde End Wokingham 65 F8
Hyde Heath Bucks 84 E6
Hyde Lea Staffs 151 E8
Hyde Park S Yorks 198 G5
Hydestile Surrey 50 E3
Hylton Castle Tyne/Wear 243 F9
Hylton Red House Tyne/Wear 243 F9
Hyndburn Bridge Lancs 203 G11
Hyndford Bridge S Lanarks 269 G8
Hynish Arg/Bute 288 F1
Hyssington Powys 130 E6
Hystfield Glos 79 F11
Hythe Hants 32 F6
Hythe Kent 55 G7
Hythe Som'set 44 C3
Hythe Surrey 66 E4
Hythe End Bucks 66 E4
Hythie Aberds 303 D10
Hyton Cumb 210 B1

I

Iarsiadar W Isles 304 E3
Ibberton Dorset 30 F3
Ible Derby 170 D3
Ibrox Glasg C 267 C11
Ibsley Hants 31 F11
Ibstock Leics 153 G8
Ibstone Bucks 84 G3
Ibthorpe Hants 47 C11
Iburndale N Yorks 227 D7
Ibworth Hants 48 C5
Icelton N Som'set 59 F11
Ichrachan Arg/Bute 284 D4
Ickburgh Norfolk 140 D6
Ickenham London 66 B5
Ickenthwaite Cumb 210 B6
Ickford Bucks 83 D10
Ickham Kent 55 B8
Ickleford Herts 104 E3
Icklesham E Sussex 38 D5
Ickleton Cambs 105 C9
Icklingham Suffolk 124 C5
Ickornshaw N Yorks 204 E5
Ickwell Beds 104 B3
Ickwell Green Beds 104 B3
Ickworth House Suffolk 124 E6
Icomb Glos 100 G4
Icy Park Devon 8 F3
Idbury Oxon 82 B2
Iddesleigh Devon 25 F9
Ide Devon 14 C3
Ide Hill Kent 52 C3
Ideford Devon 14 F3
Iden E Sussex 38 B6
Iden Green Kent 53 G10
Iden Green Kent 53 F8
Idle W Yorks 205 F9
Idle Moor W Yorks 205 F9
Idless Cornw'l 4 F6
Idlicote Warwick 100 C5
Idmiston Wilts 47 F7
Idole Carms 74 B6
Idridgehay Derby 170 F3
Idrigill H'land 298 C3
Idstone Oxon 63 C9
Idvies Angus 287 C9
Iet-y-bwlch Carms 92 F3
Iffley Oxon 83 E8
Ifield W Sussex 51 F9
Ifieldwood W Sussex 51 F8
Ifold W Sussex 50 G4
Iford Bournem'th 19 C8
Iford E Sussex 36 F6
Ifton Monmouths 60 B3
Ifton Heath Shrops 148 B6
Ightfield Shrops 149 B11
Ightfield Heath Shrops 149 B11
Ightham Kent 52 B5
Ightham Common Kent 52 B5
Ightham Mote, Sevenoaks Kent 52 C5
Iken Suffolk 127 F9
Ilam Staffs 169 E10
Ilchester Som'set 29 C8
Ilderton Northum 264 E2
Ilford London 68 B2
Ilford Som'set 28 D5
Ilfracombe Devon 40 D4
Ilkeston Derby 171 G7
Ilketshall St. Andrew Suffolk 143 F7
Ilketshall St. Lawrence Suffolk 143 G7
Ilketshall St. Margaret Suffolk 143 F7
Ilkley W Yorks 205 D8
Illand Cornw'l 11 F11
Illey W Midlands 133 G9
Illington Norfolk 141 F8
Illingworth W Yorks 196 B5
Illogan Cornw'l 4 G3
Illogan Highway Cornw'l 4 G3
Ilmer Bucks 84 D3
Ilmington Warwick 100 C4
Ilminster Som'set 28 D5
Ilshaw Heath W Midlands 118 C2
Ilsington Devon 13 F11
Ilston Swan 75 G9
Ilston on the Hill Leics 136 D4
Ilton N Yorks 214 D3
Ilton Som'set 28 D4
Imachar N Ayrs 255 C9
Imber Wilts 46 D3
Imeraval Arg/Bute 254 C4
Immervoulin Stirl 285 F9
Immingham NE Lincs 201 E7
Immingham Dock NE Lincs 201 D8
Imperial War Museum London 67 D10
Imperial War Museum North Gtr Man 184 B4
Impington Cambs 123 E8
Ince Ches 182 F6
Ince Blundell Mersey 193 G10
Ince-in-Makerfield Gtr Man 194 G5
Inch of Arnhall Aberds 293 F8
Inchbae Lodge H'land 300 C4
Inchbare Angus 293 G8
Inchberry Moray 302 D3
Inchbraoch Angus 287 B11
Inchbrook Glos 80 E4
Inchcape H'land 309 J6
Incheril H'land 299 C10
Inchgrundle Angus 292 F6
Inchina H'land 307 K4
Inchinnan Renf 267 B9
Inchkinloch H'land 308 E5
Inchlaggan H'land 290 C3
Inchlumpie H'land 300 B5
Inchmore H'land 300 E3
Inchmore H'land 300 E5
Inchnacardoch Hotel H'land 290 B5
Inchnadamph H'land 307 G7
Inchock Angus 287 C10
Inchree H'land 290 G2
Inchrory Moray 292 C3
Inchture Perth/Kinr 286 E6
Inchyra Perth/Kinr 286 E5
Indian Queens Cornw'l 5 D8
Inerval Arg/Bute 254 C4
Ingatestone Essex 87 F11
Ingbirchworth S Yorks 197 F8
Ingerthorpe N Yorks 214 F5
Ingestre Staffs 151 E9
Ingham Lincs 188 E6
Ingham Norfolk 161 D7
Ingham Suffolk 125 C7
Ingham Corner Norfolk 161 D7
Ingleborough Norfolk 157 F9
Ingleby Derby 152 D6
Ingleby Lincs 188 F5
Ingleby Arncliffe N Yorks 225 E9
Ingleby Barwick Stockton 225 C8
Ingleby Cross N Yorks 225 E9
Ingleby Greenhow N Yorks 225 D11
Ingleigh Green Devon 25 F10
Inglemire Kingston/Hull 209 G7
Inglesbatch Bath/NE Som'set 61 G8
Inglesham Swindon 82 F2
Inglestone Common S Glos 61 B9
Ingleton Durham 233 G9
Ingleton N Yorks 212 E3
Inglewhite Lancs 202 F6
Ingliston C/Edinb 280 G2
Ingoe Northum 242 C2
Ingol Lancs 202 G6
Ingoldmells Lincs 175 B9
Ingoldsby Lincs 155 C10
Ingoldisthorpe Norfolk 158 C3
Ingon Warwick 118 F4
Ingram Northum 264 F2
Ingrave Essex 87 G10
Ingrow W Yorks 204 F6
Ings Cumb 221 F8
Ingst S Glos 60 B5
Ingthorpe Rutl'd 137 B9
Ingworth Norfolk 160 D3
Inham's End Cambs 138 D5
Inhurst Hants 64 G5
Inkberrow Worcs 117 F10
Inkerman Durham 233 D8
Inkersall Derby 186 G6
Inkersall Green Derby 186 G6
Inkford Worcs 117 C11
Inkpen W Berks 63 G11
Inkstack H'land 310 B6
Inlands W Sussex 34 F3
Inmarsh Wilts 62 G2
Innellan Arg/Bute 276 G2
Inner Hope Devon 8 H3
Innerleithen Scot Borders 261 B8
Innerleven Fife 287 G7
Innermessan Dumf/Gal 236 C2
Innerwick E Loth 282 G4
Innerwick Perth/Kinr 285 C9
Innie Arg/Bute 275 B9
Inninbeg H'land 289 E8
Innis Chonain Arg/Bute 284 E5
Innistrynich Arg/Bute 284 E5
Innox Hill Som'set 45 D9
Innsworth Glos 99 G7
Insch Aberds 302 G6
Insh H'land 291 C10
Inshegra H'land 306 D7
Inshore H'land 308 C3
Inskip Lancs 202 F5
Inskip Moss Side Lancs 202 F5
Instoneville S Yorks 198 E5
Instow Devon 40 G3
Insworke Cornw'l 7 E8
Intack Blackb'n 195 B8
Intake S Yorks 199 G6
Intake S Yorks 186 E5
Inver Aberds 292 D4
Inver H'land 311 L2
Inver Perth/Kinr 286 C4
Inver Mallie H'land 290 E3
Inveralort H'land 295 G9
Inveraldie Angus 287 D8
Inveralivaig H'land 298 E4
Inverallign H'land 299 D8
Inverallochy Aberds 303 C10
Inveran H'land 299 B8
Inveran H'land 309 K5
Inveraray Arg/Bute 284 G4
Inveraray Jail Arg/Bute 284 G4
Inverarish H'land 295 B7
Inverarity Angus 287 C8
Inverarnan Stirl 285 F7
Inverasdale H'land 307 L3
Inverawe Ho. Arg/Bute 284 D4
Inverbeg Arg/Bute 276 B6
Inverbervie Aberds 293 F10
Inverboyndie Aberds 302 C6
Inverbroom H'land 307 L6
Invercarron Mains H'land 309 K5
Invercassley H'land 309 J4
Invercauld House Aberds 292 D3
Inverchaolain Arg/Bute 275 F11
Invercharnan H'land 284 C5
Inverchoran H'land 300 D2
Invercreran Arg/Bute 284 C4
Inverdruie H'land 291 B11
Inverebrie Aberds 303 F9
Inverernan Ho. Aberds 292 B5
Invereshie House H'land 291 C10
Inveresk E Loth 280 G6
Inverewe Garden, Gairloch H'land 307 L3
Inverey Aberds 292 E2
Inverfarigaig H'land 300 G5
Invergarry H'land 290 C5
Invergelder Aberds 292 D4
Invergeldie Perth/Kinr 285 E11
Invergordon H'land 301 C7
Invergowrie Perth/Kinr 287 D7
Inverguseran H'land 295 E9
Inverhadden Perth/Kinr 285 B10
Inverhaggernie Stirl 285 E7
Inverharroch Moray 302 F3
Inverherive Stirl 285 E7
Inverie H'land 295 F9
Inverinan Arg/Bute 275 B10
Inverinate H'land 295 C11
Inverkeilor Angus 287 C10
Inverkeithing Fife 280 E2
Inverkeithny Aberds 302 E6
Inverkip Invercl 276 G4
Inverkirkaig H'land 307 H5
Inverlael H'land 307 L6
Inverleith C/Edinb 280 F4
Inverliever Lodge Arg/Bute 275 C9
Inverliver Arg/Bute 284 D4
Inverlochlarig Stirl 285 F8
Inverlochy Arg/Bute 284 E5
Inverlochy H'land 290 F3
Inverlochy Moray 301 G11
Inverlussa Arg/Bute 275 E7
Invermark Lodge Angus 292 E6
Invermoidart H'land 289 B8
Invermoriston H'land 290 B6
Invernaver H'land 308 C7
Inverneill Arg/Bute 275 E9
Inverness H'land 300 E6
Inverness Airport H'land 301 D7
Invernettie Aberds 303 E11
Invernoaden Arg/Bute 276 B2
Inveronich Arg/Bute 284 G6
Inveroran Hotel Arg/Bute 284 C6
Inverpolly Lodge H'land 307 H5
Inverquharity Angus 287 B8
Inverquhomery Aberds 303 E10
Inverroy H'land 290 E4
Inversanda H'land 289 D11
Invershiel H'land 295 D11
Invershin H'land 309 K5
Invershore H'land 310 F6
Inversnaid Hotel Stirl 285 G7
Invertrossachs Stirl 285 G9
Inverugie Aberds 303 E11
Inveruglas Arg/Bute 285 G7
Inveruglass H'land 291 C10
Inverurie Aberds 303 G7
Invervar Perth/Kinr 285 C10
Inverythan Aberds 303 E7
Inwardleigh Devon 12 B7
Inworth Essex 88 B5
Iochdar W Isles 297 G3
Iolyn Park Conwy 180 F3
Iona Abbey and Cathedral Arg/Bute 288 G4
Iping W Sussex 34 C5
Ipplepen Devon 8 B6
Ipsden Oxon 64 B6
Ipstones Staffs 169 F8
Ipswich Suffolk 108 C3
Ir Wyddgrug = Mold Flints 166 C2
Irby Mersey 182 E3
Irby Hill Mersey 182 D3
Irby in the Marsh Lincs 175 C7
Irby upon Humber NE Lincs 201 G7
Irchester Northants 121 D8
Ireby Cumb 229 D10
Ireby Lancs 212 D3
Ireland Beds 104 C2
Ireland Orkney 313 H4
Ireland Shetl'd 315 L5
Ireland Wood W Yorks 205 F11
Ireland's Cross Shrops 168 G2
Ireleth Cumb 210 D4
Ireshopeburn Durham 232 D3
Ireton Wood Derby 170 F3
Irlam Gtr Man 184 C2
Irlams o' th' Height Gtr Man 184 B3
Irnham Lincs 155 D10
Iron Acton S Glos 61 C7
Iron Bridge Cambs 139 D9
Iron Cross Warwick 117 G11
Iron Lo. H'land 299 G10
Ironbridge Telford 132 C3
Ironbridge Gorge Museum, Telford Shrops 132 C3
Ironmacannie Dumf/Gal 237 B8
Irons Bottom Surrey 51 D9
Ironside Aberds 303 D8
Ironville Derby 170 E6
Irstead Norfolk 161 E7
Irstead Street Norfolk 161 F7
Irthington Cumb 239 E11
Irthlingborough Northants 121 C8
Irton N Yorks 217 C10
Irvine N Ayrs 257 B8
Irwell Vale Lancs 195 C9
Isabella Northum 253 G8
Isauld H'land 310 C3
Isbister Orkney 312 F3
Isbister Orkney 312 G4
Isbister Shetl'd 314 D5
Isbister Shetl'd 315 G7
Isel Cumb 229 E9
Isfield E Sussex 36 D6
Isham Northants 121 C7
Ishriff Arg/Bute 289 F8
Isington Hants 49 E9
Island Carr N Lincs 200 F3
Islawr-dref Gwyn 146 F3
Islay Airport Arg/Bute 254 B4
Islay Ho Arg/Bute 274 G4
Isle Abbotts Som'set 28 C5
Isle Brewers Som'set 28 C5
Isle of Man Dumf/Gal 238 B2
Isle of Man Airport I/Man 192 F3
Isle of Man Steam Railway I/Man 192 E4
Isle of Whithorn Dumf/Gal 236 F6
Isleham Cambs 124 C2
Isleornsay H'land 295 D9
Islesburgh Shetl'd 314 G5
Islesteps Dumf/Gal 237 B11
Isleworth London 67 D7
Isley Walton Leics 153 D8
Islibhig W Isles 304 F1
Islington London 67 B10
Islip Northants 121 B9
Islip Oxon 83 C8
Istead Rise Kent 68 F6
Itchen S'thampton 32 E6
Itchen Abbas Hants 48 G4
Itchen Stoke Hants 48 G5
Itchingfield W Sussex 35 B10
Itchington S Glos 61 B7
Itteringham Norfolk 160 C2
Itteringham Common Norfolk 160 D3
Itton Common Monmouths 79 F7
Ivegill Cumb 230 C4
Ivelet N Yorks 223 F8
Iver Bucks 66 C4
Iver Heath Bucks 66 C4
Iveston Durham 242 G4
Ivetsy Bank Staffs 150 G6
Ivinghoe Bucks 84 B6
Ivinghoe Aston Bucks 85 B7
Ivington Heref'd 115 F9
Ivington Green Heref'd 115 F9
Ivy Chimneys Essex 87 E7
Ivy Cross Dorset 30 C5
Ivy Hatch Kent 52 C5
Ivy Todd Norfolk 141 B7
Ivybridge Devon 8 D2
Ivychurch Kent 39 B8
Iwade Kent 70 F2
Iwerne Courtney Dorset 30 E4
Iwerne Minster Dorset 30 E5
Iwood N Som'set 60 G3
Ixhill Bucks 83 C11
Ixworth Suffolk 125 C8
Ixworth Thorpe Suffolk 125 C8

J

Jack Bridge W Yorks 196 B3
Jack Hill N Yorks 205 C10
Jackfield Shrops 132 C3
Jack-in-the-Green Devon 14 B6
Jack's Green Essex 105 G11
Jack's Green Glos 80 D5
Jack's Hatch Essex 86 D6
Jacksdale Notts 170 E6
Jackson Bridge W Yorks 197 F7
Jackstown Aberds 303 F7
Jackton E Renf 267 E11
Jacobs Well Surrey 50 C4
Jacobstow Cornw'l 11 B9
Jacobstowe Devon 25 G9
Jagger Green W Yorks 196 D5
Jameston Pembs 73 F9
Jamestown Dumf/Gal 249 D7
Jamestown Fife 280 E2
Jamestown H'land 300 D4
Jamestown W Dunb 277 E7
Jamphlars Fife 280 B4
Janetstown H'land 310 C4
Janke's Green Essex 107 F8
Jarlshof Prehistoric Site Shetl'd 315 N5
Jarman Park Herts 85 D9
Jarrow Tyne/Wear 243 D8
Jarvis Brook E Sussex 37 B8
Jasper's Green Essex 106 F4
Java Arg/Bute 289 F9
Jaw Hill W Yorks 197 C9
Jawcraig Falk 278 F6
Jaywick Essex 89 C10
Jealott's Hill Brackn'l 65 E11
Jedburgh Scot Borders 262 E5
Jeffreyston Pembs 73 D9
Jellyhill E Dunb 278 G2
Jemimaville H'land 301 C7
Jennett's Hill W Berks 64 E5
Jericho Gtr Man 195 E10
Jersey Marine Neath P Talb 76 F2
Jesmond Tyne/Wear 243 D7
Jevington E Sussex 23 E9
Jewell's Cross Devon 24 G3
Jingle Street Monmouths 79 C7
Jockey End Herts 85 C8
Jodrell Bank Ches 184 F4
Jodrell Bank Visitor Centre, Holmes Chapel Ches 168 A3
John o'Gaunt Leics 136 B4
John O'Gaunts W Yorks 197 B11
John o'Groats H'land 310 B7
Johnby Cumb 230 E4
John's Cross E Sussex 38 C3
Johnshaven Aberds 293 G9
Johnson Fold Gtr Man 195 E7
Johnson Street Norfolk 161 F7
Johnston Pembs 72 C6
Johnstone Renf 267 C8
Johnstone Mains Aberds 293 F9
Johnstonebridge Dumf/Gal 248 E4
Johnstown Carms 74 B5
Johnstown Wrex 166 F4
Joppa C/Edinb 280 G6
Joppa S Ayrs 257 F10
Jordan Green Norfolk 159 E11
Jordanhill Glasg C 267 B10
Jordans Bucks 85 G7
Jordanston Pembs 91 E8
Jordanthorpe S Yorks 186 E5
Jordon S Yorks 186 C6
Jorvik Viking Centre C/York 207 C8
Joyden's Wood Kent 68 E4
Joyford Glos 79 C9
Joy's Green Glos 79 B10
Jubilee Gtr Man 196 E2
Judges Lodging, Presteigne Powys 114 E6
Jugbank Staffs 150 B5
Jump S Yorks 197 G11
Jumper's Common Dorset 19 C8
Jumper's Town E Sussex 52 G3
Juniper Green C/Edinb 270 B4
Jurby East I/Man 192 C4
Jurby South Motor Racing Circuit I/Man 192 C4
Jurby West I/Man 192 C4

K

Kaber Cumb 222 C5
Kaimend S Lanarks 269 F9
Kaimes C/Edinb 270 B5
Kame Fife 287 G7
Kames Arg/Bute 275 B9
Kames Arg/Bute 275 F10
Kames E Ayrs 258 D5
Kea Cornw'l 4 G6
Keadby N Lincs 199 E10
Keal Cotes Lincs 174 C5
Kearsley Gtr Man 195 G9
Kearsney Kent 55 E9
Kearstwick Cumb 212 D2
Kearton N Yorks 223 F9
Kearvaig H'land 306 B7
Keasden N Yorks 212 F4
Keason Cornw'l 6 B6
Keaton Devon 8 E2
Kebroyd W Yorks 196 C4
Keckwick Halton 183 E9
Keddington Lincs 190 D4
Keddington Corner Lincs 190 D5
Kedington Suffolk 106 B4
Kedleston Derby 170 G3
Kedleston Hall Derby 170 G4
Keekle Cumb 219 B10
Keelars Tye Essex 107 G11
Keelby Lincs 201 F7
Keele Staffs 168 F4
Keeley Green Beds 103 B10
Keelham W Yorks 205 G7
Keeres Green Essex 87 C9
Keeston Pembs 72 B6

Keevil Wilts 46 B2
Kegworth Leics 153 D9
Kehelland Cornw'l 4 G2
Keig Aberds 293 B8
Keighley W Yorks 205 E7
Keighley and Worth Valley Railway W Yorks 205 F7
Keil H'land 289 D11
Keilarsbrae Clack 279 C7
Keilhill Aberds 303 D7
Keillmore Arg/Bute 275 E7
Keillor Perth/Kinr 286 C6
Keillour Perth/Kinr 286 E3
Keills Arg/Bute 274 G5
Keils Arg/Bute 274 G6
Keinton Mandeville Som'set 44 G5
Keir Mill Dumf/Gal 247 E9
Keirsleywell Row Northum 241 G7
Keisby Lincs 155 D10
Keisley Cumb 231 G10
Keiss H'land 310 C7
Keistle H'land 298 D4
Keith Moray 302 D4
Keith Hall Aberds 303 G7
Keith Inch Aberds 303 E11
Keithock Angus 293 G8
Kelbrook Lancs 204 E4
Kelburn Invercl 276 G6
Kelby Lincs 173 G8
Kelcliffe W Yorks 205 E9
Keld Cumb 221 C11
Keld N Yorks 223 E7
Keld Head N Yorks 216 C5
Keldholme N Yorks 216 B4
Kelfield N Lincs 199 G10
Kelfield N Yorks 207 F7
Kelham Notts 172 D3
Kellacott Devon 12 D4
Kellan Arg/Bute 289 E7
Kellas Angus 287 D8
Kellas Moray 301 D11
Kellaton Devon 9 G11
Kellaways Wilts 62 D3
Kelleth Cumb 222 D3
Kelling Norfolk 177 E9
Kellingley N Yorks 198 C4
Kellington N Yorks 198 C5
Kelloe Durham 234 D2
Kelloholm Dumf/Gal 258 G6
Kells Cumb 219 B9
Kelly Devon 12 E3
Kelly Bray Cornw'l 12 G3
Kelmarsh Northants 120 B4
Kelmscott Oxon 82 F3
Kelsale Suffolk 127 E7
Kelsall Ches 167 B8
Kelsall Hill Ches 167 B8
Kelsay Arg/Bute 254 B2
Kelshall Herts 104 D6
Kelsick Cumb 238 G5
Kelso Scot Borders 262 C6
Kelso Racecourse Scot Borders 262 B6
Kelstedge Derby 170 C4
Kelstern Lincs 190 C3
Kelsterton Flints 182 G3
Kelston Bath/NE Som'set 61 F8
Keltneyburn Perth/Kinr 285 C11
Kelton Dumf/Gal 237 B11
Kelton Durham 232 G4
Kelty Fife 280 C2
Keltybridge Fife 280 B2
Kelvedon Essex 88 B5
Kelvedon Hatch Essex 87 F9
Kelvin S Lanarks 268 E2
Kelvindale Glasg C 267 B11
Kelvinside Glasg C 267 B11
Kelynack Cornw'l 1 C3
Kemacott Devon 41 D7
Kemback Fife 287 F8
Kemberton Shrops 132 C4
Kemble Glos 81 F7
Kemerton Worcs 99 D8
Kemeys Commander Monmouths 78 E5
Kemeys Inferior Monmouths 78 G5
Kemnay Aberds 293 B9
Kemp Town Brighton/Hove 36 G4
Kempe's Corner Kent 54 D4
Kempie H'land 308 D4
Kempley Glos 98 F3
Kempley Green Glos 98 F3
Kemp's Green Warwick 118 C2
Kempsey Worcs 99 B7
Kempsford Glos 81 F11
Kempshott Hants 48 D6
Kempston Beds 103 B10
Kempston Church End Beds 103 B10
Kempston Hardwick Beds 103 C10
Kempston West End Beds 103 B10
Kempton Shrops 131 G7
Kempton Park Racecourse Surrey 66 E6
Kemsing Kent 52 B4
Kemsley Kent 70 F2
Kemsley Street Kent 69 G10
Kenardington Kent 54 G3
Kenchester Heref'd 97 C8
Kencot Oxon 82 E3
Kendal Cumb 221 G10
Kendal End Worcs 117 C10
Kendleshire S Glos 61 D7
Kendoon Dumf/Gal 246 F4
Kendray S Yorks 197 G11
Kenfig Bridg 57 E10
Kenfig Bridg 57 E10
Kenfig Hill Bridg 57 E10
Kengharair Arg/Bute 288 E6
Kenilworth Warwick 118 C5
Kenilworth Castle Warwick 118 C5
Kenknock Stirl 285 D8
Kenley London 51 B10
Kenley Shrops 131 C11
Kenmore Arg/Bute 284 G4
Kenmore H'land 299 D7
Kenmore Perth/Kinr 285 C11
Kenmure Dumf/Gal 237 B8
Kenn Devon 14 D4
Kenn N Som'set 60 F2
Kennacley W Isles 305 J3
Kennacraig Arg/Bute 275 G9
Kennards House Cornw'l 11 E11
Kenneggy Cornw'l 2 D3
Kenneggy Downs Cornw'l 2 D3
Kennerleigh Devon 26 F4
Kennet Clack 279 C8
Kennet End Cambs 124 D3
Kennethmont Aberds 302 G5
Kennetpans Falk 279 D8
Kennett Cambs 124 D3
Kennford Devon 14 D4
Kenninghall Norfolk 141 F10
Kenninghall Heath Norfolk 141 G10
Kennington Kent 54 E4
Kennington London 67 D10
Kennington Oxon 83 E8
Kennishead Glasg C 267 C10
Kennoway Fife 287 G7
Kenny Som'set 28 D4
Kennyhill Suffolk 140 G3
Kennythorpe N Yorks 216 F5
Kenovay Arg/Bute 288 E1
Kensal Green London 67 C8
Kensal Rise London 67 C8
Kensal Town London 67 C8
Kensaleyre H'land 298 D4
Kensary H'land 310 E6
Kensington London 67 D9
Kenson V/Glam 58 F5
Kenstone Shrops 149 D11
Kensworth Beds 85 B8
Kent End Wilts 81 G9
Kent Hatch Kent 52 C2
Kent International Airport Kent 71 F10
Kent Street E Sussex 38 D3
Kent Street Kent 53 C7
Kent Street W Sussex 36 C2
Kentallen H'land 284 B4
Kentchurch Heref'd 97 F8
Kentford Suffolk 124 D4
Kentisbeare Devon 27 G9
Kentisbury Devon 40 E6
Kentisbury Ford Devon 40 E6
Kentish Town London 67 C9
Kentmere Cumb 221 E9
Kenton Devon 14 E5
Kenton London 67 B7
Kenton Suffolk 126 D3
Kenton Tyne/Wear 242 D6
Kenton Bankfoot Tyne/Wear 242 D6
Kenton Bar Tyne/Wear 242 D6
Kenton Corner Suffolk 126 D4
Kenton Green Glos 80 C3
Kentra H'land 289 C8
Kentrigg Cumb 221 G10
Kents Bank Cumb 211 D7
Kent's Green Glos 98 G4
Kents Hill M/Keynes 103 D7
Kent's Oak Hants 32 C4
Kenwick Shrops 149 C8
Kenwyn Cornw'l 4 F6
Kenyon Warrington 183 B10
Keoldale H'land 308 C3
Keonchulish Ho H'land 307 K6
Kepnal Wilts 63 G7
Keppanach H'land 290 G2
Keppoch H'land 295 C11
Keprigan Arg/Bute 255 F7
Kepwick N Yorks 225 G9
Kerchesters Scot Borders 263 B7
Kerdiston Norfolk 159 E11
Keresley W Midlands 134 G6
Keresley Newlands Warwick 134 G6
Kerley Downs Cornw'l 4 G5
Kernborough Devon 8 G5
Kerne Bridge Heref'd 79 B9
Kernsary H'land 299 B8
Kerridge Ches 184 F6
Kerridge-end Ches 184 G6
Kerris Cornw'l 1 D4
Kerry Powys 130 F3
Kerrycroy Arg/Bute 266 C2
Kerrycrusach Arg/Bute 266 C1
Kerrylamont Arg/Bute 266 D2
Kerry's Gate Heref'd 97 E7
Kerrysdale H'land 299 B8
Kerrytonlia Arg/Bute 266 D2
Kersal Gtr Man 195 G10
Kersall Notts 172 C2
Kersbrook Devon 15 E7
Kerscott Devon 25 B10
Kersey Suffolk 107 C9
Kersey Tye Suffolk 107 C9
Kersey Upland Suffolk 107 C9
Kershopefoot Cumb 249 G11
Kerswell Devon 27 G9
Kerswell Green Worcs 99 B7
Kerthen Wood Cornw'l 2 C3
Kesgrave Suffolk 108 B4
Kessingland Suffolk 143 F11
Kessingland Beach Suffolk 143 F11
Kestle Cornw'l 3 D7
Kestle Cornw'l 5 F9
Kestle Mill Cornw'l 4 D6
Keston London 68 G2
Keston Mark London 68 G2
Keswick Cumb 229 G11
Keswick Norfolk 142 C4
Keswick Norfolk 161 C7
Ketley Telford 150 G3
Ketley Bank Telford 150 G3
Ketsby Lincs 190 F5
Kettering Northants 121 B7
Ketteringham Norfolk 142 C3
Kettins Perth/Kinr 286 D6
Kettle Corner Kent 53 C8
Kettle Green Herts 86 B6
Kettlebaston Suffolk 125 G9
Kettlebridge Fife 287 G7
Kettlebrook Staffs 134 C4
Kettleburgh Suffolk 126 E5
Kettlehill Fife 287 G7
Kettleholm Dumf/Gal 238 B4
Kettleness N Yorks 226 B6
Kettleshulme Ches 185 F7
Kettlesing N Yorks 205 B10
Kettlesing Bottom N Yorks 205 B10
Kettlestone Norfolk 159 C9
Kettlethorpe Lincs 188 F4
Kettletoft Orkney 312 E7
Kettlewell N Yorks 213 E9
Ketton Rutl'd 137 C9
Kevingtown London 68 F3
Kew London 67 D7
Keward Som'set 44 E4
KewRoyal Botanic Gardens London 67 D7
Kewstoke N Som'set 59 G10
Kexbrough S Yorks 197 F10
Kexby C/York 207 C10
Kexby Lincs 188 D5
Key Green Ches 168 C5
Key Green N Yorks 226 E6
Key Street Kent 69 G11
Keycol Kent 69 G11
Keyford Som'set 45 D9
Keyham Leics 136 B3
Keyhaven Hants 20 C2
Keyingham ER Yorks 201 B8
Keymer W Sussex 36 E4
Keynsham Bath/NE Som'set 61 F7
Key's Green Kent 53 F7
Keysers Estate Essex 86 D5
Keysoe Beds 121 E11
Keysoe Row Beds 121 E11
Keyston Cambs 121 B10
Keyworth Notts 154 C2
Khantore Aberds 292 D4
Kibblesworth Tyne/Wear 242 F6
Kibworth Beauchamp Leics 136 E3
Kibworth Harcourt Leics 136 E3
Kidbrooke London 68 D2
Kiddal Lane End W Yorks 206 F4
Kiddemore Green Staffs 133 B7
Kidderminster Worcs 116 B6
Kiddington Oxon 101 G8
Kidland Devon 26 C4
Kidlington Oxon 83 C7
Kidmore End Oxon 65 D7
Kidnal Ches 167 F7
Kidsdale Dumf/Gal 236 F6
Kidsgrove Staffs 168 E4
Kidstones N Yorks 213 C9
Kidwelly = Cydweli Carms 74 D6
Kiel Crofts Arg/Bute 289 F11
Kielder Northum 250 E4
Kielder Castle Visitor Centre Northum 250 E4
Kierfiold Ho Orkney 312 G3
Kilbagie Clack 279 C8
Kilbarchan Renf 267 C8
Kilbeg H'land 295 E8
Kilberry Arg/Bute 275 G8
Kilbirnie N Ayrs 266 E6
Kilbowie W Dunb 277 G10
Kilbraur H'land 311 H2
Kilbride Arg/Bute 254 C4
Kilbride Arg/Bute 275 D9
Kilbride Arg/Bute 289 G10
Kilbride Arg/Bute 289 G11
Kilbride H'land 295 C7
Kilbridemore Arg/Bute 275 D11
Kilbryde Castle Stirl 285 G11
Kilburn Angus 292 G5
Kilburn Derby 170 F5
Kilburn London 67 C8
Kilburn N Yorks 215 D10
Kilby Leics 136 D2
Kilchamaig Arg/Bute 275 G9
Kilchattan Arg/Bute 274 D4
Kilchattan Bay Arg/Bute 266 D2
Kilchenzie Arg/Bute 255 E7
Kilcheran Arg/Bute 289 F10
Kilchiaran Arg/Bute 274 G3
Kilchoan Arg/Bute 275 B8
Kilchoan H'land 288 C6
Kilchoman Arg/Bute 274 G3
Kilchrenan Arg/Bute 284 E4
Kilconquhar Fife 287 G8
Kilcot Glos 98 F3
Kilcoy H'land 300 D5
Kilcreggan Arg/Bute 276 E4
Kildale N Yorks 226 D2
Kildalloig Arg/Bute 255 F8
Kildary H'land 301 B7
Kildaton Ho Arg/Bute 254 C5
Kildavanan Arg/Bute 275 G11
Kildermorie Lodge H'land 300 B5
Kildonan Dumf/Gal 236 D2
Kildonan H'land 298 D3
Kildonan N Ayrs 256 E2
Kildonan Lodge H'land 311 G3
Kildonnan H'land 294 G6
Kildrum N Lanarks 278 F5
Kildrummy Aberds 292 B6
Kildwick W Yorks 204 D6
Kilfinan Arg/Bute 275 F10
Kilfinnan H'land 290 D4
Kilgetty Pembs 73 D10
Kilgour Fife 286 G6
Kilgrammie S Ayrs 244 C7
Kilgwrrwg Common Monmouths 79 F7
Kilhallon Cornw'l 5 E11
Kilham ER Yorks 217 G11
Kilham Northum 263 C9
Kilkeddan Arg/Bute 255 E8
Kilkenneth Arg/Bute 288 E1
Kilkerran Arg/Bute 255 F8
Kilkhampton Cornw'l 24 E3
Killamarsh Derby 187 E7
Killay Swan 75 G10
Killbeg Arg/Bute 289 E8
Killean Arg/Bute 255 C7
Killearn Stirl 277 D10
Killegruer Arg/Bute 255 D7
Killellan Arg/Bute 266 B2
Killen H'land 300 D6
Killerby D'lington 224 B3
Killerton House, Exeter Devon 14 A5
Killichonan Perth/Kinr 285 B9
Killiechoinich Arg/Bute 289 G10
Killiechonate H'land 290 E4
Killiechronan Arg/Bute 289 E7
Killiecrankie Perth/Kinr 291 G11
Killiemor Arg/Bute 288 F6
Killiemore House Arg/Bute 288 G6
Killigorrick Cornw'l 6 C4
Killilan H'land 295 B11
Killimster H'land 310 D7
Killin Stirl 285 D9
Killin Lodge H'land 291 C7
Killinallan Arg/Bute 274 F4
Killinghall N Yorks 205 B11
Killington Cumb 212 B2
Killington Devon 41 D7
Killingworth Tyne/Wear 243 C7
Killingworth Moor Tyne/Wear 243 C7
Killingworth Village Tyne/Wear 243 C7
Killmahumaig Arg/Bute 275 D8
Killochyett Scot Borders 271 F9
Killocraw Arg/Bute 255 D7
Killundine H'land 289 E7
Kilmacolm Invercl 267 B7
Kilmaha Arg/Bute 275 C10
Kilmahog Stirl 285 G10
Kilmalcolm Invercl 277 G7
Kilmalieu H'land 289 D10
Kilmaluag H'land 298 B4
Kilmany Fife 287 E7
Kilmarie H'land 295 D7
Kilmarnock E Ayrs 257 B10
Kilmaron Castle Fife 287 F7
Kilmartin Arg/Bute 275 D9
Kilmaurs E Ayrs 267 G8
Kilmelford Arg/Bute 275 B9
Kilmeny Arg/Bute 274 G4
Kilmersdon Som'set 45 C7
Kilmeston Hants 33 B9
Kilmichael Arg/Bute 255 E7
Kilmichael Arg/Bute 275 F10
Kilmichael Glassary Arg/Bute 275 D9
Kilmichael of Inverlussa Arg/Bute 275 E8
Kilmington Devon 15 B11
Kilmington Wilts 45 F9
Kilmington Common Wilts 45 F9
Kilmington Street Wilts 45 F9
Kilmoluaig Arg/Bute 288 E1
Kilmonivaig H'land 290 E3
Kilmorack H'land 300 E4
Kilmore Arg/Bute 289 G10
Kilmore H'land 295 E8
Kilmory Arg/Bute 275 F8
Kilmory H'land 289 B7
Kilmory H'land 294 E5
Kilmory N Ayrs 255 E10
Kilmory Lodge Arg/Bute 275 C8
Kilmote H'land 311 H3
Kilmuir H'land 298 B3
Kilmuir H'land 298 E2
Kilmuir H'land 300 E6
Kilmuir H'land 301 B7
Kilmun Arg/Bute 275 B10
Kilmun Arg/Bute 275 B10
Kilmun Arg/Bute 276 E3
Kiln Farm M/Keynes 102 D6
Kiln Green Heref'd 79 B10
Kiln Green Wokingham 65 D10
Kiln Pit Hill Northum 242 F2
Kilnave Arg/Bute 274 F3
Kilncadzow S Lanarks 269 F7
Kilndown Kent 53 F8
Kilnhill Cumb 229 E10
Kilnhurst S Yorks 187 B7
Kilninian Arg/Bute 288 E5
Kilninver Arg/Bute 289 G10
Kilnsea ER Yorks 201 D12
Kilnsey N Yorks 213 F9
Kilnwick ER Yorks 208 D5
Kilnwick Percy ER Yorks 208 C2
Kiloran Arg/Bute 274 D4
Kilpatrick N Ayrs 255 E10
Kilpeck Heref'd 97 E8
Kilphedir H'land 311 H3
Kilpin ER Yorks 199 B9
Kilpin Pike ER Yorks 199 B9
Kilrenny Fife 287 G9
Kilsby Northants 119 C11
Kilspindie Perth/Kinr 286 E6
Kilsyth N Lanarks 278 F4
Kiltarlity H'land 300 E5
Kilton Notts 187 D9
Kilton Redcar/Clevel'd 226 B3
Kilton Som'set 43 E7
Kilton Thorpe Redcar/Clevel'd 226 B3
Kiltyrie Perth/Kinr 285 D10
Kilvaxter H'land 298 C3
Kilve Som'set 42 E6
Kilvington Notts 172 G4
Kilwinning N Ayrs 266 G6
Kimberley Notts 171 G7
Kimberley Street Norfolk 141 C11
Kimberworth S Yorks 186 C6
Kimberworth Park S Yorks 186 C6
Kimble Wick Bucks 84 D4
Kimblesworth Durham 233 B11
Kimbolton Cambs 122 D2
Kimbolton Heref'd 115 E10
Kimbridge Hants 32 B4
Kimcote Leics 135 F11
Kimmeridge Dorset 18 F4
Kimmerston Northum 263 B11
Kimpton Hants 47 D9
Kimpton Herts 85 B11
Kimworthy Devon 24 E4
Kinabus Arg/Bute 254 C3
Kinbeachie H'land 300 C6
Kinbrace H'land 310 F2
Kinbuck Stirl 285 G11
Kincaidston S Ayrs 257 F8
Kincaple Fife 287 F8
Kincardine Fife 279 D8
Kincardine H'land 309 L6
Kincardine Bridge Fife 279 D8
Kincardine O'Neil Aberds 293 D7
Kinclaven Perth/Kinr 286 D5
Kincorth Aberd C 293 C11
Kincorth Ho. Moray 301 C10
Kincraig H'land 291 C10
Kincraigie Perth/Kinr 286 C3
Kindallachan Perth/Kinr 286 C3
Kinderland, Scarborough N Yorks 227 G10
Kineton Glos 99 F11
Kineton Warwick 118 G6
Kineton Green W Midlands 134 G2
Kinfauns Perth/Kinr 286 E5
King Edward Aberds 303 D7
King Sterndale Derby 185 G9
King Street Essex 87 E9
Kingairloch H'land 289 D10
Kingarth Arg/Bute 255 B11
Kingarth Arg/Bute 266 D2
Kingates I/Wight 20 F6
Kingcoed Monmouths 78 D6
Kingdown N Som'set 60 G4
Kingerby Lincs 189 C9
Kingfield Surrey 50 B4
Kingford Devon 24 F3
Kingham Oxon 100 G5
Kingholm Quay Dumf/Gal 237 B11
Kinghorn Fife 280 D5
Kingie H'land 290 C3
Kinglassie Fife 280 B4
Kingoodie Perth/Kinr 287 E7
King's Acre Heref'd 97 C9
King's Bank E Sussex 38 C5
King's Bromley Staffs 152 F2
King's Broom Warwick 117 G11
King's Caple Heref'd 97 F11
King's Cliffe Northants 137 D10
Kings College Chapel, Cambridge Cambs 123 F9
King's Coughton Warwick 117 F11
King's End Oxon 101 G11
Kings Farm Kent 69 E7
Kings Furlong Hants 48 C6
King's Green Glos 98 E5
King's Heath Northants 120 E4
King's Heath W Midlands 133 G11
Kings Hedges Cambs 123 E8
King's Hill Kent 53 B7
King's Hill W Midlands 133 D9
Kings Langley Herts 85 E9
King's Lynn Norfolk 158 E2
King's Meaburn Ches 231 G8
King's Mills Wrex 166 F4
King's Moss Gtr Man 194 G4
Kings Muir Scot Borders 261 B7
Kings Newnham Warwick 119 B9
Kings Newton Derby 153 D7
Kings Norton Leics 136 C3
Kings Norton W Midlands 117 B11
King's Nympton Devon 25 D11
King's Park Glasg C 267 C11
Kings Pyon Heref'd 115 G8
Kings Ripton Cambs 122 B5
King's Somborne Hants 47 G11
King's Stag Dorset 30 E2
King's Stanley Glos 80 E4
King's Sutton Oxon 101 D9
King's Tamerton Plym'th 7 D9
King's Thorne Heref'd 97 E10
King's Walden Herts 104 G3
Kings Worthy Hants 48 G3
Kingsand Cornw'l 7 E8
Kingsash Bucks 84 D5
Kingsbarns Fife 287 F9
Kingsbridge Devon 8 G4
Kingsbridge Som'set 42 F3
Kingsburgh H'land 298 D3
Kingsbury London 67 B7
Kingsbury Warwick 134 D4
Kingsbury Episcopi Som'set 28 C6
Kingsbury Regis Wilts 29 D11
Kingscauseway H'land 301 B7
Kingscavil W Loth 279 F10
Kingsclere Hants 48 B4
Kingscote Glos 80 F4
Kingscote Wokingham 65 E10
Kingscott Devon 25 D8
Kingscourt Glos 80 E4
Kingscross N Ayrs 256 D3
Kingsditch Glos 99 G8
Kingsdon Som'set 29 B8
Kingsdown Kent 55 D11
Kingsdown Swindon 63 B7
Kingsdown Wilts 61 F10
Kingseat Fife 280 C2
Kingseathill Fife 280 D2
Kingsey Bucks 84 D2
Kingsfold Lancs 194 B4
Kingsfold W Sussex 51 F7
Kingsford Aberds 293 B7
Kingsford E Ayrs 267 F8
Kingsford Worcs 132 G6
Kingsgate Kent 71 E11
Kingshall Green Suffolk 125 E8
Kingshall Street Suffolk 125 E8
Kingsheanton Devon 40 F5
Kingshill Glos 80 F2
Kingsholm Glos 80 B4
Kingshouse Hotel H'land 284 B6
Kingshurst W Midlands 134 F3
Kingside Hill Cumb 238 G5
Kingskerswell Devon 9 B7
Kingskettle Fife 287 G7
Kingsland Dorset 16 B5
Kingsland Heref'd 115 E9
Kingsland Angl 178 E2
Kingsland Shrops 149 G9
Kingsley Ches 183 G9
Kingsley Hants 49 F9
Kingsley Staffs 169 F8
Kingsley Green W Sussex 49 G11
Kingsley Holt Staffs 169 F8
Kingsley Park Northants 120 E5
Kingsmead Ches 183 G11
Kingsmead Hants 33 E9
Kingsmoor Essex 86 D6
Kingsmuir Angus 287 C8
Kingsmuir Fife 287 G9
Kingsnorth Kent 54 F4
Kingstanding W Midlands 133 E11
Kingsteignton Devon 14 G3
Kingsteps H'land 301 D9
Kingsthorpe Northants 120 E5
Kingsthorpe Hollow Northants 120 E4
Kingston Cambs 122 F6
Kingston Cornw'l 12 F3
Kingston Dorset 18 F5
Kingston Dorset 30 F3
Kingston Devon 8 F2
Kingston E Loth 281 E10
Kingston Gtr Man 184 B6
Kingston Hants 31 G11
Kingston I/Wight 20 E5
Kingston Kent 55 C7
Kingston Moray 302 C3
Kingston W Sussex 35 G9
Kingston Bagpuize Oxon 82 F6
Kingston Blount Oxon 84 F2
Kingston by Sea W Sussex 36 F2
Kingston Deverill Wilts 45 F10
Kingston Gorse W Sussex 35 G9
Kingston Lacy, Wimborne Minster Dorset 31 G7
Kingston Lisle Oxon 63 B10
Kingston Maurward Dorset 17 C10
Kingston near Lewes E Sussex 36 F5
Kingston on Soar Notts 153 D10
Kingston Park Tyne/Wear 242 D6
Kingston Russell Dorset 17 C7
Kingston St. Mary Som'set 28 B2
Kingston Seymour N Som'set 60 F2
Kingston Stert Oxon 84 E2
Kingston upon Hull Kingston/Hull 200 B6
Kingston upon Thames London 67 F7
Kingston Vale London 67 E8
Kingstone Heref'd 97 D8
Kingstone Heref'd 98 G2
Kingstone Som'set 28 E5
Kingstone Staffs 151 D11
Kingstone S Yorks 197 F10
Kingstone Winslow Oxon 63 B9
Kingstonia N Yorks 214 F6
Kingstonridge E Sussex 36 F5
Kingstown Cumb 239 F9
Kingstreet Gtr Man 184 E5
Kingsway Halton 183 D8
Kingswear Devon 9 E7
Kingswells Aberd C 293 C10
Kingswinford W Midlands 133 F7
Kingswood Bucks 83 B11
Kingswood Ches 183 G8
Kingswood Glos 80 G2
Kingswood Heref'd 114 G5
Kingswood Herts 85 E10
Kingswood Kent 53 C10
Kingswood Powys 130 C4
Kingswood S Glos 61 E7
Kingswood Som'set 42 F6
Kingswood Surrey 51 B8
Kingswood Warwick 118 C3
Kingswood Warrington 183 C9
Kingswood Warren Surrey 51 B8
Kingthorpe Lincs 189 F10
Kington Heref'd 114 F5
Kington S Glos 79 G10
Kington Worcs 117 F9
Kington Langley Wilts 62 D2
Kington Magna Dorset 30 C3
Kington St. Michael Wilts 62 D2
Kingussie H'land 291 C9
Kingweston Som'set 44 G4
Kinhrive H'land 301 B7
Kininvie Ho. Moray 302 E3
Kinkell Bridge Perth/Kinr 286 F3
Kinknockie Aberds 303 E10
Kinknockie Aberds 303 G9
Kinkry Hill Cumb 240 B2
Kinlet Shrops 132 G4
Kinloch Fife 286 F6
Kinloch H'land 289 D8
Kinloch H'land 294 F5
Kinloch H'land 295 D8
Kinloch H'land 308 F3
Kinloch Perth/Kinr 286 C5
Kinloch Perth/Kinr 286 C6
Kinloch Damph H'land 299 E8
Kinloch Hourn H'land 295 E11
Kinloch Laggan H'land 291 E7
Kinloch Lodge H'land 308 D5
Kinloch Rannoch Perth/Kinr 285 B10
Kinlochan H'land 289 C10
Kinlochard Stirl 285 G8
Kinlochbeoraid H'land 295 G10
Kinlochbervie H'land 306 D7
Kinlocheil H'land 289 B11
Kinlochewe H'land 299 C10
Kinlochleven H'land 290 G3
Kinlochmoidart H'land 289 B9
Kinlochmorar H'land 295 F10
Kinlochmore H'land 290 G3
Kinlochspelve Arg/Bute 289 G8
Kinloid H'land 295 G8
Kinloss Moray 301 C10
Kinmel Bay = Bae Cinmel Conwy 181 E7
Kinmuck Aberds 293 B10
Kinmundy Aberds 293 B10
Kinnadie Aberds 303 E9
Kinnaird Perth/Kinr 286 B3
Kinnaird Perth/Kinr 286 E6
Kinnaird Castle Angus 287 B10
Kinnauld H'land 309 J7
Kinneff Aberds 293 F10
Kinneil Falk 279 E9
Kinnelhead Dumf/Gal 248 C2
Kinnell Angus 287 B10
Kinnerley Shrops 148 E6
Kinnersley Heref'd 96 B6
Kinnersley Worcs 99 C7
Kinnerton Powys 114 E4
Kinnesswood Perth/Kinr 286 G5
Kinninvie Durham 233 G7
Kinnordy Angus 287 B7
Kinoulton Notts 154 C3
Kinross Perth/Kinr 286 G5
Kinrossie Perth/Kinr 286 D5
Kinsbourne Green Herts 85 B10
Kinsey Heath Ches 167 G11
Kinsham Worcs 99 D8
Kinsley W Yorks 198 E2
Kinson Bournem'th 19 B7
Kintallan Arg/Bute 275 E8
Kintbury W Berks 63 F11
Kintbury Cross Ways W Berks 63 F11
Kintessack Moray 301 C9
Kintillo Perth/Kinr 286 F5
Kintocher Aberds 293 C7
Kinton Heref'd 115 C8
Kinton Shrops 149 F7
Kintore Aberds 293 B9
Kintour Arg/Bute 254 B5
Kintra Arg/Bute 254 C4
Kintra Arg/Bute 288 G5
Kintradwell H'land 311 J3
Kintraw Arg/Bute 275 C9
Kinuachdrachd Arg/Bute 275 D8
Kinveachy H'land 291 B11
Kinver Staffs 132 G6
Kinwarton Warwick 118 F2
Kip Hill Durham 242 G6
Kiplin N Yorks 224 F5
Kippax W Yorks 198 B2
Kippen Stirl 278 C3
Kippford or Scaur Dumf/Gal 237 D10
Kipping's Cross Kent 52 F6
Kippington Kent 52 C4
Kirbister Orkney 312 F7
Kirbister Orkney 312 G3
Kirbister Orkney 313 H4
Kirbuster Orkney 312 F3
Kirby Bedon Norfolk 142 B5
Kirby Bellars Leics 154 F4
Kirby Cane Norfolk 143 E7
Kirby Corner W Midlands 118 B5
Kirby Cross Essex 108 G4
Kirby Fields Leics 135 C10
Kirby Grindalythe N Yorks 217 F8
Kirby Hill N Yorks 215 F7
Kirby Hill N Yorks 224 D2
Kirby Knowle N Yorks 215 B9
Kirby Misperton N Yorks 216 D5
Kirby Muxloe Leics 135 C10
Kirby Row Norfolk 143 E7
Kirby Sigston N Yorks 225 G8
Kirby Underdale ER Yorks 208 B2
Kirby Wiske N Yorks 215 C7
Kirby-le-Soken Essex 108 G4
Kirdford W Sussex 35 B8
Kirk H'land 310 D6
Kirk Bramwith S Yorks 198 E6
Kirk Deighton N Yorks 206 C3
Kirk Ella ER Yorks 200 B4
Kirk Hallam Derby 171 G7
Kirk Hammerton N Yorks 206 B5
Kirk Ireton Derby 170 E3
Kirk Langley Derby 152 B5
Kirk Merrington Durham 233 E11
Kirk Michael I/Man 192 C4
Kirk of Shotts N Lanarks 268 C6
Kirk Sandall S Yorks 198 F6
Kirk Smeaton N Yorks 198 D4
Kirk Yetholm Scot Borders 263 D8
Kirkabister Shetl'd 314 G6
Kirkabister Shetl'd 315 K6
Kirkandrews Dumf/Gal 237 E8
Kirkandrews-on-Eden Cumb 239 F9
Kirkapol Arg/Bute 288 E2
Kirkbampton Cumb 239 F8
Kirkbean Dumf/Gal 237 D11
Kirkbrae Orkney 312 D5
Kirkbride Cumb 238 F6
Kirkbridge N Yorks 224 G5
Kirkbuddo Angus 287 C9
Kirkburn Scot Borders 261 B7
Kirkburn ER Yorks 208 B5
Kirkburton W Yorks 197 E8
Kirkby Lincs 189 C9
Kirkby Mersey 182 B6
Kirkby N Yorks 225 D10
Kirkby W Yorks 197 E8
Kirkby Fenside Lincs 174 C4
Kirkby Fleetham N Yorks 224 G5
Kirkby Green Lincs 173 D9
Kirkby in Ashfield Notts 171 D7
Kirkby la Thorpe Lincs 173 F9
Kirkby Lonsdale Cumb 212 D2
Kirkby Malham N Yorks 213 G7
Kirkby Mallory Leics 135 C9
Kirkby Malzeard N Yorks 214 E4
Kirkby Mills N Yorks 216 B4
Kirkby on Bain Lincs 174 C2
Kirkby Overblow N Yorks 206 D2
Kirkby Park Mersey 182 B6
Kirkby Stephen Cumb 222 D5
Kirkby Thore Cumb 231 F8
Kirkby Underwood Lincs 155 D11
Kirkby Village Leics 136 D2
Kirkby Wharfe N Yorks 206 E6
Kirkby Woodhouse Notts 171 E7
Kirkby-in-Furness Cumb 210 C4
Kirkbymoorside N Yorks 216 B3
Kirkcaldy Fife 280 C5
Kirkcambeck Cumb 240 D2
Kirkcarswell Dumf/Gal 237 E9
Kirkcolm Dumf/Gal 236 C2
Kirkconnel Dumf/Gal 258 G6
Kirkconnell Dumf/Gal 237 C11
Kirkcowan Dumf/Gal 236 C5
Kirkcudbright Dumf/Gal 237 D8
Kirkdale Mersey 182 C4
Kirkfieldbank S Lanarks 269 G7
Kirkforthar Feus Fife 286 G6
Kirkgunzeon Dumf/Gal 237 C10
Kirkham Lancs 202 G4
Kirkham N Yorks 216 F4
Kirkhamgate W Yorks 197 C9
Kirkhams Gtr Man 195 G10
Kirkharle Northum 252 G2
Kirkheaton Northum 242 B2
Kirkheaton W Yorks 197 D7
Kirkhill Angus 293 G8
Kirkhill E Renf 267 D11
Kirkhill H'land 300 E5
Kirkhill Midloth 270 C4
Kirkhill Moray 302 F2
Kirkholt Gtr Man 195 E11
Kirkhope Scot Borders 261 E9
Kirkhouse Scot Borders 261 C8
Kirkhouse Cumb 240 F3
Kirkhouse Green S Yorks 198 D6
Kirkiboll H'land 308 D5
Kirkibost H'land 295 D7
Kirkinch Angus 287 C7
Kirkinner Dumf/Gal 236 D6
Kirkintilloch E Dunb 278 G3
Kirkland Cumb 219 B11
Kirkland Cumb 231 E8
Kirkland Cumb 229 B11
Kirkland Dumf/Gal 247 E8
Kirkland Dumf/Gal 258 G6
Kirkland Fife 281 A7
Kirkland Guards Cumb 229 C9
Kirkleatham Redcar/Clevel'd 235 G7
Kirklees Gtr Man 195 E9
Kirklevington Stockton 225 D8
Kirkley Suffolk 143 E10
Kirklington Notts 171 E10
Kirklington N Yorks 214 C6
Kirklinton Cumb 239 D10
Kirkliston C/Edinb 280 G3
Kirkmaiden Dumf/Gal 236 F3
Kirkmichael Perth/Kinr 286 B4
Kirkmichael S Ayrs 245 B8
Kirkmuirhill S Lanarks 268 G5
Kirknewton Northum 263 C10
Kirknewton W Loth 270 B2
Kirkney Aberds 302 F5
Kirkoswald Cumb 231 C7

Kirkoswald S Ayrs 244 B6
Kirkpatrick Dumf/Gal 247 E10
Kirkpatrick Durham Dumf/Gal 237 B9
Kirkpatrick-Fleming Dumf/Gal 239 C7
Kirksanton Cumb 210 C2
Kirkshaw N Lanarks 268 C4
Kirkstall W Yorks 205 F11
Kirkstile Aberds 302 F5
Kirkstyle H'land 310 B7
Kirkthorpe W Yorks 197 C11
Kirkton Aberds 302 E6
Kirkton Aberds 302 G6
Kirkton Angus 286 C6
Kirkton Angus 287 C8
Kirkton Angus 287 D8
Kirkton Arg/Bute 275 C8
Kirkton Scot Borders 262 G2
Kirkton Dumf/Gal 247 G11
Kirkton Fife 287 E7
Kirkton Fife 280 D4
Kirkton H'land 295 C10
Kirkton H'land 299 E9
Kirkton H'land 301 D7
Kirkton H'land 309 K7
Kirkton N Ayrs 266 D3
Kirkton Perth/Kinr 286 F3
Kirkton Stirl 285 G9
Kirkton S Lanarks 259 E10
Kirkton W Loth 269 B10
Kirkton Manor Scot Borders 260 B6
Kirkton of Airlie Angus 287 B7
Kirkton of Auchterhouse Angus 287 D7
Kirkton of Auchterless Aberds 303 E7
Kirkton of Barevan H'land 301 E8
Kirkton of Bourtie Aberds 303 G8
Kirkton of Collace Perth/Kinr 286 D5
Kirkton of Craig Angus 287 B11
Kirkton of Culsalmond Aberds 302 F6
Kirkton of Durris Aberds 293 D9
Kirkton of Glenbuchat Aberds 292 B5
Kirkton of Glenisla Angus 292 G4
Kirkton of Kingoldrum Angus 287 B7
Kirkton of Largo Fife 287 G8
Kirkton of Lethendy Perth/Kinr 286 C5
Kirkton of Logie Buchan Aberds 303 G9
Kirkton of Maryculter Aberds 293 D10
Kirkton of Menmuir Angus 293 G7
Kirkton of Monikie Angus 287 D9
Kirkton of Oyne Aberds 302 G6
Kirkton of Rayne Aberds 302 G6
Kirkton of Skene Aberds 293 C10
Kirkton of Tough Aberds 293 B8
Kirktonhill Scot Borders 271 E9
Kirktonhill W Dunb 277 G7
Kirktoun E Ayrs 267 G8
Kirktown Aberds 303 D10
Kirktown of Alvah Aberds 302 C6
Kirktown of Deskford Moray 302 C5
Kirktown of Fetteresso Aberds 293 E10
Kirktown of Mortlach Moray 302 F3
Kirktown of Slains Aberds 303 G10
Kirkud Scot Borders 270 G2
Kirkwall Orkney 312 G5
Kirkwall Airport Orkney 313 H5
Kirkwhelpington Northum 251 G11
Kirkwood Dumf/Gal 238 B4
Kirkwood N Lanarks 268 C4
Kirmington N Lincs 200 E6
Kirmond le Mire Lincs 189 C11
Kirn Arg/Bute 276 F3
Kirriemuir Angus 287 B7
Kirstead Green Norfolk 142 D5
Kirtlebridge Dumf/Gal 238 C6
Kirtleton Dumf/Gal 249 G7
Kirtling Cambs 124 F3
Kirtling Green Cambs 124 F3
Kirtlington Oxon 83 B7
Kirtomy H'land 308 C7
Kirton Lincs 156 B6
Kirton Notts 171 B11
Kirton Suffolk 108 D5
Kirton End Lincs 156 B5
Kirton Holme Lincs 174 G3
Kirton in Lindsey N Lincs 188 B6
Kiskin Cumb 210 B1
Kislingbury Northants 120 F4
Kitchenroyd W Yorks 197 F8
Kites Hardwick Warwick 119 D9
Kit's Coty Kent 69 G8
Kitt Green Gtr Man 194 F5
Kittisford Som'set 27 C9
Kittisford Barton Som'set 27 C9
Kittle Swan 56 D5
Kitt's End Herts 86 F2
Kitt's Green W Midlands 134 F3
Kitt's Moss Gtr Man 184 E5
Kittwhistle Dorset 28 G5
Kittybrewster Aberd C 293 C11
Kitwood Hants 49 G7
Kivernoll Heref'd 97 E9
Kiveton Park S Yorks 187 E7
Knackers Hole Dorset 30 E3
Knaith Lincs 188 E4
Knaith Park Lincs 188 D4
Knap Corner Dorset 30 C4
Knaphill Surrey 50 B3
Knapp Hants 32 C6
Knapp Perth/Kinr 286 D6
Knapp Som'set 28 B3
Knapthorpe Notts 172 D2
Knapton C/York 207 C7
Knapton Norfolk 160 C6
Knapton Green Heref'd 115 G8
Knapwell Cambs 122 E6
Knaresborough N Yorks 206 B3
Knarsdale Northum 240 G5
Knatts Valley Kent 68 G5
Knauchland Moray 302 D5
Knaven Aberds 303 E8
Knave's Ash Kent 71 G8
Knaves Green Suffolk 126 D2
Knavesmire C/York 207 D7
Knayton N Yorks 215 B8
Knebworth Herts 104 G5
Knebworth House, Stevenage Herts 104 G4
Knedlington ER Yorks 199 B8
Kneesall Notts 172 C2
Kneesworth Cambs 104 B6
Kneeton Notts 172 F2
Knelston Swan 56 D3
Knenhall Staffs 151 B8
Knettishall Suffolk 141 G9
Knightacott Devon 41 F6
Knightcote Warwick 119 G7
Knightcott N Som'set 43 B11
Knightley Staffs 150 D6
Knightley Dale Staffs 150 E6
Knighton Dorset 29 E10
Knighton Devon 7 F10
Knighton Leics C 136 C2
Knighton Oxon 63 B9
Knighton Poole 19 B7
Knighton Som'set 43 E7
Knighton Staffs 150 D4
Knighton Staffs 168 G2
Knighton = Tref-y-Clawdd Powys 114 C5
Knighton Wilts 63 E9
Knighton Worcs 117 F10
Knighton Fields Leics C 135 C11
Knighton on Teme Worcs 116 C2
Knight's End Cambs 139 E8
Knights Enham Hants 47 D11
Knight's Green Glos 98 E4
Knightshayes Court Devon 27 D7
Knightsridge W Loth 269 B10
Knightswood Glasg C 267 B10
Knill Heref'd 114 E5
Knipoch Arg/Bute 289 G10
Knipton Leics 154 C6
Knitsley Durham 233 B8
Kniveton Derby 170 E2
Knocharthur H'land 309 J7
Knock Arg/Bute 289 F7
Knock Cumb 231 F9
Knock Moray 302 D5
Knockally H'land 311 G5
Knockan H'land 307 H7
Knockandhu Moray 302 G2
Knockando Moray 301 E11
Knockando Ho. Moray 302 E2
Knockandoo H'land 301 G7
Knockbain H'land 300 D6
Knockbreck H'land 298 C2
Knockbrex Dumf/Gal 237 E7
Knockcarrach H'land 290 B6
Knockdee H'land 310 C5
Knockdolian S Ayrs 244 F4
Knockdow Arg/Bute 276 G2
Knockdown Wilts 61 B10
Knockenbaird Aberds 302 G6
Knockenkelly N Ayrs 256 E2
Knockentiber E Ayrs 257 B9
Knockespock Ho. Aberds 302 G5
Knockfarrel H'land 300 D5
Knockglass Dumf/Gal 236 D2
Knockhall Kent 68 E5
Knockhall Castle Aberds 303 G9
Knockhill Motor Racing Circuit Fife 279 C11
Knockholt London 52 B3
Knockholt Pound London 52 B3
Knockie Lodge H'land 290 B6
Knockin Shrops 148 E6
Knockinlaw E Ayrs 257 B10
Knockinnon H'land 310 F5
Knocklearn Dumf/Gal 237 B9
Knocklearoch Arg/Bute 274 G4
Knockmill Kent 68 G5
Knocknaha Arg/Bute 255 F7
Knocknain Dumf/Gal 236 C1
Knockothie Aberds 303 F9
Knockrome Arg/Bute 274 F6
Knocksharry I/Man 192 D3
Knockstapplemore Arg/Bute 255 F7
Knockvologan Arg/Bute 288 H5
Knodishall Suffolk 127 E8
Knokan Arg/Bute 288 G6
Knole Som'set 29 B7
Knole House & Gardens Kent 52 C4
Knoll Green Som'set 43 F8
Knollbury Monmouths 60 B2
Knolls Green Ches 184 F4
Knolton Wrex 149 B7
Knolton Bryn Wrex 149 B7
Knook Wilts 46 E2
Knossington Rutl'd 136 B6
Knotbury Staffs 169 B8
Knotlow Derby 169 B10
Knott End-on-Sea Lancs 202 D3
Knott Lanes Gtr Man 196 G2
Knott Side N Yorks 214 F3
Knotting Beds 121 E10
Knotting Green Beds 121 E10
Knottingley W Yorks 198 C4
Knotts Cumb 230 G4
Knotty Ash Mersey 182 C6
Knotty Green Bucks 84 G6
Knowbury Shrops 115 C11
Knowe Dumf/Gal 236 B5
Knowe Shetl'd 315 G5
Knowefield Cumb 239 F10
Knowehead Aberds 302 D5
Knowehead Aberds 293 C7
Knowehead Dumf/Gal 246 E4
Knowes of Elrick Aberds 302 D6
Knowesgate Northum 251 F11
Knoweton N Lanarks 268 D5
Knowhead Aberds 303 D9
Knowl Green Essex 106 C5
Knowl Hill Flints 166 C3
Knowl Hill Windsor 65 D10
Knowl Wood W Yorks 196 C2
Knowle Bristol 60 E6
Knowle Devon 27 F8
Knowle Devon 15 E7
Knowle Devon 26 G3
Knowle Devon 40 F3
Knowle Shrops 115 C11
Knowle Som'set 42 E3
Knowle Som'set 43 F10
Knowle Wilts 63 G7
Knowle W Midlands 118 B3
Knowle Cross Devon 14 B6
Knowle Green Lancs 203 F8
Knowle Green Surrey 66 E4
Knowle Hill Surrey 66 F3
Knowle Park W Yorks 205 E7
Knowle St. Giles Som'set 28 E4
Knowle Top S Yorks 186 D4
Knowle Village Hants 33 F9
Knowles Hill Devon 14 G3
Knowlton Kent 55 C9
Knowsley Mersey 182 B6
Knowsley Industrial Estate Mersey 182 B6
Knowsley Safari Park Mersey 183 C7
Knowsthorpe W Yorks 206 G2
Knowstone Devon 26 C4
Knox N Yorks 205 B11
Knox Bridge Kent 53 E9
Knuckas Powys 114 C5
Knuston Northants 121 D8
Knutsford Ches 184 F3
Knutton Staffs 168 F4
Knuzden Brook Lancs 195 B8
Knypersley Staffs 168 D5
Kraiknish H'land 294 C5
Krumlin W Yorks 196 E4
Kuggar Cornw'l 2 F6
Kyle of Lochalsh H'land 295 C9
Kyleakin H'land 295 C9
Kylepark S Lanarks 268 C3
Kylerhea H'land 295 C9
Kylesknoydart H'land 295 F10
Kylesku H'land 306 F7
Kylesmorar H'land 295 F10
Kylestrome H'land 306 F7
Kyllachy House H'land 301 G7
Kymin Monmouths 79 C8
Kynaston Heref'd 97 F10
Kynaston Heref'd 98 D2
Kynaston Shrops 149 E7
Kynnersley Telford 150 F3
Kyre Green Worcs 116 E2
Kyrewood Worcs 116 D2
Kyrle Som'set 27 C9

L

Labost W Isles 304 D4
Lacasaidh W Isles 304 F5
Lacasdal W Isles 304 E6
Laceby NE Lincs 201 F8
Lacey Green Bucks 84 F4
Lacey Green Ches 184 E4
Lach Dennis Ches 184 G2
Lache Ches 166 C5
Lackenby Redcar/Clevel'd 225 B11
Lackford Suffolk 124 C5
Lacock Wilts 62 F2
Ladbroke Warwick 119 F8
Laddingford Kent 53 D7
Lade Bank Lincs 174 E5
Ladock Cornw'l 5 E7
Ladwood Kent 55 E8
Lady Orkney 312 D7
Lady Balk W Yorks 198 C3
Lady Green Mersey 193 G10
Lady Hall Cumb 210 B3
Lady House Gtr Man 196 E2
Ladybank Fife 287 F7
Ladybrook Notts 171 C8
Ladyburn Invercl 276 F6
Ladycross Cornw'l 12 D2
Ladykirk Scot Borders 273 F7
Ladyridge Heref'd 97 E11
Lady's Green Suffolk 124 F5
Ladysford Aberds 303 C9
Ladywell London 67 E11
Ladywell W Loth 269 B10
Ladywood W Midlands 133 F11
Ladywood Worcs 117 E7
Laga H'land 289 C8
Lagafater Lodge Dumf/Gal 236 B3
Lagalochan Arg/Bute 275 B9
Lagavulin Arg/Bute 254 C5
Lagg Arg/Bute 274 F6
Lagg N Ayrs 255 E10
Laggan Arg/Bute 254 B3
Laggan H'land 289 B9
Laggan H'land 290 D4
Laggan H'land 291 D8
Laggan Lodge Arg/Bute 289 G8
Lagganlia H'land 291 C10
Lagganmullan Dumf/Gal 237 D7
Lagganulva Arg/Bute 288 E6
Lagness W Sussex 34 G5
Laide H'land 307 K3
Laig H'land 294 G6
Laigh Fenwick E Ayrs 267 G9
Laigh-Glengall S Ayrs 257 F8
Laighmuir E Ayrs 267 F9
Laighstonehall S Lanarks 268 E4
Laindon Essex 69 B7
Lair H'land 299 E10
Lair Perth/Kinr 292 G3
Laira Plym'th 7 D10
Lairg H'land 309 J5
Lairg Lodge H'land 309 J5
Lairg Muir H'land 309 J5
Lairgmore H'land 300 F5
Laisterdyke W Yorks 205 G9
Laithes Cumb 230 E5
Laithkirk Durham 232 G5
Laity Moor Cornw'l 3 B7
Lake Devon 40 G5
Lake I/Wight 21 E7
Lake Poole 18 C5
Lake Wilts 46 F6
Lake End Windsor 66 D2
Lakenham Norfolk 142 B4
Lakenheath Suffolk 140 G4
Lakesend Norfolk 139 D10
Lakeside Cumb 211 B7
Lakeside Worcs 117 D11
Lakeside and Haverthwaite Railway Cumb 210 B6
Laleham Surrey 66 F5
Laleston Bridg 57 F11
Lamarsh Essex 107 D7
Lamas Norfolk 160 E4
Lamb Corner Essex 107 E10
Lamb Roe Lancs 203 F10
Lambden Scot Borders 272 G4
Lamberhead Green Gtr Man 194 G4
Lamberhurst Kent 53 F7
Lamberhurst Quarter Kent 53 F7
Lamberton Scot Borders 273 D9
Lambert's End W Midlands 133 E9
Lambeth London 67 D10
Lambfair Green Suffolk 124 G4
Lambfoot Cumb 229 E9
Lambhill Glasg C 267 B11
Lambley Notts 171 G10
Lambley Northum 240 F5
Lambourn W Berks 63 D10
Lambourn Woodlands W Berks 63 D10
Lambourne Cornw'l 4 E5
Lambourne End Essex 87 G7
Lambridge Bath/NE Som'set 61 F9
Lamb's Green Dorset 18 B5
Lambs Green W Sussex 51 F8
Lambston Pembs 72 B6
Lambton Tyne/Wear 243 G7
Lamellion Cornw'l 6 C4
Lamerton Devon 12 F5
Lamesley Tyne/Wear 243 F7
Laminess Orkney 312 E7
Lamington H'land 301 B7
Lamington S Lanarks 259 C11
Lamlash N Ayrs 256 C2
Lamledra Cornw'l 5 G10
Lamloch Dumf/Gal 246 D2
Lamonby Cumb 230 D4
Lamorick Cornw'l 5 C10
Lamorna Cornw'l 1 E4
Lamorran Cornw'l 5 G7
Lampardbrook Suffolk 126 E5
Lampen Cornw'l 6 B3
Lampeter = Llanbedr Pont Steffan Ceredig'n 93 B11
Lampeter Velfrey Pembs 73 C11
Lamphey Pembs 73 E8
Lamplugh Cumb 229 G7
Lamport Northants 120 C5
Lampton London 66 D6
Lamyatt Som'set 45 F7
Lana Devon 12 B2
Lana Devon 24 F4
Lanark S Lanarks 269 G7
Lancaster Lancs 211 G9
Lancaster Leisure Park Lancs 202 A5
Lanchester Durham 233 B9
Lancing W Sussex 35 F11
Land Gate Gtr Man 194 G5
Land Side Gtr Man 183 B11
Landbeach Cambs 123 D9
Landcross Devon 25 C7
Landerberry Aberds 293 C9
Landford Wilts 32 D3
Landford Common Wilts 32 D3
Landfordwood Wilts 32 C3
Landican Mersey 182 D3
Landimore Swan 75 G7
Landkey Devon 40 G5
Landkey Newland Devon 40 G5
Landore Swan 75 F11
Landport E Sussex 36 E6
Landport Portsm'th 33 G10
Landrake Cornw'l 7 C7
Land's End Cornw'l 1 D2
Land's End Airport Cornw'l 1 D3
Landscove Devon 8 B5
Landshipping Pembs 73 C8
Landulph Cornw'l 7 C8
Landwade Cambs 124 D2
Landywood Staffs 133 B9
Lane Cornw'l 4 C6
Lane Bottom Lancs 204 F3
Lane End Bucks 84 G4
Lane End Cumb 220 G2
Lane End Derby 170 C6
Lane End Dorset 18 C3
Lane End Flints 166 C3
Lane End Gtr Man 184 C5
Lane End Gtr Man 195 F11
Lane End Hants 33 B9
Lane End Heref'd 79 B10
Lane End I/Wight 21 D9
Lane End Kent 68 E5
Lane End Lancs 204 D3
Lane End N Yorks 225 F8
Lane End Surrey 49 E10
Lane End Wilts 45 D10
Lane End W Yorks 204 F6
Lane Ends Ches 185 E7
Lane Ends Derby 152 C4
Lane Ends Derby 170 E5
Lane Ends Gtr Man 185 C7
Lane Ends Lancs 203 G8
Lane Ends Lancs 203 G11
Lane Ends Lancs 203 C10
Lane Ends Lancs 194 D6
Lane Ends N Yorks 204 E5
Lane Ends W Yorks 205 F10
Lane Green Staffs 133 C7
Lane Head Derby 185 F11
Lane Head Durham 233 F7
Lane Head Durham 224 C2
Lane Head Gtr Man 183 B10
Lane Head W Midlands 133 C9
Lane Head W Yorks 197 E7
Lane Head W Yorks 197 F7
Lane Heads Lancs 202 F4
Lane Side Lancs 195 C9
Lane Side Lancs 195 C9
Laneast Cornw'l 11 E10
Lane-end Cornw'l 5 B10
Laneham Notts 188 F4
Lanehead Durham 232 C2
Lanehead Northum 251 F7
Lanercost Cumb 240 E3
Lanescot Cornw'l 5 D11
Lanesend Pembs 73 D9
Lanesfield W Midlands 133 D8
Laneshaw Bridge Lancs 204 E4
Laney Green Staffs 133 B9
Langaford Devon 12 B4
Langal H'land 289 C9
Langaller Som'set 28 B3
Langar Notts 154 C4
Langbank Renf 277 G7
Langbar N Yorks 205 C7
Langbaurgh N Yorks 225 C11
Langbridge I/Wight 21 D7
Langburnshiels Scot Borders 250 C2
Langcliffe N Yorks 212 G6
Langdale H'land 308 E6
Langdon Cornw'l 12 D2
Langdon Beck Durham 232 E3
Langdon Hills Essex 69 B7
Langdown Hants 32 F6
Langdyke Fife 287 G7
Langeitho Ceredig'n 112 F2
Langenhoe Essex 89 B8
Langford Beds 104 C3
Langford Devon 27 G8
Langford Essex 88 D4
Langford Notts 172 D4
Langford Oxon 82 E2
Langford Som'set 28 B2
Langford Budville Som'set 27 C10
Langford Green N Som'set 44 B3
Langham Dorset 30 B3
Langham Essex 107 E10
Langham Norfolk 177 E8
Langham Rutl'd 154 G6
Langham Suffolk 125 D9
Langhaugh Scot Borders 260 C6
Langho Lancs 203 G10
Langholm Dumf/Gal 249 G9
Langlees Falk 279 E7
Langley Ches 184 G6
Langley Derby 170 F6
Langley Essex 105 D8
Langley Glos 99 F10
Langley Gtr Man 195 F11
Langley Hants 32 G6
Langley Herts 104 G4
Langley Kent 53 C9
Langley Northum 241 E8
Langley Slough 66 D4
Langley Som'set 27 B9
Langley Warwick 118 E3
Langley W Midlands 133 F9
Langley Burrell Wilts 62 D2
Langley Common Derby 152 B5
Langley Common Wokingham 65 G9
Langley Corner Bucks 66 B4
Langley Green Derby 152 B5
Langley Green Essex 107 G7
Langley Green Norfolk 143 C7
Langley Green W Sussex 51 F9
Langley Heath Kent 53 C10
Langley Marsh Som'set 27 B9
Langley Mill Derby 170 F6
Langley Moor Durham 233 C10
Langley Park Durham 233 C10
Langley Street Norfolk 143 C7
Langley Vale Surrey 51 B8
Langleyfield Telford 132 B3
Langloan N Lanarks 268 C4
Langmere Norfolk 142 G3
Langney E Sussex 23 E10
Langold Notts 187 D9
Langore Cornw'l 11 D11
Langport Som'set 28 B6
Langrick Lincs 174 F3
Langridge Bath/NE Som'set 61 F8
Langridgeford Devon 25 C9
Langrigg Cumb 222 C5
Langrigg Cumb 229 B9
Langrish Hants 34 C2
Langsett S Yorks 197 G8
Langshaw Scot Borders 262 B2
Langside Glasg C 267 C11
Langside Perth/Kinr 285 F11
Langskaill Orkney 312 D5
Langstone Hants 34 F2
Langstone Newp 59 B11
Langthorne N Yorks 224 G5
Langthorpe N Yorks 215 F7
Langthwaite N Yorks 223 E10
Langtoft ER Yorks 217 F10
Langtoft Lincs 156 G2
Langton Durham 224 B3
Langton Lincs 174 B2
Langton Lincs 190 G5
Langton N Yorks 216 F5
Langton by Wragby Lincs 189 F10
Langton Green Kent 52 F4
Langton Green Suffolk 126 C2
Langton Herring Dorset 17 E8
Langton Long Blandford Dorset 30 F5
Langton Matravers Dorset 18 F5
Langtree Devon 24 D7
Langtree Week Devon 25 D7
Langwathby Cumb 231 E7
Langwell Ho. H'land 311 G5
Langwell Lodge H'land 307 J6
Langwith Derby 171 B8
Langwith Junction Derby 171 B8
Langworth Lincs 189 F9
Lanham Green Essex 106 G5
Lanhydrock House, Bodmin Cornw'l 5 C11
Lanivet Cornw'l 5 C10
Lanjeth Cornw'l 5 E9
Lank Cornw'l 11 F7
Lanlivery Cornw'l 5 D11
Lanmack Blackb'n 195 B7
Lanner Cornw'l 2 B6
Lanoy Cornw'l 11 F11
Lanreath Cornw'l 6 D3
Lanrick Stirl 285 G10
Lansallos Cornw'l 6 E3
Lansbury Park Caerph 59 B7
Lansdown Bath/NE Som'set 61 F8
Lansdown Glos 99 G8
Lansdown Glos 100 G3
Lanstephan Cornw'l 12 D2
Lanteglos Cornw'l 11 E7
Lanton Scot Borders 262 E4
Lanton Northum 263 C10
Lanvean Cornw'l 5 B7
Lapal W Midlands 133 G9
Lapford Devon 26 F2
Laphroaig Arg/Bute 254 C4
Lapley Staffs 151 G7
Lapworth Warwick 118 C3
Larachbeg H'land 289 E8
Larbert Falk 279 E7
Larbreck Lancs 202 E4
Larches Lancs 202 G6
Larden Green Ches 167 E9
Larg H'land 292 B2
Largie Aberds 302 F6
Largiebaan Arg/Bute 255 F7
Largiemore Arg/Bute 275 E10
Largoward Fife 287 G8
Largs N Ayrs 266 D4
Largue Aberds 302 E6
Largybeg N Ayrs 256 E3
Largymeanoch N Ayrs 255 E11
Largymore N Ayrs 256 E2
Larkbeare Devon 15 B7
Larkfield Invercl 276 F4
Larkfield Kent 53 B8
Larkhall Bath/NE Som'set 61 F9
Larkhall S Lanarks 268 E5
Larkhill Wilts 46 E6
Larkhill Worcs 116 B6
Larklands Derby 171 G7
Larling Norfolk 141 F9
Larport Heref'd 97 D11
Larrick Cornw'l 12 F2
Larriston Scot Borders 250 E2
Lartington Durham 223 B10
Lary Aberds 292 C5
Lasborough Glos 80 G4
Lasham Hants 49 E7
Lashenden Kent 53 E11
Laskill N Yorks 225 G11
Lassington Glos 98 G5
Lasswade Midloth 270 B6
Lastingham N Yorks 226 G4
Latcham Som'set 44 D2
Latchford Herts 105 G7
Latchford Oxon 83 E11
Latchford Warrington 183 D10
Latchingdon Essex 88 E5
Latchley Cornw'l 12 G4
Latchmore Bank Essex 87 B7
Latchmore Green Hants 48 B6
Lately Common Warrington 183 B11
Lathallan Mill Fife 287 G8
Lathbury Durham 223 B10
Lathbury M/Keynes 103 B7
Latheron H'land 310 F5
Latheronwheel H'land 310 F5
Latheronwheel Ho. H'land 310 F5
Lathones Fife 287 G8
Latimer Bucks 85 F7
Latteridge S Glos 61 C7
Lattersey Hill Cambs 138 D5
Lattiford Som'set 29 B11
Latton Wilts 81 F9
Latton Bush Essex 87 D7
Lauchintilly Aberds 293 B9
Laudale Ho H'land 289 D9
Lauder Scot Borders 271 F10
Laugharne = Talacharn Carms 74 C4
Laugherton Lincs 188 F4
Laughton E Sussex 37 E7
Laughton Leics 136 F3
Laughton Lincs 155 C11
Laughton Lincs 188 B4
Laughton Common E Sussex 37 E7
Laughton Common S Yorks 187 D9
Laughton en le Morthen S Yorks 187 D9
Launcells Cornw'l 24 F2
Launceston Cornw'l 12 E2
Launcherley Som'set 44 E5
Laund Lancs 195 C10
Laund Lancs 204 F3
Launton Oxon 102 G2
Laurel Street Som'set 44 F4
Laurencekirk Aberds 293 F9
Laurieston Dumf/Gal 237 C8
Laurieston Falk 279 F8
Lavendon M/Keynes 121 G8
Lavenham Suffolk 107 B8
Laverackloch Moray 301 C11
Laverhay Dumf/Gal 248 D4
Laversdale Cumb 239 E11
Laverstock Wilts 47 G7
Laverstoke Hants 48 D3
Laverton Glos 99 D11
Laverton N Yorks 214 E4
Laverton Som'set 45 C9
Lavister Wrex 166 D5
Law S Lanarks 268 E6
Law Hill S Lanarks 268 E6
Lawers Perth/Kinr 285 D10
Lawers Perth/Kinr 285 E11
Lawford Essex 107 E11
Lawford Som'set 42 F6
Lawhill Perth/Kinr 286 F3
Lawhitton Cornw'l 12 E3
Lawkland N Yorks 212 F5
Lawkland Green N Yorks 212 F5
Lawley Telford 132 B3
Lawn Swindon 63 C7
Lawnhead Staffs 150 D6
Lawnswood W Yorks 205 F11
Lawrence Weston Bristol 60 D4
Lawrenny Pembs 73 D8
Lawshall Suffolk 125 G7
Lawshall Green Suffolk 125 G7
Lawson Street Kent 70 G3
Lawton Heath End Ches 168 D3
Lawtongate Ches 168 D4
Laxey I/Man 192 D5
Laxey Wheel and Mines I/Man 192 D5
Laxfield Suffolk 126 C5
Laxfirth Shetl'd 315 H6
Laxfirth Shetl'd 315 J6
Laxford Bridge H'land 306 E7
Laxo Shetl'd 315 G6
Laxobigging Shetl'd 314 F6
Laxton ER Yorks 199 B9
Laxton Northants 137 D9
Laxton Notts 172 B2
Laycock W Yorks 204 E6
Layer Breton Essex 88 B6
Layer Breton Heath Essex 88 B6
Layer de la Haye Essex 89 B7
Layer Marney Essex 88 B6
Layerthorpe C/York 207 C8
Layham Suffolk 107 C10
Laymore Dorset 28 G5
Layter's Green Bucks 85 G7
Laytham ER Yorks 207 F10
Layton Blackp'l 202 F2
Lazenby Redcar/Clevel'd 225 B11
Lazonby Cumb 231 D7
Lea Derby 170 D4
Lea Devon 15 B10
Lea Heref'd 98 G3
Lea Lancs 202 G5
Lea Lincs 188 D4
Lea Shrops 131 F7
Lea Shrops 131 B8
Lea Warwick 134 E4
Lea Wilts 62 B3
Lea Bridge London 67 B11
Lea Brook S Yorks 186 B6
Lea End Worcs 117 B10
Lea Green Mersey 183 C8
Lea Hall Derby 170 D4
Lea Hall W Midlands 134 F2
Lea Heath Staffs 151 D10
Lea Marston Warwick 134 E3
Lea Town Lancs 202 G5
Lea Yeat Cumb 212 B5
Leabrooks Derby 170 E6
Leac a Li W Isles 305 J3
Leacainn W Isles 305 H3
Leachkin H'land 300 E6
Leacnasaide H'land 299 B7
Leadburn Midloth 270 D4
Leaden Roding Essex 87 C9
Leadenham Lincs 173 E7
Leaderfoot Scot Borders 262 C3
Leadgate Cumb 231 C10
Leadgate Durham 242 G4
Leadgate Northum 242 F4
Leadhills S Lanarks 259 F9
Leadingcross Green Kent 53 C11
Leadmill Flints 166 C2
Leadmill S Yorks 186 E2
Leafield Oxon 82 B4
Leafield Wilts 61 F11
Leagrave Luton 103 G10
Leake N Yorks 225 G8
Leake Commonside Lincs 174 E5
Leake Fold Hill Lincs 174 E6
Leake Gride Lincs 174 E5
Leake Hurn's End Lincs 174 F6
Lealholm N Yorks 226 D5
Lealholm Side N Yorks 226 D5
Lealt Arg/Bute 275 D7
Lealt H'land 298 C5
Leam Derby 186 F2
Leam Lane Tyne/Wear 243 E7
Leamington Hastings Warwick 119 D8
Leamonsley Staffs 134 B2
Leamoor Common Shrops 131 F8
Leamore W Midlands 133 C9
Leamside Durham 234 C2
Leanach Arg/Bute 275 D11
Leanachan H'land 290 F4
Leanaig H'land 300 D5
Leargybreck Arg/Bute 274 F6
Lease Rigg N Yorks 226 E6
Leasgill Cumb 211 C9
Leasingham Lincs 173 F9
Leasingthorne Durham 233 F11
Leasowe Mersey 182 C3
Leatherhead Surrey 51 B7
Leatherhead Common Surrey 51 B7
Leathern Bottle Glos 80 E2
Leathley N Yorks 205 D10
Leaths Dumf/Gal 237 C9
Leaton Shrops 149 F9
Leaton Telford 150 G2
Leaveland Kent 54 C4
Leavenheath Suffolk 107 D9
Leavening N Yorks 216 G5
Leaves Green London 68 G2
Leavesden Green Herts 85 E9
Leazes Durham 242 F5
Leazes Northum 241 E10
Lebberston N Yorks 217 C11
Lechlade-on-Thames Glos 82 F2
Leck Lancs 212 D2
Leckford Hants 47 F11
Leckfurin H'land 308 D7
Leckgruinart Arg/Bute 274 G3
Leckhampstead Bucks 102 D4
Leckhampstead W Berks 64 D2
Leckhampstead Street W Berks 64 D2
Leckhampstead Thicket W Berks 64 D2
Leckhampton Glos 80 B6
Leckie H'land 299 C10
Leckmelm H'land 307 K6
Leckuary Arg/Bute 275 D9
Leckwith V/Glam 59 E7
Leconfield ER Yorks 208 E6
Ledaig Arg/Bute 289 F11
Ledburn Bucks 103 G8
Ledbury Heref'd 98 D4
Ledcharrie Stirl 285 E9
Ledgemoor Heref'd 115 G8
Ledgowan H'land 299 D11
Ledicot Heref'd 115 E8
Ledmore Angus 293 G7
Ledmore H'land 307 H7
Lednagullin H'land 308 C7
Ledsham Ches 182 G5
Ledsham W Yorks 198 B3
Ledston W Yorks 198 B2
Ledstone Devon 8 F4
Ledwell Oxon 101 F8
Lee Arg/Bute 288 G6
Lee Devon 40 D3
Lee Devon 40 D5
Lee Devon 26 B4
Lee Hants 32 D5
Lee Lancs 203 B7
Lee London 67 E11
Lee Northum 241 F10
Lee Shrops 149 C8
Lee Brockhurst Shrops 149 D10
Lee Chapel Essex 69 B7
Lee Clump Bucks 84 E6
Lee Green Medway 69 E8
Lee Ground Hants 33 F8
Lee Head Derby 185 C8
Lee Mill Devon 7 D11
Lee Moor Devon 7 C11
Leeans Shetl'd 315 J5
Leebotten Shetl'd 315 L6
Leebotwood Shrops 131 D9
Leece Cumb 210 F4
Leech Pool Pembs 73 B7
Leechpool Monmouths 60 B4
Leeden Beds 103 F8
Leeds Kent 53 C10
Leeds W Yorks 206 F2
Leeds Bradford International Airport W Yorks 205 E10
Leeds Castle Kent 53 C10
Leeds City Art Gallery W Yorks 206 G2
Leedstown Cornw'l 2 C4
Leeford Devon 41 D9
Leegomery Telford 150 G3
Leeholme Durham 233 E10
Leek Staffs 169 D7
Leek Wootton Warwick 118 D5
Leekbrook Staffs 169 E7
Leeming N Yorks 214 B5
Leeming W Yorks 204 G6
Leeming Bar N Yorks 224 G5
Lee-on-the-Solent Hants 33 G9
Lee-over-Sands Essex 89 C10
Lees Derby 152 B5
Lees Gtr Man 196 G3

Lees W Yorks 204 F6
Lees Hill Cumb 240 D3
Leesthorpe Leics 154 G5
Leeswood Flints 166 D3
Leetown Perth/Kinr 286 E6
Leftwich Ches 183 G11
Legar Powys 78 B2
Legbourne Lincs 190 E5
Legburthwaite Cumb 220 B6
Legerwood Scot Borders 271 G11
Legoland Windsor 66 E2
Legsby Lincs 189 D10
Leicester Leics C 136 B2
Leicester Forest East Leics 135 C10
Leicester Racecourse Leics 136 C2
Leigh Dorset 29 F10
Leigh Dorset 30 F3
Leigh Devon 26 D2
Leigh Gtr Man 195 G7
Leigh Kent 52 D5
Leigh Shrops 130 C6
Leigh Surrey 51 D8
Leigh Wilts 81 G9
Leigh Worcs 116 G5
Leigh Beck Essex 69 B10
Leigh Common Som'set 45 G8
Leigh Delamere Wilts 61 D11
Leigh End Glos 99 F7
Leigh Green Kent 54 G2
Leigh Park Dorset 18 B6
Leigh Park Hants 34 F2
Leigh Sinton Worcs 116 G5
Leigh Street Kent 54 G2
Leigh upon Mendip Som'set 45 D7
Leigh Woods N Som'set 60 E5
Leigham Plym'th 7 D10
Leighland Chapel Som'set 42 F4
Leigh-on-Sea Southend 69 B10
Leighswood W Midlands 133 C11
Leighterton Glos 80 G4
Leighton N Yorks 214 D3
Leighton Powys 130 B4
Leighton Shrops 132 B2
Leighton Som'set 45 E8
Leighton Bromswold Cambs 122 B2
Leighton Buzzard Beds 103 F8
Leinthall Earls Heref'd 115 D8
Leinthall Starkes Heref'd 115 D8
Leintwardine Heref'd 115 C8
Leire Leics 135 E10
Leirinmore H'land 308 C4
Leiston Suffolk 127 E8
Leitfie Perth/Kinr 286 C6
Leith C/Edinb 280 F5
Leitholm Scot Borders 272 G5
Lelant Cornw'l 2 B2
Lelant Downs Cornw'l 2 B2
Lelly ER Yorks 209 G10
Lem Hill Shrops 116 B4
Lemington Tyne/Wear 242 E5
Lempitlaw Scot Borders 263 C7
Lemsford Herts 86 C2
Lenborough Bucks 102 E3
Lenchwick Worcs 99 B10
Lendalfoot S Ayrs 244 E4
Lendrick Lodge Stirl 285 G9
Lengthwaite Cumb 230 G4
Lenham Kent 53 C11
Lenham Forstal Kent 54 C2
Lenham Heath Kent 54 D2
Lennel Scot Borders 272 G7
Lennoxtown E Dunb 278 F2
Lent Bucks 66 C2
Lent Rise Slough 66 C2
Lenton Nott'ham 153 B10
Lenton Lincs 155 C10
Lentran H'land 300 E5
Lenwade Norfolk 159 F11
Leny Ho. Stirl 285 G10
Lenzie E Dunb 278 G3
Lenziemill N Lanarks 278 G5
Leoch Angus 287 D7
Leochel-Cushnie Aberds 293 B7
Leominster Heref'd 115 F9
Leonard Stanley Glos 80 E4
Leonardslee Gardens W Sussex 36 B2
Leorin Arg/Bute 254 C4
Lepe Hants 20 B5
Lephin H'land 297 G7
Lephinchapel Arg/Bute 275 D10
Lephinmore Arg/Bute 275 D10
Leppington N Yorks 216 G5
Lepton W Yorks 197 D8
Lerigoligan Arg/Bute 275 C9
Lerrocks Stirl 285 G11
Lerryn Cornw'l 6 D2
Lerwick Shetl'd 315 J6
Lerwick (Tingwall) Airport Shetl'd 315 J6
Lesbury Northum 264 G6
Leschangie Aberds 293 B9
Leslie Aberds 302 G5
Leslie Fife 286 G6
Lesmahagow S Lanarks 268 G6
Lesnewth Cornw'l 11 C8
Lessendrum Aberds 302 E5
Lessingham Norfolk 161 D7
Lessness Heath London 68 D3
Lessonhall Cumb 238 G6
Leswalt Dumf/Gal 236 C2
Letchmore Heath Herts 85 F11
Letchworth Herts 104 D4
Letcombe Bassett Oxon 63 B11
Letcombe Regis Oxon 63 B11
Letham Angus 287 C9
Letham Fife 287 F7
Letham Falk 279 D7
Letham Perth/Kinr 286 E4
Letham Grange Angus 287 C10
Lethen Ho H'land 301 D9
Lethenty Aberds 303 E8
Lethenty Aberds 303 G7
Letheringham Suffolk 126 F5
Letheringsett Norfolk 159 B10
Lettaford Devon 13 D10
Lettan Orkney 312 D8
Letter Aberds 293 B9
Letterewe H'land 299 B9
Letterfearn H'land 295 C10
Letterfinlay H'land 290 D4
Lettermay Arg/Bute 284 G5
Lettermorar H'land 295 G9
Lettermore Arg/Bute 288 E6
Letters H'land 307 L6
Letterston = Treletert Pembs 91 F8
Lettoch H'land 292 B2
Lettoch H'land 301 F10
Lettoch Moray 302 F3
Lettoch Perth/Kinr 291 G11
Letton Heref'd 96 B6
Letton Heref'd 115 C7
Letton Green Norfolk 141 B9
Letty Green Herts 86 C3
Letwell S Yorks 187 D9
Leuchars Fife 287 E8
Leuchars Ho. Moray 302 C2
Leumrabhagh W Isles 305 G5
Leusdon Devon 13 G10
Levalsa Meor Cornw'l 5 F10
Levan Invercl 276 F4
Levaneap Shetl'd 315 G6
Levedale Staffs 151 F8
Level's Green Essex 105 G9
Leven ER Yorks 209 D8
Leven Fife 287 G7
Leven Seat W Loth 269 D8
Levencorroch N Ayrs 256 E2
Levenhall E Loth 281 G7
Levens Cumb 211 B9
Levens Green Herts 105 G7
Levenshulme Gtr Man 184 C5
Leventhorpe W Yorks 205 G8
Levenwick Shetl'd 315 L6
Lever Edge Gtr Man 195 F8
Leverburgh = An t-Ob W Isles 296 C6
Leverington Cambs 157 G8
Leverstock Green Herts 85 D9
Leverton Lincs 174 F5
Leverton Highgate Lincs 174 F6
Leverton Ings Lincs 174 F5
Leverton Lucasgate Lincs 174 F6
Leverton Outgate Lincs 174 F6
Levington Suffolk 108 D4
Levisham N Yorks 226 G6
Levishie H'land 290 B6
Lew Oxon 82 E4
Lewannick Cornw'l 11 E11
Lewdown Devon 12 D4
Lewes E Sussex 36 E6
Leweston Pembs 91 G8
Lewisham London 67 E11
Lewiston H'land 300 G5
Lewistown Bridg 58 B2
Lewknor Oxon 84 F2
Leworthy Devon 41 F7
Lewsey Farm Beds 103 G10
Lewth Lancs 202 F5
Lewthorn Cross Devon 13 F11
Lewtrenchard Devon 12 D4
Lexden Essex 107 F9
Ley Aberds 293 B7
Ley Cornw'l 6 B3
Ley Green Herts 104 G3
Ley Hey Park Gtr Man 185 D7
Ley Hill Bucks 85 E7
Leybourne Kent 53 B7
Leyburn N Yorks 224 G2
Leycett Staffs 168 F3
Leyfields Notts 171 B11
Leyfields Staffs 134 B3
Leyhill S Glos 79 G11
Leyland Lancs 194 C4
Leyland's Green W Berks 63 F11
Leylodge Aberds 293 B9
Leymoor W Yorks 196 D6
Leys Aberds 292 C6
Leys Aberds 303 D10
Leys Cumb 219 B11
Leys Perth/Kinr 286 D6
Leys Castle H'land 300 E6
Leys of Cossans Angus 287 C7
Leysdown-on-Sea Kent 70 E4
Leysmill Angus 287 C10
Leysters Heref'd 115 E11
Leysthorpe N Yorks 216 D2
Leyton London 67 B11
Leytonstone London 67 B11
Lezant Cornw'l 12 F2
Lezerea Cornw'l 2 C5
Leziate Norfolk 158 F3
Lhanbryde Moray 302 C2
Liatrie H'land 300 F2
Libanus Powys 95 F9
Libberton S Lanarks 269 G9
Liberton C/Edinb 270 B5
Liberton Dams C/Edinb 280 G5
Liceasto W Isles 305 J3
Lichfield Staffs 134 B2
Lichfield Cathedral Staffs 134 B2
Lick Perth/Kinr 286 B2
Lickey Worcs 117 B9
Lickey End Worcs 117 C9
Lickey Rock Worcs 117 C9
Lickfold W Sussex 34 B6
Lickhills Worcs 116 C5
Lickleyhead Castle Aberds 302 G6
Liddaton Devon 12 E5
Liddel Orkney 313 K5
Liddesdale H'land 289 D9
Liddeston Pembs 72 D5
Liddington Swindon 63 C8
Liden Swindon 63 C7
Lidgate Derby 186 F4
Lidgate Suffolk 124 F4
Lidget S Yorks 199 G7
Lidget Green W Yorks 205 G8
Lidgett Notts 171 B11
Lidlington Beds 103 D9
Lidsey W Sussex 34 G6
Lidsing Kent 69 G9
Lidstone Oxon 101 G7
Lidwell Cornw'l 12 G3
Lieurary H'land 310 C4
Liff Angus 287 D7
Lifford W Midlands 117 B11
Lifton Devon 12 D3
Liftondown Devon 12 D3
Light Oaks Stoke 168 E6
Lightcliffe W Yorks 196 B6
Lighthorne Warwick 118 F6
Lightmoor Aqueduct Telford 132 B3
Lightpill Glos 80 E4
Lightwater Surrey 66 G2
Lightwater Valley N Yorks 214 D5
Lightwood Derby 186 E5
Lightwood Stoke 168 G6
Lightwood Staffs 169 G8
Lightwood Green Ches 167 G10
Lightwood Green Wrex 166 G5
Lilbourne Northants 119 B11
Lillesdon Som'set 28 C4
Lilleshall Telford 150 F4
Lilley Herts 104 F2
Lilley W Berks 64 D2
Lilliesleaf Scot Borders 262 D2
Lillingstone Dayrell Bucks 102 D4
Lillingstone Lovell M/Keynes 102 C4
Lillington Dorset 29 E10
Lillington Warwick 118 D6
Lilliput Poole 18 D6
Lily Green N Yorks 214 G2
Lily Lake Devon 27 G7
Lilybank Invercl 276 G6
Lilyhurst Shrops 150 G4
Lilyvale Kent 54 F5
Limbrick Lancs 194 D6
Limbury Luton 103 G11
Lime Side Gtr Man 196 G2
Lime Street Worcs 98 E6
Lime Tree Park W Midlands 118 B5
Limefield Gtr Man 195 E10
Limehouse London 67 C11
Limehurst Gtr Man 196 G2
Limekiln Field Derby 187 G7
Limekilnburn S Lanarks 268 E4
Limekilns Fife 279 E11
Limerigg Falk 279 G7
Limerstone I/Wight 20 E4
Limestone Brae Northum 231 B11
Limington Som'set 29 C8
Limlow Hill Cambs 104 C6
Limmerhill Wokingham 65 F9
Limpenhoe Norfolk 143 C8
Limpenhoe Hill Norfolk 143 C8
Limpley Stoke Bath/NE Som'set 61 G9
Limpsfield Surrey 52 C2
Limpsfield Chart Surrey 52 C2
Linburn W Loth 270 B2
Linby Notts 171 E8
Linchmere W Sussex 49 G11
Lincluden Dumf/Gal 237 B11
Lincoln Lincs 189 G7
Lincoln Castle Lincs 189 G7
Lincoln Cathedral Lincs 189 G7
Lincomb Worcs 116 D6
Lincombe Devon 40 D4
Lindal in Furness Cumb 210 D5
Lindale Cumb 211 C9
Lindean Scot Borders 261 C11
Linden Glos 80 B4
Lindfield W Sussex 36 B4
Lindford Hants 49 F10
Lindifferon Fife 287 F7
Lindisfarne Priory, Holy Island Northum 273 B11
Lindley N Yorks 205 D10
Lindley W Yorks 196 D6
Lindores Fife 286 F6
Lindow End Ches 184 F4
Lindridge Worcs 116 D3
Lindsell Essex 106 F2
Lindsey Suffolk 107 C9
Lindsey Tye Suffolk 107 B9
Lindwell W Yorks 196 C5
Lineholt Worcs 116 D6
Liney Som'set 43 F11
Linfit W Yorks 197 E8
Linfitts Gtr Man 196 F3
Linford Hants 31 F11
Linford Thurr'k 69 D7
Lingague I/Man 192 E3
Lingbob W Yorks 205 F7
Lingdale Redcar/Clevel'd 226 B3
Lingen Heref'd 115 D7
Lingfield D'lington 224 C6
Lingfield Surrey 51 E11
Lingfield Common Surrey 51 E11
Lingfield Park Racecourse Surrey 51 E11
Lingley Green Warrington 183 D9
Lingreabhagh W Isles 296 C6
Linguards Wood W Yorks 196 E5
Lingwood Norfolk 143 B7
Linhope Northum 263 F11
Linicro H'land 298 C3
Link N Som'set 44 B3
Linkend Worcs 98 E6
Linkenholt Hants 47 B11
Linkhill Kent 38 B4
Linkinhorne Cornw'l 12 G2
Linklater Orkney 313 K5
Linklet Orkney 312 C8
Linkness Orkney 312 G6
Linksness Orkney 313 H3
Linktown Fife 280 C5
Linley Shrops 132 D3
Linley Green Heref'd 116 G3
Linlithgow W Loth 279 F10
Linlithgow Bridge W Loth 279 F9
Linndhu Ho. Arg/Bute 289 D7
Linneraineach H'land 307 J6
Linns Angus 292 F3
Linnyshaw Gtr Man 195 G8
Linsiadar W Isles 304 E4
Linsidemore H'land 309 K5
Linslade Beds 103 F8
Linstead Parva Suffolk 126 B6
Linstock Cumb 239 F10
Lint Northum 263 B10
Linthorpe Middlesbro 225 B9
Linthurst Worcs 117 C9
Linthwaite W Yorks 196 E6
Lintmill Moray 302 C5
Linton Scot Borders 263 D7
Linton Cambs 105 B11
Linton Derby 152 F5
Linton Heref'd 98 F3
Linton Kent 53 C8
Linton Northum 253 E7
Linton N Yorks 213 G9
Linton W Yorks 206 D3
Linton Hill Heref'd 98 G3
Linton-on-Ouse N Yorks 215 G9
Lintz Durham 242 F5
Lintzford Tyne/Wear 242 F4
Lintzgarth Durham 232 C4
Linwood Hants 31 F11
Linwood Lincs 189 D10
Linwood Renf 267 C8
Lionacleit W Isles 297 G3
Lional W Isles 304 B7
Lions Green E Sussex 37 D9
Liphook Hants 49 G10
Lipley Shrops 150 C4
Lipyeate Som'set 45 C7
Liquo N Lanarks 269 D7
Liscard Mersey 182 C4
Liscombe Som'set 41 G11
Liskeard Cornw'l 6 C5
Liss Hants 34 B3
Liss Forest Hants 34 B3
Lissett ER Yorks 209 B8
Lissington Lincs 189 E10
Listerdale S Yorks 187 C7
Listoft Lincs 191 G8
Liston Essex 107 C7
Liston Garden Essex 106 B6
Lisvane Card 59 C7
Liswerry Newp 59 B10
Litcham Norfolk 159 F7
Litchard Bridg 58 C2
Litchborough Northants 120 G2
Litchfield Hants 48 C3
Litherland Mersey 182 B4
Litlemoss Gtr Man 184 B6
Litlington Cambs 104 B6
Litlington E Sussex 23 E8
Little Abington Cambs 105 B10
Little Addington Northants 121 C9
Little Airmyn N Yorks 199 B8
Little Almshoe Herts 104 F4
Little Alne Warwick 118 E2
Little Altcar Mersey 193 F10
Little Ann Hants 47 E10
Little Arowry Wrex 167 G7
Little Ashby Cumb 222 D3
Little Assynt H'land 307 G6
Little Aston Staffs 133 C11
Little Atherfield I/Wight 20 E5
Little Ayre Orkney 313 J4
Little Ayton N Yorks 225 C11
Little Baddow Essex 88 D3
Little Badminton S Glos 61 C10
Little Ballinluig Perth/Kinr 286 B3
Little Bampton Cumb 239 F7
Little Bardfield Essex 106 E3
Little Barford Beds 122 F2
Little Barningham Norfolk 160 C2
Little Barrington Glos 82 C2
Little Barrow Ches 183 G7
Little Barugh N Yorks 216 D5
Little Bavington Northum 241 B11
Little Bayham E Sussex 52 F6
Little Bayton Warwick 135 F7
Little Bealings Suffolk 108 B4
Little Bedwyn Wilts 63 F9
Little Bentley Essex 108 F2
Little Berkhamsted Herts 86 D3
Little Billing Northants 120 E6
Little Billington Beds 103 G8
Little Birch Heref'd 97 E10
Little Bispham Blackp'l 202 E2
Little Blakenham Suffolk 108 B2
Little Blencow Cumb 230 E5
Little Bloxwich W Midlands 133 C10
Little Bognor W Sussex 35 C8
Little Bolehill Derby 170 E3
Little Bollington Ches 184 D2
Little Bolton Gtr Man 184 B3
Little Bookham Surrey 50 C6
Little Bourton Oxon 101 C9
Little Bowden Leics 136 F4
Little Boys Heath Bucks 84 F6
Little Bradley Suffolk 124 G3
Little Braithwaite Cumb 229 G10
Little Brampton Shrops 131 G7
Little Brechin Angus 293 G7
Little Brickhill M/Keynes 103 E8
Little Bridgeford Staffs 151 D7
Little Brington Northants 120 E3
Little Bristol S Glos 80 G2
Little Britain Warwick 118 G2
Little Bromley Essex 107 F11
Little Bromwich W Midlands 134 F2
Little Broughton Cumb 229 E7
Little Budworth Ches 167 B9
Little Burdon D'lington 224 B6
Little Burstead Essex 87 G11
Little Burton ER Yorks 209 D8
Little Bytham Lincs 155 F10
Little Cambridge Essex 106 F2
Little Canford Dorset 18 B7
Little Carleton Blackp'l 202 F2
Little Carlton Lincs 190 D5
Little Carlton Notts 172 D3
Little Casterton Rutl'd 137 B10
Little Catwick ER Yorks 209 E8
Little Catworth Cambs 121 C11
Little Cawthorpe Lincs 190 E5
Little Chalfont Bucks 85 F8
Little Charlinch Som'set 43 F8
Little Chart Kent 54 D2
Little Chell Stoke 168 E5
Little Chesterford Essex 105 C10
Little Chesterton Oxon 101 G11
Little Cheverell Wilts 46 C3
Little Chishill Cambs 105 D8
Little Clacton Essex 89 B11
Little Clanfield Oxon 82 E3
Little Clegg Gtr Man 196 E2
Little Clifton Cumb 228 F6
Little Coates NE Lincs 201 F8
Little Colesborne Glos 81 C8
Little Colp Aberds 303 E7
Little Comberton Worcs 99 C9
Little Comfort Cornw'l 12 E2
Little Common E Sussex 38 F2
Little Compton Warwick 100 E5
Little Conghurst Kent 38 B3
Little Corby Cumb 239 F11
Little Cornard Suffolk 107 D8
Little Cowarne Heref'd 116 G2
Little Coxwell Oxon 82 G3
Little Crakehall N Yorks 224 G4
Little Cransley Northants 120 B6
Little Crawley M/Keynes 103 B8
Little Creaton Northants 120 C4
Little Creich H'land 309 L6
Little Cressingham Norfolk 141 C7
Little Croft West Cornw'l 4 F5
Little Crosby Mersey 193 G10
Little Crosthwaite Cumb 229 F10
Little Cubley Derby 152 B3
Little Dalby Leics 154 G5
Little Dawley Telford 132 B3
Little Dens Aberds 303 E10
Little Dewchurch Heref'd 97 E10
Little Ditton Cambs 124 F3
Little Doward Heref'd 79 B8
Little Down Hants 47 B11
Little Downham Cambs 139 G10
Little Drayton Shrops 150 C3
Little Driffield ER Yorks 208 B6
Little Drybrook Glos 79 D9
Little Dunham Norfolk 159 G7
Little Dunkeld Perth/Kinr 286 C4
Little Dunmow Essex 106 G3
Little Durnford Wilts 46 G6
Little Easton Essex 106 G2
Little Eaton Derby 170 G5
Little Eccleston Lancs 202 E4
Little Ellingham Norfolk 141 D10
Little Elm Som'set 45 D8
Little End Cambs 122 F3
Little End Essex 87 E8
Little End ER Yorks 208 F2
Little Everdon Northants 119 F11
Little Eversden Cambs 123 G7
Little Eyton Telford 132 B3
Little Faringdon Oxon 82 E2
Little Fencote N Yorks 224 G5
Little Fenton N Yorks 206 F6
Little Finborough Suffolk 125 G10
Little Forest Hants 33 E10
Little Fransham Norfolk 159 G8
Little Gaddesden Herts 85 C7
Little Garway Heref'd 97 G8
Little Gidding Cambs 138 G2
Little Gight Aberds 303 F8
Little Givendale ER Yorks 208 C2
Little Glemham Suffolk 126 F6
Little Glenshee Perth/Kinr 286 D3
Little Gorsley Heref'd 98 G3
Little Gransden Cambs 122 F5
Little Grays Kent 71 F8
Little Green Cambs 104 C5
Little Green Notts 172 G2
Little Green Suffolk 125 C11
Little Green Suffolk 125 C11
Little Green Som'set 45 D8
Little Green Wrex 167 G7
Little Grimsby Lincs 190 C4
Little Gringley Notts 188 E2
Little Gruinard H'land 307 L4
Little Habton N Yorks 216 D4
Little Hadham Herts 105 G8
Little Hale Lincs 173 G10
Little Hale Norfolk 141 B8
Little Hallam Derby 171 G7
Little Hallingbury Essex 87 B8
Little Hampden Bucks 84 E5
Little Hanford Dorset 30 E4
Little Haresfield Glos 80 D4
Little Harrowden Northants 121 C7
Little Harwood Blackb'n 195 B7
Little Haseley Oxon 83 E10
Little Hatfield ER Yorks 209 E9
Little Hautbois Norfolk 160 E5
Little Haven Pembs 72 C5
Little Hay Staffs 134 C2
Little Hayfield Derby 185 D8
Little Haywood Staffs 151 E10
Little Heath Ches 167 G11
Little Heath Herts 86 E3
Little Heath Herts 85 D8
Little Heath London 68 B3
Little Heath Surrey 66 G6
Little Heath W Berks 65 E7
Little Heath W Midlands 134 G6
Little Herbert's Glos 99 G9
Little Hereford Heref'd 115 D10
Little Hill Heref'd 97 F9
Little Holbury Hants 32 G6
Little Horkesley Essex 107 E9
Little Hormead Herts 105 F8
Little Horsted E Sussex 37 D7
Little Horton Wilts 62 G4
Little Horton W Yorks 205 F9
Little Horwood Bucks 102 E5
Little Houghton Northants 120 F6
Little Houghton S Yorks 198 F2
Little Hucklow Derby 185 F11
Little Hulton Gtr Man 195 G8
Little Humber ER Yorks 201 C7
Little Hungerford W Berks 64 E4
Little Hutton N Yorks 215 D9
Little Ickford Bucks 83 D11
Little Inkberrow Worcs 117 F10
Little Irchester Northants 121 D8
Little Island W Midlands 133 D9
Little Kelk ER Yorks 218 G2
Little Keyford Som'set 45 D8
Little Kimble Bucks 84 D4
Little Kineton Warwick 118 G6
Little Kingshill Bucks 84 F5
Little Knowle Devon 15 E7
Little Knowles Green Suffolk 124 F5
Little Langdale Cumb 220 E6
Little Langford Wilts 46 F4
Little Laver Essex 87 D8
Little Lawford Warwick 119 B9
Little Layton Blackp'l 202 F2
Little Leigh Ches 183 F10
Little Leighs Essex 88 B2
Little Lepton W Yorks 197 E8
Little Leven ER Yorks 209 D7
Little Lever Gtr Man 195 F9
Little Linford M/Keynes 102 C6
Little Load Som'set 29 C7
Little London Bucks 83 C10
Little London Cambs 139 D8
Little London E Sussex 37 D9
Little London Essex 106 D3
Little London Glos 80 B2
Little London Hants 47 D11
Little London Hants 48 B6
Little London Kent 54 D6
Little London Lincs 156 E4
Little London Lincs 157 E8
Little London Lincs 190 F4
Little London Lincs 189 D10
Little London NE Lincs 201 E7
Little London Norfolk 140 D5
Little London Norfolk 160 C2
Little London Norfolk 160 C5
Little London Norfolk 160 E3
Little London Oxon 83 E8
Little London Powys 129 F10
Little London Suffolk 125 F10
Little London Suffolk 125 E10
Little London Som'set 44 D6
Little London Wilts 62 E5
Little London W Yorks 205 F10
Little Longstone Derby 185 G11
Little Lynturk Aberds 293 B7
Little Madeley Staffs 168 F3
Little Malvern Worcs 98 C5
Little Mancot Flints 166 B4
Little Maplestead Essex 106 E6
Little Marcle Heref'd 98 D3
Little Marlow Bucks 65 B11
Little Marsden Lancs 204 F3
Little Marsh Wilts 45 B10
Little Marton Blackp'l 202 G3
Little Massingham Norfolk 158 E5
Little Melton Norfolk 142 B3
Little Milford Pembs 73 C7
Little Mill Kent 53 D7
Little Mill Monmouths 78 E4
Little Milton Oxon 83 E10
Little Minster Oxon 82 C4
Little Missenden Bucks 84 F6
Little Mongeham Kent 55 C10
Little Moor Gtr Man 184 D6
Little Moor Lancs 203 E10
Little Moor Som'set 43 G10
Little Moor End Lancs 195 B8
Little Morrell Warwick 118 F6
Little Mountain Flints 166 C3
Little Musgrave Cumb 222 C5
Little Ness Shrops 149 F8
Little Neston Ches 182 F3
Little Newcastle Pembs 91 F9
Little Newsham Durham 224 B2
Little Norton Som'set 29 D7
Little Oakley Essex 108 F4
Little Oakley Northants 137 F7
Little Odell Beds 121 F9
Little Offley Herts 104 F2
Little Onn Staffs 150 F6
Little Ormside Cumb 222 B4
Little Orton Cumb 239 F9
Little Orton Leics 134 B6
Little Ouse Cambs 140 F2
Little Ouseburn N Yorks 215 G8
Little Oxney Green Essex 87 D11
Little Packington Warwick 134 G4
Little Parndon Essex 86 C6
Little Pattenden Kent 53 D8
Little Paxton Cambs 122 E3
Little Petherick Cornw'l 10 G4
Little Pill Devon 40 G5
Little Pitlurg Moray 302 E4
Little Plumpton Lancs 202 G3
Little Plumstead Norfolk 160 G6
Little Ponton Lincs 155 C8
Little Preston Northants 119 G11
Little Preston W Yorks 206 G3
Little Raveley Cambs 122 B5
Little Reedness ER Yorks 199 C10
Little Reynoldston Swan 56 D3
Little Ribston N Yorks 206 C3
Little Rissington Glos 81 B11
Little Rogart H'land 309 J7
Little Rollright Oxon 100 E5
Little Ryburgh Norfolk 159 D9
Little Ryle Northum 264 G2
Little Ryton Shrops 131 C9
Little Salkeld Cumb 231 D7
Little Sampford Essex 106 E2
Little Sandhurst Brackn'l 65 G10
Little Saredon Staffs 133 B8
Little Sarnesfield Heref'd 115 G7
Little Saxham Suffolk 124 E6
Little Scatwell H'land 300 D3
Little Scotland Gtr Man 194 E6
Little Sessay N Yorks 215 E9
Little Shelford Cambs 123 F9
Little Shellwood Surrey 51 D8
Little Shurdington Glos 80 B6
Little Silver Devon 26 G5
Little Silver Devon 26 F6
Little Silver Devon 27 E7
Little Silver Devon 27 G8
Little Singleton Lancs 202 F3
Little Skillymarno Aberds 303 D9
Little Skipwith N Yorks 207 F9
Little Smeaton N Yorks 198 D4
Little Smeaton N Yorks 224 E6
Little Snoring Norfolk 159 C9
Little Sodbury S Glos 61 C9
Little Sodbury End S Glos 61 C8
Little Somborne Hants 47 G11
Little Somerford Wilts 62 C3
Little Soudley Shrops 150 D4
Little Stainforth N Yorks 212 F6
Little Stainton D'lington 234 G2
Little Stanmore London 85 G11
Little Stanney Ches 182 G6
Little Staughton Beds 122 E2
Little Steeping Lincs 174 B6
Little Stoke S Glos 60 C6
Little Stoke Staffs 151 C8
Little Stonham Suffolk 126 F2
Little Stretton Leics 136 C3
Little Stretton Shrops 131 E8
Little Strickland Cumb 221 B11
Little Stukeley Cambs 122 B4
Little Sugnall Staffs 150 C6
Little Sutton Ches 182 F5
Little Swinburne Northum 241 B11
Little Tarrington Heref'd 98 C2
Little Tew Oxon 101 F7
Little Tey Essex 107 G7
Little Thetford Cambs 123 B10
Little Thirkleby N Yorks 215 D9
Little Thornage Norfolk 159 B11
Little Thornton Lancs 202 E3
Little Thorpe Durham 234 C4
Little Thorpe W Yorks 197 C7
Little Thurlow Suffolk 124 G3
Little Thurlow Green Suffolk 124 G3
Little Thurrock Thurr'k 68 D6
Little Torboll H'land 309 K7
Little Torrington Devon 25 D7
Little Tosson Northum 252 C2
Little Totham Essex 88 C5
Little Toux Aberds 302 D5
Little Town Cumb 220 B4
Little Town Lancs 203 F9
Little Town Warrington 183 C10
Little Turnberry S Ayrs 244 B6
Little Twycross Leics 134 B6
Little Urswick Cumb 210 E5
Little Wakering Essex 70 B2
Little Walden Essex 105 C10
Little Waldingfield Suffolk 107 B8
Little Walsingham Norfolk 159 B8
Little Waltham Essex 88 C2
Little Warley Essex 87 G10
Little Washbourne Glos 99 E9
Little Watersend Kent 55 E9
Little Weighton ER Yorks 208 G4
Little Welland Worcs 98 D6
Little Welnetham Suffolk 125 E7
Little Welton Lincs 190 D4
Little Wenham Suffolk 107 D11
Little Wenlock Telford 132 B2
Little Weston Som'set 29 B10
Little Whittingham Green Suffolk 126 B5
Little Wilbraham Cambs 123 F10
Little Wishford Wilts 46 F5
Little Witcombe Glos 80 B6
Little Witley Worcs 116 E5
Little Wittenham Oxon 83 G9
Little Wolford Warwick 100 E5
Little Woodcote London 67 G9
Little Woolgarston Dorset 18 E5
Little Wratting Suffolk 106 B3
Little Wymington Beds 121 D9
Little Wymondley Herts 104 F4
Little Wyrley Staffs 133 B10
Little Yeldham Essex 106 D5
Little-ayre Shetl'd 315 G5
Littleborough Devon 26 E4
Littleborough Gtr Man 196 D2
Littleborough Notts 188 E4
Littlebourne Kent 55 B7
Littlebredy Dorset 17 D7
Littlebury Essex 105 D10
Littlebury Green Essex 105 D9
Littlecott Wilts 62 D4
Littlecott Wilts 46 C6
Littledean Glos 79 C11
Littledown Bournem'th 19 C8
Littleferry H'land 311 K2
Littlefield NE Lincs 201 F9
Littlefield Green Windsor 65 D11
Littleham Devon 14 E6
Littleham Devon 24 C6
Littlehampton W Sussex 35 G8
Littlehempston Devon 8 C6
Littlehoughton Northum 264 F6
Littlemill Aberds 292 D5
Littlemill E Ayrs 257 F11
Littlemill H'land 301 D9
Littlemoor Derby 170 C5
Littlemoor Dorset 17 E9
Littlemore Oxon 83 E8
Littleover Derby C 152 C6
Littleport Cambs 139 F11
Littleport Norfolk 158 B4
Littler Ches 167 B10
Littlestead Green Oxon 65 D8
Littlestone-on-Sea Kent 39 C9
Littlethorpe Leics 135 D10
Littlethorpe N Yorks 214 F6
Littleton Bath/NE Som'set 60 G5
Littleton Ches 166 B6
Littleton Dorset 30 G5
Littleton Hants 48 G3
Littleton Perth/Kinr 286 D6
Littleton Som'set 44 G3
Littleton Surrey 50 D3
Littleton Surrey 66 F5
Littleton Wilts 62 G2
Littleton Drew Wilts 61 C10
Littleton on Severn S Glos 60 B5
Littleton Pannell Wilts 46 C3
Littletown Durham 234 C2
Littletown Devon 15 B9
Littletown I/Wight 20 C6
Littletown W Yorks 197 C8
Littlewick Green Windsor 65 D10
Littlewindsor Dorset 28 G6
Littlewood Staffs 133 B9
Littlewood Green Warwick 117 E11
Littleworth Beds 103 C11
Littleworth Glos 80 E5
Littleworth Glos 100 D2
Littleworth Oxon 82 F4
Littleworth Oxon 83 D9
Littleworth Oxon 83 G10
Littleworth Staffs 151 E8
Littleworth Staffs 151 G10
Littleworth S Yorks 187 B10
Littleworth Worcs 117 G7
Littleworth Worcs 117 E9
Littleworth W Sussex 35 C11
Littleworth Cross Surrey 49 D11
Littley Green Essex 87 B11
Litton Derby 185 F11
Litton N Yorks 213 E8
Litton Som'set 44 C5
Litton Cheney Dorset 17 C7
Liurbost W Isles 304 F5
Livermead Torbay 9 C8
Liverpool Mersey 182 C4
Liverpool Airport Mersey 182 E6
Liverpool Cathedral (C of E) Mersey 182 D5
Liverpool Cathedral (RC) Mersey 182 C5
Liverpool John Lennon Airport Mersey 182 E6
Liversedge W Yorks 197 C7
Liverton Devon 14 F2
Liverton Redcar/Clevel'd 226 B4
Liverton Mines Redcar/Clevel'd 226 B4
Liverton Street Kent 53 C11
Livesey Street Kent 53 C8
Livingston W Loth 269 B10
Livingston Village W Loth 269 B10
Lix Toll Stirl 285 D9

Lixwm Flints 181 G11
Lizard Cornw'l 2 G6
Llaingarreglwyd Ceredig'n 111 F8
Llaingoch Angl 178 E2
Llaithddu Powys 129 G11
Llampha V/Glam 58 D2
Llan Powys 129 C7
Llan Rh Cyn Taff 58 B4
Llan Ffestiniog Gwyn 164 G2
Llanaber Gwyn 146 F2
Llanaelhaearn Gwyn 162 G5
Llanaeron Ceredig'n 111 E9
Llanafan Ceredig'n 112 C3
Llanafan-fawr Powys 113 F9
Llanallgo Angl 179 D8
Llanandras = Presteigne Powys 114 E6
Llananno Powys 113 C11
Llanarmon Gwyn 145 B8
Llanarmon Dyffryn Ceiriog Wrex 148 C3
Llanarmon Mynydd-Mawr Powys 148 D2
Llanarmon-yn-Ial Denbs 165 D11
Llanarth Ceredig'n 111 F8
Llanarth Monmouths 78 C5
Llanarthne Carms 93 G10
Llanasa Flints 181 E10
Llanbabo Angl 178 D5
Llanbad Bridg 58 C3
Llanbadarn Fawr Ceredig'n 128 G2
Llanbadarn Fynydd Powys 113 B11
Llanbadarn-y-garreg Powys 96 B2
Llanbadoc Monmouths 78 E5
Llanbadrig Angl 178 C5
Llanbeder Newp 78 G5
Llanbedr Gwyn 145 D11
Llanbedr Powys 96 B2
Llanbedr Powys 96 G4
Llanbedr Pont Steffan = Lampeter Ceredig'n 93 B11
Llanbedr-Dyffryn-Clwyd Denbs 165 D10
Llanbedrgoch Angl 179 E8
Llanbedrog Gwyn 144 C6
Llanbedr-y-cennin Conwy 164 B3
Llanberis Gwyn 163 C9
Llanbethery V/Glam 58 F4
Llanbister Powys 114 C3
Llanblethian V/Glam 58 E3
Llanboidy Carms 92 G4
Llanbradach Caerph 77 G10
Llanbrynmair Powys 129 C7
Llancadle V/Glam 58 F4
Llancaiach Merth Tyd 77 F10
Llancarfan V/Glam 58 E5
Llancayo Monmouths 78 E5
Llancloudy Heref'd 97 G9
Llancoch Powys 114 C4
Llancynfelyn Ceredig'n 128 E2
Llan-dafal Bl Gwent 77 E11
Llandaff Card 59 D7
Llandaff North Card 59 D7
Llandanwg Gwyn 145 D11
Llandarcy Rh Cyn Taff 76 F2
Llandawke Carms 74 C3
Llanddaniel Fab Angl 179 G7
Llanddarog Carms 75 B8
Llanddeiniol Ceredig'n 111 C11
Llanddeiniolen Gwyn 163 B8
Llandderfel Gwyn 147 B9
Llanddeusant Carms 94 G5
Llanddeusant Angl 178 D4
Llanddew Powys 95 E11
Llanddewi Swan 56 D3
Llanddewi Brefi Ceredig'n 112 F3
Llanddewi Rhydderch Monmouths 78 C4
Llanddewi Velfrey Pembs 73 B10
Llanddewi Ystradenni Powys 114 D2
Llanddewi'r-Cwm Powys 95 B10
Llanddoged Conwy 164 C4
Llanddona Angl 179 F9
Llanddowror Carms 74 C3
Llanddulas Conwy 180 F6
Llanddwywe Gwyn 145 E11
Llanddyfgael Hir Angl 178 C5
Llandecwyn Gwyn 146 B2
Llandefaelog Powys 95 E10
Llandefaelogtre'r-graig Powys 96 F2
Llandefalle Powys 96 D2
Llandegfan Angl 179 G9
Llandegla Denbs 165 E11
Llandegley Powys 114 E2
Llandegveth Monmouths 78 F4
Llandegwning Gwyn 144 D5
Llandeilo'r-Fan Powys 95 E7
Llandeilo Carms 94 G2
Llandeilo Graban Powys 95 C11
Llandeloy Pembs 91 F7
Llandenny Monmouths 78 E6
Llandevaud Newp 78 G6
Llandevenny Monmouths 60 B2
Llandilo Carms 92 F2
Llandinabo Heref'd 97 F10
Llandinam Powys 129 F10
Llandissilio Pembs 92 G2
Llandogo Cleddon Monmouths 79 E8
Llandough V/Glam 58 E3
Llandough V/Glam 59 E7
Llandovery = Llanymddyfri Carms 94 E5
Llandow V/Glam 58 E2
Llandre Carms 94 C3
Llandre Ceredig'n 128 F2
Llandrillo Denbs 147 B10
Llandrillo-yn-Rhôs Conwy 180 E4
Llandrindod = Llandrindod Wells Powys 113 E11
Llandrindod Wells = Llandrindod Powys 113 E11
Llandrinio Powys 148 F5
Llandudno Conwy 180 E3
Llandudno Junction = Cyffordd Llandudno Conwy 180 F4
Llandudoch = St. Dogmaels Pembs 92 B3
Llandwrog Gwyn 163 D7
Llandybie = Llandybïe Carms 75 B10
Llandybïe = Llandybie Carms 75 B10
Llandyfaelog Carms 74 C6
Llandyfan Carms 75 B10
Llandyfriog Ceredig'n 92 C6
Llandyfrydog Angl 178 D6
Llandygai Gwyn 179 G9
Llandygwydd Ceredig'n 92 C4
Llandynan Denbs 165 G11
Llandyrnog Denbs 165 B10
Llandyry Carms 74 E6
Llandysilio Powys 148 F5
Llandyssil Powys 130 D3
Llandysul Ceredig'n 93 C8
Llanedeyrn Card 59 C8
Llanedi Carms 75 D9
Llaneglwys Powys 95 D11
Llanegryn Gwyn 110 B2
Llanegwad Carms 93 G10
Llaneilian Angl 179 C7
Llanelian-yn-Rhos Conwy 180 F5
Llanelidan Denbs 165 E10
Llanelieu Powys 96 E3
Llanellen Monmouths 78 C4
Llanelli Carms 75 E8
Llanelltyd Gwyn 146 F4
Llanelly Monmouths 78 C2
Llanelly Hill Monmouths 78 C2
Llanelwedd Powys 113 G11
Llanelwy = St. Asaph Denbs 181 G8
Llanenddwyn Gwyn 145 E11
Llanengan Gwyn 144 D5
Llanerch Emrys Powys 148 E4
Llanerchymedd Angl 178 E6
Llanerch-y-môr Flints 181 F11
Llanerfyl Powys 129 B10
Llaneuddog Angl 179 D7
Llan-eurgain = Northop Flints 166 B2
Llanfach Caerph 78 F2
Llanfachraeth Angl 178 E4
Llanfachreth Gwyn 146 E5
Llanfaelog Angl 178 G4
Llanfaelrhys Gwyn 144 D4
Llanfaenor Monmouths 78 B6
Llanfaes Angl 179 F10
Llanfaes Powys 95 F10
Llanfaethlu Angl 178 D4
Llanfaglan Gwyn 163 C7
Llanfair Gwyn 145 D11
Llanfair Caereinion Powys 130 B2
Llanfair Clydogau Ceredig'n 112 G2
Llanfair Dyffryn Clwyd Denbs 165 D10
Llanfair Kilgeddin Monmouths 78 D4
Llanfair Talhaiarn Conwy 180 G6
Llanfair Waterdine Shrops 114 B4
Llanfairfechan Conwy 179 F11
Llanfair-Nant-Gwyn Pembs 92 D3
Llanfairpwllgwyngyll Angl 179 G8
Llanfair-ym-Muallt = Builth Wells Powys 113 G10
Llanfairyneubwll Angl 178 F4
Llanfairynghornwy Angl 178 C4
Llanfallteg Carms 73 B11
Llanfaredd Powys 113 G11
Llanfarian Ceredig'n 111 B11
Llanfechain Powys 148 E3
Llanfechan Powys 113 G9
Llanfechell Angl 178 C5
Llanfendigaid Gwyn 110 C2
Llanferres Denbs 165 C11
Llanfflewyn Angl 178 D5
Llanfihangel Crucorney Monmouths 96 G6
Llanfihangel Glyn Myfyr Conwy 165 F7
Llanfihangel Nant Bran Powys 95 E8
Llanfihangel Rhydithon Powys 114 D3
Llanfihangel Tal-y-llyn Powys 96 F2
Llanfihangel yn Nhowyn Angl 178 F4
Llanfihangel-ar-arth Carms 93 D9
Llanfihangel-helygen Powys 113 E10
Llanfihangel-nant-Melan Powys 114 F3
Llanfihangel-y-Creuddyn Ceredig'n 112 B3
Llanfihangel-yng-Ngwnfa Powys 147 F11
Llanfihangel-y-pennant Gwyn 128 B3
Llanfihangel-y-pennant Gwyn 163 G8
Llanfilo Powys 96 E2
Llanfoist Monmouths 78 C3
Llanfor Gwyn 147 B8
Llanfrechfa Torf 78 G4
Llanfrothen Gwyn 163 G10
Llanfrynach Powys 95 F11
Llanfwrog Denbs 165 D10
Llanfwrog Angl 178 E4
Llanfyllin Powys 148 F2
Llanfynydd Carms 93 F11
Llanfynydd Flints 166 D3
Llanfyrnach Pembs 92 E4
Llangadfan Powys 147 G10
Llangadog Carms 74 D6
Llangadog Carms 94 F4
Llangadwaladr Angl 162 B5
Llangadwaladr Powys 148 C3
Llangaffo Angl 162 B6
Llangain Carms 74 B5
Llangammarch Wells Powys 95 B8
Llangan V/Glam 58 D3
Llangarron Heref'd 97 G10
Llangasty-Talyllyn Powys 96 F2
Llangathen Carms 93 G11
Llangattock Powys 78 B2
Llangattock Lingoed Monmouths 97 F7
Llangedwyn Powys 148 E3
Llangefni Angl 179 F7
Llangeinor Bridg 58 B2
Llangeler Carms 93 D7
Llangelynnin Gwyn 110 B2
Llangendeirne Carms 75 C7
Llangennech Carms 75 E9
Llangennith Carms 74 G6
Llangenny Powys 78 B2
Llangernyw Conwy 164 B5
Llangeview Monmouths 78 E6
Llangian Gwyn 144 D5
Llangiwg Neath P Talb 76 D2
Llangloffan Pembs 91 E8
Llanglydwen Carms 92 F3
Llangoed Angl 179 F10
Llangoedmor Ceredig'n 92 B4
Llangollen Denbs 166 G2
Llangolman Pembs 92 F2
Llangors Powys 96 F2
Llangorwen Ceredig'n 128 G2
Llangovan Monmouths 79 D7
Llangower Gwyn 147 C8
Llangrannog Ceredig'n 110 G6
Llangristiolus Angl 178 G6
Llangrove Heref'd 79 B8
Llangua Monmouths 97 F7
Llangunllo Powys 114 C4
Llangunnor Carms 93 G8
Llangurig Powys 129 G8
Llangwm Conwy 165 G7
Llangwm Monmouths 78 F6
Llangwm Pembs 73 D7
Llangwnnadl Gwyn 144 C4
Llangwyfan Denbs 165 B10
Llangwyllog Angl 178 F6
Llangwyryfon Ceredig'n 112 C2
Llangybi Ceredig'n 112 G2
Llangybi Gwyn 162 G6
Llangybi Monmouths 78 F5
Llangyfelach Swan 75 F10
Llangynhafal Denbs 165 C10
Llangynidr Powys 77 B11
Llangynin Carms 74 B3
Llangynllo Ceredig'n 93 C7
Llangynog Carms 74 B4
Llangynog Powys 147 D11
Llangynwyd Bridg 57 D11
Llanhamfach Powys 95 F11
Llanharan Rh Cyn Taff 58 C4
Llanharry Rh Cyn Taff 58 C4
Llanhennock Monmouths 78 G5
Llanhilleth Bl Gwent 78 E2
Llanidloes Powys 129 G9
Llaniestyn Gwyn 144 C5
Llanifihangel-uwch-Gwili Carms 93 G9
Llanifyny Powys 129 G7
Llanigon Powys 96 C4
Llanilar Ceredig'n 112 B2
Llanilid Rh Cyn Taff 58 C3
Llanion Pembs 73 E7
Llanishen Card 59 C7
Llanishen Monmouths 79 E7
Llanllawddog Carms 93 F9
Llanllechid Gwyn 163 B10
Llanllowell = Llanllywell Monmouths 78 F5
Llanllugan Powys 129 C11
Llanllwch Carms 74 B5
Llanllwchaiarn Powys 130 E2
Llanllwni Carms 93 D9
Llanllyfni Gwyn 163 E7
Llanllywell = Llanllowell Monmouths 78 F5
Llanmadoc Carms 74 G6
Llanmaes V/Glam 58 F3
Llanmartin Newp 59 B11
Llanmihangel V/Glam 58 E3
Llan-mill Pembs 73 C10
Llanmiloe Carms 74 D3
Llanmorlais Swan 75 G8
Llannant Swan 75 E9
Llannefydd Conwy 181 G7
Llannon Carms 75 D8
Llan-non = Llanon Ceredig'n 111 D10
Llannor Gwyn 145 B7
Llanon = Llan-non Ceredig'n 111 D10
Llanover Monmouths 78 D4
Llanpumpsaint Carms 93 F8
Llanreath Pembs 73 E7
Llanreithan Pembs 91 F7
Llanrhaeadr Denbs 165 C9
Llanrhaeadr-ym-Mochnant Powys 148 D2
Llanrhian Pembs 90 E6
Llanrhidian Swan 75 G7
Llanrhos Conwy 180 E3
Llanrhyddlad Angl 178 D4
Llanrhystud Ceredig'n 111 D10
Llanrosser Heref'd 96 D5
Llanrothal Heref'd 79 B7
Llanrug Gwyn 163 C8
Llanrumney Card 59 C8
Llanrwst Conwy 164 C4
Llansadurnen Carms 74 C3
Llansadwrn Carms 94 E3
Llansadwrn Angl 179 F9
Llansaint Carms 74 D5
Llansanffraid Glan Conwy Conwy 180 F4
Llansannan Conwy 164 B6
Llansannor V/Glam 58 D3
Llansantffraed Ceredig'n 111 D10
Llansantffraed Powys 96 G2
Llansantffraed-Cwmdeuddwr Powys 113 D9
Llansantffraed-in-Elwel Powys 113 G11
Llansantffraid-ym-Mechain Powys 148 E4
Llansawel = Briton Ferry Rh Cyn Taff 76 G2
Llansawel Carms 94 D2
Llansilin Powys 148 D4
Llansoy Monmouths 78 E6
Llanspyddid Powys 95 F10
Llanstadwell Pembs 73 D7
Llansteffan Carms 74 C5
Llanstephan Powys 96 C2
Llantarnam Torf 78 G4
Llanteg Pembs 73 C11
Llanteglos Pembs 73 D11
Llanthony Monmouths 96 F5
Llantilio Crossenny Monmouths 78 C5
Llantilio Pertholey Monmouths 78 B4
Llantood Pembs 92 C3
Llantrisant Angl 178 E5
Llantrisant Monmouths 78 F5
Llantrisant Rh Cyn Taff 58 C4
Llantrithyd V/Glam 58 E4
Llantwit Fardre Rh Cyn Taff 58 C5
Llantwit Major V/Glam 58 F3
Llanuwchllyn Gwyn 147 C7
Llanvaches Newp 78 G6
Llanvair Discoed Monmouths 78 G6
Llanvapley Monmouths 78 C5
Llanvetherine Monmouths 78 B5
Llanveynoe Heref'd 96 E6
Llanvihangel Gobion Monmouths 78 D4
Llanvihangel Pontymoel Torf 78 E4
Llanvihangel-Ystern-Llewern Monmouths 78 C6
Llanwarne Heref'd 97 F10
Llanwddyn Powys 147 F10
Llanwenarth Monmouths 78 C3
Llanwenog Ceredig'n 93 B9
Llanwern Newp 59 B11
Llanwinio Carms 92 F5
Llanwnda Gwyn 163 D7
Llanwnda Pembs 91 D8
Llanwnnen Ceredig'n 93 B10
Llanwnog Powys 129 E10
Llanwonno Rh Cyn Taff 77 F8
Llanwrda Carms 94 E4
Llanwrin Powys 128 C5
Llanwrthwl Powys 113 E9
Llanwrtud = Llanwrtyd Wells Powys 95 B7
Llanwrtyd Powys 95 B7
Llanwrtyd Wells = Llanwrtud Powys 95 B7
Llanwryglyn Powys 129 E8
Llanwyddelan Powys 129 C11
Llanyblodwel Shrops 148 E4
Llanybri Carms 74 C4
Llanybydder Carms 93 C10
Llanycefn Pembs 91 G11
Llanychaer Pembs 91 D9
Llanycil Gwyn 147 C8
Llanycrwys Carms 94 B2
Llanymawddwy Gwyn 147 F8
Llanymddyfri = Llandovery Carms 94 E5
Llanymynech Shrops 148 E5
Llanynghenedl Angl 178 E4
Llanynys Denbs 165 C10
Llan-y-pwll Wrex 166 E5
Llanyrafon Torf 78 F4
Llanyre Powys 113 E10
Llanystumdwy Gwyn 145 B9
Llanywern Powys 96 F2
Llawhaden Pembs 73 B9
Llawndy Flints 181 E10
Llawnt Shrops 148 C5
Llay Wrex 166 D4
Llechcynfarwy Angl 178 E5
Llecheiddior Gwyn 163 G7
Llechfaen Powys 95 F11
Llechfraith Gwyn 146 F3
Llechryd Caerph 77 D10
Llechryd Ceredig'n 92 C4
Llechwedd Conwy 180 F3
Llechwedd Slate Caverns, Blaenau Ffestiniog Gwyn 164 F2
Lledrod Ceredig'n 112 C2
Llenmerewig Powys 130 E3
Llethrid Swan 75 G8
Lletty Brongu Bridg 57 D11
Llidiadnenog Carms 93 D10
Llidiardau Gwyn 147 B7
Llidiart-y-Parc Denbs 165 G10
Llidiartywaen Powys 129 G10
Llingattock-Vibon-Avel Monmouths 79 B7
Llithfaen Gwyn 162 G5
Lloc Flints 181 F10
Llong Flints 166 C3
Llowes Powys 96 C3
Lloyney Powys 114 B4
Llugwy Gwyn 128 C4
Llundain-fach Ceredig'n 111 F11
Llwydcoed Rh Cyn Taff 77 E7
Llwyn Gwyn 146 B3
Llwyncelyn Ceredig'n 111 F8
Llwyndafydd Ceredig'n 111 F7
Llwynderw Powys 130 C4
Llwyndrain Carms 92 E5
Llwyn-du Monmouths 78 B3
Llwyn-du Swan 76 E2
Llwyndyrys Gwyn 162 G5
Llwyneinion Wrex 166 F3
Llwyngwril Gwyn 110 B2
Llwynhendy Carms 75 E8
Llwynmawr Wrex 148 B4
Llwyn-on-village Merth Tyd 77 C8
Llwyn-y-brain Carms 73 B11
Llwyn-y-Groes Ceredig'n 111 F11
Llwynymaen Shrops 148 D5
Llwynypia Rh Cyn Taff 77 G7
Llynclys Shrops 148 E5
Llynfaes Angl 178 F6
Llyn-y-Pandy Flints 166 B2
Llysdinam Powys 113 F10
Llysfaen Conwy 180 F5
Llysnewydd Carms 93 D7
Llyswen Powys 96 D2
Llysworney V/Glam 58 E3
Llys-y-Fran Pembs 91 G10
Llywel Powys 95 E7
Llywernog Ceredig'n 128 G4
Loan Falk 279 F9
Loandhu H'land 301 B8
Loanhead Aberds 302 D6
Loanhead Midloth 270 B5
Loanhead Perth/Kinr 286 D5
Loanreoch H'land 300 B6
Loans S Ayrs 257 C8
Loans of Tullich H'land 301 B8
Loansdean Northum 252 G5
Lobb Devon 40 F3
Lobhillcross Devon 12 D5
Lobley Hill Tyne/Wear 242 E6
Lobthorpe Lincs 155 E9
Loch a Charnain W Isles 297 G4
Loch a'Ghainmhich W Isles 304 F4
Loch Baghasdail = Lochboisdale W Isles 297 K3
Loch Choire Lodge H'land 308 F6
Loch Eil H'land 290 F2
Loch Euphoirt W Isles 296 E4
Loch Head Dumf/Gal 236 E5
Loch Loyal Lodge H'land 308 E6
Loch nam Madadh = Lochmaddy W Isles 296 E5
Loch Ness Monster Exhibition, Drumnadrochit H'land 300 F5
Loch Sgioport W Isles 297 H4
Lochailort H'land 295 G9
Lochaline H'land 289 E8
Lochanhully H'land 301 G9
Lochans Dumf/Gal 236 D2
Locharbriggs Dumf/Gal 247 G11
Lochassynt Lodge H'land 307 G6
Lochavich Ho Arg/Bute 275 B10
Lochawe Arg/Bute 284 E5
Lochboisdale = Loch Baghasdail W Isles 297 K3
Lochbuie Arg/Bute 289 G8
Lochbuie Ho Arg/Bute 289 G8
Lochcallater Lodge Aberds 292 E3
Lochcarron H'land 295 B10
Lochdhu H'land 310 E4
Lochdochart House Stirl 285 E8
Lochdon Arg/Bute 289 F9
Lochdrum H'land 300 B2
Lochead Arg/Bute 275 E11
Lochead Arg/Bute 275 F8
Lochearnhead Stirl 285 E9
Lochee Dundee C 287 D7
Lochend H'land 300 F5
Lochend H'land 310 C6
Lochend Ho. Stirl 285 H9
Lochetive Ho. H'land 284 C5
Lochfoot Dumf/Gal 237 B10
Lochgair Arg/Bute 275 D10
Lochgarthside H'land 291 B7
Lochgelly Fife 280 C3
Lochgilphead Arg/Bute 275 E9
Lochgoilhead Arg/Bute 284 G6
Lochhill Moray 302 C2
Lochhussie H'land 300 D4
Lochinch Castle Dumf/Gal 236 C3
Lochindorb Lodge H'land 301 F9
Lochinver H'land 307 G5
Lochlane Perth/Kinr 286 E2
Lochletter H'land 300 G4
Lochluichart H'land 300 C3
Lochmaben Dumf/Gal 248 G3
Lochmaddy = Loch nam Madadh W Isles 296 E5
Lochmore Cottage H'land 310 E4
Lochmore Lodge H'land 306 F7
Lochnell Ho Arg/Bute 289 F10
Lochore Fife 280 B3
Lochorodale Arg/Bute 255 F7
Lochportain W Isles 296 D5
Lochranza N Ayrs 255 B10
Lochs Crofts Moray 302 C3
Lochside Aberds 293 G9
Lochside Dumf/Gal 247 H11
Lochside H'land 301 D8
Lochside H'land 308 D4
Lochside H'land 310 F2
Lochslin H'land 311 L2
Lochstack Lodge H'land 306 E7
Lochton Aberds 293 D9
Lochton Scot Borders 263 B7
Lochty Angus 293 G7
Lochty Fife 287 G9
Lochty Perth/Kinr 286 E4
Lochuisge H'land 289 D9
Lochurr Dumf/Gal 247 F7
Lochwinnoch Renf 267 D7
Lochwood Glasg C 268 B3
Lochwood Dumf/Gal 248 D3
Lochyside H'land 290 F3
Lockengate Cornw'l 5 C10
Lockerbie Dumf/Gal 248 G4
Lockeridge Wilts 62 F6
Lockerley Hants 32 B3
Lockhills Cumb 230 B6
Locking N Som'set 43 B11
Locking Stumps Warrington 183 C10
Lockington ER Yorks 208 D5
Lockington Leics 153 D9
Lockleaze Bristol 60 D6
Lockleywood Shrops 150 D3
Locks Heath Hants 33 F8
Locksbottom London 68 G2
Locksbrook Bath/NE Som'set 61 F8
Locksgreen I/Wight 20 C4
Lockton N Yorks 216 B6
Lockwood W Yorks 196 D6
Lockwood W Yorks 196 D6
Locomotion Museum, Shildon Durham 233 F10
Loddington Leics 136 C5
Loddington Northants 120 B6
Loddiswell Devon 8 F4
Loddon Norfolk 143 D7
Lode Cambs 123 E10
Lode Heath W Midlands 134 G3
Loders Dorset 16 C5
Lodge Green W Midlands 134 G5
Lodge Hill Cornw'l 6 C4
Lodge Hill W Midlands 133 G10
Lodge Lees Kent 55 D8
Lodsworth W Sussex 34 C6
Lodway N Som'set 60 D4
Lofthouse N Yorks 214 E2
Lofthouse W Yorks 197 B10
Lofthouse Gate W Yorks 197 C10
Loftus Redcar/Clevel'd 226 B4
Logan E Ayrs 258 E3
Logan Mains Dumf/Gal 236 E2
Loganlea W Loth 269 C9
Logaston Heref'd 114 G6
Loggerheads Staffs 150 B4
Logie Angus 293 G8
Logie Fife 287 E8
Logie Moray 301 D10
Logie Coldstone Aberds 292 C6
Logie Hill H'land 301 B7
Logie Newton Aberds 302 F6
Logie Pert Angus 293 G8
Logiealmond Lodge Perth/Kinr 286 D3
Logierait Perth/Kinr 286 B3
Login Carms 92 G3
Loidse Mhorsgail W Isles 304 F3
Lolworth Cambs 123 E7
Lonbain H'land 298 D6
Londesborough ER Yorks 208 D3
London Apprentice Cornw'l 5 E10
London Beach Kent 53 F11
London City Airport London 68 C2
London Colney Herts 85 E11
London Fields W Midlands 133 E8
London Gatwick Airport W Sussex 51 E9
London Heathrow Airport London 66 D5
London Luton Airport Luton 104 G2
London Minstead Hants 32 E3
London Stansted Airport Essex 105 G10
London Zoo London 67 C9
Londonderry N Yorks 214 B6
Londonderry W Midlands 133 F10
Londonthorpe Lincs 155 B9
Londubh H'land 307 L3
Lonemore H'land 299 B7
Lonemore H'land 309 L7
Long Ashton N Som'set 60 E4
Long Bank Worcs 116 C5
Long Bennington Lincs 172 G4
Long Bredy Dorset 17 C7
Long Buckby Northants 120 D2
Long Buckby Wharf Northants 120 D2
Long Clawson Leics 154 D4
Long Common Hants 33 E8
Long Compton Staffs 151 E7
Long Compton Warwick 100 E5
Long Crendon Bucks 83 D11
Long Crichel Dorset 31 E7
Long Cross N Som'set 60 F4
Long Cross Wilts 45 G9
Long Dean Wilts 61 D11
Long Ditton Surrey 67 F7
Long Drax N Yorks 199 B7
Long Duckmanton Derby 186 G6
Long Eaton Derby 153 C9
Long Gardens Essex 106 D6
Long Green Ches 183 G7
Long Green Worcs 98 E6
Long Hanborough Oxon 82 C6
Long Honeyborough Pembs 73 D7
Long Itchington Warwick 119 D8
Long John's Hill Norfolk 142 B4
Long Lane Telford 150 F2
Long Lawford Warwick 119 B9
Long Load Som'set 29 C7
Long Marston Herts 84 B5
Long Marston N Yorks 206 C6
Long Marston Warwick 100 B3
Long Marton Cumb 231 G9
Long Meadow Cambs 123 E10
Long Meadowend Shrops 131 G8
Long Melford Suffolk 107 B7
Long Moor Wokingham 65 G9
Long Newnton Glos 80 G6
Long Newton E Loth 271 C10
Long Park Hants 48 G2
Long Preston N Yorks 204 B2
Long Riston ER Yorks 209 E8
Long Sandall S Yorks 198 F6
Long Sight Gtr Man 196 F2
Long Stratton Norfolk 142 E3
Long Street M/Keynes 102 B5
Long Sutton Hants 49 D8
Long Sutton Lincs 157 E8
Long Sutton Som'set 29 B7
Long Thurlow Suffolk 125 D10
Long Whatton Leics 153 E9
Long Wittenham Oxon 83 G8
Longbar N Ayrs 266 E6
Longbenton Tyne/Wear 243 D7
Longborough Glos 100 F3
Longbridge Plym'th 7 D10
Longbridge Staffs 151 F8
Longbridge Warwick 118 E5
Longbridge W Midlands 117 B10
Longbridge Deverill Wilts 45 E11
Longburgh Cumb 239 F8
Longburton Dorset 29 E10
Longcause Devon 8 C5
Longcliffe Derby 170 D2
Longcombe Devon 8 D6
Longcot Oxon 82 G3
Longcroft Cumb 238 F6
Longcroft Falk 278 F5
Longcross Surrey 66 F3
Longdale Cumb 222 D2
Longdales Cumb 230 C6
Longden Shrops 131 B8
Longden Common Shrops 131 C8
Longdenwood Shrops 131 B9
Longdon Staffs 151 G11
Longdon Worcs 98 D6
Longdon Green Staffs 151 G11
Longdon Heath Worcs 98 D6
Longdon-on-Tern Telford 150 F2
Longdown Devon 14 C3
Longdowns Cornw'l 2 C6
Longdrum Angus 292 G4
Longfield Kent 68 F6
Longfield Shetl'd 315 M5
Longfield Wilts 45 B10
Longfield Hill Kent 68 F6
Longfleet Poole 18 C6
Longford Derby 152 B4
Longford Glos 98 G6
Longford Kent 52 B4
Longford London 66 D5
Longford Shrops 150 C2
Longford Telford 150 F4
Longford W Midlands 135 G7
Longford Warrington 183 C10
Longforgan Perth/Kinr 287 E7
Longformacus Scot Borders 272 D3
Longframlington Northum 252 C4
Longham Dorset 19 B7
Longham Norfolk 159 F8
Longhaven Aberds 303 F11
Longhedge Wilts 45 E10
Longhill Aberds 303 D9
Longhill S Ayrs 257 F8
Longhirst Northum 252 F6
Longhope Glos 79 B11
Longhope Orkney 313 J4
Longhorsley Northum 252 E5
Longhoughton Northum 264 F6
Longlands Cumb 229 D11
Longlands Lincs 191 E7
Longlands London 68 E3
Longlane Derby 152 B5
Longlane W Berks 64 E4
Longleat House Wilts 45 E10
Longlevens Glos 99 G7
Longley W Yorks 196 F6
Longley W Yorks 196 C4
Longley Estate S Yorks 186 C5
Longley Green Worcs 116 G4
Longleys Perth/Kinr 286 C6
Longmanhill Aberds 303 C7
Longmoor Camp Hants 49 G9
Longmorn Moray 302 D2
Longmoss Ches 184 G5
Longnewton Scot Borders 262 D3
Longnewton Stockton 225 B7
Longney Glos 80 C3
Longniddry E Loth 281 F8
Longnor Shrops 131 C9
Longnor Staffs 169 C9
Longparish Hants 48 E2
Longpark Cumb 239 E10
Longpark E Ayrs 257 B10
Longport Stoke 168 F5
Longridge Glos 80 D5
Longridge Lancs 203 F8
Longridge W Loth 269 C8
Longridge End Glos 98 G6
Longrigg N Lanarks 278 G6
Longriggend N Lanarks 278 G6
Longrock Cornw'l 1 C5
Longsdon Staffs 169 E7
Longshaw Gtr Man 194 G4
Longside Aberds 303 E10
Longsight Gtr Man 184 C5
Longslow Shrops 150 B3
Longsowerby Cumb 239 G9
Longstanton Cambs 123 D7
Longstock Hants 47 F11
Longstone C/Edinb 280 G4
Longstone Cornw'l 11 G7
Longstone Cornw'l 2 B2
Longstone Pembs 73 D10
Longstowe Cambs 122 G6
Longstreet Wilts 46 C6
Longthorpe Peterbro 138 D3
Longton Lancs 194 B3
Longton Stoke 168 G6
Longton Hill End Worcs 98 D6
Longtown Cumb 239 D9
Longtown Heref'd 96 F6
Longtownmail Orkney 313 H5
Longview Mersey 182 C6
Longville in the Dale Shrops 131 E10
Longwell Green S Glos 61 E7
Longwick Bucks 84 D3
Longwitton Northum 252 F3
Longwood W Yorks 196 D6
Longwood Edge W Yorks 196 D6
Longworth Oxon 82 F5
Longyester E Loth 271 B10
Lon-las Rh Cyn Taff 76 F2
Lonmay Aberds 303 D10
Lonmore H'land 298 E2
Looe Cornw'l 6 E5
Looe Mills Cornw'l 6 C4
Loose Kent 53 C9
Loosebeare Devon 26 F2
Loosegate Lincs 156 D6
Loosley Row Bucks 84 E4
Lopcombe Corner Wilts 47 F9
Lopen Som'set 28 E6
Loppington Shrops 149 D9
Lopwell Devon 7 B9
Lord's Cricket Ground London 67 C9
Lord's Hill S'thampton 32 D5
Lords Wood Medway 69 G9
Lordsbridge Norfolk 157 G11
Lornty Perth/Kinr 286 C5
Loscoe Derby 170 F6
Loscombe Dorset 16 B6
Losgaintir W Isles 305 J2
Lossiemouth Moray 302 B2
Lossit Arg/Bute 254 B2
Lossit Lodge Arg/Bute 274 G5
Lostock Gralam Ches 183 F11
Lostock Green Ches 183 G11
Lostock Hall Lancs 194 B4
Lostock Junction Gtr Man 195 F7
Lostwithiel Cornw'l 6 D2
Loth Orkney 312 E7
Lothbeg H'land 311 H3
Lothersdale N Yorks 204 D5
Lothianbridge Midloth 270 B6
Lothmore H'land 311 H3
Lottisham Som'set 44 G5
Loudwater Bucks 84 G6
Loudwater Herts 85 F9
Loughborough Leics 153 F10
Loughor Swan 75 F9
Loughton Essex 86 F6
Loughton Lincs 155 C11
Loughton M/Keynes 102 D6
Loughton Shrops 132 G2
Louis Tussaud's Waxworks Blackp'l 202 F2
Lound Lincs 155 F11
Lound Notts 187 D11
Lound Suffolk 143 D10
Lount Leics 153 F7
Lour Angus 287 C8
Louth Lincs 190 D4
Lovat H'land 300 E5
Love Clough Lancs 195 B10
Love Green Bucks 66 C4
Lovedean Hants 33 E11
Lover Wilts 32 C2
Loversall S Yorks 187 B9
Loves Green Essex 87 E10
Loveston Pembs 73 D9
Lovington Som'set 44 G5
Low Ackworth W Yorks 198 D3
Low Angerton Northum 252 G3
Low Bentham N Yorks 212 F3
Low Biggins Cumb 212 D2
Low Blantyre S Lanarks 268 D3
Low Bolton N Yorks 223 F10
Low Borrowbridge Cumb 222 E2
Low Bradfield S Yorks 186 B3
Low Bradley N Yorks 204 D6
Low Braithwaite Cumb 230 C4
Low Brunton Northum 241 D10
Low Burnham N Lincs 199 G9
Low Catton ER Yorks 207 C10
Low Clanyard Dumf/Gal 236 F3
Low Common Norfolk 141 G11
Low Common Norfolk 142 E2
Low Common Norfolk 160 C4
Low Compton Gtr Man 196 F2
Low Conscliffe N Yorks 224 C5
Low Cotehill Cumb 239 G11

410 Low – Man

Low Coylton S Ayrs 257 F10
Low Crosby Cumb 239 F10
Low Dalby N Yorks 217 B7
Low Dinsdale D'lington 224 C6
Low Dyke Cumb 230 E5
Low Eighton Tyne/Wear 243 F7
Low Ellingham N Yorks 214 C4
Low Entercommon N Yorks 224 D6
Low Etherley Durham 233 F9
Low Fell Tyne/Wear 243 E7
Low Fold W Yorks 205 F10
Low Fremington N Yorks 223 F10
Low Fulney Lincs 156 E5
Low Garth N Yorks 226 D4
Low Gate Northum 241 E10
Low Gate N Yorks 214 F5
Low Gatherley N Yorks 224 E4
Low Geltbridge Cumb 240 F2
Low Grantley N Yorks 214 E4
Low Green N Yorks 205 B10
Low Green Suffolk 125 E7
Low Green W Yorks 205 F10
Low Greenfield Durham 233 F9
Low Greenside Tyne/Wear 242 E4
Low Habberley Worcs 116 B6
Low Ham Som'set 28 B6
Low Hameringham Lincs 174 B4
Low Harker Cumb 239 E9
Low Hauxley Northum 253 C7
Low Hawkser N Yorks 227 D8
Low Hesket Cumb 230 B5
Low Hutton N Yorks 216 F5
Low Knipe Cumb 230 G6
Low Laithe N Yorks 214 G3
Low Laithes S Yorks 197 G11
Low Lands Durham 233 G8
Low Langton Lincs 189 F11
Low Leighton Derby 185 D8
Low Lorton Cumb 229 F9
Low Marishes N Yorks 216 D6
Low Marnham Notts 172 B4
Low Mill N Yorks 226 F3
Low Moor Lancs 203 E10
Low Moor W Yorks 197 B7
Low Moorsley Tyne/Wear 234 B2
Low Moresby Cumb 228 G5
Low Newbiggin Tyne/Wear 242 D5
Low Newton Cumb 211 C9
Low Newton-by-the-Sea Northum 264 E6
Low Prudhoe Northum 242 E4
Low Risby N Lincs 200 D2
Low Row Cumb 229 C9
Low Row Cumb 240 E3
Low Row N Yorks 223 F9
Low Salchrie Dumf/Gal 236 C2
Low Smerby Arg/Bute 255 E8
Low Street Norfolk 141 B10
Low Street Thurr'k 69 D7
Low Tharston Norfolk 142 D3
Low Torry Fife 279 D10
Low Town Northum 252 C4
Low Town N Yorks 225 C7
Low Toynton Lincs 190 G3
Low Valley S Yorks 198 G2
Low Valleyfield Fife 279 D10
Low Walworth D'lington 224 B4
Low Waters S Lanarks 268 E4
Low Westwood Durham 242 F4
Low Whinnow Cumb 239 G8
Low Whita N Yorks 223 F10
Low Wood Cumb 210 C6
Low Worsall N Yorks 225 D7
Lowbands Glos 98 E5
Lowca Cumb 228 G5
Lowcote Gate Derby 170 G6
Lowcross Hill Ches 167 E7
Lowden Wilts 62 E2
Lowdham Notts 171 G10
Lowdham Grange Notts 171 G10
Lowe Shrops 149 C10
Lowedges S Yorks 186 E4
Lower Achachenna Arg/Bute 284 E4
Lower Airsholt Som'set 43 F8
Lower Altofts W Yorks 197 C11
Lower Ansty Dorset 30 G3
Lower Apperley Glos 99 F7
Lower Ardtun Arg/Bute 288 G5
Lower Arncott Oxon 83 B10
Lower Ashtead Surrey 51 B7
Lower Ashton Devon 14 E2
Lower Assendon Oxon 65 C8
Lower Badcall H'land 306 E6
Lower Ballam Lancs 202 G3
Lower Bartle Lancs 202 G5
Lower Basildon W Berks 64 D6
Lower Bassingthorpe Lincs 155 D9
Lower Bearwood Heref'd 115 F7
Lower Bebington Mersey 182 E4
Lower Beeding W Sussex 36 B2
Lower Benefield Northants 137 F9
Lower Bentley Worcs 117 D9
Lower Berry Hill Glos 79 C9
Lower Bevendean Brighton/Hove 36 F4
Lower Bitchet Kent 52 C5
Lower Black Moss Lancs 204 E2
Lower Blandford St. Mary Dorset 30 F5
Lower Bobbingworth Green Essex 87 D8
Lower Boddington Northants 119 G9
Lower Bodham Norfolk 160 B2
Lower Bordean Hants 33 B11
Lower Boscaswell Cornw'l 1 C3
Lower Bourne Surrey 49 E10
Lower Brailes Warwick 100 D6
Lower Breakish H'land 295 C8
Lower Bredbury Gtr Man 184 C6
Lower Breinton Heref'd 97 D9
Lower Broadheath Worcs 116 F6
Lower Broughton Gtr Man 184 B4
Lower Broxwood Heref'd 115 G7
Lower Brynamman Neath P Talb 76 C2
Lower Buckland Hants 20 B2
Lower Bullingham Heref'd 97 D10
Lower Bunbury Ches 167 D9
Lower Burgate Hants 31 D10
Lower Burrow Som'set 28 C6
Lower Cadsden Bucks 84 E4
Lower Caldecote Beds 104 B3
Lower Cam Glos 80 E3
Lower Cambourne Cambs 122 F6
Lower Canada N Som'set 43 B11
Lower Catesby Northants 119 F10
Lower Chapel Powys 95 D10
Lower Cheriton Devon 27 G10
Lower Chicksgrove Wilts 46 G3
Lower Chute Wilts 47 C10
Lower Clapton London 67 B11
Lower Clent Worcs 117 B8
Lower Cokeham W Sussex 35 G11
Lower Common Hants 48 E6
Lower Common Hants 65 G9
Lower Cotburn Aberds 303 D7
Lower Cox Street Kent 69 G10
Lower Cragabus Arg/Bute 254 C4
Lower Crossings Derby 185 E8
Lower Cumberworth W Yorks 197 F8
Lower Darwen Blackb'n 195 B7
Lower Dean Beds 121 D11
Lower Dell H'land 292 B2
Lower Denby W Yorks 197 F8
Lower Deuchries Aberds 302 D6
Lower Diabaig H'land 299 C7
Lower Dicker E Sussex 37 E9
Lower Drift Cornw'l 1 D4
Lower Dunsforth N Yorks 215 G8
Lower Earley Wokingham 65 E9
Lower Edmonton London 86 G4
Lower Egleton Heref'd 98 B2
Lower Elkstone Staffs 169 D9
Lower Ellastone Staffs 169 G10
Lower Elsted W Sussex 34 C4
Lower End Beds 103 D8
Lower End Beds 103 G9
Lower End Bucks 83 D11
Lower End Bucks 102 E4
Lower End Devon 27 E9
Lower End Glos 81 E7
Lower End Northants 120 F6
Lower End Northants 121 E7
Lower Ensden Kent 54 B5
Lower Everleigh Wilts 47 C7
Lower Exbury Hants 20 B2
Lower Eythorne Kent 55 D9
Lower Failand N Som'set 60 E4
Lower Faintree Shrops 132 F3
Lower Falkenham Suffolk 108 D5
Lower Farringdon Hants 49 F8
Lower Feltham London 66 E6
Lower Fittleworth W Sussex 35 D8
Lower Ford Lancs 195 B9
Lower Foxdale I/Man 192 E3
Lower Freystrop Pembs 73 C7
Lower Froyle Hants 49 E9
Lower Gabwell Devon 9 B8
Lower Gledfield H'land 309 K5
Lower Godney Som'set 44 E3
Lower Goldstone Kent 71 G9
Lower Gornal W Midlands 133 E8
Lower Grange W Yorks 205 G8
Lower Gravenhurst Beds 104 D2
Lower Green Essex 105 E8
Lower Green Essex 88 E2
Lower Green Essex 106 E4
Lower Green Gtr Man 184 B2
Lower Green Herts 104 E3
Lower Green Herts 105 E8
Lower Green Kent 52 E5
Lower Green Kent 52 E6
Lower Green Norfolk 143 B8
Lower Green Norfolk 159 B9
Lower Green Suffolk 124 D4
Lower Green Suffolk 125 F8
Lower Green Surrey 66 F6
Lower Green Staffs 133 B8
Lower Green Warwick 119 D9
Lower Green W Berks 63 G11
Lower Grove Common Heref'd 97 F11
Lower Hacheston Suffolk 126 F6
Lower Halistra H'land 298 D2
Lower Halliford Surrey 66 F5
Lower Halstock Leigh Dorset 29 F8
Lower Halstow Kent 69 F11
Lower Hamswell S Glos 61 E8
Lower Hamworthy Poole 18 C6
Lower Hardres Kent 55 C7
Lower Harpton Heref'd 114 E5
Lower Hartlip Kent 69 G10
Lower Hartwell Bucks 84 C3
Lower Hawthwaite Cumb 210 B4
Lower Hayne Som'set 29 C8
Lower Hayton Shrops 131 G10
Lower Hazel S Glos 60 B6
Lower Heath Ches 168 C5
Lower Hempriggs Moray 301 C11
Lower Heppington Kent 55 C7
Lower Hergest Heref'd 114 F5
Lower Herne Kent 71 F7
Lower Heyford Oxon 101 G9
Lower Heysham Lancs 211 G8
Lower Higham Kent 69 E8
Lower Holbrook Suffolk 108 D3
Lower Holloway London 67 B10
Lower Hook Worcs 98 C6
Lower Hopton W Yorks 197 D7
Lower Hordley Shrops 149 D7
Lower Horncroft W Sussex 35 D8
Lower Horsebridge E Sussex 37 E9
Lower Houses W Yorks 197 D7
Lower Howsell Worcs 98 B5
Lower Illey W Midlands 133 G9
Lower Island Kent 70 F6
Lower Kersal Gtr Man 195 G10
Lower Kilcott Glos 61 B9
Lower Killeyan Arg/Bute 254 C3
Lower Kingcombe Dorset 17 B7
Lower Kingswood Surrey 51 C9
Lower Kinnerton Ches 166 C4
Lower Kinsham Heref'd 115 E7
Lower Knapp Som'set 28 B4
Lower Knowle Bristol 60 E5
Lower Langford N Som'set 60 G3
Lower Largo Fife 287 G8
Lower Leigh Staffs 151 B10
Lower Leighton Powys 130 B4
Lower Lemington Glos 100 E4
Lower Lenie H'land 300 G5
Lower Ley Glos 80 B2
Lower Lovacott Devon 25 B8
Lower Loxhore Devon 40 F6
Lower Luggy Powys 130 C4
Lower Lydbrook Glos 79 B9
Lower Lye Heref'd 115 D8
Lower Machen Newp 59 B8
Lower Maes-coed Heref'd 96 E6
Lower Mains Clack 279 B9
Lower Mannington Dorset 31 F9
Lower Marston Som'set 45 E9
Lower Mayland Essex 88 E6
Lower Meend Glos 79 E9
Lower Merridge Som'set 43 G8
Lower Middleton Cheney Northants 101 C10
Lower Midway Derby 152 E6
Lower Milovaig H'land 296 F7
Lower Milton Som'set 44 D4
Lower Moor Worcs 99 B9
Lower Morton S Glos 79 G10
Lower Mountain Flints 166 D4
Lower Nash Pembs 73 E8
Lower Nazeing Essex 86 D5
Lower Nobut Staffs 151 C10
Lower North Dean Bucks 84 F5
Lower Noverton Glos 99 G9
Lower Nyland Dorset 30 C2
Lower Oakfield Fife 280 C2
Lower Oddington Glos 100 F4
Lower Ollach H'land 295 B7
Lower Penarth V/Glam 59 E7
Lower Penn Staffs 133 D7
Lower Pennington Hants 20 C2
Lower Penwortham Lancs 194 B4
Lower Peover Ches 184 G2
Lower Pexhill Ches 184 G5
Lower Pitkerrie H'land 311 L2
Lower Place Gtr Man 196 E2
Lower Porthpean Cornw'l 5 E10
Lower Pothkerry V/Glam 58 F5
Lower Quinton Warwick 100 B3
Lower Race Torf 78 E3
Lower Rainham Medway 69 F10
Lower Ratley Hants 32 C4
Lower Raydon Suffolk 107 D10
Lower Redbrook Glos 79 D8
Lower Roadwater Som'set 42 F4
Lower Row Dorset 31 G8
Lower Sapey Worcs 116 E3
Lower Seagry Wilts 62 C3
Lower Sheering Essex 87 C7
Lower Shelton Beds 103 C9
Lower Shiplake Oxon 65 D9
Lower Shuckburgh Warwick 119 E9
Lower Slackstead Hants 32 B5
Lower Slade Devon 40 D4
Lower Slaughter Glos 100 G3
Lower Soothill W Yorks 197 C9
Lower Soudley Glos 79 C11
Lower Spoad Shrops 130 G5
Lower Stanton St. Quintin Wilts 62 C2
Lower Stoke Medway 69 D10
Lower Stondon Beds 104 D3
Lower Stone Glos 79 G11
Lower Stonnal Staffs 133 C11
Lower Stow Bedon Norfolk 141 E9
Lower Stratton Swindon 63 B7
Lower Street Dorset 18 B2
Lower Street E Sussex 38 E2
Lower Street Norfolk 160 F6
Lower Street Norfolk 160 C3
Lower Street Norfolk 160 B5
Lower Street Suffolk 108 B5
Lower Strensham Worcs 99 C8
Lower Stretton Warrington 183 E10
Lower Strode Dorset 16 B5
Lower Strode N Som'set 60 G4
Lower Studley Wilts 45 B10
Lower Sundon Beds 103 F11
Lower Swainswick Bath/NE Som'set 61 F9
Lower Swanwick Hants 33 F7
Lower Swell Glos 100 F3
Lower Sydenham London 67 E11
Lower Tadmarton Oxon 101 D8
Lower Tale Devon 27 G9
Lower Tasburgh Norfolk 142 D3
Lower Tean Staffs 151 B10
Lower Thorpe Northants 101 B10
Lower Thurlton Norfolk 143 D8
Lower Thurnham Lancs 202 B5
Lower Thurvaston Derby 152 B4
Lower Tote H'land 298 C5
Lower Town Devon 13 G10
Lower Town Devon 27 E8
Lower Town Heref'd 98 C2
Lower Town Pembs 91 D9
Lower Town Som'set 29 D7
Lower Town W Yorks 204 G6
Lower Trebullett Cornw'l 12 F2
Lower Tuffley Glos 80 C4
Lower Turmer Hants 31 F10
Lower Twydall Medway 69 F10
Lower Tysoe Warwick 100 C6
Lower Upham Hants 33 D8
Lower Upnor Medway 69 E9
Lower Vexford Som'set 42 F6
Lower Walton Warrington 183 D10
Lower Wanborough Swindon 63 C8
Lower Waterhay Wilts 81 G9
Lower Waterston Dorset 17 C10
Lower Weald M/Keynes 102 D5
Lower Wear Devon 14 D4
Lower Weare Som'set 44 C2
Lower Welson Heref'd 114 G5
Lower Westmancote Worcs 99 D8
Lower Whatcombe Dorset 30 G4
Lower Whatley Som'set 45 D8
Lower Whitley Ches 183 F10
Lower Wick Glos 80 F2
Lower Wield Hants 48 E6
Lower Willingdon E Sussex 23 E9
Lower Winchendon Bucks 84 C2
Lower Woodend Aberds 293 B8
Lower Woodend Bucks 65 B10
Lower Woodford Wilts 46 F6
Lower Woon Cornw'l 5 C10
Lower Wraxall Dorset 29 G9
Lower Wraxall Som'set 44 F6
Lower Wych Ches 167 G7
Lower Wyche Worcs 98 C5
Lower Wyke W Yorks 197 B7
Lowerford Lancs 204 F3
Lowerhouse Ches 184 G6
Lowerhouse Lancs 204 G2
Lowertown Cornw'l 2 D5
Lowes Barn Durham 233 C11
Lowesby Leics 136 B4
Lowestoft Suffolk 143 E10
Loweswater Cumb 229 G8
Lowfield S Yorks 186 D5
Lowfield Heath W Sussex 51 F9
Lowford Hants 33 E7
Lowgill Cumb 222 F2
Lowgill Lancs 212 G3
Lowick Cumb 210 B5
Lowick Northants 137 G9
Lowick Northum 264 B2
Lowick Bridge Cumb 210 B5
Lowick Green Cumb 210 B5
Lowlands Torf 78 F3
Lowna N Yorks 226 G3
Lownie Moor Angus 287 C8
Lowood Scot Borders 262 B2
Lowsonford Warwick 118 D3
Lowther Cumb 230 G6
Lowther Town Dumf/Gal 238 D6
Lowthorpe ER Yorks 217 G11
Lowthwaite Cumb 230 G4
Lowton Devon 25 G11
Lowton Gtr Man 183 B10
Lowton Som'set 27 D11
Lowton Common Gtr Man 183 B10
Lowton Heath Warrington 183 B10
Lowton St. Mary's Gtr Man 183 B10
Loxbeare Devon 26 D6
Loxford London 68 B2
Loxhill Surrey 50 F4
Loxhore Devon 40 F6
Loxhore Cott Devon 40 F6
Loxley S Yorks 186 D4
Loxley Warwick 118 G5
Loxley Green Staffs 151 C11
Loxton N Som'set 43 B11
Loxwood W Sussex 50 G4
Loyter's Green Essex 87 C8
Lozells W Midlands 133 F11
Lubachlaggan H'land 300 B3
Lubachoinnich H'land 309 K4
Lubberland Shrops 116 B2
Lubcroy H'land 309 J3
Lubenham Leics 136 F3
Lubinvullin H'land 308 C5
Lucas End Herts 86 E4
Luccombe Som'set 42 E2
Luccombe Village I/Wight 21 F7
Lucker Northum 264 C5
Luckett Cornw'l 12 G3
Lucking Street Essex 106 E6
Luckington Wilts 61 C10
Lucklawhill Fife 287 E8
Luck's Bridge Lincs 156 F4
Luckwell Bridge Som'set 42 F2
Lucton Heref'd 115 E8
Ludag W Isles 297 K3
Ludborough Lincs 190 B3
Ludbrook Devon 8 E3
Ludchurch Pembs 73 C10
Luddenden W Yorks 196 B4
Luddenden Foot W Yorks 196 C4
Ludderburn Cumb 221 G8
Luddesdown Kent 69 F7
Luddington N Lincs 199 D10
Luddington Warwick 118 G3
Luddington in the Brook Northants 138 G2
Lude House Perth/Kinr 291 G10
Ludford Lincs 189 D10
Ludford Shrops 115 C10
Ludgershall Bucks 83 B11
Ludgershall Wilts 47 C9
Ludgvan Cornw'l 2 C2
Ludham Norfolk 161 F7
Ludlow Shrops 115 C10
Ludlow Racecourse Shrops 115 B9
Ludney Lincs 190 B5
Ludney Som'set 28 E5
Ludsden Oxon 84 D2
Ludstock Heref'd 98 D3
Ludwell Wilts 30 C6
Ludworth Durham 234 C3
Luffenhall Herts 104 F5
Luffincott Devon 12 C2
Lufton Som'set 29 D8
Lugate Scot Borders 271 G8
Lugg Green Heref'd 115 E9
Luggate Burn E Loth 281 G11
Luggiebank N Lanarks 278 G5
Lugsdale Halton 183 D8
Lugton E Ayrs 267 E8
Lugwardine Heref'd 97 C10
Luib H'land 295 C7
Luibeilt H'land 290 G4
Lulham Heref'd 97 C8
Lullington Derby 152 G5
Lullington Som'set 45 C9
Lulsgate Bottom N Som'set 60 F3
Lulsley Worcs 116 F4
Lulworth Camp Dorset 18 E2
Lulworth Castle Dorset 18 E3
Lumb Lancs 195 D9
Lumb Lancs 195 C10
Lumb W Yorks 196 C4
Lumbutts W Yorks 196 C2
Lumby N Yorks 206 G5
Lumley W Sussex 34 F3
Lumloch E Dunb 268 B2
Lumphanan Aberds 293 C7
Lumphinnans Fife 280 C3
Lumsden Aberds 302 G4
Lunan Angus 287 B10
Lunanhead Angus 287 B8
Luncarty Perth/Kinr 286 E4
Lund ER Yorks 208 D5
Lund N Yorks 207 G9
Lund Shetl'd 314 C7
Lund W Isles 304 E3
Lundavra H'land 290 G2
Lunderton Aberds 303 E11
Lundie Angus 286 D6
Lundie H'land 290 B3
Lundin Links Fife 287 G8
Lundwood S Yorks 197 F11
Lundy Green Norfolk 142 E4
Lunga Arg/Bute 275 C8
Lunna Shetl'd 314 G6
Lunning Shetl'd 314 G7
Lunnister Shetl'd 314 F5
Lunnon Swan 56 D4
Lunsford Kent 53 B8
Lunsford's Cross E Sussex 38 E2
Lunt Mersey 193 G10
Lunts Heath Halton 183 D8
Lupbridge Devon 8 E4
Luppitt Devon 27 F11
Lupset W Yorks 197 D10
Lupton Cumb 211 C11
Lurg Aberds 293 C8
Lurgashall W Sussex 34 B6
Lurignich Arg/Bute 289 D11
Lurley Devon 26 E6
Lusby Lincs 174 B4
Luscombe Devon 8 D5
Luson Devon 8 E2
Luss Arg/Bute 277 C7
Lussagiven Arg/Bute 275 E7
Lusta H'land 298 D2
Lustleigh Devon 13 E11
Luston Heref'd 115 E9
Lusty Som'set 45 G7
Luthermuir Aberds 293 G8
Luthrie Fife 287 F7
Luton Devon 14 F4
Luton Devon 27 G9
Luton Luton 103 G11
Luton Medway 69 F9
Lutsford Devon 24 D3
Lutterworth Leics 135 G10
Lutton Dorset 18 E4
Lutton Devon 7 D11
Lutton Devon 8 C3
Lutton Lincs 157 D8
Lutton Northants 138 F2
Luxborough Som'set 42 F3
Luxted London 68 G2
Luxton Devon 28 E2
Luxulyan Cornw'l 5 D10
Luzley Gtr Man 196 G3
Luzley Brook Gtr Man 196 F2
Lybster H'land 310 F6
Lydbury North Shrops 131 F7
Lydcott Devon 41 F7
Lydd Kent 39 C8
Lydden Kent 71 F11
Lydden Kent 55 D9
Lydden Motor Racing Circuit Kent 55 D8
Lyddington Rutl'd 137 D7
Lydd-on-Sea Kent 39 D9
Lyde Orkney 312 G4
Lyde Cross Heref'd 97 C10
Lyde Green Hants 49 B8
Lyde Green S Glos 61 D7
Lydeard St. Lawrence Som'set 42 G6
Lydford Devon 12 E6
Lydford Fair Place Som'set 44 G5
Lydford-on-Fosse Som'set 44 G5
Lydgate Gtr Man 196 G3
Lydgate Gtr Man 196 D3
Lydgate W Yorks 196 B2
Lydham Shrops 130 E6
Lydiard Green Wilts 62 B5
Lydiard Millicent Wilts 62 B5
Lydiard Tregoze Swindon 62 C6
Lydiate Mersey 193 G11
Lydiate Ash Worcs 117 B9
Lydlinch Dorset 30 E2
Lydmarsh Som'set 28 F5
Lydney Glos 79 E10
Lydstep Pembs 73 F9
Lye W Midlands 133 G8
Lye Green Bucks 85 E7
Lye Green E Sussex 52 G4
Lye Green Warwick 118 D3
Lye Head Worcs 116 C5
Lye Hole N Som'set 60 G4
Lye's Green Wilts 45 D10
Lyford Oxon 82 G5
Lymbridge Green Kent 54 E6
Lyme Park, Disley Ches 185 E7
Lyme Regis Dorset 16 C2
Lyminge Kent 55 E7
Lymington Hants 20 B2
Lyminster W Sussex 35 G8
Lymm Warrington 183 D11
Lymore Hants 19 C11
Lympne Kent 54 F6
Lympsham Som'set 43 C10
Lympstone Devon 14 E5
Lynbridge Devon 41 D8
Lynch Hants 48 D4
Lynch Som'set 42 D2
Lynchat H'land 291 C9
Lyncombe Som'set 41 F11
Lyndale Ho. H'land 298 D3
Lyndhurst Hants 32 F4
Lyndon Rutl'd 137 C8
Lyndon Green W Midlands 134 F2
Lyne Scot Borders 270 G4
Lyne Surrey 66 F4
Lyne Down Heref'd 98 E2
Lyne of Gorthleck H'land 300 G5
Lyne of Skene Aberds 293 B9
Lyneal Shrops 149 C8
Lyneham Oxon 100 G5
Lyneham Wilts 62 D4
Lynemore H'land 301 G10
Lynemouth Northum 253 E7
Lynesack Durham 233 F7
Lyness Orkney 313 J4
Lynford Norfolk 140 E6
Lyng Norfolk 159 F11
Lyng Som'set 28 B4
Lyngate Norfolk 160 C5
Lyngate Norfolk 160 D6
Lyngford Som'set 28 B2
Lynmore H'land 301 F10
Lynmouth Devon 41 D8
Lynn Staffs 133 C11
Lynsore Bottom Kent 55 D7
Lynsted Kent 70 G2
Lynstone Cornw'l 24 F2
Lynton Devon 41 D8
Lynton & Lynmouth Cliff Railway Devon 41 D8
Lynwilg H'land 291 B10
Lynworth Glos 99 G9
Lyons Tyne/Wear 234 B3
Lyon's Gate Dorset 29 F11
Lyon's Green Norfolk 159 G8
Lyonshall Heref'd 114 F6
Lyrabus Arg/Bute 274 G3
Lytchett Matravers Dorset 18 B4
Lytchett Minster Dorset 18 C5
Lyth H'land 310 C6
Lytham Lancs 193 B11
Lytham St. Anne's Lancs 193 B10
Lythbank Shrops 131 B9
Lythe N Yorks 226 C6
Lythes Orkney 313 K5
Lythmore H'land 310 C4

M

Maam Arg/Bute 284 F5
Mabe Burnthouse Cornw'l 3 C7
Mabie Dumf/Gal 237 B11
Mablethorpe Lincs 191 D8
Macclesfield Ches 184 G6
Macduff Aberds 303 C7
Mace Green Suffolk 108 C2
Macedonia Fife 280 A5
Machan S Lanarks 268 E5
Macharioch Arg/Bute 255 G8
Machen Caerph 59 B8
Machrie N Ayrs 255 D9
Machrie Hotel Arg/Bute 254 C4
Machrihanish Arg/Bute 255 E7
Machroes Gwyn 144 D6
Machynlleth Powys 128 C4
Machynys Carms 75 E8
Mackerel's Common W Sussex 35 B8
Mackerye End Herts 85 B11
Mackney Oxon 64 B5
Mackworth Derby 152 B6
Macmerry E Loth 281 G8
Madame Tussaud's London 67 C9
Madderty Perth/Kinr 286 E3
Maddington Wilts 46 E5
Maddiston Falk 279 F8
Maddox Moor Pembs 73 C7
Madehurst W Sussex 35 E7
Madeley Staffs 168 G3
Madeley Telford 132 C4
Madeley Heath Staffs 168 F3
Madeley Heath Worcs 117 B8
Madeleywood Telford 132 C3
Maders Cornw'l 12 G2
Madford Devon 27 E11
Madingley Cambs 123 E7
Madley Heref'd 97 D8
Madresfield Worcs 98 B6
Madron Cornw'l 1 C5
Maen Porth Cornw'l 3 D7
Maenaddwyn Angl 179 E7
Maenclochog Pembs 91 F11
Maendy Card 59 D7
Maendy V/Glam 58 D4
Maenorbŷr = Manorbier Pembs 73 F9
Maentwrog Gwyn 163 G11
Maen-y-groes Ceredig'n 111 F7
Maer Staffs 150 B5
Maerdy Conwy 165 G8
Maerdy Monmouths 78 E6
Maerdy Monmouths 97 F7
Maerdy Rh Cyn Taff 77 F7
Maes Pennant Flints 181 F11
Maes Treylow Powys 114 D5
Maesbrook Shrops 148 E6
Maesbury Shrops 148 D6
Maesbury Marsh Shrops 148 D6
Maesgeichen Gwyn 179 G9
Maes-glas Newp 59 B10
Maesgwn-Isaf Powys 148 G3
Maesgwyn Ganol Powys 148 G3
Maeshafn Denbs 166 C2
Maesllyn Ceredig'n 93 C7
Maesmawr Powys 129 E11
Maesmynis Powys 95 B10
Maesteg Brig 76 G5
Maesybont Carms 75 B9
Maesycrugiau Carms 93 C9
Maes-y-cwmmer Caerph 77 G11
Maesydd Powys 148 G5
Maes-y-facrell Conwy 180 E3
Maesygwartha Monmouths 78 C2
Maesyrhandir Powys 129 E11
Magdalen Laver Essex 87 D8
Maggieknockater Moray 302 E3
Maggots End Essex 105 G9
Magham Down E Sussex 37 E10
Maghull Mersey 193 G11
Magna Science Adventure Centre, Rotherham S Yorks 186 C6
Magor Monmouths 60 B2
Magpie Green Suffolk 125 B11
Mahaar Dumf/Gal 236 B2
Maida Vale London 67 C9
Maiden Bradley Wilts 45 F10
Maiden Head N Som'set 60 F5
Maiden Law Durham 233 B9
Maiden Newton Dorset 17 B7
Maiden Wells Pembs 73 F7
Maidencombe Torbay 9 B8
Maidenhall Suffolk 108 C3
Maidenhayne Devon 15 B11
Maidenhead Windsor 65 C11
Maidenmarsh W Sussex 34 C3
Maidenpark Falk 279 E9
Maidens S Ayrs 244 B6
Maiden's Green Brackn'l 65 E11
Maidensgrave Suffolk 108 B5
Maidenwell Lincs 190 F4
Maidford Northants 120 G2
Maidford Wilts 61 C11
Maids Moreton Bucks 102 D4
Maidstone Kent 53 B9
Maidwell Northants 120 B4
Mail Shetl'd 315 L6
Mailand Shetl'd 314 C8
Main Powys 148 F3
Maindee Newp 59 B10
Mainholm S Ayrs 257 E9
Mains of Airies Dumf/Gal 236 C1
Mains of Allardice Aberds 293 F10
Mains of Annochie Aberds 303 E9
Mains of Ardestie Angus 287 D9
Mains of Arnage Aberds 303 F9
Mains of Auchoynanie Moray 302 E4
Mains of Baldoon Dumf/Gal 236 D6
Mains of Balhall Angus 293 G7
Mains of Ballindarg Angus 287 B8
Mains of Balnakettle Aberds 293 F8
Mains of Birness Aberds 303 F9
Mains of Blackhall Aberds 303 G7
Mains of Burgie Moray 301 D10
Mains of Cairnbrogie Aberds 303 G8
Mains of Cairnty Moray 302 D3
Mains of Clunas H'land 301 E8
Mains of Crichie Aberds 303 E9
Mains of Daltulich H'land 301 E7
Mains of Dalvey H'land 301 F11
Mains of Dellavaird Aberds 293 E9
Mains of Drum Aberds 293 D10
Mains of Edingight Moray 302 D5
Mains of Fedderate Aberds 303 E8
Mains of Flichity H'land 300 G6
Mains of Hatton Aberds 303 D9
Mains of Hatton Aberds 303 E7
Mains of Inkhorn Aberds 303 F9
Mains of Innerpeffray Perth/Kinr 286 F3
Mains of Kirktonhill Aberds 293 G8
Mains of Lathers Aberds 302 E6
Mains of Mayen Moray 302 E5
Mains of Melgund Angus 287 B9
Mains of Taymouth Perth/Kinr 285 C11
Mains of Thornton Aberds 293 F8
Mains of Towie Aberds 303 E7
Mains of Ulbster H'land 310 E7
Mains of Watten H'land 310 D6
Mainsforth Durham 234 E2
Mainsriddle Dumf/Gal 237 D11
Mainstone Plym'th 7 D10
Mainstone Shrops 130 F5
Maisemore Glos 98 G6
Major's Green Worcs 117 B11
Makeney Derby 170 G5
Makerstoun Scot Borders 262 C5
Malacleit W Isles 296 D3
Malborough Devon 9 G9
Malborough Lincs 172 C6
Malcoff Derby 185 E9
Malden Rushett London 67 G7
Maldensgrove Oxon 65 B8
Maldon Essex 88 D5
Malham N Yorks 213 G8
Maligar H'land 298 C4
Malinbridge S Yorks 186 D4
Malins Lee Telford 132 B3
Mallaig H'land 295 F8
Mallaig Bheag H'land 295 F8
Malleny Mills C/Edinb 270 B3
Malling Stirl 285 G9
Mallory Park Motor Racing Circuit Leics 135 C8
Mallows Green Essex 105 G9
Malltraeth Angl 162 B6
Mallwyd Gwyn 147 G7
Malmesbury Wilts 62 B2
Malmsmead Devon 41 D9
Malpas Ches 167 F7
Malpas Cornw'l 4 G6
Malpas Newp 78 G4
Malswick Glos 98 F4
Maltby Stockton 225 C9
Maltby S Yorks 187 B8
Maltby le Marsh Lincs 191 E7
Malting End Suffolk 124 G4
Maltings Angus 293 G9
Maltman's Hill Kent 54 E2
Malton N Yorks 216 E5
Malvern Common Worcs 98 C5
Malvern Link Worcs 98 B5
Malvern Wells Worcs 98 C5
Mamble Worcs 116 C3
Mamhilad Monmouths 78 E4
Manaccan Cornw'l 3 D7
Manadon Plym'th 7 D9
Manafon Powys 130 C2
Manais W Isles 296 C7
Manar Ho. Aberds 303 G7
Manaton Devon 13 E11
Manby Lincs 190 D5
Mancetter Warwick 134 D6
Manchester Gtr Man 184 B5
Manchester Airport Gtr Man 184 E4
Manchester Airport Gtr Man 184 E4
Manchester National Velodrome Gtr Man 184 B5
Mancot Royal Flints 166 B4
Mandally H'land 290 C4
Manea Cambs 139 F9
Maney W Midlands 134 D2
Manfield N Yorks 224 C4
Mangaster Shetl'd 314 F5
Mangerton Dorset 16 B5
Mangotsfield S Glos 61 D7
Mangrove Green Herts 104 G2
Mangurstadh W Isles 304 E2
Mankinholes W Yorks 196 C3
Manley Ches 183 G8
Manley Devon 27 E7
Manmoel Caerph 77 E11
Mannal Arg/Bute 288 E1
Mannamead Plym'th 7 D9
Mannerston W Loth 279 F10
Manningford Abbots Wilts 46 B6
Manningford Bohune Wilts 46 B6

Manningford Bruce Wilts 46 B6
Manningham W Yorks 205 G9
Manning's Common Devon 28 E2
Mannings Heath W Sussex 36 B2
Mannington Dorset 31 F9
Manningtree Essex 108 E2
Mannofield Aberd C 293 C11
Manor Bourne Devon 7 F9
Manor Estate S Yorks 186 D5
Manor Park Bucks 84 C4
Manor Park Ches 167 B11
Manor Park Halton 183 E8
Manor Park London 68 B2
Manor Park Notts 153 C11
Manor Park Slough 66 C3
Manor Park S Yorks 186 D5
Manor Parsley Cornw'l 4 F4
Manor Powis Stirl 278 B6
Manorbier = Maenorbŷr Pembs 73 F9
Manorbier Newton Pembs 73 F8
Manordeifi Pembs 92 C4
Manordeilo Carms 94 F3
Manselfield Swan 56 D5
Mansell Gamage Heref'd 97 C7
Mansell Lucy Heref'd 97 B8
Manselton Swan 75 F11
Mansergh Cumb 212 C2
Mansewood Glasg C 267 C11
Mansfield E Ayrs 258 G4
Mansfield Notts 171 C8
Mansfield Woodhouse Notts 171 C8
Manson Green Norfolk 141 C10
Mansriggs Cumb 210 C5
Manston Dorset 30 D4
Manston Kent 71 F11
Manston W Yorks 206 F3
Manswood Dorset 31 F7
Manthorpe Lincs 155 F11
Mantles Green Bucks 85 F7
Manton Notts 187 G10
Manton Rutl'd 137 C7
Manton Wilts 63 F7
Manuden Essex 105 G9
Manwood Green Essex 87 C8
Manx Electric Railway I/Man 192 C5
Maperton Som'set 29 B11
Maple Cross Herts 85 G8
Maple End Essex 105 D11
Maplebeck Notts 172 C2
Mapledurham Oxon 65 D7
Mapledurwell Hants 49 C7
Maplehurst W Sussex 35 C11
Maplescombe Kent 68 G4
Mapleton Derby 169 F11
Mapleton Kent 52 D3
Mapperley Nott'ham 171 G9
Mapperley Derby 170 G6
Mapperley Park Nott'ham 171 G9
Mapperton Dorset 16 B6
Mapperton Dorset 18 B4
Mappleborough Green Warwick 117 D11
Mappleton ER Yorks 209 E10
Mapplewell S Yorks 197 F10
Mappowder Dorset 30 F2
Mar Lodge Aberds 292 D2
Maraig W Isles 305 H3
Marazanvose Cornw'l 4 E6
Marazion Cornw'l 2 C3
Marbhig W Isles 305 G6
Marbury Ches 167 F9
March Cambs 139 D8
March S Lanarks 259 G11
Marcham Oxon 83 F7
Marchamley Shrops 149 D11
Marchamley Wood Shrops 149 C11
Marchington Staffs 152 C2
Marchington Woodlands Staffs 152 D2
Marchwiel Wrex 166 F5
Marchwood Hants 32 E5
Marcle Hill Heref'd 98 E2
Marcross V/Glam 58 F2
Marden Heref'd 97 B10
Marden Kent 53 E8
Marden Tyne/Wear 243 C9
Marden Wilts 46 B5
Marden Ash Essex 87 E9
Marden Beech Kent 53 E8
Marden Thorn Kent 53 E9
Marden's Hill E Sussex 52 G4
Mardleybury Herts 86 B3
Mardon Northum 263 B10
Mardu Shrops 130 G5
Mardy Monmouths 78 B4
Marefield Bucks 65 B10
Marefield Leics 136 B4
Mareham Gate Lincs 174 D3
Mareham le Fen Lincs 174 C3
Mareham on the Hill Lincs 174 B3
Marehay Derby 170 F5
Marehill W Sussex 35 D9
Maresfield E Sussex 37 C7
Marfleet Kingston/Hull 200 B6
Marford Wrex 166 D5
Margam Neath P Talb 57 D9
Margaret Marsh Dorset 30 D4
Margaret Roding Essex 87 C9
Margaretta Norfolk 157 F11
Margaretting Essex 87 E11
Margaretting Tye Essex 87 E11
Margate Kent 71 E11
Margery Surrey 51 C9
Margnaheglish N Ayrs 256 C2
Margreig Dumf/Gal 237 B10
Margrove Park Redcar/Clevel'd 226 B3
Marham Norfolk 140 B4
Marhamchurch Cornw'l 24 G2
Marholm Peterbro 138 C2
Marian Denbs 181 F9
Marian Cwm Denbs 181 F9
Marian Ffrith Denbs 181 F9
Marianglas Angl 179 E8
Mariansleigh Devon 26 C2
Marian-y-de Gwyn 145 C7
Marian-y-mor Gwyn 145 C7
Marine Town Kent 70 E2
Marionburgh Aberds 293 C9
Marishader H'land 298 C4
Marjoriebanks Dumf/Gal 248 G3
Mark Dumf/Gal 236 D3
Mark Dumf/Gal 237 C7
Mark S Ayrs 236 B2
Mark Som'set 43 D11
Mark Causeway Som'set 43 D11
Mark Cross E Sussex 37 E7
Mark Cross E Sussex 52 G5
Mark Hall North Essex 87 C7
Mark Hall South Essex 87 C7
Markbeech Kent 52 E3
Markby Lincs 191 F7
Markeaton Derby C 152 B6
Market Bosworth Leics 135 C8
Market Deeping Lincs 156 G2
Market Drayton Shrops 150 C3
Market End Warwick 134 F6
Market Harborough Leics 136 F4
Market Lavington Wilts 46 C4
Market Overton Rutl'd 155 F7
Market Rasen Lincs 189 D10
Market Rasen Racecourse Lincs 189 D10
Market Stainton Lincs 190 F2
Market Warsop Notts 171 B9
Market Weighton ER Yorks 208 E3
Market Weston Suffolk 125 B9
Markethill Perth/Kinr 286 D6
Markfield Leics 153 G9
Markham Caerph 77 E11
Markham Moor Notts 188 G2
Markinch Fife 286 G6
Markington N Yorks 214 G5
Markland Hill Gtr Man 195 F7
Marks Gate London 87 G7
Marks Tey Essex 107 G8
Marksbury Bath/NE Som'set 61 G7
Markyate Herts 85 B9
Marl Bank Worcs 98 C5
Marland Gtr Man 195 E11
Marlas Heref'd 97 F8
Marlborough Wilts 63 F7
Marlbrook Heref'd 115 G10
Marlbrook Worcs 117 C9
Marlcliff Warwick 117 G11
Marldon Devon 9 C7
Marle Green E Sussex 37 D9
Marle Hill Glos 99 G8
Marlesford Suffolk 126 F6
Marley Kent 55 C7
Marley Kent 55 C10
Marley Green Ches 167 F9
Marley Hill Tyne/Wear 242 F6
Marlingford Norfolk 142 B2
Marloes Pembs 72 D3
Marlow Bucks 65 B11
Marlow Heref'd 115 B8
Marlow Bottom Bucks 65 B10
Marlpit Hill Kent 52 D2
Marlpits E Sussex 38 E2
Marlpits E Sussex 37 B7
Marlpool Derby 170 F6
Marnhull Dorset 30 D3
Marnoch Aberds 302 D5
Marnock N Lanarks 268 B4
Marple Gtr Man 185 D7
Marple Bridge Gtr Man 185 D7
Marpleridge Gtr Man 185 D7
Marr S Yorks 198 F4
Marrel H'land 311 H4
Marrick N Yorks 223 F11
Marridge Hill Wilts 63 E9
Marrister Shetl'd 315 G7
Marros Carms 74 D2
Marsden Tyne/Wear 243 E9
Marsden W Yorks 196 E4
Marsden Hall Lancs 204 F3
Marsden Height Lancs 204 F3
Marsett N Yorks 213 B8
Marsh Bucks 84 D4
Marsh Devon 28 E3
Marsh W Yorks 196 D6
Marsh W Yorks 204 F6
Marsh W Yorks 197 B7
Marsh Baldon Oxon 83 F9
Marsh Benham W Berks 64 F2
Marsh End Worcs 98 D6
Marsh Gibbon Bucks 102 G2
Marsh Green Ches 183 F8
Marsh Green Devon 14 C6
Marsh Green Gtr Man 194 F5
Marsh Green Kent 52 E2
Marsh Green Staffs 168 D5
Marsh Green Telford 150 G2
Marsh Lane Derby 186 F6
Marsh Lane Glos 79 D9
Marsh Leys Beds 103 B10
Marsh Street Som'set 42 E3
Marshall's Cross Mersey 183 C8
Marshall's Elm Som'set 44 G3
Marshall's Heath Herts 85 C11
Marshalswick Herts 85 D11
Marsham Norfolk 160 E3
Marshaw Lancs 203 C7
Marshborough Kent 55 B10
Marshbrook Shrops 131 F8
Marshchapel Lincs 190 B5
Marshfield Newp 59 C9
Marshfield S Glos 61 E9
Marshgate Cornw'l 11 C9
Marshland St. James Norfolk 139 B10
Marshside Kent 71 F8
Marshside Mersey 193 D11
Marshwood Dorset 16 B3
Marske N Yorks 224 E2
Marske-by-the-Sea Redcar/Clevel'd 235 G8
Marsland Green Gtr Man 183 B11
Marston Ches 183 F11
Marston Heref'd 115 F7
Marston Lincs 172 G5
Marston Oxon 83 D8
Marston Staffs 150 G6
Marston Staffs 151 D8
Marston Warwick 134 E4
Marston Wilts 46 B3
Marston Bigot Som'set 45 E9
Marston Doles Warwick 119 F9
Marston Green W Midlands 134 F3
Marston Hill Glos 81 F10
Marston Jabbett Warwick 135 F7
Marston Junction Warwick 135 F7
Marston Magna Som'set 29 C9
Marston Meysey Wilts 81 F10
Marston Montgomery Derby 152 B2
Marston Moretaine Beds 103 C9
Marston on Dove Derby 152 D4
Marston St. Lawrence Northants 101 C10
Marston Trussell Northants 136 F3
Marstow Heref'd 79 B9
Marsworth Bucks 84 C6
Marten Wilts 63 G9
Marthall Ches 184 F4
Martham Norfolk 161 F9
Marthwaite Cumb 222 G2
Martin Hants 31 D9
Martin Kent 55 D10
Martin Lincs 174 B2
Martin Lincs 173 C10
Martin Drove End Hants 31 C9
Martin Hussingtree Worcs 117 F7
Martin Mill Kent 55 D10
Martindale Cumb 221 B8
Martinhoe Devon 41 D7
Martinscroft Warrington 183 D10
Martinslade Wilts 62 G3
Martinstown Dorset 17 D8
Martlesham Suffolk 108 B5
Martlesham Heath Suffolk 108 B5
Martletwy Pembs 73 C8
Martley Worcs 116 F5
Martock Som'set 29 D7
Marton Ches 168 B5
Marton Cumb 210 D4
Marton ER Yorks 209 F9
Marton Lincs 188 E4
Marton Middlesbro 225 B10
Marton N Yorks 215 G8
Marton N Yorks 216 C4
Marton Shrops 130 C5
Marton Shrops 149 E8
Marton Warwick 119 D8
Marton Grove Middlesbro 225 B9
Marton Moss Side Blackp'l 202 G2
Marton-in-the-Forest N Yorks 216 F2
Marton-le Moor N Yorks 215 E7
Martyr Worthy Hants 48 G4
Martyr's Green Surrey 50 B5
Marus Bridge Gtr Man 194 G5
Marwell Zoo, Bishop's Waltham Hants 33 C8
Marwick Orkney 312 F3
Marwood Devon 40 F4
Mary Arden's House, Wilmcote Warwick 118 F3
Mary Rose Portsm'th 33 G10
Mary Tavy Devon 12 F6
Marybank H'land 300 D4
Marybank H'land 301 B7
Maryburgh H'land 300 D5
Maryfield Aberds 293 D7
Maryfield Cornw'l 7 D8
Maryhill Glasg C 267 B11
Marykirk Aberds 293 G8
Maryland Monmouths 79 D8
Marylebone Gtr Man 194 F5
Marylebone London 67 C9
Marypark Moray 301 F11
Maryport Cumb 228 D6
Maryport Dumf/Gal 236 F3
Marystow Devon 12 E4
Maryton Angus 287 B10
Maryton Angus 287 B7
Marywell Aberds 293 D11
Marywell Aberds 293 D7
Marywell Angus 287 C10
Masbrough S Yorks 186 C6
Masham N Yorks 214 C4
Mashbury Essex 87 C11
Mason Tyne/Wear 242 C6
Masongill N Yorks 212 D2
Masonhill S Ayrs 257 E9
Mastin Moor Derby 187 F7
Mastrick Aberd C 293 C10
Matchborough Worcs 117 D11
Matching Essex 87 C8
Matching Green Essex 87 C8
Matching Tye Essex 87 C8
Matfen Northum 242 C2
Matfield Kent 53 E7
Mathern Monmouths 79 G8
Mathon Heref'd 98 B4
Mathrafal Powys 148 G2
Mathry Pembs 91 E7
Matlaske Norfolk 160 C3
Matlock Derby 170 C4
Matlock Bank Derby 170 C3
Matlock Bath Derby 170 D3
Matlock Bridge Derby 170 D3
Matlock Dale Derby 170 D3
Matlock Moor Derby 170 C4
Matravers Dorset 16 C6
Matshead Lancs 202 E6
Matson Glos 80 B4
Matterdale End Cumb 230 G3
Mattersey Notts 187 D11
Mattersey Thorpe Notts 187 C11
Matthewsgreen Wokingham 65 F10
Mattingley Hants 49 B8
Mattishall Norfolk 159 G10
Mattishall Burgh Norfolk 159 G11
Mauchline E Ayrs 258 D2
Maud Aberds 303 E9
Maudlin Cornw'l 5 C11
Maudlin W Sussex 34 F5
Maugersbury Glos 100 F4
Maughold I/Man 192 C5
Mauld H'land 300 F4
Maulden Beds 103 D11
Maulds Meaburn Cumb 222 B2
Maunby N Yorks 215 B7
Maund Bryan Heref'd 115 G10
Maundown Som'set 27 B8
Mautby Norfolk 161 G9
Mavesyn Ridware Staffs 151 F11
Mavis Enderby Lincs 174 B5
Maviston H'land 301 D9
Maw Green Ches 168 D2
Mawbray Cumb 229 B7
Mawdesley Lancs 194 E3
Mawdlam Bridg 57 E10
Mawgan Cornw'l 2 E6
Mawgan Porth Cornw'l 4 B6
Mawla Cornw'l 4 F4
Mawnan Cornw'l 3 D7
Mawnan Smith Cornw'l 3 D7
Mawsley Northants 120 B6
Mawthorpe Lincs 191 G7
Maxey Peterbro 138 B2
Maxstoke Warwick 134 F4
Maxted Street Kent 54 E6
Maxton Scot Borders 262 C4
Maxton Kent 55 E10
Maxwellheugh Scot Borders 262 C6
Maxwelltown Dumf/Gal 237 B11
Maxworthy Cornw'l 11 C11
May Bank Staffs 168 F5
May Hill Monmouths 79 C8
Mayals Swan 75 G10
Maybole S Ayrs 245 B8
Maybury Surrey 50 B4
Maybush S'thampton 32 E5
Mayes Green Surrey 50 F6
Mayeston Pembs 73 E8
Mayfair London 67 C9
Mayfield E Sussex 37 B9
Mayfield Midloth 271 C7
Mayfield N Ayrs 266 G5
Mayfield Northum 243 B7
Mayfield Staffs 169 F11
Mayfield W Loth 269 B8
Mayford Surrey 50 B3
Mayhill Swan 75 G10
Mayland Essex 88 E6
Maylandsea Essex 88 E6
Maynard's Green E Sussex 37 D9
Mayne Ho. Moray 302 C2
Mayon Cornw'l 1 D3
Maypole Kent 71 G7
Maypole Kent 68 E4
Maypole London 68 G3
Maypole Monmouths 79 B7
Maypole W Midlands 117 B11
Maypole Green Essex 107 G9
Maypole Green Norfolk 143 D8
Maypole Green Suffolk 126 D5
Maypole Green Suffolk 125 F8
May's Green N Som'set 59 G11
Mays Green Oxon 65 D8
Mayshill S Glos 61 C7
Maythorn S Yorks 197 F7
Maywick Shetl'd 315 L5
Mead Devon 13 G11
Mead Devon 24 D2
Mead End Hants 19 B11
Mead End Hants 33 E11
Mead End Wilts 31 C8
Mead Vale Surrey 51 D9
Meadgate Bath/NE Som'set 45 B7
Meadle Bucks 84 D4
Meadow Derby 185 G10
Meadow Green Heref'd 116 F4
Meadow Head S Yorks 186 E4
Meadowbank Ches 167 B10
Meadowfield Durham 233 D10
Meadowfoot N Ayrs 266 F4
Meadowmill E Loth 281 G8
Meadows Nott'ham 153 B11
Meadowtown Shrops 130 C6
Meads E Sussex 23 F10
Meadside Oxon 83 G9
Meadwell Devon 12 E4
Meal Bank Cumb 221 F10
Mealabost W Isles 304 E6
Mealabost Bhuirgh W Isles 304 C6
Mealasta W Isles 304 F1
Mealrigg Cumb 229 B8
Mealsgate Cumb 229 C10
Mean Ham Glos 80 B4
Meanwood W Yorks 205 F11
Mearbeck N Yorks 212 G6
Meare Som'set 44 E3
Meare Green Som'set 28 C3
Meare Green Som'set 28 B4
Mearns E Renf 267 D10
Mears Ashby Northants 120 D6
Measborough Dike S Yorks 197 F11
Measham Leics 152 G6
Meath Green Surrey 51 E9
Meathop Cumb 211 C9
Meaux ER Yorks 209 F7
Meavy Devon 7 B10
Medbourne Leics 136 E5
Medburn Northum 242 C4
Meddon Devon 24 D3
Meden Vale Notts 171 B9
Medlam Lincs 174 D4
Medlar Lancs 202 F4
Medlock Vale Gtr Man 184 B6
Medlyn Cornw'l 2 C6
Medmenham Bucks 65 C10
Medomsley Durham 242 G4
Medstead Hants 49 F7
Meer Common Heref'd 115 G7
Meer End W Midlands 118 C4
Meerbrook Staffs 169 C7
Meers Bank Lincs 191 D7
Meers Bridge Lincs 191 D7
Meersbrook S Yorks 186 E4
Meesden Herts 105 E8
Meeth Devon 25 F8
Meethe Devon 25 C11
Meeting Green Suffolk 124 F4
Meeting House Hill Norfolk 160 D6
Meggernie Castle Perth/Kinr 285 C9
Meggethead Scot Borders 260 E5
Meidrim Carms 92 G5
Meifod Powys 148 G3
Meigle Perth/Kinr 286 C6
Meikle Earnock S Lanarks 268 E4
Meikle Ferry H'land 309 L7
Meikle Forter Angus 292 G3
Meikle Gluich H'land 309 L6
Meikle Obney Perth/Kinr 286 D4
Meikle Pinkerton E Loth 282 F4
Meikle Strath Aberds 293 F8
Meikle Tarty Aberds 303 G9
Meikle Wartle Aberds 303 F7
Meikleour Perth/Kinr 286 D5
Meinciau Carms 75 C7
Meir Stoke 168 G6
Meir Heath Staffs 151 B8
Melbourn Cambs 105 C7
Melbourne Derby 153 D7
Melbourne ER Yorks 207 E10
Melbourne S Lanarks 269 G11
Melbury Abbas Dorset 30 C5
Melbury Bubb Dorset 29 F9
Melbury Osmond Dorset 29 F9
Melbury Sampford Dorset 29 F9
Melby Shetl'd 315 H3
Melchbourne Beds 121 D10
Melcombe Som'set 43 G9
Melcombe Bingham Dorset 30 G3
Melcombe Regis Dorset 17 E9
Meldon Devon 13 C7
Meldon Northum 252 G4
Meldreth Cambs 105 B7
Meldrum Ho. Aberds 303 G8
Meledor Cornw'l 5 E8
Melfort Arg/Bute 275 B9
Melgarve H'land 290 D6
Meliden = Gallt Melyd Denbs 181 E9
Melin Meredydd Denbs 165 D10
Melinbyrhedyn Powys 128 D6
Melincourt Neath P Talb 76 E4
Melincryddan Rh Cyn Taff 76 F2
Melin-y-coed Conwy 164 C4
Melin-y-ddôl Powys 129 B11
Melin-y-Grogue Shrops 114 B4
Melin-y-wig Denbs 165 F8
Melkinthorpe Cumb 231 F7
Melkridge Northum 240 E6
Melksham Wilts 62 G2
Melksham Forest Wilts 62 G2
Mell Green W Berks 64 D3
Mellangaun H'land 307 L3
Melldalloch Arg/Bute 275 F10
Mellguards Cumb 230 B4
Melling Lancs 211 E11
Melling Mersey 193 G11
Melling Mount Mersey 194 G2
Mellis Suffolk 126 C2
Mellon Charles H'land 307 K3
Mellon Udrigle H'land 307 K3
Mellor Gtr Man 185 D7
Mellor Lancs 203 G9
Mellor Brook Lancs 203 G8
Mells Som'set 45 D8
Mells Green Som'set 45 D8
Melmerby Cumb 231 D8
Melmerby N Yorks 214 D6
Melmerby N Yorks 213 B11
Melon Green Suffolk 124 F6
Melplash Dorset 16 B5
Melrose Scot Borders 262 C2
Melsetter Orkney 313 K3
Melsonby N Yorks 224 D3
Meltham W Yorks 196 E5
Meltham Mills W Yorks 196 E6
Melton ER Yorks 200 B3
Melton Suffolk 126 G5
Melton Constable Norfolk 159 C10
Melton Mowbray Leics 154 F5
Melton Ross N Lincs 200 E5
Meltonby ER Yorks 207 C11
Melvaig H'land 307 L2
Melverley Shrops 148 F6
Melverley Green Shrops 148 F6
Melvich H'land 310 C2
Membland Devon 7 F11
Membury Devon 28 G3
Memsie Aberds 303 C9
Memus Angus 287 B8
Menabilly Cornw'l 6 E2
Menagissey Cornw'l 4 F4
Menai Bridge = Porthaethwy Angl 179 G9
Mendham Suffolk 142 G5
Mendlesham Suffolk 126 D2
Mendlesham Green Suffolk 125 E11
Menethorpe N Yorks 216 F5
Mengham Hants 22 D2
Menheniot Cornw'l 6 C5
Menherion Cornw'l 2 B6
Menithwood Worcs 116 D4
Menna Cornw'l 5 E8
Mennock Dumf/Gal 247 B8
Menston W Yorks 205 E9
Menstrie Clack 279 B7
Mentmore Bucks 84 B6
Meoble H'land 295 G9
Meole Brace Shrops 149 G9
Meols Mersey 182 C2
Meonstoke Hants 33 D10
Meopham Kent 68 F6
Meopham Green Kent 68 F6
Meopham Station Kent 68 F6
Mepal Cambs 139 G8
Meppershall Beds 104 D2
Merbach Heref'd 96 B6
Merchiston C/Edinb 280 G4
Mere Ches 184 E2
Mere Wilts 45 G10
Mere Brow Lancs 194 D2
Mere Green W Midlands 134 D2
Mere Green Worcs 117 E8
Mere Heath Ches 183 G11
Mereclough Lancs 204 G3
Merefield Northants 120 F4
Meresborough Medway 69 G10
Mereside Blackp'l 202 G2
Mereworth Kent 53 C7
Mergie Aberds 293 E9
Meriden W Midlands 134 G4
Merkadale H'land 294 B5
Merkland Dumf/Gal 237 B9
Merkland N Ayrs 256 B2
Merkland S Ayrs 244 E6
Merkland Lodge H'land 309 G4
Merley Poole 18 B6
Merlin Haven Glos 80 G2
Merlin's Bridge Pembs 72 C6
Merlins Cross Pembs 73 E7
Merridge Som'set 43 G8
Merrifield Devon 8 F6
Merrifield Devon 24 G3
Merrington Shrops 149 E9
Merrion Pembs 72 F6
Merriott Som'set 28 E6
Merriottsford Som'set 28 E6
Merritown Dorset 19 B8
Merrivale Devon 12 F6
Merrivale Heref'd 98 G2
Merrow Surrey 50 C4
Merry Field Corner Som'set 45 D7
Merry Field Hill Dorset 31 G8
Merry Hill Herts 85 G10
Merry Hill Staffs 133 D7
Merrybent Durham 224 C4
Merryhill Green Wokingham 65 E9
Merrylee E Renf 267 D11
Merrymeet Cornw'l 6 B5
Merseyside Maritime Museum Mersey 182 D4
Mersham Kent 54 F5
Merstham Surrey 51 C9
Merston W Sussex 34 G5
Merstone I/Wight 20 D6
Merther Cornw'l 5 G7
Merther Lane Cornw'l 5 G7
Merthyr Carms 93 G7
Merthyr Cynog Powys 95 D9
Merthyr Dyfan V/Glam 58 F6
Merthyr Mawr Bridg 57 F11
Merthyr Tudful = Merthyr Tydfil Merth Tyd 77 D9
Merthyr Tydfil = Merthyr Tudful Merth Tyd 77 D9
Merton Devon 25 E8
Merton London 67 F8
Merton Norfolk 141 D8
Merton Oxon 83 B9
Merton Park London 67 F8
Meshaw Devon 26 D3
Messing Essex 88 B5
Messingham N Lincs 199 G11
Mesty Croft W Midlands 133 D9
Metcombe Devon 15 C7
Metfield Suffolk 142 G5
Metfield Common Suffolk 126 B5
Metherell Cornw'l 7 B8
Metheringham Lincs 173 C9
Methersgate Suffolk 108 C5
Methil Fife 281 B7
Methilhill Fife 281 A7
Methley W Yorks 197 B11
Methley Junction W Yorks 197 B11
Methlick Aberds 303 F8
Methven Perth/Kinr 286 E4
Methwold Norfolk 140 E4
Methwold Hythe Norfolk 140 D4
Metroland, Gateshead Tyne/Wear 242 E6
Mettingham Suffolk 143 F7
Metton Norfolk 160 B4
Mevagissey Cornw'l 5 G10
Mewith Head N Yorks 212 F4
Mexborough S Yorks 198 G3
Mey H'land 310 B6
Meylltyern Gwyn 144 C4
Meysey Hampton Glos 81 F10
Miabhag W Isles 305 H2
Miabhag W Isles 305 J3
Miabhig W Isles 304 E2
Mial H'land 299 B7
Michaelchurch Heref'd 97 F10
Michaelchurch Escley Heref'd 96 E6
Michaelchurch-on-Arrow Powys 114 G4
Michaelston-le-pit V/Glam 58 E6
Michaelston-super-Ely Card 58 D6
Michaelston-y-Fedw Newp 59 C8
Michaelstow Cornw'l 11 F7
Michel Troy Monmouths 79 C7
Michelcombe Devon 8 B3
Micheldever Hants 48 F4
Micheldever Station Hants 48 E4
Michelmersh Hants 32 B5
Mickfield Suffolk 126 E2
Mickle Trafford Ches 166 B6
Micklebring S Yorks 187 B8
Mickleby N Yorks 226 C6
Micklefield Bucks 84 G5
Micklefield Green Herts 85 F9
Mickleham Surrey 51 C7
Micklehurst Gtr Man 196 G3
Mickleover Derby C 152 C6
Micklethwaite Cumb 239 G7
Micklethwaite W Yorks 205 E8
Mickleton Durham 232 G5
Mickleton Glos 100 C3
Mickletown W Yorks 197 B11
Mickley Derby 186 F4
Mickley N Yorks 214 D5
Mickley Green Suffolk 124 F6
Mickley Square Northum 242 E3
Mid Ardlaw Aberds 303 C9
Mid Auchinlek Invercl 276 G6
Mid Beltie Aberds 293 C8
Mid Calder W Loth 269 B11
Mid Cloch Forbie Aberds 303 D7
Mid Clyth H'land 310 F6
Mid Garrary Dumf/Gal 237 B7
Mid Lavant W Sussex 34 F5
Mid Letter Arg/Bute 284 G4
Mid Main H'land 300 F4
Mid Shandon Stirl 277 C9
Mid Urchany H'land 301 E8
Mid Walls Shetl'd 315 H4
Mid Yell Shetl'd 314 D7
Midanbury S'thampton 33 E7
Midbea Orkney 312 D5
Middle Assendon Oxon 65 B8
Middle Aston Oxon 101 F9
Middle Balnald Perth/Kinr 286 B4
Middle Barton Oxon 101 F8
Middle Bickenhill W Midlands 134 G4
Middle Bockhampton Dorset 19 B9
Middle Bridge N Som'set 60 D3
Middle Burnham Som'set 43 C10
Middle Cairncake Aberds 303 E8
Middle Chinnock Som'set 29 E7
Middle Claydon Bucks 102 F4
Middle Drums Angus 287 B9
Middle Duntisbourne Glos 81 D7
Middle Green Suffolk 124 E4
Middle Green Slough 66 C3
Middle Green Som'set 27 D10
Middle Handley Derby 186 F6
Middle Harling Norfolk 141 F9
Middle Herrington Tyne/Wear 243 G9
Middle Hill Pembs 73 C7
Middle Kames Arg/Bute 275 E10
Middle Lambrook Som'set 28 D6
Middle Littleton Worcs 99 B11
Middle Maes-coed Heref'd 96 E6
Middle Marwood Devon 40 F4
Middle Mayfield Staffs 169 G10
Middle Mill Pembs 90 F6
Middle Quarter Kent 53 F11
Middle Rainton Tyne/Wear 234 C2
Middle Rasen Lincs 189 D9
Middle Rigg Perth/Kinr 286 G4
Middle Rocombe Devon 9 B8
Middle Stoford Som'set 27 C11
Middle Stoke Medway 69 D10
Middle Stoke W Midlands 119 B7
Middle Stoughton Som'set 44 D2
Middle Street Glos 80 E3
Middle Street Norfolk 160 B5
Middle Taphouse Cornw'l 6 C3
Middle Town I/Scilly 1 F4
Middle Town Warwick 117 E11
Middle Tysoe Warwick 100 C6
Middle Wallop Hants 47 F9
Middle Weald M/Keynes 102 D5
Middle Wick Glos 80 F2
Middle Winterslow Wilts 47 G8
Middle Woodford Wilts 46 F6
Middlebie Dumf/Gal 238 B6
Middlecave N Yorks 216 E5
Middlecliffe S Yorks 198 F2
Middlecott Devon 13 D10
Middlecroft Derby 186 G6
Middlefield Falk 279 E7
Middlefield Leics 135 E8
Middleforth Green Lancs 194 B4
Middleham N Yorks 214 B2
Middlehill Cornw'l 6 B5
Middlehill Wilts 61 F10
Middlehope Shrops 131 F9
Middlemarsh Dorset 29 F11
Middlemore Devon 12 G5
Middlemuir Aberds 303 D9
Middlemuir Aberds 303 E8
Middlemuir Aberds 303 G9
Middleport Stoke 168 F5
Middlesbrough Middlesbro 225 B10
Middlesceugh Cumb 230 C3
Middleshaw Cumb 211 B11
Middleshaw Dumf/Gal 238 B4
Middlesmoor N Yorks 213 E11
Middlestone Durham 233 E11
Middlestone Moor Durham 233 E10
Middlestown W Yorks 197 D9
Middlethorpe C/York 207 D7
Middleton Aberds 293 B10
Middleton Arg/Bute 288 E1
Middleton Cumb 212 B2
Middleton Derby 170 D3
Middleton Derby 169 C11
Middleton Essex 107 D7
Middleton Gtr Man 195 F11
Middleton Hants 48 E2
Middleton Heref'd 115 D10
Middleton Hartlep'l 234 E6
Middleton I/Wight 20 D2
Middleton Lancs 202 B4
Middleton Midloth 271 D7
Middleton Norfolk 158 F3
Middleton Northants 136 E6
Middleton Northum 252 F3
Middleton Northum 264 B4
Middleton N Yorks 204 E5
Middleton N Yorks 205 D8
Middleton N Yorks 216 C5
Middleton Perth/Kinr 286 C5
Middleton Perth/Kinr 286 F2
Middleton Perth/Kinr 286 G5
Middleton Shrops 115 B10
Middleton Shrops 148 D6
Middleton Suffolk 127 D8
Middleton Swan 56 D2
Middleton Warwick 134 D3
Middleton W Yorks 197 B10
Middleton Cheney Northants 101 C10
Middleton Green Staffs 151 B9
Middleton Hall Northum 263 D11
Middleton Junction Gtr Man 195 G11
Middleton Moor Suffolk 127 D8
Middleton of Rora Aberds 303 E10
Middleton on the Hill Heref'd 115 E10
Middleton One Row D'lington 225 C7
Middleton Place Cumb 219 G11
Middleton Quernhow N Yorks 214 D6
Middleton Railway, Hunslet W Yorks 206 G2
Middleton St. George D'lington 225 C7
Middleton Scriven Shrops 132 F3
Middleton Stoney Oxon 101 G10
Middleton Tyas N Yorks 224 D4
Middleton-in-Teesdale Durham 232 F5
Middleton-on-Leven N Yorks 225 D9
Middleton-on-Sea W Sussex 35 H7
Middleton-on-the-Wolds ER Yorks 208 D4
Middletown Cumb 219 D9
Middletown N Som'set 60 E2
Middletown Powys 148 G6
Middlewich Ches 168 B2
Middlewood Ches 184 E6
Middlewood Cornw'l 11 F11
Middlewood Heref'd 96 C5
Middlewood S Yorks 186 C4
Middlewood Green Suffolk 125 E11
Middleyard Glos 80 E4
Middlezoy Som'set 43 G11
Middridge Durham 233 F11
Midfield H'land 308 C5
Midford Bath/NE Som'set 61 G9
Midge Hall Lancs 194 C4
Midgehole W Yorks 196 B3
Midgeholme Cumb 240 F4
Midgham W Berks 64 F5
Midgham Green W Berks 64 F5
Midgley W Yorks 197 E9
Midgley W Yorks 196 B4
Mid-Hants Railway (Watercress Line), New Alresford Hants 48 G5
Midhopestones S Yorks 186 B2
Midhurst W Sussex 34 C5
Midland Orkney 313 H4
Midlem Scot Borders 262 D2
Midmar Aberds 293 C8
Midmuir Arg/Bute 289 G11
Midpark Arg/Bute 255 B11
Midplaugh Aberds 302 E5
Midsomer Norton Bath/NE Som'set 45 C7
Midton Invercl 276 F4

Muddlebridge Devon 40 G4
Muddles Green E Sussex 37 E8
Mudeford Dorset 19 C9
Mudford Som'set 29 D9
Mudford Sock Som'set 29 D9
Mudgley Som'set 44 D2
Mugdock Stirl 277 F11
Mugeary H'land 294 B6
Mugginton Derby 170 G3
Muggintonlane End Derby 170 G3
Muggleswick Durham 232 B6
Muie H'land 309 J6
Muir Aberds 292 E2
Muir of Alford Aberds 293 B7
Muir of Fairburn H'land 300 D4
Muir of Fowlis Aberds 293 B7
Muir of Kinellar Aberds 293 B10
Muir of Miltonduff Moray 301 D11
Muir of Ord H'land 300 D5
Muir of Pert Angus 287 D8
Muirden Aberds 303 D7
Muirdrum Angus 287 D9
Muirend Glasg C 267 C11
Muirhead Angus 287 D7
Muirhead Glasg C 268 C3
Muirhead Fife 286 G6
Muirhead Fife 287 F8
Muirhead N Lanarks 268 B3
Muirhead S Ayrs 257 C8
Muirhouse C/Edinb 280 F4
Muirhouse N Lanarks 268 E5
Muirhouses Falk 279 E10
Muirkirk E Ayrs 258 D5
Muirmill Stirl 278 E4
Muirshearlich H'land 290 E3
Muirskie Aberds 293 D10
Muirtack Aberds 303 F9
Muirton Aberds 303 D7
Muirton H'land 301 C7
Muirton Perth/Kinr 286 E5
Muirton Perth/Kinr 286 F3
Muirton Mains H'land 300 D4
Muirton of Ardblair Perth/Kinr 286 C5
Muirton of Ballochy Angus 293 G8
Muiryfold Aberds 303 D7
Muker N Yorks 223 F8
Mulbarton Norfolk 142 C3
Mulben Moray 302 D3
Mulgrave Castle N Yorks 226 C6
Mulindry Arg/Bute 254 B4
Mulla Shetl'd 315 G6
Mullardoch House H'land 300 F2
Mullion Cornw'l 2 F5
Mullion Cove Cornw'l 2 F5
Mumby Lincs 191 G8
Mumps Gtr Man 196 F2
Muncaster Owl Trust World HQ Cumb 219 F11
Mundale Moray 301 D10
Munday Bois Kent 54 D2
Munderfield Row Heref'd 116 G3
Munderfield Stocks Heref'd 116 G3
Mundesley Norfolk 160 B6
Mundford Norfolk 140 E6
Mundham Norfolk 142 D6
Mundon Essex 88 E5
Mundurno Aberd C 293 B11
Munerigie H'land 290 C4
Muness Shetl'd 314 C8
Mungasdale H'land 307 K4
Mungrisdale Cumb 230 E3
Munlochy H'land 300 D6
Munsary Cottage H'land 310 E6
Munsley Heref'd 98 C3
Munslow Shrops 131 F10
Munstead Heath Surrey 50 E3
Munstone Heref'd 97 C10
Murch V/Glam 59 E7
Murchington Devon 13 D9
Murcot Worcs 99 C11
Murcott Oxon 83 B9
Murcott Wilts 81 G7
Murdishaw Wood Halton 183 E9
Murieston W Loth 269 C11
Murkle H'land 310 C5
Murlaggan H'land 290 D2
Murlaggan H'land 290 E5
Murra Orkney 313 H3
Murrayfield C/Edinb 280 G4
Murrayfield Stadium C/Edinb 280 G4
Murrays Motorcycle Museum I/Man 192 D4
Murrayshall Perth/Kinr 286 E5
Murraythwaite Dumf/Gal 238 C4
Murrell Green Hants 49 B8
Murrion Shetl'd 314 F4
Murrow Cambs 139 B7
Mursley Bucks 102 F6
Murston Kent 70 G2
Murthill Angus 287 B8
Murthly Perth/Kinr 286 D4
Murton Cumb 231 G10
Murton C/York 207 C9
Murton Durham 234 B3
Murton Swan 56 D5
Murton Tyne/Wear 243 C8
Musbury Devon 15 C11
Muscliff Bournem'th 19 B7
Muscoates N Yorks 216 C3
Muscott Northants 120 E2
Musdale Arg/Bute 289 G11
Museum of the Broads, Sutton Norfolk 161 E7
Musselburgh E Loth 280 G6
Musselburgh Racecourse E Loth 280 G6
Mustard Hyrn Norfolk 161 F8
Muston Leics 154 B6
Muston N Yorks 217 D11
Mustow Green Worcs 117 C7
Muswell Hill London 67 B9
Mutehill Dumf/Gal 237 E8
Mutford Suffolk 143 F9
Muthill Perth/Kinr 286 F2
Mutley Plym'th 7 D9
Mutterton Devon 27 F8
Mutton Hall E Sussex 37 C9
Muxton Telford 150 G4
Mwnt Ceredig'n 110 G3
Mybster H'land 310 D5
Mychett Surrey 49 B11
Myddfai Carms 94 E5
Myddle Shrops 149 E9
Myddlewood Shrops 149 E9
Mydroilyn Ceredig'n 111 F9
Myerscough Lancs 202 F5
Myerscough Lancs 203 G8
Mylor Bridge Cornw'l 3 B8
Mylor Churchtown Cornw'l 3 B8
Mynachlog-ddu Pembs 92 E2
Mynydd Alltir-fach Newp 78 G6
Mynydd Bach Ceredig'n 112 B4
Mynydd Cilan Gwyn 144 E5
Mynydd Isa Flints 166 C3
Mynydd Llandegai Gwyn 163 B10
Mynydd Marian Conwy 180 F5
Mynydd-bach Monmouths 79 G7
Mynydd-Bach Swan 75 F11
Mynydd-bach-y-glo Swan 75 F10
Mynyddislwyn Caerph 77 G11
Mynydd-llan Flints 181 G11
Mynydd-y-briw Powys 148 D3
Mynyddygarreg Carms 74 D6
Mynytho Gwyn 144 C6
Myrebird Aberds 293 D9
Myrelandhorn H'land 310 D6
Myreside Perth/Kinr 286 E6
Mytholm W Yorks 196 B3
Mytholmes W Yorks 204 F6
Mytholmroyd W Yorks 196 B4
Mythop Lancs 202 G3
Mytice Aberds 302 F4
Myton Warwick 118 E6
Myton-on Swale N Yorks 215 F8
Mytton Shrops 149 F8

N

Na Gearrannan W Isles 304 D3
Naast H'land 307 L3
Nab Wood W Yorks 205 F8
Nab's Head Lancs 194 B6
Naburn C/York 207 D7
Naccolt Kent 54 E5
Nackington Kent 55 C7
Nacton Suffolk 108 C4
Nacton Heath Suffolk 108 C4
Nadderwater Devon 14 C3
Nafferton ER Yorks 209 B7
Nags Head Glos 80 F5
Nailbridge Glos 79 B10
Nailsbourne Som'set 28 B2
Nailsea N Som'set 60 E3
Nailstone Leics 135 B8
Nailsworth Glos 80 F5
Nairn H'land 301 D8
Nalderswood Surrey 51 D8
Nancegollan Cornw'l 2 C4
Nancledra Cornw'l 1 B5
Nangreaves Lancs 195 D10
Nanhoron Gwyn 144 C5
Nannerch Flints 165 B11
Nannerth Powys 113 C8
Nanpantan Leics 153 F10
Nanpean Cornw'l 5 D9
Nanstallon Cornw'l 5 B10
Nant Denbs 165 D11
Nant Alyn Flints 165 B11
Nant Ddu Rh Cyn Taff 77 C7
Nant Mawr Flints 166 C3
Nant Peris = Old Llanberis Gwyn 163 D9
Nanternis Ceredig'n 111 F7
Nantffyllon Bridg 76 G5
Nantgaredig Carms 93 G9
Nantgarw Rh Cyn Taff 58 B6
Nant-glas Powys 113 D9
Nantglyn Denbs 165 C8
Nantgwyn Powys 113 B9
Nantlle Gwyn 163 E8
Nantmawr Shrops 148 E5
Nantmel Powys 113 D10
Nantmor Gwyn 163 F10
Nantwich Ches 167 E11
Nant-y-Bai Carms 94 C5
Nant-y-Bwch Bl Gwent 77 C10
Nant-y-Cafn Neath P Talb 76 D4
Nant-y-Caws Shrops 148 D5
Nant-y-derry Monmouths 78 E4
Nant-y-felin Conwy 179 G11
Nant-y-ffin Carms 93 E11
Nantyglesaid Caerph 59 B8
Nantyglo Bl Gwent 77 C11
Nant-y-gollen Shrops 148 D4
Nant-y-Moel Bridg 76 G6
Nant-y-pandy Conwy 179 G11
Napchester Kent 55 D10
Naphill Bucks 84 F5
Napleton Worcs 99 B7
Nappa N Yorks 204 C3
Napton on the Hill Warwick 119 E9
Narberth = Arberth Pembs 73 C10
Narberth Bridge Pembs 73 C10
Narborough Leics 135 D10
Narborough Norfolk 158 G4
Narkurs Cornw'l 6 D6
Narracott Devon 24 D5
Narrowgate Corner Norfolk 161 F8
Nasareth Gwyn 163 E7
Naseby Northants 120 B3
Nash Bucks 102 E5
Nash Kent 55 B9
Nash London 68 G2
Nash Newp 59 C10
Nash Shrops 116 C2
Nash Som'set 29 E8
Nash End Worcs 132 G5
Nash Lee Bucks 84 D4
Nash Street Kent 68 F6
Nashend Glos 80 E6
Nashes Green Hants 49 D7
Nassington Northants 137 D11
Nastend Glos 80 D3
Nasty Herts 105 G7
Natcott Devon 24 C3
Nateby Cumb 222 D5
Nateby Lancs 202 E5
Nately Scures Hants 49 C8
National Agricultural Centre, Stoneleigh Warwick 118 C6
National Botanic Garden of Wales Carms 75 B8
National Cycle Collection, Llandrindod Wells Powys 113 E11
National Exhibition Centre, Birmingham W Midlands 134 G3
National Fishing Heritage Centre, Grimsby NE Lincs 201 F9
National Forest Discovery Centre Leics 152 F6
National Gallery London 67 C9
National Hockey Stadium M/Keynes 102 D6
National Ice Centre Nott'ham 153 B11
National Maritime Museum London 67 D11
National Maritime Museum, Falmouth Cornw'l 3 C8
National Motor Museum, Beaulieu Hants 32 G5
National Museum of Photography, Bradford W Yorks 205 G9
National Museum of Wales Card 59 D7
National Portrait Gallery (See National Gallery) London 67 C9
National Railway Museum C/York 207 C7
National Seal Sanctuary, Gweek Cornw'l 2 D6
National Space Science Centre Leics 135 B11
National Squash Centre Gtr Man 184 B5
National Waterfront Museum Swan 57 C7
Natland Cumb 211 B10
Natural History Museum London 67 D9
Natureland Seal Sanctuary, Skegness Lincs 175 C9
Naughton Suffolk 107 B10
Naunton Glos 100 G2
Naunton Worcs 99 D7
Naunton Beauchamp Worcs 117 G9
Navarino Cornw'l 11 D11
Navenby Lincs 173 D7
Navestock Essex 87 F9
Navestock Heath Essex 87 F8
Navidale H'land 311 H4
Navity H'land 301 C7
Nawton N Yorks 216 C3
Nayland Suffolk 107 E9
Nazeing Essex 86 D6
Nazeing Gate Essex 86 D6
Nazeing Long Green Essex 86 E6
Nazeing Mead Essex 86 D5
Neacroft Hants 19 B9
Nealhouse Cumb 239 G8
Neal's Green Warwick 134 G6
Neames Forstal Kent 54 B4
Neap Shetl'd 315 H7
Near Sawrey Cumb 221 F7
Nearton End Bucks 102 F6
Neasden London 67 B8
Neasham D'lington 224 C6
Neat Enstone Oxon 101 G7
Neath = Castell-nedd Rh Cyn Taff 76 F3
Neath Abbey Rh Cyn Taff 76 F2
Neath Hill M/Keynes 103 C7
Neatham Hants 49 E8
Neatishead Norfolk 160 E6
Neaton Norfolk 141 C8
Nebo Conwy 164 D4
Nebo Ceredig'n 111 D10
Nebo Gwyn 163 E7
Nebo Angl 179 C7
Nechells W Midlands 133 F11
Necton Norfolk 141 B7
Nedd H'land 306 F6
Nedderton Northum 252 G6
Nedging Suffolk 107 B9
Nedging Tye Suffolk 107 B10
Needham Norfolk 142 G4
Needham Green Essex 87 B9
Needham Market Suffolk 125 F11
Needham Street Suffolk 124 D4
Needingworth Cambs 122 C6
Needwood Staffs 152 E3
Neen Savage Shrops 116 B3
Neen Sollars Shrops 116 C3
Neenton Shrops 132 F2
Neep's Bridge Norfolk 139 B11
Neeston Pembs 72 D5
Nefyn Gwyn 162 G4
Neilston E Renf 267 D9
Neithrop Oxon 101 C8
Nelly Andrews Green Powys 130 B5
Nelson Caerph 77 F10
Nelson Lancs 204 F3
Nelson Village Northum 242 B6
Nemphlar S Lanarks 269 G7
Nempnett Thrubwell Bath/NE Som'set 60 G4
Nene Terrace Lincs 138 B4
Nenthall Cumb 231 B11
Nenthead Cumb 231 C11
Nenthorn Scot Borders 262 B5
Neopardy Devon 13 B11
Nep Town W Sussex 36 D2
Nepcote W Sussex 35 F10
Nepgill Cumb 229 F7
Nerabus Arg/Bute 254 B3
Nercwys Flints 166 C2
Nerston S Lanarks 268 D2
Nesbit Northum 263 C11
Nesbitt Hill Head Northum 242 E3
Nesfield N Yorks 205 D7
Ness Ches 182 F4
Ness Orkney 312 E5
Ness Gardens, Connah's Quay Ches 182 F4
Nesscliffe Shrops 149 F7
Nessholt Ches 182 F4
Nesstoun Orkney 312 C8
Neston Ches 182 F3
Neston Wilts 61 F11
Nether Fife 280 B5
Nether Alderley Ches 184 F4
Nether Blainslie Scot Borders 271 G10
Nether Booth Derby 185 D10
Nether Broughton Leics 154 D3
Nether Burrow Lancs 212 D2
Nether Burrows Derby 152 B5
Nether Cerne Dorset 17 B9
Nether Compton Dorset 29 D9
Nether Crimond Aberds 303 G8
Nether Dalgliesh Scot Borders 249 B7
Nether Dallachy Moray 302 C3
Nether Edge S Yorks 186 E4
Nether End Derby 186 G3
Nether End Leics 154 G4
Nether End W Yorks 197 F9
Nether Exe Devon 26 G6
Nether Glasslaw Aberds 303 D8
Nether Hall Leics C 136 B2
Nether Handwick Angus 287 C7
Nether Haugh S Yorks 186 B6
Nether Headon Notts 188 F2
Nether Heage Derby 170 E5
Nether Hesleden N Yorks 213 E7
Nether Heyford Northants 120 F3
Nether Howecleuch S Lanarks 260 G2
Nether Kellet Lancs 211 F10
Nether Kinmundy Aberds 303 E10
Nether Kirkton E Renf 267 D9
Nether Langwith Notts 187 G8
Nether Leask Aberds 303 F10
Nether Lenshie Aberds 302 E6
Nether Liberton C/Edinb 280 G5
Nether Moor Derby 170 B5
Nether Padley Derby 186 F3
Nether Park Aberds 303 D10
Nether Poppleton C/York 207 C7
Nether Row Cumb 230 D2
Nether Savock Aberds 303 E10
Nether Silton N Yorks 225 G9
Nether Skyborry Shrops 114 C5
Nether Stowey Som'set 43 F7
Nether Street Essex 87 C9
Nether Street Herts 86 B6
Nether Street Suffolk 125 E8
Nether Urquhart Fife 286 G5
Nether Wallop Hants 47 F10
Nether Wasdale Cumb 220 E2
Nether Welton Cumb 230 B3
Nether Westcote Glos 100 G4
Nether Whitacre Warwick 134 E4
Nether Worton Oxon 101 E8
Nether Yeadon W Yorks 205 E10
Netheravon Wilts 46 D6
Netherbrae Aberds 303 D7
Netherbrough Orkney 312 G4
Netherburn S Lanarks 268 F6
Netherbury Dorset 16 B5
Netherby Cumb 239 C9
Netherby N Yorks 206 D2
Nethercley Som'set 28 C3
Nethercote Glos 100 G3
Nethercote Warwick 119 E10
Nethercott Devon 40 F3
Nethercott Oxon 101 G9
Netherdale Shetl'd 315 H3
Netherend Glos 79 E9
Netherfield E Sussex 38 D2
Netherfield M/Keynes 103 D7
Netherfield Notts 171 G10
Nethergate Norfolk 159 D11
Netherhall N Ayrs 266 C4
Netherhampton Wilts 31 B10
Netherhay Dorset 28 F6
Netherland Green Staffs 152 C2
Netherlaw Dumf/Gal 237 E9
Netherlee E Renf 267 D11
Netherley Aberds 293 D10
Netherley Mersey 182 D6
Nethermill Dumf/Gal 248 F2
Nethermills Moray 302 D5
Nethermuir Aberds 303 E9
Netheroyd Hill W Yorks 196 D6
Netherplace E Renf 267 D10
Netherseal Derby 152 G5
Netherthird E Ayrs 258 F3
Netherthong W Yorks 196 F6
Netherthorpe Derby 186 G6
Netherthorpe S Yorks 187 E8
Netherton Aberds 303 E8
Netherton Angus 287 B9
Netherton Ches 183 F8
Netherton Cumb 228 D6
Netherton Cornw'l 11 G11
Netherton Devon 14 G3
Netherton Hants 47 B11
Netherton Heref'd 97 F10
Netherton Mersey 193 G11
Netherton N Lanarks 268 E5
Netherton Northum 251 B11
Netherton Oxon 82 F6
Netherton Perth/Kinr 286 B5
Netherton Shrops 132 G4
Netherton Stirl 277 F11
Netherton W Midlands 133 F8
Netherton Worcs 99 C9
Netherton W Yorks 196 E6
Netherton W Yorks 197 D9
Netherton of Lonmay Aberds 303 C10
Nethertown Cumb 219 D9
Nethertown H'land 310 B7
Nethertown Lancs 203 F10
Nethertown Staffs 152 F2
Netherwitton Northum 252 E4
Netherwood E Ayrs 258 D5
Nethy Bridge H'land 301 G10
Netley Hants 33 F7
Netley Marsh Hants 32 E4
Netteswell Essex 87 C7
Nettlebed Oxon 65 B7
Nettlebridge Som'set 45 D6
Nettlecombe Dorset 16 B6
Nettlecombe I/Wight 20 F6
Nettleden Herts 85 C8
Nettleham Lincs 189 F8
Nettlehirst N Ayrs 267 E7
Nettlestead Kent 53 C7
Nettlestead Suffolk 107 B11
Nettlestead Green Kent 53 C7
Nettlestone I/Wight 21 C8
Nettlesworth Durham 233 B11
Nettleton Glos 80 C6
Nettleton Lincs 189 B10
Nettleton Wilts 61 D10
Nettleton Green Wilts 61 D10
Nettleton Shrub Wilts 61 D10
Nettleton Top Lincs 189 B10
Netton Wilts 46 F6
Neuadd Carms 94 G4
Nevendon Essex 88 G2
Nevern Pembs 91 C11
Nevill Holt Leics 136 E6
Nevilles Cross Durham 233 C11
Nevis Range Ski Centre, Torlundy H'land 290 F3
New Abbey Dumf/Gal 237 C11
New Aberdour Aberds 303 C8
New Addington London 67 G11
New Alresford Hants 48 G5
New Alyth Perth/Kinr 286 C6
New Arley Warwick 134 F5
New Arram ER Yorks 208 E6
New Ash Green Kent 68 F6
New Balderton Notts 172 E4
New Barn Kent 68 F6
New Barnet London 86 F3
New Barnetby N Lincs 200 E5
New Barton Northants 121 E7
New Basford Nott'ham 171 G9
New Beckenham London 67 E11
New Belses Scot Borders 262 D3
New Bewick Northum 264 E3
New Bilton Warwick 119 B9
New Bolingbroke Lincs 174 D4
New Bolsover Derby 187 G7
New Boston Mersey 183 B9
New Boultham Lincs 189 G7
New Bradwell M/Keynes 102 C6
New Brancepath Durham 233 C10
New Bridge ER Yorks 199 D7
New Bridge N Yorks 216 B5
New Brighton Flints 166 B3
New Brighton Hants 34 F2
New Brighton Mersey 182 C4
New Brighton N Yorks 204 C4
New Brighton Wrex 166 E3
New Brighton W Yorks 205 F8
New Brighton W Yorks 197 B9
New Brimington Derby 186 G6
New Brinsley Notts 171 E7
New Brotton Redcar/Clevel'd 235 G9
New Broughton Wrex 166 E4
New Buckenham Norfolk 141 E11
New Buildings Bath/NE Som'set 45 B7
New Bury Gtr Man 195 F8
New Byth Aberds 303 D8
New Catton Norfolk 160 G4
New Cheriton Hants 33 B9
New Chesterton Cambs 123 F8
New Costessey Norfolk 160 G3
New Coundon Durham 233 E10
New Cowper Cumb 229 B8
New Crofton W Yorks 197 D11
New Cross London 67 D11
New Cross Som'set 28 D6
New Cubbington Warwick 118 D6
New Cummock E Ayrs 258 G4
New Cut E Sussex 38 D4
New Deer Aberds 303 E8
New Delaval Northum 243 B7
New Delph Gtr Man 196 F3
New Denham Bucks 66 C4
New Duston Northants 120 E4
New Earswick C/York 207 B8
New Eastwood Notts 171 F7
New Edlington S Yorks 187 B8
New Elgin Moray 302 C2
New Ellerby ER Yorks 209 F9
New Eltham London 68 E2
New End Worcs 117 F10
New England Essex 106 C4
New England Lincs 175 D8
New England Peterbro 138 C3
New England Surrey 66 G2
New Farm Loch E Ayrs 257 B10
New Farnley W Yorks 205 G10
New Ferry Mersey 182 D4
New Fletton Peterbro 138 D3
New Fryston W Yorks 198 B3
New Galloway Dumf/Gal 237 B8
New Gilston Fife 287 G8
New Greens Herts 85 D10
New Grimsby I/Scilly 1 F3
New Hall Warrington 183 D9
New Hall Hey Lancs 195 C10
New Hartley Northum 243 B8
New Haw Surrey 66 G5
New Headington Oxon 83 D8
New Hedges Pembs 73 E10
New Herrington Tyne/Wear 243 G8
New Hinksey Oxon 83 E8
New Holkham Norfolk 176 F5
New Holland N Lincs 200 C5
New Horwich Derby 185 E8
New Houghton Derby 171 B8
New Houghton Derby 171 B7
New Houghton Norfolk 158 D5
New House Durham 233 C9
New House Green Wilts 62 D2
New Houses Gtr Man 194 G5
New Humberstone Leics C 136 B2
New Hunwick Durham 233 E9
New Hutton Cumb 221 G11
New Hythe Kent 53 B8
New Inn Carms 93 D9
New Inn Carms 94 F2
New Inn Devon 24 F6
New Inn Pembs 91 E11
New Inn Torf 78 F4
New Invention W Midlands 133 C9
New Kelso H'land 299 E9
New Kingston Notts 153 D10
New Kyo Durham 242 G5
New Lambton Tyne/Wear 243 G8
New Lanark S Lanarks 269 G7
New Lanark World Heritage Village, Lanark S Lanarks 269 G7
New Lane Lancs 194 E2
New Lane End Warrington 183 C10
New Langholm Dumf/Gal 249 G9
New Leake Lincs 174 D6
New Leaze S Glos 60 B5
New Leeds Aberds 303 D9
New Lodge S Yorks 197 F10
New Longton Lancs 194 B4
New Luce Dumf/Gal 236 C3
New Malden London 67 F8
New Marske Redcar/Clevel'd 235 G8
New Marston Oxon 83 D8
New Marton Shrops 148 C6
New Micklefield W Yorks 206 G4
New Mill Aberds 293 E9
New Mill Cumb 219 E11
New Mill Cornw'l 1 C5
New Mill Cornw'l 4 F6
New Mill Herts 84 C6
New Mill Wilts 63 G7
New Mill W Yorks 197 F7
New Mill End Beds 85 B10
New Mills Ches 184 E3
New Mills Cornw'l 5 E8
New Mills Derby 185 D7
New Mills Powys 129 C11
New Mills Powys 148 F2
New Milton Hants 19 B10
New Mistley Essex 108 E2
New Moat Pembs 91 F11
New Moston Gtr Man 195 G11
New Ollerton Notts 171 B11
New Oscott W Midlands 133 E11
New Park N Yorks 206 B2
New Parks Leics C 135 B11
New Pitsligo Aberds 303 D8
New Polzeath Cornw'l 10 F4
New Quay = Ceinewydd Ceredig'n 111 E7
New Quay Devon 8 G4
New Rackheath Norfolk 160 G5
New Radnor Powys 114 E4
New Rent Cumb 230 D5
New Ridley Northum 242 F3
New Road Side N Yorks 204 E5
New Road Side W Yorks 196 B6
New Romney Kent 39 C9
New Rossington S Yorks 187 B10
New Row Ceredig'n 112 C4
New Sawley Derby 153 C9
New Scarbro W Yorks 205 G10
New Sharlston W Yorks 197 C11
New Silksworth Tyne/Wear 243 G9
New Skelton Redcar/Clevel'd 226 B3
New Smithy Derby 185 E9
New Southgate London 86 G3
New Springs Gtr Man 194 F6
New Sprowston Norfolk 160 G4
New Stanton Derby 153 B9
New Stevenston N Lanarks 268 D5
New Street Heref'd 114 F6
New Street Staffs 169 E9
New Sulehay Northants 137 D11
New Swanage Dorset 18 E6
New Swannington Leics 153 F8
New Thirsk N Yorks 215 C8
New Thundersley Essex 69 B9
New Totley S Yorks 186 F4
New Town Bath/NE Som'set 60 G5
New Town C/Edinb 280 G5
New Town Dorset 30 D4
New Town Dorset 31 F7
New Town Dorset 31 D7
New Town Dorset 31 D7
New Town Dorset 30 C3
New Town E Loth 281 G8
New Town E Sussex 37 C7
New Town Glos 99 E10
New Town Kent 53 B7
New Town Lancs 203 F8
New Town Luton 103 G11
New Town Medway 69 G8
New Town Shetl'd 314 E6
New Town Som'set 29 D9
New Town Som'set 44 D3
New Town Swindon 63 C7
New Town Tyne/Wear 234 B2
New Town Tyne/Wear 243 E8
New Town W Berks 64 D6
New Town Wokingham 65 E8
New Town Wilts 29 D11
New Town Wilts 63 E9
New Town Wilts 61 C11
New Town W Midlands 133 E9
New Town W Sussex 51 G7
New Town W Yorks 198 C3
New Tredegar = Tredegar Newydd Caerph 77 E10
New Trows S Lanarks 259 B8
New Ulva Arg/Bute 275 E8
New Village ER Yorks 209 G7
New Village S Yorks 198 F5
New Waltham NE Lincs 201 G9
New Whittington Derby 186 F5
New Wimpole Cambs 122 G6
New Winton E Loth 281 G8
New Woodhouse Shrops 167 G9
New World Cambs 139 E7
New Yatt Oxon 82 C5
New York Lincs 174 D2
New York N Yorks 214 G3
New York Tyne/Wear 243 C8
New Zealand Derby C 152 B6
New Zealand Wilts 62 D4
Newall W Yorks 205 D10
Newall Green Gtr Man 184 D4
Newark Orkney 312 D8
Newark Peterbro 138 C4
Newark Castle Notts 172 E3
Newark-on-Trent Notts 172 E3
Newarthill N Lanarks 268 D5
Newball Lincs 189 F9
Newbarn Kent 55 F7
Newbarns Cumb 210 E4
Newbattle Midloth 270 B6
Newbiggin Cumb 210 F5
Newbiggin Cumb 219 G11
Newbiggin Cumb 230 F5
Newbiggin Cumb 231 F8
Newbiggin Cumb 231 B7
Newbiggin Durham 232 F4
Newbiggin Durham 233 B8
Newbiggin Northum 232 B5
Newbiggin N Yorks 218 C2
Newbiggin N Yorks 223 G9
Newbiggin N Yorks 213 B10
Newbiggin Hall Estate Tyne/Wear 242 D6
Newbiggin-by-the-Sea Northum 253 F8
Newbigging Aberds 303 G7
Newbigging Angus 286 C6
Newbigging Angus 287 D8
Newbigging Angus 287 D8
Newbigging S Lanarks 269 F10
Newbiggings Orkney 312 D7
Newbiggin-on-Lune Cumb 222 D4
Newbold Derby 186 G5
Newbold Gtr Man 196 E2
Newbold Leics 153 F8
Newbold Leics 136 B5
Newbold on Avon Warwick 119 B9
Newbold on Stour Warwick 100 B4
Newbold Pacey Warwick 118 F5
Newbold Verdon Leics 135 C8
Newborough = Niwbwrch Angl 162 B6
Newborough Peterbro 138 B4
Newborough Staffs 152 D2
Newbottle Northants 101 D10
Newbottle Tyne/Wear 243 G8
Newbourne Suffolk 108 C5
Newbridge C/Edinb 280 G2
Newbridge Caerph 78 F2
Newbridge Ceredig'n 111 F10
Newbridge Cornw'l 1 C4
Newbridge Cornw'l 4 G5
Newbridge Cornw'l 6 B6
Newbridge Dumf/Gal 237 B11
Newbridge E Sussex 52 G3
Newbridge Hants 32 D3
Newbridge I/Wight 20 D4
Newbridge Lancs 204 F3
Newbridge Oxon 82 E6
Newbridge Pembs 91 E8
Newbridge W Midlands 133 D7
Newbridge Wrex 166 G3
Newbridge Green Worcs 98 D6
Newbridge on Wye Powys 113 F10
Newbridge-on-Usk Monmouths 78 G5
Newbrough Northum 241 D9
Newbuildings Devon 26 G3
Newburgh Aberds 303 D9
Newburgh Aberds 303 G9
Newburgh Scot Borders 261 E8
Newburgh Fife 286 F6
Newburgh Lancs 194 E3
Newburn Tyne/Wear 242 D5
Newbury Kent 54 B2
Newbury Som'set 45 C7
Newbury W Berks 64 F3
Newbury Wilts 45 E10
Newbury Park London 68 B2
Newbury Racecourse W Berks 64 F3
Newby Cumb 231 G7
Newby Lancs 204 D2
Newby N Yorks 205 D11
Newby N Yorks 212 E4
Newby N Yorks 227 G10
Newby N Yorks 225 C10
Newby Bridge Cumb 211 B7
Newby Cote N Yorks 212 E4
Newby East Cumb 239 F11
Newby Hall & Gardens, Ripon N Yorks 214 F6
Newby Head Cumb 231 G7
Newby West Cumb 239 G9
Newby Whiske N Yorks 215 B7
Newcastle Bridg 57 F11
Newcastle Monmouths 78 B6
Newcastle Shrops 130 G4
Newcastle Emlyn = Castell Newydd Emlyn Carms 92 C6
Newcastle International Airport Tyne/Wear 242 C5
Newcastle Racecourse Tyne/Wear 243 C7
Newcastle upon Tyne Tyne/Wear 242 D6
Newcastleton = Copshaw Holm Scot Borders 249 F11
Newcastle-under-Lyme Stoke 168 F4
Newchapel Pembs 92 D4
Newchapel Powys 129 G9
Newchapel Surrey 51 E11
Newchapel Staffs 168 E5
Newchurch Bl Gwent 77 C11
Newchurch Carms 93 G7
Newchurch Heref'd 115 G7
Newchurch I/Wight 21 D7
Newchurch Kent 54 G5
Newchurch Lancs 195 C10
Newchurch Monmouths 79 F7
Newchurch Powys 114 G4
Newchurch Staffs 152 E2
Newchurch in Pendle Lancs 204 F2
Newcott Devon 28 F2
Newcraighall E Loth 280 G6
Newdigate Surrey 51 E7
Newell Green Brackn'l 65 E11
Newenden Kent 38 B4
Newent Glos 98 F4
Newerne Glos 79 E10
Newfield Durham 233 E10
Newfield Durham 242 G6
Newfield H'land 301 B7
Newfield Stoke 168 E5
Newfield Green S Yorks 186 E5
Newfound Hants 48 C5
Newgale Pembs 91 G7
Newgarth Orkney 312 G3
Newgate Derby 186 G4
Newgate Lancs 194 F4
Newgate Norfolk 177 E9
Newgate Street Herts 86 D3
Newhailes E Loth 280 G6
Newhall Ches 167 F10
Newhall Derby 152 E5
Newhall House H'land 300 C6
Newhall Point H'land 301 C7
Newham Cornw'l 4 G6
Newham Lincs 174 E3
Newham Northum 264 D5
Newhaven C/Edinb 280 F5
Newhaven Derby 169 D11
Newhaven E Sussex 36 G6
Newhey Gtr Man 196 E2
Newhill Fife 286 F6
Newhill Perth/Kinr 286 G5
Newhill S Yorks 186 B6
Newhills Aberd C 293 C10
Newholm N Yorks 227 C7
Newhouse N Lanarks 268 C5
Newhouse Shetl'd 315 G6
Newick E Sussex 36 C6
Newingreen Kent 54 F6
Newington C/Edinb 280 G5
Newington Kent 71 F11
Newington Kent 55 F7

414 New – Nor

Newington Kent 69 G11
Newington Notts 187 C11
Newington Oxon 83 F10
Newington Shrops 131 G8
Newington Bagpath Glos 80 G4
Newland Cumb 210 D5
Newland ER Yorks 199 B10
Newland Glos 79 D9
Newland Kingston/Hull 209 G7
Newland N Yorks 199 C7
Newland Oxon 82 D5
Newland Som'set 41 F10
Newland Worcs 98 B5
Newland Green Kent 54 D2
Newlandrig Midloth 271 C7
Newlands Scot Borders 250 E2
Newlands Glasg C 267 C11
Newlands Cumb 229 G10
Newlands Cumb 230 D2
Newlands Derby 170 F6
Newlands Essex 69 C10
Newlands Heref'd 115 F9
Newlands H'land 301 E7
Newlands Moray 302 D3
Newlands Notts 171 C9
Newlands Northum 242 F3
Newland's Corner Surrey 50 D4
Newlands of Geise H'land 310 C4
Newlands of Tynet Moray 302 C3
Newlands Park Angl 178 E3
Newlandsmuir S Lanarks 268 E2
Newlay W Yorks 205 F10
Newliston C/Edinb 280 G3
Newliston Fife 280 C5
Newlot Orkney 312 G6
Newlyn Cornw'l 1 D5
Newlyn East Cornw'l 4 D6
Newmachar Aberds 293 B10
Newmains N Lanarks 268 D6
Newman Street Som'set 45 E7
Newman's End Essex 87 C8
Newman's Green Suffolk 107 C7
Newmarket Glos 80 F4
Newmarket Suffolk 124 E2
Newmarket W Isles 304 E6
Newmarket Racecourse Suffolk 124 E2
Newmill Scot Borders 261 G11
Newmill Moray 302 D4
Newmill of Inshewan Angus 292 G6
Newmillerdam W Yorks 197 D10
Newmills Fife 279 D10
Newmills H'land 300 C6
Newmills of Boyne Aberds 302 D5
Newmiln Perth/Kinr 286 D5
Newmilns E Ayrs 258 B2
Newmore H'land 300 B6
Newmore H'land 300 D5
Newney Green Essex 87 D11
Newnham Cambs 123 F8
Newnham Glos 79 C11
Newnham Hants 49 C8
Newnham Herts 104 D4
Newnham Kent 54 B3
Newnham Northants 119 F11
Newnham Warwick 118 E3
Newnham Bridge Worcs 116 D2
Newnham Murren Oxon 64 B6
Newpark Fife 287 F8
Newpool Staffs 168 D5
Newport Cornw'l 12 D2
Newport Dorset 18 B3
Newport Essex 105 E10
Newport ER Yorks 199 B11
Newport Glos 79 F11
Newport H'land 311 G5
Newport I/Wight 20 D4
Newport Norfolk 161 F10
Newport Newp 59 B10
Newport Som'set 28 C4
Newport Telford 150 F4
Newport = Trefdraeth Pembs 91 D11
Newport Museum & Art Gallery Newp 59 B10
Newport Pagnell M/Keynes 103 C7
Newport Sands Pembs 91 C11
Newport-on-Tay Fife 287 E8
Newpound Common W Sussex 35 B9
Newquay Cornw'l 4 C6
Newquay Airport Cornw'l 5 C7
Newsam Green W Yorks 206 G3
Newsbank Ches 168 B4
Newseat Aberds 303 E10
Newseat Aberds 303 F7
Newsells Herts 105 D7
Newsham Lancs 202 F6
Newsham Northum 253 G7
Newsham Northum 243 B8
Newsham N Yorks 224 D2
Newsham N Yorks 215 C7
Newsholme ER Yorks 199 B8
Newsholme Lancs 204 C2
Newsholme W Yorks 204 F6
Newsome W Yorks 196 E6
Newstead Scot Borders 262 C3
Newstead Notts 171 E8
Newstead Stoke 168 G5
Newstead W Yorks 197 E11
Newstead Abbey, Kirkby in Ashfield Notts 171 E8
Newstreet Lane Shrops 150 B2
Newthorpe Notts 171 F7
Newthorpe N Yorks 206 G5
Newthorpe Common Notts 171 F7
Newtoft Lincs 189 D8
Newton Arg/Bute 275 D11
Newton Beds 104 C4
Newton Bridg 57 F10
Newton Cambs 157 G8
Newton Cambs 105 B8
Newton Card 59 D8
Newton Ches 167 D8
Newton Ches 166 B6
Newton Ches 183 F8
Newton Cumb 210 E4
Newton Derby 170 D6
Newton Dumf/Gal 239 C7
Newton Dumf/Gal 248 D4
Newton Dorset 30 E3
Newton Falk 279 E9
Newton Gtr Man 185 B7
Newton Heref'd 115 G10
Newton Heref'd 96 E6
Newton H'land 301 C7
Newton H'land 301 E7
Newton H'land 306 F7
Newton H'land 310 E7
Newton Lancs 202 F2
Newton Lancs 211 E11
Newton Lancs 203 C9
Newton Lincs 155 B10
Newton Mersey 182 D2
Newton Moray 301 C11
Newton Norfolk 158 F6
Newton Northants 137 F7
Newton Notts 171 G11
Newton Northum 242 E2
Newton Northum 252 C2
Newton Perth/Kinr 286 D2
Newton Suffolk 107 C8
Newton Shetl'd 314 E5
Newton Shetl'd 315 K5
Newton S Glos 79 G10
Newton Som'set 42 F6
Newton S Lanarks 259 C10
Newton S Lanarks 268 C3
Newton Staffs 151 D10
Newton S Yorks 198 G5
Newton Swan 56 D6
Newton Warwick 119 B10
Newton Wilts 32 C2
Newton W Midlands 133 E10
Newton W Loth 279 F11
Newton W Yorks 198 B2
Newton Abbot Devon 14 G3
Newton Abbot Racecourse Devon 9 A7
Newton Arlosh Cumb 238 F5
Newton Aycliffe Durham 233 G11
Newton Bewley Hartlep'l 234 F5
Newton Blossomville M/Keynes 121 G8
Newton Bromswold Northants 121 D9
Newton Burgoland Leics 135 B7
Newton by Toft Lincs 189 D8
Newton Court Monmouths 79 C8
Newton Cross Pembs 91 F7
Newton Farm Heref'd 97 D9
Newton Ferrers Devon 7 F10
Newton Flotman Norfolk 142 D4
Newton Green Monmouths 79 G8
Newton Hall Durham 233 C11
Newton Hall Northum 242 D2
Newton Harcourt Leics 136 D2
Newton Heath Gtr Man 195 G11
Newton Hill W Yorks 197 C10
Newton Ho. Aberds 302 G6
Newton Ketton D'lington 234 G2
Newton Kyme N Yorks 206 D5
Newton Longville Bucks 103 E7
Newton Mearns E Renf 267 D10
Newton Morrell N Yorks 224 D4
Newton Mulgrave N Yorks 226 B5
Newton Noyes Pembs 72 D6
Newton of Ardtoe H'land 289 B8
Newton of Balcanquhal Perth/Kinr 286 F5
Newton of Balcormo Fife 287 G9
Newton of Falkland Fife 286 G6
Newton of Mountblairy Aberds 302 D6
Newton of Pitcairns Perth/Kinr 286 F4
Newton on Ayr S Ayrs 257 E8
Newton on the Hill Shrops 149 E9
Newton on Trent Lincs 188 G4
Newton Park Mersey 183 C9
Newton Peveril Dorset 18 B4
Newton Poppleford Devon 15 D7
Newton Purcell Oxon 102 E2
Newton Regis Warwick 134 B5
Newton Reigny Cumb 230 E5
Newton St. Boswells Scot Borders 262 C3
Newton St. Cyres Devon 14 B3
Newton St. Faith Norfolk 160 F4
Newton St. Loe Bath/NE Som'set 61 G8
Newton St. Petrock Devon 24 E6
Newton Solney Derby 152 D5
Newton Stacey Hants 48 E2
Newton Stewart Dumf/Gal 236 C6
Newton Toney Wilts 47 E8
Newton Tracey Devon 25 B8
Newton under Roseberry Redcar/Clevel'd 225 C11
Newton Underwood Northum 252 F5
Newton upon Derwent ER Yorks 207 D10
Newton Valence Hants 49 G8
Newton Wood Gtr Man 184 B6
Newtonairds Dumf/Gal 247 G9
Newtongrange Midloth 270 C6
Newtongrange Midloth 270 C6
Newtonhill Aberds 293 D11
Newtonhill H'land 300 E5
Newtonia Ches 167 B11
Newton-in-St. Martin Cornw'l 2 E6
Newton-le-Willows Mersey 183 B9
Newton-le-Willows N Yorks 214 B4
Newtonmill Angus 293 G8
Newtonmore H'land 291 D9
Newton-on-Ouse N Yorks 206 B6
Newton-on-Rawcliffe N Yorks 226 G6
Newton-on-the-Moor Northum 252 B5
Newton-with-Scales Lancs 202 G4
Newtown Arg/Bute 284 G4
Newtown Bl Gwent 77 D11
Newtown Bridg 58 C2
Newtown Bucks 85 E7
Newtown Cambs 122 C4
Newtown Cambs 121 D11
Newtown Caerph 78 G2
Newtown Ches 167 F10
Newtown Ches 183 F8
Newtown Ches 184 E6
Newtown Cumb 229 B7
Newtown Cumb 239 F9
Newtown Cumb 230 G6
Newtown Cumb 240 E2
Newtown Cornw'l 11 F11
Newtown Cornw'l 2 D3
Newtown Cornw'l 6 E2
Newtown Derby 185 E7
Newtown Dorset 29 G7
Newtown Devon 15 B7
Newtown Devon 26 B3
Newtown Glos 79 E11
Newtown Gtr Man 195 G9
Newtown Gtr Man 194 F5
Newtown Hants 32 C4
Newtown Hants 49 G10
Newtown Hants 64 G3
Newtown Hants 32 E3
Newtown Hants 33 D8
Newtown Hants 33 F7
Newtown Hants 33 E10
Newtown Heref'd 115 F9
Newtown Heref'd 98 C2
Newtown Heref'd 97 E10
Newtown H'land 290 C5
Newtown I/Man 192 E4
Newtown I/Wight 20 C4
Newtown Mersey 183 B7
Newtown Norfolk 143 B10
Newtown Northum 264 D2
Newtown Northum 263 C11
Newtown Oxon 65 C9
Newtown Poole 18 C6
Newtown Rh Cyn Taff 77 F9
Newtown Shrops 149 E8
Newtown Shrops 149 C9
Newtown Som'set 28 E3
Newtown Som'set 43 F9
Newtown Som'set 43 D10
Newtown Som'set 28 B6
Newtown S'thampton 33 E7
Newtown Staffs 133 C9
Newtown Staffs 169 C9
Newtown Warwick 134 F5
Newtown Wilts 63 G10
Newtown Wilts 30 B6
Newtown Worcs 117 F7
Newtown Worcs 116 F5
Newtown Worcs 117 E7
Newtown = Y Drenewydd Powys 130 E2
Newtown Common Hants 64 G3
Newtown Linford Leics 153 G10
Newtown Unthank Leics 135 C9
Newtyle Angus 286 C6
Newyears Green London 66 B5
Nextend Heref'd 114 F6
Neyland Pembs 73 E7
Niarbyl I/Man 192 E3
Nib Heath Shrops 149 F8
Nibley Glos 79 D11
Nibley S Glos 61 C7
Nibley Green Glos 80 F2
Nibon Shetl'd 314 F5
Nicholashayne Devon 27 D10
Nicholaston Swan 56 D4
Nidd N Yorks 214 G6
Niddrie C/Edinb 280 G6
Nigg Aberd C 293 C11
Nigg H'land 301 B8
Nigg Ferry H'land 301 C7
Nimble Nook Gtr Man 196 G2
Nimmer Som'set 28 E4
Nine Ashes Essex 87 E9
Nine Elms London 67 D9
Nine Elms Swindon 62 B6
Nine Mile Burn Scot Borders 270 D3
Nine Wells Pembs 90 G5
Ninebanks Northum 241 G7
Nineveh N Yorks 215 E10
Nineveh Worcs 116 E2
Ninewells Glos 79 C9
Ninfield E Sussex 38 E2
Ningwood I/Wight 20 D4
Ningwood Common I/Wight 20 D3
Ninnes Bridge Cornw'l 2 B2
Ninnis Cornw'l 4 G4
Nisbet Scot Borders 262 D5
Nisbet E Loth 271 B9
Nisthouse Orkney 312 G4
Nisthouse Shetl'd 315 G7
Niton I/Wight 20 F6
Nitshill Glasg C 267 C10
Niwbwrch = Newborough Angl 162 B6
No Man's Green Shrops 132 G5
No Man's Heath Ches 167 F8
No Man's Heath Warwick 134 B5
No Man's Land Hants 33 B8
Noah's Green Worcs 117 E10
Noak Hill London 87 G8
Nob End Gtr Man 195 F9
Nobland Green Herts 86 B6
Noblehill Dumf/Gal 238 B1
Noblethorpe S Yorks 197 G9
Nobold Shrops 149 G9
Nobottle Northants 120 E3
Nobs Crook Hants 33 C7
Nocton Lincs 173 C9
Noctorum Mersey 182 D3
Noel Park London 86 G4
Nog Tow Lancs 202 G6
Nogdam End Norfolk 143 C8
Noke Oxon 83 C8
Noke Street Medway 69 E8
Nolton Pembs 72 B5
Nolton Haven Pembs 72 B5
Nomansland Devon 26 E4
Nomansland Herts 85 C11
Nomansland Wilts 32 D2
Noneley Shrops 149 D9
Noness Shetl'd 315 L6
Nonikiln H'land 300 B6
Nonington Kent 55 C9
Nook Cumb 211 C10
Nook Lancs 202 E5
Noon Nick W Yorks 205 F8
Noonsbrough Shetl'd 315 H4
Noranside Angus 292 G6
Norbiton London 67 F7
Norbiton Common London 67 F7
Norbreck Blackp'l 202 E2
Norbridge Heref'd 98 B4
Norbury Ches 167 F9
Norbury Derby 169 G10
Norbury London 67 F10
Norbury Shrops 131 E7
Norbury Staffs 150 E5
Norbury Common Ches 167 F9
Norbury Junction Staffs 150 E5
Norbury Moor Gtr Man 184 D6
Norby N Yorks 215 C8
Norby Shetl'd 315 H3
Norchard Worcs 116 D6
Norcott Brook Ches 183 E10
Norcross Blackp'l 202 E2
Nordelph Norfolk 139 C11
Norden Dorset 18 E4
Norden Gtr Man 195 E11
Nordley Shrops 132 D3
Nore Marsh Wilts 62 C5
Norham Northum 273 F8
Nork Surrey 51 B8
Norland Town W Yorks 196 C5
Norley Ches 183 G9
Norley Devon 25 G7
Norley Gtr Man 194 F4
Norleywood Hants 20 B3
Norlington E Sussex 36 E6
Normacot Stoke 168 G6
Norman Corner NE Lincs 201 G9
Norman Cross Cambs 138 E3
Normanby N Lincs 199 D11
Normanby N Yorks 216 C4
Normanby Redcar/Clevel'd 225 B11
Normanby by Stow Lincs 188 E5
Normanby le Wold Lincs 189 B10
Normanby-by-Spital Lincs 189 D8
Normandy Surrey 50 C2
Norman's Bay E Sussex 23 D11
Norman's Green Devon 27 G9
Normanston Suffolk 143 E10
Normanton Derby C 152 C6
Normanton Leics 172 G4
Normanton Lincs 173 F6
Normanton Notts 172 E2
Normanton Wilts 47 E6
Normanton W Yorks 197 C11
Normanton le Heath Leics 153 G7
Normanton on Soar Notts 153 E10
Normanton on the Wolds Notts 154 C2
Normanton on Trent Notts 172 B3
Normanton Spring S Yorks 186 E6
Normos Blackp'l 202 F2
Norney Notts 187 D11
Norney Surrey 50 E2
Norridge Common Wilts 45 D10
Norrington Common Wilts 61 G11
Norris Green Cornw'l 7 B8
Norris Green Mersey 182 C5
Norris Hill Leics 152 F6
Norris's Green Wokingham 65 E9
Norristhorpe W Yorks 197 C8
Norseman Orkney 312 G4
North America ER Yorks 208 G2
North Anston S Yorks 187 E8
North Aston Oxon 101 F9
North Ayre Shetl'd 314 F6
North Baddesley Hants 32 D5
North Baddesley Hants 32 D5
North Ballachulish H'land 290 G2
North Barrow Som'set 29 B10
North Barsham Norfolk 159 C8
North Beach Suffolk 143 E10
North Benfleet Essex 69 B9
North Bersted W Sussex 34 G6
North Berwick E Loth 281 D11
North Bitchburn Durham 233 E9
North Blyth Northum 253 G8
North Boarhunt Hants 33 E10
North Bockhampton Dorset 19 B9
North Bovey Devon 13 E10
North Bowood Dorset 16 B4
North Bradley Wilts 45 C11
North Brentor Devon 12 E5
North Brewham Som'set 45 F8
North Brook End Cambs 104 C5
North Broomage Falk 279 E7
North Buckland Devon 40 E3
North Burlingham Norfolk 161 G7
North Cadbury Som'set 29 B10
North Cairn Dumf/Gal 236 B1
North Carlton Lincs 188 F6
North Carlton Notts 187 E9
North Carrine Arg/Bute 255 G7
North Cave ER Yorks 208 G3
North Cerney Glos 81 D8
North Chailey E Sussex 36 C5
North Charford Hants 31 D11
North Charlton Northum 264 E5
North Cheam London 67 F8
North Cheriton Som'set 29 B11
North Chideock Dorset 16 C4
North Choppingham Northum 252 F6
North Cliffe ER Yorks 208 F3
North Clifton Notts 188 G4
North Close Durham 233 E11
North Cockerington Lincs 190 C5
North Coker Som'set 29 E8
North Collafirth Shetl'd 314 E5
North Common Suffolk 125 B9
North Common S Glos 61 E7
North Connel Arg/Bute 289 F11
North Cornelly Bridg 57 E10
North Corner S Glos 61 C7
North Corriegills N Ayrs 256 C2
North Corry H'land 289 D10
North Cotes Lincs 201 G10
North Country Cornw'l 4 G3
North Cove Suffolk 143 F9
North Cowton N Yorks 224 E5
North Craigo Angus 293 G8
North Crawley M/Keynes 103 C8
North Cray London 68 E3
North Creake Norfolk 159 B7
North Curry Som'set 28 B4
North Dalton ER Yorks 208 C4
North Darley Cornw'l 11 G11
North Dawn Orkney 313 H5
North Deighton N Yorks 206 C3
North Denes Norfolk 161 G10
North Dronley Angus 287 D7
North Drumachter Lodge H'land 291 F8
North Duffield N Yorks 207 F9
North Elham Kent 55 E7
North Elkington Lincs 190 C3
North Elmham Norfolk 159 E9
North Elmsall W Yorks 198 E3
North End Beds 103 B9
North End Bath/NE Som'set 60 G6
North End Bucks 102 F3
North End Bucks 102 F6
North End Cumb 239 F8
North End Dorset 30 B4
North End Durham 233 C11
North End E Sussex 36 E6
North End Essex 105 D10
North End Essex 87 B11
North End Essex 106 D5
North End ER Yorks 209 G11
North End ER Yorks 209 C9
North End ER Yorks 209 E9
North End Hants 33 B9
North End Hants 31 D10
North End Hants 64 G2
North End Leics 153 F11
North End Lincs 174 G2
North End Lincs 190 D6
North End Lincs 189 B8
North End Lincs 201 G10
North End Lincs 190 C5
North End London 68 D4
North End London 67 B9
North End Mersey 193 G10
North End Norfolk 141 E10
North End N Lincs 200 C6
North End N Som'set 60 F2
North End Northum 252 C4
North End Portsm'th 33 G11
North End Som'set 28 B3
North End Wilts 81 G8
North End W Sussex 35 F10
North End W Sussex 51 F11
North Erradale H'land 307 L2
North Evington Leics C 136 C2
North Fambridge Essex 88 F5
North Fearns H'land 295 B7
North Featherstone W Yorks 198 C2
North Feorline N Ayrs 255 E10
North Ferriby ER Yorks 200 B3
North Finchley London 86 G3
North Flobbets Aberds 303 F7
North Frodingham ER Yorks 209 C7
North Gluss Shetl'd 314 F5
North Gorley Hants 31 E11
North Green Norfolk 141 B10
North Green Norfolk 142 F4
North Green Suffolk 126 B6
North Green Suffolk 126 E6
North Green Suffolk 127 D7
North Greetwell Lincs 189 G8
North Grimston N Yorks 216 F6
North Gyle C/Edinb 280 G3
North Halley Orkney 313 H6
North Halling Medway 69 F8
North Harby Notts 188 G5
North Hayling Hants 34 G2
North Hazelrigg Northum 264 C3
North Heasley Devon 41 G8
North Heath W Berks 64 E3
North Heath W Sussex 35 C9
North Hill Cornw'l 11 F11
North Hill Dorset 17 C8
North Hillingdon London 66 C5
North Hinksey Oxon 83 D7
North Holmwood Surrey 51 D7
North Houghton Hants 47 G10
North Ho Shetl'd 315 J5
North Huish Devon 8 D4
North Hykeham Lincs 172 B6
North Hylton Tyne/Wear 243 F9
North Johnston Pembs 72 C6
North Kelsey Lincs 200 G4
North Kelsey Moor Lincs 200 G5
North Kessock H'land 300 E6
North Killingholme N Lincs 200 D6
North Kilvington N Yorks 215 B8
North Kilworth Leics 136 G2
North Kingston Hants 31 G11
North Kirkton Aberds 303 D11
North Kiscadale N Ayrs 256 D2
North Kyme Lincs 173 E11
North Laggan H'land 290 D4
North Lancing W Sussex 35 F11
North Leazes Durham 233 F9
North Lee Bucks 84 D4
North Lees N Yorks 214 E5
North Leigh Kent 54 D6
North Leigh Oxon 82 C5
North Leverton with Habblesthorpe Notts 188 E3
North Littleton Worcs 99 B11
North Lobb Devon 40 F3
North Looe Surrey 67 G8
North Lopham Norfolk 141 G10
North Luffenham Rutl'd 137 C8
North Marden W Sussex 34 D4
North Marston Bucks 102 G5
North Middleton Midloth 271 D7
North Middleton Northum 264 E2
North Millbrex Aberds 303 E8
North Molton Devon 26 B2
North Moreton Oxon 64 B5
North Morte Devon 40 D3
North Mosstown Aberds 303 D10
North Motherwell N Lanarks 268 D4
North Moulsecoomb Brighton/Hove 36 F4
North Mundham W Sussex 34 G5
North Muskham Notts 172 D3
North Newbald ER Yorks 208 F4
North Newington Oxon 101 D8
North Newnton Wilts 47 B6
North Newton Som'set 43 G9
North Nibley Glos 80 F2
North Norfolk Railway, Sheringham Norfolk 177 E10
North Oakley Hants 48 C4
North Ockendon London 68 C5
North Ormesby Middlesbro 225 B10
North Ormsby Lincs 190 C3
North Otterington N Yorks 215 B7
North Owersby Lincs 189 C9
North Perrott Som'set 29 F7
North Petherton Som'set 43 G9
North Petherwin Cornw'l 11 D11
North Pickenham Norfolk 141 B7
North Piddle Worcs 117 G9
North Pool Devon 8 G5
North Poorton Dorset 16 B6
North Port Arg/Bute 284 E4
North Poulner Hants 31 F11
North Quarme Som'set 42 F2
North Queensferry Fife 280 E2
North Radworthy Devon 41 G9
North Rauceby Lincs 173 F8
North Reddish Gtr Man 184 C5
North Reston Lincs 190 E5
North Riddingwood Dumf/Gal 247 F11
North Rigton N Yorks 205 D11
North Ripley Hants 19 B9
North Rode Ches 168 B5
North Roe Shetl'd 314 E5
North Ronaldsay Airport Orkney 312 C8
North Row Cumb 229 E10
North Runcton Norfolk 158 F2
North Saltwick Northum 252 G5
North Sandwick Shetl'd 314 D7
North Scale Cumb 210 F3
North Scarle Lincs 172 B5
North Seaton Northum 253 F7
North Sheen London 67 D7
North Shian Arg/Bute 289 E11
North Shields Tyne/Wear 243 D9
North Shoebury Southend 70 B2
North Shore Blackp'l 202 F2
North Side Cumb 228 F6
North Side Peterbro 138 D5
North Skelmanae Aberds 303 D9
North Skelton Redcar/Clevel'd 226 B3
North Somercoates Lincs 190 B6
North Stainley N Yorks 214 D5
North Stainmore Cumb 222 B6
North Stifford Thurr'k 68 C6
North Stoke Bath/NE Som'set 61 F8
North Stoke Oxon 64 B6
North Stoke W Sussex 35 E8
North Street Hants 48 G6
North Street Hants 31 D11
North Street Kent 54 B4
North Street Medway 69 E10
North Street W Berks 64 E6
North Sunderland Northum 264 C6
North Tamerton Cornw'l 12 B2
North Tawton Devon 25 G11
North Thoresby Lincs 190 B3
North Tidworth Wilts 47 D8
North Togston Northum 252 C6
North Town Devon 25 F8
North Town Som'set 44 E5
North Town Som'set 29 B10
North Town Surrey 49 C11
North Town Windsor 65 C11
North Tuddenham Norfolk 159 G10
North Walbottle Tyne/Wear 242 D5
North Walsham Norfolk 160 D5
North Waltham Hants 48 D5
North Warnborough Hants 49 C8
North Water Bridge Angus 293 G8
North Watten H'land 310 D6
North Weald Bassett Essex 87 E8
North Weirs Hants 32 G3
North Wembley London 67 B7
North Weston N Som'set 60 D3
North Wheatley Notts 188 D3
North Whilborough Devon 9 B7
North Whiteley Moray 302 E4
North Wick Bath/NE Som'set 60 F5
North Widcombe Bath/NE Som'set 44 B5
North Willingham Lincs 189 D10
North Wingfield Derby 170 C6
North Witham Lincs 155 E8
North Woods S Glos 60 C6
North Wootton Dorset 29 E11
North Wootton Norfolk 158 E2
North Wootton Som'set 44 E5
North Wraxall Wilts 61 D10
North Wroughton Swindon 62 C6
North Yorkshire Moors Railway, Pickering N Yorks 216 B6
Northacre Norfolk 141 D9
Northall Beds 103 G9
Northall Green Norfolk 159 G9
Northallerton N Yorks 225 G7
Northam Devon 24 B6
Northam S'thampton 32 E6
Northampton Northants 120 E5
Northaw Herts 86 E3
Northay Som'set 28 E3
Northbeck Lincs 173 G9
Northborough Peterbro 138 B3
Northbourne Bournem'th 19 B7
Northbourne Kent 55 C10
Northbridge Street E Sussex 38 C2
Northbrook Hants 48 F4
Northbrook Oxon 101 G9
Northchapel W Sussex 35 B7
Northchurch Herts 85 D7
Northcott Devon 27 E9
Northcott Hamlet Devon 12 C2
Northcourt Oxon 83 F8
Northdown Kent 71 F11
Northdyke Orkney 312 F3
Northedge Derby 170 C5
Northend Bath/NE Som'set 61 F9
Northend Bucks 84 G2
Northend Essex 89 E7
Northend Warwick 119 G7
Northend Woods Bucks 66 B2
Northenden Gtr Man 184 C4
Northern Moor Gtr Man 184 C4
Northfield Aberd C 293 C11
Northfield Scot Borders 273 B8
Northfield ER Yorks 200 B4
Northfield H'land 301 B7
Northfield Som'set 43 F9
Northfield Som'set 29 B7
Northfield W Midlands 117 B10
Northfields Lincs 137 B10
Northfleet Kent 68 E6
Northfleet Green Kent 68 E6
Northgate Lincs 156 D3
Northgate Som'set 27 B9
Northgate W Sussex 51 F9
Northhouse Scot Borders 249 B10
Northiam E Sussex 38 C4
Northill Beds 104 B2
Northington Glos 80 D2
Northington Hants 48 F5
Northlands Lincs 174 E4
Northlea Durham 243 G10
Northleach Glos 81 C10
Northleigh Devon 15 B9
Northlew Devon 12 B6
Northmoor Oxon 82 E6
Northmoor Corner Som'set 43 G10
Northmoor Green Som'set 43 G10
Northmostown Devon 15 D7
Northmuir Angus 287 B7
Northney Hants 34 G2
Northolt London 66 C6
Northop = Llan-eurgain Flints 166 B2
Northop Hall Flints 166 B3
Northorpe Lincs 156 B4
Northorpe Lincs 188 B5
Northorpe Lincs 155 F11
Northorpe W Yorks 197 C8
Northover Som'set 44 F3
Northover Som'set 29 C8
Northowram W Yorks 196 B6
Northpark Arg/Bute 275 G11
Northport Dorset 18 D4
Northpunds Shetl'd 315 L6
Northrepps Norfolk 160 B4
Northside Aberds 303 D8
Northside Orkney 312 F3
Northton Aberds 293 C9
Northtown Orkney 313 J5
Northtown Shetl'd 315 M5
Northumberland Heath London 68 D4
Northumbria Craft Centre, Morpeth Northum 252 F5
Northward I/Scilly 1 F3
Northway Glos 99 E8
Northway Som'set 27 B10
Northway Swan 56 D5
Northwich Ches 183 G11
Northwick S Glos 60 B5
Northwick Som'set 43 D11
Northwick Worcs 116 F6
Northwold Norfolk 140 D5
Northwood Derby 170 C3
Northwood Glos 80 B2
Northwood I/Wight 20 C5
Northwood Kent 71 F11
Northwood London 85 G9
Northwood Mersey 182 B6
Northwood Shrops 149 C9
Northwood Stoke 168 F5
Northwood Staffs 168 G5
Northwood Green Glos 80 B2
Northwood Hills London 85 G9
Norton Devon 9 E7
Norton E Sussex 37 G7
Norton Glos 99 G7
Norton Halton 183 E9
Norton Herts 104 D4
Norton I/Wight 20 D2
Norton Northants 120 E2
Norton N Som'set 59 G10
Norton Notts 187 G9
Norton Powys 114 D6
Norton Shrops 131 G9
Norton Shrops 131 B11
Norton Shrops 132 C4
Norton Suffolk 125 D9
Norton Stockton 234 G4
Norton S Yorks 198 D4
Norton S Yorks 186 E5
Norton Swan 56 D6
Norton Wilts 61 C11
Norton Worcs 117 G7
Norton Worcs 99 B10
Norton W Sussex 22 D5
Norton W Sussex 34 F6
Norton Ash Kent 70 G3
Norton Bavant Wilts 46 E2
Norton Bridge Staffs 151 C7
Norton Bury Herts 104 D4
Norton Canes Staffs 133 B10
Norton Canon Heref'd 97 B7
Norton Corner Norfolk 159 D11
Norton Disney Lincs 172 D5
Norton East Staffs 133 B10
Norton Ferris Wilts 45 F9
Norton Fitzwarren Som'set 27 B11
Norton Green Herts 104 G4
Norton Green I/Wight 20 D2
Norton Green Kent 69 G11
Norton Green Stoke 168 E5
Norton Green W Midlands 118 C3
Norton Hawkfield Bath/NE Som'set 60 G5
Norton Heath Essex 87 E10
Norton Hill Bath/NE Som'set 45 C7
Norton in Hales Shrops 150 B4
Norton Juxta Twycross Leics 134 B6
Norton Lindsey Warwick 118 E4
Norton Little Green Suffolk 125 D9
Norton Malreward Bath/NE Som'set 60 F6
Norton Mandeville Essex 87 E9
Norton St. Philip Som'set 45 B9
Norton sub Hamdon Som'set 29 D7
Norton Wood Heref'd 97 B7
Norton Woodseats S Yorks 186 E5

Norton-in-the-Moors Stoke 168 E5
Norton-le-Clay N Yorks 215 E8
Norton-on-Derwent N Yorks 216 E6
Norwell Notts 172 C3
Norwell Woodhouse Notts 172 C2
Norwich Norfolk 142 B4
Norwich Castle Museum Norfolk 142 B4
Norwich Cathedral Norfolk 142 B4
Norwich International Airport Norfolk 160 G4
Norwick Shetl'd 314 B8
Norwood Derby 187 E7
Norwood End Essex 87 D9
Norwood Green London 66 D6
Norwood Green W Yorks 196 B6
Norwood Hill Surrey 51 E8
Norwood Park Som'set 44 F4
Norwoodside Cambs 139 D8
Noseley Leics 136 D4
Noss H'land 310 D7
Noss Shetl'd 315 M5
Noss Mayo Devon 7 F11
Nosterfield N Yorks 214 C5
Nosterfield End Cambs 106 C2
Nostie H'land 295 C10
Notgrove Glos 100 G2
Nothe Fort, Weymouth Dorset 17 F9
Nottage Bridg 57 F10
Notter Cornw'l 7 C7
Notting Hill London 67 C8
Nottingham Nott'ham 171 G9
Nottingham Castle Museum Nott'ham 153 B11
Nottingham East Midlands Airport Leics 153 D8
Nottingham Racecourse Nott'ham 153 B11
Nottington Dorset 17 E9
Notton Wilts 62 F2
Notton W Yorks 197 E10
Nounsley Essex 88 C3
Noutard's Green Worcs 116 D6
Nova Scotia Ches 167 B10
Novar House H'land 300 C6
Novers Park Bristol 60 F5
Noverton Glos 99 G9
Nowton Suffolk 125 E7
Nox Shrops 149 G8
Noyadd Trefawr Ceredig'n 92 B5
Nuffield Oxon 65 B7
Nun Hills Lancs 195 C11
Nun Monkton N Yorks 206 B6
Nunburnholme ER Yorks 208 D2
Nuncargate Notts 171 E8
Nunclose Cumb 230 B5
Nuneaton Warwick 135 E7
Nuneham Courtenay Oxon 83 F8
Nuney Green Oxon 65 D7
Nunhead London 67 E11
Nunney Som'set 45 D8
Nunney Catch Som'set 45 D8
Nunnington N Yorks 216 D3
Nunnington Park Som'set 27 B9
Nunsthorpe NE Lincs 201 F9
Nunthorpe C/York 207 D7
Nunthorpe Middlesbro 225 C10
Nunton Wilts 31 B11
Nunwick N Yorks 214 E6
Nup End Bucks 84 B5
Nup End Herts 86 B2
Nupdown S Glos 79 F10
Nupend Glos 80 D3
Nupend Glos 80 F4
Nuptown Brackn'l 65 E11
Nursling Hants 32 D5
Nursted Hants 34 C3
Nursteed Wilts 62 G4
Nurston V/Glam 58 F5
Nut Grove Mersey 183 C7
Nutbourne W Sussex 34 F3
Nutbourne W Sussex 35 D9
Nutbourne Common W Sussex 35 D9
Nutburn Hants 32 D5
Nutfield Surrey 51 C10
Nuthall Notts 171 F8
Nuthampstead Herts 105 E8
Nuthurst Warwick 118 C2
Nuthurst W Sussex 35 B11
Nutley E Sussex 36 B6
Nutley Hants 48 E6
Nuttall Gtr Man 195 D9
Nutwell S Yorks 198 G6
Nybster H'land 310 C7
Nyetimber W Sussex 22 D5
Nyewood W Sussex 34 C4
Nyland Som'set 44 C3
Nymans Garden, Crawley W Sussex 36 B3
Nymet Rowland Devon 26 F2
Nymet Tracy Devon 26 G2
Nympsfield Glos 80 E4
Nynehead Som'set 27 C10
Nythe Som'set 44 G2
Nythe Swindon 63 B7
Nyton W Sussex 34 F6

O

Oad Street Kent 69 G11
Oadby Leics 136 C2
Oak Bank Gtr Man 195 F10
Oak Hill Suffolk 109 B7
Oak Hill Stoke 168 G5
Oak Tree Durham 225 C7
Oakamoor Staffs 169 G9
Oakbank W Loth 269 B11
Oakdale Caerph 77 F11
Oakdale Poole 18 C6
Oake Som'set 27 B11
Oake Green Som'set 27 B11
Oaken Staffs 133 C7
Oakenclough Lancs 202 D6
Oakengates Telford 150 G4
Oakenholt Flints 182 G3
Oakenshaw Durham 233 D9
Oakenshaw Lancs 203 G11
Oakenshaw Worcs 117 D10
Oakenshaw W Yorks 197 B7
Oakerthorpe Derby 170 E5
Oakes W Yorks 196 D6
Oakfield I/Wight 21 C7
Oakfield Torf 78 G3
Oakford Ceredig'n 111 F9
Oakford Devon 26 C6
Oakfordbridge Devon 26 C6
Oakgrove Ches 168 B6
Oakhall Green Worcs 116 E6
Oakham Rutl'd 137 B7
Oakham W Midlands 133 F9
Oakhanger Hants 49 F9
Oakhill Som'set 44 D6
Oakhill W Sussex 51 G7
Oakhurst Kent 52 C5
Oakington Cambs 123 E8
Oaklands Flints 182 G2
Oaklands Herts 86 B2
Oaklands Powys 113 G10
Oakle Street Glos 80 B3
Oakleigh Park London 86 G3
Oakley Beds 121 G10
Oakley Bucks 83 C10
Oakley Fife 279 D10
Oakley Glos 99 G9
Oakley Hants 48 C5
Oakley Oxon 84 E2
Oakley Poole 18 B6
Oakley Suffolk 126 B3
Oakley Staffs 133 B7
Oakley Green Windsor 66 D2
Oakley Park Powys 129 F9
Oakmere Ches 167 B9
Oakridge Glos 80 E6
Oakridge Hants 48 C6
Oaks Shrops 131 C8
Oaks Green Derby 152 C3
Oaks in Charnwood Leics 153 F9
Oaksey Wilts 81 G7
Oakshaw Ford Cumb 240 B2
Oakshott Hants 34 B2
Oakthorpe Leics 152 G6
Oakwell W Yorks 197 B8
Oakwood Derby C 153 B7
Oakwood London 86 F3
Oakwood Northum 241 D10
Oakwood Warrington 183 B10
Oakwood W Yorks 206 F2
Oakwood Adventure Park, Narberth Pembs 73 C9
Oakwoodhill Surrey 50 F6
Oakworth W Yorks 204 F6
Oape H'land 309 J4
Oare Kent 70 G4
Oare Som'set 41 D10
Oare W Berks 64 E4
Oare Wilts 63 G7
Oareford Som'set 41 D10
Oasby Lincs 155 B10
Oat Hill Ches 167 F7
Oatfield Glos 80 D3
Oath Som'set 28 B5
Oathill Dorset 28 F6
Oathlaw Angus 287 B8
Oatlands Glasg C 267 C11
Oatlands N Yorks 206 C2
Oatlands Park Surrey 66 F5
Oban Arg/Bute 289 G10
Oban H'land 295 G10
Oban W Isles 305 H3
Oborne Dorset 29 D11
Obridge Som'set 28 B2
Obthorpe Lincs 155 F11
Occold Suffolk 126 C3
Ocean Beach Amusement Park, Rhyl Denbs 181 E7
Ochiltree E Ayrs 258 E2
Ochrwyth Caerph 59 B8
Ochr-y-foel Denbs 181 F9
Ochtermuthill Perth/Kinr 286 F2
Ochtertyre Perth/Kinr 286 E2
Ochtow H'land 309 J4
Ockbrook Derby 153 B8
Ocker Hill W Midlands 133 E9
Ockeridge Worcs 116 E5
Ockford Ridge Surrey 50 E3
Ockham Surrey 50 B5
Ockle H'land 289 B7
Ockley Kent 53 G9
Ockley Surrey 50 F6
Ocle Pychard Heref'd 97 B11
Octon ER Yorks 217 F10
Odcombe Som'set 29 D8
Odd Down Bath/NE Som'set 61 G8
Oddendale Cumb 221 C11
Odder Lincs 188 F6
Oddingley Worcs 117 F8
Oddington Oxon 83 C9
Odell Beds 121 F9
Odgen Gtr Man 196 E3
Odham Devon 25 G7
Odie Orkney 312 F7
Odiham Hants 49 C8
Odsal W Yorks 197 B7
Odsey Cambs 104 D5
Odstock Wilts 31 B10
Odstone Leics 135 B7
Offchurch Warwick 119 D7
Offenham Worcs 99 B11
Offenham Cross Worcs 99 B11
Offerton Gtr Man 184 D6
Offerton Tyne/Wear 243 F8
Offerton Green Gtr Man 184 D6
Offham E Sussex 36 E5
Offham Kent 53 B7
Offham W Sussex 35 F8
Offley Chase Herts 104 G2
Offley Hoo Herts 104 F3
Offleyhay Staffs 150 D5
Offleymarsh Staffs 150 D5
Offleyrock Staffs 150 D5
Offmore Farm Worcs 116 B6
Offord Cluny Cambs 122 D4
Offord D'Arcy Cambs 122 D4
Offton Suffolk 107 B11
Offwell Devon 15 B9
Ogbourne Maizey Wilts 63 E7
Ogbourne St. Andrew Wilts 63 E7
Ogbourne St. George Wilts 63 E7
Ogden W Yorks 205 G7
Ogdens Hants 31 E11
Ogden's Purlieu Hants 31 E11
Ogil Angus 292 G6
Ogle Northum 242 B4
Ogmore V/Glam 57 F11
Ogmore Vale Bridg 58 B2
Ogmore-by-Sea = Aberogwr V/Glam 57 G11
Okeford Fitzpaine Dorset 30 E4
Okehampton Devon 13 C7
Okehampton Camp Devon 13 C7
Oker Derby 170 C3
Okle Green Glos 98 F5
Okraquoy Shetl'd 315 K6
Olchfa Swan 75 G10
Old Northants 120 C5
Old Aberdeen Aberd C 293 C11
Old Alresford Hants 48 G5
Old Arley Warwick 134 E5
Old Basford Notts 171 G9
Old Basing Hants 49 C7
Old Belses Scot Borders 262 D3
Old Bewick Northum 264 E3
Old Blacksmith's Shop Centre, Gretna Green Dumf/Gal 239 D8
Old Blair Perth/Kinr 291 G10
Old Bolingbroke Lincs 174 B5
Old Boston Mersey 183 B9
Old Bramhope W Yorks 205 E10
Old Brampton Derby 186 G4
Old Bridge of Tilt Perth/Kinr 291 G10
Old Bridge of Urr Dumf/Gal 237 C9
Old Buckenham Norfolk 141 E11
Old Burdon Tyne/Wear 243 G9
Old Burghclere Hants 48 B3
Old Byland N Yorks 215 B10
Old Cambus Scot Borders 272 B6
Old Carlisle Cumb 229 B11
Old Cassop Durham 234 D2
Old Castleton Scot Borders 250 E2
Old Catton Norfolk 160 G4
Old Chalford Oxon 100 F6
Old Church Stoke Powys 130 D5
Old Clee NE Lincs 201 F9
Old Cleeve Som'set 42 E4
Old Clipstone Notts 171 C9
Old Colwyn Conwy 180 F5
Old Corry H'land 295 C8
Old Coulsdon London 51 B10
Old Craig Aberds 303 G9
Old Craig Angus 292 G4
Old Craighall E Loth 280 G6
Old Crombie Aberds 302 D5
Old Cullen Moray 302 C5
Old Dailly S Ayrs 244 D6
Old Dalby Leics 154 E3
Old Dam Derby 185 F10
Old Deer Aberds 303 E9
Old Denaby S Yorks 187 B7
Old Dilton Wilts 45 D11
Old Ditch Som'set 44 D4
Old Dolphin W Yorks 205 G8
Old Down S Glos 60 B6
Old Down Som'set 44 C6
Old Duffus Moray 301 C11
Old Edlington S Yorks 187 B8
Old Eldon Durham 233 F10
Old Ellerby ER Yorks 209 F9
Old Fallings W Midlands 133 C8
Old Farm Park M/Keynes 103 D8
Old Felixstowe Suffolk 108 D6
Old Field Shrops 115 B9
Old Field Carr Lancs 202 F3
Old Fletton Peterbro 138 D3
Old Fold Tyne/Wear 243 E7
Old Ford London 67 C11
Old Forge Heref'd 79 B9
Old Furnace Heref'd 97 G9
Old Furnace Torf 78 E3
Old Gate Lincs 157 E8
Old Glossop Derby 185 C8
Old Goginan Ceredig'n 128 G3
Old Goole ER Yorks 199 C8
Old Gore Heref'd 98 F2
Old Graitney Dumf/Gal 239 D8
Old Grimsbury Oxon 101 C9
Old Grimsby I/Scilly 1 F3
Old Hall Powys 129 G8
Old Hall Green Herts 105 G7
Old Hall Street Norfolk 160 C6
Old Hatfield Herts 86 D2
Old Heath Essex 107 G10
Old Heathfield E Sussex 37 C9
Old Hill W Midlands 133 F9
Old House, Rochford Essex 88 G5
Old Hunstanton Norfolk 175 G11
Old Hurst Cambs 122 B6
Old Hutton Cumb 211 B11
Old Hyton Cumb 210 B2
Old Kea Cornw'l 4 G6
Old Kilpatrick W Dunb 277 G9
Old Kinnernie Aberds 293 C9
Old Knebworth Herts 104 G4
Old Langho Lancs 203 F10
Old Laxey I/Man 192 D5
Old Leake Lincs 174 E6
Old Lindley W Yorks 196 D5
Old Linslade Beds 103 F8
Old Llanberis = Nant Peris Gwyn 163 D9
Old Malden London 67 F8
Old Malton N Yorks 216 E5
Old Micklefield W Yorks 206 G4
Old Milton Hants 19 C10
Old Milverton Warwick 118 D5
Old Monkland N Lanarks 268 C4
Old Netley Hants 33 F7
Old Newton Suffolk 125 E11
Old Oak Common London 67 C8
Old Passage S Glos 60 B5
Old Pentland Midloth 270 B5
Old Philipstoun W Loth 279 F11
Old Quarrington Durham 234 D2
Old Radnor Powys 114 F5
Old Rattray Aberds 303 D10
Old Rayne Aberds 302 G6
Old Romney Kent 39 B8
Old Sarum, Salisbury Wilts 46 G6
Old Shirley S'thampton 32 E5
Old Sodbury S Glos 61 C9
Old Somerby Lincs 155 C9
Old Stillington Stockton 234 G3
Old Stratford Northants 102 C5
Old Struan Perth/Kinr 291 G10
Old Swan Mersey 182 C5
Old Swarland Northum 252 C5
Old Swinford W Midlands 133 G9
Old Tame Gtr Man 196 F3
Old Tebay Cumb 222 D2
Old Thirsk N Yorks 215 C8
Old Toll S Ayrs 257 E9
Old Town C/Edinb 280 G5
Old Town Cumb 211 C11
Old Town Cumb 230 C5
Old Town E Sussex 23 F9
Old Town ER Yorks 218 F3
Old Town I/Scilly 1 G4
Old Town Northants 101 D11
Old Town Som'set 28 F4
Old Town S Yorks 197 F10
Old Town W Yorks 196 B3
Old Trafford Gtr Man 184 B4
Old Tree Kent 71 G8
Old Tupton Derby 170 B5
Old Warden Beds 104 C2
Old Weston Cambs 122 B2
Old Whittington Derby 186 G5
Old Wick H'land 310 D7
Old Windsor Windsor 66 E3
Old Wingate Durham 234 D3
Old Wives Lees Kent 54 C5
Old Woking Surrey 50 B4
Old Wolverton M/Keynes 102 C6
Old Woodbury Beds 122 G4
Old Woodhall Lincs 174 B2
Old Woodhouse Shrops 167 G9
Old Woods Shrops 149 E9
Old Woodstock Oxon 82 B6
Oldany H'land 306 F6
Oldberrow Warwick 118 D2
Oldborough Devon 26 F3
Oldbury Kent 52 B5
Oldbury Shrops 132 E4
Oldbury Warwick 134 E6
Oldbury W Midlands 133 F9
Oldbury Naite S Glos 79 G10
Oldbury on Severn S Glos 79 G10
Oldbury on the Hill Glos 61 B10
Oldcastle Bridg 58 D2
Oldcastle Monmouths 96 G6
Oldcastle Heath Ches 167 F7
Oldcotes Notts 187 E8
Oldcroft Glos 79 D10
Oldeamere Cambs 138 D6
Oldend Glos 80 D3
Oldfallow Staffs 151 G9
Oldfield Mersey 182 E3
Oldfield Shrops 132 F3
Oldfield Worcs 116 D6
Oldfield W Yorks 196 E6
Oldfield W Yorks 204 F6
Oldfield Brow Gtr Man 184 D2
Oldford Som'set 45 C9
Oldfurnace Staffs 169 G8
Oldhall Renf 267 B10
Oldhall Green Suffolk 125 F7
Oldhall Ho H'land 310 D6
Oldham Gtr Man 196 G2
Oldham Edge Gtr Man 196 F2
Oldhamstocks E Loth 282 G4
Oldland S Glos 61 E7
Oldland Common S Glos 61 E7
Oldmeldrum Aberds 303 G8
Oldmill Cornw'l 12 G3
Oldmixon N Som'set 43 B10
Oldpark Telford 132 B3
Oldridge Devon 14 B2
Oldshore Beg H'land 306 D6
Oldshoremore H'land 306 D7
Oldstead N Yorks 215 C10
Oldtown Aberds 293 C7
Oldtown Aberds 302 G5
Oldtown H'land 309 L5
Oldtown of Ord Aberds 302 D6
Oldwall Cumb 239 E11
Oldwalls Swan 75 G7
Oldway Swan 56 D5
Oldway Torbay 9 C7
Oldways End Devon 26 C5
Oldwhat Aberds 303 D8
Oldwich Lane W Midlands 118 C4
Olgrinmore H'land 310 D4
Oliver's Battery Hants 33 B7
Ollaberry Shetl'd 314 E5
Ollag W Isles 297 G3
Ollerbrook Booth Derby 185 E10
Ollerton Ches 184 F3
Ollerton Notts 171 B11
Ollerton Shrops 150 D3
Olmarch Ceredig'n 112 F2
Olmstead Green Cambs 106 C2
Olney M/Keynes 121 G7
Olrig Ho. H'land 310 C5
Olton W Midlands 134 G2
Olveston S Glos 60 B6
Ombersley Worcs 116 E6
Ompton Notts 171 B11
Omunsgarth Shetl'd 315 J5
Onchan I/Man 192 E4
Onecote Staffs 169 D8
Onehouse Suffolk 125 F10
Onen Monmouths 78 C6
Ongar Street Heref'd 115 D7
Ongley Kent 53 F10
Onibury Shrops 115 B9
Onich H'land 290 G2
Onllwyn Neath P Talb 76 C4
Onneley Staffs 168 G3
Onslow Village Surrey 50 D3
Onston Ches 183 G9
Onthank E Ayrs 267 G8
Onziebust Orkney 312 F5
Openshaw Gtr Man 184 C5
Openwoodgate Derby 170 F5
Opinan H'land 299 B7
Opinan H'land 307 K3
Orange Lane Scot Borders 272 G5
Orange Row Norfolk 157 E10
Orasaigh W Isles 305 G5
Orbiston N Lanarks 268 D4
Orbliston Moray 302 D3
Orbost H'land 298 E2
Orby Lincs 175 B7
Orchard Hill Devon 24 B6
Orchard Leigh Bucks 85 E7
Orchard Portman Som'set 28 C2
Orcheston Wilts 46 D5
Orcop Heref'd 97 F9
Orcop Hill Heref'd 97 F9
Ord H'land 295 D8
Ordale Shetl'd 314 C8
Ordhead Aberds 293 B8
Ordie Aberds 292 C6
Ordiequish Moray 302 D3
Ordiqhill Aberds 302 D5
Ordley Northum 241 F10
Ordsall Gtr Man 184 B4
Ordsall Notts 188 F2
Ore E Sussex 38 E4
Oreston Plym'th 7 E10
Oreton Shrops 132 G3
Orford Lincs 190 C2
Orford Suffolk 109 B8
Orford Warrington 183 C10
Organford Dorset 18 C4
Orgreave Staffs 152 F3
Oridge Street Glos 98 F5
Orleton Heref'd 115 D9
Orleton Worcs 116 D3
Orlingbury Northants 121 C7
Ormacleit W Isles 297 H3
Ormathwaite Cumb 229 F11
Ormesby Redcar/Clevel'd 225 B10
Ormesby St. Margaret Norfolk 161 G9
Ormesby St. Michael Norfolk 161 G9
Ormiclate Castle W Isles 297 H3
Ormidale Lodge Arg/Bute 275 F11
Ormiscaig H'land 307 K3
Ormiston E Loth 271 B8
Ormsaigbeg H'land 288 C6
Ormsaigmore H'land 288 C6
Ormsary Arg/Bute 275 F8
Ormsgill Cumb 210 E3
Ormskirk Lancs 194 F2
Ornsby Hill Durham 233 B9
Orpington London 68 F3
Orrell Gtr Man 194 G4
Orrell Mersey 182 B4
Orrell Post Gtr Man 194 F4
Orrisdale I/Man 192 C4
Orrock Fife 280 D4
Orroland Dumf/Gal 237 E9
Orsett Thurr'k 68 C6
Orsett Heath Thurr'k 68 E6
Orslow Staffs 150 F6
Orston Notts 172 G2
Orthwaite Cumb 229 E11
Ortner Lancs 202 C6
Orton Cumb 222 D2
Orton Northants 120 B6
Orton Staffs 133 D7
Orton Brimbles Peterbro 138 D2
Orton Goldhay Peterbro 138 D3
Orton Longueville Peterbro 138 D3
Orton Malborne Peterbro 138 D3
Orton on the Hill Leics 134 C6
Orton Rigg Cumb 239 G8
Orton Waterville Peterbro 138 D3
Orton Wistow Peterbro 138 D2
Orwell Cambs 123 G7
Osbaldeston Lancs 203 G8
Osbaldeston Green Lancs 203 G8
Osbaldwick C/York 207 C8
Osbaston Leics 135 C8
Osbaston Telford 150 F2
Osbaston Hollow Leics 135 B8
Osborne House I/Wight 20 C6
Osbournby Lincs 155 B11
Oscroft Ches 167 B8
Ose H'land 298 E3
Osgathorpe Leics 153 F8
Osgodby Lincs 189 C9
Osgodby N Yorks 207 G8
Osgodby N Yorks 217 C11
Osidge London 86 G3
Oskaig H'land 295 B7
Oskamull Arg/Bute 288 E6
Osleston Derby 152 B4
Osmaston Derby 169 G11
Osmaston Derby C 153 C7
Osmington Dorset 17 E10
Osmington Mills Dorset 17 E10
Osmondthorpe W Yorks 206 G2
Osmotherley N Yorks 225 F9
Osney Oxon 83 D7
Ospisdale H'land 309 L7
Ospringe Kent 70 G3
Ossett W Yorks 197 C9
Ossett Spa W Yorks 197 D9
Ossett Street Side W Yorks 197 C9
Ossington Notts 172 C3
Ostend Essex 88 F6
Ostend Norfolk 161 C7
Osterley London 66 D6
Oswaldkirk N Yorks 216 D2
Oswaldtwistle Lancs 195 B8
Oswestry Shrops 148 D5
Otby Lincs 189 C10
Otford Kent 52 B4
Otham Kent 53 C9
Otham Hole Kent 53 C9
Othery Som'set 43 G11
Otley Suffolk 126 F4
Otley W Yorks 205 E9
Otter Ferry Arg/Bute 275 E10
Otter Ho Arg/Bute 275 F10
Otterbourne Hants 33 C7
Otterburn Northum 251 E9
Otterburn N Yorks 204 B3
Otterburn Camp Northum 251 D9
Otterham Cornw'l 11 C9
Otterham Quay Kent 69 F10
Otterhampton Som'set 43 E8
Ottershaw Surrey 66 G4
Otterspool Mersey 182 D5
Otterswick Shetl'd 314 E7
Otterton Devon 15 D7
Otterwood Hants 32 G6
Ottery St. Mary Devon 15 B8
Ottinge Kent 55 E7
Ottringham ER Yorks 201 C9
Oughterby Cumb 239 F7
Oughtershaw N Yorks 213 C7
Oughterside Cumb 229 C8
Oughtibridge S Yorks 186 C4
Oughtrington Warrington 183 D11
Oulston N Yorks 215 E10
Oulton Cumb 238 G6
Oulton Norfolk 160 D2
Oulton Suffolk 143 E10
Oulton Staffs 151 B8
Oulton W Yorks 197 B11
Oulton Broad Suffolk 143 E10
Oulton Heath Staffs 151 B8
Oulton Park Motor Racing Circuit Ches 167 C9
Oulton Street Norfolk 160 D3
Oultoncross Staffs 151 C8
Oundle Northants 137 F10
Ousby Cumb 231 E8
Ousdale H'land 311 G4
Ousden Suffolk 124 F4
Ousefleet ER Yorks 199 C10
Ouston Durham 243 G7
Ouston Northum 241 G7
Ouston Northum 242 C3
Out Elmstead Kent 55 C8
Out Gate Cumb 221 F7
Out Newton ER Yorks 201 C11
Out Rawcliffe Lancs 202 E4
Outchester Northum 264 C4
Outer Hope Devon 8 G3
Outertown Orkney 312 G3
Outhgill Cumb 222 E5
Outhill Warwick 118 D2
Outhills Aberds 303 D10
Outlane W Yorks 196 D5
Outwell Norfolk 139 C10
Outwick Hants 31 D10
Outwood Gtr Man 195 F9
Outwood Surrey 51 D10
Outwood W Yorks 197 C10
Outwoods Leics 153 F8
Outwoods Staffs 150 F5
Outwoods Warwick 134 G4
Ouzlewell Green W Yorks 197 B10
Ovenden W Yorks 196 B5
Ovenden Wood W Yorks 196 B5
Ovenscloss Scot Borders 261 C11
Over Cambs 123 C7
Over Ches 167 B10
Over Glos 80 B4
Over S Glos 60 C5
Over Burrow Lancs 212 D2
Over Burrows Derby 152 B5
Over Compton Dorset 29 D9
Over End Cambs 137 D11
Over End Derby 186 G3
Over Green W Midlands 134 E3
Over Haddon Derby 170 B2
Over Hall Suffolk 108 D4
Over Hulton Gtr Man 195 F7
Over Kellet Lancs 211 F10
Over Kiddington Oxon 101 G8
Over Knutsford Ches 184 F3
Over Leck Lancs 212 D3
Over Monnow Monmouths 79 C8
Over Norton Oxon 100 F6
Over Silton N Yorks 225 G9
Over Stowey Som'set 43 F7
Over Stratton Som'set 28 D6
Over Tabley Ches 184 E2
Over Town Lancs 195 B11
Over Wallop Hants 47 F9
Over Whitacre Warwick 134 E5
Over Worton Oxon 101 F8
Overbister Orkney 312 D7
Overbury Worcs 99 D9
Overcombe Dorset 17 E9
Overend W Midlands 133 G8
Overgreen Derby 186 G4
Overleigh Som'set 44 F3
Overpool Ches 182 F5
Overscaig Hotel H'land 309 G4
Overseal Derby 152 F5
Overslade Warwick 119 C9
Oversland Kent 54 B5
Oversley Green Warwick 117 F11
Overstone Northants 120 D6
Overstrand Norfolk 160 A4
Overthorpe Northants 101 C9
Overthorpe W Yorks 197 D8
Overthwaite Cumb 211 C10
Overton Aberds 293 B9
Overton Aberd C 293 B10
Overton Ches 183 F8
Overton Dumf/Gal 237 C11
Overton Glos 80 C2
Overton Hants 48 D4
Overton Lancs 202 B4
Overton N Yorks 207 B7
Overton = Owrtyn Wrex 166 G5
Overton Shrops 115 C10
Overton Staffs 151 B11
Overton Swan 56 D3
Overton W Yorks 197 D9
Overtown Lancs 212 D2
Overtown N Lanarks 268 E6
Overtown Swindon 63 D7
Overy Oxon 83 G9
Oving Bucks 102 G5
Oving W Sussex 34 F6
Ovingdean Brighton/Hove 36 G5
Ovingham Northum 242 E3
Ovington Durham 224 C2
Ovington Essex 106 C5
Ovington Hants 48 G5
Ovington Norfolk 141 C8
Ovington Northum 242 E3
Ower Hants 32 D4
Owermoigne Dorset 17 D11
Owl End Cambs 122 B4
Owlcotes Derby 170 B6
Owler Bar Derby 186 F3
Owlerton S Yorks 186 D4
Owlet W Yorks 205 F9
Owletts End Worcs 99 C10
Owl's Green Suffolk 126 D5
Owlsmoor Brackn'l 65 G11
Owlswick Bucks 84 D3
Owlthorpe S Yorks 186 E6
Owmby Lincs 200 G5
Owmby-by-Spital Lincs 189 D8
Ownham W Berks 64 E2
Owrtyn = Overton Wrex 166 G5
Owslebury Hants 33 C8
Owston Leics 136 B5
Owston S Yorks 198 E4
Owston Ferry N Lincs 199 G10
Owstwick ER Yorks 209 G11
Owthorne ER Yorks 201 B10
Owthorpe Notts 154 C3
Owton Manor Hartlep'l 234 F5
Oxborough Norfolk 140 C4
Oxburgh Hall Norfolk 140 C4
Oxclose S Yorks 186 E6
Oxclose Tyne/Wear 243 F7
Oxcombe Lincs 190 F4
Oxcroft Derby 187 G7
Oxen End Essex 106 F3
Oxen Park Cumb 210 B6
Oxenhall Glos 98 F4
Oxenholme Cumb 221 G10
Oxenhope W Yorks 204 F6
Oxenpill Som'set 44 E2
Oxenton Glos 99 E9
Oxenwood Wilts 47 B10
Oxford Oxon 83 D8
Oxford University Botanic Garden Oxon 83 D8
Oxgang E Dunb 278 G3
Oxgangs C/Edinb 270 B4
Oxhey Herts 85 F10
Oxhill Durham 242 G5
Oxhill Warwick 100 B6
Oxlease Herts 86 D2
Oxley W Midlands 133 C8
Oxley Green Essex 88 C6
Oxley's Green E Sussex 37 C11
Oxlode Cambs 139 F9
Oxnam Scot Borders 262 F5
Oxnead Norfolk 160 E4
Oxshott Surrey 66 G6
Oxspring S Yorks 197 G9
Oxted Surrey 51 C11
Oxton Scot Borders 271 E9
Oxton Mersey 182 D3
Oxton Notts 171 E11
Oxton N Yorks 206 E6
Oxwich Swan 56 D3
Oxwich Green Swan 56 D3
Oxwick Norfolk 159 D8
Oykel Bridge H'land 309 J3
Oyne Aberds 302 G6
Oystermouth Swan 56 D6
Ozleworth Glos 80 G3

P

Pabail Iarach W Isles 304 E7
Pabail Uarach W Isles 304 E7
Packers Hill Dorset 30 E2
Packington Leics 153 G7
Packmoor Stoke 168 E5
Packmores Warwick 118 D5
Packwood Warwick 118 C3
Padanaram Angus 287 B8
Padbury Bucks 102 E4
Paddington London 67 C9
Paddington Warrington 183 D10
Paddlesworth Kent 55 E7
Paddlesworth Kent 69 G7
Paddock Kent 54 C3
Paddock W Yorks 196 D6
Paddock Wood Kent 53 E7
Paddockhaugh Moray 302 D2
Paddockhole Dumf/Gal 248 G6
Paddolgreen Shrops 149 C10
Padfield Derby 185 B8
Padgate Warrington 183 C10
Padham's Green Essex 87 F10
Padiham Lancs 203 G11
Padog Conwy 164 E4
Padside N Yorks 205 B9
Padside Green N Yorks 205 B9
Padstow Cornw'l 10 F4
Padworth W Berks 64 F6
Paganhill Glos 80 D4
Page Bank Durham 233 D10
Page Moss Mersey 182 C6
Page's Green Suffolk 126 D2
Pagham W Sussex 22 D5
Paglesham Churchend Essex 88 G6
Paglesham Eastend Essex 88 G6
Paibeil W Isles 296 E3
Paible W Isles 305 J2
Paignton Devon 9 C7
Paignton Zoo Devon 9 D7
Pailton Warwick 135 G9
Painleyhill Staffs 151 C10
Pains Hill Surrey 52 C2
Painscastle Powys 96 B3
Painshawfield Northum 242 E3
Painsthorpe ER Yorks 208 B2
Painswick Glos 80 D5
Painter's Forstal Kent 54 B3
Painter's Green Herts 86 B3
Painthorpe W Yorks 197 D10
Pairc Shiabost W Isles 304 D4
Paisley Renf 267 C9
Pakefield Suffolk 143 E10
Pakenham Suffolk 125 D8
Palace House, Beaulieu Hants 32 G5
Palace of Holyroodhouse C/Edinb 280 G5
Palacefields Halton 183 E9
Pale Gwyn 147 B9
Pale Green Essex 106 C3
Palehouse Common E Sussex 37 D7
Palestine Hants 47 E9
Paley Street Windsor 65 D11
Palfrey W Midlands 133 D10
Palgowan Dumf/Gal 245 G9
Palgrave Suffolk 126 B2
Palla Flat Cumb 219 C9
Pallion Tyne/Wear 243 F9
Palmarsh Kent 54 G6
Palmers Devon 28 G3
Palmers Cross Staffs 133 C7
Palmer's Flat Glos 79 D9
Palmer's Green Kent 53 E7
Palmer's Green London 86 G4
Palmerstown V/Glam 58 F6
Palmersville Tyne/Wear 243 C7
Palnackie Dumf/Gal 237 D10
Palnure Dumf/Gal 236 C6
Palterton Derby 171 B7
Pamber End Hants 48 B6
Pamber Green Hants 48 B6
Pamber Heath Hants 64 G6
Pamington Glos 99 E8
Pamphill Dorset 31 G7
Pampisford Cambs 105 B8
Pan Orkney 313 J4
Panborough Som'set 44 D3
Panbride Angus 287 D9
Pancakehill Glos 81 C9
Pancrasweek Devon 24 F4
Pancross V/Glam 58 F4
Pandy Gwyn 128 C2
Pandy Gwyn 147 D7
Pandy Monmouths 96 G6
Pandy Powys 129 C8
Pandy Wrex 148 B3
Pandy Tudur Conwy 164 C5
Pandy'r Capel Denbs 165 E9
Panfield Essex 106 F4
Pangbourne W Berks 64 D6
Pangelly Cornw'l 11 E7
Panhall Fife 280 C6
Pannal N Yorks 206 C2
Pannal Ash N Yorks 205 C11
Panshanger Herts 86 C3
Pant Caerph 78 F2
Pant Denbs 166 E2
Pant Flints 181 G10
Pant Gwyn 144 C4
Pant Merth Tyd 77 D9
Pant Shrops 148 E5
Pant Wrex 166 F3
Pant Mawr Powys 129 G7
Panta Monmouths 79 F7
Pantasaph Flints 181 F11
Panteg Ceredig'n 111 E9
Panteg Torf 78 F4
Pantersbridge Cornw'l 6 B3

Pant-Glas Gwyn 163 F7
Pantglas Powys 128 D5
Pantglas Shrops 130 F4
Pant-glas Shrops 148 C5
Pantgwyn Carms 93 F11
Pantgwyn Ceredig'n 92 B4
Pantgwyn Rh Cyn Taff 58 C4
Pant-lasau Swan 75 F11
Pantmawr Card 59 C7
Panton Lincs 189 F11
Pant-pastynog Denbs 165 C8
Pant-teg Carms 93 F9
Pant-y-Caws Carms 92 F3
Pant-y-dwr Powys 113 C9
Pant-y-Fenni Carms 74 B2
Pant-y-ffridd Powys 130 C3
Pantyffynnon Carms 75 C10
Pantygasseg Torf 78 F3
Pant-y-llyn Carms 75 B10
Pant-y-mwyn Flints 165 C11
Pant-y-pyllau Bridg 58 C2
Pant-yr-awel Bridg 58 B2
Pantyscallog Merth Tyd 77 D9
Pant-y-Wacco Flints 181 F10
Panxworth Norfolk 160 G6
Papa Westray Airport Orkney 312 C5
Papcastle Cumb 229 E8
Papigoe H'land 310 D7
Papil Shetl'd 315 K5
Papley Northants 138 F2
Papley Orkney 313 J5
Papley Grove Cambs 122 E5
Papple E Loth 281 G11
Papplewick Notts 171 E8
Papworth Everard Cambs 122 E5
Papworth St. Agnes Cambs 122 E5
Papworth Village Settlement Cambs 122 E5
Par Cornw'l 5 E11
Paradise Glos 80 C5
Paradise Wildlife Park, Broxbourne Herts 86 D4
Paramoor Cornw'l 5 F9
Parbold Lancs 194 E3
Parbrook Som'set 44 F5
Parbrook W Sussex 35 B9
Parc Gwyn 147 C7
Parchey Som'set 43 F11
Parciau Angl 179 E7
Parcllyn Ceredig'n 110 G4
Parc-Seymour Newp 78 G6
Parc-y-rhos Carms 93 B11
Pardown Hants 48 D5
Pardshaw Cumb 229 G7
Parford Devon 13 D10
Parham Suffolk 126 E6
Park Dumf/Gal 247 E10
Park N Lincs 199 F8
Park Swindon 63 C7
Park Barn Surrey 50 C3
Park Bottom Cornw'l 4 G3
Park Bridge Gtr Man 196 G2
Park Broom Cumb 239 F10
Park Close Lancs 204 E3
Park Common Norfolk 141 F11
Park Corner Bath/NE Som'set 45 B9
Park Corner E Sussex 52 F4
Park Corner E Sussex 37 E8
Park Corner Oxon 65 B7
Park Corner Windsor 65 C11
Park End Beds 121 G9
Park End Cambs 123 E11
Park End Middlesbro 225 B10
Park End Northum 241 B9
Park Farm Inverci 276 G6
Park Farm Kent 54 F4
Park Farm Worcs 117 D11
Park Gate Hants 33 F8
Park Gate Kent 55 D7
Park Gate Suffolk 124 F4
Park Gate Worcs 117 C8
Park Green Suffolk 126 E2
Park Head Cumb 231 C7
Park Head W Yorks 197 F7
Park Lane Bucks 84 G4
Park Lane Gtr Man 195 G9
Park Lidget Notts 172 C3
Park Mains Renf 277 G9
Park Mill W Yorks 197 E9
Park North Swindon 63 C7
Park Rose Pottery and Leisure Park, Bridlington ER Yorks 218 G3
Park Royal London 67 C7
Park South Swindon 63 C7
Park Street Herts 85 E10
Park Street W Sussex 50 G6
Park Town Luton 104 G2
Park Town Oxon 83 D8
Park Village Northum 240 E5
Park Village W Midlands 133 C8
Park Villas W Yorks 206 F2
Park Wood Kent 53 C9
Park Wood Medway 69 G10
Parkend Glos 79 D10
Parkend Glos 80 C3
Parkend S Glos 79 G11
Parkeston Essex 108 E4
Parkfield Bucks 84 E4
Parkfield Cornw'l 6 B6
Parkfield S Glos 61 D7
Parkfield W Midlands 133 D8
Parkfoot Falk 278 F6
Parkgate Ches 182 F3
Parkgate Ches 184 G3
Parkgate Cumb 229 B10
Parkgate Dumf/Gal 248 F2
Parkgate Essex 106 F3
Parkgate Kent 53 G11
Parkgate Surrey 51 E8
Parkgate S Yorks 186 B6
Parkhall W Dunb 277 G9
Parkham Devon 24 C5
Parkham Ash Devon 24 C5
Parkhead Glasg C 268 B2
Parkhead Cumb 230 C2
Parkhead S Yorks 186 E4
Parkhill Aberds 303 E10
Parkhill Notts 171 E11
Parkhill Ho. Aberds 293 B10
Parkhouse Monmouths 79 E7
Parkhouse Green Derby 170 C6
Parkhurst I/Wight 20 C5
Parkmill Swan 56 D4
Parkneuk Aberds 293 F9
Parkneuk Fife 279 D11
Parkside Cumb 219 B10
Parkside Durham 234 B4
Parkside N Lanarks 268 D5
Parkside Staffs 151 D8
Parkstone Poole 18 C6
Parkway Heref'd 98 D4
Parkway Som'set 29 C9
Parkwood Springs S Yorks 186 D4
Parley Cross Dorset 19 B7
Parley Green Dorset 19 B7
Parliament Heath Suffolk 107 C9
Parmoor Bucks 65 B9
Parmour Street Kent 71 G9
Parr Mersey 183 B8
Parr Brow Gtr Man 195 G8
Parracombe Devon 41 D7
Parrog Pembs 91 D10
Parsley Hay Derby 169 B10
Parslow's Hillock Bucks 84 E4
Parson Cross S Yorks 186 C5
Parson Drove Cambs 139 B7
Parsonage Green Essex 88 D2
Parsonby Cumb 229 D8
Parsons Green London 67 D9
Parson's Heath Essex 107 F10
Partick Glasg C 267 B11
Partington Gtr Man 184 C2
Partney Lincs 174 B6
Parton Cumb 228 G5
Parton Cumb 239 G7
Parton Dumf/Gal 237 B8
Parton Heref'd 96 B6
Partridge Green W Sussex 35 D11
Parwich Derby 169 E11
Paslow Wood Common Essex 87 E9
Passenham Northants 102 D5
Passfield Hants 49 G10
Passmore Essex 86 D6
Paston Norfolk 160 C6
Paston Peterbro 138 C3
Paston Green Norfolk 160 C6
Patchacott Devon 12 B5
Patcham Brighton/Hove 36 F4
Patchett's Green Herts 85 F10
Patching W Sussex 35 F9
Patchole Devon 40 E6
Patchway S Glos 60 C6
Pategill Cumb 230 F6
Pateley Bridge N Yorks 214 F3
Paternoster Heath Essex 88 B6
Path Head Tyne/Wear 242 E5
Path of Condie Perth/Kinr 286 F4
Pathe Som'set 43 G11
Pathhead Aberds 293 G9
Pathhead E Ayrs 258 G4
Pathhead Fife 280 C5
Pathhead Midloth 271 C7
Pathlow Warwick 118 F3
Pathstruie Perth/Kinr 286 F4
Patient End Herts 105 F8
Patna E Ayrs 257 G10
Patney Wilts 46 B5
Patrick I/Man 192 D3
Patrick Brompton N Yorks 224 G4
Patricroft Gtr Man 184 B3
Patrington ER Yorks 201 C10
Patrington Haven ER Yorks 201 B10
Patrixbourne Kent 55 C7
Patterdale Cumb 221 B7
Pattiesmuir Fife 279 E11
Pattingham Staffs 132 D6
Pattishall Northants 120 G3
Pattiswick Essex 106 G6
Patton Bridge Cumb 221 F11
Paul Cornw'l 1 D5
Paulerspury Northants 102 B4
Paull ER Yorks 201 B7
Paull Holme ER Yorks 201 C7
Paulsgrove Portsm'th 33 F10
Paulton Bath/NE Som'set 44 B7
Paultons Park, Totton Hants 32 D4
Paulville W Loth 269 B9
Pave Lane Telford 150 F5
Pavenham Beds 121 F9
Pawlett Som'set 43 E10
Pawston Northum 263 C9
Paxford Glos 100 D3
Paxton Scot Borders 273 E8
Paxton Park Cambs 122 E3
Payden Street Kent 54 C2
Payhembury Devon 27 G9
Paynter's Cross Cornw'l 7 C7
Paynter's Lane End Cornw'l 4 G3
Paythorne Lancs 204 C2
Payton Som'set 27 C10
Peacehaven E Sussex 36 G6
Peacemarsh Dorset 30 B4
Peak Dale Derby 185 F9
Peak Forest Derby 185 F10
Peakirk Peterbro 138 B3
Pean Kent 55 F7
Pean Hill Kent 70 G6
Pear Tree Derby C 153 C7
Pearsie Angus 287 B7
Pearson's Green Kent 53 E7
Peartree Herts 86 C2
Peartree Green Essex 87 F9
Peartree Green Heref'd 98 E2
Peartree Green S'thampton 32 E6
Peas Hill Cambs 139 D8
Pease Pottage W Sussex 51 G9
Peasedown St. John Bath/NE Som'set 45 B8
Peaseland Green Norfolk 159 F11
Peasemore W Berks 64 D3
Peasenhall Suffolk 127 D7
Peaslake Surrey 50 E5
Peasley Cross Mersey 183 C8
Peasmarsh E Sussex 38 C5
Peasmarsh Som'set 28 E4
Peasmarsh Surrey 50 D3
Peaston E Loth 271 B8
Peastonbank E Loth 271 B8
Peat Inn Fife 287 G8
Peathill Aberds 303 C9
Peatling Magna Leics 135 E11
Peatling Parva Leics 135 F11
Peaton Shrops 131 F10
Peat's Corner Suffolk 126 E3
Pebble Hill Oxon 83 F9
Pebmarsh Essex 106 E6
Pebsham E Sussex 38 F3
Pebworth Worcs 100 B2
Pecket Well W Yorks 196 B3
Peckforton Ches 167 D8
Peckham London 67 D10
Peckham Bush Kent 53 C7
Peckleton Leics 135 C9
Pedair-ffordd Powys 148 E2
Pedham Norfolk 160 G6
Pedlinge Kent 54 F6
Pedmore W Midlands 133 G8
Pednormead End Bucks 85 E7
Pedwell Som'set 44 F2
Peebles Scot Borders 270 G5
Peel I/Man 192 D3
Peel Lancs 202 G3
Peel Common Hants 33 G9
Peel Green Gtr Man 184 B2
Peel Hall Gtr Man 184 D4
Peel Park S Lanarks 268 E2
Peening Quarter Kent 38 B5
Pegg's Green Leics 153 F8
Pegsdon Beds 104 E2
Pegswood Northum 252 F6
Pegwell Kent 71 G11
Peinaha H'land 298 D4
Peinchorran H'land 295 B7
Peingown H'land 298 B4
Peinlich H'land 298 D4
Peinmore H'land 298 E4
Pelaw Tyne/Wear 243 E7
Pelcomb Pembs 72 B6
Pelcomb Bridge Pembs 72 B6
Pelcomb Cross Pembs 72 B6
Peldon Essex 89 B7
Pell Green E Sussex 52 G6
Pellon W Yorks 196 B5
Pelsall W Midlands 133 C10
Pelsall Wood W Midlands 133 C10
Pelton Durham 243 G7
Pelton Fell Durham 243 G7
Pelutho Cumb 229 B8
Pelynt Cornw'l 6 D4
Pemberton Carms 75 E8
Pemberton Gtr Man 194 G5
Pembles Cross Kent 53 D11
Pembre = Pembrey Carms 74 E6
Pembrey = Pembre Carms 74 E6
Pembrey Motor Racing Circuit Carms 74 E6
Pembridge Heref'd 115 F7
Pembroke = Penfro Pembs 73 E7
Pembroke Castle Pembs 73 E7
Pembroke Dock = Doc Penfro Pembs 73 E7
Pembroke Ferry Pembs 73 E7
Pembury Kent 52 E6
Pen Mill Som'set 29 D9
Pen Rhiwfawr Neath P Talb 76 C2
Pen y mynydd Flints 166 C4
Penallt Monmouths 79 C8
Penallt Monmouths 79 C8
Penally = Penalun Pembs 73 F10
Penalt Heref'd 97 F11
Penalun = Penally Pembs 73 F10
Penare Cornw'l 5 G10
Penarlâg = Hawarden Flints 166 B4
Penarth V/Glam 59 E7
Penbeagle Cornw'l 2 B2
Penberth Cornw'l 1 E4
Penbidwal Monmouths 96 G6
Penbodlas Gwyn 144 C5
Pen-bont-Rhydybeddau Ceredig'n 128 G3
Penboyr Carms 93 D7
Penbryn Ceredig'n 110 G5
Pencader Carms 93 D8
Pen-cae Ceredig'n 111 F8
Pencaenewydd Gwyn 162 G6
Pencaerau Neath P Talb 76 F3
Pen-caer-fenny Swan 75 F8
Pencaitland E Loth 271 B8
Pencarnisiog Angl 178 G5
Pencarreg Carms 93 B10
Pencarrow Cornw'l 11 E8
Penceiliogi Carms 75 E8
Pencelli Powys 95 F11
Pen-clawdd Swan 75 F8
Pencoed Bridg 58 C3
Pencoedtre V/Glam 58 E6
Pencombe Heref'd 115 G11
Pencoyd Heref'd 97 F10
Pencoys Cornw'l 2 B5
Pencraig Heref'd 97 G11
Pencraig Angl 179 F7
Pencraig Powys 147 D10
Pencroesoped Monmouths 78 D4
Pendas Fields W Yorks 206 F3
Pendeen Cornw'l 1 C3
Pendeford W Midlands 133 C7
Pendennis Castle Cornw'l 3 C8
Penderyn Rh Cyn Taff 76 D6
Pendinas Ceredig'n 128 G1
Pendine = Pentwyn Carms 74 D2
Pendlebury Gtr Man 195 G9
Pendleton Gtr Man 184 B4
Pendleton Lancs 203 F11
Pendock Worcs 98 E5
Pendoggett Cornw'l 10 F6
Pendomer Som'set 29 E8
Pendoylan V/Glam 58 D5
Pendre Bridg 58 C3
Pendre Gwyn 110 C2
Pengoes Powys 128 C5
Penelewey Cornw'l 4 G6
Penenden Heath Kent 53 B9
Penfeidir Pembs 91 E7
Penffordd Pembs 91 G11
Penfro = Pembroke Pembs 73 E7
Pengam Card 59 D8
Pengam Caerph 77 F11
Penge London 67 E10
Pengenffordd Powys 96 E3
Pengersick Cornw'l 2 D3
Pen-gilfach Gwyn 163 C9
Pengorffwysfa Angl 179 C7
Pengover Green Cornw'l 6 B5
Penhale Cornw'l 10 G5
Penhale Cornw'l 2 F5
Penhale Cornw'l 5 D8
Penhale Camp Cornw'l 4 D5
Penhallow Cornw'l 4 E5
Penhalurick Cornw'l 2 B6
Penhelig Gwyn 128 D2
Penhellick Cornw'l 4 G3
Penhill Swindon 63 B7
Penhole Cornw'l 11 F11
Penhosfeilw Angl 178 E2
Penhow Newp 78 G6
Penhurst E Sussex 37 D11
Peniarth Gwyn 128 B2
Peniarth Powys 148 F3
Penicuik Midloth 270 C4
Peniel Carms 93 G8
Peniel Denbs 165 C8
Penifiler H'land 298 E4
Peninver Arg/Bute 255 E8
Penisa'r-Waun Gwyn 163 C9
Penistone S Yorks 197 G8
Penjerrick Cornw'l 3 C7
Penketh Warrington 183 D9
Penkill S Ayrs 244 D6
Penkridge Staffs 151 G8
Pen-lan Swan 75 F11
Penley Wrex 149 B8
Penllech Gwyn 144 C4
Penllergaer Swan 75 F10
Penllwyn Caerph 77 F11
Pen-llyn Angl 178 E5
Penllyn V/Glam 58 D3
Pen-lôn Angl 162 C6
Penmachno Conwy 164 E3
Penmaen Caerph 77 F11
Penmaen Swan 56 D4
Penmaen Rhôs Conwy 180 F5
Penmaenan Conwy 180 F2
Penmaenmawr Conwy 180 F2
Penmaenpool Gwyn 146 F3
Penmark V/Glam 58 F5
Penmarth Cornw'l 2 B6
Penmayne Cornw'l 10 F4
Penmon Angl 179 E10
Penmore Mill Arg/Bute 288 D6
Penmorfa Ceredig'n 110 G6
Penmorfa Gwyn 163 G8
Penmynydd Angl 179 G8
Penn Bucks 84 G6
Penn Dorset 16 B2
Penn W Midlands 133 D7
Penn Bottom Bucks 84 G6
Penn Cross Dorset 16 C2
Penn Hill Dorset 30 D5
Penn Street Bucks 84 F6
Pennal Gwyn 128 C3
Pennal-isaf Gwyn 128 C4
Pennan Aberds 303 C8
Pennance Cornw'l 4 G4
Pennant Ceredig'n 111 E10
Pennant Denbs 147 C10
Pennant Gwyn 147 E8
Pennant Gwyn 163 F8
Pennant Powys 129 D7
Pennant-Melangell Powys 147 D10
Pennar Pembs 73 E7
Pennard Swan 56 D5
Pennerley Shrops 131 D7
Pennington Cumb 210 D5
Pennington Gtr Man 183 B11
Pennington Hants 20 C2
Pennington Green Gtr Man 194 F6
Pennorth Powys 96 F2
Pennsylvania Devon 14 C4
Pennsylvania S Glos 61 E8
Penny Bridge Cumb 210 C6
Penny Hill Lincs 157 D7
Penny Hill W Yorks 196 D5
Pennycross Arg/Bute 289 G7
Pennycross Devon 7 D9
Pennygate Norfolk 160 E6
Pennygown Arg/Bute 289 E7
Pennyland M/Keynes 103 C7
Pennylands Lancs 194 F3
Pennymoor Devon 26 E5
Penny's Green Norfolk 142 D3
Pennywell Tyne/Wear 243 F9
Penparc Ceredig'n 92 B4
Penparcau Ceredig'n 128 G1
Penpedairheol Caerph 77 F10
Penpedairheol Monmouths 78 E4
Penperlleni Monmouths 78 E4
Penpethy Cornw'l 11 D7
Penpillick Cornw'l 5 D11
Penpol Cornw'l 3 B8
Penpoll Cornw'l 3 D7
Penpoll Cornw'l 6 E2
Penponds Cornw'l 2 B4
Penpont Cornw'l 11 G7
Penpont Dumf/Gal 247 E8
Penprysg Bridg 58 C3
Penquit Devon 8 E2
Penrest Cornw'l 12 F2
Penrherber Carms 92 D5
Penrhiwceiber Rh Cyn Taff 77 F9
Penrhiw-llan Ceredig'n 93 C7
Pen-rhiw-newydd Ceredig'n 128 G3
Penrhiwpal Ceredig'n 93 B6
Penrhiwtyn Rh Cyn Taff 76 F2
Penrhos Gwyn 144 C6
Penrhos Monmouths 78 C6
Penrhos Powys 76 C4
Penrhos-garnedd Gwyn 179 G9
Penrhyn Bay = Bae Penrhyn Conwy 180 E4
Penrhyn Castle Gwyn 179 G10
Penrhyn Castle Pembs 92 B2
Penrhyncoch Ceredig'n 128 G2
Penrhyndeudraeth Gwyn 146 B2
Penrhynside Conwy 180 E4
Penrhys Rh Cyn Taff 77 F8
Penrice Swan 56 D3
Penrith Cumb 230 E6
Penrose Cornw'l 10 G3
Penrose Cornw'l 11 F7
Penrose Hill Cornw'l 2 D4
Penruddock Cumb 230 F4
Penryn Cornw'l 3 C7
Pensarn Carms 74 B6
Pensarn Conwy 181 F7
Pen-sarn Gwyn 145 D11
Pensax Worcs 116 D4
Pensby Mersey 182 E3
Penselwood Som'set 45 G9
Pensford Bath/NE Som'set 60 G6
Pensham Worcs 99 C8
Penshaw Tyne/Wear 243 G8
Penshurst Kent 52 E4
Pensilva Cornw'l 6 B5
Pensnett W Midlands 133 F8
Penston E Loth 281 G8
Penstone Devon 26 G3
Penstraze Cornw'l 4 F5
Penstrowed Powys 129 E11
Pentewan Cornw'l 5 F10
Penthryn Fechan Powys 148 F4
Pentir Gwyn 163 B9
Pentire Cornw'l 4 C5
Pentlepoir Pembs 73 D10
Pentlow Essex 106 C6
Pentney Norfolk 158 G4
Penton Grafton Hants 47 D10
Penton Mewsey Hants 47 D10
Pentonville London 67 C10
Pentraeth Angl 179 F8
Pentrapeod Caerph 77 E11
Pentre Flints 166 B4
Pentre Monmouths 78 C4
Pentre Pembs 92 C4
Pentre Powys 148 G3
Pentre Powys 114 F4
Pentre Powys 130 E5
Pentre Rh Cyn Taff 77 F7
Pentre Shrops 149 F7
Pentre Wrex 148 C2
Pentre Wrex 166 G3
Pentre Berw Angl 179 G7
Pentre Cilgwyn Wrex 148 B4
Pentre Dolau-Honddu Powys 95 C9
Pentre Ffwrndan Flints 182 G3
Pentre Gwenlais Carms 75 B10
Pentre Gwynfryn Gwyn 145 D11
Pentre Halkyn Flints 181 G11
Pentre Llanrhaeadr Denbs 165 C9
Pentre Llifior Powys 130 D2
Pentre llwyn-llwyd Powys 113 G9
Pentre llyn Ceredig'n 112 B2
Pentre Meyrick V/Glam 58 D3
Pentre Saron Denbs 165 C8
Pentrebach Carms 94 E6
Pentrebach Ceredig'n 93 B11
Pentre-bach Gwyn 162 G5
Pentrebach Merth Tyd 77 E9
Pentre-bach Powys 95 E8
Pentrebach Rh Cyn Taff 58 B5
Pentrebach Swan 75 D10
Pentre-bont Conwy 164 E2
Pentre-cagal Carms 92 C6
Pentre-cefn Shrops 148 D4
Pentre-celyn Denbs 165 E11
Pentre-chwyth Swan 75 F11
Pentre-cwrt Carms 93 D7
Pentre-du Conwy 164 D3
Pentredwr Denbs 165 F11
Pentre-dwr Swan 75 F11
Pentrefelin Carms 93 G11
Pentrefelin Conwy 180 G4
Pentrefelin Ceredig'n 94 B2
Pentrefelin Denbs 166 G2
Pentrefelin Gwyn 145 B10
Pentrefelin Angl 178 C6
Pentrefelin Powys 148 E3
Pentrefoelas Conwy 164 E5
Pentre-Galar Pembs 92 E3
Pentregat Ceredig'n 111 G7
Pentreheyling Shrops 130 E4
Pentre-Isaf Conwy 164 B5
Pentre-llyn-cymmer Conwy 165 E7
Pentre-newydd Shrops 148 B5
Pentre-Poeth Carms 75 E8
Pentre-poeth Newp 59 B9
Pentre-Poid Torf 78 E3
Pentre'r beirdd Powys 148 G3
Pentre'r Felin Conwy 164 B4
Pentre'r-felin Powys 95 E8
Pentre'r-gof Powys 148 G3
Pentre-rhew Ceredig'n 112 G3
Pentre-ty-gwyn Carms 94 E6
Pentre-uchaf Gwyn 145 B7
Pentrich Derby 170 E5
Pentridge Dorset 31 D8
Pentwyn Carms 75 C9
Pen-twyn Caerph 78 E2
Pentwyn Caerph 77 E10
Pen-twyn Monmouths 79 D8
Pentwyn = Pendine Carms 74 D2
Pen-twyn Torf 78 E3
Pentwyn Berthlwyd Merth Tyd 77 F10
Pentwyn-mawr Caerph 77 F11
Pentyrch Card 58 C6
Pen-Ucha'r Plwyf Flints 181 G11
Penuwch Ceredig'n 111 E11
Penwartha Cornw'l 4 E5
Penwartha Coombe Cornw'l 4 E5
Penweathers Cornw'l 4 G5
Penwithick Cornw'l 5 D10
Penwood Hants 64 G2
Penwortham Lane Lancs 194 B4
Penwyllt Powys 76 B5
Pen-y-banc Carms 75 C10
Pen-y-banc Carms 94 G2
Pen-y-Bont Bl Gwent 78 D2
Pen-y-bont Carms 92 F6
Penybont Ceredig'n 128 F2
Penybont Powys 114 E2
Pen-y-bont Llanerch Emrys Powys 148 E4
Penybontfawr Powys 147 E11
Penybryn Caerph 77 F10
Pen-y-bryn Gwyn 146 F3
Pen-y-bryn Pembs 92 C3
Pen-y-bryn Wrex 166 G3
Pen-y-cae Bridg 58 C2
Pen-y-cae Powys 76 C4
Penycae Wrex 166 F3
Pen-y-cae-mawr Monmouths 78 F6
Penycaerau Gwyn 144 D3
Pen-y-cefn Flints 181 F10
Pen-y-clawdd Monmouths 79 D7
Penycoed Caerph 77 F11
Pen-y-coed Gwyn 146 F4
Pen-y-coed Powys 148 F4
Pen-y-coed Shrops 148 E5
Pen-y-coedcae Rh Cyn Taff 58 B5
Penycwm Pembs 91 G7
Pen-y-darren Merth Tyd 77 D9
Penydre Swan 75 E11
Pen-y-fai Bridg 57 E11
Pen-y-Fan Carms 75 F8
Pen-y-fan Monmouths 79 D8
Penyfeidr Pembs 91 F7
Pen-y-felin Flints 165 B11
Pen-y-ffordd Flints 181 E10
Penyffordd Flints 166 C4
Penyffridd Gwyn 163 D8
Pen-y-Garn Carms 93 E11
Pen-y-garn Ceredig'n 128 F2
Penygarn Torf 78 E3
Pen-y-garnedd Angl 179 F8
Penygarnedd Powys 148 E2
Pen-y-graig Gwyn 144 C4
Penygraig Rh Cyn Taff 77 G7
Pen-y-groes Card 59 C8
Penygroes Carms 75 C9
Penygroes Gwyn 163 E7
Penygroes Pembs 92 D3
Pen-y-groeslon Gwyn 144 C4
Pen-y-lan Card 59 D7
Pen-y-lan Newp 59 B9
Pen-y-lan V/Glam 58 D3
Pen-y-maes Flints 181 F11
Pen-y-Parc Flints 166 D3
Penyraber Pembs 91 D9
Pen-yr-englyn Rh Cyn Taff 77 F6
Pen-yr-heol Bridg 58 C3
Penyrheol Caerph 58 B6
Pen-yr-heol Monmouths 78 C6
Penyrheol Swan 75 F9
Penyrheol Swan 75 G9
Penyrheol Torf 78 F3
Penysarn Angl 179 C7
Pen-y-stryt Denbs 165 E11
Penywaun Rh Cyn Taff 77 E7
Penzance Cornw'l 1 C5
Penzance Heliport Cornw'l 1 C5
People's Palace Glasg C 268 C2
Peopleton Worcs 117 G8
Peover Ches 184 G3
Peover Heath Ches 184 G3
Peper Harow Surrey 50 E2
Pepperly Hill Notts 187 F11
Pepper's Green Essex 87 C10
Peppershill Bucks 83 D11
Pepperstock Beds 85 B9
Perceton N Ayrs 267 G7
Percie Aberds 293 D7
Percy Main Tyne/Wear 243 D8
Percyhorner Aberds 303 C9
Perham Downs Wilts 47 D9
Periton Som'set 42 D3
Perivale London 67 C7
Perkhill Aberds 293 C7
Perkin's Village Devon 14 C6
Perkinsville Durham 243 G7
Perlethorpe Notts 187 G11
Perran Downs Cornw'l 2 C3
Perran Wharf Cornw'l 3 B7
Perranarworthal Cornw'l 3 B7
Perrancoombe Cornw'l 4 E5
Perranporth Cornw'l 4 E5
Perranuthnoe Cornw'l 2 D2
Perranwell Cornw'l 3 B7
Perranwell Cornw'l 4 E5
Perranwell Station Cornw'l 3 B7
Perranzabuloe Cornw'l 4 E5
Perry Kent 55 B9
Perry Som'set 42 E6
Perry Barr W Midlands 133 E11
Perry Beeches W Midlands 133 E11
Perry Common W Midlands 133 E11
Perry Crofts Staffs 134 B4
Perry Green Devon 26 F5
Perry Green Essex 106 G6
Perry Green Herts 86 B6
Perry Green Som'set 43 F9
Perry Green Wilts 62 B3
Perry Street Kent 68 E6
Perry Street Som'set 28 F4
Perryfoot Derby 185 E10
Perrymead Bath/NE Som'set 61 G8
Perrywood Kent 54 B4
Pershall Staffs 150 D6
Pershore Worcs 99 B8
Pert Angus 293 G8
Pertenhall Beds 121 D11
Perth Perth/Kinr 286 E5
Perth Racecourse Perth/Kinr 286 E5
Perthcelyn Rh Cyn Taff 77 F9
Perthy Shrops 149 C7
Perton Heref'd 97 C11
Perton Staffs 133 D7
Pertwood Wilts 45 F11
Pested Kent 54 C4
Peter Tavy Devon 12 F6
Peterborough Peterbro 138 D3
Peterborough Cathedral Peterbro 138 D3
Peterburn H'land 307 L2
Peterchurch Heref'd 96 D6
Peterculter Aberd C 293 C10
Peterhead Aberds 303 E11
Peterlee Durham 234 C4
Peters Green Herts 85 B10
Peters Marland Devon 25 E7
Petersburn N Lanarks 268 C5
Petersfield Hants 34 C2
Petersfinger Wilts 31 B11
Petersham London 67 E7
Petershill Glasg C 268 B2
Peterstone Wentlooge Newp 59 C9
Peterston-super-Ely V/Glam 58 D5
Peterstow Heref'd 97 G11
Petertown Orkney 313 H4
Peterville Cornw'l 4 E4
Petham Kent 54 C6
Petherwin Gate Cornw'l 11 D11
Petre Bank Ches 184 E6
Petrockstowe Devon 25 F8
Petsoe End M/Keynes 103 B7
Pett E Sussex 38 E5
Pett Bottom Kent 54 E6
Pett Street Kent 54 D5
Pettaugh Suffolk 126 F3
Petteridge Kent 53 E7
Pettinain S Lanarks 269 G9
Pettistree Suffolk 126 G5
Petton Devon 27 C8
Petton Shrops 149 D8
Petts Wood London 68 F2
Petty Aberds 303 F7
Petty France S Glos 61 B9
Pettycur Fife 280 D5
Pettymuick Aberds 303 G9
Petworth W Sussex 35 C7
Petworth House W Sussex 35 C7
Pevensey E Sussex 23 E11
Pevensey Bay E Sussex 23 E11
Peverell Plym'th 7 D9
Pew Hill Wilts 62 E2
Pewsey Wilts 63 G7
Pewterspear Warrington 183 E10
Pheasants Bucks 65 B9
Pheasant's Hill Bucks 65 B9
Pheasey W Midlands 133 D11
Philadelphia Tyne/Wear 243 G8
Philiphaugh Scot Borders 261 D10
Philipstoun W Loth 279 F10
Phillack Cornw'l 2 B3
Philleigh Cornw'l 3 B9
Phillip's Town Caerph 77 E10
Phocle Green Heref'd 98 F2
Phoenix Green Hants 49 B9
Phorp Moray 301 D10
Pibsbury Som'set 28 B6
Pibwrlwyd Carms 74 B6
Pica Cumb 228 G6
Piccadilly Corner Norfolk 142 F5
Piccott's End Herts 85 D8
Pickburn S Yorks 198 F4
Picken End Worcs 98 C6
Pickering N Yorks 216 C5
Pickering Nook Durham 242 F5
Picket Hill Hants 31 F11
Picket Piece Hants 47 D11
Pickford W Midlands 134 G5
Pickhill N Yorks 214 C6
Pickle Fen Cambs 139 G7
Picklenash Glos 98 F4
Picklescott Shrops 131 D8
Pickletillem Fife 287 E8
Pickley Green Gtr Man 195 G7
Pickmere Ches 183 F11
Pickney Som'set 27 B11
Pickstock Telford 150 E4
Pickup Bank Blackb'n 195 C8
Pickwell Devon 40 E3
Pickwell Leics 154 G5
Pickwood Scar W Yorks 196 C5
Pickworth Lincs 155 C10
Pickworth Rutl'd 155 G9
Picton Ches 182 G6
Picton Flints 181 E10
Picton N Yorks 225 D8
Pict's Cross Heref'd 97 F11
Picts Hill Som'set 28 B6
Piddinghoe E Sussex 36 G6
Piddington Bucks 84 G4
Piddington Northants 120 G6
Piddington Oxon 83 B10
Piddlehinton Dorset 17 B10
Piddletrenthide Dorset 17 B10
Pidley Cambs 122 B6
Pidney Dorset 30 F2
Piece Cornw'l 2 B5
Piece Hall Art Gallery, Halifax W Yorks 196 B5
Pield Heath London 66 C5
Piercebridge D'lington 224 B4
Pierowall Orkney 312 D5
Pierremont D'lington 224 C5
Piff's Elm Glos 99 F8
Pig Oak Dorset 31 G8
Pig Street Heref'd 97 B7
Pigdon Northum 252 F5
Pightley Som'set 43 F8
Pike Hill Lancs 204 G3
Pikehall Derby 169 D11
Pikeshill Hants 32 F3
Pilford Dorset 31 G8
Pilgrim Oak Notts 171 E9
Pilgrims Hatch Essex 87 F9
Pilham Lincs 188 C5
Pill N Som'set 60 D4
Pill Pembs 72 D6
Pillaton Cornw'l 7 C7
Pillatonmill Cornw'l 7 C7
Pillerton Hersey Warwick 100 B6
Pillerton Priors Warwick 100 B5
Pilleth Powys 114 D5
Pilley Glos 81 B7
Pilley Hants 20 B2
Pilley S Yorks 197 G10
Pillgwenlly Newp 59 B10
Pillhead Devon 25 B7
Pilling Lancs 202 D4
Pilling Lane Lancs 202 D3
Pillowell Glos 79 D10
Pillows Green Glos 98 F6
Pillwell Dorset 30 D3
Pilning S Glos 60 B5
Pilsdon Dorset 16 B4
Pilsgate Peterbro 137 B11
Pilsley Derby 186 G2
Pilsley Derby 170 C6
Pilsley Green Derby 170 C6
Pilson Green Norfolk 161 G7
Piltdown E Sussex 36 C6
Pilton C/Edinb 280 F4
Pilton Devon 40 G5
Pilton Northants 137 G10
Pilton Rutl'd 137 C8
Pilton Som'set 44 E5
Pilton Swan 56 D2
Pilton Green Swan 56 D2
Piltown Som'set 44 F5
Pimbo Lancs 194 G3
Pimhole Gtr Man 195 E10
Pimlico Herts 85 D9
Pimlico Lancs 203 E10
Pimlico London 67 D9
Pimperne Dorset 30 F6
Pin Green Herts 104 F5
Pin Mill Suffolk 108 D4
Pinchbeck Lincs 156 D4
Pinchbeck West Lincs 156 E4
Pincheon Green S Yorks 199 D7
Pincock Lancs 194 D5
Pineham Kent 55 D10
Pineham M/Keynes 103 C7
Pinehurst Swindon 63 B7
Pinfarthings Glos 80 E5
Pinfold Lancs 193 E11
Pinford End Suffolk 125 F7
Pinged Carms 74 E6
Pinhoe Devon 14 C5
Pinkett's Booth W Midlands 134 G5
Pinkney Wilts 61 B11
Pinkneys Green Windsor 65 C11
Pinley W Midlands 119 B7
Pinley Green Warwick 118 D4
Pinminnoch Dumf/Gal 236 D2
Pinminnoch S Ayrs 244 E5
Pinmore S Ayrs 244 E6
Pinmore Mains S Ayrs 244 E6
Pinn Devon 15 D7
Pinnacles Essex 86 D6
Pinner London 85 G10
Pinner Green London 85 G10
Pinnerwood Park London 85 G10
Pin's Green Worcs 98 B6
Pinsley Green Ches 167 F9
Pinvin Worcs 99 C9
Pinwall Leics 134 D6
Pinwherry S Ayrs 244 F5
Pinxton Derby 171 D7
Pipe and Lyde Heref'd 97 C10
Pipe Gate Shrops 168 G2
Pipe Ridware Staffs 151 F11
Pipehill Staffs 133 B11
Piperhill H'land 301 D8
Piper's Ash Ches 166 B6
Piper's Corner Bucks 84 F5
Piper's End Worcs 98 D6

Rockland St. Mary Norfolk 142 C6
Rockland St. Peter Norfolk 141 D9
Rockley Notts 188 G2
Rockley Wilts 63 E7
Rockliffe Lancs 195 C11
Rockness Glos 80 F4
Rockrobin E Sussex 52 G6
Rocks Park E Sussex 37 C7
Rocksley M/Keynes 102 D6
Rockstowes Glos 80 F3
Rockwell Cornw'l 12 D2
Rockwell End Bucks 65 B9
Rockwell Green Som'set 27 B10
Rodborough Glos 80 E4
Rodbourne Swindon 62 B6
Rodbourne Wilts 62 C2
Rodbourne Cheney Swindon 62 B6
Rodbridge Corner Suffolk 107 C7
Roddam Northum 264 E2
Rodden Dorset 17 E8
Roddymoor Durham 233 D9
Rode Som'set 45 C10
Rode Heath Ches 168 D4
Rode Hill Som'set 45 C10
Rodeheath Ches 168 B5
Roden Telford 149 F11
Rodford S Glos 61 C8
Rodhuish Som'set 42 F4
Rodington Telford 149 G11
Rodington Heath Telford 149 G11
Rodley Glos 80 C2
Rodley W Yorks 205 F10
Rodmarton Glos 80 F6
Rodmell E Sussex 36 F6
Rodmersham Kent 70 G2
Rodmersham Green Kent 70 G2
Rodney Stoke Som'set 44 C3
Rodsley Derby 170 G2
Rodway Som'set 43 E9
Rodwell Dorset 17 F9
Roe Cross Gtr Man 185 B7
Roe End Herts 85 B8
Roe Green Gtr Man 195 G9
Roe Green Herts 86 D2
Roe Green Herts 104 E6
Roe Lee Blackb'n 203 G9
Roebuck Low Gtr Man 196 F3
Roecliffe N Yorks 215 F7
Roedean Brighton/Hove 36 G4
Roehampton London 67 E8
Roesound Shetl'd 314 G5
Roestock Herts 86 D2
Roffey W Sussex 51 G7
Rogart H'land 309 J7
Rogart Station H'land 309 J7
Rogate W Sussex 34 C4
Roger Ground Cumb 221 F7
Rogerstone Newp 59 B9
Rogerton S Lanarks 268 D2
Roghadal W Isles 296 C6
Rogiet Monmouths 60 B3
Rogues Alley Cambs 139 B7
Roke Oxon 83 G10
Rokemarsh Oxon 83 G10
Roker Tyne/Wear 243 F10
Rollesby Norfolk 161 F8
Rolleston Leics 136 C4
Rolleston Notts 172 E2
Rolleston on Dove Staffs 152 D4
Rollestone Wilts 46 E5
Rolls Park Essex 86 G6
Rolston ER Yorks 209 D10
Rolstone N Som'set 59 G11
Rolvenden Kent 53 G10
Rolvenden Layne Kent 53 G11
Romaldkirk Durham 232 G5
Roman Bank Shrops 131 E10
Roman Baths & Pump Room, Bath Bath/NE Som'set 61 F9
Roman Hill Suffolk 143 E10
Romanby N Yorks 225 G7
Romannobridge Scot Borders 270 F3
Romansleigh Devon 26 C2
Rome Angus 293 G7
Romesdal H'land 298 D4
Romford Dorset 31 F9
Romford Kent 52 E6
Romford London 68 B4
Romiley Gtr Man 184 C6
Romney, Hythe and Dymchurch Light Railway Kent 54 G6
Romney Street Kent 68 G4
Rompa Shetl'd 315 L6
Romsey Hants 32 C4
Romsey Town Cambs 123 F9
Romsley Shrops 132 G5
Romsley Worcs 117 B9
Ronachan Ho Arg/Bute 255 B8
Ronague I/Man 192 E3
Ronkswood Worcs 117 F7
Rood Ashton Wilts 45 B11
Rood End W Midlands 133 F10
Rook Devon 8 C2
Rook End Essex 105 E11
Rookhope Durham 232 C4
Rooking Cumb 221 B8
Rookley I/Wight 20 E6
Rookley Green I/Wight 20 E6
Rooks Bridge Som'set 43 C11
Rook's Nest Som'set 42 G5
Rook's Street Wilts 45 G10
Rooksmoor Glos 80 E4
Rookwith N Yorks 214 B4
Rookwood W Sussex 22 D3
Roos ER Yorks 209 G11
Roose Cumb 210 F4
Roosebeck Cumb 210 F5
Roosecote Cumb 210 F4
Roost End Essex 106 C4
Rootham's Green Beds 122 G2
Rooting Street Kent 54 D3
Rootpark S Lanarks 269 E9
Ropley Hants 48 G6
Ropley Dean Hants 48 G6
Ropley Stoke Hants 49 G7
Ropsley Lincs 155 C9
Rora Aberds 303 D10
Rorandle Aberds 293 B8
Rorrington Shrops 130 C6
Rosarie Moray 302 E3
Roscroggan Cornw'l 4 G2
Rose Cornw'l 4 E5
Rose Ash Devon 26 C3
Rose Green Essex 107 F8
Rose Green Suffolk 107 C9
Rose Green Suffolk 107 D8
Rose Green W Sussex 22 D6
Rose Grove Lancs 204 G2
Rose Hill Derby C 153 B7
Rose Hill E Sussex 37 D7
Rose Hill Gtr Man 195 F8
Rose Hill Lancs 204 G2
Rose Hill Oxon 83 E8
Rose Hill Suffolk 108 C3
Rose Hill Surrey 51 D7
Rose Hill Stockton 225 C8
Roseacre Kent 53 B9
Roseacre Lancs 202 F4
Rose-an-Grouse Cornw'l 2 B2
Rosebank E Dunb 278 G3
Rosebank S Lanarks 268 F6
Rosebrae Moray 301 C11
Rosebush Pembs 91 F11
Rosecare Cornw'l 11 B9
Rosedale Abbey N Yorks 226 F4
Roseden Northum 264 E2
Rosedinnick Cornw'l 5 B8
Rosedown Devon 24 C3
Rosefield H'land 301 D8
Rosehall H'land 309 J4
Rosehall N Lanarks 268 C4
Rosehaugh Mains H'land 300 D6
Rosehearty Aberds 303 C9
Rosehill Blackb'n 195 C8
Rosehill Cornw'l 4 E5
Rosehill London 67 F9
Rosehill Shrops 149 F9
Rosehill Tyne/Wear 243 D8
Roseisle Moray 301 C11
Roseland Cornw'l 6 C5
Roselands E Sussex 23 E10
Rosemarket Pembs 73 D7
Rosemarkie H'land 301 D7
Rosemary Lane Devon 27 E11
Rosemount Perth/Kinr 286 C5
Rosenannon Cornw'l 5 B9
Rosenithon Cornw'l 3 E8
Roser's Cross E Sussex 37 C9
Rosevean Cornw'l 5 D10
Rosevidney Cornw'l 2 C2
Roseville W Midlands 133 E8
Rosevine Cornw'l 3 B9
Rosewarne Cornw'l 4 G2
Rosewarne Cornw'l 2 B4
Rosewell Midloth 270 C5
Roseworth Stockton 234 G4
Roseworthy Cornw'l 4 F5
Roseworthy Cornw'l 2 B4
Rosgill Cumb 221 B10
Roshven H'land 289 B9
Roskhill H'land 298 E2
Roskill House H'land 300 D6
Roskorwell Cornw'l 3 E7
Rosley Cumb 230 B2
Roslin Midloth 270 C5
Rosliston Derby 152 F4
Rosneath Arg/Bute 276 E5
Ross Dumf/Gal 237 E8
Ross Northum 264 B4
Ross Perth/Kinr 285 E11
Ross Green Worcs 116 E5
Ross on Wye Heref'd 98 G2
Rossett Wrex 166 D4
Rossett Green N Yorks 206 C2
Rossie Ochill Perth/Kinr 286 F4
Rossie Priory Perth/Kinr 286 D6
Rossington S Yorks 187 B11
Rosskeen H'land 300 C6
Rossland Renf 277 G8
Rossmore Poole 19 C7
Roster H'land 310 F6
Rostherne Ches 184 E2
Rostholme S Yorks 198 F5
Rosthwaite Cumb 210 B4
Rosthwaite Cumb 220 C5
Roston Derby 169 G10
Rosudgeon Cornw'l 2 D3
Rosyth Fife 280 E2
Rotcombe Bath/NE Som'set 45 B7
Rothbury Northum 252 C3
Rotherby Leics 154 F3
Rotherfield E Sussex 37 B9
Rotherfield Greys Oxon 65 C8
Rotherfield Peppard Oxon 65 C8
Rotherham S Yorks 186 C6
Rotherhithe London 67 D11
Rothersthorpe Northants 120 F4
Rotherwas Heref'd 97 D10
Rotherwick Hants 49 B8
Rothes Moray 302 E2
Rothesay Arg/Bute 275 G11
Rothiebrisbane Aberds 303 F7
Rothiemay Crossroads Moray 302 E5
Rothiemurchus Estate Visitor Centre H'land 291 C11
Rothiemurchus Lodge H'land 291 C11
Rothienorman Aberds 303 F7
Rothiesholm Orkney 312 F7
Rothley Leics 153 G11
Rothley Northum 252 F2
Rothmaise Aberds 302 F6
Rothwell Lincs 189 B11
Rothwell Northants 136 G6
Rothwell W Yorks 197 B10
Rothwell Haigh W Yorks 197 B10
Rotsea ER Yorks 209 C7
Rottal Angus 292 G5
Rotten End Suffolk 127 D7
Rotten Green Hants 49 B9
Rotten Row Norfolk 159 G11
Rottingdean Brighton/Hove 36 G5
Rottington Cumb 219 C9
Rotton Row W Berks 64 E5
Rotton Row W Midlands 118 B3
Rotunda, Folkestone Kent 55 F8
Roud I/Wight 20 E6
Rough Close Staffs 151 B8
Rough Common Kent 54 B6
Rough Haugh H'land 308 E7
Rough Hay Staffs 152 E4
Rougham Norfolk 158 E6
Rougham Suffolk 125 E8
Rougham Green Suffolk 125 E8
Roughbirchworth S Yorks 197 G9
Roughburn H'land 290 E5
Roughlee Lancs 204 E2
Roughley W Midlands 134 D2
Roughrigg N Lanarks 278 F6
Roughsike Cumb 240 B2
Roughton Lincs 174 C2
Roughton Norfolk 160 B4
Roughton Shrops 132 E5
Roughway Kent 52 C6
Round Bush Herts 85 F11
Round Maple Suffolk 107 C9
Round Oak Shrops 131 G7
Round Oak W Berks 64 F6
Round Oak W Midlands 133 F8
Round Spinney Northants 120 D5
Round Street Kent 69 F7
Roundbush Essex 88 E5
Roundbush Glos 98 F5
Roundbush Green Essex 87 C9
Roundham Som'set 28 F6
Roundhay W Yorks 206 F2
Roundstonefoot Dumf/Gal 248 B4
Roundstreet Common W Sussex 35 B9
Roundswell Devon 40 G4
Roundthorn Gtr Man 184 D4
Roundthwaite Cumb 222 E2
Roundway Wilts 62 G4
Roundyhill Angus 287 B7
Rous Lench Worcs 117 G10
Rousdon Devon 15 C11
Rousham Oxon 101 G9
Routenburn N Ayrs 266 C3
Routh ER Yorks 209 D7
Rout's Green Bucks 84 F3
Row Cumb 219 E11
Row Cumb 211 B9
Row Cumb 231 E8
Row Cornw'l 11 F7
Row Ash Hants 33 E8
Row Brow Cumb 229 D7
Row Green Essex 106 G4
Row Heath Essex 89 B10
Row Town Surrey 66 G4
Rowanburn Dumf/Gal 239 B10
Rowanfield Glos 99 G8
Rowardennan Stirl 277 B7
Rowarth Derby 185 D8
Rowbarns Surrey 50 C6
Rowbarton Som'set 28 B2
Rowberrow Som'set 44 B3
Rowde Wilts 62 G3
Rowden N Yorks 205 B11
Rowden Down Wilts 62 E2
Rowell Cumb 211 C10
Rowen Conwy 180 G3
Rowfoot Northum 240 E5
Rowford Som'set 28 B2
Rowhedge Essex 107 G10
Rowhill Surrey 66 G4
Rowhook W Sussex 50 G6
Rowington Warwick 118 D4
Rowington Green Warwick 118 C4
Rowland Derby 186 G2
Rowlands Castle W Sussex 34 E2
Rowlands Gill Tyne/Wear 242 F5
Rowledge Surrey 49 E10
Rowlestone Heref'd 97 F7
Rowley Durham 233 B7
Rowley ER Yorks 208 G5
Rowley Shrops 130 B6
Rowley Hill W Yorks 197 E7
Rowley Park Staffs 151 E8
Rowley Regis W Midlands 133 F9
Rowley's Green Warwick 134 G6
Rowly Surrey 50 E4
Rowmore Arg/Bute 276 D4
Rowner Hants 33 G9
Rowney Green Worcs 117 C10
Rownhams Hants 32 D5
Row-of-Trees Ches 184 F4
Rowrah Cumb 219 B11
Rowsham Bucks 84 B5
Rowsley Derby 170 B3
Rowstock Oxon 64 B3
Rowston Lincs 173 D9
Rowthorn Derby 171 C7
Rowton Ches 166 C6
Rowton Shrops 149 G7
Rowton Telford 150 F2
Roxburgh Scot Borders 262 C5
Roxby N Lincs 200 D2
Roxby N Yorks 226 B5
Roxeth London 66 B6
Roxton Beds 122 G3
Roxwell Essex 87 D10
Royal Botanic Gardens C/Edinb 280 F4
Royal British Legion Village Kent 53 B8
Royal Leamington Spa Warwick 118 E6
Royal Museum of Scotland C/Edinb 280 G5
Royal Oak Durham 233 G10
Royal Oak Lancs 194 G2
Royal Oak N Yorks 218 D2
Royal Pavilion, Brighton Brighton/Hove 36 G4
Royal Tunbridge Wells = Tunbridge Wells Kent 52 F5
Royal Welch Fusiliers Regimental Museum (See Caernarfon Castle) Gwyn 163 C7
Royal Worcester Porcelain, Worcester Worcs 117 G7
Royal's Green Ches 167 G10
Roybridge H'land 290 E4
Roydhouse W Yorks 197 E8
Roydon Essex 86 C6
Roydon Norfolk 141 G11
Roydon Norfolk 158 E4
Roydon Hamlet Essex 86 D6
Royston Herts 105 C7
Royston S Yorks 197 E11
Royston Water Som'set 28 E2
Royton Gtr Man 196 F2
Ruabon = Rhiwabon Wrex 166 G4
Ruaig Arg/Bute 288 E2
Ruan High Lanes Cornw'l 3 B10
Ruan Lanihorne Cornw'l 5 G7
Ruan Major Cornw'l 2 F6
Ruan Minor Cornw'l 2 F6
Ruarach H'land 295 C11
Ruardean Glos 79 B10
Ruardean Hill Glos 79 B10
Ruardean Woodside Glos 79 B10
Rubery Worcs 117 B9
Rubha Ghaisinis W Isles 297 G4
Rubha Stoer H'land 306 F5
Ruchazie Glasg C 268 B3
Ruchill Glasg C 267 B11
Ruckcroft Cumb 230 C6
Ruckhall Heref'd 97 D8
Ruckinge Kent 54 G4
Ruckland Lincs 190 F4
Rucklers Green Herts 85 E9
Rudbaxton Pembs 91 G9
Rudby N Yorks 225 D9
Rudddle Glos 79 C11
Ruddington Notts 153 C11
Ruddlemoor Cornw'l 5 D10
Rudford Glos 98 G5
Rudge Shrops 132 D6
Rudge Som'set 45 C10
Rudgeway S Glos 60 B6
Rudgwick W Sussex 50 G5
Rudhall Heref'd 98 F2
Rudheath Ches 183 G11
Rudhja Garbh Arg/Bute 289 E11
Rudley Green Essex 88 E4
Rudloe Wilts 61 E10
Rudry Caerph 59 B7
Rudston ER Yorks 217 F11
Rudyard Staffs 168 D6
Ruffets Monmouths 60 B4
Rufford Lancs 194 D3
Rufforth C/York 206 C6
Ruffs Notts 171 F8
Ruffside Durham 241 G11
Rugby Warwick 119 C10
Rugeley Staffs 151 F11
Ruggin Som'set 27 D11
Ruglen S Ayrs 245 C7
Ruilick H'land 300 E5
Ruishton Som'set 28 C3
Ruisigearraidh W Isles 296 C5
Ruislip London 66 B5
Ruislip Common London 66 B5
Ruislip Gardens London 66 B5
Ruislip Manor London 66 B6
Ruiton W Midlands 133 E8
Rumach H'land 295 G8
Rumbling Bridge Perth/Kinr 279 B10
Rumburgh Suffolk 142 G6
Rumer Hill Staffs 133 B9
Rumford Cornw'l 10 G3
Rumford Falk 279 F8
Rumney Card 59 D8
Rumsam Devon 40 G5
Rumwell Som'set 27 C11
Runcorn Halton 183 E8
Runcton W Sussex 34 G5
Runcton Bottom Norfolk 140 B2
Runcton Holme Norfolk 140 B2
Rundlestone Devon 13 F7
Runfold Surrey 49 D11
Runhall Norfolk 141 B11
Runham Norfolk 143 B10
Runham Norfolk 161 G9
Running Waters Durham 234 C2
Runnington Som'set 27 C10
Runsell Green Essex 88 E3
Runshaw Moor Lancs 194 D4
Runswick Bay N Yorks 226 B6
Runwell Essex 88 G3
Ruscombe Glos 80 D4
Ruscombe Wokingham 65 D10
Ruscote Oxon 101 C8
Rush Green Essex 89 B11
Rush Green Herts 104 G4
Rush Green Herts 104 F6
Rush Green London 68 B4
Rush Green Norfolk 141 B11
Rush Hill Bath/NE Som'set 61 G8
Rushall Heref'd 98 E2
Rushall Norfolk 142 G3
Rushall Wilts 46 B6
Rushall W Midlands 133 C10
Rushbrooke Suffolk 125 E7
Rushbury Shrops 131 E10
Rushden Herts 104 E6
Rushden Northants 121 D9
Rushenden Kent 70 E2
Rusher's Cross E Sussex 37 B10
Rushey Mead Leics C 136 B2
Rushford Devon 12 F4
Rushford Norfolk 141 G8
Rushgreen Warrington 183 D11
Rush-head Aberds 303 E8
Rushington Hants 32 E5
Rushlake Green E Sussex 37 D10
Rushley Green Essex 106 D5
Rushmere Beds 103 F8
Rushmere Suffolk 143 F9
Rushmere St. Andrew Suffolk 108 B3
Rushmere Street Suffolk 108 B4
Rushmoor Surrey 49 E11
Rushock Worcs 117 C7
Rusholme Gtr Man 184 B5
Rushton Northants 136 G6
Rushton Shrops 132 B2
Rushton Spencer Staffs 168 C6
Rushwick Worcs 116 G6
Rushy Green E Sussex 23 B7
Rushyford Durham 233 F11
Ruskie Stirl 285 G10
Ruskington Lincs 173 E9
Rusland Cumb 210 B6
Rusper W Sussex 51 F8
Ruspidge Glos 79 C11
Russ Hill Surrey 51 E8
Russel H'land 299 E8
Russell's Green E Sussex 38 E2
Russell's Hall W Midlands 133 F8
Russell's Water Oxon 65 B8
Russel's Green Suffolk 126 C5
Rusthall Kent 52 F5
Rustington W Sussex 35 G9
Ruston N Yorks 217 C9
Ruston Parva ER Yorks 217 G11
Ruswarp N Yorks 227 D7
Rutherglen Glasg C 268 C2
Ruthernbridge Cornw'l 5 B10
Ruthin Denbs 165 D10
Ruthin V/Glam 58 D3
Ruthin Craft Centre Denbs 165 D10
Ruthrieston Aberd C 293 C11
Ruthven Aberds 302 E5
Ruthven Angus 286 C6
Ruthven H'land 291 D9
Ruthven H'land 301 F8
Ruthven House Angus 287 C7
Ruthvoes Cornw'l 5 C8
Ruthwaite Cumb 229 D10
Ruthwell Dumf/Gal 238 D4
Ruxley London 68 E3
Ruxton Green Heref'd 79 B8
Ruyton-XI-Towns Shrops 149 E7
Ryal Northum 242 C2
Ryall Worcs 99 C7
Ryarsh Kent 69 G7
Rychraggan H'land 300 F4
Rydal Cumb 221 D7
Ryde I/Wight 21 C7
Rye E Sussex 38 C6
Rye Foreign E Sussex 38 C6
Rye Harbour E Sussex 38 D6
Rye Hill Essex 87 D7
Rye Park Herts 86 C5
Rye Street Worcs 98 D5
Ryebank Shrops 149 C10
Ryecroft W Yorks 205 F7
Ryeford Glos 80 E4
Ryeford Heref'd 98 G2
Ryehill ER Yorks 201 B8
Ryeish Green Wokingham 65 F8
Ryeworth Glos 99 G9
Ryhall Rutl'd 155 G10
Ryhill W Yorks 197 E11
Ryhope Tyne/Wear 243 G10
Ryhope Colliery Tyne/Wear 243 G10
Rylah Derby 171 B7
Rylands Notts 153 B10
Rylstone N Yorks 204 B5
Ryme Intrinseca Dorset 29 E9
Ryther N Yorks 207 F7
Ryton Glos 98 E4
Ryton N Yorks 216 D5
Ryton Shrops 132 C5
Ryton Tyne/Wear 242 E5
Ryton Warwick 135 F7
Ryton on Dunsmore Warwick 119 C7
Ryton Woodside Tyne/Wear 242 E4

S

Saasaig H'land 295 E8
Sabden Lancs 203 F11
Sabine's Green Essex 87 F8
Sackers Green Suffolk 107 D8
Sacombe Herts 86 B4
Sacombe Green Herts 86 B4
Sacriston Durham 233 B10
Sadberge D'lington 224 B6
Saddell Arg/Bute 255 D8
Saddell Ho Arg/Bute 255 D8
Saddington Leics 136 E3
Saddle Bow Norfolk 158 F2
Saddlescombe W Sussex 36 E3
Sadgill Cumb 221 D9
Saffron Walden Essex 105 D10
Sageston Pembs 73 E9
Saham Grove Norfolk 141 B8
Saham Hill Norfolk 141 C8
Saham Toney Norfolk 141 C8
Saighdinis W Isles 296 E4
Saighton Ches 166 C6
St. Abbs Scot Borders 273 B8
St. Abb's Haven Scot Borders 273 B8
St. Agnes Cornw'l 4 E4
St. Albans Herts 85 D10
St Alban's Abbey Herts 85 D10
St. Allen Cornw'l 4 E6
St. Andrews Fife 287 F9
St. Andrew's Major V/Glam 58 E6
St. Andrew's Well Dorset 16 C5
St. Anne's Lancs 193 B10
St. Anne's Park Bristol 60 E6
St. Ann's Nott'ham 171 G9
St. Ann's Dumf/Gal 248 E3
St. Ann's Chapel Cornw'l 12 G4
St. Ann's Chapel Devon 8 F3
St. Anthony Cornw'l 3 C9
St. Anthony-in-Meneage Cornw'l 3 D7
St. Anthony's Tyne/Wear 243 E7
St. Anthony's Hill E Sussex 23 E10
St. Arvans Monmouths 79 F8
St. Asaph = Llanelwy Denbs 181 G8
St. Athan V/Glam 58 F4
St. Austell Cornw'l 5 E10
St. Bartholomew's Hill Wilts 30 B5
St. Bees Cumb 219 C9
St. Blazey Cornw'l 5 E11
St. Blazey Gte Cornw'l 5 E11
St. Boswells Scot Borders 262 C3
St. Breock Cornw'l 10 G5
St. Breward Cornw'l 11 F7
St. Briavels Glos 79 E9
St. Briavels Common Glos 79 E8
St. Brides Pembs 72 C3
St. Bride's Major = Saint-y-Brid V/Glam 57 G11
St. Bride's Netherwent Monmouths 60 B2
St. Bride's Wentlooge Newp 59 C9
St. Bride's-super-Ely V/Glam 58 D5
St. Budeaux Plym'th 7 D8
St. Buryan Cornw'l 1 D4
St. Catherine Bath/NE Som'set 61 E9
St. Catherine's Arg/Bute 284 G5
St. Chloe Glos 80 E4
St. Clears = Sanclêr Carms 74 B3
St. Cleer Cornw'l 6 B4
St. Clement Cornw'l 5 G6
St Clement's Caves, Hastings E Sussex 38 F4
St. Clether Cornw'l 11 E10
St. Colmac Arg/Bute 275 G11
St. Columb Major Cornw'l 5 C8
St. Columb Minor Cornw'l 4 C6
St. Columb Road Cornw'l 5 D8
St. Combs Aberds 303 C10
St. Cross Hants 33 B7
St. Cross South Elmham Suffolk 142 G6
St. Cyrus Aberds 293 G9
St. David's Perth/Kinr 286 E3
St. David's = Tyddewi Pembs 90 F5
St. Day Cornw'l 4 G4
St. Decumans Som'set 42 E5
St. Dennis Cornw'l 5 D9
St. Denys S'thampton 32 E6
St. Dials Torf 78 G3
St. Dogmaels = Llandudoch Pembs 92 B3
St. Dominick Cornw'l 7 B8
St. Donats V/Glam 58 F2
St. Edith's Marsh Wilts 62 G3
St. Endellion Cornw'l 10 F5
St. Enoder Cornw'l 5 D7
St. Erme Cornw'l 4 F6
St. Erney Cornw'l 7 D7
St. Erth Cornw'l 2 B3
St. Erth Praze Cornw'l 2 B3
St. Ervan Cornw'l 10 G3
St. Eval Cornw'l 5 B7
St. Ewe Cornw'l 5 F9
St. Fagans Card 58 D6
St Fagans Museum of Welsh Life Card 58 D6
St. Fergus Aberds 303 D10
St. Fillans Perth/Kinr 285 E10
St. Florence Pembs 73 E9
St. Gennys Cornw'l 11 B8
St. George Bristol 60 E6
St. George Conwy 181 F7
St. George's N Som'set 59 G11
St. George's Telford 150 G4
St. George's V/Glam 58 D5
St. George's Hill Surrey 66 G5
St. Germans Cornw'l 7 D7
St. Giles Lincs 189 G7
St Giles Cathedral C/Edinb 280 G5
St. Giles in the Wood Devon 25 D8
St. Giles on the Heath Devon 12 C3
St. Giles's Hill Hants 33 B7
St. Gluvias Cornw'l 3 C7
St. Harmon Powys 113 C9
St. Helen Auckland Durham 233 F9
St. Helena Warwick 134 C5
St. Helens Cumb 228 E6
St. Helen's E Sussex 38 E4
St. Helen's I/Wight 21 D8
St. Helens Mersey 183 C9
St. Helen's S Yorks 197 F11
St. Helen's Wood E Sussex 38 E4
St. Helier London 67 F9
St. Hilary Cornw'l 2 C3
St. Hilary V/Glam 58 E4
St. Hill Devon 27 G9
St. Ibbs Herts 104 F3
St. Illtyd Bl Gwent 78 E2
St. Ippollitts Herts 104 F4
St. Ishmael Carms 74 D5
St. Ishmael's Pembs 72 D4
St. Issey Cornw'l 10 G4
St. Ive Cornw'l 6 B6
St. Ive Cross Cornw'l 6 B6
St. Ives Cambs 122 C6
St. Ives Cornw'l 2 A2
St. Ives Dorset 31 G10
St. James Dorset 30 C5
St. James Norfolk 160 E5
St. James South Elmham Suffolk 142 G6
St. James's End Northants 120 E4
St. James's Park Notts 154 B3
St. Jidgey Cornw'l 5 B8
St. John Cornw'l 7 E8
St. John's E Sussex 52 G4
St. John's I/Man 192 D3
St. John's Kent 52 B4
St. John's London 67 D11
St. John's Suffolk 108 C3
St. John's Surrey 50 B3
St. John's W Yorks 206 F4
St. John's Chapel Durham 232 D3
St. John's Fen End Norfolk 157 G10
St. John's Highway Norfolk 157 G10
St. John's Town of Dalry Dumf/Gal 246 G4
St. John's Wells Aberds 303 F7
St. John's Wood London 67 C9
St. Judes I/Man 192 C4
St. Julians Herts 85 D10
St. Julian's Newp 59 B10
St. Just Cornw'l 1 C3
St. Just in Roseland Cornw'l 3 B9
St Just In Roseland Cornw'l 3 B9
St. Katherine's Aberds 303 F7
St. Keverne Cornw'l 3 E7
St. Kew Cornw'l 10 F6
St. Kew Highway Cornw'l 10 F6
St. Keyne Cornw'l 6 C4
St. Lawrence Essex 89 E7
St. Lawrence I/Wight 20 F6
St. Lawrence Kent 71 F11
St. Leonards Bucks 84 D6
St. Leonards Dorset 31 G10
St. Leonards E Sussex 38 F4
St. Leonards S Lanarks 268 E2
St. Leonard's Street Kent 53 B7
St. Levan Cornw'l 1 E3
St. Loy Cornw'l 1 E4
St. Lukes Derby C 152 B6
St. Lythans Card 58 E6
St. Mabyn Cornw'l 10 G6
St. Madoes Perth/Kinr 286 E5
St. Margaret South Elmham Suffolk 142 G6
St. Margaret's Heref'd 97 E7
St. Margarets Herts 86 C5
St. Margaret's Wilts 63 F7
St. Margaret's at Cliffe Kent 55 E11
St. Margaret's Hope Orkney 313 J5
St. Mark's Glos 99 G8
St. Mark's I/Man 192 E3
St. Martin Cornw'l 6 D5
St. Martin Cornw'l 2 E6
St. Martins Perth/Kinr 286 D5
St. Martin's Shrops 148 B6
St. Martin's Wilts 63 F7
St. Martin's Moor Shrops 148 B6
St. Martin's Plain Kent 55 F7
St. Mary Bourne Hants 48 C2
St. Mary Church V/Glam 58 E4
St. Mary Cray London 68 F3
St. Mary Hill V/Glam 58 D3
St. Mary Hoo Medway 69 D10
St. Mary in the Marsh Kent 39 B9
St. Marychurch Torbay 9 B8
St. Mary's Orkney 313 H5
St. Mary's Bay Kent 39 B9
St Mary's Church Warwick 118 D5
St. Mary's Grove N Som'set 60 F3
St. Maughans Monmouths 79 B7
St. Maughans Green Monmouths 79 B7
St. Mawes Cornw'l 3 C8
St. Mawgan Cornw'l 5 B7
St. Mellion Cornw'l 7 B7
St. Mellons Card 59 C8
St. Merryn Cornw'l 10 G3
St. Mewan Cornw'l 5 E9
St. Michael Caerhays Cornw'l 5 G9
St. Michael Church Som'set 43 G10
St. Michael Penkevil Cornw'l 5 G7
St. Michael South Elmham Suffolk 142 G6
St. Michaels Kent 53 F11
St. Michael's Torbay 9 C7
St. Michael's Worcs 115 D11
St. Michael's Hamlet Mersey 182 D5
St. Michael's Mead Herts 87 B7
St Michael's Mount, Penzance Cornw'l 2 D2
St. Michael's-on-Wyre Lancs 202 E5
St. Minver Cornw'l 10 F5
St. Monans Fife 287 G9
St. Neot Cornw'l 6 B3
St. Neots Cambs 122 F2
St. Nicholas Pembs 91 D8
St. Nicholas V/Glam 58 E5
St. Nicholas at Wade Kent 71 F9
St. Nicholas South Elmham Suffolk 142 G6
St. Nicolas Park Warwick 135 E7
St. Ninians Stirl 278 C6
St. Olaves Norfolk 143 D9
St. Osyth Essex 89 B10
St. Osyth Heath Essex 89 B10
St. Owen's Cross Heref'd 97 G10
St Paul's Cathedral London 67 C10
St. Paul's Cray London 68 F3
St. Paul's Walden Herts 104 G4
St. Peter South Elmham Suffolk 142 G6
St. Peter The Great Worcs 117 G7
St. Peters Glos 99 G8
St. Peters Kent 71 F11
St. Peter's Tyne/Wear 243 E7
St. Petrox Pembs 73 F7
St. Pinnock Cornw'l 6 C4
St. Quivox S Ayrs 257 E9
St. Ruan Cornw'l 2 F6
St. Stephen Cornw'l 5 E8
St. Stephens Cornw'l 12 D2
St. Stephen's Cornw'l 7 D8
St. Stephen's Herts 85 D10
St. Teath Cornw'l 11 E7
St. Thomas Devon 14 C4
St. Tudy Cornw'l 11 F7
St. Twynnells Pembs 73 F7
St. Veep Cornw'l 6 D2
St. Vigeans Angus 287 C10
St. Vincent's Hamlet Essex 87 G9
St. Wenn Cornw'l 5 C9
St. Weonards Heref'd 97 G9
St. Winnow Cornw'l 6 D2
Saintbridge Glos 80 B5
Saintbury Glos 100 D2
Saint-y-Brid = St. Bride's Major V/Glam 57 G11
Saith Ffynnon Flints 181 F11
Salcombe Devon 9 G9
Salcombe Regis Devon 15 D8
Salcott Essex 89 C7
Sale Gtr Man 184 C3
Sale Ees Gtr Man 184 C3
Sale Green Worcs 117 F8
Saleby Lincs 191 F7
Salehurst E Sussex 38 C2
Salem Carms 94 F2
Salem Ceredig'n 128 G3
Salem Cornw'l 4 G4
Salen Arg/Bute 289 E7
Salen H'land 289 C8
Salendine Nook W Yorks 196 D6
Salesbury Lancs 203 G9
Saleway Worcs 117 F8
Salford Beds 103 D8
Salford Gtr Man 184 B4
Salford Oxon 100 F5
Salford Priors Warwick 117 G11
Salford Quays Gtr Man 184 B4
Salfords Surrey 51 D9
Salhouse Norfolk 160 G6
Saline Fife 279 C10
Salisbury Wilts 47 G7
Salisbury Cathedral Wilts 31 B10
Salisbury Racecourse Wilts 31 B10
Salisbury Street Dorset 30 D3
Salkeld Dykes Cumb 230 D6
Sallachan H'land 289 C11
Sallachy H'land 295 B11
Sallachy H'land 309 J5
Salle Norfolk 160 E2
Salmonby Lincs 190 G4
Salmond's Muir Angus 287 D9
Salperton Glos 99 G11
Salph End Beds 121 G11
Salsburgh N Lanarks 268 C6
Salt Staffs 151 D9
Salt Cotes Cumb 238 G5
Salt Hill Slough 66 C3
Salta Cumb 229 B7
Saltaire W Yorks 205 F8
Saltaire 1853 Gallery W Yorks 205 F8
Saltash Cornw'l 7 D8
Saltburn H'land 301 C7
Saltburn-by-the-Sea Redcar/Clevel'd 235 G9
Saltby Leics 155 D7
Saltcoats Cumb 219 F11
Saltcoats E Loth 281 E9
Saltcoats N Ayrs 266 G4
Saltcotes Lancs 193 B11
Saltdean Brighton/Hove 36 G5

Salter Street W Midlands 118 C2
Salterbeck Cumb 228 F5
Salterforth Lancs 204 D3
Saltergate N Yorks 227 G7
Saltergate Hill N Yorks 205 B11
Salters Heath Hants 48 B6
Salters Heath Kent 52 C4
Salters Lode Norfolk 139 C11
Salterswall Ches 167 B10
Salterton Wilts 46 F6
Saltfleet Lincs 191 C7
Saltfleetby All Saints Lincs 191 C7
Saltfleetby St. Clements Lincs 191 C7
Saltfleetby St. Peter Lincs 190 D6
Saltford Bath/NE Som'set 61 F7
Salthouse Cumb 210 F4
Salthouse Norfolk 177 E9
Saltley W Midlands 133 F11
Saltmarsh Newp 59 C11
Saltmarshe ER Yorks 199 C9
Saltmead Card 59 D7
Saltness Orkney 313 J3
Saltness Shetl'd 315 J4
Saltney Flints 166 C5
Salton N Yorks 216 C4
Saltrens Devon 25 C7
Saltwell Tyne/Wear 243 E7
Saltwick Northum 242 B5
Saltwood Kent 55 F7
Salum Arg/Bute 288 E2
Salvington W Sussex 35 F10
Salwarpe Worcs 117 E7
Salwayash Dorset 16 B5
Salwick Lancs 202 G5
Sambourne Warwick 117 E11
Sambourne Wilts 45 E11
Sambrook Telford 150 E4
Samhla W Isles 296 E3
Samlesbury Lancs 203 G7
Samlesbury Bottoms Lancs 194 B6
Sammy Miller Motorcycle Museum Hants 19 B10
Sampford Arundel Som'set 27 D10
Sampford Brett Som'set 42 E5
Sampford Chapple Devon 25 G10
Sampford Courtenay Devon 25 G10
Sampford Moor Som'set 27 D10
Sampford Peverell Devon 27 E8
Sampford Spiney Devon 12 G7
Samuel's Corner Essex 70 B3
Samuelston E Loth 281 G9
Sanachan H'land 299 E8
Sanaigmore Arg/Bute 274 F3
Sanclêr = St. Clears Carms 74 B3
Sancreed Cornw'l 1 D4
Sancton ER Yorks 208 F4
Sand H'land 307 K4
Sand Shetl'd 315 J5
Sand Som'set 44 D2
Sand Acre Cottages Lincs 156 C3
Sand Beds W Midlands 133 D9
Sand Hill ER Yorks 199 D10
Sand Hole ER Yorks 208 F2
Sand Hutton N Yorks 207 B9
Sand Side Cumb 210 C4
Sandaig H'land 295 E9
Sandal Magna W Yorks 197 D10
Sandale Cumb 229 C11
Sandavore H'land 294 G6
Sanday Airport Orkney 312 D7
Sandbach Ches 168 C3
Sandbach Heath Ches 168 C3
Sandbank Arg/Bute 276 E3
Sandbanks Poole 18 D6
Sandbraes Lincs 200 G6
Sandend Aberds 302 C5
Sanderstead London 67 G10
Sandfields Rh Cyn Taff 76 G2
Sandfields Staffs 134 B2
Sandford Cumb 222 B4
Sandford Dorset 18 D4
Sandford Devon 26 G4
Sandford Hants 31 G11
Sandford I/Wight 20 E6
Sandford N Som'set 44 B2
Sandford Shrops 148 E6
Sandford Shrops 149 C11
Sandford S Lanarks 268 G4
Sandford Hill Stoke 168 G6
Sandford on Thames Oxon 83 E8
Sandford Orcas Dorset 29 C10
Sandford St. Martin Oxon 101 F8
Sandfordhill Aberds 303 E11
Sandgate Kent 55 F8
Sandgreen Dumf/Gal 237 D7
Sandhaven Aberds 303 C9
Sandhead Dumf/Gal 236 E2
Sandhill Bucks 102 F4
Sandhill Cambs 139 F11
Sandhill S Yorks 186 B6
Sandhill S Yorks 198 F2
Sandhills Dorset 29 G9
Sandhills Dorset 29 E11
Sandhills Oxon 83 D9
Sandhills Surrey 50 F2
Sandhills W Yorks 206 F3
Sandhoe Northum 241 D11
Sandhole Arg/Bute 275 D11
Sandholme ER Yorks 208 G2
Sandholme Lincs 156 B6
Sandholme Landing ER Yorks 208 G2
Sandhurst Brackn'l 65 G10
Sandhurst Glos 98 G6
Sandhurst Kent 38 B3
Sandhurst Cross Kent 38 B3
Sandhutton N Yorks 215 C7
Sandiacre Derby 153 B9
Sandilands Lincs 191 E8
Sandilands S Lanarks 259 B9
Sandiway Ches 183 G10
Sandleford Close W Berks 64 F3
Sandleheath Hants 31 E10
Sandling Kent 53 B9
Sandlow Green Ches 168 B3
Sandness Shetl'd 315 H3
Sandon Essex 88 E2
Sandon Herts 104 E6
Sandon Staffs 151 D8
Sandown I/Wight 21 E7
Sandown Park Kent 52 E6
Sandown Park Surrey 66 F6
Sandown Park Racecourse Surrey 66 F6
Sandplace Cornw'l 6 D5
Sandridge Herts 85 C11
Sandringham Norfolk 158 D3
Sands Bucks 84 G4
Sandsend N Yorks 227 C7
Sandside Cumb 211 C9
Sandside Orkney 313 H3
Sandside Ho. H'land 310 C3
Sandsound Shetl'd 315 J5
Sandtoft N Lincs 199 F8
Sandvoe Shetl'd 314 D5
Sandway Dorset 45 G9
Sandway Kent 53 C11
Sandwell W Midlands 133 F10
Sandwich Kent 55 B10
Sandwich Bay Est Kent 55 B11
Sandwick Cumb 221 B8
Sandwick Orkney 313 K5
Sandwick Shetl'd 315 L6
Sandwith Cumb 219 C9
Sandwith Newton Cumb 219 C9
Sandy Beds 104 B3
Sandy Carms 75 E7
Sandy Bank Lincs 174 D3
Sandy Bank Shrops 149 B10
Sandy Carrs Durham 234 C3
Sandy Cross E Sussex 37 C9
Sandy Cross Surrey 49 D11
Sandy Gate Devon 14 C5
Sandy Haven Pembs 72 D5
Sandy Lane Wilts 62 F3
Sandy Lane Wrex 166 G6
Sandy Lane W Yorks 205 F8
Sandy Way I/Wight 20 E5
Sandybank Orkney 312 E6
Sandycroft Flints 166 B4
Sandyford Dumf/Gal 248 E6
Sandyford Stoke 168 E5
Sandygate Devon 14 G3
Sandygate I/Man 192 C4
Sandygate S Yorks 186 D4
Sandyhills Dumf/Gal 237 D10
Sandylake Cornw'l 6 C2
Sandylands Lancs 211 G8
Sandylane Swan 56 D5
Sandypark Devon 13 D10
Sandysike Cumb 239 D9
Sandystones Scot Borders 262 D3
Sandyway Heref'd 97 F9
Sanford Batch N Som'set 44 B2
Sangobeg H'land 308 C4
Sangomore H'land 308 C4
Sanham Green W Berks 63 F10
Sankey Bridges Warrington 183 D9
Sankyn's Green Worcs 116 D5
Sanna H'land 288 C6
Sanndabhaig W Isles 297 G4
Sanndabhaig W Isles 304 E6
Sannox N Ayrs 255 C11
Sanquhar Dumf/Gal 247 B7
Santa Barbara W Midlands 118 B3
Santa Pod Raceway Beds 121 E9
Santon Cumb 220 E2
Santon N Lincs 200 E2
Santon Bridge Cumb 220 E2
Santon Downham Norfolk 140 F6
Sapcote Leics 135 E9
Sapey Common Worcs 116 E4
Sapiston Suffolk 125 B8
Sapley Cambs 122 C4
Sapperton Glos 80 E6
Sapperton Lincs 155 C10
Saracen's Head Lincs 156 D6
Sarclet H'land 310 E7
Sardis Carms 75 E9
Sardis Pembs 73 D7
Sardis Mountain Pembs 73 D10
Sarisbury Hants 33 F8
Sarn Bridg 58 C2
Sarn Flints 181 F10
Sarn Powys 130 E4
Sarn Bach Gwyn 144 D6
Sarn Meyllteyrn Gwyn 144 C4
Sarnau Ceredig'n 110 G6
Sarnau Gwyn 147 B9
Sarnau Powys 148 F4
Sarnau Powys 95 E10
Sarnesfield Heref'd 115 G7
Saron Carms 93 D7
Saron Carms 75 C9
Saron Gwyn 163 B8
Saron Gwyn 163 D7
Sarratt Herts 85 F8
Sarratt Bottom Herts 85 F8
Sarre Kent 71 F9
Sarsden Oxon 100 G5
Sarsgrum H'land 308 C3
Satley Durham 233 C8
Satmar Kent 55 F9
Satran H'land 294 B6
Satron N Yorks 223 F8
Satterleigh Devon 25 C11
Satterthwaite Cumb 220 G6
Satwell Oxon 65 C8
Sauchen Aberds 293 B8
Saucher Perth/Kinr 286 D5
Sauchie Clack 279 C8
Sauchieburn Aberds 293 G8
Saughall Ches 182 G5
Saughall Massie Mersey 182 D3
Saughton C/Edinb 280 G4
Saughtree Scot Borders 250 D3
Saul Glos 80 D2
Saundby Notts 188 D3
Saundersfoot Pembs 73 E10
Saunderton Bucks 84 E3
Saunderton Lee Bucks 84 F3
Saunton Devon 40 F3
Sausthorpe Lincs 174 B5
Saval H'land 309 J5
Savary H'land 289 E8
Saveock Cornw'l 4 F5
Saverley Green Staffs 151 B9
Savile Park W Yorks 196 C5
Savile Town W Yorks 197 C8
Sawbridge Warwick 119 D10
Sawbridgeworth Herts 87 B7
Sawdon N Yorks 217 C8
Sawley Derby 153 C9
Sawley Lancs 203 D11
Sawley N Yorks 214 F4
Sawston Cambs 105 B9
Sawtry Cambs 138 G3
Saxby Leics 154 F6
Saxby Lincs 189 D8
Saxby All Saints N Lincs 200 D3
Saxelbye Leics 154 E4
Saxham Street Suffolk 125 E11
Saxilby Lincs 188 F5
Saxlingham Norfolk 159 B10
Saxlingham Green Norfolk 142 D4
Saxlingham Nethergate Norfolk 142 D4
Saxlingham Thorpe Norfolk 142 D4
Saxmundham Suffolk 127 E7
Saxon Street Cambs 124 F3
Saxondale Notts 154 B3
Saxtead Suffolk 126 D5
Saxtead Green Suffolk 126 E5
Saxtead Little Green Suffolk 126 D5
Saxthorpe Norfolk 160 C2
Saxton N Yorks 206 F5
Sayers Common W Sussex 36 D3
Scackleton N Yorks 216 E2
Scadabhagh W Isles 305 J3
Scaftworth Notts 187 C11
Scagglethorpe N Yorks 216 E6
Scaitcliffe Lancs 195 B9
Scaladal W Isles 305 G3
Scalan Moray 292 B4
Scalasaig Arg/Bute 274 D4
Scalby ER Yorks 199 B10
Scalby N Yorks 227 G10
Scalby Mills N Yorks 227 G10
Scald End Beds 121 F10
Scaldwell Northants 120 C5
Scale Hall Lancs 211 G9
Scaleby Cumb 239 E11
Scaleby Hill Cumb 239 E10
Scales Cumb 210 E5
Scales Cumb 230 F2
Scales Lancs 202 G5
Scalford Leics 154 E5
Scaling Redcar/Clevel'd 226 C4
Scaling Dam Redcar/Clevel'd 226 C4
Scaliscro W Isles 304 F3
Scallasaig H'land 295 D10
Scallastle Arg/Bute 289 F8
Scalloway Shetl'd 315 K6
Scalpay W Isles 305 J4
Scalpay Ho. H'land 295 C8
Scalpsie Arg/Bute 255 B11
Scamadale H'land 295 F9
Scamblesby Lincs 190 F3
Scammadale Arg/Bute 289 G10
Scamodale H'land 289 B10
Scampston N Yorks 217 D7
Scampton Lincs 189 F7
Scaniport H'land 300 F6
Scapa Orkney 313 H5
Scapegoat Hill W Yorks 196 D5
Scar Orkney 312 D7
Scarborough N Yorks 217 B10
Scarborough Sea Life Centre N Yorks 227 G10
Scarcewater Cornw'l 5 E8
Scarcliffe Derby 171 B7
Scarcroft W Yorks 206 E3
Scardroy H'land 300 D2
Scarff Shetl'd 314 E4
Scarfskerry H'land 310 B6
Scargill Durham 223 C11
Scarinish Arg/Bute 288 E2
Scarisbrick Lancs 193 E11
Scarletts Wokingham 65 D10
Scarness Cumb 229 E10
Scarning Norfolk 159 G9
Scarrington Notts 172 G3
Scarth Hill Lancs 194 F2
Scarthin Nick Derby 170 D3
Scarthingwell N Yorks 206 F5
Scartho NE Lincs 201 F9
Scarvister Shetl'd 315 J5
Scarwell Orkney 312 F3
Scatness Shetl'd 315 M5
Scatraig H'land 301 F7
Scatwell Ho H'land 300 D3
Scawby N Lincs 200 F3
Scawby Brook N Lincs 200 F3
Scawsby S Yorks 198 G4
Scawthorpe S Yorks 198 F5
Scawton N Yorks 215 C11
Scayne's Hill W Sussex 36 C5
Scethrog Powys 96 F2
Scholar Green Ches 168 D4
Scholemoor W Yorks 205 G8
Scholes Gtr Man 194 F5
Scholes S Yorks 186 B5
Scholes W Yorks 197 F7
Scholes W Yorks 204 F6
Scholes W Yorks 197 B7
Scholes W Yorks 206 F3
Scholey Hill W Yorks 197 B11
School Aycliffe Durham 233 G11
School Green Ches 167 C10
School Green Essex 106 E4
School Green I/Wight 20 D2
School House Dorset 28 G5
School Lane Lancs 194 B5
Schoolgreen Wokingham 65 F8
Schoolhill Aberds 293 D11
Sciberscross H'land 309 H7
Science & Industry Museum, Manchester Gtr Man 184 B4
Science Centre Glasg C 267 B11
Science Museum London 67 D9
Scilly Bank Cumb 219 B9
Scissett W Yorks 197 E9
Scleddau Pembs 91 E8
Sco Ruston Norfolk 160 E5
Scofton Notts 187 D11
Scole Norfolk 126 B3
Scole Common Norfolk 142 G2
Scolpaig W Isles 296 D3
Scone Perth/Kinr 286 E5
Scone Palace, Perth Perth/Kinr 286 E5
Sconser H'land 295 B7
Scoonie Fife 287 G7
Scoor Arg/Bute 288 H6
Scopwick Lincs 173 D9
Scoraig H'land 307 K5
Scorborough ER Yorks 208 D6
Scorrier Cornw'l 4 G4
Scorriton Devon 8 B4
Scorton Lancs 202 D6
Scorton N Yorks 224 E5
Scot Hay Staffs 168 F4
Scot Lane End Gtr Man 194 F6
Scotbheinn W Isles 296 F4
Scotby Cumb 239 G10
Scotch Corner N Yorks 224 D4
Scotforth Lancs 202 B5
Scothern Lincs 189 F8
Scotland Leics 136 D3
Scotland Lincs 155 C10
Scotland End Oxon 100 E6
Scotland Gate Northum 253 G7
Scotlandwell Perth/Kinr 286 G5
Scotney Castle Garden Kent 53 F7
Scot's Gap Northum 252 F2
Scotsburn H'land 301 B7
Scotscalder Station H'land 310 D4
Scotscraig Fife 287 E8
Scotsdike Cumb 239 C9
Scotston Aberds 293 F9
Scotston Perth/Kinr 286 C3
Scotstoun Glasg C 267 B10
Scotstown H'land 289 C10
Scotswood Tyne/Wear 242 E6
Scott Willoughby Lincs 155 B11
Scottas H'land 295 E9
Scotter Lincs 199 G11
Scotterthorpe Lincs 199 G11
Scottish Sea Life Sanctuary, Barcaldine Arg/Bute 284 C3
Scottlethorpe Lincs 155 E11
Scotton Lincs 188 B5
Scotton N Yorks 206 B2
Scotton N Yorks 224 F3
Scottow Norfolk 160 E5
Scoughall E Loth 282 E2
Scoulag Arg/Bute 266 D2
Scoulton Norfolk 141 C9
Scounslow Green Staffs 151 D11
Scourie H'land 306 E6
Scourie More H'land 306 E6
Scousburgh Shetl'd 315 M5
Scout Dike S Yorks 197 F8
Scout Green Cumb 221 D11
Scouthead Gtr Man 196 F3
Scowles Glos 79 C9
Scrabster H'land 310 B4
Scrafield Lincs 174 B4
Scragged Oak Kent 69 G10
Scrainwood Northum 251 B11
Scrane End Lincs 174 G5
Scrapsgate Kent 70 E2
Scraptoft Leics 136 B2
Scratby Norfolk 161 F10
Scrayingham N Yorks 216 G4
Scredington Lincs 173 G9
Scremby Lincs 174 B6
Scremerston Northum 273 F10
Screveton Notts 172 G2
Scrivelsby Lincs 174 B3
Scriven N Yorks 206 B3
Scriventon Kent 52 E5
Scronkey Lancs 202 D4
Scrooby Notts 187 C11
Scropton Derby 152 C3
Scrub Hill Lincs 174 D2
Scruton N Yorks 224 G6
Scrwgan Powys 148 E3
Scuddaborg H'land 298 C3
Scuggate Cumb 239 C10
Sculcoates Kingston/Hull 209 G7
Sculthorpe Norfolk 159 C7
Scunthorpe N Lincs 199 F11
Scupholme Lincs 190 C6
Scurlage Swan 56 D3
Sea Som'set 28 E4
Sea Mills Bristol 60 D5
Sea Palling Norfolk 161 D8
Seaborough Dorset 28 F6
Seabridge Staffs 168 G4
Seabrook Kent 55 G7
Seaburn Tyne/Wear 243 F10
Seacombe Mersey 182 C4
Seacox Heath Kent 53 G8
Seacroft Lincs 175 C9
Seacroft W Yorks 206 F3
Seadyke Lincs 156 B6
Seafar N Lanarks 278 G5
Seafield H'land 311 L3
Seafield Midloth 270 C5
Seafield S Ayrs 257 E8
Seafield W Loth 269 B10
Seaford E Sussex 23 F7
Seaforth Mersey 182 B5
Seagrave Leics 154 F2
Seagry Heath Wilts 62 C3
Seaham Durham 234 B4
Seahouses Northum 264 C6
Seal Kent 52 B5
Sealand Flints 166 B5
Seale Surrey 49 D11
Seamer N Yorks 217 C10
Seamer N Yorks 225 C10
Seamill N Ayrs 266 F3
Searby Lincs 200 F5
Seasalter Kent 70 F5
Seascale Cumb 219 E10
Seaside Carms 75 F8
Seathorne Lincs 175 B9
Seathwaite Cumb 220 F4
Seathwaite Cumb 220 C4
Seatle Cumb 211 C7
Seatoller Cumb 220 C4
Seaton Cumb 228 E6
Seaton Cornw'l 6 E6
Seaton Devon 15 C10
Seaton ER Yorks 209 D9
Seaton Kent 55 B8
Seaton Northum 243 B8
Seaton Rutl'd 137 D8
Seaton Burn Tyne/Wear 242 C6
Seaton Carew Hartlep'l 234 E6
Seaton Delaval Northum 243 B8
Seaton Junction Devon 15 B10
Seaton Ross ER Yorks 207 E11
Seaton Sluice Northum 243 B8
Seaton Terrace Northum 243 B8
Seatown Aberds 302 C5
Seatown Aberds 303 D11
Seatown Dorset 16 C4
Seave Green N Yorks 225 E11
Seaview I/Wight 21 C8
Seaville Cumb 238 G5
Seavington St. Mary Som'set 28 E5
Seavington St. Michael Som'set 28 D6
Seawick Essex 89 C10
Sebastopol Torf 78 F3
Sebay Orkney 313 H6
Sebergham Cumb 230 C3
Sebiston Velzian Orkney 312 F3
Seckington Warwick 134 B5
Second Coast H'land 307 K4
Sector Devon 16 B2
Sedbergh Cumb 222 G3
Sedbury Glos 79 G8
Sedbusk N Yorks 223 G7
Seddington Beds 104 B3
Sedgeberrow Worcs 99 D10
Sedgebrook Lincs 155 B7
Sedgecroft Devon 28 G4
Sedgefield Durham 234 F3
Sedgefield Racecourse Durham 234 F2
Sedgeford Norfolk 158 B4
Sedgehill Wilts 30 B5
Sedgemere W Midlands 118 B4
Sedgley W Midlands 133 E8
Sedgley Park Gtr Man 195 G10
Sedgwick Cumb 211 B10
Sedlescombe E Sussex 38 D3
Seed Kent 54 B2
Seedley Gtr Man 184 B4
Seend Wilts 62 G2
Seend Cleeve Wilts 62 G2
Seend Row Wilts 62 G2
Seer Green Bucks 85 G7
Seething Norfolk 142 D6
Sefton Mersey 193 G11
Seggat Aberds 303 E7
Seghill Northum 243 C7
Seighford Staffs 151 E7
Seilebost W Isles 305 J2
Seion Gwyn 163 B8
Seisdon Staffs 132 E6
Seisiadar W Isles 304 E7
Selattyn Shrops 148 C5
Selborne Hants 49 G8
Selby N Yorks 207 G8
Selham W Sussex 34 C6
Selhurst London 67 F10
Selkirk Scot Borders 261 D11
Selkirk Glass Scot Borders 261 D11
Sellack Heref'd 97 F11
Sellack Marsh Heref'd 97 F11
Sellafirth Shetl'd 314 D7
Sellibister Orkney 312 D8
Sellick's Green Som'set 28 D2
Sellindge Kent 54 F6
Selling Kent 54 B4
Sells Green Wilts 62 G3
Selly Hill N Yorks 227 D7
Selly Oak W Midlands 133 G10
Selly Park W Midlands 133 G11
Selmeston E Sussex 23 D8
Selsdon London 67 G11
Selsey Glos 80 E4
Selsey W Sussex 22 E5
Selsfeild Common W Sussex 51 G10
Selside Cumb 221 F10
Selside N Yorks 212 D5
Selsmore Hants 22 D2
Selson Kent 55 B10
Selstead Kent 55 E8
Selston Notts 171 E7
Selston Common Notts 171 E7
Selston Green Notts 171 E7
Selwick Orkney 313 H3
Selworthy Som'set 42 D2
Semblister Shetl'd 315 H5
Semer Suffolk 107 B9
Semere Green Norfolk 142 G3
Semington Wilts 61 G11
Semley Wilts 30 B5
Send Surrey 50 B4
Send Marsh Surrey 50 B4
Senghenydd Caerph 77 G10
Sennen Cornw'l 1 D3
Sennen Cove Cornw'l 1 D3
Sennicotts W Sussex 34 F4
Sennybridge = Pont Senni Powys 95 F8
Serbly Notts 187 D11
Serrington Wilts 46 F5
Sessay N Yorks 215 D9
Setchey Norfolk 158 G2
Setley Hants 32 G4
Seton E Loth 281 G8
Seton Mains E Loth 281 F8
Setter Shetl'd 314 E6
Setter Shetl'd 315 H5
Setter Shetl'd 315 J7
Setter Shetl'd 315 L6
Settiscarth Orkney 312 G4
Settle N Yorks 212 G6
Settrington N Yorks 216 E6
Seven Ash Som'set 43 G7
Seven Kings London 68 B3
Seven Sisters = Blaendulais Neath P Talb 76 D4
Seven Springs Glos 81 B7
Seven Star Green Essex 107 F8
Sevenhampton Glos 99 G10
Sevenhampton Swindon 82 G2
Sevenoaks Kent 52 B4
Sevenoaks Weald Kent 52 C4
Severn Beach S Glos 60 C4
Severn Bridges Visitor Centre S Glos 60 B4
Severn Stoke Worcs 99 C7
Severn Valley Railway Worcs 116 B5
Sevick End Beds 121 G11
Sevington Kent 54 E4
Sevington Wilts 61 D11
Sewards End Essex 105 D11
Sewardstone Essex 86 F5
Sewardstonebury Essex 86 F5
Sewell Beds 103 G10
Sewerby ER Yorks 218 F3
Sewerby Hall and Gardens, Bridlington ER Yorks 218 F4
Seworgan Cornw'l 2 C6
Sewstern Leics 155 E7
Sexhow N Yorks 225 D9
Sgarasta Mhor W Isles 305 J2
Sgiogarstaigh W Isles 304 B7
Shabbington Bucks 83 D11
Shackerley Shrops 132 B6
Shackerstone Leics 135 B7
Shacklecross Derby 153 C8
Shackleford Surrey 50 D2
Shacklewell London 67 B10
Shade W Yorks 196 C2
Shadforth Durham 234 C2
Shadingfield Suffolk 143 G8
Shadoxhurst Kent 54 F3
Shadsworth Blackb'n 195 B8
Shadwell Glos 80 F3
Shadwell London 67 C11
Shadwell Norfolk 141 G8
Shadwell W Yorks 206 F2
Shaftenhoe End Herts 105 D8
Shaftesbury Dorset 30 C5
Shaftholme S Yorks 198 F5
Shafton S Yorks 197 E11
Shafton Two Gates S Yorks 197 E11
Shaggs Dorset 18 E3
Shakerley Gtr Man 195 G7
Shakesfield Glos 98 E3
Shakespeare's Birthplace, Stratford-upon-Avon Warwick 118 G3
Shalbourne Wilts 63 G10
Shalcombe I/Wight 20 D3
Shalden Hants 49 E7
Shalden Green Hants 49 E7
Shaldon Devon 14 G4
Shalfleet I/Wight 20 D4
Shalford Essex 106 F4
Shalford Som'set 45 G8
Shalford Surrey 50 D4
Shalford Green Essex 106 F4
Shalloch Moray 302 D3
Shallowford Devon 13 F9
Shallowford Staffs 151 D7
Shalmsford Street Kent 54 C5
Shalstone Bucks 102 D2
Shamley Green Surrey 50 E4
Shandon Arg/Bute 276 D5
Shandwick H'land 301 B8
Shangton Leics 136 D4
Shankhouse Northum 243 B7
Shanklin I/Wight 21 E7
Shanklin Chine I/Wight 21 E7
Shannochie N Ayrs 255 E10
Shanquhar Aberds 302 F5
Shanwell Fife 287 E8
Shanzie Perth/Kinr 286 B6
Shap Cumb 221 B11
Shapridge Glos 79 B11
Shapwick Dorset 30 G6
Shapwick Som'set 44 F2
Sharcott Wilts 46 B7
Shard End W Midlands 134 F3
Shardlow Derby 153 C8
Shareshill Staffs 133 B8
Sharlston W Yorks 197 D11
Sharlston Common W Yorks 197 E11
Sharman's Cross W Midlands 118 B2
Sharnal Street Medway 69 E9
Sharnbrook Beds 121 F9
Sharneyford Lancs 195 C11
Sharnford Leics 135 E9
Sharnhill Green Dorset 30 F2
Sharoe Green Lancs 202 G6
Sharow N Yorks 214 E6
Sharp Street Norfolk 161 E7
Sharpenhoe Beds 103 E11
Sharperton Northum 251 C11
Sharples Gtr Man 195 E8
Sharpness Glos 79 E11
Sharp's Corner E Sussex 37 D9
Sharpsbridge E Sussex 36 C6
Sharpstone Bath/NE Som'set 45 B9
Sharpthorne W Sussex 51 G11
Sharptor Cornw'l 11 G11
Sharpway Gate Worcs 117 D9
Sharrington Norfolk 159 B10
Sharrow S Yorks 186 D4
Sharston Gtr Man 184 D4
Shatterford Worcs 132 G5
Shatterling Kent 55 B9
Shatton Derby 185 E11
Shaugh Prior Devon 7 C10
Shave Cross Dorset 16 B4
Shavington Ches 168 E2
Shaw Gtr Man 196 F2
Shaw Swindon 62 B6
Shaw W Berks 64 F3
Shaw Wilts 61 F11
Shaw W Yorks 204 F6
Shaw Common Glos 98 F3
Shaw Green Herts 104 E5
Shaw Green Lancs 194 D4
Shaw Green N Yorks 205 C11
Shaw Heath Ches 184 F3
Shaw Heath Gtr Man 184 D5
Shaw Lands S Yorks 197 F10
Shaw Mills N Yorks 214 G5
Shaw Side Gtr Man 196 F2
Shawbirtch Telford 150 G2
Shawbury Shrops 149 E11
Shawclough Gtr Man 195 E11
Shawell Leics 135 G10
Shawfield Gtr Man 195 E11
Shawfield Head N Yorks 205 C11
Shawford Hants 33 C7
Shawforth Lancs 195 C11
Shawhead Dumf/Gal 237 B10
Shawhead N Lanarks 268 C4
Shawhill Dumf/Gal 238 D6
Shawlands Glasg C 267 C11
Shawsburn S Lanarks 268 F5
Shawton S Lanarks 268 F3
Shawtonhill S Lanarks 268 F3
Sheandow Moray 302 F2
Shear Cross Wilts 45 E11
Shearington Dumf/Gal 238 D2
Shearsby Leics 136 E2
Shearston Som'set 43 G9
Shebbear Devon 24 F6
Shebdon Staffs 150 D5
Shebster H'land 310 C4
Sheddens E Renf 267 D11
Shedfield Hants 33 E9
Sheen Staffs 169 C10
Sheep Hill Durham 242 F5
Sheepbridge Derby 186 G5
Sheepcote Close N Yorks 225 F7
Sheepplane Beds 103 E8
Sheepridge W Yorks 196 D6
Sheepscar W Yorks 206 G2
Sheepscombe Glos 80 C5
Sheepstor Devon 7 B10
Sheeptick End Beds 103 D9
Sheepwash Devon 25 F7
Sheepwash Northum 253 F7
Sheepway N Som'set 60 D3
Sheepy Magna Leics 134 C6
Sheepy Parva Leics 134 C6
Sheering Essex 87 C8
Sheerness Kent 70 D2
Sheerwater Kent 71 G9
Sheerwater Surrey 66 G4
Sheet Hants 34 C3
Sheet Shrops 115 C10
Sheets Heath Surrey 50 B3
Sheffield Cornw'l 1 D5
Sheffield S Yorks 186 D5
Sheffield Bottom W Berks 65 F7
Sheffield Common Essex 87 G9
Sheffield Green E Sussex 36 B6
Sheffield Park S Yorks 186 D5
Sheffield Park, Uckfield E Sussex 36 C6
Shefford Beds 104 D2
Shefford Woodlands W Berks 63 E11
Sheigra H'land 306 C6
Sheinton Shrops 132 C2
Shelderton Shrops 115 B8
Sheldon Derby 169 B11
Sheldon Devon 27 F10
Sheldon W Midlands 134 G3
Sheldwich Kent 54 B4
Sheldwich Lees Kent 54 B4
Shelf Bridg 58 C2
Shelf W Yorks 196 B6
Shelfanger Norfolk 142 G2
Shelfield Warwick 118 E2
Shelfield W Midlands 133 C10
Shelfield Green Warwick 118 E2
Shelfleys Northants 120 F4
Shelford Notts 171 G11
Shelford Warwick 135 F8
Shell Green Halton 183 D8
Shelley Essex 87 D9
Shelley Suffolk 107 D10
Shelley W Yorks 197 E8
Shellingford Oxon 82 G4
Shellow Bowells Essex 87 D10
Shellthorn Som'set 43 G8
Shelly Green W Midlands 118 B2
Shelsley Beauchamp Worcs 116 E4
Shelsley Walsh Worcs 116 E4
Shelthorpe Leics 153 F10
Shelton Beds 121 D10
Shelton Norfolk 142 E4
Shelton Notts 172 G3
Shelton Shrops 149 G9
Shelton Common Norfolk 142 E4
Shelton Green Norfolk 142 E4
Shelton Lock Derby C 153 C7
Shelton under Harley Staffs 150 B6
Shelve Shrops 130 D6
Shelvingford Kent 71 F8
Shelwick Heref'd 97 C10
Shelwick Green Heref'd 97 C10
Shenfield Essex 87 G9
Shenington Oxon 101 C7
Shenley Herts 85 E11
Shenley Brook End M/Keynes 102 E6
Shenley Church End M/Keynes 102 D6
Shenley Fields W Midlands 133 G10
Shenley Lodge M/Keynes 102 D6
Shenleybury Herts 85 E11
Shenmore Heref'd 97 D7
Shennanton Dumf/Gal 236 C5
Shennanton Ho. Dumf/Gal 236 C5
Shenstone Staffs 134 C2
Shenstone Worcs 117 C7
Shenstone Woodend Staffs 134 C2
Shenton Leics 135 C7
Shenval H'land 300 G4
Shenval Moray 302 G2
Shenvault Moray 301 E10
Shepard Hill N Yorks 225 E9
Shepard Hill W Yorks 197 C9
Shepeau Stow Lincs 156 G6
Shephall Herts 104 G5
Shepherds Cornw'l 4 E6
Shepherd's Bush London 67 C8
Shepherd's Gate Norfolk 157 F11
Shepherd's Green Oxon 65 C8
Shepherd's Patch Glos 80 E2
Shepherd's Port Norfolk 158 C3
Shepherdswell or Sibertswold Kent 55 D9
Shepley W Yorks 197 F7
Shepperdine S Glos 79 F10
Shepperton Surrey 66 F5
Shepperton Green Surrey 66 F5
Shepreth Cambs 105 B7
Shepshed Leics 153 F9
Shepton Beauchamp Som'set 28 D6
Shepton Mallet Som'set 44 E6
Shepton Montague Som'set 45 G7
Shepway Kent 53 C9
Sheraton Durham 234 D4
Sherborne Dorset 29 D10
Sherborne Glos 81 C11
Sherborne Causeway Dorset 30 C4
Sherborne St. John Hants 48 B6
Sherborne Street Suffolk 107 C9
Sherbourne Warwick 118 E5
Sherburn Durham 234 C2
Sherburn N Yorks 217 D9
Sherburn Hill Durham 234 C2
Sherburn in Elmet N Yorks 206 G5
Shere Surrey 50 D5
Shereford Norfolk 159 D7
Sherfield English Hants 32 C3
Sherfield Hill Hants 49 B7
Sherfield on Loddon Hants 49 B7
Sherfin Lancs 195 B9
Sherford Devon 8 G5
Sherford Som'set 28 C2
Sheriff Hill Tyne/Wear 243 E7
Sheriff Hutton N Yorks 216 F3
Sheriffhales Shrops 150 G5
Sheringham Norfolk 177 E11
Sherington M/Keynes 103 B7
Sheringwood Norfolk 177 E11
Shernal Green Worcs 117 E8
Shernborne Norfolk 158 C4
Sherrard's Green Worcs 98 B6
Sherrardspark Herts 86 C2
Sherrington Wilts 46 F3
Sherston Wilts 61 B11
Sherston Parva Wilts 61 B11
Sherwood Nott'ham 171 G9
Sherwood Lancs 202 G6
Sherwood Park Kent 52 E6
Shettleston Glasg C 268 C2
Shevington Gtr Man 194 F4
Shevington Moor Gtr Man 194 E4
Shevington Vale Gtr Man 194 F4

Sheviock Cornw'l 7 D7
Shewalton N Ayrs 257 B8
Shibden Head W Yorks 196 B5
Shide I/Wight 20 D5
Shiel Aberds 292 B4
Shiel Bridge H'land 295 D11
Shield Row Durham 242 G6
Shieldaig H'land 299 B8
Shieldaig H'land 299 D8
Shieldhall Glasg C 267 B10
Shieldhall Falk 279 F7
Shieldhill Dumf/Gal 248 F2
Shieldhill S Lanarks 269 G10
Shieldmuir N Lanarks 268 D5
Shielfoot H'land 289 C8
Shielhill Angus 287 B8
Shifford Oxon 82 E5
Shifnal Shrops 132 B5
Shilbottle Northum 252 B5
Shilbottle Grange Northum 252 B6
Shildon Durham 233 F10
Shillford E Renf 267 D8
Shillingford Devon 27 C7
Shillingford Oxon 83 G9
Shillingford Abbot Devon 14 D4
Shillingford St. George Devon 14 D4
Shillingstone Dorset 30 E4
Shillington Beds 104 D2
Shillmoor Northum 251 B9
Shilton Oxon 82 D3
Shilton Warwick 135 G8
Shilvinghampton Dorset 17 E8
Shilvington Northum 252 G5
Shimpling Norfolk 142 G3
Shimpling Suffolk 125 G7
Shimpling Street Suffolk 125 G7
Shincliffe Durham 233 C11
Shiney Row Tyne/Wear 243 G8
Shinfield Wokingham 65 F8
Shingay Cambs 104 B6
Shingham Norfolk 140 B5
Shingle Street Suffolk 109 C7
Shinner's Bridge Devon 8 C5
Shinness H'land 309 H5
Shipbourne Kent 52 C5
Shipbrookhill Ches 183 G11
Shipdham Norfolk 141 B9
Shipham Som'set 44 B2
Shiphay Torbay 9 B7
Shiplake Oxon 65 D9
Shiplake Bottom Oxon 65 C8
Shiplake Row Oxon 65 D9
Shiplate N Som'set 43 B11
Shipley Northum 264 F4
Shipley Shrops 132 D6
Shipley W Sussex 35 C10
Shipley W Yorks 205 F8
Shipley Bridge Surrey 51 E10
Shipley Common Derby 171 G7
Shipmeadow Suffolk 143 F7
Shipmeadow Common Suffolk 143 F7
Shippon Oxon 83 F7
Shipston on Stour Warwick 100 C5
Shipton Bucks 102 F5
Shipton Glos 81 B8
Shipton N Yorks 207 B7
Shipton Shrops 131 E11
Shipton Bellinger Hants 47 D8
Shipton Gorge Dorset 16 C5
Shipton Green W Sussex 22 D3
Shipton Moyne Glos 61 B11
Shipton Oliffe Glos 81 B8
Shipton on Cherwell Oxon 83 B7
Shipton Solers Glos 81 B8
Shipton under Wychwood Oxon 82 B3
Shiptonthorpe ER Yorks 208 E3
Shirburn Oxon 84 F2
Shirdley Hill Lancs 193 E11
Shire Cumb 231 D8
Shire Horse Centre, Stratford-upon-Avon Warwick 118 G4
Shire Oak W Midlands 133 C11
Shirebrook Derby 171 B8
Shirecliffe S Yorks 186 C4
Shiregreen S Yorks 186 C5
Shirehampton Bristol 60 D4
Shiremoor Tyne/Wear 243 C8
Shirenewton Monmouths 79 G7
Shireoaks Notts 187 E9
Shirkoak Kent 54 F2
Shirl Heath Heref'd 115 F8
Shirland Derby 170 D5
Shirlett Shrops 132 D3
Shirley Derby 170 G2
Shirley Hants 19 B9
Shirley S'thampton 32 E6
Shirley W Midlands 118 B2
Shirley Heath W Midlands 118 B2
Shirley Warren S'thampton 32 E6
Shirrell Heath Hants 33 E9
Shirwell Devon 40 F5
Shirwell Cross Devon 40 F5
Shiskine N Ayrs 255 E10
Shittlehope Durham 232 D6
Shobdon Heref'd 115 E7
Shobley Hants 31 F11
Shobnall Staffs 152 E4
Shobrooke Devon 26 G5
Shoby Leics 154 E3
Shocklach Ches 166 F6
Shocklach Green Ches 166 F6
Shoeburyness Southend 70 C2
Sholden Kent 55 C11
Sholing S'thampton 33 E7
Sholing Common S'thampton 33 E7
Sholver Gtr Man 196 F2
Shoot Hill Shrops 149 G8
Shootash Hants 32 C4
Shooter's Hill London 68 D2
Shootersway Herts 85 D7
Shop Cornw'l 10 G3
Shop Cornw'l 24 E2
Shop Devon 24 E5
Shop Corner Suffolk 108 D4
Shopford Cumb 240 C3
Shopnoller Som'set 43 G7
Shore Gtr Man 196 D2
Shore W Yorks 196 B2
Shore Mill H'land 301 C7
Shoreditch London 67 C10
Shoreditch Som'set 28 C2
Shoregill Cumb 222 E5
Shoreham Kent 68 G4
Shoreham Airport W Sussex 36 F2
Shoreham Beach W Sussex 36 G2
Shoreham-by-Sea W Sussex 36 G2
Shoresdean Northum 273 F9
Shoreside Shetl'd 315 J4
Shoreswood Northum 273 F8
Shoreton H'land 300 C6
Shorley Hants 33 B9
Shorncote Glos 81 F8
Shorne Kent 69 E7
Shorne Ridgeway Kent 69 E7
Short Cross W Midlands 133 G9
Short Heath Leics 152 G6
Short Heath W Midlands 133 E11
Short Street Wilts 45 D10
Shorta Cross Cornw'l 6 D5
Shortacombe Devon 12 D6
Shortbridge E Sussex 36 C6
Shortfield Common Surrey 49 E10
Shortgate E Sussex 37 D7
Shorthampton Oxon 100 G6
Shortheath Hants 49 F9
Shortheath Surrey 49 E10
Shortlands London 67 F11
Shortlanesend Cornw'l 4 F6
Shortlees E Ayrs 257 B10
Shorton Torbay 9 C7
Shortroods Renf 267 B9
Short's Corner Lincs 174 E4
Shortstanding Glos 79 C9
Shortstown Beds 103 B11
Shortwood Glos 80 F4
Shortwood S Glos 61 D7
Shorwell I/Wight 20 E5
Shoscombe Bath/NE Som'set 45 B8
Shoscombe Vale Bath/NE Som'set 45 B8
Shotesham Norfolk 142 D5
Shotford Heath Suffolk 142 G4
Shotgate Essex 88 G3
Shotley Northants 137 D8
Shotley Suffolk 108 D4
Shotley Bridge Northum 242 G3
Shotley Gate Suffolk 108 D4
Shotleyfield Northum 242 G3
Shottenden Kent 54 C4
Shottermill Surrey 49 G11
Shottery Warwick 118 F3
Shotteswell Warwick 101 B8
Shottisham Suffolk 108 C6
Shottle Derby 170 F4
Shottlegate Derby 170 F4
Shotton Durham 234 D4
Shotton Durham 234 F3
Shotton Flints 166 B4
Shotton Northum 242 B6
Shotton Northum 263 C8
Shotton Colliery Durham 234 C3
Shotts N Lanarks 269 C7
Shotwick Ches 182 G4
Shouldham Norfolk 140 B3
Shouldham Thorpe Norfolk 140 B3
Shoulton Worcs 116 F6
Shover's Green E Sussex 52 G6
Shraleybrook Staffs 168 F3
Shrawardine Shrops 149 F8
Shrawley Worcs 116 E6
Shreding Green Bucks 66 C4
Shrewley Warwick 118 D4
Shrewsbury Shrops 149 G10
Shrewton Wilts 46 E5
Shripney W Sussex 34 G6
Shrivenham Oxon 63 B8
Shropham Norfolk 141 E9
Shroton Dorset 30 E4
Shrub End Essex 107 G9
Shrubs Hill Surrey 66 F3
Shuart Kent 71 F9
Shucknall Heref'd 97 C11
Shudy Camps Cambs 106 C2
Shulishadermor H'land 298 E4
Shulista H'land 298 B4
Shuna Ho Arg/Bute 275 C8
Shurdington Glos 80 B6
Shurlock Row Windsor 65 E10
Shurnock Worcs 117 E10
Shurrery H'land 310 D4
Shurrery Lodge H'land 310 D4
Shurton Som'set 43 E8
Shustoke Warwick 134 E4
Shute Devon 15 B11
Shute Devon 26 G5
Shute End Wilts 31 B11
Shutford Oxon 101 C7
Shutheath Staffs 151 E7
Shuthonger Glos 99 D7
Shutlanger Northants 102 B4
Shutta Cornw'l 6 E5
Shuttington Warwick 134 B5
Shuttlesfield Kent 55 E7
Shuttlewood Derby 187 G7
Shuttleworth Lancs 195 D10
Shwt Bridg 57 D11
Siabost bho Dheas W Isles 304 D4
Siabost bho Thuath W Isles 304 D4
Siadar W Isles 304 C5
Siadar Iarach W Isles 304 C5
Siadar Uarach W Isles 304 C5
Sibbaldbie Dumf/Gal 248 F4
Sibbertoft Northants 136 G3
Sibdon Carwood Shrops 131 G8
Sibford Ferris Oxon 101 D7
Sibford Gower Oxon 101 D7
Sible Hedingham Essex 106 E5
Sibley's Green Essex 106 F2
Sibsey Lincs 174 E5
Sibsey Fen Side Lincs 174 E4
Sibson Cambs 137 D11
Sibson Leics 135 C7
Sibster H'land 310 D7
Sibthorpe Notts 172 F3
Sibthorpe Notts 188 G2
Sibton Suffolk 127 D7
Sibton Green Suffolk 127 C7
Sicklesmere Suffolk 125 E7
Sicklinghall N Yorks 206 D3
Sid Devon 15 D8
Sidbrook Som'set 28 B3
Sidbury Devon 15 C8
Sidbury Shrops 132 F3
Sidcot N Som'set 44 B2
Sidcup London 68 E3
Siddal W Yorks 196 C6
Siddick Cumb 228 E6
Siddington Ches 184 G4
Siddington Glos 81 F8
Side of the Moor Gtr Man 195 E8
Sidemoor Worcs 117 C8
Sidestrand Norfolk 160 B5
Sideway Stoke 168 G5
Sidford Devon 15 C8
Sidlesham W Sussex 22 D5
Sidley E Sussex 38 F2
Sidlow Surrey 51 D9
Sidmouth Devon 15 D8
Siefton Shrops 131 G9
Sigford Devon 13 G11
Sigglesthorne ER Yorks 209 D9
Sighthill C/Edinb 280 G3
Sigingstone V/Glam 58 E3
Signet Oxon 82 C2
Silchester Hants 64 G6
Sildinis W Isles 305 G4
Sileby Leics 154 F2
Silecroft Cumb 210 C2
Silfield Norfolk 142 D2
Silford Devon 24 B6
Silian Ceredig'n 111 G11
Silk Willoughby Lincs 173 G9
Silkstead Hants 32 C6
Silkstone S Yorks 197 F9
Silkstone Common S Yorks 197 G9
Sill Field Cumb 211 B11
Sillaton Cornw'l 7 C7
Sillerhole Fife 281 A7
Silloth Cumb 238 G4
Sillyearn Moray 302 D5
Siloh Carms 94 D4
Silpho N Yorks 227 G9
Silsden W Yorks 204 D6
Silsoe Beds 103 D11
Silver End Essex 88 B4
Silver Green Norfolk 142 E5
Silver Hill E Sussex 38 B2
Silver Street Glos 80 E3
Silver Street Kent 69 G11
Silver Street Som'set 27 C11
Silver Street Som'set 44 G4
Silver Street Worcs 117 B11
Silverburn Midloth 270 C4
Silverdale Lancs 211 D9
Silverdale Staffs 168 F4
Silverdale Green Lancs 211 E9
Silvergate Norfolk 160 D3
Silverhill E Sussex 38 E4
Silverhill Park E Sussex 38 E4
Silverknowes C/Edinb 280 F4
Silverlace Green Suffolk 126 E6
Silverley's Green Suffolk 126 B5
Silverstone Northants 102 C3
Silverstone Motor Racing Circuit Northants 102 C3
Silverton Devon 27 G7
Silverton W Dunb 277 F8
Silvertonhill S Lanarks 268 E4
Silvertown London 68 C2
Silverwell Cornw'l 4 F4
Silvington Shrops 116 B2
Silwick Shetl'd 315 J4
Simister Gtr Man 195 F10
Simmondley Derby 185 C8
Simm's Cross Halton 183 D8
Simm's Lane End Mersey 194 G4
Simonburn Northum 241 C9
Simonsbath Som'set 41 F9
Simonside Tyne/Wear 243 E8
Simonstone Lancs 203 G11
Simonstone N Yorks 223 G7
Simprim Scot Borders 273 F7
Simpson M/Keynes 103 D7
Simpson Pembs 72 B5
Simpson Cross Pembs 72 B5
Simpson Green W Yorks 205 F9
Sinclair's Hill Scot Borders 272 E6
Sinclairston E Ayrs 257 F11
Sinclairtown Fife 280 C5
Sinderby N Yorks 214 C6
Sinderhope Northum 241 G8
Sinderland Green Gtr Man 184 C2
Sindlesham Wokingham 65 F9
Sinfin Derby C 152 C6
Singdean Scot Borders 250 C3
Singleborough Bucks 102 E5
Singledge Kent 55 D9
Singleton Lancs 202 G2
Singleton W Sussex 34 E5
Singlewell Kent 69 E7
Singret Wrex 166 D4
Sinkhurst Green Kent 53 E10
Sinnahard Aberds 292 B6
Sinnington N Yorks 216 B4
Sinton Worcs 116 E6
Sinton Green Worcs 116 E6
Sion Hill Bath/NE Som'set 61 F8
Sion Hill N Yorks 215 C7
Sipson London 66 D5
Sirhowy Bl Gwent 77 D10
Sisland Norfolk 142 D6
Sissinghurst Kent 53 F9
Sissinghurst Castle Garden Kent 53 F10
Siston S Glos 61 D7
Sithney Cornw'l 2 D4
Sithney Green Cornw'l 2 D4
Sitterton Dorset 18 C2
Sittingbourne Kent 70 G2
Sitwell Grange Derby 170 C6
Six Ashes Staffs 132 F5
Six Bells Bl Gwent 78 E2
Six Mile Bottom Cambs 123 F10
Sixhills Lincs 189 D10
Sixmile Kent 54 E6
Sixpenny Handley Dorset 31 D7
Sizewell Suffolk 127 E9
Skail H'land 308 E7
Skaill Orkney 312 E5
Skaill Orkney 312 G3
Skaill Orkney 313 H6
Skara Brae Orkney 312 G3
Skares E Ayrs 258 F2
Skateraw E Loth 282 F4
Skaw Shetl'd 314 B8
Skaw Shetl'd 314 G7
Skeabost H'land 298 E4
Skeabrae Orkney 312 F3
Skeeby N Yorks 224 E4
Skeete Kent 54 E6
Skeffington Leics 136 C4
Skeffling ER Yorks 201 D11
Skegby Notts 171 C8
Skegness Lincs 175 C9
Skelberry Shetl'd 315 G6
Skelberry Shetl'd 315 M5
Skelbo H'land 309 K7
Skelbo Street H'land 309 K7
Skelbrooke S Yorks 198 E4
Skeldyke Lincs 156 B6
Skelfhill Scot Borders 249 C11
Skellingthorpe Lincs 188 G6
Skellister Shetl'd 315 H6
Skellorn Green Ches 184 E6
Skellow S Yorks 198 E4
Skelmanthorpe W Yorks 197 E8
Skelmersdale Lancs 194 F3
Skelmonae Aberds 303 F8
Skelmorlie N Ayrs 266 B3
Skelmuir Aberds 303 E9
Skelpick H'land 308 D7
Skelton Cumb 230 D4
Skelton C/York 207 B7
Skelton ER Yorks 199 B9
Skelton N Yorks 215 F7
Skelton N Yorks 223 E11
Skelton Redcar/Clevel'd 226 B3
Skelton Green Redcar/Clevel'd 226 B3
Skelton Wood End Cumb 230 D4
Skelwick Orkney 312 D5
Skelwith Bridge Cumb 220 E6
Skendleby Lincs 174 B6
Skendleby Psalter Lincs 190 G6
Skene Ho. Aberds 293 C9
Skenfrith Monmouths 97 G9
Skerne ER Yorks 208 B6
Skeroblingarry Arg/Bute 255 E8
Skerray H'land 308 C6
Skerricha H'land 306 D7
Skerton Lancs 211 G9
Sketchley Leics 135 E8
Sketchley Hill Leics 135 E8
Sketty Swan 75 G10
Skewen Rh Cyn Taff 76 F2
Skewsby N Yorks 216 E2
Skeyton Norfolk 160 D4
Skeyton Corner Norfolk 160 D5
Skiag Bridge H'land 307 G7
Skibo Castle H'land 309 L7
Skidbrooke Lincs 190 C6
Skidbrooke North End Lincs 190 B6
Skidby ER Yorks 208 G6
Skilgate Som'set 27 B7
Skillington Lincs 155 E7
Skinburness Cumb 238 F4
Skinflats Falk 279 E8
Skinidin H'land 298 E2
Skinnand Lincs 172 D6
Skinner's Bottom Cornw'l 4 F4
Skinners Green W Berks 64 F3
Skinnet H'land 308 C5
Skinningrove Redcar/Clevel'd 226 B4
Skipness Arg/Bute 255 B9
Skippool Lancs 202 E2
Skiprigg Cumb 230 B3
Skipsea ER Yorks 209 C9
Skipsea Brough ER Yorks 209 C9
Skipton N Yorks 204 C5
Skipton-on-Swale N Yorks 215 D7
Skipwith N Yorks 207 F9
Skirbeck Lincs 174 G4
Skirbeck Quarter Lincs 174 G4
Skireholme N Yorks 213 G11
Skirethorns N Yorks 213 G9
Skirlaugh ER Yorks 209 F8
Skirling Scot Borders 260 B3
Skirmett Bucks 65 B9
Skirpenbeck ER Yorks 207 B10
Skirwith N Yorks 212 E4
Skirwith Cumb 231 E8
Skirza H'land 310 C7
Skitby Cumb 239 D10
Skitham Lancs 202 E4
Skittle Green Bucks 84 E3
Skrinkle Pembs 73 F9
Skulamus H'land 295 C8
Skullomie H'land 308 C6
Skyborry Green Shrops 114 C5
Skye Green Essex 107 G7
Skye of Curr H'land 301 G9
Skyfog Pembs 90 F6
Slack W Yorks 196 B3
Slack Head Cumb 211 D9
Slackcote Gtr Man 196 F3
Slackhall Derby 185 E9
Slackhead Moray 302 C4
Slackholme End Lincs 191 G8
Slacks of Cairnbanno Aberds 303 E8
Slad Glos 80 D5
Slade Kent 54 C2
Slade Pembs 72 B6
Slade Swan 56 D3
Slade End Oxon 83 G9
Slade Green London 68 D4
Slade Heath Staffs 133 B8
Slade Hooton S Yorks 187 E9
Slades Green Worcs 99 E7
Sladesbridge Cornw'l 10 G6
Slaggyford Northum 240 G5
Slaid Hill W Yorks 206 E2
Slaidburn Lancs 203 C10
Slaithwaite W Yorks 196 E5
Slaley Derby 170 D3
Slaley Northum 241 F11
Slamannan Falk 279 G7
Slapeworth Redcar/Clevel'd 226 B2
Slapton Bucks 103 G8
Slapton Devon 8 F6
Slapton Northants 102 B2
Slate Haugh Moray 302 C4
Slatepit Dale Derby 170 B4
Slattocks Gtr Man 195 F11
Slaugham W Sussex 36 B3
Slaughterford Wilts 61 E10
Slawston Leics 136 E5
Slay Pits S Yorks 199 F7
Slea View Lincs 173 F9
Sleaford Hants 49 F10
Sleaford Lincs 173 F9
Sleagill Cumb 221 B11
Sleap Shrops 149 D9
Sleapford Telford 150 F2
Sleapshyde Herts 86 D2
Sleastary H'land 309 K6
Sledge Green Worcs 98 E6
Sledmere ER Yorks 217 G8
Sleeches Cross E Sussex 52 G5
Sleet Moor Derby 170 E6
Sleight Dorset 18 B5
Sleights N Yorks 227 D7
Slepe Dorset 18 C4
Slerra Devon 24 C4
Sliabhna h-Airde W Isles 296 F3
Slickly H'land 310 C6
Sliddery N Ayrs 255 E10
Sligachan Hotel H'land 294 C6
Sligneach Arg/Bute 288 G4
Slimbridge Glos 80 E2
Slimbridge Wildfowl & Wetlands Centre, Frampton on Severn Glos 80 E2
Slindon Staffs 150 C6
Slindon W Sussex 35 F7
Slindon Common W Sussex 35 F7
Slinfold W Sussex 50 G6
Sling Glos 79 D9
Sling Gwyn 163 B10
Slingsby N Yorks 216 D4
Slioch Aberds 302 F5
Slip End Beds 85 B9
Slip End Herts 104 D5
Slipper's Hill Cornw'l 11 F11
Slipton Northants 121 B9
Slitting Mill Staffs 151 F10
Sloadlane Derby 186 E5
Slochd H'land 301 G8
Slockavullin Arg/Bute 275 D9
Slogan Moray 302 E3
Sloley Norfolk 160 E5
Sloncombe Devon 13 D10
Sloothby Lincs 191 G7
Slough Windsor 66 C3
Slough Green Som'set 28 C3
Slough Green W Sussex 36 B3
Sluggan H'land 301 G8
Sluggans H'land 298 E4
Slumbay H'land 295 B10
Slyfield Surrey 50 C3
Slyne Lancs 211 F9
Smailholm Scot Borders 262 B4
Small Dole W Sussex 36 E2
Small End Lincs 174 D6
Small Heath W Midlands 133 F11
Small Hythe Kent 53 G11
Small Way Som'set 44 G6
Smallbridge Gtr Man 196 E2
Smallbrook Devon 14 B3
Smallbrook Glos 79 E9
Smallburgh Norfolk 160 E6
Smallburn Aberds 303 E10
Smallburn E Ayrs 258 D5
Smalldale Derby 185 F9
Smalldale Derby 185 E11
Smalley Derby 170 G6
Smalley Common Derby 170 G6
Smalley Green Derby 170 G6
Smallfield Surrey 51 E10
Smallford Herts 85 D11
Smallholm Dumf/Gal 238 B3
Smallridge Devon 28 G3
Smallshaw Gtr Man 196 G2
Smallwood Worcs 117 D10
Smallwood Green Suffolk 125 F8
Smallwood Hey Lancs 202 D3
Smallworth Norfolk 141 G10
Smannell Hants 47 D11
Smardale Cumb 222 D4
Smarden Kent 53 E11
Smarden Bell Kent 53 E11
Smart's Hill Kent 52 E4
Smaull Arg/Bute 274 G3
Smeatharpe Devon 27 E11
Smeaton Fife 280 C5
Smeeth Kent 54 F5
Smeeton Westerby Leics 136 E3
Smelthouses N Yorks 214 G3
Smercleit W Isles 297 K3
Smerral H'land 310 F5
Smestow Staffs 133 E7
Smethcott Shrops 131 D8
Smethwick W Midlands 133 F10
Smirisary H'land 289 B8
Smisby Derby 153 F7
Smith End Green Worcs 116 G5
Smith Green Lancs 202 B5
Smithaleigh Devon 7 D11
Smithbrook W Sussex 34 C6
Smithfield Cumb 239 D10
Smithies S Yorks 197 F11
Smithincott Devon 27 E9
Smithley S Yorks 197 G11
Smith's End Herts 105 D7
Smith's Green Essex 105 G11
Smith's Green Essex 106 C3
Smithston Aberds 302 G5
Smithstown H'land 299 B7
Smithton H'land 301 E7
Smithwood Green Suffolk 125 G8
Smithy Bridge Gtr Man 196 D2
Smithy Gate Flints 181 F11
Smithy Green Ches 184 G2
Smithy Green Cumb 210 C6
Smithy Green Gtr Man 184 D5
Smithy Hill Derby 185 E11
Smithy Lane Ends Lancs 194 E2
Smockington Leics 135 F8
Smoky Row Bucks 84 D4
Smoogro Orkney 313 H4
Smythe's Green Essex 88 B6
Snaefell Mountain Railway I/Man 192 D5
Snaigow House Perth/Kinr 286 C4
Snailbeach Shrops 131 C7
Snailswell Herts 104 E3
Snailwell Cambs 124 D2
Snainton N Yorks 217 C8
Snaisgill Durham 232 F5
Snaith ER Yorks 198 C6
Snape N Yorks 214 C5
Snape Suffolk 127 F7
Snape Green Lancs 193 E11
Snape Hill Derby 186 F5
Snape Hill S Yorks 198 G2
Snape Watering Suffolk 127 F7
Snapper Devon 40 G6
Snaresbrook London 67 B11
Snarestone Leics 134 B6
Snarford Lincs 189 E9
Snargate Kent 39 B7
Snarraness Shetl'd 315 H4
Snatchwood Torf 78 E3
Snave Kent 39 B8
Sneachill Worcs 117 G8
Snead Common Heref'd 116 D4
Sneath Common Norfolk 142 F3
Sneaton N Yorks 227 D7
Sneatonthorpe N Yorks 227 D8
Sneedham's Green Glos 80 C4
Sneinton Nott'ham 153 B11
Snelland Lincs 189 E9
Snelston Derby 169 G11
Snetterton Norfolk 141 E9
Snetterton Motor Racing Circuit Norfolk 141 F10
Snettisham Norfolk 158 C3
Sneyd Green Stoke 168 F5
Sneyd Park Bristol 60 D5
Snibston Discovery Park, Coalville Leics 153 G8
Snig's End Glos 98 F5
Snipeshill Kent 70 G2
Sniseabhal W Isles 297 H3
Snitter Northum 252 C2
Snitterby Lincs 189 C7
Snitterfield Warwick 118 F4
Snittlegarth Cumb 229 D10
Snodhill Heref'd 96 C6
Snodland Kent 69 G7
Snods Edge Northum 242 G3
Snow End Herts 105 E8
Snow Hill W Yorks 197 C10
Snow Lea W Yorks 196 D5
Snow Street Norfolk 141 G11
Snowden Hill S Yorks 197 G9
Snowdon Mountain Railway, Llanberis Gwyn 163 D9
Snowdown Kent 55 C8
Snowhill Telford 150 G4
Snowshill Glos 99 E11
Snowshill Manor Glos 99 E11
Snydale W Yorks 198 C2
Soake Hants 33 E11
Soar Card 58 C5
Soar Carms 94 F2
Soar Gwyn 146 B2
Soar Angl 178 G5
Soar Powys 95 E9
Soar-y-Mynydd Ceredig'n 112 G5
Soberton Hants 33 D10
Soberton Heath Hants 33 E10
Sockbridge Cumb 230 F5
Sockburn N Yorks 224 D6
Sodom Shetl'd 315 G7
Sodom Wilts 62 C4
Soham Cambs 123 C11
Soham Cotes Cambs 123 B11
Soho London 67 C9
Soho Som'set 45 D7
Solas W Isles 296 D4
Soldon Cross Devon 24 E4
Soldridge Hants 49 G7
Sole Street Kent 54 D5
Sole Street Kent 69 F7
Solent Breezes Hants 33 G8
Solfach = Solva Pembs 90 G5
Solihull W Midlands 118 B2
Solihull Lodge W Midlands 117 B11
Sollers Dilwyn Heref'd 115 F8
Sollers Hope Heref'd 98 E2
Sollom Lancs 194 D3
Solva = Solfach Pembs 90 G5
Somerby Leics 154 G5
Somerby Lincs 200 F5
Somercotes Derby 170 E6
Somerford Dorset 19 C9
Somerford Keynes Glos 81 F8
Somerley W Sussex 22 D4
Somerleyton Suffolk 143 D9
Somersal Herbert Derby 152 B2
Somersby Lincs 190 G4
Somersham Cambs 123 B7
Somersham Suffolk 107 B11
Somerton Newp 59 B10
Somerton Oxon 101 F9
Somerton Suffolk 124 G6
Somerton Som'set 29 B7
Somerwood Shrops 149 G11
Sompting W Sussex 35 G11
Sompting Abbots W Sussex 35 F11
Sonning Wokingham 65 D9
Sonning Common Oxon 65 C8
Sonning Eye Oxon 65 D9
Sookholme Notts 171 B8
Sopley Hants 19 B9
Sopwell Herts 85 D11
Sopworth Wilts 61 B10
Sorbie Dumf/Gal 236 E6
Sordale H'land 310 C5
Sorisdale Arg/Bute 288 C4
Sorley Devon 8 F4
Sorn E Ayrs 258 D3
Sornhill E Ayrs 258 B2
Sortat H'land 310 C6
Sotby Lincs 190 F2
Sothell S Yorks 186 E6
Sots Hole Lincs 173 C10
Sotterley Suffolk 143 G9
Soudley Shrops 150 D4
Soughton = Sychdyn Flints 166 B2
Soulbury Bucks 103 F7
Soulby Cumb 230 F5
Soulby Cumb 222 C4
Souldern Oxon 101 E10
Souldrop Beds 121 E9
Sound Shetl'd 315 H5
Sound Shetl'd 315 J6
Sound Heath Ches 167 F10
Soundwell S Glos 61 D7
Sourhope Scot Borders 263 E8
Sourin Orkney 312 E5
Sourton Devon 12 C6
Soutergate Cumb 210 C4
South Acre Norfolk 158 G6
South Acton London 67 D8
South Alkham Kent 55 E9
South Allington Devon 9 G10
South Alloa Falk 279 C7
South Ambersham W Sussex 34 C6
South Anston S Yorks 187 E9
South Ascot Windsor 66 F2
South Ashford Kent 54 E4
South Auchmachar Aberds 303 E9
South Baddesley Hants 20 B3
South Ballachulish H'land 284 B4
South Balloch S Ayrs 245 D8
South Bank C/York 207 C7
South Bank Redcar/Clevel'd 234 G6
South Barham Kent 55 D7
South Barrow Som'set 29 B10
South Beddington London 67 G10
South Benfleet Essex 69 B9
South Bents Tyne/Wear 243 E10
South Bersted W Sussex 34 G6
South Bockhampton Dorset 19 B9
South Bowood Dorset 16 B4
South Bramwith S Yorks 198 E6
South Brent Devon 8 C3
South Brewham Som'set 45 F8
South Broomhill Northum 252 D6
South Burlingham Norfolk 143 B7
South Cadbury Som'set 29 B10
South Cairn Dumf/Gal 236 C1
South Carlton Lincs 189 F7
South Carlton Notts 187 E9
South Cave ER Yorks 208 G4
South Cerney Glos 81 F8
South Chailey E Sussex 36 D5
South Chard Som'set 28 F4
South Charlton Northum 264 E5
South Cheriton Som'set 29 C11
South Church Durham 233 F10
South Cleatlam Durham 224 B2
South Cliffe ER Yorks 208 F3
South Clifton Notts 188 G4
South Clunes H'land 300 E5
South Cockerington Lincs 190 D5
South Common Devon 28 G4
South Cornelly Bridg 57 E10
South Corriegills N Ayrs 256 C2
South Cove Suffolk 143 G9
South Creagan Arg/Bute 289 E11
South Creake Norfolk 159 B7
South Crosland W Yorks 196 E6
South Croxton Leics 154 G3
South Croydon London 67 G10
South Cuil H'land 298 C3
South Dalton ER Yorks 208 D5
South Darenth Kent 68 F5
South Devon Railway Devon 8 C5
South Duffield N Yorks 207 G9
South Dunn H'land 310 D5
South Elkington Lincs 190 D3
South Ella ER Yorks 200 B4
South Elmsall W Yorks 198 E3
South End Beds 103 B10
South End Bucks 103 G7
South End ER Yorks 201 D11
South End ER Yorks 209 E9
South End Hants 31 E10
South End Leics 153 G11
South End Norfolk 141 E9
South End N Lincs 200 C6
South End W Berks 64 E5
South Erradale H'land 299 B7
South Fambridge Essex 88 F5
South Fawley W Berks 63 C11
South Ferriby N Lincs 200 C3
South Field ER Yorks 200 B4
South Flobbets Aberds 303 F7
South Garth Shetl'd 314 D7
South Garvan H'land 289 B11
South Glendale W Isles 297 K3
South Gluss Shetl'd 314 F5
South Godstone Surrey 51 D11
South Gorley Hants 31 E11
South Gosforth Tyne/Wear 242 D6
South Green Essex 87 G11
South Green Essex 89 B8
South Green Kent 69 G10
South Green Norfolk 157 F10
South Green Norfolk 142 G4
South Green Norfolk 159 G11
South Green Norfolk 159 G9
South Green Suffolk 126 C3
South Ham Hants 48 C6
South Hanningfield Essex 88 F2
South Harefield London 66 B5
South Harrow London 66 B6
South Harting W Sussex 34 D3
South Hatfield Herts 86 D2
South Hayling Hants 22 D2
South Hazelrigg Northum 264 C3
South Heath Bucks 84 E6
South Heighton E Sussex 37 G7
South Hetton Durham 234 B3
South Hiendley W Yorks 197 E11
South Hill Cornw'l 12 G2
South Hill Som'set 29 B7
South Hinksey Oxon 83 E8
South Hole Devon 24 D2
South Holme N Yorks 216 D3
South Holmwood Surrey 51 D7
South Hornchurch London 68 C4
South Huish Devon 8 G3
South Hykeham Lincs 172 C6
South Hylton Tyne/Wear 243 F9
South Kelsey Lincs 189 B8
South Kensington London 67 D9
South Kessock H'land 300 E6
South Killingholme N Lincs 200 D6
South Kilvington N Yorks 215 C8
South Kilworth Leics 136 G2
South Kirkby W Yorks 198 E3
South Kirkton Aberds 293 C9
South Kiscadale N Ayrs 256 D2
South Knighton Devon 14 G2
South Knighton Leics C 136 C2
South Kyme Lincs 173 F11
South Lambeth London 67 D10
South Lancing W Sussex 35 G11
South Lane S Yorks 197 F9
South Leigh Oxon 82 D5
South Leverton Notts 188 E3
South Littleton Worcs 99 B11
South Loftus Redcar/Clevel'd 226 B4
South Lopham Norfolk 141 G10
South Luffenham Rutl'd 137 C8
South Malling E Sussex 36 E6
South Marston Swindon 63 B7
South Merstham Surrey 51 C9
South Middleton Northum 263 E11
South Milford N Yorks 206 G5

422 Sou – Sto

South Millbrex Aberds 303 E8
South Milton Devon 8 G3
South Mimms Herts 86 E2
South Molton Devon 26 C2
South Moor Durham 242 G5
South Moor N Yorks 224 G2
South Moreton Oxon 64 B5
South Mundham W Sussex 34 G5
South Muskham Notts 172 D3
South Newbald ER Yorks 208 F4
South Newbarns Cumb 210 F4
South Newington Oxon 101 E8
South Newsham Northum 243 B8
South Newton Wilts 46 G5
South Normanton Derby 170 D6
South Norwood London 67 F10
South Nutfield Surrey 51 D10
South Ockendon Thurr'k 68 C5
South of Gyle C/Edinb 280 G3
South Ormsby Lincs 190 F5
South Ossett W Yorks 197 D9
South Otterington N Yorks 215 B7
South Owersby Lincs 189 C9
South Oxhey Herts 85 G10
South Park Surrey 51 D8
South Parks Fife 280 A5
South Pelaw Durham 243 G7
South Perrot Dorset 29 F7
South Petherton Som'set 28 D6
South Petherwin Cornw'l 12 E2
South Pickenham Norfolk 141 C7
South Pill Cornw'l 7 D8
South Pool Devon 8 G5
South Poorton Dorset 16 B6
South Port Arg/Bute 284 E4
South Quilquox Aberds 303 F8
South Radworthy Devon 41 G8
South Rauceby Lincs 173 F8
South Raynham Norfolk 159 E7
South Reddish Gtr Man 184 C5
South Reston Lincs 190 E6
South Row Oxon 64 B3
South Ruislip London 66 B6
South Runcton Norfolk 140 B2
South Scarle Notts 172 C4
South Shian Arg/Bute 289 E11
South Shields Tyne/Wear 243 E8
South Shields Museum Tyne/Wear 243 D9
South Shore Blackp'l 202 G2
South Side Durham 233 F8
South Side Orkney 312 F6
South Somercotes Lincs 190 B6
South Stainley N Yorks 214 G6
South Stainmore Cumb 222 C6
South Stanley Durham 242 G5
South Stifford Thurr'k 68 D5
South Stoke Bath/NE Som'set 61 G8
South Stoke Oxon 64 C6
South Stoke W Sussex 35 F8
South Stour Kent 54 F4
South Street E Sussex 36 D5
South Street Kent 54 B5
South Street Kent 68 G6
South Street Kent 69 G10
South Street Kent 70 F6
South Street London 52 B2
South Tawton Devon 13 C9
South Tehidy Cornw'l 4 G3
South Thoresby Lincs 190 F6
South Tidworth Hants 47 D8
South Town Devon 14 E5
South Town Hants 49 F7
South Twerton Bath/NE Som'set 61 G8
South View Hants 48 C6
South Voxter Shetl'd 315 G5
South Walsham Norfolk 161 G7
South Warnborough Hants 49 D8
South Weald Essex 87 G9
South Weirs Hants 32 G3
South Weston Oxon 84 F2
South Wheatley Cornw'l 11 C10
South Wheatley Notts 188 D3
South Whiteness Shetl'd 315 J5
South Widcombe Bath/NE Som'set 44 B5
South Wigston Leics 135 D11
South Willesborough Kent 54 E4
South Willingham Lincs 189 E11
South Wimbledon London 67 E9
South Wingate Durham 234 D4
South Wingfield Derby 170 D5
South Witham Lincs 155 F8
South Wonford Devon 24 F5
South Wonston Hants 48 F3
South Woodford London 68 B2
South Woodham Ferrers Essex 88 F4
South Wootton Norfolk 158 E2
South Wraxall Wilts 61 G10
South Yardley W Midlands 134 G2
South Yarrows H'land 310 E7
South Zeal Devon 13 C9
Southall London 66 C6
Southam Glos 99 F9
Southam Warwick 119 E8
Southampton S'thampton 32 E6
Southampton International Airport Hants 33 D7
Southborough Kent 52 E5
Southborough London 67 F7
Southborough London 68 F2
Southbourne Bournem'th 19 C8
Southbourne W Sussex 34 F3
Southbrook Dorset 18 C2
Southbrook Wilts 45 G10
Southburgh Norfolk 141 C9
Southburn ER Yorks 208 C5
Southchurch Southend 70 B2
Southcote Reading 65 E7
Southcott Beds 103 G8
Southcott Devon 24 D6
Southcott Devon 25 B7
Southcott Wilts 47 B7
Southcourt Bucks 84 C4
Southcrest Worcs 117 D10
Southdean Scot Borders 250 B4
Southdene Mersey 182 B6
Southdown Bath/NE Som'set 61 G8
Southease E Sussex 36 F6
Southend Arg/Bute 255 G7
Southend Bucks 65 B9
Southend Glos 80 F2
South-end Herts 86 B6
Southend London 67 E11
Southend Oxon 83 E9
Southend Wilts 63 E7
Southend Airport Essex 69 B11
Southend Sea Life Centre Essex 69 C11
Southend-on-Sea Southend 69 B11
Southerhouse Shetl'd 315 K5
Southern Green Herts 104 E6
Southernby Cumb 230 D3
Southernden Kent 53 D11
Southerndown V/Glam 57 G11
Southerness Dumf/Gal 237 D11
Southerton Devon 15 C7
Southery Norfolk 140 E2
Southey Green Essex 106 E5
Southfield Fife 280 B5
Southfield Northum 243 B7
Southfield Thurr'k 69 C7
Southfields London 67 E9
Southfleet Kent 68 E6
Southgate Ceredig'n 111 B11
Southgate London 86 G4
Southgate Norfolk 158 C3
Southgate Norfolk 159 B7
Southgate Norfolk 160 E2
Southgate Swan 56 D5
Southgate W Sussex 51 F9
South-haa Shetl'd 314 E5
South-heog Shetl'd 314 E5
Southill Beds 104 C3
Southington Hants 48 D4
Southleigh Devon 15 C10
Southmarsh Som'set 45 G8
Southmead Bristol 60 D5
Southminister Essex 89 F7
Southmoor Oxon 82 F5
Southoe Cambs 122 E3
Southolt Suffolk 126 D3
Southorpe Peterbro 137 C11
Southover Dorset 16 D5
Southover Dorset 17 C8
Southover E Sussex 37 B11
Southowram W Yorks 196 C6
Southport Mersey 193 D10
Southpunds Shetl'd 315 L6
Southrepps Norfolk 160 B5
Southrey Lincs 173 B10
Southrop Glos 82 D2
Southrope Hants 49 E7
Southsea Portsm'th 21 B9
Southsea Wrex 166 E4
Southtown Norfolk 143 B10
Southtown Orkney 313 J5
Southtown Som'set 28 D4
Southtown Som'set 44 F5
Southwaite Cumb 230 C5
Southwark London 67 D10
Southwater W Sussex 35 B11
Southwater Street W Sussex 35 B11
Southway Plym'th 7 C9
Southway Som'set 44 E4
Southwell Dorset 17 G9
Southwell Notts 171 E11
Southwell Minster Notts 172 E2
Southwell Racecourse Notts 172 E2
Southwick Hants 33 F10
Southwick Northants 137 E10
Southwick Som'set 43 D11
Southwick Tyne/Wear 243 F9
Southwick Wilts 45 B10
Southwick W Sussex 36 F2
Southwold Suffolk 127 B10
Southwood Hants 49 B10
Southwood Norfolk 143 B7
Southwood Som'set 44 G5
Soval Lodge W Isles 304 F5
Sowden Devon 14 E5
Sower Carr Lancs 202 E3
Sowerby N Yorks 215 C8
Sowerby W Yorks 196 C4
Sowerby Bridge W Yorks 196 C5
Sowerby Grange N Yorks 225 G8
Sowerby Row Cumb 230 C3
Sowley Green Suffolk 124 G4
Sowood W Yorks 196 D5
Sowood Green W Yorks 196 D5
Sowton Devon 14 C5
Soyal H'land 309 K5
Soyland Town W Yorks 196 C4
Spa Common Norfolk 160 C5
Spacey Houses N Yorks 206 C2
Spalding Lincs 156 E4
Spaldington ER Yorks 207 G11
Spaldwick Cambs 122 C2
Spalford Notts 172 B4
Spanby Lincs 155 B11
Spanish Green Hants 49 B7
Sparham Norfolk 159 F11
Sparhamhill Norfolk 159 F11
Spark Bridge Cumb 210 C6
Sparket Cumb 230 F4
Sparkford Som'set 29 B10
Sparkhill W Midlands 133 G11
Sparkwell Devon 7 D11
Sparl Shetl'd 314 G5
Sparnon Gate Cornw'l 4 G3
Sparrow Green Norfolk 159 G9
Sparrowpit Derby 185 E9
Sparrow's Green E Sussex 52 G6
Sparsholt Hants 48 G2
Sparsholt Oxon 63 B10
Spartylea Northum 232 B3
Spath Staffs 151 B11
Spaunton N Yorks 216 B4
Spaxton Som'set 43 F8
Spean Bridge H'land 290 E4
Spear Hill W Sussex 35 D10
Spearywell Hants 32 B4
Speedwell Bristol 60 E6
Speen Bucks 84 F4
Speen W Berks 64 F3
Speen Hill W Berks 64 F3
Speeton N Yorks 218 E3
Speke Mersey 182 E6
Speke Hall Mersey 182 E6
Speldhurst Kent 52 E5
Spellbrook Herts 87 B7
Spelsbury Oxon 101 G7
Spelter Bridg 76 G5
Spen W Yorks 197 B8
Spen Green Ches 168 C4
Spencer's Wood Wokingham 65 F8
Spennells Worcs 116 C6
Spennithorne N Yorks 214 B2
Spennymoor Durham 233 E10
Spernall Warwick 117 E11
Spetchley Worcs 117 G7
Spetisbury Dorset 30 G6
Spexhall Suffolk 143 G7
Spey Bay Moray 302 C3
Speybank H'land 291 C10
Speybridge H'land 301 G10
Speyview Moray 302 E2
Spillardsford Aberds 303 D10
Spilsby Lincs 174 B6
Spinkhill Derby 187 F7
Spinney Hill Northants 120 E5
Spinney Hills Leics C 136 C2
Spinningdale H'land 309 L6
Spion Kop Notts 171 B8
Spirit of the West, St Columb Major Cornw'l 5 B8
Spirthill Wilts 62 D3
Spital Mersey 182 E4
Spital Windsor 66 D3
Spital in the Street Lincs 189 C7
Spital Tongues Tyne/Wear 242 D6
Spitfire and Hurricane Memorial, Manston Kent 71 F10
Spithurst E Sussex 36 D6
Spittal Dumf/Gal 236 D5
Spittal E Loth 281 F9
Spittal ER Yorks 207 C11
Spittal H'land 310 D5
Spittal Northum 273 E10
Spittal Pembs 91 G9
Spittal of Glenmuick Aberds 292 E5
Spittal of Glenshee Perth/Kinr 292 F3
Spittalfield Perth/Kinr 286 C5
Spittlegate Lincs 155 B8
Spixworth Norfolk 160 F4
Splatt Cornw'l 11 D10
Splatt Cornw'l 10 F4
Splatt Som'set 43 F8
Splayne's Green E Sussex 36 C6
Splottlands Card 59 D7
Spodegreen Ches 184 D2
Spofforth N Yorks 206 C3
Spon End W Midlands 118 B6
Spon Green Flints 166 C3
Spondon Derby C 153 B8
Spooner Row Norfolk 141 D11
Sporle Norfolk 158 G6
Spotland Bridge Gtr Man 195 E11
Spott E Loth 282 F3
Spratton Northants 120 C4
Spreakley Surrey 49 E10
Spreyton Devon 13 B10
Spriddlestone Devon 7 E10
Spridlington Lincs 189 E8
Spring Bank Gtr Man 194 F5
Spring Bank W Midlands 133 D9
Spring Gardens Durham 233 F9
Spring Gardens Shrops 149 G10
Spring Grove London 67 D7
Spring Head Kent 68 E6
Spring Hill Gtr Man 196 F2
Spring Hill Lancs 195 B8
Spring Hill Staffs 133 B11
Spring Hill W Midlands 133 D7
Spring Park London 67 F11
Spring Vale I/Wight 21 C8
Spring Vale S Yorks 197 G9
Spring Valley I/Man 192 E4
Springbank Glos 99 G8
Springboig Glasg C 268 C3
Springburn Glasg C 268 B2
Springfield Arg/Bute 275 F11
Springfield Caerph 77 F11
Springfield Dumf/Gal 239 D8
Springfield Essex 88 D2
Springfield Fife 287 F7
Springfield Gtr Man 194 F5
Springfield H'land 300 C6
Springfield M/Keynes 103 D7
Springfield Moray 301 D10
Springfield W Midlands 133 F9
Springfield W Midlands 133 G11
Springhill E Renf 267 D10
Springhill N Lanarks 269 D7
Springhill Shrops 130 G5
Springhill Staffs 133 C9
Springhill Staffs 133 B11
Springholm Dumf/Gal 237 C10
Springkell Dumf/Gal 239 B7
Springside N Ayrs 257 B9
Springthorpe Lincs 188 D5
Springwell Tyne/Wear 243 F9
Springwell Tyne/Wear 243 F7
Sproatley ER Yorks 209 G9
Sproston Green Ches 168 B2
Sprotbrough S Yorks 198 G4
Sproughton Suffolk 108 C2
Sprouston Scot Borders 263 B7
Sprowston Norfolk 160 G5
Sproxton Leics 155 E7
Sproxton N Yorks 216 C2
Sprunston Cumb 230 B3
Sprytown Devon 12 D4
Spurlands End Bucks 84 F5
Spurstow Ches 167 D9
Spynie Moray 302 C2
Squires Gate Blackp'l 202 G2
Sraid Ruadh Arg/Bute 288 E1
Srannda W Isles 296 C6
Sronphadruig Lodge Perth/Kinr 291 F9
SS Great Britain Bristol 60 E5
Stable Green Devon 25 E10
Stableford Shrops 132 D5
Stacey Bank S Yorks 186 C3
Stackhouse N Yorks 212 F6
Stackpole Pembs 73 F7
Stackpole Elidor Pembs 73 F7
Stacksford Norfolk 141 E11
Stacksteads Lancs 195 C11
Stackyard Green Suffolk 107 B9
Staddiscombe Devon 7 E10
Staddlethorpe ER Yorks 199 B10
Staden Derby 185 G9
Stadhampton Oxon 83 F10
Stadhlaigearraidh W Isles 297 H3
Staffield Cumb 230 C6
Staffin H'land 298 C4
Stafford Staffs 151 E8
Stafford Park Telford 132 B4
Staffordlake Surrey 50 B2
Stafford's Green Dorset 29 C10
Stagden Cross Essex 87 C10
Stag's Head Devon 25 B11
Stag's Holt Cambs 139 C8
Stagsden Beds 103 B9
Stagsden West End Beds 103 B9
Stain H'land 310 C7
Stainburn Cumb 228 F6
Stainburn N Yorks 205 D10
Stainby Lincs 155 E8
Staincliffe W Yorks 197 C8
Staincross S Yorks 197 E10
Staindrop Durham 233 G8
Staines Surrey 66 E5
Staines Green Herts 86 C4
Stainfield Lincs 155 D11
Stainfield Lincs 189 G10
Stainforth N Yorks 212 F6
Stainforth S Yorks 198 E6
Staining Lancs 202 F3
Stainland W Yorks 196 D5
Stainsacre N Yorks 227 D8
Stainsby Derby 170 B6
Stainton Cumb 211 B10
Stainton Cumb 230 F5
Stainton Cumb 239 F9
Stainton Durham 223 B11
Stainton Middlesbro 225 C9
Stainton N Yorks 224 F2
Stainton S Yorks 187 C9
Stainton by Langworth Lincs 189 F9
Stainton le Vale Lincs 189 C11
Stainton with Adgarley Cumb 210 E4
Staintondale N Yorks 227 F9
Stair Cumb 229 G10
Stair E Ayrs 257 E10
Stairfoot S Yorks 197 G11
Stairhaven Dumf/Gal 236 D4
Staithe Norfolk 143 E9
Staithes N Yorks 226 B5
Stake Hill Gtr Man 195 F11
Stake Pool Lancs 202 D4
Stakeford Northum 253 F7
Stakes Portsm'th 33 F11
Stalbridge Dorset 30 D2
Stalbridge Weston Dorset 30 D2
Stalham Norfolk 161 D7
Stalham Green Norfolk 161 E7
Stalisfield Green Kent 54 C2
Stalland Common Norfolk 141 D10
Stallen Dorset 29 D10
Stalling Busk N Yorks 213 B8
Stallingborough NE Lincs 201 E8
Stalmine Lancs 202 D3
Stalmine Moss Side Lancs 202 D3
Stalybridge Gtr Man 185 B7
Stambermill W Midlands 133 G8
Stambourne Essex 106 D4
Stambourne Green Essex 106 D4
Stamford Lincs 137 B10
Stamford Northum 264 F6
Stamford Bridge Ches 167 B7
Stamford Bridge ER Yorks 207 B10
Stamford Hill London 67 B10
Stamfordham Northum 242 C3
Stamperland E Renf 267 D11
Stamshaw Portsm'th 33 G11
Stanah Lancs 202 E3
Stanborough Herts 86 C2
Stanbridge Beds 103 G9
Stanbridge Dorset 31 G8
Stanbrook Essex 106 F2
Stanbrook Worcs 98 B6
Stanbury W Yorks 204 F6
Stand Gtr Man 195 F9
Stand N Lanarks 268 B5
Standburn Falk 279 G8
Standeford Staffs 133 B8
Standen Kent 53 E11
Standen, East Grinstead W Sussex 51 F11
Standen Manor W Berks 63 F10
Standen Street Kent 53 G10
Standerwick Som'set 45 C10
Standford Hants 49 G10
Standingstone Cumb 229 B11
Standish Glos 80 D4
Standish Gtr Man 194 E5
Standish Lower Ground Gtr Man 194 F5
Standish Moreton Glos 80 D3
Standlake Oxon 82 E5
Standon Hants 32 B6
Standon Herts 105 G7
Standon Staffs 150 C6
Standon Green End Herts 86 B5
Stane N Lanarks 269 D7
Stanecastle N Ayrs 266 G6
Stanfield Norfolk 159 E8
Stanfield Stoke 168 E5
Stanford Beds 104 C3
Stanford Kent 54 F6
Stanford Bishop Heref'd 116 G3
Stanford Bridge Worcs 116 D4
Stanford Dingley W Berks 64 E5
Stanford End Wokingham 65 G8
Stanford in the Vale Oxon 82 G4
Stanford on Avon Northants 119 B11
Stanford on Soar Notts 153 E10
Stanford Rivers Essex 87 E8
Stanford-le-Hope Thurr'k 69 C7
Stanfree Derby 187 G7
Stanghow Redcar/Clevel'd 226 B3
Stanground Peterbro 138 D4
Stanhill Lancs 195 B8
Stanhoe Norfolk 158 B6
Stanhope Scot Borders 260 D4
Stanhope Durham 232 D5
Stanion Northants 137 F8
Stanley Derby 170 G6
Stanley Durham 242 G5
Stanley Lancs 194 F3
Stanley Notts 171 C7
Stanley Perth/Kinr 286 D5
Stanley Shrops 132 G5
Stanley Staffs 168 E6
Stanley Wilts 62 E3
Stanley W Yorks 197 C10
Stanley Common Derby 170 G6
Stanley Crook Durham 233 D9
Stanley Downton Glos 80 E4
Stanley Gate Lancs 194 F2
Stanley Green Gtr Man 184 E5
Stanley Green Poole 18 C6
Stanley Green Shrops 149 B10
Stanley Hill Heref'd 98 C3
Stanley Pontlarge Glos 99 E9
Stanleytown Rh Cyn Taff 77 G8
Stanlow Ches 182 F6
Stanmer Brighton/Hove 36 F4
Stanmore Hants 33 B7
Stanmore London 85 G11
Stanmore W Berks 64 D3
Stanner Powys 114 F5
Stannergate Dundee C 287 D8
Stannersburn Northum 250 F6
Stanningfield Suffolk 125 F7
Stanningley W Yorks 205 G10
Stannington Northum 242 B6
Stannington S Yorks 186 D4
Stanpit Dorset 19 C9
Stansbatch Heref'd 115 E6
Stansfield Suffolk 124 G5
Stanshope Staffs 169 E10
Stanstead Suffolk 106 B6
Stanstead Abbotts Herts 86 C5
Stanstead Street Suffolk 106 B6
Stansted Kent 68 G6
Stansted Airport Essex 105 G10
Stansted Mountfitchet Essex 105 G10
Stanton Derby 152 F5
Stanton Glos 99 E11
Stanton Monmouths 96 G6
Stanton Northum 252 E4
Stanton Suffolk 125 C9
Stanton Staffs 169 F10
Stanton by Bridge Derby 153 D7
Stanton Chare Suffolk 125 C9
Stanton Drew Bath/NE Som'set 60 G5
Stanton Fitzwarren Swindon 81 G11
Stanton Gate Notts 153 B9
Stanton Harcourt Oxon 82 D6
Stanton Hill Notts 171 C7
Stanton in Peak Derby 170 C2
Stanton Lacy Shrops 115 B9
Stanton Lees Derby 170 C3
Stanton Long Shrops 131 E11
Stanton on the Wolds Notts 154 C2
Stanton Prior Bath/NE Som'set 61 G7
Stanton St. Bernard Wilts 62 G5
Stanton St. John Oxon 83 D9
Stanton St. Quintin Wilts 62 D2
Stanton Street Suffolk 125 D9
Stanton under Bardon Leics 153 G9
Stanton upon Hine Heath Shrops 149 E11
Stanton Wick Bath/NE Som'set 60 G6
Stantonbury M/Keynes 102 C6
Stanton-by-Dale Derby 153 B9
Stantway Glos 80 C2
Stanwardine in the Fields Shrops 149 E8
Stanwardine in the Wood Shrops 149 D8
Stanway Essex 107 G8
Stanway Glos 99 E11
Stanway Green Essex 107 G9
Stanway Green Suffolk 126 C4
Stanwell Surrey 66 E5
Stanwell Moor Surrey 66 E4
Stanwick Northants 121 C9
Stanwick-St.-John N Yorks 224 C3
Stanwix Cumb 239 F9
Stanycliffe Gtr Man 195 F11
Stanydale Shetl'd 315 H4
Staoinebrig W Isles 297 H3
Stape N Yorks 226 G5
Stapehill Dorset 31 G9
Stapeley Ches 167 F11
Stapeley Water Gardens, Nantwich Ches 167 E11
Stapenhill Staffs 152 E5
Stapford on Teme Worcs 116 D4
Staple Kent 55 B9
Staple Som'set 42 E6
Staple Cross Devon 27 C8
Staple Fitzpaine Som'set 28 D3
Staple Hill S Glos 61 D7
Staple Hill Worcs 117 C9
Staplecross E Sussex 38 C3
Staplefield W Sussex 36 B3
Stapleford Cambs 123 F9
Stapleford Herts 86 B4
Stapleford Leics 154 F6
Stapleford Lincs 172 D5
Stapleford Notts 153 B9
Stapleford Wilts 46 F5
Stapleford Abbots Essex 87 G8
Stapleford Tawney Essex 87 F8
Staplegrove Som'set 28 B2
Staplehay Som'set 28 C2
Staplehurst Kent 53 E9
Staplers I/Wight 20 D6
Staples Hill W Sussex 35 B8
Staplestreet Kent 70 G5
Stapleton Bristol 60 D6
Stapleton Cumb 240 C2
Stapleton Heref'd 114 D6
Stapleton Leics 135 D8
Stapleton N Yorks 224 C4
Stapleton N Yorks 198 D4
Stapleton Shrops 131 C9
Stapleton Som'set 29 C7
Stapley Som'set 27 E10
Staploe Beds 122 E2
Staplow Heref'd 98 C3
Stapness Shetl'd 315 J4
Star Fife 287 G7
Star Angl 179 G8
Star Pembs 92 D4
Star Som'set 44 B2
Stara Orkney 312 F3
Starbeck N Yorks 206 B2
Starbotton N Yorks 213 E9
Starcross Devon 14 E5
Stareton Warwick 118 C6
Stargate Tyne/Wear 242 E5
Starkholmes Derby 170 D4
Starling Gtr Man 195 E9
Starling's Green Essex 105 E9
Starr's Green E Sussex 38 E3
Starston Norfolk 142 G4
Start Devon 8 F6
Startforth Durham 223 B10
Startley Wilts 62 C3
Startop's End Bucks 84 C6
Start's Green Staffs 132 G6
Starve Acre Hants 49 B10
Statenborough Kent 55 B10
Statham Warrington 183 D11
Stathe Som'set 28 B5
Stathern Leics 154 C5
Station Hill Cumb 229 B11
Station Town Durham 234 D4
Staughton Green Cambs 122 D2
Staughton Highway Cambs 122 E2
Staughton Moor Cambs 122 E2
Staunton Glos 79 C8
Staunton Glos 98 F5
Staunton Green Heref'd 115 E7
Staunton in the Vale Notts 172 G4
Staunton on Arrow Heref'd 115 E7
Staunton on Wye Heref'd 97 B7
Staupes N Yorks 205 B10
Staveley Cumb 221 F9
Staveley Derby 186 G6
Staveley N Yorks 215 G7
Staveley-in-Cartmel Cumb 211 B7
Staverton Devon 8 C5
Staverton Glos 99 G7
Staverton Northants 119 E10
Staverton Wilts 61 G11
Staverton Bridge Glos 99 G7
Stawell Som'set 43 F11
Stawley Som'set 27 C9
Staxigoe H'land 310 D7
Staxton N Yorks 217 D10
Staylittle Powys 129 E7
Staynall Lancs 202 E3
Staythorpe Notts 172 E3
Stead W Yorks 205 D8
Stean N Yorks 213 E11
Steanbow Som'set 44 F5
Steane Northants 101 D11
Stearsby N Yorks 216 E2
Steart Som'set 43 E9
Stebbing Essex 106 G3
Stebbing Green Essex 106 G3
Stebbing Park Essex 106 G3
Stechford W Midlands 134 F2
Stede Quarter Kent 53 F11
Stedham W Sussex 34 C5
Steel Northum 241 F10
Steel Bank S Yorks 186 D4
Steel Cross E Sussex 52 G4
Steel Green Cumb 210 D3
Steel Heath Shrops 149 B10
Steel Lane Head W Yorks 196 D5
Steele Road Scot Borders 250 E2
Steelend Fife 279 C10
Steen's Bridge Heref'd 115 F10
Steep Hants 34 B2
Steep Lane W Yorks 196 C4
Steep Marsh Hants 34 B3
Steephill I/Wight 21 F7
Steeple Dorset 18 E4
Steeple Essex 88 E6
Steeple Ashton Wilts 46 B2
Steeple Aston Oxon 101 F9
Steeple Barton Oxon 101 F8
Steeple Bumpstead Essex 106 C3
Steeple Claydon Bucks 102 F4
Steeple Gidding Cambs 138 G2
Steeple Langford Wilts 46 F4
Steeple Morden Cambs 104 C5
Steeplechase Suffolk 106 B4
Steeton W Yorks 204 E6
Stein H'land 298 D2
Steinmanhill Aberds 303 E7
Stella Tyne/Wear 242 E5
Stelling Minnis Kent 54 D6
Stelvio Newp 59 B10
Stembridge Som'set 28 C6
Stemster H'land 310 C5
Stemster Ho. H'land 310 C5
Stenalees Cornw'l 5 D10
Stenaquoy Orkney 312 E6
Stenhill Devon 27 E9
Stenhouse C/Edinb 280 G4
Stenhousemuir Falk 279 E7
Stenigot Lincs 190 E3
Stennack Cornw'l 2 B2
Stenness Shetl'd 314 F4
Stenscholl H'land 298 C4
Stenso Orkney 312 F4
Stenson Staffs 152 D6
Stenton E Loth 282 F2
Stenton Fife 280 B5
Stenwith Lincs 154 B6
Stepaside Cornw'l 5 E8
Stepaside Pembs 73 D10
Stepaside Powys 129 F11
Stepney London 67 C11
Stepping Hill Gtr Man 184 D6
Steppingley Beds 103 D10
Stepps N Lanarks 268 B3
Sterndale Moor Derby 169 B10
Sternfield Suffolk 127 E7
Sterridge Devon 40 D5
Stert Wilts 46 B4
Sterte Poole 18 C6
Stetchworth Cambs 124 F2
Stetchworth Ley Cambs 124 F2
Stevenage Herts 104 G4
Stevenston N Ayrs 266 G5
Steventon Hants 48 D4
Steventon Oxon 83 G7
Steventon End Essex 105 C11
Stevington Beds 121 G9
Stewards Essex 87 D7
Stewartby Beds 103 C10
Stewarton Arg/Bute 255 F7
Stewarton E Ayrs 267 F8
Stewkley Bucks 103 F7
Stewley Som'set 28 D4
Stewton Lincs 190 D5
Steyne Cross I/Wight 21 D8
Steyning W Sussex 35 E11
Steynton Pembs 72 D6
Stibb Cornw'l 24 E2
Stibb Cross Devon 24 E6
Stibb Green Wilts 63 G8
Stibbard Norfolk 159 D9
Stibbington Cambs 137 D11
Stichill Scot Borders 262 B6
Stick Hill Kent 52 E3
Sticker Cornw'l 5 E9
Stickford Lincs 174 D5
Sticklepath Devon 13 C8
Sticklepath Devon 40 G5
Sticklepath Som'set 42 F4
Sticklinch Som'set 44 F5
Stickling Green Essex 105 E9
Stickney Lincs 174 D4
Stiff Street Kent 69 G11
Stiffkey Norfolk 177 E7
Stifford's Bridge Heref'd 98 B4
Stileway Som'set 44 E3
Stillingfleet N Yorks 207 E7
Stillington N Yorks 215 F11
Stillington Stockton 234 G3
Stilton Cambs 138 F3
Stinchcombe Glos 80 F2
Stinsford Dorset 17 C10
Stiperstones Shrops 131 C7
Stirchley Telford 132 B4
Stirchley W Midlands 133 G11
Stirkoke Ho. H'land 310 D7
Stirling Aberds 303 E11
Stirling Stirl 278 C6
Stirling Castle Stirl 278 C5
Stirtloe Cambs 122 D3
Stirton N Yorks 204 C5
Stisted Essex 106 G6
Stitchcombe Wilts 63 F8
Stithians Cornw'l 2 B6
Stittenham H'land 300 B6
Stivichall W Midlands 118 B6
Stixwould Lincs 173 B11
Stoak Ches 182 G6
Stobhill Northum 252 F6
Stobhill Gate Northum 252 F6
Stobieside S Lanarks 258 B4
Stobo Scot Borders 260 B5
Stoborough Dorset 18 D4
Stoborough Green Dorset 18 D4
Stobs Castle Scot Borders 250 B2
Stobshiel E Loth 271 C9
Stobswood Northum 252 E6
Stock Essex 87 F11
Stock Lancs 204 D3
Stock N Som'set 60 G3
Stock Green Worcs 117 F9
Stock Wood Worcs 117 F10
Stockbridge Hants 47 F11
Stockbridge W Sussex 34 G5
Stockbridge W Yorks 205 E7
Stockbridge Village Mersey 182 C6
Stockbury Kent 69 G10
Stockcross W Berks 64 F2
Stockdalewath Cumb 230 C3
Stocken Hall Rutl'd 155 F9
Stocker's Head Kent 54 C3
Stockerston Leics 136 D6
Stockham Oxon 63 B11
Stockheath Hants 34 F2
Stockholes Turbary N Lincs 199 F9
Stockiemuir Stirl 277 E9
Stocking Heref'd 98 E2
Stocking Farm Leics C 135 B11
Stocking Green Essex 105 D11
Stocking Green M/Keynes 102 B6
Stocking Pelham Herts 105 F8
Stockingford Warwick 134 E6
Stockland Card 58 D6
Stockland Devon 28 G2
Stockland Bristol Som'set 43 E8
Stockland Green Kent 52 E5
Stockleigh English Devon 26 F4
Stockleigh Pomeroy Devon 26 G5
Stockley Wilts 62 F4
Stocklinch Som'set 28 D5
Stocklinch Ottersey Som'set 28 D5
Stockport Gtr Man 184 C6
Stocks Green Kent 52 D5
Stocksbridge S Yorks 186 B3
Stocksfield Northum 242 E2
Stocksmoor W Yorks 197 E7
Stockton Heref'd 115 E10
Stockton Norfolk 143 E7
Stockton Shrops 132 D4
Stockton Shrops 130 C5
Stockton Warwick 119 E8
Stockton Wilts 46 F3
Stockton Heath Warrington 183 D10
Stockton on Tees Stockton 225 B8
Stockton on Teme Worcs 116 D4
Stockton on the Forest C/York 207 B9
Stockwell London 67 D10
Stockwell End W Midlands 133 C7
Stockwell Heath Staffs 151 E11
Stockwitch Cross Som'set 29 C8
Stockwood Bristol 60 F6
Stockwood Dorset 29 F9
Stockwood Craft Museum Luton 85 B9
Stockwood Vale Bath/NE Som'set 60 F6
Stodday Lancs 202 B5
Stodmarsh Kent 71 G8
Stody Norfolk 159 B11
Stoer H'land 307 G5
Stoford Som'set 29 E9
Stoford Wilts 46 F5
Stogumber Som'set 42 F5
Stogursey Som'set 43 E8
Stoke Devon 13 G9
Stoke Devon 24 C2
Stoke Hants 34 G2
Stoke Hants 48 C2
Stoke Medway 69 D10
Stoke Plym'th 7 D9
Stoke Suffolk 108 C3
Stoke W Midlands 119 B7
Stoke Abbott Dorset 28 G7
Stoke Albany Northants 136 F6
Stoke Aldermoor W Midlands 119 B7
Stoke Ash Suffolk 126 C2
Stoke Bardolph Notts 171 G11
Stoke Bishop Bristol 60 D5
Stoke Bliss Worcs 116 E3
Stoke Bruerne Northants 120 G4
Stoke by Clare Suffolk 106 C4

Stoke Cannon Devon 14 B4
Stoke Charity Hants 48 F3
Stoke Climsland Cornw'l 12 G3
Stoke Common Hants 33 C7
Stoke Cross Heref'd 116 G2
Stoke D'Abernon Surrey 50 B6
Stoke Doyle Northants 137 F10
Stoke Dry Rutl'd 137 D7
Stoke Edith Heref'd 98 C2
Stoke Farthing Wilts 31 B9
Stoke Ferry Norfolk 140 C4
Stoke Fleming Devon 9 F7
Stoke Gabriel Devon 8 D6
Stoke Gifford S Glos 60 C6
Stoke Golding Leics 135 D8
Stoke Goldington M/Keynes 102 B6
Stoke Green Bucks 66 C3
Stoke Hammond Bucks 103 F7
Stoke Heath Shrops 150 D3
Stoke Heath W Midlands 135 G7
Stoke Heath Worcs 117 D8
Stoke Hill Devon 14 C4
Stoke Holy Cross Norfolk 142 C4
Stoke Lacy Heref'd 98 B2
Stoke Lyne Oxon 101 F11
Stoke Mandeville Bucks 84 C4
Stoke Newington London 67 B10
Stoke on Tern Shrops 150 D2
Stoke Orchard Glos 99 F8
Stoke Park Suffolk 108 C2
Stoke Poges Bucks 66 C3
Stoke Pound Worcs 117 D9
Stoke Prior Heref'd 115 F10
Stoke Prior Worcs 117 D9
Stoke Rivers Devon 41 G6
Stoke Rochford Lincs 155 D8
Stoke Row Oxon 65 C7
Stoke St. Gregory Som'set 28 B4
Stoke St. Mary Som'set 28 C3
Stoke St. Michael Som'set 45 D7
Stoke St. Milborough Shrops 131 G11
Stoke sub Hamdon Som'set 29 D7
Stoke Talmage Oxon 83 F11
Stoke Trister Som'set 30 B2
Stoke Villice Bath/NE Som'set 60 G5
Stoke Wake Dorset 30 F3
Stoke-by-Nayland Suffolk 107 D9
Stokeford Dorset 18 D3
Stokeham Notts 188 F3
Stokeinteignhead Devon 14 G4
Stokenchurch Bucks 84 F3
Stokenham Devon 8 G6
Stoke-on-Trent Stoke 168 F5
Stokesay Shrops 131 G8
Stokesby Norfolk 161 G8
Stokesley N Yorks 225 D10
Stolford Som'set 43 D8
Ston Easton Som'set 44 C6
Stondon Massey Essex 87 E9
Stone Bucks 84 C3
Stone Glos 79 F11
Stone Kent 68 E5
Stone Som'set 44 G5
Stone Staffs 151 C8
Stone Worcs 117 C7
Stone Allerton Som'set 44 C2
Stone Bridge Corner Peterbro 138 C5
Stone Chair W Yorks 196 B6
Stone Common Suffolk 127 F7
Stone Cross E Sussex 23 E10
Stone Cross E Sussex 37 B8
Stone Cross E Sussex 52 G6
Stone Cross Kent 55 B10
Stone Cross Kent 54 F4
Stone Cross Kent 52 F4
Stone Cross W Midlands 133 E10
Stone End Glos 80 B3
Stone Fold Lancs 195 B9
Stone Head N Yorks 204 E4
Stone Hill Kent 54 F5
Stone Hill S Glos 60 E6
Stone Hill S Yorks 199 F7
Stone Hill S Yorks 187 E7
Stone House Cumb 212 B5
Stone in Oxney Kent 38 B6
Stone Street Kent 52 C5
Stone Street Suffolk 143 G7
Stone Street Suffolk 107 D9
Stonea Cambs 139 E9
Stonebridge Essex 70 B2
Stonebridge London 67 C8
Stonebridge M/Keynes 102 C6
Stonebridge N Som'set 43 B11
Stonebridge Surrey 51 D7
Stonebridge Warwick 134 G4
Stonebridge Green Kent 54 D2
Stonebroom Derby 170 D6
Stoneclough Gtr Man 195 F9
Stonecross Green Suffolk 124 F6
Stone-edge-Batch N Som'set 60 E3
Stoneferry Kingston/Hull 209 G8
Stonefield Arg/Bute 289 F11
Stonefield S Lanarks 268 D3
Stonefield Staffs 151 C7
Stonefield Castle Hotel Arg/Bute 275 F9
Stonegate E Sussex 37 B11
Stonegate N Yorks 226 D5
Stonegrave N Yorks 216 D3
Stonegravels Derby 186 G5
Stonehall Worcs 99 B7
Stonehaugh Northum 241 B7
Stonehaven Aberds 293 E10
Stonehenge, Amesbury Wilts 46 E6
Stonehill Surrey 66 G4
Stonehill Green Kent 68 E4
Stonehouse Aberds 303 F8
Stonehouse Glos 80 D4
Stonehouse Northum 240 F5
Stonehouse Plym'th 7 E9
Stonehouse S Lanarks 268 F5
Stoneleigh Surrey 67 G8
Stoneleigh Warwick 118 C6
Stoneless Kent 71 G10
Stonely Cambs 122 D2
Stonequarry W Sussex 51 F11
Stoner Hill Hants 34 B2
Stones Green Essex 108 F3
Stonesby Leics 154 E6
Stonesfield Oxon 82 B5
Stonestreet Green Kent 54 F5
Stonethwaite Cumb 220 C5
Stonewells Moray 302 C2
Stonewood Kent 68 E5
Stoney Cross Hants 32 E3
Stoney Middleton Derby 186 F2
Stoney Pound Shrops 130 G4
Stoney Royd W Yorks 196 C6
Stoney Stanton Leics 135 E9
Stoney Stoke Som'set 45 G8
Stoney Stratton Som'set 45 F7
Stoney Stretton Shrops 131 B7
Stoneyard Green Heref'd 98 C4
Stoneybank E Loth 280 G6
Stoneybreck Shetl'd 315 N2
Stoneyburn W Loth 269 C9
Stoneycroft Mersey 182 C5
Stoneydelph Staffs 134 C4
Stoneyfield Gtr Man 195 E11
Stoneyfield Moray 301 D11
Stoneyford Derby 170 F6
Stoneyford Devon 15 D7
Stoneygate Aberds 303 F10
Stoneygate Leics C 136 C2
Stoneyholme Lancs 204 G2
Stoneykirk Dumf/Gal 236 D2
Stoneywood Aberd C 293 B10
Stoneywood Falk 278 E5
Stonganess Shetl'd 314 C7
Stonham Aspal Suffolk 126 F2
Stonor Oxon 65 B8
Stonton Wyville Leics 136 D4
Stony Cross Devon 25 B8
Stony Cross Heref'd 98 B4
Stony Dale Notts 172 G2
Stony Gate Tyne/Wear 243 G9
Stony Green Bucks 84 F5
Stony Houghton Derby 171 B7
Stony Knaps Dorset 28 G5
Stony Lea Staffs 151 G9
Stony Stratford M/Keynes 102 C5
Stonyfield H'land 300 B6
Stonyford Hants 32 D4
Stoodham Som'set 28 D6
Stoodleigh Devon 26 D6
Stopes S Yorks 186 D3
Stopham W Sussex 35 D8
Stopper Lane Lancs 204 D2
Stopsley Luton 103 G11
Stoptide Cornw'l 10 F4
Stores Corner Suffolk 109 B7
Storeton Mersey 182 E4
Storiths N Yorks 205 C7
Stormontfield Perth/Kinr 286 E5
Stormore Wilts 45 D10
Stormsdown Devon 13 G11
Stornoway W Isles 304 E6
Stornoway Airport W Isles 304 E6
Storridge Heref'd 98 B5
Storrington W Sussex 35 E9
Storrs Cumb 221 G7
Storrs S Yorks 186 D3
Stortford Park Herts 105 G9
Storth Cumb 211 D9
Storwood ER Yorks 207 E10
Stotfield Moray 302 B2
Stotfold Beds 104 D4
Stottesdon Shrops 132 G3
Stoughton Leics 136 C2
Stoughton Surrey 50 C3
Stoughton W Sussex 34 E4
Stoughton Cross Som'set 44 D2
Stoul H'land 295 F9
Stoulton Worcs 99 B8
Stour Provost Dorset 30 C3
Stour Row Dorset 30 C4
Stourbridge W Midlands 133 G7
Stourhead Garden Wilts 45 G9
Stourpaine Dorset 30 F5
Stourport on Severn Worcs 116 C6
Stourton Staffs 133 G7
Stourton Warwick 100 D5
Stourton Wilts 45 G9
Stourton W Yorks 206 G2
Stourton Caundle Dorset 30 D2
Stout Som'set 44 G2
Stove Orkney 312 E7
Stove Shetl'd 315 L6
Stoven Suffolk 143 G8
Stover S Glos 61 C7
Stow Scot Borders 271 G9
Stow Lincs 155 C11
Stow Lincs 188 E5
Stow Bardolph Norfolk 140 B2
Stow Bedon Norfolk 141 D9
Stow Cum Quy Cambs 123 E10
Stow Lawn W Midlands 133 D8
Stow Longa Cambs 122 C2
Stow Maries Essex 88 F4
Stow Park Lincs 188 E5
Stow Pasture Lincs 188 E5
Stowbridge Norfolk 139 B11
Stowe Glos 79 D9
Stowe Heref'd 96 B5
Stowe Shrops 114 C6
Stowe Staffs 152 G2
Stowe Green Glos 79 D9
Stowe House and Gardens, Buckingham Bucks 102 D3
Stowe-by-Chartley Staffs 151 D10
Stowehill Northants 120 F2
Stowell Som'set 29 C11
Stowey Bath/NE Som'set 44 B6
Stowfield Glos 79 B9
Stowford Devon 12 D4
Stowford Devon 15 D8
Stowford Devon 25 B10
Stowford Devon 41 E7
Stowlangtoft Suffolk 125 D9
Stowmarket Suffolk 125 F10
Stow-on-the-Wold Glos 100 F3
Stowting Kent 54 E6
Stowting Common Kent 54 E6
Stowting Hill Kent 54 E6
Stowupland Suffolk 125 F11
Straad Arg/Bute 275 G11
Strachan Aberds 293 D8
Strachurmore Arg/Bute 284 G5
Stradbroke Suffolk 126 C4
Stradbrook Wilts 46 C2
Stradishall Suffolk 124 G4
Stradley Castle Carms 75 E7
Stradsett Norfolk 140 B3
Stragglethorpe Lincs 172 E6
Stragglethorpe Notts 154 B3
Straid S Ayrs 244 E4
Straight Soley Wilts 63 E10
Straith Dumf/Gal 247 F8
Straiton C/Edinb 270 B5
Straiton S Ayrs 245 C9
Straloch Aberds 303 G8
Straloch Perth/Kinr 292 G2
Stramshall Staffs 151 B11
Strand Glos 80 C2
Strands Cumb 210 C3
Strang I/Man 192 E4
Strangeways Gtr Man 184 B4
Strangford Heref'd 97 F11
Strangways Wilts 46 E6
Stranog Aberds 293 D10
Stranraer Dumf/Gal 236 C2
Strata Florida Ceredig'n 112 D4
Stratfield Mortimer W Berks 65 G7
Stratfield Saye Hants 65 G7
Stratfield Turgis Hants 49 B7
Stratford Beds 104 B3
Stratford London 67 C11
Stratford Worcs 99 D7
Stratford Castle Wilts 46 G6
Stratford Racecourse Warwick 118 G3
Stratford St. Andrew Suffolk 127 E7
Stratford St. Mary Suffolk 107 D10
Stratford Tony Wilts 31 B9
Stratford-upon-Avon Warwick 118 F4
Strath H'land 299 B7
Strath H'land 310 D6
Strathallan Castle Perth/Kinr 286 F3
Strathan H'land 295 F11
Strathan H'land 307 G5
Strathan H'land 308 C5
Strathan Skerray H'land 308 C6
Strathaven S Lanarks 268 G4
Strathavon Lo. Moray 301 G11
Strathblane Stirl 277 F11
Strathbungo Glasg C 267 C11
Strathcanaird H'land 307 J6
Strathcarron H'land 299 E9
Strathcoil Arg/Bute 289 F8
Strathcoul H'land 310 D5
Strathdon Aberds 292 B5
Strathellie Aberds 303 C10
Strathgarve Lodge H'land 300 C4
Strathkinness Fife 287 F8
Strathmashie House H'land 291 D7
Strathmiglo Fife 286 F6
Strathmore Lodge H'land 310 E5
Strathpeffer H'land 300 D4
Strathrannoch H'land 300 B3
Strathtay Perth/Kinr 286 B3
Strathvaich Lodge H'land 300 B3
Strathwhillan N Ayrs 256 B2
Strathy H'land 300 B6
Strathy H'land 310 C2
Strathyre Stirl 285 F9
Stratton Cornw'l 24 F2
Stratton Dorset 17 C8
Stratton Glos 81 E8
Stratton Audley Oxon 102 F2
Stratton St. Margaret Swindon 63 B7
Stratton St. Michael Norfolk 142 E4
Stratton Strawless Norfolk 160 E4
Stratton-on-the-Fosse Som'set 45 C7
Stravithie Fife 287 F9
Strawberry Bank Cumb 211 B8
Strawberry Hill W Yorks 198 C2
Stream Som'set 42 F5
Streat E Sussex 36 D5
Streatham London 67 E10
Streatham Vale London 67 E9
Streatley Beds 103 F11
Streatley W Berks 64 C5
Street Devon 15 D9
Street Lancs 202 C6
Street N Yorks 226 E4
Street Som'set 28 F5
Street Som'set 44 F3
Street Som'set 45 C7
Street S Yorks 186 B7
Street Ashton Warwick 135 G9
Street Dinas Shrops 148 B6
Street End Hants 49 B8
Street End Kent 54 C6
Street End N Som'set 44 B3
Street End W Sussex 22 D5
Street Gate Tyne/Wear 242 F6
Street Houses N Yorks 206 D6
Street Lydan Wrex 149 B8
Street of Kincardine H'land 291 B11
Street on the Fosse Som'set 44 F6
Streethay Staffs 152 G2
Streethouse W Yorks 197 C11
Streetlam N Yorks 224 F6
Streetly W Midlands 133 D11
Streetly End Cambs 106 B2
Streetway Lane Dorset 30 G3
Strefford Shrops 131 F8
Strelley Notts 171 G8
Strensall C/York 216 G2
Strensall Camp C/York 207 B8
Stretch Down Devon 26 E4
Stretcholt Som'set 43 E9
Strete Devon 8 F6
Stretford Gtr Man 184 B4
Strethall Essex 105 D9
Stretham Cambs 123 C10
Strettington W Sussex 34 F5
Stretton Derby 170 C5
Stretton Rutl'd 155 F8
Stretton Staffs 151 G7
Stretton Staffs 152 D5
Stretton Warrington 183 E10
Stretton en le Field Leics 152 G6
Stretton Grandison Heref'd 98 C2
Stretton Heath Shrops 149 G7
Stretton on Dunsmore Warwick 119 C8
Stretton on Fosse Warwick 100 D4
Stretton Sugwas Heref'd 97 C9
Stretton under Fosse Warwick 135 G8
Stretton Westwood Shrops 131 D11
Strichen Aberds 303 D9
Strines Gtr Man 185 D7
Stringston Som'set 43 E7
Strixton Northants 121 E8
Stroat Glos 79 F9
Strom Shetl'd 315 J5
Stromeferry H'land 295 B10
Stromemore H'land 295 B10
Stromness Orkney 313 H3
Stronaba H'land 290 E4
Stronachlachar Stirl 285 F8
Stronachullin Lodge Arg/Bute 275 F9
Stroncheggan H'land 290 F2
Stronchrubie H'land 307 H7
Strone Arg/Bute 255 F7
Strone Arg/Bute 274 G6
Strone Arg/Bute 276 E3
Strone H'land 290 E3
Strone H'land 291 D9
Strone H'land 300 G5
Strone Inverc! 276 G5
Stronelairg Lodge H'land 291 C7
Stroneskar Arg/Bute 275 C9
Strongstry Lancs 195 D9
Stronmachair Stirl 285 G8
Stronmilchan Arg/Bute 284 E5
Stronord Dumf/Gal 236 C6
Stronsay Airport Orkney 312 F7
Strontian H'land 289 C10
Stronvar Stirl 285 E9
Strood Kent 53 G11
Strood Medway 69 F8
Strood Green Surrey 51 D8
Strood Green W Sussex 50 G6
Strood Green W Sussex 35 C8
Strothers Dale Northum 241 F11
Stroud Glos 80 D4
Stroud Hants 34 C2
Stroud Green Essex 88 G5
Stroud Green Glos 80 D4
Stroud Green London 67 B10
Stroud Green W Berks 64 F3
Stroude Surrey 66 F4
Stroupster H'land 310 C7
Stroxton Lincs 155 C8
Struan H'land 294 B5
Struan Perth/Kinr 291 G10
Strubby Lincs 191 E7
Strubby Lincs 189 F11
Struggs Hill Lincs 156 B5
Strumpshaw Norfolk 143 B7
Strutherhill S Lanarks 268 F5
Struthers Fife 287 G7
Struy H'land 300 F3
Stryd Angl 178 E2
Stryt-cae-rhedyn Flints 166 C3
Stryt-issa Wrex 166 F3
Stuartfield Aberds 303 E9
Stubb Norfolk 161 E8
Stubber's Green W Midlands 133 C10
Stubbing's Green Suffolk 125 C11
Stubbington Hants 33 G8
Stubbins Lancs 195 D9
Stubble Green Cumb 219 F11
Stubbles W Berks 64 D5
Stubbs Cross Kent 54 F3
Stubb's Green Norfolk 142 D5
Stubbs Green Norfolk 143 D7
Stubhampton Dorset 30 E6
Stubhampton Down Dorset 30 E6
Stubshaw Cross Gtr Man 194 G5
Stubton Lincs 172 F5
Stubwood Staffs 152 B2
Stuckgowan Arg/Bute 285 G7
Stuckton Hants 31 E11
Stud Green Windsor 65 D11
Studd Hill Kent 71 F7
Studdal Kent 55 D10
Studham Beds 85 B8
Studland Dorset 18 E6
Studley Warwick 117 E11
Studley Wilts 62 E3
Studley Roger N Yorks 214 E5
Stump Cross W Yorks 196 B5
Stuntney Cambs 123 B11
Stunts Green E Sussex 37 E10
Sturbridge Staffs 150 C6
Sturmer Essex 106 C3
Sturminster Common Dorset 30 E3
Sturminster Marshall Dorset 18 B5
Sturminster Newton Dorset 30 E3
Sturry Kent 71 G7
Sturton N Lincs 200 G3
Sturton by Stow Lincs 188 E5
Sturton-le-Steeple Notts 188 E3
Stuston Suffolk 126 B2
Stutton N Yorks 206 E5
Stutton Suffolk 108 D3
Styal Ches 184 E4
Styants Bottom Kent 52 B5
Stydd Lancs 203 F9
Styrrup Notts 187 C11
Suainebost W Isles 304 B7
Suardail W Isles 304 E6
Succoth Aberds 302 F4
Succoth Arg/Bute 284 G6
Suckley Worcs 116 G4
Suckley Green Worcs 116 G4
Suckley Knowl Worcs 116 G4
Suckquoy Orkney 313 K5
Sucksted Green Essex 105 F11
Sudborough Northants 137 G9
Sudbourne Suffolk 127 G8
Sudbrook Lincs 173 G7
Sudbrook Monmouths 60 B4
Sudbrooke Lincs 189 F8
Sudbury Derby 152 C3
Sudbury London 67 B7
Sudbury Suffolk 107 C7
Sudden Gtr Man 195 E11
Suddie H'land 300 D6
Sudeley Castle and Gardens Glos 99 F10
Suffield Norfolk 160 C4
Suffield N Yorks 227 G9
Sugnall Staffs 150 C5
Sugwas Pool Heref'd 97 C8
Suisnish H'land 295 D7
Suladale H'land 298 D3
Sulaisiadar W Isles 304 E7
Sulby I/Man 192 C4
Sulgrave Northants 101 B11
Sulgrave Tyne/Wear 243 F8
Sulham W Berks 64 E6
Sulhamstead W Berks 64 F6
Sulhamstead Abbots W Berks 64 F6
Sulhamstead Bannister W Berks 64 F6
Sulland Orkney 312 D6
Sullington W Sussex 35 E10
Sullom Shetl'd 314 F5
Sullom Voe Oil Terminal Shetl'd 314 F5
Sully V/Glam 59 F7
Sumburgh Shetl'd 315 N6
Sumburgh Airport Shetl'd 315 M5
Summer Hill W Midlands 133 E9
Summerbridge N Yorks 214 G3
Summercourt Cornw'l 5 D7
Summerfield Kent 55 B9
Summerfield Norfolk 158 B4
Summerfield Worcs 116 C6
Summerfield Park W Midlands 133 F10
Summergangs Kingston/Hull 209 G8
Summerhill Norfolk 158 B3
Summerhill Pembs 73 D11
Summerhill Worcs 116 B6
Summerhill Wrex 166 E4
Summerhouse D'lington 224 B4
Summerlands Cumb 211 B10
Summerlands Som'set 29 D8
Summerleaze Newp 60 C2
Summerlee Heritage Centre, Coatbridge N Lanarks 268 B4
Summerley Derby 186 F5
Summersdale W Sussex 34 F5
Summerseat Gtr Man 195 E9
Summerston Glasg C 277 G11
Summerstown London 67 E9
Summertown Oxon 83 D8
Summit Gtr Man 195 E10
Summit Gtr Man 196 F2
Summit Gtr Man 196 D2
Sun Green Gtr Man 185 B7
Sunbiggin Cumb 222 D3
Sunbury Surrey 66 F5
Sunbury Common Surrey 66 E5
Sunbury Court Surrey 66 E6
Sundaywell Dumf/Gal 247 G8
Sunderland Arg/Bute 274 G3
Sunderland Cumb 229 D9
Sunderland Lancs 202 B4
Sunderland Tyne/Wear 243 F10
Sunderland Bridge Durham 233 D11
Sundhope Scot Borders 261 D8
Sundon Park Luton 103 F11
Sundown Adventure Land, Rampton Notts 188 F3
Sundridge Kent 52 B3
Sunipol Arg/Bute 288 D5
Sunk Island ER Yorks 201 D9
Sunningdale Windsor 66 F3
Sunninghill Windsor 66 F2
Sunningwell Oxon 83 E8
Sunniside Durham 233 D8
Sunniside Tyne/Wear 242 F6
Sunniside Tyne/Wear 243 G8
Sunny Bank Gtr Man 195 F10
Sunny Bower Blackb'n 203 G10
Sunny Brow Durham 233 E9
Sunny Hill Derby C 152 C6
Sunnyfields S Yorks 198 F4
Sunnyhurst Blackb'n 195 C7
Sunnylaw Stirl 278 B5
Sunnymead Oxon 83 D8
Sunnyside Essex 87 G11
Sunnyside N Lanarks 268 B4
Sunnyside S Yorks 187 B7
Sunnyside W Sussex 51 F11
Sunrising Estate Cornw'l 6 E5
Sunton Wilts 47 B8
Surbiton London 67 F7
Surby I/Man 192 E3
Surfleet Lincs 156 D4
Surfleet Seas End Lincs 156 D5
Surlingham Norfolk 142 B6
Surrex Essex 107 G7
Sustead Norfolk 160 B3
Susworth Lincs 199 G10
Sutcombe Devon 24 E4
Sutcombemill Devon 24 E4
Sutherland Grove Arg/Bute 289 E11
Suton Norfolk 141 D11
Sutors of Cromarty H'land 301 C8
Sutterby Lincs 190 G5
Sutterton Lincs 156 B5
Sutterton Dowdyke Lincs 156 C5
Sutton Beds 104 B4
Sutton Bucks 66 D4
Sutton Cambs 123 B8
Sutton Cornw'l 11 G11
Sutton Devon 8 G4
Sutton E Sussex 23 F7
Sutton Kent 55 D10
Sutton London 67 G9
Sutton Mersey 183 C9
Sutton Norfolk 161 E7
Sutton Notts 154 B5
Sutton Notts 172 E5
Sutton Notts 187 E11
Sutton Oxon 82 D6
Sutton Peterbro 138 D2
Sutton Pembs 72 B6
Sutton Shrops 132 F4
Sutton Shrops 149 D7
Sutton Shrops 149 G10
Sutton Suffolk 108 B6
Sutton Som'set 44 G6
Sutton Staffs 150 E5
Sutton S Yorks 198 E5
Sutton W Sussex 35 D7
Sutton Abinger Surrey 50 D6
Sutton Bassett Northants 136 E5
Sutton Benger Wilts 62 D2
Sutton Bingham Som'set 29 E8
Sutton Bonington Notts 153 D10
Sutton Bridge Lincs 157 E9
Sutton Cheney Leics 135 C8
Sutton Coldfield W Midlands 134 D2
Sutton Common Hants 49 D8
Sutton Courtenay Oxon 83 G8
Sutton Crosses Lincs 157 E8
Sutton End W Sussex 35 D7
Sutton Farm Worcs 116 B6
Sutton Gault Cambs 123 B8
Sutton Green Ches 182 F5
Sutton Green Oxon 82 D6
Sutton Green Surrey 50 C4
Sutton Green Wrex 166 F6
Sutton Heath Mersey 183 C8
Sutton Hill Shrops 132 C4
Sutton Howgrave N Yorks 214 D6
Sutton in Ashfield Notts 171 E7
Sutton in the Elms Leics 135 E10
Sutton Ings Kingston/Hull 209 G8
Sutton Lakes Heref'd 97 B10
Sutton Lane Ends Ches 184 G6
Sutton Leach Mersey 183 C8
Sutton Maddock Shrops 132 C4
Sutton Mallet Som'set 43 F11
Sutton Mandeville Wilts 31 B7
Sutton Manor Mersey 183 C8
Sutton Marsh Heref'd 97 C11
Sutton Montis Som'set 29 C10
Sutton on the Hill Derby 152 C4
Sutton Poyntz Dorset 17 E10
Sutton Row Wilts 31 B7
Sutton St. Edmund Lincs 157 G7
Sutton St. Edmund's Common Cambs 138 B6
Sutton St. James Lincs 157 F7
Sutton St. Michael Heref'd 97 B10
Sutton St. Nicholas Heref'd 97 B10
Sutton Scarsdale Derby 170 B6
Sutton Scotney Hants 48 F3
Sutton under Brailes Warwick 100 D6
Sutton upon Derwent ER Yorks 207 D10
Sutton Valence Kent 53 D10
Sutton Veny Wilts 45 E11
Sutton Waldron Dorset 30 D5
Sutton Warblington Hants 49 D8
Sutton Weaver Ches 183 F8
Sutton Wick Bath/NE Som'set 44 B5
Sutton Wick Oxon 83 G7
Sutton-at-Home Kent 68 F5
Sutton-in-Craven N Yorks 204 E6
Sutton-on-Hull Kingston/Hull 209 G8
Sutton-on-Sea Lincs 191 E8
Sutton-on-the-Forest N Yorks 215 G11
Sutton-on-Trent Notts 172 B3
Sutton-under-Whitestonecliffe N Yorks 215 C9
Swaby Lincs 190 F5
Swadlincote Derby 152 F6
Swaffham Norfolk 140 B6
Swaffham Bulbeck Cambs 123 E11
Swaffham Prior Cambs 123 E11
Swafield Norfolk 160 C5
Swainby N Yorks 225 E9
Swainshill Heref'd 97 C9
Swainsthorpe Norfolk 142 C4
Swainswick Bath/NE Som'set 61 F9
Swaithe S Yorks 197 G11
Swalcliffe Oxon 101 D7
Swalecliffe Kent 70 F6
Swaledale N Yorks 223 F9
Swallow Lincs 201 G7
Swallow Beck Lincs 173 B7
Swallowcliffe Wilts 31 B7
Swallowfield Wokingham 65 F8
Swallowfields Devon 8 C5
Swallowhurst Cumb 220 G2
Swallownest S Yorks 186 E6
Swallows Cross Essex 87 F10
Swalwell Tyne/Wear 242 E6
Swampton Hants 48 C2
Swan Green Ches 184 G2
Swan Green Suffolk 126 C5
Swan Street Essex 107 F7
Swan Street Kent 54 D2
Swan Village W Midlands 133 E9
Swanage Dorset 18 F6
Swanage Railway Dorset 18 F5
Swanbach Ches 167 G11
Swanbister Orkney 313 H4
Swanbourne Bucks 102 F6
Swanbridge V/Glam 59 F7
Swanland ER Yorks 200 B3
Swanley Glos 80 F2
Swanley Kent 68 F4
Swanley Bar Herts 86 E3
Swanley Village Kent 68 F4
Swanmore Hants 33 D9
Swanmore I/Wight 21 C7
Swannay Orkney 312 F3
Swannery, Abbotsbury Dorset 17 E7
Swannington Leics 153 F8
Swannington Norfolk 160 F2
Swanpool Lincs 188 G6
Swanscombe Kent 68 E6
Swansea = Abertawe Swan 75 G11
Swanside Mersey 182 C6
Swanston C/Edinb 270 B4
Swanton Abbott Norfolk 160 D5
Swanton Morley Norfolk 159 F10
Swanton Novers Norfolk 159 C10
Swanton Street Kent 53 B11
Swanwick Derby 170 E6
Swanwick Hants 33 F8
Swanwick Green Ches 167 F9
Swarby Lincs 173 G8
Swarcliffe W Yorks 206 F3
Swardeston Norfolk 142 C3
Swarister Shetl'd 314 E7
Swarkestone Derby 153 D7
Swarland Northum 252 C5
Swarraton Hants 48 F5
Swartha W Yorks 205 D7
Swarthmoor Cumb 210 D5
Swartland Orkney 312 F3
Swathwick Derby 170 B5
Swaton Lincs 156 B2
Swavesey Cambs 123 D7
Sway Hants 19 B11
Swayfield Lincs 155 E9
Swaythling S'thampton 32 D6
Sweeney Mountain Shrops 148 D5
Sweet Green Worcs 116 E3
Sweetham Devon 14 B3
Sweethaws E Sussex 37 B8
Sweetholme Cumb 221 B11
Sweets Cornw'l 11 B9
Sweetshouse Cornw'l 5 C11
Sweffling Suffolk 126 E6
Swell Som'set 28 C5
Swepstone Leics 153 G7
Swerford Oxon 101 E7
Swettenham Ches 168 B3
Swetton N Yorks 214 E3
Swffryd Bl Gwent 78 F2
Swift's Green Kent 53 E11
Swiftsden E Sussex 38 B2
Swilland Suffolk 126 G3
Swillbrook Lancs 202 G5
Swillington W Yorks 206 G3
Swillington Common W Yorks 206 G3
Swimbridge Devon 40 G6
Swimbridge Newland Devon 40 G6
Swinbrook Oxon 82 C3
Swincliffe W Yorks 197 B8
Swinden N Yorks 204 B2
Swinderby Lincs 172 C5
Swindon Glos 99 F8
Swindon Staffs 133 E7
Swindon Swindon 63 B7
Swine ER Yorks 209 F8
Swinefleet ER Yorks 199 C9
Swineford S Glos 61 F7
Swineshead Beds 121 D11
Swineshead Lincs 174 G2
Swineshead Bridge Lincs 174 G2
Swineshed Worcs 117 G7
Swineside N Yorks 213 C11
Swinethorpe Lincs 172 B5
Swiney H'land 310 F6
Swinford Leics 119 B11
Swinford Oxon 82 D6
Swingbrow Cambs 139 F7
Swingfield Minnis Kent 55 E8
Swingfield Street Kent 55 E8
Swingleton Green Suffolk 107 B9
Swinhoe Northum 264 D6
Swinhope Lincs 190 B2
Swining Shetl'd 314 G6
Swinister Shetl'd 314 E5
Swinister Shetl'd 315 L6
Swinithwaite N Yorks 213 B10
Swinley Green Worcs 98 E6
Swinmore Common Heref'd 98 C3
Swinnow Moor W Yorks 205 G10
Swinscoe Staffs 169 F10
Swinside Cumb 229 G10
Swinstead Lincs 155 E10
Swinthorpe Lincs 189 E9
Swinton Scot Borders 272 F6
Swinton Glasg C 268 C3
Swinton Gtr Man 195 G9
Swinton N Yorks 214 D4
Swinton N Yorks 216 E5
Swinton S Yorks 187 B7
Swinton Bridge S Yorks 187 B7
Swinton Green N Yorks 214 D4
Swinton Park Gtr Man 195 G9
Swiss Valley Carms 75 E8
Swithland Leics 153 G10
Swordale H'land 300 C5
Swordale H'land 309 K6
Swordland H'land 295 F9
Swordly H'land 308 C7
Sworton Heath Ches 183 E11
Swyddffynnon Ceredig'n 112 D3
Swynnerton Staffs 150 B6
Swyre Dorset 16 D6
Sycharth Powys 148 D4
Sychdyn = Soughton Flints 166 B2
Sychnant Powys 113 B9
Sydallt Flints 166 D4
Syde Glos 81 C7
Sydenham Oxon 84 E2
Sydenham Som'set 43 F10
Sydenham Damerel Devon 12 F4
Syderstone Norfolk 158 C6
Sydling St. Nicholas Dorset 17 B8
Sydmonton Hants 48 B3
Sydney Ches 168 D2
Syerston Notts 172 F2
Syke Gtr Man 195 D11
Syke Side Lancs 203 G11
Sykehouse S Yorks 198 D6
Sykemoor Pembs 73 E7
Syleham Suffolk 126 B4
Sylen Carms 75 D8
Sylfaen Powys 130 B3
Symbister Shetl'd 315 G7
Symington S Ayrs 257 C9
Symington S Lanarks 259 C11
Symonds Yat Heref'd 79 B9
Symondsbury Dorset 16 C4
Synderford Dorset 28 G5
Synod Inn Ceredig'n 111 G8
Synton Scot Borders 261 E11
Syon Park & House London 67 D7
Syre H'land 308 E6
Syreford Glos 99 G10
Syresham Northants 102 C2
Syster H'land 310 C6
Syston Leics 154 G2
Syston Lincs 172 G6
Sytchampton Worcs 116 D6
Sywell Northants 120 D6

T

Taagan H'land 299 C10
Tabley Ches 184 F2
Tabley Hill Ches 184 F2
Tabost W Isles 305 G5
Tachbrook Mallory Warwick 118 E6
Tackley Oxon 101 G9
Tacleit W Isles 304 E3
Tacolneston Norfolk 142 E2
Tadcaster N Yorks 206 E5
Tadden Dorset 31 G7
Taddington Derby 185 G10
Taddington Glos 99 E11
Taddiport Devon 25 D7
Tadhill Som'set 45 D7
Tadley Hants 64 G6
Tadley Oxon 64 B4
Tadlow Cambs 104 B5
Tadmarton Oxon 101 D7
Tadwick Bath/NE Som'set 61 E8
Tadworth Surrey 51 B8

Tafarnaubach Bl Gwent 77 C10
Tafarn-y-Bwlch Pembs 91 E11
Tafarn-y-Gelyn Denbs 165 C11
Taff Merthyr Garden Village Merth Tyd 77 F10
Taff's Well Card 58 C6
Tafolwern Powys 129 C7
Tàbost W Isles 304 B7
Tai Conwy 164 C3
Taibach Neath P Talb 57 D9
Tai-bach Powys 148 D3
Taicynhaeaf Gwyn 146 F3
Taigh a Ghearraidh W Isles 296 D3
Taigh Bhalaigh W Isles 296 D3
Taillwyd Rh Cyn Taff 76 F2
Tai-morfa Gwyn 144 D5
Tain H'land 309 L7
Tain H'land 310 C6
Tai'n Lon Gwyn 162 E6
Tairbeart = Tarbert W Isles 305 H3
Tai'r-Bull Powys 95 F9
Tairgwaith Neath P Talb 76 C2
Tai'r-heol Caerph 77 G10
Tai'r-waun Caerph 77 G10
Tai'r-ysgol Swan 75 F11
Takeley Essex 105 G11
Takeley Street Essex 105 G10
Talacharn = Laugharne Carms 74 C4
Talachddu Powys 95 E11
Talacre Flints 181 E10
Talardd Gwyn 147 D7
Talaton Devon 15 B7
Talbenny Pembs 72 C4
Talbot Green Rh Cyn Taff 58 C4
Talbot Village Bournem'th 19 C7
Talbot's End S Glos 80 G2
Talerddig Powys 129 C8
Talewater Devon 15 B7
Talgarreg Ceredig'n 111 G8
Talgarth Powys 96 E3
Taliesin = Tre Taliesin Ceredig'n 128 E3
Talisker H'land 294 B5
Talke Staffs 168 E4
Talke Pits Stoke 168 E4
Talkin Cumb 240 F2
Talladale H'land 299 B9
Tallarn Green Wrex 166 G6
Tallentire Cumb 229 D8
Talley Carms 94 E2
Tallington Lincs 137 B11
Tallistown Bl Gwent 77 D11
Talmine H'land 308 C5
Talog Carms 92 F6
Talsarn Carms 94 F5
Tal-sarn Ceredig'n 111 F10
Talsarnau Gwyn 146 B2
Talskiddy Cornw'l 5 B8
Talwrn Angl 179 F7
Talwrn Wrex 166 F3
Talwrn Wrex 166 E3
Tal-y-Bont Conwy 164 B3
Tal-y-bont Ceredig'n 128 F3
Tal-y-bont Gwyn 145 E11
Tal-y-bont Gwyn 179 G10
Talybont-on-Usk Powys 96 G2
Tal-y-cafn Conwy 180 G3
Tal-y-coed Monmouths 78 B6
Talyllin Powys 96 F2
Tal-y-llyn Gwyn 128 B4
Talysarn Gwyn 163 E7
Tal-y-Waenydd Gwyn 163 F11
Talywain Torf 78 E3
Tamanabhagh W Isles 304 F2
Tame Bridge N Yorks 225 D10
Tame Water Gtr Man 196 F3
Tamer Lane End Gtr Man 194 G6
Tamerton Foliot Plym'th 7 C9
Tamfourhill Falk 279 F7
Tamworth Staffs 134 C4
Tamworth Green Lincs 174 G5
Tan Hills Durham 233 B11
Tan Office Suffolk 126 E2
Tan Office Green Suffolk 124 F5
Tandem W Yorks 197 E7
Tandlehill Renf 267 C8
Tandridge Surrey 51 C10
Tanerdy Carms 93 G8
Tanfield Durham 242 F5
Tanfield Lea Durham 242 G5
Tang N Yorks 205 B10
Tang Hall C/York 207 C8
Tangasdal W Isles 297 M2
Tangier Som'set 28 C2
Tangiers Pembs 73 B7
Tangley Hants 47 C10
Tanglwst Carms 92 E6
Tangmere W Sussex 34 F6
Tangwick Shetl'd 314 F4
Tangy Arg/Bute 255 E7
Tanhouse Lancs 194 F3
Tanis Wilts 62 G3
Tank Museum, Bovington Dorset 18 D2
Tankersley S Yorks 186 B4
Tankerton Kent 70 F6
Tan-lan Conwy 164 C3
Tan-lan Flints 181 E10
Tan-lan Gwyn 163 G10
Tannach H'land 310 E7
Tannachie Aberds 293 E9
Tannadice Angus 287 B8
Tanner's Green Worcs 117 C11
Tannington Suffolk 126 D4
Tannington Green Suffolk 126 D4
Tannochside N Lanarks 268 C4
Tanshall Fife 280 A5
Tansley Derby 170 D4
Tansley Hill W Midlands 133 F9
Tansley Knoll Derby 170 C4
Tansor Northants 137 E11
Tanterton Lancs 202 G6
Tantobie Durham 242 G5
Tanton N Yorks 225 C10
Tanvats Lincs 173 C10
Tanworth in Arden Warwick 118 C2
Tan-y-Bwlch Gwyn 163 B10
Tan-y-bwlch Gwyn 163 G11
Tan-y-coed Gwyn 163 C8
Tan-y-fron Conwy 165 C7
Tan-y-fron Wrex 166 E3
Tanygrisiau Gwyn 163 F11
Tan-y-groes Ceredig'n 92 B5
Tan-y-Lôn Gwyn 179 G10
Tan-yr-allt Denbs 181 E9
Tan-yr-allt Gwyn 163 E7
Taobh a Chaolais W Isles 297 K3
Taobh a Thuath Loch Aineort W Isles 297 J3
Taobh a Tuath Loch Baghasdail W Isles 297 J3
Taobh a'Ghlinne W Isles 305 G5
Taobh Siar W Isles 305 H3
Taobh Tuath W Isles 296 C5
Taplow Bucks 66 C2
Tapton Derby 186 G5
Tapton Hill S Yorks 186 D4
Tarbat Ho. H'land 301 B7
Tarbert Arg/Bute 255 B7
Tarbert Arg/Bute 275 E7
Tarbert Arg/Bute 275 G9
Tarbert = Tairbeart W Isles 305 H3
Tarbet Arg/Bute 285 G7
Tarbet H'land 295 F9
Tarbet H'land 306 E6
Tarbock Green Mersey 183 D7
Tarbolton S Ayrs 257 D10
Tarbrax S Lanarks 269 D10
Tardebigge Worcs 117 D9
Tardy Gate Lancs 194 B4
Tarfside Angus 292 F6
Tarland Aberds 292 C6
Tarleton Lancs 194 C2
Tarlogie H'land 309 L7
Tarlscough Lancs 194 E2
Tarlton Glos 81 F7
Tarn W Yorks 205 F9
Tarnbrook Lancs 203 B7
Tarnock Som'set 43 C11
Tarns Cumb 229 B8
Tarnside Cumb 221 G8
Tarporley Ches 167 C9
Tarpots Essex 69 B9
Tarr Som'set 42 G6
Tarraby Cumb 239 F10
Tarrant Crawford Dorset 30 G6
Tarrant Gunville Dorset 30 E6
Tarrant Hinton Dorset 30 E6
Tarrant Keyneston Dorset 30 G6
Tarrant Launceston Dorset 30 F6
Tarrant Monkton Dorset 30 F6
Tarrant Rawston Dorset 30 F6
Tarrant Rushton Dorset 30 F6
Tarrel H'land 311 L2
Tarring Neville E Sussex 36 G6
Tarrington Heref'd 98 C2
Tarryblake Ho. Moray 302 E5
Tarsappie Perth/Kinr 286 E5
Tarskavaig H'land 295 E7
Tarves Aberds 303 F8
Tarvie H'land 300 D4
Tarvie Perth/Kinr 292 G2
Tarvin Ches 167 B7
Tarvin Sands Ches 167 B7
Tasburgh Norfolk 142 D3
Tasley Shrops 132 E3
Taston Oxon 101 G7
Tat Bank W Midlands 133 F9
Tate Gallery London 67 D9
Tate Gallery, Albert Dock Mersey 182 D4
Tate Modern London 67 C10
Tate St Ives Cornw'l 2 A2
Tatenhill Staffs 152 E4
Tathall End M/Keynes 102 B6
Tatham Lancs 212 F2
Tathwell Lincs 190 E4
Tatling End Bucks 66 B4
Tatlingbury Kent 52 D6
Tatmore Place Herts 104 F3
Tatsfield Surrey 52 B2
Tattenhall Ches 167 D7
Tattenhoe M/Keynes 102 E6
Tatterford Norfolk 159 D7
Tattersett Norfolk 158 D6
Tattershall Lincs 174 D2
Tattershall Bridge Lincs 173 D11
Tattershall Thorpe Lincs 174 D2
Tattingstone Suffolk 108 D2
Tattingstone White Horse Suffolk 108 D2
Tatton Dale Ches 184 E2
Tatton Park Ches 184 E2
Tatworth Som'set 28 F4
Taunton Gtr Man 196 G2
Taunton Som'set 28 B2
Taunton Racecourse Som'set 28 C2
Taverham Norfolk 160 G3
Taverners Green Essex 87 B9
Tavernspite Pembs 73 C11
Tavistock Devon 12 G5
Taw Green Devon 13 B9
Tawd Bridge Lancs 194 F3
Tawstock Devon 25 B8
Taxal Derby 185 F8
Tay Bridge Dundee C 287 E8
Tayinloan Arg/Bute 255 C7
Taymouth Castle Perth/Kinr 285 C11
Taynish Arg/Bute 275 E8
Taynton Glos 98 G4
Taynton Oxon 82 C2
Taynuilt Arg/Bute 284 D4
Tayport Fife 287 E8
Tayvallich Arg/Bute 275 E8
Tea Green Herts 104 G2
Tealby Lincs 189 C11
Tealby Thorpe Lincs 189 C10
Tealing Angus 287 D8
Team Valley Tyne/Wear 242 E6
Teams Tyne/Wear 242 E6
Teanford Staffs 169 G8
Teangue H'land 295 E8
Teanna Mhachair W Isles 296 E3
Tebay Cumb 222 E2
Tebworth Beds 103 F9
Tedburn St. Mary Devon 14 C2
Teddington Glos 99 E9
Teddington London 67 E7
Tedstone Delamere Heref'd 116 F3
Tedstone Wafre Heref'd 116 F3
Teesport Redcar/Clevel'd 234 G6
Teesville Redcar/Clevel'd 225 B10
Teeton Northants 120 C3
Teffont Evias Wilts 46 G3
Teffont Magna Wilts 46 G3
Tegiskey Cornw'l 5 F10
Tegryn Pembs 92 E4
Teigh Rutl'd 155 F7
Teign Village Devon 14 E2
Teigncombe Devon 13 D9
Teigngrace Devon 14 G3
Teignmouth Devon 14 G4
Telford Shrops 150 G4
Telham E Sussex 38 E3
Tellisford Som'set 45 B9
Telscombe E Sussex 36 G6
Telscombe Cliffs E Sussex 36 G5
Templand Dumf/Gal 248 F3
Temple Glasg C 267 B10
Temple Cornw'l 11 G8
Temple Midloth 270 D6
Temple Wilts 45 E10
Temple Windsor 65 C10
Temple Balsall W Midlands 118 B4
Temple Bar Carms 75 B9
Temple Bar Ceredig'n 111 F11
Temple Bar Pembs 91 D11
Temple Bar W Sussex 34 F6
Temple Bruer Lincs 173 E8
Temple Cloud Bath/NE Som'set 44 B6
Temple Cowley Oxon 83 E8
Temple End Suffolk 124 G3
Temple Ewell Kent 55 E9
Temple Fields Essex 87 C7
Temple Grafton Warwick 118 G2
Temple Guiting Glos 99 F11
Temple Herdewyke Warwick 119 G7
Temple Hill Kent 68 D4
Temple Hirst N Yorks 198 C6
Temple Normanton Derby 170 B6
Temple Sowerby Cumb 231 F8
Templeborough S Yorks 186 C6
Templecombe Som'set 30 C2
Templehall Fife 280 C5
Templeton Devon 26 E5
Templeton Pembs 73 C10
Templeton Bridge Devon 26 E5
Templetown Durham 233 B8
Tempsford Beds 122 G3
Ten Acres W Midlands 133 G11
Ten Mile Bank Norfolk 139 D11
Tenandry Perth/Kinr 291 G11
Tenbury Wells Worcs 115 D11
Tenby = Dinbych-y-Pysgod Pembs 73 E10
Tendring Essex 108 G2
Tendring Green Essex 108 F2
Tendring Heath Essex 108 F2
Tenston Orkney 312 G3
Tenterden Kent 53 G11
Terfyn Conwy 180 F6
Terhill Som'set 43 G7
Terling Essex 88 B3
Ternhill Shrops 150 C2
Terpersie Castle Aberds 302 G5
Terras Cornw'l 5 E8
Terregles Banks Dumf/Gal 237 B11
Terrick Bucks 84 D4
Terrick Shrops 167 G8
Terrier's End Bucks 84 D6
Terrington N Yorks 216 E3
Terrington St. Clement Norfolk 157 E10
Terrington St. John Norfolk 157 G10
Terryhorn Aberds 302 F4
Terry's Green Warwick 118 C2
Terwick Common W Sussex 34 C4
Teston Kent 53 C7
Testwood Hants 32 E5
Tetbury Glos 80 G5
Tetbury Upton Glos 80 F5
Tetchill Shrops 149 C7
Tetchwick Bucks 83 B11
Tetcott Devon 12 B2
Tetford Lincs 190 G4
Tetney Lincs 201 G10
Tetney Lock Lincs 201 G10
Tetsworth Oxon 83 E11
Tettenhall W Midlands 133 C7
Tettenhall Wood W Midlands 133 D7
Tetworth Cambs 122 G4
Tetworth Windsor 66 F2
Teuchan Aberds 303 F10
Teversal Notts 171 C7
Teversham Cambs 123 F9
Teviothead Scot Borders 249 B10
Tevorrick Cornw'l 10 G4
Tewel Aberds 293 E10
Tewin Herts 86 C3
Tewitfield Lancs 211 E10
Tewkesbury Glos 99 E7
Tewkesbury Abbey Glos 99 E7
Teynham Kent 70 G2
Teynham Street Kent 70 G3
Thackley W Yorks 205 F9
Thackley End W Yorks 205 F9
Thackthwaite Cumb 229 G8
Thackthwaite Cumb 230 F4
Thainston Aberds 293 F8
Thakeham W Sussex 35 D10
Thame Oxon 84 D2
Thames Ditton Surrey 66 F6
Thames Haven Thurr'k 69 C8
Thamesmead London 68 C3
Thankerton S Lanarks 259 B11
Thannington Kent 54 B6
Tharbies Herts 87 B7
Tharston Norfolk 142 E3
Thatcham W Berks 64 F4
Thatto Heath Mersey 183 C8
Thaxted Essex 106 E2
The Aird H'land 298 D4
The All England Jumping Course, Hickstead W Sussex 36 D3
The Bage Heref'd 96 C5
The Balloch Perth/Kinr 286 F2
The Bank Ches 168 D4
The Bank Shrops 132 D2
The Banks Gtr Man 185 D7
The Banks Wilts 62 D4
The Barony Orkney 312 F3
The Barton Wilts 62 D5
The Batch S Glos 61 E7
The Batch Som'set 44 C4
The Bell Gtr Man 194 F4
The Bent Derby 152 C4
The Bluebell Railway, Sheffield Park E Sussex 36 C6
The Blyth Staffs 151 D11
The Bourne Surrey 49 D10
The Bourne Worcs 117 F9
The Bows Stirl 285 G11
The Braes H'land 295 B7
The Bratch Staffs 133 E7
The Breaches Worcs 117 D11
The Breck Orkney 313 H4
The Brushes Derby 186 F5
The Bryn Monmouths 78 D4
The Burf Worcs 116 D6
The Burrell Collection Glasg C 267 C11
The Bury Herts 104 F4
The Butts Som'set 45 D9
The Camp Glos 80 D6
The Camp Herts 85 D11
The Cape Warwick 118 D5
The Chequer Wrex 167 G7
The Children's Village E Loth 271 C9
The Chuckery W Midlands 133 D10
The City Beds 122 F2
The City Bucks 84 F3
The City Suffolk 143 F7
The Cleaver Heref'd 97 F10
The Common Bucks 102 E5
The Common Oxon 100 F5
The Common Surrey 51 G7
The Common Wilts 47 G8
The Common Wilts 62 B4
The Corner Kent 53 E8
The Corner Shrops 131 F8
The Craigs H'land 309 K4
The Cronk I/Man 192 C4
The Dams Cambs 139 E9
The Dell Suffolk 143 D9
The Delves W Midlands 133 E10
The Den N Ayrs 266 E6
The Dene Durham 242 G4
The Dicker E Sussex 23 D9
The Dinosaur Museum, Dorchester Dorset 17 C9
The Down Kent 53 F7
The Dunks Wrex 166 E4
The Eaves Glos 79 D10
The Fall W Yorks 197 B10
The Fence Glos 79 D8
The Flat Glos 80 B3
The Folly Som'set 44 C5
The Folly W Berks 64 F3
The Ford Bucks 84 E3
The Forstal E Sussex 52 F4
The Forstal Kent 54 F5
The Four Alls Shrops 150 C3
The Fox Wilts 62 B6
The Foxholes Shrops 116 B2
The Frenches Hants 32 C4
The Friars, Aylesford Kent 53 B8
The Garths Shetl'd 314 B8
The Gibb Wilts 61 D10
The Graig Monmouths 79 D8
The Green Beds 85 B8
The Green Cambs 122 D5
The Green Cumb 210 C3
The Green Essex 88 B3
The Green Flints 166 B2
The Green Glos 99 F9
The Green Hants 32 B3
The Green M/Keynes 103 C7
The Green Norfolk 141 C11
The Green Norfolk 159 B11
The Green Northants 102 C5
The Green Notts 188 G4
The Green Oxon 84 E3
The Green S Glos 61 E7
The Green S Yorks 197 G8
The Green Warwick 118 F4
The Green Wilts 45 G11
The Grove Dumf/Gal 237 B11
The Grove Durham 242 G3
The Grove Worcs 99 C7
The Hall Suffolk 126 F4
The Hall Shetl'd 314 D8
The Hallands N Lincs 200 C5
The Ham Wilts 45 C11
The Haven W Sussex 50 G5
The Hawkhills N Yorks 215 F10
The Headland Hartlep'l 234 E6
The Heath Norfolk 159 D8
The Heath Norfolk 160 E3
The Heath Norfolk 160 E4
The Heath Suffolk 108 D2
The Heath Staffs 151 C11
The Heavens Notts 153 D11
The Hem Shrops 132 B4
The Herberts V/Glam 58 E4
The High Essex 86 C6
The Highlands E Sussex 38 F2
The Hill Cumb 210 C3
The Hill Worcs 98 D6
The Holt Hants 64 G5
The Holt W Berks 63 E10
The Holt Wokingham 65 D10
The Hoo Glos 100 D3
The Hook Worcs 98 C6
The Howe Cumb 211 B9
The Howe I/Man 192 F2
The Hundred Heref'd 115 E10
The Hyde London 67 B8
The Hythe Essex 107 G10
The Kendals Dorset 30 B4
The Knapp S Glos 79 G11
The Knowle W Midlands 133 F9
The Lake Dumf/Gal 237 E8
The Lakes Worcs 116 B5
The Lawe Tyne/Wear 243 D9
The Leacon Kent 54 G3
The Lee Bucks 84 E6
The Lees Kent 54 C4
The Leigh Glos 99 F7
The Leys Staffs 134 C4
The Lhen I/Man 192 B4
The Lindens Lincs 201 F7
The Lindens W Midlands 133 D11
The Ling Norfolk 142 D6
The Lings Norfolk 141 B10
The Lings S Yorks 199 F7
The Linleys Wilts 61 F11
The Living RainForest W Berks 64 D4
The Lodge Wrex 166 E3
The Long Man of Wilmington E Sussex 37 G8
The Lost Gardens of Heligan, Mevagissey Cornw'l 5 F9
The Lowry, Salford Gtr Man 184 B4
The Lunt W Midlands 133 D9
The Marsh Heref'd 115 F9
The Marsh Powys 130 D6
The Marsh Shrops 150 D3
The Marsh Suffolk 125 B11
The Marsh Wilts 62 C5
The Middles Durham 242 G6
The Moor Cambs 105 B7
The Moor E Sussex 38 D4
The Moor Kent 38 B3
The Moors Heref'd 97 E10
The Moors Centre, Danby N Yorks 226 D4
The Mount Dorset 16 B5
The Mount Hants 64 G2
The Mount London 52 B3
The Mount Reading 65 E8
The Mount Worcs 116 C6
The Mumbles = Y Mwmbwls Swan 56 D6
The Murray S Lanarks 268 E2
The Mythe Glos 99 E7
The Nant Wrex 166 E3
The Narth Monmouths 79 D8
The National Archives, Kew London 67 D7
The Needles Old Battery I/Wight 20 E1
The Neuk Aberds 293 D9
The Node Herts 104 G4
The Oval Bath/NE Som'set 61 G8
The Oval Cricket Ground London 67 D10
The Oxford Story, Oxford Oxon 83 D8
The Park Glos 99 G8
The Park Glos 99 F8
The Park N Som'set 60 E2
The Parks S Yorks 198 F6
The Pentre Monmouths 78 B3
The Pill Monmouths 60 B3
The Pitts Wilts 31 B9
The Platt Kent 52 G5
The Point Devon 14 E5
The Pole of Itlaw Aberds 302 D6
The Pound Glos 98 E4
The Pound Powys 114 C3
The Purlieu Glos 79 D11
The Quarry Glos 80 F2
The Quarter Kent 53 E11
The Ramplings Worcs 99 E7
The Reddings Glos 99 G8
The Rhos Pembs 73 C8
The Rhydd Heref'd 97 E9
The Ridge Wilts 61 F11
The Rise Windsor 66 F2
The Rock Shrops 132 B3
The Rocks Kent 53 B8
The Rocks S Glos 61 C8
The Rookery Herts 85 F10
The Rookery Staffs 168 D5
The Roundabout S Glos 60 B6
The Row Lancs 211 D9
The Row Oxon 82 C6
The Rowe Staffs 150 B6
The Ryde Herts 86 D2
The Sale Staffs 152 G3
The Sands Surrey 49 D11
The Scarr Glos 98 F4
The Shoe Wilts 61 E10
The Shruggs Staffs 151 C8
The Slack Durham 233 F8
The Slade W Berks 64 F4
The Spa Wilts 62 G2
The Square Torf 78 F3
The Stocks Kent 38 B6
The Stocks Wilts 62 G2
The Straits W Midlands 133 E8
The Strand Wilts 46 B2
The Swillett Herts 85 G8
The Tales of Robin Hood Nott'ham 153 B11
The Thorn Heref'd 97 G11
The Three Crossways Suffolk 126 F2
The Thrift Herts 104 D6
The Throat Wokingham 65 F10
The Turves Cambs 138 D6
The Tutankhamun Exhibition, Dorchester Dorset 17 C9
The Tynings Glos 80 B6
The Vale W Sussex 35 F10
The Valley Ches 167 D11
The Valley Kent 54 C3
The Valley Pembs 73 D10
The Verne Dorset 17 G9
The Village Newp 78 G4
The Village Surrey 66 E3
The Village W Midlands 133 F7
The Vyne Hants 48 B6
The Walshes Worcs 116 C6
The Warren Flints 181 E10
The Warren Reading 65 D7
The Wern Wrex 166 E3
The Willows NE Lincs 201 F8
The Woodlands Suffolk 107 C11
The Woods W Midlands 133 D10
The World of Beatrix Potter, Bowness-on-Windermere Cumb 221 F8
The Wrangle Bath/NE Som'set 44 B4
The Wrythe London 67 F9
The Wyke Shrops 132 B4
Theakston N Yorks 214 B6
Thealby N Lincs 199 D11
Theale Som'set 44 D3
Theale W Berks 64 E6
Theale Green W Berks 64 E6
Thearne ER Yorks 209 F7
Theberton Suffolk 127 D8
Theddingworth Leics 136 F3
Theddlethorpe All Saints Lincs 191 D7
Theddlethorpe St. Helen Lincs 191 D7
Thelnetham Suffolk 125 B10
Thelveton Norfolk 142 G3
Thelwall Warrington 183 D10
Themelthorpe Norfolk 159 E11
Thenford Northants 101 C10
Theobald's Green Wilts 62 F4
Therfield Herts 104 D6
Thetford Lincs 156 G2
Thetford Norfolk 141 G7
Thethwaite Cumb 230 C3
Theydon Bois Essex 86 F6
Thick Hollins W Yorks 196 E6
Thicket Mead Bath/NE Som'set 45 B7
Thickwood Wilts 61 E10
Thimble End W Midlands 134 E2
Thimbleby Lincs 174 B2
Thimbleby N Yorks 225 F9
Thingwall Mersey 182 E3
Third Dumf/Gal 248 F3
Thirdpart N Ayrs 266 F3
Thirkleby N Yorks 215 D9
Thirlby N Yorks 215 C9
Thirlestane Scot Borders 271 F11
Thirn N Yorks 214 B4
Thirsk N Yorks 215 C8
Thirsk Racecourse N Yorks 215 C8
Thirtleby ER Yorks 209 G9
Thisleton Lancs 202 F4
Thistleton Rutl'd 155 F8
Thistley Green Essex 88 B2
Thistley Green Suffolk 124 B3
Thixendale N Yorks 216 G6
Thockrington Northum 241 B11
Tholomas Drove Cambs 139 B8
Tholthorpe N Yorks 215 F9
Thomas Chapel Pembs 73 D10
Thomas Close Cumb 230 C4
Thomas Town Warwick 117 E11
Thomastown Aberds 302 F5
Thomastown Rh Cyn Taff 58 B4
Thompson Norfolk 141 D8
Thomshill Moray 302 D2
Thong Kent 69 E7
Thongsbridge W Yorks 197 F7
Thoralby N Yorks 213 B10
Thoresby Notts 187 G11
Thoresthorpe Lincs 191 F7
Thoresway Lincs 189 B11
Thorganby Lincs 190 B2
Thorganby N Yorks 207 E9
Thorgill N Yorks 226 F4
Thorington Suffolk 127 C8
Thorington Street Suffolk 107 D10
Thorlby N Yorks 204 C5
Thorley Herts 87 B7
Thorley I/Wight 20 D3
Thorley Houses Herts 105 G9
Thorley Street Herts 87 B7
Thorley Street I/Wight 20 D3
Thormanby N Yorks 215 E9
Thorn Beds 103 G10
Thorn Powys 114 E5
Thorn Green Northum 232 B2
Thornaby-on-Tees Stockton 225 B9
Thornage Norfolk 159 B11
Thornaugh Peterbro 137 C11
Thornborough Bucks 102 E4
Thornborough N Yorks 214 D5
Thornbury Devon 24 F6
Thornbury Heref'd 116 F2
Thornbury S Glos 79 G10
Thornbury W Yorks 205 G9
Thornbury Park S Glos 79 G10
Thornby Cumb 239 G7
Thornby Northants 120 B3
Thornby Wood Stockton 225 C8
Thorncliff Staffs 169 D8
Thorncliff W Yorks 197 E8
Thorncombe Street Surrey 50 E4
Thorncote Green Beds 104 B3
Thorncross I/Wight 20 E4
Thorndon Suffolk 126 D2
Thorndon Cross Devon 12 C6
Thorne S Yorks 199 E7
Thorne Abbotts Norfolk 126 B3
Thorne Coffin Som'set 29 D8
Thorne St. Margaret Som'set 27 C9
Thornecombe Dorset 28 G5
Thornend Wilts 62 D3
Thorner W Yorks 206 E3
Thornes Staffs 133 C11
Thornes W Yorks 197 D10
Thorney Bucks 66 D4
Thorney Notts 188 G5
Thorney Peterbro 138 C5
Thorney Som'set 28 C6
Thorney Close Tyne/Wear 243 G9
Thorney Crofts ER Yorks 201 C8
Thorney Green Suffolk 125 E11
Thorney Hill Hants 19 B10
Thorney Toll Cambs 138 C6
Thorneywood Notts 171 G9
Thornfalcon Som'set 28 C3
Thornford Dorset 29 E10
Thorngill N Yorks 213 B11
Thorngrafton Northum 241 D7
Thorngrove Som'set 43 G11
Thorngumbald ER Yorks 201 B8
Thornham Norfolk 176 E2
Thornham Fold Gtr Man 195 F11
Thornham Magna Suffolk 126 C2
Thornham Parva Suffolk 126 C2
Thornhill Caerph 59 C7
Thornhill Cumb 219 D10
Thornhill Derby 185 E11
Thornhill Dumf/Gal 247 D9
Thornhill Stirl 278 B3
Thornhill S'hampton 33 E7
Thornhill Wilts 62 D5
Thornhill W Yorks 197 D9
Thornhill Edge W Yorks 197 D9
Thornhill Head Devon 24 D6
Thornhill Lees W Yorks 197 D8
Thornhill Park S'hampton 33 E7
Thornhills W Yorks 197 C7
Thornholme ER Yorks 218 G2
Thornicombe Dorset 30 G5
Thornington Northum 263 C9
Thornley Durham 233 D8
Thornley Durham 234 D3
Thornley Gate Northum 241 F8
Thornliebank E Renf 267 D11
Thornly Park Renf 267 C9
Thornroan Aberds 303 F8
Thorns N Yorks 223 E7
Thorns Suffolk 124 F4
Thorns Beach Hants 20 B4
Thorns Green Ches 184 E3
Thornsett Derby 185 D8
Thornship Cumb 221 C11
Thornthwaite Cumb 229 F10
Thornthwaite N Yorks 205 B9
Thornton Angus 287 C7
Thornton Bucks 102 D5
Thornton E Loth 282 G4
Thornton ER Yorks 207 D11
Thornton Fife 280 B5
Thornton Lancs 202 E2
Thornton Leics 135 B9
Thornton Lincs 174 B2
Thornton Middlesbro 225 C9
Thornton Mersey 193 G10
Thornton Northum 273 F9
Thornton Pembs 72 D6
Thornton W Yorks 205 G8
Thornton Curtis N Lincs 200 D5
Thornton Heath London 67 F10
Thornton Hough Mersey 182 E4
Thornton in Craven N Yorks 204 D4
Thornton in Lonsdale N Yorks 212 E3
Thornton Rust N Yorks 213 B9
Thornton Steward N Yorks 214 B3
Thornton Watlass N Yorks 214 B4
Thorntonhall S Lanarks 267 D11
Thornton-le-Beans N Yorks 225 G7
Thornton-le-Clay N Yorks 216 F3
Thornton-le-Dale N Yorks 216 C6
Thornton-le-Moor Lincs 189 B8
Thornton-le-Moor N Yorks 215 B7
Thornton-le-Moors Ches 182 G6
Thornton-le-Street N Yorks 215 B8
Thorntonloch E Loth 282 G5
Thornwood Common Essex 87 E7
Thoroton Notts 172 G3
Thorp Gtr Man 196 F2
Thorp Arch W Yorks 206 D4
Thorpe Cumb 230 F5
Thorpe Derby 169 E11
Thorpe ER Yorks 208 D5
Thorpe Lincs 191 E7
Thorpe Norfolk 143 D8
Thorpe Notts 172 F3
Thorpe N Yorks 213 G10
Thorpe Surrey 66 F4
Thorpe Acre Leics 153 E10
Thorpe Arnold Leics 154 E5
Thorpe Audlin W Yorks 198 D3
Thorpe Bassett N Yorks 217 E7
Thorpe Bay Southend 70 B2
Thorpe by Water Rutl'd 137 D7
Thorpe Common Suffolk 108 D5
Thorpe Constantine Staffs 134 B5
Thorpe Culvert Lincs 175 C7
Thorpe Edge W Yorks 205 F9
Thorpe End Norfolk 160 G5
Thorpe Fendykes Lincs 175 C7
Thorpe Green Essex 108 G3
Thorpe Green Suffolk 125 G8
Thorpe Green Surrey 66 F4
Thorpe Hamlet Norfolk 142 B4
Thorpe Hesley S Yorks 186 B5
Thorpe in Balne S Yorks 198 E5
Thorpe Langton Leics 136 E4
Thorpe Larches Durham 234 F3
Thorpe le Fallows Lincs 188 E6
Thorpe le Street ER Yorks 208 E2
Thorpe le Vale Lincs 190 C2
Thorpe Lea Surrey 66 E4
Thorpe Malsor Northants 120 B6
Thorpe Mandeville Northants 101 B10
Thorpe Market Norfolk 160 B4
Thorpe Marriot Norfolk 160 G3
Thorpe Morieux Suffolk 125 G8
Thorpe on the Hill Lincs 172 B6
Thorpe on the Hill W Yorks 197 B10
Thorpe Park, Chertsey Surrey 66 F4
Thorpe Row Norfolk 141 B9
Thorpe St. Andrew Norfolk 142 B5
Thorpe St. Peter Lincs 175 C7
Thorpe Salvin S Yorks 187 E9
Thorpe Satchville Leics 154 G4
Thorpe Street Suffolk 125 B10
Thorpe Thewles Stockton 234 G4
Thorpe Tilney Lincs 173 D10
Thorpe Tilney Dales Lincs 173 D11
Thorpe Underwood Northants 136 G5
Thorpe Underwood N Yorks 206 B5
Thorpe Waterville Northants 137 G10
Thorpe Willoughby N Yorks 207 G7
Thorpe-le-Soken Essex 108 G3
Thorpeness Suffolk 127 F9
Thorpland Norfolk 140 B2
Thorrington Essex 89 B9
Thorverton Devon 26 G6
Thrandeston Suffolk 126 B2
Thrapston Northants 121 B9
Thrashbush N Lanarks 268 B5
Threapland Cumb 229 D9
Threapland N Yorks 213 G9
Threapwood Staffs 169 G8
Threapwood Wrex 166 F6
Threave Gardens Dumf/Gal 237 C9
Three Ashes Hants 64 G6
Three Ashes Heref'd 97 G10
Three Ashes Som'set 45 D7
Three Bridges Arg/Bute 284 F4
Three Bridges Lincs 190 D6
Three Bridges W Sussex 51 F9
Three Burrows Cornw'l 4 F4
Three Chimneys Kent 53 F10
Three Cocks Powys 96 D3
Three Counties Showground, Malvern Worcs 98 C5
Three Crosses Swan 75 G9
Three Cups Corner E Sussex 37 C10
Three Gates Shrops 130 F5
Three Hammers Cornw'l 11 D10
Three Holes Norfolk 139 C10
Three Horse Shoes Devon 14 B4
Three Leg Cross E Sussex 53 G7
Three Legged Cross Dorset 31 F9
Three May Poles W Midlands 118 B2
Three Mile Cross Wokingham 65 F8
Three Oaks E Sussex 38 E4
Threehammer Common Norfolk 160 F6
Threekingham Lincs 155 B11

Threemilestones Cornw'l 4 G5
Threemiletown W Loth 279 F11
Threewaters Cornw'l 5 B10
Threlkeld Cumb 230 F2
Threshers Bush Essex 87 D8
Threshfield N Yorks 213 G9
Thrigby Norfolk 161 G9
Thrimby Cumb 231 G7
Thringarth Durham 232 G4
Thringstone Leics 153 F8
Thrintoft N Yorks 224 G6
Thriplow Cambs 105 B8
Throapham S Yorks 187 E9
Throckenholt Lincs 139 B7
Throcking Herts 104 E6
Throckley Tyne/Wear 242 D5
Throckmorton Worcs 99 B9
Throop Dorset 18 C2
Throphill Northum 252 F4
Thropton Northum 252 C2
Throsk Stirl 279 C7
Throughgate Dumf/Gal 247 G9
Throwleigh Devon 13 C9
Throwley Kent 54 B3
Throwley Forstal Kent 54 C3
Thrumpton Notts 153 C10
Thrumpton Notts 188 E2
Thrumster H'land 310 E7
Thrunton Northum 264 G3
Thrupe Som'set 44 D6
Thrupp Glos 80 E5
Thrupp Oxon 82 F3
Thrupp Oxon 83 B7
Thruscross N Yorks 205 B9
Thrushelton Devon 12 D4
Thrussington Leics 154 F3
Thruxted Kent 54 C6
Thruxton Hants 47 D9
Thruxton Heref'd 97 E8
Thruxton Motor Racing Circuit Hants 47 D9
Thrybergh S Yorks 187 B7
Thulston Derby 153 C8
Thunder Bridge W Yorks 197 E7
Thundergay N Ayrs 255 C9
Thundersley Essex 69 B9
Thundridge Herts 86 B5
Thurcaston Leics 153 G11
Thurcroft S Yorks 187 E7
Thurdon Cornw'l 24 E3
Thurgarton Notts 171 G11
Thurgaton Norfolk 160 C3
Thurgoland S Yorks 197 G9
Thurlaston Leics 135 D10
Thurlaston Warwick 119 C9
Thurlbear Som'set 28 C3
Thurlby Lincs 191 F7
Thurlby Lincs 155 F11
Thurlby Lincs 172 C6
Thurleigh Beds 121 F11
Thurlestone Devon 8 G3
Thurloxton Som'set 43 G9
Thurlstone S Yorks 197 G8
Thurlton Norfolk 143 D8
Thurlwood Ches 168 D5
Thurmaston Leics 136 B2
Thurnby Leics 136 C2
Thurne Norfolk 161 F8
Thurnham Kent 53 B10
Thurning Norfolk 159 D11
Thurning Northants 137 F11
Thurnscoe S Yorks 198 F3
Thurnscoe East S Yorks 198 F3
Thursby Cumb 239 G8
Thursden Lancs 204 F4
Thursford Norfolk 159 C9
Thursford Collection, Fakenham Norfolk 159 C9
Thursford Green Norfolk 159 C9
Thursley Hants 50 F2
Thurso H'land 310 C5
Thurso East H'land 310 C5
Thurstaston Mersey 182 E2
Thurston Pembs 73 D7
Thurston Suffolk 125 D8
Thurston Clough Gtr Man 196 F3
Thurston End Suffolk 124 G5
Thurston Planche Suffolk 125 E8
Thurstonfield Cumb 239 F8
Thurstonland W Yorks 197 E7
Thurton Norfolk 142 C6
Thurvaston Derby 152 B4
Thuxton Norfolk 141 B10
Thwaite Durham 223 C10
Thwaite N Yorks 223 F7
Thwaite Suffolk 126 D2
Thwaite Head Cumb 220 G6
Thwaite St. Mary Norfolk 142 D6
Thwaites W Yorks 205 E7
Thwaites Brow W Yorks 205 E7
Thwing ER Yorks 217 E11
Tibbermore Perth/Kinr 286 E4
Tibberton Glos 98 G5
Tibberton Telford 150 E3
Tibberton Worcs 117 F8
Tibenham Norfolk 142 F2
Tibshelf Derby 170 C6
Tibthorpe ER Yorks 208 B5
Ticehurst E Sussex 53 G7
Tichborne Hants 48 G5
Tickencote Rutl'd 137 B9
Tickenham N Som'set 60 E3
Tickenhurst Kent 55 C9
Tickford End M/Keynes 103 C7
Tickhill S Yorks 187 B9
Ticklerton Shrops 131 E9
Tickmorend Glos 80 F4
Ticknall Derby 153 E7
Tickton ER Yorks 209 D7
Tidbury Green W Midlands 118 B2
Tidcombe Wilts 47 B9
Tiddington Oxon 83 E11
Tiddington Warwick 118 F4
Tiddleywink Wilts 61 D11
Tidebrook E Sussex 37 B10
Tideford Cornw'l 6 D6
Tideford Cross Cornw'l 6 C6
Tidenham Glos 79 F9
Tideswell Derby 185 F11
Tidmarsh W Berks 64 E6
Tidmington Warwick 100 D5
Tidnor Heref'd 97 D11
Tidpit Hants 31 D9
Tidworth Wilts 47 D8
Tiers Cross Pembs 72 C6
Tiffield Northants 120 G3
Tifty Aberds 303 E7
Tigerton Angus 293 G7
Tigh-na-Blair Perth/Kinr 285 F11
Tighnabruaich Arg/Bute 275 F10
Tighnacachla Arg/Bute 274 G3
Tighnafiline H'land 307 L3
Tighness Arg/Bute 284 G6
Tigley Devon 8 C5
Tilbrook Cambs 121 D11
Tilbrook M/Keynes 103 E8
Tilbrook Grange Cambs 121 C11
Tilbury Thurr'k 68 D6
Tilbury Green Essex 106 C4
Tile Cross W Midlands 134 F3
Tile Hill W Midlands 118 B5
Tilegate Green Essex 87 D8
Tilehouse Green W Midlands 118 B3
Tilehurst Reading 65 E7
Tilekiln Essex 106 E4
Tilekiln Green Essex 105 G10
Tilford Surrey 49 E11
Tilgate W Sussex 51 G9
Tilgate Forest Row W Sussex 51 G9
Tilkey Essex 106 G6
Tilland Cornw'l 6 C6
Tillathrowie Aberds 302 F4
Tillcoultry Clack 279 B8
Tillers Green Glos 98 E3
Tilley Shrops 149 D10
Tilley Green Shrops 149 D10
Tillingham Essex 89 E7
Tillington Heref'd 97 B9
Tillington Staffs 151 E8
Tillington W Sussex 35 C7
Tillington Common Heref'd 97 B9
Tilly Lo. Aberds 293 C7
Tillyarblet Angus 293 G7
Tillybirloch Aberds 293 C8
Tillycorthie Aberds 303 G9
Tillydrine Aberds 293 D8
Tillyfour Aberds 293 B7
Tillyfourie Aberds 293 B8
Tillygarmond Aberds 293 D8
Tillygreig Aberds 303 G8
Tillykerrie Aberds 303 G8
Tillynaught Aberds 302 C5
Tilmanstone Kent 55 C10
Tiln Notts 188 E2
Tilney All Saints Norfolk 157 F11
Tilney Cum Islington Norfolk 157 G11
Tilney Fen End Norfolk 157 G10
Tilney High End Norfolk 157 F11
Tilney St. Lawrence Norfolk 157 G10
Tilsdown Glos 80 F3
Tilshead Wilts 46 D4
Tilsmore E Sussex 37 C9
Tilstock Shrops 149 B10
Tilston Ches 167 E7
Tilstone Bank Ches 167 D9
Tilstone Fearnall Ches 167 C9
Tilsworth Beds 103 G9
Tilton on the Hill Leics 136 B4
Tiltups End Glos 80 F4
Tilty Essex 105 F11
Timbercombe Som'set 43 G8
Timberden Bottom Kent 68 G4
Timberland Lincs 173 D10
Timbersbrook Ches 168 C5
Timberscombe Som'set 42 E3
Timble N Yorks 205 C9
Timperley Gtr Man 184 D3
Timsbury Bath/NE Som'set 45 B7
Timsbury Hants 32 C4
Timsgearraidh W Isles 304 E2
Timworth Suffolk 125 D7
Timworth Green Suffolk 125 D7
Tincleton Dorset 17 C11
Tindale Cumb 240 F4
Tindale Crescent Durham 233 F9
Tingewick Bucks 102 E3
Tingley W Yorks 197 B9
Tingon Shetl'd 314 E4
Tingrith Beds 103 E10
Tingwall Orkney 312 F4
Tinhay Devon 12 D3
Tinkers End Bucks 102 F5
Tinkers Hill Hants 47 D11
Tinshill W Yorks 205 F11
Tinsley S Yorks 186 C6
Tinsley Green W Sussex 51 F9
Tintagel Cornw'l 11 D7
Tintagel Castle Cornw'l 11 D7
Tintern Abbey Monmouths 79 E8
Tintern Parva Monmouths 79 E8
Tintinhull Som'set 29 D7
Tintwistle Derby 185 B8
Tinwald Dumf/Gal 248 G2
Tinwell Rutl'd 137 B10
Tipperty Aberds 302 C6
Tipperty Aberds 303 G9
Tip's Cross Essex 87 E9
Tips End Norfolk 139 E10
Tiptoe Hants 19 B11
Tipton W Midlands 133 E8
Tipton Green W Midlands 133 E9
Tipton St. John Devon 15 C7
Tiptree Essex 88 B5
Tiptree Heath Essex 88 C5
Tirabad Powys 95 C7
Tiraghoil Arg/Bute 288 G5
Tircanol Swan 75 F11
Tirdeunaw Swan 75 F10
Tiree Airport Arg/Bute 288 E1
Tirinie Perth/Kinr 291 G10
Tirley Glos 98 F6
Tiroran Arg/Bute 288 G6
Tirphil Caerph 77 E10
Tirril Cumb 230 F6
Tirryside H'land 309 H5
Tir-y-dail Carms 75 C10
Tir-y-fron Flints 166 D3
Tisbury Wilts 30 B6
Tisman's Common W Sussex 50 G5
Tissington Derby 169 E11
Titchberry Devon 24 B2
Titchfield Hants 33 F8
Titchfield Common Hants 33 F8
Titchmarsh Northants 121 B10
Titchwell Norfolk 176 E3
Titcomb W Berks 63 F11
Tithby Notts 154 B3
Tithe Barn Hillock Mersey 183 B9
Tithebarn Staffs 169 G9
Tithill Som'set 27 B11
Titley Heref'd 114 F6
Titmore Green Herts 104 F4
Titsey Surrey 52 C2
Titson Cornw'l 24 G2
Tittenhurst Windsor 66 F2
Tittensor Staffs 151 B7
Tittleshall Norfolk 159 E7
Titton Worcs 116 D6
Tiverton Ches 167 C9
Tiverton Devon 27 E7
Tivetshall Norfolk 142 F3
Tivetshall St. Margaret Norfolk 142 F3
Tividale W Midlands 133 E9
Tivington Som'set 42 D2
Tivoli Cumb 219 B9
Tixall Staffs 151 E9
Tixover Rutl'd 137 C9
Toab Orkney 313 H6
Toab Shetl'd 315 M5
Toad Row Suffolk 143 F10
Toadmoor Derby 170 E5
Tobermory Arg/Bute 289 D7
Toberonochy Arg/Bute 275 C8
Tobha Beag W Isles 296 D5
Tobha Mor W Isles 297 H3
Tobhtarol W Isles 304 E3
Tobson W Isles 304 E3
Toby's Hill Lincs 191 C7
Tocher Aberds 302 F6
Tockenham Wilts 62 D4
Tockenham Wick Wilts 62 C4
Tockholes Blackb'n 195 C7
Tockington S Glos 60 B6
Tockwith N Yorks 206 C5
Todber Dorset 30 C3
Todding Heref'd 115 B8
Toddington Beds 103 F10
Toddington Glos 99 E10
Toddington W Sussex 35 G8
Toddlehills Aberds 303 E10
Todd's Green Herts 104 F4
Todenham Glos 100 D4
Todhill Angus 287 D8
Todhills Cumb 239 E9
Todhills Durham 233 E10
Todlachie Aberds 293 B8
Todmorden W Yorks 196 C2
Todrig Scot Borders 261 F10
Todwick S Yorks 187 E7
Toft Cambs 123 F7
Toft Lincs 155 F11
Toft Shetl'd 314 F6
Toft Warwick 119 C9
Toft Hill Durham 233 F9
Toft Hill Lincs 174 C2
Toft Monks Norfolk 143 E8
Toft next Newton Lincs 189 D8
Toftrees Norfolk 159 D7
Tofts H'land 310 C7
Tofts Northum 241 D8
Toftwood Norfolk 159 G9
Tog Hill S Glos 61 E8
Togston Northum 252 B6
Tokavaig H'land 295 D8
Tokers Green Oxon 65 D8
Tolastadh a Chaolais W Isles 304 E3
Tolastadh bho Thuath W Isles 304 D7
Tolborough Cornw'l 11 F9
Toldish Cornw'l 5 D8
Tolgus Mount Cornw'l 4 G3
Tolhurst E Sussex 53 G7
Toll Bar Mersey 183 C7
Toll Bar S Yorks 198 F5
Toll End W Midlands 133 E9
Toll of Birness Aberds 303 F10
Tolladine Worcs 117 F7
Tolland Som'set 42 G6
Tollard Farnham Dorset 31 D7
Tollard Royal Wilts 30 D6
Tollbar End W Midlands 119 B7
Toller Fratrum Dorset 17 B7
Toller Porcorum Dorset 17 B7
Toller Whelme Dorset 29 G8
Tollerford Dorset 17 B7
Tollerton Notts 154 C2
Tollerton N Yorks 215 G10
Tollesbury Essex 89 C7
Tollesby Middlesbro 225 B10
Tolleshunt D'Arcy Essex 88 C6
Tolleshunt Knights Essex 88 B6
Tolleshunt Major Essex 88 C5
Tollie H'land 300 D5
Tollingham ER Yorks 208 F2
Tolm W Isles 304 E6
Tolpuddle Dorset 17 C11
Tolvah H'land 291 D10
Tolworth London 67 F7
Tom an Fhuadain W Isles 305 G5
Tomaknock Perth/Kinr 286 E2
Tomatin H'land 301 G8
Tombreck H'land 300 F6
Tombui Perth/Kinr 286 B2
Tomchrasky H'land 290 B4
Tomdoun H'land 290 C3
Tomich H'land 300 B6
Tomich H'land 300 G3
Tomich House H'land 300 E5
Tomintoul Aberds 292 D3
Tomintoul Moray 292 B3
Tomlow Warwick 119 E9
Tomnaven Moray 302 F4
Tomnavoulin Moray 302 G2
Tomsleibhe Arg/Bute 289 F8
Ton Monmouths 78 F5
Tonbridge Kent 52 D5
Tonderghie Dumf/Gal 236 F6
Tondu Bridg 57 E11
Tone Som'set 27 C10
Tone Green Som'set 27 C11
Tonedale Som'set 27 C10
Tonfanau Gwyn 110 C2
Tong Kent 53 D10
Tong Shrops 132 B5
Tong W Yorks 205 G10
Tong End Lancs 195 D11
Tong Green Kent 54 C3
Tong Norton Shrops 132 B5
Tong Park W Yorks 205 F9
Tong Street W Yorks 205 G9
Tongdean Brighton/Hove 36 F3
Tonge Leics 153 E8
Tonge Fold Gtr Man 195 F8
Tonge Moor Gtr Man 195 E8
Tongham Surrey 49 D11
Tongland Dumf/Gal 237 D8
Tongue H'land 308 D5
Tongue End Lincs 156 F3
Tongwell M/Keynes 103 C7
Tongwynlais Card 58 C6
Tonmawr Rh Cyn Taff 76 F4
Tonna = Tonnau Rh Cyn Taff 76 F3
Tonnau = Tonna Rh Cyn Taff 76 F3
Ton-Pentre Rh Cyn Taff 77 F7
Ton-teg Rh Cyn Taff 58 B5
Tontine Lancs 194 G4
Ton-ty'r-bel Caerph 78 F2
Tonwell Herts 86 B4
Tonypandy Rh Cyn Taff 77 G7
Ton-y-pistyll Caerph 77 F11
Tonyrefail Rh Cyn Taff 58 B4
Toot Baldon Oxon 83 E9
Toot Hill Essex 87 E8
Toothill Hants 32 D5
Toothill Swindon 62 C6
Toothill W Yorks 196 C6
Tooting Graveney London 67 E9
Top End Beds 121 E10
Top Green Notts 172 F3
Top Lock Gtr Man 194 F6
Top of Hebers Gtr Man 195 F11
Top o'th'Lane Lancs 194 C5
Top Valley Nott'ham 171 G9
Topcliffe N Yorks 215 D8
Topcliffe W Yorks 197 B9
Topcroft Norfolk 142 E5
Topcroft Street Norfolk 142 E5
Topham S Yorks 198 D6
Toppesfield Essex 106 D4
Toppings Gtr Man 195 E8
Toprow Norfolk 142 D3
Topsham Devon 14 D5
Top-y-rhos Flints 166 D3
Torbay Torbay 9 C8
Torbeg N Ayrs 255 E10
Torboll Farm H'land 309 K7
Torbothie N Lanarks 269 D7
Torbreck H'land 309 J7
Torbrex Stirl 278 C5
Torbryan Devon 8 B6
Torbush N Lanarks 268 D6
Torcross Devon 8 G6
Torcroy H'land 291 D9
Tore H'land 300 D6
Torfrey Cornw'l 6 E2
Torgyle H'land 290 B5
Torinturk Arg/Bute 275 G9
Torkington Gtr Man 184 D6
Torksey Lincs 188 F4
Torlum W Isles 296 F3
Torlundy H'land 290 F3
Tormarton S Glos 61 D9
Tormisdale Arg/Bute 254 B2
Tormitchell S Ayrs 244 E6
Tormore H'land 295 E8
Tormore N Ayrs 255 D9
Tornagrain H'land 301 E7
Tornahaish Aberds 292 C4
Tornapress H'land 299 E8
Tornaveen Aberds 293 C8
Torness H'land 300 G5
Toronto Durham 233 E9
Torpenhow Cumb 229 D10
Torphichen W Loth 279 G9
Torphin Midloth 270 B4
Torphins Aberds 293 C8
Torpoint Cornw'l 7 D8
Torquay Torbay 9 C8
Torquhan Scot Borders 271 F8
Torr Devon 7 E11
Torr Devon 8 C2
Torra Arg/Bute 254 B4
Torran Arg/Bute 275 C9
Torran H'land 298 E5
Torran H'land 301 B7
Torrance E Dunb 278 G2
Torrans Arg/Bute 288 G6
Torranyard N Ayrs 267 G7
Torre Som'set 42 E4
Torre Torbay 9 B8
Torridon H'land 299 D9
Torridon Ho. H'land 299 D8
Torries Aberds 293 B8
Torrin H'land 295 C7
Torrisdale H'land 308 C6
Torrisdale Castle Arg/Bute 255 D8
Torrisdale-Square Arg/Bute 255 D8
Torrish H'land 311 H3
Torrisholme Lancs 211 G9
Torroble H'land 309 J5
Torroy H'land 309 K5
Torry Aberds 302 F4
Torry Aberd C 293 C11
Torryburn Fife 279 D10
Torterston Aberds 303 E10
Torthorwald Dumf/Gal 238 B2
Tortington W Sussex 35 F7
Torton Worcs 116 C6
Tortworth S Glos 80 G2
Torvaig H'land 298 E4
Torver Cumb 220 G5
Torwood Falk 278 D6
Torworth Notts 187 E11
Tosberry Devon 24 C3
Toscaig H'land 295 B9
Toseland Cambs 122 E4
Tosside N Yorks 203 B11
Tostock Suffolk 125 E9
Totaig H'land 295 C10
Totaig H'land 298 D2
Totardor H'land 294 B5
Tote H'land 298 E4
Totegan H'land 310 C2
Totford Hants 48 F5
Totgarrick Cornw'l 5 E8
Totham Hill Essex 88 C5
Totham Plains Essex 88 C5
Tothill Lincs 190 E6
Totland I/Wight 20 D2
Totley Bents S Yorks 186 E4
Totley Brook S Yorks 186 E4
Totley Rise S Yorks 186 E4
Totnell Dorset 29 F10
Totnes Devon 8 C6
Toton Notts 153 C10
Totronald Arg/Bute 288 D3
Totscore H'land 298 C3
Tottenham London 86 G4
Tottenhill Norfolk 158 G2
Tottenhill Row Norfolk 158 G2
Totteridge Bucks 84 G5
Totteridge Park London 86 G2
Totternhoe Beds 103 G9
Totties W Yorks 197 F7
Tottington Gtr Man 195 E9
Tottlebank Cumb 210 C6
Totton Hants 32 E5
Touchen-end Windsor 65 D11
Touches Som'set 28 F4
Toulton Som'set 43 G7
Toulvaddie H'land 311 L2
Tournaig H'land 307 L3
Toux Aberds 303 D9
Tovil Kent 53 C8
Tow House Northum 241 E7
Tow Law Durham 233 D8
Towan Cornw'l 10 G3
Towan Cross Cornw'l 4 F4
Toward Arg/Bute 266 B2
Towcester Northants 102 B3
Towcester Racecourse Northants 102 B4
Towednack Cornw'l 1 B5
Tower End Norfolk 158 F3
Tower Hamlets Kent 55 E10
Tower Hill Ches 184 F6
Tower Hill Essex 108 E5
Tower Hill Herts 85 E8
Tower Hill Mersey 194 G2
Tower Hill W Midlands 133 E11
Tower Hill W Sussex 35 B11
Tower Knowe Visitor Centre, Kielder Water Northum 250 F5
Tower of London London 67 C10
Towerhead N Som'set 44 B2
Towersey Oxon 84 D2
Towie Aberds 292 B6
Towie Aberds 302 G5
Towie Aberds 303 C8
Towiemore Moray 302 E3
Town Bent Lancs 195 B8
Town End Bucks 84 F3
Town End Cambs 139 D8
Town End Cumb 211 B7
Town End Cumb 221 F7
Town End Cumb 220 D6
Town End Cumb 211 C8
Town End Cumb 221 E8
Town End Cumb 212 C2
Town End Cumb 230 F6
Town End Cumb 231 F8
Town End Derby 185 F11
Town End Lincs 173 G7
Town End Mersey 183 D7
Town End W Yorks 196 D5
Town End Farm Tyne/Wear 243 F8
Town Fields Ches 167 B10
Town Green Gtr Man 183 B9
Town Green Lancs 194 F2
Town Green Norfolk 160 C4
Town Green Norfolk 161 G7
Town-head Arg/Bute 275 G11
Town Head Cumb 222 C3
Town Head Cumb 220 D6
Town Head Cumb 221 E8
Town Head Cumb 231 F7
Town Head Cumb 222 C2
Town Head Cumb 231 F8
Town Head Derby 185 F11
Town Head N Yorks 212 F5
Town Head N Yorks 204 B2
Town Hill N Yorks 213 G10
Town Kelloe Durham 234 D3
Town Lane Gtr Man 195 G7
Town Littleworth E Sussex 36 D6
Town of Lowton Gtr Man 183 B10
Town Park Telford 132 B4
Town Row E Sussex 52 G5
Town Street Glos 98 F6
Town Yetholm Scot Borders 263 D8
Townend Derby 185 E9
Townend W Dunb 277 F7
Townend W Dunb 277 F8
Townfield Durham 232 B5
Towngate Cumb 230 B6
Towngate Lincs 156 G2
Townhead Arg/Bute 266 C1
Townhead Cumb 229 D7
Townhead Cumb 230 D6
Townhead Cumb 231 E8
Townhead Dumf/Gal 237 E8
Townhead Lancs 203 C10
Townhead N Lanarks 268 B4
Townhead S Ayrs 244 C6
Townhead S Yorks 197 G7
Townhead S Yorks 186 E4
Townhead of Greenlaw Dumf/Gal 237 C9
Townhill Fife 280 D2
Townhill Swan 75 G10
Townhill Park Hants 33 E7
Townlake Devon 12 F4
Townland Green Kent 54 G2
Town's End Bucks 84 D2
Town's End Bucks 102 G2
Town's End Dorset 18 B3
Town's End Dorset 18 E5
Town's End Dorset 29 F9
Towns End Hants 48 B5
Town's End Som'set 42 E6
Town's End Som'set 45 D7
Towns End Som'set 30 D2
Townsend Bath/NE Som'set 44 B5
Townsend Herts 85 D10
Townsend Oxon 63 B11
Townsend S Glos 60 C5
Townsend Stoke 168 F6
Townsend Som'set 44 C4
Townsend Som'set 28 E5
Townsend Som'set 43 G11
Townsend Wilts 46 B3
Townsend Fold Lancs 195 C10
Townshend Cornw'l 2 C3
Townwell S Glos 79 G11
Towthorpe C/York 207 B8
Towthorpe ER Yorks 217 G8
Towton N Yorks 206 F5
Towyn Conwy 181 F7
Toxteth Mersey 182 D5
Toynton All Saints Lincs 174 C5
Toynton Fen Side Lincs 174 C5
Toynton Ings Lincs 174 C6
Toynton St. Peter Lincs 174 C6
Toy's Hill Kent 52 C3
Trabboch E Ayrs 257 E10
Traboe Cornw'l 2 E6
Tracebridge Som'set 27 C9
Tradespark H'land 301 D8
Tradespark Orkney 313 H5
Trafford Park Gtr Man 184 B3
Trago Mills, Newton Abbot Devon 14 G2
Traigh Ho H'land 295 F8
Trallong Powys 95 F9
Trallwn Swan 75 F11
Tram Inn Heref'd 97 E9
Tranch Torf 78 E3
Tranent E Loth 281 G8
Tranmere Mersey 182 D4
Trantlebeg H'land 310 D2
Trantlemore H'land 310 D2
Tranwell Northum 252 G5
Trapp Carms 75 B11
Traprain E Loth 281 F11
Trap's Green Warwick 118 D2
Trapshill W Berks 63 G11
Traquair Scot Borders 261 C8
Trash Green W Berks 65 F7
Travellers Rest Carms 74 B5
Travelmond Cornw'l 6 C4
Trawden Lancs 204 F4
Trawscoed Powys 95 E11
Trawsfynydd Gwyn 146 B4
Trawsmawr Carms 93 G7
Trawsnant Ceredig'n 111 D11
Tre Taliesin = Taliesin Ceredig'n 128 E3
Treaddow Heref'd 97 G10
Trealaw Rh Cyn Taff 77 G8
Treales Lancs 202 G4
Treamble Cornw'l 4 D5
Trearddur Angl 178 F3
Treaslane H'land 298 D3
Treator Cornw'l 10 F4
Tre-Aubrey V/Glam 58 E4
Trebah Garden, Mawnan Smith Cornw'l 3 D7
Trebahwartha Cornw'l 3 D7
Trebanog Rh Cyn Taff 76 D6
Trebanog Rh Cyn Taff 77 G8
Trebanos Neath P Talb 76 E2
Trebarber Cornw'l 5 C7
Trebartha Cornw'l 11 F11
Trebarvah Cornw'l 2 D2
Trebarvah Cornw'l 2 C6
Trebarwith Cornw'l 11 D7
Trebeath Cornw'l 11 D11
Tre-Beferad V/Glam 58 F3
Trebehor Cornw'l 1 E3
Trebetherick Cornw'l 10 F4
Treble's Holford Som'set 42 G6
Tre-boeth Swan 75 F11
Treborough Som'set 42 F4
Trebudannon Cornw'l 5 C7
Trebullett Cornw'l 12 F2
Treburley Cornw'l 12 F2
Treburrick Cornw'l 10 G3
Trebyan Cornw'l 5 C11
Trecastle Powys 95 F7
Trecenydd Caerph 58 B6
Trecrogo Cornw'l 12 E2
Trecwn Pembs 91 E9
Trecynon Rh Cyn Taff 77 E7
Tredarrup Cornw'l 11 C9
Tredaule Cornw'l 11 E10
Tredavoe Cornw'l 1 D5
Tredegar Bl Gwent 77 D10
Tredegar Newydd = New Tredegar Caerph 77 E10
Trederwen Powys 148 F5
Tredington Glos 99 F8
Tredington Warwick 100 C5
Tredinnick Cornw'l 1 C4
Tredinnick Cornw'l 6 B3
Tredinnick Cornw'l 6 D4
Tredogan V/Glam 58 F5
Tredomen Powys 96 E2
Tredrizzick Cornw'l 10 F5
Tredunnock Monmouths 78 G5
Tredustan Powys 96 E2
Tredworth Glos 80 B4
Treen Cornw'l 1 E3
Treen Cornw'l 1 B4
Treesmill Cornw'l 5 D11
Tre-Essey Heref'd 97 G10
Treeton S Yorks 186 D6
Trefaes Gwyn 144 C5
Trefaldwyn = Montgomery Powys 130 D4
Trefasser Pembs 91 D7
Trefdraeth Angl 178 G6
Trefdraeth = Newport Pembs 91 D11
Trefeca Powys 96 E2
Trefechan Ceredig'n 128 G1
Trefechan Merth Tyd 77 D8
Trefeglwys Powys 129 E9
Trefeitha Powys 96 E2
Trefelyn Pembs 91 F7
Trefenter Ceredig'n 112 D2
Treffanney Powys 148 F4
Treffany Hill Cornw'l 6 D4
Treffgarne Pembs 91 G9
Treffynnon Pembs 90 F6
Treffynnon = Holywell Flints 181 F11
Trefgarn Owen Pembs 91 F7
Trefil Bl Gwent 77 C10
Trefilan Ceredig'n 111 F10
Trefin = Trevine Pembs 90 E6
Treflach Shrops 148 D5
Trefnant Denbs 181 G8
Trefonen Shrops 148 D5
Trefor Gwyn 162 F5
Trefor Angl 178 E5
Trefor Angl 179 F8
Treforest Rh Cyn Taff 58 B5
Tre-Forgan Neath P Talb 76 D3
Treforys = Morriston Swan 75 F11
Trefriw Conwy 164 C3
Tref-y-Clawdd = Knighton Powys 114 C5
Tref-y-nant Wrex 166 G3
Tregada Cornw'l 12 E2
Tregadillet Cornw'l 11 E11
Tre-gagle Monmouths 79 D8
Tregaian Angl 179 F7
Tregajorran Cornw'l 4 G3
Tregare Monmouths 78 C6
Tregarland Cornw'l 6 D5
Tregarne Cornw'l 3 E7
Tregaron Ceredig'n 112 E3
Tregarth Gwyn 163 B10
Tregaswith Cornw'l 5 C7
Tregatta Cornw'l 11 D7
Tregavarras Cornw'l 5 G9
Tregear Cornw'l 5 E7
Tregeare Cornw'l 11 D10
Tregeiriog Wrex 148 C3
Tregele Angl 178 C5
Tregellist Cornw'l 10 F6
Tregenna Cornw'l 11 G7
Tregeseal Cornw'l 1 C3
Tre-Gibbon Rh Cyn Taff 77 D7
Tregonce Cornw'l 10 G4
Tregonetha Cornw'l 5 C9
Tregonhawke Cornw'l 7 E8
Tregonna Cornw'l 10 G4
Tregony Cornw'l 5 G8
Tregoodwell Cornw'l 11 E8
Tregorrick Cornw'l 5 E10
Tregoss Cornw'l 5 C9
Tregowris Cornw'l 3 E7
Tregoyd Powys 96 D3
Tregoyd Mill Powys 96 D3
Tregrehan Mills Cornw'l 5 E10
Tregroes Ceredig'n 93 C8
Tregullon Cornw'l 5 C11
Tregunna Cornw'l 10 G5
Tregunnon Cornw'l 11 E10
Tregurrian Cornw'l 5 B7
Tre-Gwyr = Gowerton Swan 75 F9
Tregynon Powys 129 D11
Tre-gynwer Carms 74 B6
Trehafod Rh Cyn Taff 77 G8
Trehan Cornw'l 7 D8
Treharris Merth Tyd 77 F9
Trehemborne Cornw'l 10 G3
Treherbert Rh Cyn Taff 77 F6
Treheveras Cornw'l 4 F6
Trehill V/Glam 58 E5
Trehilyn Pembs 91 D8
Trehunist Cornw'l 6 C6
Tre-Ifon Rh Cyn Taff 77 D7
Trekeivesteps Cornw'l 6 B4
Trekelland Cornw'l 11 F11
Trekelland Cornw'l 12 E2
Trekenner Cornw'l 12 F2
Treknow Cornw'l 11 D7
Trelan Cornw'l 2 F6
Tre-lan Flints 165 B11
Trelash Cornw'l 11 C9
Trelassick Cornw'l 5 E7
Trelawnyd Flints 181 F9
Trelech Carms 92 E5
Trelech-a'r-Bettws Carms 92 F6
Treleddyd fawr Pembs 90 F5
Treleigh Cornw'l 4 G4
Treletert = Letterston Pembs 91 F8
Trelewis Merth Tyd 77 F10
Treligga Cornw'l 10 E7
Trelights Cornw'l 10 F5
Trelill Cornw'l 10 F6
Trelinnoe Cornw'l 12 E2
Trelion Cornw'l 5 E8
Trelissick Cornw'l 3 B8
Trelissick Garden, Feock Cornw'l 3 B8
Trellech Monmouths 79 D8
Trelleck Cross Monmouths 79 E8
Trelleck Grange Monmouths 79 E7
Trelogan Flints 181 E10
Trelonk Cornw'l 5 G7
Trelowia Cornw'l 6 D5
Trelowth Cornw'l 5 E9
Trelowthas Cornw'l 5 F7
Treluggan Cornw'l 3 B9
Trelydan Powys 148 G4
Tremadog Gwyn 163 G9
Tremail Cornw'l 11 D9
Tremain Ceredig'n 92 B4
Tremaine Cornw'l 11 D10
Tremar Cornw'l 6 B5
Trematon Cornw'l 7 D7
Trembraze Cornw'l 6 B5
Tremeirchion Denbs 181 G9
Tremollett Cornw'l 11 F11
Tremore Cornw'l 5 C10
Tremorfa Card 59 D8
Tre-Mostyn Flints 181 F10
Trenale Cornw'l 11 D7
Trenance Cornw'l 10 G4
Trenance Cornw'l 5 C6
Trenant Cornw'l 6 B4
Trenarren Cornw'l 5 F10
Trenarrett Cornw'l 11 E10
Trenault Cornw'l 11 E11
Trench Telford 150 G3
Trench Green Oxon 65 D7
Trench Wood Kent 52 D5
Trencreek Cornw'l 4 C6
Trendeal Cornw'l 5 E7
Trendrean Cornw'l 4 D6
Treneague Cornw'l 10 G5
Trenear Cornw'l 2 C5
Treneglos Cornw'l 11 D10
Trenewan Cornw'l 6 E3
Trengune Cornw'l 11 C9
Trenhorne Cornw'l 11 F11
Treninnick Cornw'l 4 C6
Trenode Cornw'l 6 D5
Trenoweth Cornw'l 3 C7
Trent Dorset 29 D9
Trent Vale Stoke 168 G5
Trentham Staffs 168 G5
Trentham Gardens, Newcastle-under-Lyme Staffs 168 G5
Trentishoe Devon 40 D6
Trentlock Derby 153 C9
Trenwheal Cornw'l 2 C4
Treoes V/Glam 58 D2
Treopert = Granston Pembs 91 E7
Treorchy = Treorci Rh Cyn Taff 77 F7
Treorci = Treorchy Rh Cyn Taff 77 F7
Treowen Caerph 78 F2
Treowen Powys 130 E2
Trequite Cornw'l 10 F6
Trerank Moor Cornw'l 5 D9
Tre'r-ddol Ceredig'n 128 E3
Trerhyngyll V/Glam 58 D4
Trerose Cornw'l 3 D7
Trerulefoot Cornw'l 6 D6
Tresaith Ceredig'n 110 G5
Tresawle Cornw'l 5 F7
Tresawsen Cornw'l 4 F5
Trescott Staffs 132 D6
Trescowe Cornw'l 2 C3
Tresean Cornw'l 4 D5
Tresevern Croft Cornw'l 2 B6
Tresham S Glos 80 G3
Tresillian Cornw'l 5 F7
Treskillard Cornw'l 2 B5
Treskinnick Cross Cornw'l 11 B10
Tresmeer Cornw'l 11 D10
Tresowes Green Cornw'l 2 D3
Tresoweshill Cornw'l 2 D3
Tresparrett Cornw'l 11 C8
Tresparrett Posts Cornw'l 11 C8
Trespeane Cornw'l 11 E10
Tressady H'land 309 J7
Tressait Perth/Kinr 291 G10
Tressinney Cornw'l 11 E8
Tresta Shetl'd 314 D8
Tresta Shetl'd 315 H5
Treswell Notts 188 F3
Treswithian Cornw'l 4 G2
Treswithian Downs Cornw'l 4 G2
Trethevy Cornw'l 11 D7
Trethewey Cornw'l 1 E3
Trethomas Caerph 59 B7
Trethosa Cornw'l 5 E8
Trethowel Cornw'l 5 E10

Trethurgy Cornw'l 5 D10
Tretio Pembs 90 F5
Tretire Heref'd 97 G10
Tretower Powys 96 G3
Treuddyn Flints 166 D3
Trevadlock Cornw'l 11 F11
Trevalga Cornw'l 11 C7
Trevalyn Wrex 166 D5
Trevance Cornw'l 10 G4
Trevanger Cornw'l 10 F5
Trevanson Cornw'l 10 G5
Trevarrack Cornw'l 1 C5
Trevarren Cornw'l 5 C8
Trevarrick Cornw'l 5 B7
Trevaughan Carms 73 B11
Trevaughan Carms 93 G8
Treveal Cornw'l 4 D5
Treveddw Monmouths 96 G6
Treveighan Cornw'l 11 F7
Trevellas Cornw'l 4 E4
Trevemper Cornw'l 4 D6
Treverbyn Cornw'l 5 D10
Treverbyn Cornw'l 6 B4
Treverva Cornw'l 3 C7
Trevescan Cornw'l 1 E3
Trevethan Cornw'l 4 G4
Trevethin Torf 78 E3
Trevia Cornw'l 11 E7
Trevigro Cornw'l 12 G2
Trevilla Cornw'l 3 B8
Trevillian Cornw'l 11 C9
Trevine = Trefin Pembs 90 E6
Treviscoe Cornw'l 5 D8
Treviscoe Barton Cornw'l 5 D8
Trevithal Cornw'l 1 D5
Trevivian Cornw'l 11 D9
Trevoll Cornw'l 4 D6
Trevone Cornw'l 10 F3
Trevor Wrex 166 G3
Trevor Gardens E Sussex 37 F7
Trevor Uchaf Denbs 166 G2
Trevowah Cornw'l 4 D5
Trew Cornw'l 2 D4
Trewalder Cornw'l 11 E7
Trewarlett Cornw'l 12 E2
Trewarmett Cornw'l 11 D7
Trewassa Cornw'l 11 D8
Treween Cornw'l 11 E10
Trewellard Cornw'l 1 C3
Trewen Cornw'l 11 E11
Trewennack Cornw'l 2 D5
Tre-wern Powys 148 D2
Trewern Powys 114 F4
Trewern Powys 148 G5
Trewetha Cornw'l 10 E6
Trewethern Cornw'l 10 E6
Trewidland Cornw'l 6 D5
Trewint Cornw'l 11 B9
Trewint Cornw'l 11 E10
Trewint Cornw'l 6 C5
Trewithian Cornw'l 3 B9
Trewoodloe Cornw'l 12 G2
Trewoofe Cornw'l 1 D4
Trewoon Cornw'l 5 E9
Treworga Cornw'l 5 G7
Treworlas Cornw'l 3 B9
Treworthal Cornw'l 3 B9
Tre-wyn Monmouths 96 G6
Treyarnon Cornw'l 10 G3
Treyford W Sussex 34 D4
Triangle Staffs 133 B10
Triangle W Yorks 196 C6
Trickett's Cross Dorset 31 G9
Tricombe Devon 15 B10
Trill Devon 15 B11
Trimdon Durham 234 E3
Trimdon Colliery Durham 234 D3
Trimdon Grange Durham 234 D3
Trimingham Norfolk 160 B5
Trimley Lower Street Suffolk 108 D5
Trimley St. Martin Suffolk 108 D5
Trimley St. Mary Suffolk 108 D5
Trimpley Worcs 116 B5
Trims Green Herts 87 B7
Trimsaran Carms 74 E7
Trimstone Devon 40 E3
Trinafour Perth/Kinr 291 G9
Trinant Caerph 78 F2
Tring Herts 84 C6
Tring Wharf Herts 84 C6
Tringford Herts 84 C6
Trinity Angus 293 G8
Trinity C/Edinb 280 F4
Trinity Devon 27 F7
Trinity Fields Staffs 151 D8
Trisant Ceredig'n 112 B4
Triscombe Som'set 43 F7
Trislaig H'land 290 F2
Trispen Cornw'l 4 E6
Tritlington Northum 252 E6
Troan Cornw'l 5 D7
Trochry Perth/Kinr 286 C3
Trodigal Arg/Bute 255 G2
Troedrhiwfuwch Powys 113 G9
Troedrhiwgwair Caerph 77 E10
Troedrhiwgwair Bl Gwent 77 D11
Troedyraur Ceredig'n 92 B6
Troed-y-rhiw Ceredig'n 111 G10
Troedyrhiw Merth Tyd 77 E9
Trofarth Conwy 180 G5
Trolway Heref'd 97 G9
Tromode I/Man 192 E4
Trondavoe Shetl'd 314 F6
Troon Cornw'l 2 B5
Troon S Ayrs 257 C8

Trosaraidh W Isles 297 K3
Trossachs Hotel Stirl 285 G9
Troston Suffolk 125 C8
Trostre Carms 75 F8
Trostrey Common Monmouths 78 E5
Troswell Cornw'l 11 C11
Trotten Marsh W Sussex 34 B4
Trottiscliffe Kent 68 G6
Trotton W Sussex 34 C4
Trough Gate Lancs 195 C11
Troutbeck Cumb 221 E8
Troutbeck Cumb 230 F3
Troutbeck Bridge Cumb 221 E7
Trow Devon 15 D9
Trow Green Glos 79 D9
Troway Derby 186 F5
Trowbridge Card 59 C8
Trowbridge Wilts 45 B10
Trowell Notts 153 B9
Trowle Common Wilts 45 B10
Trowley Bottom Herts 85 C9
Trowse Newton Norfolk 142 B4
Troy N Yorks 205 F10
Troy Town Kent 52 D2
Troydale W Yorks 205 G10
Trub Gtr Man 195 F11
Trubshaw Staffs 168 D5
Trudoxhill Som'set 45 E9
Trueman's Heath Worcs 117 B11
Trull Som'set 28 C2
Trumaisgearraidh W Isles 296 D4
Trumfleet S Yorks 198 E6
Trumpan H'land 298 C2
Trumpet Heref'd 98 D3
Trumpington Cambs 123 F8
Trumps Green Surrey 66 F4
Trunch Cornw'l 160 C5
Trunnah Lancs 202 E2
Truro Cornw'l 4 G6
Truro Cathedral Cornw'l 4 G6
Truscott Cornw'l 12 D2
Trusham Devon 14 E3
Trusley Derby 152 B5
Trusthorpe Lincs 191 E8
Truthwall Cornw'l 2 C2
Tryfil Angl 178 E6
Trysull Staffs 133 E7
Trythogga Cornw'l 1 C5
Tubney Oxon 82 F6
Tuckenhay Devon 8 D6
Tuckermarsh Devon 7 B8
Tuckhill Staffs 132 F5
Tuckingmill Cornw'l 11 C10
Tuckingmill Cornw'l 4 G3
Tuckingmill Wilts 30 B6
Tuckton Bournem'th 19 C8
Tuddenham Suffolk 124 C4
Tuddenham St. Martin Suffolk 108 B3
Tudeley Kent 52 D6
Tudeley Hale Kent 52 D6
Tudhoe Durham 233 D11
Tudhoe Grange Durham 233 E11
Tudor Hill W Midlands 134 D2
Tudorville Heref'd 97 G11
Tudweiliog Gwyn 144 B4
Tuebrook Mersey 182 C5
Tuffley Glos 80 B4
Tufnell Park London 67 B9
Tufton Hants 48 D3
Tufton Pembs 91 F10
Tugby Leics 136 C5
Tugford Shrops 131 F11
Tughall Northum 264 D6
Tulchan Lodge Angus 292 F3
Tullibardine Perth/Kinr 286 F3
Tullibody Clack 279 B7
Tullich Arg/Bute 284 F4
Tullich H'land 299 E10
Tullich H'land 300 G6
Tullich Muir H'land 301 B7
Tullie House Museum, Carlisle Cumb 239 F9
Tulliemet Perth/Kinr 286 B3
Tulloch Aberds 293 F9
Tulloch Aberds 303 F8
Tulloch H'land 291 E8
Tulloch Perth/Kinr 286 E4
Tulloch Castle H'land 300 C5
Tulloch-gribban H'land 301 G10
Tullochgorm Arg/Bute 275 D10
Tullochroisk Perth/Kinr 285 B11
Tullochvenus Aberds 293 C7
Tulloes Angus 287 C9
Tullybannocher Perth/Kinr 285 E11
Tullybelton Perth/Kinr 286 D4
Tullyfergus Perth/Kinr 286 C6
Tullymurdoch Perth/Kinr 286 B5
Tullynessle Aberds 293 B7
Tulse Hill London 67 E10
Tumble = Y Tymbl Carms 75 C8
Tumblers Green Essex 106 F6
Tumby Lincs 174 C2
Tumby Woodside Lincs 174 D3
Tummel Bridge Perth/Kinr 285 B11
Tumpy Green Glos 80 E2
Tunbridge Wells Kent 52 F5
Tunbridge Wells = Royal Tunbridge Wells Kent 52 F5
Tunga W Isles 304 E6
Tungate Norfolk 160 D5
Tunley Bath/NE Som'set 45 B7
Tunnel End N Yorks 196 E4
Tunnel Hill Worcs 98 C6
Tunshill Gtr Man 196 E2
Tunstall ER Yorks 209 G12
Tunstall Kent 70 G2

Tunstall Lancs 212 E2
Tunstall Norfolk 143 B8
Tunstall N Yorks 224 F4
Tunstall N Yorks 225 C10
Tunstall Suffolk 127 F7
Tunstall Stoke 168 E5
Tunstall Tyne/Wear 243 G9
Tunstall Hills Tyne/Wear 243 G9
Tunstead Gtr Man 196 G4
Tunstead Norfolk 160 E5
Tunstead Milton Derby 185 E8
Tunworth Hants 49 D7
Tupsley Heref'd 97 C10
Tupton Derby 170 B5
Tur Langton Leics 136 E4
Turf Hill Gtr Man 196 E2
Turfdown Cornw'l 5 B11
Turfholm S Lanarks 259 B8
Turfmoor Devon 28 G3
Turgis Green Hants 49 B8
Turin Angus 287 B9
Turkdean Glos 81 B10
Turkey Island Hants 33 E9
Turkey Island W Sussex 34 D3
Turleigh Wilts 61 G10
Turleygreen Shrops 132 F5
Turlin Moor Poole 18 C5
Turmer Hants 31 F10
Turn Lancs 195 D10
Turnalt Arg/Bute 275 C9
Turnant Heref'd 96 F6
Turnastone Heref'd 97 D7
Turnberry S Ayrs 244 B6
Turnchapel Plym'th 7 E9
Turnditch Derby 170 F3
Turner Green Lancs 203 G8
Turnerheath Ches 184 F6
Turner's Green E Sussex 37 D10
Turner's Green Warwick 118 D3
Turner's Green W Berks 64 F4
Turners Hill W Sussex 51 F10
Turners Puddle Dorset 18 C2
Turner's Tump Glos 79 B10
Turnford Herts 86 E5
Turnhouse C/Edinb 280 G3
Turnhurst Stoke 168 E5
Turnworth Dorset 30 F4
Turrerrich Perth/Kinr 286 D2
Turriff Aberds 303 D7
Tursdale Durham 234 D2
Turton Bottoms Blackb'n 195 D8
Turves Green W Midlands 117 B10
Turvey Beds 121 G8
Turville Bucks 84 G3
Turweston Bucks 102 D2
Tushielaw Scot Borders 261 F8
Tutbury Staffs 152 D4
Tutnall Worcs 117 C9
Tutnalls Glos 79 E10
Tutshill Glos 79 F8
Tutt Hill Kent 54 D3
Tuttington Norfolk 160 D4
Tutts Clump W Berks 64 E5
Tutwell Cornw'l 12 F3
Tuxford Notts 188 G2
Twatt Orkney 312 F3
Twatt Shetl'd 315 H5
Twechar E Dunb 278 F4
Tweedmouth Northum 273 D7
Tweedsmuir Scot Borders 260 E3
Tweenaways Torbay 9 D7
Twelve Oaks E Sussex 37 C11
Twelveheads Cornw'l 4 G5
Twemlow Green Ches 168 B3
Twenty Lincs 156 D3
Twerton Bath/NE Som'set 45 B8
Twickenham London 66 E6
Twickenham Stadium London 66 E7
Twig Side Bucks 84 G3
Twigworth Glos 98 G6
Twineham W Sussex 36 D3
Twineham Green W Sussex 36 C3
Twinhoe Bath/NE Som'set 45 B8
Twinstead Essex 107 D7
Twinstead Green Essex 107 D7
Twiss Green Warrington 183 B11
Twiston Lancs 204 E2
Twitchen Devon 41 G9
Twitchen Shrops 115 B7
Twitham Kent 55 B9
Twitton Kent 52 B4
Two Bridges Devon 13 G9
Two Burrows Cornw'l 4 F4
Two Dales Derby 170 C3
Two Gates Staffs 134 C4
Two Mile Ash M/Keynes 102 D6
Two Mile Oak Cross Devon 8 B6
Two Mills Ches 182 G5
Two Waters Herts 85 D9
Twycross Leics 134 C6
Twycross Zoo, Ashby-de-la-Zouch Leics 134 B6
Twydall Medway 69 F9
Twyford Bucks 102 F3
Twyford Dorset 30 D5
Twyford Hants 33 C7
Twyford Leics 154 G4
Twyford Lincs 155 E8
Twyford Norfolk 159 D10
Twyford Oxon 101 D9
Twyford Staffs 152 D6
Twyford Wokingham 65 D9
Twyford Common Heref'd 97 D10
Twyn Allwws Monmouths 78 C3
Twyn Shon-Ifan Caerph 77 G11
Twyn Nervet W Berks 64 F6
Twywardreath Cornw'l 5 D11
Twyn-gwyn Torf 78 E3

Twynholm Dumf/Gal 237 D8
Twyning Glos 99 D7
Twyning Green Glos 99 D8
Twynllanan Carms 94 G5
Twynmynydd Carms 75 C11
Twynrodyn Merth Tyd 77 D9
Twyn-yr-odyn V/Glam 58 E6
Twyn-y-Sheriff Monmouths 78 D6
Twywell Northants 121 B9
Tyberton Heref'd 97 D7
Tyburn W Midlands 134 E2
Tyby Norfolk 159 D11
Tycroes Carms 75 C10
Tycrwyn Powys 148 F2
Tydd Gote Lincs 157 F9
Tydd St. Giles Cambs 157 F8
Tydd St. Mary Lincs 157 F8
Tyddewi = St. David's Pembs 90 F5
Tyddyn Powys 129 F9
Tyddyn Dai Angl 178 C6
Tyddyn Llwely Gwyn 145 C7
Tyddyn Sieffre Gwyn 146 G2
Tye Hants 34 G2
Tye Common Essex 87 G11
Tye Green Essex 87 D7
Tye Green Essex 105 G10
Tye Green Essex 105 D11
Tye Green Essex 87 C10
Tye Green Essex 106 G5
Tyes Cross E Sussex 51 G11
Ty-hen Carms 92 G6
Tŷ-gwyn Powys 148 E5
Tyldesley Gtr Man 195 G7
Tyler Hill Kent 70 G6
Tylers Causeway Herts 86 D3
Tyler's Green Bucks 84 G6
Tyler's Green Essex 87 D8
Tyler's Green Surrey 51 C10
Tyllwyd Ceredig'n 92 B5
Tylorstown Rh Cyn Taff 77 F8
Tylwch Powys 129 G9
Ty-Mawr Carms 93 C10
Ty-mawr Denbs 181 F7
Ty-mawr Angl 179 D7
Ty'n Coed Angl 179 F7
Ty-nant Conwy 165 G2
Ty-nant Denbs 165 F9
Tyn Dock Tyne/Wear 243 D9
Tyne Tunnel Tyne/Wear 243 D8
Tyneham Dorset 18 E3
Tynehead Midloth 271 D7
Tynemouth Tyne/Wear 243 C9
Tynewydd Rh Cyn Taff 76 F6
Tyning Bath/NE Som'set 45 B7
Tyningham E Loth 282 F2
Tyn-lôn Gwyn 163 D7
Tynron Dumf/Gal 247 E8
Tyntesfield N Som'set 60 E4
Tyntetown Rh Cyn Taff 77 F9
Ty'n-y-bryn Rh Cyn Taff 58 B4
Tyn-y-ffridd Powys 148 C2
Ty'n-y-garn Bridg 57 E11
Tynygongl Angl 179 E8
Tynygraig Ceredig'n 112 D3
Ty'n-y-graig Powys 95 B10
Ty'n-y-groes Conwy 180 G3
Ty'n-y-maes Gwyn 163 D10
Ty'n-y-maes Powys 148 D2
Ty'n-y-Pistyll Conwy 165 F7
Ty'n-yr-eithin Ceredig'n 112 E3
Tyn-y-Rhos Shrops 148 B5
Tynywaun Powys 114 D3
Tyrie Aberds 303 C9
Tyringham M/Keynes 103 B7
Tyrrell's Wood Surrey 51 B7
Tyseley W Midlands 134 G2
Ty-Sign Caerph 78 G2
Tythe Luton 103 G10
Tythecott Devon 24 D6
Tythegston Bridg 57 F11
Tytherington Ches 184 F6
Tytherington S Glos 61 B7
Tytherington Som'set 45 D9
Tytherington Wilts 46 E2
Tytherleigh Devon 28 G4
Tyttenhanger Herts 85 D11
Tywardreath Cornw'l 5 E11
Tywardreath Highway Cornw'l 5 D11
Tywyn Conwy 180 F3
Tywyn Gwyn 110 C2

U

Uachdar W Isles 296 F3
Uags H'land 295 B9
Ubberley Stoke 168 F6
Ubbeston Green Suffolk 126 C6
Ubley Bath/NE Som'set 44 B4
Uckerby N Yorks 224 E4
Uckfield E Sussex 37 C7
Uckinghall Worcs 99 D7
Uckington Glos 99 F8
Uddingston S Lanarks 268 C3
Uddington S Lanarks 259 C9
Udimore E Sussex 38 D5
Udley N Som'set 60 G3
Udny Green Aberds 303 G8
Udny Station Aberds 303 G9
Udston S Lanarks 268 D3
Udstonhead S Lanarks 268 F4
Uffcott Wilts 62 D6
Uffculme Devon 27 E9
Uffington Lincs 137 B11
Uffington Oxon 63 B10
Uffington Shrops 149 G10
Ufford Peterbro 137 C11
Ufford Suffolk 126 G5
Ufton Warwick 119 E7
Ufton Nervet W Berks 64 F6
Ugadale Arg/Bute 255 E8
Ugborough Devon 8 D3

Ugford Wilts 46 G5
Uggeshall Suffolk 105 C10
Ugglebarnby N Yorks 227 D7
Ugley Essex 105 F10
Ugley Green Essex 105 F10
Ugthorpe N Yorks 226 C5
Uidh W Isles 297 M2
Uig Arg/Bute 288 D3
Uig Arg/Bute 276 E2
Uig H'land 296 F7
Uig H'land 298 C3
Uigen W Isles 304 E2
Uigshader H'land 298 E4
Uisken Arg/Bute 288 H5
Ulaw Aberds 303 G9
Ulbster H'land 310 E7
Ulcat Row Cumb 230 G4
Ulceby Lincs 190 G6
Ulceby N Lincs 200 E6
Ulceby Skitter N Lincs 200 D6
Ulcombe Kent 53 D10
Uldale Cumb 229 D10
Uley Glos 80 F3
Ulgham Northum 252 E6
Ullapool H'land 307 K6
Ullenhall Warwick 118 D2
Ullenwood Glos 80 B6
Ulleskelf N Yorks 206 F6
Ullesthorpe Leics 135 G10
Ulley S Yorks 187 D7
Ullingswick Heref'd 97 B11
Ullinish H'land 294 B5
Ullock Cumb 229 G7
Ullock Cumb 229 G10
Ulnes Walton Lancs 194 D4
Ulpha Cumb 220 G3
Ulrome ER Yorks 209 B9
Ulsta Shetl'd 314 E6
Ulva House Arg/Bute 288 F6
Ulverley Green W Midlands 134 G2
Ulverston Cumb 210 D5
Ulwell Dorset 18 E6
Umberleigh Devon 25 C10
Unapool H'land 306 F7
Unasary W Isles 297 J3
Uncleby ER Yorks 208 B2
Under Tofts S Yorks 186 D4
Underbarrow Cumb 221 G9
Undercliffe W Yorks 205 G9
Underdale Shrops 149 G10
Underdown Devon 13 C10
Underhill London 86 F3
Underhoull Shetl'd 314 C7
Underling Green Kent 53 D9
Underriver Kent 52 C5
Underwood Newp 59 B11
Underwood Notts 171 E7
Underwood Plym'th 7 D10
Undley Suffolk 140 G3
Undy Monmouths 60 B2
Ungisiadar W Isles 304 F3
Unifirth Shetl'd 315 H4
Union Cottage Aberds 293 D10
Union Mills I/Man 192 E4
Union Street E Sussex 53 G8
University Museum, Oxford Oxon 83 D8
Unst Airport Shetl'd 314 C8
Unstone Derby 186 F5
Unstone Green Derby 186 F5
Unsworth Gtr Man 195 F10
Unthank Cumb 230 D4
Unthank Cumb 230 B3
Unthank Cumb 231 C8
Unthank Derby 186 F4
Unthank End Cumb 230 D5
Up Cerne Dorset 29 G11
Up End M/Keynes 103 B8
Up Exe Devon 26 G6
Up Green Hants 65 G9
Up Hatherley Glos 99 G8
Up Holland Lancs 194 G4
Up Marden W Sussex 34 E3
Up Mudford Som'set 29 D9
Up Nately Hants 49 C7
Up Somborne Hants 47 G11
Up Sydling Dorset 29 G10
Upavon Wilts 46 C7
Upchurch Kent 69 F10
Upcott Devon 25 F9
Upcott Heref'd 114 G6
Upcott Som'set 26 B6
Upcott Som'set 27 C11
Upend Cambs 124 F3
Upgate Norfolk 160 F2
Upgate Street Norfolk 141 E10
Upgate Street Norfolk 142 E5
Uphall Dorset 29 G9
Uphall W Loth 279 G11
Uphall Station W Loth 279 G11
Upham Devon 26 F5
Upham Hants 33 C8
Uphampton Heref'd 115 E8
Uphampton Worcs 116 E6
Uphempston Devon 8 B6
Uphill N Som'set 43 B10
Uplands Glos 80 D5
Uplands Swan 75 G10
Uplawmoor E Renf 267 D8
Upleadon Glos 98 F5
Uplees Kent 70 G3
Uploders Dorset 16 B6
Uplowman Devon 27 D8
Uplyme Devon 16 C2
Upminster London 68 B5
Uppottery Devon 28 F2

Upper Ardgrain Aberds 303 F9
Upper Ardroscadale Arg/Bute 275 G11
Upper Arley Worcs 132 G5
Upper Armley W Yorks 205 G11
Upper Arncott Oxon 83 B10
Upper Astley Shrops 149 F10
Upper Astrop Northants 101 D10
Upper Badcall H'land 306 E6
Upper Bangor Gwyn 179 G9
Upper Basildon W Berks 64 D5
Upper Batley W Yorks 197 B8
Upper Battlefield Shrops 149 F10
Upper Beeding W Sussex 35 E11
Upper Benefield Northants 137 F9
Upper Bentley Worcs 117 D9
Upper Bighouse H'land 310 D2
Upper Birchwood Derby 170 E6
Upper Boat Rh Cyn Taff 58 B6
Upper Boddam Aberds 302 F6
Upper Boddington Northants 119 G9
Upper Bogrow H'land 309 L7
Upper Bogside Moray 302 D2
Upper Booth Derby 185 E10
Upper Borth Ceredig'n 128 F2
Upper Boyndlie Aberds 303 C9
Upper Brailes Warwick 100 D6
Upper Breakish H'land 295 C8
Upper Breinton Heref'd 97 C9
Upper Broadheath Worcs 116 F6
Upper Broughton Notts 154 D3
Upper Broxwood Heref'd 115 G7
Upper Brynamman Carms 76 C2
Upper Buckenhill Heref'd 97 E11
Upper Bucklebury W Berks 64 F4
Upper Burgate Hants 31 D10
Upper Burnhaugh Aberds 293 D10
Upper Caldecote Beds 104 B3
Upper Canada N Som'set 43 B11
Upper Canterton Hants 32 E3
Upper Catesby Northants 119 F10
Upper Catshill Worcs 117 C9
Upper Chapel Powys 95 C10
Upper Cheddon Som'set 52 C5
Upper Chicksgrove Wilts 31 B7
Upper Chute Wilts 47 B9
Upper Clapton London 67 B10
Upper Clatford Hants 47 E11
Upper Coberley Glos 81 B7
Upper Cokeham W Sussex 35 C11
Upper Colwall Heref'd 98 C5
Upper Common Hants 48 D6
Upper Cotburn Aberds 303 D7
Upper Cotton Staffs 169 E9
Upper Coullie Aberds 293 B9
Upper Cound Shrops 131 C10
Upper Cudworth S Yorks 197 G11
Upper Culphin Aberds 302 D6
Upper Cumberworth W Yorks 197 F8
Upper Cwmbran Torf 78 F3
Upper Dallachy Moray 302 C3
Upper Deal Kent 55 C10
Upper Dean Beds 121 D10
Upper Denby W Yorks 197 F8
Upper Denton Cumb 240 D4
Upper Derraid H'land 301 F10
Upper Diabaig H'land 299 C8
Upper Dicker E Sussex 37 E9
Upper Dounreay H'land 310 C4
Upper Dovercourt Essex 108 E4
Upper Druimfin Arg/Bute 289 D7
Upper Dunsforth N Yorks 215 G8
Upper Eashing Surrey 50 E3
Upper Eastwood W Yorks 196 B3
Upper Eathie H'land 301 C7
Upper Edmonton London 86 G5
Upper Egleton Heref'd 98 B2
Upper Elkstone Staffs 169 D9
Upper Ellastone Staffs 169 G10
Upper Elmers End London 67 F11
Upper End Derby 185 F9
Upper End Glos 98 G4
Upper End Leics 154 G4
Upper Enham Hants 47 C11
Upper Farringdon Hants 49 F8
Upper Feorlig H'land 298 E3
Upper Fivehead Som'set 28 C4
Upper Framilode Glos 80 C2
Upper Froyle Hants 49 E9
Upper Gills H'land 310 B7
Upper Glenfintaig H'land 290 E4
Upper Godney Som'set 44 E3
Upper Goldstone Kent 71 G9
Upper Gornal W Midlands 133 E8
Upper Gravenhurst Beds 104 D2
Upper Green Essex 105 D8
Upper Green Monmouths 78 B5
Upper Green Suffolk 124 E4
Upper Green W Berks 63 G11
Upper Green W Yorks 197 B9

Upper Grove Common Heref'd 97 F11
Upper Guist Norfolk 159 D10
Upper Hackney Derby 170 C3
Upper Hale Surrey 49 D10
Upper Halistra H'land 298 D2
Upper Halliford Surrey 66 F5
Upper Halling Medway 69 G7
Upper Ham Worcs 99 D7
Upper Ham Worcs 99 B7
Upper Hambleton Rutl'd 137 B8
Upper Harbledown Kent 54 B6
Upper Hartfield E Sussex 52 G3
Upper Hartshay Derby 170 E5
Upper Haugh S Yorks 186 C6
Upper Hawkhillock Aberds 303 F10
Upper Haysden Kent 52 E5
Upper Hayton Shrops 131 G10
Upper Heaton W Yorks 197 D7
Upper Hellesdon Norfolk 160 G4
Upper Helmsley N Yorks 207 B9
Upper Hengoed Shrops 148 C5
Upper Hergest Heref'd 114 G5
Upper Heyford Northants 120 F3
Upper Heyford Oxon 101 F9
Upper Hiendley W Yorks 197 E11
Upper Hill Heref'd 115 G9
Upper Hill S Glos 79 F11
Upper Holloway London 67 B9
Upper Holton Suffolk 127 B8
Upper Hopton W Yorks 197 D7
Upper Horsebridge E Sussex 37 E9
Upper Howsell Worcs 98 B5
Upper Hoyland S Yorks 197 G11
Upper Hulme Staffs 169 C8
Upper Ifield Kent 69 E7
Upper Ifold Surrey 50 G4
Upper Inglesham Swindon 82 F2
Upper Kergord Shetl'd 315 H6
Upper Kilcott S Glos 61 B9
Upper Killay Swan 75 G9
Upper Killeyan Arg/Bute 254 C3
Upper Kinsham Heref'd 115 D7
Upper Kirton N Ayrs 266 D3
Upper Knockando Moray 301 E11
Upper Lambourn W Berks 63 C10
Upper Landywood Staffs 133 B9
Upper Langford N Som'set 44 B3
Upper Langwith Derby 171 B8
Upper Leigh Staffs 151 B10
Upper Lenie H'land 300 G5
Upper Lochton Aberds 293 D8
Upper Longdon Staffs 151 G11
Upper Longwood Shrops 131 B11
Upper Lybster H'land 310 F6
Upper Lydbrook Glos 79 B10
Upper Maes-coed Heref'd 96 E6
Upper Marsh W Yorks 204 F6
Upper Midhope S Yorks 186 B2
Upper Midway Derby 152 E5
Upper Miloviag H'land 297 G2
Upper Milton Oxon 82 B3
Upper Milton Som'set 44 D4
Upper Minety Wilts 81 G8
Upper Moor Worcs 99 B9
Upper Moor Side W Yorks 205 G10
Upper Morton S Glos 79 G11
Upper Nash Pembs 73 E8
Upper Newbold Derby 186 G5
Upper Nobut Staffs 151 B10
Upper North Dean Bucks 84 F5
Upper Norwood London 67 G10
Upper Norwood W Sussex 34 D6
Upper Obney Perth/Kinr 286 D4
Upper Oddington Glos 100 F4
Upper Ollach H'land 295 B7
Upper Outwoods Staffs 152 D4
Upper Padley Derby 186 F6
Upper Pennington Hants 20 B2
Upper Pollicott Bucks 84 C2
Upper Poppleton C/York 207 C7
Upper Port H'land 301 G10
Upper Quinton Warwick 100 B3
Upper Race Torf 78 F3
Upper Ratley Hants 32 C4
Upper Ridinghill Aberds 303 D10
Upper Rochford Worcs 116 D2
Upper Sandaig H'land 295 D9
Upper Sanday Orkney 313 H6
Upper Saxondale Notts 154 B3
Upper Seagry Wilts 62 D2
Upper Shelton Beds 103 B9
Upper Sheringham Norfolk 177 B10
Upper Shirley London 67 F11
Upper Shirley S'thampton 32 E5
Upper Shuckburgh Warwick 119 E9

Upper Slackstead Hants 32 B5
Upper Slaughter Glos 100 G3
Upper Soudley Glos 79 C11
Upper Spond Heref'd 114 G6
Upper Stanton Drew Bath/NE Som'set 60 G6
Upper Stoke Norfolk 142 C4
Upper Stoke W Midlands 119 B7
Upper Stondon Beds 104 D3
Upper Stonnall Staffs 133 C11
Upper Stowe Northants 120 F2
Upper Stratton Swindon 63 B7
Upper Street Hants 31 D10
Upper Street Norfolk 126 B3
Upper Street Norfolk 160 E7
Upper Street Norfolk 160 F6
Upper Street Norfolk 161 F7
Upper Street Suffolk 108 D2
Upper Street Suffolk 124 G5
Upper Street Suffolk 124 D5
Upper Strensham Worcs 99 D8
Upper Studley Wilts 45 B10
Upper Sundon Beds 103 F10
Upper Swell Glos 100 F3
Upper Sydenham London 67 E10
Upper Tean Staffs 151 B10
Upper Threapwood Ches 166 E6
Upper Thurnham Lancs 202 C5
Upper Tillyrie Perth/Kinr 286 G5
Upper Tooting London 67 E9
Upper Tote H'land 298 D5
Upper Town Derby 170 E2
Upper Town Durham 233 D7
Upper Town Heref'd 97 B11
Upper Town N Som'set 60 F4
Upper Town Suffolk 125 D8
Upper Town Wilts 62 D3
Upper Town N Yorks 204 G6
Upper Treverward Shrops 114 B5
Upper Tysoe Warwick 100 C6
Upper Upham Wilts 63 D8
Upper Upnor Medway 69 E9
Upper Vobster Som'set 45 D8
Upper Walthamstow London 67 B11
Upper Wardington Oxon 101 B9
Upper Waterhay Wilts 81 G9
Upper Weald M/Keynes 102 D5
Upper Weedon Northants 120 F2
Upper Welland Worcs 98 C5
Upper Wellingham E Sussex 36 D6
Upper Welson Heref'd 114 G5
Upper Weston Bath/NE Som'set 61 F8
Upper Weybread Suffolk 126 B4
Upper Whiston S Yorks 187 D7
Upper Wick Glos 80 F2
Upper Wick Worcs 116 G6
Upper Wield Hants 48 F6
Upper Wilcove Cornw'l 7 D8
Upper Winchendon Bucks 84 C2
Upper Witton W Midlands 133 E11
Upper Wolvercote Oxon 83 C7
Upper Woodend Aberds 293 B8
Upper Woodford Wilts 46 F6
Upper Woolhampton W Berks 64 F5
Upper Wootton Hants 48 C5
Upper Wraxall S Glos 61 E10
Upper Wyche Worcs 98 C5
Upperby Cumb 239 G10
Uppermill Gtr Man 196 F3
Uppersound Shetl'd 315 J6
Upperthong W Yorks 196 F6
Upperthorpe Derby 187 E7
Upperthorpe N Lincs 199 G9
Upperton E Sussex 23 E10
Upperton W Sussex 35 C7
Uppertown Derby 170 B4
Uppertown H'land 300 F4
Uppertown H'land 310 B7
Uppertown Northum 241 C9
Uppertown Orkney 313 J5
Uppincott Devon 26 G5
Uppingham Rutl'd 137 D7
Uppington Dorset 31 F8
Uppington Shrops 131 B11
Upsall N Yorks 215 B9
Upsettlington Scot Borders 273 F7
Upsher Green Suffolk 107 C8
Upshire Essex 86 E6
Upstreet Kent 71 G8
Upthorpe Glos 80 E3
Upthorpe Suffolk 125 C9
Upton Cambs 122 B3
Upton Ches 166 B6
Upton Cumb 230 D2
Upton Cornw'l 11 G11
Upton Cornw'l 24 G2
Upton Devon 8 G5
Upton Devon 27 G9
Upton Dorset 17 E10
Upton Dorset 18 C5
Upton ER Yorks 209 C8
Upton Hants 31 D10
Upton Hants 47 B11
Upton Hants 32 D5
Upton Halton 183 D7
Upton Kent 71 F11
Upton Leics 135 D7
Upton Lincs 188 E5
Upton London 68 C2
Upton Mersey 182 D3
Upton Norfolk 161 G7
Upton Northants 120 E4
Upton Notts 172 E2
Upton Notts 188 F2

Upton Oxon 64 B4
Upton Oxon 82 C2
Upton Peterbro 138 C2
Upton Pembs 73 D8
Upton Redcar/Clevel'd 226 B4
Upton Slough 66 D3
Upton Som'set 27 B7
Upton Som'set 29 B7
Upton Warwick 118 F2
Upton Wilts 45 G11
Upton W Yorks 198 E3
Upton Bishop Heref'd 98 F3
Upton Cheyney S Glos 61 F7
Upton Cressett Shrops 132 E3
Upton Crews Heref'd 98 F2
Upton Cross Cornw'l 11 G11
Upton Dinton Bucks 84 C3
Upton End Beds 104 D2
Upton Field Notts 172 E2
Upton Green Norfolk 161 G7
Upton Grey Hants 49 D7
Upton Heath Ches 166 B6
Upton Hellions Devon 26 F4
Upton House Warwick 101 B7
Upton Lovell Wilts 46 E2
Upton Magna Shrops 149 G11
Upton Noble Som'set 45 F8
Upton Park London 68 C2
Upton Pyne Devon 14 B4
Upton Rocks Halton 183 D8
Upton St. Leonards Glos 80 C5
Upton Scudamore Wilts 45 D11
Upton Snodsbury Worcs 117 G8
Upton upon Severn Worcs 99 C7
Upton Warren Worcs 117 D8
Upton Wood Kent 55 D9
Upwaltham W Sussex 34 E6
Upware Cambs 123 C10
Upwell Norfolk 139 C9
Upwey Dorset 17 D9
Upwick Green Herts 105 G9
Upwood Cambs 138 G5
Uradale Shetl'd 315 K6
Urafirth Shetl'd 314 F5
Uragaig Arg/Bute 274 D4
Urchfont Wilts 46 B4
Ure Shetl'd 314 F4
Ure Bank N Yorks 214 E6
Urgha W Isles 305 J3
Urgha Beag W Isles 305 H3
Urlar Perth/Kinr 286 C2
Urlay Nook Stockton 225 C8
Urmston Gtr Man 184 C3
Urpeth Durham 243 G7
Urquhart H'land 300 D5
Urquhart Moray 302 C2
Urquhart Castle, Drumnadrochit H'land 300 G5
Urra N Yorks 225 E11
Urray H'land 300 D5
Ushaw Moor Durham 233 C10
Usk Monmouths 78 E5
Uskmouth Newp 59 C10
Usselby Lincs 189 C9
Usworth Tyne/Wear 243 F8
Utkinton Ches 167 C8
Utley W Yorks 205 E7
Uton Devon 14 B2
Utterby Lincs 190 C4
Uttoxeter Staffs 151 C11
Uttoxeter Racecourse Staffs 152 C2
Uwchmynydd Gwyn 144 D2
Uxbridge London 66 C5
Uyea Shetl'd 314 D5
Uyeasound Shetl'd 314 C7
Uzmaston Pembs 73 C7

V

V & A Museum of Childhood London 67 C10
Vachelich Pembs 90 F5
Vadlure Shetl'd 315 J4
Vaila Hall Shetl'd 315 J4
Vaivoe Shetl'd 314 G7
Vale W Yorks 196 B2
Valeswood Shrops 149 E7
Valley = Y Fali Angl 178 F3
Valley End Surrey 66 G3
Valley Truckle Cornw'l 11 E7
Valleyfield Dumf/Gal 237 D8
Valsgarth Shetl'd 314 B8
Valtos H'land 298 C5
Van Caerph 59 B7
Vange Essex 69 B8
Vanlop Shetl'd 315 M5
Varteg Torf 78 D3
Vassa Shetl'd 315 H6
Vatsetter Shetl'd 314 E7
Vatsetter Shetl'd 315 L5
Vatten H'land 298 E2
Vaul Arg/Bute 288 E2
Vauxhall London 67 D10
Vauxhall W Midlands 133 F11
Vaynor Merth Tyd 77 C9
Vaynor Merth Tyd 77 C8
Veensgarth Shetl'd 315 J6
Velindre Powys 96 D3
Vellanoweth Cornw'l 2 C2
Vellow Som'set 42 F5
Velly Devon 24 C3
Veness Orkney 312 F6
Venn Devon 8 F4
Venn Devon 24 C4
Venn Green Devon 24 E5
Venn Ottery Devon 15 C7
Vennington Shrops 130 B6
Venny Tedburn Devon 14 B2
Venterdon Cornw'l 12 G3
Ventnor I/Wight 21 F7
Ventnor Botanic Garden I/Wight 20 F6
Venton Devon 7 D11
Venton Devon 13 C9
Ventongimps Mill Cornw'l 4 E5
Venus Hill Herts 85 E8
Vementry Shetl'd 315 H5
Verney Junction Bucks 102 F4
Vernham Dean Hants 47 B10
Vernham Row Hants 47 B10
Vernham Street Hants 47 B11
Vernolds Common Shrops 131 G9
Vertington Som'set 30 B2
Verwood Dorset 31 F9
Veryan Cornw'l 3 B10
Veryan Green Cornw'l 5 G8
Vickerstown Cumb 210 F3
Victoria Cornw'l 5 C9
Victoria S Yorks 197 F7
Victoria and Albert Museum London 67 D9
Victoria Park Bucks 84 C4
Victoria Park Dorset 17 D9
Victoria Park Gtr Man 184 B5
Victory Gardens Renf 267 B10
Vidlin Shetl'd 314 G6
Viewland Fife 280 A5
Viewpark N Lanarks 268 C4
Vigo Tyne/Wear 243 G7
Vigo W Midlands 133 C10
Vigo Village Kent 68 G6
Vinegar Hill Monmouths 60 B2
Vinehall Street E Sussex 38 C3
Vines Cross E Sussex 37 D9
Viney Hill Glos 79 D11
Vinny Green S Glos 61 D7
Virginia Water Surrey 66 F3
Virginstow Devon 12 C3
Virley Essex 88 C6
Viscar Cornw'l 2 C6
Vivod Denbs 165 G11
Vobster Som'set 45 D8
Voe Shetl'd 314 E5
Voe Shetl'd 315 G6
Vole Som'set 43 C11
Vowchurch Heref'd 97 D7
Vowchurch Common Heref'd 97 D7
Voxter Shetl'd 314 F5
Voy Orkney 312 G3
Vron Gate Shrops 130 B6
Vulcan Village Mersey 183 C9

W

Waberthwaite Cumb 220 G2
Wackerfield Durham 233 G9
Wacton Norfolk 142 E3
Wacton Common Norfolk 142 E3
Wadbister Shetl'd 315 J6
Wadborough Worcs 99 B8
Waddesdon Bucks 84 B2
Waddesdon Manor, Aylesbury Bucks 84 B2
Waddeton Devon 9 D7
Waddicar Mersey 182 B5
Waddicombe Devon 26 B5
Waddingham Lincs 189 B7
Waddington Lancs 203 E10
Waddington Lincs 173 C7
Waddingworth Lincs 189 G11
Waddon Dorset 17 D8
Waddon Devon 14 F3
Wade Hall Lancs 194 C4
Wadebridge Cornw'l 10 G5
Wadeford Som'set 28 E4
Wadenhoe Northants 137 G10
Wadesmill Herts 86 B5
Wadhurst E Sussex 52 G6
Wadhurst Park E Sussex 37 B10
Wadshelf Derby 186 G4
Wadsley S Yorks 186 C4
Wadsley Bridge S Yorks 186 C5
Wadswick Wilts 61 F10
Wadwick Hants 48 C2
Wadworth S Yorks 187 B9
Waen Denbs 165 C7
Waen Denbs 165 B10
Waen Flints 181 G11
Waen Powys 148 F4
Waen Aberwheeler Denbs 165 B9
Waen Fach Powys 148 F4
Waen Goleugoed Denbs 181 G9
Waen-dymarch Flints 181 G11
Waen-pentir Gwyn 163 B9
Waen-wen Gwyn 163 B9
Wag H'land 311 G4
Wagbeach Shrops 131 B7
Wagg Som'set 28 B6
Waggersley Staffs 151 B7
Waggs Plot Devon 28 G4
Wainfelin Torf 78 E3
Wainfleet All Saints Lincs 175 D7
Wainfleet Bank Lincs 175 D7
Wainfleet St. Mary Lincs 175 D8
Wainfleet Tofts Lincs 175 D7
Wainford Norfolk 142 E6
Waingroves Derby 170 F6
Wainhouse Corner Cornw'l 11 B9
Wainscott Medway 69 E8
Wainstalls W Yorks 196 B4
Waitby Cumb 222 D5
Waithe NE Lincs 201 G9
Wake Green W Midlands 133 G11
Wakefield W Yorks 197 C10
Wakeham Devon 8 F3
Wakehurst Place Garden, Crawley W Sussex 51 G10
Wakerley Northants 137 D9
Wakes Colne Essex 107 F7
Wakes Colne Green Essex 107 E7
Walberswick Suffolk 127 C9
Walberton W Sussex 35 F7
Walbottle Tyne/Wear 242 D5
Walby Cumb 239 E10
Walcombe Som'set 44 D5
Walcot Lincs 155 B11
Walcot N Lincs 199 C11
Walcot Shrops 130 D5
Walcot Swindon 63 C7
Walcot Telford 149 G11
Walcot Warwick 118 F2
Walcot Green Norfolk 142 G2
Walcot West Swindon 63 C7
Walcote Leics 135 G11
Walcott Lincs 173 D10
Walcott Norfolk 161 C7
Walden N Yorks 213 C10
Walden Head N Yorks 213 C9
Walden Stubbs N Yorks 198 D5
Walderslade Medway 69 G9
Walderslade Bottom Medway 69 G9
Walderton W Sussex 34 E3
Walditch Dorset 16 C5
Waldley Derby 152 B2
Waldridge Durham 243 G7
Waldringfield Suffolk 108 C5
Waldringfield Heath Suffolk 108 C5
Waldron E Sussex 37 D9
Wales Som'set 29 B9
Wales S Yorks 187 E7
Wales Bar S Yorks 187 E7
Walesby Lincs 189 C10
Walesby Notts 187 G11
Walford Heref'd 115 C7
Walford Heref'd 97 G11
Walford Shrops 149 E8
Walford Heath Shrops 149 F8
Walgherton Ches 167 F11
Walgrave Northants 120 C6
Walham Glos 98 G6
Walham Green London 67 D9
Walhampton Hants 20 B2
Walk Mill Lancs 204 G3
Walkden Gtr Man 195 G8
Walker Tyne/Wear 243 D7
Walker Art Gallery Mersey 182 C5
Walker Fold Lancs 203 E9
Walkerburn Scot Borders 261 B9
Walkergate Tyne/Wear 243 D7
Walkeringham Notts 188 C3
Walkerith Lincs 188 C3
Walkern Herts 104 F5
Walker's Green Heref'd 97 B10
Walker's Heath W Midlands 117 B11
Walkerville N Yorks 224 F4
Walkford Dorset 19 C10
Walkhampton Devon 7 B10
Walkington ER Yorks 208 F5
Walkley S Yorks 186 D4
Walkley Clogs, Hebden Bridge W Yorks 196 B4
Walkwood Worcs 117 E10
Wall Cornw'l 2 B4
Wall Northum 241 D10
Wall Staffs 134 B2
Wall Bank Shrops 131 E10
Wall End Cumb 210 C4
Wall End Kent 71 G8
Wall Heath W Midlands 133 F7
Wall Hill Gtr Man 196 F3
Wall Houses Northum 242 D2
Wall Mead Bath/NE Som'set 45 B7
Wall Nook Durham 233 B10
Wall under Heywood Shrops 131 E10
Wallacestone Falk 279 F8
Wallaceton Dumf/Gal 247 F8
Wallacetown S Ayrs 245 C7
Wallacetown S Ayrs 257 E8
Wallacetown Shetl'd 315 H5
Wallands Park E Sussex 36 E6
Wallasey Mersey 182 C3
Wallbank Lancs 195 D11
Wallbrook W Midlands 133 E8
Wallcrouch E Sussex 53 G7
Wallend London 68 C2
Waller's Green Heref'd 98 D3
Wallingford Oxon 64 B6
Wallingswells Notts 187 E9
Wallington Hants 33 F9
Wallington Herts 104 D5
Wallington London 67 G9
Wallington Bury Herts 104 D5
Wallington Heath W Midlands 133 C9
Wallington House, Ponteland Northum 252 G2
Wallis Pembs 91 F10
Wallisdown Poole 19 C7
Walliswood Surrey 50 F6
Wallow Green Glos 80 F4
Walls Shetl'd 315 J4
Wall's Green Essex 87 D10
Wallsend Tyne/Wear 243 D7
Wallston V/Glam 58 E6
Wallsuches Gtr Man 195 E7
Wallsworth Glos 98 G6
Wallyford E Loth 281 G7
Walman's Green Herts 104 G5
Walmer Kent 55 C11
Walmer Bridge Lancs 194 C3
Walmersley Gtr Man 195 E9
Walmestone Kent 55 B9
Walmley W Midlands 134 E2
Walmley Ash W Midlands 134 E2
Walmsgate Lincs 190 F5
Walney Island Airport, Barrow Cumb 210 E3
Walnut Grove Perth/Kinr 286 E5
Walnut Tree M/Keynes 103 D7
Walpole Suffolk 127 C7
Walpole Som'set 43 E10
Walpole Cross Keys Norfolk 157 E10
Walpole Highway Norfolk 157 G10
Walpole Marsh Norfolk 157 F9
Walpole St. Andrew Norfolk 157 F10
Walpole St. Peter Norfolk 157 F9
Walrow Som'set 43 D10
Walsall W Midlands 133 D10
Walsall Arboretum W Midlands 133 D10
Walsall Wood W Midlands 133 C10
Walsden W Yorks 196 C2
Walsgrave on Sowe W Midlands 135 G7
Walsham le Willows Suffolk 125 C10
Walshaw Gtr Man 195 E9
Walshford N Yorks 206 C4
Walsoken Norfolk 157 G8
Walston S Lanarks 269 F11
Walsworth Herts 104 E4
Walter's Ash Bucks 84 F4
Walterston V/Glam 58 E5
Walterstone Heref'd 96 F6
Walterstone Common Heref'd 96 F6
Waltham Kent 54 D6
Waltham NE Lincs 201 G9
Waltham Abbey Essex 86 E5
Waltham Chase Hants 33 D9
Waltham Cross Herts 86 E5
Waltham on the Wolds Leics 154 D6
Waltham St. Lawrence Windsor 65 D10
Waltham's Cross Essex 106 E3
Walthamstow London 67 B11
Walton Bucks 84 C4
Walton Cumb 240 E2
Walton Derby 170 B5
Walton Derby 170 B5
Walton Leics 135 F11
Walton Mersey 182 B5
Walton M/Keynes 103 D7
Walton Peterbro 138 C3
Walton Powys 114 F5
Walton Shrops 115 B9
Walton Suffolk 108 D5
Walton Som'set 44 F3
Walton Staffs 151 C7
Walton Telford 149 F11
Walton Warwick 118 G5
Walton W Yorks 197 D11
Walton W Yorks 206 D4
Walton Cardiff Glos 99 E8
Walton Court Bucks 84 C4
Walton East Pembs 91 G10
Walton Elm Dorset 30 D3
Walton Hall Warrington 183 E9
Walton Highway Norfolk 157 G8
Walton on Thames Surrey 66 F6
Walton on the Hill Surrey 51 C8
Walton on the Hill Staffs 151 E9
Walton on the Wolds Leics 153 F11
Walton on Trent Derby 152 F4
Walton Park N Som'set 60 E2
Walton St. Mary N Som'set 60 E2
Walton Summit Lancs 194 B5
Walton Warren Norfolk 158 F4
Walton West Pembs 72 C5
Walton-in-Gordano N Som'set 60 E2
Walton-le-Dale Lancs 194 B5
Walton-on-the-Naze Essex 108 G5
Walwen Flints 181 F10
Walwen Flints 182 F2
Walwick Northum 241 C10
Walworth D'lington 224 B4
Walworth London 67 D10
Walworth Gate D'lington 233 G10
Walwyn's Castle Pembs 72 C5
Wambrook Som'set 28 F3
Wampool Cumb 238 G6
Wanborough Surrey 50 D2
Wanborough Swindon 63 C8
Wanderwell Dorset 16 C5
Wandon End Herts 104 G2
Wandsworth London 67 E9
Wandylaw Northum 264 D4
Wangford Suffolk 127 B9
Wangford Suffolk 140 G5
Wanlip Leics 153 G11
Wanlockhead Dumf/Gal 259 G9
Wannock E Sussex 23 E9
Wansford ER Yorks 209 B7
Wansford Peterbro 137 D11
Wanshurst Green Kent 53 D9
Wanson Cornw'l 24 G1
Wanstead London 68 B2
Wanstrow Som'set 45 E8
Wanswell Glos 79 E11
Wantage Oxon 64 B2
Wapley S Glos 61 D8
Wappenbury Warwick 119 D7
Wappenham Northants 102 B2
Wapping London 67 C10
Warbleton E Sussex 37 D10
Warblington Hants 34 F2
Warborough Oxon 83 G9
Warboys Cambs 138 G6
Warbreck Blackp'l 202 F2
Warbstow Cornw'l 11 C10
Warbstow Cross Cornw'l 11 C10
Warburton Ches 183 D11
Warburton Green Gtr Man 184 D3
Warburton Park Gtr Man 184 C2
Warcop Cumb 222 B4
Ward End W Midlands 134 F2
Ward Green Suffolk 125 E10
Ward Green S Yorks 197 G10
Ward Green Cross Lancs 203 F8
Warden Kent 70 E4
Warden Northum 241 D10
Warden Hill Beds 122 G2
Warden Hill Glos 99 G8
Warden Street Beds 104 C2
Wardhedges Beds 103 D11
Wardhill Orkney 312 F7
Wardington Oxon 101 B9
Wardlaw Scot Borders 261 F7
Wardle Ches 167 D10
Wardle Gtr Man 196 D2
Wardley Gtr Man 195 G9
Wardley Rutl'd 136 C6
Wardley Tyne/Wear 243 E7
Wardley W Sussex 34 B4
Wardlow Derby 185 G11
Wardpark N Lanarks 278 F5
Wardsend Ches 184 E6
Wardy Hill Cambs 139 G9
Ware Devon 16 C2
Ware Herts 86 C5
Ware Kent 71 G9
Ware Street Kent 53 B9
Wareham Dorset 18 D4
Warehorne Kent 54 G3
Warenford Northum 264 D4
Warenton Northum 264 C4
Wareside Herts 86 B5
Waresley Cambs 122 G5
Waresley Worcs 116 C6
Warfield Brackn'l 65 E11
Warfleet Devon 9 E7
Wargate Lincs 156 C4
Wargrave Mersey 183 C9
Wargrave Wokingham 65 D9
Warham Heref'd 97 D9
Warham Norfolk 176 E6
Warhill Gtr Man 185 B7
Waring's Green W Midlands 118 C2
Wark Northum 241 B9
Wark Northum 263 B8
Warkleigh Devon 25 C10
Warkton Northants 137 F7
Warkworth Northants 101 C9
Warkworth Northum 252 B6
Warlaby N Yorks 224 G6
Warland W Yorks 196 C2
Warleggan Cornw'l 6 B3
Warleigh Bath/NE Som'set 61 G9
Warley Essex 87 G9
Warley W Midlands 133 F10
Warley Town W Yorks 196 B5
Warley Woods W Midlands 133 F10
Warlingham Surrey 51 B11
Warmbrook Derby 170 E3
Warmfield W Yorks 197 C11
Warmingham Ches 168 C2
Warminghurst W Sussex 35 D10
Warmington Northants 137 E11
Warmington Warwick 101 B8
Warminster Wilts 45 E11
Warminster Common Wilts 45 E11
Warmlake Kent 53 C10
Warmley S Glos 61 E7
Warmley Hill S Glos 61 E7
Warmonds Hill Northants 121 D9
Warmsworth S Yorks 198 G4
Warmwell Dorset 17 D11
Warndon Worcs 117 F7
Warners End Herts 85 D8
Warnford Hants 33 C10
Warnham W Sussex 51 G7
Warningcamp W Sussex 35 F8
Warninglid W Sussex 36 B3
Warren Ches 184 G5
Warren Pembs 72 F6
Warren S Yorks 186 B5
Warren Corner Hants 34 B2
Warren Corner Hants 49 D10
Warren Heath Suffolk 108 C3
Warren Knoll Beds 103 G9
Warren Mill Northum 264 C4
Warren Row Windsor 65 C10
Warren Street Kent 54 C2
Warrenby Redcar/Clevel'd 235 G7
Warren's Green Herts 104 F5
Warrington M/Keynes 121 G7
Warrington Warrington 183 D10
Warriston C/Edinb 280 F5
Warsash Hants 33 F7
Warslow Staffs 169 D9
Warsop Vale Notts 171 B9
Warstock W Midlands 117 B11
Warter ER Yorks 208 C3
Warthermarske N Yorks 214 D4
Warthill N Yorks 207 B9
Wartle Aberds 293 C7
Wartling E Sussex 23 D11
Wartnaby Leics 154 E4
Warton Lancs 194 B2
Warton Lancs 211 E9
Warton Northum 252 C2
Warton Warwick 134 C5
Warton Bank Lancs 194 B2
Warwick Cumb 239 F11
Warwick Warwick 118 D5
Warwick Bridge Cumb 239 F11
Warwick Castle Warwick 118 E5
Warwick Racecourse Warwick 118 D5
Warwick Wold Surrey 51 C10
Warwicksland Cumb 239 B11
Wasbister Orkney 312 E4
Wasdale Head Cumb 220 D3
Wash Derby 185 E9
Wash Common W Berks 64 G3
Wash Dyke Norfolk 157 F10
Washall Green Herts 105 E8
Washaway Cornw'l 5 B10
Washbourne Devon 8 E5
Washbrook Suffolk 108 C2
Washbrook Som'set 44 C2
Washbrook Street Suffolk 108 C2
Washerwall Staffs 168 F6
Washfield Devon 26 D6
Washfold N Yorks 223 E11
Washford Som'set 42 E4
Washford Warwick 117 E11
Washford Pyne Devon 26 F4
Washingborough Lincs 189 G8
Washington Tyne/Wear 243 F8
Washington W Sussex 35 E10
Washington Village Tyne/Wear 243 F8
Washmere Green Suffolk 107 B8
Washpit W Yorks 196 F6
Washwood Heath W Midlands 134 F2
Waskerley Durham 233 B7
Wasp Green Surrey 51 D10
Wasperton Warwick 118 F5
Wasps Nest Lincs 173 C9
Wass N Yorks 215 D11
Waste Green Warwick 118 D4
Watch House Green Essex 106 G3
Watchet Som'set 42 E5
Watchfield Oxon 63 B8
Watchfield Som'set 43 D10
Watchgate Cumb 221 F10
Watchhill Cumb 229 C9
Watchhill Dumf/Gal 238 D6
Watchill Dumf/Gal 248 G3
Watcombe Torbay 9 B8
Watendlath Cumb 220 B5
Water Devon 13 E11
Water Lancs 195 B10
Water Eaton M/Keynes 103 E7
Water Eaton Oxon 83 C8
Water End Beds 103 D11
Water End Beds 104 B5
Water End Beds 104 B2
Water End Essex 105 C11
Water End ER Yorks 207 F11
Water End Hants 49 C7
Water End Herts 86 E2
Water End Herts 85 C8
Water Fryston W Yorks 198 B3
Water Gate N Yorks 215 D11
Water Newton Cambs 138 D2
Water Orton Warwick 134 E3
Water Stratford Bucks 102 E3
Water Swallows Derby 185 F9
Water Yeat Cumb 210 B5
Waterbeach Cambs 123 D9
Waterbeck Dumf/Gal 238 B6
Watercombe Dorset 17 E11
Watercress Line (Mid Hants Railway), Alton Hants 49 F7
Waterdale Herts 85 E10
Waterditch Hants 19 B9
Waterend Bucks 84 F3
Waterend Cumb 229 G8
Waterend Glos 80 C3
Waterend Herts 86 C2
Waterfall Staffs 169 E9
Waterfoot Arg/Bute 255 D9
Waterfoot E Renf 267 D11
Waterfoot Lancs 195 C10
Waterford Hants 20 C2
Waterford Herts 86 C4
Watergate Cornw'l 11 E8
Watergore Som'set 28 D6
Waterham Kent 70 G5
Waterhead Angus 292 F6
Waterhead Cumb 221 E7
Waterhead Dumf/Gal 248 E5
Waterhead Devon 8 F3
Waterheads Scot Borders 270 E4
Waterheath Norfolk 143 E8
Waterhouses Durham 233 C9
Waterhouses Staffs 169 E9
Wateringbury Kent 53 C7
Waterlane Glos 80 E6
Waterlip Som'set 45 E7
Waterloo Blackb'n 195 B7
Waterloo Caerph 59 B7
Waterloo Cornw'l 11 G8
Waterloo Derby 170 C6
Waterloo Gtr Man 196 G2
Waterloo H'land 295 C8
Waterloo Mersey 182 B5
Waterloo Norfolk 143 E8
Waterloo N Lanarks 268 E6
Waterloo N Yorks 214 F5
Waterloo Pembs 73 E7
Waterloo Perth/Kinr 286 D4
Waterloo Poole 18 C6
Waterloo Powys 148 E3
Waterloo Shrops 149 C10
Waterloo Worcs 99 D8
Waterloo Park Mersey 182 B5
Waterloo Port Gwyn 163 C7
Waterlooville Hants 33 F11
Waterlow Norfolk 142 B6
Waterman Quarter Kent 53 E10
Watermeetings S Lanarks 259 G11
Watermillock Cumb 230 G4
Watermoor Glos 81 E8
Watermouth Castle Devon 40 D5
Watermouth Castle, Ilfracombe Devon 40 D5
Waterperry Oxon 83 D10
Waterrow Som'set 27 B9
Water's Nook Gtr Man 195 F7
Waters Upton Telford 150 F2
Watersfield W Sussex 35 D8
Watershed Mill Visitor Centre, Settle N Yorks 212 G6
Watersheddings Gtr Man 196 F2
Waterside Aberds 292 B5
Waterside Aberds 303 G10
Waterside Blackb'n 195 C8
Waterside Bucks 85 E7
Waterside Cambs 124 B2
Waterside Cumb 229 B10
Waterside E Ayrs 245 B10
Waterside E Ayrs 267 G9
Waterside E Dunb 278 G3
Waterside E Renf 267 B10
Waterside Surrey 51 D11
Waterslack Lancs 211 D9
Waterstein H'land 297 G7
Waterstock Oxon 83 D10
Waterston Pembs 72 D6
Waterthorpe S Yorks 186 E6
Waterton Aberds 303 F9
Waterton V/Glam 58 D2
Watford Caerph 59 B7
Watford Herts 85 F10
Watford Northants 120 D2
Watford Heath Herts 85 G10
Wath Cumb 222 D3
Wath N Yorks 214 F2
Wath N Yorks 214 D6
Wath N Yorks 216 D3
Wath Brow Cumb 219 C10
Wath upon Dearne S Yorks 198 G2
Watledge Glos 80 E4
Watley's End S Glos 61 C7
Watlington Norfolk 158 G2
Watlington Oxon 83 G11
Watnall Notts 171 F8
Watsness Shetl'd 315 H3
Watten H'land 310 D6
Wattisfield Suffolk 125 C10
Wattisham Suffolk 125 G10
Wattisham Stone Suffolk 125 G10
Wattlesborough Heath Shrops 149 G7
Watton Dorset 16 C5
Watton ER Yorks 208 C6
Watton Norfolk 141 C8
Watton at Stone Herts 86 B4
Watton Green Norfolk 141 C8
Watton's Green Essex 87 F8
Watt's Cross Kent 52 D5
Wattston N Lanarks 278 G5
Wattstown Rh Cyn Taff 77 G8
Wattsville Caerph 78 G2
Wauchan H'land 295 G11
Waulkmill Lodge Orkney 313 H4
Waun Gwyn 163 C9
Waun Powys 130 C2
Waun Baglam Carms 74 E6
Waun Fawr Ceredig'n 128 G2
Waun y Clyn Carms 74 E7
Waunarlwydd Swan 75 F10
Waunclunda Carms 94 E3
Waunfawr Gwyn 163 D8
Waungilwen Carms 92 D6
Waungron Swan 75 E9
Waun-Lwyd Bl Gwent 77 D11
Wavendon M/Keynes 103 D8
Waverbridge Cumb 229 B10
Waverley Surrey 49 D11
Waverton Ches 167 C7
Waverton Cumb 229 B10
Wavertree Mersey 182 D5
Wawcott W Berks 63 F11
Wawne ER Yorks 209 F7
Waxham Norfolk 161 D8
Waxholme ER Yorks 201 B10
Way Kent 71 F10
Way Head Cambs 139 G9
Way Village Devon 26 E5
Way Wick N Som'set 59 G11
Waye Devon 13 G11
Wayend Street Heref'd 98 D4
Wayfield Medway 69 F9
Wayford Som'set 28 F6
Waymills Shrops 167 G9
Wayne Green Monmouths 78 B6
Ways Green Ches 167 B11
Wayside Gardens W Yorks 206 E3
Waytown Dorset 16 B5
Waytown Devon 24 C5
Wdig = Goodwick Pembs 91 D8
Weachyburn Aberds 302 D6
Weacombe Som'set 42 E6
Weald Cambs 122 F4
Weald Oxon 82 E4
Weald and Downland Open Air Museum, Chichester W Sussex 34 E5
Wealdstone London 67 B7
Wearde Cornw'l 7 D8
Weardley W Yorks 205 E11
Weare Som'set 44 C2
Weare Giffard Devon 25 C7
Wearhead Durham 232 D3
Wearne Som'set 28 B6
Weasdale Cumb 222 D3
Weasenham All Saints Norfolk 158 E6
Weasenham St. Peter Norfolk 159 E7
Weaste Gtr Man 184 B4
Weatherhill Surrey 51 E10
Weatheroak Hill Worcs 117 C11
Weaverham Ches 183 G10
Weavering Street Kent 53 B9
Weaverthorpe N Yorks 217 E9
Webbington Som'set 43 B11
Webb's Green W Midlands 133 G9
Webb's Heath S Glos 61 E7
Webheath Worcs 117 D10
Webton Heref'd 97 D8
Wedderlairs Aberds 303 F8
Weddington Kent 55 B9
Weddington Warwick 135 E7
Wedge's Mill Staffs 133 B9
Wedgwood Visitor Centre, Barlaston Staffs 151 B7
Wedhampton Wilts 46 B5
Wedmore Som'set 44 D2
Wednesbury W Midlands 133 D9
Wednesbury Oak W Midlands 133 E9
Wednesfield W Midlands 133 C9
Weecar Notts 172 B4
Weedon Bucks 84 B4
Weedon Bec Northants 120 F2
Weedon Lois Northants 102 B2
Weeford Staffs 134 C2
Week Devon 8 C5
Week Devon 25 G11
Week Devon 25 B9
Week Green Cornw'l 11 B10
Week St. Mary Cornw'l 11 B10
Weeke Hants 48 G3
Weekley Northants 137 F7
Weeks I/Wight 21 C7
Weel ER Yorks 209 F7
Weeley Essex 108 G2
Weeley Heath Essex 108 G3
Weelsby NE Lincs 201 F9
Weem Perth/Kinr 286 C2
Weeping Cross Staffs 151 E8
Weethley Warwick 117 F11
Weeting Norfolk 140 F5
Weeting Heath NNR Norfolk 140 F5
Weeton ER Yorks 201 C11
Weeton Lancs 202 F3
Weeton N Yorks 205 D11
Weeton Camp Lancs 202 F3
Weetwood W Yorks 205 F11
Weir Lancs 195 B11
Weir Green Glos 80 B3
Weir Quay Devon 7 B8
Weirbrook Shrops 148 E7
Weirend Heref'd 97 G11
Welbeck Abbey Notts 187 G9
Welbeck Colliery Village Notts 187 G8
Welborne Norfolk 141 B11
Welbourn Lincs 173 E7
Welburn N Yorks 216 F4
Welburn N Yorks 216 C3
Welbury N Yorks 225 E7
Welby Lincs 155 B9
Welcombe Devon 24 D2
Weld Bank Lancs 194 D5
Weldon Northants 137 F8
Weldon Northum 252 D4
Welford Northants 136 G2
Welford W Berks 64 E2
Welford on Avon Warwick 118 G2
Welham Leics 136 E5
Welham Notts 188 E2
Welham Green Herts 86 D2
Well Hants 49 D9
Well Lincs 190 G6
Well N Yorks 214 C5
Well Bank Lancs 195 C9
Well Cross Devon 8 D3
Well End Bucks 65 B11
Well End Herts 86 F2
Well Green Gtr Man 184 D3
Well Hall London 68 E2
Well Head Wilts 45 G10
Well Hill Kent 68 G3
Well Street Kent 53 B7
Well Town Devon 26 F6
Welland Worcs 98 D5
Wellbank Angus 287 D8
Wellbrook E Sussex 37 B9
Welldale Dumf/Gal 238 D5
Weller's Town Kent 52 E4
Wellesbourne Warwick 118 F5
Wellhead Herts 104 F3
Wellheads Aberds 302 F4
Wellhouse W Berks 64 E4
Wellhouse W Yorks 196 E5
Welling London 68 D3
Wellingborough Northants 121 D7
Wellingham Norfolk 159 E7
Wellingley S Yorks 187 C9
Wellingore Lincs 173 D7
Wellington Brackn'l 65 G10
Wellington Cumb 219 E11
Wellington Heref'd 97 B9
Wellington Som'set 27 C10
Wellington Telford 150 G3
Wellington Heath Heref'd 98 C4
Wellington Hill W Yorks 206 F2
Wellington Marsh Heref'd 97 B9
Wellisford Som'set 27 C9
Wellow Bath/NE Som'set 45 B8
Wellow I/Wight 20 D3
Wellow Notts 171 B11
Wellow Wood Hants 32 C3
Wellpond Green Herts 105 G8
Wells Som'set 44 D4
Wells Cathedral Som'set 44 D5
Wells Green Ches 167 E11
Wells Green W Midlands 134 G2

Wellsborough Leics 135 C7
Wells-next-the-Sea Norfolk 176 E6
Wellstye Green Essex 87 B10
Wellswood Torbay 9 C8
Wellsworth Hants 34 E2
Wellwood Fife 279 D11
Welney Norfolk 139 E10
Welsford Devon 24 C3
Welsh Bicknor Heref'd 79 B9
Welsh End Shrops 149 B10
Welsh Frankton Shrops 149 C7
Welsh Highland Railway, Caernarfon Gwyn 163 C7
Welsh Highland Railway, Porthmadog Gwyn 163 H9
Welsh Hook Pembs 91 F8
Welsh National Velodrome Newp 59 B10
Welsh Newton Heref'd 79 B7
Welsh Newton Common Heref'd 79 B8
Welsh St. Donats V/Glam 58 D4
Welshampton Shrops 149 B8
Welshpool = Y Trallwng Powys 130 B4
Welstor Devon 13 G10
Welton Bath/NE Som'set 45 C7
Welton Cumb 230 C3
Welton ER Yorks 200 B3
Welton Lincs 189 F8
Welton Northants 119 D11
Welton Hill Lincs 189 E8
Welton le Marsh Lincs 175 B7
Welton le Wold Lincs 190 D3
Welwick ER Yorks 201 B10
Welwyn Herts 86 B2
Welwyn Garden City Herts 86 C3
Wem Shrops 149 D10
Wembdon Som'set 43 F9
Wembley London 67 B7
Wembley Park London 67 B7
Wembley Stadium London 67 B7
Wembury Devon 7 F10
Wembworthy Devon 25 F11
Wemyss Bay Inverclyde 266 B3
Wenallt Ceredig'n 112 C3
Wendens Ambo Essex 105 D10
Wendlebury Oxon 83 B9
Wendling Norfolk 159 G8
Wendover Bucks 84 D5
Wendover Dean Bucks 84 E5
Wendron Cornw'l 2 C5
Wendy Cambs 104 B6
Wenfordbridge Cornw'l 11 F7
Wenhaston Suffolk 127 B8
Wennington Cambs 122 B4
Wennington Lancs 212 E2
Wennington London 68 C4
Wensley Derby 170 C3
Wensley N Yorks 213 B11
Wentbridge W Yorks 198 D3
Wentnor Shrops 131 E7
Wentworth Cambs 123 B9
Wentworth S Yorks 186 C5
Wenvoe V/Glam 58 E6
Weobley Heref'd 115 G8
Weobley Marsh Heref'd 115 G8
Weoley Castle W Midlands 133 G10
Wepham W Sussex 35 F8
Wepre Flints 166 B3
Wereham Norfolk 140 C3
Wereton Staffs 168 E3
Wergs W Midlands 133 C7
Wern Gwyn 145 B10
Wern Powys 148 G5
Wern Powys 148 E5
Wern Shrops 148 C5
Wern Gifford Monmouths 96 G6
Wern Tarw Bridg 58 C3
Werneth Gtr Man 196 G2
Werneth Low Gtr Man 185 C7
Wernffrwd Swan 75 G8
Wern-gerhynt Powys 129 D7
Wernheolydd Monmouths 78 G5
Wern-olau Swan 75 F9
Wern-y-cwrt Monmouths 78 D5
Wern-y-gaer Flints 166 B2
Werrington Cornw'l 12 D2
Werrington Peterbro 138 C3
Werrington Staffs 168 F6
Wervin Ches 182 G6
Wescoe Cumb 230 F2
Wesham Lancs 202 G4
Wessington Derby 170 D5
West Aberthaw V/Glam 58 F4
West Acre Norfolk 158 F5
West Acton London 67 C7
West Adderbury Oxon 101 D9
West Allerdean Northum 273 F9
West Allotment Tyne/Wear 243 C8
West Alvington Devon 8 G4
West Amesbury Wilts 46 E6
West Anstey Devon 26 B4
West Appleton N Yorks 224 G4
West Ardhu Arg/Bute 288 D6
West Ardsley W Yorks 197 B9
West Ardwell Dumf/Gal 236 E2
West Arthurlie E Renf 267 D9
West Ashby Lincs 190 G3
West Ashford Devon 40 F4
West Ashling W Sussex 34 F4
West Ashton Wilts 45 B11
West Auckland Durham 233 F9
West Ayton N Yorks 217 C9
West Bagborough Som'set 43 G7
West Bank Bl Gwent 78 D2
West Bank Halton 183 E8
West Barkwith Lincs 189 E11
West Barnby N Yorks 226 C6
West Barnes London 67 F8
West Barns E Loth 282 F3
West Bay Dorset 16 C5
West Beckham Norfolk 160 B2
West Bedfont Surrey 66 E5
West Benhar N Lanarks 269 C7
West Bergholt Essex 107 F9
West Bexington Dorset 16 D6
West Bilney Norfolk 158 F4
West Blackdene Durham 232 D3
West Blatchington Brighton/Hove 36 F3
West Boldon Tyne/Wear 243 E9
West Bourton Dorset 30 B3
West Bowling W Yorks 205 G9
West Bradford Lancs 203 E10
West Bradley Som'set 44 F5
West Brasham Norfolk 159 C8
West Bretton W Yorks 197 E9
West Bridgford Notts 153 B11
West Brigg's Norfolk 158 G3
West Bromwich W Midlands 133 E10
West Buckland Devon 41 G7
West Buckland Som'set 27 C11
West Burnside Aberds 293 F8
West Burrafirth Shetl'd 315 H4
West Burton N Yorks 213 B10
West Burton W Sussex 35 E8
West Butsfield Durham 233 C8
West Butterwick N Lincs 199 F10
West Byfleet Surrey 66 G4
West Caister Norfolk 161 G10
West Calder W Loth 269 C10
West Camel Som'set 29 C9
West Carr Kingston/Hull 209 G7
West Carr N Lincs 199 F8
West Chadsmoor Staffs 151 G9
West Chaldon Dorset 17 E11
West Challow Oxon 63 B11
West Charleton Devon 8 G5
West Chelborough Dorset 29 F8
West Chevington Northum 252 D6
West Chiltington W Sussex 35 D9
West Chiltington Common W Sussex 35 D9
West Chinnock Som'set 29 E7
West Chirton Tyne/Wear 243 D8
West Chisenbury Wilts 46 C6
West Clandon Surrey 50 C4
West Cliff N Yorks 227 C7
West Cliffe Kent 55 E11
West Clyne H'land 311 J2
West Clyth H'land 310 F6
West Coker Som'set 29 E8
West Cornforth Durham 234 E2
West Common Hants 32 G6
West Compton Dorset 17 C7
West Compton Som'set 44 E5
West Cowick ER Yorks 198 C6
West Creech Dorset 18 E3
West Cross Kent 53 G10
West Cross Swan 56 D6
West Cullery Aberds 293 C9
West Curry Cornw'l 11 C11
West Curthwaite Cumb 230 B2
West Darlochan Arg/Bute 255 E7
West Dean Wilts 32 B3
West Dean W Sussex 34 E5
West Deeping Lincs 138 B2
West Dennant Pembs 72 C6
West Denton Tyne/Wear 242 D5
West Derby Mersey 182 C6
West Dereham Norfolk 140 C2
West Didsbury Gtr Man 184 C4
West Down Devon 40 E4
West Drayton London 66 D5
West Drayton Notts 188 G2
West Dulwich London 67 E10
West Ealing London 67 C7
West Ella ER Yorks 200 B4
West End Beds 121 G9
West End Beds 122 E2
West End Brackn'l 65 E11
West End Bucks 102 F3
West End Caerph 78 F2
West End Cumb 239 F8
West End Dorset 30 G6
West End ER Yorks 201 B9
West End ER Yorks 208 G4
West End ER Yorks 209 G9
West End ER Yorks 217 G11
West End ER Yorks 209 B9
West End Glos 80 F5
West End Hants 48 F6
West End Hants 33 E7
West End Hants 33 F9
West End Herts 86 D3
West End Kent 54 B2
West End Kent 71 F7
West End Lancs 195 B8
West End Lancs 211 G8
West End Leics 153 F8
West End Lincs 174 F5
West End Lincs 190 B5
West End Norfolk 141 B8
West End Norfolk 161 G9
West End Northants 102 C3
West End N Som'set 60 F3
West End N Yorks 206 E6
West End N Yorks 205 B8
West End Oxon 82 E6
West End Oxon 64 B5
West End Suffolk 143 G9
West End S Glos 61 B8
West End Som'set 28 E5
West End Som'set 29 B7
West End Som'set 45 F7
West End Som'set 44 C5
West End S Lanarks 269 F9
West End Surrey 66 G2
West End Surrey 66 G6
West End S Yorks 199 F7
West End Wilts 30 C6
West End Wilts 31 C7
West End Wilts 62 D3
West End Windsor 65 D10
West End Worcs 99 D11
West End W Sussex 36 D2
West End W Yorks 197 B7
West End W Yorks 205 F10
West End Green Hants 65 G7
West Ewell Surrey 67 G8
West Farleigh Kent 53 C8
West Farndon Northants 119 G10
West Felton Shrops 148 D6
West Fenton E Loth 281 E9
West Ferry Dundee C 287 D8
West Firle E Sussex 37 F7
West Fleetham Northum 264 D5
West Garforth W Yorks 206 G3
West Gillibrands Lancs 194 F3
West Ginge Oxon 64 B2
West Grafton Wilts 63 G8
West Green Hants 49 B8
West Green London 67 B10
West Green W Sussex 51 F9
West Greenskares Aberds 303 C7
West Grimstead Wilts 32 B2
West Grinstead W Sussex 35 C11
West Haddlesey N Yorks 198 B5
West Haddon Northants 120 C2
West Hagbourne Oxon 64 B4
West Hagley Worcs 117 B8
West Hale N Lincs 199 F8
West Hall Cumb 240 D3
West Hallam Derby 170 G6
West Halton N Lincs 200 C2
West Ham London 68 C2
West Hampstead London 67 B9
West Handley Derby 186 F5
West Hanney Oxon 82 G6
West Hanningfield Essex 88 F2
West Hardwick W Yorks 198 D2
West Harnham Wilts 31 B10
West Harptree Bath/NE Som'set 44 B5
West Harrow London 66 B6
West Harting W Sussex 34 C3
West Harton Tyne/Wear 243 E9
West Hatch Som'set 28 C3
West Hatch Wilts 30 B6
West Hay N Som'set 60 G3
West Head Norfolk 139 B11
West Heath Ches 168 C4
West Heath Hants 48 B5
West Heath Hants 49 B11
West Heath London 68 D3
West Heath W Midlands 117 B10
West Helmsdale H'land 311 H4
West Hendon London 67 B8
West Hendred Oxon 64 B2
West Herrington Tyne/Wear 243 G8
West Heslerton N Yorks 217 D8
West Hewish N Som'set 59 G11
West Hill Devon 15 C7
West Hill ER Yorks 218 F3
West Hill London 67 E8
West Hill N Som'set 60 E3
West Hill N Som'set 60 D3
West Hill Staffs 151 G9
West Hill Wilts 61 F11
West Hill W Sussex 51 G10
West Hoathly W Sussex 51 G11
West Holme Dorset 18 D3
West Holywell Tyne/Wear 243 C8
West Horndon Essex 68 B6
West Horrington Som'set 44 D5
West Horsley Surrey 50 C5
West Horton Northum 264 C2
West Hougham Kent 55 E9
West Houlland Shetl'd 315 H4
West Houses Lincs 174 E4
West Howe Bournem'th 19 B7
West Howetown Som'set 42 F2
West Huntspill Som'set 43 E10
West Hurn Dorset 19 B8
West Hyde Herts 85 G8
West Hynish Arg/Bute 288 F1
West Hythe Kent 54 G6
West Ilsley W Berks 64 C3
West Itchenor W Sussex 34 G3
West Jesmond Tyne/Wear 243 D7
West Keal Lincs 174 C5
West Kennett Wilts 62 F6
West Kilbride N Ayrs 266 F4
West Kingsdown Kent 68 G5
West Kington Wilts 61 D10
West Kington Wick Wilts 61 D10
West Kinharrachie Aberds 303 F9
West Kirby Mersey 182 D2
West Knapton N Yorks 217 D7
West Knighton Dorset 17 D10
West Knoyle Wilts 45 G11
West Kyo Durham 242 G5
West Lambrook Som'set 28 D6
West Langdon Kent 55 D10
West Langwell H'land 309 J6
West Lavington Wilts 46 C4
West Lavington W Sussex 34 C5
West Layton N Yorks 224 D2
West Lea Durham 234 B4
West Leake Notts 153 D10
West Learmouth Northum 263 B8
West Leigh Devon 25 F11
West Leigh Hants 34 F2
West Lexham Norfolk 158 F6
West Lilling N Yorks 216 F2
West Linton Scot Borders 270 E3
West Liss Hants 34 B3
West Littleton S Glos 61 D9
West Lockinge Oxon 64 B2
West Looe Cornw'l 6 E5
West Luccombe Som'set 42 D2
West Lulworth Dorset 18 E3
West Lutton N Yorks 217 F8
West Lydford Som'set 44 G5
West Lydiatt Heref'd 97 C11
West Lyn Devon 41 D8
West Lyng Som'set 28 B4
West Lynn Norfolk 158 E2
West Mains S Lanarks 268 E2
West Malling Kent 53 B7
West Malvern Worcs 98 B5
West Marden W Sussex 34 E3
West Marina E Sussex 38 F3
West Markham Notts 188 G2
West Marsh NE Lincs 201 F9
West Marton N Yorks 204 C3
West Mathers Aberds 293 G9
West Melbury Dorset 30 C5
West Melton S Yorks 198 G2
West Meon Hants 33 C10
West Meon Woodlands Hants 33 B10
West Merkland H'land 308 F3
West Mersea Essex 89 C8
West Midland Safari Park, Kidderminster Worcs 116 B6
West Mill Herts 104 E3
West Milton Dorset 16 B6
West Minster Kent 70 E2
West Molesey Surrey 66 F6
West Monkseaton Tyne/Wear 243 C8
West Monkton Som'set 28 B3
West Moor Tyne/Wear 243 C7
West Moors Dorset 31 G9
West Morden Dorset 18 B4
West Morriston Scot Borders 271 G11
West Morton W Yorks 205 E7
West Mudford Som'set 29 C9
West Muir Angus 293 G7
West Myreriggs Perth/Kinr 286 C6
West Ness N Yorks 216 D3
West Newton ER Yorks 209 F9
West Newton Norfolk 158 D3
West Newton Som'set 28 B3
West Norwood London 67 E10
West Ogwell Devon 14 G2
West Orchard Dorset 30 D4
West Overton Wilts 62 F6
West Panson Devon 12 C2
West Park Hartlep'l 234 E5
West Park Mersey 183 B7
West Park Tyne/Wear 243 D9
West Park W Yorks 205 F11
West Parley Dorset 19 B7
West Peckham Kent 52 C6
West Pelton Durham 242 G6
West Pennard Som'set 44 F4
West Pentire Cornw'l 4 C5
West Perry Cambs 122 D2
West Poringland Norfolk 142 C5
West Porlock Som'set 41 D11
West Pulham Dorset 30 F2
West Putford Devon 24 D5
West Quantoxhead Som'set 42 E6
West Rainton Durham 234 B2
West Rasen Lincs 189 D9
West Ravendale NE Lincs 190 B2
West Raynham Norfolk 159 D7
West Retford Notts 187 E11
West Rounton N Yorks 225 E8
West Row Suffolk 124 B3
West Royd W Yorks 205 F9
West Rudham Norfolk 158 D6
West Ruislip London 66 B5
West Runton Norfolk 177 E11
West Saltoun E Loth 271 B9
West Sandford Devon 26 G4
West Sandwick Shetl'd 314 E6
West Scholes W Yorks 205 G7
West Scrafton N Yorks 213 C11
West Shepton Som'set 44 E6
West Side Orkney 312 E6
West Sleekburn Northum 253 F7
West Somerset Railway, Minehead Som'set 42 E4
West Somerton Norfolk 161 F9
West Stafford Dorset 17 D10
West Stockwith Notts 188 B3
West Stoke Som'set 29 D7
West Stoke W Sussex 34 F4
West Stonesdale N Yorks 223 E7
West Stoughton Som'set 44 D2
West Stour Dorset 30 C3
West Stourmouth Kent 71 G9
West Stow Suffolk 124 C6
West Stowell Wilts 62 G6
West Strathan H'land 308 C5
West Stratton Hants 48 E4
West Street Kent 55 B10
West Street Kent 54 C2
West Street Medway 69 D8
West Street Suffolk 125 C9
West Street Suffolk 125 C10
West Tanfield N Yorks 214 D5
West Taphouse Cornw'l 6 C3
West Tarbert Arg/Bute 275 G9
West Tarring W Sussex 35 G10
West Third Scot Borders 262 B4
West Thirston Northum 252 D5
West Thorney W Sussex 34 G3
West Thurrock Thurr'k 68 D5
West Tilbury Thurr'k 69 D7
West Tisted Hants 33 B10
West Tofts Norfolk 140 E6
West Tofts Perth/Kinr 286 D5
West Tolgus Cornw'l 4 G3
West Torrington Lincs 189 E10
West Town Bath/NE Som'set 60 G4
West Town Bucks 66 C2
West Town Devon 14 B3
West Town Devon 24 C4
West Town Hants 22 D2
West Town Heref'd 115 E8
West Town N Som'set 60 F3
West Town Som'set 44 F4
West Town W Sussex 36 D3
West Tytherley Hants 32 B3
West Tytherton Wilts 62 E3
West Vale W Yorks 196 C5
West View Hartlep'l 234 D5
West Village V/Glam 58 E3
West Walton Norfolk 157 G9
West Wellow Hants 32 D3
West Wembury Devon 7 F10
West Wemyss Fife 280 C6
West Wick N Som'set 59 G11
West Wickham Cambs 106 B2
West Wickham London 67 F11
West Williamston Pembs 73 D8
West Willoughby Lincs 173 G7
West Winch Norfolk 158 F2
West Winterslow Wilts 47 G8
West Wittering W Sussex 22 D3
West Witton N Yorks 213 C10
West Woodburn Northum 251 F9
West Woodhay W Berks 63 G11
West Woodlands Som'set 45 E9
West Worldham Hants 49 F8
West Worlington Devon 26 E3
West Worthing W Sussex 35 G10
West Wratting Cambs 124 G2
West Wycombe Bucks 84 G4
West Wylam Northum 242 E4
West Yatton Wilts 61 D11
West Yell Shetl'd 314 E6
West Yeo Som'set 43 G10
Westbere Kent 71 G7
Westborough Lincs 172 G5
Westbourne Bournem'th 19 C7
Westbourne Suffolk 108 B2
Westbourne W Sussex 34 F3
Westbrook Heref'd 96 C5
Westbrook Kent 71 F11
Westbrook Surrey 50 E3
Westbrook W Berks 64 E2
Westbrook Wilts 62 F3
Westbrook Warrington 183 C9
Westbrook Green Norfolk 142 G2
Westburn S Lanarks 268 C3
Westbury Bucks 102 D2
Westbury Shrops 131 B7
Westbury Wilts 45 C11
Westbury Leigh Wilts 45 C11
Westbury on Trym Bristol 60 D5
Westbury Park Bristol 60 D5
Westbury-on-Severn Glos 80 C2
Westbury-sub-Mendip Som'set 44 D4
Westby Lancs 202 G3
Westby Lincs 155 D9
Westcliff I/Wight 20 F6
Westcliff-on-Sea Southend 69 B11
Westcombe Som'set 29 B7
Westcombe Som'set 45 F7
Westcot Oxon 63 B10
Westcote Glos 100 G4
Westcott Bucks 84 B2
Westcott Devon 13 D11
Westcott Devon 27 G8
Westcott Surrey 50 D6
Westcott Barton Oxon 101 F8
Westcourt Wilts 63 G8
Westcraigs W Loth 269 B8
Westcroft M/Keynes 102 E6
Westdean E Sussex 23 F8
Westdene Brighton/Hove 36 F3
Westdowns Cornw'l 10 E7
Wester Aberchalder H'land 300 G5
Wester Arboll H'land 311 L2
Wester Auchinloch N Lanarks 278 G3
Wester Auchnagallin H'land 301 F10
Wester Balgedie Perth/Kinr 286 G5
Wester Brae H'land 300 C6
Wester Craiglands H'land 301 D7
Wester Culbeuchly Aberds 302 C6
Wester Dalvoult H'land 291 B11
Wester Dechmont W Loth 279 G10
Wester Denoon Angus 287 C7
Wester Ellister Arg/Bute 254 B2
Wester Essendy Perth/Kinr 286 C5
Wester Feddal Perth/Kinr 286 G2
Wester Fintray Aberds 293 B10
Wester Galgantray H'land 301 E8
Wester Gospetry Fife 286 G5
Wester Gruinards H'land 309 K5
Wester Hailes C/Edinb 270 B4
Wester Lealty H'land 300 B6
Wester Lix Stirl 285 E9
Wester Milton H'land 301 D9
Wester Mosshead Aberds 302 F5
Wester Newburn Fife 287 G8
Wester Ord Aberds 293 C10
Wester Quarff Shetl'd 315 K6
Wester Skeld Shetl'd 315 J4
Wester Strath H'land 300 D6
Wester Watten H'land 310 D6
Westerdale H'land 310 D5
Westerdale N Yorks 226 D3
Westerfield Suffolk 108 B3
Westerfield Shetl'd 315 H5
Westerfolds Moray 301 C11
Westergate W Sussex 34 F6
Westerham Kent 52 C2
Westerhope Tyne/Wear 242 D5
Westerleigh S Glos 61 D8
Westerleigh Common S Glos 61 C8
Westerleigh Hill S Glos 61 D8
Western Bank Cumb 229 B10
Western Downs Staffs 151 E8
Western Heights Kent 55 E10
Western Hill Durham 233 C11
Western Point Halton 183 E7
Westerton Aberds 293 B9
Westerton Aberds 302 E5
Westerton Angus 287 B10
Westerton Durham 233 E10
Westerton Moray 302 D3
Westerton Stirl 278 B5
Westerton W Sussex 34 F5
Westertown Aberds 303 F7
Westerwick Shetl'd 315 J4
Westfield Bath/NE Som'set 45 C7
Westfield Cumb 228 F5
Westfield E Sussex 38 D4
Westfield Hants 22 D2
Westfield Heref'd 98 B4
Westfield H'land 310 C4
Westfield Norfolk 141 B9
Westfield N Lanarks 278 G4
Westfield N Lincs 200 D6
Westfield Redcar/Clevel'd 235 G7
Westfield Surrey 50 B4
Westfield S Yorks 186 E6
Westfield W Loth 279 G8
Westfield W Yorks 205 E9
Westfield W Yorks 197 C8
Westfield Sole Kent 69 G9
Westfields Dorset 30 F2
Westfields Heref'd 97 C10
Westfields of Rattray Perth/Kinr 286 C5
Westford Som'set 27 C10
Westgate Durham 232 D4
Westgate Norfolk 177 E7
Westgate N Lincs 199 F9
Westgate Hill W Yorks 197 B8
Westgate on Sea Kent 71 E10
Westgate Street Norfolk 160 E3
Westhall Aberds 302 G6
Westhall Suffolk 143 G8
Westhall Hill Oxon 82 C2
Westham Dorset 17 F9
Westham E Sussex 23 E10
Westham Som'set 44 D2
Westhampnett W Sussex 34 F5
Westhay Som'set 44 E2
Westhead Lancs 194 F2
Westhide Heref'd 97 C11
Westhill Aberds 293 C10
Westhill H'land 301 E7
Westholme Som'set 44 E5
Westhope Heref'd 115 G9
Westhope Shrops 131 F9
Westhorp Northants 119 G10
Westhorpe Derby 187 F7
Westhorpe Lincs 156 C4
Westhorpe Suffolk 125 D10
Westhoughton Gtr Man 195 F7
Westhouse N Yorks 212 E3
Westhouses Derby 170 D6
Westhumble Surrey 51 C7
Westing Shetl'd 314 C7
Westlake Devon 8 E2
Westland Arg/Bute 275 G11
Westland Green Herts 105 G8
Westlands Cambs 139 F10
Westlands Staffs 168 G4
Westlands Worcs 117 E7
Westlea Swindon 62 C6
Westleigh Devon 27 D9
Westleigh Devon 25 B7
Westleigh Gtr Man 195 G7
Westleigh Gtr Man 194 G6
Westleton Suffolk 127 D8
Westley Shrops 131 B7
Westley Suffolk 124 E6
Westley Heights Essex 69 B7
Westley Waterless Cambs 124 G2
Westlington Bucks 84 C3
Westlinton Cumb 239 E9
Westmancote Worcs 99 D8
Westmarsh Kent 71 G9
Westmeston E Sussex 36 E4
Westmill Herts 105 F7
Westminster London 67 D9
Westminster Cathedral London 67 D9
Westmoor End Cumb 229 D8
Westmuir Angus 287 B7
Westness Orkney 312 F4
Westnewton Cumb 229 C8
Westnewton Northum 263 C10
Westoe Tyne/Wear 243 D9
Weston Bath/NE Som'set 61 F8
Weston Ches 168 E2
Weston Ches 184 G5
Weston Dorset 17 G9
Weston Devon 15 D9
Weston Devon 27 G10
Weston Hants 34 C2
Weston Heref'd 115 F7
Weston Halton 183 E8
Weston Herts 104 E5
Weston Lincs 156 D5
Weston Northants 101 B11
Weston Notts 172 B3
Weston N Yorks 205 D9
Weston Shrops 114 C6
Weston Shrops 131 E11
Weston Shrops 149 D11
Weston S Lanarks 269 F10
Weston S'thampton 32 E6
Weston Staffs 151 D9
Weston W Berks 63 E11
Weston Bampfylde Som'set 29 B10
Weston Beggard Heref'd 97 C11
Weston by Welland Northants 136 E5
Weston Colley Hants 48 F4
Weston Colville Cambs 124 G2
Weston Corbett Hants 49 D7
Weston Coyney Stoke 168 G6
Weston Ditch Suffolk 124 B3
Weston Favell Northants 120 E5
Weston Green Cambs 124 G2
Weston Green Norfolk 160 G2
Weston Green Surrey 67 F7
Weston Heath Shrops 149 D11
Weston Heath Shrops 150 G5
Weston Hills Lincs 156 E5
Weston in Arden Warwick 135 F7
Weston Jones Staffs 150 E5
Weston Longville Norfolk 160 F2
Weston Lullingfields Shrops 149 E8
Weston Mill Plym'th 7 D9
Weston on the Green Oxon 83 B8
Weston on Trent Derby 153 D8
Weston Park Bath/NE Som'set 61 F8
Weston Park Staffs 150 G6
Weston Patrick Hants 49 D7
Weston Point Halton 183 E7
Weston Rhyn Shrops 148 B5
Weston Subedge Glos 100 C2
Weston Town Som'set 45 E8
Weston Turville Bucks 84 C5
Weston under Lizard Staffs 150 G6
Weston under Penyard Heref'd 98 G2
Weston under Wetherley Warwick 119 D7
Weston Underwood Derby 170 G3
Weston Underwood M/Keynes 121 G7
Westonbirt Glos 61 B11
Westonbirt Arboretum, Tetbury Glos 61 B11
Westoning Beds 103 E10
Weston-in-Gordano N Som'set 60 E2
Weston-on-Avon Warwick 118 G3
Weston-super-Mare N Som'set 59 G10
Westonzoyland Som'set 43 F11
Westover Hants 47 E11
Westow N Yorks 216 F5
Westowe Som'set 42 G6
Westown Devon 27 E10
Westown Perth/Kinr 286 E6
Westport Arg/Bute 255 E7
Westport Som'set 28 C5
Westquarter Falk 279 F8
Westra V/Glam 58 E6
Westray Airport Orkney 312 C5
Westridge Green W Berks 64 D5
Westrigg W Loth 269 B8
Westrip Glos 80 D4
Westrop Swindon 82 G2
Westrop Wilts 61 E11
Westruther Scot Borders 272 F2
Westry Cambs 139 D8
Westvale Mersey 182 B6
Westville Notts 171 F8
Westward Cumb 229 B11
Westward Ho! Devon 24 B6
Westwell Kent 54 D3
Westwell Oxon 82 C2
Westwell Leacon Kent 54 D3
Westwells Wilts 61 F11
Westwick Cambs 123 D8
Westwick Durham 223 B11
Westwick Norfolk 160 D5
Westwood Devon 26 G4
Westwood Devon 14 B6
Westwood Kent 71 F10
Westwood Kent 68 E5
Westwood Notts 171 E7
Westwood Peterbro 138 D3
Westwood S Lanarks 268 E2
Westwood Wilts 45 B10
Westwood Wilts 46 G6
Westwood Heath W Midlands 118 B5
Westwood Park Gtr Man 184 B3
Westwoodside N Lincs 188 B2
Westy Warrington 183 D10
Wetham Green Kent 69 F10
Wetheral Cumb 239 F11
Wetheral Plain Cumb 239 F11
Wetherby W Yorks 206 D4
Wetherby Racecourse W Yorks 206 D4
Wetherden Suffolk 125 E10
Wetheringsett Suffolk 126 D2
Wethersfield Essex 106 E4
Wethersta Shetl'd 314 G5
Wetherup Street Suffolk 126 E2
Wetley Rocks Staffs 169 F7
Wetmore Staffs 152 E5
Wetreins Green Ches 166 E6
Wettenhall Ches 167 C10
Wetton Staffs 169 D10
Wetwang ER Yorks 208 B4
Wetwood Staffs 150 C5
Wexcombe Wilts 47 B9
Wexham Street Bucks 66 C3
Weybourne Norfolk 177 E10
Weybourne Surrey 49 D11
Weybread Suffolk 142 G4
Weybridge Surrey 66 G5
Weycroft Devon 28 G4
Weydale H'land 310 C5
Weyhill Hants 47 D10
Weymouth Dorset 17 F9
Weymouth Sea Life Park Dorset 17 E9
Weythel Powys 114 F4
Whaddon Bucks 102 E6
Whaddon Cambs 104 B6
Whaddon Glos 80 C4
Whaddon Glos 99 G9
Whaddon Wilts 31 B11
Whaddon Wilts 61 G11
Whaddon Gap Cambs 104 B6
Whale Cumb 230 G6
Whalecombe Pembs 73 D8
Whaley Derby 187 G8
Whaley Bridge Derby 185 E8
Whaley Thorns Derby 187 G8
Whaligoe H'land 310 E7
Whalley Lancs 203 F10
Whalley Banks Lancs 203 F10
Whalley Range Gtr Man 184 C4
Whalleys Mersey 194 F3
Whalsay Airport Shetl'd 314 G7
Whalton Northum 252 G4
Whaplode Lincs 156 E6
Whaplode Drove Lincs 156 G6
Whaplode St. Catherine Lincs 156 E6
Wharf Warwick 119 G8
Wharfe N Yorks 212 F5
Wharles Lancs 202 F4
Wharley End Beds 103 C8
Wharmley Northum 241 D9
Wharncliffe Side S Yorks 186 C3
Wharram le Street N Yorks 217 F7
Wharton Ches 167 B11
Wharton Lincs 188 C4
Wharton Green Ches 167 B11
Whashton N Yorks 224 D3
Whashton Green N Yorks 224 D2
Whasset Cumb 211 C10
Whatcote Warwick 100 C6
Whateley Warwick 134 D4
Whatfield Suffolk 107 B10
Whatley Som'set 28 F5
Whatley Som'set 45 D8
Whatlington E Sussex 38 D3
Whatsole Street Kent 54 E6
Whatstandwell Derby 170 E4
Whatton Notts 154 B4
Whauphill Dumf/Gal 236 E6
Whaw N Yorks 223 E9
Wheal Baddon Cornw'l 4 G5
Wheal Busy Cornw'l 4 G4
Wheal Frances Cornw'l 4 E5
Wheal Rose Cornw'l 4 G4
Wheal Vor Cornw'l 2 C4
Wheatacre Norfolk 143 E9
Wheatcroft Derby 170 D5
Wheatenhurst Glos 80 D3
Wheatfield Oxon 83 F11
Wheathampstead Herts 85 C11
Wheathill Shrops 132 G2
Wheathill Som'set 44 G5
Wheatley Devon 14 C4
Wheatley Hants 49 E9
Wheatley Oxon 83 D9
Wheatley S Yorks 198 G5
Wheatley W Yorks 196 B5
Wheatley Hill Durham 234 D3
Wheatley Hill W Yorks 197 F9
Wheatley Hills S Yorks 198 G6
Wheatley Lane Lancs 204 F2
Wheatley Park S Yorks 198 G5
Wheaton Aston Staffs 150 G6
Wheatridge Glos 80 B5
Wheddon Cross Som'set 42 F2
Wheedlemont Aberds 302 G4
Wheelbarrow Town Kent 54 D6
Wheelerend Common Bucks 84 G4
Wheelerstreet Surrey 50 E2
Wheelock Ches 168 D3
Wheelock Heath Ches 168 D3
Wheelton Lancs 194 C6
Wheen Angus 292 F5
Wheldale W Yorks 198 B3

Wheldrake C/York 207 D9
Whelford Glos 81 F11
Whelley Gtr Man 194 F5
Whelp Street Suffolk 107 B8
Whelpley Hill Bucks 85 E7
Whelpo Cumb 230 D2
Whelprigg Cumb 212 C2
Whelston Flints 182 F2
Whenby N Yorks 216 F2
Whepstead Suffolk 124 F6
Wherry Town Cornw'l 1 D5
Wherstead Suffolk 108 C3
Wherwell Hants 47 E11
Wheston Derby 185 F10
Whetley Cross Dorset 29 G7
Whetsted Kent 53 D7
Whetstone Leics 135 D11
Whetstone London 86 G3
Whicham Cumb 210 C2
Whichford Warwick 100 E6
Whickham Tyne/Wear 242 E6
Whickham Fell Tyne/Wear 242 F6
Whiddon Devon 40 G5
Whiddon Down Devon 13 C9
Whifflet N Lanarks 268 C4
Whigstreet Angus 287 C8
Whilton Northants 120 E2
Whiltonlocks Northants 120 E2
Whimble Devon 24 G5
Whimple Devon 14 B6
Whimpwell Green Norfolk 161 D7
Whin Lane End Lancs 202 E3
Whinburgh Norfolk 141 B10
Whinfield D'lington 224 B6
Whinhall N Lanarks 268 B5
Whinmoor W Yorks 206 F3
Whinney Hill S Yorks 187 C7
Whinnieliggate Dumf/Gal 237 D9
Whinny Heights Blackb'n 195 B7
Whinny Hill D'lington 225 B7
Whinny Hill Notts 171 B9
Whinnyfold Aberds 303 F10
Whins of Milton Stirl 278 C5
Whins Wood W Yorks 205 F7
Whipcott Devon 27 D9
Whippingham I/Wight 20 C6
Whipps Cross London 67 B11
Whipsiderry Cornw'l 4 C6
Whipsnade Beds 85 B8
Whipsnade Wild Animal Park, Dunstable Beds 85 B8
Whipton Devon 14 C4
Whirley Grove Ches 184 F5
Whirlow S Yorks 186 E4
Whirlow Brook S Yorks 186 E4
Whisby Lincs 172 B6
Whissendine Rutl'd 154 G6
Whissenthorpe Leics 154 G5
Whissonsett Norfolk 159 E8
Whisterfield Ches 184 G4
Whistlefield Arg/Bute 276 C4
Whistley Green Wokingham 65 E10
Whiston Mersey 183 C7
Whiston Northants 121 E7
Whiston Staffs 151 G7
Whiston Staffs 169 F8
Whiston S Yorks 187 D7
Whiston Cross Mersey 183 C7
Whitacre Heath Warwick 134 E4
Whitbeck Cumb 210 C2
Whitbourne Heref'd 116 F4
Whitbourne Ford Heref'd 116 F4
Whitbread Hop Farm, Beltring Kent 53 D7
Whitburn Tyne/Wear 243 E10
Whitburn W Loth 269 C8
Whitburn Colliery Tyne/Wear 243 E10
Whitby Ches 182 F5
Whitby N Yorks 227 C8
Whitby Abbey N Yorks 227 C8
Whitbyheath Ches 182 G5
Whitchurch Bucks 102 G6
Whitchurch Bristol 60 F6
Whitchurch Card 59 D7
Whitchurch Devon 12 G5
Whitchurch Hants 48 D3
Whitchurch Heref'd 79 B8
Whitchurch Oxon 64 D6
Whitchurch Pembs 90 F5
Whitchurch Shrops 167 G8
Whitchurch Warwick 100 B4
Whitchurch Cannonicorum Dorset 16 B3
Whitchurch Hill Oxon 64 D6
Whitcombe Dorset 17 D10
Whitcott Keysett Shrops 130 G5
White Ball Devon 27 D9
White Colne Essex 107 F7
White Cross Bath/NE Som'set 44 B6
White Cross Cornw'l 2 E5
White Cross Cornw'l 5 D7
White Cross Heref'd 97 C9
White Cross Wilts 45 G9
White End Glos 98 F6
White Gate Gtr Man 195 G11
White Hill Wilts 45 G10
White Hills Northants 120 E4
White Horse Common Norfolk 160 D6
White House Suffolk 108 B2
White Houses Notts 188 F2
White Kirkley Durham 232 D6
White Lackington Dorset 17 B10
White Ladies Aston Worcs 117 G8
White Lee W Yorks 197 B8
White Lund Lancs 211 G8
White Mill Carms 93 G9
White Moor Derby 170 F5
White Moss Cumb 239 E11
White Ness Shetl'd 315 J5
White Notley Essex 88 B3
White Ox Mead Bath/NE Som'set 45 B8
White Pit Lincs 190 F5
White Post Notts 171 D10
White Post Farm Centre, Farnsfield Notts 171 D10
White Rocks Heref'd 97 G8
White Roding Essex 87 C9
White Stake Lancs 194 B4
White Stone Heref'd 97 C11
White Waltham Windsor 65 D11
Whiteacen Moray 302 E2
Whiteacre Kent 54 D6
Whiteash Green Essex 106 E5
Whitebirk Blackb'n 195 B8
Whitebog H'land 301 C7
Whitebridge H'land 290 B6
Whitebrook Monmouths 79 D8
Whiteburn Scot Borders 271 F11
Whitecairn Dumf/Gal 236 D4
Whitecairns Aberds 293 B11
Whitecastle S Lanarks 269 G10
Whitechapel Lancs 203 E7
Whitechapel London 67 C10
Whitechurch Som'set 30 C2
Whitecleat Orkney 313 H6
Whitecliff Glos 79 C9
Whiteclosegate Cumb 239 F10
Whitecote W Yorks 205 F10
Whitecraigs E Renf 267 D11
Whitecroft Glos 79 D10
Whitecrook Renf 267 B10
Whitecross Cornw'l 10 G5
Whitecross Cornw'l 2 C2
Whitecross Dorset 16 B5
Whitecross Falk 279 F9
Whitecross Staffs 151 E7
Whitecross Green Oxon 83 C9
Whiteface H'land 309 L7
Whitefarland N Ayrs 255 C9
Whitefaulds S Ayrs 245 B7
Whitefield Aberds 303 G7
Whitefield Dorset 18 C4
Whitefield Gtr Man 195 F10
Whitefield Perth/Kinr 286 D5
Whitefield Som'set 27 B9
Whitefield Lane End Mersey 183 D7
Whitefield Lane End Mersey 183 D7
Whiteford Aberds 303 G7
Whitegate Ches 167 B10
Whitehall Devon 27 E10
Whitehall Devon 40 F4
Whitehall Hants 49 C8
Whitehall Herts 104 E6
Whitehall Lancs 195 C7
Whitehall W Sussex 35 C10
Whitehall Village Orkney 312 F7
Whitehaven Cumb 219 B9
Whitehaven Shrops 148 E5
Whiteheath Gate W Midlands 133 F9
Whitehill E Sussex 37 B8
Whitehill Hants 49 G9
Whitehill Kent 54 B4
Whitehill Midloth 271 B7
Whitehill Moray 302 D5
Whitehill S Lanarks 268 D4
Whitehills Aberds 302 C6
Whitehills S Lanarks 268 E2
Whitehills Tyne/Wear 243 E7
Whitehough Derby 185 E8
Whitehouse Aberds 293 B8
Whitehouse Arg/Bute 275 G9
Whitehouse Common W Midlands 134 D2
Whitehouse Green W Berks 65 F7
Whiteinch Glasg C 267 B10
Whitekirk E Loth 281 E11
Whiteknights Reading 65 E8
Whiteknowes Aberds 293 C7
Whitelackington Som'set 28 D5
Whitelaw S Lanarks 268 G2
Whiteleaf Bucks 84 E4
Whiteleas Tyne/Wear 243 E9
Whiteleaved Oak Heref'd 98 D5
White-le-Head Durham 242 G5
Whiteless S Ayrs 257 C9
Whiteley Bank I/Wight 21 E7
Whiteley Green Ches 184 F6
Whiteley Village Surrey 66 G5
Whitelye Monmouths 79 E8
Whitemans Green W Sussex 36 B4
Whitemire Moray 301 D9
Whitemoor Nott'ham 171 G8
Whitemoor Cornw'l 5 D9
Whitenap Hants 32 C5
Whiteoak Green Oxon 82 C4
Whiteparish Wilts 32 C3
Whiterashes Aberds 303 G8
Whiterow H'land 310 E7
Whites Som'set 43 G10
Whiteshill Glos 80 D4
Whiteshill S Glos 60 D6
Whiteside W Loth 269 B9
Whitesmith E Sussex 37 E8
Whitestaunton Som'set 28 E3
Whitestone Devon 14 C3
Whitestone Aberds 293 D8
Whitestone Devon 40 D3
Whitestone Warwick 135 F7
Whitestone Cross Devon 14 C4
Whitestones Aberds 303 D8
Whitestreet Green Suffolk 107 D9
Whitewall Common Monmouths 60 B2
Whitewall Corner N Yorks 216 E5
Whiteway Bath/NE Som'set 61 G8
Whiteway Glos 80 F4
Whiteway Glos 80 C6
Whitewayhead Shrops 115 C11
Whitewell Aberds 303 C9
Whitewell H'land 291 C11
Whitewell Lancs 203 D9
Whitewell Bottom Lancs 195 C10
Whiteworks Devon 13 G8
Whitfield Heref'd 97 G11
Whitfield Kent 55 D10
Whitfield Northants 102 D2
Whitfield Northum 241 F7
Whitfield S Glos 79 G11
Whitfield Stoke 168 E4
Whitford Devon 15 B11
Whitford Flints 181 F10
Whitgift ER Yorks 199 C10
Whitgreave Staffs 151 D7
Whithebeir Orkney 312 E6
Whithorn Dumf/Gal 236 E6
Whiting Bay N Ayrs 256 D2
Whitkirk W Yorks 206 G3
Whitland = Hendy-Gwyn Carms 73 B11
Whitle Derby 185 D7
Whitlea Northum 243 B7
Whitleigh Plym'th 7 C9
Whitletts S Ayrs 257 E9
Whitley Gtr Man 194 F5
Whitley N Yorks 198 C5
Whitley Reading 65 E8
Whitley Wilts 61 F11
Whitley W Midlands 119 B7
Whitley Bay Tyne/Wear 243 C9
Whitley Chapel Northum 241 F10
Whitley Heath Staffs 150 D6
Whitley Lower W Yorks 197 D8
Whitley Reed Ches 183 E10
Whitley Row Kent 52 C4
Whitley Thorpe N Yorks 198 C5
Whitley Woood Reading 65 F8
Whitlock's End W Midlands 118 B2
Whitminster Glos 80 D3
Whitmoor Devon 27 E9
Whitmore Dorset 31 F9
Whitmore Staffs 168 G4
Whitmore Heath Staffs 168 G3
Whitmore Park W Midlands 134 G6
Whitnage Devon 27 D8
Whitnash Warwick 118 E6
Whitnell Som'set 43 F8
Whitney Bottom Som'set 28 E4
Whitney-on-Wye Heref'd 96 B5
Whitrigg Cumb 229 D10
Whitrigg Cumb 238 F6
Whitsbury Hants 31 D10
Whitsome Scot Borders 273 E7
Whitsomehill Scot Borders 273 F7
Whitson Newp 59 C11
Whitstable Kent 70 F6
Whitstone Cornw'l 11 B11
Whittaker Gtr Man 196 D2
Whittingham Northum 264 G3
Whittingslow Shrops 131 F8
Whittington Glos 99 G10
Whittington Lancs 212 D2
Whittington Norfolk 140 D4
Whittington Shrops 148 C6
Whittington Staffs 133 G7
Whittington Staffs 134 B3
Whittington Warwick 134 D5
Whittington Moor Derby 186 G5
Whittle Hill Gtr Man 195 F10
Whittlebury Northants 102 C3
Whittleford Warwick 134 E6
Whittle-le-Woods Lancs 194 C5
Whittlesey Cambs 138 D5
Whittlesford Cambs 105 B9
Whittlestone Head Blackb'n 195 D8
Whitton Scot Borders 263 E7
Whitton London 66 E6
Whitton N Lincs 200 C2
Whitton Northum 252 C3
Whitton Powys 114 D5
Whitton Shrops 115 C11
Whitton Suffolk 108 B2
Whitton Stockton 234 G3
Whittonditch Wilts 63 E9
Whittonstall Northum 242 F3
Whitway Hants 48 B3
Whitwell Derby 187 G9
Whitwell Herts 104 G3
Whitwell I/Wight 20 F6
Whitwell N Yorks 224 F5
Whitwell Rutl'd 137 B8
Whitwell Common Norfolk 159 E11
Whitwell Street Norfolk 160 E2
Whitwell-on-the-Hill N Yorks 216 F4
Whitwick Leics 153 F8
Whitwood W Yorks 198 C2
Whitworth Lancs 195 D11
Whixall Shrops 149 C10
Whixley N Yorks 206 B4
Whoberley W Midlands 118 B6
Wholeflats Falk 279 E8
Whome Orkney 313 J4
Whorlton Durham 224 C2
Whorlton N Yorks 225 E9
Whydown E Sussex 38 F2
Whyke W Sussex 34 G5
Whyle Heref'd 115 E11
Whyteleafe Surrey 51 B11
Wibsey W Yorks 205 G8
Wibtoft Warwick 135 F9
Wichenford Worcs 116 E5
Wichling Kent 54 B2
Wick Bournem'th 19 C9
Wick Devon 27 G11
Wick H'land 310 D7
Wick Shetl'd 315 K6
Wick S Glos 61 E8
Wick Som'set 43 E8
Wick Som'set 28 B6
Wick Som'set 44 F4
Wick Som'set 43 C10
Wick V/Glam 58 E2
Wick Wilts 31 C11
Wick Worcs 99 B9
Wick W Sussex 35 G8
Wick Airport H'land 313 N4
Wick End Beds 121 G9
Wick Hill Brackn'l 65 E11
Wick Hill Kent 53 E10
Wick Hill Wokingham 65 G10
Wick Hill Wilts 62 E3
Wick St. Lawrence N Som'set 59 F11
Wick Street Glos 80 D5
Wicken Cambs 123 C11
Wicken Northants 102 D4
Wicken Bonhunt Essex 105 E10
Wicken Green Village Norfolk 158 C6
Wickenby Lincs 189 E9
Wicker Street Green Suffolk 107 C9
Wickersley S Yorks 187 C7
Wickford Essex 88 G2
Wickham Hants 33 E9
Wickham W Berks 63 E11
Wickham Bishops Essex 88 C4
Wickham Green Suffolk 125 D11
Wickham Green W Berks 63 E11
Wickham Heath W Berks 64 F2
Wickham Market Suffolk 126 F5
Wickham St. Paul Essex 106 D6
Wickham Skeith Suffolk 125 D11
Wickham Street Suffolk 125 D11
Wickham Street Suffolk 124 G5
Wickhambreaux Kent 55 B8
Wickhambrook Suffolk 124 G4
Wickhamford Worcs 99 C11
Wickhampton Norfolk 143 B8
Wicklane Bath/NE Som'set 45 B7
Wicklewood Norfolk 141 C11
Wickmere Norfolk 160 C3
Wickridge Street Glos 98 F6
Wicksgreen Glos 80 C3
Wicksteed Park, Kettering Northants 121 B7
Wickstreet E Sussex 23 D8
Wickwar S Glos 61 B8
Widcombe Bath/NE Som'set 61 G9
Widcombe Som'set 28 D2
Widdenham Wilts 61 E10
Widdington Essex 105 E10
Widdop W Yorks 204 G4
Widdrington Northum 253 D7
Widdrington Station Northum 252 E6
Wide Open Tyne/Wear 242 C6
Widecocmbe in the Moor Devon 13 F10
Widegate's Cornw'l 6 D5
Widemarsh Heref'd 97 C10
Widemouth Bay Cornw'l 24 G2
Widewall Orkney 313 J5
Widewell Plym'th 7 C9
Widford Essex 87 E11
Widford Herts 86 B6
Widford Oxon 82 C3
Widham Wilts 62 B5
Widley Hants 33 F11
Widmer End Bucks 84 F5
Widmerpool Notts 154 D2
Widnes Halton 183 E8
Widworthy Devon 15 B10
Wig Powys 130 F2
Wigan Gtr Man 194 F5
Wigan Pier Gtr Man 194 G5
Wigbeth Dorset 31 F8
Wigborough Som'set 28 D6
Wig-Fach Bridg 57 F10
Wiggaton Devon 15 C8
Wiggenhall St. Germans Norfolk 157 G11
Wiggenhall St. Mary Magdalen Norfolk 157 G11
Wiggenhall St. Mary the Virgin Norfolk 157 G11
Wiggenhall St. Peter Norfolk 158 G2
Wiggens Green Essex 106 C3
Wigginton C/York 207 B7
Wigginton Herts 84 C6
Wigginton Oxon 101 E7
Wigginton Staffs 134 B4
Wigginton Bottom Herts 84 D6
Wigglesworth N Yorks 204 B2
Wiggonby Cumb 239 G7
Wiggonholt W Sussex 35 D9
Wighill N Yorks 206 D5
Wighton Norfolk 176 E6
Wightwick W Midlands 133 D7
Wigley Hants 32 D4
Wigmore Heref'd 115 D8
Wigmore Medway 69 G10
Wigsley Notts 188 G5
Wigsthorpe Northants 137 G10
Wigston Leics 136 D2
Wigston Fields Leics C 135 C11
Wigston Harcourt Leics 136 D2
Wigston Magna Leics 136 D2
Wigston Parva Leics 135 F9
Wigthorpe Notts 187 E9
Wigtoft Lincs 156 B5
Wigton Cumb 229 B11
Wigtown Dumf/Gal 236 D6
Wîg Powys 147 G11
Wike W Yorks 206 E2
Wike Well End S Yorks 199 E7
Wilbarston Northants 136 F6
Wilberfoss ER Yorks 207 C10
Wilberlee W Yorks 196 E5
Wilburton Cambs 123 C9
Wilby Norfolk 141 F10
Wilby Northants 121 D7
Wilby Suffolk 126 C4
Wilcot Wilts 62 G6
Wilcot Green Wilts 62 G6
Wilcott Shrops 149 F7
Wilcrick Newp 60 B2
Wild Mill Bridg 58 C2
Wildboarclough Ches 169 B7
Wilde Street Suffolk 124 B4
Wilden Beds 121 F11
Wilden Worcs 116 C6
Wildern Hants 33 E7
Wildernesse Kent 52 B4
Wilderspool Warrington 183 D10
Wildfowl and Wetland Centre, Martin Mere Lancs 194 E2
Wildhern Hants 47 C11
Wildhill Herts 86 D3
Wildlife & Dinosaur Park, Combe Martin Devon 40 E6
Wildmanbridge S Lanarks 268 E6
Wildmoor Hants 49 B7
Wildmoor Oxon 83 F7
Wildmoor Worcs 117 B9
Wildridings Brackn'l 65 F11
Wildsworth Lincs 188 B4
Wildwood Staffs 151 E8
Wilford Notts 153 B11
Wilkesley Ches 167 G10
Wilkhaven H'land 311 L3
Wilkieston W Loth 270 B2
Wilkin Throop Som'set 29 C11
Wilksby Lincs 174 C3
Willacy Lane End Lancs 202 F5
Willand Devon 27 E8
Willand Som'set 27 E11
Willand Moor Devon 27 E8
Willards Hill E Sussex 38 C2
Willaston Ches 167 E11
Willaston Ches 182 F4
Willaston Shrops 149 B11
Willen M/Keynes 103 C7
Willenhall W Midlands 133 D9
Willenhall W Midlands 119 B7
Willerby ER Yorks 208 G6
Willerby N Yorks 217 D10
Willersey Glos 100 D2
Willersley Heref'd 96 B6
Willesborough Kent 54 E4
Willesborough Lees Kent 54 E4
Willesden London 67 B8
Willesden Green London 67 C8
Willesleigh Devon 40 G5
Willesley Glos 61 B11
Willestrew Devon 12 F4
Willett Som'set 42 G6
Willey Shrops 132 D3
Willey Warwick 135 G9
Willey Green Surrey 50 C3
William Herts 104 E4
William's Green Suffolk 107 C9
Williamscot Oxon 101 B9
Williamstown Rh Cyn Taff 77 G8
Williamthorpe Derby 170 B6
Williamwood E Renf 267 D11
Willingale Essex 87 D9
Willingcott Devon 40 E3
Willingdon E Sussex 23 E9
Willingham Cambs 123 B8
Willingham by Stow Lincs 188 D5
Willingham Green Cambs 124 G2
Willington Beds 104 B2
Willington Derby 152 D5
Willington Durham 233 D9
Willington Kent 53 C9
Willington Tyne/Wear 243 D8
Willington Warwick 100 D5
Willington Corner Ches 167 B8
Willington Quay Tyne/Wear 243 D8
Willisham Suffolk 125 G11
Willisham Tye Suffolk 125 G11
Willitoft ER Yorks 207 F10
Williton Som'set 42 E5
Willoughbridge Staffs 168 G2
Willoughby Lincs 191 G7
Willoughby Warwick 119 D10
Willoughby Hills Lincs 174 F5
Willoughby on the Wolds Notts 154 D2
Willoughby Waterleys Leics 135 E11
Willoughton Lincs 188 C6
Willoughton Cliff Lincs 188 C6
Willow Green Ches 183 F10
Willow Holme Cumb 239 F9
Willowbank Bucks 66 B5
Willows Gtr Man 195 F8
Willows Green Essex 88 B2
Willsbridge S Glos 61 E7
Willslock Staffs 151 C11
Willtown Som'set 28 C5
Wilmcote Warwick 118 F3
Wilmington Bath/NE Som'set 61 G7
Wilmington Devon 15 B10
Wilmington E Sussex 23 E9
Wilmington Kent 68 E4
Wilminstone Devon 12 F5
Wilmslow Ches 184 E4
Wilmslow Park Ches 184 E5
Wilnecote Staffs 134 C4
Wilney Green Norfolk 141 G11
Wilpshire Lancs 203 G9
Wilsden W Yorks 205 F7
Wilsford Lincs 173 G8
Wilsford Wilts 46 F6
Wilsford Wilts 46 B5
Wilshaw W Yorks 196 F6
Wilsill N Yorks 214 G3
Wilsley Green Kent 53 F9
Wilsley Pound Kent 53 F9
Wilsom Hants 49 F8
Wilson Heref'd 97 G11
Wilson Leics 153 E8
Wilsontown S Lanarks 269 D8
Wilstead Beds 103 C11
Wilsthorpe Derby 153 C9
Wilsthorpe Lincs 155 G11
Wilstone Herts 84 C6
Wilstone Green Herts 84 C6
Wilthorpe S Yorks 197 F10
Wilton Scot Borders 261 G11
Wilton Cumb 219 C10
Wilton Heref'd 97 G11
Wilton N Yorks 217 C7
Wilton Redcar/Clevel'd 225 B11
Wilton Som'set 28 C2
Wilton Wilts 63 G9
Wilton Wilts 46 G5
Wilton House, Salisbury Wilts 46 G5
Wiltown Devon 27 D11
Wimbish Essex 105 D11
Wimbish Green Essex 106 D2
Wimblebury Staffs 151 G10
Wimbledon London 67 E8
Wimbledon All England Tennis Club London 67 E8
Wimblington Cambs 139 E8
Wimborne Minster Dorset 18 B6
Wimborne Minster Dorset 18 B6
Wimborne St. Giles Dorset 31 E8
Wimbotsham Norfolk 140 B2
Wimpole Hall and Home Farm, Royston Cambs 122 G6
Wimpson S'thampton 32 E5
Wimpstone Warwick 100 B4
Wincanton Som'set 30 B2
Wincanton Racecourse Som'set 45 G8
Winceby Lincs 174 B4
Winch Fawr Merth Tyd 77 D8
Wincham Ches 183 F11
Winchburgh W Loth 279 F11
Winchcombe Glos 99 F10
Winchelsea E Sussex 38 D6
Winchelsea Beach E Sussex 38 D6
Winchester Hants 33 B7
Winchester Cathedral Hants 33 B7
Winchestown Bl Gwent 77 C11
Winchet Hill Kent 53 E8
Winchfield Hants 49 C9
Winchmore Hill Bucks 84 F6
Winchmore Hill London 86 G4
Wincle Ches 169 B7
Wincobank S Yorks 186 C5
Wincombe Wilts 30 C5
Wind Mill Durham 233 F8
Windcross Glos 98 E3
Winder Cumb 219 B10
Windermere Cumb 221 F8
Winderton Warwick 100 C6
Windfallwood Common W Sussex 34 B6
Windhill H'land 300 E5
Windhill S Yorks 198 G3
Windhill W Yorks 205 F9
Windhouse Shetl'd 314 D6
Windle Hill Ches 182 F4
Windlehurst Gtr Man 185 D7
Windlesham Surrey 66 G2
Windley Derby 170 F4
Windmill Cornw'l 10 G3
Windmill Derby 185 F11
Windmill Hill Bristol 60 E5
Windmill Hill E Sussex 37 E11
Windmill Hill Halton 183 E9
Windmill Hill Kent 69 F10
Windmill Hill Som'set 28 D4
Windmill Hill S Yorks 198 F2
Windmill Hill Worcs 99 B8
Windmill Hill W Yorks 197 E11
Windrush Glos 81 C11
Windsor N Lincs 199 E9
Windsor Windsor 66 D2
Windsor Castle Windsor 66 D3
Windsor Green Suffolk 125 G7
Windsor Racecourse Windsor 66 D2
Windsoredge Glos 80 E4
Windy Arbor Mersey 183 D7
Windy Arbour Warwick 118 C5
Windy Hill Wrex 166 E4
Windy Nook Tyne/Wear 243 E7
Windygates Fife 287 G7
Windyharbour Ches 184 G4
Windyknowe W Loth 269 B9
Windywalls Scot Borders 263 C7
Wineham W Sussex 36 C2
Winestead ER Yorks 201 C9
Winewall Lancs 204 F4
Winfarthing Norfolk 142 F2
Winford I/Wight 21 E7
Winford N Som'set 60 F4
Winforton Heref'd 96 B5
Winfrith Newburgh Dorset 18 E2
Wing Bucks 103 G7
Wing Rutl'd 137 C7
Wingate Durham 234 D3
Wingates Gtr Man 195 F7
Wingates Northum 252 D4
Wingerworth Derby 170 B5
Wingfield Beds 103 F10
Wingfield Suffolk 126 B4
Wingfield S Yorks 186 C6
Wingfield Wilts 45 B10
Wingfield Green Suffolk 126 B4
Wingfield Park Derby 170 E5
Wingham Kent 55 B8
Wingham Green Kent 55 B8
Wingham Well Kent 55 B8
Wingmore Kent 55 D7
Wingrave Bucks 84 B5
Winkburn Notts 172 D2
Winkfield Brackn'l 66 E2
Winkfield Row Brackn'l 65 E11
Winkfield Street Brackn'l 66 E2
Winkhill Lincs 173 F10
Winkhill Staffs 169 E9
Winkhurst Green Kent 52 D3
Winklebury Hants 48 C6
Winkleigh Devon 25 F10
Winksley N Yorks 214 E4
Winkton Dorset 19 B9
Winkton Common Dorset 19 C9
Winlaton Tyne/Wear 242 E5
Winlaton Mill Tyne/Wear 242 E5
Winless H'land 310 D7
Winmarleigh Lancs 202 D5
Winnal Heref'd 97 E9
Winnal Common Heref'd 97 E9
Winnall Worcs 116 D6
Winnersh Wokingham 65 E9
Winnington Ches 183 G10
Winnington Shrops 148 G6
Winnothdale Staffs 169 G8
Winscales Cumb 228 F6
Winscombe N Som'set 44 B2
Winsdon Hill Luton 103 G11
Winsford Ches 167 B11
Winsford Som'set 42 G2
Winsham Devon 40 F3
Winsham Som'set 28 F5
Winshill Staffs 152 E5
Winsh-wen Swan 75 F11
Winsick Derby 170 B6
Winskill Cumb 231 E7
Winslade Hants 48 D6
Winsley N Yorks 214 G4
Winsley Wilts 61 G10
Winslow Bucks 102 F5
Winson Glos 81 D9
Winson Green W Midlands 133 F10
Winsor Hants 32 E4
Winstanley Gtr Man 194 G5
Winster Cumb 221 G8
Winster Derby 170 C2
Winston Durham 224 B2
Winston Suffolk 126 E3
Winston Green Suffolk 126 E3
Winstone Glos 81 D7
Winswell Devon 25 E7
Winter Gardens Essex 69 C9
Winter Well Som'set 28 C3
Winterborne Clenston Dorset 30 G4
Winterborne Herrington Dorset 17 D9
Winterborne Houghton Dorset 30 G4
Winterborne Kingston Dorset 18 B3
Winterborne Monkton Dorset 17 D9
Winterborne Stickland Dorset 30 G4
Winterborne Whitechurch Dorset 30 G4
Winterborne Zelston Dorset 18 B3
Winterbourne S Glos 60 B6
Winterbourne W Berks 64 E2
Winterbourne Abbas Dorset 17 C8
Winterbourne Bassett Wilts 62 D5
Winterbourne Dauntsey Wilts 47 G7
Winterbourne Down S Glos 61 D7
Winterbourne Earls Wilts 47 G7
Winterbourne Gunner Wilts 47 F7
Winterbourne Monkton Wilts 62 E5
Winterbourne Steepleton Dorset 17 D8
Winterbourne Stoke Wilts 46 E5
Winterbrook Oxon 64 B5
Winterburn N Yorks 204 B4
Winterhay Green Som'set 28 D5
Winteringham N Lincs 200 C2
Winterley Ches 168 D2
Wintersett W Yorks 197 E11
Wintershill Hants 33 D8
Winterton N Lincs 200 D2
Winterton-on-Sea Norfolk 161 F9
Winthorpe Lincs 175 B9
Winthorpe Notts 172 D4
Winton Bournem'th 19 C7
Winton Cumb 222 C5
Winton E Sussex 23 E8
Winton Gtr Man 184 B3
Winton N Yorks 225 F8
Wintringham N Yorks 217 E7
Winwick Cambs 138 G2
Winwick Northants 120 C2
Winwick Warrington 183 C10
Winwick Quay Warrington 183 C9
Winyates Worcs 117 D11
Winyates Green Worcs 117 D11
Wirksworth Derby 170 E3
Wirksworth Moor Derby 170 E4
Wirswall Ches 167 G8
Wisbech Cambs 139 B9
Wisbech St. Mary Cambs 139 B8
Wisborough Green W Sussex 35 B8
Wiseton Notts 188 D2
Wishanger Glos 80 D6
Wishaw N Lanarks 268 E5
Wishaw Warwick 134 E2
Wisley Surrey 50 B5
Wispington Lincs 190 G2
Wissenden Kent 54 E2
Wissett Suffolk 127 B7
Wistanstow Shrops 131 F8
Wistanswick Shrops 150 D3
Wistaston Ches 167 E11
Wistaston Green Ches 167 E11
Wiston Pembs 73 B8
Wiston S Lanarks 259 C11
Wiston W Sussex 35 E10
Wistow Cambs 138 G5
Wistow Leics 136 D2
Wistow N Yorks 207 F7
Wistow Lordship N Yorks 207 F8
Wiswell Lancs 203 F10
Witcham Cambs 123 B9
Witchampton Dorset 31 F7
Witchford Cambs 123 B9
Witcombe Som'set 29 C7
Withacott Devon 24 D6
Witham Essex 88 C4
Witham Friary Som'set 45 E8
Witham on the Hill Lincs 155 F11
Witham St. Hughes Lincs 172 C5
Withcall Lincs 190 E3
Withdean Brighton/Hove 36 F4
Withecombe Devon 13 D9
Witherenden Hill E Sussex 37 B10
Withergate Norfolk 160 D5
Witheridge Devon 26 E4
Witheridge Hill Oxon 65 C7
Witherley Leics 134 D6
Withermarsh Green Suffolk 107 D10
Withern Lincs 190 E6
Withernsea ER Yorks 201 B10
Withernwick ER Yorks 209 E9
Withersdale Street Suffolk 142 G5
Withersdane Kent 54 D5
Withersfield Suffolk 106 B3
Witherslack Cumb 211 C9
Witherwack Tyne/Wear 243 F9
Withiel Cornw'l 5 B9
Withiel Florey Som'set 42 G3
Withielgoose Mills Cornw'l 5 B10
Withington Ches 168 B4
Withington Glos 81 B8
Withington Gtr Man 184 C5
Withington Heref'd 97 C11
Withington Shrops 149 G11
Withington Staffs 151 B10
Withington Green Ches 184 G4
Withington Marsh Heref'd 97 C11
Withleigh Devon 26 E6
Withnell Lancs 194 C6
Withnell Fold Lancs 194 C6
Withybrook Som'set 45 D7
Withybrook Warwick 135 G8
Withybush Pembs 73 B7
Withycombe Som'set 42 E4
Withycombe Raleigh Devon 14 E6
Withyditch Bath/NE Som'set 45 B8
Withyham E Sussex 52 F3
Withymoor Village W Midlands 133 F8
Withypool Som'set 41 F10
Withywood Bristol 60 F5
Witley Surrey 50 F2
Witnell's End Worcs 132 G5
Witnesham Suffolk 126 G3
Witney Oxon 82 C5
Witney Green Essex 87 D9
Wittensford Hants 32 E3
Wittering Peterbro 137 C11
Wittersham Kent 38 B5
Witton Angus 293 F7
Witton Norfolk 142 B6
Witton Worcs 117 E7
Witton Bridge Norfolk 160 C6
Witton Gilbert Durham 233 B10
Witton le Wear Durham 233 E8
Witton Park Durham 233 E9
Wiveliscombe Som'set 27 B9
Wivelrod Hants 49 F7
Wivelsfield E Sussex 36 C4
Wivelsfield Green E Sussex 36 D5
Wivenhoe Essex 107 G10
Wivenhoe Cross Essex 107 G10
Wiveton Norfolk 177 E8
Wix Essex 108 F3
Wixford Warwick 117 G11

Wixhill Shrops 149 D11
Wixhoe Suffolk 106 C4
Woath Dorset 16 B5
Woburn Beds 103 E8
Woburn Abbey, Woburn Beds 103 E9
Woburn Sands M/Keynes 103 D8
Woburn Wild Animal Kingdom Beds 103 E9
Wofferwood Common Heref'd 116 G3
Woking Surrey 50 B4
Wokingham Wokingham 65 F10
Wolborough Devon 14 G3
Wold Newton ER Yorks 217 E10
Wold Newton NE Lincs 190 B2
Woldingham Surrey 51 B11
Woldingham Garden Village Surrey 51 B11
Wolferlow Heref'd 116 E3
Wolferton Norfolk 158 D3
Wolfhampcote Warwick 119 D10
Wolfhill Perth/Kinr 286 D5
Wolf's Castle Pembs 91 F9
Wolfsdale Pembs 91 G8
Woll Scot Borders 261 E11
Wollaston Northants 121 E8
Wollaston Shrops 148 G6
Wollaston W Midlands 133 G7
Wollaton Nott'ham 153 B10
Wollaton Hall Nott'ham 153 B10
Wolleigh Devon 14 F2
Wollescote W Midlands 133 G8
Wolsingham Durham 233 D7
Wolstanton Staffs 168 F5
Wolstenholme Gtr Man 195 E11
Wolston Warwick 119 B8
Wolsty Cumb 238 G4
Wolterton Norfolk 160 C3
Wolvercote Oxon 83 D7
Wolverham Ches 182 F6
Wolverhampton W Midlands 133 D8
Wolverhampton Racecourse W Midlands 133 C8
Wolverley Shrops 149 C9
Wolverley Worcs 116 B6
Wolverstone Devon 27 G10
Wolverton Hants 48 B5
Wolverton Kent 55 E9
Wolverton M/Keynes 102 C6
Wolverton Shrops 131 F9
Wolverton Warwick 118 E4
Wolverton Wilts 45 G9
Wolverton Common Hants 48 B5
Wolverton Mill M/Keynes 102 C6
Wolvesnewton Monmouths 79 F7
Wolvey Warwick 135 F8
Wolvey Heath Warwick 135 F8
Wolviston Stockton 234 F4
Womaston Powys 114 E5
Wombleton N Yorks 216 C3
Wombourn Staffs 133 E7
Wombridge Telford 150 G3
Wombwell S Yorks 197 G11
Womenswold Kent 55 C8
Womersley N Yorks 198 D4
Wonderstone N Som'set 43 B10
Wonersh Surrey 50 D4
Wonford Devon 14 C4
Wonson Devon 13 D9
Wonston Dorset 30 F2
Wonston Hants 48 F3
Wooburn Bucks 66 B2
Wooburn Common Bucks 66 B2
Wooburn Green Bucks 66 B2
Wooburn Moor Bucks 66 B2
Wood Pembs 91 G7
Wood Som'set 28 D4
Wood Bevington Warwick 117 G11
Wood Burcote Northants 102 B3
Wood Dalling Norfolk 159 D11
Wood Eaton Staffs 150 F6
Wood End Beds 103 B9
Wood End Beds 103 C9
Wood End Beds 121 F11
Wood End Bucks 102 E5
Wood End Bucks 102 E5
Wood End Gtr Man 196 E2
Wood End Heref'd 98 C2
Wood End Herts 104 F6
Wood End London 66 C5
Wood End London 66 C5
Wood End Warwick 118 C2
Wood End Warwick 134 F5
Wood End Warwick 134 D4
Wood End W Midlands 135 G7
Wood End W Midlands 133 C8
Wood End Green London 66 C5
Wood Enderby Lincs 174 C3
Wood Field Surrey 51 B7
Wood Gate Staffs 152 D2
Wood Green Essex 86 F6
Wood Green London 86 G4
Wood Green Norfolk 142 E4
Wood Green W Midlands 133 D9
Wood Green Worcs 116 D6
Wood Hayes W Midlands 133 C8
Wood Hill Kent 55 D11
Wood Kirk W Yorks 197 C9
Wood Laithes S Yorks 197 G11
Wood Lane Staffs 168 E4
Wood Lanes Ches 184 E6
Wood Linkin Derby 170 F6
Wood Nook W Yorks 196 E6
Wood Norton Norfolk 159 D10
Wood Road Gtr Man 195 E9
Wood Row W Yorks 197 B11
Wood Stanway Glos 99 E11
Wood Street Norfolk 161 E7
Wood Street Surrey 50 C3
Wood Street Wilts 62 D5
Woodacott Devon 24 F5
Woodacott Cross Devon 24 F5
Woodale N Yorks 213 D10
Woodall S Yorks 187 E7
Woodbank Arg/Bute 255 F7
Woodbastwick Norfolk 160 G6
Woodbeck Notts 188 F3
Woodborough Notts 171 G11
Woodborough Wilts 46 B6
Woodbridge Dorset 30 E2
Woodbridge Devon 15 B9
Woodbridge Northum 253 F7
Woodbridge Suffolk 108 B5
Woodbridge Hill Surrey 50 C3
Woodbrook Heref'd 114 G6
Woodbury Devon 14 D6
Woodbury Salterton Devon 14 D6
Woodchester Glos 80 E4
Woodchurch Kent 54 G2
Woodchurch Mersey 182 D3
Woodcock Wilts 45 E11
Woodcock Hill Herts 85 G9
Woodcock Hill W Midlands 133 G10
Woodcombe Som'set 42 D2
Woodcote London 67 G10
Woodcote Oxon 64 C6
Woodcote Green Worcs 117 C8
Woodcott Hants 48 C2
Woodcroft Glos 79 F8
Woodcutts Dorset 31 D7
Woodditton Cambs 124 F3
Woodeaton Oxon 83 C8
Woodend Beds 103 E10
Woodend Ches 185 D7
Woodend Cumb 229 F10
Woodend Cumb 220 F3
Woodend Cumb 219 C10
Woodend Essex 87 C9
Woodend Fife 280 B4
Woodend Hants 33 E9
Woodend Halton 183 D7
Woodend Northants 102 B2
Woodend Notts 171 D7
Woodend Notts 187 G8
Woodend Staffs 152 D3
Woodend W Loth 279 F11
Woodend W Sussex 34 F4
Woodend Green Essex 105 F11
Woodend Green Northants 102 B2
Woodend Ho Arg/Bute 275 G11
Woodfalls Wilts 31 C11
Woodfield Glos 80 E2
Woodfield Oxon 101 G11
Woodfield S Ayrs 257 E8
Woodford Cornw'l 24 E2
Woodford Devon 8 E5
Woodford Glos 79 F11
Woodford Gtr Man 184 E5
Woodford London 86 G6
Woodford Northants 121 B9
Woodford Plym'th 7 D10
Woodford Som'set 42 F5
Woodford Som'set 44 E4
Woodford Bridge London 86 G6
Woodford Green London 86 G6
Woodford Halse Northants 119 G10
Woodford Wells London 86 G6
Woodgate Devon 27 D10
Woodgate Norfolk 159 F10
Woodgate W Midlands 133 G9
Woodgate Worcs 117 D9
Woodgate W Sussex 34 G6
Woodgate Hill Gtr Man 195 E10
Woodgate Valley W Midlands 133 G10
Woodgates End Essex 105 F11
Woodgreen Hants 31 D11
Woodgreen Animal Shelter, Godmanchester Cambs 122 D5
Woodhall Herts 86 C2
Woodhall Invercl 276 G6
Woodhall N Yorks 223 G9
Woodhall Hills W Yorks 205 F10
Woodhall Spa Lincs 173 C11
Woodham Durham 233 F11
Woodham Surrey 66 G4
Woodham Ferrers Essex 88 F3
Woodham Mortimer Essex 88 E4
Woodham Walter Essex 88 D4
Woodhatch Surrey 51 D9
Woodhaven Fife 287 E8
Woodhead Aberds 303 F7
Woodhey Gtr Man 195 D9
Woodhey Mersey 182 D4
Woodhey Green Ches 167 E9
Woodhill Essex 88 E3
Woodhill N Som'set 60 D3
Woodhill Shrops 132 G4
Woodhill Som'set 28 B5
Woodhorn Northum 253 F8
Woodhouse Cumb 211 C10
Woodhouse Cumb 219 B9
Woodhouse Hants 47 D11
Woodhouse Leics 153 F10
Woodhouse N Lincs 199 F9
Woodhouse S Yorks 186 D6
Woodhouse W Yorks 205 E7
Woodhouse W Yorks 197 C7
Woodhouse W Yorks 205 F11
Woodhouse W Yorks 197 C11
Woodhouse Down S Glos 60 B6
Woodhouse Eaves Leics 153 G10
Woodhouse Mill S Yorks 186 D6
Woodhouse Park Gtr Man 184 D4
Woodhouselee Midloth 270 C4
Woodhouselees Dumf/Gal 239 C9
Woodhouses Ches 183 F8
Woodhouses Cumb 239 G8
Woodhouses Durham 233 F9
Woodhouses Gtr Man 184 C3
Woodhouses Gtr Man 196 G2
Woodhouses Staffs 133 B11
Woodhouses Staffs 152 F3
Woodhurst Cambs 122 B6
Woodingdean Brighton/Hove 36 F5
Woodington Hants 32 C4
Woodlake Dorset 18 C3
Woodland Cumb 210 B4
Woodland Durham 233 F7
Woodland Devon 8 D2
Woodland Devon 8 B4
Woodland Kent 54 E6
Woodland Head Devon 13 B11
Woodland Leisure Park, Dartmouth Devon 8 E6
Woodlands Aberds 293 D9
Woodlands Aberds 303 G8
Woodlands Aberd C 293 B10
Woodlands Dumf/Gal 238 B3
Woodlands Dorset 31 F9
Woodlands Gtr Man 185 B7
Woodlands Hants 32 E4
Woodlands H'land 300 C5
Woodlands Kent 68 G5
Woodlands London 67 D7
Woodlands N Yorks 206 C2
Woodlands Som'set 43 E7
Woodlands Som'set 44 F4
Woodlands S Yorks 198 F4
Woodlands W Yorks 196 B5
Woodlands Park Windsor 65 D11
Woodlands St. Mary W Berks 63 D10
Woodlane Shrops 150 D3
Woodlane Staffs 152 E2
Woodleigh Devon 8 F4
Woodlesford W Yorks 197 C11
Woodley Devon 12 F4
Woodley Gtr Man 184 C6
Woodley Hants 32 C5
Woodley Wokingham 65 E9
Woodley Green Wokingham 65 E9
Woodleys Beds 121 E11
Woodloes Warwick 118 D5
Woodmancote Glos 80 F3
Woodmancote Glos 81 D8
Woodmancote Glos 99 F9
Woodmancote W Sussex 34 F3
Woodmancote W Sussex 36 E2
Woodmancott Hants 48 E5
Woodmansey ER Yorks 208 F7
Woodmansgreen W Sussex 34 B5
Woodmansterne Surrey 67 G9
Woodmanton Devon 14 D6
Woodmarsh Wilts 45 B10
Woodmill Staffs 152 E2
Woodminton Wilts 31 C8
Woodmoor Shrops 130 C5
Woodnesborough Kent 55 B10
Woodnewton Northants 137 E10
Woodnook Lancs 195 B9
Woodperry Oxon 83 C9
Woodplumpton Lancs 202 G6
Woodrising Norfolk 141 C9
Woodrow Cumb 229 B10
Woodrow Dorset 30 F2
Woodrow Dorset 30 E3
Woodrow Worcs 117 D11
Woods Bank W Midlands 133 D9
Wood's Corner E Sussex 37 D11
Woods Eaves Heref'd 96 B5
Woods End Gtr Man 184 B2
Wood's Green E Sussex 52 G6
Woods Hill W Sussex 35 D9
Woods Moor Gtr Man 184 D6
Woodsden Kent 53 G9
Woodseaves Shrops 150 C3
Woodseaves Staffs 150 D5
Woodsend Wilts 63 D8
Woodsetton W Midlands 133 E8
Woodsetts S Yorks 187 E9
Woodsfold Lancs 202 F5
Woodsford Dorset 17 C11
Woodside Aberds 303 E10
Woodside Aberd C 293 C11
Woodside Beds 85 B9
Woodside Beds 121 G11
Woodside Brackn'l 66 E2
Woodside Ches 183 G8
Woodside Cumb 228 E6
Woodside Derby 187 G7
Woodside Dumf/Gal 238 B2
Woodside Durham 233 F9
Woodside Essex 87 E7
Woodside Fife 280 A5
Woodside Fife 287 G8
Woodside Hants 20 C2
Woodside Herts 86 D3
Woodside Herts 85 E10
Woodside London 67 F10
Woodside Perth/Kinr 286 D6
Woodside Telford 132 C3
Woodside W Midlands 133 F8
Woodside W Yorks 196 B6
Woodside Farm and Wildfowl Park, Luton Beds 85 B9
Woodside Green Essex 87 B8
Woodside Green Kent 54 C2
Woodside of Arbeadie Aberds 293 D9
Woodside Park London 86 G2
Woodspeen W Berks 64 F2
Woodstock Kent 70 G2
Woodstock Oxon 82 B6
Woodstock Pembs 91 F10
Woodston Peterbro 138 D3
Woodthorpe C/York 207 D7
Woodthorpe Derby 187 G7
Woodthorpe Leics 153 F10
Woodthorpe Lincs 190 E6
Woodthorpe Notts 171 G9
Woodton Norfolk 142 E5
Woodtown Devon 24 C6
Woodvale Mersey 193 E10
Woodville Derby 152 F6
Woodville Dorset 30 C4
Woodville Kent 55 E9
Woodville Feus Angus 287 C10
Woodwall Green Staffs 150 C5
Woodwalls Dorset 29 F8
Woodwalton Cambs 138 G4
Woodwick Orkney 312 F4
Woodworth Green Ches 167 D9
Woody Bay Devon 41 D7
Woodyates Dorset 31 D8
Woofferton Shrops 115 D10
Wookey Som'set 44 D4
Wookey Hole Som'set 44 D4
Wookey Hole Caves & Papermill, Wells Som'set 44 D4
Wool Dorset 18 D2
Woolacombe Devon 40 E3
Woolage Green Kent 55 D8
Woolage Village Kent 55 C8
Woolaston Glos 79 F9
Woolaston Common Glos 79 E9
Woolaston Slade Glos 79 E9
Woolaston Woodside Glos 79 E9
Woolavington Som'set 43 E11
Woolbeding W Sussex 34 C5
Woolbridge E Sussex 37 B9
Wooldale W Yorks 197 F7
Wooler Northum 263 D11
Wooley Northum 241 G8
Woolfall Heath Mersey 182 C6
Woolfardisworthy Devon 26 F4
Woolfardisworthy Devon 24 C4
Woolfold Gtr Man 195 E9
Woolfords Cottages S Lanarks 269 D10
Woolgarston Dorset 18 E5
Woolgreaves W Yorks 197 D10
Woolhampton W Berks 64 F5
Woolhope Heref'd 98 D2
Woolhope Cockshoot Heref'd 98 D2
Woolland Dorset 30 F3
Woollard Bath/NE Som'set 60 G6
Woollaton Devon 25 E7
Woollensbrook Herts 86 D5
Woolley Bath/NE Som'set 61 F8
Woolley Cambs 122 C3
Woolley Cornw'l 24 D3
Woolley Derby 170 C5
Woolley Wilts 61 G10
Woolley W Yorks 197 E10
Woolley Green Wilts 61 G10
Woolley Green Windsor 65 C11
Woolmer Green Herts 86 B3
Woolmere Green Worcs 117 E9
Woolmersdon Som'set 43 G9
Woolminstone Som'set 28 F6
Woolpit Suffolk 125 E9
Woolpit Green Suffolk 125 E9
Woolpit Heath Suffolk 125 E9
Woolridge Glos 98 G6
Woolsbridge Dorset 31 F10
Woolscott Warwick 119 D9
Woolsgrove Devon 26 G3
Woolsington Tyne/Wear 242 D5
Woolstaston Shrops 131 D9
Woolsthorpe Lincs 154 C6
Woolsthorpe-by-Colsterworth Lincs 155 E8
Woolston Cornw'l 6 B5
Woolston Devon 8 G4
Woolston Shrops 148 E6
Woolston Som'set 42 F5
Woolston Som'set 29 B10
Woolston S'thampton 32 E6
Woolston Warrington 183 D10
Woolston Green Devon 8 B5
Woolstone Glos 99 E9
Woolstone M/Keynes 103 D7
Woolstone Oxon 63 B9
Woolton Mersey 182 D6
Woolton Hill Hants 64 G2
Woolvers Hill N Som'set 59 G11
Woolverstone Suffolk 108 D3
Woolverton Som'set 45 C9
Woolwell Devon 7 C10
Woolwich London 68 D2
Woolwich Ferry London 68 D2
Woon Cornw'l 5 D10
Woonton Heref'd 114 G6
Woonton Ash Heref'd 115 G6
Wooperton Northum 264 E2
Woore Shrops 168 G2
Wooton Heref'd 97 D11
Wootten Green Suffolk 126 C4
Wootton Beds 103 C10
Wootton Hants 19 B10
Wootton Heref'd 114 G6
Wootton Heref'd 97 B9
Wootton I/Wight 20 C6
Wootton Kent 55 D8
Wootton Northants 120 F5
Wootton N Lincs 200 D5
Wootton Oxon 83 E7
Wootton Oxon 82 B6
Wootton Shrops 115 B9
Wootton Shrops 148 D6
Wootton Staffs 169 F10
Wootton Bassett Wilts 62 C5
Wootton Bridge I/Wight 20 C6
Wootton Broadmead Beds 103 C10
Wootton Common I/Wight 20 C6
Wootton Courtney Som'set 42 E2
Wootton Fitzpaine Dorset 16 B3
Wootton Green Beds 103 C9
Wootton Rivers Wilts 63 G7
Wootton St. Lawrence Hants 48 C5
Wootton Wawen Warwick 118 E3
Worcester Worcs 117 F7
Worcester Cathedral Worcs 116 G6
Worcester Park Surrey 67 F8
Worcester Racecourse Worcs 116 F6
Wordsley W Midlands 133 F7
Worfield Shrops 132 D5
Worgret Dorset 18 D4
Work Orkney 312 G5
Workhouse Common Norfolk 141 E10
Workhouse Common Norfolk 160 E7
Workhouse Green Suffolk 107 D7
Workhouse Hill Essex 107 E9
Workington Cumb 228 F5
Worksop Notts 187 G9
Worlaby N Lincs 200 E4
World Museum Liverpool Mersey 182 C4
World of James Herriot N Yorks 215 C8
World's End Bucks 84 D5
World's End Hants 33 E10
World's End London 86 F4
World's End Suffolk 125 F9
World's End W Berks 64 D3
World's End W Midlands 134 G2
World's End W Sussex 36 D4
Worle N Som'set 59 G11
Worlebury N Som'set 59 G10
Worleston Ches 167 D11
Worley Glos 80 F4
Worlingham Suffolk 143 F8
Worlington Suffolk 124 C3
Worlingworth Suffolk 126 D4
Wormadale Shetl'd 315 J5
Wormald Green N Yorks 214 F6
Wormbridge Heref'd 97 E8
Wormegay Norfolk 158 G3
Wormelow Tump Heref'd 97 E9
Wormhill Derby 185 G10
Wormhill Heref'd 97 D8
Wormingford Essex 107 E8
Worminghall Bucks 83 D10
Wormington Glos 99 D10
Worminster Som'set 44 E5
Wormiston Ho Fife 287 G10
Wormit Fife 287 E7
Wormleighton Warwick 119 G8
Wormley Herts 86 D5
Wormley Surrey 50 F3
Wormley West End Herts 86 D4
Wormleybury Herts 86 D5
Wormshill Kent 53 B11
Wormsley Heref'd 97 B8
Worplesdon Surrey 50 C3
Worrall S Yorks 186 C4
Worrall Hill Glos 79 C10
Worsbrough S Yorks 197 G11
Worsbrough Bridge S Yorks 197 G11
Worsbrough Common S Yorks 197 F10
Worsley Gtr Man 195 G8
Worsley Hall Gtr Man 194 F5
Worsley Mesnes Gtr Man 194 G5
Worstead Norfolk 160 D5
Worsthorne Lancs 204 G3
Worston Devon 7 E11
Worston Lancs 203 E11
Worten Kent 54 E3
Worth Devon 25 G7
Worth Devon 27 G7
Worth Kent 55 B10
Worth Som'set 41 G10
Worth Som'set 44 D4
Worth W Sussex 51 F9
Worth Matravers Dorset 18 F5
Wortham Suffolk 125 B11
Worthen Shrops 130 C6
Worthenbury Wrex 166 F6
Worthing Norfolk 159 F9
Worthing W Sussex 35 G11
Worthington Leics 153 E8
Worthy Som'set 41 D11
Worting Hants 48 C6
Wortley Glos 80 G3
Wortley S Yorks 186 B4
Wortley W Yorks 205 G11
Worton N Yorks 223 G9
Worton Wilts 46 B3
Wortwell Norfolk 142 G5
Wothorpe Peterbro 137 B10
Wotter Devon 7 C11
Wotton Glos 80 B4
Wotton Surrey 50 D6
Wotton Bourne End Beds 103 B9
Wotton under Edge Glos 80 G3
Wotton Underwood Bucks 83 B11
Woughton on the Green M/Keynes 103 D7
Woughton Park M/Keynes 103 D7
Wouldham Kent 69 G8
Wrabness Essex 108 E3
Wraes Aberds 302 F5
Wrafton Devon 40 F3
Wragby Lincs 189 F10
Wragby W Yorks 198 D2
Wragholme Lincs 190 B5
Wramplingham Norfolk 142 B2
Wrangaton Devon 8 D3
Wrangbrook W Yorks 198 E3
Wrangham Aberds 302 F6
Wrangle Lincs 174 E6
Wrangle Bank Lincs 174 E6
Wrangle Common Lincs 174 E6
Wrangle Low Ground Lincs 174 E6
Wrangle Lowgate Lincs 174 E6
Wrangway Som'set 27 D10
Wrantage Som'set 28 C4
Wrawby N Lincs 200 F4
Wraxall N Som'set 60 E3
Wraxall Som'set 44 F6
Wray Lancs 212 F2
Wray Common Surrey 51 C9
Wraysbury Windsor 66 E4
Wrayton Lancs 212 E2
Wrea Green Lancs 202 G4
Wreaks End Cumb 210 B4
Wreay Cumb 230 G4
Wreay Cumb 230 B4
Wrecclesham Surrey 49 D10
Wrecsam = Wrexham Wrex 166 E4
Wrekenton Tyne/Wear 243 F7
Wrelton N Yorks 216 B5
Wrenbury Ches 167 F9
Wreningham Norfolk 142 D3
Wrentham Suffolk 143 G9
Wrenthorpe W Yorks 197 C10
Wrentnall Shrops 131 C8
Wressle ER Yorks 207 G10
Wressle N Lincs 200 F3
Wrestlingworth Beds 104 B5
Wretham Norfolk 141 F8
Wretton Norfolk 140 D3
Wrexham = Wrecsam Wrex 166 E4
Wrexham Industrial Estate = Ystad Diwydiannol Wrecsam Wrex 166 F5
Wribbenhall Worcs 116 B5
Wrightington Bar Lancs 194 E4
Wrigwell Hill Devon 8 B5
Wrinehill Staffs 168 F3
Wrington N Som'set 60 G3
Writhlington Bath/NE Som'set 45 B8
Writtle Essex 87 D11
Wrockwardine Telford 150 G2
Wrockwardine Wood Telford 150 G3
Wroot N Lincs 199 G8
Wrose W Yorks 205 F9
Wrotham Kent 52 B6
Wrotham Heath Kent 52 B6
Wroughton Swindon 63 C7
Wroxall I/Wight 21 F7
Wroxall Warwick 118 C4
Wroxeter Shrops 131 B11
Wroxham Norfolk 160 F6
Wroxham Barns, Hoveton Norfolk 160 E6
Wroxton Oxon 101 C8
Wyaston Derby 169 G11
Wyastone Leys Heref'd 79 B8
Wyatt's Green Essex 87 F10
Wyberton Lincs 174 G4
Wyborn's Charity Kent 55 B8
Wyboston Beds 122 F2
Wybunbury Ches 167 F11
Wych Dorset 16 C5
Wych Cross E Sussex 52 G2
Wychbold Worcs 117 D8
Wychnor Staffs 152 F3
Wychnor Bridges Staffs 152 F3
Wyck Hants 49 F9
Wyck Rissington Glos 100 G3
Wycliffe Durham 224 C2
Wycoller Lancs 204 F4
Wycomb Leics 154 E5
Wycombe Marsh Bucks 84 G5
Wyddial Herts 105 E7
Wye Kent 54 D5
Wyegate Green Glos 79 D9
Wyesham Monmouths 79 C8
Wyfordby Leics 154 F5
Wyham Lincs 190 B3
Wyke Dorset 30 B3
Wyke Shrops 132 C3
Wyke Surrey 50 C2
Wyke W Yorks 197 B7
Wyke Champflower Som'set 45 G7
Wyke Green Devon 16 B2
Wyke Regis Dorset 17 F9
Wykeham N Yorks 216 D6
Wykeham N Yorks 217 C9
Wyken Shrops 132 E5
Wyken W Midlands 135 G7
Wyken Green W Midlands 135 G7
Wykey Shrops 149 E7
Wykin Leics 135 D8
Wylam Northum 242 E4
Wylde Green W Midlands 134 E2
Wyllie Caerph 77 G11
Wylye Wilts 46 F4
Wymans Brook Glos 99 G8
Wymering Portsm'th 33 F11
Wymeswold Leics 154 E2
Wymington Beds 121 E9
Wymondham Leics 154 F7
Wymondham Norfolk 142 C2
Wymondley Bury Herts 104 F4
Wynard Village Stockton 234 F4
Wyndham Bridg 76 G6
Wyndham Park V/Glam 58 D5
Wynford Eagle Dorset 17 B7
Wyng Orkney 313 J4
Wynn's Green Heref'd 98 B2
Wyre Piddle Worcs 99 B9
Wysall Notts 154 D2
Wyson Heref'd 115 D10
Wythall Worcs 117 C11
Wytham Oxon 83 D7
Wythburn Cumb 220 C6
Wythenshawe Gtr Man 184 D4
Wythop Cumb 229 F9
Wyton Cambs 122 B5
Wyton ER Yorks 209 G9
Wyverstone Suffolk 125 D10
Wyverstone Green Suffolk 125 D11
Wyverstone Street Suffolk 125 D10
Wyville Lincs 155 D7
Wyvis Lodge H'land 300 B4

Y

Y Bala = Bala Gwyn 147 B8
Y Borth = Borth Ceredig'n 128 E2
Y Drenewydd = Newtown Powys 130 E2
Y Fali = Valley Angl 178 F3
Y Fan Powys 129 F8
Y Felinheli = Port Dinorwic Gwyn 163 B8
Y Fflint = Flint Flints 182 G2
Y Ffôr Gwyn 145 B7
Y Gelli Gandryll = Hay on Wye Powys 96 C4
Y Mwmbwls = The Mumbles Swan 56 D6
Y Pîl = Pyle Bridg 57 E10
Y Rhyl = Rhyl Denbs 181 E8
Y Trallwng = Welshpool Powys 130 B4
Y Tymbl = Tumble Carms 75 C8
Y Waun = Chirk Wrex 148 B5
Yaddlethorpe N Lincs 199 F11
Yafford I/Wight 20 E4
Yafforth N Yorks 224 G6
Yalberton Torbay 9 D7
Yalding Kent 53 C8
Yalway Som'set 43 G8
Yanley N Som'set 60 E5
Yanwath Cumb 230 F6
Yanworth Glos 81 C9
Yapham ER Yorks 207 C11
Yapton W Sussex 35 G7
Yarberry N Som'set 43 B11
Yarborough NE Lincs 201 F9
Yarbridge I/Wight 21 D8
Yarburgh Lincs 190 C4
Yarcombe Devon 28 F2
Yardey Gobion Northants 102 C5
Yardley W Midlands 134 F2
Yardley Hastings Northants 121 F7
Yardley Wood W Midlands 117 B11
Yardro Powys 114 F4
Yarford Som'set 28 B2
Yarkhill Heref'd 98 C2
Yarley Som'set 44 D4
Yarlington Som'set 29 B11
Yarlside Cumb 210 F4
Yarm Stockton 225 C8
Yarmouth I/Wight 20 D3
Yarmouth Racecourse Norfolk 161 G10
Yarnacott Devon 40 G6
Yarnbrook Wilts 45 C11
Yarner Devon 13 F11
Yarnfield Staffs 151 C7
Yarnscombe Devon 25 B9
Yarnton Oxon 83 C7
Yarpole Heref'd 115 E9
Yarrow Scot Borders 261 D9
Yarrow Northum 250 F6
Yarrow Som'set 43 D11
Yarsop Heref'd 97 B8
Yarwell Northants 137 D11
Yate S Glos 61 C8
Yate Rocks S Glos 61 C8
Yatehouse Green Ches 168 B2
Yateley Hants 65 G10
Yatesbury Wilts 62 E5
Yattendon W Berks 64 E5
Yatton Heref'd 115 D8
Yatton N Som'set 60 F2
Yatton Keynell Wilts 61 D11
Yaverland I/Wight 21 D8
Yawl Devon 16 C2
Yawthorpe Lincs 188 C5
Yaxham Norfolk 159 G10
Yaxley Cambs 138 E3
Yaxley Suffolk 126 C2
Yazor Heref'd 97 B8
Yeabridge Som'set 28 D6
Yeading London 66 C6
Yeadon W Yorks 205 E10
Yealand Conyers Lancs 211 E9
Yealand Redmayne Lancs 211 D10
Yealand Storrs Lancs 211 D9
Yealmpton Devon 7 E11
Yearby Redcar/Clevel'd 235 G8
Yearngill Cumb 229 C8
Yearsett Heref'd 116 G4
Yearsley N Yorks 215 E11
Yeaton Shrops 149 F8
Yeaveley Derby 169 G11
Yeavering Northum 263 C10
Yedingham N Yorks 217 D7
Yelden Beds 121 D10
Yelford Oxon 82 E5
Yelland Devon 40 G3
Yelling Cambs 122 E5
Yelsted Kent 69 G10
Yelvertoft Northants 120 B2
Yelverton Devon 7 B10
Yelverton Norfolk 142 C5
Yenston Som'set 30 C2
Yeo Mill Devon 26 B4
Yeo Park Devon 7 E11
Yeoford Devon 13 B11
Yeolmbridge Cornw'l 12 D2
Yeovil Som'set 29 D9
Yeovilton Som'set 29 C8
Yerbeston Pembs 73 D9
Yesnaby Orkney 312 G3
Yetlington Northum 252 B2
Yetminster Dorset 29 E9
Yett N Lanarks 268 D5
Yett S Ayrs 257 E10
Yettington Devon 15 D7
Yetts o'Muckhart Clack 286 G4
Yew Green Warwick 118 D4
Yew Tree W Midlands 133 D10
Yewtree Cross Kent 55 E7
Y-Ffrith Denbs 181 E8
Yieldshields S Lanarks 269 E7
Yiewsley London 66 C5
Yinstay Orkney 312 G6
Ynsforgan Swan 75 F11
Ynys Gwyn 145 B11
Ynys Gwyn 145 B7
Ynys Tachwedd Ceredig'n 128 E2
Ynysboeth Rh Cyn Taff 77 F9
Ynysddu Caerph 77 G11
Ynyshafren Carms 75 D7
Ynys-hir Ceredig'n 128 D3
Ynyshir Rh Cyn Taff 77 G8
Ynyslas Ceredig'n 128 E2
Ynysmaengwyn Gwyn 110 C2
Ynysmaerdy Neath P Talb 76 F2
Ynysmaerdy Rh Cyn Taff 58 C4
Ynysmeudwy Neath P Talb 76 D2
Ynystawe Swan 75 E11
Ynyswen Powys 76 C4
Ynys-wen Rh Cyn Taff 77 F7
Ynysybwl Rh Cyn Taff 77 G9
Yockenthwaite N Yorks 213 D8
Yockleton Shrops 149 G7
Yokefleet ER Yorks 199 C10
Yoker Glasg C 267 B10
Yonder Bognie Aberds 302 E5
Yondertown Devon 7 D11
Yondover Dorset 16 C5
Yopps Green Kent 52 C6
York C/York 207 C8
York Lancs 203 G10
York Castle Museum C/York 207 C8
York Minster C/York 207 C8
York Racecourse C/York 207 D7
York Town Surrey 49 B11
Yorkhill Glasg C 267 B11
Yorkletts Kent 70 G5
Yorkley Glos 79 D10
Yorkley Slade Glos 79 D10
Yorkshire Air Museum C/York 207 D9
Yorkshire Sculpture Park, Wakefield W Yorks 197 E9
Yorton Shrops 149 E10
Yorton Heath Shrops 149 E10
Youlecote ER Yorks 207 B11
Youlgreave Derby 170 C2
Youlton N Yorks 215 G9
Young Wood Lincs 189 G10
Young's End Essex 88 B2
Yoxford Suffolk 127 D7
Yoxhall Staffs 152 F2
Yr Hôb = Hope Flints 166 D4
Ysbyty Cynfyn Ceredig'n 112 B5
Ysbyty Ifan Conwy 164 F4
Ysbyty Ystwyth Ceredig'n 112 C4
Ysceifiog Flints 181 G11
Ysgeibion Denbs 165 D9
Ysgubor-y-coed Ceredig'n 128 D3
Yspitty Carms 75 F9
Ystad Diwydiannol Wrecsam = Wrexham Industrial Estate Wrex 166 F5
Ystalyfera Neath P Talb 76 D3
Ystrad Rh Cyn Taff 77 F7
Ystrad Aeron Ceredig'n 111 F10
Ystrad Mynach Caerph 77 G11
Ystradfellte Powys 76 C6
Ystradffin Carms 94 B5
Ystradgynlais Powys 76 C3
Ystradmeurig Ceredig'n 112 D4
Ystradowen Carms 76 C3
Ystradowen V/Glam 58 D4
Ystumtuen Ceredig'n 112 B4
Ythanbank Aberds 303 F9
Ythanwells Aberds 302 F6
Ythsie Aberds 303 F8

Z

Zeal Monachorum Devon 26 G2
Zeals Wilts 45 G9
Zelah Cornw'l 4 E6
Zennor Cornw'l 1 B5
Zoar Cornw'l 3 F7

County and unitary authority boundaries

Greater London

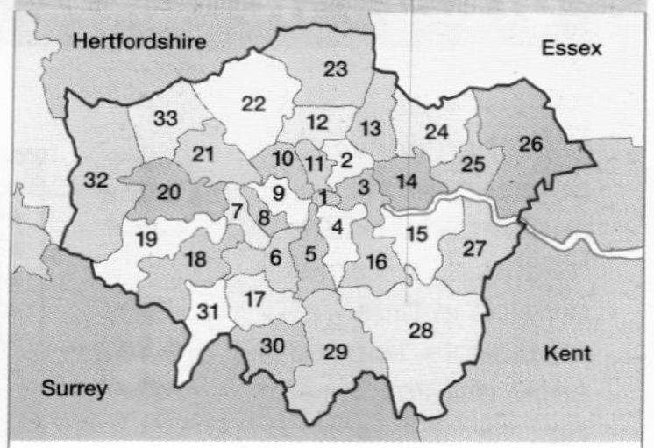

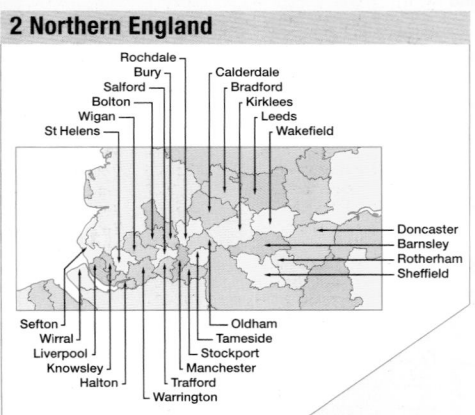

Hertfordshire
Essex
Surrey
Kent
1 2 3 4 5 6 7 8 9 10 11 12 13 14 15 16 17 18 19 20 21 22 23 24 25 26 27 28 29 30 31 32 33

1 City and County of the City of London	16 Lewisham
2 Hackney	17 Merton
3 Tower Hamlets	18 Richmond upon Thames
4 Southwark	19 Hounslow
5 Lambeth	20 Ealing
6 Wandsworth	21 Brent
7 Hammersmith and Fulham	22 Barnet
8 Royal Borough of Kensington and Chelsea	23 Enfield
9 City of Westminster	24 Redbridge
10 Camden	25 Barking and Dagenham
11 Islington	26 Havering
12 Haringey	27 Bexley
13 Waltham Forest	28 Bromley
14 Newham	29 Croydon
15 Greenwich	30 Sutton
	31 Kingston upon Thames
	32 Hillingdon
	33 Harrow

1 Central Scotland

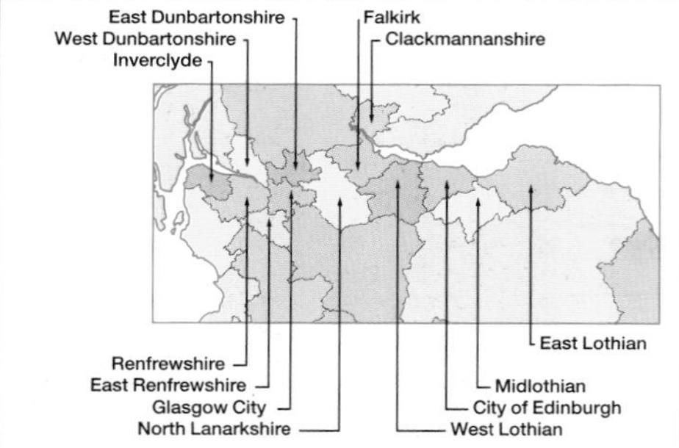

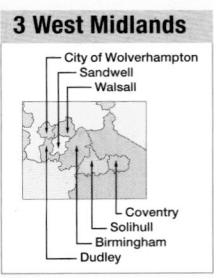

East Dunbartonshire
West Dunbartonshire
Inverclyde
Falkirk
Clackmannanshire
Renfrewshire
East Renfrewshire
Glasgow City
North Lanarkshire
East Lothian
Midlothian
City of Edinburgh
West Lothian

2 Northern England

Rochdale
Bury
Salford
Bolton
Wigan
St Helens
Calderdale
Bradford
Kirklees
Leeds
Wakefield
Doncaster
Barnsley
Rotherham
Sheffield
Sefton
Wirral
Liverpool
Knowsley
Halton
Oldham
Tameside
Stockport
Manchester
Trafford
Warrington

3 West Midlands

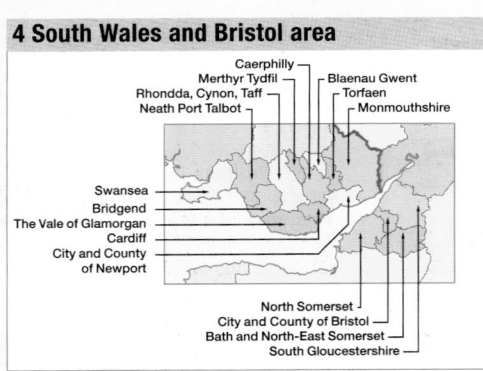

City of Wolverhampton
Sandwell
Walsall
Coventry
Solihull
Birmingham
Dudley

4 South Wales and Bristol area

Caerphilly
Merthyr Tydfil
Rhondda, Cynon, Taff
Neath Port Talbot
Blaenau Gwent
Torfaen
Monmouthshire
Swansea
Bridgend
The Vale of Glamorgan
Cardiff
City and County of Newport
North Somerset
City and County of Bristol
Bath and North-East Somerset
South Gloucestershire

5 Thames Valley

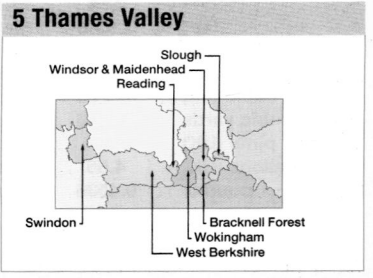

Slough
Windsor & Maidenhead
Reading
Swindon
Bracknell Forest
Wokingham
West Berkshire

Ordnance Survey National Grid

The blue lines which divide the Navigator map pages into squares for indexing match the Ordnance Survey National Grid and correspond to the small squares on the boundary map below. Each side of a grid square measures 10km on the ground.

The National Grid 100-km square letters and kilometre values are indicated for the grid intersection at the outer corners of each page. For example, the intersection SP1020 at the lower right corner of page 99 is 10km East and 20km North of the south-west corner of National Grid square SP.

SP 10 20
Warwickshire
Northamptonshire
Milton Keynes
Buckinghamshire
Oxfordshire
SP
20km
10km

A436
NOTGROVE LONG BARROW
SP
20
10
Pountwell

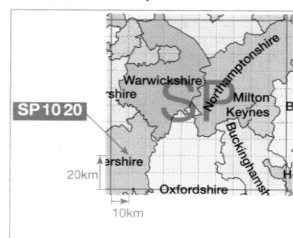

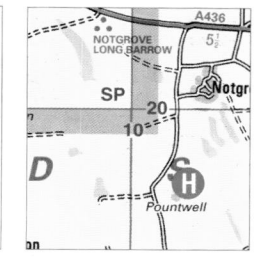

Using GPS with Navigator mapping

Since Navigator Britain is based on Ordnance Survey mapping, and rectified to the National Grid, it can be used with in-car or handheld GPS for locating identifiable waypoints such as road junctions, bridges, railways and farms, or assessing your position in relation to any of the features shown on the map.

On your receiver, choose British Grid as the location format and for map datum select Ordnance Survey (this may be described as Ord Srvy GB or similar, or more specifically as OSGB36). Your receiver will automatically convert the latitude/longitude co-ordinates transmitted by GPS into compatible National Grid data.

Positional accuracy of any particular feature is limited to 50–100m, due to the limitations of the original survey and the scale of Navigator mapping.

For further information see *www.gps.gov.uk*

1000
900
800
700
600
500
400
300
200
100
0
0 100 200 300 400 500 600 700
NA NB NC ND
NF NG NH NJ NK
NL NM NN NO
NR NS NT NU
NW NX NY NZ
SC SD SE TA
SH SJ SK TF TG
SM SN SO SP TL TM
SQ SR SS ST SU TQ TR
SV SW SX SY SZ TV
Western Isles
Moray
Highland
Aberdeen City
Aberdeenshire
Angus
Perth and Kinross
Dundee City
Argyll and Bute
Fife
Stirling
North Ayrshire
South Lanarkshire
Scottish Borders
East Ayrshire
South Ayrshire
Dumfries and Galloway
Northumberland
Newcastle upon Tyne
North Tyneside
South Tyneside
Tyne and Wear
Sunderland
Gateshead
Cumbria
Durham
Hartlepool
Redcar and Cleveland
Middlesbrough
Stockton-on-Tees
Darlington
Isle of Man
North Yorkshire
York
East Riding of Yorkshire
Blackpool
Lancashire
West Yorkshire
City of Kingston upon Hull
Blackburn with Darwen
North Lincolnshire
Flintshire
Greater Manchester
Denbighshire
South Yorkshire
North East Lincolnshire
Merseyside
Isle of Anglesey
Cheshire
Derbyshire
Lincolnshire
City of Stoke-on-Trent
City of Nottingham
City of Derby
City of Leicester
City of Peterborough
Conwy
Nottinghamshire
Wrexham
Gwynedd
Staffordshire
Leicestershire
Rutland
Norfolk
Telford and Wrekin
Shropshire
Ceredigion
Powys
West Midlands
Northamptonshire
Cambridgeshire
Warwickshire
Suffolk
Worcestershire
Milton Keynes
Bedfordshire
Herefordshire
Carmarthenshire
Luton
Pembrokeshire
Gloucestershire
Buckinghamshire
Hertfordshire
Essex
Oxfordshire
Southend-on-Sea
London
Thurrock
Medway
Wiltshire
Surrey
Kent
Somerset
Hampshire
West Sussex
East Sussex
Devon
Dorset
City of Brighton and Hove
Isle of Wight
Cornwall
Bournemouth
Poole
City of Portsmouth
City of Southampton
Torbay
City of Plymouth
Isles of Scilly

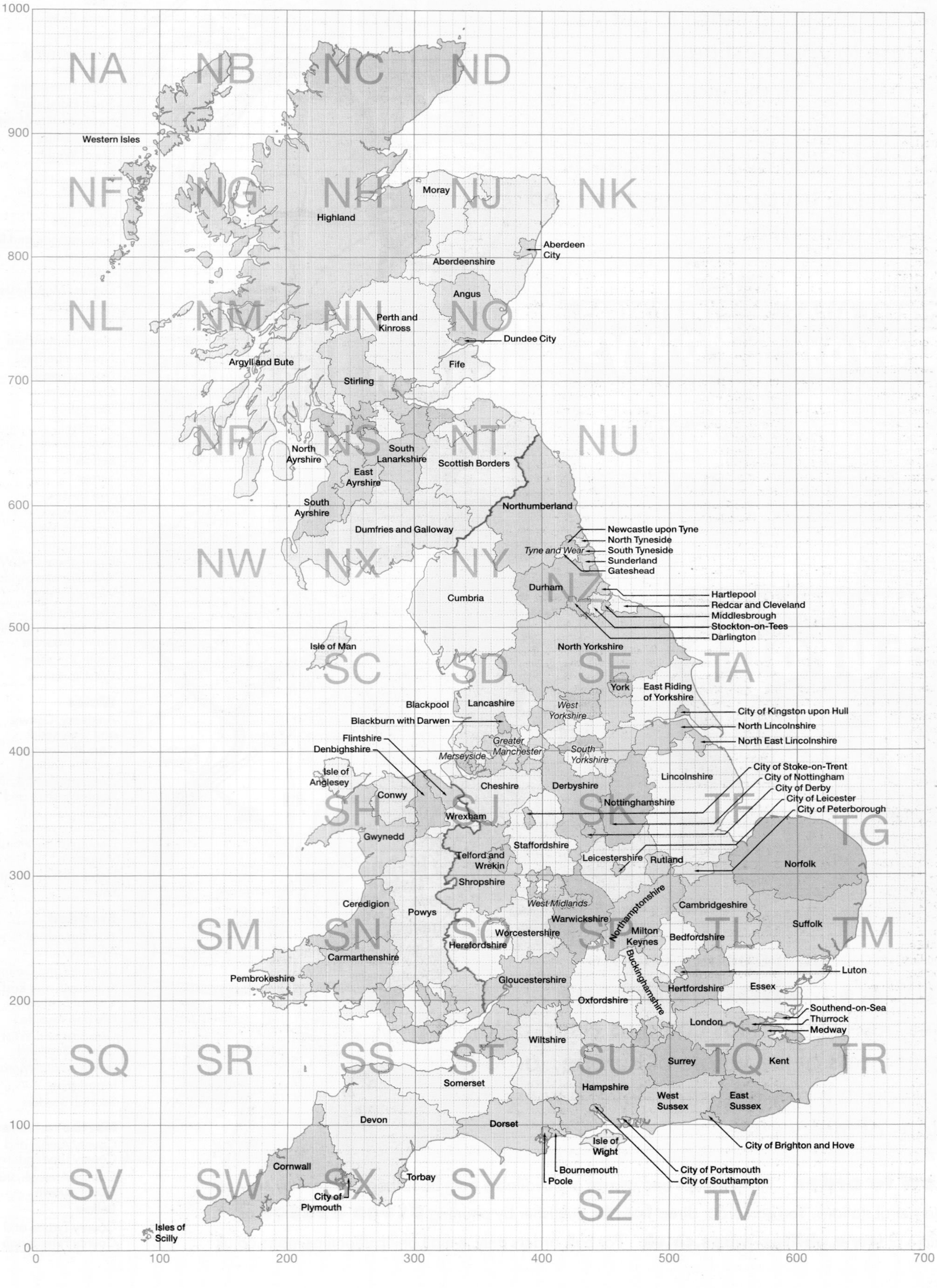